Lecture Notes in Computer Science 6184

Commenced Publication in 1973
Founding and Former Series Editors:
Gerhard Goos, Juris Hartmanis, and Jan van Leeuwen

Lei Chen Changjie Tang Jun Yang
Yunjun Gao (Eds.)

Web-Age Information Management

11th International Conference, WAIM 2010
Jiuzhaigou, China, July 15-17, 2010
Proceedings

Springer

Volume Editors

Lei Chen
Hong Kong University of Science and Technology
Department of Computer Science
Clear Water Bay, Kowloon, Hong Kong, China
E-mail: leichen@cs.ust.hk

Changjie Tang
Sichuan University, Computer Department
Chengdu 610064, China
E-mail: cjtang@scu.edu.cn

Jun Yang
Duke University, Department of Computer Science
Box 90129, Durham, NC 27708-0129, USA
E-mail: junyang@cs.duke.edu

Yunjun Gao
Zhejiang University, College of Computer Science
388 Yuhangtang Road, Hangzhou 310058, China
E-mail: gaoyj@zju.edu.cn

Library of Congress Control Number: 2010929625

CR Subject Classification (1998): H.3, H.4, I.2, C.2, H.2, H.5

LNCS Sublibrary: SL 3 – Information Systems and Application, incl. Internet/Web and HCI

ISSN 0302-9743
ISBN-10 3-642-14245-1 Springer Berlin Heidelberg New York
ISBN-13 978-3-642-14245-1 Springer Berlin Heidelberg New York

springer.com

Printed in Germany

Typesetting: Camera-ready by author, data conversion by Scientific Publishing Services, Chennai, India
Printed on acid-free paper 06/3180

Preface

WAIM is a leading international conference on research, development, and applications of Web technologies, database systems, and information management. Traditionally, WAIM has drawn the strongest participation from the Asia-Pacific region. The previous WAIM conferences were held in Shanghai (2000), Xi'an (2001), Beijing (2002), Chengdu (2003), Dalian (2004), Hangzhou (2005), Hong Kong (2006), Huangshan (2007), Zhangjiajie (2008), and Suzhou (2009). In 2010, WAIM was held in Jiuzhaigou, Sichuan, China.

This high-quality program would not have been possible without the authors who chose WAIM for disseminating their contributions. Out of 205 submissions from 16 countries and regions, including Australia, Canada, France, Germany, Hong Kong, Japan, Korea, Macau, Malaysia, Mainland China, Saudi Arabia, Singapore, Taiwan, Thailand, UK, and USA, we selected 58 full papers and 11 short papers for publication. The acceptance rate for regular full papers was 28%. The contributed papers addressed a wide range of topics such as Web, XML, and multimedia data, data processing in the cloud or on new hardware, data mining and knowledge discovery, information integration and extraction, networked data and social networks, graph and stream processing, similarity search, etc. We are also grateful to our distinguished keynote speakers Prof. Jianzhong Li, Dr. Divesh Srivastava, Prof. Katsumi Tanaka, and Prof. Xiaofang Zhou.

A conference like WAIM can only succeed as a team effort. We want to thank the Program Committee members and the reviewers for their invaluable efforts. Special thanks go to the local Organizing Committee headed by Changjie Tang, Aoying Zhou, and Lei Duan. Many thanks also go to our Workshop Co-chairs (Jian Pei and Hengtao Shen), Tutorial Co-chairs (Liu Wenyin and Jian Yang), Publicity Co-chairs (Hua Wang and Shuigeng Zhou), Industrial Chairs (Qiming Chen and Haixun Wang), Registration Chair (Chuan Li), and Finance Co-chairs (Howard Leung and Yu Chen). Last but not least, we wish to express our gratitude for the hard work of our webmaster Jie Zuo, and for our sponsors who generously supported the smooth running of our conference.

Lei Chen
Changjie Tang
Jun Yang
Masaru Kitsuregawa
Qing Li

WAIM 2010 Conference Organization

Honorary Chair

Yi Zhang — Sichuan University, China

Conference Co-chairs

Masaru Kitsuregawa — University of Tokyo, Japan
Qing Li — City University of Hong Kong, Hong Kong

Program Committee Co-chairs

Lei Chen — Hong Kong University of Science and Technology, Hong Kong
Changjie Tang — Sichuan University, China
Jun Yang — Duke University, USA

Local Organization Co-chairs

Aoying Zhou — East China Normal University, China
Lei Duan — Sichuan University, China

Workshops Co-chairs

Jian Pei — Simon Fraser University, Canada
Hengtao Shen — University of Queensland, Australia

Tutorial/Panel Co-chairs

Wenyin Liu — City University of Hong Kong, Hong Kong
Jian Yang — Macquarie University, Australia

Industrial Co-chairs

Qiming Chen — HP Labs, Palo Alto, USA
Haixun Wang — Microsoft Research Asia, China

Publication Chair

Yunjun Gao	Zhejiang University, China

Publicity Co-chairs

Hua Wang	University of Southern Queensland, Australia
Shuigeng Zhou	Fudan University, China

Finance Co-chairs

Howard Leung	Hong Kong Web Society, Hong Kong
Yu Chen	Sichuan University, China

Registration Chair

Chuan Li	Sichuan University, China

CCF DB Society Liaison

Xiaofeng Meng	Renmin University of China, China

Steering Committee Liaison

Zhiyong Peng	Wuhan University, China

Web Master

Jie Zuo	Sichuan University, China

Program Committee

James Bailey	University of Melbourne, Australia
Gang Chen	Zhejiang University, China
Hong Chen	Chinese Univeristy of Hong Kong, Hong Kong
Yu Chen	Sichuan University, China
Reynold Cheng	The University of Hong Kong, Hong Kong
David Cheung	The University of Hong Kong, Hong kong
Dickson Chiu	Dickson Computer Systems, Hong Kong
Byron Choi	Hong Kong Baptist University, Hong Kong
Bin Cui	Peking University, China
Alfredo Cuzzocrea	University of Calabria, Italy

Guozhu Dong	Wright State University, USA
Xiaoyong Du	Renmin University of China, China
Lei Duan	Sichuan University, China
Ling Feng	Tsinghua University, China
Johann Gamper	Free University of Bozen-Bolzano, Italy
Bryon Gao	Texas State University at San Marcos, USA
Yong Gao	Univeristy of British Columbia, Canada
Jihong Guan	Tongji University, China
Giovanna Guerrini	Università di Genova, Italy
Bingsheng He	Chinese Univeristy of Hong Kong, Hong Kong
Jimmy Huang	York Univeristy, Canada
Seung-won Hwang	Pohang University of Science and Technology, Korea
Wee Hyong	Microsoft
Yoshiharu Ishikawa	Nagoya University, Japan
Yan Jia	National University of Defence Technology, China
Ruoming Jin	Kent State University, USA
Ning Jing	National University of Defence Technology, China
Ben Kao	The University of Hong Kong, Hong Kong
Yong Kim	Korea Education & Research Information Service, Korea
Nick Koudas	Univeristy of Toronto, Canada
Wu Kui	Victoria University, Canada
Carson Leung	University of Manitoba, Canada
Chengkai Li	University of Texas at Arlington, USA
Chuan Li	Sichuan University, China
Feifei Li	Florida State University, USA
Tao Li	Florida International University, USA
Tianrui Li	Southwest Jiaotong University, China
Zhanhuai Li	Northwestern Polytechnical University, China
Zhoujun Li	Beihang University, China
Xiang Lian	Hong Kong University of Science and Technology, Hong Kong
Lipeow Lim	University of Hawaii at Manoa, USA
Xuemin Lin	University of New South Wales, Australia
Huan Liu	Arizona State University, USA
Lianfang Liu	Computing Center of Guangxi, China
Qizhi Liu	Nanjing University, China
Weiyi Liu	Yunnan University, China
Wenyin Liu	City Univeristy of Hong Kong
Eric Lo	Hong Kong Polytechnic University, Hong Kong
Zongmin Ma	Northeastern University, China
Weiyi Meng	State University of New York at Binghamton, USA
Mohamed Mokbel	University of Minnesota, USA
Yang-Sae Moon	Kangwon National University, Korea
Akiyo Nadamoto	Konan University, Japan
Miyuki Nakano	University of Tokyo, Japan

Raymond Ng	University of British Columbia, Canada
Anne Ngu	Texas State University at San Marcos, USA
Tadashi Ohmori	University of Electro Communications, Japan
Olga Papaemmanouil	Brandeis University, USA
Zhiyong Peng	Wuhan University, China
Evaggelia Pitoura	University of Ioannina, Greece
Tieyun Qian	Wuhan University, China
Shaojie Qiao	Southwest Jiaotong University, China
Markus Schneider	University of Florida, USA
Hengtao Shen	University of Queensland, Australia
Yong Tang	Sun Yat-sen University, China
David Taniar	Monash University, Australia
Maguelonne Teisseire	University Montpellier 2, France
Anthony Tung	National University of Singapore, Singapore
Shunsuke Uemura	Nara Sangyo University, Japan
Jianyong Wang	Tsinghua University, China
Ke Wang	Simon Fraser University, Canada
Tengjiao Wang	Peking University, China
Wei Wang	University of New South Wales, Australia
Raymond Wong	University of New South Wales, Australia
Raymond Chi-Wing Wong	Hong Kong University of Science and Technology, Hong Kong
Xintao Wu	University of North Carolina at Charlotte, USA
Yuqing Wu	Indiana University at Bloomington, USA
Junyi Xie	Oracle Corp., USA
Li Xiong	Emory University, USA
Jianliang Xu	Hong Kong Baptist University, Hong Kong
Jian Yang	Macquaire University, Australia
Xiaochun Yang	Northeastern University, China
Ke Yi	Hong Kong University of Science and Technology, Hong Kong
Hwanjo Yu	Pohang University of Science and Technology, Korea
Jeffrey Yu	Chinese Univeristy of Hong Kong, Hong Kong
Lei Yu	State University of New York at Binghamton, USA
Philip Yu	University of Illinois at Chicago, USA
Ting Yu	North Carolina State University, USA
Xiaohui Yu	York University, Canada
Demetris Zeinalipour	University of Cyprus, Cyprus
Donghui Zhang	Microsoft Jim Gray Systems Lab, USA
Ji Zhang	University of Southern Queensland, Australia
Baihua Zheng	Singapore Management University, Singapore
Aoying Zhou	East China Normal University, China
Shuigeng Zhou	Fudan University, China
Xiangmin Zhou	CSIRO, Australia
Qiang Zhu	University of Michigan at Dearborn, USA
Lei Zou	Peking University, China

Organized by

Sichuan University

Sponsored by

国家自然科学基金委员会
National Natural Science Foundation of China
NSFC

华东师范大学
EAST CHINA NORMAL UNIVERSITY

四川大學
SICHUAN UNIVERSITY

川大智胜
WISESOFT
www.wisesoft.com.cn

Table of Contents

Social Networks

Cloud Computing

Data Mining I

Stream Processing

Graph Processing

Query Processing

Potpourri

Web Data II

Data Mining II

XML and Images

New Hardware

Similarity Search

Information Extraction

Knowledge Discovery

Information Integration

Extending Databases

Analyzing Data Quality Using Data Auditor

Divesh Srivastava

AT&T Labs− Research
divesh@research.att.com

Abstract. Monitoring databases maintain configuration and measurement tables about computer systems, such as networks and computing clusters, and serve important business functions, such as troubleshooting customer problems, analyzing equipment failures, planning system upgrades, etc. These databases are prone to many data quality issues: configuration tables may be incorrect due to data entry errors, while measurement tables may be affected by incorrect, missing, duplicate and delayed polls.

We describe Data Auditor, a system for analyzing data quality and exploring data semantics of monitoring databases. Given a user-supplied constraint, such as a boolean predicate expected to be satisfied by every tuple, a functional dependency, or an inclusion dependency, Data Auditor computes "pattern tableaux", which are concise summaries of subsets of the data that satisfy or fail the constraint. We discuss the architecture of Data Auditor, including the supported types of constraints and the tableau generation mechanism. We also show the utility of our approach on an operational network monitoring database.

L. Chen et al. (Eds.): WAIM 2010, LNCS 6184, p. 1, 2010.

Rebuilding the World from Views

Xiaofang Zhou and Henning Köhler

School of Information Technology and Electrical Engineering
The University of Queensland, Australia
{zxf,henning}@itee.uq.edu.au

Abstract. With the ever-increasing growth of the internet, more and more data sets are being made available. Most of this data has its origin in the real world, often describing the same objects or events from different viewpoints. One can thus consider data sets obtained from different sources as different (and possibly inconsistent) views of our world, and it makes sense to try to integrate them in some form, e.g. to answer questions which involve data from multiple sources. While data integration is an old and well-investigated subject, the nature of the data sets to be integrated is changing. They increase in volume as well as complexity, are often undocumented, relationships between data sets are more fuzzy, and representations of the same real-word object differ. To address these challenges, new methods for rapid, semi-automatic, loose and virtual integration, exploration and querying of large families of data sets must be developed.

In an ongoing project we are investigating a framework for sampling and matching data sets in an efficient manner. In particular, we consider the problem of creating and analyzing samples of relational databases to find relationships between string-valued attributes [1]. Our focus is on identifying attribute pairs whose value sets overlap, a pre-condition for typical joins over such attributes. We deal with the issue of different representation of objects, i.e., 'dirty' data, by employing new similarity measures between sets of strings, which not only consider set based similarity, but also similarity between string instances. To make the measures effective, especially in light of data sets being large and distributed, we developed efficient algorithms for distributed sample creation and similarity computation. Central to this is that sampling is *synchronized*. For clean data this means that the same values are sampled for each set, if present [2,3]. For dirty data one must ensure that similar values are sampled for each set, if present, and we manage to do so in a probabilistic manner.

The next step of our research is to extend such a sampling and matching approach to multiple attributes and semi-structured data, and to construct search and query systems which make direct use of the matches discovered.

References

1. Köhler, H., Zhou, X., Sadiq, S., Shu, Y., Taylor, K.: Sampling dirty data for matching attributes. In: SIGMOD (2010)
2. Broder, A.: On the resemblance and containment of documents. In: SEQUENCES: Proceedings of the Compression and Complexity of Sequences, p. 21 (1997)
3. Dasu, T., Johnson, T., Muthukrishnan, S., Shkapenyuk, V.: Mining database structure; or, how to build a data quality browser. In: SIGMOD, pp. 240–251 (2002)

L. Chen et al. (Eds.): WAIM 2010, LNCS 6184, p. 2, 2010.

Approximate Query Processing in Sensor Networks

Jianzhong Li

Institute of Computer Science and Technology
Harbin Institute of Technology, 150001 Harbin, China
ljz@hit.edu.cn

Abstract. Many emerging applications are collecting massive volumes of sensor data from networks of distributed devices, such as sensor networks and cyber-physical systems. These environments are commonly characterized by the intrinsic volatility and uncertainty of the sensor data, and the strict communication (energy) constraints of the distributed devices. Approximate query processing is important methodology that exploits the tolerance of many applications to inaccuracies in reported data in order to reserve communication overhead. The research challenge is how to ensure communication efficiency without sacrificing result usefulness.

Many prior work depends on users to impose preferences or constraints on approximate query processing, such as result inaccuracies, candidate set size, and response time. We argue that the pre-determined user preferences may turn out to be inappropriate and become a substantial source of i) jeopardized query results, ii) prohibitive response time, and iii) overwhelming communication overhead.

Our work '*Probing Queries in Wireless Sensor Networks*' (ICDCS 2008) studies a scenario where empty sets may be returned as accurate query results, yet users may benefit from approximate answer sets not exactly conforming the specified query predicates. The approximate answer sets can be used not only to answer the query approximately but also to guide users to modify their queries for further probing the monitored objects. The distance between sensing data and a query and the dominating relationship between sensing data are first defined. Then, three algorithms for processing probing queries are proposed, which compute the best approximate answer sets that consist of the sensing data with the smallest distance from given queries. All the algorithms utilize the dominating relationship to reduce the amount of data transmitted in sensor networks by filtering out the unnecessary data. Experimental results on real and synthetic data sets show that the proposed algorithms have high performance and energy efficiency.

Our work '*Enabling ε-Approximate Querying in Sensor Networks*' (VLDB 2009) studies the scenario where, due to the dynamic nature of sensor data, users are unable to determine *in advance* what error bounds can lead to affordable cost in approximate query processing. We propose a novel ε-approximate querying (EAQ) scheme to resolve the problem. EAQ is a uniform data access scheme underlying various queries in sensor networks. The core idea of EAQ is to introduce run-time iteration and refinement mechanisms to enable efficient, ε-approximate query processing in sensor networks. Thus it grants more flexibility to in-network query processing and minimizes energy

L. Chen et al. (Eds.): WAIM 2010, LNCS 6184, pp. 3–4, 2010.

consumption through communicating data up to a *just-sufficient* level. To ensure bounded overall cost for the iteration and refinement procedures of the EAQ scheme, we develop a novel *data shuffling* algorithm. The algorithm converts sensed datasets into special representations called MVA. From prefixes of MVA, we can recover approximate versions of the entire dataset, where all individual data items have guaranteed error bounds. The EAQ scheme supports efficient and flexible processing of various queries including *spatial window* query, *value range* query, and queries with QoS constraints. The effectiveness and efficiency of the EAQ scheme are evaluated in a real sensor network testbed.

Even in case the users know exactly what result inaccuracies they can tolerate, many prior query processing techniques still cannot meet arbitrary precision requirements given by users. Most notably, many aggregational query processing methods can only support fixed error bounds.

In '*Sampling based (ε, δ)-Approximate Aggregation Algorithm in Sensor Networks*' (ICDCS 2009), we propose a uniform sampling based aggregation algorithm. We prove that for any ε ($\varepsilon \leq 0$) and δ ($0 \leq \delta \leq 1$), this algorithm returns the approximate aggregation result satisfying that the probability of the relative error of the results being larger than ε is less than δ. However, this algorithm is only suitable for static network. Considering the dynamic property of sensor networks, we further proposed a Bernoulli sampling based algorithm in '*Bernoulli Sampling based (ε, δ)-Approximate Aggregation in Large-Scale Sensor Networks*' (INFOCOM 2010). We prove that this algorithm also can meet the requirement of any precision, and is suitable for both static and dynamic networks. Besides, two sample data adaptive algorithms are also provided. One is to adapt the sample with the varying of precision requirement. The other is to adapt the sample with the varying of the sensed data in networks. The theoretical analysis and experiments show that all proposed algorithms have high performance in terms of accuracy and energy cost.

Duplicate Identification in Deep Web Data Integration

Wei Liu[1], Xiaofeng Meng[2], Jianwu Yang[1], and Jianguo Xiao[1]

[1] Institute of Computer Science & Technology, Peking University,
Beijing, China
[2] School of Information, Renmin University of China,
Beijing, China
gue1976@gmail.com, xfmeng@ruc.edu.cn,
{yangjianwu,xjg}@icst.pku.edu.cn

Abstract. Duplicate identification is a critical step in deep web data integration, and generally, this task has to be performed over multiple web databases. However, a customized matcher for two web databases often does not work well for other two ones due to various presentations and different schemas. It is not practical to build and maintain C_n^2 matchers for *n* web databases. In this paper, we target at building one universal matcher over multiple web databases in one domain. According to our observation, the similarity on an attribute is dependent of those of some other attributes, which is ignored by existing approaches. Inspired by this, we propose a comprehensive solution for duplicate identification problem over multiple web databases. The extensive experiments over real web databases on three domains show the proposed solution is an effective way to address the duplicate identification problem over multiple web databases.

Keywords: duplicate identification, deep web data integration, web database.

1 Introduction

Survey[6] revealed deep web is being the largest information depository on the web. Deep web data integration is becoming a hot area for both research and industry. There is often high redundancy among web databases, so it is a necessary step to match duplicates for data cleaning or further applications, such as price comparison services and the information merging.

Duplicate identification(a.k.a. de-duplication, record linkage, etc.) is the process of identifying different representations of one entity, which is always a challenging task in heterogeneous data sources integration. To the best of our knowledge, lots of solutions have been proposed to address this issue[7]. However, most of them focus on the problem only between two sources. Due to the large scale of deep web, lots of web databases are integrated in practice. As a result, C_n^2 matchers have to be built for *n* web databases if traditional approaches were applied.

Fig.1 shows three movies records from web databases W_A, W_B and W_C. M(W_A, W_B) is the customized duplicate matcher for W_A and W_B, and an example rule requires *title* similarity of two duplicate records is larger than 0.85. The threshold is high due to the

L. Chen et al. (Eds.): WAIM 2010, LNCS 6184, pp. 5–17, 2010.

W_A

Title	Actor	Director	...
E T the Extra Terrestrial	Henry Thomas	Steven Spielberg	...

W_B

Title	Actor	Genre	...
E T the Extra Terrestrial	Henry Thomas	Sci-Fi	...

W_C

Title	Actor	Genre	...
E T	H Thomas	Fantasy, Sci-Fi	...

M(W_A, W_B)

title	actor	...
>0.85	>0.9	...

Fig. 1. An example to illustrate the limitation of most traditional approaches

full *titles* given by W_A and W_B. But M(W_A, W_B) is not applicable for W_C and W_B because the *title* similarity is smaller than the threshold though the two records are matched in fact. More importantly, the new shared attribute, *genre*, cannot be handled by M(W_A, W_B). As a result, M(W_A, W_C) and M(W_B, W_C) have to be built. Several works[5][13] have realized this fact, and they try to select the best matching technique or combine multiple matching algorithms to improve matching performance. But it is a challenging problem to build and maintain the library of matching algorithm and select the optimal one.

In this paper, we study the problem of duplicate identification over multiple web databases. There are a large number of web databases in one domain and usually lots of web databases are integrated, and it is not practical to build and maintenance lots of matchers. The proposed approach is based on two interesting observations. First, the presentation variations of an attribute are finite, which means an instance of it can be transformed into other forms according to some variation rules(e.g. the person name "Jim Gray" has limited variations, such as "J. Gray", "Gray J.".). Second, there exists similarity dependency among attributes, i.e. the similarity of one attribute can be improved by the similarities of other attributes. For example, if having known the actors and the publication dates of two movie records are same, we are more certain the titles are same too. However, previous works only calculate the attribute similarity independently without considering their dependency.

In summary, the contributions of this paper are present as follows. First, we believe this is the first attempt to build one matcher for multiple web databases, which is an interesting issue in deep Web data integration. Second, we identify the similarity dependencies among attributes, and proposed an inference-based method to improve the record similarity by exploiting the similarity dependencies. Third, an efficient approach is proposed to building the universal matcher, which can greatly reduce the cost of manual labeling.

The rest of this paper is organized as follows. Section 2 introduces the variation rules to handle various representations of attribute values, and further give the uniform representation of record similarity. An inference-based method to improve the record similarity is described in Section 3. Section 4 introduces the approach of building the universal matcher. Section 5 presents the experiments. Section 6 contains the related works. Section 7 is the conclusion.

2 Uniform Representation for Attribute Similarity and Record Similarity

This section first presents the variation rules of attributes, and then gives the uniform representation of record similarity based on the variation rules.

Table 1. Classification of variation rules

Classification	Rule	Example
Character Level Rules	*Prefix*	"Johnson" vs. "J."
	Suffix	"2008" vs. "08"
	Prefix+Suffix	"Dept" vs. "Department"
	Plural	"university" vs. "universities"
Token Level Rules	*Prefixes Concatenation*	"Caltech" vs. "California Institute of Technology"
	Acronym	"UCSD" vs. "University of California, San Diego"
	Subsequence	"Java 2 Bible" vs. "Java 2 (JSEE 1.4) Bible"
	Rearrangement	"2/18/2008" vs. "18/2/2008"
Semantic Level Rules	*Synonymy*	"Automobile" vs. "Car"
	Hypernymy/Hyponymy	"Vehicle" vs. "Car"

2.1 Variation Rules

Different representations would be found for the same object from different web databases. A number of methods have been developed to calculate the attribute similarity by assigning a 0-1 real number. Such real-value based approaches are not applicable for our task , just like the example shown in Fig.1. Therefore, a uniform similarity metric is needed to represent the attribute similarity. In fact, the presentations of an attribute follow finite variation rules. We summarize and classify all the observed variation rules in Table 1, and the examples are also given.

For each attribute, one or several rules are assigned to it by domain experts. For instance, four rules, "*Prefix*", "*Acronym*", "*Subsequence*" and "*Rearrangement*", are assigned to the person name related attributes(e.g. "actor" and "director") in movie domain. Though being a manual task, the assignments are universal and stable on domain level. In practice, assigning rules to about 25 popular attributes in one domain is enough because the "rare" attributes have little contribution.

2.2 Representations of Attribute Similarity and Record Similarity

An important characteristic of our approach is using three logic values (Yes, Maybe and No) instead of 0-1 real values to represent attribute similarity. Different to the probabilistic-based approaches, the three logic values are based on the variation rules defined below (suppose v_1 and v_2 are two compared values):

(1) YES (Y). If v_1 and v_2 are absolutely same, their similarity is "YES".
(2) MAYBE (M). If v_1 and v_2 are not same, but $v_1$could be transformed into v_2 using the assigned variation rules. For example, "John Smith" can be transformed into "S. John" with "*Rearrangement*" and "*Prefix*" rules. In this situation, it is uncertain whether v_1 and v_2 are the same semantic, and "MAYBE" is labeled.
(3) NO (N). If v_1 cannot be transformed into v_2 by applying the assigned rules, "NO" is labeled, such as "John Smith" and "S. Jensen".

Based on the three logic values, attribute similarity can be represented as "Y", "M" or "N". And record similarity can be represented as $S(r_1, r_2) = \{<a_1, s_1>,<a_2, s_2>,\ldots,<a_k, s_k>\}$, where a_i $(1 \le i \le k)$ are their shared attributes, and $s_i \in \{Y, M, N\}$ Table 2 shows an example to illustrate the representation of record similarity.

Table 2. An example of record similarity

	Title	Actor	Director	Publication date
r_1	E.T.: The Extra-Terrestrial	Henry Thomas	S. Spielberg	1982
r_2	E.T.	Henry Thomas	Steven Spielberg	1982
$S(r_1, r_2)$	M	Y	M	Y

3 Record Similarity Improvement

"M" is the obstacle to duplicate identification, and it must be "Y" or "N" in fact. Hence, if "M" is transformed into "Y" or "N" with more evidences, duplicates can be identified more accurately. Existing approaches do not catch sight of the inherent similarity dependency among attributes. In this section, we first propose the concept of attribute similarity dependency and then present a novel method to improve record similarity by using Markov Logic Networks to exploit the attribute similarity dependency.

3.1 Attribute Similarity Dependency

Table 3. Several examples to illustrate the attribute similarity dependency

First-logic Formulas	Weights(importance)
Y(actor) ∧ Y(publication date) ∧ M(director) → Y(director)	3.872
Y(director) ∧ Y(publication date) ∧ M(title) → Y(title)	3.551
Y(director) ∧ Y(actor) ∧ M(genre) → Y(genre)	2.394

Previous approaches do not give insight into attribute similarity dependency. Actually, there exists potential similarity dependency among attributes. For example, it is difficult to determine the titles of the two records in Table 2 are same no matter which current similarity function is applied. But intuitively, we will be sure the titles are same if having known both actors and publication dates are same.

Definition. *Attribute similarity dependency.* We say the similarity on attribute a_0 is dependent of those on attributes $\{a_1,\ldots,a_m\}$ *iff* $P(a_0 = s_0) \neq P(a_0 = s_0 | a_1 = s_1, \ldots, a_m = s_m)$ Where $s_i \in \{Y, M, N\}$ denotes the similarity on a_i. Otherwise, the attribute a_0 is independent of attributes $\{a_1,\ldots,a_m\}$.

In fact, this is an interactive and propagating process. Table 3 shows three examples which are represented in form of the first-logic formulas to illustrate this process. Formula 1 means the similarity M on *director* can be improved to Y if the similarities on *actor* and *publication date* are Y. As we have seen, Formula 1 and Formula 2 illustrate the interactive process, while Formula 1 and Formula 2 illustrate the propagating process. To discover attribute similarity dependency, we employ Markov Logic Networks(MLNs)[11] to model the graph-like dependency. The basic concept of MLNs is introduced first, and then the method of exploiting the attribute similarity dependency using this model is presented.

3.2 Markov Logic Networks

MLNs are a combination of probabilistic graph model and first-order logic to handle the uncertainty in the real world. In a first-order logic, if a world violates one constraint it will have probability zero. MLNs soften the constraints of the first-order logic. If a world violates one formula it is less probable, but not impossible. Thus, MLNs is a more sound framework since the real world is full of uncertainty and violation. In MLNs, each formula has an associated weight to show its importance: higher the weight is, the greater the difference in log probability between a world that satisfies the formula.

MLNs is a template for constructing Markov Network [10]. With a set of formulas and constants, MLNs define a Markov network with one node per ground atom and one feature per ground formula. The probability of a state x in such a network is:

$$P(X = x) = \frac{1}{Z} \prod_i \emptyset_i (x_{\{i\}})^{n_i\{x\}} \tag{1}$$

where Z is a normalization constant, $n_i(x)$ is the number of true groundings of formula F_i in x, $x_{\{i\}}$ is the state of the atoms appearing in F_i, and $\emptyset_i(x_{\{i\}}) = e^{wi}$, w_i is the weight of F_i. Eq. (1) is a generative MLNs model, that is, it defines the joint probability of all the predicates. More details of MLNs is discussed in [11].

3.3 Automatic Formulas Generation

The formulas of first-order logic are constructed using four types of symbols: constants, variables, functions, and predicates. The predications are the three logic values {Y, M, N}. The constants are the attributes of one domain. In existing works(e.g. [19]), the formulas of MLNs are written manually by experts. It is time-consuming and difficult to find the important formulas. Alternatively, we generate formulas automatically based on the following formula templates.

Thus, the formula templates in a given domain can be represented as the following form:

$$\forall a_0, a_1 \ldots, a_m \ \mathrm{Y}(a_1) \wedge \mathrm{Y}(a_2) \ldots \wedge \mathrm{Y}(a_m) \wedge \mathrm{M}(a_0) \rightarrow \mathrm{Y}(a_0) \quad (2)$$

where a_i is an attribute, m is the number of attributes are involved in this formula. The example formulas shown in Table 2 are generated with the formula templates, and their weights are trained with MLNs. A large number of formulas will be produced by Eq. (2)

The dependencies of two attributes are found first, then the dependencies of i attributes are found by extending the dependencies of i-1 attributes. The whole process of the formulas generation includes two stages. In the first stage, all formulas involving two attributes, such as $\forall x_1\ A_i(x_1) \wedge A_j(M) \rightarrow A_j(Y)\ (i \neq j)$, are exhausted as the initial formula set, and further, weights are assigned by MLNs through training. In the second stage, high-weight(>1) formulas are selected, and the two formulas whose query predicates are same are merged into one two-evidence-predicate formula. And further three-evidence-predicate formulas are generated by merging two-evidence-predicate formulas and one-evidence-predicate formulas.

4 Efficient Approach to Building Universal Matcher

In the traditional way, the training set for n web databases is times the training set for two web databases. It is not practical to label such large a training set. To reduce the labeling cost, this section proposes an efficient approach for building the universal matcher for n web databases.

The basic idea of our approach is that, given n web databases $\{W_1, W_2, \ldots, W_n\}$, the initial matcher is built for W_1 and W_2, and then it is evolved into a new one when W_3 is incorporated. The evolvement process stops until all web databases have been incorporated. The flowchart of building the universal matcher is shown in Fig. 2, which consists of three stages. The rest of this section introduces them in turn.

4.1 Training Set Generation

Two types of training sets are generated: labeled training set for Stage II and unlabeled training set for Stage III. The labeled training set is the record pairs that have been labeled as matched or not. For each record pair, one record is from W_1 and the other is from W_2. For each record pair in the unlabeled training set, two records are from different web databases except W_1 and W_2. All the record pairs have been processed by the uniform representation component and the record similarity improvement component and transformed into the form of the example shown in Table 1.

4.2 Initial Matcher Building

An initial matcher is built with the labeled training set for W_1 and W_2. We still use MLNs to build the initial matcher. The evidence predicates are the shared attributes of the two web databases, and the only query predicate is the match decision for the record pairs. The formulas can be represented as follows:

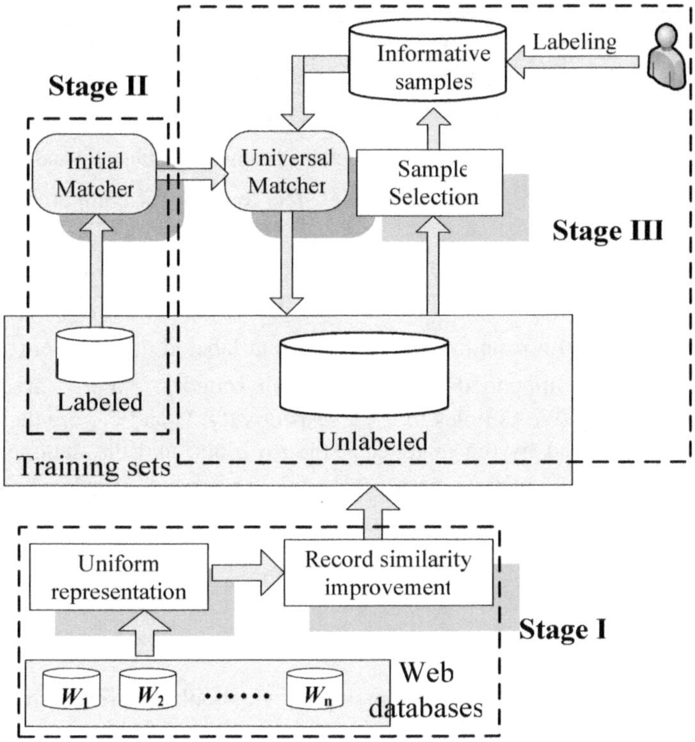

Fig. 2. Flowchart of building universal matcher

$$\forall x_1, x_2 \ldots, x_m, r_1, r_2 \quad S_1(a_1) \wedge S_2(a_2) \ldots \wedge S_m(a_m) \rightarrow \text{Match}(r_1, r_2) \tag{3}$$

where a_i is an attribute of the two records shared, $S_i \in \{Y, M, N\}$. The record pair (r_1,r_2) is matched if Match(r_1,r_2) is true, otherwise not matched. Considering the efficiency, the low-weight formulas (say, less than 0.3) can be pruned at this stage because they have little contributions to the performance.

4.3 Matcher Evolving

When the initial matcher has been built, it still cannot get a better performance over all web databases because the labeled training set is only from W_1 and W_2. We propose an evolving strategy to reduce the labeling cost. As shown in Fig. 3, the evolving strategy is a cycle process. In each round, some informative samples are selected automatically by the current matcher and are labeled. And then the matcher is improved with the labeled record pairs. The process stops until the matcher cannot be improved anymore.

In this process, the key issue is how to automatically select the informative samples from the unlabeled training set for labeling. The informative samples can be classified into two types. The first type is the record pairs that contain new attributes, and the second type is the ones that cannot be determined with a high probability. The first type are easy to detect. For the second type, a sample is selected if its probability assigned by the current matcher is in the range $[1-\alpha, \alpha]$ $(0.5 < \alpha < 1)$, which means this sample cannot be determined by the current matcher with high probabilities. To avoid too many samples are labeled in each round, at the *t*+1th round is computed using at the *t*th round. The matcher at the first round is the initial matcher obtained in Stage II, and at the second round is set as 0.65 based on the experience. The formula for computing at the *t*+1th round is:

$$\alpha_{t+1} = \alpha_t + \frac{\sum_{s_i^+ \in TS_{lab}}(P_t(s_i^+) - P_{t-1}(s_i^+)) + \sum_{s_i^- \in TS_{lab}}(P_{t-1}(s_i^-) - P_t(s_i^-))}{|TS_{lab}|} \quad (4)$$

where α_t are α at the *t*th round, TS_{lab} is the current labeled training set (because some labeled samples are appended to TS_{lab} in each round), and are the positive samples and the negative samples of TS_{lab} respectively, P_t and P_{t-1} are the probabilities of an sample predicted by the matcher at the *t*th round and the matcher at the *t*-1th round respectively. When $\alpha_{t+1} < \alpha_t$, the evolving process stops, which means the current matcher be improved when more samples are labeled.

5 Experiments

5.1 Experiment Setup

Our data set includes three popular domains: movie, book, and research paper.
For each domain, we select five popular web databases. Table 4 shows the details about the date set. The records in the data set are extracted by the customized

Table 4. The Data Set used in the Experiments

Domain	Web database	URL	The number of records
Movie	IMDB	uk.imdb.com	62793
	Yahoo	movies.yahoo.com	10288
	the-numbers	www.the-numbers.com	5486
	aol	movies.aol.com	6541
	listentoamovie	power.listentoamovie.com	554
Book	Amazon	www.amazon.com	18623
	abebooks	www.abebooks.com	10039
	Bookpool	www.bookpool.com	3881
	collinsbooks	www.collinsbooks.com.au	2020
	Chapters	www.chapters.indigo.ca	1051
Research paper	DBLP	dblp.uni-trier.de/xml	38738
	Libra	libra.msra.cn	3459
	ACM	portal.acm.org	2738
	citeseer	citeseer.ist.psu.edu	1207
	springer	www.springerlink.com	189

wrappers for the web databases. The whole data set is divided into two parts averagely. One is as the training set, and the other is as the test set.

We use traditional *precision*, *recall* and *F-measure* metrics to evaluate our solution. precision is defined as the ratio of the total number of correctly matched record pairs and the total number of matched record pairs, and *recall* is defined as the total number of correctly matched record pairs and the total number of actual matched record pairs. *F-measure* is the harmonic mean of *precision* and *recall.*

5.2 Performance

The performance of our approach is evaluated on the three domains respectively, and the order of web databases coincides with the order shown in Table 2. We also implemented a rule-based matcher as the baseline for comparison, i.e., , one rule like that in Fig. 1 for each domain is trained. For the attributes of person name and organization, the *Smith*-Waterman *distance* algorithm [15] is adopted. For other attributes, the traditional edit distance is adopted. We use the popular tool Weka to learn the thresholds of the attributes. The experimental results are shown in Fig. 5. We explain the experimental results on two aspects. (1) The performance of our approach is much better than the rule-based approach on all the three measures. This proves our approach is superior than existing solutions to perform duplicate identification for multiple web databases. (2) The performance in research paper domain is better than those in other two domains. The main reason is that spelling errors in research paper domain are much less than the other two domains. Since once a spelling error occurs, the attribute similarity is "N", and the duplicates this record will have little chance to be matched.

Table 5. The performances comparison between the rule-based approach and our approach

		Our approach	**rule-based approach**
precision	Book	92.7%	57.3%
	Movie	93.5%	68.7%
	Research paper	96.8%	78.4%
recall	Book	85.3%	42.9%
	Movie	88.4%	59.1%
	Research paper	91.2%	73.5%
F	Book	88.8%	48.7%
	Movie	90.9%	63.5%
	Research paper	93.4%	75.9%
AVG-F		91.0%	62.7%

5.3 Evaluation of Record Similarity Improvement

The goal of this experiment is to evaluate the contribution of record similarity improvement to the performance of the matcher. We turned off the record similarity improvement component is and then carry out the experiment again. As it can be seen from Fig. 3, the performance can improved greatly by the record similarity improvement component in all the three domains(especially book domain).

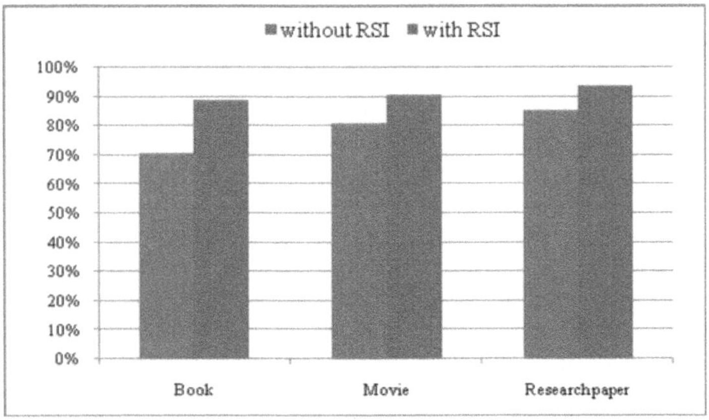

Fig. 3. Evaluation results of record similarity improvement(RSI) on *F measure*

5.4 Labeling Cost

In this part, we evaluate the labeling cost during the evolving process. Fig. 4 shows the labeling costs on the three domains. y axis refers to the number of labeled samples. From the experimental results indicate that the number of labeled samples drops significantly as the evolving rounds increasing. When the evolving rounds are more than 9, no samples need labeling for research paper domain (the evolving process stops), while only about 100 samples are required to label for other two domains. In addition, the curve of book domain is not as regular as those of other two domains. This phenomenon is caused by two reasons. The first reason is spelling errors occurs in this domain, and it is useless for improving the matcher even if a spelling-error record pair is labeled,. Second, the involved attributes of unlabeled training set contain some new ones compared to those of labeled training set, which makes more samples be labeled at the first time of the evolving process.

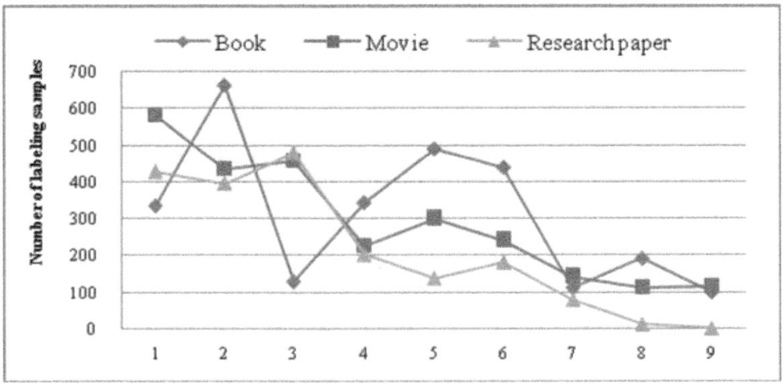

Fig. 4. Trend of the labeling cost during the evolving process

5.5 Scalability

Our ultimate goal is "one matcher, one domain", i.e. only one duplicate identification matcher is competent for one domain. In this way, no training is needed when new web databases are incorporated. To verify this hypothesis, we use the record pairs from W_1, W_2, W_3 and W_4 as the training set to build the matcher, and the test set is the record pairs in which one record is from W_5 and the other is from W_1, W_2, W_3 or W_4. In this way, W_5 can be viewed as the new incorporated web database. The experimental results in Fig. 5 are very close to those in Table 5. This indicates that the matcher can still achieve a good performance without training when a new web database(W_5) is incorporated.

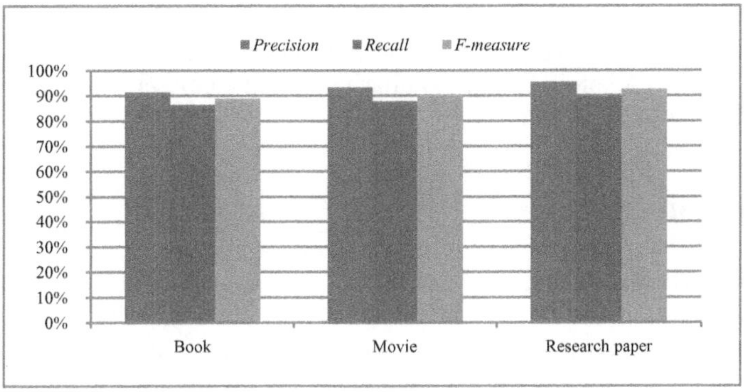

Fig. 5. The experimental results on robustness

6 Related Work

Duplication identification has been a thriving area of data integration surveyed in [9] and [7]. Previous researches mainly focused on similarity functions. They can be classified into two kinds according to the tasks they engaged in.

Attribute similarity. The most common reason of mismatches is the presentation variations of shared attributes. Therefore, duplicate detection typically relies on string comparison techniques to deal with presentation variations. Multiple methods have been developed for this task. Edit distance and its variations [9], jaccard similarity, tf-idf based cosine similarity [10] are the most popular similarity functions. Some of them are semantic-specific, such as the Jaro distance [6] and Jaro Winkler distance [7] for person names, and functions used by tools such as Trillium [8] for addresses.

Duplicate identification. The records usually consist of multiple attributes, making the duplicate detection problem more complicated. There are multiple techniques for duplicate detection, such as Bayesian-inference based techniques[16], active-learning based techniques[2], distance based techniques[4], rule based approaches[8], etc. A recent trend is to investigate algorithms that compute the similarity join exactly. Recent advances include inverted index-based methods[14], prefix filtering-based techniques[3,18], and signature-based methods[1]. Most of them focused on designing an appropriate similarity function. However, no similarity function can conciliate all presentation variations of an entity(record). Bayesian-inference-based techniques are the most similar approach with ours. They also represent record similarity as a vector $\{x_1,x_2,\ldots,x_n\}$ on the shared attributes, and 0 and 1 are used to denote the similarity on x_i. So assigning 0 or 1 to x_i properly is the basis of this approach. But in the context of deep web integration, many web databases will incur more presentation variations, which makes this task very challenging and further impacts on the accuracy of inference. Our approach supplements "Maybe" to accept the uncertainty and eliminate the uncertainty as far as possible by exploring the similarity dependency among attributes.

Overall, our solution includes both the two tasks above, and the closely coupled solutions are proposed for them respectively. The main differences of our solution and previous works are on two aspects. First, we put forward three logic values coupled with predefined variation rules instead of traditional similarity functions. Second, we first discover and exploiting the similarity dependency among attributes, while previous works loose insight of this.

7 Conclusion

In this paper, we studied the duplicate identification problem in the context of deep web data integration. The proposed solution can build one universal matcher for multiple web databases in one domain instead of ones. We believe this is the first try to address the duplicate identification problem by building one universal matcher. Our solution shows better performance when web databases have little spell errors and have rich schemas.

Acknowledgement

This work was supported in part by the China Postdoctoral Science Foundation funded project under grant 20080440256 and 200902014, NSFC (60833005 and 60875033), National High-tech R&D Program (2009AA011904 and 2008AA01Z421), the Doctoral Fund of Ministry of Education of China (200800020002), and National Development and Reform Commission High-tech Program of China (2008-2441). The authors would also like to express their gratitude to the anonymous reviewers for providing some very helpful suggestions.

References

1. Arasu, A., Ganti, V., Kaushik, R.: Efficient exact set-similarity joins. In: VLDB 2006 (2006)
2. Bilenko, M., Mooney, R.J., Cohen, W.W.: Adaptive Name Matching in Information Integration. IEEE Intelligent Systems 18(5) (2003)
3. Bayardo, R.J., Ma, Y.: Scaling up all pairs similarity search. In: WWW 2007 (2007)

4. Cohen, W.W.: Data Integration Using Similarity Joins and a Word-Based Information Representation Language. ACM Trans. Information Systems (3) (2000)
5. Chaudhuri, S., Chen, B., Ganti, V.: Example-driven design of efficient record matching queries. In: VLDB 2007 (2007)
6. Chang, K.C., He, B., Li, C., Patel, M., Zhang, Z.: Structured Databases on the web: Observations and Implications. SIGMOD Record 33(3) (2004)
7. Elmagarmid, A.K., Ipeirotis, P.G., Verykios, V.S.: Duplicate record detection: A survey. IEEE Trans. Knowl. Data Eng. 19(1) (2007)
8. Galhardas, H., Florescu, D., Shasha, D., Simon, E., Saita, C.: Declarative Data Cleaning: Language, Model, and Algorithms. In: VLDB 2001 (2001)
9. Koudas, N., Sarawagi, S., Srivastava, D.: Record linkage: similarity measures and algorithms. In: SIGMOD 2006 (2006)
10. Poon, H., Domingos, P.: Joint inference in information extraction. In: AAAI 2007 (2007)
11. Richardson, M., Domingos, P.: Markov logic networks. Machine Learning 62(1-2) (2006)
12. `http://www.cs.utexas.edu/users/ml/riddle/index.html`
13. Shen, W., DeRose, P., Vu, L.: Source-aware Entity Matching: A Compositional Approach. In: ICDE 2007 (2007)
14. Sarawagi, S., Kirpal, A.: Efficient set joins on similarity predicates. In: SIGMOD (2004)
15. Smith, T.-F., Waterman, M.-S.: Identification of common molecular subsequences. Journal of Molecular Biology (1981)
16. Winkler, W.E.: Methods for Record Linkage and Bayesian Networks. Technical Report Statistical Research Report Series RRS2002/05, US Bureau of the Census (2002)
17. Winkler, W.E.: The state of record linkage and current research problems. US Bureau of Census (1999)
18. Xiao, C., Wang, W., Lin, X.: Efficient similarity joins for near duplicate detection. In: WWW 2008 (2008)

Learning to Detect Web Spam by Genetic Programming

Xiaofei Niu[1,3], Jun Ma[1,*], Qiang He[1], Shuaiqiang Wang[2], and Dongmei Zhang[1,3]

[1] School of Computer Science and Technology, Shandong University, Jinan 250101, China
[2] Department of Computer Science, Texas State University, San Marcos, US
[3] School of Computer Science & Technology of Shandong Jianzhu University, Shandong 250101, China
xiaofein@sdjzu.edu.cn, majun@sdu.edu.cn

Abstract. Web spam techniques enable some web pages or sites to achieve undeserved relevance and importance. They can seriously deteriorate search engine ranking results. Combating web spam has become one of the top challenges for web search. This paper proposes to learn a discriminating function to detect web spam by genetic programming. The evolution computation uses multi-populations composed of some small-scale individuals and combines the selected best individuals in every population to gain a possible best discriminating function. The experiments on WEBSPAM-UK2006 show that the approach can improve spam classification recall performance by 26%, F-measure performance by 11%, and accuracy performance by 4% compared with SVM.

Keywords: Web Spam; Information Retrieval; Genetic Programming; Machine Learning.

1 Introduction

With the explosive growth of information on the web, search engine has become an important tool to help people find their desired information in daily lives. The page ranking is highly important in the search engine design. So some techniques are employed to enable some web pages or sites to achieve undeserved relevance and importance. All the deceptive actions that try to increase the ranking of a page illogically are generally referred to as Web spam [1]. People who make spam are called spammers. A spam page is a page that is either made by spammer or receives a substantial amount score for its ranking from other spam pages. Web spam seriously deteriorates search engine ranking results. Detecting web spam is considered as one of the top challenges in the research of web search engines.

Web spam can be broadly classified into term (content) spam and link spam [2]. Term spam refers to deliberate changes in the content of special HTML text fields in the pages in order to make spam pages relevant to some queries. Link spam refers to unfairly gaining a high ranking on search engines for a web page by means of trickily manipulating the link graph to confuse the hyper-link structure analysis algorithms. Previous work on web spam identification mostly focused on these two categories.

* Corresponding author.

L. Chen et al. (Eds.): WAIM 2010, LNCS 6184, pp. 18–27, 2010.

In the previous research, Ntoulas et al. [3] proposed to detect spam pages by building up a classification model which combines multiple heuristics based on page content analysis. Gyongyi et al. [4] proposed the TrustRank algorithm to separate normal pages from spam. Their work was followed by much effort in spam page link analysis such as Anti-Trust Rank [5] and Truncated PageRank [1]. C. Castillo et al. [6], which is the first paper that integrates link and content attributes to build a system to detect Web spam, extracted transformed link-based features with PageRank, TrustRank , and Truncated PageRank etc. G. G. Geng et al.[7] proposed a predicted spamicity-based ensemble under-sampling strategy for spamdexing detection. Within this strategy, many existing learning algorithms, such as C4.5, bagging and adaboost, can be applied; distinguishing information involved in the massive reputable websites were fully explored and solved the class-imbalance problem well. Yiqun Liu et al. [8] proposed three user behavior features to separate web spam from ordinary ones. Na Dai et al. [9] used content features from historical versions of web pages to improve spam classification.

However, once a type of spam is detected and banned, usually new Web spam techniques will be created instantly. Therefore to study how to detect Web spam automatically based on machine learning is very meaningful. In this paper we discuss how to detect web spam by Genetic Programming (GP) [10]. Since GP has been used in binary classification problem [11], it inspires us to use GP to detect Web spam because detecting Web spam is a special binary classification, where Web pages are labeled spam or normal.

We define an individual as a discriminating function for detecting Web spam. The individuals are evolved based on the feature values of training set of the Web pages. Further the individuals are combined based on GP to generate an optimized discriminant for Web spam detection. We study the key techniques in using GP to detect Web Spam, which include the representation of individual, e.g. the architecture and the GP operation in an individual, the features of Web pages that can be used in detecting Web spam and using multi-populations and combination to generate the discriminating function, where we study the effect of the depth of the binary trees representing the individual in the GP evolution process and the efficiency of the combination. We carried out the experiments on WEBSPAM-UK2006 to evaluate the validity of the approach. The experimental results show that the new method can improve spam classification recall performance by 26%, F-measure performance by 11%, and accuracy performance by 4% compared with SVM.

2 GP Adapted to Web Spam Detection

2.1 Individual Representation and Population

Usually the tree-based structure is used to represent genetic programs [10]. In this paper we let an individual be represented as a binary tree. We use two kinds of terminals: feature terminals and numeric/constant terminals. Feature terminals are the transformed link-based features of a web spam, such as log of in-degree, log of out-degree/pagerank and so on. Constants are 11 predefined floating numbers which are 0.0, 0.1, 0.2, 0.3, 0.4, 0.5, 0.6, 0.7, 0.8, 0.9, 1.0. The internal nodes denote the simple arithmetic operations, which include $\{+, -, \times, \div\}$. The $+$, $-$, and $\times$ operators have their usual meanings, while ÷ represents "protected" division, which is the usual division operator except that a divide by zero gives a result of zero. Although we can use more operators, e.g. *log, sin, cos* etc al, it is shown that the classification accuracy of using only simple arithmetic operators is sufficient to achieve high accuracy and using simple operators is capable of reducing computation cost [12]. In fact we did the experiment to verify the assumption in our experiment, where results show that the linear function is better than non-linear function for web spam dataset. Therefore we only use the four arithmetic operators.

Unlike decision trees that are used in data classification, e.g., ID3, C4.5 [3], GP algorithms do not directly construct a solution to a problem, but rather search for a solution in a space of possible solutions. That means that some of the individuals in a population may not be able to detect spam pages accurately, however it is well known since GP can search the space to find an optimal solution in its evolution process, the final output will be a discriminative function based on the features of example data with high probability.

The output of an individual in the standard tree-based GP system is a floating point number. In our approach for web spam detection, a population *P* is a set of individuals and denoted as $p = \{I_1, I_2, \hbar\ , I_{|p|}\}$, and for a given instance *x* and an individual *I*, we consider that *I* recognizes *x* as spam if $I(x) \geq 0$, otherwise normal.

2.2 The Features of Web Pages Considered in Web Spam Detection

The features used in our experiments are the 138 transformed link-based features [7], which are the simple combination or logarithm operation of the link-based features. The 138 features can be divided into five categories: *Degree-related features*, *PageRank-related features, TrustRank-related features, Truncated PageRank-related features* and *Supporter-related features.*

2.3 Mutation Rate and Crossover Rate

The genetic operators used in our experiments are reproduction, crossover, and mutation. They are performed according to predefined rates R_r, R_c and R_m. The reproduction operator keeps several selected individuals alive to the next generation. It mimics the natural principle of survival of the fittest. The crossover operator consists in taking two individuals from *p*, selecting a subtree from each individual randomly and exchanging the two selected subtrees to generate two new individuals. The mutation operator was implemented in such a way that a randomly selected subtree is replaced by a new tree also created randomly.

Because the mutation operator can generate individuals with new structures that have never occurred on existing individuals, it is mainly used to escape local optimum. If R_m is too high, the population tends to generate diverse individuals instead of discovering solutions from present individuals. If R_m is too low, individuals may not have sufficient opportunity to mutate and the diversity is limited. In our experiments, (R_m, R_c) is initialized to (0.2,0.8). In the *g*th generation, if the ratio of the fitness value of the best individual f_{max} to the average fitness value of all individuals $f_{average}$ is less than 2, R_m and R_c are tuned by formula 1, otherwise, R_m and R_c are not changed[13].

$$(R_m, R_c) = \begin{cases} \left(\frac{\alpha}{R_c + \alpha}, 1 - \frac{\alpha}{R_c + \alpha}\right) & \frac{f_{\max}}{f_{average}} < 2 \\ (R_m, R_c) & \text{otherwise} \end{cases} \tag{1}$$

where $\alpha = R_m \times (\frac{R_c}{R_m})^{g/G}$ and G is the maximum generation.

3 Multi-population GP and Combination

Traditionally, GP works with a single population. Recently it is shown that Multi-population GP (MGP) is better than single GP in terms of finding the optimal solution [14]. Therefore we adopt MGP in finding the optimal discriminating function for detecting spam pages. It is pointed out that it is difficult to know the proper length of an individual before finding an optimal solution [13]. Different from the normal definition of the depth of trees, the length of an individual is defined as the maximum number of available nodes of the individual. It is because the definition is more suitable according to the heuristic or empirical assumptions based on previous research. Since a long function can be viewed as a composition of a number of small GP solutions, we generate an optimal solution by the combination of sub-solutions, i.e. we make use of multi-populations composed of some small-scale individuals and combine the selected best individual in every population to gain better result.

Table 1 shows an example of the combination where F stands for features and H stands for Hosts. At first, we employ GP with two populations in which the depth of the individual is 3 and get two best discriminative functions F_1-F_4 (The first best)and F_2-(F_3+F_5)(The second Best). From Table 1, the accuracy of the first best function is 60% and the accuracy of the second best function is 80%, but the accuracy of the combination of the two best discriminating functions (F_1-F_4)+ (F_2-(F_3+F_5)) is 100%. As a result, it is likely that the combination might prove effective.

Table 1. An example of Combination

T	F1	F2	F3	F4	F5	class	First Best	Second Best	Combination
H1	0.8	0.67	0.1	0.1	0.2	Spam	0.7	0.37	1.07
H2	0.1	0.5	0.8	0.1	0.5	Normal	0	-0.8	-0.8
H3	0.6	1.14	0.7	0.9	0.3	Normal	-0.3	0.14	-0.16
H4	0.9	1	0.1	0.1	0.2	Spam	0.8	0.7	1.5
H5	1.4	0.86	0.6	0.8	0.9	Normal	0.6	-0.64	-0.04

4 The Fitness Function

The fitness function F(I_j) of an individual I_j is denoted by $Accu\ (I_j, T)$.

$$Accu(I_j, T) = \frac{\text{the number of examples of } T \text{ that are correctly classified by } I_j}{|T|} \tag{2}$$

where T is a data set. The best individual produced by a population P is denoted as BI.

5 The Evolution Computation Algorithm

The evolution algorithm is a revised basic GP with multi-populations. The Vector Space Model is used to represent every page. We let T denote the training data set, N_p be the total number of populations; the number of individuals and the maximum generation of every population are stored in array $N[N_p]$ and $G[N_p]$ respectively; K is the maximum depth of the binary trees which represent the individuals; C is the times of the combination for the found possible best individuals; N_{pc}, $Nc[N_{pc}]$, $Gc[N_{pc}]$ are the corresponding parameters of the cth combination ($1 \le c \le C$). Then the process of GP evolution can be described as follows.

Algorithm 1 (The evolution for finding the possible discriminating function)
Input: T, C, N_p, K, $N[N_p]$, $G[N_p]$
N_{pc}, $Nc[N_{pc}]$, $Gc[N_{pc}]$ of the cth combination($1 \le c \le C$)
Output: The best individual BI as the discriminating function.

(1) i=0.
(2) Initialize population P_i with randomly generated individuals according to $N[i]$ and K; let g=0, R_m=0.2 , R_c=0.8; generate an empty population P' and an empty set S.
(3) Calculate the fitness value $F(I_t)$ of every individual $I_t \in P_i$ with T.
(4) Perform genetic operators:
  (4.1) Perform reproduction operator: Compare the fitness values of the individuals in P_i and put two best individuals into P'.
  (4.2) Compute the average fitness value of all individuals in P_i and find $\max\{F(I_b) | I_b \in P_i\}$, then tune R_m and R_c according to formula 1.
  (4.3) Select the crossover or mutation operator according to R_m and R_c.
  (4.4) If $|P'|=N[i]$-1 or the mutation is selected, then perform mutation operator on a randomly selected individual, calculate the fitness value for the mutant and compare its fitness value with that of the selected individual, and put the better individual into P'.
  (4.5) If the crossover is selected and $|P'|< N[i]$-1, then perform crossover operator on selected two individuals and evaluate the fitness values of the two newly generated individuals. Compare their fitness values with those of the two selected individuals and put the best two individuals to P'.
  (4.6) Continue to perform step (4.3)-(4.5) if $|P'|< N[i]$.
(5) Store the best individual of this generation BI_g. Let $P_i = P'$, $P'=\Phi$, g=g+1.
(6) If g<$G[i]$, then repeat (3)-(5).
(7) Output $BI_j(0 \le j < G[i])$ to be the result of the population P_i if $F(BI_j)$ is equal to $\max\{F(BI_j) | 0 \le j < G[i]\}$. Let $S = S \cup BI_j$, i=i+1.
(8) if $i< N_p$, then repeat (2)-(7).
(9) Combine the best individual in every population as following if C>0
  (9.1) Let c=1.
  (9.2) With individuals in S as new features, compute a new instance e_m' for every instance e_m in T; $T'=\{ e_m' | 1 \le m \le |T|\}$
  (9.3) Let $T = T'$, $N_p=N_{pc}$, $N[N_p]=Nc[N_{pc}]$, $G[N_p]=Gc[N_{pc}]$, then repeat (1)-(8).
  (9.4) Let c=c+1
  (9.5) If c≤C, repeat (9.2)-(9.4).

Algorithm 1 is an iterative process. Starting with a labeled training data set *T*, the algorithm generates N_p populations. All initial individuals in the *i*th population are randomly generated by the ramped half-and-half method [11].

After all individuals in the *i*th population are evaluated by the fitness function, the algorithm evolves the *i*th population by applying genetic operators in order to generate the best individual of the *i*th population. As a result, there are N_p individuals. Then we can combine N_p individuals using GP to gain better discriminating functions. In the *c*th combination process, the first step is to figure out a new instance for each instance in *T* with the above N_p individuals as new features, thus all the new instances can make up of a new data set T'; the next step is to repeat step (1)-(8) according to T' and the corresponding parameters N_{pc}, $Nc[N_{pc}]$, $Gc[N_{pc}]$. We can continue to perform the next combination on the basis of the above combined result. Please note that N_p should be assigned to 1 in the last combination because we need a possible best discriminating function finally. When the single population GP is executed, *C* and N_{pc} should be assigned to 0 and N_p should be assigned to 1.

6 Experiments

6.1 Data Set

In our experiments, we use the publicly available WEBSPAM-UK2006 dataset [15]. It is based on a set of pages obtained from a crawler of the .uk domain. The set includes 77.9 million pages, corresponding to 11402 hosts, among which over 8000 hosts have been labeled as "spam", "non-spam(normal)" or "borderline". We use the labeled hosts in webspam-uk2006-set1-labels –DomainOrTwoHumans.txt and webspam-uk2006-set2-labels-DomainOrTwoHumans.txt, which can be downloaded from http://barcelona.research.yahoo.net/webspam/datasets/uk2006/, where 4948 hosts are marked normal and 674 hosts are marked spam. We select 470 spam hosts and 500 normal hosts as train set, 204 spam hosts and 300 normal hosts as test set. Each host is presented as a 139-dimensional vector including 138 features and an associated class label.

6.2 Evaluations

The evaluations used in our experiments are precision, recall, F-measure and accuracy. For the binary classification, all instances are divided into positive instances if they belong to the target class and negative instances if they do not. Our target class is web spam. The confusion matrix is as follows:

Table 2. The confusion matrix

	actual positive	actual negative
predicted positive	TP	FP
predicted negative	FN	TN

where TP represents the number of positive examples that are correctly classified as positive, FP represents the number of negative examples that are falsely classified as positive, FN represents the number of positive examples that are falsely classified as negative, TN represents the number of negative examples that are correctly classified as negative. The evaluations are defined as following:

Precision: the percentage of truly positive examples in those classified as positive by the classifier:

$$\Pr ecision = \frac{TP}{TP + FP} \tag{3}$$

Recall: the percentage of correctly classified positive examples out of all positive examples:

$$\operatorname{Re} call = \frac{TP}{TP + FN} \tag{4}$$

F-measure: a balance between Precision and Recall:

$$F\_measure = \frac{2 \times \Pr ecision \times \operatorname{Re} call}{\Pr ecision + \operatorname{Re} call} \tag{5}$$

Accuracy: the percentage of correctly classified examples out of all examples:

$$Accuracy = \frac{TP + TN}{TP + FP + FN + TN} \tag{6}$$

6.3 Experimental Results

Because of the randomicity of GP process, we perform every experiment 10 times and get the average value of every measure to compare. The experiments shown in Table 3-4 make use of 3 populations at first. They have 10, 20 and 30 individuals respectively. Their maximum generations are 50, 30 and 20 respectively. Then combinations are employed. The first combination also uses 3 populations. They have 20, 30 and 40 individuals respectively. Their maximum generations are 100, 50 and 50 respectively. The last combination uses 1 population. It has 50 individuals and its maximum generation is 50.

Table 3. Comparison between the linear function and the non-linear function

	precision_Avg	recall_Avg	F_measure_Avg	accuracy_Avg
Linear function	0.77828174	0.836764706	0.805602567	0.836706349
Non-Linear function	0.630408109	0.759313725	0.685843185	0.718253968

Table 3 shows the comparison between the linear function and the non-linear function in condition that the depth of the binary tree is eight. As we can see in Table 3, the linear function is better than the non-linear function.

Table 4. Comparison among the depth of the tree that ranges between 1 and 9

depth	precision_Avg	recall_Avg	F_measure_Avg	accuracy_Avg
1	0.505585508	0.90294118	0.646087527	0.597222222
2	0.655315651	0.76372549	0.700587373	0.733928571
3	0.716419012	0.82303922	0.764246563	0.794642857
4	0.795592113	0.81911765	0.80486974	0.839880952
5	0.712093992	0.825	0.763331324	0.793452381
6	0.739557878	0.85833333	0.794075354	0.819642857
7	0.761283597	0.84705882	0.800857247	0.829365079
8	0.77828174	0.83676471	0.805602567	0.836706349
9	0.755325083	0.82794118	0.788169917	0.819444444

In order to present the effect of the depth of the binary tree, we perform experiments with the depth of the tree that ranges between 1 and 9. Table 4 shows the results. From Table 4, when the depth of the tree is 4, the average precision and the average accuracy are the best. When the depth of the tree is 8, the average F_measure is the best, the average accuracy is the second. However from Fig. 1, the running time when the depth of the tree is 8 is six times longer than that of when the depth of the tree is 4. From Fig.1, the running time increases exponentially with the increasing of the depth of the binary tree. So the depth of the binary tree should not be too large when we use GP to learn a possible best discriminating function.

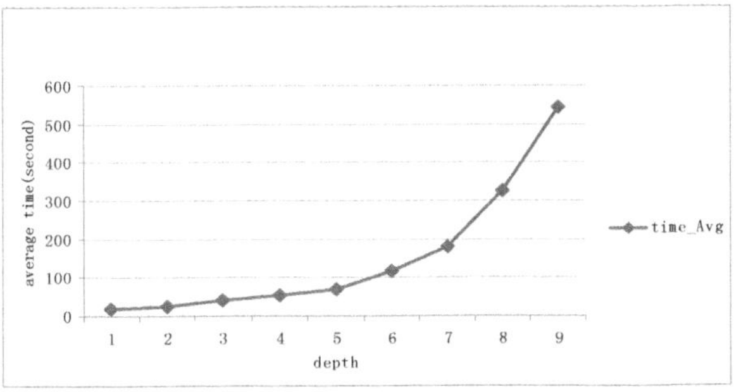

Fig. 1. Time comparison among the depth of the binary tree that ranges between 1 and 9

In order to show the effect of the combination, we perform experiments when the depth of the tree is 4. When the single population GP is carried out, both the total number of individuals and the maximum generation are 50. In the experiments of one combination, the parameters are same to those of the experiments shown in Table 3-4 except there is no the first combination. In the experiments of two combinations, all parameters are same to those of the experiments shown in Table 3-4. From Table 5, we can see that compared with the single population GP, the multi-population GP with two combinations can improve spam classification recall performance by 5.6%, F-measure performance by 2.25% and accuracy performance by 2.83%. The experimental results (the depth of the tree is 8) in Table 6 further confirm that the combination can improve the classification performance.

Table 5. Comparison between the single population and the combination(4)

	precision_Avg	recall_Avg	F_measure_Avg	accuracy_Avg	time
Single population	0.73915245	0.83480392	0.78235325	0.811507937	32.0746
One Combination	0.751195618	0.82892157	0.787326785	0.818650794	39.1965
Two Combinations	0.795592113	0.81911765	0.80486974	0.839880952	53.5418

Table 6. Comparison between the single population and the combination(8)

	precision_Avg	recall_Avg	F_measure_Avg	accuracy_Avg	time
Single population	0.763119123	0.82401961	0.791372801	0.823809524	163.0511
One Combination	0.77828174	0.83676471	0.805602567	0.836706349	324.5528

Table 7. Comparison between GP_4 and SVM

	precision_Avg	recall_Avg	F_measure_Avg	accuracy_Avg
2CGP_4	0.795592113	0.81911765	0.80486974	0.839880952
SVM	0.904761905	0.55882353	0.690909091	0.797619048

Table 7 shows the comparison between SVM and the multi-population GP with two combinations when the depth of the binary tree is 4(2CGP_4). From Table 7, we can find that 2CGP_4 improves spam classification recall performance by 26%, F-measure performance by 11% and accuracy performance by 4% compared with SVM. The precision of SVM is higher than GP_4, but the recall is too lower.

7 Conclusions and Future Work

In this paper, we propose the method using GP to learn a discriminating function to detect web spam. We study the representation of an individual, the features of Web pages that are used to detect Web spam, the effect of the depth of the binary trees in the GP evolution process and the efficiency of the combination. We performed the experiments on WEBSPAM-UK2006 collection. Experimental results show that the method can improve the web spam detection performance effectively compared with SVM. However the method does not detect content spam because only the link based features are used. We also do not consider the problem of class imbalance.

Future work involves using other proposed features in GP, e.g. the content features, finding better features by GP, considering the problem of class imbalance and proposing better classification method to detect web spam.

Acknowledgments

This work is supported by the Natural Science Foundation of China (60970047), the Natural Science Foundation of Shandong Province (Y2008G19) and the Key Science-Technology Project of Shandong Province (2007GG10001002, 2008GG10001026).

References

1. Becchetti, L., Castillo I, C., Donato I, D., Leonardi, S., Baeza-Yates, R.: Using Rank Propagation and Probabilistic Counting for Link Based Spam Detection. In: Nasraoui, O., Spiliopoulou, M., Srivastava, J., Mobasher, B., Masand, B. (eds.) WebKDD 2006. LNCS (LNAI), vol. 4811, pp. 127–146. Springer, Heidelberg (2007)
2. Gyongyi, Z., Garcia-Molina, H.: Web Spam Taxonomy. In: Proc. of First Workshop on Adversarial Information Retrieval on the Web (2005)
3. Ntoulas, A., Najork, M., Manasse, M., Fetterly, D.: Detecting spam web pages through content analysis. In: Proceedings of the 15th International Conference on World Wide Web, WWW 2006, Edinburgh, Scotland, May 23 - 26, pp. 83–92. ACM Press, New York (2006)
4. Gyöngyi, Z., Garcia-Molina, H., Pedersen, J.: Combating web spam with trustrank. In: Proceedings of the Thirtieth international Conference on Very Large Data Bases, vol. 30, pp. 576–587 (2004)
5. Krishnan, V., Raj, R.: Web Spam Detection with Anti-Trust-Rank. In: The 2nd International Workshop on Adversarial Information Retrieval on the Web (AIRWeb) (August 2006)
6. Castillo, C., Donato, D., Gionis, A., Murdock, V., Silvestri, F.: Know your Neighbors: Web Spam Detection using the Web Topology. Technologies Project (November 2006)
7. Geng, G.G., Wang, C.H., Li, Q.D., Xu, L., Jin, X.B.: Boosting the Performace of Web Spam Detection with Ensemble Under-Sampling Classification. In: Proc. of the 4th International Conference on Fuzzy Systems and Knowledge Discovery, FSKD 2007 (August 2007)
8. Liu, Y., Cen, R., Zhang, M., Ma, S., Ru, L.: Identifying Web Spam with User Behavior Analysis. In: AIRWeb 2008, Beijing, China, April 22 (2008)
9. Dai, N., Davison, B.D., Qi, X.: Looking into the Past to Better Classify Web Spam. In: AIRWeb '09, Madrid, Spain (April 21, 2009)
10. Koza, J.R.: Genetic Programming: on the Programming of Computers by Means of Natural Selection. MIT Press, Cambridge (1992)
11. Zhang, M., Wong, P.: Genetic programming for medical classification: a program simplification approach. Genet. Program. Evolvable Mach. 9, 229–255 (2008)
12. Kishore, J.K., Patnaik, L.M., Mani, V., Agrawal, V.K.: Application of genetic programming for multi-category pattern classification. IEEE Trans. Evol. Comput. 4(3), 242–258 (2000)
13. Lin, J.-Y., Ke, H.-R., Chien, B.-C., Yang, W.-P.: Designing a classifier by a layered multi-population genetic programming approach. Pattern Recognition 40, 2211–2225 (2007)
14. Fernández, F., Tomassini, M., Vanneschi, L.: An Empirical Study of Multi-population Genetic Programming. Genet. Programming Evolvable Mach. 4, 21–51 (2003)
15. Castillo, C., Donato, D., Becchetti, L., Boldi, P., Leonardi, S., Santini, M., Vigna, S.: A reference collection for web spam detection. ACM SIGIR Forum 40(2), 11–24 (2006)

Semantic Annotation of Web Objects Using Constrained Conditional Random Fields

Yongquan Dong[1,2], Qingzhong Li[1], Yongqing Zheng[1], Xiaoyang Xu[1], and Yongxin Zhang[1]

[1] School of Computer Science and Technology, Shandong University, Jinan, China
[2] School of Computer Science and Technology, Xuzhou Normal University, Xuzhou, China
dongyongquan@mail.sdu.edu.cn, lqz@sdu.edu.cn, zyq@sdu.edu.cn, xu_xiaoyang@hotmail.com, zhangyongxin@mail.sdu.edu.cn

Abstract. Semantic annotation of Web objects is a key problem for Web information extraction. The Web contains an abundance of useful semi-structured information about real world objects, and the empirical study shows that strong sequence characteristics exist for Web information about objects of the same type across different Web sites. Conditional Random Fields (CRFs) are the state of the art approaches taking the sequence characteristics to do better labeling. However, previous CRFs have their limitations and can not deal with a variety of logical constraints between Web object elements efficiently. This paper presents a Constrained Conditional Random Fields (Constrained CRFs) model to do semantic annotation of Web objects. The model incorporates a novel inference procedure based on integer linear programming and extends CRFs to naturally and efficiently support all kinds of logical constraints. Experimental results using a large number of real-world data collected from diverse domains show that the proposed approach can significantly improve the semantic annotation accuracy of web objects.

1 Introduction

The World Wide Web is a vast and rapidly growing repository of information, and various kinds of valuable information are embedded in webpages. In a webpage, all related Web information about the same object integrates as an information unit, which is called a Web object [1]. A web object can be further segmented into atomic entities called object elements. Extracting these Web objects and assigning an attribute name to each object element are necessary for Web data integration [1], which can benefit the construction of many useful applications, such as comparison shopping, meta-search etc.

The empirical study shows that strong sequence characteristics exist for Web objects of the same type across different Web sites. For example, a book's name is always ahead of its description in all the pages. Conditional Random Fields (CRFs) are the state-of-the-art approaches in information extraction taking the sequence characteristics to do better labeling[2]. But, traditional CRFs can not support a variety of logical constraints among sequence elements, which leads to the low accuracy of

L. Chen et al. (Eds.): WAIM 2010, LNCS 6184, pp. 28–39, 2010.

sequence labeling. For instance, on online bookselling sites, the existing CRFs can not guarantee the uniqueness of all semantic labels in a book object.

To improve the accuracy of semantic annotation, a Constrained Conditional Random Fields model (Constrained CRFs) has been proposed in this paper. The new model extends CRFs models to support a variety of constraints. It introduces a novel inference procedure based on integer linear programming (ILP) to replace traditional Viterbi inference. The modeling allows one to add logical constraints over the semantic labels in a natural and systematic fashion. The logical constraints are defined by general Boolean functions which can be expressed as linear (in)equalities. After the conversion of logical constraints properly, the model incorporates the ILP general optimization procedure to determine the semantic label of every object element in a Web object.

Experimental results using a large number of real-world data collected from diverse domains indicate that the proposed Constrained CRFs model performs better than traditional CRFs for semantic annotation of Web objects.

The rest of this paper is organized as follows. First, the related work is discussed in Section 2. Then, the concepts of traditional CRFs are introduced in Section 3. In Section 4, Constrained CRFs are presented, and ILP-based inference methods and the construction and utilization of logical constraints are discussed. In Section 5, the experimental setup and results are showed. Finally, the conclusion is presented.

2 Related Work

There has been much work in the field of semantic annotation for Web objects. Embley et al.[3] utilize ontologies together with several heuristics to automatically extract data in multi-record documents and label them. However, ontologies for different domains must be constructed manually. Mukherjee et al.[4]exploit the presentation styles and the spatial locality of semantically related items, but its learning process for annotation is domain-dependent. Arlotta et al.[5]basically annotate data units with the closest labels on result pages. However, this method has limited applicability because many sites do not encode data units with their labels on result pages.

CRFs[2] are the state of the art approaches in information extraction taking the sequence characteristics to do better labeling, which have been widely used in many fields, such as NLP tasks, IE etc. Although some researchers have tried to incorporate the constraints into Viterbi algorithm used for inference in CRFs, it can only support some simple constraints. Kristjannson et al.[6] proposed constrained Viterbi to deal with certain types of constraints, but the types of constraints may only disallow some labels or ensure that some object elements are assigned some labels. It can not process more complex constraints.

The idea of inference using ILP has been attempted in previous work. Dan Roth et al.[7,8] introduce ILP-CRFs to facilitate semantic role labeling in natural language understanding. But they only consider the problem of semantic role labeling and the approach does not apply to semantic annotation of web objects so far. Semantic annotation of web objects has the constraints which do not occur in natural language understanding. For example, in a book object, the value of "original price" is greater than or equal to that of "current price". So, it is necessary to further research on how to incorporate logical constraints into semantic annotation for web objects.

3 Linear-Chain Conditional Random Fields

A conditional random field is an undirected graphical model that defines a single exponential distribution over label sequences given a particular observation sequence. Let X be a random variable over the observations to be labeled, and Y be a random variable over corresponding labels. All components Y_i of Y are assumed to range over a finite label alphabet y . In a discriminative framework, CRFs construct a conditional model $p(Y \mid X)$ with a given set of features from paired observations and labels. Formally, the definition of CRFs [2] is given subsequently:

Definition 1. Let $G=(V,E)$ be an undirected graph such that $Y=\{Y_v\}_{v\in V}$. Then (X,Y) is said to be a conditional random field if, when conditioned on X , the random variables Y_v obey the Markov property with respect to the graph: $p(Y_v \mid X, Y_{V-\{v\}}) = p(Y_v \mid X, Y_{N_v})$, where $V-\{v\}$ is the set of nodes in the graph except the node v and N_v is the set of neighbors of the node v in Graph G .

Thus, Conditional Random Fields are Markov Random Fields globally conditioned on the observations X . In theory the structure of graph G can be arbitrary. Many previous applications use the Linear-chain CRFs [2], in which a first-order Markov assumption is made on the hidden variables. By the Hammersley-Clifford Theorem [9], the conditional distribution of the labels $y = y_1 \dots y_T$ given the observations $x = x_1 \dots x_T$ has the form,

$$p_\Lambda(y \mid x) = \frac{1}{Z(x)} \exp\left\{ \sum_{t=1}^{T} \sum_{k} \lambda_k f_k(y_{t-1}, y_t, x, t) \right\} \tag{1}$$

where $f_k(y_{t-1}, y_t, x, t)$ is a feature function of vertex and edge, λ_k is a learned weight associated with f_k , Λ is the weight set, $\Lambda = \{\lambda_k\}$, and $Z(x)$ is the normalization factor, also know as partition function, which has the form,

$$Z(x) = \sum_{y} \exp\left(\sum_{t=1}^{T} \sum_{k} \lambda_k f_k(y_{t-1}, y_t, x, t) \right) \tag{2}$$

Training of CRFs requires estimating the values of the weight set, Λ , which is usually done by maximizing the log-likelihood of a given training set. Popular training methods include generalized iterative scaling, conjugate-gradient and limited-memory quasi-Newton [10].

Inference in CRFs is done by finding the most probable label sequence, y^* , for an input sequence x, given the model in equation (1):

$$y^* = \arg\max_y P_\Lambda(y \mid x) \tag{3}$$

Generally speaking, $P_\Lambda(y \mid x)$ can be expressed concisely in matrix form. Let Y be the set of possible labels, where $|Y| = m$ .A set of $m \times m$ matrices $\{M_i(x) \mid i = 1,\ldots,n\}$ is defined over each pair of labels $y', y'' \in Y$

$$M_i(y', y'' \mid x) = \exp(\sum_k \lambda_k f_k(y', y'', i)) \tag{4}$$

By augmenting two special nodes y_0, y_{n+1} before and after the sequence with labels start and end respectively, the sequence probability is

$$p_\Lambda(y \mid x) = \frac{1}{Z(x)} \prod_{i=1}^{n+1} M_i(y_{i-1}, y_i \mid x) \tag{5}$$

where $Z(x)$ can be computed from the M_i 's but not needed in evaluation. Therefore, we only need to find the label sequence y^* that maximizes the product of the corresponding elements of these n+1 matrices. Viterbi algorithm can be used to compute the most likely label sequence.

4 Constrained Conditional Random Fields

CRFs are the state-of-the-art approaches in information extraction taking the sequence characteristics to do better labeling. However, traditional CRFs can not deal with a variety of logical constraints, which leads to the low accuracy of sequence labeling. To improve the performance of semantic annotation of web objects, this paper proposes a Constrained Conditional Random Fields (Constrained CRFs) to do semantic annotation of Web objects, which extends Linear-Chain CRFs and incorporates a variety of logical constraints.

4.1 Model

In this section, a Constrained CRFs model is presented, which can deal with a variety of constraints.

Definition 2. Let $G = \langle X, Y \rangle$ be a Linear-Chain CRFs, X denotes the random variable over observations, Y denotes the random variable over the corresponding labels. Logical Constraints refer to the logical relations among different Y_j . The Linear-Chain CRFs with logical constraints are called Constrained Conditional Random Fields (Constrained CRFs).

Let $x = x_1 \ldots x_T$ be an observation sequence, c be logical constraints and $y = y_1 \ldots y_T$ be a corresponding label sequence. The conditional probability for y given x and c to be

$$p_{\Lambda}(y \mid x, c) = \frac{1}{Z(x,c)} \exp\left\{ \sum_{t=1}^{T} \sum_{k} \lambda_k f_k(y_{t-1}, y_t, x, c, t) \right\} \tag{6}$$

where f_k are feature functions defined on two types of cliques (i.e. edges and vertexes) , λ_k is a learnt weight associated with f_k and $Z(x,c)$ is a normalization constant that makes the probabilities of all label sequences sum to one, which has the form,

$$Z(x,c) = \sum_{y} \exp\left(\sum_{t=1}^{T} \sum_{k} \lambda_k f_k(y_{t-1}, y_t, x, c, t) \right) \tag{7}$$

4.2 Parameter Estimation

Given a set of training samples $D = \{(x^{(j)}, y^{(j)})\}_{j=1}^{M}$, parameter estimation is to choose the feature function's weights, $\Lambda = \{\lambda_k\}$, to maximize the likelihood of the set of training samples. For Constrained CRFs, the log likelihood is given by

$$L(\Lambda) = \sum_{j=1}^{M} \log P_{\Lambda}(y^{(j)} \mid x^{(j)}, c) - \sum_{k} \frac{\lambda_k^2}{2\sigma^2} \tag{8}$$

where the term $\sum_{k} \frac{\lambda_k^2}{2\sigma^2}$ is a Gaussian prior that is used for penalizing the log-likelihood in order to avoid over-fitting, and σ^2 is a variance.

The gradient-based L-BFGS [10] is used in the experiment to optimize the concave function. Each element of the gradient vector is given by

$$\frac{\partial L(\Lambda)}{\partial \lambda_k} = E_{\tilde{p}(x,y)}[f_k] - E_{p(y|x,\Theta)}[f_k] - \frac{\lambda_k}{\sigma^2} \tag{9}$$

where $\tilde{p}(x, y)$ is the empirical distribution of training samples and $E_p[.]$ denotes expectation with respect to distribution p.

4.3 Inference

The Viterbi algorithm is often used for inference in CRFs. It has been extended, as is done with HMMs, to satisfy some types of additional constraints on the label sequence (e.g., constrained Viterbi described in [6]).But the types of constraints only disallow some labels or ensure that some object elements are assigned some labels. And it can not deal with more complex constraints, for example, no duplicate semantic labels within the same web object. Therefore, it is necessary to incorporate a new inference procedure to support a variety of logical constraints. Integer linear programming (ILP) can easily incorporate logical constraints. Logical constraints can be represented as Boolean expression and encoded as linear inequalities in ILP. In this section, we first transform the inference procedure of CRFs into the problem that ILP has modeled. Then the inference procedure is modeled by ILP. At last, the construction and incorporation approaches of logical constraints are presented.

4.3.1 Transformation of Inference Problem

As the shortest path problems have been modeled in ILP[11], the inference procedure of CRFs needs to be converted to the shortest path problems. The construction is as follows [7].

Let n be the number of object elements in the observation sequence, and m be the number of labels each object element can take. In addition to two special nodes start and end that denote the start and end positions of the path, the label of each object element is represented by a node v_{ij}, where $1 \le i \le n$ and $1 \le j \le m$. If the path passes node v_{ij}, then label j is assigned to object element i. For nodes that represent two adjacent object elements $v_{(i-1)j}$ and $v_{ij'}$, where $1 \le i \le n$ and $1 \le j, j' \le m$, there is a directed edge $x_{i,jj'}$ from $v_{(i-1)j}$ to $v_{ij'}$, with the cost $-\log(M_i(j, j' \mid x))$. $M_i(j, j' \mid x)$ represents the value of the position (j, j') in the matrix $M_i(x)$ which is introduced in section 3.

Fig. 1 illustrates the graph. As is shown in the graph, the path from start to end will pass exactly one node on position i. That is, exactly one of the nodes v_{ij}, $1 \le j \le m$, will be picked. Suppose that $y = y_0 y_1 \cdots y_{n-1}$ is the label sequence determined by the path. Then,

$$\arg\max_y \prod_{i=1}^{n} M_i(y_{i-1}, y_i \mid x) = \arg\min_y -\sum_{i=1}^{n} \log(M_i(y_{i-1}, y_i \mid x)) \tag{10}$$

Namely, the nodes in the shortest path are exactly the labels returned by the Viterbi algorithm.

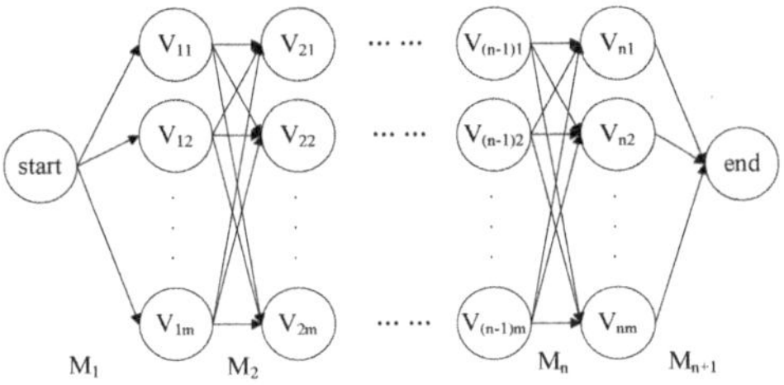

Fig. 1. The graph of the transformation from the inference problem of CRFs to shortest path problem

4.3.2 Shortest Path Problems Modelled by ILP

A general shortest path problem can be processed by integer linear programming [13]. The ILP model of shortest path problem in Fig. 1 is shown in Fig. 2.

$$\min -\sum_{\substack{1\le i\le n \\ 1\le j,j'\le m}} \log(M_i(j,j'))\cdot x_{i,jj'}$$

subject to:

$$\sum_{1\le j_1\le m} x_{i-1,j_1 j} - \sum_{1\le j_2\le m} x_{i-1,jj_2} = 0 \quad (1\le i\le n, 1\le j\le m) \tag{11.1}$$

$$\sum_{1\le j\le m} x_{1,0j} = 1 \tag{11.2}$$

$$\sum_{1\le j\le m} x_{n+1,j(n+1)} = 1 \tag{11.3}$$

$$x_{1,0j}, x_{i,j_1 j}, x_{n+1,j(n+1)} \in \{0,1\} \quad (1\le i\le n, 1\le j, j_1\le m) \tag{11.4}$$

Fig. 2. The ILP model of shortest path problem in Fig. 1

In Fig. 2, the positions of start and end nodes are 0 and n+1 respectively. And $x_{1,0j}$ and $x_{n+1,j(n+1)}$ represents special edges connected with start and end nodes. Equation (11.1) represents that for each node in the graph except start and end, the number of inward edges in the path should be the same as the number of the outward edges. Equation (11.2) denotes the number of inward edges for node start should be 1. Equation (11.3) denotes the number of outward edges for node end should also be 1. Equation (11.4) represents that the indicator variable should be 0 or 1.

Wolsey has proved that the solution to shortest path problem is integral [11]. Therefore, solving it takes only polynomial time using interior point algorithms for linear programming. Without any other constraints, the label sequence in the path of Fig. 2 corresponds to the outputs of Viterbi algorithm.

4.3.3 The Construction and Incorporation of Logical Constraints

Logical constraints refer to the logical relations among the semantic labels. Logical constraints can be described with Boolean expression. It is known that all possible Boolean expression can be represented as sets of linear (in)equalities [12].

After analyzing semantic annotation of web objects in different domain, we sum up several common Boolean expressions of logical constraints and the corresponding linear (in)equalities. This is a portion of all logical constraints and we can construct any logical constraints of interest.

Let Boolean variable a,b indicate whether the semantic labels L_a, L_b appear respectively, that is to say,

$$a = \begin{cases} 1 & L_a \textit{ appears} \\ 0 & L_a \textit{ does not appear} \end{cases} \qquad b = \begin{cases} 1 & L_b \textit{ appears} \\ 0 & L_b \textit{ does not appear} \end{cases}$$

And $v(a)$,$v(b)$ represent the value of object element marked as L_a,L_b respectively.

Table 1 lists several common Boolean expressions of logical constraints and the corresponding linear (in) equalities.

Table 1. Boolean expressions of semantic annotation and the (in)equalities in Fig.2

id	Boolean Expression	Meanings	Linear (in)equalities
1	$a \rightarrow b$	If L_a appears, then L_b must also appear.	$x_{i,ac} \le \sum_{\substack{1\le j\le m \\ 1\le k\le n}} x_{k,jb}\ (2\le i\le n, 1\le c\le m)$
2	$a \succ b$	L_a appears before L_b.	$m(i-2)x_{i,ac} \le \sum_{\substack{1\le j\le m \\ 1\le k\le i-2}} (1-x_{k,jb})$ $(2\le i\le n, 1\le c\le m)$
3	$\ddot{a}$	L_a must appear only once.	$\sum_{\substack{1\le j\le m \\ 1\le i\le n}} x_{i,ja} = 1$
4	$\hat{a}$	If L_a appears, then it only appears once.	$m(n-i)x_{i,ac} \le \sum_{\substack{1\le j\le m \\ i+1\le k\le n}} (1-x_{k,ja})$ $(2\le i\le n, c\ne a, 1\le c\le m)$
5	$v(a)\ge v(b)$	If L_a and L_b appear simultaneously, then the value of object element marked as L_a is greater than or equal to the value of object element marked as L_b.	$[v(a)\ge v(b)] \ge \sum_{\substack{1\le j_1\le m \\ 1\le i_1\le n}} x_{i_1,j_1 a} + \sum_{\substack{1\le j_2\le m \\ 1\le i_2\le n}} x_{i_2,j_2 b} - 1$

The following is the brief description of the conversion of Boolean expression to linear (in)equalities.

In Fig. 2, the Boolean expression of the first logical constraint can be represented as $x_{i,ac} \rightarrow \bigvee_{1\le k\le n \wedge k\ne i-1} x_{k,jb}$ which can be converted to $x_{i,ac} \rightarrow x_{1,jb} \vee x_{2,jb} \vee \cdots \vee x_{n,jb}$ because $x_{i-1,jb}$ is equal to zero. Since the logic rule "$x \rightarrow x_1 \vee x_2 \vee \cdots \vee x_n$" can be represented by the linear inequality "$x \le \sum_{i=1}^{n} x_i$", we can get the corresponding linear inequalities in Table 1.

The meaning of the second logical constraint is that if L_a appears, then L_b can not appear before L_a. In Fig. 2, its Boolean expression can be described as $x_{i,ac} \rightarrow \bigwedge_{1\le k\le i-2} \neg x_{k,jb}$, *where* $c \ne a,b$, that is to say, $x_{i,ac} \rightarrow \overline{x_{1,jb}} \wedge \overline{x_{2,jb}} \wedge \cdots \wedge \overline{x_{i-2,jb}}$. Since $\overline{x} = 1 - x$ and the logic rule "$x \rightarrow \overline{x_1} \wedge \overline{x_2} \wedge \cdots \wedge \overline{x_n}$" can be represented by the linear inequality "$nx \le \sum_{i=1}^{n} x_i$", we can get the corresponding linear inequalities in Table 1.

The third logical constraint represents the meaning in Fig. 2 that the number of inward edge for the node marked as L_a is equal to one in the whole graph.

The meaning of the fourth logical constraint is that if L_a appears, then L_a can not appear again. The conversion rule is similar to the second constraint.

In Fig. 2, the Boolean expression of the fifth logical constraints can be represented as $\overleftrightarrow{a} \Lambda \overleftrightarrow{b} \rightarrow [v(a) > v(b)]$ which can be converted to $[v(a) > v(b)] \geq \overleftrightarrow{a} + \overleftrightarrow{b} - 1$. Then we can get the corresponding linear inequalities in Table 1.

As is shown in Table 1, we can see that logical constraints can easily extended according to the characteristics of different domains. The approach in [12] can be used to convert the Boolean expressions to the corresponding (in)equalities. And these (in)equalities can be added to the basic program as constraint (in)equalitites in Fig. 2.

5 Experiments

5.1 Datasets

The approach is evaluated on the following datasets.

(1) Book dataset (denoted as Book)
The book dataset consists of 3000 books collected from 20 online book stores. And 1000 books are used for training and the remaining 2000 are used for testing. Books contain 7 fields: *Title*, *Author*, *ISBN*, *Publisher*, *Publication Date*, *Original Price* and *Current Price*. In addition, 20000 books are randomly crawled from http://www.goldengatebookstore.com and saved in a relational table as an external book database.

(2) Paper reference dataset (denoted as Paper)
The reference dataset was created by the Cora project (http://www.cs.umass.edu/~mccallum/data). It contains 800 references, and 300 references are used for training and the remaining 500 are used for testing. References contain 9 fields: *Author*, *Title*, *Editor*, *Booktitle*, *Date*, *Volume*, *Pages*, *Location* and *Publisher*. In addition, 30000 papers are randomly crawled from ACM Digital Library and saved in a relational table as an external database.

5.2 Evaluation Criteria

To evaluate the performance comprehensively, several criteria that were widely used before are taken: *Recall*, *Precision*, *F1* and Instance Accuracy. They measure the performance of the model on different aspects. A brief definition is given as follows.

Defining *A* as the existing total number of special object elements, *B* as the number of object elements which are correctly labeled, *C* as the number of object elements which are wrongly labeled.

(1) First, two basic measurements, *Recall* and *Precision*, are defined as:

$$Recall = \frac{B}{A}, \ Precision = \frac{B}{B+C}.$$

Then *F1* is calculated to be $F1 = \dfrac{2 \times Precision \times Recall}{Precision + Recall}$.

(2) Instance Accuracy: the percentage of instances in which all object elements is correctly labeled.

5.3 Experimental Results

5.3.1 Transformation of Inference Problem

The experimental results on the two datasets (Book and Paper) are showed. A comparison with traditional CRFs (denoted as CRFs) and Constrained CRFs is made. Table 2 and Table 3 list *Precision* (denoted as P) , *Recall* (denoted as R) and *F1* and their corresponding average value on each field, and Fig. 3 shows the Instance Accuracy on the two datasets.

From the results in Table 2 and Table 3, it can be known that Constrained CRFs achieve an obvious improvement on almost each field compared with CRFs. Constrained CRFs outperform CRFs in average *F1* on the two different datasets by 10.19%, and 12.9% respectively. This fully shows that logical constraints can certainly improve the performance of semantic annotation of web object.

Table 2. Semantic annotation results on the dataset Book

Fields	CRFs			Constrained CRFs		
	P	R	F1	P	R	F1
Title	55.68	56.63	56.15	63.83	63.83	63.83
Author	61.86	62.36	62.11	68.96	69.86	69.41
ISBN	84.35	85.56	84.95	85.69	86.58	86.13
Publisher	63.47	66.65	65.02	75.16	73.26	74.20
Publication Date	79.62	75.34	77.42	80.85	75.59	78.13
Original Price	54.26	50.65	52.39	75.35	73.28	74.30
Our Price	52.37	56.27	54.25	78.62	76.63	77.61
Average	64.52	64.78	64.61	75.49	74.15	74.80

Table 3. Semantic annotation results on the dataset Paper

Fields	CRFs			Constrained CRFs		
	P	R	F1	P	R	F1
Author	76.58	78.95	77.75	83.86	83.86	83.86
Title	60.62	63.63	62.09	67.68	67.68	67.68
Editor	58.86	55.69	57.23	63.26	60.18	61.68
Book Title	72.28	66.56	69.30	73.28	70.52	71.87
Date	78.85	75.26	77.01	79.86	76.35	78.07
Volume	83.24	80.25	81.72	88.68	85.09	86.85
Pages	70.12	73.85	71.94	70.69	72.12	71.40
Location	68.84	60.62	64.47	69.95	65.86	67.84
Publisher	75.42	70.01	72.61	86.26	82.10	84.13
Average	71.65	69.42	70.46	75.95	73.75	74.82

In Fig. 3, it shows the Instance Accuracy of four models on the two datasets. From the results, it can be found that compared with CRFs, the Instance Accuracy of Constrained CRFs achieves an obvious improvement on the two different datasets.

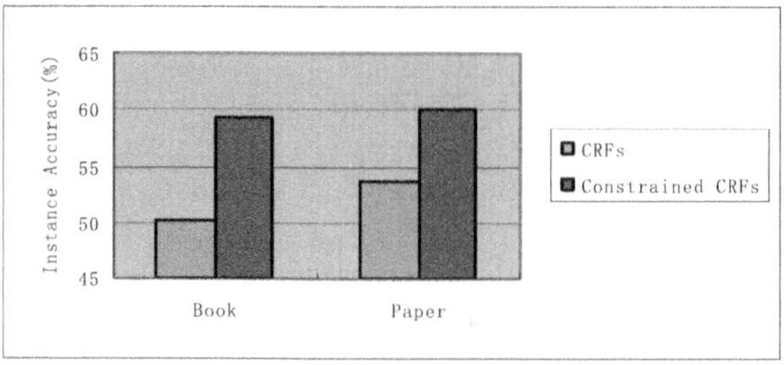

Fig. 3. Instance accuracy by CRFs and Constrained CRFs on different datasets

5.3.2 Effect of Incrementally Adding Logical Constraint

To test the effectiveness of every logical constraint, logical constraints on the dataset Book are shown in Table 4 in which semantic labels represent Boolean variables. The adding order of logical constraints conforms to the order of id in Table 4.

Fig. 4 shows the change of average *F1* when incrementally adding different logical constraint on dataset Book. The basic is CRFs. With the increase of logical constraints, the average *F1* is a gradually improvement. It shows that every logical constraint can improve the performance of semantic annotation.

Table 4. Boolean expressions of logical constraints and their meanings on dataset Book

id	Boolean Expression	Meanings
HC1	$\hat{Title}, \hat{Author}, \ldots$	All semantic labels of a web object can not be repeatable.
HC2	$Title \succ Author$	"*Title*" appears before "*Author*".
HC3	$Title \rightarrow Our\ Price$	If "*Title*" appears, then "*Our Price*" must also appear.
HC4	$\overleftrightarrow{Title}$	"*Title*" must appear only once.
HC5	$v(Origin\ Price) \geq v(Current\ Price)$	The value of "*Origin Price*" is greater than or equal to the value of "*Current Price*"

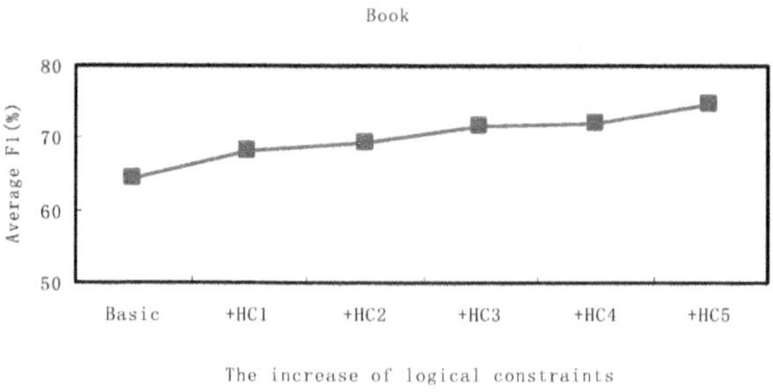

Fig. 4. Variation of average *F1* with the increase of different logical constraints on dataset Book

6 Conclusion

In this paper, a Constrained Conditional Random Fields model(Constrained CRFs) is proposed. Constrained CRFs extend traditional CRFs and use integer linear programming to inference. It incorporates logical constraints into CRFs, where logical constraints are defined by Boolean expression to describe logical relations among semantic labels. Experimental results using a large number of real-world data collected from diverse domains show that the proposed approach can significantly improve the semantic annotation accuracy of web objects.

In the future, how to collect the semantic labels automatically and how to further improve the semantic annotation accuracy of Web objects will be focused on.

Acknowledgments. This work was supported in part by the National Natural Science Foundation of China under Grant No. 90818001 and the Natural Science Foundation of Shandong Province of China under Grant No.Y2007G24, No. Y2007G38.

References

1. Haas, L.M.: Beauty and the Beast: The Theory and Practice of Information Integration. In: Schwentick, T., Suciu, D. (eds.) ICDT 2007. LNCS, vol. 4353, pp. 28–43. Springer, Heidelberg (2006)
2. Lafferty, J.D., McCallum, A., Pereira, F.C.: Conditional Random Fields: Probabilistic Models for Segmenting and Labeling Sequence Data. In: Proceedings of the Eighteenth International Conference on Machine Learning, pp. 282–289 (2001)
3. Embley, D.W., Campbell, D.M., Jiang, Y.S., Liddle, S.W., Ng, Y., Quass, D., Smith, R.D.: Conceptual-model-based data extraction from multiple-record Web pages. Data Knowl. Eng. 31(3), 227–251 (1999)
4. Mukherjee, S., Ramakrishnan, I.V., Singh, A.: Bootstrapping Semantic Annotation for Content-Rich HTML Documents. In: Proceedings of the 21st International Conference on Data Engineering, pp. 583–593 (2005)
5. Arlotta, L., Crescenzi, V., Mecca, G., Merialdo, P., Tre, U.R.: Automatic Annotation of Data Extracted from Large Web Sites. In: Proceedings of Sixth International Workshop on the Web and Databases, pp. 7–12 (2003)
6. Kristjansson, T., Culotta, A., Viola, P., McCallum, A.: Interactive information extraction with constrained conditional random fields. In: Proceedings of the 19th national conference on Artifical intelligence, pp. 412–418 (2004)
7. Roth, D., Yih, W.: Integer linear programming inference for conditional random fields. In: Proceedings of the 22nd international conference on Machine learning, pp. 736–743 (2005)
8. Punyakanok, V., Roth, D., Yih, W., Zimak, D.: Semantic role labeling via integer linear programming inference. In: Proceedings of the 20th international conference on Computational Linguistics, pp. 1346–1352 (2004)
9. Hammersley, J.M., Clifford, P.: Markov field on finite graphs and lattices (1971) (unpublished manuscript)
10. Liu, D.C., Nocedal, J.: On the limited memory BFGS method for large scale optimization. Math. Program. 45(3), 503–528 (1989)
11. Wolsey, L.: Integer Programming. John Wiley&Sons, Inc., Chichester (1998)
12. Guéret, C., Prins, C., Sevaux, M., Heipcke, S.: Applications of Optimization with XpressMP. Dash Optimization Ltd. (2002)

Time Graph Pattern Mining for Web Analysis and Information Retrieval

Taihei Oshino, Yasuhito Asano, and Masatoshi Yoshikawa

Department of Social Informatics, Graduate School of Informatics, Kyoto University
Yoshida Honmachi, Sakyo-ku, Kyoto, 606–8591 Japan
oshino@db.soc.i.kyoto-u.ac.jp, {asano,yoshikawa}@i.kyoto-u.ac.jp

Abstract. Graph patterns on the web are characteristic substructures of web graphs. Graph patterns have played important roles in web analysis and information retrieval. However, temporal characteristics of the web have not been estimated sufficiently in previously proposed graph patterns. We first propose time graph patterns, and then, we mine the patterns representing topics that are discussed extensively on the web. Conducting experiments using those mined patterns, we finally ascertain that time graph pattern opens a novel way for information retrieval and web analysis reflecting temporal characteristics.

1 Introduction

Web graphs have been studied in the fields of web analysis and information retrieval on the web. A web graph is a directed graph whose nodes and edges represent pages and links. In those studies, "graph patterns" have frequently played important roles. A *graph pattern* is a structural property that should be satisfied by specified subgraphs. Previously proposed graph patterns reflect only graph structures on the web. However, the web has been changing since its inception. Therefore, temporal characteristics of the web are also expected to be important for web analysis and information retrieval. For example, the speed of information propagation might be important, although existing graph pattern based analysis cannot distinguish whether information spreads rapidly or slowly.

In this paper, we first propose a new graph pattern type, named "time graph patterns," for estimating time-series data. A *time graph pattern* is a graph pattern whose nodes have labels representing creation and deletion times of web pages. We then examine whether time graph patterns are useful for web analysis and information retrieval. We specifically examine patterns representing topics that are discussed extensively on the web because they represent the temporal characteristics of the web fairly well.

For this examination, we first confirm that time graph patterns can be mined in practical time. By assigning proper labels reflecting the process of discussing topics, a previously proposed graph-mining algorithm, "gSpan", becomes able to mine patterns representing topics that are discussed extensively. The gSpan [1] is a graph mining algorithm to enumerate frequent graph patterns from a set of

L. Chen et al. (Eds.): WAIM 2010, LNCS 6184, pp. 40–46, 2010.

labeled graphs. The inputs of gSpan are a set of graphs and minimum support as *minSup*. Then, gSpan outputs all patterns in more than *minSup* graphs. We then analyze blog sites using the mined patterns. We enumerate subgraphs matching specified time graph patterns, and construct a matrix, each element of which represents how many of a specified pattern exists in a specified site. We perform a principal component analysis (PCA) of the matrix, which can classify the sites into several clusters reflecting their structural characteristics. Based on results of the PCA, we automatically identify important patterns representing extensively discussed topics. Therefore, we ascertain that time graph patterns opens a novel way for web analysis and information retrieval reflecting temporal characteristics.

2 Related Work

In this section, we introduce studies using time-series data of the web. Then, we introduce studies related to graph patterns.

2.1 Web Analysis Using Time-Series Data

In recent years, several studies have been made of temporal properties of the web. For example, several models have been proposed [2,3,4] for simulating the growth of a social network, a community of sites, and the whole web. The "forest fire model" proposed by Leskovec et al.[2] can simulate properties of the web such that their degree distribution follows a power law [5]; their diameter shrinks over time [2]. Kumar et al.[6] introduced a "web time graph" to track the bursty growth of communities. A *web time graph* is an extension of a web graph showing nodes as pages and edges as links: in a web time graph, each node is given the creation and deletion time of the corresponding page; each link between two pages is regarded as valid for the duration that both pages exist. Their studies analyze the temporal variation of the number of pages statistically, but our study analyzes the time variation of graph structures.

2.2 Web Analysis Using Graph Patterns

Many researchers have examined information retrieval and web analysis using graph patterns. The HITS algorithm proposed by Kleinberg [7] uses the two concepts of "hub" and "authority" in the web graph. The HITS finds better pages on a specific topic using the pattern by which a good hub page links many good authoritative pages and by which a good authoritative page is linked by many good hub pages. Trawling, as proposed by Kumar [8] discovers communities by finding subgraphs matching patterns called complete bipartite graphs. Leskovec et al. [9] utilized graph patterns to analyze how information is propagated among blogs. They consider that links between blogs propagates information on them, and proposed "cascade" graph patterns representing various shapes of link structures in blogs. A *cascade* consists of all the nodes reachable to the unique starting node which has no out-links. McGlohon et al. [10] classified blogs by using cascades. They performed principal component analysis (PCA) on a matrix representing how many subgraphs, matching to each of different types of cascades, the link structure of each blog site contains. They ascertained that blogs are classified into conservative ones and humorous ones by using the first and the second principal components. However, cascade graph patterns do not estimate temporal characteristics of the web sufficiently.

3 Mining Time Graph Patterns

We propose time graph patterns for estimating temporal characteristics of the web. Then, we explain the process of mining time graph patterns.

3.1 Time Graph Patterns

We define a *time graph pattern* as a graph pattern whose nodes and edges have labels representing time-series data. A possible implementation of a time graph pattern is a pattern whose nodes have integer labels representing their creation periods; the nodes with label i were created before those with label j were created when $i < j$.

3.2 Construction of Web Graph Sets

First, we construct a set of graphs for the input of gSpan. To do so, we prepared some topics that have been discussed extensively on the web. For each topic, we construct a set of graphs whose nodes are the pages containing the topic. We use the Google search engine[1] to collect web pages related to the topics. We query the characteristic keywords representing a topic and an approximate time period. In this way, we can restrict results pages for our target of interests. Consequently, we can obtain the top k, say 300, web pages and their indexed time according to Google, and construct a web graph consisting of the pages and links among them. We can regard the indexed time as the creation time of the page because it almost always corresponds with its posted time in the text of the blog entry or the new page.

3.3 Labeling Method Reflecting Time-Series Data

We reflect temporal characteristics of web pages in labeling nodes. For each graph, we collect a set of web pages whose topic is discussed extensively during a specified period. In such topics, few pages present discussion of the topic at first. Subsequently, the topic spreads gradually: few pages related to the topic are created. An explosive spread then occurs: numerous pages are created in a few days. Subsequently, new pages referring to the topic do not increase much. The propagation enters a stable period. Thereafter, if some progress or change is made on this topic, then a second or third explosion of activity occurs. Fig. 1 portrays the growth process of extensively discussed topics. To use characteristics

[1] http://www.google.co.jp/

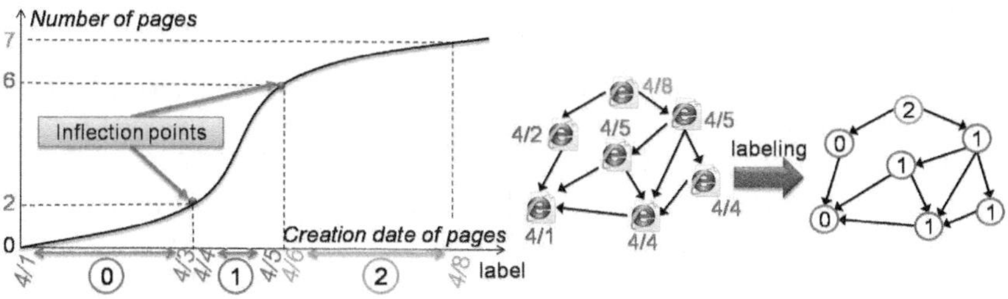

Fig. 1. Typical growth process and a labeled graph

of the spread, we assign the node labels reflecting the growth period of a graph. For example, the second sub-period for a topic might correspond to a period during which the topic spreads gradually; the same sub-period might correspond to an explosive spread for another topic. We intend to use the same label for periods with the same temporal characteristics, such as how the topic spreads, as possible. Therefore, we use inflection points as labeling boundaries. We find the time points at which the graph of growth changes drastically as inflection points. Subsequently, we label the nodes of the graph in the order of periods whose boundaries are these time points such as Fig. 1.

3.4 Extracting Frequent Graph Patterns

We enumerate frequent time graph patterns from the set of labeled graphs. Particularly, we examine discussions found on blogs and news sites. In such discussions, once an entry about a topic is posted on a blog or news site, then bloggers discuss the topic by creating links to the entry and posting their personal comments. We choose and investigate the 7 topics, which have been discussed in the past. For each topic, we construct a web graph as explained in 3.2.

We apply gSpan to the constructed 7 graphs by setting *minSup* to 4. If *minSup* is too large, then the nodes in each maximal pattern become extremely few. Small patterns are usually found on almost all web graphs other than the constructed graphs, so they are not useful for finding interesting topics. In contrast, if *minSup* is too small, then the structures of enumerated patterns would depend considerably on the constructed graphs. Consequently, the patterns would not be sufficiently versatile to find new useful information for many topics. In addition, the number of patterns would be too large to compute them in practice. When *minSup* = 4, we can obtain 107 time graph patterns in a few minutes. Therefore, time graph patterns can be mined by gSpan in practical time.

4 Web Analysis and Information Retrieval Using Time Graph Patterns

In this section, we explain how useful time graph patterns are for web analysis and information retrieval. Using PCA, we first verify time graph patterns can analyze structural and temporal characteristics of the web.

4.1 PCA Dataset

McGlohon et al. [10] performed PCA using cascades and blog sites. Instead, we perform PCA using the time graph patterns, mined for extensively discussed topics, and sites related to such topics. As candidates of such sites, we collect blogs authoritative for and sensitive to hot topics, or blogs posting many entries related to daily news, and sites summarizing such blogs and news sites. We collect not only pages in the sites but also pages linking to or linked from them. We obtain a web graph consisting of 850 pages in 55 sites and 732 links.

4.2 Principal Component Analysis

McGlohon et al. performed PCA on a matrix whose element indicate how many each type of cascades is contained in each site. Instead, we construct a matrix using the dataset explained above and the time graph pattern mined in the previous section. Each row represents a site in the dataset. Each column represents a pair of a pattern and a node label. Let $e_{i,(j,\ell)}$ be the element for the i-th site and the pair of the j-th pattern and label ℓ. We define the value of $e_{i,(j,\ell)}$ be the number of pages in site i matching a node with lable ℓ in pattern j.

We have performed PCA on the matrix. Generally, the number of important PCs is determined so that the cumulative proportion is above a certain threshold, like 70%. The cumulative proportion of the third PC is 0.763. Therefore, we regard the first three PCs as important ones.

4.3 Structural and Temporal Characteristics

We investigate the obtained PCs to confirm whether time graph patterns can analyze structural and temporal characteristics of the web. We first classify the sites in the dataset using the PCs. For the classification of the sites related to topics discussed extensively, we have observed the following three classes of sites: "primary source," "triggers," and "summarizers." A *primary source* is a site reporting a topic first. If an influential blog site or a famous personal site find and link to the primary source, then the topic becomes discussed extensively. We designate these sites as *triggers.* Some sites then summarizes the topic by linking to the primary source and the triggers. We designate these sites as *summarizers.*

We have investigated the sites to construct the correct answers for the classification manually. We have decided not to distinguish primary sources from triggers, because a trigger for a topic is also the primary source for another topic frequently. Therefore, we manually classify the sites into the following two classes: (A) primary sources and triggers for topics, and (B) summarizers.

Fig. 2(a) is the scatter diagram of the sites according to the PC scores for the first and the second PCs. Similarly, Fig. 2(b) is for the second and the third PCs. In these figures, "$\circ$" represents a site of class (A); "$\times$" represents one of class (B). The two classes are separated distinctly in these figures. As a result, the first three PCs obtained from the time graph patterns are sufficient for the classification. The link structure information is sufficient for the manual

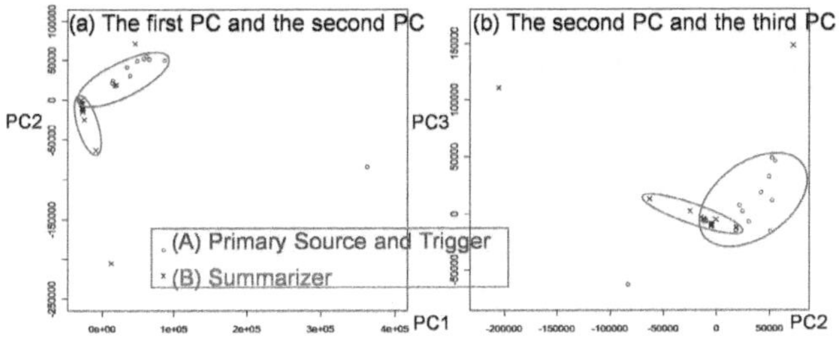

Fig. 2. Scatter diagram of PC scores

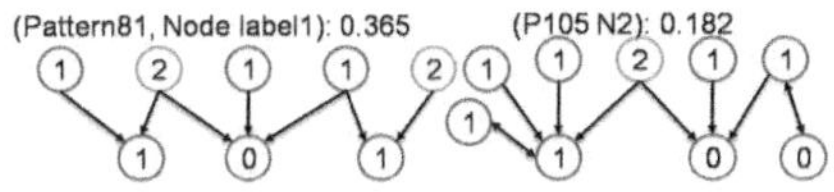

Fig. 3. P-CPs to the third PC

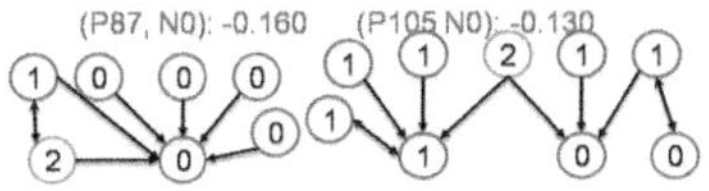

Fig. 4. N-CPs to the third PC

classification as explained above. Consequently, time graph patterns are useful for analyzing structural characteristics of the web.

We turn to factor loadings and temporal characteristics of the web. The factor loadings for our PCA are the correlation coefficients between the pattern-label pairs and the PCs. A pattern-label pair greatly contributes to a PC if the absolute value of the factor loading against the PC. Therefore, we define a *positively contributing pair* (P-CP) as a pair having the factor loading higher than 0.100. Similarly, a pair is called a *negatively contributing pair* (N-CP) if the factor loading is lower than −0.100. Fig. 3 illustrates the top two P-CPs to the third PC. Similarly, Fig. 4 illustrates the top two N-CPs. We have found that most of the P-CPs have label 2. On the other hand, most of the N-CPs have labels 0 or 1. Furthermore, we have found an interesting fact about pairs having the same pattern but having different labels. When one of them appears as P-CP, and the other might appear as N-CP. There is an example in Fig. 3 and Fig. 4. The pair of pattern 105 and label 2 is a P-CP, but the pair of the same pattern and label 0 is a N-CP.

In contrast to the third PC, each label appears uniformly in both the P-CPs and N-CPs to the the first PC and the second PC. Furthermore, the contributing pairs to them contain no example similar to the pairs of pattern 105 for the third PC. Therefore, only the third PC would reflect temporal information sufficiently. Consequently, time graph patterns, particularly pairs contributing to the third PC, would be useful for analyzing temporal characteristics of the web.

5 Conclusion

We proposed time graph patterns estimating temporal and structural characteristics. We mined actual time graph patterns and applied them to web analysis and information retrieval. Performing PCA can facilitate classification of web sites according to important characteristics of extensively discussed topics such as the primary source, trigger, and summarizer. The results demonstrate that time graph patterns are useful to analyze both structural characteristics and temporal characteristics of the web. Our future work will include analysis of other datasets, e.g. citation networks.

References

1. Yan, X., Han, J.: gSpan: Graph-based substructure pattern mining. In: Proceedings of the 2002 IEEE International Conference on Data Mining, pp. 721–724 (2002)
2. Leskovec, J., Kleinberg, J., Faloutsos, C.: Graphs over time: densification laws, shrinking diameters and possible explanations. In: Proceedings of the eleventh ACM SIGKDD International Conference on Knowledge Discovery in Data Mining, pp. 177–187 (2005)
3. Tawde, V.B., Oates, T., Glover, E.: Generating web graphs with embedded communities. Algorithms and Models for the Web-Graph, 80–91 (2004)
4. Pennock, D.M., Flake, G.W., Lawrence, S., Glover, E.J., Giles, C.L.: Winners don't take all: Characterizing the competition for links on the web. Proceedings of the National Academy of Sciences of the United States of America, National Acad. Sciences, 5207 (2002)
5. Huberman, B., Adamic, L.: Growth dynamics of the world-wide web. Nature 401, 131 (1999)
6. Kumar, R., Novak, J., Raghavan, P., Tomkins, A.: On the bursty evolution of blogspace. In: Proceedings of the 12th International World Wide Web Conference, pp. 159–178 (2005)
7. Kleinberg, J.M.: Authoritative sources in a hyperlinked environment. Journal of the ACM 46(5), 604–632 (1999)
8. Kumar, R., Raghavan, P., Rajagopalan, S., Tomkins, A.: Trawling the web for emerging cyber-communities. Computer Networks 31, 1481–1493 (1999)
9. Leskovec, J., McGlohon, M., Faloutsos, C.: Cascading behavior in large blog graphs. In: SIAM International Conference on Data Minig (2007)
10. McGlohon, M., Leskovec, J., Faloutsos, C., Hurst, M., Glance, N.: Finding patterns in blog shapes and blog evolution. In: Proceedings of ICWSM (2007)

FISH: A Novel Peer-to-Peer Overlay Network Based on Hyper-deBruijn

Ye Yuan[1,2], Guoren Wang[1,2], and Yongjiao Sun[1,2]

[1] College of Information Science and Engineering, Northeastern University, Shenyang 110004, China
[2] Key Laboratory of Medical Image Computing (Northeastern University), Ministry of Education
linuxyy@gmail.com

Abstract. Autonomy, efficiency, robustness and load balancing are four desirable features for Peer-to-Peer (P2P) systems. These four features however, are often in conflict with each other. We present a novel P2P architecture, called FISH, based on the Hyper-deBruijn topology. FISH provides flexibility in terms of connections per node and the level of fault-tolerance, and possesses a low diameter. We further address the challenge of dynamic operations of peers by introducing a novel set of algorithms. We also design two variants of Hyper-deBruijn topology for achieving an asymptotical optimal diameter. Comprehensive experiments show that FISH has a good trade-off among the four expected features.

1 Introduction

P2P overlay networks have recently emerged as a good substrate for building internet scale and robust systems. The native P2P networks are based on one or more centralized servers, such as Napster and Kazaa. The unstructured P2P networks like Gnutella [1], impose less and loose the constraints on topology and resource placement strategies. In the past few years, different structured P2P networks [2,3,4,5] are also designed. They impose a certain structure on the overlay network and control the placement of resources, thus exhibit the unique properties that unstructured P2Ps lack. Many of these structured networks are based on the Hypercube structure or the deBruijn structure, such as Pastry [4], Tapestry [6], HyperCup [7], based on Hypercube, and Koorde [8], CAN-d2B [9], Distance Halving [10], ODRI [12], based on deBruijn.

An n-cube Hypercube graph contains 2^n vertices labeled from 0 to 2^n-1. There is an edge between two vertices if and only if the binary representations of their labels differ by one bit. Given a Hypercube with N vertices, the diameter is log_2N and the average distance is $log_2N/2$. The degree of each vertex grows logarithmically with N. Hence, the Hypercube is not a constant-degree topology, but it achieves an optimal level of connectivity. There are log_2N vertex-disjoint paths between any two vertices. That is, there still exists a path of length at most log_2N between any two vertices when log_2N-1 edges are removed from the network. The fault-tolerance capacity of Hypercube is excellent since there are number of $k!$ different shortest paths between any two vertices in distance k. Drawback of the Hypercube structure is that a vertex must keep

L. Chen et al. (Eds.): WAIM 2010, LNCS 6184, pp. 47–61, 2010.

increasingly large number of connections as the number of vertices increases. Hence, Hypercube does not achieve a good tradeoff between the routing table size and the routing delay when it is utilized to implement a structured P2P network.

In contrast to Hypercube, the out-degree of each vertex in a deBruijn digraph does not increase as the increase of the number of vertices; it is a constant. The diameter of deBruijn is asymptotically optimal since it almost achieves the Moore bound. Fraigniaud and Gauron [9] proposed a famous structured P2P network based on the deBruijn topology, called D2B. Koorde [8] extends the Chord to obtain optimal deBruijn degree/diameter tradeoff. Unlike D2B, Koorde does not constrain the selection of node identifier, while it supports concurrent joins. Kaashoek and Karger [8] investigated Koorde's resilience under a rather harsh failure scenario: "If a network is still connected when all nodes fail with probability 1/2, the out-degree of some nodes must be $O(logN)$". Inspired by this observation, they proposed a mechanism to increase the node degree at the cost of losing the constant degree advantage of the deBruijn topology.

As discussed above, the structured P2P networks based on deBruijn topology inherit the advantages of deBruijn topology, including constant node degree and optimal diameter. These P2P networks however, have the following two disadvantages. First, they assume that the resources follows an uniform distribution. In practice however, this assumption does not hold. Hence, Networks based on deBruijn fail to meet the ideal load balance and search efficiency if the resource distribution is uneven even highly skewed. Secondly, they suffer from poor fault-tolerance since the node degree does not increase with the increase of network size.

Both Hypercube and deBruijn topologies possess certain unique advantages. Hyper-deBruijn topology is the a hybrid of Hypercube topology and deBruijn topology, and combining advantageous features from both models. Hyper-deBruijn was first introduced in the interconnection field [11], and later used to support wormhole routing [17]. In this work, we propose a novel P2P overlay network, called FISH, based on the Hyper-deBruijn topology. The main contributions of this paper are as follows:

1. Based on the Hyper-deBruijn topology, we design a novel structured P2P network with a good fault-tolerance capacity, a low diameter and flexible connections of each node.
2. We propose a fault-tolerant routing algorithm, combined with the features of a "small-world" network, for FISH in dynamic scenarios. We also introduce self-stabilization algorithms to deal with the dynamic operations of peers, such as *join*, *departure* and *failure*.
3. We propose a constant degree and a logarithmic degree variants of the Hyper-deBruijn topology. The diameters of the two topologies are asymptotical optimal. We also associate each new topology with an efficient routing algorithm.
4. We evaluate the major metrics of FISH by extensive experiments. The results show that FISH has a good trade-off among the four features of autonomy, efficiency, robustness and load balance.

2 General Design of FISH

2.1 Hyper-deBruijn

To introduce Hyper-deBruijn, this paper follows notations and definitions defined in [11]. Contrary to [11], in which an undirected deBruijn graph is used, a directed deBruijn graph is used. A network can be modeled as a graph $G(V_G, E_G)$, where V_G is the set of vertices and E_G is the set of edges.

For any positive k, Z_k denotes the set $\{0, 1, ..., k-1\}$. For the set Z_k and any positive integer n, Z_k^n denotes the set of all length-n strings of Z_k. The order-n Hypercube graph $H(n)$ consists of the set of Z_k^n vertices. There is an edge between two vertices if and only if their labels differ by exactly one bit. $H(n)$ is an undirected graph with k^n vertices. Consider two vertices x and y of $H(n)$. Proceeding from x, it is possible to reach y in, at most, n hops.

For a positive m, an order-m deBruijn graph $D(m)$ consists of the set Z_k^m of vertices. There is an arc from a vertex $u{=}(x_m, x_{m-1},.., x_1)$ to a vertex $v{=}(x_{m-1}, x_{m-2},.., x_1, \alpha)$ where $\alpha \in Z_k$. The order-m deBruijn is a directed graph with k^m vertices. Consider two vertices x and y of $D(m)$. Proceeding from x, it is possible to reach y in, at most, m hops.

Definition 1. *Let $G(V_G, E_G)$ and $H(V_H, E_H)$ be two graphs. The direct product graph of G and H, denoted by $G{\times}H$, has a node set $V_G{\times}V_H$. For any $u, v{\in}G$ and $x, y{\in}H$, $(<u, x>,<v, y>)$ is an edge of $G{\times}H$ if and only if either (u, v) is an edge of G and $x{=}y$, or (x, y) is an edge of H and $u{=}v$*

Definition 2. *Let $H(n)$ be an order-n Hypercube graph and $D(m)$ an order-m deBruijn digraph. Then an order-(n, m) Hyper-deBruijn graph $HD(n, m)$ is the direct product of $H(n)$ and $D(m)$, denoted as $H(n){\times}D(m)$.*

Figure 1 shows the $HD(2, 2)$ of Hyper-deBruijn.

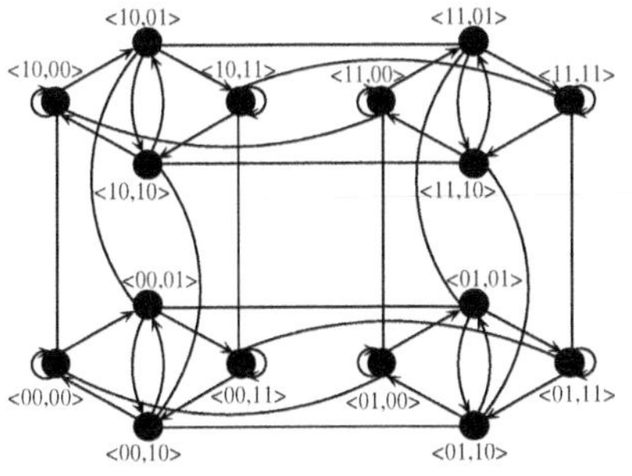

Fig. 1. Example of $HD(2, 2)$ Hyper-deBruijn

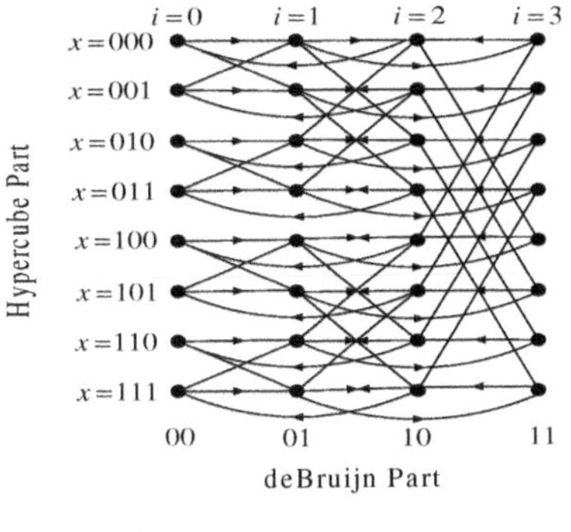

Fig. 2. Example of the Hyper-deBruijn graph with an optimal diameter

2.2 Construction of FISH

Hyper-deBruijn is a combination of Hypercube and deBruijn, thus inheriting desirable features of both topologies. However, Hyper-deBruijn is a static structure and only has desirable features with concrete number of nodes, i.e., $2^2 \times 2^2 = 16$ in Fig. 1. This requirement is difficult to meet in dynamic scenarios, and a P2P network should support arbitrary number of nodes. In this section, we present how to use the topology feature of Hyper-deruijn to construct a randomized topology that is suitable for P2P networks.

Suppose the ID of a node of Hyper-deBruijn is $< h, d >$ which represents the Hypercube part and deBruijn part respectively. Let a deBruijn have M nodes and a Hypercube have N nodes. The randomized topology can be constructed as follows:

Firstly, for d, it employs a constant routing table with multiple entries, where each entry represents a matching suffix up to a digit position in its ID. The connection from d to another d' is the same as deBruijn graph introduced in the last subsection, i.e, $d = (x_m, x_{m-1}, ..., x_1)$ connecting to $d' = (x_{m-1}, x_{m-2}, ..., x_1, \alpha)$.

Secondly, for Hypercube part $h = h_1 \cdots h_i \cdots h_k$ $(1 \leq i \leq k)$ h makes a connection with another h' as follows: h_i bit is flipped, and each of the remaining $k - 1$ bits is chosen uniformly at random.

Finally, the SHA-1 hashing function is adopted for producing an ID for each node and data evenly. To support more data than nodes, the node ID is the prefix of data ID. Then the data can be distributed across the network according to the longest prefix matching rule.

As a result, the topology of FISH becomes a deterministic deBruijn and a completely randomized Hypercube. The deBruijn graph with constant degree has an optimal autonomy and routing efficiency, but has a poor fault tolerance due to its constant degree. Hypercube can make up the disadvantage of deBruijn. However, the self-stabilization of Hypercube topology is computationally expensive. A randomized Hypercube is easy to control in dynamic scenarios since it provides a large set of possible connections for a given node ID. That also means the randomized Hypercube provides more fault tolerance than traditional Hypercube. Therefore, FISH has a good autonomy and fault tolerance.

According to [23], as the construction scheme for Hyper-deBruijn, the topology of FISH has become a "small-world percolation" network which satisfies the following condition.

Definition 3. *A "small-world percolation" network of dimension d is a graph whose vertex set is associated with the d−dimensional mesh. The probability that an edge* (u, v) *exists is* $\frac{1}{||u-v||^d}$, *where* $||u - v||$ *stands for the L1 distance between u and v. For Hyper-deBruijn,* $||u-v||$ *stands for the distance in Hyper-deBruijn hashing namespace.*

FISH can only theoretically be a "small-world percolation" network. In distributed and dynamic scenarios, it is difficult for each node of FISH to satisfy the condition (given by Definition 3) of the "small-world" network. For example, the nodes satisfying $||u - v|| = 1$ may not have an edge each other. Therefore, the traditional greedy routing for the "small-world percolation" network [23] may fail for FISH in some cases. To solve the problem, we adopt the following method.

The topology still owns the "small-world" network feature that FISH is a "power-law" network. The random "power-law" network has a degree distribution:

$$p_k = Ck^{-\gamma} \tag{1}$$

where

$$C^{-1} = \sum_{k=2}^{k_{max}} k^{-\gamma} \approx \zeta(\gamma) - 1$$

and $\zeta(\cdot)$ is the Riemann zeta function. k_{max} is the maximum degree of the network.

The "power-law" network means some fractions of the network nodes have a high degree. For any node with degree k, we say it is a high degree node if $k \geq k_{max}/2$. From the Equation (1), we can get the number of high degree nodes G given by:

$$G = N(C \sum_{k=k_{max}/2}^{k_{max}} k^{-\gamma}) \tag{2}$$

where N is the total number of nodes.

Since for all decreasing, positive function, $f(k)$ we have $\sum_{k=a}^{b} f(k) > \int_a^{b+1} f(k)dk > \int_b^a f(k)dk$ and $\sum_{k=a}^{b} f(k) < \int_{a-1}^{b} f(k)dk$, We can bound G from the above formulas:

$$G > \frac{C}{\gamma - 1}(\frac{1}{(\frac{1}{2})^{\gamma-1}} - 1)\frac{N}{k_{max}^{\gamma-1}},$$

and

$$G < \frac{C}{\gamma - 1}(\frac{1}{(\frac{1}{2})^{\gamma-1}(1 - \frac{1}{k_{max}/2})} - 1)\frac{N}{k_{max}^{\gamma-1}}$$

For $k_{max} \to \infty$, we have that $\frac{1}{k_{max}/2} \to 0$ thus:

$$G \approx \frac{C}{\gamma - 1}(2^{\gamma-1} - 1)\frac{N}{k_{max}^{\gamma-1}} \tag{3}$$

We have shown that $G = O(\frac{N}{k_{max}^{\gamma-1}})$. According to [25], the maximum value of k_{max} can reach $O(N^{\frac{1}{\gamma}})$. Thus the number of high degree nodes is at least $O(N^{\frac{1}{\gamma}})$. According to the Definition 2, Hyper-deBruijn can be viewed as a Hypercube where each node represents a deBruijn graph (deBruijn group), and symmetrically it can also be a deBruijn graph with each node having a Hypercube group. When $\gamma = 2$, there is at least one high degree node in each Hypercube or deBruijn group.

As noted above, the greedy routing algorithm used for "small-world" network may fail for FISH. The failures often happen when querying the low degree ($k < \log N$) nodes that have no connections to high degree nodes, since there is little or no information for a routing algorithm to discover such nodes. To solve this problem, the problematic nodes are forced to have an edge to the high degree nodes in its deBruijn group. According to the above analysis, there should be at least one high degree node in each deBruijn group. The high degree nodes can be found using the deBruijn part routing algorithm that will be proposed in section 2.3. As a result, high degree nodes have edges to most nodes of the network, while other nodes are connected using the Hyper-deBruijn construction rule. To apply the information, we adopt an improved routing algorithm to speed up the routing for FISH in section 2.3. Though a randomized topology may lead to imbalanced node degrees that have impacts on routing efficiency, our improved routing method can avoid this.

The construction method of FISH can guarantee that FISH obtains a good tradeoff among autonomy, efficiency, robustness and load balancing in some points.

2.3 Fault Tolerance Routing Algorithm

Since nodes often fail without notifying other nodes in the P2P network, a fully distributed routing algorithm is very important for being adaptable to one or more node failures. To address this problem, the routing algorithm should provide as many as routing paths between any pair of nodes.

Suppose a node $<h,d>$ originates a message or receives a message from a neighbor, and the destination node of the message is $<h',d'>$. This message might be used to publish or search a resource with the label of the node $<h',d'>$ as a prefix of the label of resource. A greedy routing algorithm designed for FISH is described as follows. Here, *Hyper-algorithm* represents the routing algorithm for Hypercube proposed in [6] and *De-algorithm* represents the routing algorithm for deBruijn shown in [8].

1. $(h = h')$ and $(d \neq d')$
   Under this scenario, De-algorithm is used to route the message from the node $<h,d>$ to the destination node $<h,d'>$. According to the deBruijn routing algorithm, the node $<h,d>$ can find its successor along path to the the node $<h,d'>$. If the successor node is faulty, the node $<h,d>$ forwards the message to another deBruijn neighbor if it survives. If two deBruijn neighbors of the node $<h,d>$ fail simultaneously, then the message will be forwarded to a surviving Hypercube neighbor. The node which receives the message from the node $<h,d>$ will repeat to route the message based on this greedy algorithm until the message meets its destination.
2. $(h \neq h')$ and $(d = d')$
   Under this scenario, Hyper-algorithm is used to route the message from the node $<h,d>$ to the destination node $<h',d>$. According to the Hypercube routing algorithm, the node $<h,d>$ can find its successor along the path to the the node $<h',d>$. If the successor node has failed, the node $<h,d>$ forwards the message to another Hypercube neighbor if it survives. If two Hypercube neighbors of the node $<h,d>$ fail simultaneously, then the message will be forwarded to one survival deBruijn neighbor. The node which receives the message from the node $<h,d>$ will repeat to route the message based on this greedy algorithm until the message meets its destination.
3. $(h{\neq}h')$ and $(d{\neq}d')$
   The request is routed from $< h,d >$ to $< h,d' >$ using the method in case 1. Then the request is from $< h,d' >$ to $< h',d' >$ using the method in case 2.

Next we use the features of the "power-law" network to improve the algorithm.

To make most use of features of the randomized topology, a randomized selection neighbor scheme is proposed to improve the fault-tolerant routing algorithm. Assuming node i with capacity's metric c_i has k_i edges, the randomized scheme is given by:

Node i select a neighbor j with probability: $p_{i,j} = \frac{1}{k_i} max\{1, \frac{c_j k_j}{c_i k_i}\}$.

For each scenario of the fault-tolerant routing algorithm, in every hop, suppose current node A selects a neighbor B with the random selection neighbor scheme, and the Hyper-deBruijn neighbor of node A is C. Node B checks its neighbor identifiers to see if there is a neighbor D closer to the destination node than C. If there exists such a D node, the query is forwarded to D via node B. Otherwise the query reaches node C, then C repeats to route the query based on this algorithm until the query meets its destination.

From the selection probability formula, we know the message from a node is usually forwarded to the highest degree and most powerful node among all its neighbors. The proposed routing algorithm is similar to the first max-degree search algorithm [22], which has been proven to be more efficient than other routing algorithms for "small-world" networks. The actual performance of the traditional first max-degree search algorithm is far worse than the theoretically predicted value due to the fact that the assumption that the nodes scanned during a walk are unique, i.e., no node is scanned more than once. Besides applying the principle of the first max-degree search algorithm, our improved routing algorithm also adopts the greedy routing which makes the query to be approaching the destination node more gradually. Therefore, the scheme avoids the same node being scanned twice. Furthermore, unlike the traditional greedy routing algorithm [23], the improved algorithm uses the high degree nodes to speed up the query. Note that high degree nodes have been chosen according to the node's capacity. The selection neighbor probability can guarantee that the query is forward to a powerful neighbor. Therefore, the routing scheme reduces the impact on the search efficiency due to the degree imbalance of the randomized network. The improved routing algorithm is a reasonable merge of routing algorithms for a "small-world" network and a structured network.

2.4 Self-Stabilization of FISH

Self-stabilization is important to P2P networks, since they usually suffer from highly dynamic nodes operations. We deal with these operations in the following cases.

Join. Consider that peer A wants to join the system. Peer A first finds a peer B with closest ID to A in FISH using the *fault-tolerant routing* algorithm. Then peer A updates its routing table according to peer B's. Finally peer B transfers half its data to A.

Departure. Consider that peer A wants to leave from the system. Peer A finds another peer B with closest ID to A. Peer A transfers all its data to peer B, and peer A's neighbors update their routing tables.

Failure. A super node is selected in each deBruijn group, and suppose this super node is A. Peer A constructs a local queue and a statistical model, by considering some factors such as which peers are more important nodes; which data is most frequently queried; which peers are often failed. A can get these statistical information from high degree nodes in that deBruijn group. A puts k nodes with the highest probability of failure in front of the queue after analyzing these factors using the statistical model. These k nodes may vary periodically. For each X of the k nodes, peer A periodically visits X to see if it fails. Once it fails, then peer A notices neighbors of X.

3 Optimal Diameter Design of FISH

The problem of designing an optimal diameter for a graph with a fixed degree has been extensively studied in the past. Assume that a graph has a fixed degree k and a diameter D. The minimum diameter in any graph built on the top of N nodes is given as follows [16,18]:

$$D \geq \lceil \log_k(N(k-1)+1) \rceil - 1 = D_M \tag{4}$$

When k is $\log_2 N$, the lower bound of the diameter is $O(\frac{\log_2 N}{\log_2 \log_2 N})$.

Next we first analyze the diameter of the general design of FISH, then propose an asymptotical optimal diameter design for FISH.

Suppose $N=n \times m$, n is the number of Hypercube nodes and m is for deBruijn. Then the degree of the Hyper-deBruijn is $(\log_2 n)+2$ and the diameter is $\log_2 n+\log_2 m=\log_2 nm=\log_2 N$. This means the diameter of Hyper-deBruijn is independent of the combination of Hypercube and deBruijn. Compared with the theoretical lower bound D_M given by Formula (4), it can be concluded that the diameter is not optimal.

An intuitive idea for improving the diameter design of Hyper-deBruijn is reducing n since deBruijn has optimal diameter. As n decreases, Hyper-deBruijn adopts more deBruijn protocol, and therefore getting a better diameter design. However, this solution has the following main shortcomings.

As m increases, the degree of the Hyper-deBruijn decreases. In this case, the Hyper-deBruijn cannot get a good tradeoff amongst search efficiency, fault tolerance and load balancing when the degree is less than $\log_2 N$. Since it can be proven that if a P2P network is a fault tolerant and load balancing network, then the degree is at least $\log_2 N$ [8]. Moreover, reducing n will cause the drawbacks of deBruijn to be more prominent. In the following, we show how to improve FISH so as to make the diameter be asymptotical optimal while keeping a good tradeoff amongst search efficiency, fault tolerance and load balancing.

Let $n=u^v$ and $m=v+1$. Then $N=u^v \times (v+1)$, where u and v are positive integers. In the following, we will construct the topology which has an asymptotical diameter and a good tradeoff for both the constant degree and the logarithmic degree.

3.1 Constant Degree

1. **Topology Construction**

In this case, u is a constant. A constant degree topology with an asymptotical optimal diameter can be constructed in two steps.

Firstly, u^v deBruijn groups are constructed in advance and there are $v+1$ nodes within each deBruijn group. Since deBruijn is a Hamiltonian graph, there is a cycle passing through all the nodes in the deBruijn group exactly, and all the nodes in the Hamiltonian circle are numbered as $0, 1, ..., v$.

Next, Hypercube neighbors are constructed for nodes in the deBruijn groups. For node i ($0 \leq i < v$) in a group, $u - 1$ nodes whose IDs are $i+1$ are randomly selected from the $u^v - 1$ deBruijn groups and connected to node i as the Hypercube neighbors of node i.

For the above constructed topology, the degree is $u + (u - 1) = 2u - 1$, where u and $(u - 1)$ are the degree of the deBruijn part and the Hypercube part respectively. Similarly, the diameter is $\log_u(v + 1) + v$. It can be shown that the diameter is $\log_u N$, since $u^v(v + 1) = N \Rightarrow v + \log_u(v + 1) = \log_u N$. To the best of our knowledge, the above constructed topology is a new kind of P2P overlay network with a constant degree and an asymptotical optimal diameter.

Figure 2 shows an example of the proposed topology, and the topology consists of 8 deBruijn groups within each which there are 4 nodes. In this figure, there are $N = u^v(v + 1) = 2^3 \times (3 + 1) = 32$ nodes, and the diameter and degree are 3 and 5. From the figure, we know that the diagonal lines are Hypercube connections and the lines with an arrow are deBruijn connections.

2. Routing Algorithm

Although the new topology can also use the fault tolerant routing algorithm to perform a query, the new topology is different from general Hyper-deBruijn, so a new routing algorithm is proposed to perform a query more efficiently.

We still use the SHA-1 hashing function to produce data and node IDs. The node ID is the prefix of data ID. Since all the nodes in a deBruijn group have been numbered as $0, 1 \ldots, v$, the ID of each node is denoted as $(x_0 x_1 \ldots x_{v-1}; d_0 d_1 \ldots d_m; l)$, $m = \lfloor \log_u(v + 1) \rfloor$ and $0 \leq l \leq v$. Suppose node $(x_0 x_1 \ldots x_{v-1}; d_0 d_1 \ldots d_m; l)$ requests a key whose prefix is $(y_0 y_1 \cdots y_{v-1}; h_0 h_1 \ldots, h_m; s)$. Then the routing algorithm is described as follows.

Step 1. Routing within the Hypercube section while using the sequence of Hamiltonian circle

- **if** (the routing node contains the string $y_0 y_1 \cdots y_{v-1}$) **stop**;
- **else** from the $u-1$ Hypercube neighbors find a neighbor node h with the closest ID to the requesting key, then route the request to h. During the routing, x_{l+1} is successively changed to y_{l+1} while going from l to $l+1$ in the Hamiltonian circle, x_{l+2} to y_{l+2} while going from $l+1$ to $l+2$ in the Hamiltonian circle, and so on. This process continues until the routing node contains string $y_0 y_1 \cdots y_{v-1}$;
- $i = l$

Step 2. Routing in the deBruijn group

- **if** $(i == s)$ **stop**;
- **else** the request is routed to the node containing string $(y_0 y_1 \cdots y_{v-1}; h_0 h_1 \ldots h_m; s)$ using deBruijn routing algorithm;

Step 1 is a Hypercube part routing which can find the string using at most k hops. Step 2 is deBruijn part routing using at most $\log_u(v+1)$ hops. Therefore the diameter is v+$\log_u(v+1)$=$\log_u N$ and the routing algorithm can be performed efficiently. For example, in Fig. 2, suppose the message is routed from peer $(000, 00, 0)$ to peer $(111, 00, 0)$. The step 1 is along the path $(000, 00, 0) \rightarrow (001, 01, 1) \rightarrow (011, 10, 2) \rightarrow (111, 11, 3)$, and then the message is routed down the path $(111, 11, 3) \rightarrow (111, 10, 2) \rightarrow (111, 00, 0)$.

3.2 Logarithmic Degree

1. Topology Construction

A logarithmic degree topology with an asymptotical optimal diameter is constructed as follows.

Similar to the constant degree topology, u^v deBruijn groups are constructed first resulting in $v+1$ nodes within each deBruijn group. These $v+1$ nodes are numbered as $0, 1, ..., v$ according to the hamiltonian circle.

Secondly, Hypercube neighbors are constructed for nodes in the deBruijn groups. For node i $(0 \leq i < v)$ in a group, $u-1$ nodes whose IDs are $i+1$ are randomly selected from the u^v-1 deBruijn groups and connected to node i as the Hypercube neighbors of node i.

Finally, for all u^v deBruijn groups, additional $v-u$ edges are added to every node in the same deBruijn group. In this case, each group becomes a complete connected graph. This means the diameter of every group is 1.

For the same reason of the constant degree topology, the degree of the above constructed topology is $(u-1)+v = u+v-1$. The diameter is v+1. Let v be $\frac{\log_2 N}{\log_2 \log_2 N}$. Then u=$(N/\frac{\log_2 N}{\log_2 \log_2 N})^{1/\frac{\log_2 N}{\log_2 \log_2 N}}$<$\log_2 N$. Thus, the degree is v+u−1 <$\frac{\log_2 N}{\log_2 \log_2 N}$+ $\log_2 N$−1. The diameter is v+1=$\frac{\log_2 N}{\log_2 \log_2 N}$+1 which is asymptotical optimal to the theoretical lower bound. This leads to a constructed topology that has a logarithmic degree and an asymptotical optimal diameter. An example of the topology is similar as the Fig. 2. The Hypercube part is the same, and the deBruijn part for the logarithmic degree topology is a complete graph.

2. Routing Algorithm

The node and data IDs for the logarithmic degree topology are the same as the constant degree topology. The only difference is that the node ID of the logarithmic degree topology does not need contain the deBruijn string. Let node $(x_0x_1 \ldots x_{v-1}; l)$ request a key whose prefix is $(y_0y_1 \ldots y_{v-1}; s)$. The routing algorithm for the logarithmic degree topology is described as follows.

Step 1. Hypercube domain routing while using the sequence of Hamiltonian circle

- **if** (the routing node contains the string $y_0y_1 \ldots y_{v-1}$) **stop**;
- **else** from the $u-1$ Hypercube neighbors find a neighbor node with the closest ID to the key and route the request to this neighbor. During the routing, x_{l+1} is successively changed to y_{l+1} while going from l to l+1 in the Hamiltonian

circle, x_{l+2} to y_{l+2} while going from $l+1$ to $l+2$ in the Hamiltonian circle, and so on. This process continues until the routing node contains the string $y_0 y_1 \cdots y_v$;
- $i=l$.

Step 2. Complete graph routing
- **if** $(i==s)$ **stop**;
- **else** the request is routed from the node $(y_0 y_1 \ldots y_{v-1}; i)$ to the node containing string $(y_0 y_1 \ldots y_{v-1}; s)$ using only one hop;

Step 1 is a Hypercube domain routing to find the key using at most v hops. To optimize the procedure in the situation that there is no path in the Hypercube-domain, step 2 can be run first, after which step 1 is executed. Step 2 only uses one hop. Therefore the diameter is $v+1=\frac{\log_2 N}{\log_2 \log_2 N}+1$.

4 Performance Evaluation

We use PeerSim to implement proposed algorithms of FISH. PeerSim is a P2P simulation framework aimed at developing and testing any kind of P2P protocols [24]. The experiment environment is a PC with Pentium 4-3.0G, 2 G memory.

We use FISH to denote the general design of Hyper-deBruijn and FISH+ to denote the optimal diameter design (with the logarithmic degree) of Hyper-deBruijn. We also implement Pastry [4] and Chord [5] to compare FISH, and Koorde [8] based on deBruijn and Viceroy [20] based on Butterfly to compare FISH+. For a fair comparison, we design the routing table size of each network to be $\log_2 N$ as the corresponding protocol of the network. All queries are generated randomly and uniformly at each node for each network. We evaluate these networks using the number of nodes from 256 to 1 million.

Figure 3 shows the worst case path lengths of routes (also called network diameter) taken by queries for different networks. Figure 4(a) shows the result for general designs. The result shows that the maximum number of hops required for a query is almost same for Chord and Pastry. That is because they both own a length of $\log_2 N$ diameter, but Pastry provides a more flexible and efficient routing scheme. FISH has the smallest diameter which is smaller than half of the diameter of Pastry and Chord with the help of high degree nodes. As given in Fig. 3(b), the maximum numbers of hops for optimal diameter networks are much smaller than the numbers in Fig. 3(a). When these networks have a $\log_2 N$ degree, their diameters are asymptotically optimal. In the Figure, FISH+ has the smallest diameter, since FISH+ has a deBruijn subgraph while others only have a line as subgraph.

Figure 4(a) shows the average number of hops required for a query for Chord, Pastry and FISH networks. FISH has a smaller average distance than others, which shows that it has the best search delay. From Fig. 4(b), it can be concluded that for the optimal diameter networks the average number of hops required for a query of FISH+ is smaller than Viceroy and Koorde.

Next we examine the effects of dynamic networks on the routing efficiency. In this experiment, each system initially has 16k peers, then the same number of peers begin concurrently join and (depart) in (from) the network. Thus the number of peers in the

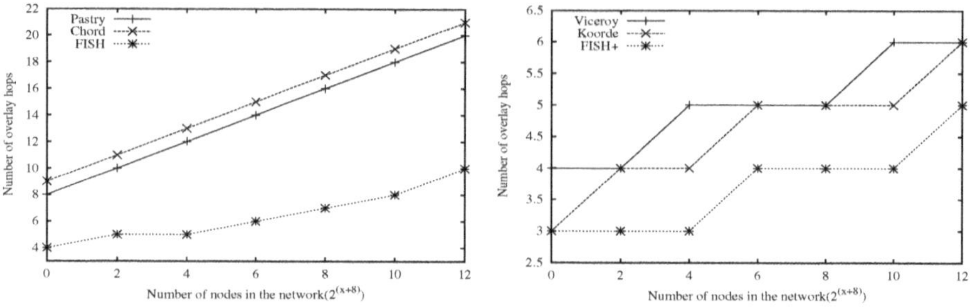

(a) General overlay network (b) Asymptotical optimal diameter network

Fig. 3. Maximum number of hops required for a query in the network

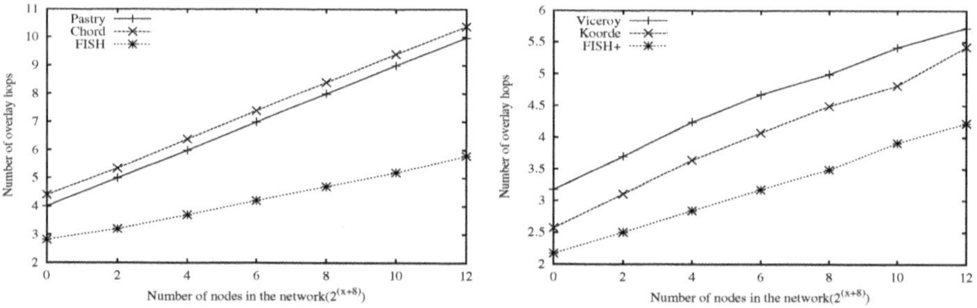

(a) General overlay network (b) Asymptotical optimal diameter network

Fig. 4. Average number of hops required for a query in the network

network hardly changes. Figure 5(a) shows the variation of the average querying path lengths of general designs. As shown in the result, the degree of the fluctuation for FISH is close to the degrees of Pastry and Chord, but FISH provides more flexible autonomy in terms of each node. Almost the same result is presented in Fig. 5(b) for the networks with optimal diameters. Though the number of querying hops have been small, the variations of Viceroy and Koorde are still serious. FISH+ adapts to the dynamic network well, which validates our design.

Figure 6 presents the degree distribution of our proposed networks consisting of 2^{12} =4k nodes. This metric reflects the load balance of topology. As our experimental configuration, the theoretical value of the degree is $\log_2 N = 12$. From the figure, for FISH+, the ratio of the node degrees equaling 12 exceeds 40%, and that of the remaining peers are close to the two side trails of the curve. The distribution of FISH spans more, since its neighbor-chosen scheme is random. However, the imbalanced node degrees do not have an effect on the routing efficiency.

Figure 7 plots the probability that a query encounters a node failure while following a path to its destination using the forwarding algorithm of the corresponding protocol. For the same percentage of node failures, the probabilities that a query in Koorde and FISH+ encounters a failure on its path are higher than other networks, but FISH+ encounters

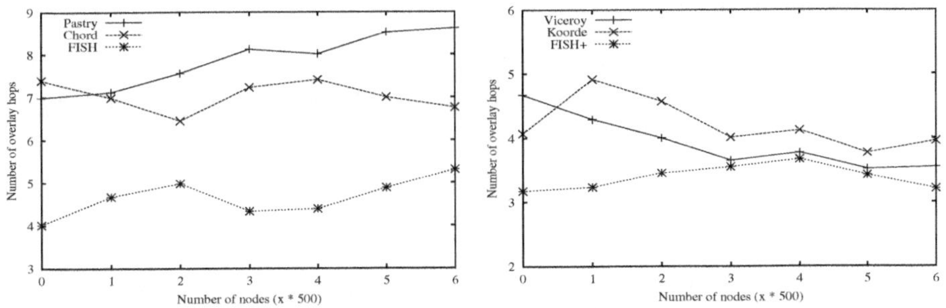

(a) General overlay network (b) Asymptotical optimal diameter network

Fig. 5. Variations of average querying path lengths in the presence of peers concurrently joining and leaving

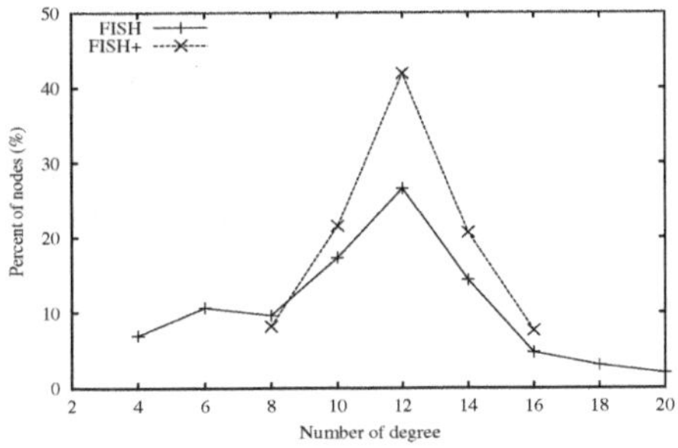

Fig. 6. Degree distribution of the network with 2^{12} nodes

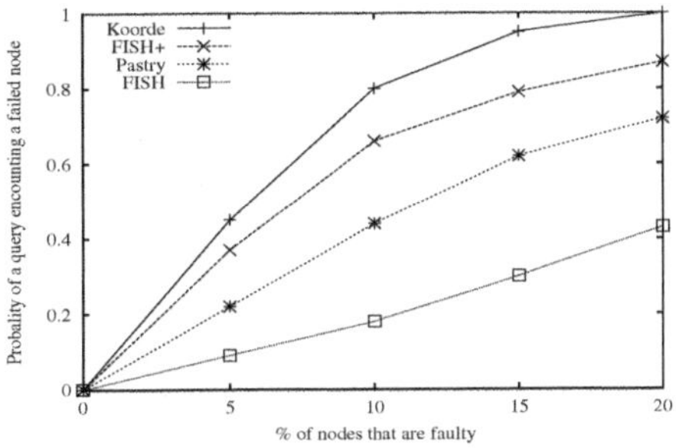

Fig. 7. Probability that a query encounters a node failure as we vary the percentage of node failures in one hundred thousand nodes overlay network

much fewer failed nodes than Koorde. The robustness of FISH is much superior over Pastry, FISH+ and Koorde with the help of the randomized construction method for the Hypercube domain.

5 Conclusions

In this paper, we present a novel P2P overlay network, FISH, based on the Hyper-deBruijn topology. It inherits advantages of Hypercube and deBruijn while strongly reducing the influence of the disadvantages. We first introduced Hyper-deBruijn topology, then gave a randomized general design of Hyper-deBruijn for P2P networks including the construction methods, self-stabilization mechanism of topology, and a fault-tolerant routing algorithm. Next, we proposed two improved Hyper-deBruijn topologies to get an asymptotically optimal diameter. Finally, we evaluated FISH using simulation. The results verify our designs for Hyper-deBruijn.

Acknowledgment

This research was supported by the National Natural Science Foundation of China (Grant Nos. 60873011,60803026 and 60933001) and National Basic Research Program of China (Grant No. 2006CB303103).

References

1. Chawathe, Y., Ratnasamy, S., Breslau, L., et al.: Making gnutella-like P2P systems scalable. In: Proceedings of ATAPCC 2003 (2003)
2. Aberer, K.: P-Grid: A self-organizing access structure for P2P information systems. In: Batini, C., Giunchiglia, F., Giorgini, P., Mecella, M. (eds.) CoopIS 2001. LNCS, vol. 2172, p. 179. Springer, Heidelberg (2001)
3. Ratnasamy, S., Francis, P., Handley, M., Karp, R., Shenker, S.: A Scalable Content-Addressable Network. In: Proceedings of the ACM SIGCOMM (2001)
4. Rowstron, A., Druschel, P.: Pastry: Scalable, distributed object ocation and routing for large-scale peer-to-peer systems. In: Guerraoui, R. (ed.) Middleware 2001. LNCS, vol. 2218, p. 329. Springer, Heidelberg (2001)
5. Stoica, I., Morris, R., Karger, D., Kaashoek, F., Balakrishnan, H.: Chord: A Scalable Peer-To-Peer Lookup Service for Internet Applications. In: Proceedings of the ACM SIGCOMM (2001)
6. Zhao, B.Y., Kubiatowicz, J., Joseph, A.D.: Tapestry: An infrastructure for fault-tolerant wide-area location and routing. In: Proceedings of the ACM SIGCOMM
7. Schlosser, M., Sintek, M., Decker, S., Nejdl, W.: HyperCuP-Hypercubes, Ontologies and P2P Networks. In: Moro, G., Koubarakis, M. (eds.) AP2PC 2002. LNCS (LNAI), vol. 2530, pp. 112–124. Springer, Heidelberg (2003)
8. Kaashoek, F., Karger, D.R.: Koorde: A simple degreeoptimal hash table. In: Kaashoek, M.F., Stoica, I. (eds.) IPTPS 2003. LNCS, vol. 2735. Springer, Heidelberg (2003)
9. Fraigniaud, P., Gauron, P.: The content-addressable network d2b. Technical Report LRI 1349, Univ. Paris-Sud (2003)
10. Naor, M., Wieder, U.: A Simple Fault Tolerant Distributed Hash Table. In: Kaashoek, M.F., Stoica, I. (eds.) IPTPS 2003. LNCS, vol. 2735. Springer, Heidelberg (2003)
11. Ganesan, E., Pradhan, D.K.: The Hyper-deBruijn Multiprocessor networks. IEEE Transaction (1991)
12. Loguinov, D., Kumar, A., Rai, V., Ganesh, S.: Graph-Theoretic Analysis of Structured Peer-to-Peer Systems: Routing Distances and Fault Resilience. Texas A&M Technical Report (2003)
13. Seitz, C.L.: The cosmic cube. Commun. ACM 28, 22–33 (1985)
14. de Bruijn, N.D.: A combinatorial problem. Koninklijke Nederlandse academie van Wetenschappen 49, 758–764 (1946)
15. Schlumberger, M.L.: De Bruijn communication networks. Doctoral Dissertation, Dept. of Computer Science, Stanford University, PALO Alto, CA (1974)
16. Imase, M., Itoh, M.: Design to minimized diameter on build-block network. IEEE Transactions on Computers C30(6), 439–443 (1981)
17. Ganesan, E., Pradhan, D.K.: Wormhole routing in de Bruijn networks and hyper-de Bruijn networks. In: Circuits and Systems, ISCAS 2003 (2003)
18. Bridges, W.G., Toueg, S.: On the Impossibility of Directed Moore Graphs. Journal of Combinatorial Theory, series B29(3) (1980)
19. Steinmetz, Wehrle: Peer-to-Peer System and Applications. Springer, Heidelberg (2005)

20. Malkhi, D., Naor, M., Ratajczak, D.: Viceroy: A scalable and dynamic emulation of the butterfly. In: Proceedings of the 21st ACM Symposium on Principles of Distributed Computing (2002)
21. Crainiceanu, A., Linga, P., et al.: P-Ring: An efficient and roubust P2P range index structure. In: Proceedings of SIGMOD 2007 (2007)
22. Adamic, L.A., Lukose, R.M., Puniyani, A.R., Huberman, B.A.: Search in power-law networks. Physical Review E 64(046135) (2001)
23. Manku, G.S., Naor, M., Wieder, U.: Know thy neighbor's neighbor: the power of lookahead in randomized P2P networks. In: STOC 2004 (2004)
24. Caro, G.D., Ducatelle, F., Heegaard, P., Jelasity, M., Montemanni, R., Montresor, A.: Evaluation of basic services in ahn, p2p and grid networks (February 2005), http://www.cs.unibo.it/bison/deliverables/D07.pdf
25. Aiello, W., Chung, F., Lu, L.: A random graph model for massive graphs. In: Proceedings of the 32nd Annual ACM Symposium on Theory of Computing, pp. 171–180. ACM Press, New York (2000)

Continuous Summarization of Co-evolving Data in Large Water Distribution Network

Hongmei Xiao[1,2], Xiuli Ma[1,2,*], Shiwei Tang[1,2], and Chunhua Tian[3]

[1] Key Laboratory of Machine Perception(Peking University), Ministry of Education
[2] School of Electronics Engineering and Computer Science, Peking University, Beijing, 100871, China
[3] IBM Research - China, Beijing, 100093, China
{xiaohm,maxl}@cis.pku.edu.cn, tsw@pku.edu.cn, chtian@cn.ibm.com

Abstract. While traditional water data stream analysis focuses mainly on single sensor node or monitoring station, having an accurate picture of the overall data patterns is more meaningful in understanding large water distribution network's behavior and characteristics, tracking important trends, and also making informed judgments about measurement or utilization operations. In this paper, we propose a continuous summarization scheme that aims to continuously provide Representative Patterns of the complete data in large water distribution network. Our core contributions are to propose to summarize Representative Pattern for describing the spatial-temporal pattern in water distribution network and employ a parameter-free algorithm based on the Minimum Description Length (MDL) Principle to automatically split data streams into episodes for generating the series of representative patterns. Moreover, we evaluate our approaches on a real water distribution network from the Battle of the Water Sensor Network (BWSN). Experiment results show that our online summarization methods are effective, scalable and interpretable; What's more, we discover interesting periodic time-evolving patterns on the chlorine data.

Keywords: Summarization, Representative Pattern, MDL.

1 Introduction

With the development of technology, chemical sensors can be deployed in the water distribution system to monitor various substances in the water such as chlorine in real-time instead of the traditional sample collecting way. All the sensor measurements need to be analyzed in real time in order to identify water quality in the distribution network. Therefore, having an accurate picture of the overall data pattern becomes more and more crucial in understanding network behavior and characteristics, tracking important trends, and making informed judgments about measurement or utilization patterns. For example, we want to know the time-evolving patterns about the chlorine concentration level to decide the re-chlorination time and location.

* Corresponding Author.

L. Chen et al. (Eds.): WAIM 2010, LNCS 6184, pp. 62–73, 2010.

Because of massive data streams coming at every timestamp, there are lots of challenges to do online summarization on multiple data streams. Most previous pattern discovery studies for data streams have focused on solving the problem in single stream [16], or choosing a sliding window size [11]. Recently, multiple streams have also attracted significant interest [8][9], but most of those methods use the PCA tools in which the results of data streams analysis may turn difficult to interpret as all the data coordinates participate in the linear combination that might mix both positive and negative weights thus partly canceling each other. Therefore, we need tools that can continuously find hidden time-evolving patterns and detect the summarization changes in a more interpretable and intuitive way. Thus, we can list the main problems that need to be solved:

– *How to summarize multiple streams continuously or incrementally to adapt to the streaming situation?*
– *How to effectively detect the summarization changes' timestamp?*
– *How to summarize in an interpretable and intuitive way?*

Here we propose the continuous summarization approach to address all of the above problems. We employ an algorithm to incrementally detect the summarization change point and split data streams into episodes, which requiring no user parameters by using the Minimum Description Length (MDL) [6]. We propose the novel Representative Pattern idea for describing the spatial-temporal pattern about water data in each episode. Thus, we find and maintain the current representative pattern continuously until the splitting point comes, then create a new representative pattern. Furthermore, we evaluate our approaches on a real water distribution network from the Battle of the Water Sensor Network (BWSN) [1]. Experiment results show that our online summarization is effective, interpretable and scalable, and can discover interesting periodic time-evolving patterns on the chlorine data.

Our contributions can be summarized as follows:

- To propose the idea of representative patterns to summarize the evolving data;
- The parameter-free cost based algorithm to detect summarization changes;
- To find the interesting periodic time-evolving pattern continuously in the streaming situation.

The rest of the paper is organized as the follows. Section 2 discusses the related work. Then Section 3 formally defines the problem and introduces the key definitions. Section 4 presents our core algorithm on summarization. In Section 5 we extensively evaluate all the proposed methods on a real water distribution network. Finally we conclude in Section 6.

2 Related Work

Next, we will discuss the related work in two aspects: data stream and water network.

Data stream. Data mining on streams have received tremendous attention in various communities. StatStream [11] employs the DFT to summarize streams within a finite window and compute the highest pairwise correlations among all pairs of streams.

BRAID [12] solves the problem of discovering lag correlations among multiple streams. The goal is on time and space efficient methods for finding the earliest and highest peak in the cross-correlation functions between all pairs of streams. But, neither StatStream nor BRAID explicitly aims to find the hidden time-evolving patterns. Lin et al. [13] performed clustering on different levels of wavelet coefficients of multiple time series which require having all the data in advance.

Recently, Papadimitriou et al. [8] designed an online algorithm that summarizes the multiple streams incrementally to find hidden variables and Sun et al. [9] did tensor analysis on graph streams. Both algorithms adopted the PCA tools, which made the results of data streams analysis difficult to interpret. Li et al. [14] employed DynaMMo for summarization of co-evolving sequences with missing values. Sun et al. [7] proposed a GraphScope algorithm to find interesting time-evolving patterns of graphs' structure on graph streams. However, GraphScope focused on the graph streams with source-destination structure, while our summarization on water quality data streams considers not only the rigid structure but also the data characteristics.

Water distribution network. For the last decade there has been increasing interest in the development of sensor networks to monitor the water quality in water distribution network. In August 2006, the Battle of Water Sensor Networks (BWSN) [1] was organized as an international challenge to find the best sensor placements for a real (but anonymized) metropolitan area water distribution network. The U.S. Environmental Protection Agency (EPA) exploited the EPANET [2] to simulate the hydraulic and chemical phenomena within drinking water distribution systems and developed CANARY [3] which analyses single stream by statistical and mathematical algorithms to identify the onset of periods of anomalous water quality. Different with them, we mainly focus on the whole picture of the spatial-temporal patterns.

Table 1. Description of notation

Symbol	Desription
S	the set of sensor node in network
SP_t	A snapshot pattern at time t
SP	A snapshot pattern stream
RP_r	The r-th representative pattern
RP	A representative pattern set
E_r	The r-th episode
l_r	The length of E_r
$conMatirx^{(SP_t)}$	The condition matrix of SP_t
$voteMatrix^{(r)}$	The vote matrix of $\mathrm{RP_r}$

3 Problem Definition

Now, we first formally define the notations of snapshot pattern, representative pattern and other relative concepts. Then we formulate the problems of summarization.

First of all, we assume the network infrastructure as following:

In a large water distribution network, there are many nodes at the pipe joints. A wireless sensor network is formed by a set of sensors S which are selected from nodes to monitoring the water quality. Each sensor in the pipeline network has a unique number, from 1 to s. Every sensor can sense a variety of attributes, such as: the residual chlorine, PH, temperature and so on. By transmitting all the sensor data to a central site, we can acquire the raw snapshot data at every time click. We mainly discuss the summarization on the chlorine attribute. Our goal is to find the hidden patterns and time-evolving trend by real-time summarization of the chlorine data.

3.1 Notation and Definition

Definition 1. *(SNAPSHOT PATTERN) A snapshot pattern* SP_t *is a clustering* C *of* s *sensor nodes at time t, which partitions the* s *sensor nodes into* k *disjoint set* $C_1, C_2....C_k$, *that is,* $\bigcup_i^k C_i = S = \{1,2,3.....s\}$ *and* $C_i \cap C_j = \varnothing$ *for all* $i \neq j$.

In our paper, we employ the snapshot pattern SP_t to depict the data distribution structure by clusters of the raw sensory data of s sensor nodes. Here, we cluster the sensor by the sensory data. Every cluster (or partition) C_i has the information of its members and the overall data feature of the cluster. The members are the sensor node ids, and the cluster data feature is the average value of the members' sensory data.

We focus on detecting the structure changing in data streams as we observed that the characteristic of water data in water distribution network changes smoothly and has strong spatial correlation. While the clustering structure changes flatly as the time goes by, there will appear an important pattern. However, we don't abandon the data feature but tag the cluster with the cluster's data feature.

Definition 2. *(CLUSTERING CONDITION MATRIX) A clustering condition matrix* $conMatirx^{(SP_t)}$ *of* SP_t *defines whether node* i *and* j *are in the same cluster or partition. Especially,* $conMatirx^{(SP_t)}[i][j]=1$, *means* C *places* i *and* j *in different clusters, otherwise in the same cluster. For each* $i \in S$, $C(i)$ *denote the label of the cluster to which the node* i *belongs, so we get the formal definition as following:*

$$conMatirx^{(SP_m)}[i][j] = \begin{cases} 0 & \text{if } C(i)=C(j) \\ 1 & \text{otherwise} \end{cases}$$

*Example 1.*We will take an example considering the sensor nodes set $S = \{1,2,3,4,5,6\}$ that consists of six nodes, the data at t =1:00 is $\{0.16, 0.2, 0.87, 0.85, 0.45, 0.48\}$. If $C = \{\{1, 2\}, \{3, 4\}, \{5, 6\}\}$ then the cluster number k =3, and the member of C_1 is {1, 2}, while data feature is 0.18(average of 0.16 and 0.2). It is easy to get the clustering condition matrix of snapshot pattern as Fig.1. A value 0 in the left matrix entry (i, j) means i and j in the same cluster, or vice versa. In fact, we just need the colored upper triangular matrix in Fig. 1.

Definition 3. *(DIFFCOST) A difference cost is the clustering structure difference cost between two SPs. We denote the clustering structure's difference by the XOR operation between the SPs' conMatrix. After the XOR operation, the same part of two SPs turn to 0, and the different left as 1.Therefore, the number of 1 is the diffcost between the two SP's.*

Because of the characteristic of water data changes smoothly in consecutive timestamps and we have created the structure by data feature. Thus, in our paper, we mainly focus on the structure similarity between the *SPs* instead of the detailed data feature and the significant changes, or temporal patterns, shown in structure.

	1	2	3	4	5	6
1	0	0	1	1	1	1
2	0	0	1	1	1	1
3	1	1	0	0	1	1
4	1	1	0	0	1	1
5	1	1	1	1	0	0
6	1	1	1	1	0	0

Fig. 1. An example of clustering condition matrix of Clustering $C = \{\{1, 2\}, \{3, 4\}, \{5, 6\}\}$

Definition 4. *(SNAPSHOT PATTERN STREAM) A sequence of snapshot patterns* $SP_1, SP_2......SP_n$ *, is called a snapshot pattern stream if* n *is an integer that increases with time.*

Intuitively, we can consider a snapshot pattern stream is coming incrementally over time. One of our goals is to discover the hidden patterns evolving over time of the snapshot pattern stream. To this end, we split consecutive timestamps into consecutive episodes by meeting the significant summarization change.

Definition 5. *(SNAPSHOT PATTERN EPISODE) The sequence of snapshot patterns beginning at timestamp* t_r *and ending at* t_{r+1} *make up the* r *-th episode* $E_r = \left\{SP_{t_r}, SP_{t_r+1}.....SP_{t_{r+1}}\right\}$ $r \geq 1$ *,which has length* $l_r = (t_{r+1} - t_r + 1)$.

As we see, a snapshot pattern episode is a set of consecutive snapshot patterns in a snapshot pattern stream.

Definition 6. *(REPRESENTATIVE PATTERN) A representative pattern is a typical pattern* RP_r *that can best represent the* l_r *snapshot patterns of episode* E_r .

In our paper's context, the "typical" and "best" means that the representative pattern is a constructed snapshot pattern which is the most consistent both in structure and data with a number of snapshot patterns it represents. The pattern structure and data feature of RP_r are the summarization of the l_r *snapshot patterns* in E_r .What's more, RP_r has a voteMatrix to denote structure difference of *snapshot patterns* in E_r .

Definition 7. *(VOTE MATRIX) The* $voteMatrix^{(r)}$ *presents the current clustering vote condition of episode* E_r .

The voteMatrix$^{(r)}$ of E_r is the result of summing all the condition matrices of l_r *snapshot patterns* in E_r, more details can be found out in clustering aggregation [4]. If $voteMatrix^{(r)}[i][j]$ =5, it means there are 5 *SP*s that place i and j in the different clusters in these consecutive snapshot patterns $\{SP_{t_r}......SP_{t_{r+1}}\}$.

3.2 Problem Formulation

At beginning, we point out the objective is to find out the hidden patterns on time-evolving snapshot pattern stream. Thus, we list the sub-problem as follows:

Problem 1. *(GENERATE REPRESENTATIVE PATTERN). To adapt to the streaming situation, how to incrementally generate representative pattern RP_r of episode E_r, between the timestamps t_r and t_{r+1}.*

Problem 2.*(EPISODE SPLIT). Give a snapshot pattern stream SP= {SP_1, SP_2, ...SP_n}, how can we continuously and incrementally detect the summarization change point to splitting SP into episodes.*

4 Summarization Analysis

In this section, we will describe the framework of summarization. It includes three parts: (1) get snapshot pattern; (2) generate representative pattern; (3) split the episodes. We give the detail explain as follows:

4.1 Get Snapshot Pattern

As mentioned in the definition of snapshot pattern of section 3.1, we employ the clustering algorithm in the literature [5] that finds all density connected clusters having no less than the defined dense objects' number over each attribute. We adopt the best dense threshold parameter x = 2 which is sufficient for tight clusters suggested in the literature. In fact, any clustering algorithm on numeric data is sufficient, but the algorithm based on density is more suitable in this context. After clustering on raw data, we get the *snapshot pattern* at each time click. Next, we should begin to discuss the key technology of summarization.

4.2 Representative Pattern Generation

First we will discuss our method to solve the *problem 1*. The goal is how to generate and update the representative pattern which is the summarization of episode E_r continuously in streaming situation.

In our algorithm, we employ the idea of voteMatirx and update the overall clustering structure of *RP* inspirited from the clustering aggregation [4] to generate and update the *RP*. Difference between our algorithm and clustering aggregation is: clustering aggregation solves the clustering problem of the static data, while our algorithm deals with overall clustering problem of the streaming data. Considering the clustering structure changes slowly as the time goes by, we adopt the clustering aggregation idea here to discover representative pattern.

Having the same flavor with clustering aggregation's distance matrix, we use the voteMatrix to describe correlation between two nodes. We map our problem to clustering aggregation by considering the tuples of the sensor nodes as vertices of a graph and summarizing the information provided by the input clusterings of snapshot patterns in current E_r by weights on the edges of the graph. The weight X_{uv} of the edge (u, v) is the fraction of clusterings that place u and v in different clusters. Therefore, we can compute the distance matrix by transforming the voteMatrix divided by the *SP*s number in current E_r.

The pseudo-code is listed in Algorithm 1.We compute the RP_r incrementally: firstly, initial it as the first snapshot pattern SP_{t_r} in the Episode E_r. When the next snapshot pattern SP_t comes, update the $voteMatrix^{(r)}$. The $voteMatrix^{(r)}$ presents the current clustering vote condition of E_r from SP_{t_r} to SP_t of RP_r .With the new $voteMatrix^{(r)}$ of E_r, we adopt the LocalSearch or Agglomerative algorithm in clustering aggregation to cluster nodes by the new $voteMatrix^{(r)}$.

The LocalSearch starts with some clustering of the nodes, then goes through the nodes and it considers placing them into a different cluster, or creating a new singleton cluster with this node. This operation is done to yield the minimum cost which weights the disagreements between clusterings as mentioned in clustering aggregation. While agglomerative is a standard bottom-up procedure for the correlation clustering problem. If there is no merging of current clusters can lead to a solution with improved cost, the algorithm stops.

When joining a new SP_t in the RP_r, it also has to update the data feature of RP_r .As defined in section 3.1, the data feature of each node is the average value in those *SP*s data feature which can be updated as the new cluster's data feature.

Algorithm 1. ConstructRP (Episode E_r ,l_r consecutive *SP*s)

```
1 Initial: RP_r = SP_{t_r} , voteMatrix^(r) = conMatirx^(RP_r) = conMatirx^(SP_{t_r}) ;
2 For t=t_r+1 to t_{r+1} do
      // comes the new snapshot pattern at time t
      //get the new voteMatrix^(r)
3     voteMatrix^(r) = voteMatrix^(r) + conMatirx^(SP_t) ;
      //compute RP_r the new clustering condition
4     LocalSearch(voteMatrix^(r)); //or Agglomerative( voteMatrix^(r))
5     update the RP_r's the conMatrix by the LocalSearch result
6     update the data feature of RP_r;
7 End for;
```

Output: the representative pattern of E_r.

4.3 Episodes Splitting

Now we will discuss the last problem in our framework to detect the summarization change point incrementally. In general, we wish the most similar consecutive SPs can be split into the same episode. With the idea of no-parameter, we propose a method based on cost evaluation and employ the storage cost to weigh the similarity during the snapshot pattern in episode E_r. Our problem can be rewrote as finding the best episode splitting which satisfies the whole storage cost is smallest. It formulates as:

Definition 8. *(Episode Storage Cost) Give the episode E_r, and the representative pattern RP_r, the episode storage cost is denoted as:*

$$SC_r = \sum_{i=t_r}^{i=t_{r+1}} diffCost(RP_r, SP_i) + Cost(RP_r)\ ,$$

Where the t_r and t_{r+1} are the start time and end time of E_r, respectively. Additionally, the $Cost(RP_r)$ is the storage cost of RP_r, which is the number of 1 or 0 in RP_r's $conMatrix$. We think the SC_r can weigh the episode storage cost by the sum of the storage cost of RP_r and the change cost that needs to get the SPs' original structure storage condition just with the information of RP_r's storage condition.

Definition 9. *(STREAMS SUMMARIZATION) A representative pattern set R=* $R = \{RP_1, RP_2 ......RP_m\}$ *can best describe the original snapshot pattern stream by minimizing the whole storage cost function*

$$SC = \sum_{i=1}^{i=m} SC_i\ .$$

Where the SC is the whole storage cost of snapshot pattern stream and SC_i is the storage cost in the episode E_i, and m is the number of episodes.

Find the best episodes to make the whole storage cost minimum is our ultimate goal, however getting the optimal solution is NP-hard[1].We propose an algorithm based on one form of the Minimum Description Length (MDL) principle to split the snapshot pattern stream into episodes incrementally when the new snapshot pattern arrives. Consider when new snapshot pattern SP_t arrives at every timestamps, how to split the episode incrementally. We will put SP_t in the current episode E_r and update E_r's $RP_r^{(old)}$ as $RP_r^{(new)}$ if SP_t is similar with the SPs in E_r which shown in Fig.2. (a) .Otherwise like the Fig.2. (b) split the episode E_r at time t, start a new episode E_{r+1}, and SP_t is the first snapshot pattern in E_{r+1}. More intuitively, we see the visual explanation in the Fig. 2.

To make the storage cost small, we need to compare the cost for joining with that of splitting at time t. Recall the storage cost definition, following is the detail formula of the two choices' cost:

$$Cost(join) = SC_r^{(new)} = \sum_{i=t_r}^{i=t} diffCost(RP_r^{(new)}, SP_i) + Cost(RP_r^{(new)})$$

$$Cost(split) = SC_r^{(old)} + SC_{r+1} = \sum_{i=t_r}^{i=t-1} diffCost(RP_r^{(old)}, SP_i) + Cost(RP_r^{(old)}) + Cost(RP_{r+1})$$

Since there is only one SP in Episode E_{r+1}, and the RP_{r+1} is equal to this SP, then diffCost in E_{r+1} is 0. So, we avoid this cost part in Cost (split).

Specifically, the major point is to reduce the storage point. Thus, our algorithm will combine the arrived snapshot pattern with the current episode E_r if we get a storage benefit; otherwise we split at current time tick and start a new episode E_{r+1}. The main steps are listed in Algorithm 2.

---

[1] This problem is NP-hard, you can find a reduction to the TSP problem in D. S. Johnson [15].

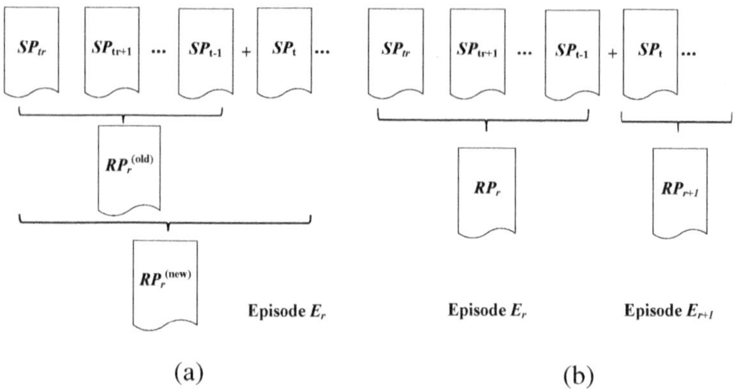

Fig. 2. (a) Choose to put SP_t into the current episode E_r; (b) Split the episode E_r at time t , new an episode E_{r+1}

Algorithm 2. SplitEpisode (current episode E_r,new coming SP_t,)

1. **Employ** algorithm 1 $E_r \cup \{SP_t\}$ to construct $RP_r^{(new)}$
2. Compute the storage cost of SP_t
3. Compute the *Cost(join)* and *Cost(split)* respectively
4. **If** *Cost(join)*<*Cost(split)* **then**
   //join the SP_t into E_r
5. Update $E_r = E_r \cup \{SP_t\}$
6. Update $RP_r = RP_r^{(new)}$
7. **Else** //start a new episode
8. $E_{r+1}=\{SP_t\}$
9. **End if**;

Output: updated episodes set, updated representative set

5 Experiments

In this section, we evaluate the proposed methods on real water distribution network which is provided by BWSN. Section 5.1 introduces the datasets and Section 5.2 studies the effectiveness interpretability and scalability of our methods. Every experiments were conducted on a Windows system equipped with an Intel Core 2G processor and 1 GB of RAM. Our algorithm is implemented in JAVA.

5.1 Datasets

Here, we describe the datasets in our experiments. The water distribution network we used is a real water distribution system referred to in BWSN (The Battle of the Water Sensor Network).This network (Fig.3 (a)) is comprised of 128 nodes, one constant head source, two tanks, 168 pipes, two pumps, eight values, and is subject to two variable demand patterns (time tick is half an hour) which are collection of multipliers that can be applied to a quantity to allow it to vary over time, and the major demand pattern is in Fig.3 (b).

The dataset of water distribution network was generated by EPANET 2.0 that accurately simulates the hydraulic and chemical phenomena within drinking water

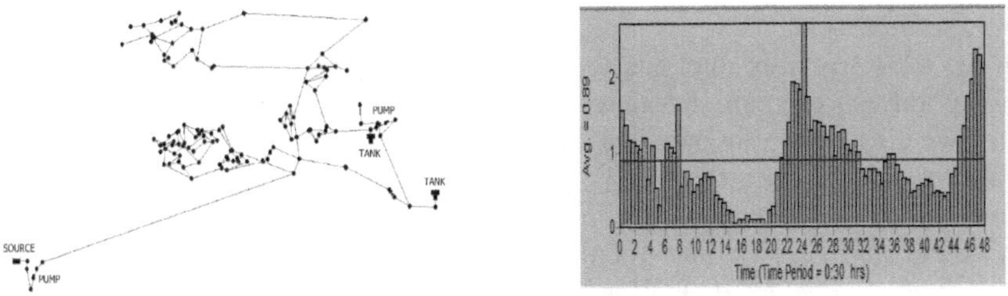

(a) (b)

Fig. 3. (a) The distribution water network (b) The major demand pattern

distribution systems. And in our experiments, we monitor the chlorine concentration level at all 128 nodes for 288 timestamps during 16 days (one time tick every 1 hour).

5.2 Evaluations

(1) Effectiveness

We first discuss the effectiveness of our methods about summarization on chlorine concentration. With the knowledge from literature [10], the chlorine concentration in pipe correlates significantly with demand, flow velocity and some other factors. Here, we use the relationship with demand to interpret effective of our methods. Since in first 4 days, the distribution water network is just initialized and not stable. Thus, we discuss the last 12 days of 16 days in Fig.4. Refers to analysis the representative patterns that be generated automatically by our algorithms, we are surprised to discover four hidden periodic representative patterns in purple color in table 2.

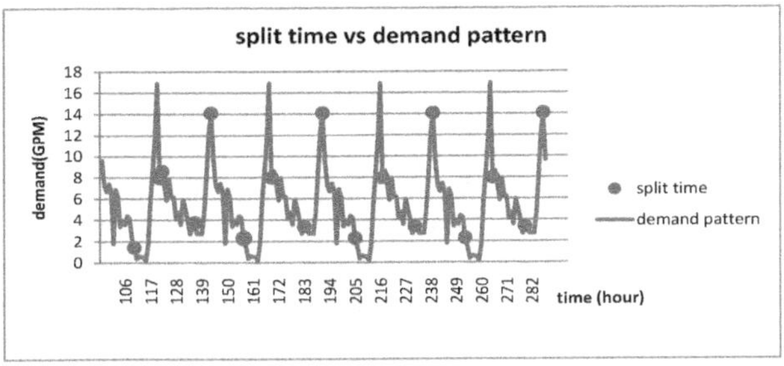

Fig. 4. Representative pattern split time vs. the major demand pattern (96-288)

Table 2. The *RP*s' start time, end time and the interval it represents

Start	End	Interval	Start	End	interval
96	110	15	192	205	14
111	121	11	206	217	12
122	122	1	218	231	14
123	136	14	232	239	8
137	143	7	240	253	14
144	157	14	254	265	12
158	169	12	266	279	14
170	183	14	280	287	8
184	191	8	288	~	~

(2)Interpretability
With the *RP*'s structure and data feature we recorded in algorithm, we draw the spatial-temporal representative pattern in map. The four *RP*s in Fig.5 are the periodic pattern we discover in the network of 16 days. For every point on the map, we think its value should be estimated by the pipe whose distance to the point is minimal. Assume that the point is *p*, its corresponding pipe *l*'s two end points are *p1* and *p2*. With the value *v1* and *v2* which are monitored by sensors, then the value of point p is $v = d2/(d1 + d2)*v1 + d1/(d1+d2)*v2$($d1$ and $d2$ is the distance between *p* and *p1*,*p2*). Thus, it becomes a convenient thing to interpret the overall situation water quality. What's more, users can get to know the chlorine information of the network easily and quickly, while others use PCA methods that need the statistics knowledge and result transforming support.

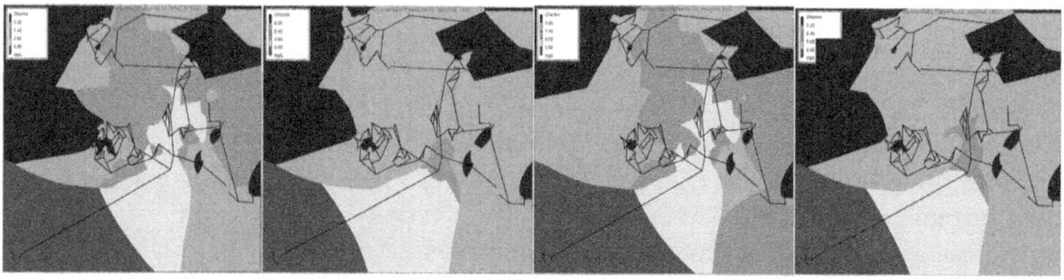

Fig. 5. Four hidden representative pattern in map form

(3) Scalability
Finally, we illustrate scalability of our online summarization which weighs by the CPU time. As shown in Fig.6. (a), we can see the CPU time (per snapshot) curve is smooth over time in the whole summarization when adopting LocalSearch or Agglomerative algorithm to generate the new RP and the LocalSearch is much faster and timesaving. In Fig.6. (b), we do experiments with 1000 nodes which picked from Wolf network provided by University of Exeter . The experiment result is the average value of six experiments' CPU time (per node). We can see the CPU time (per node) curve grows approximately linear when increasing the network size. Therefore, we have the reason to believe that our methods are scalable to streaming environments.

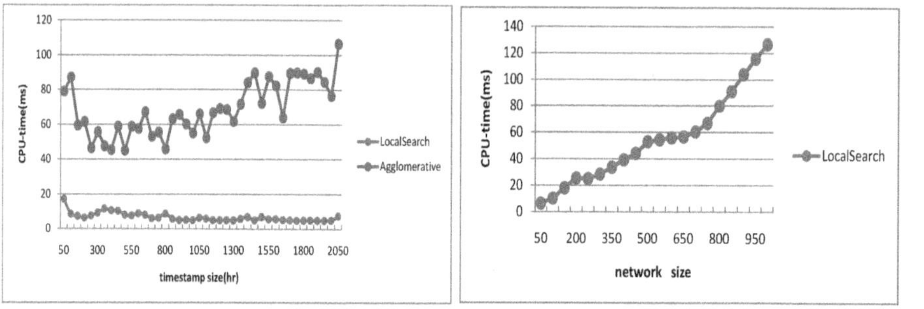

(a)Timestamp size (LocalSearch vs. Agglomerative) (b) Network size (LocalSearch)

Fig. 6. CPU time for online summarization

6 Conclusions

In this paper, we discussed a continuous summarization framework which incrementally mines and summarizes representative patterns of the multiple data streams in large water distribution network. We propose the representative patterns idea for describing summarization and employ a fully-automatic algorithm based on the Minimum Description Length (MDL) Principle to incrementally detect the summarization change point .We also provide experiments on chlorine concentration from a real water distribution network of BWSN. According to experiment results, we find out the interesting periodic time-evolving patterns on the chlorine data, and our online summarization is effective, interpretable and scalable.

Moreover, we look forward to create hierarchical structure and index on representative patterns for event detection in large water distribution network.

Acknowledgements. We are pleased to acknowledge the Centre for Water Systems at the University of Exeter for providing the BWSN's dataset.

References

1. Ostfeld, A., Uber, J.G., Salomons, E.: Battle of water sensor networks: A design challenge for engineers and algorithms. In: WDSA (2006)
2. Rossman, L.A.: EPANET2 user's manual. National Risk Management Research Laboratory: U.S. Environmental Protection Agency (2000)
3. Hart, D.B., Klise, K.A., McKenna, S.A., Wilson, M.P.: CANARY User's Manual Version 4.1. Sandia National Laboratories. U.S. Environmental Protection Agency (2009)
4. Gionis, A., Mannila, H., Tsaparas, P.: Clustering aggregation. TKDD 1(1) (2007)
5. Ester, M., Peter Kriegel, H., Sander, J.: A density-based algorithm for discovering clusters in large spatial databases with noise. In: KDD 1996 (1996)
6. Rissanen, J.: Modeling by the shortest data description. Automatica 14, 465–471 (1978)
7. Sun, J., Papadimitriou, S., Yu, P.S., Faloutsos, C.: Graphscope: Parameter-free mining of large time-evolving graphs. In: KDD (2007)
8. Papadimitriou, S., Sun, J.: Streaming Pattern Discovery in Multiple Time-Series. In: VLDB 2005 (2005)
9. Sun, J., Tao, D.: Beyond streams and graphs: dynamic tensor analysis. In: KDD (2006)
10. Silja, T., Helena, R., Didia, C.: Water Supply System Performance for Different Pipe Materials Part I: Water Quality Analysis. Water Resour. Manage. (2008)
11. Zhu, Y., Shasha, D.: Statstream: Statistical monitoring of thousands of data streams in real time. In: VLDB (2002)
12. Sakurai, Y., Papadimitriou, S., Faloutsos, C.: Braid: Stream mining through group lag correlations. In: SIGMOD (2005)
13. Lin, J., Vlachos, M., Keogh, E., Gunopulos, D.: Iterative incremental clustering of time series. In: Bertino, E., Christodoulakis, S., Plexousakis, D., Christophides, V., Koubarakis, M., Böhm, K., Ferrari, E. (eds.) EDBT 2004. LNCS, vol. 2992, pp. 106–122. Springer, Heidelberg (2004)
14. Li, L., McCann, J., Pollard, N., Faloutsos, C.: DynaMMo: Mining and Summarization of
15. Johnson, D.S., Krishnan, S., Chhugani, J., Kumar, S., Venkatasubramanian, S.: Compressing large Boolean matrices using reordering techniques. In: VLDB (2004)
16. Muthukrishnan, S.: Data Streams: Algorithms and Applications (Foundations and Trends in Theoretical Computer Science), vol. 1 (2005)

Proactive Replication and Search for Rare Objects in Unstructured Peer-to-Peer Networks

Guoqiang Gao, Ruixuan Li*, Kunmei Wen, Xiwu Gu, and Zhengding Lu

Intelligent and Distributed Computing Lab, College of Computer Science and Technology, Huazhong University of Science and Technology, Wuhan 430074, P.R. China
ggq@smail.hust.edu.cn, {rxli,kmwen,xwgu,zdlu}@hust.edu.cn

Abstract. The search efficiency problem in unstructured peer-to-peer network has not been adequately addressed so far, especially concerning search for rare objects. In this paper, we propose a proactive replication strategy to improve the search efficiency for rare objects. It uses object probing technique for peers to decide whether to establish replications for their objects or not when they join the network. This strategy can effectively increase the popularity of rare objects so as to enhance the search efficiency. We also present a rare object search algorithm. When a peer forwards a search request, forward probability is calculated according to its neighbors' degree and the number of neighbors' objects. Therefore, the search request is forwarded to the peers more likely containing target objects. Simulations show that the proactive replication strategy greatly improves the search efficiency for rare objects with moderate communication overhead. The rare object search algorithm not only improves search efficiency for rare objects, but also achieves load balance in search.

Keywords: peer-to-peer network, search, rare object, replication, object popularity.

1 Introduction

The peer-to-peer (P2P) networks can be broadly categorized into two types: structured P2P networks and unstructured P2P networks. Structured P2P networks [1] implement a Distributed Hash Table (DHT) and provide one basic operation: given a key, they map the key to a node. These systems are efficient and have a low traffic cost, but it is not clear which system is best suited to provide a reliable, load-balanced, and fault-tolerant network. Unstructured P2P networks account for millions of users dynamically connected in an ad hoc fashion, and queries, which are done through a path, are selected randomly according to a uniform distribution. They are suited to retrieve highly replicated data, but have limitations for rare information retrieval.

The typical unstructured P2P network is Gnutella [2], which implements search through using a flooding technique with a certain scope. This type of network has excessive traffic forms that account for more than 50% of network traffic [3]. Moreover, unstructured P2P has poor search efficiency, especially for rare objects. Such a

* Corresponding author.

L. Chen et al. (Eds.): WAIM 2010, LNCS 6184, pp. 74–85, 2010.

problem has been addressed by various algorithms, such as flooding, expanding ring [5] and random walks [7]. Most of these algorithms are in fact very effective for locating popular objects. However when it comes to find rare objects in unstructured P2P networks, the similar operations using these algorithms become less effective and less efficient [17]. As shown in [4], as much as 18% of all queries return no response even when results are available in the widely used Gnutella network.

This paper introduces a mechanism to address the above problems of unstructured P2P networks. Our main idea results from taking the proactive replication strategy to increase rare object proportion over unstructured P2P network and using our search scheme to improve search efficiency to the rare objects. The unstructured P2P networks such as Gnutella are power-law distribution networks. That is, the majority of the network nodes have low degrees, while a few other nodes have high degrees. Moreover, some nodes have a lot of resources, and some nodes have fewer objects. Therefore, searching the nodes with high degree and many objects is more likely to hit the target. In the search, we can take advantage of these features to forward queries to those peers more likely containing target objects in order to achieve the goal-oriented routing, which is similar to that of the structured P2P network. As we know, if an item is very rare, any query mechanism can hardly find it with limited number of steps. To alleviate this situation, we propose an object probing technique. Peers search the objects they own in the network at a certain frequency. If there are no hits, they will duplicate the objects at the terminative nodes they reach. The objective of this strategy is to increase the number of rear objects and the probability of search success. It obviously improves search efficiency for rare objects with lower popularity. The experiments show that it not only reduces the communication overhead of the search, but also minimizes the overhead of the replication.

The rest of this paper is organized as follows. Section 2 compares our strategy to related work. Section 3 presents the proposed methods. Section 4 demonstrates our algorithm through simulation. Finally, we summarize our contribution and outline items for future work.

2 Related Work

To find an object, a node queries its neighbors in unstructured P2P networks. The most typical query method is flooding, where the query is propagated to all neighbors within a certain radius. Flooding introduces duplicate messages and duplicate queries, which create pure overhead. Since flooding has inherent limitations, some improved methods have been proposed, such as expanding ring [5]. Although this approach has less message duplication than overall flooding, it does produce many extra traffic messages, especially for querying rare objects. Studies [7], [8] have shown random walk to be significantly more efficient than flooding, which forwards a query message to some randomly chosen neighbors at each step until the object is found. The query cache strategy [6] can also reduce the communication overhead, but shortens the length of the queries. With this strategy, nodes cache the results of the successful queries so that the same subsequent queries can quickly hit the target through the cache. This mechanism not only improves the search efficiency, but also reduces the communication overhead. The search efficiency of these improvements is significantly increased for those hot resources or more replicated resources, but the efficiency remains small for rare objects.

Published measurements of unstructured P2P networks such as Gnutella show that they have power-law degree distributions [9]. This distribution reflects the existence of a few nodes with very high degree and many with low degree. Adamic [10] proposed a high degree seeking strategy, in which a search request is forwarded to the high degree node because they have more neighbors. However, this method easily leads to information gathering, and harms the distribution of the search. Based on power-law characteristics, we improve the high degree seeking strategy through the probability forward. Our scheme tries to balance the load of each node in the search with the similarity search efficiency.

Replication will increase search efficiency of popular objects through storing the object at the requester or all nodes along searching path when a search is successful. Presently, replication strategy is mainly passive, as this method cannot help rare objects. Cohen [12] studied a replication strategy to improve search efficiency in unstructured P2P network in which target objects establish replication with the square root of the number of visits. This strategy can greatly improve the search efficiency of hot resources, but for rare objects the efficiency of the search has not improved much.

When searching for rare objects, the researchers put forward the strategy of object replication. When a peer joins a P2P network, it actively installs its object's references at a set with $O(\gamma n^{1/2})$ of randomly selected peers [13]. This strategy can improve the searching efficiency for rare objects, but it can introduce a high communication cost. Moreover, it is hard to estimate the network peer number n, especially for dynamical P2P networks. Krishna et al. [11] uses Supernode-Constrined Random Walk (SCRW) to search rare objects with two-hop index replication, and proposes three two-hop index replication strategies: full replication, square-root replication and constant replication. In SCRW, nodes always forward the query to one of it randomly selected supernode neighbors. Although this strategy can improve the search efficiency for rare objects, it needs the P2P network with supernode and will incur heavy overheads. Shen et al. [16] put forward an adaptive replication strategy. Compared to existing algorithms, this strategy requires the replication popularity to be relatively low. To achieve better search efficiency, the replication location is not random, but on the so-called network routing node. It can improve the search hit rate, and reduce the search latency as well.

In this paper, we propose a proactive replication strategy which can replicate the rare objects at the nodes of P2P network, and also propose a rare object search algorithm. By doing this, we can not only enhance the search efficiency for rare objects, but also reduce the unnecessary communication overhead for replication. In the next section, we will introduce our strategy in detail.

3 Replication and Search Strategy

To improve the search efficiency of rare objects, we must replicate the rare objects and improve the searching algorithm. In this section, we will first describe the object popularity and the proactive replication (PR) strategy for replicating the rare objects, and then discuss the rare objects searching (ROS) algorithm.

3.1 Object Popularity and Object Value

Object popularity is the proportion of the number of the nodes with an object to the network size. Object popularity is very important, and it directly determines the efficiency of search in unstructured P2P networks.

Let N represent the number of nodes in an unstructured P2P network, and an object R in this network has r copies, then object R's popularity is refined as $P=r/N$. In unstructured P2P network, the job of search algorithms is an exploratory attempt. Therefore, the popularity of target objects directly affects the search efficiency. If an object R is searched at a peer in the P2P network, then the search hit probability is P. Using standard random walk as the search algorithm, the maximum number of hops is k, and then the search hit probability Pr for object R is refined as $Pr(R)=kP$.

To make the standard random walk search successfully for object R, we need to ensure that $Pr(R)$ is equal to 1. According to Equation (1), it can be seen that the object R can be searched successfully if the number r of object R in the P2P network is up to a certain standard.

$$Pr(R)=1 \Rightarrow r=\frac{N}{k} \qquad (1)$$

In unstructured P2P networks, the object popularity directly affects the search efficiency, especially for rare objects. Therefore, we can build replication based on the object popularity. How to obtain the object popularity will be discussed in the next section.

Although the object popularity can be used as a basis for replication, some rare objects in the P2P network are valueless. For example, the node owner accidentally shares a private image, but it has no value to other users in the network. The overhead of replication can be reduced through the introduction of object value. The object R's value V_R at a time 't' in Equation (2) is refined to:

$$V_R(t+1)=\mu V_R(t)+\eta\frac{R_q(t)}{N_q(t)}*100 \qquad (2)$$

where $0 \le \mu, \eta \le 1$, the larger the value of μ, the more importance of the historical requests to V_R, while the larger the value of η, the more importance of the recent requests to V_R. $R_q(t)$ is the number of requests received for the object R and $N_q(t)$ is the total number of requests received by the node at a time 't'. We can take V_R as another basis for replication.

3.2 Proactive Replication

From the analysis above, we know that we can improve object R search hit rate through increasing the popularity of object R. However, in a distributed environment, each node only has the partial information, so to obtain the object popularity is very difficult. Therefore, it is not certain which objects should be replicated and how much copies should be made. The existing rare objects replication strategy is to replicate all objects to build the same number of replication, although this can improve the hit rate of the search algorithm, it also brings unnecessary communication overhead.

To address this issue, this paper presents a simple solution: When a node joins a P2P network, the node initiates a random walk to search its own objects, and the hit can be defined by success probe or failure probe. The node *i*'s proactive probe function for object *R proactiveProbe(i, R)* is refined in Equation (3).

$$proactive\,Probe(i,R)=\begin{cases}1 & i\ successfully\ search\ R\\ -1 & else\end{cases} \tag{3}$$

The node establishes a copy for those objects who fails to probe. The replication method is replicating the object in the last node during the proactive probe. The basic idea of this strategy is this: If one fails to find the source, the same thing may happen to the others. This strategy is not to obtain an accurate popularity of an object, but whether the popularity is less than the minimum value with which search can be done successfully. In order to ensure the minimum objects popularity and which object can be searched successfully, each node must pass on a regular probe to maintain objects popularity. The node for the next probe time for object *R* is refined in Equation (4).

$$T(x)=g\times 2^{l},\ l=\begin{cases}m+x & m+x>0\\ 0 & else\end{cases} \tag{4}$$

where g is configuration interval value, x is the return value of *proactiveProbe*(*i*, *R*), m is the last l values and the initial value of m is 0.

By defining the above probe time, we can effectively reduce the number of probes. In the meantime, the network maintains the minimum popularity of objects through the joint efforts of the network nodes. The detail cost analysis will be described in the experimental section.

The biggest cost of the proactive replication comes from the regular probe. To reduce this cost, object value can be introduced in regular probe of proactive replication. However, it is very difficult to compute the visit frequency of an object R_q in the distributed environment. In this article, we introduce a simple mechanism: Each object owner only computes the visit frequency of this object and its replication. Since the node's own object value V_R is 0, when it joins the network, in order to enhance the popularity of valuable objects, the node must be allowed to run a certain number of times before the factor of object value is introduced into regular probe. When the node's running times is greater than a predefined threshold *Tp*, and the object value of V_R is less than a certain threshold *Vt*, the probe is not triggered, and its next probe time is set to *T(1)*.

Node *i*'s proactive replication algorithm for object *R* is shown in Algorithm 1.

Algorithm 1. Node *i*'s proactive replication algorithm for object *R*

```
Procedure proactiveReplication(i, R, t)
Begin
  If (t > Tp and V_R(t) < Vt) Then
    After T(1), call proactiveReplication(i, R) again;
  Else
    k = proactiveProbe(i, R);
    If (k = -1) Then
      Replicate R in the last peer;
    End If
    After T(k), call proactiveReplication(i, R) again;
  End If
End
```

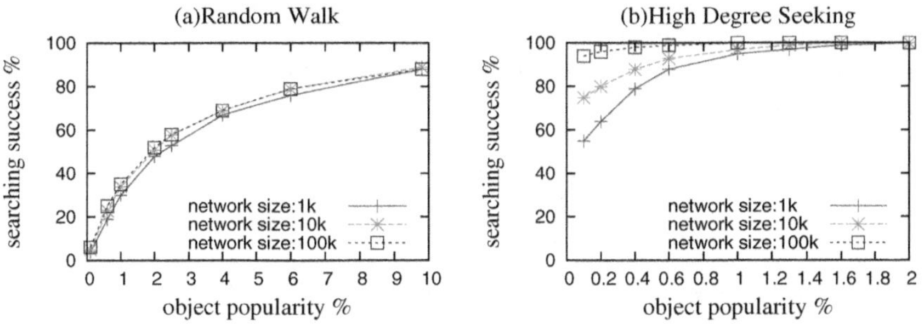

Fig. 1. The RW and HDS hit rate with different object popularity

3.3 Analyze of Search Efficiency

Random walk (RW) significantly reduces the network overhead, and the search hit rates are as well reduced. In the same hit rate, taking high degree seeking (HDS) strategy requires a lower popularity of objects than random walk. To analyze search efficiency, we design simulation experiment with different network sizes for RW and HDS. Fig. 1(a) depicts a diagram for the search hit rate and object popularity using the RW under different networks, and Fig. 1(b) describes the efficiency of HDS. Fig. 1 and 2 shows that the search hit rate of RW only reaches about 90% under 10% objects popularity, whereas HDS only requires 0.5% objects' popularity in the same search hit rate. At the same time, the correlation of the search hit rate and the objects popularity do not change in different network sizes. As we discussed earlier, the higher popularity objects have a higher hit rate of search. In subsequent experiments, this paper will only use a relatively large network size, because it is resembled to the actual network.

Since random walk is essentially a complete blind detection, it is ideal that the object popularity is relatively high, which is not suitable to our strategy characterized by the minimum object popularity. The high degree seeking search only forwards search to neighbor nodes with relatively large degree, because these nodes have more neighbors and are more likely to contain the target resources. However, there is also the issue of information gathering when high degree seeking and high degree nodes may become a routing node, which results in network bottlenecks. Furthermore, there is the problem of fixed routing for high degree seeking. If we always choose high degree neighbor as the forwarding node, the search routing is fixed, which could lead to some nodes in the network not being covered. Therefore, we need a search algorithm that can utilizes some characteristic of P2P networks such as the degree of nodes to improve efficiency, meanwhile, the algorithm is able to avoid some problems of arising from itself such as the heavy load of the high degree nodes.

3.4 Rare Object Search

In order to more effectively search for rare objects, this paper proposes a search scheme which combine with the degree and the object number of neighbors to obtain forward decision. Experimental results show that this strategy has good search efficiency for rare objects. Each node in the network keeps the object number r and the degree k of its neighbors. j_r and j_k represent the object number and the degree of neighbor node j, respectively. When a node i forwards the query to neighbor j, the forwarding probability Pr_{ij} and Pk_{ij} respectively based on the object number and the degree of neighbor are defined by Equation (5).

$$Pr_{ij} = \frac{j_r}{\sum_{p \in K} p_r}; Pk_{ij} = \frac{j_k}{\sum_{p \in K} p_k} \tag{5}$$

where K is the set of i's neighbors, p is the node of the set K, and p_r and p_k represent the object number and the degree of the node p, respectively.

Based on the above analysis, the high degree seeking can improve the search efficiency, but it will bring the load problem. The probability Pk_{ij} defined here is similar to the high degree seeking. In order to reduce the load of high degree nodes, we introduce the probability Pr_{ij} based on the object number of nodes. A node cannot contain all information of its neighbors' resources. For example, in some P2P applications, the node builds the index based on terms of its documents. The index may be very big, so the nodes cannot store it each other. Therefore, the number of objects, which may be the number of terms in some applications, can be used as an important factor in guiding query route. Pr_{ij}, like Pk_{ij}, can lead the query to those power nodes which are more likely to contain the target objects. The experiments show that this strategy is available. Node i forwards query to neighbor j with the forward probability defined by Equation (6).

$$P_{ij} = \lambda Pr_{ij} + (1-\lambda)Pk_{ij}, \quad 0 < \lambda < 1 \tag{6}$$

where λ is an adjustable parameter with the initial value being 0.5. The parameter λ can be automatically adjusted in the running system. For example, since search success is due to the factor of objects, you can increase the value of λ. The above forwarding strategy not only finds rare objects more effectively, but also enables search distribution. This strategy solves the problem of fixed routing in high degree forward and will be conducive to explore new objects.

In the rare object search strategy, the node i's forwarding algorithm is shown as Algorithm 2.

Algorithm 2. Node i's forwarding algorithm

```
Procedure Forward (i)
Begin
  For (each neighbor j in peer i);
    Calculate Pr_ij;
    Calculate Pk_ij;
  End For
  For (each neighbor j in peer i)
    Calculate P_ij;
    Forward query to neighbor j according P_ij;
  End For
End
```

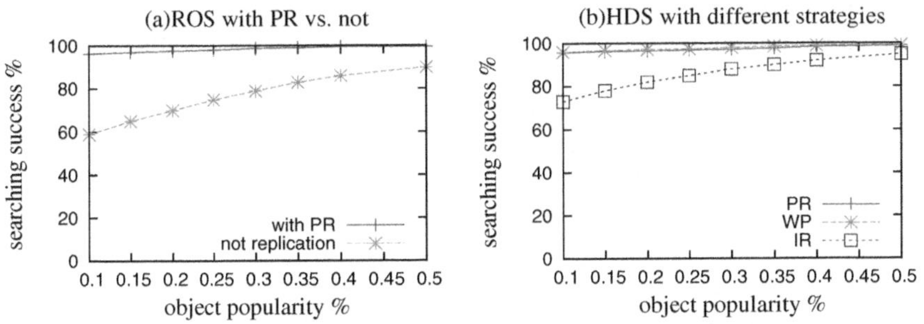

Fig. 2. Effectiveness of Proactive Replication

4 Experimental Evaluation

In this section, we analyze the efficiency of proactive replication (PR) strategy and rare object search (ROS) algorithm presented in this paper through the experiment. In order to obtain a more realistic experimental environment, the size of the node in network is in the magnitude of 100,000. Taking PeerSim [14] as the simulation-driven kernel, the initial topology is generated by Brite [15], and the distribution of network resources is defined by Zipf. In the simulations, we set Tp as 20 cycle times, $Vt = 100$, $\mu = \eta = 1$, $g = 2$ cycle times, $\lambda = 0.5$, and don't change the value of these parameters for simplicity.

4.1 Effectiveness of Proactive Replication

To assess the efficiency of proactive replication strategy and rare object search algorithm, we run rare object search (ROS) algorithm proposed in this paper in the network which proactive replication strategy is applied to and the network without any replication strategies. Fig. 2 depicts the correlation of object popularity and search hit rate in the networks in which ROS is run. Experiments show that the search efficiency of ROS has been greatly improved as proactive replication strategy is applied in the P2P network. The object popularity of the horizontal axis in Fig. 2(a) represents the system initialization popularity of the object itself, rather than the object popularity after using proactive replication strategy. This is to visually show the efficiency of the search for rare objects. The rare object search algorithms forward queries to those power nodes, so it has high search efficiency with the proactive replication strategy which provides the necessary popularity of objects for successful search. Therefore, our proactive replication strategy is available to improve the search efficiency for rare objects according to the experimental results.

Table 1. The amount of message in different replication strategies

	WP	PR
Average message processed in each node	2162	1391
Factor	1	1.55

Due to object probe, the proactive replication strategy will produce some additional communication overhead compared to other algorithms. In order to analyze these overhead, we collect the messages of objects probe and replication in the P2P network with proactive replication strategy. The average number of each node objects is 10 in the experiment. We take the replication strategy with probability (WP) proposed by Ronaldo [13] to conduct a comparative analysis. WP replicates $\gamma n^{1/2}$ copy for each object of node, n is the number of network nodes. WP has the query success rate at 85% when γ=1. The success rate of ROS reaches 95% after using PR strategy. To be fair, we take γ as 1 in the experiment. Table 1 shows the average amount of messages processed by the two kinds of replication strategies in each node in the simulation. The proactive replication proposed in this paper reduces the communication traffic by a factor of 1.55 compared to the existing WP algorithms. Obviously, the traffic of PR algorithm will be increased with the simulation cycles. However, if the object probe cycle interval is properly handled, we can maintain low communication overhead and in the meantime we can achieve a reasonable popularity of objects.

To analyze the performance of PR, we introduce another replication strategy: two-hop index replication (IR) similar to the strategy proposed in [11]. In IR, each node sends its index to all of it two-hop neighbors in its routing table. Fig. 2(b) shows the efficiency of high degree seeking (HDS) strategies with three different replication strategies. As you can see, IR has the least effective, the efficiency of PR and WP for rare objects is similar. However, the proactive replication strategy generates less communication overhead, so the proactive replication strategy PR is superior to the replication strategy with probability WP in overall performance.

4.2 Effective of Rare Object Search

We can see, from the Fig. 2, the search efficiency of rare object search (ROS) presented by this paper is similar to the high degree seeking (HDS) for searching rare objects. However, HDS forward routing is fixed, which can easily lead to information gathering; while the ROS uses the probability of forwarding, which can improve the problem of load balancing posed by query. The system with high degree forward strategy may lead the high degree nodes to become a bottleneck. To alleviate the load of high degree nodes, we can firstly run random walk and HDS after search failure to improve HDS. We call this strategy as improved HDS (IHDS). Although IHDS could improve the problem of load, it increases latency for rare objects, and brings additional communication overhead as well. Therefore, taking ROS as search scheme can not only ease the network traffic load, but also lessen the search delay of rare objects. Fig. 3(a) describes the search delay of ROS and IHDS for rare objects in P2P network with PR strategy. The vertical axis shows the maximum number of hops for successful search to target objects. IHDS firstly use random walk to search an object. However, random walk generally fails with the specified TTL value for rare objects with low popularity. Therefore, IHDS has high latency overhead.

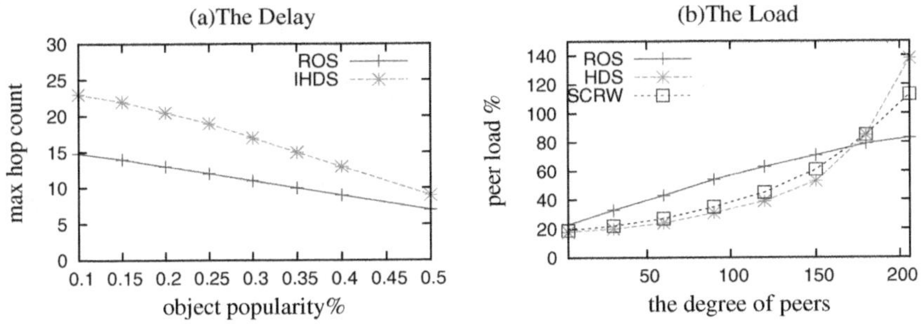

Fig. 3. Effectiveness of Rare Object Search

In order to carry out the analysis about load, we design an experiment to discuss the load balance of nodes with different degrees as follows: The network topology is generated by Brite [15], the minimum degree of nodes is 3, the maximum degree is 206, and the degree distribution of nodes obeys power-law distribution. Fig. 3(b) is the simulated results of ROS, HDS and SCRW (Supernode-Constrained Random Walk) proposed in [11] in which nodes always forward the query to one of it randomly selected supernode neighbors. As you can see, the load of ROS is balanced, and the load of the node with the greatest degree is lower than 100%. While the high load of the HDS and SCRW is mainly concentrated in the high degree nodes, the utilization of the nodes with small degree is relatively lower. Therefore, ROS algorithm presented in this paper not only has a better search efficiency, but also improve the load balance of node compared to existing algorithms.

4.3 Performance in Churn

The proactive replication can withstand the high rate of nodes dynamics. Churn arises from continued and rapid arrival and failure (or departure) of a large number of peers in the P2P network. We evaluated the efficiency of the proactive replication in unstructured P2P network in churn. Experiment results verified the resilience of the proactive replication in churn. In the simulation, node join and voluntary departures are modeled by a Poisson process with a mean rate of R, which ranges from 0.05 to 0.5. A rate of R=0.05 corresponds to one node joining and leaving every 20 seconds on average. Fig. 4(a) plots the average lookup path length versus node join/leave rate. We can see that the proactive replication has the best effect because the cycle probes of the nodes with PR which ensure the objects popularity.

Churn not only appears in the network, but also exists in the content. We take another experiment to analyze the dynamicity of the content (popularity changing over time). In the simulation, the set of search objects varies with time period, that is, the popular objects in a time period will become unpopular in another time period. We can adjust μ in equation (2) to increase the replication of popular rare objects. The proactive replication ensures high resistance to content churn and this is evident from Fig. 4(b) in which the system generates a good success rate.

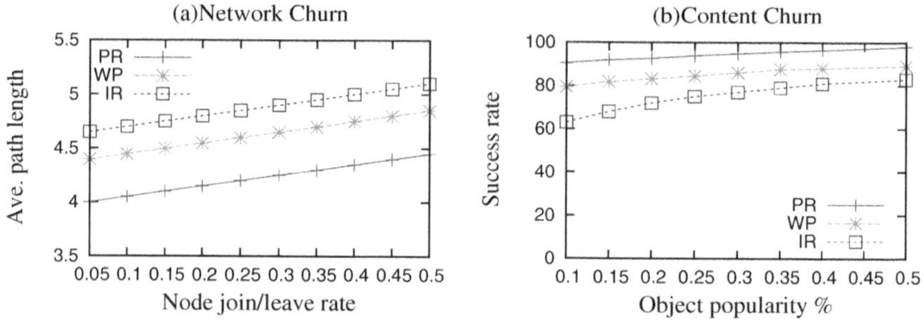

Fig. 4. Performance in churn

5 Conclusions

This paper presents a new proactive replication strategy for rare objects, as well as proposes a rare object search algorithm through the improvement of the high degree seeking strategy. Through the proposed algorithms, we can greatly improve the search efficiency for rare objects, and keep the communication cost associated with search relatively low. Experiments showed that there is a significant improvement in efficiency for rare objects after using proactive replication strategy, and the communication overhead brought by search is lower than other replication strategies. We design the comparative experiment with other search algorithms, and the results show that the search algorithm in this article has better efficiency for rare objects, and ensures load balance of search. In order to reduce unnecessary communication overhead, the replication strategy proposed by this paper is the algorithms of the least amount replication, which can decide whether to create a replication through the probe of objects. This will result in the communication overhead in probe. However, experiments have shown that the overhead is less than replication strategy of a constant amount. As a result, it will be interesting to see if the communication overhead brought by probing can be further reduced by fine-tuning the interval between detection cycles. The dynamical adjustment for the proportion of degree and objects in the rare object search algorithm is also a place worth exploring. The future work will focus on the cycle of object probing and the optimization of search strategy.

Acknowledgments. This work is supported by National Natural Science Foundation of China under Grant 60873225, 60773191, 70771043, National High Technology Research and Development Program of China under Grant 2007AA01Z403, Natural Science Foundation of Hubei Province under Grant 2009CDB298, Wuhan Youth Science and Technology Chenguang Program under Grant 200950431171, Open Foundation of State Key Laboratory of Software Engineering under Grant SKLSE20080718, Innovation Fund of Huazhong University of Science and Technology under Grant Q2009021.

References

1. Ratnasamy, S., Francis, P., Handley, M., Karp, R.M., Shenker, S.: A scalable content-addressable network. In: The 2001 annual conference of the Special Interest Group on Data Communication (SIGCOMM 2001), pp. 161–172. ACM Press, San Diego (2001)
2. Gnutella_protocol, `http://gnunet.org/papers/gnutella_protocol.pdf/`
3. Ripeanu, M.: Peer-to-Peer Architecture Case Study: Gnutella Network. In: The 1st International Conference on Peer-to-Peer Computing (P2P 2001), pp. 99–100. IEEE Press, Linköping (2001)
4. Loo, B.T., Hellerstein, J.M., Huebsch, R., Shenker, S., Stoica, I.: Enhancing p2p file-sharing with an internet-scale query processor. In: The thirtieth International Conference on Very Large Data Bases (VLDB 2004), pp. 432–443. Morgan Kaufmann, Toronto (2004)
5. Lv, Q., Cao, P., Cohen, E., Li, K., Shenker, S.: Search and replication in unstructured peer-to-peer networks. In: The 16th Annual ACM International Conference on Supercomputing (ICS 2002), pp. 84–95. ACM Press, New York (2002)
6. Yin, Z., Jin, H., Zhang, C., Yuan, Q., Zhao, C.: Adaptive Query-Caching in Peer-to-Peer Systems. In: The 2nd IFIP International Conference on Network and Parallel Computing (NPC 2005), pp. 97–104. Springer Press, Beijing (2005)
7. Gkantsidis, C., Mihail, M., Saberi, A.: Random Walks in Peer-to-Peer Networks. In: The 23rd Annual Joint Conference of the IEEE Computer and Communications Societies (INFOCOM 2004). IEEE Press, HongKong (2004)
8. Gkantsidis, C., Mihail, M., Saberi, A.: Hybrid search schemes for unstructured peer-to-peer networks. In: The 24th Annual Joint Conference of the IEEE Computer and Communications Societies (INFOCOM 2005), pp. 1526–1537. IEEE Press, Miami (2005)
9. Adamic, L.A., Lukose, R.M., Puniyani, A.R., Huberman, B.A.: Search in Power-Law Networks. Phys. Rev. E 64, 046135 (2001)
10. Adamic, L.A., Lukose, R.M., Huberman, B.A.: Local search in unstructured networks. In: Bornholdt, S., Schuster, H.G. (eds.) Handbook of Graphs and Networks. Wiley-VCH, Berlin (2003)
11. Puttaswamy, K.P.N., Sala, A., Zhao, B.Y.: Searching for Rare Objects using Index Replication. In: The 27th Annual Joint Conference of the IEEE Computer and Communications Societies (INFOCOM 2008), pp. 1723–1731. IEEE Press, Phoenix (2008)
12. Cohen, E., Shenker, S.: Replication strategies in unstructured peer-to-peer networks. In: The 2002 annual conference of the Special Interest Group on Data Communication (SIGCOMM 2002), pp. 177–190. ACM Press, Pittsburgh (2002)
13. Ferreira, R.A., Ramanathan, M.K., Awan, A., Jagannathan, S.: Search with Probabilistic Guarantees in Unstructured Peer-to-Peer Networks. In: The 5th International Conference on Peer-to-Peer Computing (P2P 2005), pp. 165–172. IEEE Press, Konstanz (2005)
14. PeerSim, `http://peersim.sourceforge.net/`
15. Brite, `http://www.cs.bu.edu/brite/`
16. Shen, H.: EAD: An Efficient and Adaptive Decentralized File Replication Algorithm in P2P File Sharing Systems. In: The 8th International Conference on Peer-to-Peer Computing (P2P 2008), pp. 99–108. IEEE Press, Aachen (2008)
17. Qiao, Y., Bustamante, F.E.: Structured and Unstructured Overlays under the Microscope: A Measurement-based View of Two P2P Systems That People Use. In: The 2006 USENIX Annual Technical Conference (USENIX 2006), pp. 341–355. USENIX Press, Boston (2006)

SWORDS: Improving Sensor Networks Immunity under Worm Attacks

Nike Gui, Ennan Zhai, Jianbin Hu, and Zhong Chen

Institute of Software, School of Electronics Engineering and Computer Science, Peking University, China
Key Laboratory of High Confidence Software Technologies (Peking University), Ministry of Education, China
{guink,zhaien,hjbin,chen}@infosec.pku.edu.cn

Abstract. Since sensor nodes are implemented in embedded computer systems, which do not have complicated hardware architecture and operating system. Therefore, worm attacks, which exploit buffer-overflow vulnerabilities, could compromise the entire sensor network by sending a single mal-packet. To address the severe problem, the technique of software diversity has been leveraged to defend against sensor worms. In this paper, we encompass *random sensor node scheduling* and *software diversity* to propose a novel sensor worm defense scheme. Our scheme can effectively improve the sensor network defensive capability. Then some practical considerations for its real application is proposed. Finally, analytical and simulation results confirm the effectiveness of our scheme in sensor worm defense.

1 Introduction

To address security problems in sensor networks, many mechanisms have been proposed to defend against various kinds of attacks in sensor networks. However, a potentially more severe attack has not yet drawn too much attention, which is called *sensor worm* attack [1]. More specifically, sensor worms are defined as crafted messages that exploit software vulnerability of sensor nodes in a sensor network, causing sensor nodes to crash or taking control of them.

Since the Harvard architecture has separated memories for program and data [2], injected mal-codes that are commonly found in worm packets are hard to be executed in sensor nodes. However, an experiment on Mica2 motes has been conducted and a buffer overflow vulnerability has been found in the work of [1]. The vulnerability could result in the transfer of program flow to a transmission component in the code space. Therefore, this leads to the propagation of the worm packet over the entire network. In addition, it is even easier for sensor nodes to be compromised by worm attacks compared with regular computer systems, because sensor nodes in the same network are mostly using homogeneous devices and software, and an attacker can capture one sensor node and read application codes out from a JTAG interface (which can be found in most embedded systems). As a result, if one sensor can be compromised due to a

L. Chen et al. (Eds.): WAIM 2010, LNCS 6184, pp. 86–96, 2010.

vulnerability, all other sensors that use the same devices and codes in the same network can be compromised due to the same vulnerability. Therefore, sensor worm is a serious threat.

The most important related work we know to defend against sensor worm attack is the software diversity-based sensor worm immunity approach [1]. It designed an backtracking color algorithm to assign the appropriate software version to sensor nodes, and examined the impact of sensor node deployment errors on worm propagation. However, the time complexity of the algorithm is $O(sN^2)$, s is the number of software versions and N is the total number of cells in the deployment area. Here, cell denotes a set of nodes assigned with the same software version. However, N can be a large number since the number of sensor nodes in one cell should be kept smaller by selecting a larger number of N. Moreover, the cell size L should be chosen carefully, since the maximum number of node compromised that could happen at one time varies as a function of L. This is not easy to be applied in some sensor networks, e.g., sensor networks deployed in critical or hostile areas.

To address the problems in sensor worm defense, this paper aims to answer the following central question:

Is it possible to propose an provable and effective sensor worm defense scheme, which is easy to be applied in sensor networks?

To answer this question, we encompass two key techniques, *random sensor node scheduling* [3] and *software diversity* [1], to propose a novel Sensor WORm Defense Scheme, namely SWORDS. On one hand, we leverage random sensor node scheduling to achieve lower active node density under guaranteed connectivity, which could improve defensive capability against sensor worm attacks; on the other hand, we explore software diversity to combat sensor worms in spirit of the survivability through heterogeneity philosophy. We can analyze the efficiency of SWORDS through a small example: a deployed sensor node may have ten or twenty neighboring nodes, but only two or three of them are working at the same time due to random sensor scheduling. If we choose three or four software versions in our scheme, the number of neighboring nodes assigned with the same software version could be limited blow one, which means that the probability of sensor worm propagation through neighboring nodes is quite small. We will give the details of proof in Section III.

To the best of our knowledge, this paper is the first research work that introduces the node scheduling into sensor worm defense scheme. SWORDS has the following salient features:

- SWORDS can defend against sensor worm effectively and can be applied in sensor networks easily.
- SWORDS makes the sensor network more energy efficient due to introducing sensor node scheduling.
- SWORDS is totally distributed, and does not need accurate location information.
- SWORDS provides guarantee that all the active sensor nodes are connected, even though random scheduling is utilized.

The rest of this paper is organized as follows. We present the related work in Section II. Section III describes the details of SWORDS, and provides analysis to illustrate SWORDS's efficiency clearly. Then, the simulation methodology and evaluation results are discussed in Section IV. Finally, we present conclusion in Section V.

2 Related Work

2.1 Worm Defense

In [4], node compromise spread in wireless sensor networks is modeled utilizing epidemic theory, and key factors determining potential outbreaks are also identified. In [2], a range of attack approaches are proposed to illustrate that a mal-packet, which only carries specially crafted data, can exploit memory-related vulnerabilities. And the mal-packet utilizes existing application codes in a sensor node to propagate itself without disrupting sensor's functionality. To improve the security of sensor nodes, a memory protection system that prevents many forms of memory corruption is proposed in [5]. And in [6], code obfuscation and randomization are combined to protect the secret keys of sensor nodes. Specifically, a systematic way to enhance sensor network immunity under worm attack is proposed in [1] recently, which explores the technique of software diversity to combat sensor worms and examines the impact of sensor node deployment errors on worm propagation. However, the node deployment method is much complex and the cell size should be chosen carefully, these shortcomings make its application in sensor networks not quite realistic.

2.2 Sensor Node Scheduling

Sensor node scheduling is a traditional research area for energy efficiency of sensor networks. SPAN is proposed in [7], which is a power saving technique for multi-hop ad hoc wireless networks that reduces energy consumption without significantly diminishing the capacity or connectivity of the network. ASCENT [8] chooses some sensor nodes to be active as routers while allows others to sleep to save energy, it selects an active router depending on local connectivity and the observed data loss rates. STEM [9] puts sensor nodes into sleep state more aggressively. Sensor nodes wake up only when they have data to transfer or they receive requests from their neighbors. Therefore, STEM trades latency for further energy saving. In [10], it is proved that to ensure that a full coverage of a convex area also guarantees the connectivity of the active nodes inside the area, the communication range should be at least twice of the sensing range. And in [11], the authors enhance the work in [10] by releasing the constraint. Specifically, the approach in [3] utilizes an integrated method that provides statistical sensing coverage and guaranteed network connectivity. The method is totally distributed, and is able to dynamically adjust sensing coverage with guaranteed network connectivity.

Table 1. Notations

Symbol	Description
n	the total number of deployed sensor nodes
v	the number of software versions, e.g., v = 3 or 4, ...
A	the size of the whole field
S	the size of communication area of each sensor node
q	the probability that a node's communication area covers another sensor node, $q = \frac{S}{A}$
c	the connectivity intensity for a specific node, which is defined as the probability that a sensor node has neighbor(s)
C	the network connectivity intensity, which is define as the expectation of c
k	the probability that a sensor node is working in a time slot, $0 < k < 1$
l	the expectation of number of neighboring nodes without sensor worm defense scheme
m	the expectation of number of neighboring nodes after applying SWORDS
s	the expectation of maximum number of node compromises that could happen at one time

2.3 Software Diversity

Inspired by diversity in biological system, software diversity becomes an important source of robustness in computer system. Several methods of achieving software diversity based on randomization are discussed in [12], such randomization could potentially increase the robustness of software systems with minimal impact on convenience, usability and efficiency. The research work in [13] assumes the availability of diverse software package for each system and then seeks to increase the intrinsic value of available diversity by considering the entire computer network. A variety of techniques have been proposed in [14] to enhance the intrusion resistance of computer systems by increasing software diversity. The research work in [15] describes the danger posed by P2P worms and initiates the study of possible mitigation mechanisms. Moreover, it suggests that diversity is an effective deterrence to P2P worms.

3 Sensor Worm Defense

3.1 Notations and Scheme

As described in [16], we consider stationary sensor networks in a two-dimensional field. Before deployment, each sensor node is randomly assigned only one software version from v software versions. We assume that sensor nodes are randomly and independently deployed in a field, and that a sensor node's radio transmission range is fixed. But we do not assume accurate global time synchronization, which is an extremely hard task for large-scale sensor networks.

For ease reference, all notations used in SWORDS are listed in Table 1. In our scheme, time is divided into slots, and in each time slot, $k \times n$ nodes are randomly selected to work, while the other nodes will be turned off. When the network is sufficiently dense, working nodes will be connected with a high probability. This random scheduling method was stimulated by the work in [3]. There is a trade-off here: a larger value of k guarantees higher connectivity probability; however, a larger value of k results in more neighboring nodes for worm propagation. As a result, we should select a proper value of k for both sensor worm defense and guaranteed connectivity intensity. Thus, we need to clearly define the *connectivity intensity.*

Definition 1. *Connectivity Intensity for a Specific Node: c. For a given node in the deployment field, we define c as the probability that at least one active sensor node locates in the given node's communication area.*

It is obvious that c depends on both the number of sensor nodes deployed in the neighborhood and our scheduling scheme. We assume that there are i nodes located in a given node's communication area, then the probability that these i nodes are all sleeping is $(1-k)^i$. Therefore, the probability that at least one neighboring node is working is $1-(1-k)^i$. So, we prove that $c = 1-(1-k)^i$.

Due to the randomness in the sensor deployment strategy and our scheduling scheme, c is a random variable. Notably, the expectation of c for any node inside the field is equal, since nodes are independently and uniformly distributed and scheduled (For simplicity, we ignore the edge effect for large deployment area). Therefore, the expectation of c is a network-wide consistent metric and could be used to evaluate the connectivity quality of the whole network.

Definition 2. *Network Connectivity Intensity: C. We define C as the expectation of c. That is* $C = E[c]$.

C could be calculated as

$$\begin{aligned} C = E[c] &= E[1-(1-k)^i] \\ &= 1-\sum_{i=0}^{n}(1-k)^i \times C_n^i \times q^i \times (1-q)^{n-i} \\ &= 1-\sum_{i=0}^{n} C_n^i \times (q-qk)^i \times (1-q)^{n-i} \\ &= 1-(1-qk)^n \end{aligned}$$

Since sensor nodes should not be separated from the network after applying scheduling scheme, the ideal value of C is 1, which indicates that every node in the field has at least one neighboring node. However, achieving this ideal value may require very dense deployment and is extremely expensive. Because different applications have different requirements on acceptable connectivity intensity, a good scheduling scheme should select a proper value of k. For a given n, the lower bound on the value of k to provide a network connectivity intensity value of C is

$$k = \frac{1 - \sqrt[n]{1-C}}{q} \tag{1}$$

For example, we set $C = 0.9$, $n = 2000$, $q = \frac{\pi}{400}$, we can get $k = 0.1466$ with Equation 1. From this example, we could see that our random scheduling scheme can achieve a reasonably high connectivity requirement by selecting a proper value of k.

3.2 Analysis on Sensor Worm Defense Capability

So far we have been focusing on random software assignment and random scheduling scheme; we have not yet discussed whether SWORDS can effectively improve the sensor network defensive capability. To prove it, we first analyze the number of neighboring nodes due to its importance in sensor worm propagation.

Theorem 1. *Without SWORDS, the expectation of number of neighboring nodes $l = nq$.*

Proof. If a sensor node is deployed inside a specific node's communication area, this node is the specific node's neighboring node. Due to the randomness in node deployment, the number of neighboring nodes is a random number. Therefore, its expectation, l, could be calculated as

$$\begin{aligned}
l &= \sum_{i=0}^{n} i \times C_n^i \times q^i \times (1-q)^{n-i} \\
&= \sum_{i=1}^{n} n \times C_{n-1}^{i-1} \times q^i \times (1-q)^{n-i} \\
&= (1-q)^{n-1} \times n \times \sum_{i=1}^{n} C_{n-1}^{i-1} \times q^i \times (\frac{1}{1-q})^{i-1} \\
&= (1-q)^{n-1} \times n \times q \times \sum_{i=1}^{n} C_{n-1}^{i-1} \times q^{i-1} \times (\frac{1}{1-q})^{i-1} \\
&= (1-q)^{n-1} \times n \times q \times \sum_{i=1}^{n} C_{n-1}^{i-1} \times (\frac{q}{1-q})^{i-1} \times 1^{n-1-i} \\
&= (1-q)^{n-1} \times n \times q \times \sum_{i=0}^{n-1} C_{n-1}^{i} \times (\frac{q}{1-q})^{i} \times 1^{n-1-i} \\
&= (1-q)^{n-1} \times n \times q \times (\frac{q}{1-q} + 1)^{n-1} \\
&= (1-q)^{n-1} \times n \times q \times (\frac{1}{1-q})^{n-1} \\
&= nq
\end{aligned}$$

After applying random scheduling scheme with guaranteed connectivity, the number of neighboring nodes can be reduced. In addition, we explore software

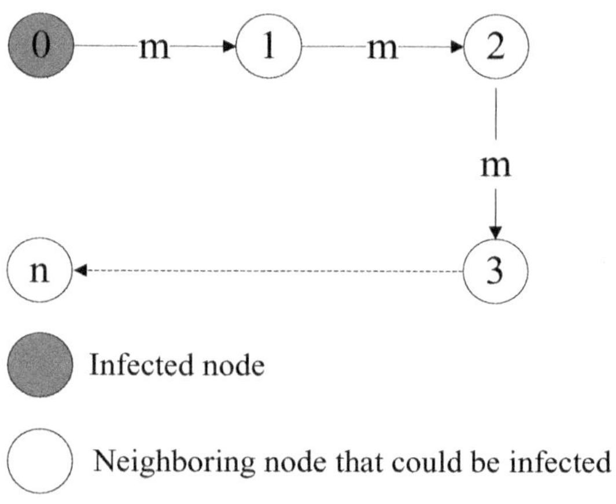

Fig. 1. Node Propagation

diversity to combat sensor worms, since different versions of the same functionality will not have the same vulnerability for the attacker to exploit. As a result, the number of neighboring nodes, which could be infected, is further limited.

Theorem 2. *After applying SWORDS, the expectation of the number of neighboring nodes that could be infected* $m = \frac{n(1-\sqrt[n]{1-C})}{v}$.

Proof. Based on Equation 1 and Theorem 1, m could be calculated as

$$\begin{aligned} m &= \frac{l \times k}{v} = \frac{n \times q \times k}{v} \\ &= \frac{n \times q \times \frac{1-\sqrt[n]{1-C}}{q}}{v} \\ &= \frac{n(1-\sqrt[n]{1-C})}{v} \end{aligned}$$

For example, we set $C = 0.9$, $n = 2000$, $v = 4$, we can get $m = 0.5753$. From this example, we could see that the number of neighboring nodes, which could be infected, is quite small (usually smaller than one) after applying SWORDS. To evaluate the effectiveness of sensor worm defense scheme, we can analyze *the number of sensor nodes that can be compromised at one time by the worm attack* as described in [1].

Theorem 3. *The maximum number of node compromises that could happen at one time* $s = \frac{m}{(1-m)^2}$.

Proof. Since the value of m is usually smaller than one, for simplicity, we take m as the probability that a specific infected node could find a neighboring node, which is assigned with the same software version. As shown in Figure 1, an infected node (node 0) has a probability of m to find a neighboring node (node

1) for worm propagation; and node 1 also has a probability of m to find another neighboring node (node 2) for worm propagation, and so on. Hence, the probability of compromising one node at one time is m; and the probability of compromising two nodes at one time is m^2, and so on. Now we calculate s as

$$s = \sum_{i=0}^{n} i \times m^i$$

So

$$s_n = m + 2 \times m^2 + 3 \times m^3 + ... + n \times m^n$$
$$s_{n-1} = m + 2 \times m^2 + 3 \times m^3 + ... + (n-1) \times m^{n-1}$$

We can get

$$s_n - s_{n-1} = n \times m^n$$
$$s_n - m \times s_{n-1} = m + m^2 + m^3 + ... + m^n = \frac{m}{1-m}$$

Finally, we calculate

$$s = s_n = \frac{m}{(1-m)^2}$$

For example, we set $C = 0.9$, $n = 2000$, $v = 4$, we can get $s = 3.1896$. That means in a sensor network with the required connectivity intensity value of 0.9, containing 2000 nodes and assigned with 4 software versions, only about three nodes could be compromised averagely in one sensor worm attack after applying SWORDS.

3.3 Practical Issue

After applying SWORDS, sensor nodes have the probability of k to be working in each time slot, and these working nodes consist of a *subnetwork*. To guarantee all the sensor nodes in the subnetwork are connected with each other, we borrow the idea of *extra-on rule* from the study in [3]. It is assumed that the original network before applying SWORDS is connected and each sensor node knows its minimal hop count to the sink node. A sensor node A is called the upstream node of another sensor node B, if node A and node B are neighboring nodes and the minimal hop count of node A to the sink node is one less than that of node B. Node B is also called node A's downstream node.

Extra-on Rule: In a specific time slot, if a sensor node A has a downstream node B, and none of node B's upstream nodes is active, then node A should also work. In other words, besides working in the duty time slots (randomly scheduled time slots), node A is required to work in extra time slots (scheduled time slots due to guaranteed connectivity).

In [3], it is proved that applying the extra-on rule to each subnetwork could ensure its connectivity. And the number of extra nodes needed to turn on for connectivity maintenance is very small, compared to the total number of active nodes.

4 Evaluation

In this section, we will validate our analytical model and show the performance of our scheme under different parameter settings.

4.1 Simulation Setup

In the simulation, the sensor nodes are randomly deployed over the deployment area of 100m $\times$100m. The total number of sensor nodes in the entire network varies from 2000 to 10000. The transmission range is 10m, and the number of available software versions is 3 or 4. Finally, the connectivity intensity changes from 0.85 to 0.95. Note that each point in the following figures is averaged over 100 rounds, each of which contains 2000 sensor worm attacks.

4.2 Simulation Results

We study the maximum number of node compromises (s) that could happen at one time. As shown in Figure 2, 3 and Figure 4, s changes as a function of the network connectivity intensity (C), the number of software versions (v), and the total number of deployed sensor node (n). Under a certain number of v and n, when C is larger, the maximum number of node compromises s becomes larger. When C is larger than a threshold and v is relatively small, s are increased rapidly. In reality, this means that we should keep C to be a relatively small value, e.g. about 0.92, so that sensor worms can not propagate over the deployment area. Under a certain number of C and n, when v is larger, the maximum number of node compromises s becomes smaller. In reality, this means that applying more software versions could improve the defensive capability against sensor worm. However, we find that s is not changed dramatically, when the value of n varies from 2000 to 10000. In summary, the above results indicate that our scheme with proper parameters can effectively prevent the propagation of sensor worms, and the simulation results match our analytical results well.

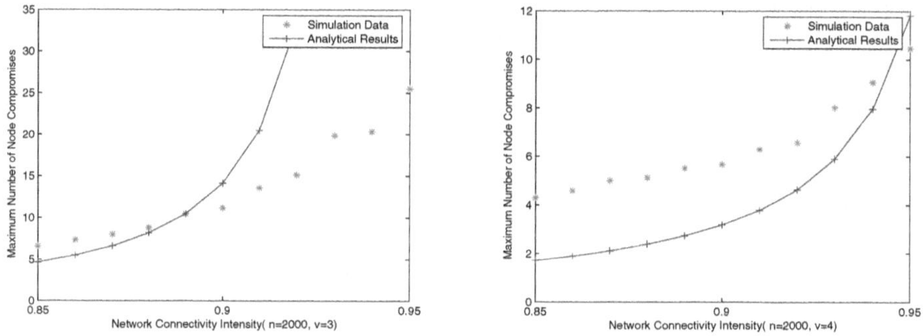

(a) v = 3 (b) v = 4

Fig. 2. Maximum Number of Node Compromises (n = 2000)

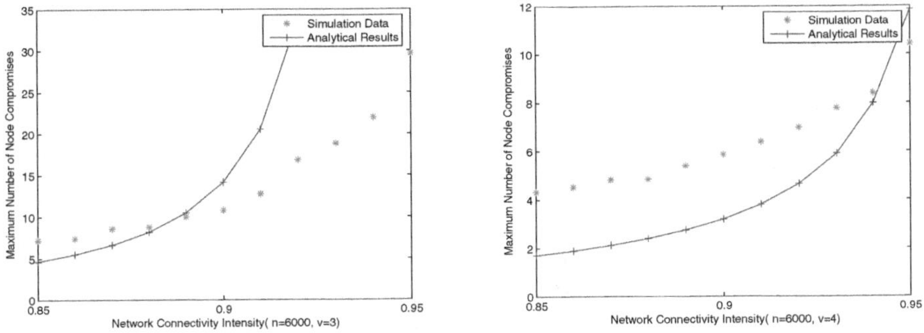

(a) v = 3 **(b)** v = 4

Fig. 3. Maximum Number of Node Compromises (n = 6000)

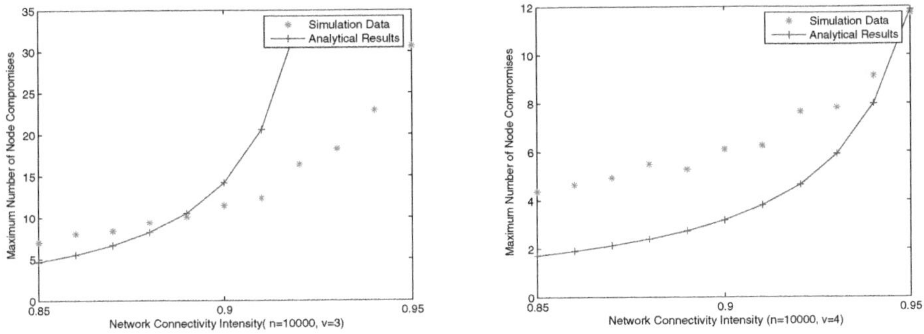

(a) v = 3 **(b)** v = 4

Fig. 4. Maximum Number of Node Compromises (n = 10000)

5 Conclusion

In this paper, we propose SWORDS, an effective and provable sensor worm defense scheme, based on the idea of random sensor node scheduling and software diversity. We are the first to introduce the node scheduling method into sensor worm defense scheme. We have proved that SWORDS can significantly increase the immunity of sensor networks under worm attacks, and our simulation results match the analytical results well.

References

1. Yang, Y., Zhu, S., Cao, G.: Improving sensor network immunity under worm attacks: a software diversity approach. In: MobiHoc, pp. 149–158 (2008)
2. Gu, Q., Noorani, R.: Towards self-propagate mal-packets in sensor networks. In: WISEC, pp. 172–182 (2008)

3. Liu, C., Wu, K., Xiao, Y., Sun, B.: Random coverage with guaranteed connectivity: Joint scheduling for wireless sensor networks. IEEE Trans. Parallel Distrib. Syst. 17(6), 562–575 (2006)
4. De, P., Liu, Y., Das, S.K.: Modeling node compromise spread in wireless sensor networks using epidemic theory. In: WOWMOM, pp. 237–243 (2006)
5. Kumar, R., Kohler, E., Srivastava, M.B.: Harbor: software-based memory protection for sensor nodes. In: IPSN, pp. 340–349 (2007)
6. Alarifi, A., Du, W.: Diversify sensor nodes to improve resilience against node compromise. In: SASN, pp. 101–112 (2006)
7. Chen, B., Jamieson, K., Balakrishnan, H., Morris, R.: Span: An energy-efficient coordination algorithm for topology maintenance in ad hoc wireless networks. In: MOBICOM, pp. 85–96 (2001)
8. Cerpa, A., Estrin, D.: Ascent: Adaptive self-configuring sensor networks topologies. In: INFOCOM (2002)
9. Schurgers, C., Tsiatsis, V., Ganeriwal, S., Srivastava, M.B.: Topology management for sensor networks: exploiting latency and density. In: MobiHoc, pp. 135–145 (2002)
10. Zhang, H., Hou, J.C.: Maintaining sensing coverage and connectivity in large sensor networks. Ad Hoc & Sensor Wireless Networks 1(1-2) (2005)
11. Tian, D., Georganas, N.D.: Connectivity maintenance and coverage preservation in wireless sensor networks. Ad Hoc Networks 3(6), 744–761 (2005)
12. Forrest, S., Somayaji, A., Ackley, D.H.: Building diverse computer systems. In: Workshop on Hot Topics in Operating Systems, pp. 67–72 (1997)
13. O'Donnell, A.J., Sethu, H.: On achieving software diversity for improved network security using distributed coloring algorithms. In: ACM Conference on Computer and Communications Security, pp. 121–131 (2004)
14. Kc, G.S., Keromytis, A.D., Prevelakis, V.: Countering code-injection attacks with instruction-set randomization. In: ACM Conference on Computer and Communications Security, pp. 272–280 (2003)
15. Zhou, L., Zhang, L., McSherry, F., Immorlica, N., Costa, M., Chien, S.: A first look at peer-to-peer worms: Threats and defenses. In: Castro, M., van Renesse, R. (eds.) IPTPS 2005. LNCS, vol. 3640, pp. 24–35. Springer, Heidelberg (2005)
16. Younis, M.F., Akkaya, K.: Strategies and techniques for node placement in wireless sensor networks: A survey. Ad Hoc Networks 6(4), 621–655 (2008)

Efficient Multiple Objects-Oriented Event Detection Over RFID Data Streams

Shanglian Peng[1], Zhanhuai Li[1], Qiang Li[2], Qun Chen[1], Hailong Liu[1], Yanming Nie[1], and Wei Pan[1]

[1] School of Computer Science and Technology, Northwestern Polytechnical University
[2] College of Software and Microelectronics, Northwestern Polytechnical University, Xi'an 710072, China
pengshanglian@mail.nwpu.edu.cn, powerqy@163.com
{lizhh,chenbenben,liuhailong,panwei1002}@nwpu.edu.cn
nymcoon@gmail.com

Abstract. Complex event processing has been extensively applied in areas such as RFID tracking for supply chain management, fluctuation detection in stock trading, real-time intrusion detection in network monitoring,etc. Most existing research works focus on specification, formalization and evaluation of single-object oriented complex event processing. In this paper, we investigate complex event processing problems over multiple correlated RFID objects. We study multiple correlated RFID event detection problems. We present two kinds of evaluation algorithms: SEquence Join Algorithm(SEJA) and Stream Join Algorithm(SJA). Experimental studies demonstrate that our proposed algorithms are effective and scalable.

Keywords: complex event processing, NFA, data stream, RFID.

1 Introduction

Radio Frequency IDentification(RFID) is an automatic information collection technology that is widely used in areas such as supply chain management [1], retail store monitoring [2], asset tracking and surveillance [3] and pervasive computing [4]. Complex event processing(CEP) is the process of extracting higher level information from lower level events. CEP over RFID streams faces challenges such as high speed and huge RFID readings, real time process and response and rich information specification(spatial, temporal, causality and similarity) between correlated events. CEP has been extensively studied in active database [5]. Existing CEP works [6,7,8,9] mainly focus on pattern definition, optimizations of query plan and evaluation optimizations. These works pay little attention to relationships between events of the same event types. In fact, there exist many event queries that involve correlated events of the same event type in applications such as asset tracking, task alignment and automatic auto assemble, etc. Here we take IT asset tracking for example.

IT asset tracking. IT assets such as laptop computers, blade servers, disks are vital for enterprise. RFID tags can be attached to IT assets and personnel for

L. Chen et al. (Eds.): WAIM 2010, LNCS 6184, pp. 97–102, 2010.

IT asset tracking tasks. An event query in IT asset tracking application can be defined as Query1:

PATTERN SEQ(A_2; B_2; C_2; D_2; F_2)
WHERE $A_2^1.id = B_2^1.id = C_2^1.id = D_2^1.id = F_2^1.id$
AND $A_2 A^2.id = B_2^2.id = C_2^2.id = D_2^2.id = F_2^2.id$
AND $|A_2^1.time - A_2^2.time| \leq \varepsilon_1$
AND $|B_2^1.time - B_2^2.time| \leq \varepsilon_2$
AND $|C_2^1.time - C_2^2.time| \leq \varepsilon_3$
AND $|D_2^1.time - D_2^2.time| \leq \varepsilon_4$
AND $|F_2^1.time - F_2^2.time| \leq \varepsilon_5$
WITHIN 20 minutes

In an RFID-enabled office, personnel can carry authenticated objects moving from one RFID reading point to another RFID reading point. Query 1 finds pattern of one RFID-enabled asset with authenticated personnel that have passed through five RFID reading points A, B, C, D and F within 20 minutes.

In this paper, we focus on evaluations and optimizations of event queries which involve multiple correlated RFID tagged objects, our works include: (1)we propose event detection problems over multiple correlated event objects which are generalization of one object-oriented event detection problems; (2)we propose effective sequence join and stream join algorithms to evaluate this kind of queries; (3)we perform extensive experiments to validate effectiveness and scalability of the proposed algorithms. The rest of the paper is organized as follows: Section 2 introduces related work of CEP. Section 3 introduces event preliminaries and event model. In section 4, we present algorithms and optimizations to evaluate multiple correlated-object event queries. In section 5, we present performance studies of the proposed algorithms. We conclude this paper in section 6.

2 Related Work

CEP has been extensively studied in active database [5]. These works focused on evaluation of complex patterns in traditional databases which can not accommodate real time and streaming requirements of current applications. In [6], a declarative event language–SASE is proposed to define, filter, aggregate and correlate events from stream data. However, NFA(non-deterministic finite automata) implementation of SASE event queries can not work efficiently when domain size in event definition is large and event objects of the same type are considered. Cayuga [9] is a CEP system developed from a pub/sub system which is focused on common sub-expressions searching amongst multiple patterns. In Cayuga, a SQL-style event definition language is proposed. Objects involved in Cayuga event queries are single object-oriented. SAMOS [10] is a petri Nets-based systems which are able to support concurrency but are very complex to express and evaluate. CEDR [11] is an event streaming system with a declarative query language which can not define multiple object-oriented event queries.

3 Event Preliminaries and Event Query Specification

Primitive event is occurrence of interest at a point in time which is instantaneous and can not be decomposed into subevents. Primitive event occurrence is an instance of an **event type**. In this paper, we use E_n to represent event type of E involving n primitive/composite events. We use E_n^m to denote the m-th event of E_n. **Composite event** is combination of **primitive(composite) events** by appliance of event operators (such as `and(&)`, `or(|)`, `not(!)`, `SEQ(;)`, etc.).

In our event model, each event(primitive or composite) is associated with a *start-timestamp* and an *end-timestamp*. As primitive event occurs instantaneously, the start time(ts) and end time(te) of primitive event is the same. For composite event, occurrence time is determined by constituent events and semantics of event operators. We present formal semantics of event operators involving multiple event objects as following:

Conjunction.(E=A_n&B_m): $E(ts,te) \Leftrightarrow \exists\ ts_A^1,..., ts_A^n, te_A^1,..., te_A^n, ts_B^1,..., ts_B^m, te_B^1,..., te_B^m (A_n^1 \wedge ... \wedge A_n^n \wedge B_m^1 \wedge ... B_m^m \wedge ts=\min\{ts_A^1,...,ts_A^n,ts_B^1,...,ts_B^m\} \wedge te =\max\{te_A^1,...,te_A^n,te_B^1,...,te_B^m\})$.
Disjunction.(E=$A_n|B_m$): $E(ts,te) \Leftrightarrow \exists\ ts_A^1,..., ts_A^n, te_A^1,..., te_A^n, ts_B^1,.., ts_B^m, te_B^1,.., te_B^m (A_n^1 \wedge .. \wedge A_n^n \wedge ts=\min\{ts_A^1,...,ts_A^n\} \wedge te=\max\{te_A^1,...,te_A^n\}) \vee (B_m^1 \wedge ... \wedge B_m^m \wedge ts=\min\{ts_B^1,...,ts_B^m\} \wedge te=\max\{te_B^1,...,te_B^m\})$.
Sequence. (E=SEQ(A_n;B_m)): $E(ts,te) \Leftrightarrow \exists\ ts_A^1,..., ts_A^n, te_A^1,..., te_A^n, ts_B^1,..., ts_B^m, te_B^1,.., te_B^m (A_n^1 \wedge .. \wedge A_n^n \wedge B_m^1 \wedge ... \wedge B_m^m \wedge ts=\min\{ts_A^1,...,ts_A^n\} \wedge te=\max\{te_B^1,...,te_B^m\} \wedge (\max\{te_A^1,...,te_A^n\} < \min\{ts_B^1,...,ts_B^m\}))$.

The event language adopted in this paper is similar to state-of-the-art event definition languages used in other CEP systems and research works [6,8,12].Overall structure of event definition language is:

```
EVENT  <event pattern>
[WHERE  <qualification>]
[WITHIN  <window>]
```

The `EVENT` clause contains an event sequence construct. The `WHERE` clause specifies constraints for event matching. The `WITHIN` clause applies a sliding window to the event stream. Note that constraints specifications and sliding window are optional.

4 Event Detection Algorithm and Optimization

In this paper, we utilize the NFA-based representation to transform and evaluate the event queries. As we consider multiple events of the same event type, to directly transform an event query into an NFA or tree model is difficult to evaluate. We classify the complex pattern into linear pattern and non-linear pattern and take linear pattern as basic evaluation structure–linear pattern is transformed into linear patterns and NFA-based evaluation is carried on these linear patterns. The complex pattern is composed of output results of these linear patterns.

4.1 Sequence Join Algorithm, SEJA

One evaluation algorithm is to transform the objective complex pattern into primitive patterns and evaluate these primitive patterns over RFID data streams. As there exists some constraints between event types and events of the same type, these constraints must be kept and evaluated after detection of the transformed partial complex patterns to form the objective complex pattern. Take query 1 for example. The objective complex pattern is E=SEQ(A_2; B_2; C_2; D_2; F_2). First, SEJ is to transform E into to primitive patterns E_1 = SEQ(A_2^1; B_2^1; C_2^1; D_2^1; F_2^1) and E_2 = SEQ(A_2^2; B_2^2; C_2^2; D_2^2; F_2^2) according to the event specification, then evaluate E_1 and E_2 over RFID data streams respectively and check time constraints over all possible event pairs of E_1 and E_2, merge these event pairs and output detected composite patterns.

Push check point validation down. We observed that in an RFID application, there exists RFID reading points which we call **check points** that at some moments relationship between objects passing through these reading points are certain, for example, in an asset monitoring place, only authorized people can take assets moving through check points. These checkpoints can be used to reduce evaluation intermediate results. So an improved SEJA(ISEJA) is to push `check points` validation down when one object patterns are evaluated. ISEJA reduce some event pairs validation especially when complex pattern is long and detected primitive patterns are numerous. In fact, number of primitive patterns is related to time constraints(ε) of event pair in the complex event specification. If time constraints are large, there exists many primitive sequences in RFID data stream, ISEJA reduces number of primitive sequences beforehand and is more efficient than SEJA.

4.2 Stream Join Algorithm, STJA

Another evaluation method of a complex pattern is stream join algorithm. Take query 1. Complex pattern of query 1 is E=SEQ(A_2; B_2; C_2; D_2; F_2). Basic stream join evaluation functions as: take an event pair from stream A that satisfies the time constraints of the query, check whether this event pair appears at B, C, D and F respectively and verify the time constraints of the query. STJA needs to keep many partial matches of the event query due to pattern match characteristics of multiple correlated event objects. Check points can also be used to speed up evaluation of a complex pattern. First we push down event pair validation first at check points. If event event pair validation satisfy the constraints of the objective complex pattern, the algorithm continues event detection process over remaining event types, else stops and begins another event detection process. Push down event pair validation at check points greatly reduces event attribute comparisons thus optimizes CPU and memory usages.

5 Performance Evaluation

We have implemented our proposed algorithms in a prototype system using C++. Experiments are run on a Pentium 2.8GHz machine with 1GB RAM on

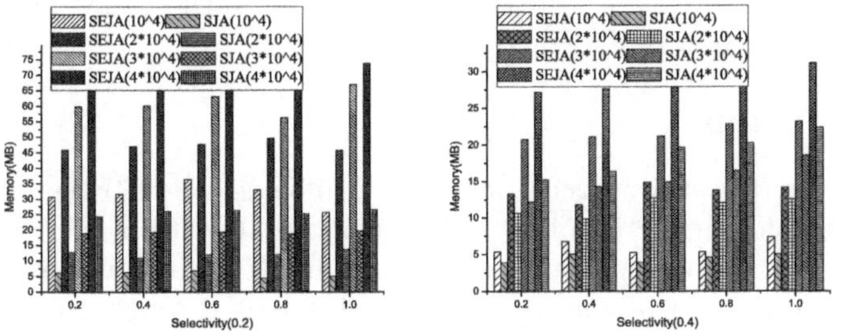

(a) selectivity: 0.2 (b) selectivity: 0.4

Fig. 1. Memory comparisons with different selectivity, window sizes(10^4–$4 * 10^4$)

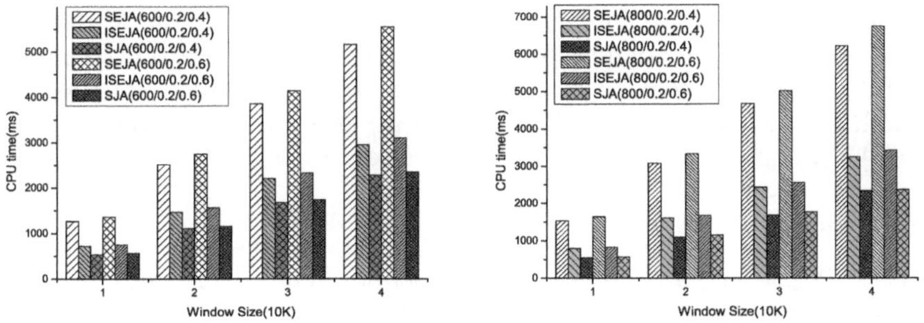

(a) ε=600, selectivity:0.2/0.4 and 0.2/0.6 (b) ε=800, selectivity:0.2/0.4 and 0.2/0.6

Fig. 2. CPU comparisons with different ε's, selectivity and window sizes

Windows XP. Because there is no public RFID test data, we generated RFID data sets of an RFID asset tracking scenario with a simulator. Number of event types in the simulator is 10. The generated event stream contains a percentage of noisy events. Events generated follow uniform distribution.

Memory Comparison. To evaluate sequence join algorithms, we use hash table to store state information of primitive events. For SJA evaluation, because time interval comparisons between primitive events are needed, so we use B+tree(event timestamp as key) to store and retrieve events. Memory comparisons of SEJA and SJA are shown in Fig. 1. As we can see from Fig. 1, with different selectivity, SJA outperform SEJA up to 5 times in memory usage.

CPU time. To evaluation CPU performances of the proposed algorithms, we generate RFID data sets with different parameters such as ε, selectivity, window size. CPU comparisons are shown in Fig. 2. As we can see from Fig. 2, when selectivity changes from 0.2/0.4 to 0.2/0.6, ε varies from 600 to 800, window size changes from 10^4 to $4 * 10^4$, ISEJA consumes less CPU time than SEJA because less intermediate results generation. SJA pushes event pair checking down at check points which generates fewer redundant results. From Fig. 2 we can see

SJA outperforms ISEJA two–five times; SJA still outperforms ISEJA although not so apparent than SEJA.

6 Conclusion

In this paper, we study event detection problems over RFID streams which involve multiple correlated objects. We propose algorithms SJA and SEJA to evaluate these complex patterns which are able to reduce intermediate results greatly in the process of complex event evaluations through optimization techniques such as state propagation and pushing time constraints down at some event types. Extensive experiments demonstrate effectiveness and efficiency of our algorithms.

Acknowledgments. This work is sponsored by the NSFC-JST Major International(Regional) Joint Research Project under Grant No. 60720106001, National Natural Science Foundation of China under Grant No. 60803043, National Natural Science Foundation of China under Grant No. 60873196 and the National High-Tech Research and Development Plan of China under Grant No. 2009AA1Z134.

References

1. Lee, Y.M., Cheng, F.: Exploring the impact of rfid on supply chain dynamics. In: Winter Simulation Conference, pp. 1145–1152 (2004)
2. Tellkamp, C., Wiechert, T., Thiesse, F., Fleisch, E.: The adoption of rfid-based self-check-out-systems at the point-of-sale. In: I3E, pp. 153–165 (2006)
3. Dickman, P., McSorley, G.P., Liddell, J., Glen, J., Green, J.: The design and development of an rfid-enabled asset tracking system for challenging environments. IJIPT 2(3/4), 232–239 (2007)
4. Roussos, G., Kostakos, V.: Rfid in pervasive computing: State-of-the-art and outlook. Pervasive and Mobile Computing 5(1), 110–131 (2009)
5. Zimmer, D., Unland, R.: On the semantics of complex events in active database management systems. In: ICDE, pp. 392–399 (1999)
6. Wu, E., Diao, Y., Rizvi, S.: High-performance complex event processing over streams. In: SIGMOD Conference, pp. 407–418 (2006)
7. Wang, F., Liu, S., Liu, P., Bai, Y.: Bridging physical and virtual worlds: Complex event processing for rfid data streams. In: Ioannidis, Y., Scholl, M.H., Schmidt, J.W., Matthes, F., Hatzopoulos, M., Böhm, K., Kemper, A., Grust, T., Böhm, C. (eds.) EDBT 2006. LNCS, vol. 3896, pp. 588–607. Springer, Heidelberg (2006)
8. Mei, Y., Madden, S.: Zstream: a cost-based query processor for adaptively detecting composite events. In: SIGMOD Conference, pp. 193–206 (2009)
9. Demers, A.J., Gehrke, J., Panda, B., Riedewald, M., Sharma, V., White, W.M.: Cayuga: A general purpose event monitoring system. In: CIDR, pp. 412–422 (2007)
10. Gatziu, S., Dittrich, K.R.: Detecting composite events in active database systems using petri nets. In: RIDE-ADS, pp. 2–9 (1994)
11. Barga, R.S., Goldstein, J., Ali, M.H., Hong, M.: Consistent streaming through time: A vision for event stream processing. In: CIDR, pp. 363–374 (2007)
12. Agrawal, J., Diao, Y., Gyllstrom, D., Immerman, N.: Efficient pattern matching over event streams. In: SIGMOD Conference, pp. 147–160 (2008)

CW2I: Community Data Indexing for Complex Query Processing

Mei Hui, Panagiotis Karras, and Beng Chin Ooi

National University of Singapore
{huimei,karras,ooibc}@comp.nus.edu.sg

Abstract. The increasing popularity of Community Web Management Systems (CWMSs) calls for tailor-made data management approaches for them. Still, existing CWMSs have mostly focused on simple similarity-based queries; they do not provide a framework for the efficient processing of more complex queries over community web data. In this paper, we propose a two-way indexing scheme that facilitates efficient and scalable retrieval and complex query processing with community data. A thorough experimental comparison, based on real-world data and practical queries, illustrates the advantages of our scheme compared to other approaches for community web data management. Besides, our double-indexing scheme provides an attractive solution to the storage problem as well.

1 Introduction

Community Web Management Systems (CWMSs) are effective in collecting and organizing the wisdom of crowds [13]. They provide a platform in which users of a community can interact and collaborate. Users can contribute to, and take ownership of, the content so as to display their collective knowledge. In general, a CWMS stores information on a wide-ranging set of entities, such as products, commercial offers, or persons. Due to diverse product specifications, user expectations, or personal interests, the data set can be very sparse when rendered as a table. Thus, such systems also raise design requirements that differ from those of conventional database systems.

For instance, the data set of the CNET e-commerce system examined in [10] comprises of a total of 2,984 attributes and 233,304 products; still,a product is described by only ten attributes on average. Likewise, most community-based data publishing systems allow users to define metadata and store information in the way they prefer (see Figure 1). For example, a subset of GoogleBase [1] that we downloaded comprises of 1,147 attributes over 779,019 items, while on average 16 attributes are defined per tuple.

A popular storage structure for CWMSs is the Sparse Wide Table (SWT). Sparse wide tables were independently proclaimed in [18] and [10] as a useful component of self-managing database systems; they free users from a potentially ineffective schema-design phase when managing sparse data sets. Furthermore,

L. Chen et al. (Eds.): WAIM 2010, LNCS 6184, pp. 103–114, 2010.

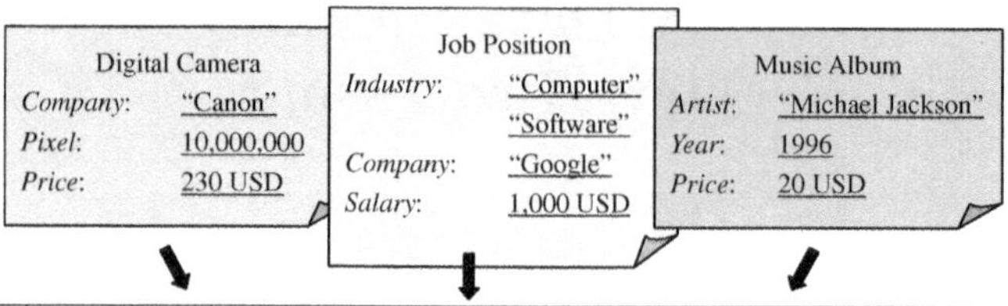

tid	Type	Industry	Year	Price	Company	Salary	Pixel	Artist
1	"Job Position"	"Computer" "Software"			"Google"	1,000		
2	"Digital Camera"			230	"Canon"		10,000,000	
3	"Music Album"		1996	20				"Michael Jackson"

A sparse wide table

Fig. 1. Submission of user-defined meta data to sparse wide table

[18] was the first work to propose a type of inverted indexing scheme for sparse table data management.

Nevertheless, most existing CWMSs either are disadvantaged by a lack of scalability to large data sets, or offer good performance only for specialized kinds of queries. None of the solutions has provided to date a scheme that can handle ever-increasing amounts of data as well as allow efficient processing of general-purpose complex queries.

In this paper, we combine two effective indexing methods: First, an *inverted* index for each attribute gathers a list of tuples, sorted by tuple ID, for each attribute value; the inverted index is sorted by the attribute value itself. Second, a separate *direct* index for each attribute provides fast access to those tuples for which the given attribute is defined, sorted by tuple ID, following a column-oriented architecture inspired by [8,9,16]. We adopt conventional query optimization techniques to our framework and discuss the benefit gained by *uniting* the inverted indexes of less-frequent attributes. We conduct a performance evaluation using the GoogleBase dataset and compare our proposed method to existing ones. The results confirm that the indexing scheme we propose outperforms the systems based on a monolithic vertical-oriented or horizontal-oriented representation. Our proposed CW2I scheme can efficiently handle complex queries over Community Data.

Outline. The remainder of this paper is structured as follows. Section 2 presents related work on SWT storage and discusses the deficiencies of previous approaches. In Section 3 we introduce our two-way indexing solution for SWT data management and a typology of queries defined over such a system. Section 4 presents our experimental results using real-world data sets. Finally, in Section 5 we outline our conclusions.

2 Background and Related Work

It has been long observed that conventional horizontal-schema database representations are not suited for emerging applications with sparsely populated and rapidly evolving data schemas. In this section we present an overview of existing approaches to handling such data by existing Community Web Management Systems.

2.1 Binary Vertical Representation

A natural approach to handling sparse relational data is to split a sparse horizontal table into as many binary (2-ary) tables as the number of attributes (columns) in the sparse table. This idea was fist suggested in the context of database machines [14] and was brought up again with the decomposition storage model [11,12]. This type of column-store model has been followed by MonetDB, along with an algebra to hide the decomposition [8,9], as well as C-Store [16], gaining benefits of compressibility [3] and performance [5]. Furthermore, in a visionary paper [2], Abadi suggested that, apart from data warehouses and OLAP workloads, column-stores may also be well suited for storing extremely sparse and wide tables.

2.2 Ternary Vertical Representation

Agrawal et al. [6] discerned that a ternary (3-ary) vertical representation offers a middle design point between the n-ary horizontal representation of conventional RDBMSs for non-sparse data and the binary vertical representation outlined above. They found that this vertical representation does uniformly outperform the horizontal representation for sparse data, yet the binary representation performs better. In response, [6] suggested the use of multiple, *partial indexes*, i.e., one index on each of the three columns of the ternary vertical table, along the lines of [15]. A premonition of a multiple-indexing approach is also contained in this suggestion.

2.3 Interpreted Storage Format

Beckmann et al. [7] suggests a storage format that attains independence from schema width. Unfortunately, as [7] observed, this renders the retrieval of values from attributes in tuples significantly more complex. To ameliorate this problem, [7] suggests an *extract* operator that returns the offsets to the referenced interpreted attribute values. Still, as [2,4,17] have noted, handling sparse tables in such a way incurs a significant performance overhead.

3 CW2I: Two-Way Indexing of Community Web Data

In order to address the aforementioned difficulties, we propose the combination of *three* design approaches for complex query processing on SWTs. *First,* we espouse a binary vertical representation for each attribute *Aid* defined in the data at hand, which collects a *sorted* vector of *Tid* (tuple identifier) entries. Each of these entries is appended with an associated sorted list of attribute values *Val*. We call this binary representation *direct* index. The binary vertical representation of [11,12,8,2] can be seen as a manifestation of our *direct* index. *Second*, we argue for an inverted index built over each *frequent* attribute. An attribute identifier *Aid* is linked to an *inverted* index, consisting of a sorted vector of *Val* (attribute value) entries, appended with their associated sorted lists of *Tids* $<Tid_1, Tid_2, \ldots, Tid_n>$ that match the given value for the *Aid* attribute. In case an attribute value consists of several short strings, these are independently indexed by our inverted index. String separators prevalent during data entry are used for this purpose. *Third*, we store a single list of attribute-value pairs for each tuple, as in [7]. This design amounts to double indexing scheme for Community Web data, which we call CW2I. It is capable to address both lookup and aggregation queries, as well as more complex queries involving several join operations. In effect, it robustly handles all ways of querying the data.

3.1 The Unified Inverted Index

The main problem arising out of attribute frequency skewness is that, if we are supposed to build both a *direct* and an *inverted* index for each attribute, then we raise unreasonable storage requirements without much of a benefit arising from them. After all, if an attribute is defined for only a few tuples, then not much stands to be gained by indexing the few values it assumes over the whole data set in both a *direct* and an *inverted* manner. Furthermore, most users are not expected to express queries using the names of thousands of lesser-used attributes. Therefore, we suggest that *less frequent attributes* may best be seen as repositories of *unstructured* information about tuples. As far as *text* attributes are concerned, this information can be appropriately considered as a collection of keywords related to the tuples in question. Thus, we propose to handle lesser used *text* attributes in a *unified* manner, gathering all of them together in a *unified inverted index*. This index provides a powerful keyword-search-like functionality over these attributes, while it increases both the storage-efficiency and the user-friendliness of our system. In particular, the unified inverted index gathers a sorted vector of attribute value entries, regardless of the attribute they correspond to; each entry is associated to a list $<$*Tid* (tuple identifier), *Aid* (attribute identifier)$>$ pairs.

It remains to be decided how attributes are to be divided into *more frequent* and *less frequent* ones, so as to decide which should receive their own separate inverted indexes, and which are to be managed by the unified inverted index. After experimentation, we decided that the following rule of thumb provides a reasonable dividing line: The top *quartile* of *text* attributes, sorted by decreasing frequency value, have a separate inverted index built for them. The rest $\frac{3}{4}$ of attributes are to be treated by the unified inverted index.

Numerical attributes are excluded from the unified inverted index; this discussion pertains to *text* attributes only. However, numerical attributes that fall below the frequency threshold to receive their own inverted index, are not indexed in this manner at all. Given the sparsity of such attributes, an inverted index is redundant for them. A lookup to their direct index is sufficient to detect any tuples that match a given value-based predicate. Besides, such numerical values do not offer anything in terms of keyword-search. Users are expected to refer to such attributes by name. The same reasoning applies to the case when a user needs to refer to a specific lesser-used text attribute by name; again, the low density of the attribute itself renders a lookup for values matches in the direct index practicable enough.

The usage of this unified inverted index addresses a problem that is particular to the community web data we examine. Moreover, it confers the following advantages to our CW2I system:

- Storage efficiency, as it is not efficient from a storage point of view to have a separate inverted index on each of the myriads of less-frequent attributes.
- Facilitation of keyword-search queries, in which a given string is to be found in *any* less frequent attribute. Resorting to a unified index of all less-frequent attributes for keyword-search is more efficient than checking many small indexes. Besides, lesser-used text attributes can be validly seen as collecting keywords related to the specific domain where an entry belongs.
- User-friendliness, users are not expected, or required, to know obscure attribute by name. Users are mostly familiar with the names of the most commonly-used attributes, but, naturally, they cannot easily figure out by what name the others are entered. These lesser-used attributes are usually domain-specific and their appearance depends on the values of other attributes.
- Functionality and practical sense: for rarely used attributes, the direct index is already good enough for a lookup, hence the inverted index can be spared. Thus, while the said benefits are gained by unifying of what could be several smaller indexes, not much is significantly lost.
- Safeguard against user inconsistency. Different users are likely to define the same lesser-used concept with differently-named attributes. Thus, it makes sense to collect the values they provide under one unified index. A keyword search on the values of such attributes is guaranteed to return the tuples related to them (i.e., there are no false negatives).

3.2 Query Typology

As we have discussed, several attribute values in Community Web systems usually appear as collections of short strings. Such strings are usually distinguished by separators. Each user may employ diverse separators (such as '>', '/', ':', ';',) to delimit short strings. Our inverted index distinguishes these short strings and creates a separate entry for each of them. A string match during query processing can be satisfied either in an *exact* or a *fuzzy* manner. Exact string matching is straightforward. For the case of fuzzy matching, we still wish to take advantage of lexicographic order for fast query processing. Thus, we say that a query string s_q of length L and an indexed string s_i satisfy a *fuzzy string match* when there is an *exact* match of the first half of the query string and a similarity between their other parts. Thus, if prefix(K, s) is the length-K prefix of string s, we define a fuzzy mach as:

$$\text{prefix}\left(\left\lceil\frac{L}{2}\right\rceil, s_q\right) = \text{prefix}\left(\left\lceil\frac{L}{2}\right\rceil, s_i\right) \wedge \quad \text{suffix}\left(\left\lfloor\frac{L}{2}\right\rfloor, s_q\right) \approx \text{suffix}\left(\left\lfloor\frac{L}{2}\right\rfloor, s_i\right)$$

Where $\approx$ denotes an approximate string similarity measure. According to this kind of fuzzy matching, short strings like 'accessories' would match with 'accessorize' and 'accessory', but not with 'access, windows version'. In the case of text match, we define the fuzzy match score between two text values s_i and s_j as:

$$\text{Score}(s_i, s_j) = N/min(len(s_i), len(s_j))$$

where N is the number of matched words in s_i and s_j, $len(s_i)$ is the number of words in text value s_i and $len(s_j)$ is the number of words in text value s_j. We set a threshold τ, when Score$(s_i, s_j) \geq \tau$, we say s_i matches s_j. This rule of thumb operates well in practice, allowing for the identification of related strings with tolerance to orthographic and terminological variations.

We distinguish four different types of queries that CW2I can process, based on their exploitation of inverted indexes, unified inverted index, and fuzzy string matching, as follows. A general *complex query*, covering all four types, is defined as follows.

$$Q\{p_1(G_1), p_2(G_2), \ldots, p_n(G_n), r_1(G_{r_1}, G'_{r_1}), \quad r_2(G_{r_2}, G'_{r_2}), \ldots, r_m(G_{r_m}, G'_{r_m})\}$$

where $p_i(G_i)$ is set of (select) predicates that define a group of tuples G_i and $r_i(G_{r_i}, G'_{r_i})$ is a (join) relation among the tuples in groups G_{r_i}, G'_{r_i} which satisfy their respective predicates. For instance, consider the query "find the black-color jewelry and purple-color jewelry such that their price difference is less than 10$". Then G_1 is 'black color jewelry', hence the predicate that defines this group is

$$\text{Product} = \textit{jewelery} \wedge \text{Color} = \textit{black}$$

Likewise, G_2 is 'purple color jewelry', hence the predicate that defines it is

$$\text{Product} = \textit{jewelery} \wedge \text{Color} = \textit{purple}$$

The relation that should be satisfied among any item $t_1 \in G_1$ and any item $t_2 \in G_2$ is

$$|t_1.\textit{price} - t_2.\textit{price}| \leq 10\$$$

We can then classify the basic join queries that satisfy this general-purpose definition in to four distinct classes as follows.

1. ***Exact* join query *without* keyword.** In such a query, the select predicates are all on most-frequent, *indexed* (i.e., having their own inverted index) attributes. The join relation operates on a *simple* (i.e., numerical or single-string) attributes (e.g., price, name, but not multiple-short-string or text attributes, on which no exact match can be done).

2. ***Exact* join query *with* keyword.** In this type of query, the select predicates may be defined on published attributes or may be just keyword-specified, referring to less-frequent attributes, lacking their own *inverted index*. The join relation is defined on a simple attributes, as in Type 1.
3. ***Fuzzy join* query *without* keyword.** In this case, the select predicates are on indexed attributes. However, the join operation is a *fuzzy join* on *text* or multiple-short-string attributes. For example, consider the query "Find a cellphone and a laptop of the same brand.". Then G1 is "cellphone", G2 is "laptop", the predicate defines G1 is:

   $$\mathsf{Product} = \mathit{cellphone}$$

   Similarly the predicate defines G2 is:

   $$\mathsf{Product} = \mathit{laptop}$$

   The join operation on G1 and G2 is:

   $$t1.brand = t2.brand$$

   Given that *brand* is a text attribute, the value of *brand* consists of several short strings. Thus the join operation on this attribute should not be done with exact match. We call this type of query *fuzzy join* query.
4. ***Fuzzy* join query *with* keyword.** A query of this type may have both a select predicate defined by a non-indexed attribute, as well as a *fuzzy* join operation on a *text* attribute.

4 Experimental Evaluation

In this section we discuss experimental studies of the scalability and performance of CW2I scheme. We compare the performance of CW2I in answering Type-1 queries with the straightforward horizontal storage scheme (HORIZ) and vertical storage scheme (VERTI). The query processing time is recorded for Type-2, Type-3 and Type-4 queries which are not evaluated in existing systems. We study the performance and the scalability of CW2I on them.

4.1 Experiment Setup

In VERTI, we store each attribute as a separate table and build index on the tuple_id column. This is same as the direct index in CW2I. The difference of implementation between CW2I and VERTI is that we create one inverted index for each of the indexed attributes and a unified index for each of the other attributes. We build a B^+ tree index on the keyword column of the inverted index and the unified index. In HORIZ, we store the indexed attributes in one relational table and the other un-indexed attributes in the vertical storage format. We build a B^+ tree index on TID (tuple id) column. Our experimental environment is a Intel Core2 Duo 1.8GHz machine with 2GB memory, 160GB hard disk, running Windows XP Professional with SP2.

4.2 Description of Data

We downloaded published data items from GoogleBase, and set up our experimental evaluation on this dataset. It consists of 30 thousands tuples which are described by 1319 attributes out of which 1217 are text attributes and others are numerical attributes. According to our statistics, the average number of attributes per tuple is 16. To test the storage cost of the three methods, we initially insert 10k tuples. We measure the additional disk space cost by incrementally inserting 5K tuples each time, as shown in Figure2. We observe that the storage space linearly increases with the number of tuples inserted. CW2I consumes about 25% more disk space than VERTI and HORIZ.

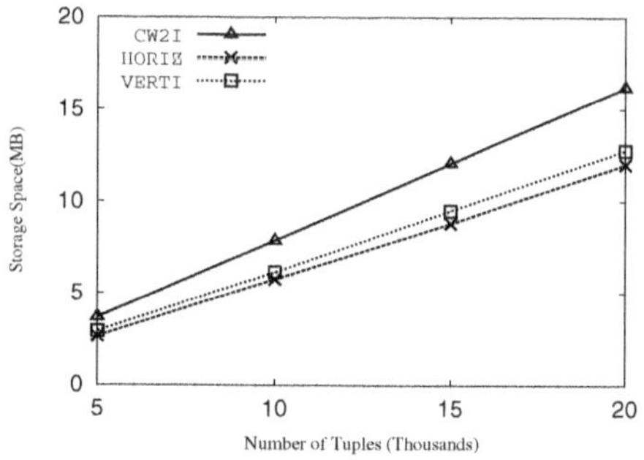

Fig. 2. Disk Space Cost of the Three Methods

4.3 Description of Queries

We discuss the four types of queries in Section 3.2. In our experiment we generate several queries for each query type. For Type-1 queries, i.e. exact join query without keyword, we compare the execution time of CW2I to VERTI and HORIZ. We describe the queries and the implementation details below.

Type-1 Queries. We first outline the Type-1 queries we have included in our experimental study.

- **Query 1.** Find the number of products that belong to the mp3 type.
- **Query 2.** Find the stores which sale both mp3 and computer products.
- **Query 3.** Find pairs of an mp3 and a headphone of the same color.
- **Query 4.** Find a black jewelry item and a purple jewelry item such that the difference of their price is less than 20$.
- **Query 5.** Find a keyboard and a mouse of the same condition(new, used, on sale etc.).
- **Query 6.** Find pairs of books and CDs such that their condition is *new* and they are both sold at the same price.

Type-2 Queries. We now define the Type-2 queries we have used for our experimental evaluation.

- **Query 1.** Find the stores which sell both an mp3 and a computer with 250GB disk.
- **Query 2.** Find pairs of two 'ipods', such that one's price is less than 200$, the other's price is more than 200$, and the difference of their prices is less than 100$.
- **Query 3.** Find the stores that sale both Mahal's CD and Dorina's CD.
- **Query 4.** Find thinkpad T41s and thinkpad T20s that the difference of their prices is less than 100$.

Type-3 Queries. We have also defined two Type-3 queries, as follows.

- **Query 1.** Find brands that make both cellphones and laptops.
- **Query 2.** Find types of products such that there exists both at least one *red* item and at least one *blue* item of that product_type.

Type-4 Queries. Lastly, we have also included two queries of the most complex type in our typology, Type-4, in our study, which are outlined below.

- **Query1.** Find *hardcover* books and Mahal's CDs with the same allowed form of payment.
- **Query2.** Find products of material 'stone' and products of material 'silver', having the same product_type.

4.4 Results

In this section we report the results of our experimental study with the queries described in Section 4.3. We use progressively larger prefixes of the experimental data set while measuring the execution time of each query. We use logarithmic y-axes for the execution time in each case. Typically, the performance of our CW2I scheme is 10 or more times better than HORIZ and VERTI.

Figure 3(a) shows the execution time results for Type-1 Query 1. In this case, CW2I largely outperforms both our prototype implementation of HORIZ and VERTI. Thanks to the availability of an inverted index in CW2I, only one B^+-tree search is required in order to find the number of qualifying items. In contrast, a whole table scan is necessitated by both HORIZ and VERTI.

Given that the size of the vertical table is smaller than that of the horizontal table, the performance of VERTI is noticeably better than that of HORIZ. Besides, the growth of execution time with the size of the data set is perceptible for both HORIZ and VERTI; on the other hand, the execution time remains relatively stable for CW2I, as new relevant items are inserted in the idlist of the inverted index and can still be easily retrieved without substantial overhead.

Our results for Query 2 of Type-1 is shown in Figure 3(b). We observe that both CW2I and HORIZ outperform VERTI, while CW2I is slightly better than

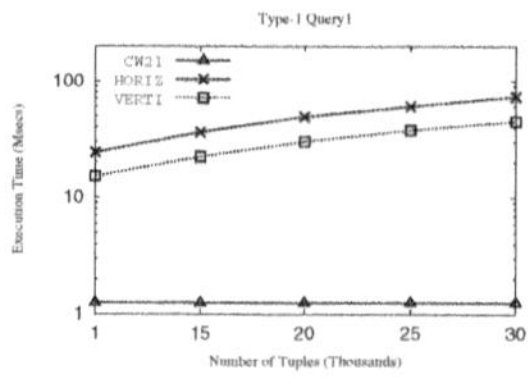

(a) Execution time, Type-1 Query1.

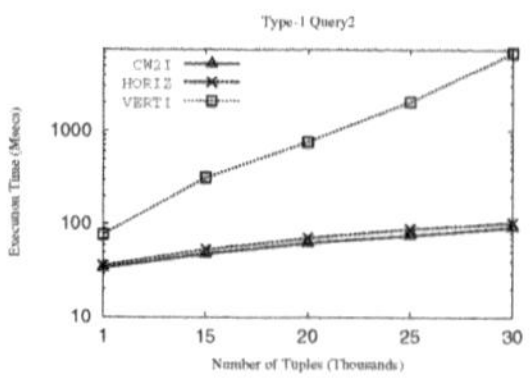

(b) Execution time, Type-1 Query2.

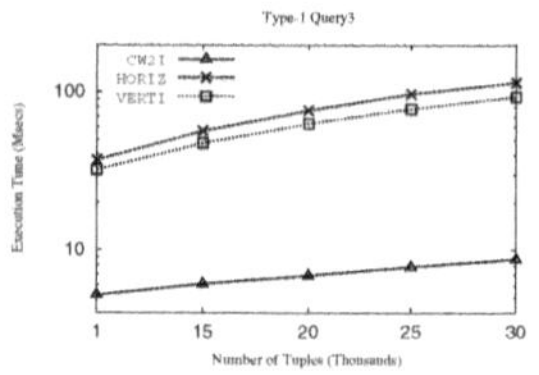

(c) Execution time, Type-1 Query3.

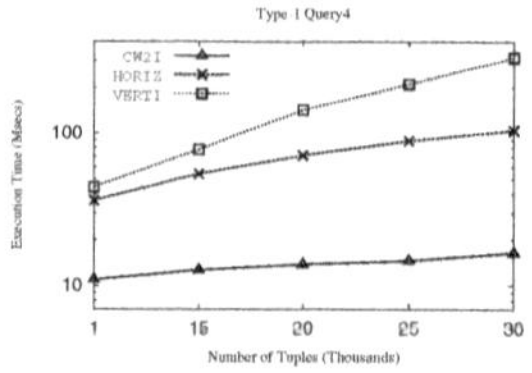

(d) Execution time, Type-1 Query4.

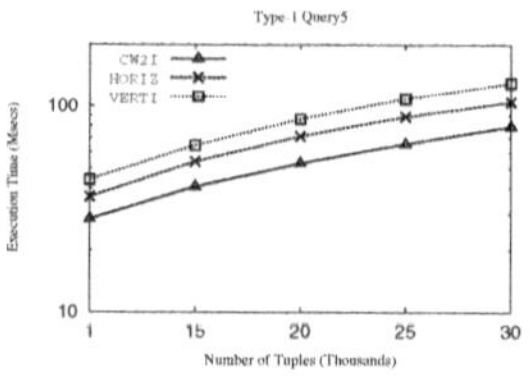

(e) Execution time, Type-1 Query5.

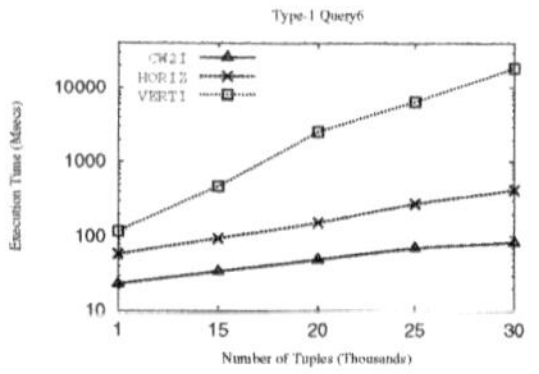

(f) Execution time, Type-1 Query6.

Fig. 3. Execution time of Type-1 Queries

HORIZ itself. Thanks to the inverted index built on attribute product_type, CW2I gets the tuple_ids of mp3 and computer with little cost. On the other hand, VERTI has to scan the vertical table of attribute product_type twice for that purpose. As far as HORIZ is concerned, a self join on attribute store_id is conducted quite efficiently in this case.

Figure 3(c) depicts our results on Type-1 Query3. Observably, CW2I gains a significant advantage over both HORIZ and VERTI. The underlying cause of this efficiency advantage is the same as in our preceding analysis for Query 2. However, now this advantage is more perceptible within the examined data set sizes.

Our results for Type-1, Query4 are illustrated in Figure 3(d). In this case, the efficiency benefit of CW2I over the other two schemes is remarkable. The reason for the advantage by CW2I remains the same as we have already analyzed in the

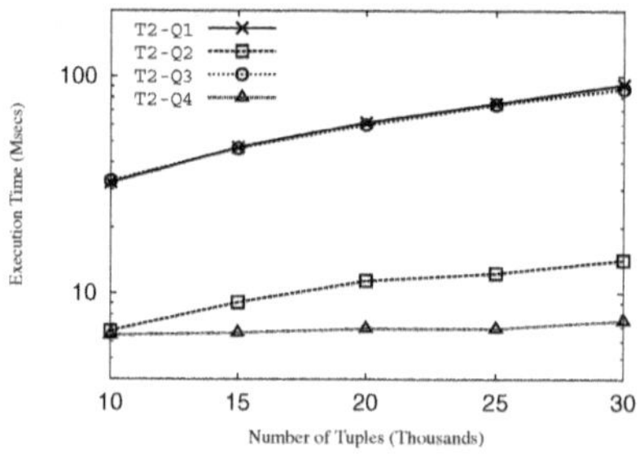

(a) Execution time, Type-2.

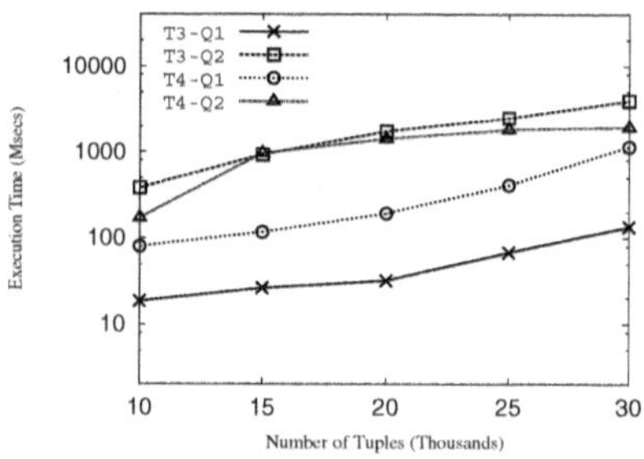

(b) Execution time, Type-3,4.

Fig. 4. Execution time of Type-2,3,4 Queries

case of Type1-Query2. However, in this case, there are two select predicates on items, instead of only one, therefore the gain becomes more noteworthy.

Likewise, Figure 3(e) shows our execution time results with the fifth query in Type 1. The advantage gap on behalf of CW2I is again due to the efficient execution of the select predicate. The cost for CW2I is again lower, even though in this case the growth is more perceptible, due to the characteristic of the data set on the specified select predicates on product_type. Still, the gain grows with the data set size in this case as well.

Figure 3(f) depicts our results for Type-1 Query6. The additional select predicates in this query reduce the number of selected results, therefore the cost of the merge step is reduced. Still, the advantages of CW2I are still salient, exactly thanks to the fact that these limited results are much more easily derived than with the other schemes. Besides, the subsequent join operation is now less demanding.

Figure 4(a) illustrates the results of the Type-2 queries. It is indicated that CW2I scales well for the queries of Type-2 with the increase of the dataset size. Q1 and Q3 are almost identical and they both join on attribute store_id, while Q2 and Q4 join on attribute price. The efficiency gap is due to the fact that the cardinality of attribute price is smaller than attribute store_id, so the second group gets better scalability. Moreover, the difference between the results of Q2 and Q4 is due to the difference of the sizes of the intermediate results.

Figure 4(b) shows our results for queries of Type-3 and Type-4. CW2I scales well for the queries of these two types. Still, compared to Type-2 queries (Figure 4(a)), those of Type-3 and Type-4 are less scalable. This difference is due to the fact that the join operations of Type-3 and Type-4 are fuzzy joins, which cost more than the exact join operations of Type-2. Besides, we observe differences among the queries of Type-3 and Type-4 themselves, which are due to variations in result set sizes.

5 Conclusions

In this paper we have proposed an architecture for the management of sparse and wide data in Community Web systems that can efficiently handle complex queries. Our proposal combines two hitherto distinct approaches. On the one hand, we employ a vertical representation scheme, whereby each attribute, no matter how frequently defined, obtains its own column-oriented *direct* index. On the other hand, we utilize an *inverted* indexing scheme, whereby the tuples that define *more frequent* attributes are indexed *by value*. Furthermore, we propose a *unified inverted* indexing scheme that gathers together all *less frequent* in a single keyword-oriented index. This additional index facilitates schema-agnostic keyword search that fits the nature of such less frequent attributes. We have defined four distinct types of join queries that our CW2I system can naturally process. Our experimental study confirms that CW2I enables fast and scalable processing of complex queries over Community Data more efficiently than systems based on a monolithic vertical-oriented or horizontal-oriented representation, and gains an advantage of several orders of magnitude over them in our prototype implementation.

References

1. Google base, `http://base.google.com/`
2. Abadi, D.J.: Column stores for wide and sparse data. In: CIDR (2007)
3. Abadi, D.J., Madden, S.R., Ferreira, M.: Integrating compression and execution in column-oriented database systems. In: SIGMOD (2006)
4. Abadi, D.J., Marcus, A., Madden, S.R., Hollenbach, K.: Scalable semantic web data management using vertical partitioning. In: VLDB (2007)
5. Abadi, D.J., Myers, D.S., DeWitt, D.J., Madden, S.: Materialization strategies in a column-oriented DBMS. In: ICDE (2007)
6. Agrawal, R., Somani, A., Xu, Y.: Storage and querying of e-commerce data. In: VLDB (2001)
7. Beckmann, J.L., Halverson, A., Krishnamurthy, R., Naughton, J.F.: Extending RDBMSs to support sparse datasets using an interpreted attribute storage format. In: ICDE (2006)
8. Boncz, P.A., Kersten, M.L.: MIL primitives for querying a fragmented world. VLDB Journal 8(2), 101–119 (1999)
9. Boncz, P.A., Zukowski, M., Nes, N.: MonetDB/X100: Hyper-pipelining query execution. In: CIDR (2005)
10. Chu, E., Beckmann, J., Naughton, J.: The case for a wide-table approach to manage sparse relational data sets. In: SIGMOD (2007)
11. Copeland, G.P., Khoshafian, S.N.: A decomposition storage model. In: SIGMOD (1985)
12. Khoshafian, S., Copeland, G.P., Jagodis, T., Boral, H., Valduriez, P.: A query processing strategy for the decomposed storage model. In: ICDE (1987)
13. Li, B., Hui, M., Li, J., Gao, H.: iVA-File: Efficiently indexing sparse wide tables in community systems. In: ICDE (2009)
14. Missikoff, M.: A domain based internal schema for relational database machines. In: SIGMOD (1982)
15. Stonebraker, M.: The case for partial indexes. SIGMOD Rec. 18(4), 4–11 (1989)
16. Stonebraker, M., Abadi, D.J., Batkin, A., Chen, X., Cherniack, M., Ferreira, M., Lau, E., Lin, A., Madden, S.R., O'Neil, E.J., O'Neil, P.E., Rasin, A., Tran, N., Zdonik, S.B.: C-store: a column-oriented DBMS. In: VLDB (2005)
17. Weiss, C., Karras, P., Bernstein, A.: Hexastore: Sextuple indexing for semantic web data management. Proc. VLDB Endowment 1(1), 1008–1019 (2008)
18. Yu, B., Li, G., Ooi, B.C., Zhou, L.-Z.: One table stores all: Enabling painless free-and-easy data publishing and sharing. In: CIDR (2007)

Clustering Coefficient Queries on Massive Dynamic Social Networks

Zhiyu Liu, Chen Wang, Qiong Zou, and Huayong Wang

IBM Research - China

Abstract. The Clustering Coefficient (CC) is a fundamental measure in social network analysis assessing the degree to which nodes tend to cluster together. While CC computation on static graphs is well studied, emerging applications have new requirements for online query of the "global" CC of a given subset of a graph. As social networks are widely stored in databases for easy updating and accessing, computing CC of their subset becomes a time-consuming task, especially when the network grows large and cannot fit in memory. This paper presents a novel method called "Approximate Neighborhood Index (ANI)" to significantly reduce the query latency for CC computation compared to traditional SQL based database queries. A Bloom-filter-like data structure is leveraged to construct ANI in front of a relational database. Experimental results show that the proposed approach can guarantee the correctness of a CC query while significantly reducing the query latency at a reasonable memory cost.

1 Introduction

Social network analysis is becoming a hot topic in the database and data mining communities with the fast growing popularity of social network applications in the web age. A social network is usually modeled as a graph with nodes representing people and edges representing their relationships, such as email communications, mobile calls, co-authorship, and replying to a blog. The analysis aims to understand the micro- and macro-characteristics inside the network. Based on the philosophy that friend's friends are also probably friends in a social network, Clustering Coefficient (CC) is one of the fundamental measures for assessing the degree to which nodes tend to cluster together. Traditionally, we use each node's local CC to characterize the node, and use a global CC to characterize the whole graph.

In social network analysis, CC is widely used to measure the closeness of people to a group , and the local "cliqueness", which is the stability of social communities to withstand the effect of link removal [17], e.g., co-authorship in the DBLP dataset [12]. Another useful application of CC is email and mobile messaging anti-spam. Some papers proposed social network based detection approaches to examine potential spammer's social behavior [7].

Technically, CC calculation boils down to the problem of triangle counting in graphs. It has been addressed in several approaches for exact calculation [2,4,11,10]. To eliminate the limitation of high memory consumption for

L. Chen et al. (Eds.): WAIM 2010, LNCS 6184, pp. 115–126, 2010.

large graphs, sampling methods [15,16] as well as stream or semi-stream based approximation methods have also been proposed [8,5]. However, all of the prior art focuses on a one-time calculation for a certain graph. Considering the scenario of spam detection, CC of the recipients in a spammer's distribution list tends to 0 while CC of normal users does not. For the requirement of online detection, CC will be calculated within the recipients of the sending batch in a certain time window. Because the incoming recipients are unknown at runtime, the spam detection scenario raises the new challenge of online CC queries of random subsets over a dynamic social network.

Another challenge is that massive social networks cannot be memory resident and are usually stored in relational databases, so disk accesses become the bottleneck for such kinds of query. However, for online applications, low latency of the query is always a key requirement. For example, under the spammer detection scenario, the sooner we detect the spammer the less damage it will cause. So the problem is: how to speed up the CC query on an extremely large graph that cannot fit in the memory?

This paper proposes a new indexing structure named Approximate Neighborhood Index (ANI) to solve the problem of online CC queries of a random subset of a dynamic social network. ANI is a memory resident index mapping each node to its approximate neighborhoods which is stored in a Bloom-filter like data structure. The space of ANI largely depends on the size of the Bloom filter used by each node, and grows linearly with number of nodes. For a sparse graph like a social network graph, ANI is very space-efficient. Although ANI will yield more accurate result with more space, our experiments demonstrate that two bytes per node are effective on a social network of millions of people. We also present the experimental formula to estimate a suitable Bloom-filter size given the concrete social network.

ANI can be built by initially traversing all the edges in social networks in a streaming manner, at can be incrementally updated when the social network changes dynamically. When querying the CC of a subset, ANI will return a CC upper bound and a much smaller edge set that needs to be further looked up in the database to get an accurate CC. Experimental results show a 2-10 times speedup while ensuring accuracy, and a 100+ times speedup if the CC upper bound is good enough for the application.

The remainder of this paper is organized as following: Section 2 introduces some related work, Section 3 gives the detailed design of ANI, Section 4 shows the performance of ANI through experimental results, and Section 5 concludes.

2 Related Work

2.1 Triangle Counting

CC can be calculated by counting number of triangles including a specific vertex. There has been work on exact triangle counting [2,4,11,10]. The brute-force algorithms examine each combination of nodes, resulting in a time complexity of $O(n^3)$. The time complexity can be reduced to $O(n^{2.376})$ using matrix multiplication [9]. However, this may still be too slow to be applicable on very large graphs.

Becchetti *et al.* [5] propose two approximation algorithms for computing the local number of triangles, which are based on the idea of min-wise independent permutations. They use $O(|V|)$ space in main memory (one of the algorithms also uses $O(|E|)$ space in external memory during computation) and perform $O(log|V|)$ sequential scans over the edges in the graph.

SparsifyingEigenTriangle [15] is proposed to count triangles in power-law networks. The main idea of the algorithm is to use a low-rank approximation of the matrix which is generated via the Achlioptas-McSherry [1] sparsification of the adjacency matrix to compute the number of triangles based on the EigenTriangle algorithm [14]

Doulion [16] is an algorithm that tosses a coin to keep an edge with a certain probability p with weight equal to $\frac{1}{p}$ in order to obtain a smaller weighted graph. Then it counts each triangle as the product of the weights of the edges comprising the triangle. They prove that the expected number of triangles in G' is the number of triangles in the initial graph G, and the variance is $\frac{\Delta(p^3-p^6)+2k(p^5-p^6)}{p^6}$, where Δ is the total number of triangles in G, and k is the number of pairs of triangles that are not edge disjoint. Any triangle counting algorithm may use the idea of Doulion as a preprocessing step.

Approximate CC computation algorithms are claimed to be a hundred times faster than accurate methods with a certain accuracy using techniques such as edge sampling [8,15,16] and min-wise independent permutations [5]. However those methods are designed for computing the global CC or every node's local CC at a time.

2.2 Bloom Filter

A Bloom filter [6] is a simple space-efficient randomized data structure for representing a set in order to support membership queries. Bloom filters allow false positives but the space savings often outweigh this drawback when the probability of an error is made sufficiently low.

A standard Bloom filter is a bit array of b bits, all set to 0. There must also be k different hash functions defined, each of which maps or hashes some set element to one of the b array positions with a uniform random distribution. To add an element, feed it to each of the k hash functions to get k array positions and set the bits at all these positions to 1. To query for an element (test whether it is in the set), feed it to each of the k hash functions to get k array positions. If any of the bits at these positions are 0, the element is not in the set. If all are 1, then either the element is in the set, or the bits have been set to 1 during the insertion of other elements. A Bloom filter may yield a false positive, where it suggests that an element $x \in S$ even though it is not. Suppose that we add i items into a Bloom filter of b bits with k hash functions, Equation (1) shows the probability of false positives.

$$p = (1 - (1 - 1/b)^{ki})^k \approx (1 - e^{-ki/b})^k \quad (1)$$

Obviously, the probability of false positives decreases as b increases, and increases as i increases. For a given b and i, the value of k that minimizes the probability is $(b/i)\ln 2 \approx 0.7 \times b/i$, which gives the false positive probability of $2^{-k} \approx 0.6185^{b/i}$. Taking the optimal number of hashes, the false positive probability (when it is not greater than 0.5) can be rewritten and bounded [13]. This means that in order to maintain a fixed false positive probability, the length of a Bloom filter must grow linearly with the number of elements being filtered.

3 Proposed Method

This section first formalizes the problem, then describes the typical database solution and its shortcomings, and finally proposes a novel index built upon the database that can greatly improve the query performance.

3.1 Formalization

Let V denote a set of vertices, and E a set of edges written as $e_{i,j} \in E$ where $v_i, v_j \in V$. A directed graph is then defined as $G = (V, E)$. The neighborhood for a vertex v_i, denoted as N_i, is defined as its immediately connected neighbors as follows: $N_i = \{v_j : e_{i,j} \in E\}$. Here we give out the definition of local CC to denote how nodes in a given subset of V cluster together, named Subset Clustering Coefficient (SCC). Suppose S is a subset of V and $|S| = M$, then

$$\mathrm{SCC}(S) = \frac{|\{e_{j,k}\}|}{M \times (M-1)}, \qquad v_j, v_k \in S, e_{j,k} \in E$$

3.2 Database Only Solution

In the database-only solution, a social network is stored in a database as a table; each edge in the graph corresponds to a record (source, destination, weight) in the table. Then we create an index on both source and destination. According to the definition of SCC, we need to count the number of edges of which the source and destination are both in the given subset. Suppose the table containing the social network is called SN_TABLE, the following SQL query calculates the numerator of SCC for a given subset $\{v_1, v_2, \ldots, v_M\}$:

```
SELECT COUNT(*) FROM SN_TABLE WHERE SOURCE IN (V1,V2,...,VM)
AND DESTINATION IN (V1,V2,...,VM) AND SOURCE<>DESTINATION
```

The execution time of the above query depends on multiple factors, including the execution path of the SQL query, the size N of the table, the size N of the given subset, and the degrees(number of neighbours of vertex v_i in the subset) D_i of each node in the given subset. For simplicity, in the following discussion, we only consider the average degree D of the given subset. Generally speaking, the time is mainly spent on three kinds of operations: scanning the index, fetching each node's neighbors from the table, and comparing the given subset with each node's neighbors. Table 1 shows the details. When N and M increase to a certain degree, the query latency begins to exceed the applications' restriction.

Table 1. Time complexity of CC query from database

Scan Index	Fetch Data	Compare
$O(M \times \log N)$	$O(M \times D)$	$O(DM^2)$

3.3 Approximate Neighborhood Index Using Bloom Filter

When memory is not sufficient to load in the entire graph index, and the latency of directly querying from the database is too long for a real-time application, we propose a balanced method that uses an Approximate Neighborhood Index (ANI) taking limited memory space to speed up the CC query.

As we analyze in database only solution, the query time increases with N and M. To decrease N, we can partition the database, query CC on each partition, and summarize them to get the final result; but considering the financial and management cost, it is beneficial to keep as much data as possible in each database instance. Here, we propose ANI to greatly reduce M. When the social network grows to an extremely large scale, database partitioning and ANI can be used together to control the query time.

Approximate Neighborhood Filter (ANF). For each node in the graph, we use a Bloom filter to store its neighbors called "Approximate Neighbor Filter (ANF)". Given an acceptable false positive probability p and the number of hash functions k, from Equation (1) we can get Equation (2) to estimate how many bits we need for each node to store one neighbor:

$$\frac{b}{i} = -\frac{k}{\ln(1 - p^{1/k})} \tag{2}$$

Table 2 shows the value of $\frac{b}{i}$ of some typical k, p combinations.

Table 2. b/i of typical k, p combinations

$k, p \rightarrow b/i$	0.05	0.01	0.001	0.0001	0.00001
3	6.5	12.4	28.5	63.1	137.7
4	6.2	10.5	20.4	38.0	69.1
5	6.3	9.8	17.3	29.0	47.5

If the false positive requirement is not that strict (say 1% is acceptable), the Bloom-filter approach needs about one to two bytes to store one edge. Answering whether a node is the neighbor of the others requires $O(1)$ time, thus reducing the time complexity of CC to $O(N)$. However, the shortcomings of using Bloom filters are also obvious. First, since one position in the Bloom filter may be set to "1" multiple times by different items, deleting an item becomes complex. Simply setting the correspondence positions to "0" may result in false negatives. One solution is to add a counter to each position; another solution is to rebuild a node's Bloom filter with the rest of its neighbors, which requires that accurate neighbors' information need to be stored somewhere. Second, the "weight" of an edge cannot be stored in a Bloom filter, so this method cannot estimate weighted CC. Third, the existence of false positives makes it only possible to estimate an upper bound of the accurate CC.

A social network is known to have the "long tail" property [3,17], which means it is a sparse graph. For subset communities containing hundreds of nodes, the CC may be as low as 10^{-4} or even 10^{-5} in practice. In order to distinguish between a spammer, whose contacts' CC is almost always 0 in any time intervals, and a normal user, the acceptable false positive probability of CC is 10^{-6}. Suppose the subset contains M nodes $v_1, v_2, \ldots, v_M$, for each node v_i, its neighbor filter's false positive is p_i, we can get the false positive of their CC by Equation (3):

$$\mathrm{FP}(CC) = \frac{(M-1)(p_1 + p_2 + \cdots + p_M)}{M(M-1)} = (p_1 + p_2 + \cdots + p_M)/M \quad (3)$$

So it requires the average false positive probability of the ANF to be less than 10^{-6}, which makes it no longer space effective to use the Bloom-filter only solution.

Furthermore, the social network is evolving with time, so deleting some nodes or edges cannot be avoided, which means the Bloom filter must be used with another data store to keep an accurate record of the social graph.

So, we propose a Bloom-filter based index called "ANI" in front of the relational database to guarantee the correctness for the CC query while significantly reducing the query latency at a reasonable memory cost.

ANI Construction. We first create a hash map for all the nodes. It maps each node to its own ANF. Then we traverse the graph in the database in a streaming way. Each time we encounter a (source, destination) pair, we insert the destination into the source's ANF. For simplicity, we use a fixed length of Bloom filters for all of the nodes. As different nodes have different degrees, the false positives will vary according to degrees. However, in a social network, most nodes have small degrees, so as long as the length of Bloom filter can control the false positives of the majority of nodes, the index will be very effective. We show the piece of code that builds the index from the database in Algorithm 1.

Query Through ANI. For a given subset $S = \{v_1, v_2, \ldots, v_M\}$, we can look up the ANI, using each node's ANF to filter out the edges that definitely do not exist and to get a set of edges that could exist in the subset. Specifically, for each

```
Input: SN_TABLE
Output:ANI
hstmt ← SQLExecDirect(SELECT * FROM SN_TABLE);
sr ← SQLFetch(hstmt);
while sr is SUCCESS do
    src ← SQLGetData(hstmt, 1, SQL_INTEGER);
    dest ← SQLGetData(hstmt, 2, SQL_INTEGER);
    itm ← ANI.Find(src);
    if src is not found then
        neighborfilter ← BMFilter();
        ANI.Insert(src, neighborfilter);
    else
        neighborfilter ← itm.neighborfilter;
    end
    neighborfilter.Add(GetMask(dest));
end
```

Algorithm 1. ANI construction

$v_i \in S$, we will first look up its ANF from the ANI, and then test whether v_j ($v_j \in S$ and $i \neq j$) is in v_i's ANF. The total size of the result set is $e + \sum_1^M p_i * d_i$, where p_i, d_i is the false positive probability and the degree of v_i, and e is the real edge number. Then we can further remove false positives using the database to get an accurate CC value. The query can be rewritten as:

```
SELECT COUNT (*) FROM SN_TABLE
  WHERE SOURCE=V1, DESTINATION IN RemainingNeighborListOfV1
     OR SOURCE=V2, DESTINATION IN RemainingNeighborListOfV2
      ...
     OR SOURCE=VP, DESTINATION IN RemainingNeighborListOfVP
```

Algorithm 2 shows the pseudo-code that transfers a subset "group" into a small graph that filters out most non-existent edges by looking up neighbor indices.

ANI Update. When the social network evolves with time, if a node or an edge is inserted into the graph, the ANF will also insert the new node or edge. If a node or edge is deleted from the graph, only the database is updated accordingly. Obviously, the false positives may increase as the social network evolves. We solve this problem by periodically rebuilding the neighbor index from the database.

Efficiency Analysis of ANI. By querying the database with hints from the ANI, we can reduce the time of index scanning, data fetching, and neighbor list comparing. In a sparse graph like a social network, one node may only connect to a few or even zero other nodes within a subset. So some nodes can be safely removed from the source list. For each source, its neighbors can also be further restricted to a relatively small area. Roughly speaking, up to $(1-CC-p)$ of query workload can be reduced. Here we can see that the efficiency of ANI is mainly

```
Input: group, ANI
Output: smallgraph, CCupperbound
for Each node n1 in group do
    neighborfilter =ANI.find(GetMask(n1).neighborfilter);
    for Each node n2 in group do
        if n2 == n1 then
            continue;
        end
        if n2 exists in neighborfilter then
            neighborlist.add(n2);
            CCupperbound ++ ;
            need = true;
        end
    end
    if need then
        smallgraph.insert(n1,neighborlist);
    end
end
```

Algorithm 2. Query through ANI

influenced by the average false positive probability p and the real CC value of the subset. Since CC is very small in sparse graphs and p can be controlled to a small value by proper ANF, the reduced workload is obvious.

4 Experiments

This section evaluates the performance of the neighbor index by measuring the percentage time reduction from using ANI in front of a database. The data set we used containing 3,091,943 users and 12,108,369 "knowing" relations between them. The data set is generated from one week's server log of a short messaging center of a city by removing private information. One person is considered to "know" another person if he/she frequently contacts him/her. Fig. 1 shows the cumulative edge degree distribution of the data set. We can see that about 80% of the nodes have a degree less than 4, and over 90% nodes have a degree less than 8.

We use two kinds of CC query series. The fist one is called "fixed size same degree" (FSSD) which contains 27 queries generated by the program. Each query in the FSSD series queries CC of a subset of 1,000 elements with the same degree. The degree varies from 1 to 27. The second query series called "real trace" (RT) is a replay of the real queries observed in the real application. If a user contacts over 10 different people in the past 10 minutes, a query of CC of his previously contactors is triggered. The RT series contains 142,848 queries and the subset size varies from 10 to 600.

In the FSSD series experiments, we mainly demonstrate how false positive influences the performance of ANI. All the queries in the FSSD series have very

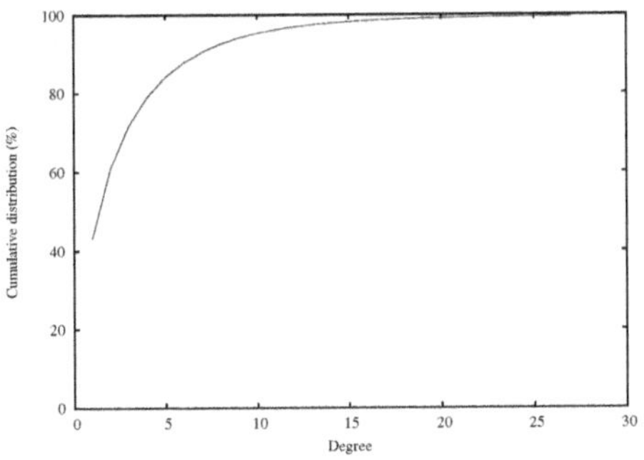

Fig. 1. Cumulative edge degree distribution of the dataset

small CC (10^{-4} to 10^{-5}) because of two reasons: first, the size of the subset is very large; and second, the elements are all randomly selected among all nodes that have a certain degree. So the main factor that differentiates the performance of ANI in different queries is the probability of false positives. Since we use a fixed-size Bloom filter for all nodes' ANF, a node's false positive probability will increase nearly exponentially with its degree. False positives are also influenced by the size of the Bloom filter, so we choose two different sizes of Bloom filter to build the ANF: 32-bit and 64-bit. With the 32-bit Bloom filter, nodes with degree no more than 4 can have a false positive probability below 0.05, and with the 64-bit Bloom filter, nodes with degree no more than 8 can have a false positive probability below 0.05. Fig. 2 shows that the 64-bit Bloom filter has better performance than the 32-bit Bloom filter, and the performance decreases as the average degree increases, as predicted by our analysis. When the average degree is less than 5, over 90% of time can be saved by using ANI of both sizes. When the degree is larger than 5, the performance of the 32-bit Bloom filter decreases sharply. But the 64-bit Bloom filter can save 70% to 99% query time in all of the queries.

Fig. 2 also plots the upper bound of CC returned when looking up ANI, which equals $(1+p) \times \text{CC}$. Consistently with our analysis, the performance curves have an opposite trend than the upper bound factor. Comparing `CC_upper_bound_64`, `CC_upper_bound_32`, and CC, we can see that the space between the upper bound and real value greatly increases as the degree increases. So in order to get an efficient ANI, we need to carefully choose the size of the Bloom filter. Our suggestion is that the size be big enough to ensure that at least 90% of nodes' ANF have a false positive probability less than 5%, thus the average false positive probability of CC can be controlled under $90\% \times 5\% + 10\% \times 1 = 15\%$.

The experiments on the RT series mainly show the effectiveness of ANI in real applications. First, we analyze how much the workload can be reduced by ANI using a 64-bit Bloom filter. In Fig. 3, 142,848 queries are grouped and ordered according to their CC on the x-axis; three curves represent the percentage of removed edges, percentage of removed sources, and cumulative distribution of query numbers. For the queries that have the same CC, we plot their average

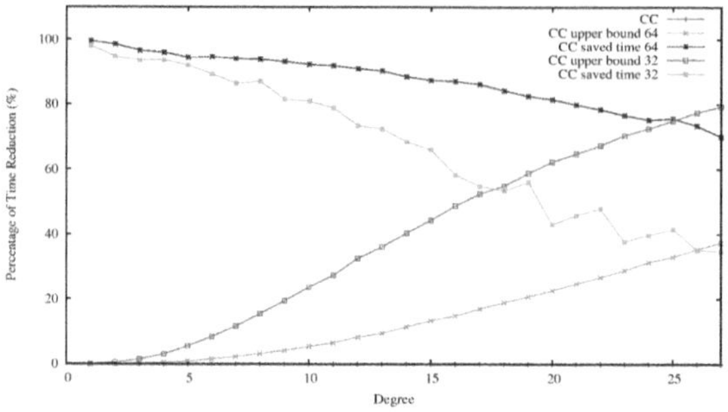

Fig. 2. Performance evaluation of FSSD series

value on the y-axis. We can see that in about 40% CC queries, we can remove over 40% source nodes that don't connect to any other node in the given subset. And totally in about 80% queries, 80% edges can be filtered out by ANI.

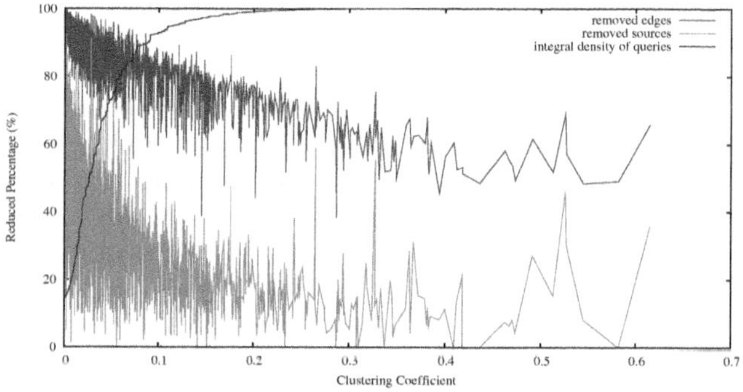

Fig. 3. Workload analysis of RT series

Comparing CC and `CC_upper_bound` in Fig. 4, we can see that most false positives probabilities are less than 20%, and the average false positive probability is 8.77% . The saved time also shows the same trend as we see in the FSSD experiments: it goes in the opposite direction of `CC_upper_bound`. By using a neighbor index with a 64-bit Bloom filter, we can save 67.25% time on average. In some rare case, the false positive probability is nearly 0.5. The reason is that there are many supernodes (having very high degree) in the subset, so the false positives of such queries are much higher than the average level. In some other rare cases, using a neighbor index doesn't save any time or even costs more time. We call such cases "time-out" cases. The overhead of looking up the index is a reason but not the main reason, because the neighbor index is small enough to be loaded into main memory and looking up the index costs no more than several milliseconds, which is a very small part of the whole query time. And in

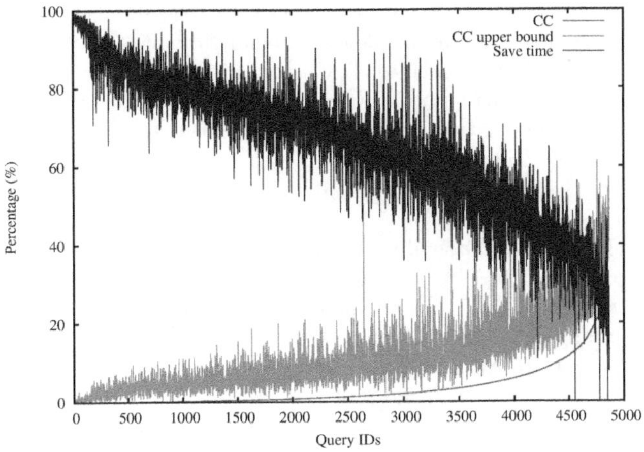

Fig. 4. Performance evaluation of RT series

each repeated run, we have about 1% "time-out" cases, but none of them are the same. One possible explanation is that the unusual latency is caused by random factors in the system, like a buffer flush just happened.

Finally, we measure the time to build the index. The average time to build an index for the dataset in the above tests is 48.1s. The time is mainly spent on reading data from the database, so it will be linearly increased with the size of the data set. And in practical applications, rebuilding the index daily or weekly is enough for a social network.

5 Conclusion

In this paper, we present a Bloom-filter based index "ANI" built upon a relational database to improve the performance of the subset CC query on extreme-scale social networks. We can get 2-10 times speedup while ensuring the accuracy and 100+ times speedup if a certain false positive is acceptable. We also present the experimental formula to estimate a suitable Bloom-filter size given the concrete social network. Although the design of ANI is triggered by the CC query, it could further be used in many other graph queries like sub-graph matching and reachability queries.

References

1. Achlioptas, D., Mcsherry, F.: Fast computation of low-rank matrix approximations. J. ACM 54(2), 9 (2007)
2. Alon, N., Yuster, R., Zwick, U.: Finding and counting given length cycles. Algorithmica 17(3), 209–223 (1997)
3. Anderson, C.: The Long Tail: Why the Future of Business Is Selling Less of More. Hyperion, vol. 12 (2004)

4. Batagelj, V., Mrvar, A.: A subquadratic triad census algorithm for large sparse networks with small maximum degree. Social Networks 23, 237–243 (2001)
5. Becchetti, L., Boldi, P., Castillo, C., Gionis, A.: Efficient semi-streaming algorithms for local triangle counting in massive graphs. In: KDD 2008: Proceeding of the 14th ACM SIGKDD international conference on Knowledge discovery and data mining, pp. 16–24. ACM, New York (2008)
6. Bloom, B.H.: Space/time trade-offs in hash coding with allowable errors. Commun. ACM 13(7), 422–426 (1970)
7. Oscar Boykin, P., Roychowdhury, V.P.: Leveraging social networks to fight spam, vol. 38, pp. 61–68. IEEE Computer Society Press, Los Alamitos (2005)
8. Buriol, L.S., Frahling, G., Leonardi, S., Marchetti-Spaccamela, A., Sohler, C.: Counting triangles in data streams. In: PODS 2006: Proceedings of the twenty-fifth ACM SIGMOD-SIGACT-SIGART symposium on Principles of database systems, pp. 253–262. ACM, New York (2006)
9. Coppersmith, D., Winograd, S.: Matrix multiplication via arithmetic progressions. In: STOC 1987: Proceedings of the nineteenth annual ACM symposium on Theory of computing, pp. 1–6. ACM, New York (1987)
10. Coppersmith, D., Winograd, S.: Matrix multiplication via arithmetic progressions. Journal of Symbolic Computation 9(3), 251–280 (1990)
11. Itai, A., Rodeh, M.: Finding a minimum circuit in a graph. SIAM Journal on Computing 7(4), 413–423 (1978)
12. Ley, M.: Dblp bibliography
13. Starobinski, D., Trachtenberg, A., Agarwal, S.: Efficient pda synchronization. IEEE Transactions on Mobile Computing 2(1), 40–51 (2003)
14. Tsourakakis, C.E.: Fast counting of triangles in large real networks without counting: Algorithms and laws. In: ICDM 2008: Proceedings of the 2008 Eighth IEEE International Conference on Data Mining, pp. 608–617. IEEE Computer Society, Washington (2008)
15. Tsourakakis, C.E., Drineas, P., Michelakis, E., Koutis, I., Faloutsos, C.: Spectral counting of triangles in power-law networks via element-wise sparsification. In: ASONAM, pp. 66–71 (2009)
16. Tsourakakis, C.E., Kang, U., Miller, G.L., Faloutsos, C.: Doulion: counting triangles in massive graphs with a coin. In: KDD 2009: Proceedings of the 15th ACM SIGKDD international conference on Knowledge discovery and data mining, pp. 837–846. ACM, New York (2009)
17. Watts, D.J., Strogatz, S.H.: Collective dynamics of'small-world'networks. Nature 393(6684), 409–410 (1998)

Predicting Best Answerers for New Questions in Community Question Answering

Mingrong Liu, Yicen Liu, and Qing Yang

National Laboratory of Pattern Recognition
Institute of Automation, Chinese Academy of Sciences
95 Zhongguancun East Road, Beijing 100190, China
{mrliu,ycliu,qyang}@nlpr.ia.ac.cn

Abstract. Community question answering (CQA) has become a very popular web service to provide a platform for people to share knowledge. In current CQA services, askers post their questions to the system and wait for answerers to answer them passively. This procedure leads to several drawbacks. Since new questions are presented to all users in the system, the askers can not expect some experts to answer their questions. Meanwhile, answerers have to visit many questions and then pick out only a small part of them to answer. To overcome those drawbacks, a probabilistic framework is proposed to predict best answerers for new questions. By tracking answerers' answering history, interests of answerers are modeled with the mixture of the Language Model and the Latent Dirichlet Allocation model. User activity and authority information is also taken into consideration. Experimental results show the proposed method can effectively push new questions to the best answerers.

Keywords: Community Question Answering, Language Model, LDA.

1 Introduction

Community question answering (CQA) services such as Yahoo! Answers[1], Baidu Zhidao[2] and Sina Iask[3] have become more and more popular during recent years in providing platforms for people to share knowledge online. Actually, CQA has existed for decades as part of bulletin board systems and Usernet, but has recently been popularized within web portals in which users answer questions posted by other users. CQA has proven to be more effective since users can post full natural language questions rather than issuing several word queries to search engines. The question answering content in online communities provides an alternative for users to obtain information in the form of answers authored by other users, rather than as lists of results or documents from search engines. In CQA, people are supposed to find the answer of any question once all people fully participate into community and share their knowledge.

Typically, a CQA service is organized in categories. When an asker has a question in his mind, he first chooses a proper category in the service system, and post the question

[1] http://answers.yahoo.com
[2] http://zhidao.baidu.com
[3] http://iask.sina.com.cn

L. Chen et al. (Eds.): WAIM 2010, LNCS 6184, pp. 127–138, 2010.

in that category, then waits others (answerers) to answer his question. With existing CQA systems, askers must passively wait for other users to visit the system, read their questions, and provide answers. It may take hours or days from asking a question in a CQA system before a user can expect to receive answers. Besides, the asker may expect some "experts" in the system to answer his question so that he has a relatively more chance to get correct answer. On the other hand, a user who knows well the answer to a particular question may not answer the question because the user may not visit the system frequently or the user may be faced with many open questions. While a user who answers a question may just happen to see the question, but is not an expert on the questions subject. To improve on this arrangement, it's a natural idea to push new questions to the right persons in a CQA system to obtain quick, high-quality answers. The reduced waiting time and improvements in the quality of answers are expected to improve user satisfaction.

In this paper, we are interested in predicting best answerers for new questions proposed in the question answering community. Generally speaking, when a new question is posted to the CQA system by an asker, we try to find the best answerers who can give correct answers to that question which may satisfy the asker. We model interests of the answerers by tracking users' answering history in the community. For a specific answerer, those questions the answerer has given best answers in the history make up the profile of that answerer. Based on the user profile, the relationship between the answerer and a new question is measured by traditional language model and the latent dirichlet allocation (LDA) model. Besides, user authority and user activity are also taken into consideration. The basic assumption is that more authoritative answerers may give more accurate answers, and more active answerers may be more willing to answer the new-coming questions.

The rest of this paper is organized as follows. Section 2 introduces some prior research related to our work. Section 3 discusses the proposed framework for predicting best answerers for new questions. Experimental results are presented in Section 4. We conclude this paper and point out future work in Section 5.

2 Related Work

Community-based Question Answering(CQA) services such as Yahoo! Answers, Baidu Zhidao and Sina Iask have been building very large archives of questions and their answers during the past few years. There is a large body of work conducted on the archives([1],[5],[7],[8],[11],[15]).

Lata et al. [1] studied Yahoo Answer! question answering system, and investigated user behavior and the quality of user generated content in the system.

Kevin K. Nam et al. [15] analyzed the characteristics of knowledge generation and user participation behavior in the largest question-answering online community in South Korea, Naver KnowledgeCiN, and found that altruism, learning, and competency are frequent motivations for top answerers to participate.

In order to avoid the lag time involved with waiting for a personal response, a Q&A service will typically automatically search the whole QA archive to see if the same question has previously been asked. In question search, given a question as query, the task is to find similar solved questions in CQA. Jeon et al. in [13] proposed an approach to estimate the question semantic similarity based on their answers. Additionally, Jeon et al. proposed a translate model to find similar questions in large question-answer archives in [12]. Besides searching for similar questions, recommending related questions in CQA, proposed by Y. Cao in [14] recently, is an alternative to similar question search.

Recently, E. Agichtein et al. proposed method in [9] to distinguish high-quality content, both questions and answers, from the rest. P. Jurczyk and E. Agichtein [8] exploited link analysis to identify authoritative users in community question answering, while M. Bouguessa et al. [6] use an alternative method to identify authoritative actors in question-answering forums.

There are relatively fewer work which aims to tackle the problem of predicting best answerers for new questions in community question answering. Y.H. Zhou et.al [3] present three approaches based on language models to represent the expertise of users based on their previous question answering activities, and then "push" the right questions to the right persons in online forums. Guo et.al [5] focus on recommending answer providers in order to increase the participation rate of users in CQA service.

Our work mostly relates to the work done in [3], [5] and [7], however, we propose to use different methods to model user interests. The prior information such as user activity and user authority is incorporated into the probabilistic framework for the first time when predicting best answerers for new questions.

3 Framework of Predicting Best Answerers

In this section, we predict best answerers for news questions in community question answering. A framework is proposed to find the top-k users for a given new question based on probabilistic model. Formally, given a new question q, the probability of user u being the best answerer for the question is measured as

$$P(u|q) = \frac{P(u)P(q|u)}{P(q)} \tag{1}$$

where $P(u)$ is the prior probability of user u, $P(q|u)$ models the probability of generating q from the profile of user u and $P(q)$ is the probability of generating the question q, which is the same for all candidate users. In this study, our main task is therefore to compute $P(q|u)$ and $P(u)$. Generally, $P(q|u)$ models the degree of interest of user u on question q, and the prior information $P(u)$ includes activity and authority of user u. Best answerers for the question q are ranked according to the combination of $P(q|u)$ and $P(u)$.

3.1 Modeling Interests of Answerers

The fact that an answerer will give the best answer to a given question typically indicates that the answerer has some degree of interest on that question. Thus, to predict the best answerer for a given new question, it's natural to model users's interests. Generally speaking, users' interests can be learned from his answering history, such as all the questions the answerer has given best answers to. In this section, two models are utilized to describe users' interests.

Language Model. Suppose a question $q = \{w_1, w_2, ..., w_N\}$, where w_i is a non-stop word in the question, $i = 1, 2, ...N$. In our approach, each word in question q is supposed to be generated independently, and the interest of user u on question q is represented by a multinomial probability distribution over the vocabulary of words. Therefore, the degree of interest of user u on question q can be obtained by taking the product of all the words in the question:

$$P(q|u) = \prod_{w} P(w|\theta_u)^{n(w,q)} \tag{2}$$

where $P(w|\theta_u)$ is the probability of a word given θ_u — the profile of user u, and $n(w, q)$ is number of times word w occurs in question q. User profile θ_u is composed of questions that are answered by user u and u is chosen as the best answerer for each of those questions. To calculate $P(w|\theta_u)$, one straight way is to compute the fraction of word w in θ_u. However, typically many users only answer a small number of questions, thus, due to sparsity, $P(w|\theta_u)$ is zero when w does not occur in θ_u, which leads to the result that user u will never be predicted as best answerer for any question containing word w. Thus, we need to do smoothing on $P(w|\theta_u)$, so that we can avoid zero probability of $P(w|\theta_u)$ to unseen words and also make the estimated model more accurate. For example, the Dirichlet smoothing method can be used to smooth $P(w|\theta_u)$, called the language model (LM)[10]:

$$P_{LM}(w|\theta_u) = \lambda P(w|\theta_u) + (1 - \lambda)P(w) \tag{3}$$

where $P(w)$ denotes the background language model built on the entire question collection Q and $\lambda \in$[0, 1] is a coefficient to control the influence of the background model, which is calculated as

$$\lambda = \frac{\Sigma_{w \in \theta_u} tf(w, \theta_u)}{\Sigma_{w \in \theta_u} tf(w, \theta_u) + \mu} \tag{4}$$

where $tf(w, \theta_u)$ is the frequency of w in the profile of user u, and the empirical parameter μ is manually set to 1000 , which can lead to relatively better results in the experiment. The background model $P(w)$ is computed through a maximum likelihood estimation:

$$P(w) = \frac{n(w, Q)}{|Q|} \tag{5}$$

where $n(w, Q)$ denotes the frequency of word w occurring in the question collection Q and $|Q|$ is the number of all words in collection Q.

Topic Model Based on Latent Dirichlet Allocation. The lexical gap problem is very important for problems related to natural language processing[16]. However, the language model is based on words matching only, and does not represent any semantic information, thus does not address the problem of lexical gaps between new questions and user profiles. In a typical question answering cycle, users always answer questions by first choosing a specific topic in an implicit way which the user has interest, and then picking out a question on that topic to answer. Note that one may have several or many interests, representing that the user should be modeled by different topics. To analyze a user's interest by investigating his previously asked questions, the set of those questions is viewed as the profile of that user. The user profile has some latent topics within it. To describe those topics, we utilize the latent dirichlet allocation (LDA, [2]) model, a topic model already used in the literature of documental information retrieval[4], which has the ability to model topics in large corpus(user profiles). The LDA model for generating user profile is represented as a probabilistic graphical model in Figure 1.

In LDA, the topic mixture is drawn from a conjugate Dirichlet prior that remains the same for all users. The process of generating user profile θ_u for a specific user u is as follows: 1) choose a multinomial distribution ϕ_z for each topic z from a Dirichlet distribution with parameter β, ϕ_z describes words distribution within topic z; 2) for the user profile θ_u, pick a multinomial distribution θ_U[4] from a Dirichlet distribution with parameter α, θ_u models topic distribution of u; 3) for each word token w in user profile θ_u, select a topic $z \in \{1, ..., K\}$[5] from the multinomial distribution θ_U; 4) pick word w from the mulitnomial distribution ϕ_z. Repeat this procedure for N_U(number of words in θ_u) times, then the user profile for u is generated.

For all of N users in the system, their profiles can be generated by repeating above procedure for N times, thus the likelihood L of the whole user profile collection is

$$P(u_1,..,u_N|\alpha,\beta)=\int\int\prod_{z=1}^{K}P(\phi_z|\beta)\prod_{U=1}^{N}P(\theta_U|\alpha)(\prod_{i=1}^{N_U}\sum_{z_i=1}^{K}P(z_i|\theta)P(w_i|z_i,\phi))d\theta d\phi \tag{6}$$

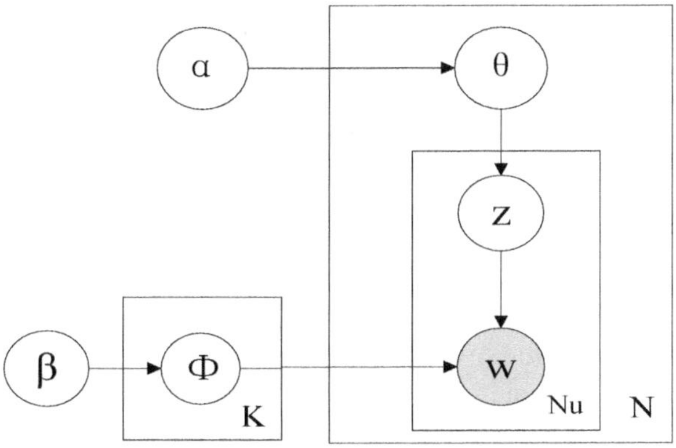

Fig. 1. User profile corpus generated by Latent Dirichlet Allocation

Compared to the simple language model, the LDA model has a new representation for a user profile based on topics. Note that the LDA model allows multiple topics per user, reflecting the fact that each user has multiple interest, which may be more reasonable in real world. After the posterior estimation of θ and ϕ, the probability of generating a word in a user profile is calculated as following,

[4] To distinguish from user profile θ_u, we use θ_U to represent this distribution.
[5] The topic number K is typically chosen empirically.

$$P_{LDA}(w|\widehat{\theta}, \widehat{\phi}, \theta_u) = \sum_{z=1}^{K} P(w|z, \widehat{\phi}) P(z|\widehat{\theta}, \theta_u) \tag{7}$$

where $\widehat{\theta}$ and $\widehat{\phi}$ are the posterior estimates of θ and ϕ respectively.

It can be seen that when measuring correlations between a word and a specific user profile, the LDA model does not require the word to appear in the user profile, since the LDA model measures their relations in the topic space rather than based on word matching. Thus, with LDA model the lexical gap problem[16] is alleviated.

Combining LM and LDA. It's natural to combine Language Model and LDA together to predict best answerers based on user profile. For example, LM and LDA can be linearly combined as

$$P_{LM+LDA}(w|\theta_u) = \pi P_{LM}(w|\theta_u) + (1 - \pi) P_{LDA}(w|\theta_u) \tag{8}$$

Here π is set to 0.5 empirically, which gives equal weights to both LM and LDA model when combining them.

3.2 The Prior Information of Answerers

To this end, in order to predict the best answerer u for a given new question q, we have calculated the likelihood, $P(q|u)$, based on user profile. In this section, we model the prior information of u as $P(u)$, which is made up of two parts: user authority and user activity. Later on we will find that the prior information will also play an important role when predicting best answerers.

User Authority. The underlying idea is that more authoritative users will probably give more authoritative answers to new questions in the future. And more authoritative answers will have a higher probability to be selected as the best answers by askers or other voters[6]. Thus, user authority is helpful to best answerer prediction. The problem of identifying authoritative users in question answering community has been well studied in the literature of community question answering ([6][8]). A common approach is to use link analysis techniques similar to the PageRank and Hub algorithm[8] for web page ranking, which are based on a large graph representing the discovered relationships between all of the askers and answerers in the community. However, more recently, M. Bouguessa et al. [6] pointed out that there were many drawbacks within the link-based methods. Furthermore, they found the Indegree technique can be used to rate the authority of users in the Q&A community effectively, where the InDegree of a user is simply the number of best answers given by that user. Here, with the same spirit of InDegree, we model the authority of users as,

$$authority(u) = log(1 + numans_u) \tag{9}$$

where $numans_u$ is the number of best answers user u has authored during his life in the question answering community. We use its log value to smooth the influence of user authority on best answerer prediction.

[6] If the asker does not select the best answer, other users can decide the best one among all candidate answers by means of voting.

User Activity. From the point of view of the asker, when posting a new question, besides the correctness of the expected answer, typically the asker would like the question to be answered as soon as possible. However, users may be quite different from each other in the degree of their activity. Some users could be active for a long time, while others may keep silent (don't give best answer to any question) for a very long time. Thus, more "active" users may be preferred, and it's reasonable to take user activity into consideration when predicting best answerers for questions in real Q&A services. For example, a user answered lots of questions in the first half year of 2008, but in the second half of that year, he gave no answer to any question at all. The activity of a user may be influenced by lots of facts, such as he may lose interest on a specific topic, or he may be quite involved in his work and have no spare time to serve as an expert in the Q&A community[15]. In this paper, we measure user's activity for a given question q as

$$activity(u) = exp^{-(t_q - t_u)} \tag{10}$$

where t_q is the posting time of the question, t_u is the most recent time when the user authored an answer to a question.

With user authority and user activity, the prior information in the probabilistic framework is calculated as the combination of them,

$$P(u) = authority(u) \times activity(u) \tag{11}$$

and the probability that user u will provide the best answer to the question q is

$$P(u|q) \propto P(u)P(q|u) \tag{12}$$

Given a test question q, all candidate users(answerers) are ranked according to $P(u|q)$, and the top ones are "pushed" (recommended) to the asker of q, who are considered as the best answerers for that question.

4 Experimental Study

4.1 Dataset

The experimental dataset is collected from a community-based question answering site, Iask[7], one of the leading web 2.0 sites in China. Overtime, the service has built up a very large archive of questions and answers written in Chinese. Topics of questions are very diverse, ranging from computer problems to restaurant recommendations. In this paper, our experiments are based on two top-level categories, Computer/Networks/IT and Health/Medical. Questions in both categories are resolved questions, thus each question has a best answer[8] corresponding to one best answerer. For the first category, the time span is from January 1, 2007 to February 18, 2009, and for the second category, the time span is from August 13,2004 to February 18, 2009. Table 1 shows the statistical information of the dataset. Numbers of resolved questions (best answers) in each of the

[7] http://iask.sina.com.cn

[8] There may be some other answers for a question, but they are ignored in this study.

Table 1. Data Statistic for two categories. Numbers in the parentheses are related to candidate best answerers for best answerer prediction.

Category	Questions	Askers	Best Answerers
Computer/Network/IT	461,712(369,490)	167,398	51,379(4,798)
Health/Medical	501,735(349,989)	219,586	86,569(5,613)

100 weeks before January 1, 2009 are depicted in Fig.3, from which we can see that user participation rate is relatively higher in the category of Computer/Network/IT than in the Health/Medical category.

For best answerer prediction, those answerers who have authored at least N(say 10) best answers are considered. Specifically, in the category of Computer/Network/IT, up to 51,379 users have given at least one best answer, while only 4,798 of them give at least ten best answers. Those 4,798 best answerers are very important to the question answering community, in fact, they have given best answers to 369,490 questions out of the total 461,712 questions. In the Health/Medical category, 5,613 active answerers contributed best answers to 349,989 questions out of 501,735 questions.

All questions are segmented using a Chinese word segmentation tool. After removing stop words, questions with less than two Chinese characters are ignored.

Test questions are drawn from the questions answered by these active users after a specific time stamp. Fig.2 shows how user profile and test questions are separated by the time stamp for an active user. To keep balance, not all questions answered by the user

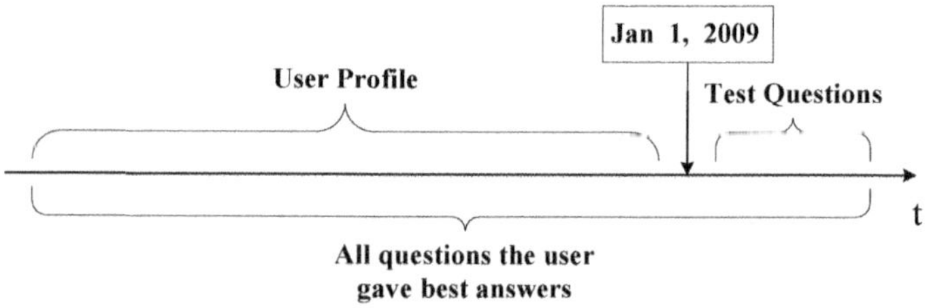

Fig. 2. An answerer's life in the Q&A community. User profile and test questions are separated by the time stamp January 1, 2009.

after the time stamp are picked out as test questions, in this study, we limit the number of test questions picked out from one answerer to 10 at most. Also note that some best answerers give no best answer to questions after the time stamp in the corpus, thus there isn't any test question drawn from them, however, they are still candidate answerers when predicting best answerers for a given question. As a result, there are 3,126 test questions for the first category, and 1,693 test questions for the other category. For each of these test questions, they are recommended to 4,798 and 5,631 answerers, respectively. The answerer who actually gave the best answer to a test question is viewed as the ground truth for that question.

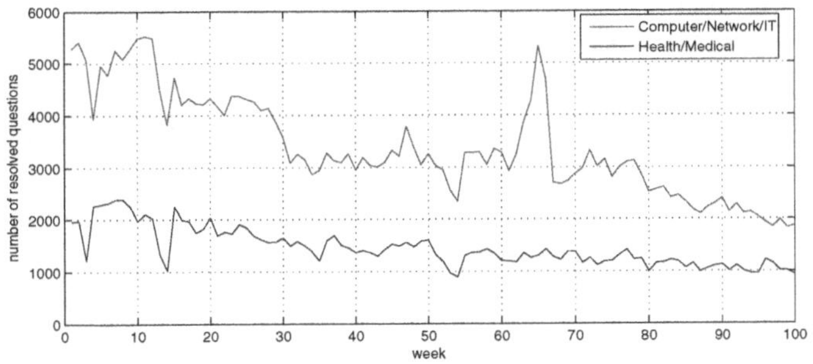

Fig. 3. Number of resolved questions(best answers) in each week before January 1, 2009

4.2 Experimental Setup

The parameter estimation and inference of the LDA model is based on Gibbs sampling, and the code implementation by X. Phan and C. Nguyen[9] is utilized. The number of topics in the LDA model is set to 100 empirically, and the Dirichlet prior parameters are set to the default values, which are typical in many other previous work. The iteration number is set to 2000. Note that the result will change with different iterations, however, in our experiment we found that the difference is slight when the iteration times is relatively large (say above 100).

4.3 Evaluation Method

Evaluation of predicting best answerers for news questions is not a trivial task. Here we propose a new metric for the evaluation which is different from the method used in [7]. In [7], each new question is recommended to the users who actually answered it(including the best answerer and other answerers whose answers were not chosen as the best finally), and those users are ranked according to their ranking method, the ranking position of the best answerer of the question is taken to measure the correctness of the recommendation of that question. Unlike [7], for a given news question, instead of only recommending it to the users who actually answered it, we "push" the question to all possible users who may answer it. When candidate users are ranked according to our model, if the "real" best answerer of the question is among the top N (say 1,10 or 100) predicted users, the prediction for that question is considered to be successful. We call this metric a success-at-N (S@N) metric, which has actually been widely used in the literature of information retrieval. Take S@1 for example, for each question in the test set, if its best answerer is the top one among the users predicted, the S@1 value is 1, otherwise its S@1 value is 0. The S@1 value of the whole test set is averaged by the S@1 value of all the test questions. Note that if there are many candidate users, the S@N value could be very small when N is relatively small.

[9] http://gibbslda.sourceforge.net/

Table 2. Four topics found in the category of Computer/Network/IT. In each topic, 15 words are shown with their weights. The English translations are listed in the brackets.

Topic 3	Topic 8	Topic 12	Topic 26
手机 (mobile phone) 0.1594	刻录 (burn) 0.0922	病毒 (virus) 0.0584	打印机 (printer) 0.1063
诺基亚 (Nokia) 0.0524	光盘 (compact disc) 0.0467	杀毒软件 (Antivirus) 0.0278	打印 (display) 0.0600
索爱 (Sony) 0.0175	盘 (disk) 0.0325	卡巴斯基 (Kaspersky) 0.0215	惠普 (HP) 0.0254
下载 (download) 0.0146	电脑 (computer) 0.0270	瑞星 (Rising) 0.0201	激光 (laser) 0.0180
三星 (SamSung) 0.0135	视频 (video) 0.0131	杀 (kill) 0.0184	墨盒 (ink box) 0.0152
摩托罗拉 (Motorola) 0.0107	光驱 (drive) 0.0130	木马 (trojan) 0.0162	纸 (paper) 0.0134
买 (buy) 0.0093	刻录机 (recorder) 0.0107	杀毒 (kill virus) 0.0153	加 (add) 0.0093
功能 (function) 0.0091	播放 (play) 0.0099	电脑 (computer) 0.0146	墨 (ink) 0.0091
支持 (support) 0.0088	文件 (file) 0.0098	密码 (password) 0.0143	彩色激光 (color laser) 0.0085
短信 (short message) 0.0074	会声会影 (UVS) 0.0088	安全 (safe) 0.0125	安装 (install) 0.0072
款 (style) 0.0067	使用 (use) 0.0077	防火墙 (firewall) 0.0113	粉 (powder) 0.0071
上网 (internet surfing) 0.0066	电影 (movie) 0.0072	删除 (delete) 0.0102	出现 (appear) 0.0070
蓝牙 (bluetooth) 0.0064	内容 (content) 0.0068	软件 (software) 0.0101	硒鼓 (toner) 0.0065
软件 (software) 0.0064	张 (a piece) 0.0065	下载 (download) 0.0092	台 (a (printer)) 0.0063
内存卡 (memory cards) 0.0062	成 (to be) 0.0060	升级 (upgrade) 0.0078	买 (buy) 0.0061

Table 3. Four topics found in the category of Medical/Health. In each topic, 15 words are shown with their weights. The English translations are listed in the brackets.

Topic 3	Topic 8	Topic 12	Topic 78
癌症 (cancer) 0.0198	糖尿病 (diabetes) 0.0543	乙肝 (hepatitis) 0.0674	锻炼 (exercise) 0.0463
白血病 (leukemia) 0.0180	血糖 (glucose) 0.0124	检查 (check) 0.0191	体检 (medical) 0.0361
癌 (cancer) 0.0167	高血压 (hypertension) 0.0117	阳性 (masculine) 0.0171	健身 (exercise) 0.0153
肺癌 (lung) 0.0150	糖尿病人 (diabetes) 0.0112	大三阳 (HBeAg) 0.0142	保健 (health care) 0.0114
化疗 (chemotherapy) 0.0148	失眠 (insomnia) 0.0104	小三阳 (HBsAg) 0.0137	运动 (movement) 0.0113
晚期 (late) 0.0137	治疗 (treatment) 0.0097	肝 (liver) 0.0125	肌肉 (muscle) 0.0102
乳腺癌 (breast cancer) 0.0108	胰岛素 (insulin) 0.0087	体检 (medical) 0.0120	保健品 (health products) 0.0087
肝癌 (cancer of the liver) 0.0066	睡觉 (sleep) 0.0085	传染 (infection) 0.0119	睡 (sleep) 0.0071
胃癌 (gastric) 0.0066	糖尿病患者 (diabetes) 0.0079	抗体 (antibody) 0.0118	晚上 (evening) 0.0066
食道癌 (esophagus) 0.0054	晚上 (night) 0.0078	正常 (normal) 0.0105	锻炼身体 (exercise) 0.0065
转移 (migrate) 0.0048	药 (drug) 0.0074	结果 (result) 0.0102	跑步 (run) 0.0065
鳞 (pangolin) 0.0035	脂肪肝 (fatty liver) 0.0069	项 (item) 0.0094	效果 (effect) 0.0060
造血 (haemopoiesis) 0.0032	注意 (attention) 0.0063	高 (high) 0.0091	健康 (healthy) 0.0058
放疗 (radiotherapy) 0.0031	专家 (expert) 0.0061	疫苗 (vaccine) 0.0089	提高 (increase) 0.0049
白血病患者 (leukemia) 0.0031	磨牙 (molar) 0.0054	肝炎 (hepatitis) 0.0088	睡眠 (sleep) 0.0044

4.4 Topics Found in User Profile by LDA

Table 2 and table 3 show several typical topics found in user profile by the LDA model in categories of Computer/Network/IT and Medical/Health, respectively. For example, in table 2, topic 3 focuses on mobile phone, topic 12 relates to computer virus, while topic 26 talks about printer. In table 3, topic 3,8 and 12 mainly focuses on diseases of cancer, diabetes and hepatitis, respectively, while topic 78 centers with exercising.

4.5 Results of Best Answerer Prediction

Experimental results are organized into three groups. The language model method is used as the baseline, and the number in the parenthesis are improvements over the baseline by different methods. In the first group, the results are based on the user profile only, while in the second group, user authorities are taken into consideration, and in the third group, both user authorities and user activities are utilized besides user profiles.

Table 4. Results of best answerers prediction for questions in the category of Computer/Network/IT. S@N is used as the evaluation metric, LM is the baseline, numbers in the parentheses are improvements(in percent) over the baseline by different methods. LM:Language Model, LDA:Latent Dirichlet Allocation, AU:user authority, AC:user activity.

Method	S@1	S@5	S@10	S@20	S@30	S@50	S@100
LM(Baseline)	0.0227	0.0605	0.0921	0.1270	0.1491	0.1862	0.2463
LDA	0.0112	0.0406	0.0669	0.1036	0.1280	0.1625	0.2281
LM+LDA	**0.0234(3.1)**	**0.0633(4.6)**	**0.0969(5.2)**	**0.1299(2.3)**	**0.1593(6.8)**	**0.2067(11.0)**	**0.2754(11.8)**
LM+AC	0.0234	0.0694	0.0956	0.1353	0.1670	0.2127	0.3081
LDA+AC	0.0243	0.0739	**0.1065(15.6)**	**0.1555(22.4)**	**0.1916(28.5)**	**0.2508(34.7)**	**0.3484(41.5)**
LM+LDA+AC	**0.0269(18.5)**	**0.0742(22.6)**	0.1036	0.1484	0.1791	0.2284	0.3346
LM+AC+AU	0.0221	0.0688	0.0947	0.1356	0.1679	0.2147	0.3084
LDA+AC+AU	**0.0278(22.5)**	0.0742	**0.1081(17.4)**	**0.1580(24.4)**	**0.1910(28.1)**	**0.2527(35.7)**	**0.3519(42.9)**
LM+LDA+AC+AU	0.0259	**0.0755(24.8)**	0.1040	0.1484	0.1795	0.2290	0.3346

Table 5. Results of best answerers prediction for questions in the category of Health/Medical. S@N is used as the evaluation metric, the result of LM is the baseline. Improvements(in percent) over the baseline by different methods are shown in the parentheses. LM:Language Model, LDA:Latent Dirichlet Allocation, AU:user authority, AC:user activity.

Method	S@1	S@5	S@10	S@20	S@30	S@50	S@100
LM(Baseline)	0.0195	0.0520	0.0732	0.1004	0.1217	0.1524	0.2132
LDA	0.0100	0.0437	0.0667	0.1063	0.1264	0.1636	0.2126
LM+LDA	**0.0195(0.0)**	**0.0555(6.7)**	**0.0797(8.9)**	**0.1122(11.8)**	**0.1411(15.9)**	**0.1784(17.1)**	**0.2386(11.9)**
LM+AC	0.0337	0.0916	0.1323	0.1837	0.2156	0.2758	0.4170
LDA+AC	0.0354	0.1022	0.1453	**0.2091(108.3)**	**0.2504(105.8)**	**0.3207(110.4)**	**0.4513(111.7)**
LM+LDA+AC	**0.0366(87.7)**	**0.1093(110.2)**	**0.1483(102.6)**	0.2020	0.2404	0.3048	0.4377
LM+AC+AU	0.0331	0.0933	0.1305	0.1843	0.2156	0.2711	0.4200
LDA+AC+AU	0.0331	0.1004	**0.1447(97.7)**	**0.2073(106.5)**	**0.2546(109.2)**	**0.3207(110.4)**	**0.4525(112.2)**
LM+LDA+AC+AU	**0.0372(90.8)**	**0.1063(104.4)**	0.1424	0.1973	0.2422	0.3036	0.4377

Table 4 shows the results of predicting best answerers for questions in the category of Computer/Network/IT. From table 4 we can see that without consideration of user authority and user activity, the combination of Language Model and LDA performed best. When taking user authority into consideration, the prediction accuracy become better, which is based on the combination of LM and LDA model or LDA model alone. The best performance is got when both user authority and user activity are involved, which is typically based on the LDA model alone. Since there are many candidate users which may give best answer to a specific question, and there are probably some users who indeed are "experts" to the question, but they did not give best answers to that question due to some reasons, the prediction accuracy could be reasonably small. Note that for the measure of S@1, a random-guess method will lead to a low accuracy of less than 0.021%.

Table 5 shows the results of predicting best answerers for questions in the category of Medical/Health. Similar to the case in the Computer/Network/IT category, we can also see that without consideration of user authority and user activity, the combination of Language Model and LDA performed better than either alone. Much better performance is reached when taking both user authority and user activity into consideration.

Generally speaking, to predict best answerers for new questions, we need semantic model such as LDA besides the language model. Additionally, the prior information such as user authority and user activity also makes great contributions to the prediction.

5 Conclusions and Future Work

In this paper, we have proposed a framework for predicting best answerers for new questions in the question answering community. By tracking answerers's answering history, interests of answerers are modeled with the mixture of the Language Model and the LDA model. User activity and authority levels are also incorporated into the probabilistic framework. Experimental results show that our proposed method can effectively predict the best answerers for new questions.

As future work, we intend to investigate the performance of the proposed framework in a larger scale dataset besides the two categories used in this study. We also plan to investigate more accurate user authority and user activity models, and more precise prediction results are expected.

References

1. Adamic, L.A., Zhang, J., Bakshy, E., Ackerman, M.S.: Knowledge sharing and yahoo answers: everyone knows something. In: Proc. of WWW, pp. 665–674 (2008)
2. Blei, D.M., Ng, A.Y., Jordan, M.I.: Latent dirichlet allocation. The Journal of Machine Learning Research 3, 993–1022 (2003)
3. Zhou, Y., Cong, G., Cui, B., Jensen, C.S., Yao, J.: Routing questions to the right users in online communities. In: Proc. of ICDE, pp. 700–711 (2009)
4. Wei, X., Croft, B.W.: LDA-based document models for ad-hoc retrieval. In: Proc. of ACM SIGIR, pp. 178–185 (2006)
5. Guo, J., Xu, S., Bao, S., Yu, Y.: Tapping on the potential of q&a community by recommending answer providers. In: Proc. of ACM CIKM, pp. 921–930 (2008)
6. Bouguessa, M., Dumoulin, B., Wang, S.: Identifying authoritative actors in question-answering forums: The case of Yahoo! Answers. In: Proc. of ACM SIGKDD, pp. 866–874 (2008)
7. Qu, M., Qiu, G., He, X., Zhang, C., Wu, H., Bu1, J., Chen, C.: Probabilistic question recommendation for question answering communities. In: Proc. of WWW, pp. 1229–1230 (2009)
8. Jurczyk, P., Agichtein, E.: Discovering authorities in question answer communities by using link analysis. In: Proc. of ACM CIKM, pp. 919–922 (2007)
9. Agichtein, E., Castillo, C., Donato, D., Gionis, A., Mishne, G.: Finding High-Quality Content in Social Media. In: Proc. of WSDM, pp. 183–194 (2008)
10. Zhai, C., Lafferty, J.: A study of smoothing methods for language models applied to information retrieval. ACM Transactions on Information Systems 22, 179–214 (2004)
11. Liu, X., Croft, W.B., Koll, M.: Finding experts in community-based questionanswering services. In: Proc. of ACM CIKM, pp. 315–316 (2005)
12. Jeon, J., Bruce Croft, W., Lee, J.H.: Finding Similar Questions in Large Question and Answer Archives. In: Proc. of CIKM, pp. 84–90 (2005)
13. Jeon, J., Bruce Croft, W., Lee, J.H.: Finding Semantically Similar Questions Based on Their Answers. In: Proc. of SIGIR, pp. 617–618 (2005)
14. Cao, Y., Duan, H., Lin, C.-Y., Yu, Y., Hon, H.-W.: Recommending Questions Using the MDL-based Tree Cut Model. In: Proc. of WWW, pp. 81–90 (2008)
15. Nam, K.K., Ackerman, M.S., Adamic, L.A.: Questions in, Knowledge iN? A Study of Naver's Question Answering Community. In: Proc. of international conference on Human factors in computing systems, pp. 779–788 (2009)
16. Berger, A., Caruana, R., Cohn, D., Freitag, D., Mittal, V.: Bridging the Lexical Chasm: Statistical Approaches to Answer-Finding. In: Proc. of ACM SIGIR, pp. 192–199 (2000)

Semantic Grounding of Hybridization for Tag Recommendation

Yan'an Jin[1,2], Ruixuan Li[1,⋆], Yi Cai[3], Qing Li[3], Ali Daud[4], and Yuhua Li[1]

[1] College of Computer Science and Technology, Huazhong University of Science and Technology, Wuhan 430074, China
jin.yan.an@smail.hust.edu.cn, rxli@hust.edu.cn, idcliyuhua@hust.edu.cn
[2] School of Information and Management, Hubei University of Economics, Wuhan 430205, China
[3] Department of Computer Science, City University of Hong Kong, Hong Kong, China
yicai3@cityu.edu.hk, itqli@cityu.edu.hk
[4] Department of Computer Science and Technology, Tsinghua University, Beijing 100084 ,China
ali_msdb@hotmail.com

Abstract. Tag recommendation for new resources is one of the most important issues discussed recently. Many existing approaches ignore text semantics and can not recommend new tags which are not in the training dataset (e.g., FolkRank). Some exceptional semantic approaches use a probabilistic latent semantic method to recommend tags in terms of topic knowledge (e.g., ACT model). However, they do not perform well because many entities in these models result in much noise. In this paper, we propose hybrid approaches in folksonomy to challenge these problems. Hybrid approaches are combination of Language Model (LM) for keyword based approach and Latent Dirichlet Allocation (LDA), Tag-Topic (TT) model and User-Tag-Topic (UTT) model for topic based approaches. Our approaches can recommend meaningful tags and can be used to discover resource implicit correlations. Experimental results on Bibsonomy dataset show that LM performs better than all other hybrid and non-hybrid approaches. Also the hybrid approaches with less number of entities (e.g., LDA with only one entity) perform better than those approaches having more entities (e.g., UTT with three entities) for tag recommendation task.

1 Introduction

As a promptly emerged popular way, social tags allow users to annotate, categorize and find web resources by assigning one or more descriptive words (called tags) in folksonomies, such as Flickr[1], Bibsonomy[2]. Thus, the tags assigned to each resource create a bridge between heterogeneous data and users who are accustomed to keyword-based search and browsing. To create this association, social tagging systems demand users to manually annotate tags for each resource [1]. However, manual assignment of

⋆ Corresponding author.

[1] http://www.flickr.com

[2] http://www.bibsonomy.org

L. Chen et al. (Eds.): WAIM 2010, LNCS 6184, pp. 139–150, 2010.

tags results in the following problems: 1) Tags assigned by users are sometime very specific and sometime very general; 2) There may exist cold start problem for new resources, as new resources do not acquire enough tags quickly; 3) Tag assignment is potentially time-consuming. Therefore, many researchers try to work on proposing some tag recommendation methods for addressing the above problems [2,3,4].

In current folksonomy services, there are four major frameworks used for tag recommendation: a) Graph connectivity based approaches, e.g., FolkRank [5,3], a variation of PageRank; b) Keywords matching based collaborative filtering approaches like [4,6,7] by using similar tags and contents of similar resources; c) topic layer (semantically related cluster of words) based approaches [8]; d) Mixture of many existing approaches and additional context component [9]. The first approach only works on a dense core of folksonomy while folksonomy usually has a sparse structure. The second approach is an essential method of keywords extraction based on word frequency but not on word semantic. Both of them can only recommend tags with highest scores from the collection of tags which have been posted previously, and can not recommend tags for new resources. The third approach is suitable for sparse kind of data and can recommend tags for newly arriving resources, but it still does not perform well because it simultaneously models many entities such as words, tags and users. What is more, it creates much noise [10]. The forth hybrid approach can do better recommendations to some extent, but its applications are limited to many context factors.

Previously, we investigate tag recommendation on Bibsonomy dataset[3] by hybrid approaches of keyword and semantic (i.e., topic-related) knowledge. Keyword based approaches are precise presentation of words, while topic modeling approaches may be not. Intuitively, topic modeling approaches represent a combination of related words as a topic. Only using topic modeling itself is too loutish for tag recommendation [11]. In this paper, we individually use keyword based and semantic based approaches as baselines to predict tags at first. Then we propose hybrid approaches to combine them pairwise. For keyword based approach, we use Language Model (LM). For semantic based approach, we employ Latent Dirichlet Allocation (LDA) [12], Tag-Topic model (TT, which is adapted from Author Topic model [13]) and User-Tag-Topic model (UTT, which is adapted from Author-Conference-Topic model [14]), respectively. The experimental result shows that LM can perform better than other approaches, and hybrid approaches with fewer entities outperform the hybrid approaches with more entities.

The novelty of this work lies in: 1) We propose hybrid approaches which combine keyword based approach and topic layer based approach to deal with the tag recommendation issue; 2) We use both description words and tags associated with a resource as the candidate set individually in hybrid approach; 3) We verify the effectiveness of our approach through experiments conducted on a real-world dataset. To the best of our knowledge, we are the first to compare the effectiveness of tag recommendation approaches by using both words and tags in hybrid approaches.

The rest of the paper is organized as follows. Section 2 provides related work. Section 3 illustrates baselines and the proposed hybrid approaches for tag recommendation. In Section 4, experiments and performance evaluation about the proposed approaches are conducted. Section 5 brings this paper to the conclusions.

[3] The dataset include two parts: tags and descriptive words associated with a resource.

2 Related Work

With the emergence of social tagging systems, tag recommendation has become an attractive area of research. Some important characteristics of social tagging systems are studied. 1) Keywords appeared in a resource are usually selected as tags by users; 2) Similar kind of tags is assigned to similar kind of resources; 3) Users with the similar interests influence each other's annotation activities [15,16].

Usually, tags are recommended on the basis of tags posted to similar posts. AutoTag [4] and TagAssist [6] use some information retrieval skills to recommend tags for web blog posts. Co-occurrence of tags was used to complement user-defined tags of photographs in Flickr [17]. An association rule mining approach is proposed for tag recommendation utilizing the association structure of tags [18]. Recently, FolkRank, an adaption of famous PageRank [10], is proposed to recommend tags on the basis of graph connectivity. Although aforementioned methods are always seen in most current social tagging systems, they are unable to perform well because of not sharing tags in the candidate set.

In addition, tag recommendation approaches based on posted tags are always doubted by the requirements of sufficient annotations for a target resource and have cold-start problem for newly arriving resources, which are highlighted by Hsu and Chen [2]. Therefore, they propose a supervised tag recommendation model to predict the stabilized tag for a target resource. Meanwhile, as a major task of RSDC2008 challenge[4], tag recommendation using semantic information is proposed. In that challenge, Zhang et al [8] propose a hybrid approach based on LM and ACT model using content information to label a new resource. Tags and users of resources are modeled together by using the topic layer to capture the semantics of text. Their main assumption is that words are responsible for generating tags and users of those tags do not match with the real world situation in which users usually generate tags for resources. As shown in [10], modeling more objects together in topic layer based approaches results in poor performance. Intuitively, we propose simpler hybrid approaches by using just description words or tags that can perform better than complex topic modeling based non-hybrid approaches.

3 Hybridization for Tag Recommendation

3.1 Keyword Based Approaches

LM is widely used in natural language processing applications such as speech recognition and information retrieval. Its goal is to try to characterize, capture, and exploit regularities in the collection of documents, and assign a reasonable probability distribution to all words. Accordingly, it can score all the words in the candidate set and recommends words with highest scores for tags.

The basic idea of LM is to interpret the relevance between a document and a query as a generative probability for the query from the document model:

$$P_{LM}(q|d) = \prod_{w \in q} P(w|d) \tag{1}$$

[4] http://www.kde.cs.uni-kassel.de/ws/rsdc08: a ECML PKDD Discovery Challenge.

where w is a query word token in q. $P(q|d)$ is the probability of the document model generating the query words under the Bag of Words (BoW) assumption[19]. $P(w|d)$ is the probability for generating word w from the document model d, which is usually specified by using the smoothing techniques (like Dirichlet smoothing [20]). The probability is a score, calculated by following Eq.2:

$$P(w|d) = \frac{N_d}{N_d + \lambda}\frac{tf(\dot{w}, d)}{|d|} + (1 - \frac{N_d}{N_d + \lambda})\frac{tf(\dot{w}, \mathbf{D})}{|\mathbf{D}|} \tag{2}$$

where $|d|$ is the length of document d, $tf(w,d)$ is the word frequency (i.e. number of words) of word w in d, $|\mathbf{D}|$ is the number of word tokens in the whole collection, and $tf(w,\mathbf{D})$ is the word frequency of word w in the whole collection $\mathbf{D}$. λ is the Dirichlet prior and its value is set according to the average document length in the document collection, which is set to 10 in our case.

In this paper, we propose three keyword based tag recommendation approaches in terms of different candidate sets: Word Language Model (**wLM**), Tag Language Model (**tLM**) and **CombLM**, which are variants of Language Model.

Word Language Model (wLM). **wLM** uses description words posted by all users for a specific resource as the candidate set. In **wLM**, a resource is viewed as a composition of the description words written by all tagging users. Symbolically, for a resource r we can write it as: $r = \{u_1w_1 + u_2w_2 + \ldots + u_iw_i\}$, where u_iw_i is the description written by a user u_i on a specific resource. According to original LM, the probability for generating a word w_i from the resource r is:

$$P_{wLM}(w|r) = \frac{N_r}{N_r + \lambda}\frac{tf(\dot{w}, r)}{|r|} + (1 - \frac{N_r}{N_r + \lambda})\frac{tf(\dot{w}, \mathbf{R})}{|\mathbf{R}|} \tag{3}$$

Tag Language Model (tLM). **tLM** uses tags posted by all users for a specific resource as the candidate set. In **tLM**, a resource is viewed as a collection of the tags for a specific resource given by all users. Symbolically, for a resource r we can write it as: $r = \{u_1t_1 + u_2t_2 + \ldots + u_it_i\}$, where u_it_i is the tag posted by a user u_i about a specific resource r. Like as **wLM**, we calculate the probability for a tag t_i from the collection by Eq.4:

$$P_{tLM}(t|r) = \frac{N_r}{N_r + \lambda}\frac{tf(\dot{t}, r)}{|r|} + (1 - \frac{N_r}{N_r + \lambda})\frac{tf(\dot{t}, \mathbf{R})}{|\mathbf{R}|} \tag{4}$$

CombLM. In fact, there are both description words and tags for a given resource in a social tagging system. Description words can be considered as summary for a resource, and tags can be thought as semantic annotation for a resource. Consequently, both can be used as the candidate set for tag recommendation. We propose a simple approach for tag recommendation combining description words and tags on **wLM** and **tLM**. The score of a tag for a given resource by **CombLM** can be calculated by Eq.5:

$$P_{CombLM}(t|r) = P_{wLM}(w|r)P_{tLM}(t|r) \tag{5}$$

3.2 Topic Modeling Approaches

Topic models are based upon the idea that documents are mixtures of topics, where a topic is a probability distribution over words. Now, there are many variants or extensions of topic model. In this paper, we use four adaptive topic models for our task: wLDA (LDA over description), tLDA (LDA over tags), TT model [13], UTT model [14].

As a basic topic model, LDA is widely used to model documents. It specifies a simple probabilistic procedure by which documents can be generated. First, for each document d, a multinomial distribution θ_d over topics is randomly sampled from a Dirichlet distribution with parameter α. Second, for each word w, a topic z is chosen from this topic distribution. Finally, the word w is generated by randomly sampling from a topic-specific multinomial distribution ϕ_z. The generating probability of word w from document **D** for LDA is given as:

$$P(w|d,\theta,\phi) = \sum_z P(w|z,\phi_z)P(z|d,\theta_d) \tag{6}$$

Word Latent Dirichlet Allocation (wLDA). wLDA uses description words posted by all users for a specific resource. In **wLDA**, a resource is viewed as a composition of the description words written by all tagging users. Symbolically, for a resource r we can write it as: $r = \{u_1w_1 + u_2w_2 + \cdots + u_iw_i\}$, where u_iw_i is the description written by a user u_i about a specific resource r. According to basic LDA equation, the generating probability of word w from resources for LDA is given as Eq.7.

$$P_{wLDA}(w|r,\theta,\phi) = \sum_z P(w|z,\phi_z)P(z|r,\theta_r) \tag{7}$$

Tags Latent Dirichlet Allocation (tLDA). tLDA uses tags posted by all users for a specific resource. In tLDA a resource is viewed as a collection of the tags given by all users to a specific resource. Symbolically, for a resource r we can write it as: $r = \{u_1t_1 + u_2t_2 + \cdots + u_it_i\}$, where u_it_i is a tag posted by a user about a specific resource. Like as **wLDA**, we calculate the probability for a tag t from the collection by Eq. 8.

$$P_{tLDA}(t|r,\theta,\phi) = \sum_z P(t|z,\phi_z)P(z|r,\theta_r) \tag{8}$$

Tag-Topic Model (TT). LDA is extended to model words and authors simultaneously by using latent topics, named Author-Topic Model [13]. We propose its variation in which, each tag of a resource r is associated with a multinomial distribution θ_t over topics is sampled from Dirichlet α, and each topic is associated with a multinomial distribution ϕ_z sampled from Dirichlet β over description words of a resource for that topic. The generating probability of word w for tag t of a resource r is given in Eq. 9.

$$P(w|t,r,\phi,\theta) = \sum_z P(w|z,\phi_z)P(z|t,\theta_t) \tag{9}$$

In **TT** model, both words and tags of a resource are modeled together to get their combined influence. It assumes that description words can be real representatives of tags. In its generative process, it considers that words of a resource are responsible for generating some topics which in turn generates the tags for that resource.

User-Tag-Topic Model (UTT). Recently, Author-Topic model is extended to model authors and conferences simultaneously by using latent topics, named Author-Conference-Topic Model (ACT) [14]. Its variation is provided by [8], in which each description word is represented by the probability distribution description over topics, and each topic is represented as a probability distribution over tags and users for each word of a resource for that topic. The generative probability of the tag t with user u for word w of resource r is given as:

$$P(w, u|t, r, \phi, \psi, \theta) = \sum_{z} P(w|z, \phi_z) P(u|z, \psi_z) P(z|t, \theta_t) \tag{10}$$

In UTT, words, tags and users are modeled together to get their combined influence, with assumption that all three components are interdependent and should be modeled together. In its generative process, it considers that words of a resource are responsible for generating some topics which in turn generates the tags and user for that resource.

3.3 Hybrid Approaches

We propose two different approaches to recommend tags: keyword based approach (KBA) and topic modeling based approach (TMBA). These two approaches focus on two different aspects. KBA will recommend some keywords extracted from the candidate set while TMBA tends to recommend some conceptual knowledge as tags. In detail, LM can only model word specific information and cannot model the topic information. LDA models can be used to model the topic distributions of documents, which eliminates the limitation of LM. Consequently, the combination of LM and LDA is an necessary and intuitive better way to improve tag recommendation performance.

Thus, in our hybrid method, we will select and recommend top k ranked tags from a probability list. We define the probability of a tag for the specific resource as an aggregation of KBA and TMBA:

$$\eta(r, t) = \gamma(\delta(r, t), \vartheta(r, t)) \tag{11}$$

where $\delta(r, t) \in [0,1]$ is the probability of a tag for the specific resource by KBA and $\vartheta(r, t) \in [0,1]$ is the probability of a tag for the specific resource by TMBA. γ is an aggregation function used to combing the effects of KBA and TMBA, which should observe the following axioms.

Axiom 1 *For a tag* t *and a resource* r,

- *if* $\delta(\mathrm{r,t})=0$, $\eta(\mathrm{r,t})=\vartheta(\mathrm{r,t})$.
- *if* $\vartheta(\mathrm{r,t})=0$, $\eta(\mathrm{r,t})=\delta(\mathrm{r,t})$.

Axiom 2 *For a tag* t *and a resource* r, *function* γ *should guarantee* $\eta(\mathrm{r,t})\in[0,1]$.

Axiom 3 *For a resource* r, *two tags* t_1 *and* t_2.

- *if* $\delta(\mathrm{r},t_1)=\delta(\mathrm{r},t_2)$ *and* $\vartheta(\mathrm{r},t_1) \geq \vartheta(\mathrm{r},t_2)$, *then* $\eta(\mathrm{r},t_1) \geq \eta(\mathrm{r},t_2)$.
- *if* $\delta(\mathrm{r},t_1) \geq \delta(\mathrm{r},t_2)$ *and* $\vartheta(\mathrm{r},t_1)=\vartheta(\mathrm{r},t_2)$, *then* $\eta(\mathrm{r},t_1) \geq \eta(\mathrm{r},t_2)$.

Axiom 1 specifies the boundary cases of the probability. When $\delta(r,t)=0$, it means that a tag t is in the training file but not in the candidate set of KBA. Thus, $\eta(r,t)$ should be equal to $\vartheta(r,t)$. When $\vartheta(r,t)=0$, it means that a tag t is in the candidate of KBA but not in the training file. Thus, $\eta(r,t)$ should be equal to $\delta(r,t)$. Axiom 2 indicates aggregation function γ should constrain $\eta(r,t) \in [0,1]$. Axiom 3 shows the interrelationship between KBA and TMBA. The aggregation γ is application-dependent [21]. The choice of aggregation function γ in a specific application is out of the scope of this paper[5]. In our paper, we present a possible function as an example to aggregate KBA and TMBA.

$$\eta(r,t) = \xi\delta(r,t) + (1-\xi)\vartheta(r,t) \tag{12}$$

where ξ is a weight to balance KBA and TMBA.

Based on these foundations mentioned-above, we propose several hybrid approaches for tag recommendation on the basis of KBA and TMBA. We instance the KBA as LM and TMBA as LDA, TT and UTT, respectively. Therefore, We consider several forms of combination including **wLM + wLDA** (Eq.13), **wLM + tLDA** (Eq.14), **wLM + TT** (Eq.15), **wLM + UTT** (Eq.16), **tLM + wLDA** (Eq.21), **tLM + tLDA** (Eq.18), **tLM + TT** (Eq.19) and **tLM + UTT** (Eq.20).

$$P(t|r) = \xi P_{wLM}(t|r) + (1-\xi)P_{wLDA}(t|r) \tag{13}$$

$$P(t|r) = \xi P_{wLM}(t|r) + (1-\xi)P_{tLDA}(t|r) \tag{14}$$

$$P(t|r) = \xi P_{wLM}(t|r) + (1-\xi)P(w|t,r,\phi,\theta) \tag{15}$$

$$P(t|r) = \xi P_{wLM}(t|r) + (1-\xi)P(w,u|t,r,\phi,\psi,\theta) \tag{16}$$

$$P(t|r) = \xi P_{tLM}(t|r) + (1-\xi)P_{wLDA}(t|r) \tag{17}$$

$$P(t|r) = \xi P_{tLM}(t|r) + (1-\xi)P_{tLDA}(t|r) \tag{18}$$

$$P(t|r) = \xi P_{tLM}(t|r) + (1-\xi)P(w|t,r,\phi,\theta) \tag{19}$$

$$P(t|r) = \xi P_{tLM}(t|r) + (1-\xi)P(w,u|t,r,\phi,\psi,\theta) \tag{20}$$

where $P_{wLM}(t|r)$ and $P_{tLM}(t|r)$ is the generating probability of word w and tag t from resource r by language model (as defined in Eq.3 and Eq.4), $P_{wLDA}(t|r)$ and $P_{tLDA}(t|r)$ is the probability of word w or tag t from resource r obtained by the LDA model (as defined in Eq.7 and Eq.8), $P(w|t,r,\phi,\theta)$ is the generating probability of word w for tag t of a resource r, and $P(w,u|t,r,\phi,\psi,\theta)$ is the probability of the tag t with user u for word w of resource r.

4 Experiments

4.1 Experimental Settings

Data sets. Bibsonomy is a social tagging tool which allows user to manage a personal collection of links to the websites and describe those links with one or more words. We selected a subset of Bibsonomy dataset provided by ECML/PKDD 2008 organizers for Discovery Challenge. There are 33,256 words, 13,276 tags, 1,185 users, 14,443 resources and 262,445 bookmarks in total. We then preprocessed dataset by a) removing stop-words, punctuations and numbers, b) lower-casing the obtained words, tags, user names and c) removing words and tags that appear less than three times in the corpus. This creates 18,450 words, 10,702 tags, 861 users, 13,179 resources and 181,491 bookmarks in the dataset.

[5] Please refer to [21] for more detail.

Baseline Approaches. We conducted experiments on Bibsonomy dataset to evaluate the recommendation quality of proposed hybrid and non-hybrid approaches using top-k recommendations metric. We use **wLM**, **tLM**, **CombLM**, **wLDA**, **tLDA**, **TT**, and **UTT** as the baseline methods.

Parameter settings. For keyword based methods we used $\lambda = 10$, as using different values does not have any impact on the performance. For topic modeling methods, one can estimate the optimal values of hyper-parameters α, β and λ by using Expectation Maximization (EM) method [22] or Gibbs sampling algorithm [23]. EM algorithm is susceptible to local maxima and computationally inefficient [12]. Consequently, Gibbs sampling algorithm is fit to use. In our experiments, for 100 topics z the hyper-parameters α, β and λ were set at 50/z, 0.01 and 0.1, respectively, by following values used in [14]. The number of topics z was fixed at 100 on the basis of human judgment of meaningful topics plus measured perplexity [24,25] on held out test dataset for different number of topics z from 20 to 200. For combination, we set $\xi = 0.15$.

Evaluation Measure. Our ultimate goal is to measure the effectiveness of suggesting top-ranked tags for a resource to a user. Thus, to fairly compare their performance, we employ the top-*k* recommendations performance measure. That is, each ranking algorithm needs to recommend the top *k* tags to a resource. This evaluation method is used for community recommendation using LDA by Chen et al [26], in which they ranked randomly withhold communities and recommended top *k* communities.

4.2 Results and Discussions

Topic Related Tags for Resources. We recommend tags with respect to specific kind of resources on the basis of topic layer. Table 1 illustrates 4 different topic related tags out of 100 by LM combined with LDA, discovered from the 1000th iteration of the particular Gibbs sampler run. Each topic shows top 10 tags that are most likely to be produced for topic related resources. The tags associated with each topic are quite intuitive and precise in the sense of conveying a semantic summary of a specific kind of resources. One can see that top ranked tags for different topics are quite informative. For example, in case of topic *Internet Security*, all tags are semantically related and show that resources will have some information about internet security issues. Similarly topics *Music*, *Semantic Web* and *Browser Extension* have tags that are real representatives of specific kind of resources. Our proposed approach discovers several other topics related to *folksonomy*, *graphics*, *data mining*, *web services*, *web tools*, *java*, *book marking*, *business*, *jobs* and also other topics that span the full range of areas encompassed in the dataset. The discovered tag results can be used to suggest meaningful tags for resources and to solve cold start problem by predicting tags, when a user wants to tag new resources to speed up the tagging process by suggesting several tags for each resource.

Top-k Recommendations. In Table 2, we show the performance of proposed approaches and baseline methods, which includes words based, tags based and combined methods. We can see that LM approaches perform better than others, the hybrid approaches is better than non-hybrid approaches except LM. The best average ranking

Table 1. An illustration of top 10 recommended tags for 4 topics(out of 100). Each tag is shown with its probability conditioned on that topic. Topic titles are assigned manually by us to represent the class of tags.

Topic "Internet Security"	Topic "Music"	Topic "Semantic Web"	Topic "Browsers Extension"
security 0.104911	music 0.139098	semanticweb 0.225512	firefox 0.187719
ittechnology 0.041783	audio 0.093745	rdf 0.103874	extension 0.097383
privacy 0.037503	mp3 0.062511	ontology 0.099498	browser 0.055331
hack 0.020918	media 0.040690	semantic 0.063911	mozilla 0.037030
firewall 0.017173	podcast 0.039406	semweb 0.039992	extensions 0.034304
hacking 0.011823	radio 0.029565	owl 0.034450	bookmarks 0.028853
proxy 0.010753	ipod 0.018013	ontologies 0.020740	greasemonkey 0.024570
safetysecurityprivacy 0.007543	podcasting 0.015018	semantics 0.016948	firefoxextension 0.016393
antivirus 0.007543	itunes 0.013307	sparql 0.014322	best 0.014446
password 0.007008	player 0.010739	semanticmarkup 0.006447	plugin 0.012110

accuracy (k = 2,4,6,8, and 10) of hybrid approach, wLM + tLDA is 65% that is 5% less than the best LM approach, wLM, 70%. We can see that better results can be obtained when keyword and topic layer based approaches are combined to build hybrid approaches. Hybrid approaches having fewer entities, such as wLM + tLDA, tLM + tLDA, perform better, while hybrid approaches modeling more entities, e.g. tLM + TT and tLM + UTT, perform worse than others. It shows that the performance can be increased when keyword and topic layer based methods for words or tags are combined, though LM as individual is still the best. It is assumed that words of resources generate tags of resources in TT approach, and words of resources simultaneously generate tags and users who tagged the resources in UTT approach. We can see that wLDA (55%) and tLDA (57%) perform better than both TT (52%) and UTT (47%), and TT performs better than UTT. It also shows that additional information used for tag recommendation results in poor performance for topic layer based approach, such as users, words and tags are modeled together in case of UTT, and words and tags are modeled together in case of TT. When tLM is combined with wLM, only 60% accuracy is obtained which is lower than that of the original accuracy obtained by tLM (68%) and wLM (70%). That means the hybridization is not useful when both approaches are keyword based ones in the hybrid.

Correlation between Resources. Hybrid approaches can be used for automatic correlation discovery between resources, including keyword and topic layer based approaches influence, simultaneously. Discovered correlations can be utilized to recommend resources to the users with similar interests. To illustrate how it can be used in this respect, the distance between resources i and j is defined as symmetric KL (sKL) divergence [27] between the topic distributions conditioned on each of the resource distribution as:

$$sKL(i,j) = \sum_{z}[\theta_{iz}\log\frac{\theta_{iz}}{\theta_{jz}} + \theta_{jz}\log\frac{\theta_{jz}}{\theta_{iz}}] \tag{21}$$

where θ_{iz} and θ_{jz} are the probability of topic z in resource i and resource j, respectively.

Table 2. Top-k recommendations performance in terms of accuracy by LM plus LDA

Approach	2	4	6	8	10	Average Accuracy
wLM	0.8249148	0.7649713	0.675038	0.633667	0.602264	0.700171
tLM	0.8550615	0.7373653	0.6684583	0.577326	0.600002	0.687643
wLM + tLDA	0.87460833	0.5661024	0.669767	0.6161768	0.567611	0.658853
tLM + tLDA	0.864880	0.5687551	0.669856	0.6127162	0.567574	0.656756
wLM + wLDA	0.8588170	0.7317167	0.657802	0.4472075	0.515749	0.642259
wLM + TT	0.7693678	0.6126987	0.622016	0.6695815	0.480619	0.630857
tLM + TT	0.7622995	0.6210024	0.61584	0.6688483	0.482262	0.63005
tLM + wLDA	0.8074751	0.7160438	0.638026	0.4335037	0.503258	0.619661
CombLM	0.740045	0.6575767	0.5449767	0.55638	0.537967	0.607389
wLM + UTT	0.7862674	0.61301507	0.575937	0.5876752	0.450426	0.602664
tLDA	0.7923222	0.4158538	0.610341	0.5590527	0.519596	0.579433
tLM + UTT	0.7586219	0.5275542	0.557271	0.5871157	0.434969	0.573104
wLDA	0.7068484	0.6338285	0.6252108	0.5582102	0.460180	0.556856
TT	0.50319819	0.4833695	0.558752	0.6289924	0.437467	0.522356
UTT	0.5102204	0.4654382	0.4878531	0.5367335	0.369267	0.473902

Table 3. Top 10 sKL based related resources with Resource "Macintosh"

Resource "Macintosh"	Description Words	Tags
http://desktop.google.com/mac	Google Desktop Download for Mac	mac 07system applications bar interface
http://www.google.com/mac.html	Google Pack	google mac software freeware
http://www.apple.com/downloads-/macosx/automator/	Apple - Downloads - Mac OS X - Automator Actions	apple mac macintosh news technology techapplemac
http://osx.iusethis.com/	iusethis mac software: New Releases	mac aggregator apple
http://www.mecheng.adelaide.edu.-au/ will/texstart/	What do I need for TeX on Mac OS X?	apple latex mac osx tex
http://www.opensourcemac.org/	Open-Source software for OS X applications directory freeware	mac opensource osx
http://www.delicious-monster.com	Delicious Library	digital apple tool software library macosx
http://www.wilber-loves-apple.org/	Wilber loves Apple.We bring the Gimp to the Mac	dmg download gimp macos
http://www.digital-web.com/articles/mac-screencast-capturing/	Digital Web Magazine Capture a Screen cast with a Mac how to capture a screen cast on mac	mac screencast
http://firefoxmac.furbism.com/	Firefox: Mac PPC Optimized Builds	apple browser firefox mac mozilla
http://bibdesk.sourceforge.net/	BibDesk JabRef for Mac OS X	mac bibtex osx

We calculated the dissimilarity between the resources by using Eq.21. The smaller dissimilarity value means the higher correlation between resources. Table 3 shows semantic-based correlation of resource *Macintosh* which is Google desktop download for Mac and tagged by *mac 07 system applications bar interface*. Here, it is obligatory to mention that top 10 resources related to resource *Macintosh* are not the necessary resources which are tagged by similar users, but rather the resources that tend to produce most tags or words for the same topics. Again the results are quite promising and realistic as most of the resources related to resource *Macintosh* are also topic related.

5 Conclusions

This study deals with the problem of tag recommendation using several hybrid and non-hybrid approaches. The approaches are proposed by combining keyword based (no-semantics) and topic layer (semantics) based approaches. In our experiments the performance difference between words and tags based approaches, e.g. tLDA and wLDA, is not very different. Although tLDA is a bit better than wLDA but we can say that both description words and tags can be a good choice for tagging resources. We find that combination of keyword and topic layer based approaches is significantly effective in many cases when there are fewer entities are modeled in topic model. The proposed approaches are simple, but the experiments show that they produced quite intuitive results. We also show that the performance decreases if the number of entities (e.g. words, tags and users) is simultaneously modeled in topic layer based approach. Moreover, through using our approaches, the correlations between the resources can be identified quite precisely.

Acknowledgements. This work is supported by NSFC (60873225, 60773191, 70771043), 863 Program (2007AA01Z403), NSF of Hubei (2009CDB298), Wuhan Chenguang Program (200950431171), Open Foundation of SKLSE (SKLSE20080718), Innovation Fund of HUST (Q2009021), Youth Fund of HBUE (XJ2009013), Humanities and Social Sciences Program of Hubei (2010Q094), Hong Kong RGC (CityU 117608).

References

1. Lipczak, M.: Tag recommendation for folksonomies oriented towards individual users. In: ECML PKDD Discovery Challenge, pp. 84–95 (2008)
2. Hsu, M., Chen, H.: A method to predict social annotations. In: CIKM, pp. 1375–1376 (2008)
3. Jäschke, R., Marinho, L.B., Hotho, A., Schmidt-Thieme, L., Stumme, G.: Tag recommendations in folksonomies. In: Kok, J.N., Koronacki, J., Lopez de Mantaras, R., Matwin, S., Mladenič, D., Skowron, A. (eds.) PKDD 2007. LNCS (LNAI), vol. 4702, pp. 506–514. Springer, Heidelberg (2007)
4. Mishne, G.: Autotag: a collaborative approach to automated tag assignment for weblog posts. In: WWW, pp. 953–954 (2006)
5. Hotho, A., Jäschke, R., Schmitz, C., Stumme, G.: Folkrank: A ranking algorithm for folksonomies. In: LWA, pp. 111–114 (2006)
6. Sood, S., Owsley, S., Hammond, K., Birnbaum, L.: Tagassist: Automatic tag suggestion for blog posts. In: ICWSM (2007)
7. Tatu, M., Srikanth, M., DSilva, T.: Tag recommendations using bookmark content. In: RSDC, pp. 96–107 (2008)

8. Zhang, N., Zhang, Y., Tang, J.: A tag recommendation system based on contents. In: RSDC (2008)
9. Chen, Z., Cao, J., Song, Y., Guo, J., Zhang, Y., Li, J.: Context-oriented web video tag recommendation. In: WWW (to appear, 2010)
10. Daud, A., Li, J., Zhou, L., Muhammad, F.: A generalized topic modeling approach for maven search. In: Li, Q., Feng, L., Pei, J., Wang, S.X., Zhou, X., Zhu, Q.-M. (eds.) APWeb/WAIM 2009. LNCS, vol. 5446, pp. 138–149. Springer, Heidelberg (2009)
11. Wei, X., Croft, W.B.: Lda-based document models for ad-hoc retrieval. In: SIGIR, pp. 178–185 (2006)
12. Blei, D.M., Ng, A.Y., Jordan, M.I.: Latent dirichlet allocation. In: NIPS, pp. 601–608 (2001)
13. Steyvers, M., Smyth, P., Rosen-Zvi, M., Griffiths, T.L.: Probabilistic author-topic models for information discovery. In: KDD, pp. 306–315 (2004)
14. Tang, J., Zhang, J., Yao, L., Li, J., Zhang, L., Su, Z.: Arnetminer: extraction and mining of academic social networks. In: KDD, pp. 990–998 (2008)
15. Bao, S., Xue, G., Wu, X., Yu, Y., Fei, B., Su, Z.: Optimizing web search using social annotations. In: WWW, pp. 501–510 (2007)
16. Halpin, H., Robu, V., Shepherd, H.: The complex dynamics of collaborative tagging. In: WWW, pp. 211–220 (2007)
17. Sigurbjörnsson, B., van Zwol, R.: Flickr tag recommendation based on collective knowledge. In: WWW, pp. 327–336 (2008)
18. Schmitz, C., Hotho, A., Jäschke, R., Stumme, G.: Mining association rules in folksonomies. In: IFCS, pp. 261–270 (2006)
19. Ruch, P., Baud, R.H., Geissbühler, A.: Evaluating and reducing the effect of data corruption when applying bag of words approaches to medical records. I. J. Medical Informatics 67(1-3), 75–83 (2002)
20. Zhai, C., Lafferty, J.D.: A study of smoothing methods for language models applied to ad hoc information retrieval. In: SIGIR, pp. 334–342 (2001)
21. Lesot, M.J., Mouillet, L., Bouchon-Meunier, B.: Fuzzy prototypes based on typicality degrees. In: Fuzzy Days, pp. 125–138 (2004)
22. Hofmann, T.: Probabilistic latent semantic analysis. In: UAI, pp. 289–296 (1999)
23. Griffiths, T., Steyvers, M.: Finding scientific topics. PNAS 101, 5228–5235 (2004)
24. Azzopardi, L., Girolami, M., van Rijsbergen, K.: Investigating the relationship between language model perplexity and ir precision-recall measures. In: SIGIR, pp. 369–370 (2003)
25. Daud, A., Li, J., Zhou, L., Muhammad, F.: Knowledge discovery through parametric directed probabilistic topic models. Journal of Frontiers of Computer Science in China (2009)
26. Chen, W., Chu, J.C., Luan, J., Bai, H., Wang, Y., Chang, E.Y.: Collaborative filtering for orkut communities: discovery of user latent behavior. In: WWW, pp. 681–690 (2009)
27. Rosen-Zvi, M., Griffiths, T.L., Steyvers, M., Smyth, P.: The author-topic model for authors and documents. In: UAI, pp. 487–494 (2004)
28. Jarvelin, K., Kekalainen, J.: Cumulated gain-based evaluation of IR techniques. ACM TOIS 4(20), 422–446 (2002)
29. Koren, Y.: Factorization meets the neighborhood: a multifaceted collaborative filtering model. In: KDD, pp. 426–434 (2008)
30. Yager, R.R.: On ordered weighted averaging aggregation operators in multicriteria decision-making. IEEE Trans. Syst. Man Cybern. 18(1), 183–190 (1988)

Rich Ontology Extraction and Wikipedia Expansion Using Language Resources

Christian Schönberg*, Helmuth Pree, and Burkhard Freitag

University of Passau, Department of Informatics and Mathematics
94030 Passau, Germany
{Christian.Schoenberg,Burkhard.Freitag}@uni-passau.de,
pree@fim.uni-passau.de

Abstract. Existing social collaboration projects contain a host of conceptual knowledge, but are often only sparsely structured and hardly machine-accessible. Using the well known Wikipedia as a showcase, we propose new and improved techniques for extracting ontology data from the wiki category structure. Applications like information extraction, data classification, or consistency checking require ontologies of very high quality and with a high number of relationships. We improve upon existing approaches by finding a host of additional relevant relationships between ontology classes, leveraging multi-lingual relations between categories and semantic relations between terms.

Keywords: Ontology extraction, Semantic web, Web ontology.

1 Introduction

Background knowledge and standardised vocabularies in the form of ontologies have become important factors in current knowledge management applications. Information extraction tasks make use of controlled vocabularies to increase precision and recall by focussing their efforts on known relevant terms [1], which is especially important if the source documents are of poor quality [2]. Classification of documents requires background knowledge about terms of interest when constructing feature vectors [3].

In general, it is difficult to obtain ontologies of sufficient quality and range for complex tasks. Wikis with a community large enough to act both normative and statistically self-correcting like Wikipedia have become a source for harvesting ontologies [4,5]. Knowledge that is implicitly modelled in a wiki is made explicit in the extracted ontology. Using the well known web ontology language OWL for representation, categories are mapped onto classes, articles onto objects, and various forms of references onto different relationships. Yet such wikis usually have a structure that is optimised for browsing, not for reasoning. They are also often incomplete in the sense that relevant relationships are missing in

* This work is partially funded by the German Research Foundation (Deutsche Forschungsgemeinschaft, DFG) under grant number FR 1021/7-2.

L. Chen et al. (Eds.): WAIM 2010, LNCS 6184, pp. 151–156, 2010.

their structure. In this paper, we present a new approach to improve ontology extraction from wikis by enriching the ontology structure in two dimensions, and by increasing its structural cohesion.

The rest of this paper is organised as follows: Section 2 describes the problem addressed in this paper, Sect. 3 describes our approach to ontology extraction and expansion from wikis, while Sect. 4 shows evaluation results for this approach. Section 5 discusses related work, and Sect. 6 concludes this paper.

2 Problem Statement

As obtaining large ontologies of high quality is an expensive task, either in terms of work or in terms of money, one approach is to generate such ontologies automatically. But even ontologies generated from human-engineered sources like wikis lack the quality of human-created ontologies like WordNet [6] or Open-GALEN [7]. In order to reduce the gap between generated and manually created ontologies, we propose an approach to enhance ontologies generated from wikis.

A wiki $W_L = (C_L, s_L, r_L, A_L, m_L, n_L)$ in a language L, i.e., the English Wikipedia, consists of a set of categories C_L, a sub-category relation $s_L : C_L \times C_L$ that defines a graph of sub-category relationships on C_L, a reference relation $r_L : C_L \times C_L$ that defines a graph of non-sub-category relationships on C_L, a set of articles A_L, a category-membership relation $m_L : A_L \times C_L$ that defines to which categories any given article belongs, and a naming function n_L that assigns a unique name to each category $c \in C_L$ and to each article $a \in A_L$. All articles consist solely of a descriptive text, i.e., their wiki content. The graph defined by s_L and r_L is also called the *category graph*. A complete wiki $W = (\mathcal{L}, \mathcal{W}_\mathcal{L}, tc, ta)$, e.g., Wikipedia, consists of a set of languages $\mathcal{L}$, a set of language-dependent wiki instances $\mathcal{W}_\mathcal{L} = \{W_L \mid L \in \mathcal{L}\}$, and two translation relations $tc : C_{L1} \times C_{L2}$ and $ta : A_{L1} \times A_{L2}$, where $L1 \neq L2 \in \mathcal{L}$, that define any known translations for both categories and articles. Note that category and article redirects have been omitted here for reasons of clarity.

Recall that in OWL an ontology $\mathbf{O} = (\mathbf{C}, \mathbf{subClassOf}, \mathbf{R}, \mathbf{I}, \mathbf{type}, \mathbf{P})$ consists of a set of classes $\mathbf{C}$, a relation $\mathbf{subClassOf} : \mathbf{C} \times \mathbf{C}$ that defines sub-class relationships on $\mathbf{C}$, a set of relations $\mathbf{R}$ on classes that define relationships between two classes that are not sub-class relationships, a set of individuals $\mathbf{I}$, a class-membership relation $\mathbf{type} : \mathbf{I} \times \mathbf{C}$ that defines the classes any individual belongs to, and a set of property relations $\mathbf{P}$ on individuals, where each $\mathbf{p} \in \mathbf{P}$ defines a property for an individual, e.g., $\mathbf{P} \ni \mathbf{birthdate} : \mathbf{I} \times \mathit{date}$.

The simplest way to generate an ontology $\mathbf{O}$ from a wiki W is to select a language L and to define a mapping ϵ_L from C_L onto $\mathbf{C}$, from A_L onto $\mathbf{I}$, from r_L onto $\mathbf{R}$, from s_L onto $\mathbf{subClassOf}$, from m_L onto $\mathbf{type}$, and from a set of attributes (e.g., names or birth dates) extracted from A_L onto $\mathbf{P}$. L is called *primary language* and determines the language of the names for classes and individuals. In the context of this paper, all names are unique identifiers. One of the contributions of this paper is a refinement of the two mappings from s_L and from r_L, which do not seem to have been considered before.

The simple mapping process described above can result in a highly fragmented ontology. Rather than relying on this "raw" ontology, one might strive for an ontology with missing relationships added and redundant classes eliminated. We propose to obtain this desired ontology by taking the following steps:

1. extract the category graph from the wiki,
2. expand the graph with additional references,
3. remove superfluous categories,
4. list articles and extract attributes (this is beyond the scope of this paper),
5. map the wiki structure to an ontology structure.

3 Extraction Approach

To test our approach we selected the well known online resource Wikipedia, using the complete sets of categories C_L and articles A_L for eleven languages: $\mathcal{L}$ = {Chinese, Dutch, English, French, German, Italian, Japanese, Russian, Serbian, Spanish, Ukrainian}, with English as the primary language. With the help of language experts, a set of keywords was created for each language, such as indicators used by Wikipedia to separate category names from article names (e.g., "Category:" in English).

3.1 Extraction of Category Graph

Using the keywords provided by language experts, the categories along with their sub-categories, references, and translations are detected in the Wikipedia data for all languages in $\mathcal{L}$, thereby constructing a category graph for each language.

3.2 Expansion and Optimisation of Category Graph

With English as the primary language for the ontology generation, the category graph of the other ten languages is analysed to find similarities and additional relationships.

In the first step we look at the structure of different language versions and try to infer hidden structural relationships such as sub-category relationships. Let c and d be two categories in the English category graph for which no structural relationship is known. Let t_c and t_d be their translations into some other language L. If t_c and t_d have a relationship in L we infer a new relationship of the same kind between c and d. Runtime performance for this process is enhanced by maintaining an indexed lookup table for the translations in main memory, one language at a time.

The second enrichment step is to regard semantic similarities between category names. To this end, a lexical database of the primary language is required (e.g., WordNet [6] for English). For each pair of categories, a score is calculated. If it exceeds a predefined threshold, a new reference between the two categories is created. The score value $s(n_1, n_2)$ for two category names n_1 and n_2 can be calculated based on the frequency of terms appearing in both names or based on a known relationship between terms from both category names, derived from the lexical database:

$$s(n_1, n_2) = \frac{\sum_{i=1}^{l(n_1)} s_t(n_1[i], n_2)}{\frac{l(n_1)+l(n_2)}{2}}$$

where $n[i]$ denotes the ith term occurring in name n, and $l(n)$ denotes the number of terms in name n. The score $s_t(t, n)$ of a term t w.r.t. a name n, and the semantic distance $s_d(t_1, t_2)$ between two terms are defined as:

$$s_t(t, n) = \sum_{i=1}^{l(n)} s_d(t, n[i]) \qquad s_d(t_1, t_2) = \begin{cases} 0.8 \text{ if } t_1 = t_2 \\ 0.5 \text{ if } t_1 \text{ related to } t_2 \\ 0.0 \text{ otherwise} \end{cases}$$

The threshold used to filter potential category relationships based on their score varies between different languages. To enhance runtime performance, the process employs an inverted index on all occurring terms. It is used to find pairs of category names with similar terms, so that a name does not have to be checked against all other names.

Categories whose purpose is simply to provide a more convenient way to display the information contained within are removed by merging them with a more general category that contains the same information. The two most prominent kinds of such categories are *order-by* categories and *list* categories. They are detected by means of keywords provided by language experts.

3.3 Creating the Ontology

After the category graph of W_{en} has been expanded with additional references and pruned of superfluous categories, W_{en} is mapped onto an ontology structure. Both sub-category and sub-class relationships are often used to define the structure of the category graph or the ontology graph, respectively. While the sub-category relationship is modelled as a sub-class relationship, it could also be expressed as the *narrower-than* relationship of the SKOS[1] vocabulary. The semantics of the sub-category relationship are broad enough to allow for both interpretations. The relationships introduced by the second enrichment step are modelled as SKOS *related* relationships.

4 Evaluation

In addition to using English as the primary language, the approach is shown to be transferrable to other languages by providing evaluation results for an alternative setting where German is selected as the primary language. German is the language of the second largest Wikipedia in terms of articles. Table 1 shows the number of relationships that were added to the original category graph in the two enrichment steps (*Exp1* and *Exp2*) and the number of categories and relationships that were removed in the third step (*Merge*) for both languages.

[1] SKOS: http://www.w3.org/2004/02/skos, last visited 04/2010

Table 1. Changes in category and relationship numbers for English and German

	Exp1 (en)	*Exp1* (de)	*Exp2* (en)	*Exp2* (de)	*Merge* (en)	*Merge* (de)
Categories	0	0	0	0	−22,702	−1,278
Relationships	+146,912	+59,514	+144,318	+3,723	−92,773	−55,803

The results show that the expansion based on language versions already provides substantial improvements over the original category references: an increase of 14 % in 178 *s* for the English version, and an increase of 46 % in 111 *s* for the German version, respectively. The latter rather large increment can be explained by the fact that *Exp1* for German could make use of the English Wikipedia, which is by far the largest language version and thus provides the highest absolute number of relationships to learn from.

The expansion based on lexical databases on the other hand requires much more time for the English version, but results in a similarly large addition of new category references in addition to the first step: an increase of 14 % in 15 *hrs*. For the German version, both the expansion time and the resulting number of references are considerably lower: an increase of 3 % in 8 *s*. The cause for this discrepancy is the lower quality and size of the German lexical database used[2]. However, the low results for *Exp2* are offset by the high results for *Exp1*. The merging step took 68 *s* and 3 *s* for English and German, respectively.

As there exists no predefined "complete" version of the ontology, no absolute recall value can be computed. However, a relative increase of 28 % and 49 % for English and German, respectively, show the effectiveness of the method. The good results for different primary languages also indicate the generality of the proposed methods.

For a qualitative evaluation, a number of independent testers were asked to rate the validity of the newly generated relationships in different random samples of 200 entries each. The resulting precision values lie between 96 % and 99 %, which is an indication of the general high quality of our results. Values still closer to 100 % are rarely encountered in ontology evaluation, because different people usually have different opinions on how an ontology should be modelled to represent the actual world more closely. Few factual errors in the Wikipedia content which slightly affect the precision values for the first expansion step are outside of our control and are hopefully corrected by the community.

5 Related Work

[5] propose extending the MediaWiki framework by adding semantic information to wiki pages during the process of authoring. Links and information carrying text fragments are enriched by annotating semantic data.

In [8] a knowledge base derived from Wikipedia is presented. Articles that use infobox templates are treated as individuals, and attributes contained in the

[2] OpenThesaurus: http://www.openthesaurus.de, last visited 04/2010

template are extracted as properties. Additional relationships between entities are detected by using different types of indicators like similarity of attributes, Google query results, and WordNet relationships.

YAGO uses an extended RDFS OWL model consisting of individuals, classes and properties [4]. It uses Wikipedia and WordNet as sources, modelling categories and WordNet synsets as classes, articles as individuals, and category and synset relationships as class relationships. Properties are derived from articles.

6 Conclusion

In this paper, we have presented an approach to ontology extraction from wikis that improves upon existing methods by enriching the ontology structure with relationships inferred from different language versions and from semantic similarities between OWL classes. By removing classes with no inherent meaning of their own, the reduced ontology provides a more concise knowledge base. An increase of almost 30 % more relevant relationships for English and just under 50 % for German has been achieved during an evaluation using Wikipedia in eleven languages – including English, German, and Chinese – and with two different primary languages. The evaluation shows that the approach is effective, of sufficient generality, and can indeed deliver high quality results.

References

1. Nédellec, C., Nazarenko, A.: Ontology and Information Extraction: a necessary symbiosis. In: Buitelaar, P., Philipp Cimiano, B.M. (eds.) Ontology Design and Population, pp. 155–170. IOS Press, Amsterdam (2005)
2. Marko, K., Schulz, S., Hahn, U.: MorphoSaurus - Design and evaluation of an interlingua-based, cross-language document retrieval engine for the medical domain. Methods of Information in Medicine 44(4), 537–545 (2005)
3. Chang, Y.: Automatically constructing a domain ontology for document classification. In: Int. Conf. on Machine Learning and Cybernetics, vol. 4 (2007)
4. Suchanek, F.M., Kasneci, G., Weikum, G.: Yago: a core of semantic knowledge. In: WWW 2007: Proc. of the 16th intern. conference on World Wide Web, pp. 697–706. ACM Press, New York (2007)
5. Krötzsch, M., Vrandecic, D., Völkel, M., Haller, H., Studer, R.: Semantic Wikipedia. Journal of Web Semantics 5, 251–261 (2007)
6. Miller, G.A.: WordNet – a lexical database for the English language (2006), `http://wordnet.princeton.edu/`
7. Rogers, J.E., Roberts, A., Solomon, W.D., van der Haring, E., Wroe, C.J., Zanstra, P.E., Rector, A.L.: GALEN ten years on: Tasks and supporting tools. In: Proceedings of MEDINFO 2001, pp. 256–260. IOS Press, Amsterdam (2001)
8. Wu, F., Weld, D.S.: Automatically refining the Wikipedia infobox ontology. In: WWW 2008: Proceeding of the 17th international conference on World Wide Web, pp. 635–644. ACM, New York (2008)

Fine-Grained Cloud DB Damage Examination Based on Bloom Filters

Min Zhang, Ke Cai, and Dengguo Feng

National Key Laboratory of Information Security,
Institute of Software, Chinese Academy of Sciences
Beijing, P.R. China
{mzhang,caik,feng}@is.iscas.ac.cn

Abstract. More and more cloud database services have emerged recently which is economical, convenient and highly scalable. However the security concerns in these services are more prominent than ever before. The users should not rely on the Cloud Service Providers(CSPs) only to protect the integrity and retrievability of their cloud databases. We argue that it is not enough for the cloud db owners to know the existence of damage, but more importantly, they should be able to locate the damages precisely for the recovery afterwards. In this paper we provide fine-grained cloud DB damage examination methods by checking the results of sampling queries. The examination process support element/tuple level damage identification and is cost-efficient based on bloom filters. The process is also server transparent and imperceptible which prevent the CSP be inconsistent to different users.

1 Introduction

With the rapid development of cloud computing technology, more and more cloud database services have emerged such as Amazon's SimpleDB [1] and Relational Database Service (RDS)[2], Google's Datastore [3], Microsoft's SQL Azure [4] etc. Despite the great difference in the data model, system architecture and query interface, they all promise to provide users with reliable, economical and highly scalable database services due to the underlying cloud computing platforms. Therefore users are entitled to database services without the purchase and maintenance of DBMS software.

However, the security and privacy concerns in these services are more prominent than ever before, especially when the databases are critical to the users. Several recent cloud computing platform security incidents occurred in Amazon and Microsoft remind the users that, due to the variety of risks such as the attacks from the hackers, the failure of the cloud computing platform, and even the closedowns of the Cloud Service Providers(CSPs), the probability of data loss and damage of cloud DB is quite significant. Therefore the users should not rely on the CSPs only to protect the integrity and retrievability of their cloud databases.

L. Chen et al. (Eds.): WAIM 2010, LNCS 6184, pp. 157–168, 2010.

The integrity protection problem of cloud DB is similar to that of the Outsourced Database (ODB) which was of considerably concern to many researchers. Currently many ODB verification methods have been proposed which have a different verification goal to that of the cloud DB. Many of them [5][6][7][8][9][10][12][13] are designed to support the ODB users to verify the correctness, completeness and freshness of their queries. They only provide users with the verification result as "yes" or "no", while the type of damages and their positions are not concerned. Some works[11],[7] delicate to provide owners with the probability analysis of ODB damages, either by checking the number of fake tuples inserted into the ODB [11] or by inserting some challenge queries whose answers are already known into a sequence of real queries [7]. They help the user/owner to understand ODB's overall damage degree, but still cannot precisely locate them. The closest work to our goal is [14] which supports ODB damage identification by embedding fragile watermark into the ODB. But their result is a superset of the real damages. Therefore we would argue that thus far the fine-grained ODB verification did not receive adequate attention yet, and it is not enough to only detect the existence of damages of cloud DBs, but more importantly, the user should be able to locate damages, such as identifying the lost tuples, damaged ones and superfluous ones etc, which can afterwards indicate the cloud DB recovery. Fig 1 shows one such scenario.

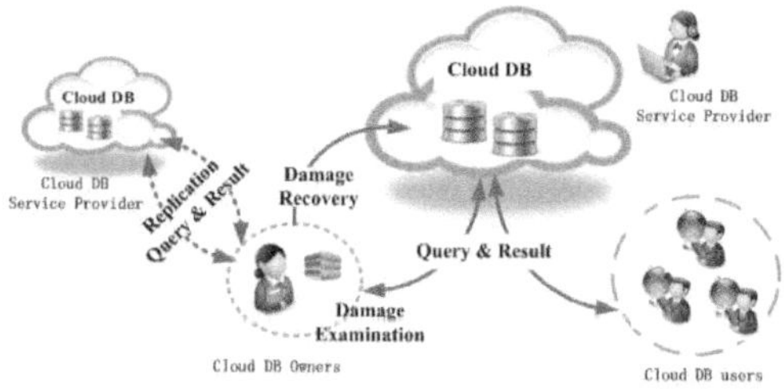

Fig. 1. Cloud DB Damage Examine and Recovery Scenario. User back up DB into multiple places, perform cloud DB damage examination constantly and recover from any damage as soon as it can be located.

To address this problem, in this paper we provide fine-grained cloud DB damage examination methods which support users to identify element/tuple level damages. In our opinion, to be efficient, the verification process should be performed by its owner instead of each user. As Fig 1 shows, occasionally the users send sampling queries to the CSP which covers a part of the DB, and based on the returned results and the verification objects stored in the user's side, the users can precisely identify the lost tuples, superfluous tuples and the damaged tuples/elements. The process is cost-efficient for the verification object is designed based on an array of bloom filters which is highly space and time efficient. Moreover, since the sampling queries are common SQL commands which is indistinguishable from the common user queries, the damage examination process is server transparent and imperceptible, which prevent the CSP be inconsistent to different users.

The rest of the paper is arranged as follows: Section 2 presents the background of bloom filter, Section 3 describes the basic method which supports the random sampling query and presents its analysis; Section 4 provides the description and analysis of the improved method which supports the range sampling query; Section 5 is the experiment analysis, and finally section 6 concludes the paper.

2 Background of Bloom Filter

The Bloom Filter [17] is a special structure used to quickly test whether one element belongs to a set. Under given error ratio, Bloom Filter enables the great saving in storage space at the price of small amount of errors. Since Bloom Filter was first presented by Burton Bloom in the 70's, it has been widely accepted in the spelling checking, web caching, network routing and database system. It is designed with l individual hash functions $h_1, h_2, ...h_l$, each hash function $h_i : \{0,1\}^* \rightarrow [1,m]$ maps a bit array of any length onto an integer between 1 and m. The Bloom Filter of set $S = \{s_1, s_2, ..., s_n\}$ is a m-bit binary array, whose initial values are all set 0s. For each element s set the position in BF represented by $h_1(s), h_2(s), ..., h_l(s)$ as 1. If a position has been set 1 by different hash functions, then only the first set works, the latter operation has no effect at all. To determine if element s belongs to set S, just applies it with the l hash functions. If in the BF all the positions stand by $h_i(s)(1 \leq i \leq l)$ are set 1, then it is regarded as the member of S, otherwise the answer is no.

A false hit occurs when a Bloom filter positively confirms the membership of an element while this element actually does not belong to this set. The false positive rate is $(1 - e^{\frac{-nl}{m}})^l$. Therefore, suppose there are n members in the set, and the maximum error rate is ε, then the length of array m should be at least $nlog_2\frac{1}{\varepsilon}$. the minimum number of hash function is $l = \frac{m}{n}ln2$.

3 Basic Method

The most primitive method to support element-level verification is to keep the original database or its variation: a hash value database of the original elements. But clearly both the storage cost and the verification requirement (DBMS) are unacceptable to the owner. In this section we provide the method based on the bloom filter, which is storage and verification efficient.

Unique Tuple IDs. To identify damage precisely, we assume each tuple in able T has an unique ID, which is continuous from 1 to N. Without the loss of generality, the ID attribute is also mentioned as A_1. We may interchangeably use the symbol $t_i.ID$ or $t_i.A_1$ to denote the ID of tuple t_i . The modification of ID is regarded as the deletion of the old tuple together with an insertion of the new tuple. Below are the major notations used in the later sections.

Table 1. Notations

Notation	*Explanation*
m	Total number of attributes in the relation
N	Total number of tuples in the relation
l	Number of individual hash functions of any bloom filter
w	Size of the bloom filter(Length of the bit array)
$Q(T)$	Sampling query Q on table T
T^o, T^s	The original table T and the real table T in the server
$Q^o/Q(T^o)$	Expected result set of query Q
$Q^s/Q(T^s)$	Real returned result set within the range of query Q
$INCR(Q)$	Incorrect element/tuple set within the range of query Q
$LOST(Q)$	Lost tuple ID set within the range of query Q
$SUP(Q)$	Superfluous tuple ID set within the range of query Q

3.1 Initialization

To support element-level verification, we apply m BFs($BF_1, ..., BF_m$) which are defined as follows:

- BF_1 records the set of hash values of all tuples in T which is denoted as: $WS_1 = \{Word(t) \mid t \in T\}$. Here, the mapping word $Word(t)$ of each tuple t is defined by the following formula:

$$WS_1 = Word(t) = H(t.A_1||t.A_2||...||t.A_m) \qquad (1)$$

  where $H(.)$ is a cryptographic hash function such as SHA-1, $||$ denotes word concatenation;
- $BF_i(2 \leq i \leq m)$ records all the elements in attribute $A_i(2 \leq i \leq m)$. Members in BF_i are described by set $WS_i = \{Word(t,i) \mid t \in T\}$, where

$$WS_i = Word(t,i) = t.A_i||t.tid \qquad (2)$$

Note. The generation of all BFs are similar: Let $h_1, h_2, ..., h_l$ be l individual hash functions, $BF_1, BF_2, ..., BF_m$ be m empty bloom filters. Then for each $BF_i(1 \leq i \leq m)$, insert all members in set WS_i into BF_i as Section 2 describes. That is, for each element x in set WS_i, computer $h_1(x), h_2(x), ..., h_l(x)$ and set the corresponding bits in BF_i as '1'. While in the tuple-level verification, only BF_1 is needed. Fig 2 illustrates the generation of 4 bloom filters for Table $TAB(ID, A_2, A_3, A_4)$.

3.2 Damage Examination

The damage examination process involves the following steps:

1. *Random Sampling Queries Generation.* Prepare a set of sampling queries $QSET = \{Q_1, Q_2, ..., Q_n\}$ whose results cover the whole table T, that is:

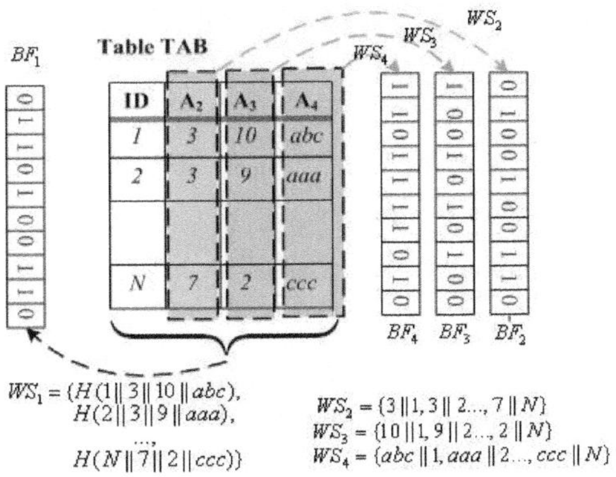

Fig. 2. Bloom Filters Initialization of table TAB

$Q_1(T) \cup Q_2(T) \cup ..., Q_n(T) = T_o \cup T_s$. Queries covering T_o indicate the lost tuples while that covering T_s help to find out the additional tuples. Each random sampling query requests for x randomly chosen tuples:

$$Q = \sigma_C(T); \quad C : A_1 \in \ SID, \ here \ SID = \{ID_1, ID_2, ...ID_x\}$$

For instance, below are two random sampling queries on table TAB:
Q1: SELECT * FROM TAB WHERE ID in (4,7,9);
Q2: SELECT * FROM TAB WHERE ID < 5 ;

2. *Random Sampling Query Processing.* For each random sampling query $Q \in QSET$ (whose returned answer from CSP is denoted as $Q(T^s)$ or Q^s) perform the following steps:
   - *Expected Tuple ID Calculation.* Apparently, the expected Tuple ID set (denoted as $Q^o.ID$) is a subset of the set $\{ID_1, ID_2, ...ID_x\}$, which includes only the tuples whose values are between 1 and N. That is: $Q^o.ID = \{ID_1, ID_2, ...ID_x\} \cap \{1, 2, ...N\}$
   - *Incorrect Tuples Identification.* For tuple level verification, a returned tuple $t \in Q^s$ is regarded as an incorrect one if $Word(t)$ is not a member of BF_1, that is: $INCR(Q) = \{t.ID|Word(t) \notin BF_1\}$, While in the element level verification, tuple t is regarded as an incorrect one with one more condition: if at least one of its $m-1$ elements is incorrect, that is: $INCR(Q) = \{t.ID|Word(t) \notin BF_1 \ OR \ \exists i \in [2, m], Word(t, i) \notin BF_i\}$.
   - *Lost and Superfluous Tuples Identification.* According to the definition, all lost and superfluous tuples within Q's scope can be identified by the following formula: $LOST(Q) = Q^o.ID - Q^s.ID$, $SUP(Q) = (SID - Q^o.ID) \cap Q^s.ID$
3. *Final Results Generation.*Given the above answers, the total lost tuples, incorrect tuples, and superfluous tuples can be achieved by the union of those in

each query's scope: $LOST = \bigcup_{Q \in QSET} LOST(Q)$, $SUP = \bigcup_{Q \in QSET} SUP(Q)$, $INCR = \bigcup_{Q \in QSET} INCR(Q)$.

3.3 Security Analysis

Since the bloom filter has certain possibility of false positive, the following Lemma describes the error bound of the basic method.

Lemma 1. *Given the random sampling query set $QSET = \{Q_1, Q_2, ..., Q_n\}$ which covers table T, The false alarm rate of $INCR$, $LOST$, and SUP are all 0; The hit rate of $LOST$, SUP, and $INCR$ are respectively* 100%, 100% *and P, which values $P = 1 - P_{Err}$ in tuple-level verification and $P = 1 - (P_{Err})^x$ in element-level verification. Here $P_{Err} = (1 - e^{\frac{-Nl}{w}})^l$ is the false positive rate of a bloom filter, x is the average number of non-ID attributes which are modified.*

Proof. In the basic method, the calculation of expected answer and $LOST(Q)$ and $SUP(Q)$ are all in strict accordance with the definition, none of bloom filter is involved whose false positive rate has no effect to them, thus for any query Q, its hit rates of $LOST(Q)$ and $SUP(Q)$ are 100% and the false alarm rates of $LOST(Q)$ and $SUP(Q)$ are all 0. Since $QSET$ covers T, this result is also applicable to that of the whole query set: $LOST$ and SUP.

The problem happens when $INCR(Q)$ is generated based on the bloom filters. Due to the false positive ratio, an non-member may be regarded as a member of the BF, which in the damage examination process means that an incorrect tuple/element is wrongly regarded as a correct one. In the tuple level identification, according to the definition, an incorrect tuple t can be regarded as a correct one if and only if $Word(t)$ is wrongly regarded as the member of BF_1, whose possibility is P_{Err}. Thus the hit rate of incorrect tuple identification is $1 - P_{Err}$. In the element level identification, according to the definition, an incorrect element $t.A_i$ can be regarded as a correct one if and only if $Word(t)$ is wrongly regarded as the member of BF_1, and at the same time, for each modified attributeA_i that $Word(t, i)$ is wrongly regarded as the member of BF_i, they are independent with each other, thus the possibility is P^x_{Err}, In this situation, the hit rate of any query $INCR(Q)$ is $P = 1 - (P_{Err})^x$. Since each query has the same hit rate, the hit rate of total table $INCR$ is the same as that of all sampling queries.

4 Improved Method

One problem of the basic method is that the query condition is on the ID attribute only, which is different for most users' queries and may be identified by the CSP. In this section we propose an improved method which use range queries whose conditions are on common attributes instead of the attribute ID. Range sampling query is difficult to be distinguished from common user's requests.

4.1 Initialization

Its initialization process includes two major steps.

1. Table Mapping Function Generation. For table $T's$ each sortable Non-ID attribute $A_i(2 \leq i \leq m)$, the owner evenly maps part of its domain into a discrete value by a mapping function $MapValue_i$:

$$MapValue_i : Dom(A_i) \rightarrow V$$

Given the mapping functions on all attributes, Table T can be mapped into T^M whose elements satisfies that, for each $1 \leq i \leq N$ and $2 \leq j \leq m$, $T^M(i,j) = MapValue_i(T(i,j))$. Apparently T^M has the same schema and scale with T.

2. Bloom Filter Initialization. In addition to the bloom filters for table T, bloom filters for mapped table T_M are built also to support the range query. The process is described as follows:

- BF_1 is filled with elements in WS_1: $WS_1 = \{Word(t) \mid t \in T\}$.
- Each $BF_i(2 \leq i \leq m)$ is filled with elements in WS_i which are defined as: $WS_i = \{(t.A_i||t.tid) \mid t \in T\}$.
- Each $BF_{m-1+i}(2 \leq i \leq m)$ is filled with elements in WS_{m-1+i} which are defined as: $WS_{m-1+i} = \{(MapValue_i(t.A_i)||t.tid) \mid t \in T\}$.

Considering the previous example table TAB. Suppose the MapValue functions are defined as follows:

$$MapValue_2(x) = MapValue_3(x) = MapValue_4(x) \triangleq H(x)(mod\ 10)$$

Then the BFs are constructed as the following figure 3 shows.

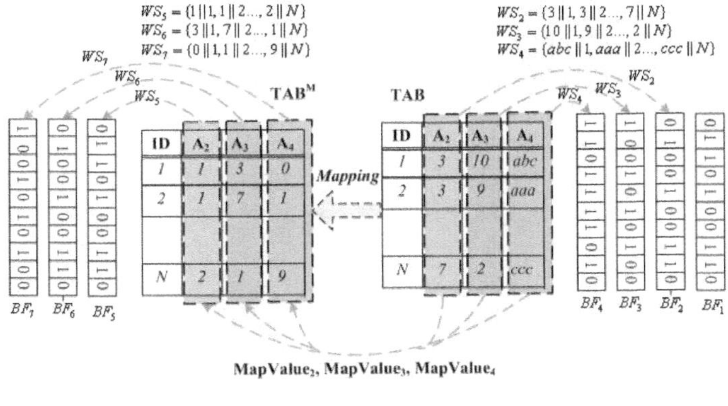

Fig. 3. Bloom Filters Initialization of table TAB

4.2 Damage Examination

The damage examination process involves the following steps:

1. *Range Sampling Queries Generation.* Prepare a set of sampling queries $QSET = \{Q_1, Q_2, ..., Q_n\}$ whose results cover the whole table T, The verifier prepares the range sampling query Q for the table T, which is equivalent to a query Q on $T's$ mapped table T^M:

$$Q = (\sigma_{P_1\ AND...\ AND\ P_x}(T));$$

where $P_j(1 \leq j \leq x)$ are conditions like: $MapValue_{kj}(A_{kj}) = v_j, (2 \leq k_j \leq m, v_j \in V)$. For instance, below are random sampling query on table TAB and its equivalent query on table TAB^M:
Q3: SELECT ID FROM TAB WHERE $MapValue(A_2) = 3$ AND $MapValue(A_3) = 4$ AND $MapValue(A_4) = 1$;
Q4: SELECT ID FROM TAB^M WHERE $A_2 = 3$ AND $A_3 = 4$ AND $A_4 = 1$;

2. *Range Sampling Query Processing.* For each random sampling query $Q \in QSET$, perform the following steps:
   - *Expected Answer Calculation.* According to the definition, $Q(T) = mapQ(T^M)$. If tuple t is an expected tuple of query Q, then for each selection attribute $A_{kj}(1 \leq j \leq x)$, it should satisfy that: $MapValue_{kj}(t.A_{kj} = v_j)$ and $Word(t, k_j)$ is a member of BF_{m-1+kj}. Thus to find out all such tuples, the verifier can transverse all tuples by their unique IDs(id from 1 to N) to see if id satisfies that:

$$(v_1||id \in BF_{m-1+k1})\ AND\ ...\ AND\ (v_x||id \in BF_{m-1+kx})\ is\ TRUE$$

     All qualified tuple IDs are added into the set EID.
   - *Lost and Superfluous Tuples Identification.* According to the definition, the verifier can generate the set $LOST(Q) = EID - Q(T^s)$, $SUP(Q) = Q(T^s) - \{1, .., N\}$.
   - *Incorrect and Correct Tuples Identification.* All returned tuples except for the superfluous ones are either correct or incorrect ones. The incorrect tuple set identification is the same as the basic method, that is, for tuple level verification, tuple $t \in Q^s$ is regarded as an incorrect one if $INCR(Q) = \{t.ID|Word(t) \notin BF_1\}$, While in the element level verification, it is defined as: $INCR(Q) = \{t.ID|Word(t) \notin BF_1\ OR\ \exists i \in [2, m], Word(t, i) \notin BF_i\}$. Otherwise it is a correct tuple, put into set CR.
3. *Final Results Generation.*Given the above answers, the total incorrect tuples and superfluous tuples can be achieved by the union of those in each query's scope: $SUP = \bigcup_{Q \in QSET} SUP(Q)$, $INCR = \bigcup_{Q \in QSET} INCR(Q)$, the lost tuples are achieved similarly: $LOST = \bigcup_{Q \in QSET} LOST(Q)$.

4.3 Security Analysis

The error bound of the improved method is described by the following Lemma.

Lemma 2. *Given the range sampling query set* $QSET = \{Q_1, Q_2, ..., Q_n\}$ *which covers table* T*, The false alarm rates of* $INCR$*,* $LOST$*, and* SUP *are respective 0,* P_{Err}*, and 0; All lost and superfluous tuples in* T^s *can be found in* $LOST$*, and* SUP*, while the hit rate of an incorrect tuple/element* $INCR$ *is same as in the basic method. Here* $P_{Err} = (1 - e^{\frac{-Nl}{w}})^l$ *is the false positive rate of a bloom filter.*

Proof. Unlike in the basic method, in the improved method the false alarm rate of $LOST(Q)$ is not 0. Due to the false positive rate of bloom filters, in the step of "Expected Answer Calculation", it is possible that one tuple ID is wrongly included in EID; thus $EID \neq Q^o$, and more precisely, $EID \subseteq Q^o$. Among all k_x selection criteria attributes, at least one attribute value A_i is wrongly regarded as a member in the bloom filter BF_{m-1+i} whose false negative rate is P_{Err}.

The computation of the hit rate of $INCR(Q)$ is rather complex due to the co-existence of three possible situations(Suppose tuple t is modified into t' by attackers):(1)$t \in Q$, but the at least one selection criteria attribute's value is modified which causes t' does not satisfies the selection criteria, that is: $t' \notin Q^s$;(2)on the contrary, $t \notin Q$, but $t' \in Q^s$; and (3) both $t \in Q$ and $t' \in Q^s$, but t' is not identified for the false positive rate of BF. Fortunately the hit rate of whole table $INCR$ is not that complex. Since $QSET$ covers T, any tuple in T will be returned in one query q: $q \in QSET$, the situation (1) and (2) will not effect the $INCR$. Only situation (3) matters. Similar to that in the basic method, due to false positive ratio of bloom filters, an incorrect tuple/element may be wrongly regarded as correct under certain possibility P. And for the same reason that $QSET$ covers T, all lost and superfluous tuples can be found in $LOST$ and SUP.

5 Experiment Evaluation

5.1 Experiment Setup

This section presents our experimental evaluation. In the experiment, we have implemented both the basic method and the improved method, and in each method we have tested the tuple level verification and element level verification.

We use a synthetic database that consists of one table with 100, 000 tuples. The experiment table contains one unique ID attribute (A1) and several string attributes which ranges from 50 byte to 500 bytes long. To test the error rate, We also build a set of error samples for the target table, which randomly modify, delete and insert specific percentage of tuples in it. The basic execution environment of the experiment is that: we build the experiment on a PC of Intel Core 2 Duo CPU E8400 with 1G Ram.

5.2 Performance

We first evaluate the storage cost of these two methods. Figure 4 shows that they both are linear to the size of the table, while the improved method is about 70% higher than that of the basic method. We also present the size of the original table and the hashed table (which is composed of the hash values of the original table)as the comparison. Figure 4 also shows that due to the characteristic of the bloom filter, both methods can greatly reduce the storage cost for about two orders of magnitude. In this experiment we choose the propitiate parameters which has the hit rate of 99.982%. Under this situation, the storage cost of the basic method and the improved method is only about 2% and 3.5% of the the original size. In fact the compression ratio can be higher when the error rate requirement can be relaxed.

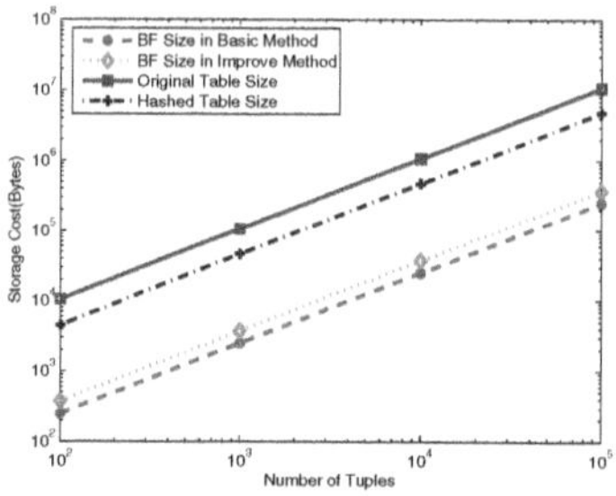

Fig. 4. Storage Cost

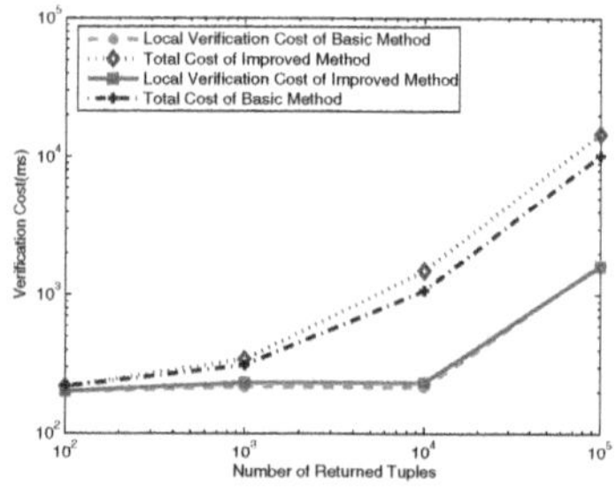

Fig. 5. Verification Cost

Figure 5 illustrates the verification time cost of both methods. For each method we measured two type of cost: the local verification time which records the processing time when the query result is received at the client's side, and the total cost which includes both the verification time and other cost such as the BF preparation time and the communication cost. As figure 5 shows, the verification cost (both the local cost and the total cost) of the improved method is only slightly higher than that of the basic method.

5.3 Error Rate and Parameter Selection

The existence of BF's false positive rate results in that the hit rate of the incorrect tuples is not 100%. Given the number of tuples N, two parameters are closely related to the hit rate: size of the BF w, and the number of hash functions l. In fact if the number of hash functions l is too small, there will be a lot of collisions which result in the increase of false positive rate; while if the value of l is too large, then there will be too much '1's in the BF which will also cause the increase of the false positive rate. According to the best number of hash functions of BF[17], in our method l is choosen approximately $l = \frac{w}{N} ln2$.

Fig 6 describes the hit rate of incorrect tuples which serves for both the basic and improved method for they have almost the same value. It's clear that the element level verification is better than the tuple level verification. Therefore instead of increase the size of the BF, user can improve the hit rate by adopting element level verification. For instance when $w/N = 10$, the hit rate of element level is 99.982% which is acceptable in most cases. Figure 7 shows the false alarm rate of both methods. As we mentioned in the paper that it is always 0 in the basic method. While for the improved method, it shows that when w/N is higher than 5 the false alarm rate will be lower than 10%. The false alarm rate has no relationship with the verification granularity.

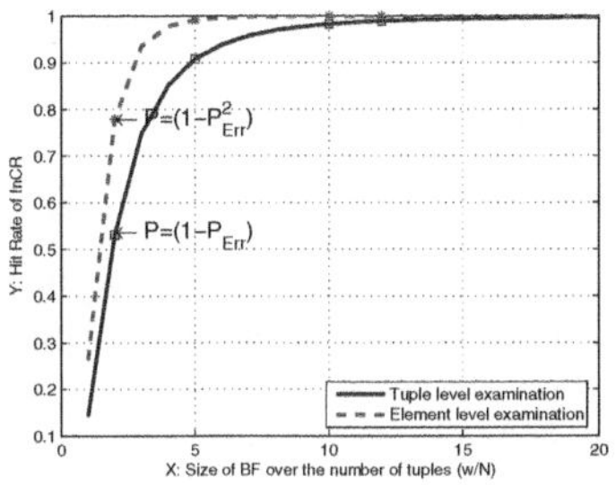

Fig. 6. Hit Rate of Incorrect tuples

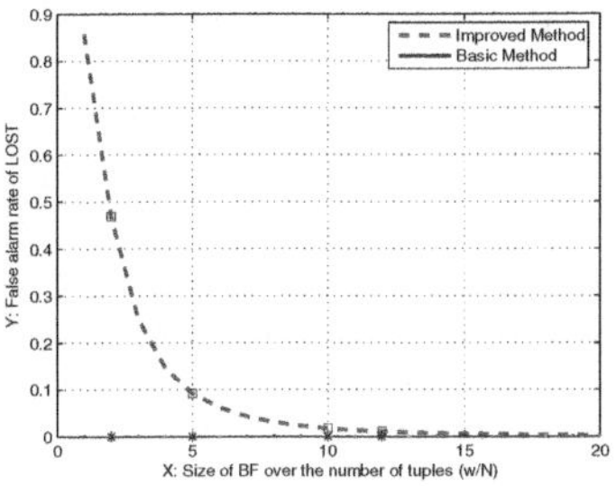

Fig. 7. False Alarm Rate of Lost Tuples

6 Summary

Due to the rapid development of cloud DB services, how to protect the integrity and availability of the cloud DB content becomes to be more and more important. In this paper we provide an efficient fine-grained cloud db damage examine method based on bloom filter arrays, which can locate the damage precisely and thus be used to for the damage recovery. Future work includes the support of cloud DB modification.

References

1. `http://aws.amazon.com/simpledb/`
2. `http://aws.amazon.com/rds/`
3. `http://code.google.com/appengine/docs/java/datastore/`
4. `https://sql.azure.com/`
5. Pang, H., Tan, K.L.: Authenticating query results in edge computing. In: Proceedings of the International Conference on Data Engineering, pp. 560–571 (2004)
6. Mykletun, E., Narasimha, M., Tsudik, G.: Authentication and Integrity in Outsourced Databases. ACM Transactions on Storage 2(2) (May 2006)
7. Sion, R.: Query execution assurance for outsourced databases. In: Proceedings of the 31st VLDB Conference, Trondheim, Norway (2005)

8. Devanbu, P., Gertz, M., Martel, C., Stubblebine, S.G.: Authentic third-party data publication. In: 14th IFIP 11.3 Working Conference in Database Security, pp. 101–112 (2000)
9. Narasimha, M., Tsudik, G.: Authentication of Outsourced Databases Using Signature Aggregation and Chaining. In: Li Lee, M., Tan, K.-L., Wuwongse, V. (eds.) DASFAA 2006. LNCS, vol. 3882, pp. 420–436. Springer, Heidelberg (2006)
10. Li, F., Hadjieleftheriou, M., Kollios, G., Reyzin, L.: Dynamic Authenticated Index Structures for Outsourced Databases. In: SIGMOD (2006)
11. Xie, M., Wang, H., Yin, J., Meng, X.: Integrity Auditing of Outsourced Data. In: VLDB 2007, pp. 782–793 (2007)
12. Cheng, W., Pang, H., Tan, K.: Authenticating Multi-dimensional Query Results in Data Publishing. In: Damiani, E., Liu, P. (eds.) Data and Applications Security 2006. LNCS, vol. 4127, pp. 60–73. Springer, Heidelberg (2006)
13. Yang, Y., Papadopoulos, S., Papadias, D., Kollios, G.: Spatial Outsourcing for Location-based Services. In: ICDE (2008)
14. Guo, H., Li, Y., Liu, A., Jajodia, S.: A fragile watermarking scheme for detecting malicious modifications of database relations. Information Sciences 176, 1350–1378 (2006)
15. Fan, L., Cao, P., Almeida, J., Broder, A.Z.: Summary Cache: A Scalable Wide-Area Web Cache Sharing Protocol. IEEE/ACM Transactions on Networking 8(3), 281–293 (2000)
16. Zhang, M., Hong, C., Chen, C.: Server Transparent Query Authentication of Outsourced Database. In: NDBC 2009 (2009) (in Chinese)
17. Bloom, B.: Space/Time Tradeoffs in Hash Coding with Allowable Errors. Communications of the ACM 13(7), 422–426 (1970)
18. Juels, A., Kaliski Jr., B.S.: Pors: proofs of retrievability for large files. In: Proc. ACM CCS, pp. 584–597 (2007)
19. Ateniese, G., Burns, R., Curtmola, R., Herring, J., Kissner, L., Peterson, Z., Song, D.: Provable data possession at untrusted stores. In: Proc. ACM CCS, pp. 598–609 (2007)
20. Shacham, H., Waters, B.: Compact proofs of retrievability. In: Pieprzyk, J. (ed.) ASIACRYPT 2008. LNCS, vol. 5350, pp. 90–107. Springer, Heidelberg (2008)

XML Structural Similarity Search Using MapReduce

Peisen Yuan[1,2], Chaofeng Sha[1,2], Xiaoling Wang[3],
Bin Yang[1,2], Aoying Zhou[2,3], and Su Yang[1,2]

[1] School of Computer Science, Fudan University, P.R.C
[2] Shanghai Key Laboratory of Intelligent Information Processing, P.R.C
[3] Shanghai Key Laboratory of Trustworthy Computing, Software Engineering Institute, East China Normal University, P.R.C
{peiseny,cfsha,byang,suyang}@fudan.edu.cn
{xlwang,ayzhou}@sei.ecnu.edu.cn

Abstract. XML is a de-facto standard for web data exchange and information representation. Efficient management of these large volumes of XML data brings challenges to conventional technique. To cope with large scale data, MapReduce computing framework as an efficient solution has attracted more and more attention in the database community recently. In this paper, an efficient and scalable framework is proposed for XML structural similarity search on large cluster with MapReduce. First, sub-structures of XML structure are extracted from large XML corpus located on a large cluster in parallel. Then Min-Hashing and locality sensitive hashing techniques are developed on the distributed and parallel computing framework for efficient structural similarity search processing. An empirical study on the cluster with real large datasets demonstrates the effectiveness and efficiency of our approach.

1 Introduction

XML has become a standard for data exchange in web application development. With the development of web and the wide usage of XML, search or query in the centralized solution cannot get satisfied result timely. To efficient manage these huge of XML data, distributed processing techniques for storing and managing the XML data in P2P or traditional distributed database techniques are developed [1,2].

Nowadays, cluster computing is broadly applied to the data explosion problem, which brings up an efficient solution by dividing the big data into small parts and processing in parallel on thousands of computers. The basic computing framework of cluster computing is MapReduce, which is a distributed programming model and software framework for rapidly writing applications that process vast amounts of data in parallel on thousands of cheap commodity computers. It has attracted much attention from many fields for processing and analyzing huge volumes of data.

Structural similarity search of XML data is an important problem in XML data management, which is related to data integration, XML classification and clustering, data cleaning etc. Tree edit distance is used for measuring the structure difference of tree-structured data, however, its complexity is rather expensive even for ordered tree [3]. Recently, Augsten et al.[4] proposes the *pq*-gram concept for tree structure comparing

L. Chen et al. (Eds.): WAIM 2010, LNCS 6184, pp. 169–181, 2010.

for the ordered tree. However, these methods are running on single machine, which cannot scale well to large cluster for big corpus.

In this paper, we propose a *filter-and-refine* framework on large cluster with the Min-Hashing and locality sensitive hashing techniques for efficient structural similarity search on large XML corpus.

First, *pq*-gram proposed in [4] is adopted for extracting XML tree-grams, which is flexible for tree data structural similarity comparing. Then Hadoop is used as a platform for storing and processing large scale of XML data in parallel. Furthermore Min-Hashing and locality sensitive hashing techniques are implemented on the cluster for efficient searching. Extensive experiments indicate that our framework is efficient and effective for XML structural similarity searching on large cluster and scales well in term of the size of corpus.

To summarize, the main contributions of this paper are outlined as follows:

- We propose an efficient framework for structural similarity searching of XML data on cluster computing platform.
- Min-Hashing and locality sensitive hashing are implemented on cluster for efficient searching.
- Extensive experiments are conducted to demonstrate the effectiveness and efficiency of our approach.

The rest of paper is organized as follows. In Section 2, the preliminaries of problem definition, XML model and MapReduce are introduced. Min-Hashing and locality sensitive hashing are presented in Section 3. Architecture and main algorithms are introduced in Section 4, and experiment evaluations are presented in Section 5. The related work is surveyed in Section 6. Conclusion and future work are presented in Section 7.

2 Preliminaries

2.1 Problem Definition

The problem of structural similarity search is to retrieve the top-*k* most similar documents. Given an XML document corpus $\mathcal{D}$, a query document $\mathcal{Q}$ and a similarity function *sim*, it retrieves the the document set $\widetilde{D_k} = \{d_i | d_i \in \widetilde{D_k}, \widetilde{D_k} \subseteq \mathcal{D}, \forall d \in \mathcal{D} \backslash \widetilde{D_k}, sim(d_i, \mathcal{Q}) \geq sim(d, \mathcal{Q}), i = 1, \cdots, k\}$.

Jaccard similarity is a set based similarity, which is a simple and effective similarity measure and defined as $sim_{jacc} = \frac{|A \cap B|}{|A \cup B|}$, where A and B are two sets. The intuitive meaning of Jaccard similarity is that the more overlapping of A and B, the higher similarity they are. In this paper, Jaccard similarity is adopted as the similarity measure for the XML structural similarity.

2.2 XML Model and Tree Gram

In this paper, an XML document is modeled as a rooted ordered labeled tree. According to this model, element nodes and attributes are considered as *structural* or *internal* nodes, and the text value and attribute value nodes are treated as *text* nodes or $leaf$

node. Only *structural* nodes are taken into consideration as the structure of XML tree, and the *element tag* and the *attribute* node name are considered as the tree node *label*.

After modeling, the *pq*-gram proposed in [4] is adopted for extracting *tree-gram* from XML tree, which is a flexible way to extract the structural information from tree structured data for approximate structural similarity comparing. The *pq*-gram is a sub-tree of the extended tree for two given integer parameters p and q.

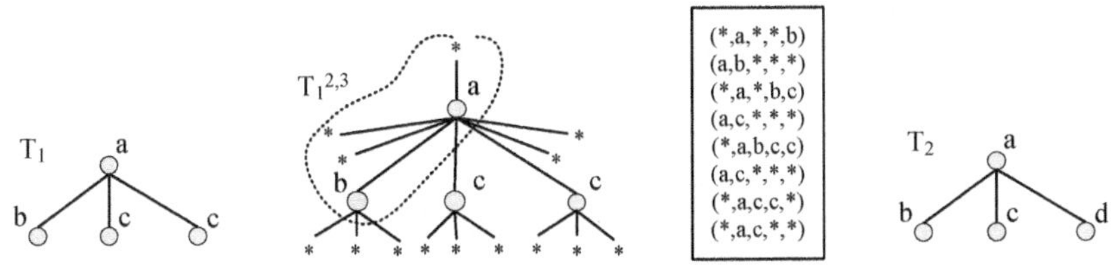

(1) Tree T_1 (2) Extended Tree of T_1 (3) *pq*-gram Tuples of T_1 (4) Tree T_2

Fig. 1. Example Trees and *pq*-gram Tuples

Example of *pq*-gram of a tree T_1 is shown in Fig. 1. According to [4], for two integers p and q, an extended tree is first built as shown in Fig.1(2), the '$*$' nodes represent the extended empty nodes. Parameters of p and q are set to 2 and 3 respectively in the example tree T_1. The sub-tree enclosed by the dotted line is the first *2,3*-gram of T_1.

Let g be a *pq*-gram with the nodes $N(g)= \{n_1, \cdots, n_p, n_{p+1}, \cdots, n_{p+q}\}$, where n_i is the i-th node in pre-order traversal of g. The $(p+q)$-tuple $L^*(g) = < l(n_1), \cdots, l(n_p), l(n_{p+1}), \cdots, l(n_{p+q}) >$ is called *pq*-gram tuple of g, where $l(n_i)$ is the node label of the tree node n_i [5].

Example 1. The first *2,3*-gram of tree T_1 is the subtree circled by the dotted line in the Fig. 1(2). After pre-order traversing of the subtree, nodes '*', 'a', '*', '*' and 'b' are visited orderly. The *2,3*-gram tuple is denoted as (*,a,*,*,b).

An example of *pq*-gram tuples of T_1 is shown in the Fig. 1(3). The *pq*-gram tuples of XML Tree T are denoted as $\mathbf{G}_T$. The *pq*-gram tuple universal of the XML corpus is noted as $\mathbf{G}_\mathcal{U}$, $\mathbf{G}_\mathcal{U} = \bigcup_{i=1} \mathbf{G}_{Ti}$. The *pq*-gram tuple is also called *tree-gram* or *pq*-gram if not confused in the following paper. Assume the universe of *pq*-gram tuples of the corpus are sorted lexicographically. Consequently, the structure of XML tree can be represented by a binary vector with dimension $|\mathbf{G}_\mathcal{U}|$.

Definition 1. *pq-Gram Binary Vector*

The binary vector $\boldsymbol{v}_T^{p,q} = (c_1, c_2, \cdots, c_{|G_\mathcal{U}|})$ *is the pq-gram binary vector of the tree* T, $c_i = 1$ *iff* g_i *occurs in* $\boldsymbol{G}_T$, *otherwise* $c_i = 0$.

Example 2. In the example trees T_1 and T_2 of Fig. 1, vectors (1, 1, 1, 0, 1, 1, 0, 0, 1, 1, 0), (1, 1, 0, 1, 0, 0, 1, 1, 1, 1, 1) are *2,3*-gram binary vectors respective to T_1 and T_2.

2.3 Hadoop and MapReduce

Hadoop is the core of Apache Hadoop project [6]. It is an open-source implementation of frameworks for cluster computing, which consists of the Hadoop Distributed File

System (HDFS) and MapReduce. HDFS is a scalable and reliable data storage system for storing the file in the distributed file system, and MapReduce is a data processing framework for distributed parallel computing.

The MapReduce programming framework is designed for fast developing applications which run on large master-slaves shared-nothing cluster in parallel. It is the basic infrastructure for cluster computing for data-intensive problems. It includes two primitives: *map* and *reduce* [7]. The *map* primitive processes *key/value* pairs and generates intermediate *key/values*. The *reduce* primitive merges all the intermediate *key/values* of the *map* output results with the same *key*. Finally the results are output to the HDFS.

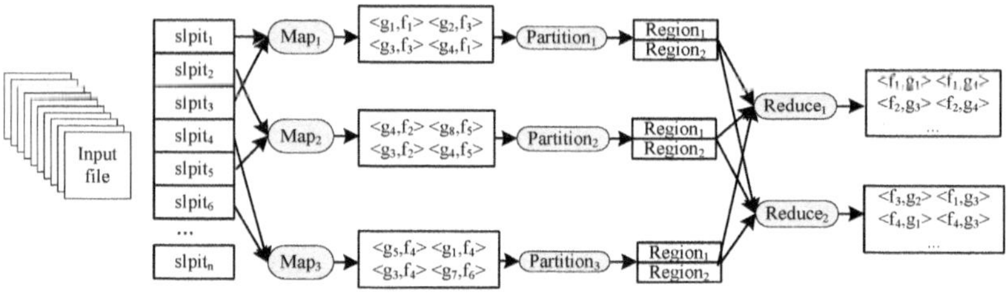

Fig. 2. MapReduce Processing Architecture

The processing architecture of MapReduce is outlined in Fig. 2. First, files to be processed are divided into equal splits. Each split is assigned to a *map* task. The *inputformat* of the application parses the data in each split into *key/value* pairs as the *map*'s input. The intermediate key value lists are obtained and sorted on each node after *map* task. Then hash-based *partition* procedure divides the intermediate key value list into R groups according to the *key* on each data node. Next, the *reduce* task is scheduled for merging value with the same *key*. Finally, the results are output into HDFS.

The advantage of MapReduce is its simple programming interface, which can be run on shared-nothing cluster without worrying about the details of parallel distributed tasks, such as task coordinating, load balancing and data storage problems etc.

3 Min-Hashing and Locality Sensitive Hashing

The structural similarity measure between XML documents is evaluated by *tree-gram* tuple set and Jaccard similarity, which is defined as: $sim_{jacc}(\mathbf{G}_{T1}, \mathbf{G}_{T2}) = \frac{|\mathbf{G}_{T1} \cap \mathbf{G}_{T2}|}{|\mathbf{G}_{T1} \cup \mathbf{G}_{T2}|}$.

Min-Hashing. (MH) is introduced in [8] and widely used in duplicate detection [9] etc, which creates compact signatures for sparse binary vectors such that the similarity can be effectively measured by their signatures. Min-Hashing is an easy way to implement *min-wise independent permutation*[10], which has the property that the probability of two sets have the same value of Min-Hashing is equal to their Jaccard similarity. The formal definition is given as follows.

Given a random hash function $h : x \longrightarrow I$, where x is an integer, and $I \subset \mathbb{N}$, the Min-Hashing function is defined as $m_h(\boldsymbol{v}) = argmin\{h(\boldsymbol{v}[i]) \mid \boldsymbol{v} \in \boldsymbol{V}_b$, $\boldsymbol{V}_b$ is binary vector set, $\boldsymbol{v}[i]$ is the i-th component of $\boldsymbol{v}$ and $\boldsymbol{v}[i] = 1, 0 \leq i \leq |\boldsymbol{v}| - 1\}$. According to the property of Min-Hashing, given two XML documents d_1, d_2, the structure of which is represented by the *tree-gram* sets $\mathbf{G}_{T_1}$ and $\mathbf{G}_{T_2}$ and their $tree\text{-}gram$ binary vector are $\boldsymbol{v}_1$ and $\boldsymbol{v}_2$ respectively, their structural similarity can be obtained by Eq. 1.

$$\mathbf{Pr}[m_h(\boldsymbol{v}_1) = m_h(\boldsymbol{v}_2)] = sim_{jacc}(\mathbf{G}_{T_1}, \mathbf{G}_{T_2}) = \frac{|\mathbf{G}_{T_1} \cap \mathbf{G}_{T_2}|}{|\mathbf{G}_{T_1} \cup \mathbf{G}_{T_2}|}. \tag{1}$$

Min-Hashing is an approximate procedure for evaluating the set similarity. Thus a random hash family $\mathcal{H} : \boldsymbol{V}_b \longrightarrow I$ is used for improving the efficiency of retrieval. Given a hash family $\mathcal{H}$, n Min-Hashing signatures are computed for each document. Thus the binary vector $d_{\boldsymbol{v}}$ of the document d is transformed into Eq. 2

$$g(d_{\boldsymbol{v}}) = \{m_{h_1}(d_{\boldsymbol{v}}), m_{h_2}(d_{\boldsymbol{v}}), \cdots, m_{h_n}(d_{\boldsymbol{v}})\}, m_{h_i} \in \mathcal{H}, i = 1, \cdots, n. \tag{2}$$

After generating n Min-Hashing value for all the documents, a signature matrix is obtained, which is a compact representation of the original binary document-gram vectors. Then pairwise similarity can be evaluated by the *signature* matrix. According to the property of Min-Hashing, Eq. 3 can be obtained.

$$\mathbf{Pr}[g(d_{\boldsymbol{v}_1}) = g(d_{\boldsymbol{v}_2})] = sim_{jacc}(d_1, d_2)^n. \tag{3}$$

Locality Sensitive Hashing. (LSH) is introduced in [11] and widely used in nearest neighbor search for high dimensional data, approximate KNN query etc, which focus on pairs of signature of the underlying similar sets. The scheme of locality sensitive hashing is a distribution on a hash function family $\mathcal{H}$, which operate on a collection of objects, such that for two objects o_1 and o_2, $\mathbf{Pr}_{h\in\mathcal{H}}[h(o_1) = h(o_2)] = sim(o_1, o_2)$ [12]. The basic idea of LSH is to hash the objects using $\mathcal{H}$, and ensures that for $\forall h \in \mathcal{H}$, the more similarity of the objects, the higher probability they are hashed to the same bucket. The LSH is a filter-and-refine framework for retrieval. For the retrieval precessing, the candidates of similar objects can be retrieved in the collision buckets, and the non-similarity objects are filtered out. The real similarity objects can be validated in the candidates set, without the need of sequential examining.

In order to improve the searching efficiency, the signature matrix is divided into b bands with r Min-Hashing signatures each band. Signatures in each band are hashed into B collision buckets, where B is a large number. Suppose the similarity of two objects is s, the probability that their LSH signatures agree in all r Min-Hashing signatures of in at least one of b bands is $1 - (1 - s^r)^b$, i.e. the probability that they can be retrieved is $1 - (1 - s^r)^b$.

In our system, r Min-Hashing values are concatenated for the hash key. The band number and the bucket number make up the key jointly of the MapReduce job. The similarity list in the bucket of each band is considered as the $value$.

4 System Architecture and Algorithms

4.1 System Architecture

The architecture of the system is shown in Fig. 3, which consists of three parts. The first part is the *parsing phase*. The structure of XML corpus stored in the HDFS are parsed and extracted into *tree-gram* tuples using the algorithm in [4] with one MapReduce job. The *key* of the result is file name and the *value* is the *tree-gram* set. The *key/value* pairs are output to HDFS by the *reduce* task finally. The processing of parsing is shown in the Fig. 2, where g_i is the *tree-gram*, f_i is the file name.

The second part is the *vector building phase*. The *tree-gram* universal $\mathbf{G}_{\mathcal{U}}$ of the corpus is obtained by the *Universal Generator* module in one MapReduce job firstly. Then $\mathbf{G}_{\mathcal{U}}$ is distributed by *DistrbutedCache* function of Hadoop to each data node. According to $\mathbf{G}_{\mathcal{U}}$ and the *pq*-gram tuple set of the XML documents, the binary document-gram vectors are built in one MapReduce job subsequently.

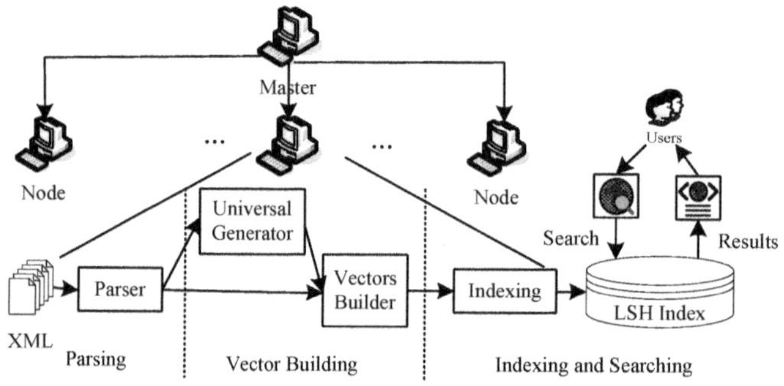

Fig. 3. Architecture of the System

The third part is the *indexing* and *searching phase*. The index is built in one MapReduce job. Given a binary document-gram vector $\boldsymbol{v}$, r Min-Hashing values of each vector are computed for each band. Then these r Min-Hashing values are concatenated to make up the hash key jointly and the keys of all the vectors are hashed into B buckets of each band. The band number and the collision bucket number make up the *key* of the index, and the candidate file list is used as the *value*. The first three part are computed in parallel on each data node.

Given a query Q, the collision bucket numbers of each band for the query are evaluated. Next the candidate set is obtained with the LSH index. Then the similarity distances of Q with candidate sets are computed. Finally the results are sorted according to their similarity and returned to the user.

After the introduction of the architecture of the system, main algorithms used in the system are presented in the following section.

4.2 Algorithms

Vector Building. The *tree-grams* are extracted from the XML documents residing on each data node in one MapReduce job using the algorithm from [4] in parallel. The *tree-*

Algorithm 1. *map* Function for Building Binary Vectors

Input: Key: *file-name*. Value: *tree-gram list. tree-gram universal* $\mathbf{G}_{\mathcal{U}}$.
Output: Key: *file-name*. Value: *doc-gram vector*.

1 Vector $\boldsymbol{v} = \emptyset$;
2 $\mathbf{G}_{\mathcal{U}}$ is distributed to each data node by $DistributedCache$;
3 **foreach** $g \in \boldsymbol{G_T}$ **do**
4   **if** $g \in \boldsymbol{G_{\mathcal{U}}}$ **then**
5         $\boldsymbol{v}$.add(1);
6   **else**
7         $\boldsymbol{v}$.add(0);
8 output_key = $file\text{-}name$;
9 output_value = $\boldsymbol{v}$;
10 **Emit**(output_key, output_value);

gram sets of the XML corpus are output into HDFS. After that, the *tree-gram* universal $\mathbf{G}_{\mathcal{U}}$ is generated in another MapReduce job.

The *map* function of the binary document-gram vector building is introduced in Algorithm 1. First $\mathbf{G}_{\mathcal{U}}$ is distributed to each data node by $DisributedCache$ (line 2). Then the binary vector is built for the XML document (line 3-7). Next the vector is emitted with the file name as the *key* and the vector as the *value* in the *map*. Finally the *reduce* algorithm outputs the binary vectors into HDFS. The *reduce* algorithm is omitted here due to its simplicity.

LSH Indexing. LSH Indexing of *map* function is presented in Algorithm 2. For each vector $\boldsymbol{v}$, the $computeMinHash()$ function compute the r Min-Hashing values for each band. These r Min-Hashing values are concatenated to make up the hash key for each band(line 4). Then the band number and the collision bucket number make up the *key* of the MapReduce, and the file name as the *value* are emitted to *reduce* (line 7).

Algorithm 2. *map* Function for LSH Indexing

Input: Key: *file-name*. Value: *binary doc-gram vectors*.
Output: Key: *collision bucket number*. Value: *file list in the bucket*.

1 MinHashClass minHash = new MinHashClass();
2 fn = $getFileName$(*file-name*); /*get the file name*/;
3 docVector = $getVector(fn)$; /*get the file vector by file name*/;
4 Band:BucketNo = minHash.computeMinHash(docVector);
5 output_key = Band:BucketNo; /*the band number and the bucket number are concatenated as the key*/
6 output_value = output_value $\cup$ $file\text{-}name$;
7 **Emit**(output_key, output_value);

Subsequently the *reduce* task of the LSH indexing merges the file list with the same *key* together, i.e. the same band and the same bucket number.

Searching Algorithm. The *map* function for structural similarity search is shown in Algorithm 3. Given a query $\mathcal{Q}$, the $minHashSimilarityQuery()$ function searches

Algorithm 3. *map* Function for Structural Similarity Searching

```
  Input: Query Q.
  Output: Key: file name pair. Value: similarity distance.
1 dist-list = minHashSimilarityQuery(Q, k); /*call algorithm 4*/
2 foreach dist ∈ dist-list do
3     output_key = file-name;
4     output_value = dist;
5     Emit(output_key, output_value);
```

the structural similarity XML documents and computes their similarity distances (line 1). Finally the similarity distance list is emitted to the *reduce* task (line 5).

The *minHashSimilarityQuery*() is introduced in Algorithm 4. Given a query Q, the *getVector*() accesses the binary vector firstly (line 4). Subsequently the collision bucket numbers for each band is computed by *computeMinHash*() for the query vector (line 5). Then for each collision number, the candidate file list is obtained (line 6-8). The Algorithm 4 can be divided into two phrases. The first phrase is the filtering phrase, which filters out the most of the non-similarity objects (line 2-8), and the second phrase is the refining phrase, which affirms the true valid similarity objects in the candidate set. The similarity distances of Q with each file in the candidate set are evaluated (line 9-12). Finally, the result list is sorted and returned (line 13-14).

Algorithm 4. Min-Hashing Structural Similarity Search on Hadoop

```
   Input: LSH index, Query Q.
   Output: Top-k result list.
1  Result = Φ;
2  C = Φ; /* list of candidate files */
3  MinHashClass minHash = new MinHashClass();
4  q'_v = getVector(Q);
5  queryCollisionBucket = minHash.computeMinHash(q'_v);
6  foreach collisionNo ∈ queryCollisionBucket do
7      c = getVectorByNo(bucketNo);
8      C = C ∪ {c};
9  foreach f ∈ C do
10     CandidateVector CV = getVector(f);
11     simi = computeSetSimilarity(q'_v, CV);
12     Result = Result ∪ {simi};
13 sort(Result);
14 return top-k result list;
```

5 Experiments

5.1 Experiment Setup

All the algorithms are implemented in Java SDK1.6 and run on Hadoop 0.19.1 and Hbase 0.19.1. The cluster is configured with 1 master node and 6 salve nodes. Each node has a duo core intel 2.33GHz processor, 2G main memory and 180GB disk, which runs on Ubuntu 9.04, and with 1G memory allocated to JVM. The cluster is organized in the LAN with 100.0 Mbps. The XML documents are stored on HDFS. Hadoop is configured with the default and the replication of the data is set to 1. Each data node is configured with 2 maps and 1 reduce. The default parameters of b and r are set to 20 and 3 respectively.

For XML datasets, data from [13,14] are used. Big XML documents such as psd7003, SwissProt, dblp, nasa and treebank in the datasets are split with the XML Twig [15] to smaller ones with size of 100KB, 200KB, 500KB and 1MB. Finally, the size of the XML corpus is 3.4G and consists of 18015 XML documents. The parameters of p and q of the pq-gram are set to 2 and 3 respectively.

The datasets are divided into 4 groups with different size which randomly choose from the 18015 XML documents. The first group D_1 is 667 XML documents with the size about 100MB. The second one D_2 is 4863 XML documents with the size about 900MB. The third group D_3 is 9382 XML documents about 1.9 GB and the forth group D_4 is 18015 XML documents with 3.4 GB size.

5.2 Time Performance

In this section, the performance of the system is studied. We mainly studied (1) Parsing of the XML corpus to generate the pq-gram profile of the XML corpus, (2) Vector building for each XML corpus, (3) LSH index building. For the comparing searching performance, 2 searching schemes are studied: (1) Sequential scan from HDFS, which evaluates the similarity by sequential scan from HDFS in one MapReduce job, (2) Using LSH index.

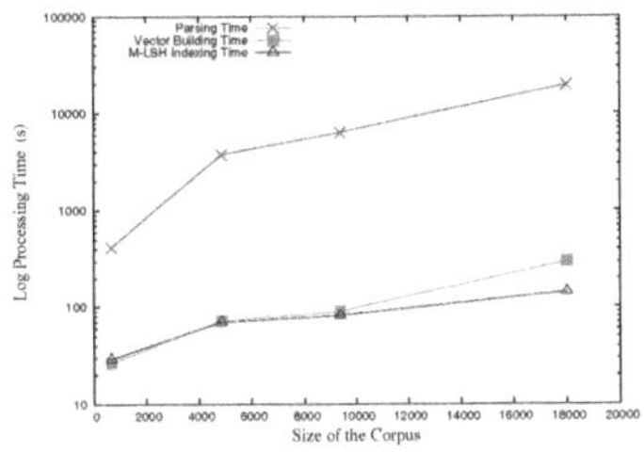

Fig. 4. Processing Time

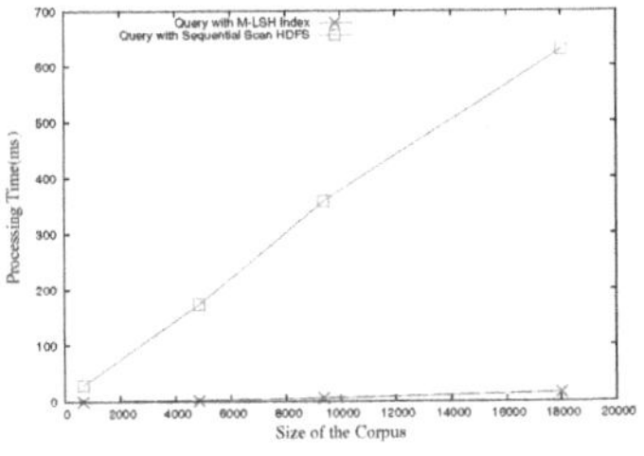

Fig. 5. Query Performance Comparison

Fig. 4 demonstrates the processing time. The time axis is logarithm time and the time unit is second. Fig. 4 indicates that (1) with the increasing of the corpus size, the parsing time increases almost linearly with the corpus size; (2) the XML parsing takes most of the time and LSH indexing takes about 150s for 18015 XML documents.

The query performance comparison is shown in Fig. 5. The time unit is millisecond. For query performance test, the number of bucket B of each band is configured to 7997. Fig. 5 indicates that the query performance with LSH index is far lower than sequential scan from HDFS, which takes time less than 0.2% of scanning from HDFS.

5.3 Precision

For precision experiment, the first group XML corpus dataset D_1 is used. The default bucket number B is set to 7997, and the *precision*, *recall* and *F-measure* are tested. The *F-measure* is defined as $2 \times \frac{precison \times recall}{precison + recall}$. 14 queries are issued in total and the average result is used as the final result.

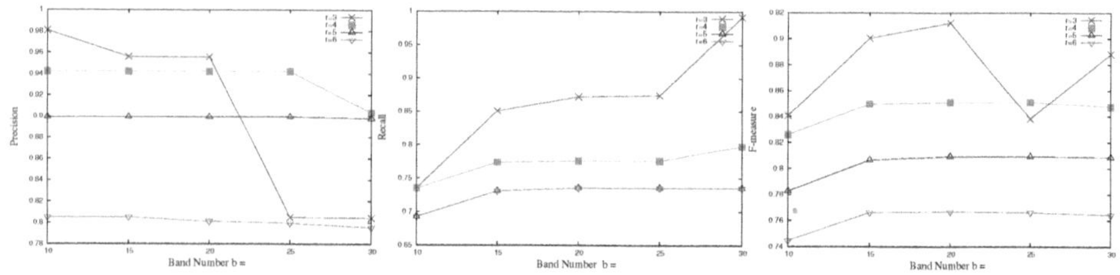

(a) Precision (b) Recall (c) F-measure

Fig. 6. Precision, Recall and F-measure

Figures in Fig. 6 show the *precision*, *recall* and the *F-measure* with different parameters b and r, $r = 3, \cdots, 6$ and $b = 10, 15, 20, 25, 30$. Fig. 6(a) shows the *precision* is decreasing with the increasing of b and r. Fig. 6(b) indicates that the *recall* is increasing the the increasing of b, however, it decreases with the increasing of r. This figure proves the principle of the LSH that the more bucket, the more relevant are retrieved. Fig. 6(c) demonstrates that (1) the *F-measure* increases with the band number b before 15, it decreases after 25; (2) it increases with the r. When $r = 3$ and $b = 20$, the *F-measure* reaches peak. From Fig. 6(a) to 6(c), when $r = 3$ and b between 15 and 20, the measures of *precision*, *recall* and *F-measure* can get the best search quality. However, when $r = 4$, the search quality is stable with different b, but is much lower than $r = 3$. Thus, conclusions can be drawn that $r = 3$ and b between 15 and 20 is a good choice for Min-Hashing LSH.

5.4 Scalability

For scalability performance test, the search time are experimented with 4 group XML corpus and different number of similarity candidates.

Fig. 7 shows the search processing time with different buckets of per band and different size of corpus. The time scale of is logarithm time and unit is millisecond. From Fig. 7, conclusion can be drawn that (1) with the size of corpus increasing, the processing time increases, (2) with the number increasing of bucket of each band, the search time decreases. However, with the increasing of the buckets, the searching time decreases tiny after a sharp decreasing. Thus a tradeoff should be made between space cost and performance.

Fig. 8 demonstrates the searching time with different corpus size and candidate set, and the time unit is millisecond. 4 queries are issued for this experiment. Q_1: OrdinaryIssue.xml, Q_2: Proceedings.xml, Q_3: customer.xml, Q_4: reed.xml. There are 99,

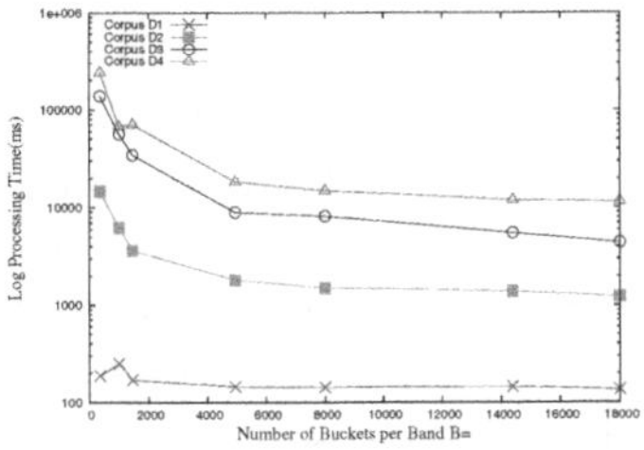

Fig. 7. Processing Time with Buckets

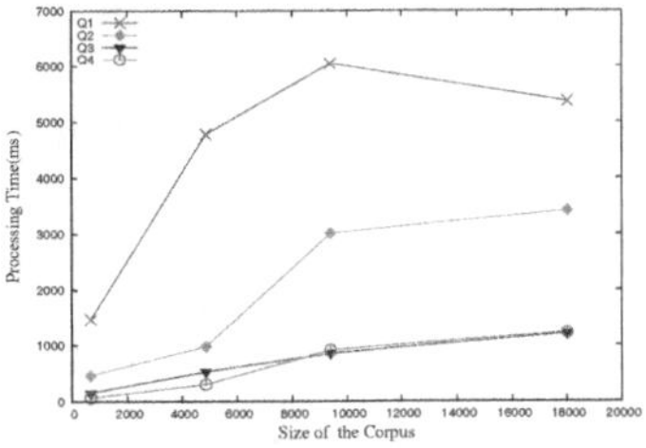

Fig. 8. Query Performance with different Candidates and Corpus Size

40, 7, 7 similarity documents respectively in each corpus. The bucket number B is set to 14389. Fig. 8 indicates that with the increasing of the size of corpus, the searching time is increasing. The reason is that the larger of the corpus size, the more candidates need to be probed. This experiment also shows that, the more similar documents in the corpus, the more time it costs for searching. However, the query time Q_1 decreases in D_4 than D_3, the reason is that the data may be distributed unevenly in the cluster. Fig. 5 and Fig. 8 indicate that our system scales well with the size of the corpus.

6 Related Work

In this section, the literatures on approximate structural similarity computing of XML data, cluster computing and the application of locality sensitive hashing are reviewed.

Approximate tree structural comparison is extensively studied which can give satisfied result. Thus researchers have proposed several approximate methods for XML structural comparison. Joshi et al. [16] proposed bag of $xpath$ based structural similarity. Recently, *tree-gram* based methods are proposed to capture the structural similarity for ordered tree [4,17], which is becoming an efficient and flexible way for tree data similarity evaluation, They also give the bound against the tree edit distance. However, they do not take large scale data collection comparison into consideration.

In term of cluster computing, extensive researches have been conducted on large scale distributed storage and computing nowadays. Such as GFS [18], MapReduce [7], Dryad [19], Hbase [20] etc. These techniques have applied in many fields and have attracted lots of attention. The performance and efficiency of these system have been shown by empirical research for big data problem in these fields. The MapReduce as the basic computing framework provides easy operations for processing massive data on thousands of machine for distributed computing.

In the last few years, the locality sensitive hashing and Min-Hashing have been well studied and applied in many fields, such as duplicate detection, large rare association rule mining, clustering, information retrieval etc. LSH is widely used for efficient nearest neighbor searching in high dimension objects etc. Google news [21] employs the Min-Hashing and locality sensitive hashing for personal news distribution. Manku et al. [22] make use of Min-Hashing for detecting the duplicate web page in the web crawler.

7 Conclusion and Future Work

We propose a *filter-and-refine* framework for searching structural similarity XML documents on the cluster with MapReduce, which is efficient and effective with high search quality. Min-Hashing and locality sensitive hashing techniques are implemented with MapReduce in the framework. Our design gives an efficient solution for large scale XML documents management in the web age. Extensive experiments on real datasets show that our framework is efficient and scales well in term of the size of the corpus for structural similarity searching for XML data. In the web age, data update is very common, so how to manage these huge amount of data incrementally is rather important. In the future, optimization of searching algorithm and incremental update functionality will be added to the system. Furthermore, data mining and analyzing functions will be incorporated into the framework for large scale XML data management problems.

Acknowledgments. This work is supported by NSFC grants (No. 60773075, No.60925008 and No. 60903014), National Hi-Tech 863 program under grant 2009A A01Z149, 973 program (No. 2010CB328106), Shanghai International Cooperation Fund Project (Project No.09530708400) and Shanghai Leading Academic Discipline Project (No. B412).

References

1. Özsu, M.T.: Distributed XML Processing. In: Li, Q., Feng, L., Pei, J., Wang, S.X., Zhou, X., Zhu, Q.-M. (eds.) APWeb/WAIM 2009. LNCS, vol. 5446, p. 1. Springer, Heidelberg (2009)
2. Abiteboul, S., Benjelloun, O., Milo, T.: The Active XML project: an overview. The VLDB Journal 17(5), 1019–1040 (2008)
3. Jiang, T., Wang, L., Zhang, K.: Alignment of Trees-An Alternative to Tree Edit. In: Crochemore, M., Gusfield, D. (eds.) CPM 1994. LNCS, vol. 807, pp. 75–86. Springer, Heidelberg (1994)
4. Augsten, N., Böhlen, M., Gamper, J.: Approximate matching of hierarchical data using pq-grams. In: VLDB, pp. 301–312 (2005)
5. Yuan, P., Wang, X., Sha, C., Gao, M., Zhou, A.: Grams^3: An efficient framework for xml structural similarity search. In: DASFAA workshop: UDM (to appear, 2010)
6. Apache Hadoop Project (2009), `http://hadoop.apache.org/`
7. Dean, J., Ghemawat, S.: MapReduce: Simplified Data Processing on Large Clusters. In: OSDI, pp. 1–13 (2004)
8. Broder, A.Z.: On the resemblance and containment of documents. In: Proceedings of Compression and Complexity of Sequences 1997, pp. 21–29 (1997)
9. Chum, O., Philbin, J., Isard, M., Zisserman, A.: Scalable near identical image and shot detection. In: ICVR, pp. 549–556. ACM, New York (2007)
10. Broder, A.Z., Charikar, M., Frieze, A.M., Mitzenmacher, M.: Min-wise independent permutations. JCSS 60(3), 630–659 (2000)
11. Indyk, P., Motwani, R.: Approximate nearest neighbors: towards removing the curse of dimensionality. In: ASTC, pp. 604–613. ACM, New York (1998)
12. Charikar, M.S.: Similarity estimation techniques from rounding algorithms. In: STOC, pp. 380–388. ACM, New York (2002)
13. XML Data Repository (2009), `http://www.cs.washington.edu/research/xmldatasets/`

14. Sigmod Record (2009), http://www.sigmod.org/publications/sigmod-record/xml-edition
15. XML Twig (2009), http://xmltwig.com/xmltwig/
16. Joshi, S., Agrawal, N., Krishnapuram, R., Negi, S.: A bag of paths model for measuring structural similarity in Web documents. In: SIGKDD, pp. 577–582. ACM, New York (2003)
17. Yang, R., Kalnis, P., Tung, A.K.H.: Similarity evaluation on tree-structured data. In: SIGMOD, pp. 754–765 (2005)
18. Ghemawat, S., Gobioff, H., Leung, S.T.: The Google file system. SIGOPS 37(5), 43 (2003)
19. Isard, M., Budiu, M., Yu, Y., Birrell, A., Fetterly, D.: Dryad: Distributed data-parallel programs from sequential building blocks. In: SIGOPS/EuroSys, pp. 59–72. ACM, New York (2007)
20. Hbase Project (2009), http://hadoop.apache.org/hbase/
21. Das, A.S., Datar, M., Garg, A., Rajaram, S.: Google news personalization: scalable online collaborative filtering. In: WWW, pp. 271–280. ACM, New York (2007)
22. Manku, G.S., Jain, A., Das Sarma, A.: Detecting near-duplicates for web crawling. In: WWW, pp. 141–150. ACM, New York (2007)

Comparing Hadoop and Fat-Btree Based Access Method for Small File I/O Applications

Min Luo[1] and Haruo Yokota[2]

[1] Department of Computer Science, Tokyo Institute of Technology 2–12–1 Ookayama, Meguro-ku, Tokyo 152–8552, Japan

[2] Global Scientific Information and Computing Center, Tokyo Instititute of Technology 2–12–1 Ookayama, Meguro-ku, Tokyo 152–8550, Japan

Abstract. Hadoop has been widely used in various clusters to build scalable and high performance distributed file systems. However, Hadoop distributed file system (HDFS) is designed for large file management. In case of small files applications, those metadata requests will flood the network and consume most of the memory in Namenode thus sharply hinders its performance. Therefore, many web applications do not benefit from clusters with centered metanode, like Hadoop. In this paper, we compare our Fat-Btree based data access method, which excludes center node in clusters, with Hadoop. We show their different performance in different file I/O applications.

Keywords: Parallel Database, Fat-Btree, Hadoop, File I/O.

1 Introduction

Recently, the "cloud" has attracted considerable attentions in high performance and scalable distributed systems research. In these systems, a large number of servers are lined up and work in parallel. Many distributed execution frameworks have been proposed, in which, Map-Reduce [2] is one of the most famous frameworks in these works. There are numerous academic and commercial implementations of Map-Reduce framework because it offers a simple, functional interface that transparently executes the computations with a good system scalability.

The most popular and public available Map-Reduce based project is Hadoop [8], an open source version under development by Apache Software Foundation. Its core components include an implementation of Map-Reduce, with a primary storage system called "Hadoop Distributed File System (HDFS)" to provide a conceptually simple programming model and abstract away any knowledge of where the data lives. Therefore, Hadoop has been widely used in both commercial and academic world, and shows high performance in many parallel processing tasks [9], [10].

On the other hand, many data access methods in parallel databases [3], [4], [5], are other choices for data processing on the "cloud". Besides the contributions made by almost all the famous database vendors that are attracted in parallel

L. Chen et al. (Eds.): WAIM 2010, LNCS 6184, pp. 182–193, 2010.

databases over the past two decades, many ongoing academic projects are also engaged to provide better performance, scalability and failure tolerance parallel database systems [11], [12], [13], [14]. Although the parallel database and Map-Reduce based systems may seem to target different applications, it is in fact possible to write the parallel processing tasks for almost all the applications with Map-Reduce jobs or database queries with these two systems, individually [15]. Therefore, it is meaningful to have some comparisons between these two systems for the users information.

In addition, in most recently, there is a new trends in the parallel processing system which tries to build a hybrid system based on Map-Reduce framework and Parallel DBMS to allow better code reusability, data independence and automatic query optimization [15]. However, almost all the forerunners do not achieve the performance of parallel databases as well as the scalability, fault tolerance of MapReduce-based systems. One of the reasons is the different the storage layers, the HDFS layer or DBMS layer, they adopted. Because these storage layers have different performance in storing different size of data, it seems interesting and necessary to compare these two basic systems in different file I/O applications, and this comparison results may be referred in the design of future hybrid Map-Reduce/DBMS systems.

The purpose of this paper is to show the different I/O performance of Hadoop in the applications of different file sizes, especially for the small file I/O case. We compare the time consumed by Hadoop and a parallel DBMS in initializing and accessing all their data, individually. The overhead for accessing files in Hadoop is then discussed. In addition, a parallel database system based on Fat-Btree index [5] is introduced and used in this comparison, whose better scalability and availability than the Hadoop's are also shown through the experiments and discussion.

The rest of the paper is organized as follows: Firstly, we present background work in Section 2. Then we outline the different maintain cost in Hadoop and parallel DBMS from architecture perspective in Section 3. In Section 4 we demonstrate and analyze the different performance in Hadoop and parallel DBMS in different file I/O applications through experimental results. Finally, we present related work in Section 5 and conclude our work in Section 6.

2 Background

2.1 Map-Reduce

Map-Reduce model (Fig. 1) consists two main functions, called Map and Reduce.

In the "Map" function, the master node reads a set of "records", chops it up into smaller intermediate records in a form of new (key, value) pairs, during this process, a "split" hash function partitions the records into R disjoint buckets. Each map bucket is written to the processing node's disk with these R output files. Since each map instance is assigned a distinct portion of input "records" by the scheduler, the total intermediate files created in this process is M*R, if there are M such distinct portions. Then, "Reduce" function transferred the

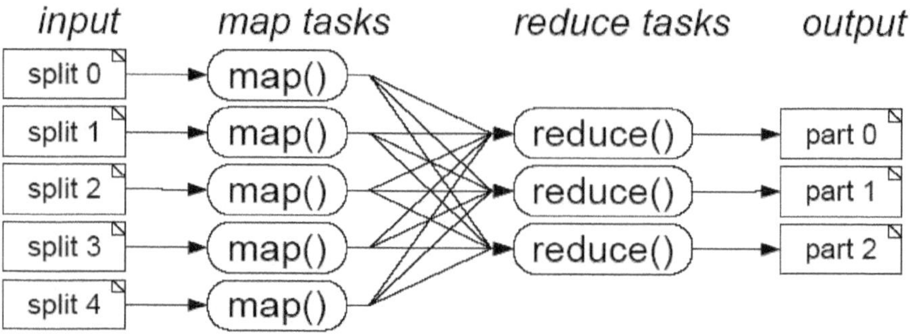

Fig. 1. Map-Reduce Model

intermediate files over network from the Map node's local disks to individual reducers, which is called "shuffle". Note that all the intermediate records with the same hash values are send into the same reducer and each reducer processes or combines the records into the final output file.

The advantage of the Map-Reduce is that the parallel and distributed processes are actuated automatically just by calling the MAP and Reduce operations provided within this model. On the contrary parallel DBMSs may require their programmers to participate into this process, like providing the Map and Reduce processers with User Defined Functions and aggregation operations in DBMS.

2.2 Hadoop

Hadoop is an open source software for reliable, scalable, distributed computing which has two main components: a freely available implementation of Map-Reduce framework and a Hadoop Distributed File System (HDFS) [8].

HDFS is a distributed file system which is suitable for distributed processing on commodity hardware. It replicas the datasets on multiple nodes to make the data available even there is a failure of nodes. There are two kinds of nodes in HDFS: a metadata server called Namenode and a large number of data storage nodes called Datanode. The Namenode is in charge of all metadata and system actions data within the HDFS. The Datanode is in charge of all read/write and data replication requests according to the direction from Namenode. Because there is only one Namenode in Hadoop and it keeps all the metadata in main memory, it appears to be the bottleneck for handling metadata requests in the applications, especially for the applications on small files [16]. In addition, this critical Namenode introduces an SPOF (Single Point of Failure) of the system, which is not easy to remove [24].

2.3 Fat-Btree

The Fat-Btree is a kind of parallel B-tree structure, which is proposed to provide dynamic data management, high throughput and efficient skew handling [5].

As shown in Fig. 2, the leaf pages of the parallel B-tree are distributed among the "Process Elements" (PEs). Each PE has a subtree of the whole B-tree containing the root node and intermediate index nodes between the root node and leaf nodes allocated to that PE. In the Fat-Btree structure, index nodes close to the root node have multiple copies but with a relatively low update frequency, on the other hand, leaf nodes have a relatively high update frequency but are not duplicated. Thus, nodes with higher update frequencies have lower synchronization overhead. Therefore, the maintain cost in Fat-Btree is much lower than the ordinary parallel Btree structure, such as Copy-Whole-Btree and Single-Index-Btree [5]. We have proposed a parallel database system based on this Fat-Btree index in [20].

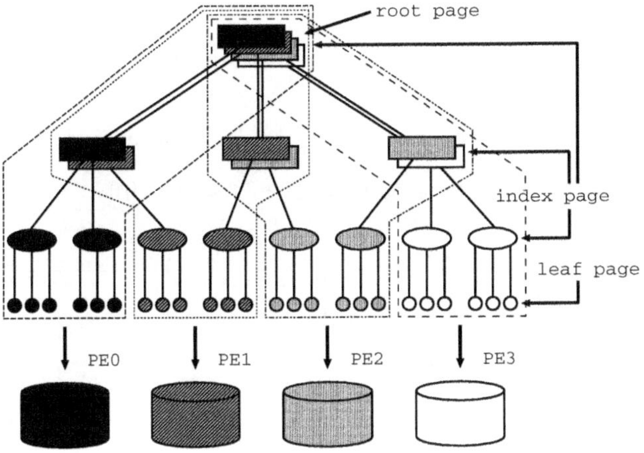

Fig. 2. A Fat-Btree

3 System Discussion

In this section, we discuss some of the system operation cost in Hadoop and Fat-Btree DBMS.

In Hadoop architecture, Map-Reduce model offers a simple, functional interface for distributed processing, while HDFS provides a reliable, shared virtual storage device.

HDFS stores the datasets and all the intermediate results which are generated during Map-Reduce processes across multiple nodes. In addition, HDFS cannot be directly mounted on an existing operating system, like Google File System (GFS), data needs to be loaded into HDFS before and after each execution in Hadoop. This can be very time consuming and we will examine this in the next section. Moreover, the HDFS store the files in each individual "Block", thus it needs to divide or unite the files and fulfill the "Block" which is 64MB by default. Therefore, extra metadata will be generated in the Namenode. This space utilization is determined by three space requirement: metadata of directories, files and blocks. In the HDFS which has 64 users:

Directory entry follows the formula as:
144 Bytes + the length of the directory name;
File entry follows the formula as:
112 Bytes + the length of the file name;
Block follows the formula as:
112 Bytes + 24 Bytes * Number of replicas;

In this paper, we assume that the directory name is in an average length of 16 characters, the file name is in an average length of 13 characters, the number of replicas is 2 in the system. The block size is the default value of 64 MB. Table 1 shows the metadata size for four different file size applications in which data volume is same as 1 GBytes. As it shows, the metadata size will increase together with the number of files or the total file size.

Table 1. An Example of Metadata Size in Hadoop

	File numbers	Size of Each File	Dir Meta	File Meta	Block Meta	Total Meta
DataSet-a	10	100M	10,240	1,250	250	11,790 Bytes
DataSet-b	100	10M	10,240	12,500	250	22,990 Bytes
DataSet-c	1,000	1M	10,240	125,000	250	135,490 Bytes
DataSet-d	5,000	200K	10,240	625,000	250	635,490 Bytes
DataSet-e	10,000	100K	10,240	1,250,000	250	1,260,490 Bytes
DataSet-f	20,000	50K	10,240	2,500,000	250	2,510,490 Bytes
DataSet-g	40,000	25K	10,240	5,000,000	250	5,010,490 Bytes
DataSet-h	80,000	12.5K	10,240	10,000,000	250	10,010,490 Bytes

On the other hand, Map-Reduce model requires the Namenode to keep all the metadata in main memory since they are regularly accessed. However, too many of these small files will exceed the addressing capacity within this node and those small file I/Os can flood the networking near Namenode, eventually. Thus, it prevents the performance of the system and leaves the remaining storage capacity unutilized. Moreover, Hadoop has to start new process for every map task. These start-up processes will occupy a great portion of time for the small file I/O application whose execution time of each task is relatively short. In addition, the Datanodes in Hadoop may have large states to checkpoint, they contend for disk and network bandwidth resources, slowing down individual checkpoints.

While for the Fat-Btree database, the metadata needed to be stored for each tuple are limited. During data accessing process, the index pages are required only for locating the leaf pages stored in each PE . Therefore, it has a high cache hit rate if the index pages are cached in each PE. Because of this high cache hit rate and low maintain cost (Section 2.3), select and update processes in Fat-Btree are much faster than other conventional parallel B-tree structures [5]. In addition, the DBMS is able to achieve high performance by using the index to accelerate join operations.

Table 2. Experimental Environment

Blade server:	Sun Fire B200x Blade Server
CPU:	AMD Athlon XP-M 1800+ (1.53 GHz)
Memory:	PC2100 DDR SDRAM 1 GB
Network:	1000BASE-T
Gigabit Ethernet Switch:	Catalyst 6505 (720GB/s backbone)
Hard Drives:	TOSHIBA MK3019GAX (30 GB, 5400 rpm, 2.5 inch)
OS:	Linux 2.4.20
Java VM:	Sun J2SE SDK 1.6.0 18 Server VM

Since there is a trade-off in Hadoop who inherits the features of high scalability and performance from Map-Reduce while contains the drawbacks mentioned above, we would like to evaluate Hadoop performance under different file I/O applications and compare it with a parallel database implemented with the open source DBMS Postgres and the Fat-Btree index [20].

4 Experiments

In this section we describe the experiments of Hadoop and our Fat-Btree database. We focus on evaluating data load (initialize) time and data accessing time, as well as system scalability.

4.1 Environmental Setup

For our experiments, we used a cluster of up to 32 nodes. Table 2 shows our experimental environment.

All the nodes run the Hadoop version 0.20.1 on JDK 1.6.0, and we deploy the system with the default configuration settings, except for changing the replicas number to 1 which is the same as that in Fat-Btree database so as to compare with it later. We do not use multiple replicas because we focus on the file I/O performance in Hadoop here. In addition, we use an individual node as the Namenode in the experiments to ensure that the performance of Datanodes will not be affected.

4.2 Data Load Performance

In this experiment, we load the same datasets as shown in TABLE 1, from the node's local disk into each system's internal storage to study their performance by examining the time it takes. Although Hadoop has been designed to run on a very large number of nodes, the Datanode number in our experiments is only up to 32 nodes. This is because by our observations, this software is typically used with significantly less instances in current computation clouds. For example, Amazon limits the number of nodes for their Hadoop application to 20 unless the respective customer passes an extended registration request [26].

We first use the dataset-{a, b, c, d, e} in this experiment to load HDFS by the command-line utility provide in Hadoop. The files in these datasets are in plain text manner to enable "wordcount" function available in later experiments.

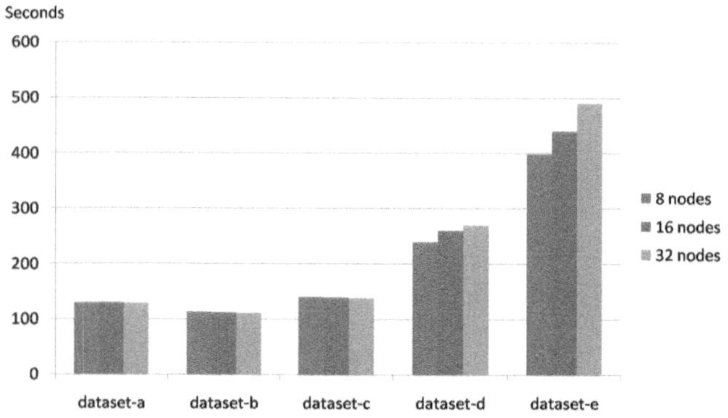

Fig. 3. Data Load Time of Different File Sizes

Fig. 3 shows the data load performance of loading the same volume of dataset-1GB. The data loading time is not same from each other if the size per each file is different. The time required for dataset-{a, b, c} are almost same. The little difference may lie in the different file split and combination cost when fill the data into blocks. For the dataset-{d, e} Hadoop consumed much larger time. This reason may be that Hadoop forces each task to run in an individual process, thus each task has to redo the same initialization in its process. When the file number is increasing, the process start-up overhead will soon come to be un-ignorable.

Now, we use dataset-{f, g, h}, a small file dataset to make a comparison between Hadoop and Fat-Btree database in the data load experiment.

In this experiment, Fat-Btree DBMS loads the data by executing the LOAD SQL command sequentially from one node. Then the Fat-Btree evenly distributes these tuples across the cluster automatically. The tuples which are inserted into Fat-Btree DBMS contain the same content as the small files that loaded into Hadoop. Fig 4 shows the time needed to load the same volume of datasets both in Hadoop and Fat-Btree DBMS. As it shows, the data load time is increased when the individual data size is decreasing in both systems. Note that when the data (file/tuple) size is larger than 100K, the load time in both Hadoop and Fat-Btree DBMS do not grow obviously, because a great portion of cost in writing one piece of data is the file I/O cost. However, when the data size becomes smaller, which means the file I/O cost in each process decreased, the extra cost turns to be dominate. Therefore, the load time in Hadoop soon overcomes that in Fat-Btree DBMS because the Hadoop has a larger process initialization, data combination and metadata management costs in storing the same volume of data, while these extra costs may be unobvious in the parallel databases, which have optimized and sophisticated process and storage management methods.

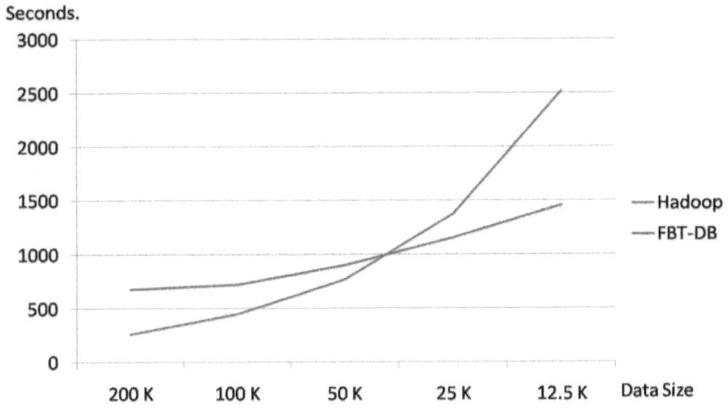

Fig. 4. Data Load Time Comparison

In a short conclusion, to load the dataset from local disk into Hadoop's virtual disk, lots of data input/split tasks will be launched as several individual processes. If the input file is in a small size (e.g. less than 50K in this experimental environment), the load performance of Hadoop will decrease dramatically, and underperform the Fat-Btree DBMS.

4.3 Data Access Performance

Now, we study the data access performance of Hadoop, including the throughput and scalability, and make a comparison with Fat-Btree DBMS.

Firstly, we modify the demonstration Map-Reduce program "wordcount" in Hadoop source code. To test Hadoop I/O performance: The Map function in "wordcount" is modified to read all the words in the small files on HDFS and write record of each word into an output file as the (key, 1) pairs, there is no calculation function in Map to get the summary of each word's appearance times. And then, we remove the Reduce function in the program, thus the output generated by each Map instance is the final output of the program. Our purpose of these modifications is to get the time required by Hadoop to read and write every word in all the files in HDFS while eliminate the extra cost of calculating, grouping and shuffling. Thus the execution time of this program is mainly the time for the file I/O process in Hadoop, then we can compare this time with that required by the Fat-Btree DBMS.

On the other hand, we use the SQL Command like: SELECT * FROM TABLE WHERE ID == 'X'; to fetch all the contents from the tuples in Fat-Btree DBMS and use the SQL Command like: UPDATE TABLE SET TEXT = 'STRING' WHERE ID == 'X' to overwrite the same data. Each node has 4 client threads to execute these commands in parallel to read and write all the data in the database.

As shown in Figure 5, Hadoop takes several hours to finish the "wordcount" transaction, while Fat-Btree outperforms Hadoop by a factor about 400, which

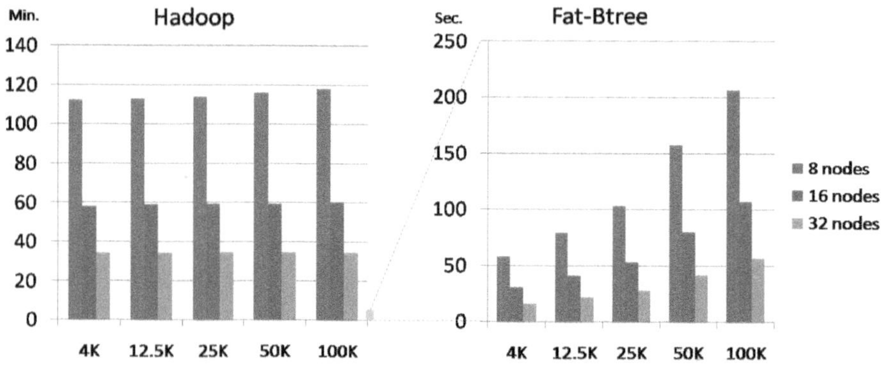

Fig. 5. Data Access Time in Hadoop and Fat-Btree

only needs several minutes to read and write all the data. This is because the start-up costs for the small file I/O applications are dominated in the execution time. On average, each task in Hadoop needs about 20 seconds to start and run at full speed.

In addition, Fig. 5 also shows the different scalabilities of Hadoop and Fat-Btree systems. We find that when the node number is increased by twice from 8 to 32, the scalability of Hadoop declines from 96% to 85% compared to that of Fat-Btree which only decreases slightly. This is because Hadoop use the job tracker to coordinate Datanode activities, and its overhead will increase as more nodes are added into the system. However, Fat-Btree DBMS does not contain these centered nodes, thus the potential bottlenecks are eliminated from the system. The reason for the slight decline may be the raise of communication cost within the Fat-Btree when the node number increasing.

In a short conclusion, for the small file I/O applications, Hadoop's performance decreased dramatically because the overhead in process start-up. It may cause every task to wait 20 seconds on average before they are executed in full speed. On the other hand, Fat-Btree DBMS does not suffer this problem and achieve a better scalability.

5 Related Works

As an open source software which implements a framework of Map-Reduce, Hadoop has been embraced by lots of data-intensive distributed applications both in commercial and academic societies. However, Hadoop seems only to be able to run large-scale analyses on big data. Almost all the applications adopt Hadoop engine for the computation on huge datasets [17], [18], because the performance for the application on small or middle size dataset in Hadoop is not as attractive as DBMS. A lot of researches that focus on these problems have been proposed. For instance, [19] optimizes the Hadoop in its branch project of HPMR, which focuses on cutting off the cost in the "Reduce" process with the High Performance Map-Reduce Engine. [17] proposes a method to reduce the metadata for the small files in Hadoop by compressing the small data which has some kind of semantic relations in the specific applications together. In [1], the small file metadata problem is slightly addressed in the original web implementation of Hadoop. However, there seem no effective solutions in these former researches for improving the small file I/O performance in Hadoop as discussed in this paper.

Therefore, recent researches, which use Hadoop as its execution engine, adopt a light database system into the system for organization the intermediate results and trial datasets, as in [21], [22], [23], [25]. These systems try to bring Map-Reduce ideas together with DBMS system and aim to integrate declarative query constructs from the database community into MapReduce-like software to allow better code reusability, data independence and automatic query optimization. Different from above interface level solutions, HadoopDB [6] integrates Hadoop with Postgres in systems-level, which may be the first practice that builds a real hybrid system of Map-Reduce and Parallel DBMS. What is more, this kind of hybrid Map-Reduce/DBMS system is looked upon as an optimal solution for parallel processing systems in recent future [15].

However, HadoopDB does not in general match the performance of parallel database systems especially in data selection. Since HadoopDB use the databases to store all the data sources similar to data blocks in HDFS, the large size of data used in [6] may be one of the reasons that hinders the data access efficiency of HadoopDB. Therefore, it is very important to choose the better storage layer, database or HDFS layer, dynamically in the future hybrid Map-Reduce/DBMS systems to store the files in the applications. To make this decision, the comparison between Hadoop and parallel DBMS in their file I/O performance on the datasets of different data size is needed for the future system design information.

As far as we know, there seems no former work that gives the comparison. In recently, there is a similar comparison work as ours [7], which compares Hadoop with other two parallel DBMSs is proposed. However, they focus on the analyses of different storage mechanism (row-based/column based) and aggregation performance in the vertical/horizontal partition DBMS with Hadoop. In addition, the size of individual data used in their experimental datasets is much larger than that of ours. What is more, the tranditional hash and clustered index used in these parallel DBMSs may hinder the database systems scalability. Note that the data load performance experiment result is hence different with ours; the scalability comparison result between our parallel DBMS and Hadoop is also different from that declared in [7].

6 Conclusion

In this paper, we focus on comparing the Hadoop, which is an implementation of map-reduce paradigm, with a parallel database system that was developed earlier at Tokyo Institute of Technology. We have taken eight different datasets to examine the data loading, accessing and modification cost of these two system especially for small file I/O. These comparison results could be a note for the information of future hybrid Map-Reduce and Parallel DBMS design.

Our results show that, Hadoop has significant overheads due to task initialization; the Namenode appears as the bottleneck when the system scales up, especially for handling the small files. Our parallel DBMS shows its higher performance, over a factor of 400 in the small file I/O performance, and shows its better scalability than that of Hadoop. Note that some of the system features in both Hadoop and DBMS are no longer the same as they used to be in former researches which mainly considered the data in large file size. As there is a great contrast in file I/O performance of Hadoop and parallel DBMS when handling the small size of data, a flexible storage layers mechanism should be considered in the design of the future hybrid Map-Reduce/DBMS systems.

Acknowledgement

This research was supported in part by MEXT Grant-in-Aid for Scientific Research on Priority Areas (#21013017).

References

1. `http://www.cloudera.com/blog/2009/02/02/the-small-files-problem`
2. Dean, J., Ghemawat, S.: MapReduce: Simplified Data Processing on Large Clusters. In: USENIX Symposium on Operating Systems Design and Implementation, OSDI 2004 (2004)
3. Boral, H., Alexander, W., Clay, L., Copeland, G., Danforth, S., Franklin, M., Hart, B., Smith, M., Valduriez, P.: Prototyping Bubba, a highly parallel database system. IEEE TKDE 2(1), 4–24 (1990)
4. Dewitt, D.J., Ghandeharizadeh, S., Schneider, D.A., Bricker, A., Hsiao, H.I., Rasmussen, R.: The Gamma database machine project. IEEE TKDE 2(1), 44–62 (1990)
5. Yokota, H., Kanemasa, Y., Miyazaki, J.: Fat-Btree: An update conscious parallel directory structure. In: ICDE 1999, March 1999, pp. 448–457. IEEE Computer Society, Los Alamitos (1999)
6. Abouzeid, A., Bajda-Pawlikowski, K., Abadi, D., Rasin, A., Silberschatz, A.: Hadoopdb: An architectural hybrid of mapreduce and dbms technologies for analytical workloads. In: VLDB 2009: Proceedings of the 2009 VLDB Endowment (2009)
7. Pavlo, A., Paulson, E., Rasin, A., Abadi, D.J., Dewitt, D.J., Madden, S., Stonebraker, M.: A comparison of approaches to large-scale data analysis. In: Proceedings of the 2009 ACM SIGMOD International Conference, June 2009. ACM, New York (2009)
8. Hadoop, `http://hadoop.apache.org/`
9. Augusto, C., Baquero, S.: Performance test of Hadoop and iRODS Distributed Storage Systems. In: Seminario De Invesigation III, Mayo 18 De (2009)
10. Delmerico, J., Byrnes, N., Bruno, A., Jones, M., Gallo, S., Chaudhary, V.: Comparing the Performance of Clusters, Hadoop and Active Disks on Microarray Correlation Computations. In: The 16th IEEE International Conference on High Performance Computing, HiPC 2009, Cochin, India (2009)

11. http://dev.mysql.com/doc/refman/5.1/en/overview.html
12. Wu, S., Kemme, B.: Postgres-R(SI): Combining Replica Control with Concurrency Control Based on Snapshot Isolation. In: Proceedings of the 21st Int'l Conf. on Data Engineering, ICDE 2005, Washington, DC, April 05 - 08, pp. 422–433 (2005)
13. Pacitti, E., Ozsu, M.T., Coulon, C.: Preventive multi-master replication in a cluster of autonomous databases. In: Kosch, H., Böszörményi, L., Hellwagner, H. (eds.) Euro-Par 2003. LNCS, vol. 2790, pp. 318–327. Springer, Heidelberg (2003)
14. http://slony.info/documentation/failover.html
15. Stonebraker, M., Abadi, D., DeWitt, D.J., Madden, S., Paulson, E., Pavlo, A., Rasin, A.: Mapreduce and parallel dbmss: friends or foes? Commun. ACM 53(1), 64–71 (2010)
16. Carns, P., Lang, S., Ross, R., Vilayannur, M., Kunkel, J., Ludwig, T.: Small-File Access in Parallel File Systems. In: Proceedings of the 23rd IEEE International Parallel and Distributed Processing Symposium (April 2009)
17. Liu, X., Han, J., et al.: Implementing WebGIS on Hadoop: A Case Study of Improving Small File IO Performance on HDFS. In: IEEE Cluster, New Orleans, LA (September 1, 2009)
18. Leo, S., Santoni, F., Zanetti, G.: Biodoop: Bioinformatics on Hadoop. In: International Conference on Parallel Processing Workshops, ICPPW 2009, September 22-25, pp. 415–422 (2009)
19. Seo, S., Jang, I., et al.: HPMR: Prefetching and pre-shuffling in shared MapReduce computation environment. In: Cluster Computing and Workshops (2009)
20. Namiki, Y., Kanbe, K., Kobayashi, D., Yokota, H.: An approach of using a parallel B-tree structure, Fat-Btree, in PostgreSQL for distributed retrieval. DBSJ Letters 6(2), 61–64 (2007)
21. Chaiken, R., Jenkins, B., Larson, P.-A., Ramsey, B., Shakib, D., Weaver, S., Zhou, J.: Scope: Easy and efficient parallel processing of massive data sets. In: Proc. of International Conference on Very Large Data Bases (2008)
22. Olston, C., Reed, B., Srivastava, U., Kumar, R., Tomkins, A.: Pig latin: a not-so-foreign language for data processing. In: Proc. of SIGMOD (2008)
23. Facebook. Hive. Web page, http://issues.apache.org/jira/browse/HADOOP-3601
24. Wang, F., Qiu, J., Yang, J., Dong, B., Li, X., Li, Y.: Hadoop high availability through metadata replication. In: CloudDB 2009: Proceeding of the First International Workshop on Cloud Data Management (2009)
25. Thusoo, A., et al.: Hive: A warehousing solution over a Map-Reduce framework. In: Proceedings of the Conference on Very Large Databases, pp. 1626–1629 (2009)
26. Amazon Web Service LLC. Amazon Elastic MapReduce (2009), http://aws.amazon.com/elasticmapreduce/

Mining Contrast Inequalities in Numeric Dataset*

Lei Duan[1], Jie Zuo[1,**], Tianqing Zhang[1], Jing Peng[2], and Jie Gong[1]

[1] School of Computer Science, Sichuan University,
Chengdu 610065, China
[2] Sci. & Tech. Department, Chengdu Municipal Public Security Bureau,
Chengdu 610017, China
{leiduan,zuojie}@scu.edu.cn

Abstract. Finding relational expressions which exist frequently in one class of data while not in the other class of data is an interesting work. In this paper, a relational expression of this kind is defined as a contrast inequality. Gene Expression Programming (GEP) is powerful to discover relations from data and express them in mathematical level. Hence, it is desirable to apply GEP to such mining task. The main contributions of this paper include: (1) introducing the concept of contrast inequality mining, (2) designing a two-genome chromosome structure to guarantee that each individual in GEP is a valid inequality, (3) proposing a new genetic mutation to improve the efficiency of evolving contrast inequalities, (4) presenting a GEP-based method to discover contrast inequalities, (5) giving an extensive performance study on real-world datasets. The experimental results show that the proposed methods are effective. Contrast inequalities with high discriminative power are discovered from the real-world datasets. Some potential works on contrast inequality mining are discussed.

Keywords: Data Mining; Contrast Mining; Gene Expression Programming.

1 Introduction

Capturing the distinguishing and important characteristics between two or more classes of data is a meaningful task in data mining. Such knowledge is very useful for scientists. For example, Emerging Patterns (EPs) [1] are itemsets whose supports change significantly between different classes of data. They have been used for understanding leukaemia and other bioinformatics applications [2]. Based on the concept of EP, other contrast pattern mining have been introduced, such as jumping EP [3], delta-discriminative EP [4], diverging pattern [5].

Similar to EP discovery, class contrast function mining is proposed in [6]. A function is called class contrast function if it is accurate in one class but not in other classes of data. The main difference between EP and class contrast function is that EPs are

* This work was supported by the National Natural Science Foundation of China under grant No. 60773169, the 11th Five Years Key Programs for Sci. &Tech. Development of China under grant No. 2006BAI05A01, and the Young Faculty Foundation of Sichuan University under grant No. 2009SCU11030.

** Corresponding author.

L. Chen et al. (Eds.): WAIM 2010, LNCS 6184, pp. 194–205, 2010.

discovered from nominal dataset while class contrast functions are discovered from numeric dataset directly. Moreover, there is another kind of contrast exists besides EP and class contrast function.

Example 1. Suppose dataset D records the average incomes of five different occupations at different cities. The samples are classified into two classes according to the city is coastal area or inland area. The samples are list as follows.

	O_1	O_2	O_3	O_4	O_5	Class
s_1	2200	1100	400	1300	2200	*coastal*
s_2	3100	1300	590	1400	1500	*coastal*
s_3	3200	1250	630	690	1600	*coastal*
s_4	2000	1500	830	1200	1400	*inland*
s_5	1900	1800	970	930	1800	*inland*
s_6	1500	1350	840	700	1300	*inland*

The dataset D shows that all samples from coastal area (s_1, s_2, s_3) hold relation $O_2 < O_5$, while samples from inland area (s_4, s_5, s_6) not. Besides $O_2 < O_5$, relation $O_1 > (O_3 + O_4)$ is held by all coastal samples while not held by inland samples.

Though Example 1 is a simple synthetic example, it reveals such significative relations in the real world. For example, a notable symptom of an influenza patient is that her/his body temperature is higher than 38 degrees centigrade. Our experimental study demonstrates that many relations of this kind exist in real-world datasets.

It is interesting to see that the relations $O_2 < O_5$ and $O_1 > (O_3 + O_4)$ in Example 1 are different from EP and class contrast function. Formally, we define this mining task as follows.

Definition 1 (Support). Given a dataset D containing numeric attributes. Let *ieq* be an inequality. Suppose the number of samples that holds *ieq* in D is n. Then the support of *ieq*, is defined as $n/|D|$, denoted as $Sup(ieq, D) = n/|D|$.

For example, the support of Inequality $O_1 > (O_3 + O_4)$ is 0.5 in Example 1. Since any multi-class problem can be converted into n two-class problems, to keep our discussion simple, we only consider two-class problem in this work. That is, given a dataset, we divide samples into positive part and negative part.

Definition 2 (Contrast Inequality). Given a dataset D, the positive part is D_p, the negative part is D_n, $D = D_p \cup D_n$ and $D_p \cap D_n = \varnothing$. Suppose support thresholds are α and β ($0.0 < \beta < \alpha < 1.0$). A ($\alpha$, β)-contrast inequality is an inequality *ieq* satisfying following support constraints: i) $Sup(ieq, D_p) \geq \alpha$ and ii) $Sup(ieq, D_n) \leq \beta$.

To the best of our knowledge, there is no previous work on finding such kind of inequalities has been done. Two contrast mining tasks that are most closely related to our work are disjunctive EP [7] and class contrast function [6]. The disjunctive EPs allows containing logical operations, such as AND, OR, XOR. So, they contain more expressive contrasts compared with EPs. In other words, disjunctive EPs are generations of traditional EPs. However, disjunctive EP is different from contrast inequality, since it cannot express the inequality relations among attributes in data. And, it does not consider the numerical operations among attributes in data. The main difference between class contrast function and contrast inequality is that contrast inequality is a relational expression, and the result of contrast inequality is a Boolean value, while the result of a class contrast function is a numeric value.

In general, we have following challenges on mining contrast inequalities:

i) How to discover one or more contrast inequalities from the numeric dataset.
ii) How to discover contrast inequalities with high discriminative power.
iii) How to discover actionable contrast inequalities for domain applications.

As the first study on contrast inequality mining, we focus on the first two challenges. The third challenge depends on expert knowledge of the application, and will be the subject of future research.

The definition of contrast inequality shows that one contrast inequality contains one relational operator, several numerical operators, and several variables. As it is hard to determine the form of inequality, it is inappropriate to apply traditional regression methods, needing user defined hypothesis, to discover such inequalities from dataset. This study applies Gene Expression Programming (GEP) [8, 9] to contrast inequality mining. GEP is the newest development of Genetic Algorithms (GA) and Genetic Programming (GP). GEP has strong evolution power, and each candidate solution (individual) in GEP is coded in a flexible structure. Moreover, we design a new individual structure in GEP to make it more suitable for contrast inequality mining. The preliminary knowledge of GEP will be introduced in Sec. 2.

The main contributions of this work include: (1) introducing the concept of contrast inequality, (2) designing a two-genome chromosome structure to guarantee that each individual in GEP is a valid inequality, (3) proposing a new genetic mutation to improve the efficiency of evolving contrast inequalities, (4) presenting a GEP-based method to discover contrast inequalities, (5) giving an extensive performance study on proposed methods and discussing some future studies.

The rest of this paper is organized as follows. Section 2 introduces related works. Section 3 presents the main ideas used by our methods and the implementation of the algorithm. Section 4 reports an experimental study on several real-world datasets. Section 5 discusses future works, and concluding remarks.

2 Related Work

2.1 Contrast Mining

As introduced in Sec. 1, EPs are itemsets whose supports change significantly from one class of data to another. The EP mining algorithm was firstly proposed in [1]. Then, several efficient methods have been designed, including: constraint-based approach [10], tree-based approach [11, 12], projection based algorithm [13], ZBDD based method [7], and equivalence classes based method [4]. The complexity of finding emerging patterns is MAX SNP-hard [14].

EPs have high discrimination power [14], many EP-based classification methods have been proposed, such as CAEP [15], DeEPs [16], JEP based method [3]. Researches on EP-classification have demonstrated that EPs are useful to construct accurate classifiers. These research results showed that EP based classification methods often out perform some well known classifiers, including C4.5 and SVM [14]. Moreover, EP has got success applications in bioinformatics. For example, it has been used for understanding leukaemia and other applications [2].

Based on the concept of EP, several variants of EP have been introduced. Jumping EPs are EPs which are found in one distinct class of data [3], disjunctive EPs generalizes EPs by introducing conjunctions for pattern description [7]. Delta-discriminative EP defines EP in a more general way [4]. Diverging patterns are itemsets whose frequencies change significantly different in two datasets [5]. Class contrast functions are functions whose accuracies change significantly between two classes [6]. Different from EP mining, class contrast functions are discovered from numeric dataset. The difference between symbolic regression and class contrast function mining is that the former just considers the accuracy while the latter not only considers the accuracy but also the accuracy changes in different classes of dataset.

2.2 Preliminary Concepts of GEP

GEP is a new evolutionary method inspired by Genetic Algorithms (GAs) and Genetic Programming (GP) [8]. The basic steps in GEP to seek the optimal solution are the same as those of GA and GP. Compared with the classical linear GA and the traditional GP, the coding of individuals (candidate solutions) in GEP is more flexible and efficient [9]. The main players in GEP are only two: the chromosomes and the expression trees. For each individual in GEP, the genotype is represented by a linear symbol string of fixed length (chromosome), and the phenotype is represented in a hierarchical structure (expression tree) that contains semantic information of the individual. So, GEP is a genotype/phenotype system that exhibits the simplicity of GA, while maintains the complexity of GP.

One or more genes compose a chromosome. Each gene is divided into a head and a tail. The head contains symbols that represent both functions and terminals, whereas the tail contains only terminals. For each problem, the length of the head h is chosen by the user, whereas the length of the tail t is a function of h and the number of arguments of the function with more arguments n, and is evaluated by the equation: $t = h(n-1) + 1$. Consider a gene for which the set of functions $F = \{+, -, *, /\}$. In this case the maximum number of arguments of the element in F is 2, then $n = 2$.

In GEP, the length of a gene and the number of genes composed in a chromosome are fixed. No matter what the gene length is, genes may code for expression trees of different sizes and shapes. Through parsing the expression tree from left to right and from top to bottom, the valid part of GEP genes, called open reading frame, can be obtained. Due to the special structure of GEP individuals, any genetic operation made in the chromosome, no matter how profound, always results in a valid expression tree. So all individuals evolved by GEP are syntactically correct.

Based on the principle of natural selection and "survival for the fittest", GEP operates iteratively evolving a population of chromosomes, encoding candidate solutions, through genetic operators, such as selection, crossover, and mutation, to find an optimum solution. The main steps of GEP consist of following steps [9]:

Step 1: Create random initial population.
Step 2: Evaluate the population with predefined fitness function.
Step 3: Select individuals according to fitness values.

Step 4: Apply genetic operations to individuals to reproduce modification.
Step 5: If evolution stop condition is not met, go to Step 2.
Step 6: Return the best-so-far candidate solution.

GEP has been widely used in data mining research fields, including symbolic regression, classification, and time series analysis [17-19].

3 Contrast Inequality Mining

In this section, we describe our proposed method for mining contrast inequalities in data. Specifically, we present a new chromosome structure in GEP to encode contrast inequalities, and introduce a genetic mutation for evolving the candidate contrast inequalities efficiently.

3.1 Two-Genome Chromosome

GEP seeks the optimal solution through evolving the population. Each individual in the population is a candidate solution to the problem. It is composed of one or more genes, and each gene can model a mathematical expression. As discussed in Section 2, the length of gene is fixed, thus the complexity of the mathematical expression presented by one gene is limited. To break this limitation, several genes are connected by linking functions, such as plus, multiplication, to express complex expressions.

When applying GEP to contrast inequality mining, one basic idea is that each GEP individual must be a valid inequality. Then, the calculation power of GEP can be fully used. To this end, a simple idea is using relational operator, such as less than, greater than, as the linking function. However, this method has an obvious disadvantage. First, the number of genes in a chromosome is fixed as two. Second, researches in [9] demonstrated that the chromosome consists of several short genes has better expression power than a single long gene. In a word, this method limits the evolution power of GEP.

We design a new GEP individual structure, called *two-genome chromosome*, in this work. A two-genome chromosome has following characteristics:

i) A two-genome chromosome is composed of two genomes, and one relational operator. The two genomes are connected by the relational operator. The genome on the left of the relational operator is called left genome, and the one on the right of the relational operator is called right genome.
ii) A genome is composed of one or more genes. Genes in genome are connected by the linking function.
iii) There is no relational operator in left or right genome.

Thus, a two-genome chromosome contains only one relational operator, several numerical operators and several variables. Moreover, the structure of two-genome guarantees that any two-genome chromosome can be decoded to a valid inequality. Example 2 gives an example of a two-genome chromosome coding an inequality.

Example 2. Given a two-genome chromosome, in which the left genome and right genome is composed of two genes, respectively. Let the function set be {+, -, *, /}, the terminal set be {a, b, c, d, e, f}, the linking function in genome be plus (+), and the relational operator be less than (<). Let the length of gene head be 4. The genes are illustrated as follows. The bold part of each gene is the valid decoding part in phenotype. The expression tree and corresponding inequality are also illustrated.

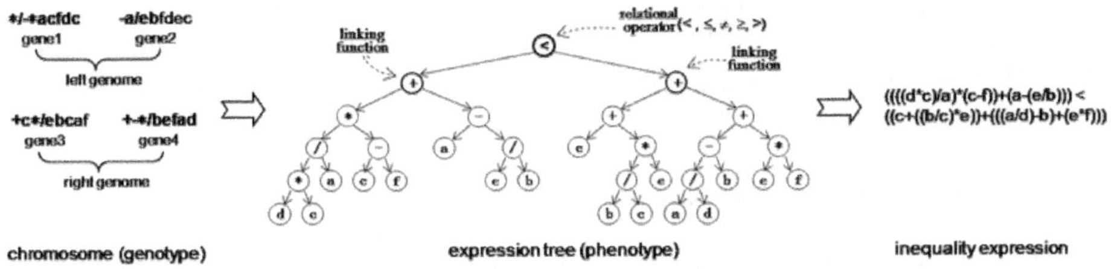

Fig. 1. An example of a two-genome chromosome coding an inequality

The gene parameters, such as head length, number of genes, linking function, for left genome and right genome are determined by the user. No matter what the values are, the individual of the two-genome structure is a valid inequality. Other relational operator, such as less than (<), less than or equal to (≤), greater than or equal to (≥), can also be used in the two-genome chromosome. In this way, the two-genome structure keeps the flexibility without losing the GEP's calculation power. Note that, when the relational operator is not-equal (≠), the contrast inequality mining can be converted to mining a function which is accurate in one class but not in other classes. The contrast inequality equals to a class contrast function in this case.

3.2 Fitness Function Design

GEP follows the principle of natural selection to evolve candidate solutions. A well-known selection method in GEP is roulette-wheel sampling [9]. Let P be the population, $P = \{g_i \mid 1 \leq i \leq |P|\}$. Given a GEP individual g_i in P, the probability of g_i being selected in the next generation is defined as:

$$Prob(g_i) = \frac{fit(g_i)}{fit(g_1) + fit(g_2) + \ldots + fit(g_{|P|})} \tag{1}$$

Based on Equation (1), the individuals with larger fitness have larger opportunity to be selected to reproduce with modification, leaving progeny with new traits.

The aim of our work is finding contrast inequalities whose supports change significantly in different classes of data. Since the fitness function evaluates all candidate solutions and guides the evolution direction, the fitness function is important in GEP application.

Given a dataset consist of positive part D_p and negative part D_n. For individual g_i, the fitness, denoted as $fit(g_i)$, is calculated as follows.

$$fit(g_i) = \frac{Sup(g, D_p) * D_p + 1}{Sup(g, D_n) * D_n + 1} \tag{2}$$

Equation (2) shows that the fitness of the individual whose support changes more significantly between positive part and negative part is larger. In addition, to avoid the zero-frequency problem, a pseudo-count of 1 is added to the fitness function.

According to Equation (2), the fitness values are all positive numbers. The maximal fitness value is $(|D_p| + 1)$, the minimal fitness value is $1/(|D_p| + 1)$. Compared with using the difference between the supports in D_p and D_n as the fitness function, Equation (2) has an advantage: it guides GEP to evolve contrast inequalities that has zero support in D_n. In EP, this kind of EP is called jumping EP, which has been proved to be very useful in constructing classifiers.

3.3 Relational Operator Mutation

Selected individuals are reproduced with modifications to create the necessary genetic diversity in population. Inspired from the nature, several modifications, like mutation, deletion and insertion, are applied during the replication of the genes. In basic GEP, the genetic operations include mutation, transposition and recombination.

Mutation is the most efficient genetic operator to introduce random modifications into a given chromosome [9]. No matter how mutation operator performs, it must keep the structural organization of individuals remain intact. To this end, any symbol in the gene heads can change into another function or terminal, while terminals in the gene tails can only change into terminals.

Functions in the basic GEP belong to the same type, they can occur anywhere at the gene head. However, in the two-genome chromosome, the relational operator cannot occur in the gene head, and functions in the gene head cannot be a relational operator. The mutation operation must remain the chromosome as a valid inequality, when applying the mutation operator to a two-genome chromosome.

There are two strategies for relational operator mutation in two-genome structure:

1. the relational operator is kept unchanged during the evolution.
2. the relational operator can randomly change into another relational operator.

For the first strategy, the mutation operator has no effect to the relational operator. As creating diverse population is helpful for evolution, we believe relational operator mutation is necessary and useful. We adopt the second strategy in the two-genome chromosome. Specifically, we define a relational operator set besides the function set and the terminal set. The relation operator set contains all available relational operators. Then, the relational operator in the individual randomly changes into another relational operator. For other symbols in the gene heads and tails, they follow the same mutation way in basic GEP. In our work, the relational operator set is $\{<, \leq, >, \geq\}$. The rate of relational operator change equals to the mutation rate.

For the other two genetic operations, transposition and recombination, we keep them as same as in the basic GEP, since their operation objects are symbols in genes. The details of transposition and recombination can be found in [9].

3.4 GEP-Based Mining Method

Algorithm 1 describes the pseudo code of contrast inequalities mining by GEP.

Algorithm 1: Contrast_Inequality_Mine(D1, D2)
Input: (1) sample set of positive class: D1; (2) sample set of negative class: D2.
Output: the individual with the highest fitness: bestIndividual.

```
begin
   1. pop ← CreateInitial( )
   2. FitEval(pop,D1,D2)
   3. bestIndividual ← GetBestIndividual(pop)
   4. Repeat
   5.    pop ← Select(pop)
   6.    RelationalOperatorMutation(pop)
   7.    Transposition(pop)
   8.    Recombination(pop)
   9.    FitEval(pop,D1,D2)
  10.    bestIndividual ← GetBestIndividual( )
  11. until StopCondition( ) = true
  12. return bestIndividual
end.
```

In Algorithm 1, Step 1 creates the initial population. In Step 2 and 9, function *FitEval*( ) evaluates each individual in *pop*. In Step 3 and 10, function *GetBestIndividual*( ) records the best individual discovered so far. From Step 5 to Step 8, selected individuals are modified by genetic operators. The relational operator in two-genome chromosome undergoes mutation operator in Step 6. The stop conditions include: the number of generations equals to the predefined value; the contrast inequalities that satisfy given thresholds are discovered; the running time equals to the predetermined value.

4 Performance Evaluation

To evaluate the performance of our GEP-based contrast inequality mining method, we implemented all proposed algorithms in Java. The experiments were performed on an Intel Pentium Dual 1.80 GHz (2 Cores) PC with 2G memory running Windows XP operating system. Table 1 lists the GEP related parameters in our experiments.

We selected two microarray datasets, Colon Tumor and ALL/AML, which were used in previous EP mining study [20]. The datasets are available at Kent Ridge Bio-medical Dataset (http://datam.i2r.a-star.edu.sg/datasets/krbd). Moreover, we applied our method to datasets selected from UCI Machine Learning Repository [21]: iris, breast cancer and wine. Both iris and wine contain three classes of samples, we divided them into three 2-class datasets, respectively. The samples containing missing values are removed from the original dataset. Table 2 lists the characteristics of datasets.

Table 1. Parameters for GEP Evolution

parameter	value	Parameter	value
Population size	100	One-point recombination rate	0.4
Relational operator set	$\{<, \leq, >, \geq\}$	Two-point recombination rate	0.2
Linking function	+	Gene recombination rate	0.1
Function set	$\{+, -, *, /\}$	IS transposition rate	0.1
Number of genes	2	IS elements length	1, 2, 3
Gene head size	4	RIS transposition rate	0.1
Selection operator	tournament	RIS elements length	1, 2, 3
Mutation rate	0.04	Gene transposition rate	0.1

Table 2. Data characteristics of experimental datasets

Dataset	# samples in pos. class	# samples in neg. class	# attributes
Colon Tumor	22 (positive)	40 (negative)	2000
ALL/AML	27 (ALL)	11 (AML)	7129
iris-virginica	50 (virginica)	100 (non-virginica)	4
iris-versicolor	50 (versicolor)	100 (non-versicolor)	4
iris-setosa	50 (setosa)	100 (non-setosa)	4
breast cancer w.	458 (benign)	241 (malignant)	9
wine-1	59 (class1)	119 (non-class1)	13
wine-2	71 (class2)	107 (non-class2)	13
wine-3	48 (class3)	130 (non-class3)	13

First of all, we compared the results of contrast inequality mining with EP mining to test the effectiveness of contrast inequality mining. In EP mining, the entropy-based discretization method [22] is used to partition numeric attributes into two disjoint intervals. Attributes are discarded if there is no cut point. As a result, 35 attributes are selected from Colon Tumor and 866 attributes are selected from ALL/AML. Though GEP can deal with as many as attributes theoretically, the large number of attributes may decrease the efficiency. Among 35 and 866 attributes that selected from Colon Tumor and ALL/AML datasets in EP mining, we selected 20 attributes with top information gains in our experiments. We set the maximal generation number of evolution is 20000, and did 20 independent running for each dataset. The results show that, for Colon Tumor dataset, the average fitness of the best individuals is 24.8, and the average generation number for evolving the best individual is 9908.7. For ALL/AML dataset, the average fitness is 28, and the average generation number for evolving the best individual is 3.2. Due to the space limits, we just list three best discovered contrast inequalities. The attributes are sorted in information gain descending order. We use the alphabet to index the attributes.

Table 3 and Table 4 show that the result of contrast inequality mining is better than that of EP mining. In Colon Tumor, the highest contrast ratio of discovered EP for positive class is 17:0, and the highest contrast ratio of discovered EP for negative class is 27:0, while the contrast ratio of discovered contrast inequality for positive class is 22:0. Moreover, it is interesting to note that given a contrast inequality with 100% frequency in positive class and 0% frequency in negative class, it is easy to convert it into a contrast inequality with 100% frequency in negative class and 0% frequency in positive class by changing the relational operator into the other direction. In ALL/AML, both EP mining and contrast inequality mining can get good results.

Table 3. Contrast inequalities discovered in Colon Tumor

contrast inequalities	fitness	# generations
$(((i+t)*l)/(k+r)+(p-s)/(n-r)) < ((c-((f*r)/s))+(b/(k/t)))$	23 (22:0)	15518
$(n+(e/((s-f)/c))) \geq ((g/t)*(f+o)+(((l-d)+s)-(c+h)))$	23 (22:0)	14507
$(((m+h)-(d+r))+(((s+n)*d)/c)) < ((o+(n-q-f))+b*(d/k))$	23 (22:0)	12828

Table 4. Contrast inequalities discovered in ALL/AML

contrast inequalities	fitness	# generations
((((o/k)/i)-c)+k) > (b+(n-j))	28 (27:0)	initial population
((((p/m)/d)/(d-m))+h) ≤ (m+e/i)	28 (27:0)	initial population
(m+(h/t)) ≥ (a+g)	28 (27:0)	1

Table 5 to Table 11 lists the discovered contrast inequalities in other datasets. The results show that many contrast inequalities with high discriminative power exist in these real-world datasets. From the fitness, we can see that most discovered inequalities close to the best solutions. So, our proposed method is effective, and it is a desirable work to discover contrast inequalities.

Table 5. Contrast inequalities discovered in iris-virginica

contrast inequalities	fitness	# generations
(((c/a)-b-b)+(((c*d)*c)*(d/c))) ≥ (d+b+b+d)	49 (48:0)	2106
((b+c)*(c/d)+d/b) < (c-b-b+c*c-d/c)	49 (48:0)	319
(d*d*d*(c-b)) > ((d+b)*c/a+d/c+a)	49 (48:0)	284

Table 6. Contrast inequalities discovered in iris-versicolor

contrast inequalities	fitness	# generations
(c/d+b+c*d+(c*b-a)*d/b) ≤ ((c*a-b)/(c-b)+c)	50 (49:0)	67
((d/b*c)-(b+c)+(a*a/d)/(c-b)) > (c+d)	50 (49:0)	18
((b-c)*d-c/b+d) ≥ ((d/a+a)/(b-c)+b-a-d+d*b)	50 (49:0)	742

Table 7. Contrast inequalities discovered in iris-setosa

contrast inequalities	fitness	# generations
(d*a+c/b/d+b/a) ≤ (a/c/d-b*d+b)	51 (50:0)	initial population
(c*a*b-(c+d)+c*c+d) ≤ (b*a/d*(a-c)+d+a+d)	51 (50:0)	initial population
(d+d+a+b+a*(c+a)/c) ≤ (a/d*a-c*c+(a/c-c)*(c+d))	51 (50:0)	Initial population

Table 8. Contrast inequalities discovered in breast cancer w.

contrast inequalities	fitness	# generations
(b*c*g-a/i+(a-b)*f-e) ≤ (g/f*b+c/d+e+g+e+e+c)	431 (430:0)	8696
((b+f+h)*c+(d-e)/g-b) ≤ (i/g+h-(i-c)+c+c+b+h+c)	429 (428:0)	3639
((a+f+a)/(i*a)+(a+a+a)/(f+c)) ≥ (a+(d*f-a)/(a+i))	428 (427:0)	1510

Table 9. Contrast inequalities discovered in wine-1

contrast inequalities	fitness	# generations
((k-l)/d*c*m+(f+i-c)*(i+g)) ≤ ((b*c-d)*a/k+k-c)	60 (59:0)	11025
((g+h)*m*c+e-m-i+e+e) ≥ ((k+g)*d*(d+d)+(d/b+a)*e)	60 (59:0)	2271
((((f-e)/c)/(g/d))+m+f-m/b) > ((d-l-a)*d+k)	59 (58:0)	1060

Table 10. Contrast inequalities discovered in wine-2

contrast inequalities	fitness	# generations
((l-d)/j*(a-e)+(c-m)/(l/c)) ≥ ((c*c-g)*(d-g)+(m-c)/(h-l))	70 (69:0)	7645
(c*b+i+d+b) > (b*(c*a-d)+(j/f*j-g/f))	68 (67:0)	1139
((j-c-i)*(b+c)+g*k-a-d/b) ≤ (b+f-(a*c-j))	67 (66:0)	2534

Table 11. Contrast inequalities discovered in wine-3

contrast inequalities	fitness	# generations
(((j+j)/l)*(c-g)+j-(i/l-b)) ≥ (e/m-(c-a)+h)	49 (48:0)	28
(j/l+i) ≥ (f*h+i+g+a/b*g*g/a)	49 (48:0)	27
(b*g-(d+j)+a*g+d*k) < (c+c*j+(k-l))	49 (48:0)	61

5 Discussions and Conclusions

Finding the distinguishing characteristics between different classes is an interesting data mining task. Based on previous contrast mining studies, we propose a new type of contrast mining, called contrast inequality mining. The concept of contrast inequality is similar to EP, while contrast inequality, containing numeric operators and relational operator, is discovered from numeric dataset directly. Contrast inequality mining is a challenging work. As GEP has many advantages on numeric calculation, we apply GEP to discover contrast inequalities in this paper. Moreover, we design a two-genome chromosome structure to guarantee that each individual in GEP population is a valid inequality, and propose the relational operator mutation to improve the efficiency of evolving contrast inequalities. The experimental results show that our proposed method is effective. Compared with EP mining, more discriminative results are discovered in contrast inequality mining. And many contrast inequalities with high discriminative power are discovered in the real-world datasets.

There are many works worth to be deeply analyzed in the future. For example, how to evaluate the discovered contrast inequalities, and how to make use of contrast inequalities to construct classifier are desirable future studies. Moreover, we will consider how to find actionable contrast inequalities by introducing domain knowledge into the mining process.

Acknowledgments. The authors thank to Guozhu Dong for his helpful comments.

References

1. Dong, G., Li, J.: Efficient Mining of Emerging Patterns: Discovering Trends and Differences. In: Zaki, M.J., Ho, C.-T. (eds.) KDD 1999. LNCS (LNAI), vol. 1759, pp. 43–52. Springer, Heidelberg (2000)
2. Li, J., Liu, H., Downing, J.R., Yeoh, A., Wong, L.: Simple Rules Underlying Gene Expression Profiles Using the Concept of Emerging Patterns. Bioinformatics 19, 71–78 (2003)
3. Li, J., Dong, G., Ramamohanarao, K.: Making Use of the Most Expressive Jumping Emerging Patterns for Classification. In: Terano, T., Chen, A.L.P. (eds.) PAKDD 2000. LNCS, vol. 1805, pp. 220–232. Springer, Heidelberg (2000)

4. Li, J., Liu, G., Wong, L.: Mining Statistically Important Equivalence Classes and Delta-Discriminative Emerging Patterns. In: Proc. of KDD 2007, pp. 430–439 (2007)
5. An, A., Wan, Q., Zhao, J., Huang, X.: Diverging Patterns: Discovering Significant Frequency Change Dissimilarities in Large Databases. In: Proc. of CIKM 2007, pp. 1473–1476 (2009)
6. Duan, L., Tang, C., Tang, L., Zhang, T., Zuo, J.: Mining Class Contrast Functions by Gene Expression Programming. In: Huang, R., Yang, Q., Pei, J., Gama, J., Meng, X., Li, X. (eds.) ADMA 2009. LNCS, vol. 5678, pp. 116–127. Springer, Heidelberg (2009)
7. Loekito, E., Bailey, J.: Fast Mining of High Dimensional Expressive Contrast Patterns Using Zero-suppressed Binary Decision Diagrams. In: Proc. of KDD 2006, pp. 307–316 (2006)
8. Ferreira, C.: Gene Expression Programming: A New Adaptive Algorithm for Solving Problems. Complex Systems 13(2), 87–129 (2001)
9. Ferreira, C.: Gene Expression Programming: Mathematical Modeling by an Artificial Intelligence. Angra do Heroismo, Portugal (2002)
10. Zhang, X., Dong, G., Ramamohanarao, K.: Exploring Constraints to Efficiently Mine Emerging Patterns from Large High-dimensional Datasets. In: Proc. of KDD 2000, pp. 310–314 (2000)
11. Bailey, J., Manoukian, T., Ramamohanarao, K.: Fast Algorithms for Mining Emerging Patterns. In: Elomaa, T., Mannila, H., Toivonen, H. (eds.) PKDD 2002. LNCS (LNAI), vol. 2431, pp. 39–50. Springer, Heidelberg (2002)
12. Fan, H., Ramamohanarao, K.: An Efficient Single-Scan Algorithm for Mining Essential Jumping Emerging Patterns for Classification. In: Chen, M.-S., Yu, P.S., Liu, B. (eds.) PAKDD 2002. LNCS (LNAI), vol. 2336, pp. 456–462. Springer, Heidelberg (2002)
13. Bailey, J., Manoukian, T., Ramamohanarao, K.: A Fast Algorithm for Computing Hypergraph Transversals and its Application in Mining Emerging Patterns. In: Proc. of ICDM 00002003, pp. 485–488 (2003)
14. Bailey, J., Dong, G.: Contrast Data Mining: Methods and Applications. Tutorial at 2007 IEEE ICDM (2007)
15. Dong, G., Zhang, X., Wong, L., Li, J.: CAEP: Classification by Aggregating Emerging Patterns. Discovery Science, 30–42 (1999)
16. Li, J., Dong, G., Ramamohanarao, K., Wong, L.: DeEPs: A New Instance-Based Lazy Discovery and Classification System. Machine Learning 54(2), 99–124 (2004)
17. Lopes, H.S., Weinert, W.R.: EGIPSYS: An Enhanced Gene Expression Programming Approach for Symbolic Regression Problems. Int'l Journal of Applied Mathematics and Computer Science 14(3), 375–384
18. Zhou, C., Xiao, W., Tirpak, T.M., Nelson, P.C.: Evolution Accurate and Compact Classification Rules with Gene Expression Programming. IEEE Transactions on Evolutionary Computation 7(6), 519–531 (2003)
19. Zuo, J., Tang, C., Li, C., et al.: Time Series Prediction based on Gene Expression Programming. In: Li, Q., Wang, G., Feng, L. (eds.) WAIM 2004. LNCS, vol. 3129, pp. 55–64. Springer, Heidelberg (2004)
20. Li, J., Wong, L.: Identifying Good Diagnostic Gene Groups from Gene Expression Profiles Using the Concept of Emerging Patterns. Bioinformatics 18, 725–734 (2002)
21. Asuncion, A., Newman, D.J.: UCI Machine Learning Repository (2007), http://www.ics.uci.edu/~mlearn/MLRepository.html
22. Fayyad, U., Irani, K.: Multi-interval Discretization of Continuous-valued Attributes for Classification Learning. In: Proc. of IJCAI 1993, pp. 1022–1029 (1993)

Users' Book-Loan Behaviors Analysis and Knowledge Dependency Mining

Fei Yan[1], Ming Zhang[1], Jian Tang[1], Tao Sun[1], Zhihong Deng[1], and Long Xiao[2]

[1] School of Electronics Engineering and Computer Science, Peking University
[2] Library of Peking University
{yanfei,mzhang,tangjian,suntao}@net.pku.edu.cn,
zhdeng@cis.pku.edu.cn, lxiao@lib.pku.edu.cn

Abstract. Book-loan is the most important library service. Studying users' book-loan behavior patterns can help libraries to provide more proactive services. Based on users' book-loan history in a university library, we could build a book-borrowing network between users and books. Furthermore, users who borrow the same books are linked together. The users and links then form a co-borrowing network which can be regarded as a knowledge sharing network. Both the book-borrowing network and the co-borrowing network can be used to study users' book-loan behavior patterns. This paper presents a study in analyzing users' book-loan behaviors and mining knowledge dependency between schools and degrees in Peking University. The mining work is based on the book-borrowing network and its corresponding co-borrowing network. To the best of our knowledge, it is the first work to mine knowledge dependency in digital library domain.

1 Introduction

Libraries are used to be storehouses for books and records. In today's globally networked information environment, where information is not rare as it used to be, the role of storehouse is becoming obsolete. Nowadays, libraries provide various kinds of items and services, e.g. electronic version of papers, multimedia learning materials and comfortable reading rooms. However, the most important service is still books loan and there exists some problems.

One problem is many libraries treat users(or readers) as if they are all the same. They don't care users' personal book-loan requirements. Users have to follow the unified steps, which may be complicated, to get their wanted books . The second problem is a lot of books brought by libraries are only useful for a few people, some of which have not even been borrowed once. Thirdly, books in the libraries are always placed in a fixed order, for example, books are placed on the shelves in the alphabetic order of standard book classification. It would be inconvenient for a user who always borrow books from two or more categories. In a word, the book-loan service is reactive rather than proactive.

Analyzing users' book-loan behaviors can help libraries to be more proactive in book-loan service. Once circulation records were saved, they could be analyzed.

L. Chen et al. (Eds.): WAIM 2010, LNCS 6184, pp. 206–217, 2010.

This analysis will turn up patterns of borrowing behavior and these patterns could be used to make suggestions (predictions) of future borrowing behavior. For example, suppose a particular set of books is consistently borrowed by a computer science students. The subject terms from this set of books could be extracted and used to suggest other books of possible use.

In Peking University library, students from different background and books of different categories are connected by book-borrowing behaviors, and they form a book-borrowing network. Besides, the students' co-borrowing relationships form a knowledge sharing network. Combining the book-borrowing network and co-borrowing network provides a basis for analyzing user behavior patterns and acquiring new understandings from user behaviors. For example, we can study the book-loan behavior similarity between groups of users by adding the users' attributes like schools and degrees to the co-borrowing network. And we can study the strength of relationships between groups of users and categories of books by adding the users' attributes and the categories of books to the book-borrowing network.

Base on these users' behavior patterns, we can study the knowledge dependency between schools. If we find students in one school has a strong book-loan similarity relationship with students in other school, then we can conclude that this school quite rely on the subjects of the other school. For example, students in school of computer science often have strong book-loan similarity with students in school of mathematics. For they often borrow mathematics related books, which provide underlying basic for computer science.

The analytical results are widely applicable. They can be used to enhance the personalized services provided by library, to find the strong correlated disciplines which tend to, or already, generate inter-disciplines. Further, this research method can be easily extended to other field such as book selling, on-line course learning and news discussion.

In this paper, following our pervious work[17], we present an in-depth analysis of the co-borrowing network and the book-borrowing network in Peking University library.

we add attributes such as school and degree to the networks to study the groups of users' book-loan behaviors by *descriptive staticstics* [9]theory. By combining these two kinds of networks, we are able to understand the users' book-loan behavior patterns more deeply. Our contributions are summarized as follows:

- We propose a novel idea to study the book-loan behavior patterns from the perspective of social network in a library.
- We confirm that students' majors and inter-disciplines are the dominant factors that affect users' book-loan behaviors.
- We gain new understandings from user behavior analysis, e.g. the widely influential disciplines, and strong correlated disciplines at Peking University.
- We have mined the knowledge dependency between schools and degrees of Peking University.

The rest of this paper is organized as follows. We study related work in Section 2. Section 3 describes the dataset, including the book-borrowing network and the students' co-borrowing network, followed by an analysis of users' book-loan behaviors based on book-borrowing network in Section 4 and mining the knowledge dependency in Section 5. Finally, Section 6 gives a conclusion.

2 Related Work

In this section we discuss the studies of data mining in digital libraries and social networks, the domains in which our method falls.

Data mining. Using data mining techniques to mine library data set has been in research for a long time. Guenther explained how libraries can use data mining techniques for more effective data collection [7]. Nicholson explored the concept of bibliomining which is the combination of bibliometrics and data mining, and presented the conceptual placement of bibliomining with other forms of evaluation in two contexts - digital library management and digital library research [12]. Web usage mining is very useful in digital library, which is the application of data mining technologies to discover usage patterns from Web data. Srivastava et al divided Web usage mining into three phases: preprocessing, pattern discovery, and pattern analysis [14]. And the technologies were applied directly to digital libraries by Bollen et al [5].

Social network. Social network is a concept derived from sociology. Researches show that the Web [4], scientific collaboration on research papers [11] and general social networks [2] have the small-world properties. Power-law distribution is another important property which has been observed to be existing in social network [2], as well as Web [4]. Wasserman and Faust, in their book [15], give an exhaustive overview of social network analysis techniques. With the increasing availability of social network data and the development of data mining technologies, social network analysis has received more and more attention by computer science researchers. Mislove et al. [10] measured and analyzed the structure of four popular online social networks. Adamic et al.[3] examined the knowledge sharing network of Yahoo! Answers and proposed a best answer prediction method. Singla and Richardson [13] verified that people who talk to each other are more likely to be similar to each other by analyzing the MSN network combining users' personal attributes. There are many other research topics in the domain of social network, such as combining the social network and semantic web technologies together [16], discovering social interests shared by groups of users [8], and community discovery method in the social network [6].

Our work differs from previous studies by combining both data mining technologies and social network technologies to study users' book loan patterns. To the best of our knowledge, this is the first work to study users' book loan patterns and knowledge dependency rules based on the hybird method in digital library.

3 Network Datasets

In this study, we use a whole year book-loan logs from Peking University library as our original dataset. A whole year is a complete cycle for university life which makes sure the analysis can minimize the influence of occurrence of particular events, and the analysis results can be easily extended to future years. We get the raw library log-files recorded from September 1, 2007 to August 31, 2008, which contains 859,735 book-loan records by 19,773 students. The original log-files contain rich information, however, we just focus on the following information: user identifier, school(department), degree, book identifier, and its category. We extract and merge the information from the log-files. Each book-borrowing event forms a record.

We set up a two-mode (bipartite graph) book-borrowing network and a one-mode co-borrowing network based on the dataset.

3.1 The Two-Mode Book-Borrowing Network

Consider a set of users borrowing a set of books in Peking University library. Users and Books are linked by the book-borrowing relationship which forms a two-mode network (bipartite graph) which can be illustrated by Figure 1(a).

We model the book-borrowing network as an undirected weighted bipartite graph. Let's define the book-borrowing network as $G_{U,B} =< U, B, E, W >$. $U = \{u_1, u_2 ... u_n\}$ and $B = \{b_1, b_2 ... b_m\}$ represent two disjoint sets of vertices in the graph. For each $e, e = (u, b)$ where $u \in U, b \in B$. And W is a mapping $W : E \rightarrow R$, where E is the set of edges, and R is the set of real number. For each $e = (u_i, b_j) \in E$, w_{ij} is the *weight* of e i.e. $W(e) = w_{ij}$. In the book-borrowing network, each user corresponds to a vertex $u_i \in U$, and each book corresponds to a vertex $b_j \in B$. An edge $e = (u_i, b_j) \in E$ indicates user u_i borrowed book b_j, and w_{ij} indicates the times user u_i borrowed book b_j in the whole year period. Table 1 presents the high-level statistics of the book-borrowing networks. *#Users*, *#Books*, *#Edges*, *Avg.Books*, *Max.Books*, *Avg.Weight* and *Max.Weight*

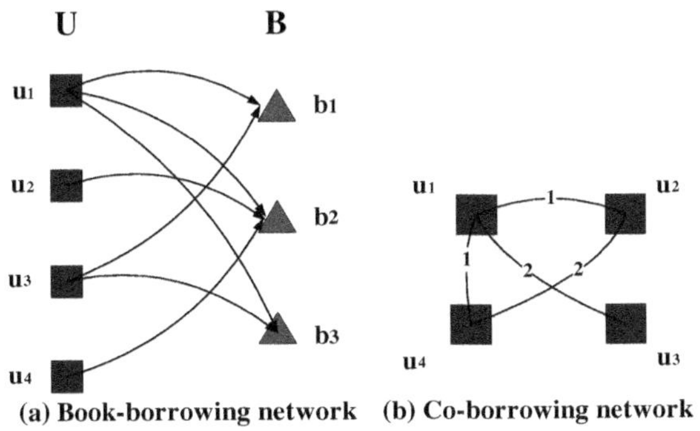

Fig. 1. A two-mode book-borrowing network and its corresponding one-mode co-borrowing network

Table 1. High-level statistics of book-borrowing networks

Network	#Users	#Books	#Edges	Max.Books	Avg.Books	Max.Weight	Avg.Weight
$G_{U,B}$	19,773	228,614	672,513	862	34.01	21	1.05

Table 2. High-level statistics of co-borrowing networks

Network	#Vertices	#Edges	Avg.Degrees
G_c	19,647	1,446,379	73.61

indicate the number of users, books and edges, the average and maximum number of books borrowed by a user, and the average and maximum weight of the edges in the network, respectively.

3.2 The One-Mode Co-borrowing Network

In a library, a book could be borrowed by more than one user. According to Figure 1(a), both u_1 and u_3 borrowed b_1 and b_3. The co-borrowing relationship linked u_1 and u_3 together. The strength of the tie can be quantified by the number of books borrowed by both two users. Figure 1(b) illustrated the co-borrowing network derived from Figure 1(a).

We model the co-borrowing network as an undirected weighted graph. Let's define the co-borrowing network as $G_C =< U, E, W >$; U is the vertex set; E is the edge set; w_{ij} is the *weight* of a edge e i.e. $W(e) = w_{ij}$, and indicates the number of books borrowed by both user u_i and user u_j in the one year period.Table 2 presents the high-level statistics of the co-borrowing networks.

3.3 The Attributes We Studied

In order to analyze the users' book-load behavior patterns, we further add users' attributes and the categories of books to the book-borrowing network and the global co-borrowing network.

In our work, we focus on users' attributes $A = \{school, degree\}$ indicating the user's school and degree respectively and the category ID of book which is referred to the *Classification for Library of the Chinese Academy of Sciences*[1]. We choose the top-level categories *A-Z* and the second level categories *TN*, *TP*, *TQ*, *TU*, *TV*, *O1*, *O2*,*O3*, *O4*, *O6* and *O7*. We define $P_i = \{p_{i_1}, p_{i_2}...p_{i_n}\}$ to denote the set of user groups divided by the value of attribute $a_i \in A$, and $C = \{c_1, c_2...c_m\}$ represents the set of book category IDs.

We apply the *descriptive statistics* theory to carry out these analytical experiments. In Section 4, we calculate the strength of borrowing relationship from users to books to analyze users' book borrowing preferences. In Section 5, we calculate the book-loan behavior similarity among groups of users to mining the knowledge dependency.

4 Analysis of Users' Book-Loan Behaviors

In the two-mode book-borrowing network, we obtain a global view by shrinking all users within a group to a new vertex representing the entire group, and shrinking all books within a category to a new vertex representing the entire category. Edges connecting shrunken vertices are replaced. The edge weight value is the sum of all original edge weight values.

We shrink $G_{U,B}$ to new networks $G_{a_k,C}$ where $a_k \in A = \{school, degree\}$. We can analyze the book-loan patterns of groups of users by calculating the strength of book-loan relationship from users to books in $G_{a_k,C}$.

Definition 1. *Let $w_{k_ic_j}$ denotes the weight of edge which connects vertex p_{k_i} and vertex c_j in $G_{a_k,C}$, and $card(p_{k_i})$ denotes cardinality of set p_{k_i}, we define the correlation between p_{k_i} and c_j as*

$$r_{k_ic_j} = \frac{w_{k_ic_j}}{card(p_{k_i})} \tag{1}$$

Actually, $r_{k_ic_j}$ represents the average number of books in category c_j borrowed by each user in group k_i. So $r_{k_ic_j}$ can reflect the strength of relationship between users in group p_{k_i} and books in category c_j.

4.1 Users' Schools VS. Categories of Books

In this part, we group the users in book-borrowing network by the value of attribute $a_1 = school$. There are students from 34 different schools involved in the book-borrowing network. Figure 2 presents an overview of the strength of borrowing relationship from schools to categories of books which varies from black at the weakest intensity to white at the strongest corresponding to the graduated scale on the right. In Figure 2 schools and categories of books are represented by IDs. The ID correspondence is shown in Table 4. The maximum strength value is hundreds of times greater than the non-zero minimum and most values are much lower than the maximum. In order to present the difference more clearly, we do base-10 logarithm calculation for all the values. For each school i, we calculate the average number of books borrowed by the users in it. Among the quantitative data, we calculate that the *mean* is 36.6, and the *standard deviation* is 17.51 according to the *descriptive statistics* theory.

First, we study how schools influence users' book category choices. We focus on the rows of Figure 2 to sort out the $Max.r_{1_ic_j}$ for every p_{1_i}. We discover that students in each school tend to borrow subject-related category. For example, students from Dept. of History borrow books in category *K: History and Geography* most. The course recommended reading lists may be an important factor accounting for this phenomenon. For example, we can see from Figure 2 that EECS has the strongest relationship with category *TP*. This may be caused by the students of EECS tending to borrow books in the reading lists of their compulsory courses, many of which are in category *TP*.

We are also interested in how categories attract students from subject unrelated disciplines. This analysis can minimize the impact of the courses reading

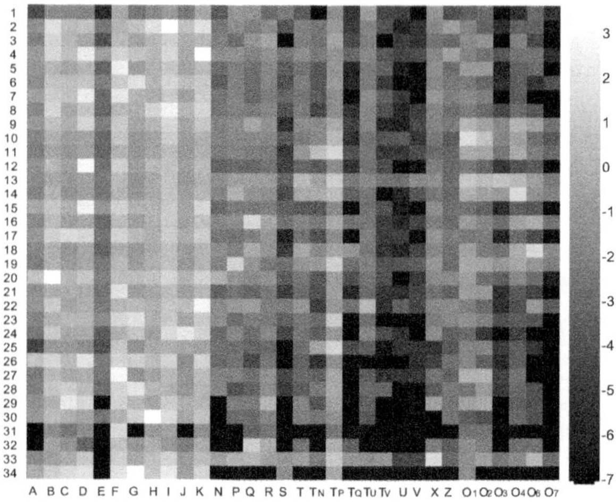

Fig. 2. Matrix of strength of relationship from Schools(Departments) to categories of books

lists. According to Figure 2, we find that the top 5 popular non-tech book categories borrowed by Science and Engineering major students are categories *F, I, K, D, and B*; while the top 5 popular non-humanity book categories borrowed by Liberal Arts and Humanities students are categories *TP, R, O2, O1, and TU*. We also observe that students in SEE, SMS and SLS, the schools of Science and Engineering disciplines, like to borrow books in non-tech categories most; while students in IM, SARC and IPR, the schools of Liberal Arts and Humanities disciplines, like to borrow books in non-humanity categories most.

Last, we find the widely influential disciplines which are studied by a large number of students from different schools. Figure 2 shows that books in categories *B: Philosophy and Religion, D: Politics and Law, Economics, I: Literature, and K: History and Geography* are widely borrowed. Therefore, they could be considered as the widely influential disciplines of Peking University.

4.2 Users' Degrees vs. Categories of Books

This part we carry on the analysis of the book-loan strength from degrees to categories of books. We find that for each book category c, the strengths from different degrees to c are almost identical which indicates that degree has tiny influence on book-borrowing behaviors.

5 Mining the Knowledge Dependency

In the one-mode co-borrowing network, we obtain a global view by shrinking the original network according to the value of users' attribute. The edges between shrunken vertices within one group are replaced by a loop.

We shrink the co-borrowing network G_C to new networks G_{p_k} where $p_k \in A = \{school, degree\}, k = 1, 2$. We define a set M_k, whose elements are also sets, as the user vertices in pair of groups. For each $m_{k_i k_j} \in M_k, m_{k_i k_j} = \{u, v | \exists e \in E(G_C), s.t. u \in p_{k_i} \bigwedge v \in p_{k_j}\}$.

Definition 2. *Let $w_{k_i k_j}$ denotes the weight of edge which connects vertex p_{k_i} and vertex p_{k_j} in G_{p_k}, and $card(m_{k_i k_j})$ denotes cardinality of set $m_{k_i k_j}$. We define the similarity between group p_{k_i} and group p_{k_j}as*

$$s_{k_i k_j} = \frac{w_{k_i k_j}}{card(m_{k_i k_j})} \tag{2}$$

Actually, $s_{k_i k_j}$ represents the average number of books co-borrowed by each pair of user in group p_{k_i} and group p_{k_j}. So $s_{k_i k_j}$ can reflect common interest between users in group p_{k_i} and p_{k_j}.

5.1 Knowledge Dependency between Schools

In this part, we group the users in the co-borrowing network by the value of attribute $p_1 = school$. Figure 3 presents an overview of the similarity between schools according to Definition 2. We also do base-10 logarithm calculation for all the values for clear display reason.

Obviously, we can see from Figure 3 that the similarity of inner-school is much greater than that of inter-schools. That verifies users' subjects affect their book-loan behaviors again.

Here we concentrate on the inter-school similarity. We focus on the rows of Figure 3 to get the knowledge dependency between schools in Peking university. First ,we define $Max.s_{1_i 1_j} = max_{1_i, 1_j} s_{1_i 1_j}$, for each $i, i \neq j$. In the global view, the maximum value of $Max.s_{1_i 1_j}$ is 14.985 when $i = 2$ and $j = 8$, which

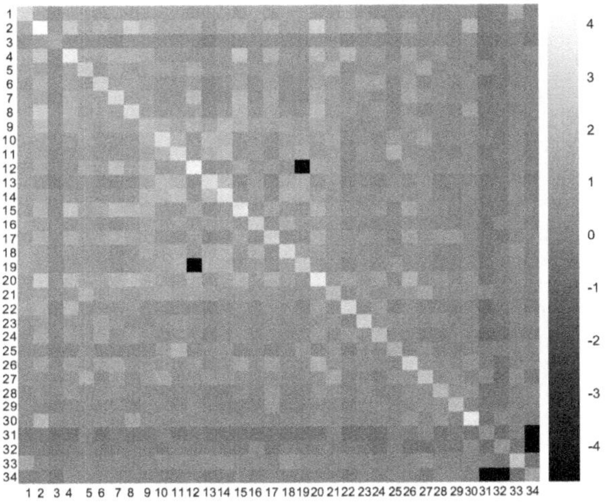

Fig. 3. Matrix of similarity between Schools(Departments)

represent the Dept. of Chinese Language and Literature (DCLL) and School of Foreign Language (SFL). Although DCLL and SFL are different disciplines, both of them are related to language study, and Peking University is good at Translation and Comparative Literature which are inter-disciplines. These factors lead to the high book-loan behavior similarity between these two schools. In the case of Science and Engineering disciplines, $Max.s_{1_i 1_j}$ is 10.205 observed between School of Electronics Engineer and Computer Science(EECS) and School of Physics(SPHY). This is because that the Electronics originally is a branch of Physics, and SPHY set a lot of basic courses about computer technologies which are important tools for the physics research.

Definition 3. *For each school p_{1_i}, we define its most dependent school p_{max_i} as the one has the largest similarity with p_{1_i}, i.e.*

$$p_{max_i} = argmax_{1_j \neq 1_i} s_{1_i 1_j} \quad (3)$$

Because $s_{1_i 1_j}$ represents the similarity between school p_{1_i} and p_{1_j}, p_{max_i} indicates the most related school of p_{1_i}. We can say that at least part of the knowledge of school p_{1_i} relies on knowledge of school p_{max_i}, so we can get each school's knowledge dependency by finding p_{max_i}.

Here, we study whether $p_{max_{p_{max_i}}} = p_{1_i}$, for each p_{1_i}, in other words, we study whether $Max.s_{1_i 1_j} = Max.s_{1_j 1_i}$, $i \neq j$. If $p_{max_{p_{max_i}}} = p_{1_i}$ $(Max.s_{1_i 1_j} = Max.s_{1_j 1_i})$, we can conclude that school p_{1_i} and school p_{max_i} have the equal status for knowledge learning. This symmetry phenomena is observed existing in five pairs of schools from Figure 3. If for school p_{1_i}, p_{max_i} is p_{1_j}, while for school p_{1_j}, p_{max_j} is not p_{1_i}. That means students in school p_{1_i} tend to share knowledge with students in school p_{1_j}, while students in school p_{1_j} have other knowledge sharing bias. Then, we could deduce that the basic knowledge of school p_{1_i} more or less depends on the basic knowledge of school p_{1_j}. For example, for the School of Life Sciences(SLS), its $p_{max_{SLS}}$ is the School of Chemistry and Molecular Engineering(SCME), but the $p_{max_{SCME}}$ is SPHY. Then we could deduce that the knowledge in SLS derives from SCME. That does make sense. Thus, we conclude the following theorem.

Theorem 1. *The knowledge dependency between schools is non-symmetric.*

Therefore, we find the knowledge dependency between schools by analyzing users' book-loan behaviors. Table 3 shows the school subject dependency where

Table 3. School (Department) Subject Dependency

Dependency			Sym.Dependency
1(SUES)→2(DCLL)	18(SCME)→14(SPHY)	27(NSD)→5(SECO)	2(DCLL)↔8(SFL)
3(DPSY)→2(DCLL)	19(SGSS)→11(EECS)	28(SEDU)→17(DSOL)	5(SECO)↔21(GSM)
4(DHIS)→2(DCLL)	20(DPHI)→2(DCLL)	29(IPR)→17(DSOL)	7(SG)↔12(SLAW)
6(SJC)→2(DCLL)	22(SARC)→4(SARC)	30(SCSL)→2(DCLL)	10(SMS)↔13(STEC)
9(SYP)→2(DCLL)	23(IM)→7(SG)	31(SZGS)→27(NSD)	11(EECS)↔14(DPSY)
15(SIS)→4(DHIS)	24(SART)→3(DPSY)	32(IMM)→16(SLS)	
16(SLS)→18(SCME)	25(SSM)→11(EECS)	26(SMP)→20(DPHI)	
17(DSOL)→2(DCLL)			

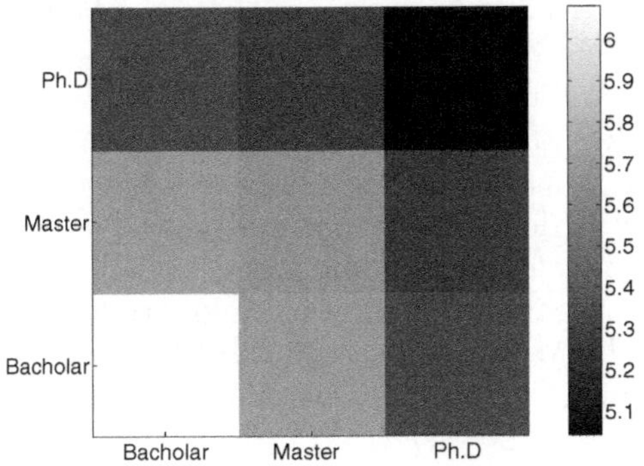

Fig. 4. Matrix of similarity between degrees

the schools is represented by IDs and abbreviations, → indicates the dependency relation, and ↔ indicates the symmetry dependency.

5.2 Knowledge Dependency between Degrees

In this part, we group the users in co-borrowing network by the value of attribute p_2 = *degree*. Figure 4 shows the similarity between degrees. We find that inner-degree similarity is greater than that of inter-degree. And the maximum similarity value is observed inner bachelors. This indicates that bachelor

Table 4. ID-School (department)and ID-Category correspondence table

ID	School (Department)	ID	Category
1	School of Urban and Environmental Sciences(SUES)	A	Marxism-Leninism
2	Dept. of Chinese Language and Literature(DCLL)	B	Philosophy and Religion
3	Dept. of Psychology(DPSY)	C	Social Science
4	Dept. of History(DHIS)	D	Politics and Law
5	School of Economics(SECO)	E	Military Affairs
6	School of Journalism and Communication(SJC)	F	Economics
7	School of Government(SG)	G	Culture, Science, Education and Sports
8	School of Foreign Language(SFL)	H	Language and Character
9	School of YuanPei(SYP)	I	Literature
10	School of Mathematics Sciences(SMS)	J	Art
11	School of Electronics Engineer and Computer Science(EECS)	K	History and Geography
12	School of Law(SLAW)	N	Natural Science
13	School of Technology(STEC)	P	Astronomy
14	School of Physics(SPHY)	Q	Bioscience
15	School of International Studies(SIS)	R	Medical Science
16	School of Life Sciences(SLS)	S	Agricultural Science
17	Dept. of Sociology(DSOL)	T	Technology
18	School of Chemistry and Molecular Engineering(SCME)	TN	Telecommunications Technology
19	School of Geoscience and Space Science(SGSS)	TP	Computer Technology
20	Dept. of Philosophy(DPHI)	TQ	Chemical Industry
21	Guanghua School of Management(GSM)	TU	Architecture Science
22	School of Archaeology(SARC)	TV	Hydraulic Engineering
23	Dept. of Information Management(IM)	U	Traffic
24	School of Arts(SART)	V	Aerospace
25	School of Software(SS)	X	Environmental Science and Safety Science
26	School of Marxist Philosophy(SMP)	Z	General Books
27	National School of Development(NSD)	O1	Mathematics
28	School of Education(SEDU)	O2	Statistics
29	Institute of Population Research(IPR)	O3	Mechanics
30	School of Chinese as a Second Language(SCSL)	O4	Physics
31	ShenZhen Graduate School(SZGS)	O6	Chemistry
32	Institute of Molecular Medicine(IMM)	O7	Crystallography
33	School of Environmental Engineering(SEE)		
34	Dept. of Physical Education and Sports Science(PESS)		

students have more reading interests in common. And this is mainly because they have more compulsory courses than other groups. The minimum similarity is between bachelor and PhD. This is because bachelor students learn more basic knowledge, while PhD students concern more about the advanced knowledge and technologies, so the sets of books they borrowed have low intersection.

For the knowledge dependency, we find that for the *Bachelor* group, its $p_{max_{Bachelor}}$ is the *Master* group, but the $p_{max_{Master}}$ is *Ph.D.* Thus we could deduce that the knowledge studied by bachelor students is part of that of Master students. And the Master group and the Ph.D group have the equal status for knowledge learning. The knowledge dependencies relation between degrees are list as follows:

$Bachelor \rightarrow Master$, $Master \leftrightarrow Ph.D$

6 Conclusions

Book-load is the most important service in library. Analyzing users' book-loan behaviors can help libraries to be more proactive in book-loan service. In this paper, we present a novel framework in studying users' book-loan behaviors and mining knowledge dependency. We set up a two-mode book-borrowing network and a one-mode co-borrowing network for analysis. We analyze the users' book-loan and co-borrowing behavior patterns by adding attributes to the vertices of the both kinds of networks. We confirm that students' majors are the dominant factors that affect users' book-loan behaviors. We also find out the widely influential disciplines and strong correlated disciplines in Peking University. Finally, we find the knowledge dependency between schools and between degrees.

In the future, we would give a more detailed analysis of knowledge dependency. This paper just concludes the knowledge dependency between schools and does not tell any information about the knowledge dependency within a specific school. For example, students majoring in computer science may be interested in whether they share any knowledge with artificial intelligence field. Moreover, we can exploit this framework to mine knowledge dependency between books. Similarly, we can build the book-borrowed network and book co-borrowed network. By combining these two kinds of networks, we can build the dependency between books. Libraries can use dependency information between books to recommend related books for users. This application exactly goes as the trend of library 2.0.

Acknowledgment

This study is partially supported by the National High Technology Research and Development Program of China (863 Program Nos. 2009AA01Z143, 2009AA01Z136 and 2009AA01Z150), as well as the Specialized Research Fund for the Doctoral Program of Higher Education of China under Grant ("FSSP" Grant No. 20090001110106).

References

1. Chinese library classification, `http://en.wikipedia.org/wiki/Chinese_Library_Classification`
2. Adamic, L.A., Buyukkokten, O., Adar, E.: A social network caught in the web. First Monday 8(6) (2003)
3. Adamic, L.A., Zhang, J., Bakshy, E., Ackerman, M.S.: Knowledge sharing and yahoo answers: Everyone knows something. In: Proceedings of ACM WWW 2008, pp. 665–674 (2008)
4. Barabasi, A.-L., Albert, R.: Emergence of scaling in random networks. Science 286(5439), 509–512 (1999)
5. Bollen, J., Luce, R., Vemulapalli, S.S., Xu, W.: Usage analysis for the identification of research trends in digital libraries. D-Lib. Magazine 9(5) (2003)
6. Chin, A., Chignell, M.H.: Identifying communities in blogs: roles for social network analysis and survey instruments. IJWBC 3(3), 345–363 (2007)
7. Guenther, K.: Applying data mining principles to library data collection. Computers in Libraries 20(4), 60–63 (2000)
8. Li, X., Guo, L., Zhao, Y.E.: Tag-based social interest discovery. In: Proceedings of ACM WWW 2008, pp. 675–684 (2008)
9. Loether, H.J., McTavish, D.G.: Descriptive and Inferential Statistics: An Introduction, 3rd edn. (1988)
10. Mislove, A., Marcon, M., Gummadi, K., Druschel, P., Bhattacharjee, B.: Measurement and analysis of online social networks. In: Proceedings of ACM IMC 2007, pp. 29–42. ACM, New York (2007)
11. Newman, M.E.J.: The structure of scientific collaboration networks. Proceedings of the National Academy of Sciences (PNAS), 409–415 (2001)
12. Nicholson, S.: The basis for bibliomining: Frameworks for bringing together usage-based data mining and bibliometrics through data warehousing in digital library services. Journal of the American Society for Information Science and Technology 42(3), 785–804 (2006)
13. Singla, P., Richardson, M.: Yes, there is a correlation: - from social networks to personal behavior on the web. In: Proceedings of ACM WWW 2008, pp. 655–664 (2008)
14. Srivastava, J., Cooley, R., Deshpande, M., Tan, P.N.: Web usage mining: discovery and applications of usage patterns from web data. SIGKDD Explor. Newsl. 1(2), 12–23 (2000)
15. Wasserman, S., Faust, K.: Social Network Analysis Methods and Applications. Cambridge University Press, Cambridge (1994)
16. Yan, F., Jiang, J., Lu, Y., Luo, Q., Zhang, M.: Community discovery based on social actors' interests and social relationships. In: SKG (2008)
17. Yan, F., Zhang, M., Sun, T., Lu, Y., Zhang, N., Xiao, L.: Analyzing user's book-loan behaviors in peking university library from social network perspective. In: JCDL 2009, pp. 461–462. ACM, New York (2009)

An Extended Predictive Model Markup Language for Data Mining

Xiaodong Zhu and Jianzheng Yang

Information Management & Electronic Business Institute,
University of Shanghai for Science and Technology,
Shanghai, China, 200093
zhuxd@usst.edu.cn

Abstract. Common data mining metadata benefits sharing, exchanging and integration among data mining applications. The Predictive Model Markup Language PMML facilitates the exchange of models among data mining applications and becomes a standard of data mining metadata. However, the evolution of models and extension of products, PMML needs large number of language elements and leads to conflicts in PMML based data mining metadata inevitably. This paper presents an extended predictive model markup language EPMML for data mining, which is designed to reduce the complexity of PMML language elements. The description logic for predictive model markup language DL4PMML that belongs to the description logic family, is the formal logical foundation of EPMML and makes it possess strong semantic expression ability. We analyze how EPMML describe data mining contents in detail. Some experiments expatiate how EPMML based data mining metadata support automatically reasoning and detect inherent semantic conflicts.

Keywords: Knowledge Engineering, Data Mining, Description Logic, Metadata, Consistency Checking.

1 Introduction

Data mining is the process of discovering latent valuable patterns and rules from large datasets. Those patterns and rules are also called knowledge which represents a higher status than chaotic data. They provide useful decision information for leaders of enterprises. In the past two decades, data mining become very attractive just because it brings large values and profits for so many corporations. With the development of data mining techniques, more and more database products providers and data analysis software corporations add abundant mining performance into their database products. An innovation in the data mining algorithms and techniques can be rapidly transformed into those products. However, as more and more data mining products are provided, different corporations look forward common data mining metadata as the data mining standards in order to realize the exchanging, sharing, integration in various data mining applications.

Currently, Common Warehouse Metamodel CWM [1][3] and Predictive Model Markup Language PMML [2] are two main data mining metamodel criteria for data mining standardization. CWM, developed by the OMG Group and focuses

L. Chen et al. (Eds.): WAIM 2010, LNCS 6184, pp. 218–231, 2010.

on business intelligence, provides detailed and sufficient graph description for data warehouse and data mining. The aim of CWM is to solve the integration and management problems of metadata, so different application can integrate each other under different conditions. However, different experiences of different corporations, different views when describing data and continual development of data mining techniques inevitably bring conflicts in metadata. But the description with natural language and graphs in CWM make it hard to automatically discover the conflicts information hidden in CWM based metadata. We proposed a description logic based inconsistence checking mechanism for data mining metamodel and metadata based on CWM, which resolved the lacks problems of semantics in CWM and acquired efficient results [3].

The Predictive Model Markup Language PMML is a XML based markup language for describing contents of data mining application [2]. The PMML facilitates the exchange of models from one data mining application to another. Exchanging models between different applications require a common understanding of the PMML specification. However, due to the evolution of models and extension of products, PMML contains large number of language elements and leads to conflicts in data mining metadata inevitably. This lacks of conformity reduces the usefulness of PMML and hampers the growth of its use by the data mining community. Efficient and consistent criteria are necessary to enhance the performance and reliability of PMML. Pechter developed a validation method that combines XSD and XSLT to guarantee the validity of PMML [7]. However, this method only discovered the syntax errors in PMML based data mining metadata. Because PMML itself lacks of formal semantics, it is difficult to automatically reason and discover inherent semantic conflicts problems in data mining metadata. While the conflicts emerge more clearly as the data mining models update and versions of PMML evolve continuously.

Above all, we give two examples about semantic problems in PMML based data mining metadata. While describing an association rules model using PMML, we can use either "AssociationRule" or "AssociationRules" to markup an association rule, however, we can not use them in the same document. For convenience, we expect that these two markup elements denotes the same semantics. Another example is the inherent semantic problems hidden in a PMML document. As we known, for an association rule, the antecedent and consequent cannot have intersection. However, PMML ignore such semantic problems. What follows shows an association rules model in PMML language, it hasn't grammatical errors but it has semantic errors because it obeys the definition of association rules.

```
<?xml version="1.0" ?>
  <PMML version="3.1" >
        <Header copyright="www.dmg.org"
              description="examplemodelforassociationrules" />
        ...
        <AssociationModel
        ...
        <AssociationRule support="0.2" confidence="0.9"
              antecedent="Beer" consequent="Beer" />
        </AssociationModel>
  </PMML>
```

Description logic, the logical basis of ontology language, is a decidable sub set of first-order predicate logic. It represents domain knowledge with structured and understandable style. In this research, we present the notion of managing data mining metadata with description logic. The idea of applying description logic into data mining metadata management derives from that metadata pattern could be expressed by description logic knowledgebase, so reasoning upon description logic could detect the inconsistency problems in data mining metadata.

The rest of this paper is organized as follows. Section 2 gives related work. In Section 3, a novel formal logic DL4PMML that belongs to the description logic family is presented, the syntax and semantics are analyzed. In section 4, we develop an extended predictive model markup language EPMML base on the DL4PMML; the elements of the language are designed in detail. Section 5 illustrate how EPMML works for data mining and we give experiments of knowledge reasoning and consistency checking upon EPMML based data mining metadata, and finally we summarize this paper.

2 Related Work

Compared with much work on developing algorithms of data mining, there is little work paid on the nature, theoretic foundation, services, platforms and stands of data mining [4][5][6]. As the development of data mining techniques, data mining standardization become a new focus problem and attract more and more attention. In the standardization of data mining, common data mining metamodel and metadata play important roles. A series of data mining criteria are proposed, such as CRISP-DM [15], PMML and CWM.

The CRISP-DM gives a process criterion of whole data mining life cycle. Now it is the standard method of the developing data mining project. However, it is described with natural language and didn't make exact criterion for data mining metadata. Common warehouse metamodel, brief for CWM, provides detailed and sufficient graph description for data warehouse and data mining. It is developed by OMG Group and focuses on business intelligence, which includes the definitions of OLAP and data mining metadata. The aim of CWM is to solve the integration and management problems of metadata, so different application programs could integrate each other under different conditions. In the CWM criteria, data mining metadata is defined in detail. However, different experiences of different corporations, different views when describing data and continual development of data mining techniques inevitably bring conflicts upon metadata. But the description with natural language and graphs in CWM make it hard to automatically discover the conflict information through reasoning. It is regretful that the problem has not been resolved well up to now. Zhu et al proposed a novel inconsistence checking mechanism based on description logic for CWM based data mining metamodel and metadata, which resolved the lacks problems of semantics in CWM precisely and successfully and acquired encouraging effects [3].

Zubcoff et al constructed a data mining metamodel for classification analysis using abundant semantic information supplied by CWM [16]. Castellano et al constructed the architecture of data mining process using CWM based meta-model [17]. Chaves et al designed a PMML based predictive engine Augustus, which can be used for data preparation and model partition [18]. However, as far as we are aware of, there is little work paid on the consistency checking upon data mining metadata using description logic.

3 Description Logic DL4PMML

Description logics are a family of knowledge representation languages which can be used to represent the concept definitions of an application domain in a structured and formally well-understood way. Description logic has formal semantics and strong expression ability. Baader point out that description logic provide essential foundation for Semantic Web [8]. Beginning from basis $\mathcal{ALC}$ description logic, adding construction operators or combining different construction operators lead to different expression ability and reasoning complexity of description logic. In fact, the stronger expression ability leads to higher reasoning complexity. For example, the OWL DL has power semantic expression ability, however, the reasoning of its logical foundation $\mathcal{SHOIN}(\mathcal{D})$ is an NEXPTIME-complete problem [9,13]. Therefore, $\mathcal{SHOIN}(\mathcal{D})$ is not a suitable description logic for description on large and variable data mining metadata. In this section, a novel fitful description logic DL4PMML is proposed as the logical foundation of EP-MML language.

3.1 Syntax and Semantics of DL4PMML

Definition 1. *DL4PMML Syntax. Let A and P denote atomic concept and atomic role respectively, the symbol " ::= " denotes a definition, then the syntax rules of any concept C or role R in DL4PMML are defined recursively as follows.*

$$C ::= \top_1|\bot_1|A|\neg C|C_1 \sqcap C_2|C_1 \sqcup C_2|\exists R.C|\forall R.C|(\geq nR)|(\leq nR)|a_1,...,a_n|(\geq nR.C)|(\leq nR.C)$$

$$R ::= \top_2|\bot_2|P|\neg R|R_1 \sqcap R_2|R_1 \sqcup R_2|R^-$$

Definition 2. *DL4PMML Semantics. The interpretation of DL4PMML is denoted by an order pair $I = (\Delta^I, \bullet^I)$, which is constituted by an nonempty interpretation domain Δ^I and an interpretation function $\bullet^I$. This function maps every concept C into a subset C^I of the domain Δ^I, and every role R into a subset R^I of the Cartesian product $(\Delta^I)^2$. Let* **card** *denotes a cardinarity of a set, the concrete semantics are listed as follows.*

(1)$\top_1^I = \Delta^I$
(2)$\bot_1^I = \varnothing$
(3)$(\neg C)^I = \Delta^I \backslash C^I$
(4)$(C_1 \sqcap C_2)^I = C_1^I \cap C_2^I$
(5)$(C_1 \sqcup C_2)^I = C_1^I \cup C_2^I$
(6)$(\exists R.C)^I = \{a \in \Delta^I | \exists b((a,b) \in R^I \wedge b \in C^I)\}$
(7)$(\forall R.C)^I = \{a \in \Delta^I | \forall b((a,b) \in R^I \rightarrow b \in C^I)\}$

(8) $(\geq nR)^I = \{a \in \Delta^I | card\{b \in \Delta^I | (a,b) \in R^I\} \geq n\}$
(9) $(\leq nR)^I = \{a \in \Delta^I | card\{b \in \Delta^I | (a,b) \in R^I\} \leq n\}$
(10) $\{a_1, ..., a_n\}^I = \{a_1^I, ..., a_n^I\}$
(11) $\top_2^I = (\Delta^I)^2$
(12) $\bot_2^I = (\varnothing)^2$
(13) $(\neg R)^I = \top_2^I \backslash R^I$
(14) $(R_1 \sqcap R_2)^I = R_1^I \cap R_2^I$
(15) $(R_1 \sqcup R_2)^I = R_1^I \cup R_2^I$
(16) $(R^-)^I = \{(b,a) \in \Delta^I \times \Delta^I | (a,b) \in R\}$

Definition 3. *The knowledge base of description logic DL4PMML is a triple:* $\mathbb{K} = \{TBox, RBox, ABox\}$.

In order to add the semantic ability on restriction on relations, Distinguishing from $\mathcal{ALC}$, A *RBox* component is added in DL4PMML knowledge base. The *RBox* is the set of axioms that describe the equivalence and subsumption between relations, denoted by $R \equiv S$ and $R \sqsubseteq S$ respectively. It is obviously that if an interpretation I satisfy the knowledge database of description logic DL4PMML $\mathbb{K}(\mathbb{K} =< TBox\ \mathcal{T}, RBox\ \mathcal{R}, ABox\ \mathcal{A} >)$, if and only if it satisfy $\mathcal{T}$, $\mathcal{R}$ and $\mathcal{A}$, written with $I \models \mathbb{K}$.

3.2 Complexity of DL4PMML

In what follows, we prove that the reasoning upon DL4PMML could be reduced to consistency checking upon *ABox*. Consequently we could discover the conflict problem of DL4PMML through reasoning of DL4PMML in reasoning engineer.

Theorem 1. *Reasoning of DL4PMML could be reduced to the satisfiability problem of DL4PMML.*

Proof. Reasoning upon DL4PMML includes five cases. First is satisfiability. It meaning is that given a knowledge base $\mathbb{K}$, if exists an interpretation I that makes $I \models \mathbb{K}$. Second is satisfiability of concepts. Its meaning is the concept C is nonempty for the *TBox* T. That is exists an interpretation I that makes $I \models T$ and $C^I \neq \varnothing$. Third is subsumption of concepts. Its meaning is that for the *TBox* T, the concept C_1 contain C_2. That is for any interpretation I, it makes $I \models T$ and $C_2^I \subseteq C_1^I$, written with $T \models C_2 \sqsubseteq C_1$. Forth is instance checking. Its meaning is given a DL4PMML knowledge base $\mathbb{K}$, if exists an individual a that belongs to the concept C. That is for any interpretation I, it makes $I \models \mathbb{K}$ and $a^I \subseteq C^I$, written with $\mathbb{K} \models C(a)$. Fifth is query retrieve. Its meaning is finding all individuals a that make$\mathbb{K} \models C(a)$ in the knowledge base $\mathbb{K}$ of DL4PMML. In the DL4PMML, considering two concept C and D, we have:

(1)D subsume $C \equiv C \sqcap \neg D$ is non-satisfiable.
(2)C is equal to $D \equiv C \sqcap \neg D$ and $\neg C \sqcap D$ are both non-satisfiable.
(3)C is disjointed with $D \equiv C \sqcap D$ is non-satisfiable.

According to the binary relation theory, a relation is a subset of Cartesian products between concepts. Therefore, the satisfiability problems upon *RBox* can be deduced from satisfiability problems upon Concepts.

General speaking, the reasoning problem upon DL4PMML could be reduced to satisfiability problem of DL4PMML. If exists algorithms determine the satisfiability, then must exists algorithms that resolve other problems.

Theorem 2. *DL4PMML is decidable, and it is Exponent-time complete problem.*

Proof. DL4PMML can be mapped into a superset of $\mathcal{ALC}$ language and the subset of $\mathcal{SHOIQ}$ language. The reasoning algorithm tableaux of $\mathcal{ALC}$ language is P-Space complete problem [10] and and $\mathcal{SHOIQ}$ language is NExponent-time complete problem respectively. Description logics that add and only add concrete domain, transitivity, reversibility, absolute quantity restriction are decidable and Exponent-time complete problems [11,12]. Therefore, DL4PMML is decidable, and it is an Exponent-time complete problem.

4 Extended Predictive Model Markup Language EPMML

DL4PMML is the foundation of EPMML, what's more, it provides strict decidable formal mechanism and support automatic reasoning. EPMML can provide standard description with semantics. Elements of EPMML include metaclass, attributes, instances of metaclass, relations between instances. Following subsections analyze the elements of EPMML in detail.

4.1 EPMML Meta Class

EPMML meta class is composed by a name and a restriction list. For example:

```
<epmml:Class rdf:ID="AssociationRules"/>
<epmml:Class rdf:ID="Itemset"/>
<epmml:Class rdf:ID="Item">
    <rdfs:subClassOf rdf:resource="#Itemset"/>
</epmml:Class>
```

Naturally, the logical bases of EPMML meta classes are concepts in the description logic DL4PMML, including atomic concepts and simple compound concepts. In the next 4.3, the logical bases of complex meta class of EPMML are complex compound concepts in DL4PMML.

4.2 EPMML Attributes

An attribute of EPMML represent a binary relation. In EPMML language, attributes are divided into object type attributes and data type attributes. Object attributes describe the relation between instances of meta classes, declared with <epmml:ObjectProperty>. At the same time, the definition domain and range are declared using <rdfs:domain>and <rdfs:range>respectively.

```
<epmml:ObjectProperty rdf:ID="HasAntecedent">
    <rdfs:domain rdf:resource="#AssociationRules"/>
    <rdfs:range ref:resource="#Antecedent"/>
</epmml:ObjectProperty>
```

Distinguished from object type attribute, the range of data type attribute are data types. In the EPMML language, the data type attributes are declared using <epmml:DataTypeProperty>. Same as object type attributes, <rdfs: domain>and <rdfs: range>indicate the domain and range of the data type attributes.

```
<epmml:DatatypeProperty rdf:ID="HasSupport">
    <rdfs:domain rdf:resource="#AssociationRules"/>
    <rdfs:range rdf:resource="http://www.dmg.org/v3-2/pmml-3-2.xsd#PROB-NUMBER"/>
</epmml:DatatypeProperty>
```

Here PROB-NUMBER denotes the positive decimal data type between 0 and 1. The logical foundation of EPMML attributes are relations of DL4PMML. In order to elaborate the semantic performance of EPMML, transitive operator and inverse operator are included in the DL4PMML. They are the logical foundation of attributes restrictions of EPMML, see subsection 4.5.

4.3 EPMML Complex Meta Class

In the EPMML language, compound concepts are constructed through intersection, union and complement. Their foundations are intersection, union and complement of concepts. They are declared using epmml:intersectionOf, epmml:unionOf and epmml:complementOf respectively. For example:

```
<epmml:Class rdf:ID="Abnormal">
    <epmml:complementOf rdf:resource="#Normal"/>
</epmml:Class>
```

Another complex meta class is the enumerative concept, which can be described by enumerating all instances of the meta class. The enumeration for enumerative meta class is a special construction, declared with epmml:oneOf. For example:

```
<epmml:Class rdf:ID="Wether">
    <epmml:oneOf rdf:parseType="Collection">
        <epmml:Thing rdf:about="#Fine"/>
        <epmml:Thing rdf:about="#Cloudy"/>
        ...
    </epmml:oneOf>
</epmml:Class>
```

4.4 EPMML Individual

Besides meta classes and attributes, EPMML should describe concrete individuals and relations between individuals. First of all, an individual is declared with <epmml:Thing>. Then use rdf:type to indicates the metaclass to which the individual belongs. For example, when we describe an association rule model, we can declare that "Cracker" is an instance of the metaclass "item".

```
<epmml:Thing rdf:ID="Cracker">
    <rdf:type rdf:resource="#Item"/>
</epmml:Thing>
```

Different from PMML, individuals of EPMML are **NOT** language elements, which reduce the complexity of PMML greatly. In order to reduce the complexity of reasoning, a resource can not be not only metaclass but also individual in the same EPMML metadata.

4.5 EPMML Attributes Restriction

Attributes are special binary relation. According to the binary relation theory, attributes has properties of reflexivity, symmetry, transitivity, reversibility and functionality. However, adding additional properties into description logic inevitably increase complexity of logical reasoning, so much as the undecidability of reasoning. Considering the characteristics of PMML based data mining metadata, in the language EPMML, we permit adding transitivity and reversibility of attributes. Reflexivity and symmetry are unnecessary and not permitted for EPMML. For instance, "Is_part_of" is a transitive attribute. We use epmml:TransitiveProperty to declare its transitivity.

```
<epmml:ObjectProperty rdf:ID="Is_part_of">
    <rdf:type rdf:resource="&epmml : TransitiveProperty"/>
</epmml:ObjectProperty>
```

We use epmml:InverseOf to declare the reversibility of an attribute. For example:

```
<epmml:ObjectProperty rdf:ID="BeAntecedentOf">
    <epmml:InverseOf rdf:resource="HasAntecedent"/>
</epmml:ObjectProperty>
```

As we known, while describing data mining models using PMML, some attributes not only indicate the domains and ranges of them, but also have determinate quantitative restriction. For instance, in order to describe that the support and confidence of an association rule are both vary between 0 and 1, in PMML based association rules models, several language elements need to be added. However, in EPMML, these language elements can be omitted. What's more, the semantics that support and confidence are both between 0 and 1 can be attached into the metadata, which can be understood by users and computers. In EPMML, we use epmml:someValuesFrom and epmml:allValueFrom to indicate the range restrictions of attributes. And we use epmml:minCardinality and epmml:maxCardinality to indicate the cardinality restrictions of attributes. The DL4PMML foundations of them are $\exists R.C$, $\forall R.C$, $(\geq nR)$ and $(\leq nR)$. For example:

```
<epmml:Restriction>
    <epmml:onProperty rdf:resource="#hasWether"/>
    <epmml:allValueFrom rdf:resource="#Wether"/>
</epmml:Restrition>
<epmml:Restriction>
    <epmml:onProperty rdf: resource ="#hasSupport"/>
    <epmml:minCardinality
        rdf:datatype="http://www.dmg.org/v3-2/pmml-3-2.xsd#PROB-NUMBER ">0.0
    </epmml:minCardinality>
    <epmml:maxCardinality
        rdf:datatype="http://www.dmg.org/v3-2/pmml-3-2.xsd#PROB-NUMBER ">1.0
    </epmml:maxCardinality>
</epmml:Restriction>
```

4.6 EPMML Assistant Language Elements

In order to reduce the complexity of reasoning and enhance the semantic understandability of EPMML, the assistant language elements such as copyright, version and namespace and so on are designed using the data type attributes of EPMML. For example:

```
<epmml:DatatypeProperty rdf:ID="HasCopyRight">
    <rdfs:domain rdf:resource="#EPMML"/>
    <rdfs:range rdf:resource="http://www.nuaa.edu.cn"/>
</epmml:DatatypeProperty>
<epmml:DatatypeProperty rdf:ID="HasVersion">
    <rdfs:domain rdf:resource="#EPMML"/>
    <rdfs:range rdf:resource="1.0.0"/>
</epmml:DatatypeProperty>
```

While designing the EPMML language, it is obvious that a resource appear in the form of only one language element. For example, if a resource is set as an individual, then it can not be set as a meta class any more, and vice versa. What's more, resources in the same namespace can not possess same names. It is allowable that resources in the different namespace have same names under the condition of adding quotations. Strict formal semantics of EPMML provide complete formal logical foundation for automatic reasoning upon EPMML based data mining metadata.

General speaking, EPMML is a markup language for data mining metadata, it is designed to describe the context of data mining process. Especially, the patterns mined by data mining systems can be described using EPMML and deployed on the Web for sharing. EPMML is like OWL language, However, it has much less complexity and is more suitable for the describing lots of data mining patterns that vary constantly.

5 EPMML Based Data Mining Metadata

Compared with PMML, the language EPMML has strong semantic representation ability. The data that describe data mining contents in EPMML is called EPMML based data mining metadata. In this section, we illustrate how EPMML guarantees the semantic consistency when describing data mining contents and supports automatically reasoning to detect the semantic conflicts in data mining metadata.

(1) Semantic Consistency Illustration.
In the PMML language, if we declare an association rule with the language element "AssociationRule", then others terminologies can not be used any more to denote the association rule. However, in the EPMML based association rules metadata, we can abolish the limitation. For example, it is allowable to denote the association rule metaclass using "AssociationRule" and "AssociationRules" at the same time, which is fit for our habits. This semantics can be realized through adding the mapping of metaclass. In EPMML, the following definition can realize the mapping of association rule metaclasses and guarantee the semantic consistency.

```
<epmml:Class rdf:ID="AssociationRules">
    <epmml:equivalentClass rdf:resource="#AssociationRule"/>
</epmml:Class>
```

(2)Conflicts Checking Illustration.
Consistency checking upon EPMML based data mining metadata includes syntax checking and semantic checking. XSD and XSLT validation upon the EPMML metadata can only discover the grammar errors and can not discover the latent inherent semantic conflicts. For example, following metadata that describes an association rule model can go through the syntax checking but can not go through the semantic checking, because it disobey the requirement that the intersection of antecedent itemset and subsequent itemset is empty set.

```
<AssociationRules rdf:ID="AssociationRules_1">
    <HasAntecedent>
        <Item rdf:ID="Beer">
            <BeAntecedentOf rdf:resource="#AssociationRules_1"/>
        </Item>
    </HasAntecedent>
    <HasConfidence rdf:datatype="http://www.dmg.org/v3-
                                        2/pmml-3-2.xsd#PROB-NUMBER">0.8
    </HasConfidence>
    <HasSupport rdf:datatype="http://www.dmg.org/v3-
                                        2/pmml-3-2.xsd#PROB-NUMBER">0.2
```

```
        </HasSupport>
        <HasSubsequent>
            <Item rdf:ID="Beer">
                <BeSubsequentOf rdf:resource="#AssociationRules_1"/>
            </Item>
        </HasSubsequent>
        <HasSubsequent>
            <Item rdf:ID="Diaper">
                <BeSubsequentOf rdf:resource="#AssociationRules_1"/>
            </Item>
        </HasSubsequent>
</AssociationRules>
```

In the section 1, we have described this semantic problem. As we know, for an association rule, the intersection of antecedent itemset and subsequent itemset should be empty set. However, in traditional PMML metadata, such semantic can not be identified. In EPMML based metadata, we can declare such requirement before describing the models. So if the nonempty intersection appears, then the metadata is conflicting. First transform the EPMML metadata into DL4PMML based knowledge base, and we can discover such conflicts through knowledge reasoning.

Now description logic has equipped with good reasoning engineer Racer. What's more, the new version RacerPro of Racer has a platform of creating knowledge base [14]. Compared with another reasoning tool LOOM, its reasoning algorithm Tableaux is reliable and complete. At the same time, the Protégé can be chosen as a constructing tool of data mining metadata, and it can invoke the racer engine for knowledge reasoning and automatically discover conflicts in data mining metadata.

There exists a grammar mapping among the DL4PMML, EPMML and RacerPro. For instance, "$C1 \sqcap C2$ "in DL4PMML maps "*epmml:intersectionOf* " in EPMML, and maps "*and C1..C2* " in RacerPro. For convenience, we illustrate the semantic conflicts checking using Protégé 3.3.1 and the Racer reasoning engineering 1.9.0. Firstly constructing the association rules metadata knowledgebase, Secondly connecting the Racer 1.9.0 engineering through the invoking button in the Protégé interface. Then we will acquire following conflicts information:
Error: The concept Antecedent is inconsistent.

The reason is that Antecedent is disjoint with Subsequent. Individual Beer is either instance of Antecedent or Subsequent. According the conflicts information, we can further derive the reason of conflicts and correct the metadata of association rules model. In above metadata, we should get rid of the description about the "Beer" in the subsequent itemsets. After eliminate the inconsistency problems, rerun the consistency checking process, the conflict is resolved. Besides, we can also construct association rules metadata knowledgebase in the new RacerPro platform, and using nRQL language to resolve above conflicts checking problems.

From the data mining metadata based on EPMML, we can further acquire the semantic graph of a data mining model. For example, we get an semantic graph amongs association rule model metaclasses, shown in Fig. 1. In the figure, the arrows denotes the $'is\_a'$ relation between two metaclasses.

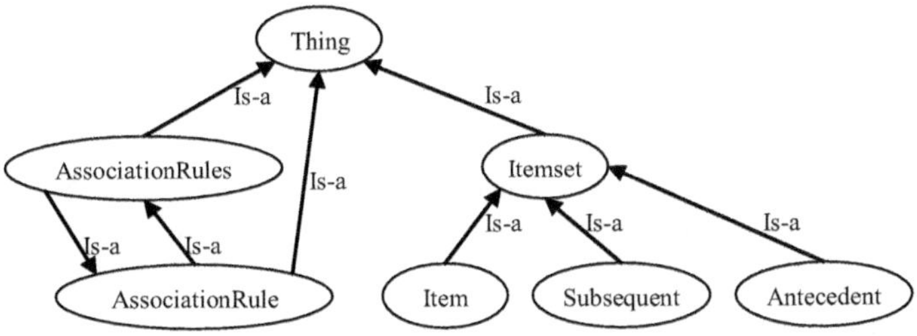

Fig. 1. Semantic Graph of Association Rules Models

On one hand, EPMML based data mining metadata possess abundant semantics expression. On the other hand, EPMML can be used as the exchanging standard between data mining applications. Fig. 2 shows how EPMML is applied into data mining systems for metadata exchanging.

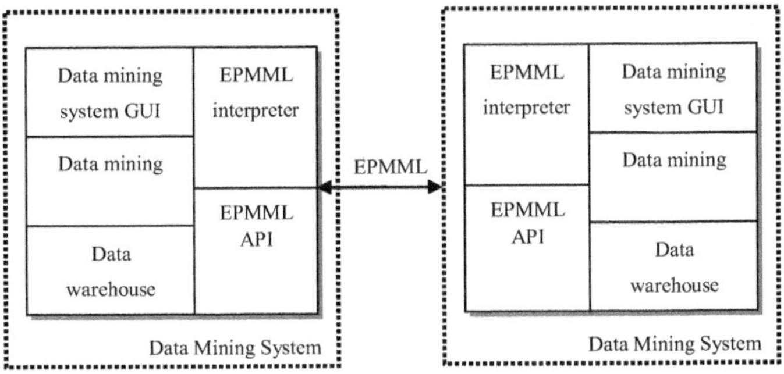

Fig. 2. EPMML based Metadata Exchanging

6 Conclusion

Currently, CWM and PMML based data mining metadata lack of formal semantics, so it is usually hard to discover the inherent conflicts in the metadata. The main contribution of this paper is developing an extended predictive model markup language EPMML based on the description logic DL4PMML for data mining. EPMML not only has strong semantic expression ability, but also reduces the complexity of language elements of PMML. We analyze the syntax and semantics of formal logic DL4PMML, and interpret how DL4PMML works for EPMML. This paper is helpful to enhance the stability of data mining metadata criteria and insure the reliability of data mining metadata integration. Future work includes investigating how to automatically revise the conflicts based on the conflicts information and enhancing the description ability of EPMML language on data mining metadata.

Acknowledgement

This research is supported by Doctoral Start Foundation of USST (No. 1D-10-303-002) and National Natural Science Foundation of China (No.70973079).

References

1. OMG, Common Warehouse Metamodel Specification, Version 1.1 (2001), http://www.omg.org
2. DMG, Data Mining Group-PMML Products (2008), http://www.dmg.org/products.html
3. Zhu, X.D., Huang, Z.Q., Shen, G.H.: Description Logic based Consistency Checking upon Data Mining Metadata. In: Wang, G., Li, T., Grzymala-Busse, J.W., Miao, D., Skowron, A., Yao, Y. (eds.) RSKT 2008. LNCS (LNAI), vol. 5009, pp. 475–482. Springer, Heidelberg (2008)
4. Zhu, X.D., Huang, Z.Q.: Conceptual Modeling Rules Extracting for Data Streams. Knowledge-based Systems 21(8), 934–940
5. DM-SSP-06: Data Mining Standards, Services and Platforms. In: DM-SSP Workshop associated with the 2006 KDD Conference, Philadelphia, PA, August 20-23 (2006), http://www.ncdm.uic.edu/dm-ssp-06.htm
6. DM-SSP-07, Data Mining Standards, Services and Platforms. In: DM-SSP Workshop associated with the 2007 KDD Conference, San Jose, California, August 12-15 (2007), http://www.opendatagroup.com/dmssp07
7. Pechter, R.: Conformance Standard for the Predictive Model Markup Language. In: The Fourth Workshop on Data Mining Standards, Services and Platforms (DM-SSP 2006), associated with 12th ACM SIGMOD International Conference on Knowledge Discovery & Data Mining (KDD 2006), Philadelphia, Pennsylvania, USA (2006)
8. Baader, F., Horrocks, I., Sattler, U.: Description Logics as Ontology Languages for the Semantic Web. In: Hutter, D., Stephan, W. (eds.) Mechanizing Mathematical Reasoning. LNCS (LNAI), vol. 2605, pp. 228–248. Springer, Heidelberg (2005)
9. Horrocks, I., Patel-Schneider, P.F.: Reducing OWL entailment to description logic satisfiability. Journal of Web Semantics 1, 345–357 (2004)
10. Horrocks, I., Sattler, U.: A Tableaux decision procedure for SHOIQ. In: The 19th International Joint Conference on Artificial Intelligence (IJCAI 2005), pp. 448–453 (2005)
11. Wessel, M.: Decidable and undecidable extensions of ALC with composition-based role inclusion axioms. University of Hamburg, Germany (2000)
12. Lutz, C.: The complexity of reasoning with concrete domains, in Teaching and Research Area for Theoretical Computer Science, Ph.D. RWTH Aachen, Germany (2002)

13. Lutz, C.: An improved NExpTime-hardness result for description logic ALC extended with inverse roles, nominals, and counting. Dresden University of Technology, Germany (2004)
14. Haarslev, V., Moller, R., Wessel, M.: RacerPro Version 1.9 (2005), `http://www.racer-systems.com`
15. CRISP-DM, CRoss Industry Standard Process for Data Mining (2007), http://www.crisp-dm.org
16. Zubcoff, J., Trujillo, J.: Conceptual Modeling for classification mining in Data Warehouses. In: Tjoa, A.M., Trujillo, J. (eds.) DaWaK 2006. LNCS, vol. 4081, pp. 566–575. Springer, Heidelberg (2006)
17. Castellano, M., Pastore, N., Arcieri, F., Summo, V., de Grecis, G.: A Model-view-controller Architecture for Knowledge Discovery. In: The 5th International Conference on Data Mining, Malaga, Spain (2004)
18. Chaves, J., Curry, C., Grossman, R.L., Locke, D., Vejcik, S.: Augustus: The design and Architecture of a PMML-based scoring engine. In: The Fourth Workshop on Data Mining Standards, Services and Platforms (DM-SSP 2006), associated with 12th ACM SIGMOD International Conference on Knowledge Discovery & Data Mining (KDD 2006), Philadelphia, Pennsylvania, USA (2006)
19. Haarslev, V., Möller, R., Wessel, M.: Querying the semantic web with Racer+nRQL (2004), `http://www.racer-systems.com/technology/contributions/2004/HaMW04.pdf`

A Cross-Media Method of Stakeholder Extraction for News Contents Analysis

Ling Xu, Qiang Ma, and Masatoshi Yoshikawa

Kyoto University, Yoshida Honmachi, Sakyo-Ku, Kyoto, Japan

Abstract. We are studying contents analysis of multimedia news as a solution to the issue of bias, which multimedia news, as a reflection of the real world, is also facing. For the contents analysis, we use a stakeholder model representing descriptions of different stakeholders, which are defined as the main participants in an event. In this paper, we propose a method of detecting stakeholders as the core component of the stakeholder-oriented analysis. In our work, a stakeholder is assumed to appear in the video clips and be mentioned in the closed captions frequently. Given a series of video clips and their closed captions reporting the same event, we extract stakeholder candidates from both textual and visual descriptions. After that, we calculate the degree of exposure for each candidate to identify stakeholders. We also present experimental results that validate our method.

1 Introduction

As the plain-text newspapers, multimedia news are also facing the issue of bias. The vivid descriptions and entertainment offered by the multimedia turn to be an obstacle that the audience may easily accept and believe what they see and hear in the multimedia news, though they are reported with bias. What to report and how to present in the video are chosen by ideological perspectives of editors, which have big effects on the audience's attitudes [2] and hardly be avoided.

Studying on analysis of multimedia news bias, we are trying to detect the contradiction (inconsistency) in the contents for each stakeholder to see if there is a danger of bias. We proposed a stakeholder model [7] representing the descriptions in the multimedia news. In the model, descriptions of a certain stakeholder (i.e., a person) are classified into objective, subjective, and relationship descriptions. Comparing these descriptions makes it possible to ascertain differences in the reporting of multimedia news items. In this paper, as one of the core technologies of news analysis mechanism based on the stakeholder model, we propose a cross-media method of stakeholder extraction. The basic idea is that, in multimedia news items, a stakeholder is expected to appear in the video and also be mentioned in the closed captions frequently. An entity that appears only in the video or is mentioned only in the text is not a stakeholder in the event. Given a series of related video clips with closed captions reporting the same event, we extract stakeholder candidates from both textual and visual descriptions, identify the faces and calculate the degrees of textual and visual exposure for each candidate

L. Chen et al. (Eds.): WAIM 2010, LNCS 6184, pp. 232–237, 2010.

for the filtering. The textual exposure degree is based on the character lengths of the textual descriptions related to the candidate. The visual exposure degree is computed using two factors: 1) the time duration of each segment in which the stakeholder candidate appears; and 2) the importance score of each face, which indicates how much it is concerned with the event. Experiment results show that our cross-media method performed better than extracting stakeholders from text or video only.

2 Related Work

The first use of the notion of stakeholder in opinion extraction was in a paper by Liu et al. [3]. There is also previous work [1] that mentions how to detect stakeholders in natural language text, where the stakeholder is an individual, group, organization, or community that has an interest or stake in a consensus-building process. In 2007, Ogasawara et al. proposed a method identifying people in broadcast news videos [6]. Their point is to identify a person who has muliple names (appellations that change according to time and circumstances) and their face matching method help merge the different names belonging to the same person.

In our work, as a more intuitive way of analyzing news, we define the stakeholders as the main participants (people, organizations, etc.) in a news event. In a particular event, the stakeholders are the entities important enough to be mentioned in all the types of media comprising multimedia news. The stakeholder set is as large as possible to avoid missing too many details in the comparison of different descriptions. In our current work, we assume that a multimedia news item consists of a video clip and its closed captions. A stakeholder should appear in or be mentioned in the video clip (and its closed captions) frequently. We are currently focusing on the people who are stakeholders in the events.

3 Stakeholder Extraction

3.1 Segmentation

We segment the video clip by using the twin comparison method [8]. After segment boundaries decided, we extract key frames representing the contents of each segment for face detection. Let n be the number of frames in the segment corresponding to the time interval. If there are camera effects during the shot change, we extract the 2nd and $(n-1)^{th}$ frames instead of the beginning and ending of each segment. We also extract the $(n/2)^{th}$ frame as the middle frame showing what the middle part is concerned with.

3.2 Extracting Stakeholder Candidates

In our method, as the main participants in an event, stakeholders should account for a sufficient fraction of the descriptions in the contents of both video and text.

Firstly, we detect faces appearing in the frames by using a Haar-like features [4] library implemented in OpenCV[1]. Candidate faces are extracted from the 2nd, $(n/2)^{th}$, and $(n-1)^{th}$ frames of each segment. After that, we calculate the importance score (IS) for each face from the face's area and position. Faces in the middle of a frame or ones that have a large area have a higher IS than other faces. Faces with high IS are assumed to belong to important people in the video clips. $IS = w_{position} \cdot w_{area}$. If $\frac{W_s}{\mu} < x_f < \frac{(\mu-1)\cdot W_s}{\mu}$ and $\frac{H_s}{\mu} < y_f < \frac{(\mu-1)\cdot H_s}{\mu}$, then $w_{position} = 1.0$, otherwise $w_{position} = \alpha$. If $W_f \cdot H_f > \frac{W_s \cdot H_s}{\omega^2}$, then $w_{area} = 1.0$, otherwise $w_{area} = \beta$. Here, μ, ω, $0 < \alpha < 1$ and $0 < \beta < 1$ are prespecified parameters; (x_f, y_f) is the midpoint of the face; (W_f, H_f) expresses the size of the face; and (W_s, H_s) expresses the size of the screen.

Secondly, we extract candidate names from closed captions and calculate their frequencies for the face matching. We treat the textual descriptions of one segment as part of the closed caption shown during the time that segment is displayed. For the identification of the faces appear in the segments, we make a list of the candidate names who may match the faces. Probability scores are computed to determine the priority of the face matching. Since the person shown in the video might be introduced a litter earlier or later than when their image appears in the video, we extend the text range used for name extraction to cover the closed captions corresponding to the $p-1^{th}$, p^{th}, and $p+1^{th}$ segments when the face is detected in the pth segment. In common cases, the probability score of candidate s_i in segment seg_p is computed as follows.

$$ps_{s_i,seg_p} = w_p \cdot f(s_i, seg_{p-1}) + w_c \cdot f(s_i, seg_p) + w_n \cdot f(s_i, seg_{p+1}) \quad (1)$$

where $0 < w_n < w_p < w_c \leq 1$ are prespecified weight parameters. High possibility is that the face detected in the frame belongs to the name mentioned in the current segment. f_{s_i,seg_p} denotes the frequency of s_i appearing in segment seg_p.

$$f(s_i, seg_p) = \sum freq(s_i, sent_j) \cdot \frac{l(sent_j, seg_p)}{l(sent_j)}, \quad sent_j \in CC \quad (2)$$

where CC are the sentences of closed captions contained in the text range; $freq(s_i, sent_j)$ is the frequency of s_i in the sentence $sent_j$; $l(sent_j)$ is the character length of sentence; and $l(sent_j, seq_p)$ is the character length of the part of $sent_j$ that belongs to seg_p.

Because of the short duration of segments, ambiguous descriptions, and the non-strict correspondence between a video clip and its closed captions, it is possible for no names to be extracted from the three segments. In such a case, we extend the text range to the beginning of the video. That is to say, let $w'_p \in (0, 1]$ be a perspecified weight parameter, we compute ps_{s_i} as follows.

$$ps_{s_i} = w'_p \cdot \sum_{t=1}^{p} f(s_i, seg_t) \quad (3)$$

[1] http://www.intel.com/research/mrl/research/opencv

After we extract the candidate names and detect the faces, we use a face-matching method to make the identification. For each face detected from video, we select from the database the faces of candidate names ranked by the probability scores (Function (1) and (3)) for those names. Comparing the detected face and the selected faces one by one, we calculate the matching number of each two faces by using Affine-SIFT [5] to represent the degree of similarity. If all the matching fail (matching number is smaller than the threshold), the face will be marked as *Unknown*. Actually, in the experiments, most of the unknown faces belong to the passers-by being interviewed in the street, or the announcers of news program, that are not the stakeholders in the event.

3.3 Candidate Union and Filtering

We merge the stakeholder candidates extracted from the news items and perform filtering to exclude those that are not so important in the contents. The news items are reporting the same event so they share the same stakeholder extraction result with each other. A stakeholder should appear frequently in both the video and text of most news items. Two standard values for filtering are the average textual exposure degree and the average visual exposure degree for each stakeholder candidate, where average exposure degrees are the averages of the exposure degrees in individual news items.

Textual Exposure Degree. We calculate the textual exposure degree by using the character length of the related closed captions. For each sentence in the text of the closed captions, if the candidate is mentioned, we consider that the sentence is related and its character length is added up for the computation. The exposure length of the textual description of candidate s_i in multimedia item c_k $T_{s_i,c_k} = l(s_i, c_k)$, where $l(s_i, c_k)$ is the length of characters related to candidate s_i in news item c_k. If s_i does not exist in the news item, $T_{s_i,c_k} = 0$. Let $l(c_k)$ be the length of characters in the closed caption of news item c_k, the textural exposure degree of candidate s_i in item c_k is computed as follows.

$$T(s_i, c_k) = \frac{T_{s_i,c_k}}{l(c_k)} \tag{4}$$

Visual Exposure Degree. We calculate visual exposure degrees by using visual information about segments in which the candidate appears. Let $d(s_i, seg_p, c_k)$ be the time duration of segment seg_p if it is related to candidate s_i; $IS(s_i, seg_p, c_k)$ be the face importance score corresponding to candidate s_i in segment seg_p; and $d(c_k)$ be the time duration of news item c_k, Visual exposure degree $V(s_i)$ of candidate s_i in item c_k is given by function below.

$$V(s_i, c_k) = \frac{\sum_{p=1}^{q} d(s_i, seg_p, c_k) \cdot IS(s_i, seg_p, c_k)}{d(c_k)} \tag{5}$$

Filtering Function. To exclude persons that have descriptions but low exposure degrees in either textual or visual descriptions, we specify two thresholds, $T_{textual}$ and T_{visual}, for textual and visual descriptions, respectively. Let $T(s_i)$ and $V(s_i)$ be the average of the textual exposure degrees and the average of the visual exposure degrees, if $T(s_i) > T_{textual}$ and $V(s_i) > T_{visual}$, then candidate s_i is a stakeholder in the event.

4 Experiments

We carried out experimental evaluation on our stakeholder extraction methods. 7 events consisting of 34 multimedia news items (video clips and their closed captions in Japanese) are selected as the test data set. Table 1 shows our parameter setting for the best-performing results after some preliminary experiments. We also built a database by saving information about person names and the (directory) paths of their faces. The database consists of 249 faces of 19 people. All the faces are in JPEG format with a size of 100 × 100 pixels.

The results for extracting stakeholders from multimedia news items are shown in Table 2. The *segment* column gives the precision and recall ratios for extracting stakeholder candidates from segments. Relevant stakeholders used for computation of precision and recall are extracted manually. The *item* columns give the experiment results for news items. The $Textual - Only$ and $Visual - Only$ columns show the performance for extracting stakeholders from only textual or visual descriptions. A comparison of the results shows the advantage of our cross-media method of stakeholder extraction. However, the recall ratio of stakeholder extraction in a segment was not high for the reasons: 1) Low recall of segmentation led to the case where some stakeholders did not appear in the key frames. 2) Face detection failed in some key frames of segments. 3) The name of the candidate was not mentioned in the closed caption, so the candidate was discarded even though the corresponding face was successfully detected.

Table 1. Parameter Setting

Face Detection	Minimal Size	56 × 56	Haar-like Features
Face Identification	Matching Number	7	A-SIFT
Calculating Importance Score	$\omega \cdot \mu$	$18 \cdot 4$	Coefficients

Table 2. Experiment Results for Stakeholder Extraction

	Both Textual and Visual		Textual-Only	Visual-Only
	Segment	Item	Item	Item
Precision	0.92	0.93	0.72	0.63
Recall	0.49	0.93	0.94	0.62

Fortunately, stakeholder determination is based on the stakeholders from all the news items. Therefore, the stakeholder might be passed over in one item, but detected in another one. The recall ratio for stakeholder extraction from news items shows that our method performed well at the multimedia news item level.

5 Conclusions and Future Work

In this paper, we introduced our method of extracting stakeholders from multimedia news items reporting the same event. We extract the candidates from not only textual descriptions but also visual descriptions. The experimental results show that the performance of the extraction method is sufficient to let us extract stakeholders from news items with higher precision and recall ratios than the methods that just use one of the textual and visual descriptions. However, there is some work left for achieving a better recall ratio at the segment level. Such an improvement would also help the precision of the calculation of the textual and visual exposure degrees. Furthermore, after we have extracted the stakeholders, we will be able to continue the inconsistency analysis in accordance with our stakeholder-oriented analysis framework. Comparing descriptions for inconsistency detection is another important task of future work.

Acknowledgment

This research is partly supported by the research for the grant of Scientific Research (No.20700084, 20300042) made available by MEXT, Japan.

References

1. Arguello, J., Callan, J.: A bootstrapping approach for identifying stakeholders in public-comment corpora. In: Proc. of the dg.o2007, pp. 20–23 (2007)
2. Lin, W.H., Haputmann, A.: Identifying news videos' ideological perspectives using emphatic patterns of visual concepts. In: Proc. of ACM MM 2009, pp. 443–452 (2009)
3. Liu, J., Birnbaum, L.: Localsavvy: aggregating local points of view about news issues. In: Proc. of the WWW 2008 Workshop on Location and the Web, pp. 33–40 (2008)
4. Mita, T., Kaneko, T., Hori, O.: Joint Haar-like features for face detection. In: Proc. of ICCV 2005, pp. 1619–1626 (2005)
5. Morel, J., Yu, G.: Asift: a new framework for fully affine invariant image comparison. SIAM Journal on Imaging Sciences 2(2), 438–469 (2009)
6. Ogasawara, T., Takahashi, T., Ide, I., Murase, H.: People identification in broadcast news video archive by face matching. Technical report of IEICE. PRMU 106(606), 55–60 (2007)
7. Xu, L., Ma, Q., Yoshikawa, M.: Stakeholder extraction for inconsistency analysis of multimedia news. In: Proc. of WebDB Forumn 2009 (2009)
8. Zhang, H.J., Kankanhalli, A., Smoliar, S.W.: Automatic partitioning of full-motion video. Multimedia Systems 1(1), 10–28 (1993)

An Efficient Approach for Mining Segment-Wise Intervention Rules in Time-Series Streams*

Yue Wang[1], Jie Zuo[1,**], Ning Yang[1], Lei Duan[1], Hong-Jun Li[1], and Jun Zhu[2]

[1] DB&KE Lab., School of Computer Science, Sichuan University, Chengdu, 610065, China
{hkharryking,zuojie,yneversky}@gmail.com
[2] China Birth Defect Monitoring Centre, Sichuan University, Chengdu, 610065, China

Abstract. Huge time-series stream data are collected every day from many areas, and their trends may be impacted by outside events, hence biased from its normal behavior. This phenomenon is referred as intervention. Intervention rule mining is a new research direction in data mining with great challenges. To solve these challenges, this study makes the following contributions: (a) Proposes a framework to detect intervention events in time-series streams, (b) Proposes approaches to evaluate the impact of intervention events, and (c) Conducts extensive experiments both on real data and on synthetic data. The results of the experiments show that the newly proposed methods reveal interesting knowledge and perform well with good accuracy and efficiency.

Keywords: Time-series stream, Intervention events, Data Mining.

1 Introduction

The modern life produces massive volumes of time-series streams. These streams are with huge quantity and keep increasing with the time evolving. To understand the rules in these streams needs to analyze their affecting factors. However, generally, only a small part of the affecting factors are known. This make many methods fail on practical data. Thus, people urge new methods to discovery knowledge in such circumstances.

Motivation. The motivation of intervention analysis comes from an observation in real life: one system keeps its status steadily if there is no outside intervention. In another words, if the system status became unstable, there must be some outside abnormal things happening; and also: If we simply treat the raw stream sequentially, the analysis result may be useless.

* Supported by the National Science Foundation of China under Grant No.60773169, the 11th Five Years Key Programs for Sci.and Tech. Development of China under grant No.2006BAI05A01.

** Corresponding author.

L. Chen et al. (Eds.): WAIM 2010, LNCS 6184, pp. 238–249, 2010.

Example 1. *Global financial crisis of 2008 is creating great panic. It is associated with banking panics, stock market crashes and the bursting of other financial bubbles, currency crisis, and so on.*

As an indicator to finance, the stock index reaches several peaks and valleys during the several-month-monitoring. This varying must have reasons. However, with the outside environment varying, the reason for market index generation is also changing. If people search the outburst of transactions in index records sequentially, the result may be useless: As transaction stops in every Saturday and Sunday, every Monday might be misrecognized as outbursts.

This observation shows that the market index records in the identical weekday (such as every Monday) vary a little. Thus, we divide original data sequence into five (one for every weekday). This method is named segment-wise way and it works to eliminate the differences caused by different weekdays.

We have proposed a new method to analyze the intervention events in traffic record stream in previous work [1]. This study extends our previous method to a segment-wise style for more general fields. The special challenges include: (1) Process stream with segment-wise intervention; (2) Detect intervention in stream adaptively; (3) Analyze the rule hidden in intervention dynamics; (4) Evaluate the impact of intervention; (5) Design efficient mining algorithms for online processing environment.

The remaining of this paper is organized as follows: Section 2 discusses the related works. Section 3 gives the concepts about intervention events, and provides a novel framework called STM for intervention mining, as well as gives the algorithms to establish our model; Section 4 provides algorithms to detect and predict intervention event; Section 5 discusses further principles about intervention events; Section 6 gives extensive experiments to evaluate our methods. Finally, section 7 concludes the paper and highlights future works.

2 Related Works

Mining base patterns in data stream. Researchers proposed many mining methods to mine base patterns in data stream [2]. Literature[3] proposed regression-based algorithms to mine frequent temporal patterns in data stream; Literature [4] studied analytically clustering data streams using one data scan K-median technique; The literature[5] gave frameworks based on regression analysis to deal with incidents detective and trends analysis in data stream. Due to the limitation of regression, it only analyzes changes in a local scope. Thus, regression is not widely applied in mining data stream. Literature [6] applied statistical methods to mine the data stream. These methods discover evolving data stream by keeping learning or updating models from the evolving data. However, these methods may remain steps behind the current trends[7]. The deep reason is that some patterns under the surface cause the varying of data, and the traditional models focus only on the rules superficially and ignore their structure change. The latter may also lead to model's overfitting problem extremely[8].

Mining high-order patterns in data stream. Many researchers tried to mine high-order patterns in stream on huge stream environment. Literatures [9] proposed some high-order models to reveal the rule behind the varying of data. Jiawei Han et al, [10] provided segment-wise algorithms for mining user specified partial periodic patterns. Based on the former works, J Yang et al, [11] introduced asynchronous periodic pattern in order to solve the periodic pattern matching problem, and intended to discover periodic automatically. Literatures [12][13] evoked the exponential or Poisson distribution to detect the abnormal running status of the processing system. Their general framework is first to generate a Hidden Markov model for the observation, then to use the Bayesian method to estimate the parameters. Literatures [14] gave some novel ways of abnormal discovering in data stream. However, these works only concerned the simple target such as email stream, and they do not step deeper to reveal the rules about the detection results.

Based on the former works, Y Wang et al, [1] provided a naive method to deal with the traffic stream in the previous work. Following the contributions on naive intervention theory, this paper combines the segment-wise and statistical method to establish a more practical model. In addition, it applies the newly provided model to discover the knowledge in real time-series stream.

3 Stream Trend Model with Segment-Wise Method

Segment-wise method for time-series stream.

Let X be a periodic time-series stream, p be the period length of X, t be the time tick (t = 0, 1, 2, 3...). Partition the subsequence in each period into d segments: Denote the nth (n=0, 1, 2..d-1) substream as $X_n(*)$, and the tth element in $X_n(*)$ is $X_n(t)$.

Example 2. *Consider a 4-week stock index records sequence X= 3.1, 12.5, 20.3, 5.2, 15.3, 3.2, 12.1, 20.1, 5.0, 16.0, 2.9, 11.7, 21.0, 4.8, 30.1, 3.3, 12.2, 19.8, 5.1, 15.7.*

(1)Sequential way: Suppose that abnormal changes are defined with numerical difference more than 10 between adjacent points on X. If X is processed sequentially, almost every point in X is with "so called" abnormal change. This result is useless.

(2) Segment-wise way: we regenerate subsequence from X for every 5 element (one sequence for every weekday), the original sequence can be partitioned into 5 subsequences as following:

$X_0(*)$ = {3.1, 3.2, 2.9, 3.3} $X_1(*)$ = {12.5, 12.1, 11.7, 12.2} $X_2(*)$ = {20.3, 20.1, 21.0, 19.8} $X_3(*)$ = {5.2, 5.0, 4.8, 5.1} $X_4(*)$ = {15.3, 16.0, 30.1, 15.7}

Note that: there is no significant change indeed inside subsequences $X_0(*)$, $X_1(*)$, $X_2(*)$, $X_3(*)$. Only in the subsequence $X_4(*)$, the third element "30.1" excess the elements around it too much, and this might be the true abnormal people wish to find.

Hidden Markov Model for Stream Processing System. Consider a stream processing system. By daily observation, if the outside conditions are fixed, then its status is satisfied certain probabilistic distribution. Formally, we have the following assumption.

Assumption 1 (Independent and identically assumption). *Data generated by stream processing system satisfy specific probability distribution under stable outside environment. Moreover, when the outside changes are within some threshold, the states of this system will satisfy a set of Independent and identically distributions (i.i.d) with different parameters.*

By the segment-wise method, the whole observation stream can be partitioned into several subsets, and according to the assumption 1: data in each subset satisfy identical distribution with same parameters. Thus, the trend of stream processing system can be described as sequences of states precisely.

When mining the rules in time-series stream, two sequences can be obtained from raw stream: (a) the feature sequence that represents the raw data, and (b) the system states sequence that describes the varying trend of the stream.

Moreover, as the current system state is only concerned with the last state, the sequence of the states satisfies the character of Markov chain. Thus, we use Hidden Markov Model (HMM) as our basic model in this paper.

3.1 Identify System States from Stream

By probability theory[17], if a random event is not affected by outside factors, its occurring times in a fixed period will satisfy the Poisson distribution with probability density function:

$$P(N;\lambda) = e^{-\lambda}\lambda^N/N! \tag{1}$$

N(N=0,1,2...) refers to the happened times of certain discrete events happened in fixed time interval, and λ represents the average occurring rate.

Non-Homogeneous Poisson Process (NHPP) is extended from Poisson distribution. NHPP can calculate the probability of observing n events in time interval (t, t + s). Suppose $\lambda(t)$ is event's occurring rate, NHPP's definition is:

Define:

$$m(t) = \int_0^t \lambda(t)\,dt. \quad m(t+s) = \int_0^{t+s} \lambda(t)\,dt. \tag{2}$$

Thus:

$$P[(N(t+s) - N(t)) = k] = \frac{e^{-(m(t+s)-m(t))}(m(t+s) - m(t))^k}{k} \tag{3}$$

In the NHPP model upon, m(t) is a function of time, and it describes the rate of event occurrence in the time interval [0, t]. N(t) refers to the occurrence times of event in the time interval [0, t], k is variable. From (E3), if the observation stream's incremental satisfies Poisson distribution, it is a NHPP. According to the concepts, we provide formal definition of system state.

Definition 1. *Let X_n be the sub-stream of the observation stream (n=0,1,2,..., d-1), t be the time tick. If $X_n(t)$ satisfies Poisson distribution with m(t), Then*

(1) System feature F(t) is denoted as a function of Poisson parameters in certain time interval, and it can be calculated as:

$$F(t) = \sum_{n=0}^{d-1}(-\log(P(X_n(t)\ m(t)))) \tag{4}$$

(2) State q is defined as set of features, and its weight w(q) is denoted as:

$$w(q) = \frac{\sum_{n=0}^{N} F(t)}{N} \tag{5}$$

(3) State Distance is defined as the weight difference between two states, and it can be calculated as:

$$Dist(q_1, q_2) = |w(q_1) - w(q_2)| \tag{6}$$

(4) For any q_1,q_2∈System state set, if Dist(q_1,q_2)<minPts, q_1 and q_2 are equivalent states;

With the concepts uppon, we provide algorithm: StateMergeClustering to do feature generation and state identification.

```
Data: O(t). M(Number of intervals to data stream values).
Result: states_queue.
begin
    foreach time t do
        foreach i in [0, M-1] do
            λ←sum_array[i] / count_observation; P_r←e^(−λ) λ^δ / δ; feature←feature - Log(P_r);
        end
        F(t)←feature;                              /* get the feature sequence */
    end
    Boolean create_new←true;
    foreach feature F(t) in F(*) do                /* cluster the similar feature */
        foreach state s in states_set do
            if dist(new state{F(t)}, s)≤minPts then
                s.add(F(t));create_new←false;
            end
        end
        if create_new = true then
            s'←newState(); s'.add(F(t)); states_queue.add(s');
        end
    end
    return states_queue;
end
```

Algorithm 1. StateMergeClustering

The main process of the algorithm StateMergeClustering can be described as: (1) Convert the observation stream into feature stream; (2) Put the similar features into one state; (3) Merge the equivalence states into one state.

3.2 Intervention Analysis Mechanics

As the description in introduction, it is the outside events' intervention changes the status of system. To discover the knowledge between these events and data, we need the following assumption.

Assumption 2. *During the process of stream processing system, if no outside intervention exists, the system will retain stable status.*

With assumption 2, we give the definition of intervention events.

Definition 2. *(Intervention events) Let t be the time point in stream system, v be the event variant. Let v (t) = true denote the event v happens at t, q_1, q_2 be the states before and after v respectively.*

(1) The event that causes states change of corresponding system is called intervention event.

(2) The impact of certain intervention event is defined as the weight difference between q_2 and q_1, and it can be calculated as:

$$Impact(v(t)) = |w_{average}(q_1) - w_{average}(q_2)| \tag{7}$$

$w_{average}(q_i)$ denotes the average weight value of state q_i(i=0,1,2,3...).

Stream Trend Model. The base framework of Stream Trend Model is weighted automation. Weighted automation model is provided in [7], which is used to deal with the burst problems in document stream. Suppose under the processing of certain stream system circumstances, several states are identified from the observation stream. Stream trend Model is defined as following:

Definition 3. *(Stream Trend Model, STM) Let N be the number of the total states, R be the number of intervention events, Pr be the prior probability vector of system states, M_t be transition matrix between system states, Mc be the confusion matrix between states and feature stream, Q be a set of system states, V be a set of intervention events then: (1) A STM is a 7-tuple Ω={N, R, P_r, M_t, M_c, Q={q_1,q_2,..q_N}, V={v_1,v_2,..v_R} }; (2) c(q_i, q_j) is denoted as the cost function when system state transfer from q_i to q_j, and it can be calculated as:*

$$c(q_i, q_j) = w(q_i) - w(q_j) \tag{8}$$

Learning Parameters

Observation 1. *Let m(t) be the Poisson parameter for non-homogeneous Poisson distribution in time interval $[0, t]$. The value of m(t) can be estimated by average recorded number of observed target in interval $[0, t]$.*

By maximum likelihood estimate m(t_0+t)-m(t_0) = N(t). As m(t_0)=0 when t_0=0, m(t) = N(t), therefore m(t) = N(t)/t. Observation 1 gives us a way to estimate current m(t) for STM.

In the experiments, our application adjusts minPts to make STM get the best analysis accuracy. Moreover, the application uses step process time and indices upon to adjust the parameter N adaptively. P_r and M_t is the prior transfer probability between the states of STM. They can be obtained with the process of stream. M_c is the relation between states and feature stream. To describe the status of feature discretely, our application set P intervals for the feature stream, and M_t can record varying probability from each state to each interval.

4 Detection and Prediction Algorithms for Intervention Events

By Definition 1, the system state is a set of features. Thus, we could obtain time character of one state through count the continue number of features in that state.

Definition 4. *If a system state of STM* $q=\{F(0),F(1),...F(n)\}$, *then*

1) The duration interval is the continuous time interval in the feature set of state q; and it is denoted as $t_{duration}(q)=\{\ [t_0,t_3],\ [t_1,t_{end}]...\}$;

2) An intervention event v happened in state q, if the event v happened in $t_{duration}(q)$;

3) Transfer point is denoted as the time point when system transfers from one state to another;

4) Adjoin state is denoted as the states next to the transfer point;

5) Intensity of intervention event v(t) is denoted as the impact varying rate in duration interval .

Based on the conceptions in Definition 4, The following algorithms are created to detect and predict the intervention events from raw stream.

(1) Detect the intervention events adaptively
We provide algorithm IntervDetect to detect intervention events.

```
Data: state_queue.
Result: interv_set.
begin
    foreach s belongs to states_set do    /* get all the transfer points */
        trans_set ←checkTransPoint(s)
    end
    foreach trans_p belong trans_set do
        if validate(trans_p) then /* if |adj − states(trans_p)|>threshold */
            Interv_set.add(trans_p);
        end
    end
end
```

Algorithm 2. IntervDetect

Note that, the detection of the unknown intervention is in the following steps: (1) Find out sets of transfer points on the STM established on the observation stream. (2) Validate the transfer points: If the number of the features in the adjoin state of the transfer points exceeds certain threshold, then we could consider some unknown events that are detected in these time points. Otherwise, we treat the transfer points with too small adjoin states as noises.

(2) Predict the future intervention events
Use the results learned from raw data, we give the IntervPredict algorithm to do predict.

```
Data: STM with parameters;
Result: Intervention intensity I, impact w, future states;
begin
    int M_states[m, t], pattern_path[t];
    foreach i in [0, m] do
        M_states[i, 0] ← Initial_Probability[i] * M_confusion[i, 0];
    end
    int MaxProb_state←MaxProb(M_states[m, 0]);
    foreach i in [0, t] do
        pattern_path[i]←ArgMax(MaxProb_state, M_c[m, i]);
        MaxProb_state ← Max(MaxProb_state× M_t[m, i]× M_c [m, t]);
        foreach j in [0, m] do
            M_states[j, i]←M_states[j, i − 1]×M_t[m, i]×M_c[m, t];
        end
    end
end
```

Algorithm 3. IntervPredict

5 Different Impact by Same Intervention Event

In practice, to certain STM, same intervention event might cause different impact in different time. To reveal this principle, we have the following theorem.

Theorem 1. *Let m(t) be the Poisson parameter of observation stream X(*), X(t) be the stream value in t. For intervention event v: if m(t)>X(t), then impact(v) is increasing with m(t); vice versa, if m(t)<X(t), then impact(v) is decreasing with m(t).*

Proof. *As the former definitions, the intervention intensity is decided by the weights of the state q in the time interval.* $w(q) = (F(t_1)+F(t_2)+...F(t_n))/n$, *and equivalence state consists of close features. Moreover, suppose* $F(t_a)$ *can represent the average feature values in q's state set, and thus, weight of q can be reduced to:* $w(q)= F(t_a)$. *By Definition 1:* $w(q) = -Log(P(X(t);m(t_a)))$. *Thus, the differentiation on variant m(t) of w(q) is:*

$$\frac{dw(q)}{dm(t)} = \frac{1}{P(X(t);m(t_a))}\frac{d(P(X(t);m(t_a))}{d(m(t_a)} = (m(t) - X(t))/m(t) \qquad (9)$$

By this equation, when m(t)>X(t), w(q) is increasing function to m(t); when m(t)<X(d), w(q) is decreasing function to m(t). Thus, when the average rate of

observation stream is higher than the current observation value, impact(v) will increase; and oppositely, impact(v) will decrease. ***This completes proof.***

Theorem 1 reveals the principles that the same intervention applied onto different data stream usually does not get the same impact. When m(t) is higher than current observation value, with the increasing of m(t), the detect program should increase the minimum point correspond so as to decrease the false alarms. The more, when m(t) is lower than the current observation value, with the increasing of m(t), detect program should decrease the minimum point in order to get enough intervention events.

6 Experiments

6.1 Date Sets and Base Framework

(1) Synthetic data set: The synthetic data sets is generate by using JSCI[18] API with parameters listed in table 1. (2) Practical data sets:"yahoo finance" data set has 3,300 records and is updated every day.(Collected from [15] stock index of yahoo [1996-4-15 ~2009-1-19]); "Dodgers" from [16]. There are totally 50,400 traffic records (288 records for one day, totally 78 recorded-events).

All of the experiments are completed on a notebook PC with a 1.7 GHZ CPU and 2 GB main memories. We implement a real time data stream processing system prototype, and a news events grabbing system by Java to collect news data for validation and training

Table 1. Parameters for Synthetic Data Sets

Data Set Name	Syn_1	Syn_2	Syn_3
Poisson parameter	50	30	40
Periodic interval	10	50	200
Data count	5,101	20,000	100,000

6.2 Experiments and Analysis

Correctness and Completeness Experiments: Test on Traffic data: As the algorithms in this study are incremental algorithms, the detection result may not be very precise at the beginning of the computation. But the accuracy of the detection result becomes more precise for a while. Figure 1 shows the result on traffic data

In this process, the precision ratio $r_p = 52.04\%$ and recall ratio $r_r = 65.38\%$. We also drill down to detect the starting and duration time in one day. As it is shown in the Figure 2, the detection result shows that during the 24 hours in 2005-9-29, there are three main intervention events happening, and the abnormal periods are "6:00-11:10", "13:30-17:30","18:30-23:16" respect. By checking the events list provided by the data set, we find that there is a game play during

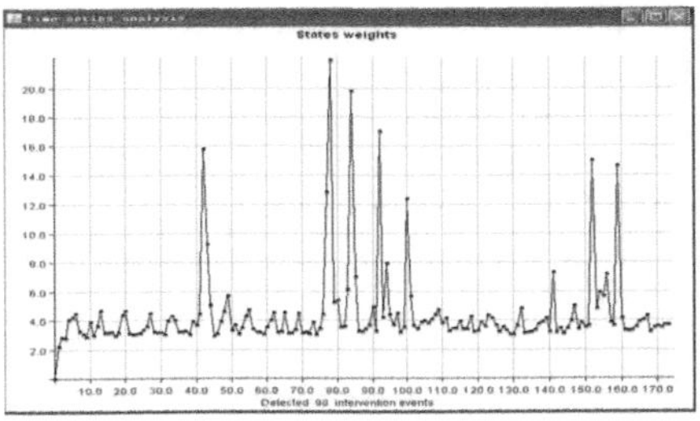

Fig. 1. features result of traffic data

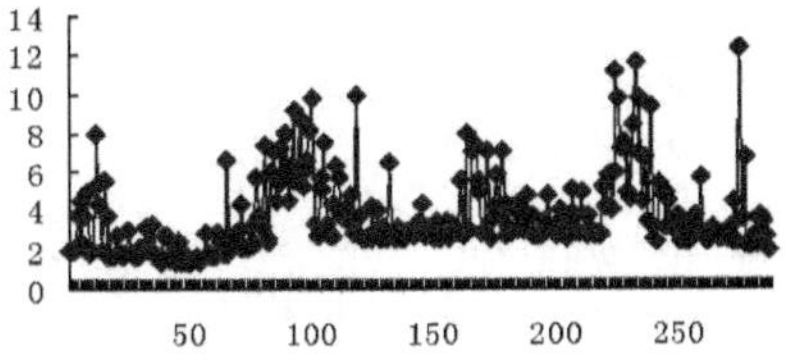

Fig. 2. feature result in 2005-9-29

19:10 to 22:24 in 2005-9-29, which is captured by our algorithm. Test on Synthetic data: The analyzing results for the relation between event occurrence rates (EOR) and detection completeness (DC) of our algorithms can be seen in figure 3. We can learn that with the rising of intervention occurrence, the algorithm detect completeness is enhanced. However, if occurrence probability exceeds 0.7, the completeness will fall quickly. This is caused by too many abnormal events (exceeds the normal states), and this should be avoid in the practical application. Empirically, our application performs well with EOR around 0.3.

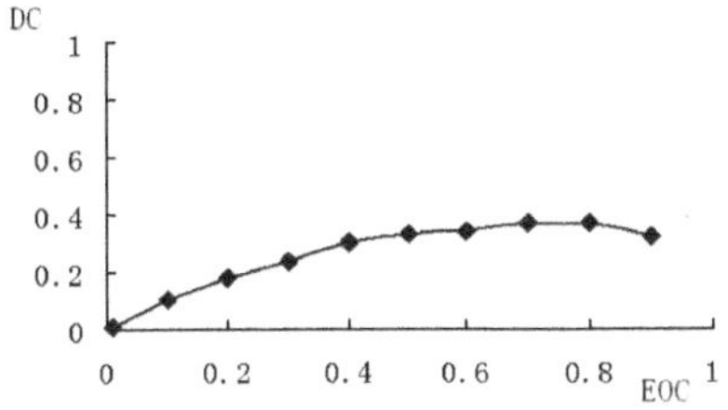

Fig. 3. EOR & DC(minPts=10)

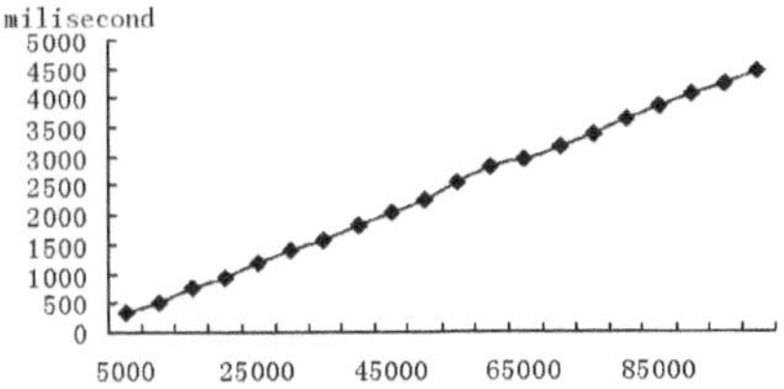

Fig. 4. Scalability of our algorithms

Scalability Experiment: This section tests the mining efficiency and scalability of our algorithms. Experiment 2 combines all the algorithms in this paper as one application to test scalability on Syn_3 data and minPts is set as 2. Figure 4 shows the scalability result of 20 running of our algorithms with almost linear performance.

Practical intervention events Detection Experiment: we apply our algorithm to detect and evaluate practical intervention events(the knowledge between the stock record data and news events.), and keep track some important financial indices to discover problem more quickly, and both, evaluate the measures taken by government or authority. (In this experiment, minPts=3.5, and all process completed with 250-milliseconds). As shown in the Table 2, our method

Table 2. Comparison of the Detected Interv. Events and News

Interv. point	*Impact*	Real News
1998-11	15	unknown
1999-09	35	Yahoo China was online
1999-11	40	unknown
2000-01~2000-07	75	Yahoo Started to use Google as its searching engine
2002-08	12	Microsoft started to use overture
2008-11	7	Google abandoned Yahoo search advertising Partnership
2008-11	27	Global financial crisis
2009-01	18	Global financial crisis

discovers eight time interval for intervention events, and according to the news grabbed from web. Six important events were detected by our algorithm. Two unknown news items may indicate some potential changes about Yahoo, which were not reported by media. By comparing the news list with the mining results, we found there are no significant changes in some events occurred time. That means, those intervention means do not reach their intention. This provides evidences quantitatively for future intervention means.

Predict the best intervention point experiment: We use the predict algorithm on "yahoo finance" data, and intend to find the future possible intervention as the possible best intervention occasion. The results show that when predict algorithm iterates more than 6 periods, the probability of system keep stable status will below 0.50. That indicates the 6th week after "2009-1-19" may be the best occasion to intervene in order to change status of the market index.

7 Conclusion

In this study, we have done the following: (1) provide models to reveal the principles between intervention events and observation stream; (2) introduce Stream Trend Model and efficient algorithms to mine the unknown intervention events adaptively; (3) give sufficient experiments to validate the rules and efficiency of our algorithms both on synthetic and practical data set.

Mining intervention events and their rules from data stream is a promising direction. It is useful in wide application area, such as medicine, economics, and meteorology. The study over intervention is just beginning, and many researches are to be done. The future works will focus on mining the intervention events on multi-sources uncertain streams in order to find interesting patterns from a global view.

Acknowledgments. Thanks to my advisor, Professor Chang-jie Tang, for all his comments and suggestions as I worked on this paper. As he is PC co-chair of WAIM2010, his name can not appear in the authors' list.

References

1. Wang, Y., Tang, C., Yang, N., Chen, Y., Li, C., Tang, R., Zhu, J.: Intervention Events Detection and Prediction in Data Streams. In: Li, Q., Feng, L., Pei, J., Wang, S.X., Zhou, X., Zhu, Q.-M. (eds.) APWeb/WAIM 2009. LNCS, vol. 5446, pp. 519–525. Springer, Heidelberg (2009)
2. La, T., Cui, B., Li, H.Y., et al.: PGG: An online pattern based approach for stream variation management. Journal Of Computer Science And Technology 23(4), 497–515 (2008)
3. Teng, W.-G., Chen, M.-S., Yu, P.S.: A regression-based temporal pattern mining scheme for data streams. In: Proc. 29th VLDB Conference (2003)
4. Aggarwal, C.C., Han, J., Wang, J., Yu, P.S.: A framework for clustering evolving data streams, pp. 81–92 (2003)
5. Chen, Y., Dong, G., Han, J., Wah, B.W., Wang, J.: MultiDimensional Regression Analysis of Time-Series Data Streams. In: Proc. VLDB (2002)
6. Zhu, Y., Shasha, D.: StatStream: Statistical Monitoring of Thousands of Data Streams in Real Time. In: VLDB 2002 (2002)
7. Chen, S., Wang, H., Zhou, S., Yu, P.S.: Stop Chasing Trends: Discovering High Order Models in Evolving Data. In: ICDE 2008 (2008)
8. Wang, H., Yin, J., Pei, J., Yu, P.S., Yu, J.X.: Suppressing Model Overfitting in Mining Concept-Drifting Data Streams. In: SIGKDD (2006)
9. Dora Cai, Y., Clustter, D., Pape, G., Han, J., Welge, M., Auvil, L.: MAIDS: Mining Alarming Incidents from Data Streams. In: Proc. ACM SIGMOD (2004)
10. Han, J., Gong, W., Yin, Y.: Mining Segment-Wise Periodic Patterns in Time-Related Databases. In: Proc. Int. Conf. on Knowledge Discovery and Data Mining (1998)
11. Yang, J., Wang, W., Yu, P.S.: Mining Asynchronous Periodic Patterns in Time Series Data. IEEE Trans. on Knowledge and Data Enginneering (2003)
12. Kleinberg, J.: Bursty and Hierarchical Structure in Streams. In: SIGKDD 2002 (2002)
13. Ihler, A., Hutchins, J., Smyth, P.: Adaptive Event Detection with TimeVarying Poisson Processes. In: SIGKDD 2006 (2006)
14. Curry, C., Grossman, R., Lockie, D., Vjcil, S., Bugajski, J.: Detecting Changes in Large Data Sets of Payment Card Data: A Case Study. In: Proc. SIGKDD (2007)
15. `http://finance.yahoo.com`
16. `http://archive.ics.uci.edu/ml/datasets/Dodgers+Loop+Sensor`
17. Consul, P.C., Jain, G.C.: A generalization of the Poisson distribution. Technometrics (1973)
18. `http://jsci.sourceforge.net/`

Automated Recognition of Sequential Patterns in Captured Motion Streams

Liqun Deng[1,2], Howard Leung[2], Naijie Gu[1], and Yang Yang[1,2]

[1] University of Science and Technology of China, Hefei, China
[2] City University of Hong Kong, Hong Kong
dlqun@mail.ustc.edu.cn, howard@cityu.edu.hk,
gunj@ustc.edu.cn, yyoung@mail.ustc.edu.cn

Abstract. Motion capture data has been frequently used in computer animation and video games. Motions are often captured in a continuous manner such that a motion contains multiple patterns joined sequentially without obvious breakpoints between them. It is challenging to learn the captured motions as it requires both segmentation and recognition. In this paper, a new method based on an extension of open-end dynamic time warping (OE-DTW) is proposed to automatically segment and recognize sequential patterns in motion streams. To enhance the performance, we introduce a global constraint of *K-Repetition* on OE-DTW and a flexible end point detection scheme. In the experiments, we applied our method on different classes of dance motions and demonstrated the effectiveness of our method by comparing with existing approach.

Keywords: Dance motion, sequential pattern, segmentation and recognition, continuous dynamic programming, global constraint, open-end DTW.

1 Introduction

Motion capture (mocap) data is a kind of multi-attribute time series, with the sample at each time instance representing a posture. Motion capture has been frequently used in computer animation, video games, etc. due to its ability to record accurate 3D information of the postures across time. The mocap data is often captured continuously such that a captured motion may contain multiple patterns (i.e. basic moves) connected in a sequential manner without obvious breakpoints between them. It is thus non-trivial to learn the patterns in the captured motions since their boundaries (start/end points) are unknown in advance. In this paper, we address the problem of segmenting and recognizing the sequential patterns in mocap data given some predefined references.

It is quite challenging to automatically segment and recognize the sequential patterns in mocap data due to three major reasons: (1) It is not known in advance which pattern is being performed as well as the start/end points of the embedded patterns; (2) The intra-class variations can be quite large as different subjects may perform the same motion with different speeds and styles. (3) Some motions from different classes may have a certain degree of similarity making it difficult to differentiate these

L. Chen et al. (Eds.): WAIM 2010, LNCS 6184, pp. 250–261, 2010.

classes. During recognition, these challenges may cause the sequential patterns to be misrecognized or the boundaries of the patterns to be wrongly detected.

For data stream segmentation, unlike the work reported in [4] and [9], where the time series is segmented according to the accumulative reconstruction error or low level kinematics features, we process the sequential patterns by comparing with predefined references. The segmentation of the patterns is determined by the matching scores between the input motion and the predefined reference motions.

Among the existing approaches on sequential patterns recognition, hidden markov model (HMM) [5][6] and dynamic time warping (DTW) [7][8] with their variants are the two main streams. With HMM, each class of patterns is trained as a separate HMM and the segmentation and recognition of the patterns is determined by the probabilities under the HMMs. Based on the complicated mathematical model, HMM based methods can handle the temporal variations of the motions and obtain good performance. The major drawback is the complexity in training each HMM and it will be problematic when there is insufficient training data.

DTW and similar methods based on dynamic programming gain significant attention for solving recognition problems due to the efficiency at aligning patterns of different durations and easy training. Continuous dynamic programming (CDP) and open-end dynamic time warping (OE-DTW) are the two most commonly used variants for solving this problem. CDP [3] relaxes the constraint on the alignment of the start points, hence maximizes the likelihood for the query sequence to find its optimally matched subsequence in the reference. On the other hand, OE-DTW [1] relaxes the constraint on the alignment of the end points, and hence it facilitates recognizing a pattern before it is completely input. In this paper, we propose a new method based on OE-DTW to segment and recognize the sequential patterns in mocap data.

The contributions of our proposed method include the followings:

1. A new global constraint, named *K-Repetition*, is introduced to apply on OE-DTW to enhance its performance on the comparison of the patterns. Although many types of locality constraint have been proposed for DTW, most of them require the knowledge of the end points of the two sequences to be matched. To the best of our knowledge, it is the first time that this constraint is applied onto OE-DTW.
2. We improve the end point detection scheme of the original OE-DTW by introducing a flexibility factor ε such that the end point of a pattern in the stream is identified within an elastic range.

The rest of the paper is organized as follows. In Section 2, we give a brief review on some important background of this work. Our proposed method is presented in Section 3. The experiments and results are provided in Section 4. Finally, Section 5 concludes the paper and discusses the future work.

2 Backgrounds

2.1 DTW and OE-DTW

DTW is a well-known distance measure in matching two signals. Given two patterns, a query pattern $Q = q_1,q_2,\ldots,q_i,\ldots,q_n$, and a reference $R = r_1,r_2,\ldots,r_j,\ldots,r_m$, DTW aims to find the optimal aligned path between them and calculate the minimal distance using dynamic programming as follows.

$$D(i,j) = d(i,j) + min(D(i-1, j), D(i, j-1), D(i-1, j-1)); \tag{1}$$

where

$$\begin{aligned} D(1,1) &= d(1,1); \\ D(i,1) &= D(i-1,1) + d(i,1); \\ D(1,j) &= D(1,j-1) + d(1,j); \end{aligned} \tag{2}$$

In the above equations, $D(i,j)$ denotes the minimum accumulative distance between the sub-patterns $Q^{(i)} = q_1,q_2,\ldots,q_i$, and $R^{(j)} = r_1,r_2,\ldots,r_j$, and $d(i,j)$ is the distance between frames q_i and r_j. Finally the expression $D_{DTW}(Q,R) = D(n,m)/N(n,m)$, where $N(n,m)$ is the normalization factor in the cell (n,m), is returned as the DTW distance between Q and R. The optimal warped path can be obtained by backtracking the recursion. An example of the DTW alignment is shown in Fig. 1.

As shown in Eq. (2), DTW has boundary constraint in which the start and end points of the two patterns must be aligned correspondingly. This will lead to undesirable result if we apply DTW to recognize an incomplete pattern. To handle this problem, OE-DTW [1] frees the constraint on end point alignment. It was demonstrated to be effective and efficient on incomplete pattern recognition. OE-DTW chooses the cell with minimal normalized distance in the last column of the distance table as the result. The process is illustrated by the following two equations:

$$D_{OE}(Q,R) = \min_{j=1,\ldots,m} D_{DTW}(Q,R^{(j)}) \tag{3}$$

$$J = \arg\min_{j=1,2,\ldots,m} D_{DTW}(Q,R^{(j)}) \tag{4}$$

where J is returned as the matched end point in the reference, meaning that the input Q matches best with the prefix $R^{(J)}$ ($R^{(J)} = r_1,r_2,\ldots,r_J$).

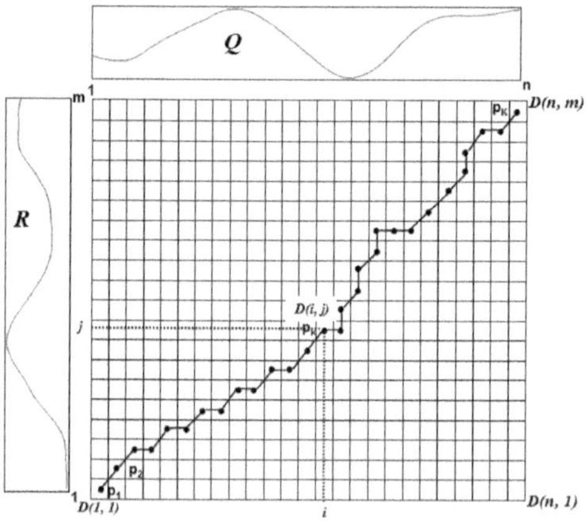

Fig. 1. An example of DTW alignment

In essence, OE-DTW computes DTW distances between Q and all the possible sub-patterns of R, $R^{(j)}$ which is truncated at time instance j. It then chooses the one with minimal distance as the final result. The solid line in Fig. 5 shows such an example.

2.2 Normalization and Global Constraint on DTW

During both DTW and OE-DTW calculation, it requires normalizing the distances in the cells to facilitate the comparison. The normalization factor $N(i,j)$ in the cell (i,j) is determined as the length of the optimal warped path from the cell (1,1) to (i,j) in the original DTW. If we take $N(i,j)$ as the sum of weights on the corresponding path, then this normalization scheme can be illustrated by Fig. 2(a). Fig. 2(b) shows another scheme of normalization, which puts more weights on the diagonal direction. In our application, we apply the latter normalization scheme because with this scheme, we can easily obtain $N(i,j)=i+j$, thus saving a lot of calculations on backtracking the optimal path to get its length as performed by the former scheme.

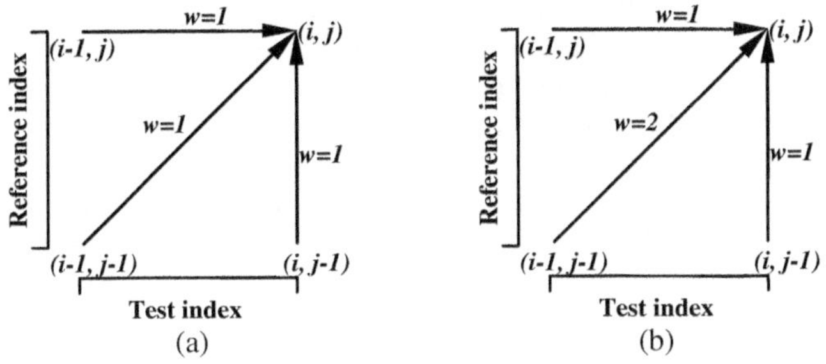

Fig. 2. Two sets of weights for DTW calculation

On the other hand, DTW may not find the desired warped path because it just tries to obtain the minimal distance without considering the shape of the path (see Fig. 3(a) for a negative example). This will deteriorate the efficiency of DTW on the classification problems [10]. To address this issue, several types of global constraints have been proposed, such as Sakoe-Chiba band [2], Itakura Parallelogram [11], and Ratanamahatana-Keogh band [12], to constrain the warped path within the shadow region as illustrated in Fig. 3(b)(c)(d).

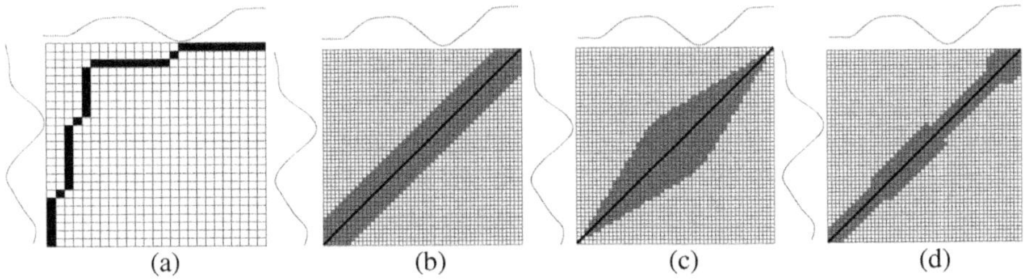

Fig. 3. (a) A negative example of the alignment between two patterns without global constraint, (b) Sakoe-Chiba band, (c) Itakura Parallelogram, and (d) Ratanamahatana-Keogh band

3 Methodology

We apply a new global constraint named *K-Repetition* on OE-DTW, and introduce a flexible scheme to improve the end point detection with OE-DTW. Based on this extended OE-DTW, an algorithm is proposed to recognize the sequential patterns in mocap data.

3.1 K-Repetition Global Constraint

As shown in Fig. 3, all the mentioned global constraints work by relying on the main diagonal of the distance table, hence the end points of the two patterns to be compared should be known in advance. As a result, these constraints cannot be applied to OE-DTW in which the end point of the warped path needs to be determined. Subsequently the main diagonal cannot be relied on.

On the other hand, after our analysis on negative DTW alignments, we find that the unwanted result often comes up when there exist many repetitions of some samples in one pattern matching with the other pattern. Subsequently there are many long vertical lines or horizontal lines in the warped path as shown in Fig. 3(a). We attempt to tackle this problem by introducing a new global constraint of *K-Repetition*.

The basic idea of *K-Repetition* is to limit the number of times that each sample in one pattern is matched by the cells in the other sequence. We impose the constraint that each sample in one pattern cannot be matched more than k times by the samples of the other pattern. Fig. 4 shows an example of DTW alignment with *K-Repetition*, where k=3.

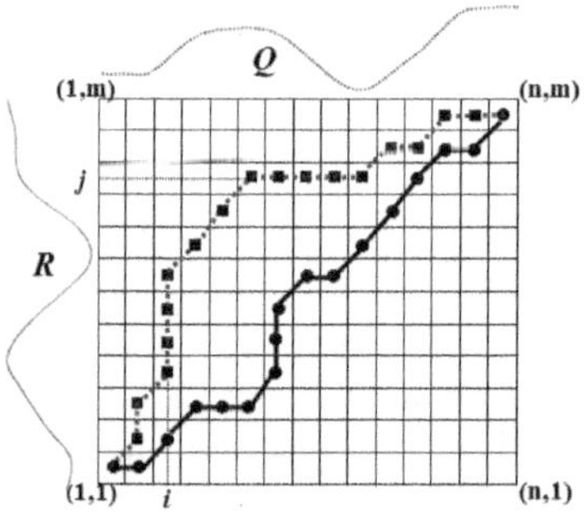

Fig. 4. An example of alignment with *K-Repetition*. The path with dotted line is illegal, as q_i matches 4 times (> k) with the samples in R, and r_j matches 5 times (> k) with the samples in Q. The solid line shows a legal path with *K-Repetition*.

With *K-Repetition*, the number of times that each sample is matched is considered. If a sample in one pattern has already been matched k times by the samples of the other pattern, then it is not allowed to be matched any more. There is no need to consider the case with the main diagonal. In other words, DTW with *K-Repetition* achieves its global performance by applying local constraint on the alignment of the samples. Due to this feature, *K-Repetition* can be applied to OE-DTW as well.

3.2 Flexible End Point Detection

As shown in Eq. (4), OE-DTW determines the forepart of the reference that matches the input best simply by the minimal distance. However, due to the variation of the patterns or the noise, this scheme is not flexible enough to obtain the optimal result. As shown in Fig. 5, it is more reasonable to take the dotted line as the alignment result.

Here we propose a flexible end point detection scheme. The rational behind the new scheme is to make the input pattern Q to be matched with the reference R with a longer path to avoid local discontinuities as shown by the solid line in Fig. 5. We make use of the result $D_{OE}(Q,R)$ and J obtained from Eq. (3) and Eq. (4), and implement our scheme by adding the following conditions:

```
J' = J;
While J'<m && DOE(Q,R)*(1+ε)<D(n,J'+1)
      J' = J'+1;
```

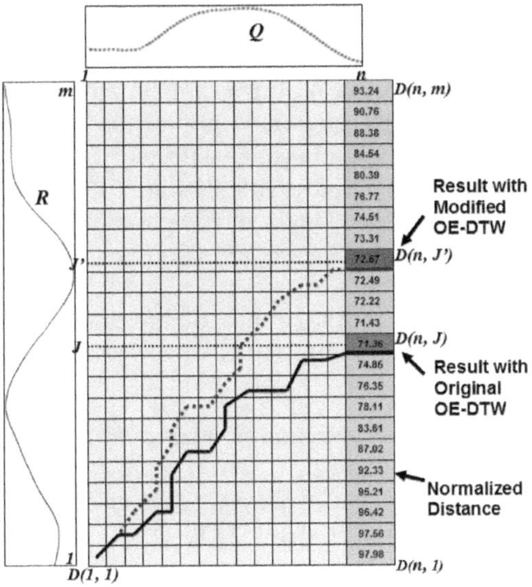

Fig. 5. An example of OE-DTW. The solid line shows the result with original OE-DTW, while the dotted line shows the result with our proposed flexible end point detection scheme with $\varepsilon = 0.02$.

3.3 Recognition Algorithm of the Sequential Patterns

In this section, we propose an algorithm based on the extended OE-DTW, namely, OE-DTW with *K-Repetition* and the flexible end point detection scheme, to recognize the sequential patterns in mocap data.

A motion can be regarded as a list of patterns connected in a continuous manner. For example, in Fig. 6, the input motion is first considered as a sequence of unknown patterns. The beginning part of the input motion is compared with each of the references using our proposed extended OE-DTW algorithm in order to find the best match. Since the reference R_A is the best match, the first pattern of the input motion is determined to be pattern *A*. The next part of the input motion is then recognized using similar technique. This process is repeated until every pattern in the motion is recognized.

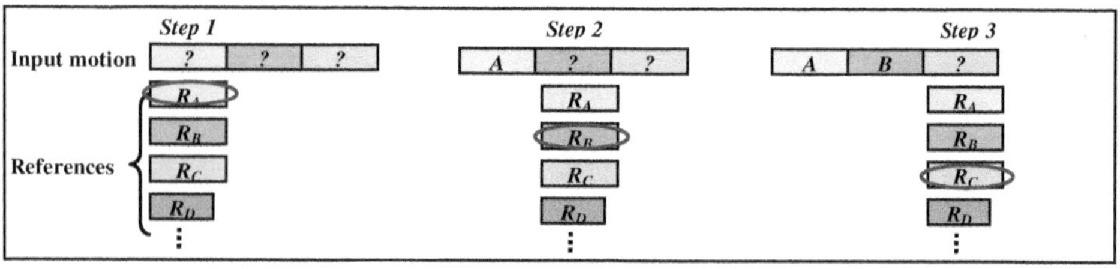

Fig. 6. An example of recognizing the sequential patterns in a continuous stream

On the other hand, as the length of any pattern in an input stream has an upper bound (say 300 samples), when processing a pattern, it does not need to take the whole motion as an input to OE-DTW. For example, in Fig. 6, when we process the first pattern, matching R_A with the beginning part of the input motion with OE-DTW can generate the same result as matching R_A with the whole motion with OE-DTW. The former condition requires much less calculation. To save the calculation, we thus define *len* as the upper bound of the length of any pattern. Each time when a pattern is being recognized, we just need to input *len* samples into the sliding window and compare them with the references.

Based on the above discussions, the proposed algorithm is presented as the following 4 steps, where *start* is used as the index of the samples in the input motion *I*. Initially, *start* is set to be 1.

1. Input *len* consecutive samples beginning at *start* from *I* into the sliding window, and denote them as *M*;
2. For each reference R_i $(i=1,2,\ldots,C$, where *C* is the number of references), calculate the distance $D_{OE}(R_i,M)$ with the extended OE-DTW, and return the corresponding end point $J(i)$.
3. If $D_{OE}(R_c,M)$ $(1\leq c \leq C)$ is the minimal distance among $D_{OE}(R_i,M)$ $(i=1,2,\ldots,C)$, then return R_c as the recognized result of *M*, and segment *I* at the point $J(c)$. Update $start = J(c)+1$.
4. If there are more samples left in *I*, return to Step 1. Otherwise end the algorithm.

For each pattern in the input stream, we can segment and recognize it with a computation complexity of $O(C\times L\times len)$, where *L* is the average length of the references.

4 Performance Evaluation

In this section, we will apply the proposed method to human motion recognition. We first introduce the acquired motion data and then present the experiments and results.

Table 1. The 19 basic moves of *A-go-go* dance used in our dataset. The average number of frames of each move pattern is shown inside the parentheses.

Move 1 *(281)*	
Move 2 *(259)*	
Move 3 *(157)*	
Move 4 *(163)*	
Move 5 *(156)*	
Move 6 *(258)*	
Move 7 *(130)*	
Move 8 *(156)*	
Move 9 *(162)*	
Move 10 *(170)*	
Move 11 *(119)*	
Move 12 *(220)*	
Move 13 *(125)*	
Move 14 *(128)*	
Move 15 *(113)*	
Move 16 *(187)*	
Move 17 *(118)*	
Move 18 *(167)*	
Move 19 *(202)*	

4.1 Data Acquisition

The dataset is captured by using a marker-based 3D optical motion capture system as shown in Fig. 7(a). An actor wears a special suit with 35 optical markers adhered to different body parts including head, torso, waist, limbs etc. From the 3D coordinates of the markers, we extract the 3D angles of the 20 joints (see Fig. 7(b), not including the end factors marked by '*') to represent each posture.

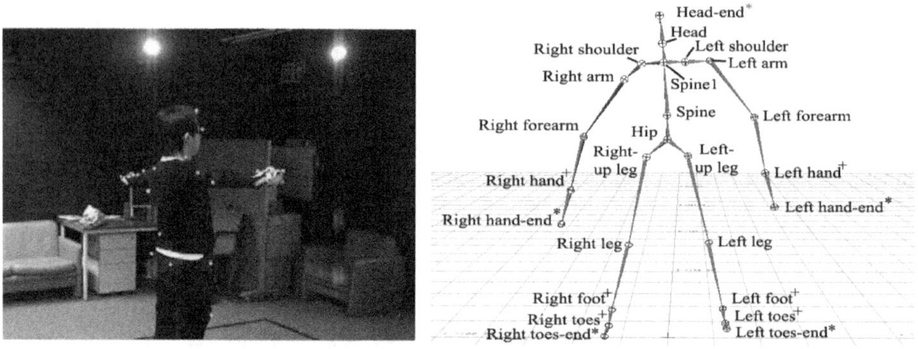

(a) (b)

Fig. 7. Data acquisition. (a) Optical motion capture system. (b) Human character model.

In our experiments, we capture the motion data with the sampling rate of 60 frames per second. There are 19 classes of patterns (basic moves) for *A-go-go* dance as shown in Table 1. It can be observed that some patterns have similar postures but with different temporal patterns and different durations. For example, Move 8 and Move 12 share a similar set of postures at the beginning part. For each class of patterns, it was performed 2 or 3 times by each of the 5 actors who have different levels of dance skills. In total, 265 isolated motions were captured in the dataset. On the other hand, we also construct 4 sets of test motion streams for later sequential patterns recognition. These streams were performed by the same 5 actors with various numbers of patterns in the streams (see Table 2 for the detail).

Table 2. Parameters of the test continuous motion sequences

	Number of streams	*Number of patterns per stream*	*Number of subjects*
Set 1	*50*	*5*	*5*
Set 2	*50*	*10*	*5*
Set 3	*50*	*20*	*5*
Set 4	*50*	*50*	*5*

4.2 Experiments and Results

The experiments include three parts: (1) evaluating the performance of DTW with *K-Repetition* on isolated moves; (2) OE-DTW with *K-Repetition* on incomplete moves; and (3) the extended OE-DTW on continuous motion streams.

In the first experiment, we applied DTW with *K-Repetition* for isolated move recognition. Among the 265 captured isolated motions, 19 motions (1 motion per class) are chosen as the references. The remaining 246 motions are used for testing. Each of the 246 motions is chosen as the input, and then DTW with *K-Repetition* is applied to recognize the class of the input motion. The total number of recognition errors among these 246 motions is recorded for different values of *k*. The result is shown in Fig. 8(a). We can see that when *k=5*, the number of recognition errors is the least (4 errors), and the result is better than that by the original DTW without applying any global constraint (5 errors). Moreover, as *k* becomes larger, the number of errors eventually becomes the same as that by DTW without *K-Repetition*. This means that if *k* is large enough, then *K-Repetition* will lose its superiority on constraining the global path.

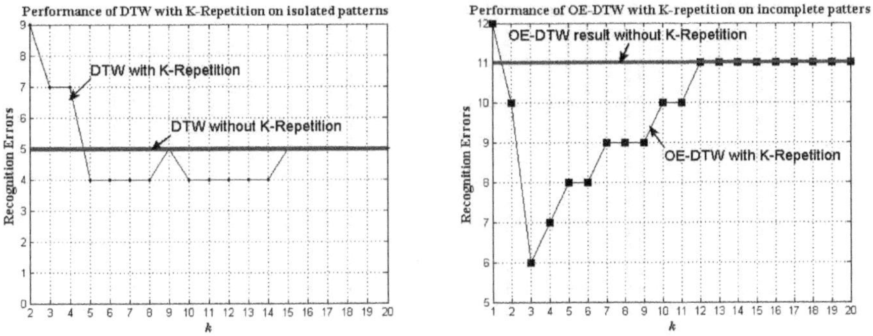

(a) (b)

Fig. 8. Evaluating the performance of *K-Repetition*. (a) Isolated pattern recognition with DTW. (b) Incomplete move recognition with OE-DTW.

In the second experiment, similar to the first experiment, 19 motions are used as the references and the others are used for testing. For each test motion, we just take its first half as the incomplete pattern input to be recognized by OE-DTW. The result is shown in Fig. 8(b). We can see that when *k=3*, OE-DTW with *K-Repetition* can get the best recognition rate with only 6 errors, outperforming OE-DTW without *K-Repetition*. Comparing the results between the first and the second experiments, the performance of the second experiment (6 errors) is worse than that of the first experiment (4 errors). This is expected since only half of the motion data are used as input for the second experiment.

In the third experiment, we apply our extended OE-DTW method for sequential pattern recognition, and compare the result with that of CDP. Since our task is to segment and recognize the patterns in the motion streams, we define the recognition accuracy of each stream as shown in Eq. (5). Moreover, there are two criteria in determining whether a pattern in a stream is correctly recognized: (1) the pattern is classified with the correct class label; (2) the detected boundary of the pattern should be close to the ground truth boundary, say within a range of 30 frames in this experiment.

$$recognition\ accuracy = \frac{\#of\ correctly\ recognized\ patterns}{\#of\ total\ patterns\ in\ input\ stream} \tag{5}$$

We test our method as well as another frequently used technique, CDP [3], on the 4 sets of captured streams. A comparison of the performance by the two methods is shown in Fig. 9.

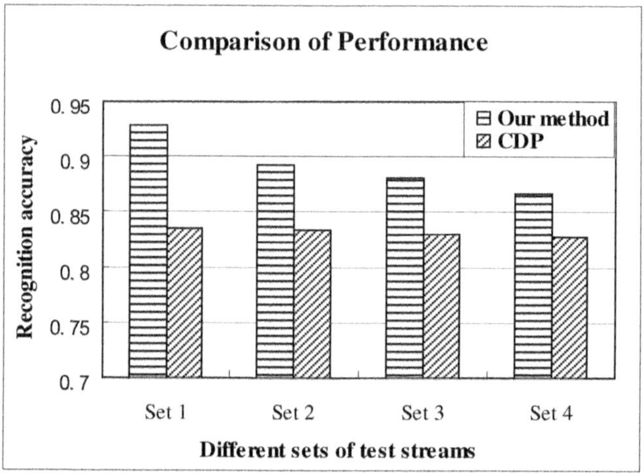

Fig. 9. Performance comparison of our method and CDP on motion stream recognition (In our method, k=5, ε=0.05)

From the result we can see that our method has higher recognition accuracy than CDP on all the 4 sets of test sequences. On the other hand, for both methods, as the number of patterns in a stream increases, the average accuracy decreases with more obvious trend with our method. This is because as there are more patterns in a stream, it is more likely to misrecognize a pattern or wrongly detect the end points, and subsequently the errors will affect the recognition of the next patterns in the stream.

5 Conclusion and Future Work

In this paper, we propose a novel method based on an extension of OE-DTW to segment and recognize the sequential patterns in mocap data. A new global constraint named *K-Repetition* is proposed to be applied with OE-DTW. A flexible end point detection scheme is also proposed to detect the end points of patterns in a more robust manner. Experimental results demonstrated the effectiveness of our methods, and showed that our method outperformed CDP on sequential pattern recognition.

In future work, the proposed method will be applied to some real applications, such as dance education and interactive dancing games. Also, we will further study the temporal alignment between motion patterns and expect to work out a real time method to segment and recognize the sequential patterns in mocap data.

Acknowledgements

The work described in this paper was fully supported by a grant from the Research Grants Councils of the Hong Kong Special Administration Region, China (Project No. CityU 1165/09E).

References

1. Tormene, P., Giorgino, T., Quaglini, S., Stefanelli, M.: Matching Incomplete Time Series with Dynamic Time Warping: An Algorithm and An Application to Post-stroke Rehabilitation. Artificial Intelligence in Medicine (ARTMED) 45(1), 11–34 (2009)
2. Sakoe, H., Chiba, S.: Dynamic Programming Algorithm Optimization for Spoken Word Recognition. IEEE Transactions on Acoustics, Speech and Signal Processing 26(1), 43–49 (1978)
3. Oka, R.: Spotting Method for Classification of Real World Data. The Computer Journal 41(8), 559–565 (1998)
4. Li, J., Wang, Y.: APCAS: An Approximate Approach to Adaptively Segment Time Series Stream. In: Dong, G., Lin, X., Wang, W., Yang, Y., Yu, J.X. (eds.) APWeb/WAIM 2007. LNCS, vol. 4505, pp. 554–565. Springer, Heidelberg (2007)
5. Kim, D., Song, J., Kim, D.: Simultaneous gesture segmentation and recognition based on forward spotting accumulative HMMs. Pattern Recognition 40, 3012–3026 (2007)
6. Park, A., Lee, S.: Gesture Spotting in Continuous Whole Body Action Sequences Using Discrete Hidden Markov Models. In: Gibet, S., Courty, N., Kamp, J.-F. (eds.) GW 2005. LNCS (LNAI), vol. 3881, pp. 100–111. Springer, Heidelberg (2006)
7. Li, H., Greenspan, M.: Continuous Time-Varying Gesture Segmentation by Dynamic Time Warping of Compound Gesture Models. In: International Workshop on Human Activity Recognition and Modeling (HARAM), pp. 35–42 (2005)
8. Blackburn, J., Ribeiro, E.: Human Motion Recognition Using Isomap and Dynamic Time Warping. In: Elgammal, A., Rosenhahn, B., Klette, R. (eds.) Human Motion 2007. LNCS, vol. 4814, pp. 285–298. Springer, Heidelberg (2007)
9. Nakata, T.: Temporal Segmentation and Recognition of Body Motion Data Based on Inter-Limb Correlation Analysis. In: Proc. of the 2007 IEEE/RSJ International Conference on Intelligent Robots and Systems, San Diego, CA, USA, October 29 - November 2 (2007)
10. Ratanamahatana, C., Keogh, E.: Three Myths about Dynamic Time Warping Data Mining. In: Proc. of 2005 SIAM International Data Mining Conference (SDM 2005), pp. 506–510 (2005)
11. Itakura, F.: Minimum Prediction Residual Principle Applied to Speech Recognition. IEEE Transactions on Acoustics, Speech and Signal Processing 23(1), 67–72 (1975)
12. Ratanamahatana, C., Keogh, E.: Making Time-series Classification More Accurate Using Learned Constraints. In: Proc. of the Fourth SIAM International Conference on Data Mining (SDM 2004), pp. 11–22 (2004)

Online Pattern Aggregation over RFID Data Streams

Hailong Liu, Zhanhuai Li, Qun Chen, and Shanglian Peng

School of Computer Science and Technology, Northwestern Polytechnical University, Xi'an, P.R.C.
{liuhailong,lizhh,chenbenben}@nwpu.edu.cn,
pengshanglian@mail.nwpu.edu.cn

Abstract. Complex events are very useful in *radio frequency identification* (*RFID*) applications. Even though many techniques have been proposed to detect RFID complex event instances online, they do not support online pattern aggregation operations. In this paper, we present an online pattern aggregation algorithm, named *RFID_PAQ*. *RFID_PAQ* divides a sliding window into several sub-windows and computes its aggregation value from those of its sub-windows. Based on the distribution characteristics of RFID data streams, we design different mapping functions to dispatch events to related sub-windows. Finally, our extensive experiments demonstrate that *RFID_PAQ* is effective and efficient.

Keywords: RFID, data stream, pattern, aggregation, sliding window.

1 Introduction

Radio frequency identification (RFID) technology enables automated and real-time information collection. It is automatic, fast and non-contact. It has great potential to be widely applied in various areas, such as supply chain monitoring [1, 2, 3], asset tracking [4, 5], anti-counterfeiting [6] and facility surveillance [7].

Raw RFID data, usually presented as a triple *<tag id, reader id, timestamp>*, contains little semantic information. Large-scale RFID implementations require raw RFID readings, *primitive events*, to be correlated and transformed into complex events that reach a semantic level appropriate for end applications. For instance, the readings from the shelves and doors in a retail store only tell us when and where tags are detected. But, if these events are correlated appropriately, a shoplifting may be found out: an item has been picked up from a shelf and then taken out of the store without being checked out.

Automatic RFID data transformation is always achieved by first devising application logic as complex events, and then detecting such complex events[8]. In this situation, aggregation information of the objects following a specific complex event pattern may be very useful. For example, let the pattern *SEQ*[9]*(HK,SH,BJ)* represent the sequence *Airport(Hong Kong)→Port(Shanghai)→Warehouse(Beijing),* the count information of the instances matching this complex event pattern can help a supply chain manager know the amount of the goods which have been transported along the path *Airport(Hong Kong)→Port(Shanghai)→Warehouse(Beijing)* quickly.

L. Chen et al. (Eds.): WAIM 2010, LNCS 6184, pp. 262–273, 2010.

In typical RFID applications, memory resource is bounded, but events streams are usually not and aggregation operations always need to be processed online. In practice, a complex event pattern usually specifies a window within which all relevant events should occur. There are three types of windows, namely *snapshot*, *landmark* and *sliding window* [10]. In this paper, we focus on the aggregation of complex event patterns specified by *sliding windows*, which is called *window pattern aggregation query (WPAQ)*.

Consider a supply chain in which items are transferred from one location to another. A *WPAQ* example is as follows.

Q1: *Find out how many items travel the path A→B→C in recent w1 period continuously and update the result every w2 interval.*

SELECT count(*)
FROM S
WHERE SEQ(A,B,C)
RANGE w1
SLIDE w2

Q1 is described by the composition of the SASE declarative language [9] and the CQL-like language [11]. *SEQ* is the operator to construct a sequential complex event from primitive events. *RANGE* specifies the size of sliding window. *SLIDE* specifies how the window moves.

Compared with traditional online window aggregations, *WPAQ* brings new challenges.

- *Composite aggregate data.* In traditional data streams, aggregation queries always only need to aggregate raw data. But, *WPAQ* aims at composite data. As we know, the composite data, complex event instances, don't exist before querying. How to integrate pattern detection and pattern aggregation efficiently is a great challenge.
- *Temporal.* Aggregate objects in XML data streams [12] are composite data, but there are no time constrains among them. Different from XML data, RFID events are temporal. As we know, traditional periodic data[13,14] is temporal and valid in a specified period. But they are not composite. How to integrate temporal attributions into pattern aggregation operations is also a great challenge.

In this paper, we present the design, implementation, and evaluation of an online window pattern aggregation method, named *RFID_PAQ*. Our contributions can be summarized as follows.

(1) We study the online window aggregation of composite data over RFID data streams which have not been studied before.

(2) We present an efficient *WPAQ* algorithm *RFID_PAQ*. *RFID_PAQ* divides a sliding window into several sub-windows and computes the aggregate value from the corresponding values of sub-windows, thus achieves high efficiency.

(3) We propose optimization techniques for *RFID_PAQ*. We design different mapping functions based on the distribution characteristics of RFID data streams.

(4) We validate our proposed techniques' effectiveness through a comprehensive empirical study. Our experimental results show that the proposed techniques are efficient.

The rest of this paper is organized as follows. We discuss related work in *Section 2*. In *Section 3*, we define valid aggregate objects and present the types of aggregate functions. The *RFID_PAQ* algorithm is described in detail in *Section 4*. We also present the optimization techniques for *WPAQ* in this section. The experimental study is presented in *Section 5*. Finally, we conclude this paper with *Section 6*.

2 Related Work

Several systems have been developed for RFID complex processing such as SASE[9] , Siemens RFID middleware[15], systems based on Path Database[16, 17]. SASE represents the structure of complex events by *non-deterministic finite automata (NFA)* and implemented event processing through sequence scan and construction. However, SASE does not support aggregation queries. Siemens RFID middleware uses an event-based framework to transform raw RFID data into semantic data. Its event processing is implemented by a graph computation model. It is an off-line system and lacks the expressiveness of the SASE language. In [17], a marvelous storage scheme is proposed to process tracking queries and path oriented queries efficiently, and in which pattern aggregate queries performs well. But as we know, [17] is based on Path Database [16] which is offline.

From *Q1*, we can see that *WPAQ* focuses on aggregations of composite data rather than raw data. There are some works on the sliding-window aggregate algorithms[11,18,19]. In [11,19], a framework for defining window semantics is presented and a one-pass algorithm is proposed to compute multiple aggregates. In [18], sharing strategies between different aggregate functions and different sliding-windows are proposed. Note that these works can only aggregate raw data in data streams. The aggregation queries over XML data streams target composite data. Unfortunately, XML data don't contain time constrains. The algorithms presented in [12] can not be applied to RFID data streams.

3 Preliminary

3.1 Valid Objects

By issuing *WPAQ* queries end users are usually interested in the aggregate information of the objects following a specified processing logic within a specified period. *For example, logistics companies want to know how many goods have been transferred from Hong Kong past Shanghai to Beijing in the past ten hours.* In RFID applications, goods movements are monitored by RFID readers. Processing logic is thus represented by RFID complex events. For a RFID complex event instance *p* contributes to a *WPAQ*, it must satisfy the following two constraints.

Constraint 1. *All the components of p have been detected.*

Constraint 2. *The start time and end time of p are in current sliding window.*

Constraint 1 guarantees that objects follow the specified processing steps. *Constraint 2* guarantees that the processing steps are accomplished within a specified time window.

A primitive RFID event has the format of *(tag id, reader id, timestamp)*, where *tag id* is an integer uniquely identifying an object, *reader id* identifies the interrogator, and *timestamp* records the reading's occurrence time.

A complex event instance is composed of a sequence of primitive events. For a complex event instance *p* with the pattern $SEQ(E_s,\ldots,E_e)$, its active period is defined to be $[e_s.timestamp,\ e_e.timestamp]$. To be a valid aggregate object for a time window *w(Start_Time, End_Time)*, *p's* active period should be included in *w*. That is

$$[e_s.timestamp, e_e.timestamp] \subseteq [w.Start\_Time, w.End\_Time],$$

as shown in Figure 1.

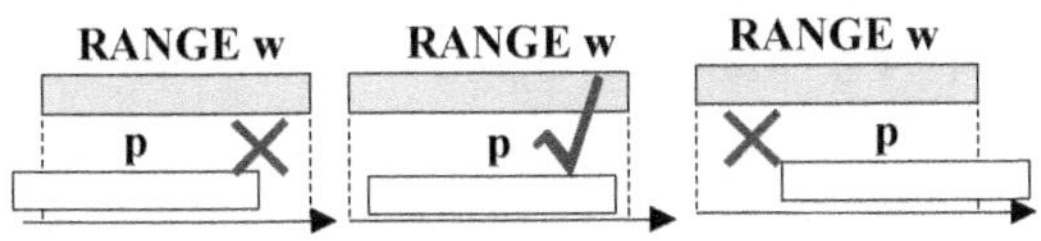

Fig. 1. Valid Aggregate Object

3.2 Aggregate Functions

In *WPAQ*, the commonly used aggregate functions include *count, sum, average, max* and *min*. In the rest of this paper, our discussion focuses on the function *count*. We will show in subsequent sections that the operations over other functions are similar.

In a *WPAQ*, multiple aggregate functions may be computed simultaneously, such as *Q2*.

Q2: *Find out the number, the average stay time, the max stay time of the items which follow the special path A→B→C in recent 24 hours and update the result every 1 hour.*

SELECT count(*),average(time),max(time)
FROM Stream
WHERE SEQ(A,B,C)
RANGE 24 hours
SLIDE 1 hour

The proposed *RFID_PAQ* algorithm supports multiple aggregate functions such as *count, average, max, sum, min,* in one query. As it will be shown later, the evaluation of multiple aggregate functions does not consume significant additional CPU time.

4 *RFID_PAQ* Algorithm

4.1 Framework of *RFID_PAQ*

We divide a sliding window into several independent sub-windows with the same size. We first sub-aggregate the stream over independent sub-streams, which we call sub-windows, and then we aggregate over the sub-window-aggregates to get window-aggregates. Let *RANGE* represent the size of the sliding window, *SLIDE* represent the size of a sub-window, *S* represent a sub-window, *R* represent a sliding window, *pattern* represent a complex event sequence, ψ represent an aggregate operator, our aggregate strategy can be described by Formula 1.

$$\psi(R_{pattern}) = \mathop{\psi}_{i=1}^{RANGE/SLIDE} (\psi(S_{i\ pattern})) \tag{1}$$

Besides saving the computational cost through sharing sub-aggregates, the sub-aggregating strategy has the following advantage.

If the data within a sub-window expire, they would not affect the aggregate values of other sub-windows.

Each primitive event will be dispatched to a sub-window. Unlike the case of traditional aggregate queries[11,18,19], in *WPAQ*, the validity of an event is not determined by its timestamp only. Consider the following example.

Example 1. *Suppose that e_s, e and e_e compose a complex event instance p but e_s has expired. In this case, no matter whether e and e_e expire or not, p is an invalid complex event instance.*

Note that a complex event instance is valid only if all its component events are valid. The first component is the starting point of a complex event instance. All its subsequent events belong to the same sub-window as which it belongs to. Let *FC* represent the first component of a complex event instance *p*. *W(RANGE,SLIDE)* specifies the size of the sliding window and its sub-window. The relationship between an event *e* and a sub-window *w* is as follows.

$$\varphi(w, E, W(RANGE,SLIDE)) = \{ e \in E \mid \\ \begin{cases} (w-1)*SLIDE \le e.timestamp < w*SLIDE & e = FC \\ (w-1)*SLIDE \le e_s.timestamp < w*SLIDE & e! = FC, e_s = p.FC \end{cases} \\ \} \tag{2}$$

Whether a complex event instance *p* belongs to a specific sub window is determined by its *FC* component. The relationship of a complex event instance *p* and a sub-window *w* can be described by the following formula.

$$\varphi(w, P, W(RANGE,SLIDE)) = \{ p \in P \mid \\ (w-1)*SLIDE \le p.FC.timestamp < w*SLIDE \\ \} \tag{3}$$

In the function φ, *FC* events are dispatched to a sub-window according to its timestamp. Other events have to identify their corresponding *FC* events so as to determine which sub-windows they belong to. It includes two steps: locating a sub-window and searching in the sub-window. Since each event needs to search for its related *FC* event in all sub-windows, the search cost is high for huge-volume data streams. The cost can be brought down from two perspectives. One is to speed up query processing in sub-windows, the other is to reduce the cost of locating the target sub-window.

To speed up query processing, we use B+ tree to store the data within a sub-window. In *WPAQ*, detailed information of primitive events does not need to be reserved. For example, in the *WPAQ* example *Q1*, we are interested in whether an instance of *SEQ(A,B,C)* has been detected or not. Other information of primitive events, such as *timestamp* and *reader id*, does not need to be reserved.

Note that searching sub-windows sequentially to identify the target sub-window is computationally prohibitive. In the movement routes of objects in RFID application scenarios, the intervals between two processing steps usually follow statistical distributions. We will use this characteristic to enhance the efficiency of locating sub-windows, as shown in next section.

Figure 2 is the framework of *RFID_PAQ*. In the framework, each event is firstly mapped to a sub-window and the state of its corresponding tag is then updated. The states of all the tags are stored in the nodes of the B+ trees. If the state code of a tag reaches the final state, the aggregate value of the sub-window will be updated accordingly. The aggregate value of a sliding window is computed from the aggregate results of all its sub-windows.

According to *Constraint 2*, every event has an expiration time. In *RFID_PAQ*, an event is considered to expire only after its corresponding sub-window falls out of the current sliding window. This expiration approach avoids frequently updating B+ trees and the aggregate values of sub-windows. When a sub-window becomes out-of-date, the aggregate value of the current sliding window has to be updated accordingly. Consider the following example.

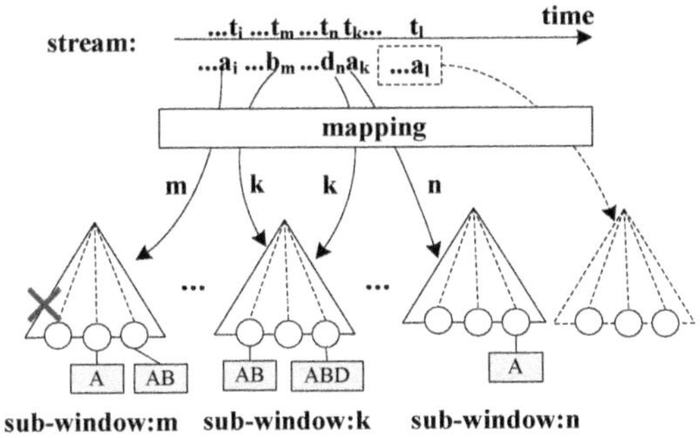

Fig. 2. Framework of *RFID_PAQ*

Example 2. *Let the punctuation PSLIDE identify the end of a sub-window. In Figure 2, processing of query SELECT count(*) FROM S WHERE SEQ(A,B,D) RANGE T hours SLIDE t hour is as follows.*

(1) When an event a_i is detected, map it to the sub-window m. Because a_i is an FC event, insert a_i into the B+ tree of sub-window m and then set the state 'A'.

(2) When an event d_n is detected, map it to the sub-window k, and then update the state from 'AB' to 'ABD'. For the pattern SEQ(A,B,D),the final state is 'ABD'. So, at that time, the aggregate value of sub-window k should be re-calculated.

(3) When PSLIDE of slide k is detected, because k<T/t, current sliding window is not full filled, no data is out-of-date.

(4) When PSLIDE of slide n is detected, because T/t=(n-m+1),current sliding window is full filled, data of sub-window m is to be out-of-date. Calculate aggregate value of current sliding window from the aggregate values of the sub-windows in the range [m , n] and then delete the B+ tree of sub-window m.

4.2 Mapping Functions

Suppose that the intervals between two processing steps satisfy statistical distributions. In this paper, we consider several common distributions: *constant distribution*, *uniform distribution* and *normal distribution*. Table 1 shows some application examples of these distributions. In a *conveyor belt system*, objects usually move with a constant speed, so time interval between two locations satisfies *constant distribution*. In a *supply chain system* or *product line*, the processing time of each step is usually pre-set in a region *[min_ProcessingTime, max_ProcessingTime]*. When the processing time is randomly distributed within the range, the intervals follow *uniform distribution*. More generally speaking, for large amounts of objects, the intervals follow *normal distribution* or *approximate normal distribution*.

Table 1. Examples of Different Distribution

Application	Distribution
conveyor belt systems	constant
supply chain	uniform, normal
product line	uniform, normal

Let T_i stand for a time interval between two steps of a processing logic. Assume that at current time *e* is detected and it is not a *FC* event. We can map RFID events to sub-windows in the following way.

(1) Constant Distribution

When the time intervals between two processing steps follow constant distribution, the distance between *e* and its *FC* event is $\sum T_i$, which is a constant value. Let *CurSLIDENo* stand for the number of current sub-window. The distance of target sub-window which contains *FC* event and *CurSLIDENo* is constant. The No. of target sub-window can be computed by Formula 4.

$$SLIDEID = CurSLIDENo - \text{int}(e.Timestamp / SLIDE) + \text{int}((e.Timestamp - \sum T_i) / SLIDE) \quad (4)$$

(2) Uniform Distribution

T_i follows $T_i \sim U(0, T_{imax})$. The largest distance between an event and its *FC* event is $\sum T_{imax}$. We can find the sub-window w_{max} which contains the point $\sum T_{imax}$ far from *e* firstly, and then set this sub-window as the start point. We search the sub-windows for *FC* events from w_{max} to the latest sub-window, instead of searching from the first sub-window. We call this method *boundary search*. The No. of w_{max} can be calculated by Formula 5.

$$w_{\max} = CurSLIDENo - \text{int}(e.Timestamp / SLIDE) + \text{int}((e.Timestamp - \sum T_{i\max}) / SLIDE) \quad (5)$$

(3) Normal Distribution (Gauss Distribution)
T_i follows $T_i \sim N(\mu_i, \sigma^2)$. Most of the distance values between RFID events and their *FC* events swarm around $\sum \mu_i$. We can find the sub-window *μ-Slide* which contains this point, and then set it as the central point. We search the sub-windows for *FC* events around *μ-Slide*. We call this method *surrounding search*. The No. of the sub-window *μ-Slide* can be calculated by Formula 6.

$$\begin{aligned}\mu - Slide = CurSLIDENo - \text{int}(e.Timestamp \,/\, SLIDE) \\ + \text{int}((e.Timestamp - \textstyle\sum \mu_i) \,/\, SLIDE)\end{aligned} \tag{6}$$

μ_i can be got from the history data of each processing step. Because it is not the focus of this article, we will not discuss the detail methods here.

4.3 State Codes

Since integer comparisons are faster, we introduce prime numbers to encode the states of tags when implementing *RFID_PAQ*. From *the fundamental theorem of arithmetic* [17], we know that any natural number greater than 1 can be uniquely expressed by the product of prime numbers. If we use different prime numbers to identify the steps of a commercial logic, a special sequence can be represented by a natural number greater than 1. Consider a processing logic described as Figure 3. Each step is monitored by a RFID reader and represented by a prime number. If a tag has gone through stepïA and step *B*, the state code of its path is *2*3=6*. Similarly, if the state code of a tag k_i is *42=2*3*7*, k_i must have gone through the path *A→B→D*.

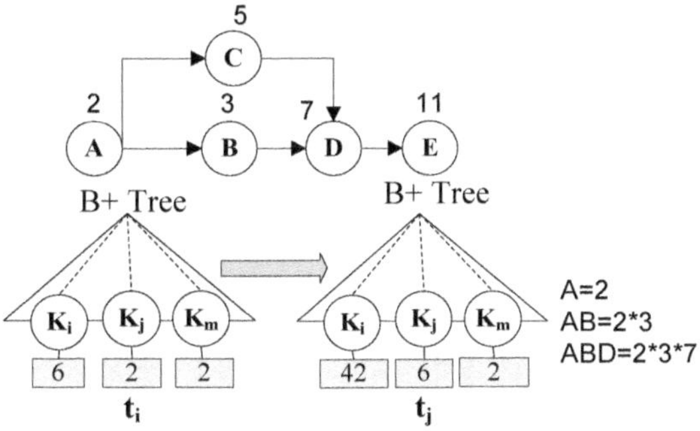

Fig. 3. State Codes in B+ Tree

5 Experiment Study

5.1 Data Sets

Since massive real-life RFID datasets are unavailable, we have conducted experiments on synthetic data. In our data generator, RFID readers are deployed as shown in Figure 4. RFID tags travel along the paths in the graph. When a tag arrives at a reader,

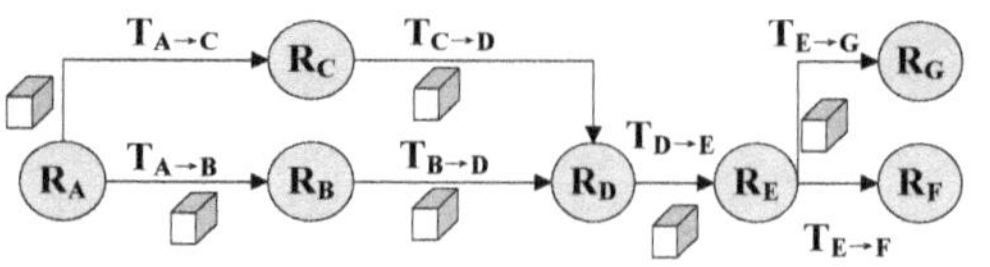

Fig. 4. Deployment of RFID Readers in RFID Data Generators

a reading is generated. Since redundant readings can be removed by cleansing process, we assume that each tag generate only one reading when it arrives at a reader.

Parameters of our data sets are shown in Table 2. $P_{x\to y}=0.5$ means that 50% tags will move from reader *X* to reader *Y*.

Table 2. Parameters

data	Tags from Reader A	$P_{X\to Y}$
S1	100000	0.5
S2	300000	0.5
S3	500000	0.5
S4	800000	0.5
S5	1000000	0.5

Timestamps of the events from reader *A* follow *t~U(0,3600)* distribution. Parameters of the intervals between two readers are as Table 3. $T_{X\to Y}$ represents intervals between reader *X* and reader *Y*.

Table 3. Distribution

Interval	Constant	uniform	normal
$T_{X\to Y}$	300	[0,300]	$\mu=300$

Our machine environment is AMD Athlon Dual Core Processor 5000B 2.61G HZ CPU, 1.87 G Memory, 250G 7200 r/s Disk.

5.2 Performance Evaluation

(1) Mapping Method vs. Directly Search

We began our study by examining the effectiveness of mapping functions.We compared two algorithms :*Direct Seach* and *Mapping*. In this set of experiments, we used the following query: *SELECT COUNT(*) FROM S WHERE SEQ(A,C,D) RANGE 4800 SLIDE 50. S* stands for a data stream,which changes from *S1* to *S5*.We considered three distributions: *constant distribution*, *uniform distribution* and *normal distribution*.

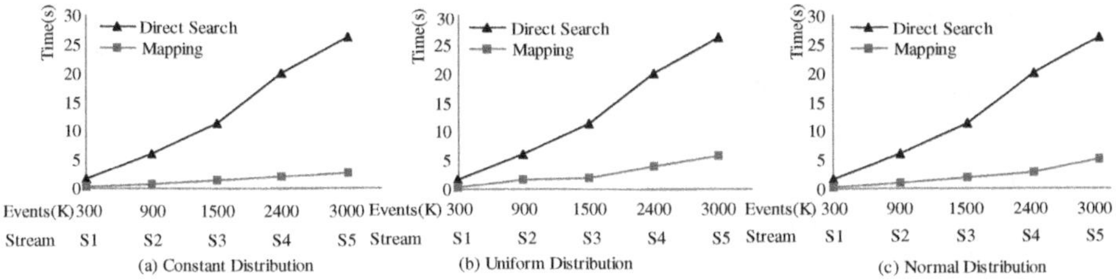

Fig. 5. Mapping vs. Direct Search

Figure 5 shows the running time of two algorithms.The mapping method performs significantly better. It effectively narrows the scope of searching target sub-window. Because the target sub-window can be fixed without searching in constant distribution situations, the gap between the two methods are more obvious.

(2) Size of Sub-windows
In this set of experiments, we used the following query: *SELECT COUNT(*) FROM S5 WHERE SEQ(A,C,D) RANGE x SLIDE var*. *Var* changes from 5 to 600.The first experiment measured the running time with *RANGE x=4800*, when there was no expiring data. The second experiment measured the running time with *RANGE x=1200*,when there was expiring data. As shown in Figure 6, no matter whether there is expiring data or not, the smaller the sub-window is, the higher efficiency *RFID_PAQ* algorithm achieves. The efficiency of *RFID_PAQ* is determined by serveral factors, such as efficiency of mapping events to sub-windows, efficiency of computing aggregate values, efficiency of eliminating out-of-dated data. In comparision with mapping events to sub-windows, the last two operations are less time-consuming. The reduction of the time to map events to sub-windows can enhance the performance of *RFID_PAQ* obviously. As we know, the smaller the size of sub-windows is, the less objects the sub-window contains, the faster B+ tree queries are, and consequently the faster *RFID_PAQ* performs.

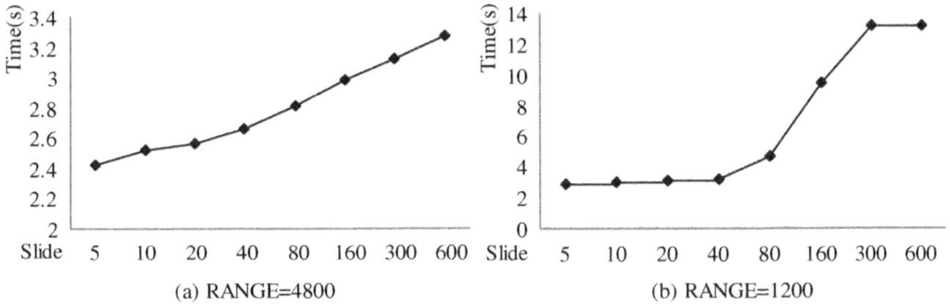

Fig. 6. Influence of Sub-window Size

(3) Multiple Aggregate Functions
In subsequent experiments, we used the following query: *SELECT Agg FROM S5 WHERE SEQ(A,C,D) RANGE 1200 SLIDE 80*. *Agg* came from the following data sets.

(a) count(*),
(b) count(*)&&sum(),
(c) count(*)&&sum()&&max(),
(d) Agg=count(*)&&sum()&&max()&&min().

We tested the running time when *Agg* varied from *(a)* to *(d)*. From the results shown in Figure 7, we can see that additional aggregate functions do not bring more running time obviously. *RFID_PAQ* aggretates sub-windows when a valid complex event came into being. By this method, the complexities of *count, sum, min* and *max* are the same. When the complex event pattern is the same, we only need to check *Constrain 1* and *Constrain 2* once. All the aggregate functions can be calculated at the same time.

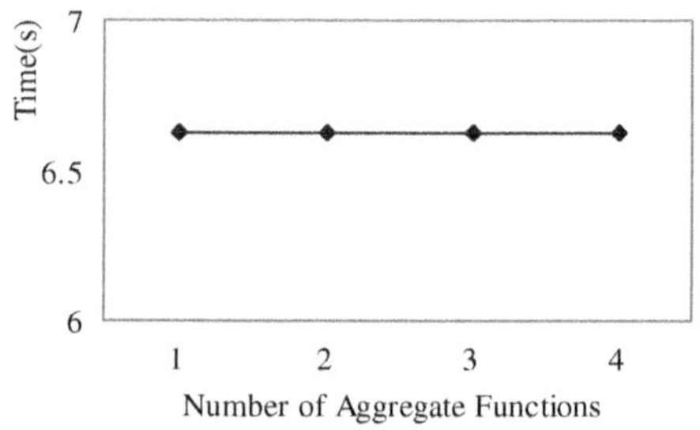

Fig. 7. Influence of Multiple Aggregate Functions

6 Conclusion

In this paper, we propose a novel online pattern aggregation approach over RFID event streams—*RFID_PAQ*. *RFID_PAQ* supports multiple aggregation functions and achieves high efficiency.

The values computed by *RFID_PAQ* are accurate. In practice, approximate values may be good enough for users. Our next work is to study online approximate pattern aggregate algorithms for RFID applications.

Acknowledgments. Our work is supported by National Science Foundation of China, with project no. 60720106001.

References

1. Doerr, K.H., Gates, W.R., Mutty, J.E.: A hybrid approach to the evaluation of RFID/MEMS technology applied to ordnance inventory. International Journal of Production Economics 103(2), 726–741 (2006)

2. Lee, Y.M., Cheng, F., Leung, Y.T.: Exploring the impact of RFID on supply chain dynamics. In: Proc. of the 36th conference on Winter simulation, pp. 1145–1152 (2004)
3. Delen, D., Hardgrave, B.C., Sharda, R.: RFID for better supply-chain management through enhanced information visibility. Production and Operations Management 16(5), 613–624 (2007)
4. Hakim, H., Renouf, R., Enderle, J.: Passive RFID asset monitoring system in hospital environments. In: Proc. of the 32nd Annual Northeast Bioengineering Conference, pp. 217–218. IEEE Press, New York (2006)
5. Rizvi, S., Jeffery, S.R., Krishnamurthy, S., Franklin, M.J., Burkhart, N., Edakkunni, A., Liang, L.: Events on the edge. In: Proc. of SIGMOD, pp. 885–887. ACM, New York (2005)
6. Zhang, X.L., King, B.: An anti-counterfeiting RFID privacy protection protocol. Journal of Computer Science and Technology 22(3), 627–644 (2007)
7. Li, Z.K., Gadh, R., Prabhu, B.S.: Applications of RFID technology and smart parts in manufacturing. In: Proc. of ASME Design Engineering Technical Conferences and Computers and Information in Engineering Conference, DETC 2004 - 57662 (2004)
8. Wang, F.S., Liu, S.R., Liu, P.Y., Bai, Y.J.: Bridging physical and virtual worlds: Complex event processing for RFID data streams. In: Ioannidis, Y., Scholl, M.H., Schmidt, J.W., Matthes, F., Hatzopoulos, M., Böhm, K., Kemper, A., Grust, T., Böhm, C. (eds.) EDBT 2006. LNCS, vol. 3896, pp. 588–607. Springer, Heidelberg (2006)
9. Wu, E., Diao, Y.L., Rizvi, S.: High-performance complex event processing over streams. In: Proc. of SIGMOD, pp. 407–418. ACM, New York (2006)
10. Chandrasekaran, S., Franklin, M.J.: Streaming queries over streaming data. In: Proc. of VLDB, pp. 203–214. Morgan Kaufmann, San Fransisco (2002)
11. Li, J., Maier, D., Tufte, K., Papadimos, V., Tucker, P.A.: Semantics and evaluation techniques for window aggregates in data streams. In: Proc. of SIGMOD, pp. 311–322. ACM, New York (2005)
12. Wang, H.Z., Li, J.Z., Luo, J.Z.: Efficient Aggregation Algorithms on XML Stream. Journal of Software 19(8), 2032–2042 (2008)
13. Timko, I., Böhlen, M.H., Gamper, J.: Sequenced Spatio-Temporal Aggregation in Road Networks. In: Proc. of the 12th International Conference on Extending Database Technology, pp. 48–59. ACM, New York (2009)
14. Zhang, D.H., Markowetz, A., Tsotras, V.J., Gunopulos, D., Seeger, B.: On computing temporal aggregates with range predicates. ACM Transactions on Database Systems 33(2), 1–39 (2008)
15. Wang, F.S., Liu, P.Y.: Temporal management of RFID data. In: Proc. of VLDB, pp. 1128–1139. ACM, New York (2005)
16. Gonzalez, H., Han, J.W., Li, X.L.: FlowCube: Constructing RFID flowcubes for multi-dimensional analysis of commodity flows. In: Proc. of VLDB, pp. 834–845. ACM, New York (2006)
17. Lee, C.H., Chung, C.W.: Efficient storage scheme and query processing for supply chain management using RFID. In: Proc. of SIGMOD, pp. 291–302. ACM, New York (2008)
18. Arasu, A., Widom, J.: Resource sharing in continuous sliding-window aggregates. In: Proc. of VLDB, pp. 336–347. Morgan Kaufmann, San Fransisco (2004)
19. Li, J., Maier, D., Tufte, K., Papadimos, V., Tucker, P.A.: No pane, no gain: efficient evaluation of sliding-window aggregates over data streams. SIGMOD Rec. 34(1), 39–44 (2005)

Cleaning Uncertain Streams by Parallelized Probabilistic Graphical Models

Qian Zhang, Shan Wang, and Biao Qin

DEKE Lab, Renmin University of China, Beijing 100872, China
{Zhangqian15,swang,qinbiao}@ruc.edu.cn

Abstract. Real-world applications generate uncertain streams due to unreliable equipments and/or data processing such as object identification. However, application context implies specific rules, which are critical in cleaning data and make them closer to the reality. In this paper, we propose a framework for cleaning uncertain streams by Parallelized Probabilistic Graphical Models (P^2GM). Making full use of multi-core processing architecture, the system processes parallelized high-volume streams efficiently. With P^2GM, users can define their own cleaning algorithms and generate specific parallelized systems. We implement a prototype of video surveillance based on P^2GM, and demonstrate the quality and performance of our approaches experimentally.

Keywords: Probabilistic graphic model, data cleaning, uncertain streams.

1 Introduction

Many applications generate uncertain streams inherently [1]. In those applications, uncertainty is mostly due to some *external* factors, such as unreliable equipments and/or imperfect computing algorithms. For example, object identification in video surveillance cannot always provide results coinciding with the fact. Such uncertainty exists widely and can not be eliminated in the near future.

Example 1. Fig. 1 (a) shows a video surveillance system, which gets video from cameras and processes by face identification and position computation. Results of those programs are probabilistic data streams, and query processing should take the uncertainty into consideration. For example, "*Person A is moving*" implies: (1) *A* appears at Position *p1* at Time *t1* and *p2* at *t2* while $t1+1 = t2$ and $p1 \neq p2$, (2) both appearances have high confidences. We make records related to *A* form a time-ordered uncertain stream named *str0* in Fig. 1 (b), where *posx* and *posy* represent two-dimensional position and *pro* is the confidence. The SQL is:

```
SQL1:
SELECT s1.t, s1.pro*s2.pro as pro, sqrt((s1.posx-
s2.posx)^2+(s1.posy-s2.posy)^2) as dis FROM str0 s1,
str0 s2 WHERE s1.t+1=s2.t and dis>0 ORDER BY pro DESC
```

L. Chen et al. (Eds.): WAIM 2010, LNCS 6184, pp. 274–279, 2010.

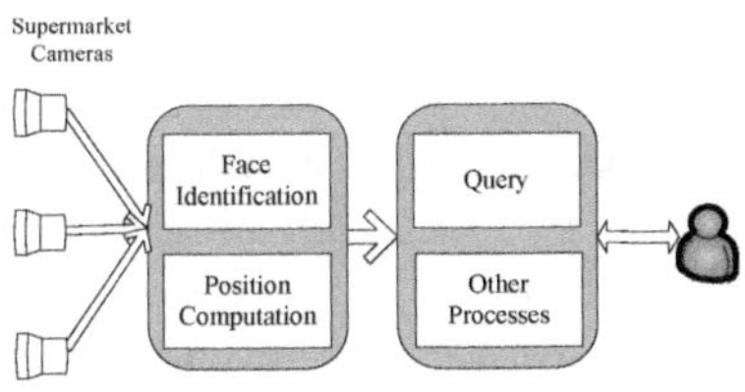

(a)

tid integer	t integer	posx integer	posy integer	pro double pre
0	0	30	87	0.9080077
1	0	98	73	0.7402804
2	0	116	87	0.7046392
3	1	149	7	0.09172698
4	1	99	73	0.07538872
5	1	96	3	0.36499622
6	2	99	73	0.21401109
7	2	85	90	0.42525476
8	2	20	36	0.83462626
9	3	3	17	0.6698783
10	3	139	70	0.86202973
11	3	99	72	0.97168815
12	4	142	37	0.8321826
13	4	108	80	0.8433741
14	4	99	72	0.999653
15	5	144	56	0.44324064

(b)

	t integer	pro double prec	dis double preci
1	275	0.9953353384	85.615419172
2	65	0.9883424401	22.847319317
3	662	0.987593643	26.172504656
4	845	0.984718977	105.6882207
5	78	0.969878268	50.289163842
6	276	0.966018640	72.124891681
7	417	0.961961434	77.82673062
8	333	0.954060265	23.706539182
9	895	0.951809644	115.4512884
10	578	0.951557405	14.866068747
11	578	0.950613502	43.046486500
12	828	0.949436367	72.567210226
13	835	0.9490474891	19.723082923
14	846	0.948117727	64.84597134
15	210	0.946117113	101.5184712
16	529	0.945780882	93.38094023
17	9	0.9416602494	106.8877916

t—second dis—centimeter

(c)

Fig. 1. (a) A simple video surveillance system. (b) Stream *Str0*. (c) Results of *SQL1*.

Results are shown in Fig. 1 (c). According to the context of supermarket environment and human beings' physical function, some results are more unreasonable, such as *Tuple 4, 9, 15* and *17* indicating that *A* moves over one meter in a second. We define them as *exception results*. To the best of our knowledge, there is no systemic solution to clean uncertain data according to application context.

In this paper, we propose a framework for cleaning uncertain streams by Parallelized Probabilistic Graphical Models (*P^2GM*). Our contributions include:

- We propose a parallelized probabilistic graphical model for high-volume stream environment by two kinds of parallelization: a single model can be executed over multiple streams in parallel; and independent models are executed simultaneously.
- We provide a general framework for users to define cleaning rules according to the applications and generate parallelized systems, and also implement an example video surveillance system with special cleaning rules based on it.
- Experiments demonstrate remarkable quality and performance of our approach.

In the rest of the paper, we overview related works in Section 2, present more details of *P^2GM* architecture in Section 3 as well as our prototype implementation in Section 4. Section 5 demonstrates the effectiveness and efficiency of our approach. Section 6 concludes the paper.

2 Related Works

Probabilistic Databases. Many recent papers relative to probabilistic databases are concerned about data structure and query processing. There are two basic types of uncertainty in probabilistic data structure: *tuple existence uncertainty* and *attribute value uncertainty* [2]. While query processing is typically based on possible world semantics, the most difficult point is the exponential increase of the number of possible worlds during processing.

We adopt *x-relation* uncertain data model [2] in our prototype. An *x-relation* is an uncertain data set consisting of *x-tuples*, where each *x-tuple* includes several alternatives with probabilities that represent a discrete probability distribution of these alternatives being selected. *X-tuples* are assumed independent from each other. That is, an *x-tuple* τ contains a finite set of tuples as *alternatives* with the constraint that $\sum_{t \in \tau} p(t) \leq 1$, where *p(t)* represent the probability of tuple *t*. X-tuple τ takes the value *t* with the probability *p(t)*, or does not exist at all with probability $1-\sum_{t \in \tau} p(t)$.

Probabilistic Data Management with Probabilistic Graphical Model (*PGM*). *PGM* has been used widely in modeling and reasoning about probabilistic data [3], and are mostly implemented as user views for hiding data details from users.

Query processing over uncertain streams gains much attention recently, with the main effort for effectiveness and efficiency [1]. Our work can be viewed as the pre-processing part of them. We aim at cleaning uncertain streams by application context to improve data quality. [1] has made similar effort, and supports SQL queries on one virtual view generated by *one HMM* over uncertain data. We propose a framework for cleaning multiple *parallelized* streams with *several PGMs*, and the proposed method is considerably efficient in multi-core environment.

3 P^2GM Architecture

P^2GM consists of five components shown in Fig. 2 (a). *Data Synchronization* buffers new-arriving data with different timestamps produced by the application, and outputs synchronized streams. Each process pair of *Stream Split & Merge* and *Cleaning Rule Deployment* implements a cleaning rule specified as *PGM*. As in video surveillance application, for uncertain streams are generated based on camera video, records for the same person may appear across streams. We choose *PersonID* as divided attribute for stream reorganization and generate new streams for individual persons respectively, which can be processed by different threads simultaneously. If there are some dependent rules, we need to define the processing order in *Deploy Order Definition*, or we execute them simultaneously. After all rules have been handled, *Output Process* generates output streams as user defined.

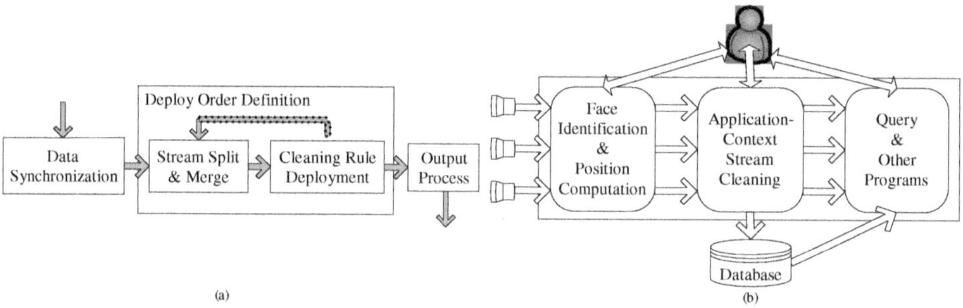

Fig. 2. (a) Dataflow and process design of *P^2GM* architecture. (b) Architecture of our prototype of video surveillance application.

We built the prototype of *P^2GM* architecture in Java over the underlying database *PostgresSQL* [4]. We also use *User Defined Functions* (*UDFs*) to realize functions inside database. Each user cleaning algorithm is proposed as a java file implementing specific APIs, and can import both system-provided algorithms and algorithms proposed before. The execution model of P^2GM can be parallelized or serial. Cleaning rules may be handled serially for the cases that dependencies exist, or be parallelized if no dependency. Parallelization inside each cleaning rule implementation requires independent partitions of original input streams.

4 Application Implementation: Video Surveillance

On the basis of P^2GM, we implement a prototype of video surveillance, and draw example cleaning rules represented as *PGMs* from application context. Fig. 2 (b) shows system architecture. While *Application-Context Data Cleaning* (*ACDC*) is implemented within *P^2GM*, it has the same structure of Fig. 2 (a).

After processes of face identification and position computation, each person-like object in a frame of surveillance video is represented by several relational records with same *t(t)*, same *pos(t)*, different *pid(t)* and *pro(t)*. Examples in Fig. 3 (a) illustrate *x-tuples* in video surveillance, composed of tuples with same *t(t)* and *pos(t)*, or tuples with same *t(t)* and *pid(t)*. A stream example is shown in Fig. 3 (b).

4.1 Probabilistic Graphical Model in Video Surveillance

Probabilistic Graphical Model consists of two components:

- Node-edge graph. Nodes represent random variables to be modeled in application, while edges represent the relationships between them. Specially, parent-child directed edge in graph represents the dependency of corresponding variables.
- *Conditional probability distribution function* (*CPD*). *CPD* is the quantized description of dependent variables' relationship. Each CPD defines a disjoint probability distribution of a node *x* by the form $\prod p(x|parent(x))$.

Example 2. Human beings' physical function restricts people's moving speed. If person *A* appears at position *I* and his possible position in the next second is *II*, the *probability distribution function* of the distance between *I* and *II* can be regarded as *Normal Distribution:* $N(\mu, \delta^2)$. $\mu = 0$ if *A* is most likely to stay still over time. Generally, if the maximum speed of people's motion is *z* metre per second, δ can be set *z/3* metre according to 3δ principle used widely in real applications. On the other hand, given *A*'s position *II* at *t+1*, his possible position *I* at *t* is also restricted by *II* in the same way. Fig. 3 (b) demonstrates the corresponding *PGM*, where each node corresponds to an *x-tuple*. Pos_T is *A*'s position at time *T*, and $Dist_{t+1}$ represents the distance of Pos_T and Pos_{T+1} as well as $Dist'_{t+1}$.

Continuous with *Example 1*, results of *SLQ1* after cleaning is shown in Fig. 4 (a). The *exception results* with large distance disappear in the top confidence group.

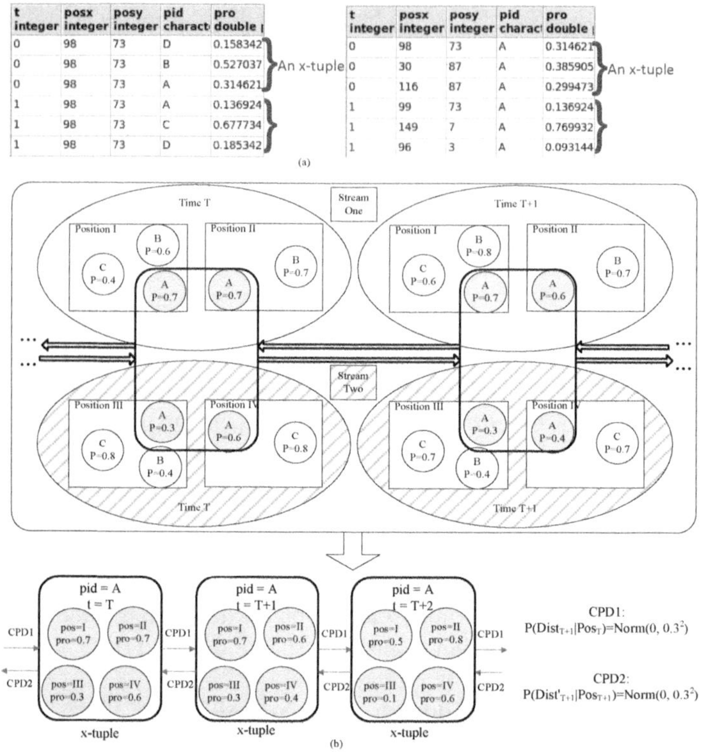

Fig. 3. (a) X-tuples in our prototype. (b) PGM in video surveillance application.

5 Evaluation

There are two datasets involved in our experiments. One is a real video surveillance dataset from CAVIAR [5], which records are annotated manually and can be regarded as fact. While CAVIAR datasets are used for effectiveness experiments, we make a simulated dataset with similar schema for efficiency experiments as well.

We initialize effectiveness experiment dataset by mixing CAVIAR datasets with noisy data, and assign artificial probabilities to the fact data. CAVIAR data occupies *32.8%* in top *500* records with the highest confidence originally, while the percent improves over *95%* after cleaning. In Fig. 4 (b), when the variance of *Normal Distribution* $N(0, \delta^2)$ used in our cleaning rule varies in X axle, the data quality curve declines slowly and is still acceptable. It not only verifies the effectiveness of our approach, but also shows that when the parameter of probability distribution function (i.e. cleaning rule) varies within a finite range, cleaning process can be still reliable.

We use three artificial uncertain streams to simulate high-volume streaming environment. Our approach is to divide streams into multiple independent sub-streams, and to process them by different threads respectively. While [1] holds similar purpose of data cleaning, it processes the whole stream at a time in traditional way (named

	t integer	pro double precision	dis double precision
1	65	0.98834244012462	22.8473193175917
2	662	0.98759364350156	26.1725046566048
3	333	0.95406026589975	23.7065391822594
4	578	0.95155740508627	14.8660687473185
5	578	0.95061350255622	43.0464865000618
6	835	0.94904748914496	19.723082923316
7	845	0.9396840997005	38.9486841883009
8	397	0.9345009081351	33.2415402771893
9	538	0.93013713867196	20.6155281280883
10	578	0.92729028008287	25
11	275	0.92703032655167	15.2315462117278
12	427	0.92499637383711	20.2484567313166
13	4	0.9240790332694	48.7031826475437
14	10	0.92238941507443	42.0594816896262
15	967	0.91861414129668	34.5253530032641
16	836	0.91691601824765	19.723082923316
17	27	0.91675120239617	15.6524758424985

(a)

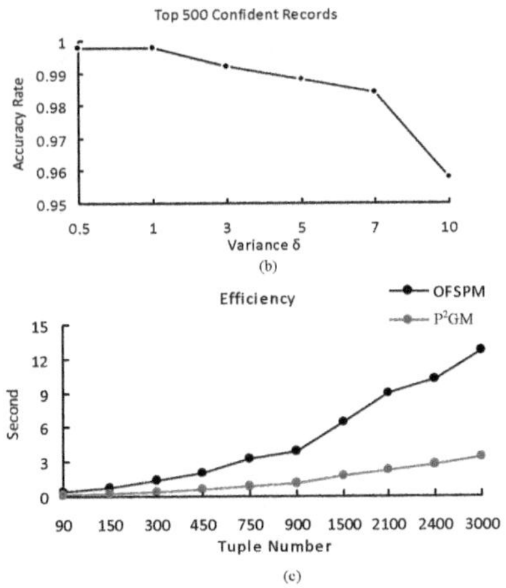

Fig. 4. (a) Results of *SQL1* after cleaning. (b) Experimental results of evaluating the effectiveness of our approach. (c) Results about efficiency experiments.

OFSPM). Results in Fig. 4 (c) illustrate that, execution time of cleaning process increases with *Tuple Number* of stream window for both execution models, while parallelized model takes about *1/3* time of serial execution (person number *3*).

6 Conclusion

Uncertain streams are generated widely in real-world applications, while most probabilities can be revised with application context restrictions. In this paper, we propose a novel system P^2GM for cleaning uncertain streams. We implement a prototype of video surveillance application over P^2GM, and demonstrate the quality and performance of our approach by experimental results.

References

1. Kanagal, B., Deshpande, A.: Online Filtering, Smoothing and Probabilistic Modeling of Streaming data. In: ICDE 2008, Cancún, Mexico (2008)
2. Benjelloun, O., Sarma, A.D., Halevy, A., Widom, J.: ULDBs: databases with uncertainty and lineage. In: VLDB 2006, Seoul, Korea (2006)
3. Sen, P., Deshpande, A.: Representing and Querying Correlated Tuples in Probabilistic Databases. In: ICDE 2007, Istanbul, Turkey (2007)
4. PostgreSQL, `http://www.postgresql.org/`
5. CAVIAR, `http://homepages.inf.ed.ac.uk/rbf/CAVIARDATA1/`

Taming Computational Complexity: Efficient and Parallel SimRank Optimizations on Undirected Graphs

Weiren Yu[1,2], Xuemin Lin[2], and Jiajin Le[1]

[1] Donghua University, Shanghai 201620, China
ywr0708@hotmail.com, lejiajin@dhu.edu.cn
[2] University of New South Wales, NSW 2052, Australia
lxue@cse.unsw.edu.au

Abstract. SimRank has been considered as one of the promising link-based ranking algorithms to evaluate similarities of web documents in many modern search engines. In this paper, we investigate the optimization problem of SimRank similarity computation on undirected web graphs. We first present a novel algorithm to estimate the SimRank between vertices in $O\left(n^3 + K \cdot n^2\right)$ time, where n is the number of vertices, and K is the number of iterations. In comparison, the most efficient implementation of SimRank algorithm in [1] takes $O\left(K \cdot n^3\right)$ time in the worst case. To efficiently handle large-scale computations, we also propose a parallel implementation of the SimRank algorithm on multiple processors. The experimental evaluations on both synthetic and real-life data sets demonstrate the better computational time and parallel efficiency of our proposed techniques.

1 Introduction

SimRank is a useful and important similarity measure exploiting the relationships between vertices (web documents) on web graphs. It has been widely studied in the literature [2,3,4,1,5,6,7]. As a multi-step generalization of co-citation [8,9], SimRank similarity is based on the recursive concept that *two different vertices are similar if their neighbors are similar*. SimRank has broad applications involving "find-similar-document" query, search engine optimization, graph clustering, etc.

Existing techniques for SimRank computation can be distinguished into two categories: (i) *probabilistic* method [3,4] that estimates SimRank by the expected value $s(a,b) = \mathbb{E}\left(c^{\tau(a,b)}\right)$, where $\tau_{(a,b)}$ is a random variable denoting the first meeting time for vertices a and b, and $c \in (0,1)$ is a decay factor; (ii) *deterministic* method [1,5,6,7] that computes SimRank iteratively for finding a fixed point of the SimRank function $s(a,b)$. Since the latter approach produces better accuracy with high time complexity compared to the probabilistic method, there has been a growing interest in SimRank deterministic optimization over the recent years. To the best of our knowledge, there are several interesting pieces of work which can efficiently reduce the time complexity of SimRank *deterministic* computation. One work [1] is mainly based on *a partial sums function* reducing the computational time from $O\left(Kn^4\right)$ to $O\left(Kn^3\right)$ in the worst case. Another work [7] oriented on *matrix representations* takes $O\left(K \min\left(mn, n^r\right)\right)$ time, where m is the number of edges, and $r \in (2, \log_2 7]$ is a positive constant. Li et al.

L. Chen et al. (Eds.): WAIM 2010, LNCS 6184, pp. 280–296, 2010.

[10] develop a novel approximate SimRank computation algorithm for static and dynamic information networks. They claim that their optimization technique is based on the non-iterative framework; however, the singular value decomposition (SVD) method they used for low-rank approximation inherently requires numerical iterations. Hence, their method is in essence iterative, not non-iterative. Details are described in the Related Work section.

Motivations: In spite of the substantial improvement achieved by these existing techniques [1,7], high performance of SimRank computation involving *fast algorithms* and *parallel implementation* is still a challenging problem. However, the time requirements of the available SimRank *deterministic* algorithms are still about cubic in the number of vertices for each iteration, which is costly over large web graphs. Additionally, in terms of *parallelization* strategies for SimRank computation, there is only one research work concerning SimRank optimization [3]. That work is based on SimRank *probabilistic* computation. As for SimRank *deterministic* computation, parallel implementation has not been addressed in scientific literature yet. This motivates our further exploration of SimRank deterministic optimization.

Contributions: In this paper, we provide efficient techniques for SimRank *deterministic* computation and parallelization on undirected graphs. The interesting aspect of our algorithm is that it uses a variant of *eigenvector centrality measure*, and we are able to prove strong theoretical guarantees on its performance. In summary, we make the following contributions:

- We present an efficient spectral decomposition based algorithm for SimRank computation over undirected graphs, which reduces the computational complexity from $O\left(Kn^3\right)$ to $O\left(n^3 + Kn^2\right)$ for K iterations in the worst case. We give theoretical results in Sect. 3.
- We develop a block partition technique in combination with the Parallel Linear Algebra Package (PLAPACK) to parallelize our SimRank algorithm on distributed memory multi-processors for achieving high parallel efficiency. We discuss these approaches in Sect. 4.
- We perform extensive evaluations of our proposed methods by using synthetic and real data sets, demonstrating the efficiency and effectiveness of our algorithms. We show experimental results in Sect. 5.

Organizations: The rest of this paper is organized as follows. Sect. 2 provides formal definition of SimRank similarity measure. Sect. 3 details optimization techniques for AUG-SimRank algorithm. Sect. 4 presents a parallel implementation of AUG-SimRank algorithm. We present experimental evaluations in Sect. 5. Sect. 6 reviews related work. And Sect. 7 concludes this paper.

2 Preliminaries

In this section, we briefly introduce the fundamental concepts, and formulate the basic problem of SimRank similarity scoring on undirected graphs. More details can be found in [2,1,7].

2.1 Problem Statement

Assume an undirected web graph $\mathcal{G} = (V, E)$, where V is the set of vertices representing web documents, and E is the set of edges. Each edge $(p, q) \in E$ between documents p and q corresponds to a reference between p and q. We denote the *derived graph* as $\mathcal{G}^2 = (V^2, E^2)$, where (a) each vertex in $V^2 = V \times V$ represents a pair (p, q) of vertices in $\mathcal{G}$, and (b) an edge $((p, q), (r, s))$ between (p, q) and (r, s) exists in E^2 *iff* the edges (p, r) and (q, s) exist in $\mathcal{G}$. Now we define a SimRank similarity function on $\mathcal{G}^2$.

Definition 1 (SimRank similarity [2]). *For two arbitrary vertices a and b, let $s : V^2 \to [0, 1] \subset \mathbb{R}$ be a real-valued function on $\mathcal{G}^2$ defined by*

$$s(a,b) = \begin{cases} 1, & a = b; \\ \frac{c}{|N(a)||N(b)|} \sum_{j=1}^{|N(b)|} \sum_{i=1}^{|N(a)|} s\left(N_i(a), N_j(b)\right), & N(a), N(b) \neq \varnothing; \\ 0, & otherwise. \end{cases} \tag{1}$$

where $c \in (0, 1)$ is a constant decay factor , $N(a)$ denotes the set of vertices neighboring to a , $|N(a)|$ is the cardinality of $N(a)$, and an individual member of $N(a)$ is referred to as $N_i(a)$ $\quad (1 \leq i \leq |N(a)|)$. The scalar $s(a, b)$ is called a SimRank similarity score between vertices a and b.

It is interesting to note that Eq.(1) has a unique solution $s(\cdot, \cdot)$ that can be reached by the following iterations to a fixed point.

Lemma 1 (SimRank iterative computation [1]). *For two arbitrary vertices a and b, let $s^{(k)}(\cdot, \cdot)$ be the SimRank value at the k-th iteration. We can use $s^{(k)}(\cdot, \cdot)$ to estimate $s(\cdot, \cdot)$ up to an error of c^{k+1} in worst-case time $O(k \cdot n^3)$, where $s^{(k)}(\cdot, \cdot)$ is generated by the following iterations:*

$$s^{(0)}(a,b) = \begin{cases} 1, \ a = b; \\ 0, \ a \neq b. \end{cases} \tag{2}$$

$$s^{(k)}(a,b) = \begin{cases} 1, & a = b; \\ \frac{c}{|N(a)||N(b)|} \sum_{j=1}^{|N(b)|} \sum_{i=1}^{|N(a)|} s^{(k-1)}\left(N_i(a), N_j(b)\right), & N(a), N(b) \neq \varnothing; \\ 0, & otherwise. \end{cases} \tag{3}$$

And the sequence $s^{(k)}$ nondecreasingly converges pointwise to a unique fixed point s, i.e.,

$$s(a,b) = \lim_{k \to +\infty} s^{(k)}(a,b) \quad \forall (a,b) \in V^2. \tag{4}$$

In matrix forms [7], Eq.(2) and Eq.(3) can be written as

$$\begin{cases} \mathbf{S}^{(0)} = \mathbf{I}_n \\ \mathbf{S}^{(k)} = \left(c \cdot \mathbf{Q} \cdot \mathbf{S}^{(k-1)} \cdot \mathbf{Q}^T\right) \bigvee \mathbf{I}_n \quad (\forall k = 1, 2, \cdots) \end{cases} \tag{5}$$

where $\mathbf{S}^{(k)}$ is the k-th iterative SimRank matrix whose entry $s_{i,j}^{(k)}$ denotes the SimRank similarity score between documents i and j at the k-th iteration.

2.2 Symbol Definitions

In Table 1, we list the notations used throughout this paper. Note that symbols defined and referenced in a local context are not listed here.

Table 1. Symbols & Notations

symbol	definition	symbol	definition
$\mathbf{Q}$	transition probability matrix of $\mathcal{G}$	c	decay factor, $0 < c < 1$
$\mathbf{S}$	SimRank matrix	n	number of vertices on $\mathcal{G}$
$\mathbf{I_n}$	$n \times n$ identity matrix	m	number of edges on $\mathcal{G}$
K	number of iterations	d	average vertex degree of $\mathcal{G}$
$\bigvee$	disjunction operator	ϵ	accuracy

3 AUG-SimRank Algorithm

In this section, we show an efficient algorithm to optimize the iterative SimRank computation over undirected graphs. We first formally introduce the notion of a graph spectrum in our paper[1].

Definition 2 (web graph spectrum). *Given a web graph $\mathcal{G}$, let $\mathbf{Q}_{\mathcal{G}}$ denote its transition probability matrix (i.e. the transpose of a column-normalized adjacency matrix). The spectrum of a web graph $\mathcal{G}$ is defined to be the set of the eigenvalues of $\mathbf{Q}_{\mathcal{G}}$. In symbols,*

$$\sigma(\mathcal{G}) := \{\lambda \in \mathbb{C} |\, \mathbf{Q}_{\mathcal{G}} \cdot \mathbf{u} = \lambda \cdot \mathbf{u}, \quad \forall \mathbf{u} \neq \mathbf{0}\}$$

Generally, for an arbitrary graph $\mathcal{G}$, the elements in $\sigma(\mathcal{G})$, given by the roots of the characteristic polynomial of the matrix $\mathbf{Q}_{\mathcal{G}}$, might be *complex* numbers. However, for *undirected* graphs, due to its *symmetric* adjacency matrix, we have the following special property of the spectrum.

Theorem 1. *Given an undirected graph $\mathcal{G}$, all the eigenvalues of its transition probability matrix $\mathbf{Q}_{\mathcal{G}}$ are real numbers associated with a complete set of orthonormal eigenvectors.*

Proof. Recall from linear algebra that an elementary row transformation on any row of $\mathbf{Q}$ corresponds to a row-multiplying operation on $\mathbf{Q}$ [11]. Therefore, $\mathbf{Q}_{\mathcal{G}}$ can be denoted as $\mathbf{Q} = \mathbf{\Lambda} \cdot \mathbf{P}$, where $\mathbf{\Lambda}$ is the real diagonal matrix normalizing $\mathbf{P}$, and $\mathbf{P}$ is the real symmetric adjacency matrix of $\mathcal{G}$.

Then we assume that $\mathbf{Q}$ contains complex eigenvalues. Let $\lambda_{\mathbf{\Lambda}}, \lambda_{\mathbf{P}}, \lambda_{\mathbf{Q}} \in \mathbb{C}$ be the eigenvalues of $\mathbf{\Lambda}$,$\mathbf{P}$ and $\mathbf{Q}$ respectively. We need to show that $\lambda_{\mathbf{Q}} = \overline{\lambda_{\mathbf{Q}}}$ for all $\lambda_{\mathbf{Q}} \in \sigma(\mathcal{G})$. By definition, we have

$$\begin{cases} \mathbf{\Lambda} \cdot \mathbf{u} = \lambda_{\mathbf{\Lambda}} \cdot \mathbf{u} \\ \mathbf{P} \cdot \mathbf{u} = \lambda_{\mathbf{P}} \cdot \mathbf{u} \end{cases} \quad (\forall \mathbf{u} \neq \mathbf{0})$$

[1] The terminology in this paper is slightly different from the traditional spectral radius of a web graph which is referred to as the dominant eigenvector of a graph *adjacency* matrix.

Taking complex conjugate of both sides, and noticing that $\mathbf{\Lambda} = \overline{\mathbf{\Lambda}^T}, \mathbf{P} = \overline{\mathbf{P}^T}$, we obtain

$$\begin{cases} \overline{\mathbf{u}^T} \cdot \mathbf{\Lambda} = \overline{\mathbf{u}^T} \cdot \overline{\lambda_{\mathbf{\Lambda}}} \\ \overline{\mathbf{u}^T} \cdot \mathbf{P} = \overline{\mathbf{u}^T} \cdot \overline{\lambda_{\mathbf{P}}} \end{cases} \quad (\forall \mathbf{u} \neq \mathbf{0})$$

Hence,

$$\overline{\mathbf{u}^T} \cdot \mathbf{Q} \cdot \mathbf{u} = \overline{\mathbf{u}^T} \cdot \mathbf{\Lambda} \cdot \underbrace{(\mathbf{P} \cdot \mathbf{u})}_{=\lambda_{\mathbf{P}} \cdot \mathbf{u}} = \lambda_{\mathbf{P}} \cdot \overline{\mathbf{u}^T} \cdot \underbrace{(\mathbf{\Lambda} \cdot \mathbf{u})}_{=\lambda_{\mathbf{\Lambda}} \cdot \mathbf{u}} = \lambda_{\mathbf{P}} \cdot \lambda_{\mathbf{\Lambda}} \cdot \left(\overline{\mathbf{u}^T} \cdot \mathbf{u}\right) = \lambda_{\mathbf{Q}} \cdot \|\mathbf{u}\|^2 \quad (\forall \mathbf{u} \neq \mathbf{0})$$

Also,

$$\overline{\mathbf{u}^T} \cdot \mathbf{Q} \cdot \mathbf{u} = \underbrace{\left(\overline{\mathbf{u}^T} \cdot \mathbf{\Lambda}\right)}_{=\overline{\mathbf{u}^T} \cdot \overline{\lambda_{\mathbf{\Lambda}}}} \cdot \mathbf{P} \cdot \mathbf{u} = \overline{\lambda_{\mathbf{\Lambda}}} \cdot \underbrace{\left(\overline{\mathbf{u}^T} \cdot \mathbf{P}\right)}_{=\overline{\mathbf{u}^T} \cdot \overline{\lambda_{\mathbf{P}}}} \cdot \mathbf{u} = \overline{\lambda_{\mathbf{\Lambda}}} \cdot \overline{\lambda_{\mathbf{P}}} \cdot \left(\overline{\mathbf{u}^T} \cdot \mathbf{u}\right) = \overline{\lambda_{\mathbf{Q}}} \cdot \|\mathbf{u}\|^2 \quad (\forall \mathbf{u} \neq \mathbf{0})$$

Thus,

$$\lambda_{\mathbf{Q}} \cdot \|\mathbf{u}\|^2 = \overline{\lambda_{\mathbf{Q}}} \cdot \|\mathbf{u}\|^2 \quad (\forall \mathbf{u} \neq \mathbf{0}) \quad \Rightarrow \quad \lambda_{\mathbf{Q}} = \overline{\lambda_{\mathbf{Q}}}$$

Therefore, for an undirected graph, every eigenvalue of the transition probability matrix $\mathbf{Q}_{\mathcal{G}}$ is a real number.

Additionally, the characteristic polynomial $\det(\mathbf{Q} - \lambda_{\mathbf{Q}} \cdot \mathbf{I}_n)$ has n roots, which implies that there exists a *complete* spectral decomposition for undirected graphs. □

Theorem 1 presents a sufficient condition that $\mathbf{Q}_{\mathcal{G}}$ has a complete real spectral decomposition, which can be applied to optimize SimRank iterative similarity computation over undirected graphs as follows.

Theorem 2. *For an undirected graph $\mathcal{G}$, let $\mathbf{Q} = \mathbf{U} \cdot \mathbf{\Lambda} \cdot \mathbf{U}^{-1}$ be a complete spectral decomposition of its transition probability matrix $\mathbf{Q}$, where $\mathbf{U}$ is an orthogonal matrix with real entities whose columns are eigenvectors of $\mathbf{Q}$, and $\mathbf{\Lambda}$ is a real diagonal matrix whose diagonal entities give the corresponding eigenvalues. Then we can construct the following iteration:*

$$\tilde{\mathbf{S}}_k = \begin{cases} \mathbf{I}_n & k = 0 \\ \left(\left[c \cdot diag(\mathbf{\Lambda}) \cdot diag(\mathbf{\Lambda})^T\right] \odot \tilde{\mathbf{S}}_{k-1}\right) \vee \mathbf{I}_n, & k = 1, 2, \cdots \end{cases} \tag{6}$$

where $diag(\mathbf{\Lambda})$ is a column vector whose elements are the main diagonal of $\mathbf{\Lambda}$, and $\odot$ is an element-wise matrix multiplication operator[2].
And SimRank similarity can be thereby obtained as follows:

$$\mathbf{S}_k = \mathbf{U} \cdot \tilde{\mathbf{S}}_k \cdot \mathbf{U}^{-1} \tag{7}$$

[2] More explicitly, for $\mathbf{A}, \mathbf{B} \in \mathbb{R}^{n \times m}$, then

$$\mathbf{A} \odot \mathbf{B} := \begin{pmatrix} a_{11}b_{11} & \ldots & a_{1m}b_{1m} \\ \vdots & \ddots & \vdots \\ a_{n1}b_{n1} & \cdots & a_{nm}b_{nm} \end{pmatrix} \in \mathbb{R}^{n \times m}$$

Proof. When $k > 0$, we substitute $\mathbf{Q} = \mathbf{U} \cdot \mathbf{\Lambda} \cdot \mathbf{U}^{-1}$ back into the naive SimRank matrix equation (5) to get

$$\begin{aligned} \mathbf{S}_k &= \left(c \cdot \mathbf{Q} \cdot \mathbf{S}_{k-1} \cdot \mathbf{Q}^T\right) \vee \mathbf{I}_n \\ &= \left(c \cdot \left(\mathbf{U} \cdot \mathbf{\Lambda} \cdot \mathbf{U}^{-1}\right) \cdot \mathbf{S}_{k-1} \cdot \left(\mathbf{U} \cdot \mathbf{\Lambda} \cdot \mathbf{U}^{-1}\right)^T\right) \vee \mathbf{I}_n \end{aligned} \tag{8}$$

Theorem 1 guarantees that the decomposition $\mathbf{Q} = \mathbf{U} \cdot \mathbf{\Lambda} \cdot \mathbf{U}^{-1}$ is complete, which implies that $\mathbf{U}$ and $\mathbf{\Lambda}$ are nonsingular. Now we premultiply and postmultiply both sides of Eq.(8), respectively, by $\mathbf{U}^{-1}$ and $\mathbf{U}$ to produce

$$\mathbf{U}^{-1} \cdot \mathbf{S}_k \cdot \mathbf{U} = (c \cdot \underbrace{\mathbf{U}^{-1} \cdot \mathbf{U}}_{=\mathbf{I}_n} \cdot \mathbf{\Lambda} \cdot \mathbf{U}^{-1} \cdot \mathbf{S}_{k-1} \cdot \mathbf{U}^{-T} \cdot \mathbf{\Lambda} \cdot \underbrace{\mathbf{U}^T \cdot \mathbf{U}}_{=\mathbf{I}_n}) \vee \underbrace{(\mathbf{U}^{-1} \cdot \mathbf{I}_n \cdot \mathbf{U})}_{=\mathbf{I}_n}$$

Applying $\mathbf{U}^{-1} \cdot \mathbf{U} = \mathbf{I}_n$ and $\mathbf{U}^{-T} = \mathbf{U}$ to the above equation yields

$$\Rightarrow \quad \underbrace{\mathbf{U}^{-1} \cdot \mathbf{S}_k \cdot \mathbf{U}}_{:=\tilde{\mathbf{S}}_k} = (c \cdot \mathbf{\Lambda} \cdot \underbrace{\mathbf{U}^{-1} \cdot \mathbf{S}_{k-1} \cdot \mathbf{U}}_{:=\tilde{\mathbf{S}}_{k-1}} \cdot \mathbf{\Lambda}) \vee \mathbf{I}_n$$

We may assume that $\tilde{\mathbf{S}}_k := \mathbf{U}^{-1} \cdot \mathbf{S}_k \cdot \mathbf{U}$, and obtain

$$\begin{cases} \mathbf{S}_k = \mathbf{U} \cdot \tilde{\mathbf{S}}_k \cdot \mathbf{U}^{-1} \\ \tilde{\mathbf{S}}_k = \left(c \cdot \mathbf{\Lambda} \cdot \tilde{\mathbf{S}}_{k-1} \cdot \mathbf{\Lambda}\right) \vee \mathbf{I}_n \end{cases} \quad (k = 1, 2, 3, \cdots) \tag{9}$$

When $k = 0$, it follows from our assumption $\tilde{\mathbf{S}}_k := \mathbf{U}^{-1} \cdot \mathbf{S}_k \cdot \mathbf{U}$ that

$$\tilde{\mathbf{S}}_0 = \mathbf{U}^{-1} \cdot \mathbf{S}_0 \cdot \mathbf{U} = \mathbf{U}^{-1} \cdot \mathbf{I}_n \cdot \mathbf{U} = \mathbf{I}_n$$

In the following, we show that $\mathbf{\Lambda} \cdot \tilde{\mathbf{S}} \cdot \mathbf{\Lambda} = \left[diag\,(\mathbf{\Lambda}) \cdot diag(\mathbf{\Lambda})^T\right] \odot \tilde{\mathbf{S}}$, which is our trick to reduce the time complexity from $O\left(n^3\right)$ to $O\left(n^2\right)$ per iteration.

As all the off-diagonal entries of $\mathbf{\Lambda}$ are zeros, then

$$\begin{aligned} \mathbf{\Lambda} \cdot \tilde{\mathbf{S}} \cdot \mathbf{\Lambda} &= \begin{pmatrix} \lambda_1 & 0 & \dots & 0 \\ 0 & \lambda_2 & \dots & 0 \\ \vdots & \vdots & \ddots & \vdots \\ 0 & 0 & \dots & \lambda_n \end{pmatrix} \cdot \begin{pmatrix} \tilde{s}_{11} & \tilde{s}_{12} & \dots & \tilde{s}_{1n} \\ \tilde{s}_{21} & \tilde{s}_{22} & \dots & \tilde{s}_{2n} \\ \vdots & \vdots & \ddots & \vdots \\ \tilde{s}_{n1} & \tilde{s}_{n2} & \dots & \tilde{s}_{nn} \end{pmatrix} \cdot \begin{pmatrix} \lambda_1 & 0 & \dots & 0 \\ 0 & \lambda_2 & \dots & 0 \\ \vdots & \vdots & \ddots & \vdots \\ 0 & 0 & \dots & \lambda_n \end{pmatrix} \\ &= \begin{pmatrix} {\lambda_1}^2 \cdot \tilde{s}_{11} & \lambda_1\lambda_2 \cdot \tilde{s}_{12} & \dots & \lambda_1\lambda_n \cdot \tilde{s}_{1n} \\ \lambda_2\lambda_1 \cdot \tilde{s}_{21} & {\lambda_2}^2 \cdot \tilde{s}_{22} & \dots & \lambda_2\lambda_n \cdot \tilde{s}_{2n} \\ \vdots & \vdots & \ddots & \vdots \\ \lambda_n\lambda_1 \cdot \tilde{s}_{n1} & \lambda_n\lambda_2 \cdot \tilde{s}_{n2} & \dots & {\lambda_n}^2 \cdot \tilde{s}_{nn} \end{pmatrix} \end{aligned}$$

On the other hand,

$$\left[diag\left(\mathbf{\Lambda}\right)\cdot diag(\mathbf{\Lambda})^T\right]\odot\tilde{\mathbf{S}}=\left[\begin{pmatrix}\lambda_1\\ \lambda_2\\ \vdots\\ \lambda_n\end{pmatrix}\cdot\left(\lambda_1\ \lambda_2\ \cdots\ \lambda_n\right)\right]\odot\begin{pmatrix}\tilde{s}_{11} & \tilde{s}_{12} & \ldots & \tilde{s}_{1n}\\ \tilde{s}_{21} & \tilde{s}_{22} & \ldots & \tilde{s}_{2n}\\ \vdots & \vdots & \ddots & \vdots\\ \tilde{s}_{n1} & \tilde{s}_{n2} & \ldots & \tilde{s}_{nn}\end{pmatrix}$$

$$=\begin{pmatrix}{\lambda_1}^2 & \lambda_1\lambda_2 & \ldots & \lambda_1\lambda_n\\ \lambda_2\lambda_1 & {\lambda_2}^2 & \ldots & \lambda_2\lambda_n\\ \vdots & \vdots & \ddots & \vdots\\ \lambda_n\lambda_1 & \lambda_n\lambda_2 & \ldots & {\lambda_n}^2\end{pmatrix}\odot\begin{pmatrix}\tilde{s}_{11} & \tilde{s}_{12} & \ldots & \tilde{s}_{1n}\\ \tilde{s}_{21} & \tilde{s}_{22} & \ldots & \tilde{s}_{2n}\\ \vdots & \vdots & \ddots & \vdots\\ \tilde{s}_{n1} & \tilde{s}_{n2} & \ldots & \tilde{s}_{nn}\end{pmatrix}=\begin{pmatrix}{\lambda_1}^2\cdot\tilde{s}_{11} & \lambda_1\lambda_2\cdot\tilde{s}_{12} & \ldots & \lambda_1\lambda_n\cdot\tilde{s}_{1n}\\ \lambda_2\lambda_1\cdot\tilde{s}_{21} & {\lambda_2}^2\cdot\tilde{s}_{22} & \ldots & \lambda_2\lambda_n\cdot\tilde{s}_{2n}\\ \vdots & \vdots & \ddots & \vdots\\ \lambda_n\lambda_1\cdot\tilde{s}_{n1} & \lambda_n\lambda_2\cdot\tilde{s}_{n2} & \ldots & {\lambda_n}^2\cdot\tilde{s}_{nn}\end{pmatrix}$$

Hence,

$$\mathbf{\Lambda}\cdot\tilde{\mathbf{S}}\cdot\mathbf{\Lambda}=\left[diag\left(\mathbf{\Lambda}\right)\cdot diag(\mathbf{\Lambda})^T\right]\odot\tilde{\mathbf{S}} \tag{10}$$

Finally, we substitute Eq.(10) back into Eq.(9), which establishes Eq.(6) and completes the proof. □

Theorem 2 provides an efficient accelerative technique for SimRank computation based on the following algorithm.

Algorithm 1. AUG-SimRank: Accelerative SimRank for Undirected Graphs

```
   Input  : adjacency matrix P = (p_{i,j}) ∈ R^{n×n}, decay factor c, accuracy ϵ
   Output : SimRank matrix S = (s_{i,j}) ∈ [0,1]^{n×n}, iteration number k
1  begin
2      Calculate transition probability matrix Q according to q_{i,j} ← p_{j,i} / Σ_{i=1}^{n} p_{j,i}
3      Decompose Q → U · Λ · U^{-1}, yielding U, orthogonal, and Λ, diagonal
4      Initialize S̃_0 ← I_n, M ← c · diag(Λ) · diag(Λ)^T, k ← 0
5      repeat                       /* each iteration takes O(n^2) time */
6          Set k ← k + 1
7          Update S̃_k ← (M ⊙ S̃_{k-1}) ∨ I_n
8      until the auxiliary matrix S̃_k converges with an error of ϵ
9      Calculate SimRank matrix S_k ← U · S̃_k · U^{-1}
10     Return S_k, k
```

Now we describe the overall idea of Algorithm 1 which involves the following three steps.

(i) **Spectral Predecomposition (Line 2-3).** The first step in our algorithm is to diagonalize the transition probability matrix $\mathbf{Q}$ in Eq.(5) by eigen-decomposition, so that we may obtain a diagonal matrix $\mathbf{\Lambda}$ which makes it much easier in the next step to compute the power series of matrices derived from the recursive substitutions of Eq.(5). An important problem underlying this step is to determine whether there exists a *full* and *real* (not singular or complex) spectral decomposition for any arbitrary web graphs. We theoretically prove in Theorem 1 that only for *undirected* graphs, all the eigenvalues of the transition probability matrix $\mathbf{Q}$ are real numbers, and the number of eigenvalues is n. Hence, in this case, $\mathbf{Q}$ can be *completely* decomposed as $\mathbf{Q} = \mathbf{U} \cdot \mathbf{\Lambda} \cdot \mathbf{U}^{-1}$. The implementation of this step requires the well-known numerical methods given in [12,11].

(ii) **Iterative Element-wise Matrix Multiplication (Line 4-8).** In this step, we develop a novel iterative method to reduce the SimRank computational complexity. The key point of our optimization technique is based on Eq.(10), where $\mathbf{\Lambda}$ is diagonal, derived from the previous step, and $\tilde{\mathbf{S}}$ is an iterative auxiliary matrix with an initial value $\mathbf{I}_n$. Note that from Eq.(10) a standard matrix multiplication $\mathbf{\Lambda} \cdot \tilde{\mathbf{S}} \cdot \mathbf{\Lambda}$ can be accelerated significantly by performing the matrix product of a column vector and a row vector (i.e. a rank-1 tensor[3] $diag\,(\mathbf{\Lambda}) \cdot diag(\mathbf{\Lambda})^T$) first, and then multiplying this rank-1 matrix *element-wise* with $\tilde{\mathbf{S}}$. Due to the diagonal structure of $\mathbf{\Lambda}$, this computation only takes $O\left(n^2\right)$ time per iteration, whereas a standard implementation of $\mathbf{\Lambda} \cdot \tilde{\mathbf{S}} \cdot \mathbf{\Lambda}$ often requires $O\left(n^3\right)$ time. Moreover, to calculate $diag\,(\mathbf{\Lambda}) \cdot diag(\mathbf{\Lambda})^T$, preconditioning techniques may be adopted, which implies that once computed, this rank-1 matrix is memorized and is therefore not recomputed when subsequently required. Hence, in Line 4, $\mathbf{M}$ is precomputed only once, and can be used in this step for K iterations.

(iii) **SimRank Matrix Computation (Line 9).** In the final step, we obtain the SimRank matrix $\mathbf{S}_k$ from the k-th iterative auxiliary matrix $\tilde{\mathbf{S}}_k$ according to Eq.(7). This computation is performed only once, taking $O\left(n^3\right)$ time in the worst case.

Analyzing the computational complexity, we now summarize the above discussion in the following result.

Theorem 3. *For undirected graphs, Algorithm 1 can perform the SimRank computation for K iterations in $O\left(n^3 + K \cdot n^2\right)$ time in the worst case, where n is the number of vertices, and $n \gg K$.*

Proof. For Algorithm 1, Step (i) and (iii) are performed only once during the whole procedure, and their computational complexities involve $O\left(n^3\right)$ operations in the worst case. In Step (ii), due to the element-wise matrix products, the computational time required for K iterations is $O\left(K \cdot n^2\right)$. Hence, the total time required for K iterations of this algorithm is $O\left(n^3 + K \cdot n^2\right)$ in the worst case. □

4 Parallel AUG-SimRank Algorithm

In this section, we parallelize the AUG-SimRank algorithm which is highly efficient on distributed multiprocessors. To implement our parallel SimRank algorithm, we utilize

[3] Here, since $diag(\mathbf{\Lambda})^T$ is a row vector, we obtain

$$diag\,(\mathbf{\Lambda}) \cdot diag(\mathbf{\Lambda})^T = diag\,(\mathbf{\Lambda}) \cdot \left(\lambda_1 \;\cdots\; \lambda_n\right) = \left(\lambda_1 \cdot diag\,(\mathbf{\Lambda}) \;\cdots\; \lambda_n \cdot diag\,(\mathbf{\Lambda})\right)$$

Thus,

$$Rank\left[diag\,(\mathbf{\Lambda}) \cdot diag(\mathbf{\Lambda})^T\right] = 1$$

the available PLAPACK [13] (Parallel Linear Algebra Package) in combination with our matrix partition techniques on distributed memory architectures. PLAPACK is a parallel ARPACK version based on MPI (Message Passing Interface) for constructing parallel linear algebra libraries. It provides a high-level object-oriented programming interface so that coding of parallel linear algebra routines becomes a straightforward translation of algorithms.

We now show how to parallelize Algorithm 1 for each step.

In the *spectral predecomposition* step, we deploy a parallel solver that is capable of spectral factorization. Several works have studied parallel eigen-decomposition [14,13]. We adopt *a PLAPACK eigen-solver* in this step to decompose matrix $\mathbf{Q}$ due to its better performance exhibited for large-scale problems.

In the *iterative element-wise matrix multiplication* step, the parallel implementation of $\tilde{\mathbf{S}}_k = \left(\mathbf{M} \odot \tilde{\mathbf{S}}_{k-1}\right) \vee \mathbf{I}_n \quad (k = 1, 2, \cdots)$ is our main concern. We first vertically partition

$$\tilde{\mathbf{S}}_k = \left(\tilde{\mathbf{S}}_k^{(1)} \middle| \cdots \middle| \tilde{\mathbf{S}}_k^{(N)}\right), \quad \mathbf{M} = \left(\mathbf{M}^{(1)} \middle| \cdots \middle| \mathbf{M}^{(N)}\right), \quad \mathbf{I} = \left(\mathbf{I}^{(1)} \middle| \cdots \middle| \mathbf{I}^{(N)}\right),$$

where $\tilde{\mathbf{S}}_k^{(i)}, \mathbf{M}^{(i)}$, and $\mathbf{I}^{(i)}$ are $n \times n_i$ submatrices satisfying $n_i < n$ and $\sum_{i=1}^{N} n_i = n \quad (i = 1, 2, \cdots, N)$, and N is the number of partitions. Then, we have

$$\begin{aligned}
\left(\tilde{\mathbf{S}}_k^{(1)} \middle| \cdots \middle| \tilde{\mathbf{S}}_k^{(N)}\right) &= \left[\left(\mathbf{M}^{(1)} \middle| \cdots \middle| \mathbf{M}^{(N)}\right) \odot \left(\tilde{\mathbf{S}}_{k-1}^{(1)} \middle| \cdots \middle| \tilde{\mathbf{S}}_{k-1}^{(N)}\right)\right] \vee \left(\mathbf{I}^{(1)} \middle| \cdots \middle| \mathbf{I}^{(N)}\right) \\
&= \left(\mathbf{M}^{(1)} \odot \tilde{\mathbf{S}}_{k-1}^{(1)} \middle| \cdots \middle| \mathbf{M}^{(N)} \odot \tilde{\mathbf{S}}_{k-1}^{(N)}\right) \vee \left(\mathbf{I}^{(1)} \middle| \cdots \middle| \mathbf{I}^{(N)}\right) \\
&= \left(\left(\mathbf{M}^{(1)} \odot \tilde{\mathbf{S}}_{k-1}^{(1)}\right) \vee \mathbf{I}^{(1)} \middle| \cdots \middle| \left(\mathbf{M}^{(N)} \odot \tilde{\mathbf{S}}_{k-1}^{(N)}\right) \vee \mathbf{I}^{(N)}\right)
\end{aligned}$$

It follows that

$$\tilde{\mathbf{S}}_k^{(i)} = \left(\mathbf{M}^{(i)} \odot \tilde{\mathbf{S}}_{k-1}^{(i)}\right) \vee \mathbf{I}^{(i)} \quad (\forall i = 1, \cdots, N, \quad k = 1, 2, \cdots) \tag{11}$$

Note that in Eq.(11), there are no dependencies among the partitions, so they can all be executed in parallel. Observe that $\tilde{\mathbf{S}}_k$ and $\mathbf{M}$ are symmetric, and therefore we only need to compute the upper (or lower) triangular portion of these matrices.

In the *SimRank matrix computation* step, we focus our attention on the parallel computation of $\mathbf{S}_k \leftarrow \mathbf{U} \cdot \tilde{\mathbf{S}}_k \cdot \mathbf{U}^{-1}$. This operation can be performed by the following substeps:

(a) $\mathbf{V}_k \leftarrow \tilde{\mathbf{S}}_k \cdot \mathbf{U}^{-1}$ as a symmetric matrix-matrix multiplication.
(b) $\mathbf{S}_k \leftarrow \mathbf{U} \cdot \mathbf{V}_k$, which requires a matrix-matrix multiplication that only updates the upper (or lower) triangular part of $\mathbf{S}_k$.

Substep (a) is a standard matrix-matrix operation which can be parallelized in PLAPACK, whereas Substep (b) is not one of those existing widely used kernels.

We now apply matrix partitioning techniques to parallelize Substep (b). We partition the matrix $\mathbf{U}$ and $\mathbf{V}_k$ as

$$\mathbf{U} = \left(\mathbf{U}^{(1)} \middle| \cdots \middle| \mathbf{U}^{(N')}\right), \quad \mathbf{V}_k = \left(\begin{array}{c} \mathbf{V}_k^{(1)} \\ \hline \vdots \\ \hline \mathbf{V}_k^{(N')} \end{array}\right), \tag{12}$$

where $\mathbf{U}^{(i)}$ and $\mathbf{V}_k^{(i)}$ are $n \times n_i{}'$ and $n_i{}' \times n$ submatrices, respectively, satisfying $n_i{}' < n$ and $\sum_{i=1}^{N'} n_i{}' = n \quad (i = 1, 2, \cdots, N')$, and N' is the number of partitions. Then, we obtain

$$\mathbf{S}_k \leftarrow \mathbf{U} \cdot \mathbf{V}_k = \left(\mathbf{U}^{(1)} \middle| \cdots \middle| \mathbf{U}^{(N')} \right) \cdot \begin{pmatrix} \mathbf{V}_k^{(1)} \\ \hline \vdots \\ \hline \mathbf{V}_k^{(N')} \end{pmatrix} = \sum_{i=1}^{N'} \mathbf{U}^{(i)} \cdot \mathbf{V}_k^{(i)}$$

Hence, Substep (b) can be parallelized by updating the upper (or lower) triangular part of $\mathbf{S}_k \leftarrow \mathbf{S}_k + \mathbf{U}^{(i)} \cdot \mathbf{V}_k^{(i)} \quad (\forall i = 1, \cdots, N')$ for each loop.

We now summarize the above parallel techniques for SimRank computation. We present the following parallel SimRank algorithm that utilizes PLAPACK and matrix partitioning techniques.

Algorithm 2 provides a parallel version of SimRank computation over undirected web graphs. In Line 2 and 12, operations can be performed in parallel by calling the corresponding PLAPACK's routines respectively. In Line 4-10 and Line 14-15, each of

---

Algorithm 2. PAUG-SimRank: Parallel Accelerative SimRank for Undirected Graphs

Input : transition probability matrix $\mathbf{Q} = (q_{i,j}) \in \mathbb{R}^{n \times n}$, decay factor c, accuracy ϵ
Output: SimRank matrix $\mathbf{S} = (s_{i,j}) \in [0, 1]^{n \times n}$

1 **begin**
`/* Step 1. Spectral Predecomposition */`
2 Use a PLAPACK eigen-solver to decompose $\mathbf{Q} \rightarrow \mathbf{U} \cdot \mathbf{\Lambda} \cdot \mathbf{U}^{-1}$ in parallel
`/* Step 2. Iterative Elementwise Matrix Multiplication */`
3 Partition the identity matrix $\mathbf{I}$ and the row vector $diag(\mathbf{\Lambda})^T$ as
$\mathbf{I} \rightarrow \left(\mathbf{I}^{(1)} \middle| \mathbf{I}^{(2)} \middle| \cdots \middle| \mathbf{I}^{(N)} \right), \quad diag(\mathbf{\Lambda})^T \rightarrow \left(\mathbf{\Lambda}^{(1)} \middle| \mathbf{\Lambda}^{(2)} \middle| \cdots \middle| \mathbf{\Lambda}^{(N)} \right)$
4 **foreach** *partition* $i \leftarrow 1 : N$ **in parallel do**
5 Initialize the upper triangular part of $\tilde{\mathbf{S}}_0^{(i)} \leftarrow \mathbf{I}^{(i)}$ and $\mathbf{M}^{(i)} \leftarrow c \cdot diag\,(\mathbf{\Lambda}) \cdot \mathbf{\Lambda}^{(i)}$
6 Fix the iteration number $k_i \leftarrow 0$
7 **repeat**
8 Set $k_i \leftarrow k_i + 1$
9 Calculate the upper triangular part of $\tilde{\mathbf{S}}_{k_i}^{(i)} \leftarrow \left(\mathbf{M}^{(i)} \odot \tilde{\mathbf{S}}_{k_i - 1}^{(i)} \right) \vee \mathbf{I}^{(i)}$
10 **until** *this auxiliary partition* $\tilde{\mathbf{S}}_{k_i}^{(i)}$ *converges with an error of* ϵ / N
`/* Step 3. SimRank Matrix Computation */`
11 Merge all the partitions of $\tilde{\mathbf{S}}$ into one matrix, i.e. $\tilde{\mathbf{S}} \leftarrow \left(\tilde{\mathbf{S}}_{k_1}^{(1)} \middle| \tilde{\mathbf{S}}_{k_2}^{(2)} \middle| \cdots \middle| \tilde{\mathbf{S}}_{k_N}^{(N)} \right)$
12 Use PLAPACK to operate $\mathbf{V} \leftarrow \tilde{\mathbf{S}} \cdot \mathbf{U}^{-1}$ as a symmetric matrix-matrix multiplication
13 Initialize $\mathbf{S} \leftarrow \mathbf{0}$, and partition the matrix $\mathbf{U}$ and $\mathbf{V}$ as in Eq.(12)
14 **foreach** *partition* $i \leftarrow 1 : N'$ **in parallel do**
15 Calculate the upper triangular part of $\mathbf{S} \leftarrow \mathbf{S} + \mathbf{U}^{(i)} \cdot \mathbf{V}^{(i)}$
16 Return $\mathbf{S}$

---

the loops is decomposed into smaller tasks which can be executed simultaneously on the different processors of a parallel computer.

5 Experimental Studies

In this section, we conduct experimental studies to evaluate the efficiency of our algorithms (i.e. AUG-SimRank and PAUG-SimRank) on both synthetic and real data sets. We compare their performances with the most efficient existing algorithms proposed in [1] and [7]. The experiments were done on 2.0GHz Pentium(R) Dual-Core CPU with 2GB main memory, running Windows Vista OS. All the algorithms were implemented in C++ and compiled using Visual C++ 6.0 compiler.

5.1 Experimental Data Sets

We use two data sets for evaluation in our experiments.

Synthetic Data Sets. We randomly generated 10 undirected web graphs with vertices ranging from 1K to 10K respectively. For each generated graph, every vertex has an average of $\lceil \xi \rceil$ links, where ξ is a random variable satisfying $\xi \sim uniform[0, 15]$. The web graphs are represented in the MATLAB sparse storage organization, using a (x, y, val) triple to describe the index and the value of the element.

Real-life Data Sets. We use a full English Wikipedia data set exported in October 2007 to show the high efficiency of our proposed algorithms. The Wikipedia link graph contains 3.2M articles (vertices) with 110M intra-wiki links (edges). SimRank computation over the Wikipedia data set has the semantics of obtaining similarity scores for encyclopedic concept pairs. We build the Wikipedia graph, choosing the relationship "*a category contains an article*" to be an edge between the category and the article.

5.2 Comparison Methods and Evaluation

We compare the performances of the following algorithms:

- **SimRank with partial sums. [1]** This algorithm employs a partial sums function to speed up SimRank computation by SimRank values clustering.
- **SOR SimRank. [7]** This algorithm develops a successive over-relaxation method for accelerating the convergence rate of SimRank computation. We take the optimal relaxation factor $\omega = 1.3$.
- **AUG SimRank.** This is our proposed algorithm based on the graph spectral decomposition.
- **PAUG SimRank.** This is a parallel version of AUG SimRank that combines PLAPACK solvers and block partitioning techniques.

Evaluation Measures. We use *CPU time* and *absolute speedup* as two measures to evaluate the computational complexity and parallel efficiency of these algorithms respectively. The definition of absolute speedup is as follows [13]:

$$S_p := \frac{T_1}{T_p} \tag{13}$$

where p is the number of processors, T_1 is the execution time of the best sequential algorithm on one processor, and T_p is the time taken on p processors.

Parameter Settings. In the experiments, we set the decay factor $c = 0.8$, and the accuracy $\epsilon = 0.05$ (unless otherwise specified).

5.3 Time Efficiency Evaluation

Figure 1(a) shows the total computational time comparison among the three methods on 10 generated graphs when we set the vertices number $n = 1\text{K}, \cdots, 10\text{K}$. For each algorithm, a least-squares polynomial is used to fit the bar series that are nonlinear. It can be seen from the chart that AUG-SimRank outperforms the other two algorithms significantly as n is growing, and CPU time value by AUG-SimRank remains a steady increase around 1.5K. This is because the time complexity of AUG-SimRank has a constant cubic coefficient that is independent of the iteration number.

Figure 1(b) and 1(c) present the results of accuracy factor that influences the computational time for our three test algorithms on a 10K synthetic graph and a Wikipedia real data set, respectively. We set the decay factor $c = 0.6$ when testing results on Wikipedia data set. Note that different scale is chosen across the vertical axis in Figure 1(b) and 1(c) for providing a more illustrative look for each data set. We notice that both SOR-SimRank and SimRank with partial sums algorithms make a massive drop in CPU time while we are varying ϵ from 0.03 to 0.15, due to the more iterations needed for achieving a high accuracy. However, the trend of AUG-SimRank computational time shows

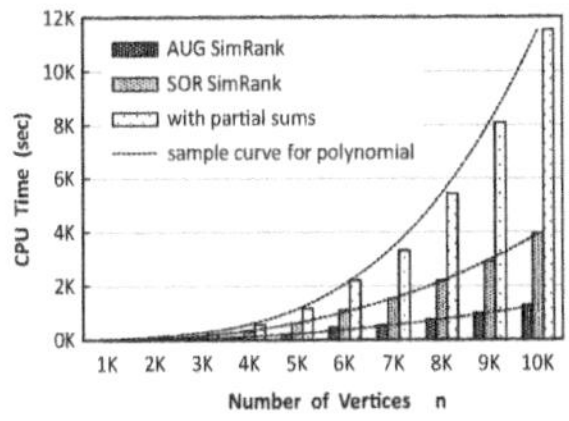

(a) CPU Time w.r.t. # of Vertices on Generated Graphs

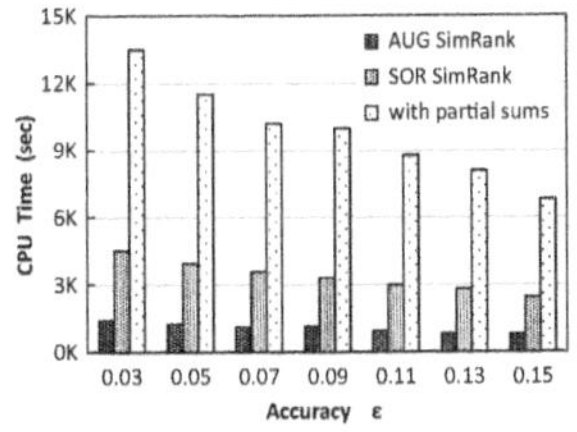

(b) CPU Time w.r.t. Accuracy on a Generated Graph (with n=10K)

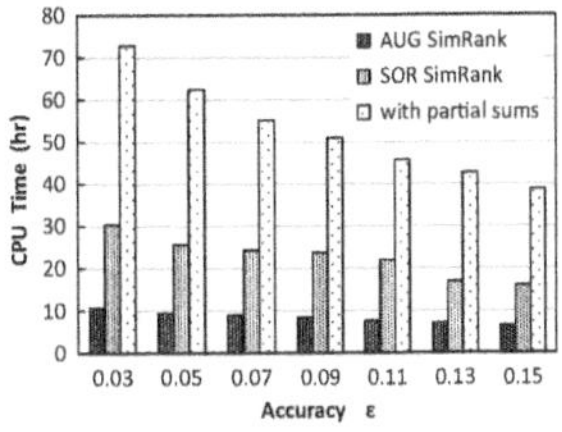

(c) CPU Time w.r.t. Accuracy on Wikipedia (with c=0.6)

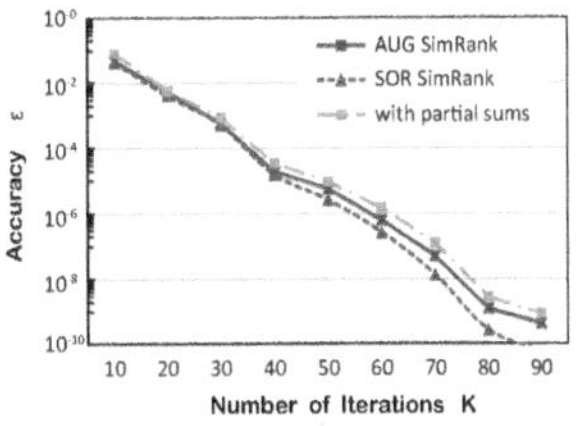

(d) Accuracy w.r.t. # of Iterations on Wikipedia (with c=0.6)

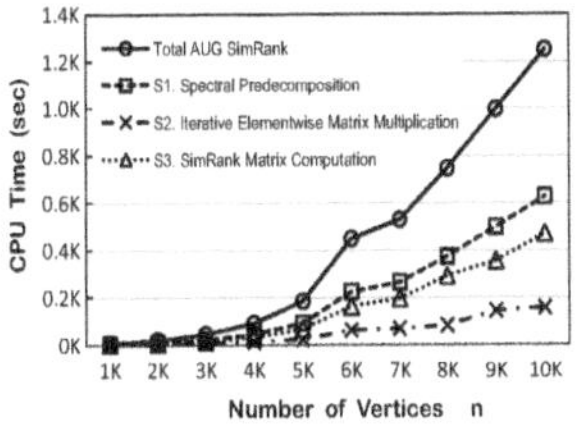

(e) AUG-SimRank Algorithm on Generated Graphs

Fig. 1. Scalability, Accuracy & Efficiency for AUG-SimRank Computation a slight downward turn as ϵ is increasing, which also implies that AUG-SimRank is insensitive to the iteration number.

Figure 1(d) compares computational accuracy with respect to the number of iterations among the three algorithms on the Wikipedia data set. It shows that for all the algorithms, ϵ decreases dramatically while the number of iterations is increasing. The accuracy values by AUG-SimRank and SimRank with partial sums algorithms are close. This demonstrates that AUG-SimRank retains the convergence power of the SimRank with partial sums algorithm. For all of the algorithms, the figure also shows a logarithmic growth in CPU time when K is growing, since Figure 1(d) is in logarithm scale, and all these algorithms approximately exhibit linear descending tendencies.

Figure 1(e) precisely visualizes the CPU time consumption of each step for AUG-SimRank algorithm on a 10K generated data set. Specifically, we plot the computational time of (a) Spectral Predecomposition, (b) Iterative Elementwise Matrix Multiplication, and (c) SimRank Matrix Computation in the same chart. Note that the time consumed by Iterative Elementwise Matrix Multiplication is minimal and remains relatively stable, whereas the operation time for the other two steps rises substantially as n is increasing. This is because $K \ll n$ so that the step of Iterative Elementwise Matrix Multiplication takes quadratic time after K iterations, whereas the other two steps require cubic time, making a large portion of the total AUG-SimRank time.

5.4 Parallel Efficiency Evaluation

We test our parallel algorithm PAUG-SimRank on a distributed memory multiprocessor over synthetic and real-life data sets respectively. We obtain the following computational results.

Table 2. CPU Time (secs) for PAUG-SimRank

# of processors p	1	2	3	4	5	6	7	8	9	10
10K Generated Graph	1,250	814	559	397	356	343	297	274	255	222
Wikipedia Data Set	27,072	18,488	11,933	10,276	8,670	7,124	6,381	5,649	5,213	5,254

The parallel efficiency E_p of PAUG-SimRank can be computed by the following equation.

$$E_p := \frac{S_p}{p} = \frac{T_1}{T_p \cdot p}$$

where S_p is the speedup on p processors defined by Eq.(13). We use the execution time of the best sequential algorithm on one processor as T_1. We present the speedup and parallel efficiency of PAUG-SimRank algorithm in the tables and charts below.

Figure 2(a) illustrates how the PAUG-SimRank implementation scales with the number of processors over a 10K generated graph and a Wikipedia data set, respectively. On both two data sets, the speedup is acceptable but not ideal due to the time required to communicate among the processors is growing. Note that there has been a dramatic increase in speedup when we have less than 4 processors. This is because of the cache effect resulting from the various memory hierarchies of a modern computer.

Table 3. PAUG-SimRank Efficiency on Generated Graph (with n=10K)

# of processors p	1	2	3	4	5	6	7	8	9	10
speedup S_p	1	1.53	2.23	3.14	3.51	3.63	4.20	4.55	4.89	5.61
efficiency E_p	1	0.76	0.74	0.78	0.70	0.60	0.60	0.56	0.54	0.56

Table 4. PAUG-SimRank Efficiency on Wikipedia

# of processors p	1	2	3	4	5	6	7	8	9	10
speedup S_p	1	1.46	2.26	2.63	3.12	3.80	4.24	4.79	5.19	5.15
efficiency E_p	1	0.73	0.75	0.65	0.62	0.63	0.60	0.59	0.57	0.51

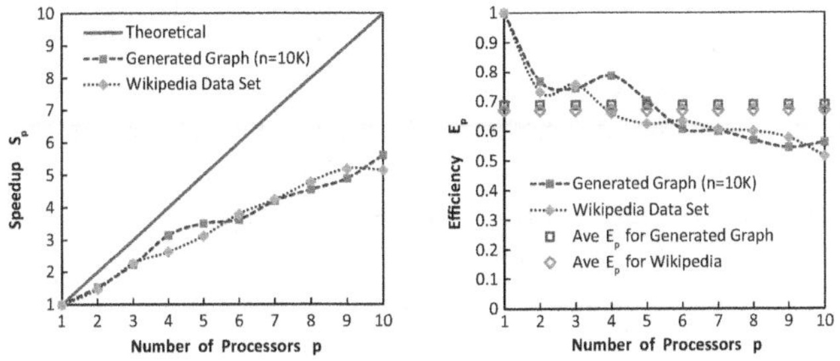

(a) Absolute Speedup (b) Parallel Efficiency

Fig. 2. PAUG-SimRank on a generated graph (with n=10K) and a Wikipedia data set

Figure 2(b) visualizes the parallel efficiency of PAUG-SimRank on two data sets. Notice that the parallel efficiency makes a general decrease due to the same arguments as for the speedup above. For each data set, we obtain a mean of approx. 67% efficiency which has been shown in the chart with hollow markers.

6 Related Work

Hyperlink-based approaches for similarity computation on web graphs have become popular since the famous result of Page et. al. [15] on Google PageRank citation ranking. Since then, there has been a surge of papers aiming at various problems in the optimization of web ranking algorithms, such as HITS [16], ReCom [17], SimRank [2], SimFusion [18], P-Rank [19], etc. In particular, there has been significant attention to computing SimRank similarities as they provide a simple and intuitive graph-theoretic model recursively refining the cocitation measure that says "*similar objects are referenced by similar objects*". Recent SimRank results include randomized approximations [3,4], estimating a precise accuracy for iterative computation [1,5,7], graph clustering [20], query rewriting for sponsored search [6], etc.

Jeh and Widom [2] first proposed a SimRank model based on the idea that "*vertices are similar if their neighbors are similar*". Unfortunately the computational time of this model is very costly as it takes $O\left(Kn^2d^2\right)$ time, where n is the number of vertices, and d is the average degree of a web graph. Hence, the naive SimRank algorithm is not suitable for practical use.

Fogaras and Racz [3,4] adopted a *probabilistic* method called *Monte Carlo* to optimize SimRank computation. The main idea of their approach is to generate a finger print tree in combination of random permutations. They estimate $s(a,b)$ by $\mathbb{E}\left(c^{\tau(a,b)}\right)$, where $\tau_{(a,b)}$ is *the first meeting time* for a pair of random walks started in nodes a and b. Though this probabilistic model can significantly reduce the computational complexity, it does not predict *deterministic* quantities of SimRank scores but rather *stochastic* estimates of these quantities.

In comparison to the work on *stochastic* SimRank approximation, the work on optimizing *deterministic* SimRank computation is limited. Recent years have witnessed a growing interest in the optimization issue of *iterative* SimRank algorithms.

A very interesting piece of work is due to Lizorkin et al. [1] who give approaches to significantly reducing the computational time complexity from $O\left(Kn^2d^2\right)$ to $O\left(Kn^2d\right)$. Their study is not under the stochastic framework; rather, they use *a partial sums function* that allows clustering $s_k(*,*)$ by the first argument to accelerate access operations. They also give the number of iterations required for achieving the desired accuracy. Given an error of ϵ and a decay factor c, the upper bound of the total number of iterations is $K = \lceil \log_c \epsilon \rceil + 1$.

There has also been work on deterministic SimRank optimization. Antonellis et al. [6] present two SimRank extensions: one exploits the *weights* of the edges in the click graph, and the other that takes into account the "*evidence*" supporting the similarity between queries. Recent work by Yu et al. [7] shows a compressed storage scheme for sparse graphs to reduce the space requirement and a fast matrix multiplication for dense graph to further reduce the time complexity from $O\left(Kn^2d\right)$ to $O\left(K\cdot\min\left(m\cdot n, n^r\right)\right)$, where r is a constant, and $r\in\left(2,\log_2 7\right]$. They also developed optimization techniques for minimizing matrix bandwidths to improve the I/O efficiency of SimRank iteration. Li et al. [10] proposed a novel approximate SimRank computation algorithm for static and dynamic information networks. They claim that their optimization technique is based on the non-iterative framework; however, the singular value decomposition (SVD) method they used for low-rank approximation inherently requires numerical iterations. Hence, their method is in essence iterative, not non-iterative. The Kronecker product in their approach is prohibitively costly in computational time and therefore is not preferable. Li et al. [21] developed a BlockSimRank algorithm that partitions the web graph into several blocks to efficiently compute similarity of each node-pair in the graph. Their approach takes $O(n^{\frac{4}{3}})$ time, which is based on the random walk model. Zhao et al. [19] proposed a new structural similarity measure called P-Rank (Penetrating Rank) that says "two entities are similar if (a) they are referenced by similar entities; and (b) they reference similar entities." This similarity takes into account of both in- and out-link relationships of entity pairs and penetrates the structural similarity computation beyond neighborhood of vertices to the entire information network.

7 Conclusions

In this paper, we study the problem of optimizing SimRank computation on undirected graphs. An efficient AUG-SimRank algorithm has been proposed to significantly reduce the SimRank computational time from $O\left(K \cdot n^3\right)$ to $O\left(n^3 + K \cdot n^2\right)$ after K iterations in the worst case. We also present a parallel version of the AUG-SimRank algorithm on distributed memory multi-processors as we combine the PLAPACK solvers with our partition techniques. Extensive experimental evaluations on synthetic and real data sets show the proposed methods outperform the existing techniques in terms of total computation cost and parallelization.

Acknowledgment

We would like to thank the anonymous reviewers for their valuable comments. The second author was supported by three ARC DPs (DP0666428, DP0881035, and DP0987557) and a Google research award.

References

1. Lizorkin, D., Velikhov, P., Grinev, M., Turdakov, D.: Accuracy estimate and optimization techniques for simrank computation. PVLDB 1(1) (2008)
2. Jeh, G., Widom, J.: Simrank: a measure of structural-context similarity. In: KDD (2002)
3. Fogaras, D., Rácz, B.: Scaling link-based similarity search. In: WWW (2005)
4. Fogaras, D., Rácz, B.: A scalable randomized method to compute link-based similarity rank on the web graph. In: Lindner, W., Mesiti, M., Türker, C., Tzitzikas, Y., Vakali, A.I. (eds.) EDBT 2004. LNCS, vol. 3268, pp. 557–567. Springer, Heidelberg (2004)
5. Cai, Y., Li, P., Liu, H., He, J., Du, X.: S-simrank: Combining content and link information to cluster papers effectively and efficiently. In: Tang, C., Ling, C.X., Zhou, X., Cercone, N.J., Li, X. (eds.) ADMA 2008. LNCS (LNAI), vol. 5139, pp. 317–329. Springer, Heidelberg (2008)
6. Antonellis, I., Garcia-Molina, H., Chang, C.C.: Simrank++: query rewriting through link analysis of the click graph. PVLDB 1(1) (2008)
7. Yu, W., Lin, X., Le, J.: A space and time efficient algorithm for simrank computation. In: APWeb (2010)
8. Weinberg, B.H.: Bibliographic coupling: A review. Information Storage and Retrieval 10(5-6) (1974)
9. Wijaya, D.T., Bressan, S.: Clustering web documents using co-citation, coupling, incoming, and outgoing hyperlinks: a comparative performance analysis of algorithms. IJWIS 2(2) (2006)
10. Li, C., Han, J., He, G., Jin, X., Sun, Y., Yu, Y., Wu, T.: Fast computation of simrank for static and dynamic information networks. In: EDBT (2010)
11. Bhatia, R.: Matrix Analysis. Springer, Heidelberg (1997)
12. Hernandez, V., Roman, J.E., Vidal, V.: Slepc: A scalable and flexible toolkit for the solution of eigenvalue problems. ACM Trans. Math. Softw. 31(3) (2005)
13. Maschhoff, K.J., Sorensen, D.C.: A portable implementation of arpack for distributed memory parallel architectures. In: CMCIM (1996)

14. Wu, K., Simon, H.: A parallel lanczos method for symmetric generalized eigenvalue problems. Technical report, Lawrence Berkeley National Laboratory (1997)
15. Page, L., Brin, S., Motwani, R., Winograd, T.: The pagerank citation ranking bringing order to the web, Technial report (1998)
16. Mendelzon, A.O.: Review - authoritative sources in a hyperlinked environment. ACM SIGMOD Digital Review 1 (2000)
17. Wang, J., Zeng, H., Chen, Z., Lu, H., Tao, L., Ma, W.: Recom: reinforcement clustering of multi-type interrelated data objects. In: SIGIR (2003)
18. Xi, W., Fox, E.A., Fan, W., Zhang, B., Chen, Z., Yan, J., Zhuang, D.: Simfusion: measuring similarity using unified relationship matrix. In: SIGIR (2005)
19. Zhao, P., Han, J., Sun, Y.: P-rank: a comprehensive structural similarity measure over information networks. In: CIKM 2009: Proceeding of the 18th ACM conference on Information and knowledge management (2009)
20. Zhou, Y., Cheng, H., Yu, J.X.: Graph clustering based on structural/attribute similarities. PVLDB 2(1) (2009)
21. Li, P., Cai, Y., Liu, H., He, J., Du, X.: Exploiting the block structure of link graph for efficient similarity computation. In: Theeramunkong, T., Kijsirikul, B., Cercone, N., Ho, T.-B. (eds.) PAKDD 2009. LNCS, vol. 5476, pp. 389–400. Springer, Heidelberg (2009)

DSI: A Method for Indexing Large Graphs Using Distance Set

Yubo Kou, Yukun Li, and Xiaofeng Meng

Renmin University of China, Beijing, China
{kouyubo,liyukun,xfmeng}@ruc.edu.cn
http://idke.ruc.edu.cn/

Abstract. Recent years we have witnessed a great increase in modeling data as large graphs in multiple domains, such as XML, the semantic web, social network. In these circumstances, researchers are interested in querying the large graph like that: Given a large graph G, and a query Q, we report all the matches of Q in G. Since subgraph isomorphism checking is proved to be NP-Complete[1], it is infeasible to scan the whole large graph for answers, especially when the query's size is also large. Hence, the "filter-verification" approach is widely adopted. In this approach, researchers first index the neighborhood of each vertex in the large graph, then filter vertexes , and finally perform subgraph matching algorithms. Previous techniques mainly focus on efficient matching algorithms, paying little attention to indexing techniques. However, appropriate indexing techniques could help improve the efficiency of query response by generating less candidates. In this paper we investigate indexing techniques on large graphs, and propose an index structure DSI(Distance Set Index) to capture the neighborhood of each vertex. Through our distance set index, more vertexes could be pruned, resulting in a much smaller search space. Then a subgraph matching algorithm is performed in the search space. We have applied our index structure to real datasets and synthetic datasets. Extensive experiments demonstrate the efficiency and effectiveness of our indexing technique.

Keywords: Graph Indexing, Distance Set.

1 Introduction

In the web age we have witnessed a great increase in modeling data as graphs in many domains, such as XML, the semantic web, biological networks, social networks, dataspace. People often need to query like that: (1) In the chemical compound database, given a specific chemical structure, we need all the compounds that contain the given chemical structure. (2) In the social network, given a specific group description, we need all the corresponding occurrences.

Actually, the database community has long been interested in querying graph databases[2, 5, 6, 7, 8, 9, 10, 11, 13, 19]. The problem previous studies mainly focus on could be defined as: Given a graph database G, and a query Q, we report all the graphs that contain Q as a subgraph. Since subgraph isomorphism

L. Chen et al. (Eds.): WAIM 2010, LNCS 6184, pp. 297–308, 2010.

checking is NP-complete[1], which means it is infeasible to scan the whole graph database for answers. To efficiently answer queries, the database community usually adopt a "filter-verification" approach, which means graph databases should be indexed at first. However, with the development of bio-informatics and social science applications, many large graphs are emerging. These graphs usually contain tens of thousands of vertexes. On large graphs there are also needs for queries which could be formalized as: Given a large graph G and a query graph Q, we report all the matches of Q in G. This problem is challenging in several aspects:

First, previous techniques about querying graph database couldn't be applied directly to this problem: previous studies aim at finding which graph contains the given query, while this problem is about the exact positions of matches in a graph. Therefore, it is challenging to figure out what to index.

Second, data mining techniques such as frequent subgraph couldn't be directly applied since it is difficult to tell what is frequent in a single graph[3,4].

Third, appropriate indexing techniques are needed for answering queries efficiently and effectively. There have already been some works[14, 15, 16, 17, 18] on this topic. Most of these works propose to first index neighborhood of each vertex in the graph, prune false vertexes through their index, and finally perform subgraph matching algorithm to find each distinct matches. In these works, most attention are paid to efficient matching, while little paid to indexing techniques. However, appropriate indexing techniques could help improve the efficiency of matching algorithm. For a query of size n(the size of a graph refers to the number of nodes), the size of candidate sets for the query nodes are k_1, k_2, .. k_n, respectively. The time cost of subgraph matching algorithm is $O(k_1 k_2..k_n)$. Thus shrinking each candidate set could help subgraph matching algorithm achieve high performance, especially when n is large.

In this paper, we propose a novel indexing technique named as distance set index(DSI). We have applied DSI to DBLP dataset and synthetic dataset. Our experiments demonstrate that our indexing technique is effective and efficient. Utilizing our indexing technique could generate much less candidates, thus accelerate query response.

To summarize, our contributions are listed as follows:

1. We introduce a new feature (distance set)to represent each vertex's neighborhood. Experiments demonstrate this feature's expressivity.

2. We propose a novel indexing technique, distance set index(DSI). This index utilize distance set for subgraph matching in a large graph, which could help accelerate the query processing.

3. We perform extensive experiments to demonstrate the effectiveness and efficiency of DSI. The experimental results also show it is quite profitable to investigate how to index vertex's neighborhood.

The remainder of this paper is organized as follows: Section 2 presents related work. Section 3 defines the preliminary concepts and problem definition. Section 4 introduces our database preprocessing step. Section 5 describes query processing. Experimental results are delivered in Section 6. Section 7 concludes our work and discusses about future work.

2 Related Work

The database community has a long-term interest in querying the graph database. Most of them investigate feature selection strategies to achieve better pruning power. [2] proposes Graphgrep to enumerate all the pathes within a given length as features. However, pathes is too simple to capture the characteristics of graphs. [13] presents node neighbor tree(NNT) to capture local structure of each vertex, and transform NNT to node projected vector(NPV) for efficient comparing. In these feature selection strategies, a frequent subgraph based approach is very popular. [5] uses gIndex to index all the frequent subgraphs as features. Later, [10] presents FG-index, [11] proves that indexing frequent trees and some special graphs are more beneficial than indexing graphs. There are also some works considering a general view. [6] considers features' relations. [7] and [8] index structures of graphs. Both works assume the graph size be small. [9] proposes to transform graphs into sequences.

There exist some works investigating querying large graphs. [18] proposes to partition the graph first, then process the partitions. [14] studies how to efficiently answer queries without database preprocessing. [15] proposes to index subgraphs composed of each vertex and its adjacent vetexes, and investigates matching algorithms. They further introduce some optimization ideas. [16] also proposes to index neighborhood. What differs is its aim at approximate subgraph matching. [17] proposes neighboring discriminating substructure(NDS) distance as a distance measure. It captures NDS for each pair of vertexes within a given distance to facilitate its matching algorithm. This approach is interesting, however, merely depending on local structures might introduce some false positives. There are also some works focusing on figuring out what is frequent in a large graph[3, 4].

3 Preliminaries

In this section, we introduce the preliminary definitions and concepts, as well as problem definition. We restrict our discussion on undirected acylic labeled graphs. However, our discussion could be easily extended to directed graphs.

Definition 1 (Labeled Graph). *A labeled graph is denoted as* $G=\langle V(G),E(G),\sum, L\rangle$*, where* $V(G)$ *is the set of vertexes,* $E(G)\subseteq V(G)\times V(G)$ *is the set of edges,* $\sum$ *is the set of labels and* L *is the injective function* $L: V(G)\rightarrow\sum$*, which assigns each vertex a label from* $\sum$*. Additionally, each vertex in the graph has a unique id.*

Definition 2 (Graph Isomorphism). *Graph isomorphism is a bijection* $f: V(G)\leftrightarrow V(G')$*. Given two labeled graph* G *and* G'*, if they are isomorphic, they satisfy such conditions: (1)* $\forall$ $u \in V(G)$, $L(u)=L'(f(u))$*; (2)* $\forall$ $u, v \in E(G) \Leftrightarrow (f(u),f(v)) \in E(G')$*.*

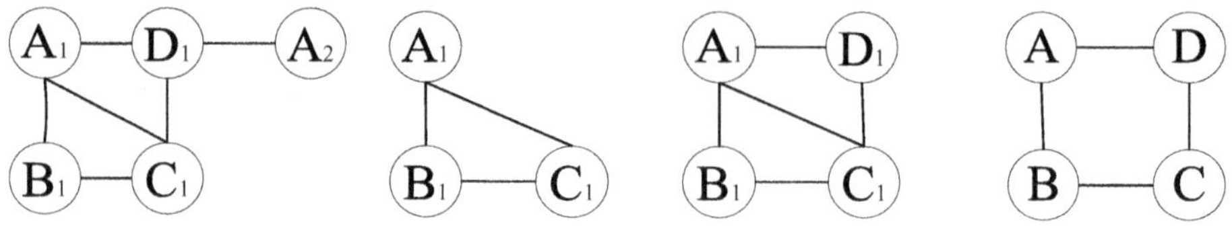

(a) Graph G (b) Induced graph of V' (c) B1's 2-neighborhood (d) query Q

Fig. 1. Examples for preliminaries

Graph S is **subgraph isomorphic** to G, if S is isomorphic to at least one subgraph G' of of G. G' is a match of S in G.

Definition 3 (Shortest Distance). *Given vertexes u and v in a graph G, the shortest distance between them is the number of edges in the shortest path between u and v.*

For example, in figure 1(a), the shortest distance between B_1 and D_1 is 2, since the shortest path between them is $B_1A_1D_1$, or $B_1C_1D_1$, both composed of 2 edges.

Definition 4 (Induced Graph). *Given a graph G, and a set of vertexes, denoted as V', V' belongs to V(G), an induced graph of V' is the subgraph composed of V' and any edge whose ends belong to V'.*

Take figure 1(b) as an instance, given V'=$\{A_1, B_1, C_1\}$, the induced graph of V' is shown in figure 1(b).

Definition 5 (K-Neighborhood). *Given a vertex v in a graph G and an integer k, the k-neighborhood of v, denoted as k-N(v), is the induced graph of a vertex set which contains v and the vertexes whose shortest distance from v is no more than k.*

For example, given k=2, B_1's 2-neighborhood is shown in figure 1(c). The graph in figure 1(c) shows the local structure of vertex B_1, which plays an important role in identifying matching vertexes.

Problem Definition(Subgraph Matching): Given a large graph G and a query graph Q, we report all the matches of Q in G.

For example, in figure 1(d), there is one match of Q, which is $\{A_1,B_1,C_1,D_1\}$.

The processing of graph queries contains two steps:

(1) Database Preprocessing. This step preprocesses the database graphs by building an index for each vertex. It is important to figure out which feature should be selected, since right feature selection strategy could achieve high pruning power, as well as low cost.

(2) query processing. This step contains two substeps. First, **Node Matching**. We retrieve candidate vertexes in G for each node in Q, respectively. These

candidates compose a search space for subgraph matching. Second, **Subgraph Matching**. we perform subgraph matching algorithm in the search space to get final matches for Q.

In this work, we mainly study graph indexing techniques to help accelerate query processing.

4 Database Preprocessing

To respond to on-line queries efficiently and effectively, it is popular to build indexes off-line, trading index space for query response time. In this section, we describe our strategy at the preprocessing step. First we introduce a new feature: distance set. Second, we extend the distance set with discriminative substructures. Finally, we describe the index structure, and how to construct the index structure.

4.1 Indexing Unit

Given a node u in Q, a node v in G, and their corresponding k-neighborhoods, the most accurate way to identify whether v is a match of u, is to perform subgraph isomorphism checking between their corresponding neighborhoods. This way takes too much computational cost, since subgraph isomorphism checking is NP-Complete[1]. Therefore, it is necessary to select appropriate features to represent k-neighborhood and prune false vertexes by these features. These features should satisfy two requirements: (1) These features should introduce as less false positives as possible, in other words, these features should have high expressivity, which implies high pruning power; (2) the cost of computing these features should be feasible. To capture the neighborhood information around vertex v, we present a new feature: distance set. First we will give the definition of distance set.

Definition 6 (Distance Set). *Given a vertex v, and a vertex u in its k-neighborhood k-N(v), the distance set between v and u record all the distinct lengths of pathes between them, denoted as DS(v, u). Here pathes do not contain repeated vertexes.*

For example in figure 2(a), given two vertexes A_1 and B_1, DS(A_1, B_1)={1, 2, 3}. Since there are three distinct pathes from A_1 to B_1: A_1B_1, $A_1C_1B_1$ and $A_1D_1C_1B_1$. To profile the neighborhood of a given vertex v, we record each neighbor vertex u's label, and DS(v, u). Suppose there is more than one path of a particular length, say 2, distance set would contain only one 2. Therefore, distance set does not contain duplicates.

Formally, the conditions for matching a query node u to a vertex v in the database graph is:

for each node u' in k-N(u), there is a vertex v' in k-N(v) such that:

(1) L(u')=L(v')
(2) DS(u,u') $\subseteq$ DS(v,v').

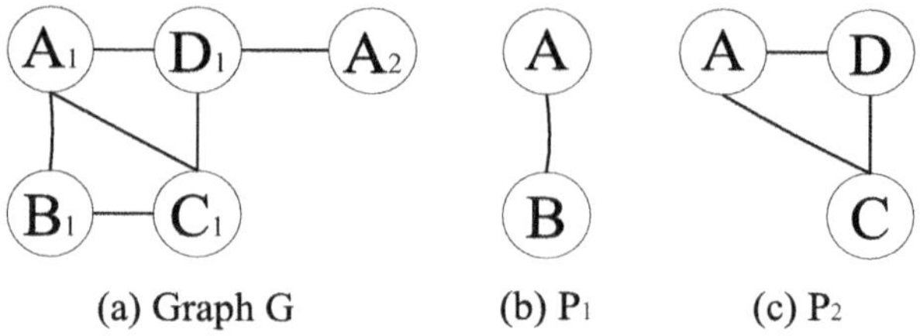

Fig. 2. Examples for distance set

For efficiency's sake, we represent DS in bit vector form, namely, distance set vector(DSV). Each position of a DSV denotes whether the DS contains the specific number. In the foregoing example, DSV(A_1, B_1)=(0, 1, 1, 1). The first position always records whether '0' exists. There is no '0' in DS(A_1, B_1), so the value of the first dimension is 0. There is one '1' in the DS, so the value of the second dimension is 1. The other dimensions' values could be computed in the same way. Thus, we change the condition (2) to that DSV(u,u') dominates DSV(v,v'). Here "dominates" means the value of each dimension in DSV(u,u') is no more than DSV(v,v').

Distance set is vertex-specific in the sense that it captures the structure between v and one vertex in its neighborhood. While vertex-specific distance set provides high expressivity, it could be further improved by utilizing a couple of neighbor vertexes which are inter-connected, in other words, a substructure. To capture more information, such as the structural information between v and one of its discriminative substructures. We extend distance set(DS) to discriminative substructure distance set(DDS). The definition of discriminative substructure could be found in [5]. With a set of k-neighborhoods, we could use frequent subgraph mining techniques to find frequent substructures and select the discriminative ones.

Definition 7 (Discriminative Substructure Distance Set). *Given a vertex v, its k-neighborhood k-N(v), and a discriminative substructure P , P belongs to k-N(v), the discriminative substructure distance set, denoted as DDS(v, P), is a set of distance sets, where each distance set contains all the distinct pathes' distance from a node in P to v. To be specific, none of these pathes contains an edge which belongs to P.*

In this definition, we emphasize the path selecting rule that given a discriminative substructure P, every path from one node of P to the root should not contain any edge of P. This property is important, since it makes discriminative substructure distance set more discriminative. For example in figure 2, let P_1 and P_2 be discriminative substructures. DDS(B_1, P_1)={A.DS'(A_1, B_1), B.DS'(B_1, B_1) }={ A.(2, 3), B.(0)}. DDS(B_1, P_2)={ A.DS'(A_1, B_1), C.DS'(C_1, B_1), D.DS'(D_1, B_1)}=(A.(1), C.(1), D.∅).

To represent the distance set of discriminative substructure in one vector, it is essential to order vertexes of discriminative substructures in a unique way.

There have been plenty of works discussing canonical form of a graph[5,6,9]. In this paper, since the discriminative substructures we deal with are generally of small size, we adopt a simple lexicographical order.

For example, in figure 2, since P_1 contains two nodes, labeled by A and B, we set A.DS'(A_1, B_1) ahead of B.DS'(B_1, B_1), since A is prior to B lexicographically. Thus we get DDSV(B_1, P_1)=(0, 0, 1, 1, 1), DDSV(B_1, P_2)=(0, 1, 0, 1). In DDSV(B_1, P_1), the first four dimensions correspond to A.DS'(A_1, B_1), while the last three dimensions correspond to B.DS'(B_1, B_1).

Given the definition of discriminative substructure distance set, the pruning condition is transformed to that: for each discriminative substructure P in k-N(u), there is a corresponding discriminative substructure P in k-N(v) such that:

(1) P' is isomorphism to P
(2) DDSV(u,P) is dominated by DDSV(v,P).

There are plenty of works discussing discriminative substructures[5, 11, 17]. In this paper, we adopt the way proposed by [17]. That is, we randomly select 100 k-neighborhoods and conduct frequent subgraph mining algorithm in these k-neighborhoods. After that, we select the most discriminative substructures of size 3 or 4.

To facilitate the process of index construction and query processing, meanwhile keep index size small, we store each DDSV in a bit vector. In the next subsection, we will introduce our index structure.

4.2 Index Structure

In this subsection we consider the index structure to implement the distance set index. We propose a bi-level index structure for distance set index. The first level of the index structure is a list of discriminative substructures. This list contains each distinct discriminative substructure as a unit. To fully cover the large graph, this list also contains each substructure of size 1, namely, each label. The second level of the index structure is bitmaps which contain bit vectors of vertexes who's k-neighborhood contains the discriminative substructure as a subgraph.

For example, given a graph G in figure 2(a), and two discriminative substructures P_1 and P_2 in figure 2(b) and 2(c), our index structure is shown in figure 3.

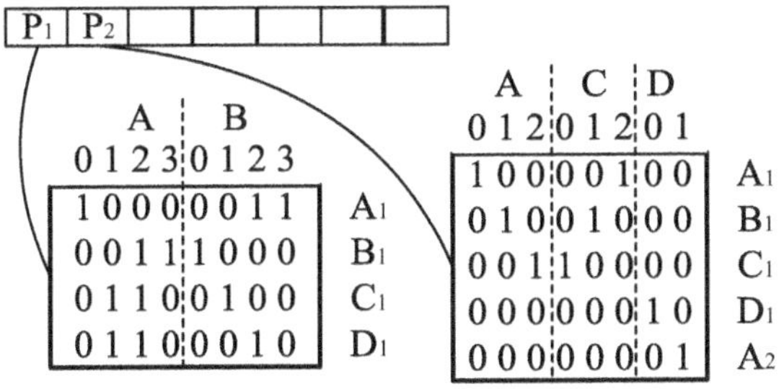

Fig. 3. Distance Set Index

Consider P_1's bitmap, since DDSV(B_1, P_1)=(0, 0, 1, 1, 1), this DDSV is recorded in the second row of the bitmap. Note that the former DDSV only has five dimensions, while in the bitmap, it has eight. We make this extension to achieve uniformity for all the bitmaps.

To index the distance set feature of each vertex, for each discriminative substructure P, we first find vertexes whose k-neighbor contains P. Then we compute the discriminative substructure distance set for each vertex, and store that vertex and its DDSV in P's bitmap.

5 Query Processing

In this section, we discuss query processing. This step contains two substeps: First, we perform node matching algorithm, which finds candidate vertexes for each node in Q. These candidate vertexes form a search space for later subgraph matching. Second, after we've prepared a set of candidate vertexes for each node, we perform subgraph matching algorithm.in the search space.

Algorithm 1. Node Matching

Input: A large graph G and its DSI, a query Q, a range value k
Output: A search space

```
1: procedure
2:     for each node u_i in query do
3:         C(u_i) ← {v| v ∈ V(G), L(v)=L(u_i)};
4:         for each discriminative substructure P in k-N(u_i) do
5:             M(u_i,P)={v| v ∈ V(G), DDSV(v, P) dominates DDSV(u_i, P)};
6:             C(u_i)=C(u_i) ∩ M(u_i,P);
7:         end for
8:     end for
9:     Output C(u_1)×C(u_2)×..×C(u_2);
10: end procedure
```

At the first substep, we first generate DSVs for each feature of node v in Q. After that, for each node v, we perform vertex matching algorithm, shown below. In Algorithm 1, C(u_i) is a set of vertexes who satisfy the matching condition of u_i. M(u_i,P) is a vertex set, where each vertex v's DDSV(v, P) dominates DDSV(u_i,P).

Algorithm 1 first initialize each node's candidate set at step 3. Then for each discriminative substructure P in k-N(u_i), we search our DSI for matching entries, and intersect with C(u). Finally, candidate set is decided when all the features are checked.

At the second substep, we adopt the subgraph matching algorithm proposed by [15]. Generally speaking, this algorithm checks the search space in a depth-first manner for matchings between the graph pattern and the graph. As stated before, our main concern is how indexing techniques could contribute to generating less candidates for each node. In a much smaller search space, the process of subgraph matching is naturally more efficient.

6 Experiments

Our method is written in Java JDK 1.6. All experiments are carried out on a machine with Intel core 2 duo CPU 2.0GHz, 2GB memory and Microsoft Windows XP.

In our experiments, we evaluate our distance set index on real large graph and synthetic graphs. We extract a real large graph from DBLP dataset[20]. In this graph, each vertex represents an author, each edge denotes the coauthor relationship between the two corresponding authors. For each author, the label is set as the conference where he has the most publications. The DBLP graph contains 776068 vertexes, 2498532 edges, and 3512 distinct labels.We also evaluate our methods on synthetic graphs. The synthetic graphs are generated with a heavy-tailed distribution by [21]. In synthetic graphs, we distribute the labels according to Zipf's law, that is, probability of the xth label is proportional to x^{-1}. The default parameter settings are: the number of vertexes is 10000, the exponent is 2.5, the minimum degree and maximum degree is 1 and 1000, the average degree is 5, and the number of labels is 100. In the experiments, we randomly select subgraphs as queries.

Table 1. Parameter Setting

k \ maxL	1	2	3
1	170.2	170.2	170.2
2		123.8	123.8
3			123.3

Next, we conduct experiments to fix the value of k. Selecting a radius of k-neighborhood involves pruning power and index construction cost. To select the most appropriate value of k, we evaluate our methods with different values on DBLP graph and synthetic graph. In our method, there is a hidden parameter, which is the max length of the distance, denoted as maxL. maxL is important in large graph circumstances, due to the special property of large graph. Large graphs are generally sparse, and locally dense. In our experiments, we randomly pick 20 vertexes and their k-neighborhood from the synthetic graph, and retrieve the candidates for each vertex. Table 1 shows the average size of the 20 candidate sets under varying k value and maxL value. According to our experimental results, the candidate set's size does not increase much with k, so we fix both k and maxL at 2.

We compare DSI's effectiveness with another feature strategy proposed by [15], which is named profile. To get the profile of a vertex, They first transform each vertex's 1-neighborhood into a sequence in lexicographic order. Thus the

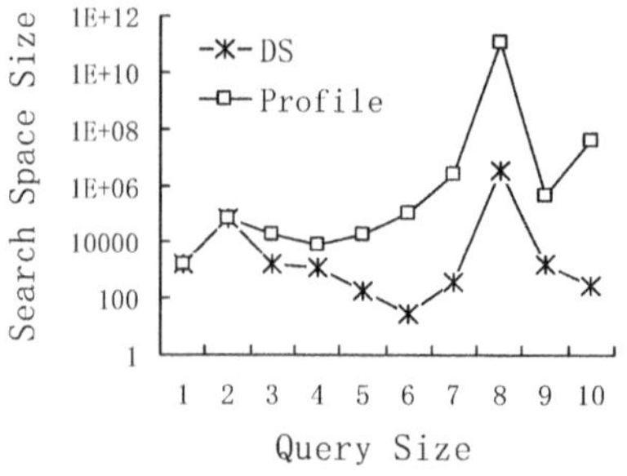

(a) Effectiveness on DBLP Dataset

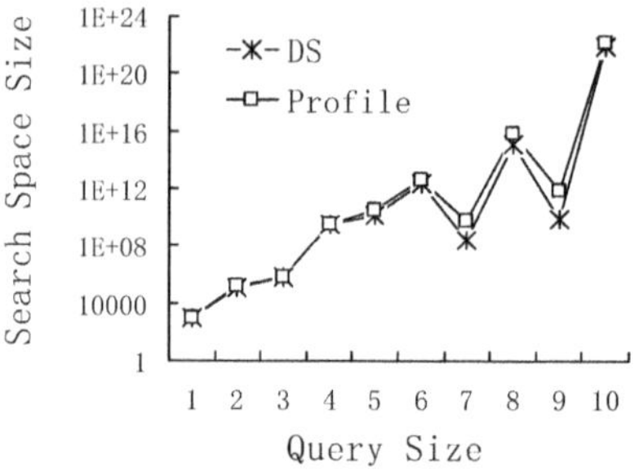

(b) Effectiveness on Synthetic Dataset

Fig. 4. Effectiveness

Table 2. Effectiveness with Different Parameters on Synthetic dataset

Graph Size	Query Size	Exponent	Min	Max	Avg. Degree	Label Number	DS	Profile
10000	5	1.5	1	1000	5	100	3.81E+5	1.04E+6
10000	5	2	1	1000	5	100	9.74E+11	1.08E+12
10000	5	2.5	1	1000	5	100	1.26E+10	3.76E+10
10000	5	4	1	1000	5	100	4.75E+6	1.69E+7
10000	5	2.5	1	100	5	100	1.06E+9	8.07E+9
10000	5	2.5	1	500	5	100	4.10E+7	1.99E+8
10000	5	2.5	1	1000	3	100	5.83E+4	4.92E+5
10000	5	2.5	1	1000	5	200	1.58E+4	3.92E+4

pruning condition is whether one vertex's profile is a subsequence of the other one's. To compare these two methods, we use search space product measure, which is defined as:

$$P=|C(u_1)| \times |C(u_2)| \times .. \times |C(u_n)|$$

In this experiment, we randomly generate 10 queries for each size in (1, 10). After retrieving the candidate set for each node in query, we compute search space product for each query, then compute the average search space product of all the 10 queries for each size. Figure 4 shows the search space product measure of different methods on two datasets. Our method greatly outperforms profile on DBLP dataset. On the synthetic dataset, our method performs slightly better than profile. This is due to the synthetic graph's particular characteristics that most vertexes whose degree is low, are usually connected to vertexes whose degree is high.

We also measure the index size and index construction time of DSI on these two datasets. The size of DSI on DBLP graph is about 1GB, and it takes us about 100 minutes to build. In synthetic graph, we spend 113 seconds building DSI, whose size is 72.3MB.

Next, we vary each parameter of the synthetic dataset at a time to conduct our method against profile. The results is shown in table 2. To specify, we don't test different graph sizes or query sizes, since the scalability has been shown on DBLP dataset. In addition, it is natural to assume that there exist leafs, therefore we don't vary the minimum degree. The last two columns show experimental results of two methods. In this experiment, we find that both methods work well while the graph is more sparse, and the label number is larger, since these characteristics would make each node more selective. Generally speaking, our method performs better.

7 Conclusion and Future Work

In the web age, large graphs are evolving in every aspect of our society, meanwhile the problem of querying large graphs has been aroused. In this paper, we investigate indexing techniques applied to large graphs. We propose distance set index to capture each vertex's local structure. We have applied our method to DBLP dataset,and a synthetic dataset. Extensive experiments show that our distance set index is efficient and effective. Although utilized in a two-way matching algorithm, our method could also be applied to dynamic matching algorithms, such as proposed by [17]. In future work, we plan to investigate utilizing discriminative substructures as basic units in the search space instead of vertexes, and compressing index size of DSI.

Acknowledgements

This research was partially supported by the grants from the Natural Science Foundation of China (No.60833005); the National High-Tech Research and Development Plan of China (No.2007AA01Z155); and the Doctoral Fund of Ministry of Education of China (No. 200800020002).

References

1. Cook, S.A.: The complexity of theorem-proving procedures. In: STOC 1971, pp. 151–158 (1971)
2. Shasha, D., Wang, J.T.L., Giugno, R.: Algorithmics and Applications of Tree and Graph Searching. In: PODS 2002, pp. 39–52 (2002)
3. Kuramochi, M., Karypis, G.: Finding Frequent Patterns in a Large Sparse Graph. In: DMKD 2004, pp. 243–271 (2004)
4. Fiedler, M., Borgelt, C.: Subgraph Support in a Single Large Graph. In: ICDM Workshops 2007, pp. 399–404 (2007)

5. Yan, X., Yu, P.S., Han, J.: Graph indexing: A frequent structure-based approach. In: SIGMOD 2004, pp. 335–346 (2004)
6. Yan, X., Yu, P.S., Han, J.: Substructure similarity search in graph databases. In: SIGMOD 2005, pp. 766–777 (2005)
7. He, H., Singh, A.K.: Closure-tree: An index structure for graph queries. In: ICDE 2006, p. 38 (2006)
8. Williams, D.W., Huan, J., Wang, W.: Graph Database Indexing Using Structured Graph Decomposition. In: ICDE 2007, pp. 976–985 (2007)
9. Jiang, H., Wang, H., Yu, P.S., Zhou, S.: GString: A Novel Approach for Efficient Search in Graph Databases. In: ICDE 2007, pp. 566–575 (2007)
10. Cheng, J., Ke, Y., Ng, W.: FG-Index: Towards Verification-Free Query Processing on Graph Databases. In: SIGMOD 2007, pp. 857–872 (2007)
11. Zhao, P., Yu, J.X., Yu, P.S.: Graph Indexing: Tree + Delta $\geq$ Graph. In: VLDB 2007, pp. 938–949 (2007)
12. Chen, C., Yan, X., Yu, P.S., Han, J., Zhang, D.-Q., Gu, X.: Towards graph containment search and indexing. In: VLDB 2007, pp. 926–937 (2007)
13. Wang, C., Chen, L.: Continuous Subgraph Pattern Search over Graph Streams. In: ICDE 2009, pp. 393–404 (2009)
14. Tong, H., Gallagher, B., Faloutsos, C., E-Rad, T.: Fast Best-Effort Pattern Matching in Large Attributed Graphs. In: SIGKDD 2007, pp. 737–746 (2007)
15. He, H., Singh, A.K.: Graphs-at-a-time Query Language and Access Methods for Graph Databases. In: SIGMOD 2008, pp. 405–418 (2008)
16. Tian, Y., Patel, J.M.: Tale A tool for approximate large graph matching. In: ICDE 2008, pp. 963–972 (2008)
17. Zhang, S., Li, S., Yang, J.: GADDI Distance Index based Subgraph Matching in Biological Networks. In: EDBT 2008, pp. 192–203 (2008)
18. Zou, L., Chen, L., Lu, Y.: Top-K Subgraph Matching Query in A Large Graph. In: First PH.D. Workshop CIKM 2007, pp. 139–146 (2007)
19. Zou, L., Chen, L., Yu, J.X., Lu, Y.: A Novel Spectral Coding in a Large Graph Database. In: EDBT 2008: pp. 181–192 (2008)
20. DBLP Dataset, http://dblp.uni-trier.de/xml/
21. Viger, F., Latapy, M.: Efficient and simple generation of random simple connected graphs with prescribed degree sequence. In: Wang, L. (ed.) COCOON 2005. LNCS, vol. 3595, pp. 440–449. Springer, Heidelberg (2005)

K-Radius Subgraph Comparison for RDF Data Cleansing

Hai Jin, Li Huang, and Pingpeng Yuan

Services Computing Technology and System Lab
Cluster and Grid Computing Lab
School of Computer Science and Technology
Huazhong University of Science and Technology, Wuhan, 430074, China
{hjin,ppyuan}@mail.hust.edu.cn, lihuang@smail.hust.edu.cn

Abstract. With the quick development of the semantic web technology, RDF data explosion has become a challenging problem. Since RDF data are always from different resources which may have overlap with each other, they could have duplicates. These duplicates may cause ambiguity and even error in reasoning. However, attentions are seldom paid to this problem. In this paper, we study the problem and give a solution, named *K-radius subgraph comparison* (KSC). The proposed method is based on RDF-Hierarchical Graph Model. KSC combines similar and comparison of *context* to detect duplicate in RDF data. Experiments on publication datasets show that the proposed method is efficient in duplicate detection of RDF data. KSC is simpler and less time-costs than other methods of graph comparison.

Keywords: RDF data cleansing, K-radius subgraph comparison.

1 Introduction

The Web enables persons to link related documents. Similarly it enables persons to link related data. Linking open data project, one of endeavors to link data, aims to use the Web to connect related data. Nowadays, according to its statistics the data sets consist of over 13.1 billion RDF triples, which are interlinked by around 142 million RDF links in November 2009[1]. Comparing with its statistics of April 2008 (2 billion RDF triples, and around 3 million RDF links) [1], the linked data have more than six times. The trends show the linked data will be even larger in the future.

However, due to diverse sources of data, it is quite possible that there exist duplicates in linked data. It may lead to many duplicate search results or wrong statistics on entities of Web. Let us take DBLP[2] which data are generally integrated from IEEE, ACM Portal et al, as an example. When we search *Jim Smith* in DBLP, DBLP returns 34 papers which DBLP thinks the single author named as *Jim Smith* wrote. But in fact those papers were written by 5 different *Jim Smith*'s. Furthermore, *Jim Smith* is generally written as *Smith, J.* in ACM database, but as *J. Smith* in IEEE database. Those

[1] http://esw.w3.org/topic/SweoIG/TaskForces/CommunityProjects/LinkingOpenData
[2] http://dblp.uni-trier.de/

L. Chen et al. (Eds.): WAIM 2010, LNCS 6184, pp. 309–320, 2010.

data make persons have to spend lots of time to explore the truth. Thus, it is highly necessary to cleanse linked data.

Linked data uses URIs and RDF to connect pieces of data, information, and knowledge on the Web. The RDF is based upon the idea of making statements about resources (in particular Web resources) in the form of subject-predicate-object expressions. A collection of RDF statements intrinsically represents a labeled, directed multi-graph. Although some solutions were proposed to cleanse relational database, few research are found on RDF data cleansing. Graph data might be transferred to relational data, but not all graph data contain uniform and enough relationship among entities. This makes the performance of traditional approaches not very well when using those approaches to cleanse graph data.

In this paper, we study the cleansing problem of linked data, and to solve the duplicate problem in linked data. The primary contributions of this paper are as follows:

- Propose a simple and intuitive graph model for RDF data, named RDF-Hierarchical Graph Model, which improves Bipartite Statement-Value Graph model [5].
- Propose a simple and efficient method for graph comparison. To avoid the time-consuming comparison of graph, we introduce a new concept of K-radius subgraph. The K-radius subgraph is the *context* of a node. We propose a *K-radius Subgraph Comparison* method, denoted KSC, to compare the *context* between two nodes in RDF-Hierarchical Graph. KSC extends subgraphs of two nodes partiwisely. The subgraphs contain the relationship-information of two nodes, partiwisely. KSC compares the two subgraphs, and calculate the similarity of them. Compared to other methods, KSC is simpler and more efficient for RDF graph comparison.
- Propose a solution for RDF data cleansing, based on above two. To the best of our knowledge, we are the first ones to study RDF data cleansing. In this solution, KSC, which is based on RDF-Hierarchical Graph model, utilizes the attribute of RDF data and the links among them, namely *context* of a node to detect duplicate.

The rest of the paper is organized as follows. The RDF-Hierarchical Graph model is defined in section 2. Section 3 describes the proposed method K-radius Subgraph comparison method. In section 4, we report the performance of our approach. Related work is discussed in section 5. Finally, we conclude this paper in section 6.

2. Hierarchical Graph Model for RDF Data

RDF (*Resource Description Framework*) proposed by WWW Consortium[1] is used to describe metadata about information resource. RDF statement is a triple which is consisted of a subject, a predicate and an object. A set of RDF triples are RDF graph. RDF graph is a sort of hypergraph. In this hypergraph, the hyperedges represent the statements, and the hypernodes denote subjects, predicates and objects.

Since hypergraph is hardly analyzed, Hayes et al. proposed bipartite graphs model to represent RDF data [5]. In a bipartite graphs model, both hyperedge and hypernode

[1] http://www.w3.org/

are represented by a node in the graph, and they are called hyperedge-node and hypernode-node respectively. Edges in bipartite graph model are used to connect hyperedges and their hypernodes. Then the hypergraph is transformed into a bipartite graph. According to RDF, subject and object are different from predicate in types. For duplicates must be of the same type, we distinguish the two parts in a triple by layers. The nodes of same type are in the same layer. Subject and object are set on the same layer, and predicate is on a different layer. We define the layer of predicate is higher. Then we get a new model of RDF graph, called RDF-hierarchical graph. We can not find that there are subject of one type and object of another type in one triple. That is because subject and object of different types could not construct a statement of RDF data. So the model graph is hierarchical.

We take a triple as a unit in RDF-hierarchical graph, for RDF-hierarchical graph is consisted of triples. Fig. 1(a) shows a unit in a subgraph of RDF-hierarchical graph. In a unit, there are four nodes, a statement node (circle nodes) and three value nodes (rectangle nodes). The three value nodes refer subject, predicate, and object, respectively. Fig. 1(b) and 1(c) shows different kinds of subgraphs in RDF-hierarchical graph.

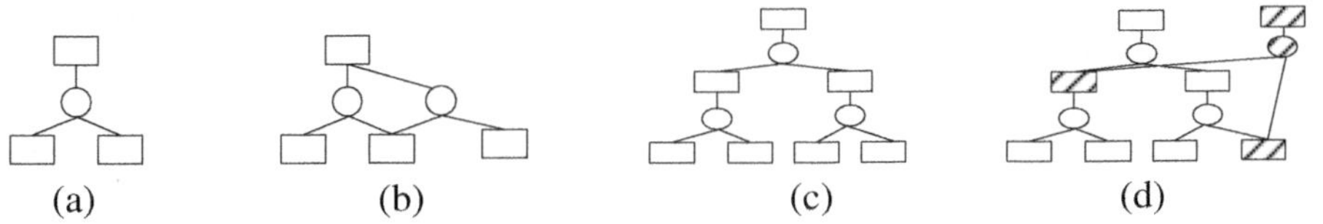

Fig. 1. Subgraphs of RDF-Hierarchical graph model

A unit is also a subgraph of RDF-hierarchical graph. Fig. 1(b) consists of two units, and Fig. 1(c) has three units. Shadowed triples in Fig. 1(d) cannot exist. The operations on RDF-hierarchical graph are most unit-oriented. We will give some definitions of concepts on RDF-hierarchical graph. Assume the target node is p, the target unit u, and G is a RDF-hierarchical graph.

Definition 1. *n*-distance. The n-distance is used to measure the distance from a unit to a node, denoted as D.

$$D(u,p)=\begin{cases} min\left(\{j|(u_1,u_2,\ldots,u_{j-1})\}\right) & p\notin u,\ \exists\, sequence\ (u_1,u_2,\ldots,u_{j-1}) \\ & \quad where\ u_i\in G,\ u_i\cap u_{i-1}\neq\phi,\ i=1,\ldots,j-1, p\in u_1,\ u\cap u_{j-1}\neq\phi \\ 1 & p\in u \\ 0 & else \end{cases}$$

Definition 2. K-radius subgraph. If the n-distance between any units in a subgraph to node P is not bigger than k, this subgraph is the k-radius subgraph of P, denoted $SG_k(P)$. If $u_i\subset SG_k(P)$, then $max(D(u_i, P))=k$.

In Fig. 2, we give a subgraph of RDF-hierarchical graph. From Fig. 2, we can get $D(u_1, A)=D(u_2, A)=D(u_3, A)=D(u_4, A)=1$, and $D(u_5, A)=D(u_6, A)=2$. We also can find all distance from units in Fig. 2 to node A is no more than 2. So the subgraph shown in Fig. 2 is a 2-radius subgraph of A.

We also introduce some operations on graph. Assume $G_1(V_1, E_1)$ and $G_2(V_2, E_2)$ are two graphs.

Operation 1. Subtraction. This operation, denoted as '-', means to subtract the nodes and edges in another graph. The result is a set calculated as G_1-G_2={V_1-V_2, E_1-E_2}. The operation of subtraction is not suitable for any pairs of graphs. If $V_1 \subseteq V_2$, V_1-V_2 is error. So V_1 should be larger than V_2.

Operation 2. Intersection. This operation, denoted as '∩', means to intersect the nodes and edges in another graph. The result is $G_1 \cap G_2$={$V_1 \cap V_2$, $E_1 \cap E_2$}.

Operation 3. Union. This operation, denoted as '∪', means to unite the nodes and edges in another graph. The result is $G_1 \cup G_2$={$V_1 \cup V_2$, $E_1 \cup E_2$}.

3 K-Radius Subgraph Comparison

Generally, in a graph, the nodes, which have smaller distance to a node *P*, have stronger relationship with *P*. These nodes restrict *P*, and help to disambiguate *P*. We call these constraints one node's *context*. If two nodes are duplicates, they would have the same or similar *context*. Thus the principle of KSC is that a node is disambiguated by the *context*, which is presented by other near nodes and edges in a graph.

The biggest difference between RDF-hierarchical graph and a general graph is the operations are unit-oriented in RDF-hierarchical instead of node-oriented. In RDF-hierarchical graph, a node is disambiguated by the units around it. The reason for using units instead of nodes is that every node has inherent neighborhoods in RDF-hierarchical graph. The nearest nodes of them are statement nodes, which cannot help for disambiguating. K-radius subgraph contains most units which the *n*-distance from the target node is no more than *K*. Thus we use K-radius subgraph to reflect the *context* around the node.

3.1 K-Radius Subgraph

From Fig. 2, we can find units are not shown clearly in RDF-hierarchical graph. To present the process of creating K-radius subgraph intuitively, we simplify the graph in this subsection. In the simple RDF-hierarchical graph, each unit in RDF-hierarchical graph is considered as a node. If two units share the same nodes, there is an edge between the two units in RDF-hierarchical graph, and the number of nodes two units shared is the weight of the edge. As the RDF-hierarchical graph is hierarchy, the simple RDF-hierarchical graph also has hierarchy. The level of the target node is level 0, and all the levels are positive. The level of a unit equals the highest level of the note in it. Fig. 3 is the result directed from Fig. 2.

According to the Definition 1 and 2, the *n*-distance from units which contain the target node is 1. So these units consist of 1-radius subgraph. If *K* is bigger than 1, the process of finding K-radius subgraph is an iteration of extending.

However, if we try to extend all the nodes, which are within *n*-distance of *K* to the target node, the result k-radius subgraph will be huge and complex. The goal of finding K-radius subgraph is to give some constraint to the target-node. Thus the units, which have stronger relationship with the target-node, have more worth.

In a simple RDF-hierarchical graph, the edge indicates the two units have overlap. The weight of the edge represents the degree of the overlap. The larger the weight is, the more overlap two units have. More overlap means stronger relationship. The hierarchy of RDF-hierarchical graph also implies the degree of the relationship. The nodes in the same layer are in the same type in RDF-hierarchical graph. The units in different layers have weaker relationship. So each time, we choose the lowest level of units. Then we conclude two properties of KSC as follows:

Assume the target node is P, $K>1$, the RDF-hierarchical graph is G.

Property 1. The set S of candidate units is $S=\{v|\max(|v\cap u_i|)$, and $u_i\in G_{k-1}(P), v\in G\}$.

Property 2. The final extending set $S'=\{t|\min(\text{level}(t)), t\in S\}$, where S is the candidate set getting from rule 1.

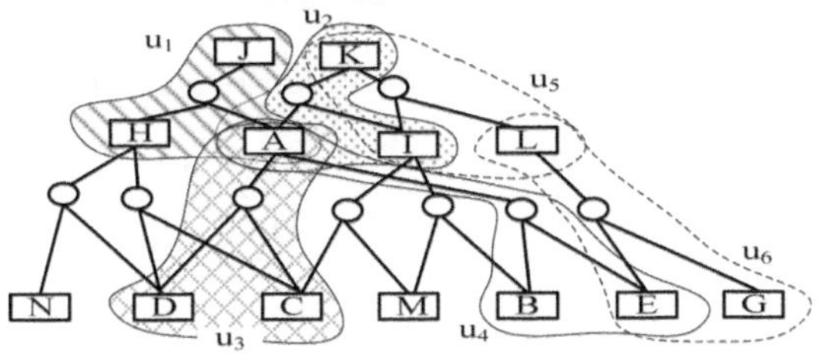

Fig. 2. Subgraph of RDF-hierarchical graph

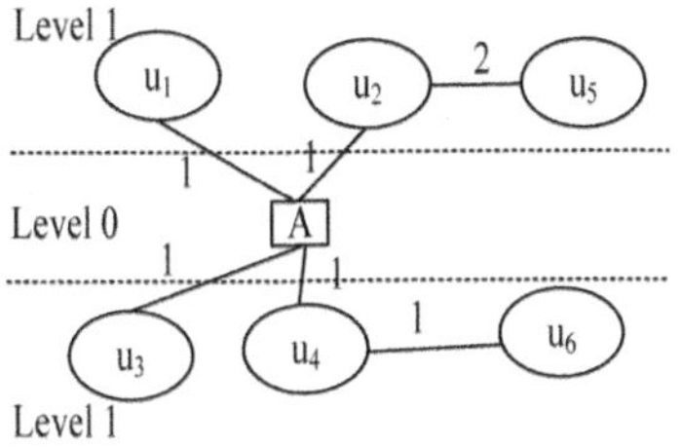

Fig. 3. Simple RDF-hierarchical graph

In each extending, KSC chooses the units having strongest relationship with the units which are already in the subgraph. Thus in Fig. 3, we will take u_6 out from the 2-radius subgraph of A.

3.2 Subgraph Comparison

In this section, we will find the K-radius subgraph of a node which not only shows information of a node but also helps disambiguating the node. Thus duplicates should have similar K-radius subgraphs. According to the above analysis, if the K-radius subgraphs of two similar nodes are similar, the two nodes have a higher probability to be duplicates. Here we will give the method of comparing two K-radius subgraphs.

There are many connections among nodes in different units. These connections contain much information. So the comparison of subgraphs is node-oriented. In general, most methods of comparing graphs are used in biology, and each edge refers to a regular bond. In that situation, they need only consider the construction of the graph without considering the values of nodes. That is a graph isomorphism problem. Many of them are complex and time-consuming. However, in RDF-hierarchical graph, the values of nodes are different and very important for duplicate detection. Both construction and value should be taken into comparing of two K-radius subgraphs. More information is supplied from K-radius subgraph. It includes the nodes, the edges, and level of the nodes, the *n*-distance from nodes to the target node. All this information help subgraph comparison. Thus, a special method for calculating similarity between two K-radius subgraphs is needed.

Let us analyze the contributions of different information implied in K-radius subgraphs. Nodes and edges are more important for comparing. However, not all the nodes in K-radius subgraphs have the same contributions. The nearer the two nodes, the stronger relationship they have. So the nodes have smaller *n*-distances from the target node are more important for identifying the target node. So the *n*-distance should be taken into calculation of similarity. The definition of *n*-distance orients units. The three value nodes in a unit are equal, so the nodes in a unit have the same *n*-distance as the unit has.

According to the above analysis, we give the calculation of similarity between two K-radius subgraphs, which is shown in formula (1).

Assume two nodes are *P* and *Q*. The K-radius subgraphs are $SG_k(P)$ and $SG_k(Q)$. $SG_0(P)=SG_0(Q)=0$.

$$\begin{aligned} SimEnv(SG_k(P), SG_k(Q)) &= \frac{1}{k}\sum_{i=1}^{k}(SimG((SG_i(P)\text{-}SG_{i-1}(P)),(SG_i(Q)\text{-}SG_{i-1}(Q))))^i \\ &= \frac{1}{k}\sum_{i=1}^{k}\left(\frac{|(SG_i(P)\text{-}SG_{i-1}(P))\cap(SG_i(Q)\text{-}SG_{i-1}(Q))|}{|(SG_i(P)\text{-}SG_{i-1}(P))\cup(SG_i(Q)\text{-}SG_{i-1}(Q))|}\right)^i \end{aligned} \quad (1)$$

In formula (1), $(SG_i(P)\text{-}SG_{i-1}(P))$ is a set which contains the nodes with *n*-distances *i* and the edges among them. Because SG_{k+1} contains SG_k, the subtract operation is valid on them. The intersection is to find the common nodes and edges. Along with *i* increasing, the nodes farther from the target-node have smaller contributions, so the similarity increase slowly.

4 Experiments and Performance Evaluation

We do some experiments and show results to examine the efficiency and accuracy of the proposed approach in this section. All experiments are performed on an IBM eServer with a 1.25GHz Power4 processor and 4GB of memory, running Suse Linux Enterprise 10.0. All approaches are implemented and tested in Java.

4.1 Dataset

We experimentally study the proposed approach on DBLP, which is a real dataset on publication. In summary, the duplicates in DBLP are mainly in two cases, author's name ambiguity and publications' title sharing. Using the traditional similarity comparison is invalid in both cases.

We store all data in DBLP in RDF triples. Since there are huge amount of triples, it is hard to measure the results by hands. So we pick up 3 groups of triples from DBLP. Each contains 5,000 triples. We use a semiautomatic method to calculate the numbers of duplications. Table 1 shows more details of the 3 groups.

Table 1. Detail of groups

	Number of triples	Number of entities	Number of duplicates
Group 1	5000	13057	73
Group 2	5000	2978	29
Group 3	5000	7843	57

In Table 1, three groups contain different numbers of entities, although they contain the same number of RDF triples. This is induced by relationships among RDF triples. The three groups we pick up for testing represent 3 typical situations. In group 1, the ratio of the number of entities to triples is close to 3. The triples have fewer relationships with each other in this situation. In group 2, the number of entities is smaller than the number of triples. This indicates most triples share entities in this situation. The number of entities in group 3 is between the above two groups. The ratios of the number of triples to entities are shown in Fig. 4.

4.2 Experimental Analysis

The process of the proposed approach can be divided into three steps. The first step is to transfer the RDF triples into RDF-hierarchical graph. Second, calculate the similarities of the data pairwisely. The similarity calculation has been studied in [6]. All the similarity calculation pairs are in the same layer. Here, we use the LFDW [6] to calculate similarity. If the similarity of the pair is higher than the threshold, the pair is a candidate. The candidate pairs need to be verified. The last step is to compare the *context* between the data. The *context* of a node is measured by the K-radius subgraph of the node. Then we combine the two similarities together as a total similarity between the two nodes. If the total similarity is bigger than the threshold, the two data are duplicates.

We first pick up two pairs of nodes in RDF-hierarchical graph to test the similarity of K-radius subgraphs. One pair has smaller similarity, and the other pair has bigger similarity. The details of the test data are as follows.

The test pairs: *pair1*(*"Thomas Cormen"*, *"Charles H. Leiserson"*), *pair2*(*"John R. Smith"*, *"Smith R. John"*). *SimString*(*pair1*)=0.098; *SimString*(*pair2*)=0.975.

The result shows both similarities increase along with K in Fig. 5. This result can be easily proved by formula (1). The similarity is a summation. We also find some interesting phenomenon in the result. Similarity of K-radius subgraphs in *pair1* increases slowly at the beginning, but quickly when K is bigger than 4. The similarity of *pair2* almost stop increasing when K is bigger than 5. After comparing strings of nodes, *pair1* has less possibility to be duplicates than *pair2*. When K is small, the two nodes in *pair2* share little nodes. Most units in subgraphs need to be extended. Along with increasing of K, more and more units are extended in subgraphs. The probability of subgraphs sharing nodes is higher. Meanwhile, most units of K-radius subgraphs in *pair2* stop extending. Small nodes are extended in the subgraphs. Thus the above phenomenon happens.

From the above test, the value of K should be smaller than 4 for distinguishing two pairs, for the different is smaller when K is bigger than 4. Then we will test the proposed approach in different K, and K is smaller than 4. The results are shown in Fig. 6 and Fig. 7. The threshold is the same in different K.

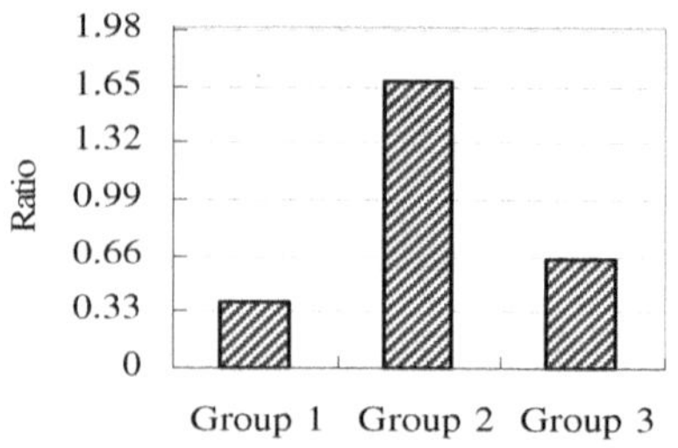

Fig. 4. Ratios of number of 3-tuples to entities

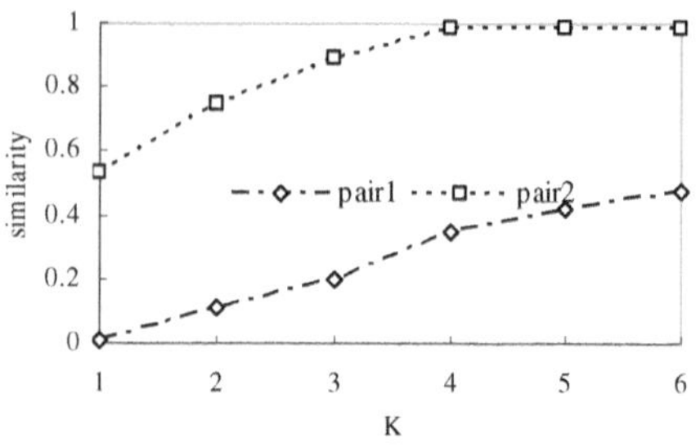

Fig. 5. Similarities of K-radius subgraphs in two pairs

Fig. 6 shows the trend of *f*-measure (denoted F_1) when *K* increases in different groups. The trends of the f-measure are the same in three groups. The *f*-measures increase quickly when *K* is small, and slow down when *K* is bigger. The critical values are reached at different *K* in three groups. In group 1, when *K* is 1, the change of *f*-measure is small. The triples in group 1 have fewer relationships with each other. There is few information of *context* around each entity. In this group, most duplicates are detected through similarity comparison between entity pairs. In group 3, triples share more entities with each other. Then more information of *context* joins to help detecting. In group 3, when *K* is 2, *f*-measure reaches critical values. We compare the *f*-measures in the three groups. Group 2 is the highest, and group 1 is the lowest. This shows that *context* is an important factor in duplicate detection.

Fig. 7 shows the running times in different *K*. In all groups, the running time increases when *K* increases. The trends are similar in the three groups. We take group 2 as an example to describe the trend in detail. The time increases slowly when *K* is small, quickly when *K* is bigger than 3, and slowly again when *K* is bigger than 4. When *K* is small, the scales of the k-radius subgraphs are small. The time cost in comparison is small. When *K* increases, more and more units are extended to the K-radius subgraph. More time are needed for comparing. When *K* is even bigger, most units in K-radius subgraphs stop extending. The scales of the K-radius subgraphs increase slowly, and then the time needed to compare is also increasing slowly. According to Fig. 6 and 7, although when *K* is 4, the *f*-measure is the highest, more time is needed. The *f*-measure is litter higher when *K* is 4 than *K* is 3, but much more time is needed when *K* is 4. Thus the optional value of *K* for group 2 is 3.

Through similar analysis on group 1 and group 3, we can get the optional values of *K* are 1 and 2, respectively. When the ratio of triples to entities is 1/3, there are no triples sharing entities with each other. In this situation, *K* equals to 0. Fig. 8 gives the relationship between the optional value of *K* and the ratio of triples to entities.

From Fig. 8, we can induce a formula to calculate *K* in a dataset. We can calculate the optional value of *K* using the formula (2).

$$k = \begin{cases} 0 & ratio = 1/3 \\ \lceil (\ln(ratio) + 1.1) * 1.8 \rceil & others \end{cases} \text{; where } ratio = \frac{Number_{triple}}{Number_{entity}} \quad (2)$$

Since RDF graph could be transferred to both entity-relationship model and simple graph model, many methods for entity-relationship model and graph model are also available for RDF graph. On entity-relationship model, many methods are proposed for duplicate detection on publication data [2, 3, 4, 9, 10]. A typical one proposed by Han [3] considers the relationship among data. For graph model, Kalashnikov proposed a domain impendent method in [7], which combines the similarity and connection for identify entities. For few methods have been proposed for RDF data cleansing, we compare the proposed method KSC with methods which are used for entity-relationship model and graph model instead. The result is shown in Fig. 9. In Fig. 9, for simplicity, we use *R* to refer to the method for entity-relationship model, and use *C* to refer to the method proposed by Kalashnikov in [7], *KSC* is the proposed approach. Here the connect-path is the shortest and least resistance path. If two units share more nodes, the connection between them is stronger. The longer the path, the bigger resistance two nodes have, the less connection they have.

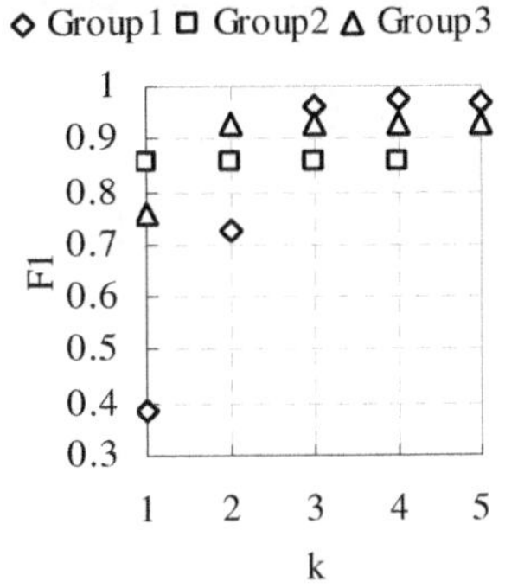

Fig. 6. Results of detection duplicate with different *K*

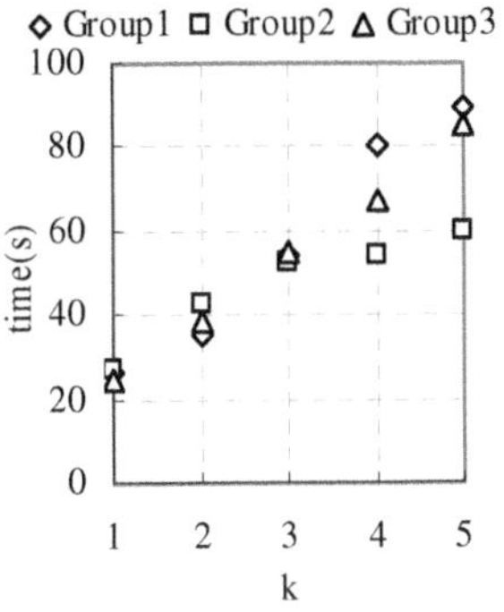

Fig. 7. Time needed in different *K*

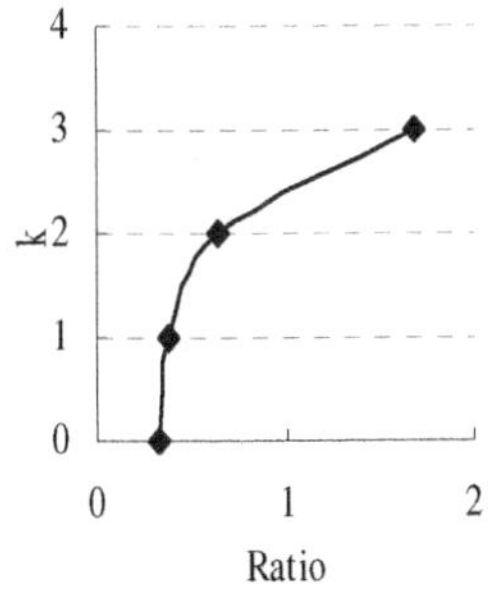

Fig. 8. Relationship between *K* and ratio of triples to entities

As KSC considers *context* of data, the more *context* the data have, the higher *f*-measure KSC gets. Thus in Fig. 9 (a-c), KSC on *Group2* gets the highest recall, precision and *f*-measure. Furthermore KSC has more advantage than other methods in *Group2*. The more relationship the entities have, the more effective KSC is. There may be missing some links when transfer RDF graph to entity-relationship model, the entity-relationship model have lowest *f*-measure. The *context* among data can better improve the precision than *connections* do, as shown in the result.

Fig. 9(d) also shows the running time of the three methods. The proposed method *KSC* costs least time. As the number of entities is the smallest in *Group2*, the least time is cost in *Group2*, although many *context* need more time to deal with. For many extra works have to do when considering the relationship between data in entity-relationship model, *R* needs most time.

To present the results intuitively, we introduce another measure, called efficiency, denoted *EFF*. The calculation of EFF is shown in formula (3).

$$EFF = F_1 * Num(duplicate) / time \tag{3}$$

EFF refers to the number of duplicates which are correctly detected in a unit time. In Fig. 9(e), we also show the *EFF*s of the three methods. By comparing EFFs, the proposed method *KSC* has the highest efficiency of duplicate detection in any situations. When there are more relationship among entities, the advantage of *KSC* is more outstanding.

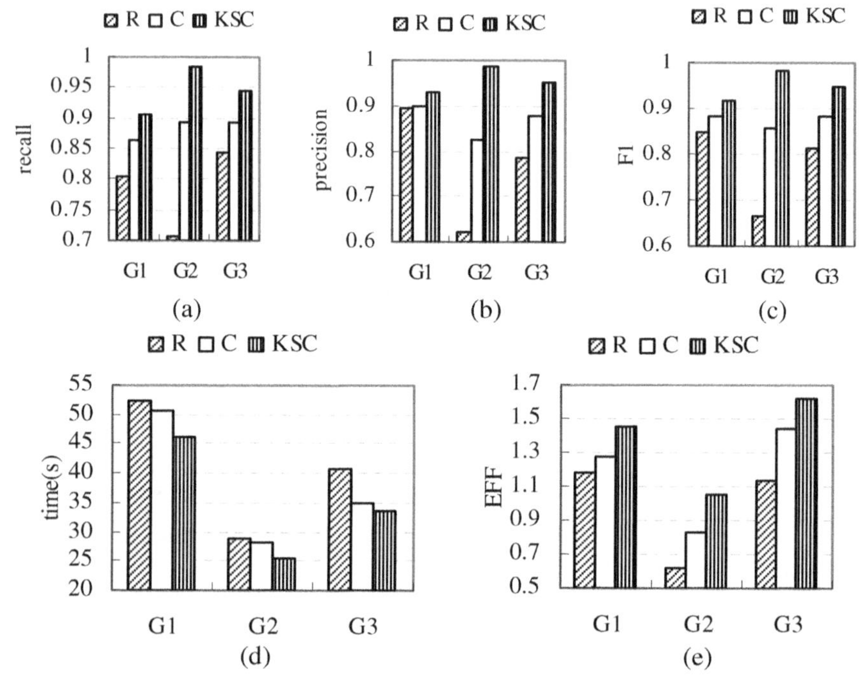

Fig. 9. Result of comparison between *R*, *C* and *KSC*. Here, *G1*, *G2*, *G3* refer to Group1, Group2, and Group3, respectively.

5 Related Works

Our work solves the duplicate detection of RDF data. This work is related to two main studies: RDF data modeling and duplicate detection.

RDF is the W3C standard model for describing metadata. The RDF data also has the problem of duplicates. RDF data represent not only the value of the data, but also the relationships among the data. In [8], Klyne et al. proposed a directed labeled graph to represent the RDF data. A triple of RDF statement is a label edges. This model is easy to implement and represents the relationship among data clearly. However, if the relationship is complex, much information would be lost. The RDF graph is different from a common graph. It is a hypergraph, because there may have more than one edge between two nodes. Morales proposed a direct hypergraph model [11]. In this model, each RDF statement is a hyperedge in the hypergraph. This model can represent the complex relationship among data. But it can not deal with the scale of RDF data, and is hard to process more on it. Hayes proposed a bipartite graph model [5]. This model transfers the hypergraph to a common bipartite graph. It is easy to manage and operate. Our model is improved from this model. All the models introduced are used for semantic retrieval, like similar query and related query. They do not focus on the duplicate detection.

Duplicate is the main inducement of data dirty. Duplicate detection belongs to data cleansing. It is an important study in data mining. The basic method to detect duplicates is to compare entities. The main issue of comparing entities is field matching [9], which could be achieved by recursive field matching algorithm [10], Smith-Waterman algorithm, and R-S-W algorithm [2] etc. The above methods all consider the records themselves and ignore the relationship among them.

Recently, researchers shifted their attention to the associations among entities. Han et al. proposed an unsupervised learning approach using K-way spectral clustering that disambiguates authors in citations [3]. It utilizes three kinds of citation attributes: co-author names, paper titles, and publication venue titles. A general object distinction methodology is introduced in [12]. The approach combines two complementary measures for relational similarity: set resemblance of neighbor tuples and random walk probability, and then analyzes subtle linkages effectively. Han et al. investigated two supervised learning approaches to disambiguate authors in the citations [4]. Kalashnikov proposed a domain-independent method [7]. This method analyzes not only object features but also inter-object relationships to improve the disambiguation quality. They use the shortest path algorithm to find the connect path connects two entities. The path is measured by the association strength between the two entities. However, it is difficult to set the association strength between two entities correctly.

6 Conclusion and Future Works

Nowadays, links among data are increasing explosively. Due to variety sources of data, RDF data have duplicates. Duplicate may cause the inference and inquire error. However, studies are seldom made on this problem. In this paper, we propose an approach to detect the duplicates in RDF data.

The proposed approach combines both similarity and *context* among RDF data to detect the duplicates. Considering the complexity of the associations among RDF data, we propose a model for RDF, called RDF-hierarchical graph, which is improved from Bipartite Statement-Value Graphs [4]. In the model, we give a K-radius subgraph comparison method to detect the *context* of the two similar nodes, to avoid the complex and high cost of graph comparison. This method explores the K-radius subgraphs of the two nodes which reflect the *context*. By comparing two K-radius subgraphs (KSC), we get the similarity of *context* between the nodes. Finally, we combine the similarity and the *context* between the two nodes to decide whether they are duplicates or not.

We implement the proposed method on publication datasets, and compare the method with the methods on entity-relationship model and graph model, for seldom methods are proposed on RDF data. The results show that the proposed method improves accuracy and efficiency in detecting duplicates obviously. KSC is convinced to be a more simple and quick method.

Acknowledgements. The work is supported by the National 973 Key Basic Research Program under grant No.2003CB317003.

References

1. Bizer, C., Heath, T., Berners-Lee, T.: Linked Data: Principles and State of the Art. In: Proceedings of 17th International World Wide Web Conference (2008)
2. Bunke, H.: On the Weighted Mean of a Pair of Strings. Pattern Analysis & Applications (5), 23–30 (2002)
3. Han, H., Zha, H., Giles, C.: Name disambiguation in author citations using a K-way spectral clustering method. In: Proceedings of the 5th ACM/IEEE-CS Joint Conference on Digital Libraries, Tools & techniques: identifying names of people and places, pp. 334–343 (2005)
4. Han, H., Giles, L., Zha, H.: Two Supervised Learning Approaches for Name Disambiguation in Author Citations. In: Proceedings of the 4th ACM/IEEE-CS Joint Conference on Digital Libraries (JCDL 2004), pp. 269–305 (2004)
5. Hayes, J., Gutierrez, C.: Bipartite Graphs as Intermediate Model for RDF. In: McIlraith, S.A., Plexousakis, D., van Harmelen, F. (eds.) ISWC 2004. LNCS, vol. 3298, pp. 47–61. Springer, Heidelberg (2004)
6. Huang, L., Jin, H., Yuan, P., Chu, F.: Duplicate Records Cleansing with Length Filtering and Dynamic Weighting. In: Proceedings of International Conference on Semantics, Knowledge and Grid 2008, December 4-6, pp. 95–102 (2008)
7. Kalashnikov, D., Mehrotra, S.: Domain-independent data cleaning via analysis of entity-relationship graph. ACM Transaction on Database Systems 31(2), 716–767 (2006)
8. Klyne, G., Carroll, J.: Resource description framework (RDF): Concepts and Abstract Syntax. W3C Recommendation. World Wide Web, February 10 (2004), `http://www.w3.org/TR/2004/REC-rdf-concepts-20040210/`
9. Minton, S.N., Nanjo, C., Knoblock, C.A., Michalowski, M., Michelson, M.: A Heterogeneous Field Matching Method for Record Linkage. In: Proceedings of the Fifth IEEE International Conference on Data Mining, pp. 314–321 (2005)
10. Monge, A.E., Elkan, C.: The field matching problem: algorithms and applications. In: Proceedings of the 2nd International Conference on Knowledge Discovery and Data Mining, pp. 267–270 (1996)
11. Morales, A., Serodio, M.: A Directed Hypergraph Model for RDF. In: Proc. of Knowledge Web PhD Symposium (2007)
12. Yin, X., Han, J., Hu, P.: Object Distinction: Distinguishing Entities with Identical Names. In: Proceedings of IEEE 23rd International Conference (ICDE 2007), pp. 1242–1246 (2007)

A Novel Framework for Processing Continuous Queries on Moving Objects

Liang Zhao, Ning Jing, Luo Chen, and Zhinong Zhong

College of Electronic Science and Engineering, National University of Defense Technology, Changsha 410073, China
liangzhao2010@gmail.com

Abstract. Traditional techniques for processing continuous queries on moving objects reduce query re-computing through single-threaded and shared execution between multiple queries, and don't make use of the parallel computing capabilities of the ubiquitous multi-core CPUs. Thus, to explore this kind of parallelism, a **M**ulti-threading based **F**ramework for **C**ontinuous **Q**ueries (MFCQ) is proposed which adopts a strategy of re-computing all of the queries periodically. The framework divides the query process into three phases:the updating, optimization and execution stages; multi-threading based methods are used in each phase. Moreover, the framework is deemed to be general, because it is compatible with various index techniques and query algorithms. By using the framework, a query index based KNN algorithm and an object index based KNN algorithm are proposed respectively. Experimental results show that the multi-threading framework executed on the multi-core platform outperforms the traditional YPK-CNN algorithm.

Keywords: multi-threading, framework, continuous queries, KNN query, grid index.

1 Introduction

Continuous queries on moving objects means to get the instantaneous query results according to the frequent changing of moving objects' positions. It is becoming increasingly important due to the wide availability of inexpensive and compact positioning devices, the evolution of mobile communications and the need for improved location-based services. Due to its complexity, several techniques (reviewed in Section 2) have been developed in the last few years for continuous range and KNN queries. Most of the proposed algorithms periodically evaluate the multiple queries, more importantly, they adopt the idea of shared execution which means to re-use the query results and re-evaluate only the queries affected by object or query updates. Therefore, they design various techniques and data structures to aid the storage and computation, which seems rather complicated and hard to understand.

With the advent of modern Chip Multi-Processors (CMPs), continuous query algorithms need to be adapted to exploit such multi-core designs. Modern CMPs

L. Chen et al. (Eds.): WAIM 2010, LNCS 6184, pp. 321–332, 2010.

integrate multiple cores and provide hardware support for parallel processing. Unlike running on single core CPUs, multithreaded program running on CMPs can implement real parallelism, because each core could support at least one thread. Based on this observation, our idea to solve the problem of multiple continuous queries is to explore this kind of parallelism. We do not use shared execution between queries, on the contrary we re-evaluate all the queries periodically. To accelerate the whole data set updates and re-evaluation, we propose a multi-threading based framework. To verify the effectiveness of the framework, we propose two KNN algorithms. So our aim is to test whether a more direct algorithm and hardware supported mechanism can provide efficient processing. Moreover, we argue that we should take the hardware development into consideration when designing new algorithms and sometimes complicated algorithms are not necessary.

Contributions of this paper can be summarized as follows:

1. We propose a general multi-threading based framework for continuous queries.
2. Based on the framework, we propose a novel query grid index based KNN algorithm (Q-KNN).
3. Based on the framework, we propose a direct moving object grid index based KNN algorithm (M-KNN).
4. We conduct extensive experiments to show the effects of different parameters to the proposed algorithms, and verify the proposed framework is more effective than the traditional YPK-CNN algorithm.

2 Related Works

Continuous queries on moving objects can be classified into two classes. The continuous range queries and the continuous K nearest neighbor(KNN) queries.

Prabhakar et al.[1-2] proposed the Q-index, which indexes range queries using an R-tree-like structure. At each evaluation step, only those objects that have moved since the previous evaluation step are evaluated against the Q-index. Mokbel et al.[3-4] proposed scalable incremental hash-based algorithms SINA and SEA-CNN for range and KNN queries. SINA and SEA-CNN index both queries and objects, and achieve scalability by employing shared execution and incremental evaluation of continuous queries.Yu et al.[5] proposed a method, hereafter referred to as YPK-CNN, for continuous monitoring of exact KNN queries. When re-evaluating an existing query q, YPK-CNN makes use of its previous result in order to restrict the search space. As an enhancement, Mouratidis et al.[6] presented a technique called CPM that defines a conceptual partitioning of the space by organizing grid cells into rectangles. Location updates are handled only when objects fall into the vicinity of queries, hence improving system throughput.

The above methods tries to minimize the execution time of algorithms, however, two other algorithms were proposed to minimize the communication cost between client and server. Hu et al.[7] first addressed the location update issue and proposed a generic framework for monitoring continuous spatial queries over moving objects which minimizes the communication cost. Hseuh et al.[8] proposed a partition-based lazy update approach that significantly reduces unnecessary location updates by maintaining a Location Information Table (LIT) on each moving object. Further, Mouratidis et al.[9] studied monitoring moving objects in road networks. By using the properties of the spatial network and the network constraint characteristic of the movements of moving objects, re-evaluation of the multiple queries could be reduced. Demiryurek et al[11] proposed a ER-CKNN method which uses the Euclidean distance to guide searching on road networks.

To summarize, most of the above-mentioned continuous query techniques adopt a memory based query processing framework and often use the grid index to store either the moving objects or the multiple queries to aid the whole query process. The core idea of most algorithms is to design the search strategy in order to minimize the access to the moving object dataset whenever updating or querying. All of them use a single thread to deal with the multiple queries although they often share the executions. None of them try to exploit the capabilities of modern CMPs, and the continuous query algorithm is often to some extent too complicated. Those are the points where our work can be distinguished from.

3 The Multi-threading Based Framework for Continuous Queries (MFCQ)

The problem to be solved can be described as: under the condition that the moving objects' positions and spatial queries' positions are continuously changing, give the up to date query results according to these changes. Compared to the traditional methods, we use multi-threading technology to re-compute all the queries in each period and try to explore the parallel capability of modern CMPs. Therefore, we propose a Multi-Threading based Framework for Continuous Queries (MFCQ), like Figure 1 shows.

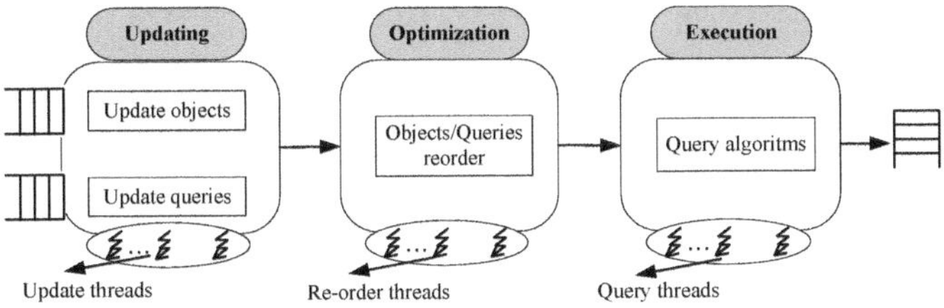

Fig. 1. The Multi-threading based Framework for Continuous Queries

The main idea of designing the framework is: on multi-core platform, we transform the continuous queries into periodically evaluated queries, in each period all queries and objects are processed through three sequential stages, i.e. the updating stage, the optimization stage and the execution stage. In each stage multi-threading is used to finish the corresponding task. MFCQ is deemed to be a general framework for the following reasons:(1) it is compatible with various query types. By using this framework, we can execute both the range query and KNN query together with other typical query types. (2) it is compatible with various index methods and optimization methods. To explain these benefits, we will present two different index based KNN algorithms respectively in section 4 and 5. Here we first give some detailed explanations on each stage in MFCQ.

3.1 The Data Updating Stage

In the problem of continuous monitoring of moving objects, the positions of the moving objects and the queries are continuously changing. Therefore, we need to update and get the latest information of objects and queries before processing the queries, making sure that the query results are instantaneous and correct.

As we adopt a periodical processing strategy, we need to buffer the updated data in a period. We use two buffer queues(as shown in the left of Figure 1)to store these updated data. In the beginning of each period, we use multiple threads to update the moving objects and queries into their corresponding data structures.

In the practical implementation, we study two data storage methods which are in accordance with the query algorithms: one is indexing the queries with grid, and using a linear list to store moving objects; the other is indexing the moving objects with grid, and using a linear list to store queries. To be concrete, when using multiple threads to update the first kind of structures we set write locks to the cells of the query grid index, only by acquiring the lock can a thread writes new data. Also we set write locks to the object list. Similar operations are set on the second kind of structures.

3.2 The Optimization Stage

Because datasets are stored directly in the main memory, we could use some techniques to optimize the cache access. Here we propose a sorting based optimization technique.

Take the first kind of data structures for example. In the query algorithm that will be explained in section 4, we use each of the objects stored in the list to search the grid index. During this process, if we store the moving objects following their arriving sequence, then the cache access hit rate of the query index based algorithm may be decreased. This phenomenon could be explained by Figure 2.

In the query index based algorithm, queries are indexed according to their spatial relation with the cells. For each object, its cell is computed and the queries that belong to the cell are accessed. Consider the example shown in Figure 2. The order in which the objects appear in the list is shown on the left of the figure in the "Unsorted list". Cell(0,3) is the first cell to be accessed for we first process object P_1. However, when we process object P_2, cell(0,0) must be accessed which means index data in cell(0,3) may be replaced outside the

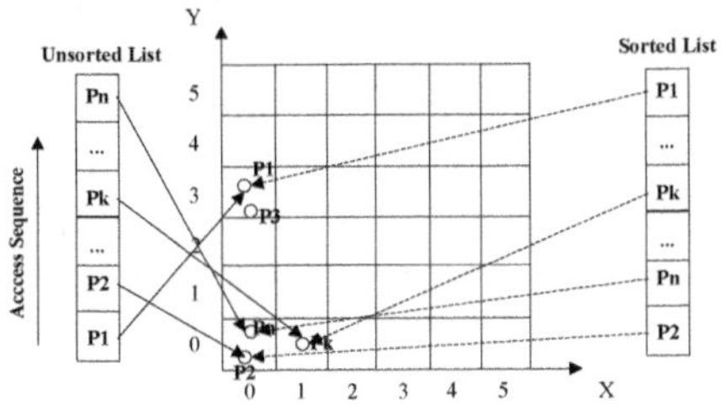

Fig. 2. Cache misses in query processing

cache, resulting in a cache miss when we process the following object P_3 as it will also access cell(0,3). This phenomenon shows us if we could sort the object list according to the objects' spatial adjacency, then the cache hit rate may be increased. On the right of Figure 2 is the sorted list. Noticing that, this kind of sorting optimization doesn't stress any constraints on objects' movement. Similar to the query index, when we use object index based query algorithm we could also sort the query list.

We use the Hilbert-curve[10] to sort the list. It maps the objects/queries that located in the same grid to a single dimensional value. We use this value as the key to sort, any famous sort algorithm can be used. In our experiment, we use multi-threaded merge sort for this optimization stage.

3.3 The Execution Stage

In fact, the first two stages in MFCQ prepare data for the last stage. In the execution stage, the framework calls the query algorithm to get the final results for each query.

In this stage, we adopt the data parallel methods that uniformly partitions the linear list to equal sized work set. Each thread takes one work set as their input. In the query index based algorithm, multiple threads may concurrently write the same query result list. In this situation, we set write locks to the result list to avoid writing conflicts.

4 Query Index Based KNN Query

In this section we propose a **Q**uery index based **KNN** Query algorithm, i.e. Q-KNN.

4.1 Building the Query Index

We build a grid index for multiple queries to help filter the massive objects. The grid index is a two dimensional space partitioned into $\delta \times \delta$ cells. In each cell we keep two lists for the storage of queries. Figure 3 is an example of the query index.

Figure 3 is a 6 × 6 grid. Each cell keeps two lists called the Mainlist and the Secondarylist storing the fully covered or partly overlapped queries. Take the cell(1,4) as an example, currently only Q_1 fully covers this cell and no other queries are overlapped with it, so the Mainlist of cell(1,4) stores Q_1 and the Secondarylist stores nothing. For cell(4,3), there doesn't exist any query that fully covers this cell, while Q_1 and Q_2 are partly overlapped with it. Thus its Mainlist stores nothing and the Secondarylist stores Q_1 and Q_2.

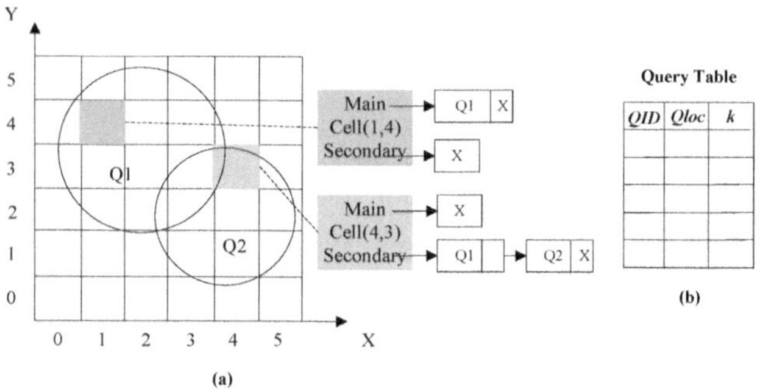

Fig. 3. The query index

For range queries, it is easy and direct to build such index according to the spatial relations between range query and the cell. However for KNN query, we need additional techniques. We first compute a histogram that keeps the number of objects in each cell. Then we judge whether the cell that a query resides in contain more than K objects, if yes, we compute the maximum distance between the query and the four corners in the cell. Using the distance as radius, we draw a circle. Finally, add the query to the lists of the cells that are covered by or overlapped with the circle. If the current cell doesn't contain enough K objects, then we add additional 8 cells around the central cell until at least K objects are found.

4.2 Q-KNN Query Algorithm

Let $Q = \{q_1, \ldots, q_{|Q|}\}$ be the query set, $X = X_1 \cup X_2 \cup \ldots \cup X_n = \{x_1, \ldots, x_{|X|}\}$be the object set. X is uniformly partitioned into subsets that are processed by each thread. For each subset X_i, algorithm 1 shows the process. The query process follows the sequence: for each object in X_i, in line 2 the algorithm identifies the cell that the object resides in by calling the function *GetCell()*. From line 3 to 7, it searches the Mainlist in the located cell, if the number of objects in the cell is less than K, then add the object to the result list, otherwise it updates the result list according to distance comparing. From line 8 to 14, the algorithm searches the Secondarylist in the above similar way. The reason why we use two iterations is that queries in the Mainlist is more like to contain the current object, so distance comparing can be reduced.

Algorithm 1. Q-KNN Queries
Input: Datasets X_i, Index GI
Output: Query Result List (QRL)

```
for j = 1 ← |X_i|
   (m,n)=GetCell(x_j)
   foreach Query q in GI(m,n).Mainlist
      if QRL[q].count < k
         QRL[q].add(x_j)
      else
         Do distance comparing and update QRL[q]
for j = 1 ← |X_i|
   (m,n)=GetCell(x_j)
   foreach Query q in GI(m,n).Secondarylist
      if QRL[q].count < k
         QRL[q].add(x_j)
      else
         Do distance comparing and update QRL[q]
```

5 Object Index Based KNN Query

In this section we propose a **M**oving object index based **KNN** Query algorithm, i.e. M-KNN.

The method to build a moving object index is direct and easy. We map the moving objects to the grid cells according to their spatial locations. In each cell we use a list to store the pointers to the moving objects.

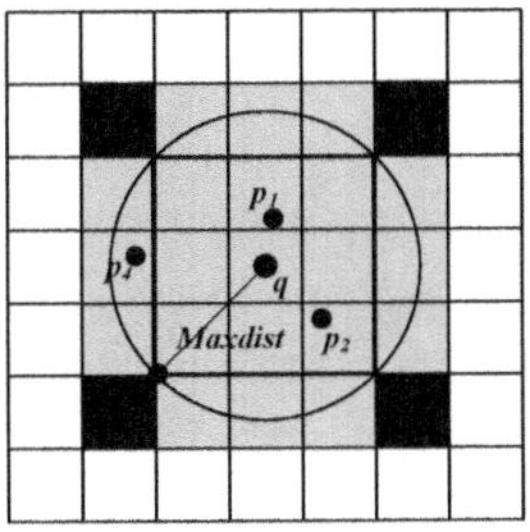

Fig. 4. Explanations to the M-KNN algorithm

The M-KNN algorithm can be explained by Figure 4. We describe the query process through a 3-NN example. First, the object list of the cell that the query resides in is searched, if the current cell doesn't contain enough K objects, then the adjacent 8 cells around the cell are searched, right now we find 3 objects and take them as the 3-NN query results. After that, we compute the maximum distance between the 3-NNs and the query. Taking the maximum distance as the radius, we then search the cells that are overlapped with the circle, and finally find that the real 3-NNs are p_1,p_2,p_4.

In the query execution stage, we uniformly partition the queries into several subsets that are processed by multiple threads. For each query, algorithm 2 shows the process. The idea of M-KNN algorithm is similar to the object index based query algorithm proposed in YPK-CNN, the difference is in the third step we only add the overlapped cells, however, in YPK-CNN additional 4 dark black cells in Figure 4 will be added into the TempCellList.

Algorithm 2. M-KNN Queries
Input: Queries Q_i, Index *GI*
Output: Query Result List (*QRL*)

1. $TempCellList = \emptyset$
//step 1 find at least k objects around q_j
2. *TempCellList*=GetCells(q_j)
//step 2 compute the maximum distance
3. maxdist=ComputeMaxDist(*TempCellList*)
//step 3 add additional cells according to maxdist
4. ComputeOverlappedCells(*TempCellList*, maxdist)
5. UpdateCells(*TempCellList*)
//step 4 compute the real KNNs in TempCellList
6. UpdateResults(*TempCellList*, $QRL(q_j)$)

6 Experimental Results

In this section, we conduct extensive experiments to evaluate the performance of our proposed two algorithms under the MFCQ framework, moreover we compare it with the YPK-CNN algorithm.

We use three different kinds of CPU platform: a single core CPU Intel Celeron 3.2GHz, a dual core CPU Intel Pentium E2200 2.2GHz with 1M L2 cache and a quad core CPU Intel Core 2 Quad Q8200 with 4M L2 cache. Each of the platforms has 1GB memory with Windows XP installed. Dual core platform is taken as the default environment. All the mentioned algorithms are implemented in C++ under the Visual Studio 2005 development environment.

The moving objects and queries are synthetically generated. Table 1 summarizes the parameters under investigation, along with their ranges and default values. The amount of the data is bigger than that of data used by the prevalent algorithms. Noticing that in Q-KNN we update all the objects periodically and define the query agility as the ratio of the changed spatial queries to the total queries. However, in M-KNN, we define the object agility as the ratio of the number of objects that move outside of their original cells to the total number of objects, and the query agility is the same with that in Q-KNN. We control the object agility through changing the objects' speed.

In the following experiments the CPU time is composed of three parts: the updating time, the optimization time and the execution time. We run the framework 10 periods and compute the average CPU time as the performance metric.

Table 1. Experimental Parameters

Parameters	Range of Parameters
Number of Objects	250K, **500K**, 750K, 1M
Number of Queries	10K, **15K**, 20K, 25K
Object agility	10, 20, 30, 40, **50**(%)
Query agility	10, 20, **30**, 40, 50(%)

6.1 Effects of the Cell Size and Object Distribution to the Framework

First, we test the effects of the cell size and object distribution to different algorithms that are used in the framework. Figure 5 and 6 show the results respectively.

Figure 5 shows the effects of the cell size to the proposed algorithms under default data amount. Performance of the Q-KNN algorithm increases with the cell size, however when the cell size is bigger than 500, the performance increases slightly. For M-KNN algorithm, there exists an optimal cell size. In the later experiments, we chose cell size 500 for Q-KNN and 600 for M-KNN.

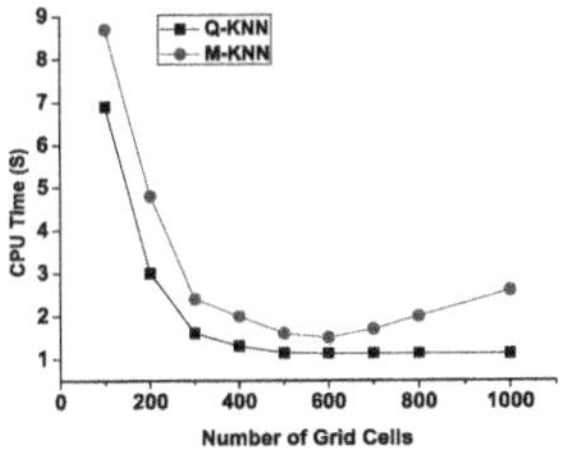

Fig. 5. Effects of cell size

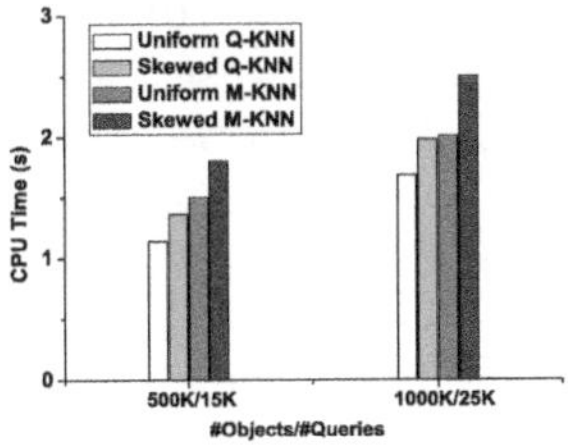

Fig. 6. Effects of data distribution

Figure 6 shows the effects of object distribution to the proposed algorithm. The skewed data set is composed of 10% of the objects distributed uniformly over the whole region and other 90% of the objects form four Gaussian clusters. Queries are uniformly distributed. For Q-KNN algorithm, data distribution has less effect to its performance. When object distribution is skewed, the performance decreased slightly. Because object distribution only affects the query index building process, however the index building accounts for a small part of the whole process. For M-KNN algorithm, data skewness has bigger effect. Because when object distribution is skewed, processing one query needs to search more cells which means more distance comparing. In the later experiments, we use the uniform data.

6.2 Effects of Data Agility to the Framework

Next, we test the effects of data agility to the framework.

Figure 7(a) shows the effects of object agility. For Q-KNN algorithm, we update all objects periodically, so object agility is not considered here. For M-KNN algorithm, object agility only affects the performance of index updating, the bigger agility the more index updating time. However for grid index, updating time is far less than the querying time, so the performance decrease is not evident.

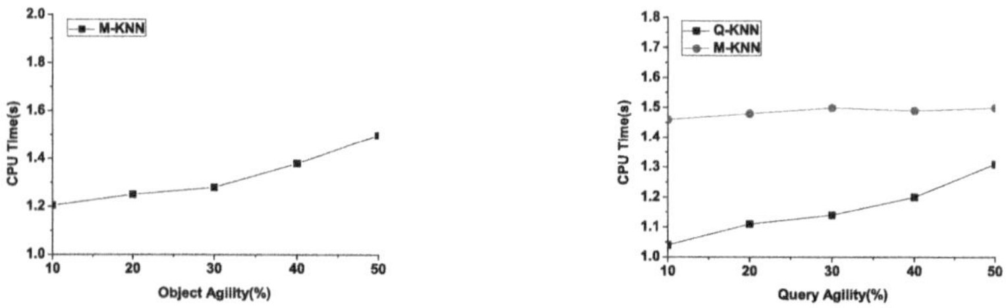

(a)Effects of object agility (b)Effects of query agility

Fig. 7. Effects of data agility

Figure 7(b) shows the effects of query agility. For Q-KNN, the bigger query agility the more query index updating time. However, for M-KNN as we keep a uniformed query dataset, and periodically re-compute all queries, so the query agility doesn't have obvious effect on the query performance.

6.3 Performance of Q-KNN under Different CPU Platforms

The following experiment tests the performance of Q-KNN under different CPU platforms. The performance curve of M-KNN is similar.

First, we use the default parameters to test the performance of Q-KNN under different CPUs by setting different thread numbers. As figure 8 shows, on single core platform, multi-threading can't bring performance improvement, on the contrary with the growth of thread numbers the CPU cost becomes larger. This is because on single core CPU, we can't realize the real parallelism, thread switch becomes a bottleneck when using multi-threading. However, on dual core or quad core CPU platform, multi-threading has very evident performance superiority. When thread number is equal to the CPU core number, the performance get optimal. However when the thread number is bigger than the core number, performance also decrease like that executed on single core CPU.

Then, we test Q-KNN on dual core and quad core CPU platforms, and set the thread numbers to 2 and 4 separately. As Figure 9 shows, with different amount of datasets, Q-KNN executed on quad core CPU platform has much better performance as much as twice the performance of that executed on dual core CPU which demonstrate that the multi-threaded framework has very good scalability.

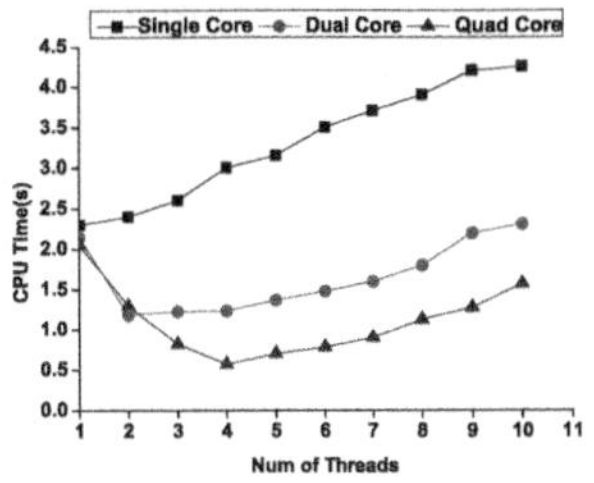

Fig. 8. Effects of thread numbers

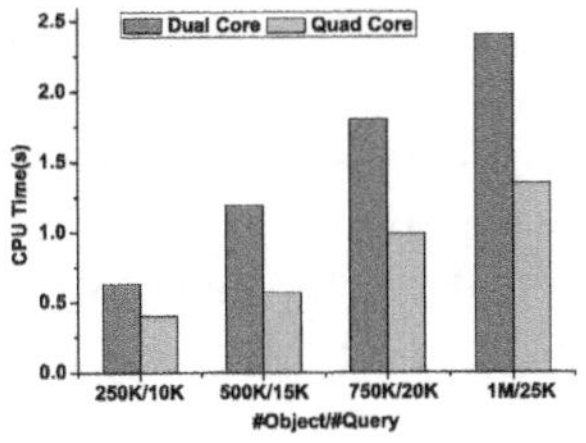

Fig. 9. Effects of different platforms

6.4 Comparisons between Different Algorithms

Finally, we test our proposed algorithms together with the YPK-CNN algorithm by using different data amount.

Figure 10 shows that under different amount of objects and queries, the proposed algorithms executed under the MFCQ framework is more efficient than the YPK-CNN algorithm. That verifies our objective which is to show the effectiveness of exploring the parallel capability of modern CMPs.

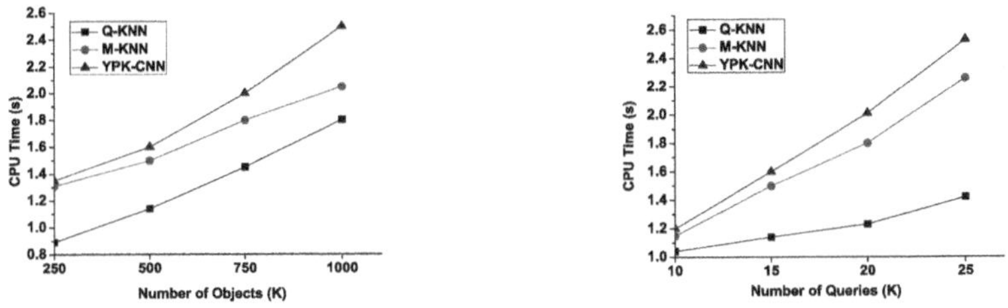

(a)Effects of objects (b)Effects of queries

Fig. 10. Effects of data amount

Figure 10 also shows that under most circumstances, the Q-KNN algorithm is better than the M-KNN algorithm, except in the case when the number of moving objects is much bigger than that of the queries.

7 Conclusion

In this paper, we reconsider the problem of continuous queries on moving objects. We want to test whether a more direct algorithm that are strengthened by multi-threading technology can outperform the traditional incremental but sophisticated algorithms. Thus, we design a multi-threading based framework for continuous queries and propose two KNN algorithms. The experimental results show that the proposed framework is more efficient than the traditional YPK-CNN algorithm, which verifies our idea. The proposed algorithms can be easily modified to support range queries. So, to summarize we deem that our proposed framework that is compatible with various indexes and query algorithms is novel and general.

We believe that future research should take fully consideration of the modern hardware capabilities. Our future research will include: comparing the framework with other algorithms such as the CPM algorithm. Further more, we will study optimization methods when mixed types of queries concurrently execute under MFCQ.

Acknowledgments. This research is supported by the National High-Tech Research and Development Plan of China (863) No.2008AA12A211, National Science Foundation China, No.40601080.

References

1. Kalashnikov, D.V., Prabhakar, S., Hambrusch, S.E.: Efficient Evaluation of Continuous Range Queries on Moving Objects. In: Hameurlain, A., Cicchetti, R., Traunmüller, R. (eds.) DEXA 2002. LNCS, vol. 2453, pp. 731–740. Springer, Heidelberg (2002)
2. Prabhakar, S., Xia, Y., Kalashnikov, D.V., et al.: Query Indexing and Velocity Constrained Indexing: Scalable Techniques for Continuous Queries on Moving Objects. IEEE Transactions on Computers 51(10), 1124–1140 (2002)
3. Mokbel, M.F., Xiong, X., Aref, W.G.: SINA: Scalable Incremental Processing of Continuous Queries in Spatiotemporal Databases. In: Proc. of SIGMOD, pp. 623–634 (2004)
4. Xiong, X., Mokbel, M.F., Aref, W.G.: SEA-CNN: Scalable Processing of Continuous K-Nearest Neighbor Queries in Spatio-temporal Databases. In: Proc. of ICDE, pp. 643–654 (2005)
5. Yu, X., Pu, K.Q., Koudas, N.: Mointoring k-Nearest Neighbor Queries over Moving Objects. In: Proc. of ICDE, pp. 631–642 (2005)
6. Mouratidis, K., Hadjieleftheriou, M., Papadias, D.: Conceptual Partitioning: An Efficient Method for Continuous Nearest Neighbor Monitoring. In: Proc. of SIGMOD, pp. 634–645 (2005)
7. Hu, H., Xu, J., Lee, D.L.: A Generic Framework for Monitoring Continuous Spatial Queries over Moving Objects. In: Proc. of SIGMOD, pp. 479–490 (2005)
8. Hsueh, Y.-L., Zimmermann, R., Wang, H., et al.: Partition-Based Lazy Updates for Continuous Queries over Moving Objects. In: Proc. of GIS (2007)
9. Mouratidis, K., Yiu, M.L., Papadias, D., Mamoulis, N.: Continuous Nearest Neighbor Monitoring in Road Networks. In: Proc. of VLDB, pp. 43–54 (2006)
10. Asano, T., Ranjan, D., Roos, T., et al.: Space filling curves and their use in the design of geometric data structures. Theoretical Computer Science 181(1), 3–15 (1997)
11. Demiryurek, U., Banaei-Kashani, F., Shahabi, C.: Efficient Continuous Nearest Neighbor Query in Spatial Networks Using Euclidean Restriction. In: Mamoulis, N., Seidl, T., Pedersen, T.B., Torp, K., Assent, I. (eds.) Advances in Spatial and Temporal Databases. LNCS, vol. 5644, pp. 25–43. Springer, Heidelberg (2009)

Group Visible Nearest Neighbor Queries in Spatial Databases

Hu Xu[1], Zhicheng Li[1], Yansheng Lu[1], Ke Deng[2], and Xiaofang Zhou[2]

[1] School of Computer Science and Technology,
Huazhong University of Science and Technology, China
{hxu,anders}@smail.hust.edu.cn, lys@mail.hust.edu.cn
[2] School of ITEE, University of Queensland, Australia
{dengke,zxf}@itee.uq.edu.au

Abstract. Traditional nearest neighbor queries and its variants, such as *Group Nearest Neighbor Query* (GNN), have been widely studied by many researchers. Recently obstacles are involved in spatial queries. The existence of obstacles may affect the query results due to the visibility of query point. In this paper, we propose a new type of query, *Group Visible Nearest Neighbor Query* (GVNN), which considers both visibility and distance as constraints. *Multiple Traversing Obstacles* (MTO) Algorithm and *Traversing Obstacles Once* (TOO) Algorithm are proposed to efficiently solve GVNN problem. TOO resolves GVNN by defining the invisible region of MBR of query set to prune both data set and obstacle set, and traverses obstacle R*-tree only once. The experiments with different settings show that TOO is more efficient and scalable than MTO.

Keywords: Group nearest neighbor, visible nearest neighbor, spatial database, query processing.

1 Introduction

The studies on *Nearest Neighbor (NN)* query have lasted for a long time in database society. As a typical variant, *Group Nearest Neighbor Queries (GNN)* [6] return an object with the minimum summed distance to all query points from the specified query objects. GNN query does not take obstacles into account. However obstacles (such as buildings, billboards etc.) do exist in real life and may affect the query results because of visibility. Although obstacles have been considered in some typical spatial queries [1,2,3,4,5], they have never been considered as a constraint in GNN query.

In this paper, we propose a new type of query, called *Group Visible Nearest Neighbor Queries (GVNN)*, which firstly involves obstacles in GNN queries. GVNN can be applied to miscellaneous real life applications such as decision support, emergency rescue, strategic planning etc. A possible scenario of a GVNN query is battle field. Obstacles can be any disused or damaged objects (e.g., civilian buildings, vehicles). During the process of a military operation, the command center may require

L. Chen et al. (Eds.): WAIM 2010, LNCS 6184, pp. 333–344, 2010.

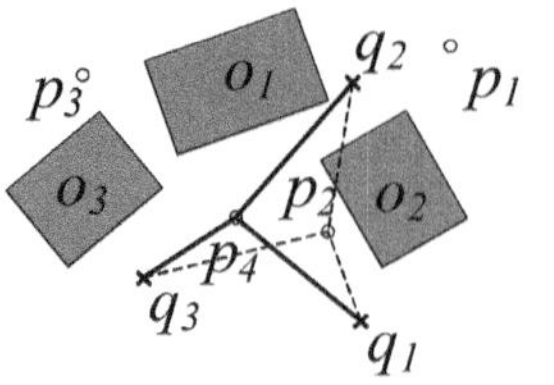

Fig. 1. Example of GVNN

all tactical teams at different locations to find a temporary assembling point so as to decide the next action. In order to guarantee the success of operation and reduce the loss to minimum, since long moving distance increases the risk of loss, the temporary assembling point should be clearly seen (not blocked) by all teams and the total distance from all teams to the gathering point should be minimized. The command center should select a best location from multiple candidates. As depicted in Fig. 1, o_i is obstacle ($1 \leq i \leq 3$) and the GNN of q_1, q_2 and q_3 is p_2 (indicated by dashed lines). As q_2 is blocked by obstacle o_2, p_4 with the second minimal summed distance is returned as the result of GVNN.

The naive method to solve GVNN problem is to check each retrieved GNN in turn and whether it is visible to each query point. It stops when a certain GNN is visible to all query points for the first time. However, this method can be inefficient because the number of GNNs needed to be checked can be huge, and the obstacle set is accessed multiple times which incurs high I/O costs.

In this paper, we propose two algorithms, *Multiple Traversing Obstacles* (MTO) Algorithm and *Traversing Obstacles Once* (TOO) Algorithm respectively. MTO solves GVNN query through constructing searching space of obstacles based on the GNN found so far. In order to overcome the main disadvantages of MTO, the obstacle line of the MBR of query set is defined and utilized by TOO to prune both obstacles and data points. TOO traverses obstacle R-tree only once while MTO needs multiple rounds. As shown in the experiments, TOO outperforms MTO in terms of both efficiency and effectiveness.

In brief, the main contributions of this paper are summarized as follows:

- We define a new type of query, called GVNN query in term, which considers both distance and visibility as constraints.
- We extend the visibility of a single query point to the MBR of query set.
- We propose a baseline algorithm MTO and an improved algorithm TOO to process GVNN query efficiently.
- Experiments with different parameter settings demonstrate the efficiency and effectiveness of our proposed algorithms.

The rest of this paper is organized as follows. Section 2 reviews the related problems. In Section 3, some important definitions are taken out. MTO and TOO are presented in Section 4. Experiments are shown in Section 5. The last section concludes this paper.

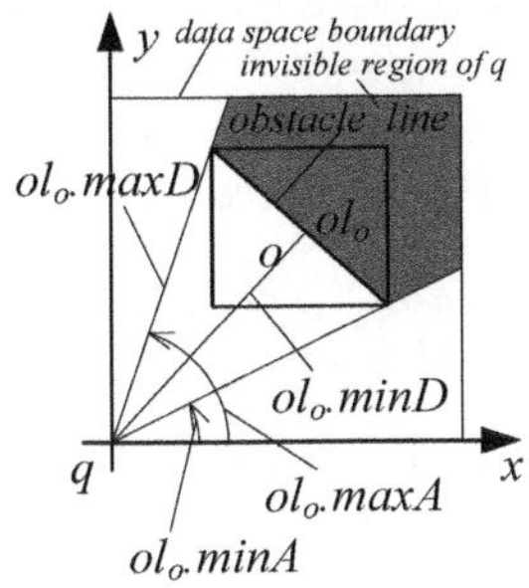

Fig. 2. Visible region of a single query point q

2 Related Work

Traditional NN query can be regarded as the special case of GNN query [6] whose query set is not a single point but multiple ones. The target is to find an object which minimizes the summed distance to all query points. MQM, SPM and MBM are proposed to solve memory-resident GNN queries. MBM treats query points as a whole, i.e., MBR of query points, and prunes unqualified data nodes as early as possible. MBM dominates MQM and SPM in both I/O and CPU costs. The case of disk resident queries is also discussed. In this paper, we only focus on memory-resident queries, i.e., the query set fits in main memory. As mentioned in Sect. 1, obstacles are not under consideration in GNN query. Therefore all aforementioned three algorithms can't be applied directly to solve our problem. Zhang et al. [9] discuss quantile based GNN query over multi-valued objects.

Visible NN [1][4][5]and obstructed NN [2][3] search have attracted a considerable number of database researchers recently. Visible NN query is first proposed in [4]. Continuous visible NN [1] and reverse visible NN [5] are studied as well. However all previous algorithms only consider single query point or multiple query points as line segment. The query points in our GVNN query are distributed arbitrarily in data space.

3 Preliminaries

In this section, we first give out the formal definition of GVNN. Then a useful concept, i.e., *obstacle line*, is introduced. Without loss of generality, we suppose that all the objects (points and obstacles) are in a 2D space. Although our discussion is under two dimensional space, extension to higher dimension is straightforward. Given a data set P, a query set Q and an obstacle set O, a data point p and a query point q are *visible* to each other if and only if the straight line segment connecting p and q does not cut through any obstacle $o \in O$. Thereupon GVNN query is formulated as follows.

Definition 1. ***(Group Visible Nearest Neighbor)*** *Given a set of data points P, a set of query points Q and a set of obstacles O, a GVNN query returns a point $p \in P$ such that (i) p is visible to all $q_i \in Q$; (ii) $\sum_{q_i \in Q} dist(p, q_i)$ is minimized where $dist(p, q)$ is the Euclidean distance between these two points.*

Definition 2. ***(Obstacle Line[5])*** *The obstacle line ol_o of an obstacle with respect to q is the line segment that obstructs the sight lines from q.*

Based on Definition 2, the *angular bound* and *distance bound* which are denoted as $[ol_o.minA,\ ol_o.maxA]$ $(0 \leq ol_o.minA \leq ol_o.maxA \leq 2\pi)$ and $[ol_o.minD, ol_o.maxD]$ $(ol_o.minD \leq ol_o.maxD)$ respectively can be derived. Here $ol_o.minA$ $(ol_o.maxA)$ represents the minimal (maximal) angle of ol_o. $ol_o.minD$ $(ol_o.maxD)$ is the minimal (maximal) distance from ol_o to q. Fig. 2 shows an instance of obstacle line and its bound. Apparently any obstacle o' with $[ol_{o'}.minD,\ ol_{o'}.maxD] \cap [ol_o.minD,\ ol_o.maxD] = \emptyset$ can't affect ol_o's visibility w.r.t. q. Then the visible region of q is the white region (Fig. 2) except the interior of o. In Section 4.1, obstacle line is used to judge the impact of an obstacle on the visibility of current GNN. In Section 4.2, we utilize obstacle line to derive our proposed *Minimum Invisible Region* (IR_{min}).

4 Processing GVNN Queries

In this section, two algorithms are presented to handle GVNN queries. Section 4.1 describes Multiple Traversing Obstacles Algorithm (MTO). A more efficient algorithm, Traversing Obstacles Once (TOO), is introduced in Section 4.2. Suppose that both data points and obstacles are indexed by R*-tree index structure [8], which are denoted as R_p and R_o respectively. The query set Q fits in main memory.

4.1 Multiple Traversing Obstacles Algorithm

In this section, we propose an algorithm called *Multiple Traversing Obstacles* (*MTO*). The basic idea of MTO is that when a new GNN p is found, we check whether it is visible to all query points. There are two ways to judge whether p is a qualified one. One way is retrieving obstacles first to find the union of p's invisible region (IR_p), and then checking whether any query point is in this union area. Another way is utilizing the search region w.r.t. p to retrieve obstacles which could affect the visibility of GNN first, and then identifying if they block any query point. According to Definition 1, not all obstacles but those making a GNN invisible to any query point should take effect. The second way can prune those unnecessarily accessed obstacles which may incur excess I/O costs. Therefore we take the second method to filter out unqualified GVNN. First of all, we define the search region of obstacles (SR_o) w.r.t. a GNN. SR_o is a sector area which consists of an angular bound and a distance bound.

Definition 3. ***(Angular Bound of*** SR_o***)*** *Considering a GNN p as an origin, the angular bound of SR_o is denoted as [p.minqa, p.maxqa] where p.minqa and* *p.maxqa are the minimum angle and maximum angle from p to q_i ($\forall q_i \in Q$) in counter-clockwise direction respectively and $0 \le p.minqa \le p.maxqa \le 2\pi$.*

Definition 4. ***(Distance Bound of** SR_o**)*** *The distance bound of SR_o, i.e., the radius of SR_o, is denoted as p.maxqd which is the maximum distance from p to any $q_i \in Q$.*

As shown in Fig. 3, p is a GNN as an origin. Two arcs with arrows correspondingly indicate $p.minqa$ and $p.maxqa$, and q_s is the farthest point in Q to p. The shadowed sector is the SR_o w.r.t. p. Apparently, all query points are visible to p without any obstacle and located in SR_o.

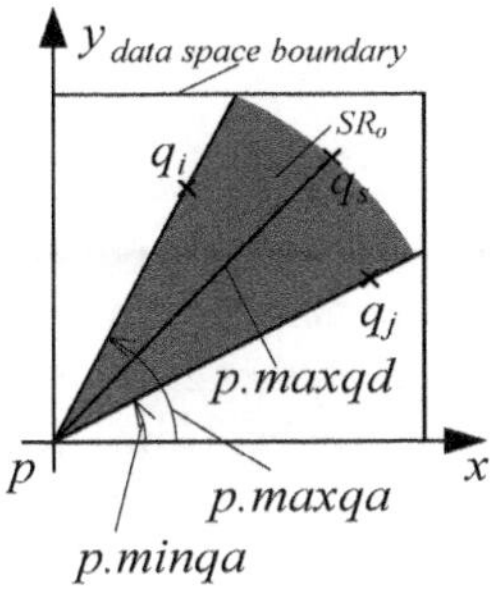

Fig. 3. Example of SR_o

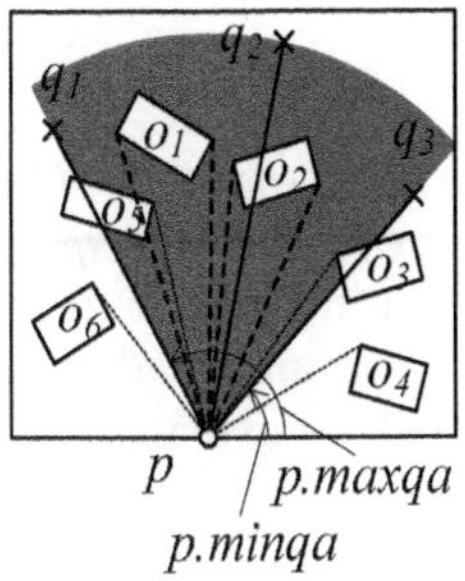

Fig. 4. Example of filtering obstacles

Before we go further into the details of our algorithm, we first enumerate the cases of obstacle impact on the visibility of GNN. The angular bound of obstacle line is applied. As depicted in Fig. 4, q_1, q_2 and q_3 are query points and o_i ($1 \le i \le 6$) are obstacles. Suppose q_2 is the farthest point to p. There are three possible cases: (i) $ol_{o_i}.maxA \le p.minqa$. (ii) $ol_{o_i}.minA \ge p.maxqa$. (iii) $[ol_{o_i}.minA,\ ol_{o_i}.maxA] \cap [p.minqa,\ p.maxqa] \ne \emptyset$. For case (i) and (ii), it is apparent that those obstacles can't affect p's visibility. E.g., obstacle o_4 ($ol_{o_4}.maxA < p.minqa$) and o_6 ($ol_{o_6}.minA > p.maxqa$). For case (iii), obstacle at least intersects with SR_o. If an obstacle partially intersects with SR_o, it definitely blocks the sight of p, such as o_5 and o_3. If an obstacle is fully contained by SR_o, it may (o_2) or may not (o_1) affect p's visibility. For this case, we should do further check with each query point q_i to confirm whether o can affect visibility of current GNN to q_i. If $[ol_o.minA,\ ol_o.maxA]$ doesn't intersect with any angle line from p to q_i (e.g., o_1), it can't affect p's visibility. Otherwise it can.

The execution framework of MTO is that whenever a new GNN is retrieved, SR_o w.r.t. current GNN is computed and obstacles are filtered from R_o. The pseudocode of MTO is given out in Algorithm 1. Data points are retrieved in a best-first manner from R_p and stored in a min heap H_p where heap entries are sorted by $\sum_{q_i \in Q} mindist(e, q_i)$ in ascending order. Here e can be either a data point or an intermediate node. When a data point is deheaped, obstacles within distance $maxdist(e, Q)$ are retrieved from R_o through function GetObs and

Algorithm 1. Multiple Traversing Obstacles (MTO)

1: $H_p \leftarrow R_p.root$
2: **while** $H_p \neq null$ **do**
3:     $e \leftarrow H_p.deheap()$
4:     **if** e is a data point entry **then** ▷ e is a GNN
5:         $Obs \leftarrow$ GETOBS$(SR_o, maxdist(e, Q))$
6:         **for** each ol_{o_i} in Obs **do**
7:             check whether ol_{o_i} blocks e
8:         **if** no obstacles in Obs block e **then return** e
9:     **else** ▷ e is an intermediate entry
10:         **for** all entries e_i in N_c **do** ▷ N_c is the child node pointed by e
11:             $H_p \leftarrow (e_i, \sum_{q_j \in Q} mindist(e_i, q_j))$

stored in a temporary set Obs (line 5). $maxdist(e, Q)$ is the maximum distance from current GNN e to q_i ($\forall q_i \in Q$). Any obstacle in Obs is considered as a candidate for further angular bound check as aforementioned three cases. For an intermediate node, all entries in e's child node with their aggregate distances are enheaped. Function GETOBS (line 5) retrieves obstacles from R_o in a best-first manner as well. For data node, obstacles are directly inserted into Obs. For intermediate node, its children nodes must be accessed if it intersects with SR_o. Due to space limitation, the pseudocode of GETOBS is omitted.

4.2 Traversing Obstacles Once Algorithm

MTO has two main disadvantages: (i) the processing time is highly dependent on the size of H_p, i.e., $|H_p|$. In the worst case, the GVNN is the last element processed by H_p, i.e., all data points must be checked. This will incur high overheads in CPU time; (ii) it accesses the same node of obstacle R*-tree R_o several times which leads to high I/O overheads.Whenever a new GNN is found, R_o needs to be traversed from the scratch in order to compute new SR_o. In this section, we propose *Traversing Obstacles Once Algorithm* (TOO) which extends the obstacle line to the MBR M of query set, utilizes it to prune both data set and obstacle set and especially traverses R_o only once.

Observe that not all of the entries in H_p are qualified candidates for GVNN. Some entries may be blocked by the obstacles having processed already. There is no need to keep such entries in H_p so as to reduce the heap size. Moreover, since obstacle line (Definition 2) can only be applied to a single query point, if obstacle line can be applied to multiple query points, or to say, the MBR of these query points, then pruning unqualified data points (or intermediate nodes) in early stage is possible. Motivated by these, we define obstacle line with respect to M.

Definition 5. *The obstacle line* ol_o^M *of an obstacle with respect to* M *is the line segment that obstructs the sight lines from all* q_i ($\forall q_i \in Q$).

Fig. 5 shows an example of the extended obstacle line. q_1 to q_4 are query points. Area painted in gray is the invisible region of M (IR_M). Similarly, the angular

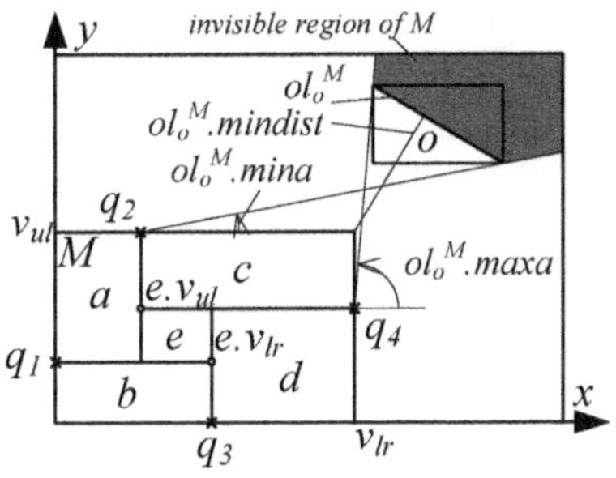

Fig. 5. Compute IR_M

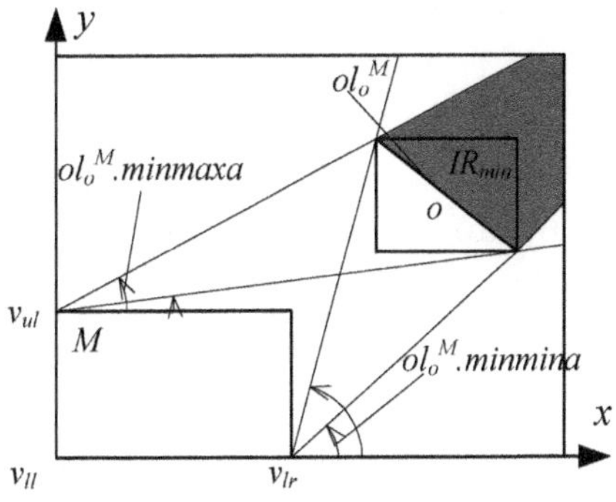

Fig. 6. Example of IR_{min}

bound of ol_o^M is $[ol_o^M.mina,\ ol_o^M.maxa]$ where $ol_o^M.mina$ and $ol_o^M.maxa$ are the minimum and maximum angle from all query points q_i to ol_o^M respectively. The distance bound of ol_o^M, denoted as $ol_o^M.mindist$, is the the minimum distance from M to ol_o^M[1]. However, computing IR_M is a non-trivial problem. Constructing each invisible region of q_i (IR_{q_i}) then finding the union of all IR_{q_i}s will surely derive IR_M. But however this method can be costly when the number of query points is large. In fact only part of query points can contribute to IR_M. We explain the details of how to compute IR_M later in this section. Here we first introduce an important conception, *Minimum Invisible Region* of M, to filter query points that contribute to IR_M.

Definition 6. *Considering the lower-left corner of M as an origin, the Minimum Invisible Region of M, IR_{min}, is a region with minimum possible area such that any point $p \in P$ located in IR_{min} is invisible to all query points.*

As depicted in Fig. 6, IR_{min} is the region painted in grey. IR_{min} includes the internal part of obstacle o. IR_{min} is formed by ol_o^M and an angular bound $[ol_o^M.minmina,\ ol_o^M.minmaxa]$. Apparently we have the following corollary.

Corollary 1. *IR_{min} must be contained by any q_i's invisible region.*

IR_{min} is used to prune both data set and obstacle set throughout the execution of TOO. Since the property of MBR doesn't guarantee that there must be a point on any corner, according to Corollary 1, IR_{min} is a *tighter* lower bound of real invisible region of M (IR_M), i.e., $IR_{min} \subseteq IR_M$. If the MBR of a node $N_p \in R_p$ is fully contained by IR_{min}, then all data points contained by N_p must be invisible to all q_i and N_p can be safely pruned. If N_p partially intersects with IR_{min}, IR_M must be retrieved to check whether N_p could contain any candidates or not. The following lemma gives out the method of how to construct IR_{min}.

Lemma 1. *Suppose the four vertices of M are v_{ll}, v_{ul}, v_{lr} and v_{ur}, i.e., the lower-left corner, upper-left corner, lower-right corner and upper-right corner.*

[1] See [7] for the details of computing minimum distance from line segment to rectangle.

Then the angular bound of IR_{min} *must be derived from two out of four corners of* M*.*

Proof. Without loss of generality, we consider the more general case that M and o do not have overlap on each dimension. Treating v_{ll} as an origin (see Fig. 6), any point q_i inside M can be regarded as first moving along positive direction of x axis then positive direction of y axis. The angular bound $q_i.minA$ and $q_i.maxA$[2] monotonously increase/decrease when only q_i's x/y coordinate grows. Hence $q_i.minA$ and $q_i.maxA$ will first increase then decrease. $q_i.minA$ ($q_i.maxA$) must reach extreme maximum and minimum value at v_{lr} and v_{ul} respectively. Then the proposed lemma holds. The proof of overlapping case is similar, we omit here. □

Lemma 1 implies a query point that contributes to IR_M should be more close to v_{ul} or v_{lr} (for case in Fig. 6). Since the monotonicity of the angular bound of points on edges, for computing IR_M, we utilize the query points on four edges of M to present our method as follows.

As depicted in Fig. 5, q_i ($1 \leq i \leq 4$) is the query point on each edge of M which is the closest one to v_{ul} or v_{lr}. In general case, suppose that there are no query points on any corner of M. Two lines which are parallel to x (y) axis are drawn from q_1 (q_2) and q_4 (q_3). Then these four lines partition M into five rectangles a, b, c, d and e. For any query point inside b and c, we have $e.v_{ul}.minA > q_2.minA$ and $e.v_{lr}.maxA < q_3.maxA$. Then there is no need to check any query point inside e. Coming to rectangle a and d, since for any query point q_i inside a (including points on the edges), we have $q_i.minA > M.v_{ul}.minA$. Similarly for any query point q_j inside d (including points on the edges), we have $q_j.maxA < M.v_{lr}.maxA$. Therefore finding a query point inside a with minimum $q_i.minA$ and a query point inside d with maximum $q_j.maxA$ will assuredly lead to IR_M.

Until now, the second disadvantage of MTO is not resolved yet, i.e., how to access R_o as less as possible. We take a method which incrementally retrieves obstacles. A basic observation is that obstacles closer to M are more possible to affect the visibility of M than farther ones. Suppose $p(\in P)$ is a certain GNN of Q. Nodes retrieved from R_o are stored in a min heap H_o. Entries in H_o are sorted in ascending order by their *mindist* value w.r.t. M. If an obstacle o with $mindist(o, M) \geq \sum_{q_i \in Q} dist(p, q_i)/|Q|$, then o can't affect M's visibility. But however, not all obstacles within distance $\sum_{q_i \in Q} dist(p, q_i)/|Q|$ should be taken into account. Only obstacles with $mindist(o, M) < mindist(p, M)$ can exactly take effect on M's visibility. If p is blocked and a new GNN is retrieved, then obstacles left in H_o within larger distance threshold are deheaped[3]. Because obstacles within smaller distance have already been processed, this makes it possible to traverse R_o only once to retrieve GVNN, which remedies the second deficiency of MTO.

[2] Without special explanation, in the rest of this paper, the angular bound of query point (including four corners of M) is the same meaning as the angular bound of obstacle line w.r.t. a single query point.

[3] Any GNN fetched behind p must have larger aggregate value.

The basic processing step of TOO is when a new GNN is retrieved, obstacles with distance no larger than average summed value w.r.t. current GNN are fetched from obstacle set, IR_{min} and IR_M are updated accordingly. If this GNN is not blocked by updated IR_M, then output this one. Otherwise it is removed and the next round begins. The main procedure of TOO is from line 1 to 13 in Algorithm 2. Nodes retrieved from R_p is stored in a min heap H_p. Entries in H_p are sorted in ascending order of their summed *mindist* value w.r.t. M. Two lists L_M and L_{min} are used to store obstacle lines which make up IR_M and IR_{min} respectively. L_o is a list for storing obstacles obtained by function RETROBS from R_o. When a data point is deheaped, derived distance constraints ($e.key/|Q|$ and $mindist(e, M)$) are passed to RETROBS. L_M and L_{min} are updated with respect to L_o. If e passes the visibility check (line 8), the whole algorithm halts. Otherwise entries (data point or intermediate node) in H_p which are blocked by current IR_{min} are removed. When an intermediate entry is encountered, insert it into H_p only if it is not blocked by IR_{min}. The procedure of updating IR_M and IR_{min} is similar to EVC in [5]. Due to space limitation, we don't discuss the details.

Function RETROBS (line 14) in Algorithm 2 describes the procedure of retrieving obstacle candidates. List $L_o^{'}$ is used to store obstacles with distance between $mindist(e, M)$ and $e.key/|Q|$. When an obstacle is deheaped, if it is within distance $mindist(e, M)$, then insert it into L_o. Otherwise insert it into $L_o^{'}$. When the next obstacle is encountered, if the new $mindist(e, M)$ value is no larger than the former one, then nothing has to be changed. Otherwise, shift obstacles from $L_o^{'}$ to L_o with respect to new $e.key/|Q|$ value (line 19). When an intermediate node is deheaped, if it is not blocked by IR_{min}, we enheap it into H_o immediately.

We judge whether an intermediate node or an object (obstacle and data point) is visible to M (line 8, 12 and 24) as follows. If it is fully contained by IR_{min}, all children nodes under it (including itself) must be invisible to all query points. An intermediate node must be accessed if it is not completely located in IR_{min}. IR_M is only used to assert whether a data point is a qualified GVNN.

5 Experimental Study

In this section, we study the performance of MTO and TOO under different parameter settings. Four real data sets, Cities, Rivers, CA and LA[4], are used. Cities and CA are 2D points which represent 5,922 cities and villages in Greece and 62,556 locations in California. Rivers and LA are 2D rectangles which represent 24,650 MBRs of rivers in Greece and 131,461 MBRs of streets in LA. All the points and rectangles are normalized to a [0, 10,000]×[0, 10,000] square. Two different combinations of data point set P and obstacle set O, CR and CL, which represent (P, O)=(Cities, Rivers) and (CA, LA) respectively, are tested. Both data points and obstacles are indexed by R*-tree with page size 1KByte. We run 100 queries and all results are average performances. The MBR of each

[4] http://www.rtreepotral.org

Algorithm 2. Traversing Obstacles Once (TOO)

$H_p \leftarrow R_p.root$
$H_o \leftarrow R_o.root$
while $H_p \neq null$ **do**
    $e \leftarrow H_p.deheap()$
    if e is a data point **then**
        RETROBS(H_o, $e.key/|Q|$, $mindist(e, M)$)
        update L_M and L_{min} w.r.t. L_o
        if e is not contained by IR_M **then return** e
        else remove invisible entries from H_p contained by IR_{min}
    else ▷ e is an intermediate entry
        for all entries e_i in N_c **do** ▷ N_c is the child node pointed by e
            if e_i is not contained by IR_{min} **then**
                $H_p \leftarrow (e_i, \sum_{q_j \in Q} mindist(e_i, q_j))$

function RETROBS(H_o, $e.key/|Q|$, $mindist(e, M)$)
    while $H_o \neq null$ **do**
        $e' \leftarrow H_o.deheap()$
        if $e'.key < e.key/|Q|$ **then**
            if e' is an obstacle **then**
                $L_o \leftarrow L_o^{'}$
                if $e'.key < mindist(e, M)$ **then** $L_o \leftarrow e'$
                else $L_o^{'} \leftarrow e'$
            else
                for all entries $e_i^{'}$ in $N_c^{'}$ **do** ▷ $N_c^{'}$ is the child node pointed by e'
                    if $e_i^{'}$ is not contained by IR_{min} **and** $e_i^{'}.key < e.key/|Q|$ **then**
                        $H_o \leftarrow (e_i^{'}, mindist(e_i^{'}, M))$
        else break

query set with area M is randomly generated in normalized data space. Here $M = Area$(MBR of Q)$/Area$(data space)$\times$100%. Query points are uniformly distributed in the MBR of query set. Algorithms are implemented in Java. All experiments are executed on a machine with 2GB memory and a 2.93Hz Intel Core2 Duo CPU. Due to space limitation, only the most important experiments are involved.

The first experiment studies the effect of $|Q|$, i.e., the number of query points. M is fixed at 10%. From Fig. 7(a) and Fig. 7(b), we can see clearly that the CPU time of both MTO and TOO increases when $|Q|$ varies. The performance of TOO varies linearly with $|Q|$ while MTO deteriorates rapidly when $|Q|$ is larger than 64. The reason is MTO can't prune entries in H_p and must access R_o multiple times. Since TOO utilizes IR_{min} to prune data points and intermediate nodes and accessed R_o only once, the processing time is less than MTO by at least an order of magnitude.

The second experiment is to test the impact of M on MTO and TOO. M varies from 2% to 30%. $|Q|$ is fixed at 64. In Fig. 8(a), M has negligible impact

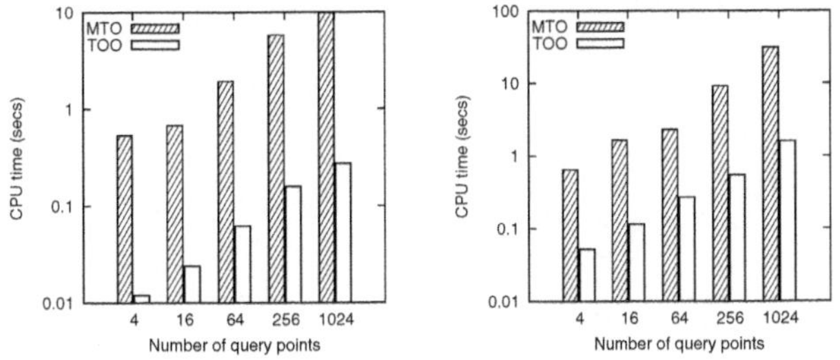

(a) CR (b) CL

Fig. 7. Effect of $|Q|$

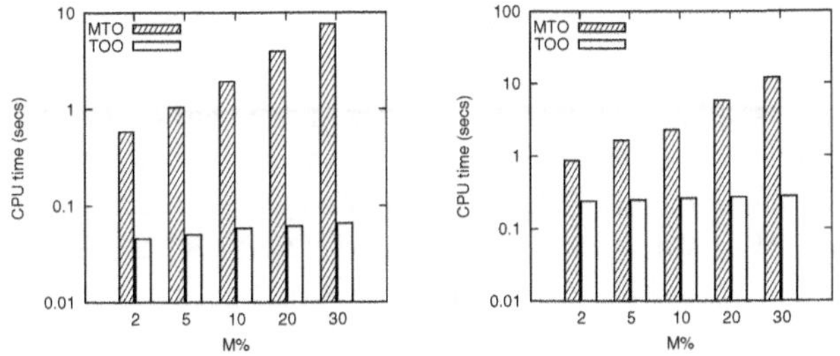

(a) CR (b) CL

Fig. 8. Effect of M

on TOO's processing time. But the CPU time of MTO increases with M. TOO beats MTO in CPU time by pruning on both data set and obstacle set. Fig. 8(b) presents similar result as Fig. 8(a).

The last experiment checks the effect of using IR_{min}. $|Q|$ varies from 4 to 1024. M is fixed at 10%. The combination of P and O is CR. When checking the visibility of M, two basic methods are taken into account in this experiment. The first one is only using IR_M to filter both data nodes and intermediate nodes (of either R_p or R_o). The second method is what TOO adopts (Section 4.2). TOOM and TOOMIN in Fig. 9 represent the first and the second method respectively. The CPU time (in Fig. 9(a)) of TOOMIN is almost 30% to 40% less than TOOM. I/O cost (in Fig. 9(b)) of TOOMIN is about 5% higher than TOOM. The decrement in CPU time of TOOMIN is caused by the computation method of IR_{min}. IR_{min} takes at most two corner points of the MBR of query set while IR_M needs filtering on query points. The increment in I/O cost of TOOMIN is incurred by $IR_{min} \subseteq IR_M$. An intermediate node intersecting with IR_{min} may be fully contained by IR_M. From this experiment, we prove that it is worth to introduce IR_{min} into TOO.

In summary, TOO is more efficient and scalable than MTO in both efficiency and effectiveness.

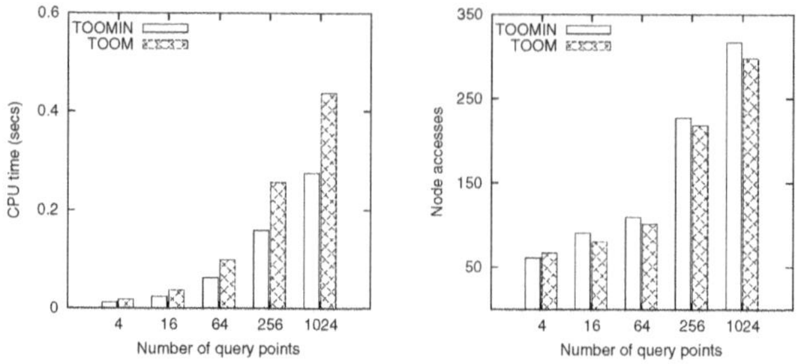

(a) CPU time (b) I/O count

Fig. 9. Effect of IR_{min} (CR)

6 Conclusion

In this paper, we study a new query type which is called GVNN in term. Two algorithms, MTO and TOO, are proposed to solve GVNN. MTO resolves GVNN from data point aspect while TOO does from query point angle. MTO reduces the search space of obstacles w.r.t. current GNN. TOO extends obstacle line to the MBR of query set so as to construct IR_{min} for pruning both data set and obstacle set. TOO accesses obstacle R*-tree only once. Experiments show that TOO is more efficient than MTO.

References

1. Gao, Y., Zheng, B., Lee, W., Chen, G.: Continuous visible nearest neighbor queries. In: EDBT (2009)
2. Gao, Y., Zheng, B.: Continuous obstructed nearest neighbor queries in spatial databases. In: SIGMOD (2009)
3. Zhang, J., Papadias, D., Mouratidis, K., Zhu, M.: Spatial Queries in the Presence of Obstacles. In: Bertino, E., Christodoulakis, S., Plexousakis, D., Christophides, V., Koubarakis, M., Böhm, K., Ferrari, E. (eds.) EDBT 2004. LNCS, vol. 2992, pp. 366–384. Springer, Heidelberg (2004)
4. Nutanong, S., Tanin, E., Zhang, R.: Visible Nearest Neighbor Queries. In: Kotagiri, R., Radha Krishna, P., Mohania, M., Nantajeewarawat, E. (eds.) DASFAA 2007. LNCS, vol. 4443, pp. 876–883. Springer, Heidelberg (2007)
5. Gao, Y., Zheng, B., Chen, G., Lee, W., Lee, K.C.K., Li, Q.: Visible Reverse k-Nearest Neighbor Query Processing in Spatial Databases. IEEE Trans. Knowl. Data Eng. in TKDE (2009)
6. Papadias, D., Shen, Q., Tao, Y., Mouratidis, K.: Group Nearest Neighbor Queries. In: ICDE (2004)
7. Frentzos, E., Gratsias, K., Pelekis, N., Theodoridis, Y.: Nearest Neighbor Search on Moving Object Trajectories. In: Bauzer Medeiros, C., Egenhofer, M.J., Bertino, E. (eds.) SSTD 2005. LNCS, vol. 3633, pp. 328–345. Springer, Heidelberg (2005)
8. Beckmann, N., Kriegel, H., Schneider, R., Seeger, B.: The R*-Tree: An Efficient and Robust Access Method for Points and Rectangles. In: SIGMOD Conference (1990)
9. Zhang, W., Lin, X., Cheema, M.A., Zhang, Y., Wang, W.: Quantile-Based KNN Over Multi-Valued Objects. In: ICDE (2010)

iPoc: A Polar Coordinate Based Indexing Method for Nearest Neighbor Search in High Dimensional Space*

Zhang Liu[1], Chaokun Wang[2,3,4], Peng Zou[2], Wei Zheng[2], and Jianmin Wang[2,3,4]

[1] Department of Computer Science and Technology, Tsinghua University
[2] School of Software, Tsinghua University, Beijing 100084, China
[3] Tsinghua National Laboratory for Information Science and Technology
[4] Key Laboratory for Information System Security, Ministry of Education
{liuzhang08,zoup04,zhengw04}@mails.tsinghua.edu.cn,
{chaokun,jimwang}@tsinghua.edu.cn

Abstract. K-nearest neighbor (KNN) search in high dimensional space is essential for database applications, especially multimedia database applications, because images and audio clips are always modeled as high dimensional vectors. However, performance of existing indexing methods degrades dramatically as the dimensionality increases. In this paper, we propose a novel polar coordinate based indexing method, called iPoc, for efficient KNN search in high dimensional space. First, data space is initially partitioned into hypersphere regions, and then each hypersphere is further refined into hypersectors via hyperspherical surface clustering. After that, a series of local polar coordinate systems can be derived from hypersectors, taking advantage of the geometric characters of hypersectors. During search processing, iPoc can effectively prune query-unrelated data points by estimating the lower and upper bounds in both radial coordinate and angle coordinate. Furthermore, we design a key mapping scheme to merge keys measured by independent local polar coordinates into the global polar coordinates. Finally, the global polar coordinates are indexed by a traditional 2-dimensional spatial index, e.g., R-tree. Extensive experiments on real audio datasets and synthetic datasets confirm the effectiveness and efficiency of our proposal and prove that iPoc is more efficient than the existing high dimensional KNN search methods.

Keywords: Nearest neighbor search, high dimensional index.

1 Introduction

K-nearest neighbor (KNN) search in high dimensional space is important in database applications, e.g., content based multimedia retrieval. Because of the

* The work is supported by the National Natural Science Foundation of China (No. 60803016), the National Basic Research Program of China (No. 2007CB310802) and the National High Technology Research and Development Program of China (No. 2008AA042301).

L. Chen et al. (Eds.): WAIM 2010, LNCS 6184, pp. 345–356, 2010.

complexity of multimedia content, images and audio clips are always modeled as high-dimensional vectors. However, performance of traditional indexing approaches, e.g., K-d-tree [1], degrades dramatically as the dimensionality increases. This phenomenon is the well-known *curse of dimensionality* [2]. There is an extensive literature [3,4,5,6,7,8,9] on the high dimensional KNN search problem, among which iDistance [10] performs as the best algorithm for exact K-nearest neighbor search [3]. iDistance indexes the Euclidean distances between data points and reference points with B-tree. However, the Euclidean distance does not have great discrimination when the dimensionality is high, because distances between any pairs of points tend to be identical. Therefore, indexing distance cannot provide great discrimination as the dimensionality increases.

Motivated by this, we propose iPoc, a **PO**lar **C**oordinate based **I**ndexing method for K-neighbor search, which adopts the polar coordinate as the indexing key of high dimensional data. The polar coordinate system locates a point with both distance and angle metrics, which can improve the discrimination of points in high dimensional space. To overcome the sparseness of high dimensional data, iPoc uses a data distribution based space partitioning approach. More specifically, data points are roughly clustered into hyperspherical regions via a generic spatial clustering algorithm, e.g., K-means or K-medoids. And then each hypersphere is further separated into hypersectors using a spherical surface clustering algorithm which takes advantage of the spherical projection. Besides, a polar coordinate system can be naturally derived in each hypersector because of the geometrical character of sectors, i.e., the vertex of sector is the *pole* and the axis of sector plays a role of the *direction* in the derived polar coordinate system. Based on the hypersector space partitioning and polar coordinate positioning, the pruning algorithms of iPoc can effectively prune unrelated data points during KNN query processing.

The primary contributions of this paper are as follows:

- We propose a novel hypersector based space partitioning method which can effectively improve the pruning performance in high dimensional space.
- We introduce polar coordinates to high dimensional indexing, which enhances the discrimination of indexing key when the dimensionality is high.
- We design a key mapping scheme, by which local keys of points in different key space can be merged into a global 2-dimensional key space. The key mapping scheme enables iPoc to index all high dimensional data by existent commercial spatial indexing methods, e.g., R-tree.
- We develop a pruning algorithm which can effectively estimate the lower and upper bounds of query regions. Therefore, most of the data points which are not related to the query can be pruned effectively.
- We conduct extensive experiments on real and synthetic datasets and experimental results show that iPoc outperforms the state-of-the-art high dimensional indexing methods.

The rest of this paper is organized as follows. In Section 2, some useful concepts and definitions are introduced. Section 3 details our indexing approach composed of the hypersector based data space partitioning and the polar coordinate based indexing. We present the query processing issues including bounds estimation and the KNN query algorithm in Section 4. Experimental results are analyzed in Section 5. Finally, we review the related work and conclude this paper in Section 6 and Section 7, respectively.

2 Preliminaries

In this section, we introduce the foundational concepts and definitions. Firstly, both distance and angle metrics in high dimensional space are reviewed, based on which we define the hypersphere and hypersector. After that, we details the polar coordinate system in high dimensional space.

Distance and Angle Metric: In this paper, we adopt the Euclidean distance as the *distance* metric. Given two points p_1, p_2 in an n-dimensional space, the distance between p_1 and p_2 can be represented as $d(p_1, p_2) = \|p_2 - p_1\|$, where $\|\cdot\|$ denotes the length of an n-dimensional vector. The *angle* between two direction vectors in an n-dimensional space is defined as the arc-cosine of the dot product between the two unit direction vectors. Formally, in an n-dimensional space, given a reference point p_o, two points p_1, p_2 ($p_1 \neq p_o$ and $p_2 \neq p_o$), the angle between directions $\overrightarrow{p_o p_1} = p_1 - p_o$ and $\overrightarrow{p_o p_2} = p_2 - p_o$, denoted as $\Theta(\overrightarrow{p_o p_1}, \overrightarrow{p_o p_2})$ or $\angle p_1 p_o p_2$, is defined as

$$\Theta(\overrightarrow{p_o p_1}, \overrightarrow{p_o p_2}) = \arccos \frac{(p_1 - p_o) \cdot (p_2 - p_o)}{\|p_1 - p_o\| \cdot \|p_2 - p_o\|}. \tag{1}$$

Polar Coordinate System: The polar coordinate system is a 2-dimensional system where coordinates of a point are determined by a fixed point and a fixed direction. Formally, given a fixed point c, a fixed direction vector ζ in an n-dimensional space, a polar coordinate system $\Psi(c, \zeta)$ can be derived where c is the *pole* and ζ is the *direction*. For any point p in $\Psi(c, \zeta)$, the polar coordinate of p is defined as (λ, θ), where λ is the distance from c to p ($\lambda = \|p - c\|$); θ represents the angle between $\overrightarrow{cp}$ and ζ ($\theta = \Theta(\overrightarrow{cp}, \zeta)$).

Hypersphere and Hypersector: Now we introduce two basic shapes in the n-dimensional space, i.e., hypersphere and hypersector, which are essential for the space partitioning of iPoc.

Definition 1 (Hypersphere). *In an n-dimensional space, given a non-negative real number r, a point c, a hypersphere, denoted as $\mathcal{S}^n$, is defined as the set of points whose distances from c are less or equal to r, i.e., $\mathcal{S}^n = \{p \mid p \in \mathbb{R}^n, \|p - c\| \leq r\}$. Especially, $\mathcal{S}^1$ is a pair of points; $\mathcal{S}^2$ and $\mathcal{S}^3$ represent a circle and a sphere respectively. Formally, an n-dimensional hypersphere $\mathcal{S}^n$ is a 2-tuple,*

$$\mathcal{S}^n := (c, r), \tag{2}$$

where c is the center of $\mathcal{S}^n$ and r is the radius of $\mathcal{S}^n$.

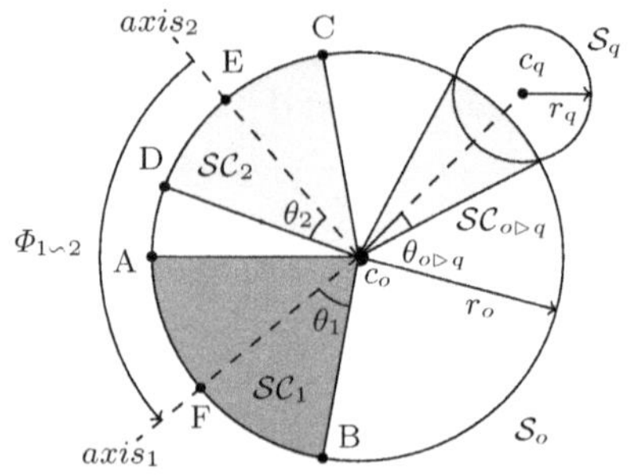

Fig. 1. Sphere

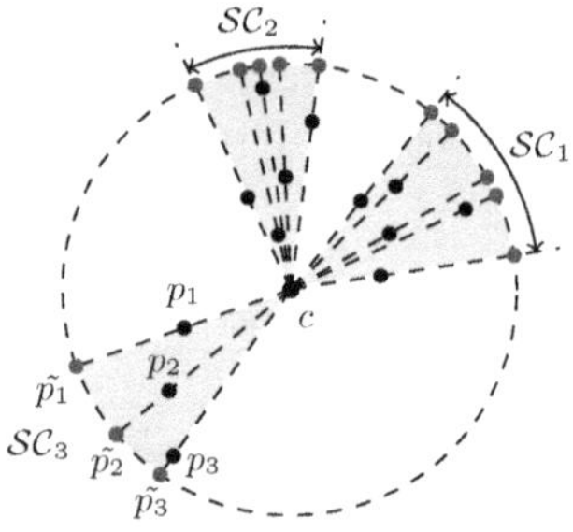

Fig. 2. Spherical surface projection

For convenience, we use $\mathcal{S}$ to represent a hypersphere when the dimensionality of data space is clear in the context. Moreover, for simplicity, we use the name *sphere* to refer to a hypersphere in general.

Definition 2 (Hypersector). *In an n-dimensional space, given an original point c, a reference point direction p_r, a non-negative real number r, an angle θ, a hypersector, denoted as $\mathcal{SC}$, is defined as the set of points whose angles w.r.t. axis, $\overrightarrow{cp_r} = (p_r - c)$, are less or equal to θ and distances w.r.t. c are less or equal to r. Formally, a hypersector is represented as a 4-tuple,*

$$\mathcal{SC} := (c, axis, \theta, r), \tag{3}$$

where c is the vertex of hypersector, $axis$ the axis ($axis = \overrightarrow{cp_r}$), r the radius, θ the angle of hypersector, $0 \leq \theta \leq \pi$.

As shown in Fig. 1, sphere $\mathcal{S}_o$, whose center point and radius are denoted as c_o and r_o, contains the sector $\mathcal{SC}_1$ (dark gray) with vertex c_o, axis $\overrightarrow{c_oF}$, angle θ_1 and radius r_o.

Definition 3 (Association Hypersector). *Given two overlapped spheres $\mathcal{S}_1(c_1, r_1)$, $\mathcal{S}_2(c_2, r_2)$ in an n-dimensional space, an association sector of $\mathcal{S}_1$ towards $\mathcal{S}_2$, denoted as $\mathcal{SC}_{1\rhd 2}$, is the minimal sector which covers the overlapped part of $\mathcal{S}_1$ and $\mathcal{S}_2$, i.e., $\mathcal{S}_1 \cap \mathcal{S}_2$. The vertex of $\mathcal{SC}_{1\rhd 2}$ is c_1 and the radius of $\mathcal{SC}_{1\rhd 2}$ equals to r_1. Besides, $\mathcal{S}_1$ is called the local sphere of $\mathcal{SC}_{1\rhd 2}$; $\mathcal{S}_2$ is defined as the outer sphere of $\mathcal{SC}_{1\rhd 2}$.*

As shown in Fig. 1, $\mathcal{SC}_{o\rhd q}$ is the association sector of $\mathcal{S}_o$ towards $\mathcal{S}_q$, denoted as $\mathcal{SC}_{o\rhd q}$. The angle of $\mathcal{SC}_{o\rhd q}$, denoted as $\theta_{o\rhd q}$, can be calculated by

$$\theta_{o\rhd q} = \begin{cases} 2\pi, & d(c_o, c_q) < r_q \\ \pi, & d(c_o, c_q) = r_q \\ \arccos \frac{{r_o}^2 + d(c_o,c_q)^2 - {r_q}^2}{2 \cdot r_q \cdot d(c_o,c_q)}, & d(c_o, c_q) > r_q \text{ and } {r_o}^2 + {r_q}^2 \geq d(c_o, c_q)^2 \\ \arcsin \frac{r_q}{d(c_o,c_q)}, & \text{otherwise} \end{cases} . \tag{4}$$

Definition 4 (Sector Distance). *Give two sectors* $\mathcal{SC}_1$ $(c, axis_1, \theta_1, r)$, $\mathcal{S}_2$ $(c, axis_2, \theta_2, r)$ *in a sphere* $\mathcal{S}$ (c, r)*, the sector distance between* $\mathcal{SC}_1$ *and* $\mathcal{SC}_2$*, denoted as* $\Phi_{1\smile 2}$*, is defined as the angle between* $axis_2$ *and* $axis_2$*. Formally,*

$$\Phi_{1\smile 2} = \Theta(axis_1, axis_2). \tag{5}$$

Considering the sectors $\mathcal{SC}_1$ and $\mathcal{SC}_2$ in Fig. 1, the sector distance between $\mathcal{SC}_1$ and $\mathcal{SC}_2$ is the degree of angle $\angle Ec_oF$.

3 Indexing Approach

In this section, we present the space partitioning strategy of iPoc, based on which a polar coordinate system is derived in each region. After that, an indexing key mapping scheme is proposed to merge all polar coordinates in different independent polar coordinate systems to global coordinates.

Algorithm 1. PARTITION-INDEXING($\mathcal{P}$)

Input : $\mathcal{P}$ — the set of all n-dimensional data points;

$\{P_0, P_1, \ldots, P_{m-1}\} \leftarrow$ Clustering $\mathcal{P}$ into m groups;
for each data point group P_i **do**
  $c_i \leftarrow$ Calculate the cluster center of data point set P_i;
  $r_i \leftarrow$ Get the maximal distance from c_i to points in P_i;
  Create sphere $\mathcal{S}_i$ using c_i as center and r_i as radius;
  $\tilde{P}_i \leftarrow$ Project all points in P_i to the surface of $\mathcal{S}_i$;
  Clustering projected data points in $\tilde{P}_i$ into s_i groups $\{\tilde{P}_{i,0}, \ldots, \tilde{P}_{i,s_i-1}\}$ and points in P_i are divided into $\{P_{i,0}, \ldots, P_{i,s_i-1}\}$ according to the clustering result of their projected counterparts;
  for each data point group $\tilde{P}_{i,j}$ **do**
    $c_{i.j} \leftarrow$ Calculate the center point of $\tilde{P}_{i,j}$;
    $axis_{i,j} \leftarrow c_{i,j} - c_i$;
    for each point p_k in $P_{i,j}$ **do**
      $(\lambda_k, \theta_k) \leftarrow$ Calculate the radius and angle coordinates of p_k using c_i as pole and $axis_{i,j}$ as polar axis;
    $\theta_{i,j} \leftarrow$ Find the maximal polar angle in $\{\theta_k \mid p_k \in P_{i,j}\}$;
    Create sector $\mathcal{SC}_{i.j}$ with vertex c_i, polar axis $axis_{i,j}$ and angle $\theta_{i.j}$;
    INDEX-DATA($P_{i,j}$, $\mathcal{SC}_{i.j}$);

3.1 Data Distribution Based Space Partitioning

To eliminate effects of sparseness of high dimensional space, iPoc divides data space into multiple spherical regions according to the data distribution, guaranteeing that any point in the data space belongs to at least one spherical region.

First, all data points in the entire dataset $\mathcal{P}$ are clustered into m groups, $P_0, \ldots, P_{m-1}$, by a generic clustering algorithm, e.g., K-means. For each data points group P_i, we want to create a sphere $\mathcal{S}_i$ which covers all data points in P_i. To simplify the process of creating spheres, the centroid of P_i can be used as the center point of $\mathcal{S}_i$ and the radius of $\mathcal{S}_i$, denoted as r_i, is the maximal distance from data points to c_i.

To further improve the index resolution of iPoc, each spherical region is separated into s_i sectors. All sectors in a sphere share the same vertex c_i and radius r_i. As shown in Fig. 2, all points in a sector are projected to a single sphere in the spherical surface space. Therefore, we take advantage of the spherical projection to create sectors. First, all data points in P_i are projected to the spherical surface of $\mathcal{S}_i$. The projected data point corresponding to p_k is denoted as $\tilde{p}_k$ (ref. to Fig. 2) and the set of projected points is represented as $\tilde{P}_i$. After that, we cluster projected points in $\tilde{P}_i$ using K-means clustering algorithm with L_2 distance metric, and the result data point groups are $\{\tilde{P}_{i,0}, \ldots, \tilde{P}_{i,s_i-1}\}$, where s_i is the number of groups clustered from $\tilde{P}_i$. The cluster center of the projected point set $\tilde{P}_{i,j}$ is denoted as $c_{i,j}$. Thereby, a local polar coordinate system is built with the pole c_i and direction $\overrightarrow{c_i c_{i,j}}$, denoted as $\Psi(c_i, \overrightarrow{c_i c_{i,j}})$. Coordinates of all points in P_i are determined by $\Psi(c_i, \overrightarrow{c_i c_{i,j}})$. In angle coordinates of all points in P_i, we find the maximal one as $\theta_{i,j}$. The sector $\mathcal{SC}_{i,j}$ covering all points in $P_{i,j}$ are created with origin point c_i, axis $\overrightarrow{c_i c_{i,j}}$, radius r_i and angle $\theta_{i,j}$.

3.2 Polar Coordinate Based Indexing

After the space partitioning, each point must belong to one and only one sector. Meanwhile, every sector belongs to one sphere. To identify different spheres and sectors, a unique identifier *cid* is assigned to each sphere. Each sector is also allocated an identifier *sid* which is unique in all identifiers of sectors belonging to the same sphere. Therefore, the 2-tuple (cid, sid) determines a unique sector and refers to one local polar coordinate system $\Psi(cid, sid)$. Formally, the position of a data point p is determined by a 4-tuple,

$$\kappa_p := (cid, sid, \lambda, \theta), \tag{6}$$

where *cid* is the identifier of the sphere which covers p, *sid* the identifier of the sector which determines the local polar coordinate system, λ the radial coordinate of p in the polar coordinate system $\Psi(cid, sid)$, θ the angle coordinate of p in $\Psi(cid, sid)$.

Because the local key κ_p is independent of keys in other polar coordinate systems, it is necessary to merge local polar coordinates to a global coordinate. Therefore, we develop a key mapping scheme. Given a point p with local key $\kappa_p(cid, sid, \lambda, \theta)$, the global key corresponding to κ_p is defined as $\kappa'_p := (\theta', \lambda')$,

$$\begin{aligned} \theta' &= \theta + sid \cdot \pi, \\ \lambda' &= \lambda + cid \cdot \Lambda, \end{aligned} \tag{7}$$

where θ' is the global angle coordinate; λ' represents the global radial coordinate and Λ is the scale factor of distance which should be larger than the maximal radius of all spheres. Besides, the range of θ is $[0, \pi]$. After key mapping, the global key κ'_p can be indexed by a 2-dimensional index, e.g., R-tree.

4 *K*-Nearest Neighbor Query Processing

In this section, we discuss the query processing issues. The pruning capability of iPoc, i.e., the upper and lower bounds estimation, is analyzed first. After that, we focus on the kNN search algorithm of iPoc.

4.1 Pruning

Potential KNN results are points which locate in the intersection of the data sphere $\mathcal{S}_i$ and the query sphere $\mathcal{S}_q$, i.e., $\mathcal{S}_i \cap \mathcal{S}_q$. There are 4 different intersection cases of the data sphere $\mathcal{S}_i$ and the query sphere $\mathcal{S}_q$: (1) Apart; (2) Wrapped; (3) Partial overlapped, and (4) Contained. Note that *Wrapped* is the case when the entire $\mathcal{S}_i$ is wrapped by $\mathcal{S}_q$. And *Contained* means the entire query sphere is wrapped by $\mathcal{S}_i$. Boundaries of both radial and angle coordinates are estimated as follows.

Lower and Upper Bound of Radial Coordinate: The upper bound of radial coordinate, denoted as $\ell_{\max}$, equals to the radius of the $\mathcal{S}_i$ — r_i, if the query sphere $\mathcal{S}_q$ is partial overlapped with $\mathcal{S}_i$; and $\ell_{\max}$ will be tighter if $\mathcal{S}_i$ contains $\mathcal{S}_q$. The lower bound of radial coordinate, denoted as $\ell_{\min}$ is decided by the relationship between the center of $\mathcal{S}_i$, c_i, and the query sphere $\mathcal{S}_q$.

$$\begin{aligned} \ell_{\min}(\mathcal{S}_i, \mathcal{S}_q) &= \max(d(c_i, c_q) - r_q,\ 0) \\ \ell_{\max}(\mathcal{S}_i, \mathcal{S}_q) &= \min(d(c_i, c_q) + r_q,\ r_i) \end{aligned} \tag{8}$$

Lower and Upper Bound of Angle Coordinate: Similar to the upper bound of radial coordinate, the upper bound of angle coordinate, denoted as $\theta_{\max}$, is the angle of data sector, $\theta_{i,j}$, if $\mathcal{SC}_{i \triangleright q}$ intersects with the conical surface of $\mathcal{SC}_{i,j}$; Otherwise, θ_{max} equals to $\Phi_{(i \triangleright q) \backsim (i,j)} + \theta_{i \triangleright q}$. The lower bound of angle coordinate, denoted as $\theta_{\min}$, is decided by whether the association sector $\mathcal{SC}_{i \triangleright q}$ contains the axis of the data sector, $axis_{i,j}$.

$$\begin{aligned} \theta_{\min}(\mathcal{SC}_{i,j}, \mathcal{SC}_{l \triangleright q}) &= \max(\Phi_{(i \triangleright q) \backsim (i,j)} - \theta_{i \triangleright q},\ 0) \\ \theta_{\max}(\mathcal{SC}_{i,j}, \mathcal{SC}_{l \triangleright q}) &= \min(\Phi_{(i \triangleright q) \backsim (i,j)} + \theta_{i \triangleright q},\ \theta_{i,j}) \end{aligned} \tag{9}$$

4.2 *K*-Nearest Neighbor Search Algorithm

In this section, we present the *K*-nearest neighbor(KNN) search algorithm of iPoc, as illustrated in Alg. 2. First, both R-tree index and information of data spheres and data sectors are loaded from the index file. The radius of query sphere is initialized, i.e., $r_q = \mu \cdot r_0$, where r_0 is the distance from query point q to the center of the nearest data sphere, and $\mu = 0.5$ in practice. After that, the overlapping types of data sphere $\mathcal{S}_i$ and query sphere $\mathcal{S}_q$ is determined and data spheres which do not intersect with the $\mathcal{S}_q$ are pruned. For the data spheres which intersect with $\mathcal{S}_q$, the association sectors towards $\mathcal{S}_q$ are created to calculate bounds of radial coordinate, $\ell_{\min}$ and $\ell_{\max}$ (ref. to Equ. 8). For each data sector in $\mathcal{S}_i$, the lower and upper bounds of angle coordinate, $\theta_{\min}$ and $\theta_{\max}$, are determined (ref. to Equ. 9). Therefore, the query range can be bounded as a rectangle $\rho((\ell_{\min}, \theta_{\min}), (\ell_{\max}, \theta_{\max}))$ in the polar coordinate system embedded in $\mathcal{SC}_{i,j}$. After that, we covert the coordinates of ρ to global coordinates representation ρ' according to Equ. 7. All rectangular queries ρ' are stored in a query list Q for batch query in the R-tree index. Finally, queries in Q are processed by the R-tree index and result points are verified, filtering all points whose distances from q are larger than r_q. If the number of points which pass the verification is less than K, the query radius r_q increases by Δr and the query process continues. Otherwise, all verified points are ranked by the distance from q in an ascending order and the algorithm returns the first K points.

Algorithm 2. KNN-SEARCH(q, k)

Input : q — the n-dimensional query point;
k — the number of the nearest neighbor result;
Output : $\mathcal{P}_{result}$ — k nearest neighbors results;

$tree, \{\mathcal{S}_0, \mathcal{S}_1, \ldots, \mathcal{S}_{m-1}\} \leftarrow$ Load R-tree and sphere list;
for each sphere $\mathcal{S}_i$ **do**
  $d_i \leftarrow$ Calculate the distance from the center point of $\mathcal{S}_i$ to query point q;
  $\{\mathcal{SC}_{i,0}, \mathcal{SC}_{i,1}, \ldots, \mathcal{SC}_{i,s_i-1}\} \leftarrow$ Load hypersector list;
Initial query radius $r_q \leftarrow \mu \cdot \min\{d_i \mid 0 \leq i < m\}$;
$\mathcal{S}_q \leftarrow$ Create query sphere $S(q, r_q)$;
while $|P_{result}| < k$ **do**
  Initial query list Q;
  for each sphere $\mathcal{S}_i$ **do**
    $overlaptype \leftarrow$ Determine the overlap type of data sphere $\mathcal{S}_i$ and query sphere $\mathcal{S}_q$;
    if $overlaptypc = Apart$ **then**
      continue;
    $(\mathcal{SC}_{i \triangleright q}, \ell_{max}, \ell_{\min}) \leftarrow$ Calculate the upper and lower bounds w.r.t. distance from the center point of sphere $\mathcal{S}_i$;
    for each sector $\mathcal{SC}_{i,j}$ belong to sphere $\mathcal{S}_i$ **do**
      $(\theta_{\min}, \theta_{\max}) \leftarrow$ Determine the upper and lower bounds w.r.t. angle in $\mathcal{SC}_{i,j}$;
      $\kappa_{low} \leftarrow (i, j, \ell_{\min}, \theta_{\min})$; $\kappa_{high} \leftarrow (i, j, \ell_{\max}, \theta_{\max})$;
      $\kappa'_{low} \leftarrow$ ENCODE-KEY(κ_{low}); $\kappa'_{high} \leftarrow$ ENCODE-KEY(κ_{high});
      Add rectangle query $\rho(\kappa'_{low}, \kappa'_{high})$ to Q;
    for each Rectangle query ρ in query list Q **do**
      $P_c \leftarrow$ RTREE-QUERY$(tree, \rho)$;
    $P_{result} \leftarrow$ Verify the distance restriction and fetch at most K points with the minimal distances from q in P_c;
  $r_q \leftarrow r_q + \Delta r$

5 Evaluation

We conduct extensive experiments on a PC with Intel Pentium D 3.0GHz processor, 2GB RAM, 160GB hard disk, running Ubuntu 9.10. Both indexing and query algorithms of iPoc are implemented in C/C++ and compiled by GCC 4.4.1. As one of the most successful high dimensional data indexing methods so far, iDistance [10] is used for comparison. Also, we implement the naive sequential scan algorithm, because it is still a powerful competitor in high dimensional KNN query algorithms. In all experiments, we focus on the criterion of average page access times and average total response time.

Datasets: Both real and synthetic datasets are used for evaluation. To examine the performance of indexing for audio retrieval task, we create a music feature database by crawlling 61,343 songs from the Internet and extracting 56-dimensional MFCC features for each song using MARSYAS. Besides, synthetic dataset with clustered distribution are adopted for scalability evaluation.

Effect of Data Size: In this set of experiments, we vary the number of points to verify the scalability of iPoc. The synthetic datasets with clustered data distribution are used. Data points are 32-dimension and we scale the number of data points from 50,000 to 100,000. 200 random generated queries are processed by iPoc and iDistance to search for the 1-NN and 5-NN. The average page access times and average total response time are illustrated in Fig. 3. iPoc takes fewer page accesses and less total response time than those of iDistance. Moreover, the total response time of iPoc increases slower than that of iDistance. Therefore, iPoc is more scalable than iDistance.

Effect of Dimensionality: To explore the effects of dimensionality, we vary the dimensionality of synthetic data from 16 to 64, using the synthetic datasets. The size of dataset is 100,000. From Fig. 4, we note that the response time and the number of page access increase linearly with the increment of dimensionality. But the total response time and page access increments are small for iPoc. The number of page access of iPoc is approximately 30% of that of iDistance.

Effect of K: Figure 5 displays results of experiment in which we vary the K, the number of nearest neighbor, from 1 to 50. The real audio MFCC feature dataset is used, which is composed of 61,343 English songs represented as 56-dimensional vectors. As shown in Fig. 5, both the page access times and total response time of iPoc and iDistance increase when K increases. This is because the increment of K leads to an enlargement of the query radius of both iPoc and iDisntance. Thus, more data points are fetched from hard disk for verification. Even though, iPoc is more efficient than iDistance.

Effect of Hypersphere Number: To discover the relationship between sphere number and the indexing performance, we vary the number of spheres from 16 to 75. Results of experiments on synthetic dataset with 100,000 points (32 dimension) and the real audio dateset are shown in Fig. 6(b) and 6(a), respectively. The optimal spheres number depends on the data distribution. And the performance

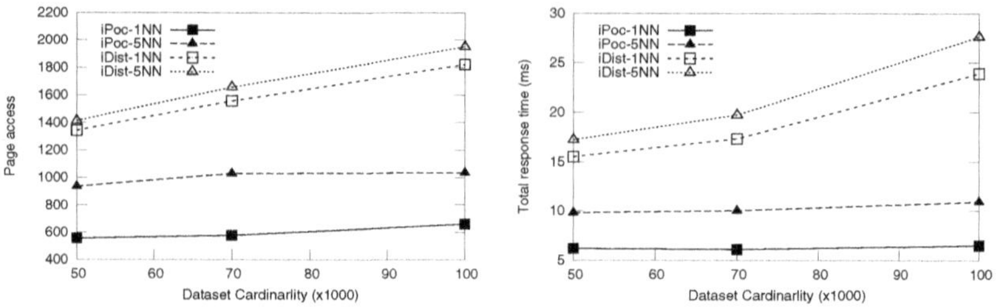

(a) Page Access (b) Total Response Time

Fig. 3. Effect of Dataset Cardinarlity (with synthetic dataset)

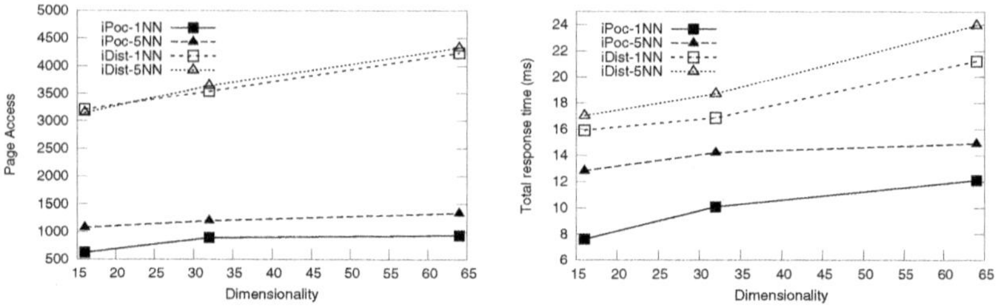

(a) Page Access (b) Total Response Time

Fig. 4. Effect of Dimensionality (with synthetic dataset)

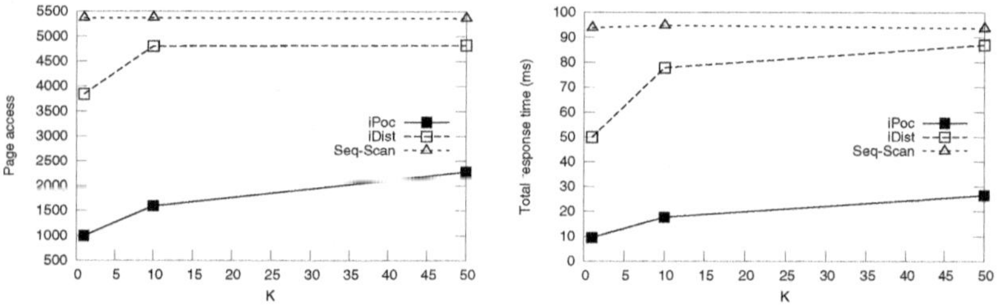

(a) Page Access (b) Total Response Time

Fig. 5. Effect of K (with real audio MFCC feature dateset)

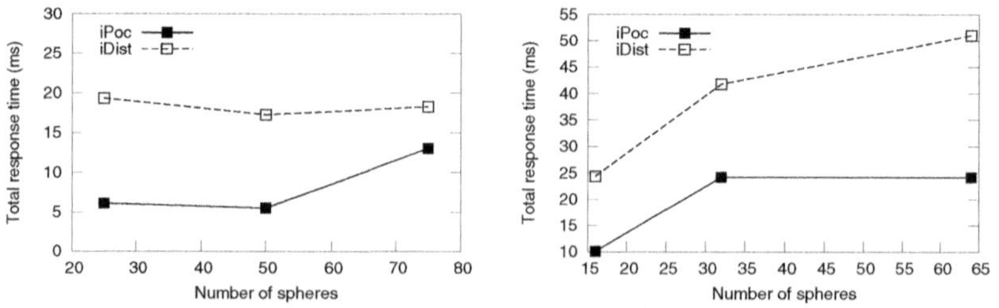

(a) Synthetic data (b) Real audio data

Fig. 6. Effect of Sphere Number

of iPoc degrades when the number of spheres is either too small or too large. The best spheres number should be identical to the actual number of data clusters.

Effect of Hypersector Number: The number of sectors in each sphere can also affect the performance of iPoc. In this set of experiments, we vary the number of sectors in each sphere from 16 to 64. As shown in Fig. 7, more sectors enhance the capability of pruning and the IOs of data points decreases. On the other hand, more sectors in each sphere increase the number of queries for R-tree and more IOs of internal nodes in R-tree degrade the performance of iPoc.

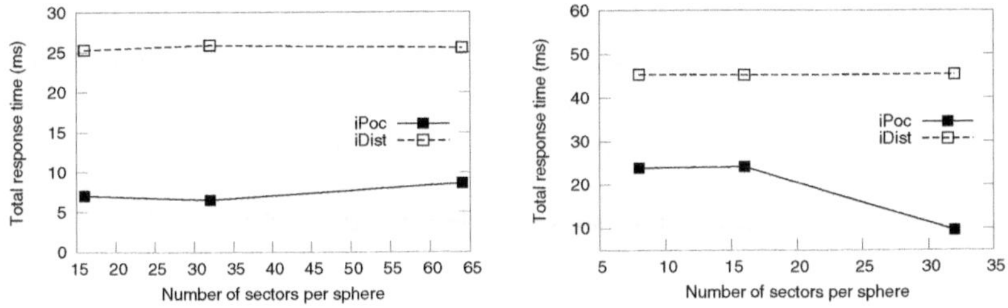

(a) Synthetic data (b) Real audio data

Fig. 7. Effect of Sector Number

6 Related Work

The database community has drawn attention to spatial indexing for a long time. Traditional spatial indexing approaches, e.g., R-tree [11], cannot efficiently index high dimensional data. Recently, Jagadish et al. [10] propose a B-tree based high dimensional indexing approach called iDistance. iDistance first clusters data points into groups and, in each cluster, a reference point is selected. For each point, the Euclidean distance from each reference point is indexed in a 1-dimensional B-tree. iDistance is considered to be the best exact KNN search algorithm [3]. However, the discrimination of Euclidean distance decreases as the dimensionality increases. As a result, performance of pruning will degrade which may increase the point verification and IO times. iPoc adopt the polar coordinate system, which has a radial coordinate and an angle coordinate, to support more precise space pruning.

Another thread of overcoming the curse of dimensionality is approximate algorithms, i.e., approximate nearest neighbor search, ANN. Medrank proposed by Fagin et al. [12] solves the high dimensional KNN search problem via aggregate ranking. Andoni et al. develop a hash function based high dimensional data indexing method called local sensitive hashing (LSH) [13]. LSH wants to find a family of hash functions, by which points close to each other are hashed to the same slot with a high probability and points which locate far away from each other are hashed to the same slot with a low probability. Most recently, locality sensitive B-tree (LSB-tree) is proposed by Tao et al. [3]. LSB-tree combines the LSH indexing and B-tree and achieves the sub-linear time complexity to the dataset cardinality. Different from iPoc, the above approximate algorithms cannot guarantee K-nearest neighbors are fetched.

7 Conclusions

KNN search in high dimensional space is an essential problem. In this paper, we proposed a novel polar coordinate based indexing method for high dimensional data, called *iPoc*. For effective space pruning, we develop a hypersector based space partitioning via a 2-phases data clustering. In the first step, data space is divided into hyperspheres. In the second step, each hypersphere is refined into hypersectors. Furthermore, local polar coordinate systems are generated to determine the position of points in each hypersectors. To merge all these independent polar coordinate systems into a global one, we design a key mapping scheme. Finally, the global coordinates are indexed in a 2-dimensional R-tree. Extensive experiments on both real and synthetic datasets demonstrate iPoc outperforms existent high dimensional indexing approaches and prove the efficiency, effectiveness and scalability of our proposal.

References

1. Bentley, J.L.: Multidimensional binary search trees in database applications. IEEE Trans. Software Eng. 5(4), 333–340 (1979)
2. Weber, R., Schek, H., Blott, S.: A quantitative analysis and performance study for similarity-search methods in high-dimensional spaces. In: VLDB, pp. 194–205 (1998)
3. Tao, Y., Yi, K., Sheng, C., Kalnis, P.: Quality and efficiency in high dimensional nearest neighbor search. In: ACM SIGMOD, pp. 563–576 (2009)
4. Andoni, A., Indyk, P.: Near-optimal hashing algorithms for approximate nearest neighbor in high dimensions. Communications of the ACM 51(1), 117–122 (2008)
5. Shen, H., Ooi, B., Zhou, X.: Towards effective indexing for very large video sequence database. In: ACM SIGMOD, p. 741 (2005)
6. Cui, B., Ooi, B.C., Su, J., Tan, K.L.: Contorting high dimensional data for efficient main memory processing. In: ACM SIGMOD, pp. 479–490 (2003)
7. Cha, G., Zhu, X., Petkovic, D., Chung, C.: An efficient indexing method for nearest neighbor searches in high-dimensional image databases. IEEE Transactions on Multimedia 4(1), 76–87 (2002)
8. Berchtold, S., Böhm, C., Kriegal, H.: The pyramid-technique: towards breaking the curse of dimensionality. In: ACM SIGMOD, pp. 142–153 (1998)
9. Apaydin, T., Ferhatosmanoglu, H.: Access structures for angular similarity queries. IEEE Transactions on Knowledge and Data Engineering, 1512–1525 (2006)
10. Jagadish, H., Ooi, B., Tan, K., Yu, C., Zhang, R.: idistance: An adaptive b+-tree based indexing method for nearest neighbor search. ACM Transactions on Database Systems (TODS) 30(2), 397 (2005)
11. Guttman, A.: R-trees: A dynamic index structure for spatial searching. In: ACM SIGMOD, pp. 47–57 (1984)
12. Fagin, R., Kumar, R., Sivakumar, D.: Efficient similarity search and classification via rank aggregation. In: ACM SIGMOD, pp. 301–312 (2003)
13. Andoni, A., Indyk, P.: Near-optimal hashing algorithms for approximate nearest neighbor in high dimensions. In: FOCS, pp. 459–468 (2006)

Join Directly on Heavy-Weight Compressed Data in Column-Oriented Database

Gan Liang[1], Li RunHeng[1], Jia Yan[1], and Jin Xin[2]

[1] School of Computer Science, Nation University of Defense Technology, 410073 ChangSha, HuNan, China
[2] School of Software, ChangSha Social Work College, 410004 ChangSha, HuNan, China
gl.nudt@gmail.com, lirunheng1982@gmail.com, jiayanjy@vip.sina.com, jx.cssw@gmail.com

Abstract. Operating directly on compressed data can decrease CPU costs. Many light-weight compressions, such as run-length encoding and bit-vector encoding, can gain this benefit easily. Heavy-Weight Lempel-Ziv (LZ) has no method to operate directly on compressed data. We proposed a join algorithm, *LZ join*, which join two relations *R* and *S* directly on compressed data when decoding. Regard *R* as probe table and *S* as build table, *R* is encoded by LZ. When *R* probing *S*, *LZ join* decreases the join cost by using *cached results* (previous join results of IDs in *R*'s LZ dictionary window when decoder find that the same *R*'s ID sequence in window). *LZ join* combines decoding and join phase into one, which reduces the memory usage for decoding the whole *R* and CPU overhead for probing those *cached results*. Our analysis and experiments show that *LZ join* is better in some cases, the more compression ratio the better.

Keywords: Heavy-weight compression join, LZ join, Column-oriented database, compression in database, LZ encoding.

1 Introduction

Compression in database systems can improve performance significantly. A column-oriented database system (or "column-store") is well-suited for more compression schemes, such as RLE (Run-length Encoding) and LZ, and achieves higher performance than traditional row-oriented database system (or "row-store")[1].

The idea of decreasing CPU costs by operating directly on compressed data was introduced by Graefe and Shapiro[2]. Each type of compression schemes will gain different effects while using direct operation method. In column-oriented database, compression algorithms are divided into two categories by encoding and decoding overhead of CPU: light-weight schemes (such as Null suppression, Dictionary Encoding, RLE, Bit-Vector Encoding) and heavy-weight schemes (LZ encoding). Some light-weight schemes can gain this benefit easily, but heavy-weight schemes need revising the execution of query to get the improvement and have never been studied yet.

L. Chen et al. (Eds.): WAIM 2010, LNCS 6184, pp. 357–362, 2010.

In this paper, we introduce a join algorithm, LZ join, which is operating directly on heavy-weight LZ compressed data as light-weight schemes do. We differ from other work on operating directly on light-weight compressed data without join in column-oriented DBMSs (Daniel et. al [1] on c-store), in which we focus on column-oriented heavy-weight compression algorithms and join directly on compressed data (whereas [2] focuses on improving join performance of standard row-based light-weight techniques).

In summary, we demonstrate several fundamental results related to join on compression in column-oriented database:

- First, operating directly on heavy-weight compressed data is feasible. And LZ join will speed up table join compare to hash join in some case.
- Secondly, the natural characteristic of data is the most important factor to select encoding scheme. Data with low run-length and high cardinality is popular, for such data, LZ join could gain more speedup than light-weight scheme for its higher compression ratio. Although sorting data to get higher run-length does good to light-weight scheme for join operation, but sorted data needs to store position of all the tuples in memory and resort join results by ID for tuple reconstruction[3] to acquire the final answer which is time-consuming.

2 Relation Work

Column-oriented database systems, such as the C-store [4] and monetDB [5] are read-optimized databases which are designed to implement sophisticated queries by storing relational data in columns (column-store) rather than in rows as in the conventional "row-store" approach. Data in column-store are easy to compress and are avoided to be read when they are useless for query.

Data compression in DBMS reduces the size of the data and improves I/O performance. For queries that are I/O limited, the CPU overhead of decompression is often compensated for by the I/O improvements. Many lossless encoding algorithm using in compressed file are exploited for database system, such as entropy encoding (Huffman encoding[6]), dictionary encoding (Simple Dictionary, RLE, LZ). Some other encoding algorithms, like frame Prefix Suppression, Frame of Reference, Bit-Vector encoding, are implemented in column-oriented database.

When data are compressed, we will gain a big improvement by operating on them directly [1][2]. But it is difficult to implement direct operation on heavy-weight compressed data. Heavy-weight LZ encoding was first proposed by Ziv and Lempel in 1977[7], which has some variants, such as LZ78, LZW, LZ77.

The input columns stored on disk must be converted to rows at some point in the query plan, called materialization. Two materialization Strategies are proposed in [3]: early materialization and late materialization. In join operation, early materialization adds all output columns before join. However, late materialization dose not form tuples until some part of the plan has been processed, that is more efficient. So, in LZ join, we use late materialization, especially for sorted column data.

3 LZ Join

We use LZ join as a type of Equi-Join: join if a certain attribute of r is equal to an attribute of s. Join operator: given relation R and S, report all pairs (r, s) , $r \in R$, $s \in S$ and the two records satisfy some given condition. In the remainder of this paper, we assume $\|R\| \geq \|S\|$ and S can be fitted in memory, R as probe table and S as build table.

1. Encoding data

Before join, R (*input stream*) has been compressed using LZ encoder yet. In the encoding process, each *attribute* (the basic data element in the relation column) was read into buffer. *Coding position* indicates the position of attribute to be encoded; *dictionary window(DW)* is the window of size W contains W attributes from the coding position backwards, i.e. the last W processed characters. When *length* attributes from *coding position* (the position of the attribute in the input stream that is currently being coded, the beginning of the *lookahead buffer*) match the attributes from *offset* in dictionary window, output (*offset*, *length*, *attribute*). When no match for the attribute, output (*0,0,attribute*). Decoding is on the reverse way.

The compression ratio that LZ method achieves is very good for many types of data, especially for data with low run-length and high cardinality. Although encoding of LZ is quite time-consuming which has a lot of comparisons to be performed between the *lookahead buffer* (from *Coding position* to the end of input stream) and the dictionary window, but decoding is very simple and fast.

2. Join operation

Time-consuming encoding has been done offline yet, joins need only simple decoding. LZ join keeps two phases: decoding and probing phase.

In decoding phase, decoder read triples from compressed data. LZ Compressed data is mainly composed of triples (*offset*, *length*, *attribute*), *offset* means dictionary window offset (and it is a flag of whether attribute match the attribute in windows, ‘0’ stands for no match, others stands for offset), *length* means it has *length* attributes matching the dictionary window from the offset, *attribute* means next attribute. From the *offset*, we know whether successive attribute(s) is (are) appearing in dictionary windows. If *offset* is no match(‘0’), we call the attribute *probing attribute*, which need to probe build table R in join operation; *offset* is match (not ‘0’), we call the attribute(s) *cached attribute*, which only copy the former join results from *cached results buffer (CRB)*, which keeps the join results of attribute in dictionary windows. When meeting probing attribute, decoder copies the *attribute* of triple to dictionary window. Otherwise, meeting cached attribute(s), decoder finds *length* number of attribute(s) from window and replicate it (them) to the successive place.

In probing phase, we choose hash join or nested-loop join at will but no sort-merge join. Hash join is recommended for its high performance.

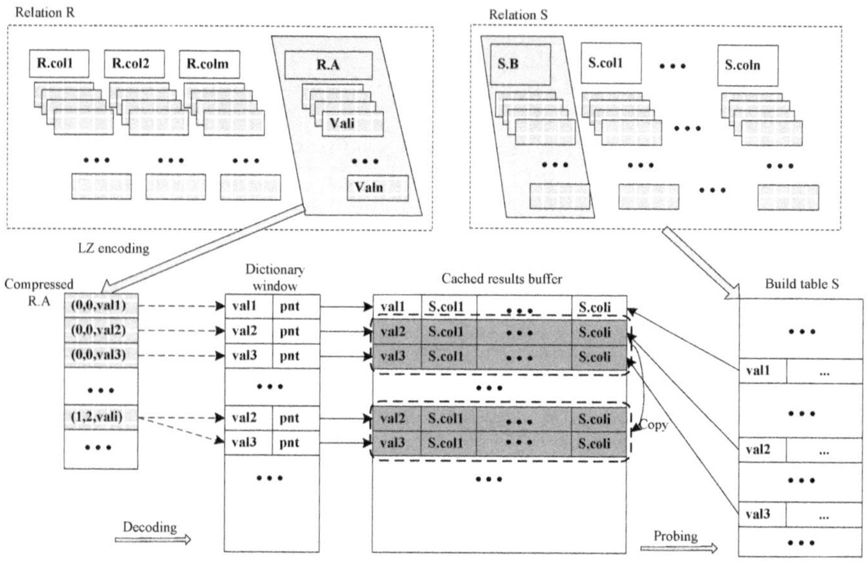

Fig. 1. Illustration of LZ join

In Fig.1, we reveal how LZ join works. LZ join adds a cached results buffer to keep join results and make a point in dictionary window for each attribute to link join result to the attribute.

For example, in Fig. 1, firstly read three probing attributes((0,0,*val1*), (0,0,*val2*) and (0,0,*val3*)), then probe build table S and keep those join results into *CRB*. If cached attribute (1,2,*vali*) arrived, LZ join read "2" cached results from offset ("1") of *CRB* and copy them into the following space of *CRB*. And then, read next probing attribute or cached attribute.

Algorithm LZ join can be easily implemented from the description above, we omit it for length restriction of the article.

Block dictionary window. For join with low selectivity, we choose another type of dictionary window, block window, because encoder with sliding window need decompress all the data no matter how many data is selected that is time-consuming and storage-wasting. Block dictionary window can overcome this problem by choose the right block. Input stream is divided into equal size of block, and each block has its own block window. On the condition of laze materialization [3] of tuple reconstruction in column-oriented database, whether data need decompress or not is indicated by its ID. So, block window can overcome the shortage of sliding window by accessing the right block directly with indication of block size and decode only part of blocks.

As shown in Fig.1, each entry of dictionary window has two elements: *value*, *point* (*value* the base element of decoding data, *point* to cached results). The *point* is an addition of LZ join for convenient replicating join results in cache results buffer. When cached attribute is arrived, LZ join finds the first cached result by *point* to it and replicates successive *length* number of cached results.

Build table *S*. Before *S* is built in memory, execution plan instructs how to load data from disk and which column is needed. Build phrase of table *S* is just like row-store do, the only difference between them is that *S* of column-store must reconstruct the vertical partitioned tuples after each column was decompressed (if compressed).

Cached results buffer. Cached results buffer is storing join results of current dictionary window. When LZ join finished, all the join results will be found in a number of cached results buffer. Finally, LZ join combine these cached results buffer, and become final join result of one join predicate. If a query has n join predicate, LZ join will integrate n final join results into query result. When memory is lack, final join result may write to disk.

Probing Phase. Probing is one of important operation of join. Sorting attribute in dictionary window must do after finish of decoding, which is no good for LZ join to operation directly on compressed data. So, sort-merge join can not apply to LZ join. The other two join methods, hash join and nested-loop join, are suited for LZ join to probe build table S. Whichever LZ join takes, it does not affect LZ join. Commonly, hash join is a good choice for its execution faster than nested-loop join.

4 Experiment

We compressed the data in each of the following four ways: Lempel-Ziv (LZ), RLE, bit-vector (BV), and no compression (NC) and use SSBM[8] which is popular in data warehouse. We use the SSBM data generator *dbgen*[1] to generate experimental data, all the tuples in fact table LO_ are order by *orderkey* and *linenumber*. The fact table LO_ at scale 10 which consists of just under 60,000,000 lineorders. Cardinality of each dimension table is *custkey* 20k, *partkey* 200k, *suppkey* 10k, *orderdate* 2406.

LZ compression has the smallest space than RLE and S-RLE, as shown in Fig. 2(a).

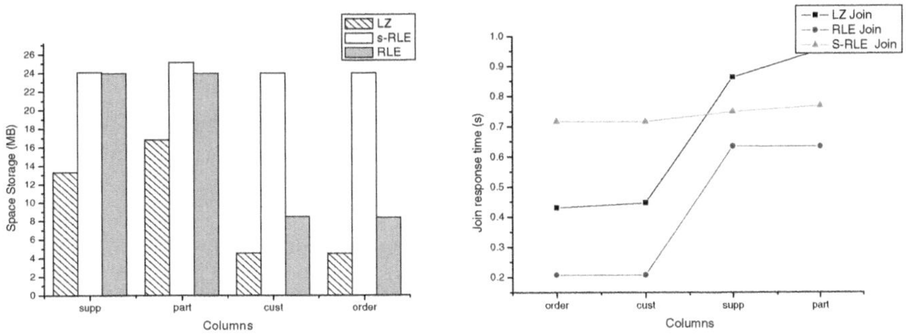

(a) (b)

Fig. 2. Performance of table LINORDER

[1] dbgen can be downloaded from: http://www.cs.umb.edu/~poneil/dbgen.zip

S-RLE is *S*orted data before *RLE,* which is commended in [9] for data with low run-length and high cardinality.

In Fig 2.(b) join phrase, decoding the compressed data take most part of join overhead, so that LZ join can not surpass RLE join in all case. Resorting results of S-RLE join waste most of its join time, so it is not good for full column join.

Although LZ join is not the best in join algorithm, but we propose a novel ideal to do join operation, and this approach can not be outstanding in all the cases.

5 Conclusion

Many light-weight schemes, such as RLE and bit-vector encoding, can operate directly on compressed data. However, heavy-weight compression is considered to be unsuited for direct operation [1]. We propose LZ join which make a change of this mind by combining join operation into decoding. Actually, LZ decoding is much faster as light-weight compression and can operate directly too. Sufficient analysis and experiments verifies this point.

In summary, vertical partition of table in column-oriented database system raises the ability of compression schemes which could not have in row-oriented database system. Under such circumstance, LZ join with high compression ratio and low join overhead make a novel approach to promote system performance.

References

1. Abadi, D.J., Madden, S.R., Ferreira, M.C.: Integrating Compression and Execution in Column-Oriented Database Systems. In: The 2006 ACM SIGMOD conference on Management of data, pp. 671–682. ACM Press, Chicago (2006)
2. Graefe, G., Shapiro, L.: Data compression and database performance. In: ACM/IEEE-CS Symp. on Applied Computing, pp. 22–27. ACM Press, New York (1991)
3. Daniel, J.A., Daniel, S.M., David, J.D., Samuel, R.M.: Materialization Strategies in a Column-Oriented DBMS. In: The 23rd International Conference on Data Engineering, pp. 466–475. IEEE Press, Turkey (2007)
4. Mike, S., Daniel, J.A., Adam, B., et al.: C-Store: A Column-oriented DBMS. In: The 31st Very Large DataBase Conference, Norway, pp. 553–564 (2005)
5. Peter, B., Zukowski, M., Nes, N.: MonetDB/X100: Hyper-Pipelining Query Execution. In: First Biennial Conference on Innovative Data Systems Research, CA, pp. 225–237 (2003)
6. Huffman, D.: A method for the construction of minimum-redundancy codes. In: Proc. IRE, pp. 1098–1101 (1952)
7. Ziv, J., Lempel, A.: A universal algorithm for sequential data compression. IEEE Transactions on Information Theory 23(3), 337–343 (1977)
8. Neil, P.E.O'., Neil, E.J.O'., Chen, X.: The Star Schema Benchmark (SSB), `http://www.cs.umb.edu/~poneil/StarSchemaB.PDF`
9. Daniel, J.A., Peter, A.B., Stavros, H.: Column-oriented Database Systems. In: Proc of the 35th Very Large DataBase Conference (VLDB), France, pp. 1644–1645 (2009)

Exploiting Service Context for Web Service Search Engine

Rong Zhang[1], Koji Zettsu[1],
Yutaka Kidawara[1], and Yasushi Kiyoki[1,2]

[1] National Institute of Information and Communications Technology,
3-5 Hikaridai, Seika-cho, Kyoto 619-0289, Japan
{rongzhang,zettsu,kidawara}@nict.go.jp
[2] Keio University, 5322 Endo, Kanagawa 252-8520, Japan
kiyoki@sfc.keio.ac.jp

Abstract. Service-oriented architecture (SOA) is rapidly becoming one of significant computing paradigms. However as the increasing of services, haphazardly of service definition makes it tedious and less efficient for service discovery. In this paper, we propose a novel context model "SPOT" to express services usage information. Based on SPOT definition, we build services' collaboration graph and propose to analyze collaboration structure to rank services by their usage goodness. The distinctive feature of our method lies on the introducing of services context model which is a new model to deal with service context information, and integrating it for supporting service search. Our experimental results indicate that: our context-based ranking is useful for good services recommendation; services' context makes up for service description heterogeneity and can help to distinguish content-"similar" services.

1 Introduction

The growing number of web services issues a new and challenging search problem: locating services. In fact, to address this problem, several search engines have recently sprung up as Seekda[1], Xmethods[2],Woogle[3], and so on, which provide simple search or service browsing functionality. However it is mentioned that there is noticeable amount of noise for service search, because of lacking of services description. As declared in [1], it has checked that 80% of services have less than 50 keys and 52% have less than 20 keys, so this is no surprising as we find that even human have difficulty assessing the functionality of these services.

To address the challenge involved with service search, much effort has been given on introducing explicit semantics for expressing the real semantic with each service, such as referring ontology[2,3], introducing service tagging or category information [4] or deducing new semantics from service description[5]. The representative query handled by these systems is like "*I want to search for services*

[1] http://webservices.seekda.com/
[2] http://www.webservicelist.com/
[3] http://db.cs.washington.edu/webService/

L. Chen et al. (Eds.): WAIM 2010, LNCS 6184, pp. 363–375, 2010.

related to keys δ". Then IR(information retrieval) method is applied to rank services' relevance to δ. However *services usefulness has seldom been considered*. An example is shown in Table.1. searching for "map location" service in services repository [6], expected services as "google earth" or "yahoo maps" is not at the top rank. So service description based method will not suggest best services to users. On the other hand, let's take a look at an example shown in Fig.1. Our query is like "*search for searvices related to* ***employee status***". We then get three services labeled as service **A,B** *and* **C**, which have high similarity value by their content information. We have tried to distinguish them by introducing ontology. Finally we can not, because they are too similar to be distinguished. Here service "A", "B" and "C" are used for checking employee class status when booking air-ticket, checking employee attendance status in public conference and checking employee daily company attendance, respectively. After we explain the application background information, we can distinguish these services easily. However *services application background or usage history has not been taken into consideration* for describing services.

Table 1. Relevant Services & Useful Serivces: We search for "location map" in Programmableweb, which just listed the services related to queried terms and did not consider about the service's usefulness. We also list the expected services related to queried terms, which are called useful services.

Content Relevant Services	Expected Useful Services
Alcatel-Lucent Open, Amazon Elastic Mapreduce, ArcWeb, BeerMapping	google maps, yahoo maps, google earth, Microsoft Virtual Earth

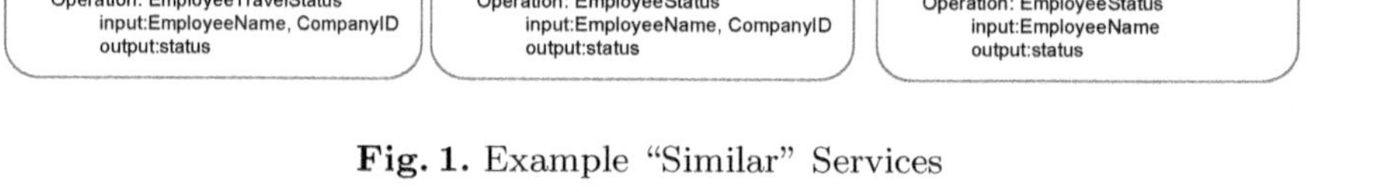

Fig. 1. Example "Similar" Services

Definition 1 (Service Context). *Service Context is represented as W2H, which represents "WHY", "WHOM" and "HOW". "WHY" is application background; "WHOM" is the story participant; "HOW" is the story plot.*

This work proposes to associate service with its "Context", defined in Def.1, to solve the problems mentioned above. We specify the context by "SPOT" data model. Based on SPOT, service collaboration graph is built up. Graph-based algorithm is designed for service ranking, which is efficient to find "useful" services, defined as service goodness. The main difference with previous work is 1) the definition and generation of "context", which is not related to ontology definition or ontology mapping[2,7]; 2) the purpose of ranking, whose intention is to return not only content-related but also good services to users.

Considering the queries mentioned above, we want to rank "google maps" higher; we want to associate "employee" services with their own applications, e.g. "A" collaborated with "air-ticket checking" (*whom*) service for "business purpose"(*why*). By the way, if we apply the context information for service comparison, these three "employee" services will be distinguished, which means we may have better performance when doing similarity search, like "find services similar to service *A*".

To evaluate our method, we conducted a set of experiments in which we compared our method with IR-based method. We find that our method yields better results for searching, ranking and clustering.

The rest of the paper is organized as follows. Section 2 describes the retrieving and formalizing of service context; Section 3 describes the context-based service ranking algorithm; Section 4 discusses the relationship between context-based and content-based methods; Section 5 presents the experimental results with result analysis; Section 6 summarizes the related work and Section 7 emphasizes our contribution points and presents the future work.

2 Context Model

2.1 Context Definition

As defined in Sec.1, service context refers to "Why", "Whom", and "How". Their triangle relationship is represented in Fig.2. **Why** is used to declare the application scenario/story background. It is decided by the task requirement, which provides a space for playing of story. **Whom** is used to declare the story participants related to the application scenario, called "collaborators" later. **How** is used to declare the story plot related to collaborators. Let's continue with "Service B" of the "employee" example in Sec.1. In such a case, WHY is "conference management"; WHOM are "hotel reservation service", "CheckingEmployeeStatus" and "transportation service"; HOW are "lodging", "registration" and "transit". Context declares the semantic relationship among collaborators by exposing their functionalities in the story background. According to the analysis above, we model context by a tetrad called SPOT, defined as:

SPOT=< *S*ubjet, *P*redict, *O*bject, *T*ask>. *Subject* is the target declaration, *Predict* is the activities for the collaboration, *Object* is the collaborated services set and *Task* is task description. Then for SPOT in Fig.3, we say: under the story

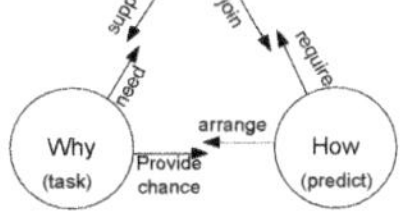

Fig. 2. Service Context Triangle Relationship

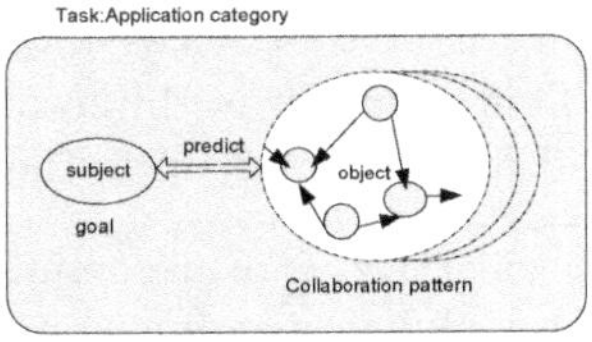

Fig. 3. Context Model: SPOT

of "Task", in order to realize the target of "Subject", "Object" collaborated by the manner of "Predict".

2.2 Context Retrieving

In order to get service context information (SPOT), we need 1) service composition environment and 2) service collaboration history.

Service composition is becoming dominant. Using of existing services modules to compose new applications has gained momentum. To support users in this effort, on one hand, composition engines are being developed. Tremendous effort has been put on standardization way in service composition area. The representative one is BPEL4WS[8] with ActiveBPEL[4], BPWS4J[5], Oracle BPEL[6] as the composition engines supporting WSDL-based[9] services composition program. In order to support free RESTful-based[10] web services composition, Mashup[11] programming environment is proposed. Its composition engines are like Yahoo Pipe[7], SnapLogic[8] and so on.

Service collaboration history is readable. The example collaboration environment is shown in Fig.4. The collaboration logic is clearly declared by these tools, presented as XML file or JSP code or Java code. We can easily get the collaboration context information by analyzing the code, because in the code, they describe in detail the collaboration logics and also with documentation description about functionalities. Additionally, these tools provide the composition logical division functionalities which separate complex composition into small logical parts. Then we can get service usage history from these tools.

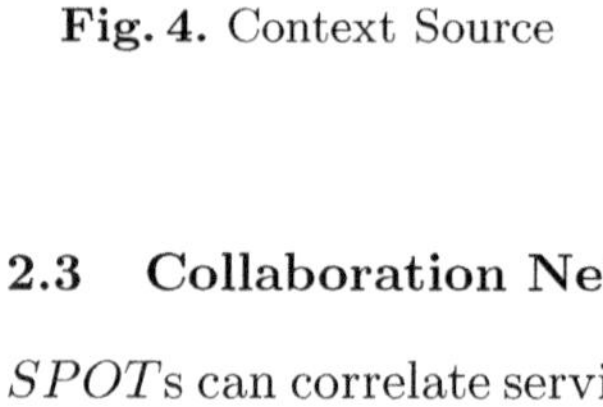

Fig. 4. Context Source

Fig. 5. Collaboration Network

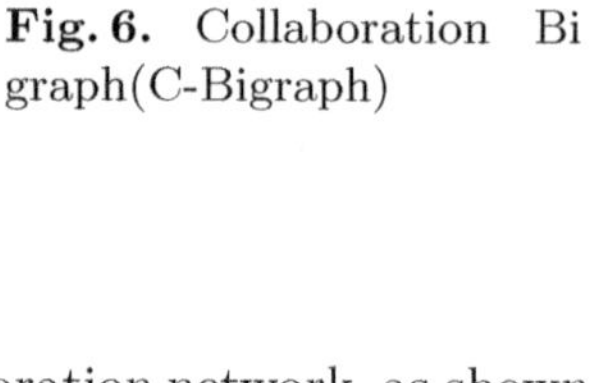

Fig. 6. Collaboration Bigraph(C-Bigraph)

2.3 Collaboration Network

*SPOT*s can correlate services and build services collaboration network, as shown in Fig.5. This network is different with the regular networks from the linkage labels. The labels along with the linkages are not linkage weight but linkage

[4] http://www.activevos.com/community-open-source.php
[5] http://www.alphaworks.ibm.com/tech/bpws4j
[6] http://www.oracle.com/technology/products/ias/bpel/index.html
[7] http://pipes.yahoo.com/pipes/
[8] http://www.snaplogic.com/

semantics representing SPOTs. Services associated with same spots are collaborators. As we have declared before, "predict" in $SPOT$ is used for building correlation between services and subject; "task" is used for declaring the application environment. In such a case, we reform Fig.5 to a semantic collaboration bipartite graph, called *C_Bigraph* as Fig. 6. In *C_Bigraph*, one side is composed of services , the other side is composed of applications $ST_j(m > j > 0)$ and they are connected by predicts $p_k(k > 0)$. Each node ST_j is composed of a two-dimension vector, related to task and subject. We suppose that each unit of task and subject corresponds to a unique set of service composition. Supposing there are n services ($V = \{s_j, 0 < j \leq n\}$) and $m(m > 0)$ composite services ($U = \{ST_i, 0 < i \leq m\}$). For each service $s_j(s_j \in V)$, its related context are $ST_j = \{s_j(st)\}(ST_j \subseteq U)$. For context st_i, its involved services are $S_i = \{st_i(s)\}(S_i \subseteq V)$.

The analysis of collaboration network with the goal of finding important/good services inspired by WWW network[12] or paper citation network[13], which verified that the linkage relationship is useful for distinguishing pages or papers. This work wants to rank the returned results by using services collaboration graph for evaluating services' goodness.

3 Context-Based Ranking

3.1 *C_Bigraph* Generation

First let's see the generation of query related services collaboration graph as shown in Algo.1[9], with input $Q_{cn}, Q_{cx}, \vartheta$ as the query string to content, context and the graph expansion stop condition. Cosine similarity is used for retrieving related services or spots based on content for R_{cn} or context for R_{cx}. Notice that here R_{cx} represents SPOTs involved services for Q_{cx}. Based on initial results S_e, we iteratively add new services and involved spots to S_e and ST_e, respectively. In this way, we generate *C_Bigraph*, which will stop expansion until the graph change is less than ϑ, line 17.

3.2 Services Goodness Ranking

We get the collaboration graph involved with nodes S_e *and* ST_e from Algo.1. Now let's rank the returned results based on the graph structure. Our algorithm, shown in Algo.2, is based on the assumption: if a service is important, it will be highly referred by ST and vise versa. On the other hand, they mutually reinforce each other, which is similar with HITS[12].

For service s_i, its goodness $G^{[s_i]}$ is defined by the goodness of its involved applications as $G^{[s_i]} = \sum_{s_i(st) \subseteq ST_e} G^{[st_j]}, with\ st_j \in s_i(st)$; For context st_j, its goodness $G^{[st_j]}$ is defined by the goodness of its involved services: $G^{[st_j]} = \sum_{st_j(s) \subseteq S_e} G^{[s_k]},\ with\ s_k \in st_j(s)$. Based on this assumption, we design the ranking algorithm in Algo.2. The initial input to this algorithm is the initial

[9] The initial rank to results is based on Cosine similarity.

Algorithm 1. Result_Graph_Generation (Q_{cn},Q_{cx}, ϑ, *join*)

```
1: Let R_cn represent the service results based on content search;
2: Let R_cx represent the service results based on context search;
3: if join then
4:     R= R_cn ∩ R_cx;
5: else
6:     R= R_cn ∪ R_cx;
7: end if
8: Set S_e=R and ST_e = ∅ and S'_e = ∅;
9: for each s_i in S_e do
10:    Let ST^[s_i] represent s_i involved SPOTs;
11:    ST_e ∪ = ST^[s_i];
12:    for each ST_j^[s_i] ∈ ST^[s_i] and ST_j^[s_i] has not been checked do
13:        Let S^[j] represent ST_j^[s_i] involved new services, which have not been in S_e;
14:        S'_e ∪ = S^[j];
15:    end for
16: end for
17: if |S'_e| / |S_e| < ϑ then
18:    return S_e ∪ S'_e and ST_e;
19: else
20:    S_e ∪ = S'_e, S'_e = ∅;
21:    go to line 9;
22: end if
```

goodness values $G^{[S_e]}$ for services in S_e and $G^{[ST_e]}$ for context nodes in ST_e. $G^{[S_e]}$ and $G^{[ST_e]}$ are both vectors with item value set to *1*. That is, for s_i, if $st_j \in s_i(st)$, its $G^{[st_j]} = 1$; for st_j, if $s_k \in st_j(s)$, its $G^{[s_k]} = 1$. Normalization in line 9 is done like this:$\sum_{s_i \in S_e} (G^{[s_i]})^2 = 1$ and $\sum_{st_j \in ST_e} (G^{[st_j]})^2 = 1$. The iteration will not stop until any goodness change is less than $\ell(\ell < 1)$.

Algorithm 2. ServiceRanking(*C_BiGraph*, ℓ, $G^{[S_e]}$, $G^{[ST_e]}$)

```
1: change = true;
2: while change do
3:    for each s_i in S_e do
4:        update G^[s_i] with the value calculated from ST_e;
5:    end for
6:    for each st_j in ST_e do
7:        update G^[st_j] with the value calculated from S_e;
8:    end for
9:    Normalize G^[S_e] and G^[ST_e] to G'^[S_e] and G'^[ST_e];
10:   change = false;
11:   for (each item in G^[S_e] and G^[ST_e]) and !change do
12:       if |G^[s_i] − G'^[s_i]| > ℓ or |G^[st_j] − G'^[st_j]| > ℓ then
13:           change=true;
14:       end if
15:   end for
16: end while
17: Order S_e and ST_e based on the goodness values to S_e' and ST_e';
```

3.3 Query Processing Based on Context

The query process is like that: 1) Keyword based method is used to find the candidates related to the query; 2) For each candidate s, we calculate the content similarity $\eta^{[s]}$; 3) We calculate context goodness score $G^{[s]}$ by Algo.2; 4) We evaluate the candidates by $\eta^{[s]} \times G^{[s]}$.

4 Discussion

Service descriptions provided by service providers are insufficient for service discovery. However we can not force the providers to provide more detailed services description. Then for returned services, we may not understand them because of lack of description. Associating services with more readable information and helping users to find useful services are urgent. This work suggests to associate services with their own usage information. This kind of information reflects services from the view of social society.

Previous work on Content-based search is focusing on the extending to query semantics by analyzing service description or query string. We cannot overlook this part of work. The motivation for this work stems from the difficulty of ontology definition or evolution. We suppose to analyze services collaboration history to rank services, which has seldom been considered in web service discovery but successfully used in social network analysis. Content analysis is important to undermine the relationship between terms, providing results candidates. Combining with goodness ranking, we suggest to provide users useful services.

By the way, our algorithm provides ranking to not only services themselves but also services' applications, which can provide users with representative services' usage. On the other side, SPOT involved Object provides a method to identify possible composite services.

One disadvantage of this work is that if we can not collect service context, the service may be ranked low. But our purpose is that we want to provide a way to make service search come out with not only related but also useful services.

5 Experiment and Evaluation

5.1 Experiment DataSet

We collected services and services related context from ProgrammableWeb[6], which records a large number of free API services (RESTful-based) and composite mashup services. For each service, we can retrieve its description; for each composite service, we can easily get its involved context and the mapping relationship is like: Subject(mashup title), Object(API list), Predict(API methods), and Task (background description). Finally, we get 1476 services and 4200 mashups. Fig.7 shows services distribution with different categories. Fig.8 shows services description terms distribution: 92% services with description terms less than 30 and 70% with description terms less than 20. Attaching new information for services are urgent. Based on the retrieved context, services collaboration network is shown in Fig.9, we have not labeled with each linkage the SPOT information because of lack of space. Service network looks like social network. We take this as the experimental dataset.

In our experiment, we compare our method with content-based method (TFIDF-based). Notice that we have not compared with some existing system like Woogle[5], because we consider about different aspect for service search and more important is that woogle-like method can also be implemented on our

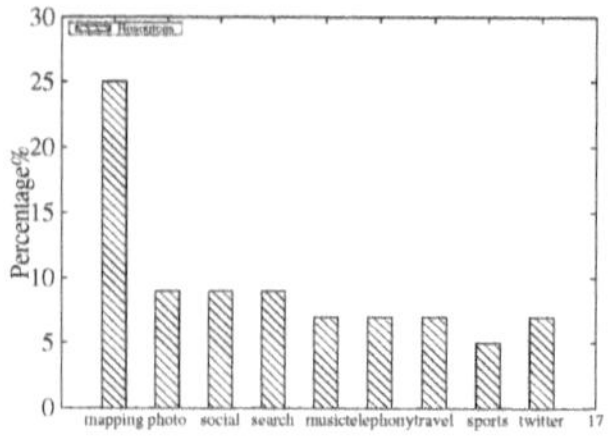

Fig. 7. Service Distribution on Different Categories

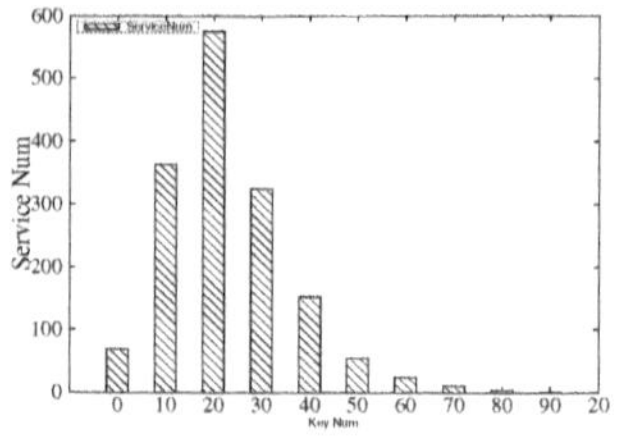

Fig. 8. Service Description Distribution

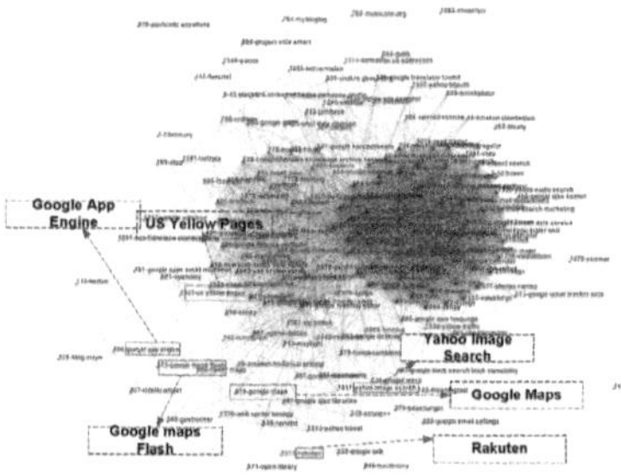

Fig. 9. Service Collaboration Network based on Context

method. From now on, we will refer our method as "Cox-Search" and TFIDF-based method as "Baseline-Search".

5.2 Experiment Results

Fundamental Result for Context

Context-based Ranking: Let's first take a look at the difference between two methods for solving the query like "*find services which related to query string* δ". The sample is shown in Table 2 which lists the top 5 results by these two methods. It is easy to see that our results are competitive to each other and they may be more trustful to users. For example, for "location map" query, Google,yahoo or Microsoft's Software will be more acceptable which have not been ranked to top list with "baseline" method.

Service Related Story Declaration: The other query from user may be like "I want a service related to δ but can be used for ζ". In such a case, user wants to know both the existence and usage information for a service. Our method can help to realize such kind of purpose, associating service together with its popular application samples, as shown in Table.3. Even you read service description of "last.fm", you will be confused about it. After shown its real joined applications, you know how to use it and what it is clearly. In this example, we can see clearly that it can be frequently used together with "google maps", "lyricsfly" and so on. And from context task, we also have a good view of this service.

Table 2. General Query and Top 5 Ranked Results

Query		Baseline	Cox-based
location map	1	Orange Location	Yahoo Maps
	2	yahoo map image	Microsoft Virtual Earth
	3	HeatMap	Google Static Maps
	4	Nac Geo-service	Google Earth
	5	Google Static Map	Google Maps Data
social community	1	Google Friend Connect	Facebook
	2	Social Entrepreneur	Delicious
	3	3jam	Myspace
	4	LiveVideo	Google Friend Connect
	5	Cogenz	LinkedIn

Table 3. Results with Highly Ranked Context

Service	Service Description	Top3 ranked SPOT-task	Top3 ranked SPOT-object
last.fm	It allows for read and write	a music mashup of lastfm...	google maps, last.fm, lyricsfly, musicbrainz, youtube
	access to the full slate of	a site about estonian music ja bands. youtube and vimeo videos are updated automatically and similar artists are shown based on last.fm similar artists feed	google maps, last.fm, lyricsfly, vimeo, youtube
	last.fm music data resources	discover music events and concerts around the world. the last.fm music map mixes last.fm music social network data with google maps	google maps, last.fm

Service Clustering: Users want to find real competitive services with respective to service s_i. In such a case, content-based search will list a set of "similar" ones based on the involved terms. Services collaboration network can help to cluster these services by context. In web search community[14], it has been proved that linkage is useful for search and organization. We detected the same thing for services environment. We generate the collaboration network $net^{[s_i]}$ for each service s_i. As shown in Fig.5, we build the collaboration network for services based on SPOTs. The services which are d-link distance away from it are called d-close neighbors represented as $net_d^{[s_i]}$. In Fig.5, supposing s_3 is current checking service, s_2, s_4 and s_5 compose the 1-close neighbors, represented as $net_1^{[s_3]}$; s_1 *and* s_6 are 2-close neighbors, represented as $net_2^{[s_3]}$. The similarity value between two services s_i and s_j is calculated as in Def.2, with $sim_{con}(s_i, s_j)$ and $sim_{cox}^{[d]}(s_i, s_j)$ as the content similarity and average d-close context similarity. we do not define some specific algorithm to calculate the similarity based on content and context, but using the simplest way shown in Def.2 to catch the values for these two parts. We take agglomerative clustering algorithm in Cluto tool[15]. Notice that, our main purpose here is not about the definition of clustering algorithm, but to see how the collaboration network affects the clustering results, as shown in Table.4. We can see link-based analysis can improve the precision of clustering results. But this is not always true and it will be evaluated in the following parts.

Definition 2. *Service* s_i *and* s_j *Similarity Value:* $Sim(s_i, s_j)$ $sim_{con}(s_i, s_j) = Cosine(V_{s_i}, V_{s_j})$, V *is the term vector of service, weighted by TFIDF;*

Table 4. Sample Clustering Results for both Systems

query keys	Baseline	Cox-based
Social community	Clustering Result Summarization	
	returned results are 58, precision for baseline system and cox-based system are 0.5 and 0.568, respectively.	
	BaseLine Samples:	Cox-based Sampels:
	wiserEarth, footPrints,GreenThings,FFwd	wiserEarth, Pownce, FFwd,Slifeshare
Service Description		
WiserEarth is a free online community space connecting people working toward a just and sustainable world;		
Pownce is a social networking platform that lets you keep up friends in interesting ways;		
Slifeshare is a lifestreaming network that makes it easy to share and discover media among friends;		
Ffwd is an online community that lets members discover new videos selected based on their interests and favorite shows, and share videos with friends;		
Green Thing is a public service that inspires people to lead a greener life,with the help of brilliant videos and inspiring stories etc;		
Footprints Network is an alliance of online e-commerce companies making a difference with a solution that supports sustainable poverty alleviation community programs.		

$sim^{[d]}_{cox}(s_i, s_j) = \frac{1}{d} \times \sum_{k=1}^{d}(\frac{net_k^{[s_i]} \bigcap net_k^{[s_j]}}{|net_k^{[s_i]} \bigcup net_k^{[s_j]}|})$, *average common context percentage* $Sim(s_i, s_j) = sim_{con}(s_i, s_j) \times sim^{[d]}_{cox}(s_i, s_j)$;

Performance Evaluation. We select a benchmark of 20 queries. When we select the queries, we ensure that they are from different categories. We manually find the relevant documents for each topic of queries by using the "Pooling" method, which has been frequently used in IR. The judgement pool is created as follows. We use baseline system, and context-based system to produce the $topK = 20$ candidates for our real candidates selection. From these merged results, we will select the most relevant results by our evaluators from the pool. To ensure $topK = 20$ is meaningful, we select the queries which can return more than 20 relevant services by each system.

We give a short description to the evaluation metrics used:

- $P@N = \frac{RetRel}{|N|}$,with $RetRel$ as the returned relevant ones and in our experiment, we select N=2,5 and 10;
- $MAP = \frac{1}{|R|} \times (\sum_{i=1}^{n}(p@i))$;

We show search precision and recall in Fig.10 and Fig.11. From Fig.10, we find that our method can provide better performance than baseline system. For example, for Top2 results, ours can have almost 20% higher precision performance. However as shown in Fig.12, our system will not improve the query processing performance when the queries are easily processed by baseline system. Here we analyze the effectiveness of our method in helping difficult queries as defined in [16]. We qualify the query difficulty by the Mean Average Precision (MAP) of the baseline search method. We order these 20 queries in a decreasing order of MAP values. We partition the queries into 4 bins with each having the equal number of queries. A higher

MAP value means the utility of the original ranking is lower. Bin 1 is with the highest MAP value in our experiment. For each bin, we compute the numbers of queries whose P@5's are improved versus decreased. Clearly, in bin 1, cox-based method decreases the performance (1 vs 3), while from bin 2, most of the queries are improved with performance, e.g. in bin 4 (4 vs 1). It is verified that our method is much useful for distinguishing the services with similar content descriptions and it also tells us this method will not help much for easy queries, thus we shall turn off the organization option for easy queries.

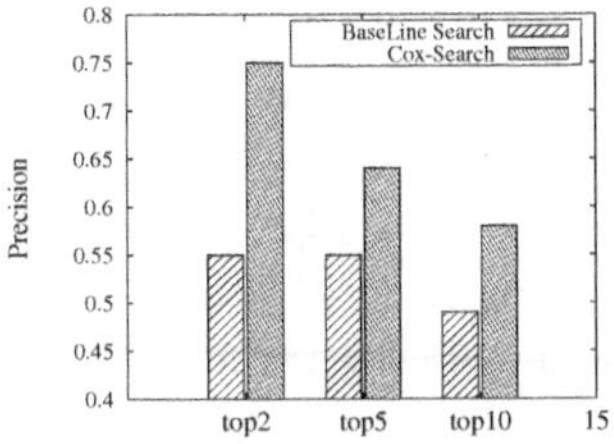

Fig. 10. P@N Precision at TopN

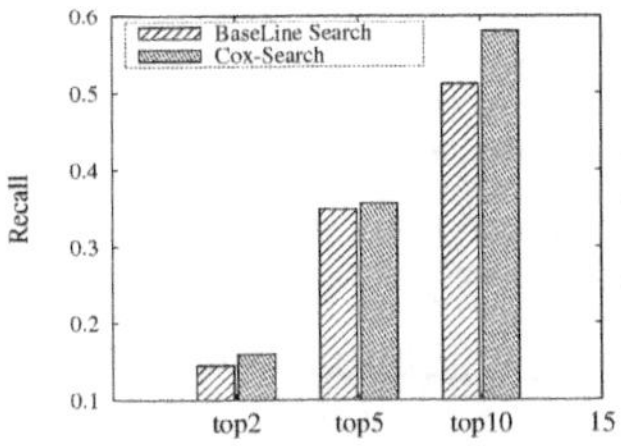

Fig. 11. Recall

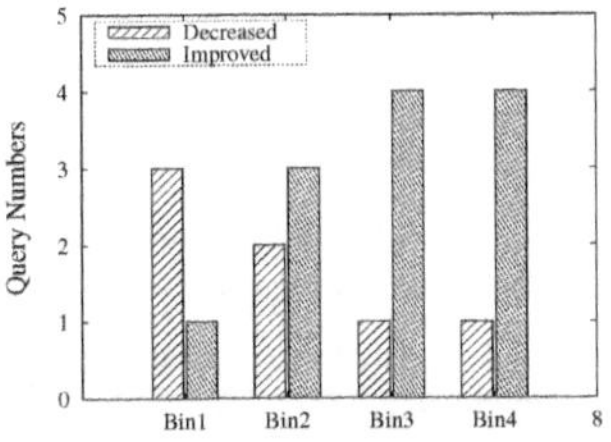

Fig. 12. Query Difficulty & Performance Improving

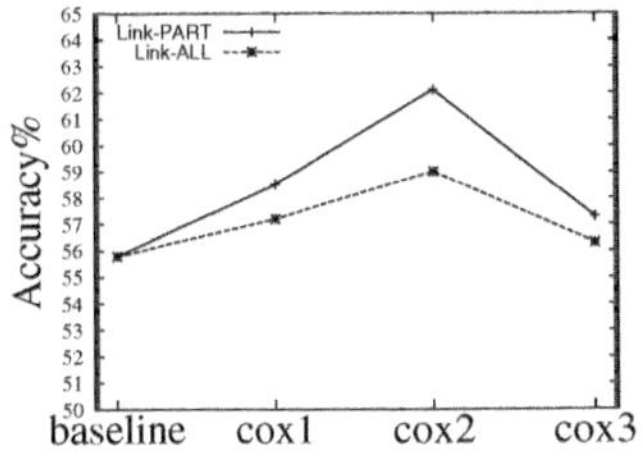

Fig. 13. Collaboration Structure Affects Clustering Performance:coxI(I=1,2,3): use the i close neighbor nodes as its attributes

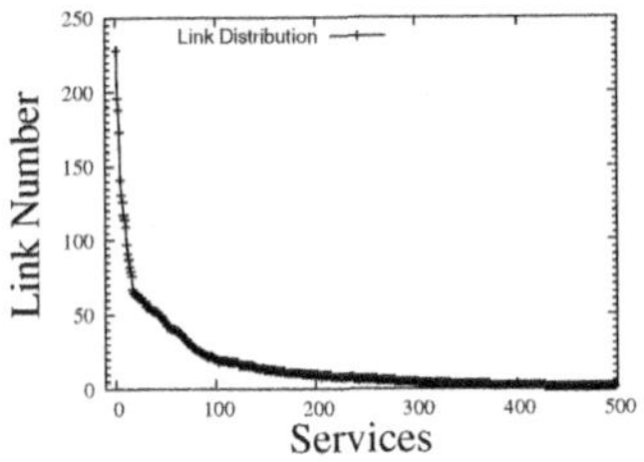

Fig. 14. Collaboration Network with Skewed Link Distribution

In Fig.13, we show the effects of introducing collaboration structure to clustering accuracy, which is defined as the number of correctly clustered services over the total number of returned results [17]. In this figure, for Link-All, we use all links(the same meaning with neighbors) associated with each returned result. And for Link-PART, we overlook the links associated with the nodes if the link number is more than 50, because such kind of services shall provide common usage, e.g. google, which can be used for traveling, for music society, for blogging and so on. We show the skewed link distribution in Fig.14. The links referred to it will be less informative. Sometimes these links can cause the clustering with lower accuracy. That is why Link-PART has better performance than Link-ALL. In Fig.13, CoxI(I=1,2,3) means to expand results (gotten from baseline system) to find the i-close neighbors. But we need not expand to find all of the i-close neighbors. When i=3, Link-PART and Link-ALL are both decreased. The main reason is that when i=3, almost all nodes which have links are linked.

6 Related Work

As the increasing of web services, desirable web service locations have increased its importance to win users. Content-based web service search has been found that there is noticeable amount of noise for service search, because of services description is short or not enough to distinguish themselves from others. Much effort has been put on solving this problem, mainly focusing on the detection or extension of service self static description. Until now, we summarize the work into 3 groups.

1. Content matching. We are supposed to compare the service functional description or functional attributes with the query to check whether advertisements support the required type of service. And we can also check the functionality capabilities of web service in terms of input and output, as used by woogle[5]. For service search and similarity calculation, it tries to include as more information as it can to characterize service. It is challenged by the length of service description, the variation of parameter names and the scale of service repository.
2. Ontology/semantics mapping [18,19,20]. These approaches require clear and formal semantic annotations to formal ontologies. But as we know most of the services those active on WWW do not contain so many ontology annotations. In order to make the work successful, it shall not contain so much semantic constraints which bound the activity of users and developers.
3. Context matching [21,22,2,7]. Recently context-aware approaches have been proposed to enhance web service location and composition. [7] proposes a context-related service discovery technique for mobile environments by defining a set of attributes to service. The search is still based on tradition search mechanism and context attributes act as filters.[2] suggests to define the context from two aspects: client-related context and provider-related context. It prefers to absorbing all the information related to service activity as the context, which makes context complicated and difficult to follow. By the way, real experiment experience has not been with the work.

7 Conclusion and Future Work

The ability to distinguish services and rank the services is crucial for SOA's prosperity. The main purpose of this work is to very the importance of services usage context, modeled by SPOT. SPOT has been proved useful for services organization: ranking, clustering or services recommendation. In this work, we suggest to rank the services by both the content relevance and usage goodness which is evaluated based on services collaboration bipartite graph building up from SPOT. Context is also useful to distinguish content similar services. However, context-related queries definition or the linkage semantics have not been tackled with yet. This part of work will be addressed in the future.

References

1. Fan, J., Kambhampati, S.: A snapshot of public web services. Journal of the ACM SIGMOD RECORD 34(1), 24–32 (2005)
2. Medjahed, B., Atif, Y.: Context-based matching for web service composition. Distributed and Parallel Databases 21(1), 5–37 (2007)
3. Segev, A., Toch, E.: Context-based matching and ranking of web services for composition. IEEE Transactions on Services Computing (2009)
4. Jones, A.B., Purao, S., et al.: Context-aware query processing on the semantic web. In: Proc. Information System (2002)
5. Dong, X., Halevy, A., et al.: Similarity search for web services. In: Proc. VLDB (2004)
6. ProgrammableWeb, `http://www.programmableweb.com/`
7. Lee, C., Helal, S.: Context attributes: an approach to enable context- awareness for service discovery. In: Proc. SAINT (2003)
8. BPEL4WS, `http://www.ibm.com/developerworks/library/specification/ws-bpel/`
9. WSDL, `http://www.w3.org/TR/wsdl`
10. RESTfull_Web_Services, `http://en.wikipedia.org/wiki/Representational_State_Transfer`
11. Mashup, `http://en.wikipedia.org/wiki/Mashup`
12. Kleinberg, J.: Authoritative sources in a hyperlinked environment. Journal of the ACM (JACM) 46(5), 668–677 (1999)
13. Small, H.: Co-citation in the scientific literature: A new measure of the relationship between two documents. J. Amer. Soc. Inform. Sci. 24(4), 265–269 (1973)
14. Wang, Y., Kitsuregawa, M.: Use link-based clustering to improve web search results. In: Proc. WISE (2001)
15. Cluto_Mining_Tool, `http://www-users.cs.umn.edu/~karypis/cluto/index.html`
16. Yom-Tov, E., Fine, S., et al.: Learning to estimate query difficulty: including applications to missing content detection and distributed information retrieval. In: Proc. SIGIR (2005)
17. Zhang, R., Zettsu, K., et al.: Context-based web service clustering. In: Proc. SKG (2009)
18. Selvi, S., Balachandar, R.A., et al.: Semantic discovery of grid services using functionality based matchmaking algorithm. In: Proc. WI (2006)
19. Paolucci, M., Kawamura, T., et al.: Semantic matching of web services capabilities. In: Horrocks, I., Hendler, J. (eds.) ISWC 2002. LNCS, vol. 2342, p. 333. Springer, Heidelberg (2002)
20. Klusch, M., Fries, B., et al.: Owls-mx: Hybrid semantic web service retrieval. In: Proc. 1st Intl. AAAI Fall Symposium on Agents and the Semantic Web (2005)
21. Morris, M.R., Teevan, J., et al.: Enhancing collaborative web search with personalization: groupization, smart splitting, and group hit-highlighting. In: Proc. CSCW (2008)
22. Wong, J., Hong, J.I.: Making mashups with marmite: Towards end-user programming for the web. In: Proc. CHI (2007)

Building Business Intelligence Applications Having Prescriptive and Predictive Capabilities

Chen Jiang, David L. Jensen, Heng Cao, and Tarun Kumar

IBM T.J.Watson Research, 1101 Kitchawan Road, Yorktown Heights, NY 10547, USA
{ChJiang,DavJen,HengCao,KTarun}@us.ibm.com

Abstract. Traditional Business Intelligence applications have focused on providing a one shop stop to integrate the enterprise information. The resulting applications are only capable of providing descriptive information viz: standard and ad-hoc reporting and drill-down capability. As part of an effort to provide prescriptive and predictive capability, we demonstrate a new architecture, methodology and implementation. Based on Cognos Business Intelligence platform and ILOG optimization engine, we showcase a truly predictive application that enables an optimal decision making in real-time analytical scenario.

Keywords: Business Intelligence, Prescriptive, Predictive, Optimization, Analytics.

1 Introduction

Business Intelligence has emerged as a key driver for growth among business organizations. The term business intelligence was first coined in an article in 1958 by IBM Researcher Hans Peter Luhn. He described a system comprising of data-processing machines for auto-abstraction of documents and creating interest profiles for each of the action points in an organization. Further, Howard Dresner in 1989 proposed that BI include concepts and methods to improve business decision making by using fact-based support systems.

Since then, numerous products and services have been rolled out by various vendors in the BI space. Each of these products fall into one of the following three categories: domain specific solutions, general purpose reporting tools, mathematical modeling products. Let us review the existing products that are currently available in the marketplace that provide BI capabilities. Domain specific solutions include the enterprise resource planning tools (ERP) from companies like SAP, Oracle etc. These tools provide an out-of-the-box functionality for some key aspects of the business function and have certain well defined analytical models that help in making business decisions. The second classes of products are commercial-off-the-shelf (COTS) data warehousing / reporting tools. These tools can be connected to an enterprise system to extract and reorganize transactional information into star schema [6] type of data models. Analysts and other decision makers can then query and analyze the information to do a trend analysis, find key bottlenecks to growth or predict future demands. They also provide online analytical processing (OLAP) capability. The third class of products is implementation of operations research methodologies viz: statistical

L. Chen et al. (Eds.): WAIM 2010, LNCS 6184, pp. 376–385, 2010.

analysis, mathematical optimization, simulation etc. These tools can be used to build mathematical models and then feed the organizational information to get specific insights e.g.: statistical models can be built to predict the demand for certain key seasonal products or an optimization model to efficiently map the rout for delivery tucks.

Each of the three classes of products comes up short of being tagged as a true BI system. Domain specific systems only provide a small subset of BI capabilities. Their main objective is to provide efficiencies in the operational systems. The off-the-shelf data warehousing tools provide the basic extract, transform & load (ETL) functionality. They enable uses to quickly transform the transactional data to create drag-drop and drill down reporting capabilities. They are very good at providing descriptive information about the enterprise but lack the capability to provide deep analytical capabilities. The products based on operations research are stand-alone tools and it is a cumbersome task to integrate them with the operational system in terms of both time and effort.

Hence there remains a need for an agile framework and tool that can overcome the deficiencies of each of the three classes of systems. Towards this end, we in IBM Research set out to design a framework and build first-of-a-kind application using the framework that showcases a truly integrated system having deep analytics embedded in it. Since the domain specific BI systems have their own proprietary architecture and interfaces, in this paper, we will focus on presenting our solution which can efficiently enable a COTS data warehousing/reporting system with prescriptive and predictive capabilities offered by the operations research methodologies. We use IBM Cognos v8 to build a reporting dashboard capability. Also, IBM ILOG OPL Studio is used to build an optimization model. These two are integrated together using analytical application integration framework (AAIF). This framework integrates predictive and optimization capabilities to an otherwise descriptive information platform. To showcase an end-to-end capability we use the Multi-Period workforce evolution model. This model enables decision makers to understand the composition of the employee's job roles and skills across the time horizon. Using this model, informed hiring and training decisions can be made to adapt the workforce to the changing business needs.

In our implementation, although we have used these two tools and AAIF to demonstrate the prescriptive and predictive capability, it should be noted that the framework and method described in this paper can be applied seamlessly to integrate a customized analytical engine to any commercial product or a custom application.

2 Business Problem and Solution Overview

Delivering predictive and prescriptive capabilities from a more generic data warehousing/reporting tool is very attractive to the business users, since they would get the combined power to understand past, as well as suggestions of future optimized actions, all from one integrated environment.

However, this is not a trivial task, as the key requirements to BI reporting tools focusing on effectively reporting on large and usually high dimensional data. To serve this purpose, the usual assumption is that the data is static, and only changes periodically. BI reporting tools usually won't have the infrastructure and capability to effectively take real-time user inputs and evaluate the changes in run time, which is often the case with optimization and what-if type of analysis. In order to accomplish this task, two levels of challenges need to be addressed: first from application middle tier and second from the back end tier. From application middle tier we need to provide mechanism to allow the system to take end user inputs and effectively invoke the backend predictive or prescriptive models; on the backend tier, we need to provide an integration between the optimization model and high dimensional BI data objects designed as a star schema type of data model.

To address the first level of challenge, various BI systems are implementing extensions to allow plug-ins into external computational processes. This implementation needs significant development effort. Further, most of the mathematical modeling tools have been developed with the assumption that the tool will be used in a stand alone mode. Hence these tools do not lend themselves easily to integration within enterprise architecture. Our approach is based on a non invasive method to address this problem by building a framework that can be applied to a host of modeling tools and is efficient to implement. The premise of our framework is based on the observation that all the existing BI reporting systems have data access via SQL through database drivers implemented using interfaces like ODBC, JDBC. In section 4, we will discuss our approach in detail which is a novel method for enabling an external computational processes being exposed as dynamic data sources through standard database interfaces, such as ODBC or JDBC. These computational processes can then be consumed by existing BI reporting systems using standard SQL queries. The framework we developed for this purpose is called Analytic Application Integration Framework (AAIF) which enables an efficient plug of an ILOG optimization solver to a query data mart cube built in Cognos reporting platform. The framework allows a bi-directional interaction between the two systems enabling reading and writing of optimization results back to data mart.

The second level of challenge which arises from the back end data integration tier is the sheer number of optimization scenarios that can be created when the user drills up and down along the high dimensional BI data space. Hence, it is impossible to build optimization models to address each possible scenario. Also, in real time, the very fine grained data existing in BI data warehouse makes the predictive and optimization models' computation time exorbitantly expensive. To address this issue, we have defined a meta-structure for the optimization model data. We have also designed an efficient binding/mapping schema between the optimization vector space and BI Star Schema's high dimensional data space. This enables an optimization model to be run on multiple scenarios regardless of the scenario being selected by the user.

Before we present the solution in detail, we are going to set the stage by first explaining briefly optimization in general and then describe the workforce use case to illustrate how optimization is used in business context. This workforce planning use case is also used through out the paper to explain the technical solution in detail. In mathematics and computer science, optimization or mathematical programming refers to choosing the best element from some set of available alternatives [1]. Below is a LP formula, which optimizes a linear objective function subject to linear equality/inequality constraints.

$$\text{LP:} \quad \text{Maximize } c^T x$$

$$\text{Subject to } Ax <= b$$

x represents the vector of variables (to be determined), while c and b are vectors of (known) coefficients and A is a (known) matrix of coefficients

Linear programming (LP) probably is one of the simplest form but with greatest practical use. For example, we are considering a workforce management business problem, the HR analyst wants to know the optimal staffing level for US by different regions for the future in terms of headcounts. This problem can be formed as a LP with variables including headcounts denoted as X(N,T), hiring H(N,T) and mandatory attritions F(N,T) where T is a vector including all the periods in the planning horizon, and N is a vector with one element corresponding to the each different regions. The object function is minimizing the overall costs including attrition costs, hiring costs and salary costs. Constrains of this LP problem come from two parts, one is external demands, we would like the headcounts be small or equal than the demands. The other set of constrains defined by the workforce its own internal structure and dynamics. We have been using Markov network to model the workforce transitions between different workforce types, e.g. junior employee evolves to be experienced with certain transition probability. For detailed mathematical treatments of this problem please refer to [2].

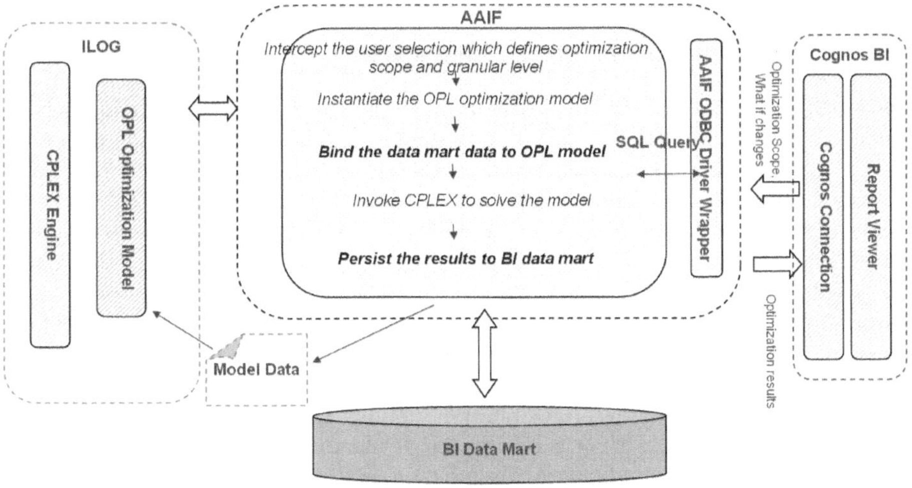

Fig. 1. Integration Diagram

One important point to be noted is that we have chosen LP here for its simplicity and ease of understanding. However the integration approach, data mapping method established in this paper can be extended to other optimization problems besides LP.

Following is a chart illustrates the information flow of the solution. As mentioned earlier ILOG has be used to provide optimization capability and Cognos is providing reporting, OLAP and dash port functionality. AAIF is used to provide the backend optimization module an ODBC wrapper and transparent to the BI reporting environment just like one of the normal data sources. AAIF helps to relieve developer from the integration effort and focus on the developing the optimization model using an optimization environment he/she is familiar with (green blocks in the chart).

3 Adaptive Application Integration Framework

AAIF is a generic architecture that helps in bringing the descriptive (Cognos) and prescriptive (OPL) applications together. AAIF enables an analytical engine to be integrated as a virtual data source. Data, parameters and results are exposed as a relational data source. This enables an existing data analysis / reporting platform to consume the analytical capabilities seamlessly, thus allowing a very simple integration path. The framework allows for integration of analytical models spanning a vast array of languages viz: C/C++, Java, Matlab, SAS, SPSS, PHP, Pearl etc. The powerful extensions built into the framework allow the application to be integrated across multiple boundaries. Applications can be integrated across the process boundaries: analytical model execution can be in-process or out-of-process; Engine boundaries: request can be marshaled to engines line MATLAB, R, SPSS, SAS etc.; Protocol Boundaries: requests can be marshaled across web services or other protocols. Note that the AAIF architecture is independent of the business problem and can be used to integrate any two component application. We now discuss the framework in detail.

3.1 Integrating External Processes Using AAIF

One of the key features of the AAIF framework is the ability to provide a bridge between applications that manipulate data sources and those that provide data analysis. ODBC[7] is the Open Database Connectivity standard. It is a standard interface supported by most tools and systems that use databases and is language and system independent. Of particular interest are tools like COGNOS, which provides a rich data access, data organization, and reporting interface. One sub-component of the AAIF is the BAMS ODBC Driver, is registered as a data source just as any other ODBC driver. It provides two dimensions of flexibility. One dimension is that it provides a proxy for another real data source through a real ODBC driver. The second dimension is that it provides a proxy for a virtual data source through a driver extension. The real data source is defined through registration of another ODBC driver and its configuration. The BAMS ODBC Driver is responsible for loading the real driver and redirecting calls from the client application through the real driver.

The extension driver is provided by the end user and is the mechanism for adding functionality into the ODBC framework. There are several forms that the extension can take. One form is to provide a binding into existing analytical models or data processing. Another form is one that provides a language binding by reflecting the ODBC interface from its native compiled environment through to an alternate target language such as Java, Perl, or PHP.

As the BAMS ODBC Driver processes requests, the user extension may manipulate both the requests, prior to their submission to the real driver, as well as post process the results of the real driver. Some of the implications of this capability are that the driver may

- augment the real data source by adding virtual tables and columns
- intercept and manipulate SQL requests from the client program before sending them on to the real driver
- redirect requests through other protocols and languages
- provide access to base operating system features such as logging, performance monitoring, network and computational services
- provide access to capabilities provided external engines such as MATLAB, SAS, SPSS, etc.

3.2 BAMS ODBC Driver

The ODBC Driver is a key component of the AAIF framework. It is, for the most part implemented by code generated from an xml encoding of the ODBC specification. An XSD is used for auto generation of the ODBC interface. The current code generation process uses an XML document and XSLT processing to generate driver code.

The default generation has two dimensions along which the core ODBC driver provides extensions. The first dimension allows the ODBC Driver to act as a proxy. That is, is provides a mechanism for deployment time registering and runtime enabling an ODBC driver to a real database. As an example, the ODBC driver provided by db2cli.dll on the Windows platform may be registered to provide access to a DB2 database. The second dimension provides a mechanism for passing ODBC requests in an extension library. The functionality of the extension library is not specified and is

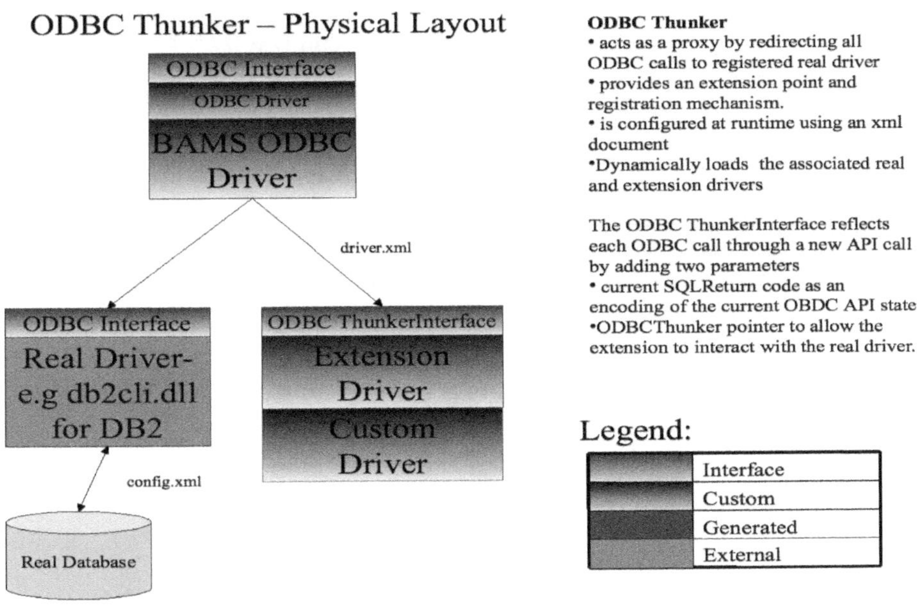

Fig. 2. ODBC Default Driver Architecture

up to the developer. The examples that we have in mind provide optimization and analytical capabilities to augment an underlying data source. We also will use this extension capability to provide extensions to the platform that cross:

- language boundaries, for example to Java, PHP, or Perl
- process boundaries so that analytical model execution may either be in-process or out-of-process
- engine boundaries so that requests may be marshaled to engines like MATLAB, R, or other analytic engines
- protocol boundaries so that requests may be marshaled across Web services or other protocols
- provide control points to implement non-functional requirements such as performance monitoring, session management, and logging.

3.3 Request / Response Interaction

This flow is implemented in generated C code for each of the methods within the ODBC interface. The pattern used is one in which an initialization method is used to set up the interface. The default implementation of the initialization method is to set up indirection tables into the real driver and extension driver at runtime on the first invocation and to do nothing on all subsequent invocations. The next call to ODBCThunkerEnter is used for performance monitoring and request tracking. The ODBCThunkerCallback call is used to invoke the corresponding extension function with additional arguments providing the current state of method call, a pointer to the methods on the real driver, and an argument indicating the current position, either on entry or exit, of the current invocation.

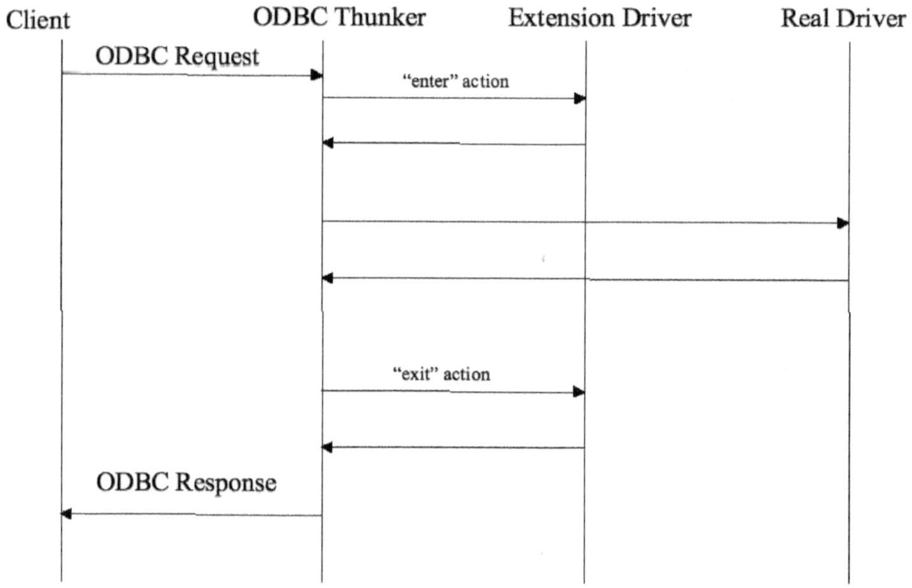

Fig. 3. Request / Response Flow in Default Extension Wrapper

If no SQLError is flagged, the real driver method is invoked. Once again, the ODBCThunkerCallback call is used to give the extension driver a chance to postprocess the results. Finally, the ODBCThunkerExit method is called to finish up the performance, logging or other generic tasks.

```
SQLRETURN SQL_API SQLPrepare(
SQLHSTMT StatementHandle,
SQLCHAR * StatementText,
SQLINTEGER TextLength
)
{
SQLRETURN ret;
ODBCThunkerInit();
ODBCThunkerEnter("SQLPrepare");
if((ret=ODBCThunkerCallback(SQL_SUCCESS,&ODBCThunker,"SQL
Prepare","enter",
StatementHandle,
StatementText,
TextLength))==SQL_SUCCESS){
ret=ODBCThunker.SQLPrepare(
StatementHandle,
StatementText,
TextLength);
```

4 Use Case Illustration

The optimization model formulation of the workforce management problem is to minimize the unmet demand of resource having specific job roles and skill sets. The formulation is parameterized by the limits on the expense in the various categories. The data that is used in the problem formulation is tabular and is available in Cognos BI data mart. The user interface we provide is a simple COGNOS report which allows uses to set parameters such as geography, salary, job category, number of planning periods, and expected change in demand and service level. When the report is run, the optimal revenue and assignment of resources are computed and displayed including the charts reflecting some of the business metrics based on the settings of these decision variables

To support the integration of the analytical models into the COGNOS platform we need to provide a mechanism for communicating the parameters and data of a workforce optimization formulation to the implementation of the linear programming problem and to capture the results of the optimization.

COGNOS uses an object model to construct potentially complex SQL queries for the user and the associated result sets to provide data for tabular and charting report components. The BAMS ODBC Driver uses this property of the COGNOS interaction with data sources and uses the semantics available through the SQL syntax. In addition to using the BAMS ODBC Driver to provide a semantic filter for generated SQL queries, we also use the driver to provide a mechanism for binding to data sources different from databases and for crossing language and process boundaries. The optimization algorithm is written in Java.

Although there are alternatives for implementing this scenario, we will use a concrete example that exploits query filters in COGNOS. The reason behind the use of query filter is two fold. First, since the objective is to tie analytical model execution to the most granular level of COGNOS user interface component, using query filters enables us to bind a COGNOS reports with the backend analytical models. Second, using query filters enables AAIF use non-invasive approach to integrate the backend analytical models. Hence a detail filter is added to the query subject in the data table of the report. The following is an example of an SQL statement generated by COGNOS to fill in the table in the report, where the query filter appears in the where clause of the select statement.

```
select
"MIDS_BAMS_RESULTS"."VALUE" "VALUE" ,
"MIDS_BAMS_RESULTS1"."INTERNET" "INTERNET" ,
"MIDS_BAMS_RESULTS"."OOH" "OOH" ,
"MIDS_BAMS_RESULTS"."DG" "DG" from "BAMS"."RESULTS"
"MIDS_BAMS_RESULTS"
where bamsFunction('Internet', '0.75..2.0', '1.00..1.00',
'OOH', '1.00..1.00', '1.00..1.00', 'DG',
'0.75..2.0', '1.00..1.00',
"MIDS_BAMS_RESULTS"."VALUE") = 0
```

The selected table is a table of results from various runs of the marketing mix optimization. The predicate of the where clause is used to communicate parameters determined by the end user to the optimization run. In order to process this request, the ODBC driver captures the select statement an SQL parser, written in Java and provided as part of the Eclipse platform, is used to parse the statement the object model provided by the parser is used to modify the statement by capturing and modifying the bamsFunction part of the where clause predicate resulting in

```
select
"MIDS_BAMS_RESULTS"."VALUE" "VALUE" ,
"MIDS_BAMS_RESULTS1"."INTERNET" "INTERNET" ,
"MIDS_BAMS_RESULTS"."OOH" "OOH" ,
"MIDS_BAMS_RESULTS"."DG" "DG" from "BAMS"."RESULTS"
"MIDS_BAMS_RESULTS" where 0 = 0
```

The bamsFunction arguments are provided to the cplex solver and the results of the optimization are stored in the table referenced by the select statement the real ODBC driver is invoked using the modified SQL to return the correct results.

In order to accomplish this, the developer can use the Java driver extension that is provided. This extension reflects all the native ODBC calls through to Java. When the Java ODBC driver is used, it is registered with the core BAMS ODBC driver through a driver registration xml document.

```
<?xml version="1.0" encoding="UTF-8"?>
      <root mlns="http://com.ibm.bams/odbcdriver/config/"
       xmlns:tns=http://com.ibm.bams/odbcdriver/config/
       xmlns:xsi="http://www.w3.org/2001/XMLSchema-
       instance"
      xsi:schemaLocation=
      "http://com.ibm.bams/odbcdriver/config /
       config.xsd ">
```

```
<library name="odbcextensionjava.dll">
      <property name="classpath"
      value="classes; /ApplicationWeb.jar; ODBCJava.jar;
            db2jcc_license_cu.jar;RunModel.jar"/>
</library>
<driver name="db2cli.dll"/>
</root>
```

This document is used to identify both the real ODBC driver, in this case provided by db2cli.dll, as well as the extension driver and properties that it requires. The extension driver is the odbcextensionjava.dll which is a generic Java extension. It is specialized to a particular purpose by specifying a class name that implements that specific purpose. The named class is responsible for extending a base class and overriding those ODBC methods required to accomplish its goals.

In the example above, only a few Java methods in the ODBC class need to be overwritten to bind the optimization method into the COGNOS platform.

5 Conclusion

In this paper, we describe a framework called AAIF which allow predictive and prescriptive capabilities on the generic BI data warehousing/reporting environments. This could provide tremendous value to the business decision makers. We are currently working on enhancing it with tooling to allow the advanced integration project be created, managed and deployed more conveniently.

References

1. Nocedal, J., Wright, S.: Numerical Optimization, 2nd edn. Springer, New York (2006) ISBN 978-0-387-30303
2. Lu, Y.D., Sharma, M., Squillante, M.: Stochastic Analytics and Optimization for Workforce Evolution, Technical Report, IBM Research (2006)
3. Kumar, T., Parija, G., Haifeng, X., Keller, D.: Strategic Planning of Preparedness Budgets for Wildland Fire Management. IBM Journal of Research and Development 51(3/4) (May/July 2007)
4. Nemhauser, G.L., Wolsey, L.A.: Integer and Combinatorial Optimization. John Wiley & Sons, Inc., Hoboken (1988)
5. IBM ILOG Optimization, http://www-01.ibm.com/software/websphere/products/optimization/
6. Cognos Business Intelligence and Financial Performance Management, http://www-01.ibm.com/software/data/cognos/
7. Star Schema, http://publib.boulder.ibm.com/infocenter/rbhelp/v6r3/index.jsp?topic=/com.ibm.redbrick.doc6.3/wag/wag32.htm
8. Open Database Connectivity Overview (ODBC), http://support.microsoft.com/kb/110093

FileSearchCube: A File Grouping Tool Combining Multiple Types of Interfile-Relationships

Yousuke Watanabe[1], Kenichi Otagiri[2], and Haruo Yokota[1,2]

[1] Global Scientific Information and Computing Center,
Tokyo Institute of Technology,
2-12-1 Ookayama, Meguro-ku, Tokyo, 152-8552 Japan
watanabe@de.cs.titech.ac.jp, yokota@cs.titech.ac.jp
[2] Graduate School of Information Science and Engineering,
Tokyo Institute of Technology
otagiri@de.cs.titech.ac.jp

Abstract. Files in computers are increasing in number, so we require file management tools to find target files and to classify large groups of files. Our research group has been developing a system that provides virtual directories made up of related files. Many methods to extract inter-file relationships are available, such as word frequency, access co-occurrence, and so on. In practice, users need to select and combine multiple types of inter-file relationships to form groups of files they want. For this purpose, we propose FileSearchCube, a tool for file group analysis that introduces the data-cube concept. FileSearchCube provides cube operations for a set of files, and helps users to find relevant file groups.

1 Introduction

Files stored in computer systems are increasing in number [1]. We have various types of files, including plain text, RTF documents, images, videos and so on. Even if the files are organized by folder, it is difficult to find target files in a large set of files. To solve this problem, we often use desktop search [8,11]. Most desktop search tools are keyword-based full-text search. They extract keywords from file paths, metadata of files (tags) and file contents. They also create an index for extracted keywords. When a user enters keywords, the tool returns a list of files associated with the keywords. Desktop search is useful when a target file includes common keywords.

Many other situations arise, however, in which desktop search tools cannot deliver satisfactory results. For example, when we need multiple files associated with different keywords, we have to choose multiple keywords and submit multiple search requests. Especially, keyword information for non-text files is limited (only file paths may be available); it is difficult for desktop search tools to find them. The difficulty arises because of limitations in keyword-based search techniques.

When we want to derive multiple target files, we would like to obtain, at one time, multiple files that have logical relationships. To achieve this, a good ap-

L. Chen et al. (Eds.): WAIM 2010, LNCS 6184, pp. 386–397, 2010.

proach is to analyze interfile relationships and group related files. When such logical file relationships are discovered, desktop search tools can expand search results more easily. And when we have forgotten files used in previous work, we can find them again by traversing file relationships. Examples of such relationships include common keywords, modified at similar times, having similar file paths, concurrently accessed by the same user, and so on. Types of interfile relationships abound, and various scoring measures for them are proposed. Which measures should we use? Can we use them together? For more precise and flexible search requirements, we need to combine multiple measures of interfile relationships to create relevant file groups. Even if files are not appropriately separated by the keyword-based grouping method, we may do that by combining other measures, such as access co-occurrence. Although file grouping tools supporting a single type of interfile relationship already exist, there are no schemes to uniformly combine multiple measures.

We propose a file grouping scheme to combine multiple interfile relationships. Its model is based on the data cube [4], which is generally used in OLAP. We call it FileSearchCube. Our scheme supports functions for generating relevant file groups: choosing appropriate relationship measures, changing granularity of grouping, selecting groups based on multiple conditions. A dimension in FileSearchCube is a list of clusters constructed from one scoring measure of interfile relationship. FileSearchCube consists of multiple lists of clusters constructed from multiple measures. A user applies cube operations to the cube, and gets the sub-cube that the user wants. Cube operations are slice and roll-up/drill-down. Slice is an operation to cut the cube based on multiple conditions for dimensions. Roll-up/drill-down are operations to change the granularity of groupings for each dimension. Our scheme analyzes a large number of files more easily than previous systems. We have developed a prototype system and include an experimental evaluation in this paper.

The remainder of this paper is organized as follows: Section 2 describes related work. Section 3 introduces interfile relationships used in this paper. Section 4 presents the proposed file-grouping framework using the data cube. Section 5 describes our prototype system. Section 7 shows experiment results. And finally the Section 8 summarizes the paper and mentions future research issues.

2 Related Work

We first introduce search engines integrating keywords and other information. Google desktop search [8] provides a timeline view to display files that are modified and where in the search result they are modified. FRIDAL[7] integrates keyword search and access co-occurrences recorded in log data of file servers. Although this technique can find more files than conventional keyword search engines, the purpose is not to group files.

Semantic File System [3] provides a logical view based on metadata attached in file attributes. In this system, files belong to virtual directories defined by multiple conditions for a file's metadata. Windows Vista provides a search folders function. These systems use only file attributes. They do not consider interfile relationships, such as path similarity and access co-occurrences.

Faceted search [5,6] explores objects with step-by-step selections. In each step, the system presents a set of selected objects and candidates of the object's attributes to give a condition for the next selection. Faceted search is similar to our scheme; it does not, however, consider interfile relationships.

Linking File Systems (LiFS)[2] can handle interfile relationships such as reference, copy/original and dependency. This system supports links to describe file relationships. Our scheme does not consider complex graph structures, but takes into account binary interfile relationships computed as numerical values.

3 Interfile Relationships

This section introduces similarity measures for interfile relationships. Of course, there are many similarity measures not described below. It is possible to introduce additional measures into FileSearchCube. We assume only that a measure returns a numeric value corresponding to an interfile relationship. In the remaining part, we assume that a similarity value between file x and file y is normalized in $[0, 1]$. The number 1 is the strongest relationship, and 0 is the weakest.

3.1 Text Similarity

Text similarity is used in document clustering. When many common keywords are contained in files, the files are strongly related to each other. Here, we assume a vector model. We extract keywords from file x and y; we then create word vectors v_x, v_y. Similarity between x and y is computed by a cosine value of two vectors. $Sim_{text}(x, y) = \frac{v_x \cdot v_y}{||v_x|| ||v_y||}$. For simplicity, we do not consider metadata (tag) information and file name to compute text similarity in this paper. We regard similarity between non-text files and other files as 0.

Although applicable only to text data, an advantage of text similarity is that the value is computed from file contents. Unlike text similarity, the three measures described below do not handle file contents. A disadvantage of this measure is that it is impossible to compute similarity for non-text files.

3.2 Modified Time Similarity

If two files are modified in close time instants, they may be processed together. This measure computes the similarity score based on the last time the two files were modified. Similarity score is computed by the following formula. $Sim_{mtime}(x, y) = 1 - \frac{|mtime(x) - mtime(y)|}{max_{a,b \in F}(|mtime(a) - mtime(b)|)}$, $mtime(f)$ expresses the last modified time of file f. The denominator in the formula is to normalize score ($\in [0, 1]$).

The advantage of modified time similarity is that it is applicable to all files. However, it is difficult to associate modified files with read-only files (their modified times are not changed).

3.3 Path Similarity

This measure regards files to be strongly related if they are located in the same folder or ancestor-descendant folders. In this paper, we use edit distance to compute path similarity. Edit distance is the distance between two strings. It is the number of operations (insert, delete, replace) to get the same string from one to another. Path similarity is computed by the following formula: $Sim_{path}(x,y) = 1 - \frac{editDistance(x,y)}{max_{a,b \in F}(editDistance(a,b))}$.

Path similarity works well when a user religiously organizes files and folders. On the other hand, when a user does not pay attention to file organization (e.g., many files are located in the same folder), this measure cannot distinguish between related files and irrelevant files.

3.4 Access Co-occurrence Similarity

When a user accesses two files at the same time, these files are processed together. If access co-occurrences are frequently observed, such files are strongly related. We can obtain access information from log data produced by file servers. [7] uses log data from a Samba server [10]. This log contains user id, file path, open/close time, and so on. In this paper, co-occurrence similarity is computed by total length of the co-occurrence time. $Sim_{cooccur}(x,y) = \frac{\Sigma t(x,y)}{max_{a,b \in F}(\Sigma t(a,b))}$, $t(x,y)$ expresses the set of co-occurrence times of files x and y.

Unlike modified time similarity, co-occurrence similarity can associate modified files with read-only files. Because of limited log data, however, it is difficult to derive precise similarity for files rarely used and files newly created.

As described above, various measures for interfile relationships have been proposed. They have advantages and disadvantages, and the effectiveness of these measures depends on user behavior and tendency. Thus, we have to choose and combine appropriate measures case by case.

4 FileSearchCube

FileSearchCube generates file groups by integrating multiple measures of inter-file relationships (Figure 1). Since its data model is based on the data cube, it consists of dimensions and hierarchies. And it supports cube operations such as slice/dice and roll-up/drill-down. Although the conventional data cube targets the presentation of aggregation results rather than groups of items, FileSearchCube aims to discover logical groups of files.

4.1 Dimension

In FileSearchCube, a dimension is a list of file clusters generated by one similarity measure. Here, we use similarity measures introduced in Section 3. Conventional clustering is used in the tool. We summarize a clustering method below. Figure 1

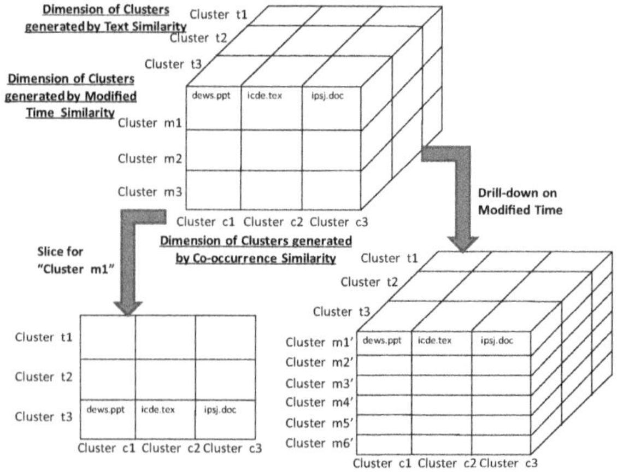

Fig. 1. FileSearchCube

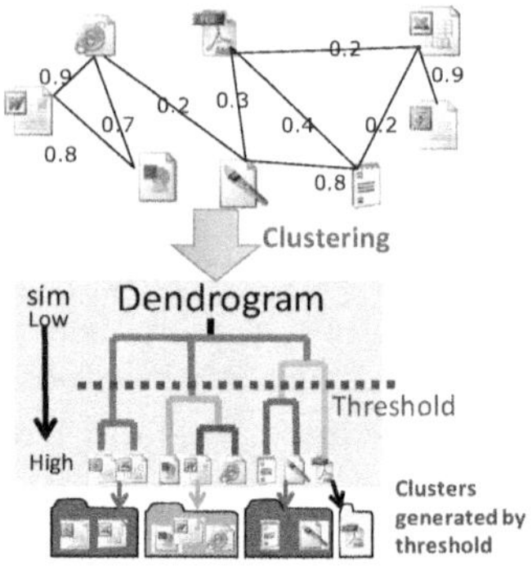

Fig. 2. Dendrogram generated by hierarchical clustering

presents a cube consisting of three dimensions. For instance, a file *dews.ppt* belongs to a cluster $t3$ generated by text similarity, $m1$ by modified time similarity, and $c1$ by co-occurrence similarity. We can use auxiliary dimensions generated by file information such as file name (dictionary order), file size, and file types (file extensions). A user groups files by combining clustering results from multiple measures and file information.

Clustering Method: By applying the formulas shown in Section 3 to N files, we can get an $N \times N$ similarity matrix. The clustering method receives this matrix as input. In this paper, we use conventional hierarchical clustering [4]. The method first makes a set of minimum clusters composed of each element; it then merges clusters that have high similarity values. It repeats merging, and finally produces one large cluster concatenating all clusters. A process in which the clustering method merges clusters is expressed as a dendrogram. Figure 2 is a dendrogram, which is the clustering result of 8 files. Clusters merged near the root of the dendrogram are regarded as having weak relationships. We can cut a dendrogram based on a threshold value and divide it into subtrees. Each pair of clusters within a subtree has larger similarities than the threshold value. A threshold value controls granularity of clusters. When a threshold value is near the root of the dendrogram, rough clusters are generated. When a threshold value is near the leaves of the dendrogram, fine clusters are generated. This property contributes to adjusting the granularity of groups in the data cube.

4.2 Hierarchy

In the conventional data cube, a concept hierarchy is used to change aggregation units in more abstracted/concreted layers. FileSearchCube also uses hierarchy information to group files. Hierarchies for dimensions corresponding to file attribute information are similar to those in the conventional method. They are defined in advance. For example, with the file extension type dimension, lower (concrete) layers are ".doc", ".txt", ".png", ".jpg" and higher (abstract) layers are "document","image". Hierarchies for dimensions corresponding to clustering results are substituted by dendrograms of clustering results. As described in Section 4.1, a dendrogram expresses the progress of merging clusters. Roll-up/drill-down cube operations change the granularity of clusters using dendrograms.

4.3 Cube Operations

Slice and Dice: Slice is a cube operation, which clips a sub-cube according to specified conditions. When conditions are defined on two or more dimensions, the operation is called dice. In this system, a user is also able to clip file groups by slicing the data cube. Beyond specifying a cluster label directly, conditions can also specify "cluster containing file A". Figure 1 is an example of slice. It clips a sub-cube with conditions that a label of modified time cluster equals $m1$.

Roll-up and Drill-down: Roll-up is an operation to regroup items by more abstract layers in the concept hierarchy. For example, roll-up changes monthly groups to yearly groups. On the other hand, drill-down is an operation to regroup items by more concrete layers. In FileSearchCube, dimensions of file attributes support conventional style roll-up/drill-down. Roll-up/drill-down for dimensions of clustering results are interpreted as an operation changing granularity of clusters. A threshold to cut a dendrogram controls granularity. When a dendrogram is cut near the root, the operation generates rough clusters. Figure 1 is an example of drill-down on a clustering result of modified time similarity.

Pivot: Pivot is an operation to change the order of dimensions and direction of axes. This is the same operation used in the conventional data cube.

5 Prototype System

A prototype system of our proposed scheme is written in Ruby (ActiveScriptRuby) and R. The architecture of the system is shown in Figure 3. The system consists of a similarity extractor, cluster generator, cube controller, and the Cube UI.

- **Similarity Extractor:** The similarity extractor obtains interfile relationships between files in a file system. The current implementation supports the text similarity, modified time similarity, path similarity and co-occurrence similarity introduced in Section 3. To compute text similarity, we use a similarity search facility provided by Hyperestraier [9], a full-text search engine. Hyperestraier has file convertor xdoc2txt, so beyond handling plain text, it can also handle .doc, .xls, .ppt, .pdf and other common file types. Path similarity and modified time similarity are computed by scanning a file system directly. Access co-occurrences are extracted from log data recorded by a

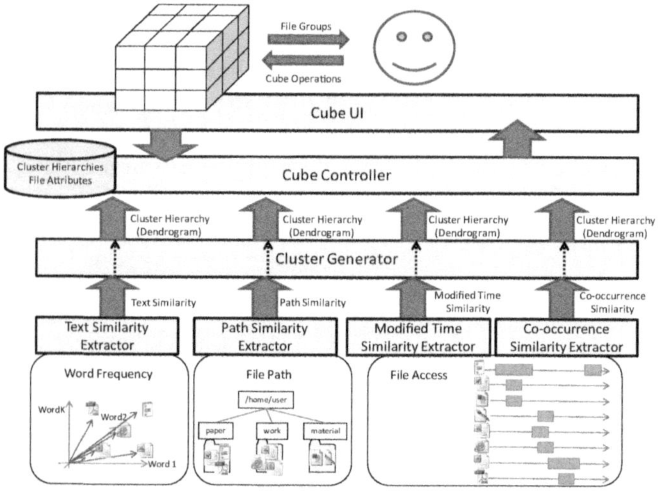

Fig. 3. System architecture

Samba file server [10]. Log data entries each contain the timestamp of file open/close, user name and file path.

- **Cluster Generator:** The cluster generator applies the hierarchical agglomerative clustering method for each similarity measure. It derives a dendrogram corresponding to the cluster merge process. This part is achieved using the hclust function in R.
- **Cube Controller:** The cube controller manages dendrograms produced by the cluster generator. It integrates clustering results and produces a multi dimensional cube. When it receives roll-up/drill-down requests from the Cube UI, it cuts dendrograms with a relevant threshold value.
- **Cube UI:** The Cube UI provides a cube-style interface and cube operations to users. The interface is based on Microsoft Excel. Since Excel has a named pivot table function similar to data cube, the Cube UI uses the Win32 OLE library and outputs Excel files that include cube data. Excel does not support Roll-up/drill-down operations, so they are performed in a separate window.

6 Examples

We show examples of the file grouping process using FileSearchCube (Figure 4). The first example is a requirement that "drill down text similarity composes groups by combining access co-occurrence similarity."

1. In Figure 4, Snapshot1 shows 10 clusters generated by the clustering method based on text similarity. Clusters of other measures are not divided (only one cluster in each dimension). A cluster text06 consists of seven files that have common keywords.

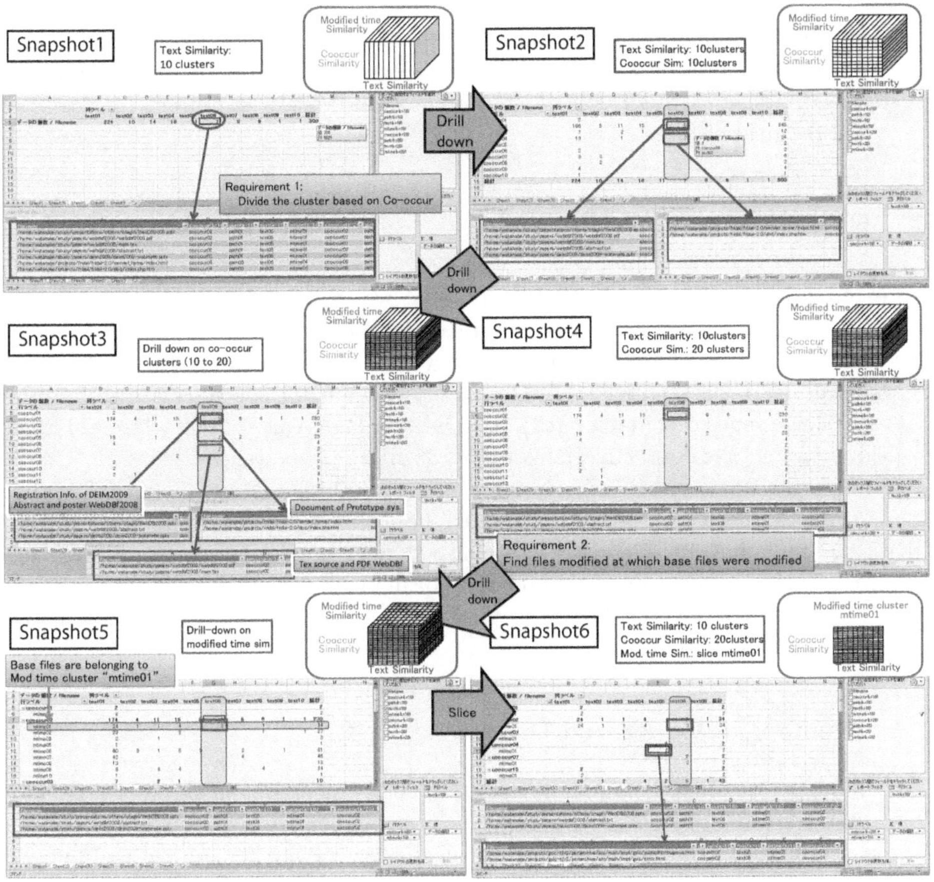

Fig. 4. Examples of file grouping

2. Snapshot2 presents a cube divided into 10 clusters on co-occurrence similarity dimension. Cluster text06 is divided into two small clusters.
3. A user who wants to divide clusters more precisely performs a drill-down operation. Snapshot3 shows a cube divided into 20 clusters on co-occurrence similarity dimension. Cluster text06 is now divided into three groups (3 files, 3 files and 2 files). Files in each group are strongly related.

The second requirement is "find files modified in the same period in which files in the group of the first requirement are modified."

1. Snapshot4 shows the same cube in Snapshot 3. Here, we suppose base files belong to both cluster text06 and cluster cooccur02. The requirement wants to get files modified in the same period in which base files are modified.
2. To get the target group, drill-down operation on the dimension of modified time similarity is required. Snapshot5 is a cube divided into 10 clusters on the

dimension of modified time similarity. Since the base files belong to cluster mtime01, we have to search target files in mtime01.

3. Snapshot6 represents a cube sliced by a condition mtime01 on the modified time dimension. Each cell of the cube includes files modified in the same period (mtime01).

7 Experimental Evaluation

To evaluate effectiveness of FileSearchCube, we experimented using our prototype system. As experiment data, we prepared 300 files from an author's home directory. We chose files with the file extensions shown in Table 1. Full-text search engine Hyperestraier can extract keywords from 200 files (the remaining 100 files are images or binary data). The Samba log (Aug. 7 2008 - Dec. 24 2008) contains 834 access co-occurrences with 135 files.

To build an answer set, we manually labeled 300 files. Table 2 shows 39 labels for 300 files. The label "Research paper" contains tex source and presentation files. "Event" contains calls for workshop papers and member lists. "Software development" contains manuals and text-based configuration files, and icon images. "Office document" contains application forms for business trips; some are created from the same template.

7.1 Number of Generated Groups

The number of groups generated by one or more measures is shown in Table 3. The first column represents the combination of measures. The second column is the number of groups. The number of clusters generated in each dimension (single measure) is fixed at 20. Files not extracted by keywords and files not recorded by any co-occurrence are grouped into the unknown group. The third column is the average number of files in one group. The fourth column is the average/maximum entropy among all groups. When a group consists of files with the same label, then the entropy of the group becomes 0. We first explain the differences in groups generated by each measure, then show combinations of two or more measures.

Single Measure

- **Text:** Text similarity generates clusters that have the highest value of average entropy among four measures. This means they are mixtures of various labels. There are interesting clusters: a cluster integrating Research paper 1 and 2 and a cluster integrating Equipment management 1 and 2. Office documents created by the same template are grouped into one cluster. A copied file and its original file become the same cluster.
- **Modified time:** Modified time similarity generates clusters classified roughly, but they are still mixtures of various labels. We think the number of clusters for this measure is too small (#cluster=20).

Table 1. Extensions of experiment files

.JPG .PNG .ai .bib .css .csv .doc .docm .docx .eml .eps .htm .html .ico .jpg .pdf .png .ppt .pptx .rtf .tex .txt .xls .xlsx

Table 2. Answer set

Category of labels	#files in the sets
Research paper 1–2	1, 29
Event 1–3	3, 8, 13
Software development 1–5	16, 24, 5, 49, 54
Meeting 1–4	6, 9, 4, 3
Equipment management 1–4	4, 3, 9, 6
Paper review 1–7	2, 2, 1, 2, 3, 3, 3
Office document 1–12	3, 4, 2, 2, 5, 3, 4, 1, 1, 1, 2, 3
etc 1–2	5, 2

Table 3. Experiment result (20 clusters in each dimension)

Measure	#groups	Average #file	Entropy(avg/max)
Sim_{text}	20	15.0	0.369 / 1.105
Sim_{mtime}	20	15.0	0.382 / 0.920
Sim_{path}	20	15.0	0.174 / 1.291
$Sim_{cooccur}$	20	15.0	0.064 / 1.270
$Sim_{text} \times Sim_{cooccur}$	47	6.38	0.137 / 1.080
$Sim_{mtime} \times Sim_{cooccur}$	48	6.25	0.112 / 1.270
$Sim_{text} \times Sim_{path}$	57	5.26	0.112 / 1.045
$Sim_{mtime} \times Sim_{path}$	63	4.76	0.092 / 0.700
$Sim_{text} \times Sim_{mtime}$	75	4.00	0.091 / 0.678
$Sim_{path} \times Sim_{cooccur}$	42	7.14	0.080 / 1.302
$Sim_{text} \times Sim_{path} \times Sim_{cooccur}$	83	3.61	0.065 / 1.073
$Sim_{mtime} \times Sim_{path} \times Sim_{cooccur}$	84	3.57	0.061 / 0.728
$Sim_{text} \times Sim_{mtime} \times Sim_{cooccur}$	100	3.00	0.053 / 0.678
$Sim_{text} \times Sim_{mtime} \times Sim_{path}$	107	2.80	0.036 / 0.602
$Sim_{text} \times Sim_{mtime} \times Sim_{path} \times Sim_{cooccur}$	126	2.38	0.022 / 0.602

- **Path:** Path similarity generates clusters reflecting folder hierarchy in a physical file system. Files located in brother folders are not divided, even if we change the granularity of clustering. The author tends to put office documents in similar locations, so they are not divided.
- **Co-occurrence:** Co-occurrence similarity generates clusters with low entropy. For "Software development 1," it generates a cluster including manual and configuration files. For "Research paper 2," it generates a cluster that includes tex source and PDF files. For "Paper review 6," a paper to review and present comments for the paper are grouped into the same cluster. There are, however, many files in which there are no co-occurrences in log data; they are included in the unknown group.

Combination of Multiple Measures

As shown in Table 3, all combinations of two measures can generate smaller groups than a single measure. Single cases contain files not classified by text similarity and co-occurrence similarity. Combinations of multiple measures, however, can classify them into relevant groups, because path and modified time similarity cover all files, unlike text and co-occurrence similarity. Groups generated by a combination of co-occurrence and path similarities have the lowest average entropy among all combinations of two measures. However, this combination marks the highest maximum entropy. This implies that generated groups are skewed.

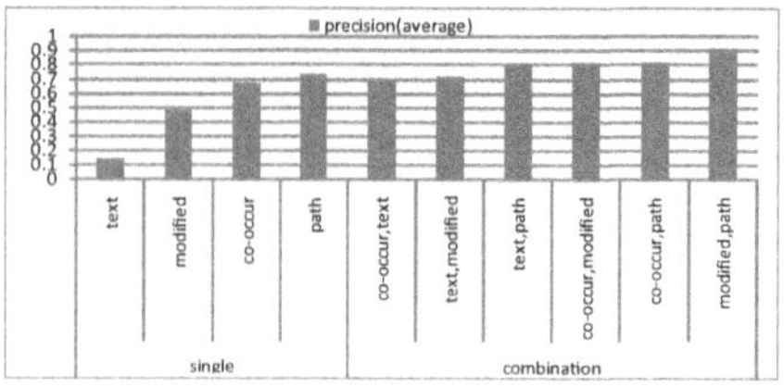

Fig. 5. Precision in type 1

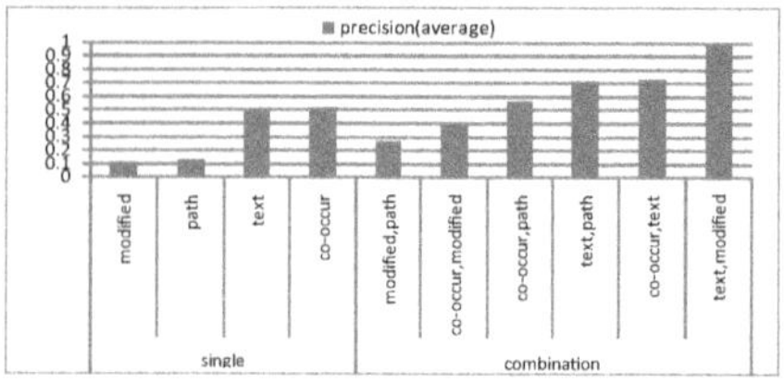

Fig. 6. Precision in type 2

Combinations of three or more measures generated more small groups. Some combinations generated over 100 groups. However, we have only 39 labels in the data set. We need a larger data set to evaluate 100 groups correctly. Evaluation with large data sets is a future research issue.

7.2 Effectiveness of Combining Multiple Measures

We consider two scenarios to evaluate the efficiency of our scheme.

Type 1: *"Group files used in the same work."*
We often access files in different folders during the same work. It is hard, however, to remember all files used in the work. This type of requirement is typical in file search. For evaluation, we use a set of files labeled "Software development1" (16 files). Figure 5 shows the result of this experiment. The vertical axis represents average precision of generated groups including files labeled "Software development1." If at least one common file exists in both a cluster C and an answer set A, we calculate precision of C by the following formula: $Precision_A(C) = \frac{|A \cap C|}{|C|}$
In single cases, the measure of path similarity is the best among four measures. Text similarity is the worst, because text information is not useful to determine which files were used in the same work. In combinations of two measures, combining path and modified time similarity is the best. And we can see that all combinations of multiple measures mark higher precision than when they are used separately.

Type 2: *"Group files created from the same template."*
When we write a new document for a paper procedure, we want to search old documents written for the same procedure. As a test data set, we used files labeled Paper review 5, 6, and 7 in Table 2 (9 files). They include reviewer's comments of the same journal, so these files are text data written in the same format. The name of the journal may be a common keyword. Results are shown in Figure 6. In a single case, co-occurrence similarity is the best. In combinations of two measures, however, combining text and modified time similarity is the best. Since content information is important in this type of requirement, combinations that include text similarity improve.

This experiment shows the effectiveness of combining multiple measures. We think the best combination may change according to a user's tendencies and requirements. Without FileSearchCube, users must manually check which combination is the best. FileSearchCube can simplify the task.

8 Conclusion

This paper proposes FileSearchCube, which provides a multidimensional cube to analyze a large number of files. It generates file groups using multiple measures of interfile relationships. To achieve roll-up/drill-down operations, FileSearchCube uses results of the hierarchical clustering method. The generated groups are useful in summarizing logical structure of file systems and expanding the results of desktop search. We implemented a prototype system and evaluated it with experiments.

Several future research issues remain. The first is to integrate more similarity measures, such as image similarity. FileSearchCube can treat a measure that returns a numeric value corresponding to an interfile relationship. The second is detailed experiments for more users and more files.

Acknowledgement

This research was supported in part by MEXT Grant-in-Aid for Scientific Research on Priority Areas (#21013017).

References

1. Agrawal, N., Bolosky, W.J., Douceur, J.R., Lorch, J.R.: A Five-Year Study of File-System Metadata. ACM Trans. Storage 3(3), 9 (2007)
2. Ames, A., Maltzahn, C., Bobb, N., Miller, E.L., Brandt, S.A., Neeman, A., Hiatt, A., Tuteja, D.: Richer File System Metadata Using Links and Attributes. In: Proc. IEEE MSST, pp. 49–60 (2005)
3. Gifford, D.K., Jouvelot, P., Sheldoon, M.A., Toole Jr., J.W.O.: Semantic File Systems. In: Proc. ACM SOSP, pp. 16–25 (1991)
4. Han, J., Kamber, M.: Data Mining: Concepts and Techniques. Morgan Kaufmann, San Francisco (2006)
5. Smith, G., Czerwinski, M., Meyers, B., Robbins, D.C., Robertson, G.G., Tan, D.S.: FacetMap: A Scalable Search and Browse Visualization Visualization and Computer Graphics. IEEE TVCG 12(5), 797–804 (2006)
6. Yee, K., Swearingen, K., Li, K., Hearst, M.: Faceted Metadata for Image Search and Browsing. In: Proc. CHI, pp. 401–408 (2003)
7. Watanabe, T., Kobayashi, T., Yokota, H.: A Method for Searching Keyword-lacking Files Based on Interfile Relationships. In: Meersman, R., Tari, Z., Herrero, P. (eds.) OTM-WS 2008. LNCS, vol. 5333, pp. 14–15. Springer, Heidelberg (2008)
8. Google Desktop, `http://desktop.google.com/`
9. Hyper Estraier, `http://hyperestraier.sourceforge.net/index.ja.html`
10. Samba, `http://us3.samba.org/samba/`
11. Windows Search, `http://www.microsoft.com/windows/desktopsearch/default.mspx`

Trustworthy Information: Concepts and Mechanisms

Shouhuai Xu[1], Haifeng Qian[2], Fengying Wang[3], Zhenxin Zhan[1], Elisa Bertino[4], and Ravi Sandhu[1]

[1] University of Texas at San Antonio (UTSA)
[2] East China Normal University (work done while visiting UTSA)
[3] Shandong University of Technology (work done while visiting UTSA)
[4] Purdue University

Abstract. We used to treating information received (from recognized sources) as trustworthy, which is unfortunately not true because of attacks. The situation can get worse with the emerging shift of information sharing paradigm from "need to know" to "need to share." In order to help information consumers make the "best" decision possible, it is imperative to formulate concepts, models, frameworks, architectures, and mechanisms to facilitate information trustworthiness management in distributed and decentralized environment. In this paper we initiate a study in this direction by proposing an abstraction called *information networks* as well as two supporting mechanisms called *provenance digital signatures* and *optimal security hardening of information network*.

1 Introduction

Suppose Alice receives a piece of information. To what extent should she trust it? Like most users, she will likely treat it as trustworthy, especially when the information is digitally signed by a peer whose public key is known to her. However, the presence of attacks such as malware and malicious insiders makes such trusting behavior questionable. This example scenario suggests the need for "trustworthy information" or "information trustworthiness management", which has been a missing piece of traditional approaches to data and information sharing. This paper is a significant first step towards addressing the problem.

Our Contributions. First, we propose the concept of "information trustworthiness management" in the context of information networks. Information networks are an abstraction we use to capture the "flow" or "movement" of information that is often in the format of messages with respect to some appropriate network protocols. Second, we formulate the abstraction of "trustworthiness graph" with respect to a piece of information. In a trustworthiness graph, a node represents a principal (e.g., a user or organization), and an arc represents the transmission of messages (containing information) between the nodes. Many mechanisms are needed for managing trustworthiness graphs. We investigate two useful mechanisms: (1) We identify a new kind of cryptographic primitive we call "provenance digital signatures" which goes beyond the standard concept of digital signatures by preserving the history of a message (i.e., a subgraph or subnetwork associated with the message). (2) We identify the need of optimal security hardening. We show that the algorithmic problem in question is NP-hard, but has a good approximation algorithm.

L. Chen et al. (Eds.): WAIM 2010, LNCS 6184, pp. 398–404, 2010.

Discussion. From a conceptual perspective, the concept of information networks as well as the resulting notion of trustworthiness graphs are reminiscent of the well-studied notion of "information flow" in computer security [7,19], which aims to ensure information secrecy and integrity. However, there are important differences. In particular, we focus on the notion of information trustworthiness, which is a broader requirement than secrecy and integrity and is, as mentioned above, about embedding security into information management at the very beginning of information lifecycle (rather than treating any given information as trustworthy). The differences are essential because, for example, an authorized user can insert a bad data item into a database, which is not trustworthy but disseminated to many other participants without violating the information-flow policy in question. While the present paper is in parallel to the recent active research that aims to inject provenance at the Operating System level and at the DataBase level (see, for example, [8,20,16,18,1] and the references therein), it is orthogonal to these studies because we take the perspective of the network that poses a new challenge that nodes in the network (e.g., OS/DB) can be compromised.

From a mechanism perspective, our notion of provenance digital signatures moves a step beyond the recent proposals for securing provenance information. Specifically, [9] investigated provenance integrity in the setting of file systems with an emphasis on the total-order operation-chain provenance of atomic objects (e.g., files). This study was extended to deal with the partial-order operation provenance of compound objects such as records and tables in database systems [22]. Compared with the integrity protection mechanisms presented in [9,22], provenance signatures offer stronger security definition and better efficiency. To see this, we note that the scheme presented in [22], when used in our setting (i.e., network), has the drawbacks of linear increasing of signature size and vulnerable to the "peeling off" attack. Intuitively, our scheme achieves strictly stronger security because signatures are always aggregated together (i.e., attacker does not "see" the individual signatures). Moreover, the "peeling off" attack has another security consequence on those schemes, which our scheme does not suffer. Specifically, a malicious user *by itself* can arbitrarily duplicate any prefix of a received signature so as to fake multiple incoming paths, which could manipulate (e.g., amplify or deflate) the trustworthiness of message it sends to downstream nodes.

From a cryptographic perspective, provenance signatures bear some similarity to (sequential) aggregate signatures [14,3]. However, we consider partial-order aggregation (i.e., with respect to information networks) whereas the later considers total-order aggregation. As such, our security definition is strictly stronger.

Other Related Work. This paper is inspired in part by a recently proposed framework for "trustworthiness-centric information sharing" [21]. The notion of trustworthiness graph was somewhat inspired by the concept of social networks [10,11].

2 Information Network and Trustworthiness Graph

We start with a simple example (Figure 1), which captures what is needed for evaluating information trustworthiness: from which principals an information item is originated; which principals have manipulated and forwarded an information item; which algorithms have been used to process an information item. Specifically, $P_1, \ldots, P_6$ in the graph represent principals, and the arcs indicate how information has moved in the information network. Specifically, suppose P_1 enters message M_1 into the system at time T_1 and P_2 enters message M_2 into the system at time T_2. At time T_3, P_3 receives M_1 from P_1 and processes M_1 to produce M_3. At time T_4, P_4 receives M_1 and M_2 from P_1 and P_2, respectively, and processes them to produce a new message M_4. At time T_5, P_5 receives M_3 and M_4 from P_3 and P_4, respectively, and processes them to produce M_5. Finally, P_6 receives M_5 at time T_6.

The goal is to help the nodes evaluate the trustworthiness of the messages. For this purpose, we first define the notion of information networks in the context of information sharing and their associated trustworthiness graphs, and then show how the goal can be achieved while requiring what support. In what follows, we assume a simple notion of time domain, that is, we assume that the domain is represented as the pair $(\mathbb{Z}; \leq)$, where each element of $\mathbb{Z}$ is referred to as a time instant and $\leq$ is a total order on $\mathbb{Z}$. Also given $T, T' \in \mathbb{Z}$, $[T, T']$ denotes a time interval starting at time instant T and ending at time instant T'. Such model is very simple but it is adequate for the purpose of the present paper. More advanced notions of time in distributed systems have been investigated [12,15] which we will consider as part of our future work.

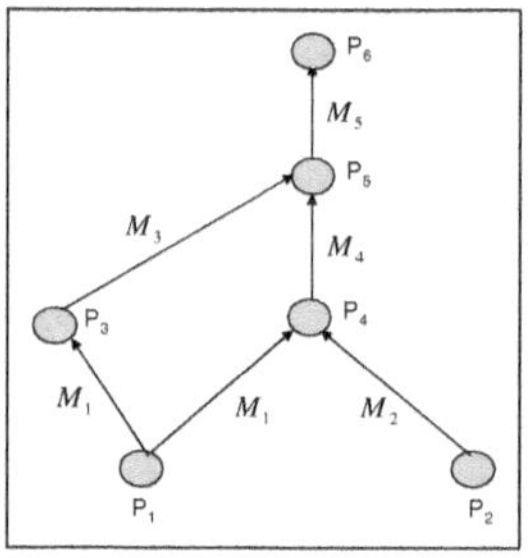

Fig. 1. Motivating example of provenance digital signatures

Definition 1. (information network) *Let $[T_1, T_2]$ be a time interval and $\mathsf{V}([T_1, T_2])$ be a set of principals (users, organizations) which exchanged information during $[T_1, T_2]$. An information network over $[T_1, T_2]$ and $\mathsf{V}([T_1, T_2])$, denoted as $\mathsf{G}([T_1, T_2])$, is a pair $(\mathsf{V}([T_1, T_2]), \mathsf{E}([T_1, T_2]))$, where $\mathsf{E}([T_1, T_2])$ is the set of edges. An edge $(u, v) \in \mathsf{E}([T_1, T_2])$ if $u \in \mathsf{V}([T_1, T_2])$ has sent a message to $v \in \mathsf{V}([T_1, T_2])$ during $[T_1, T_2]$.*

Definition 2. (trustworthiness graph of an information network) *Let $[T_1, T_2]$ be time interval and T be a time instant, where $T_1 \leq T \leq T_2$. A trustworthiness graph $G(T) = (V(T), E(T))$ at time T is defined as $\mathsf{G}(\mathsf{V}[T_1, T]) = (\mathsf{V}([T_1, T]), \mathsf{E}([T_1, T]))$ with the following annotations. If $(u, v) \in E(T)$ we say that u is an "upstream" node of v and v is a "downstream" node of u. Moreover, each $(u, v) \in E(T)$ is annotated with a pair $(w_T(u, v), \theta_T(u, v))$, where $w_T(u, v) \in [0, 1]$ is v's trustworthiness evaluation of u at time T (e.g., based on the trustworthiness of information it has so-far received from u), and $\theta_T(u, v) \in [0, 1]$ is a threshold specified by v.*

Definition 3. (most/least trustworthy path) *Given a trustworthiness graph $G(T) = (V(T), E(T))$ with annotations and a path $p = (v_1, \ldots, v_\ell)$, we can define the trustworthiness of path p as (for example) $W_T(p) = \prod_{i=1}^{\ell-1} w_T(v_i, v_{i+1})$, which is a real number in the interval $[0, 1]$. For a given pair of nodes $(u, v) \in V(T) \times V(T)$, let $P_T = \{(u, \ldots, v)\}$ denote the set of paths from u and v. We say that path $\bar{p} \in P_T$ is (one of) the most trustworthy if $W_T(\bar{p}) = \max\{W_T(p) : p \in P_T\}$ and path $\underline{p} \in P$ is (one of) the least trustworthy if $W_T(\underline{p}) = \min\{W_T(p) : p \in P_T\}$.*

3 Provenance Signatures

Let us recall the motivating example illustrated in Figure 1. At first glance, one may think that this can be achieved by letting each P_i sign the respective subgraph using a standard digital signature mechanism (as in a standard PKI) such that a new signature is attached to last signature. However, this approach has two major drawbacks. (1) The size of the resulting signatures linearly increases with the number of signers. (2) A dishonest principal could manipulate the provenance by, for example, dropping some signers who signed in the past. For example, assume that P_1, P_2, P_3 and P_4 are honest and that M_1 and M_2 are sent through private channels such that no other principals have access to them. A dishonest P_5 could convince P_6 that M_5 is derived from M_3 received P_3, M_1 received from P_1, and M_2 received from P_2 (e.g., by simply setting $M_5 = M_3||M_4$). This "peeling off" attack is undesirable at least for the sake of crediting, which may serve as incentive for information sharing. The problem cannot be solved by requiring that each signer signs the identity of next principal in the graph because, for example, P_1 may broadcast M_1 to a large population of principals, and may not know in advance that P_4 will receive or accept it.

As mentioned above, the scheme presented in [22] suffers from these problems. As we will see, our provenance signatures overcome the above two drawbacks simultaneously. The basic idea is to utilize some cryptographic aggregation technique to ensure that (1) the size of the resulting provenance signatures (not including the messages as they are needed anyway) is constant and independent of the number of signers, and (2) attacks like the above "peeling off" one are prevented. While our use of cryptographic aggregation technique can be viewed as a generalization of the recently investigated notions of multi-signature, (sequential) aggregate signatures, ordered multi-signatures [5,13,2,3], the generalization is non-trivial. This is because we have to ensure (extra) unforgeability with respect to the graph structure, which makes the security proof complicated. In contrast, existing schemes cannot assure unforgeability with respect to graph structure and are actually subject to simple attacks (e.g., two corrupt signers can arbitrarily manipulate their "positions"). Moreover, we must allow multiple aggregations of a single signature on the same message (e.g., P_1 sends the same M_1 to both P_3 and P_4). Now we describe our provenance signature scheme.

$\mathsf{Setup}(1^k)$: Generate a bilinear group $\mathbb{G}$ with order $2^{k+1} \geq p \geq 2^k$ and an associated bilinear pair $e(\cdot,\cdot) : \mathbb{G}\times\mathbb{G} :\longrightarrow \mathbb{G}_\mathsf{T}$. Return $pp = (e, \mathbb{G}, \mathbb{G}_\mathsf{T}, H)$, where $H : \{0,1\}^* \rightarrow \mathbb{G}$ a random oracle.

$\mathsf{Keygen}(pp)$: Randomly choose $x \stackrel{R}{\leftarrow} \mathbb{Z}_p$ and output a pair of private and public keys $(sk = x, pk = X = g^x)$.

$\mathsf{GraphCom}(pp, \mathsf{loc}, \{G_\lambda\}_{\lambda\in\mathcal{R}})$: On input of public parameters pp, local information string $\mathsf{loc} = (\mathsf{id}_i, m_i, t_i)$ for a local message m_i of trustworthiness t_i, and incoming $|\mathcal{R}|$ provenance subgraphs $\{G_\lambda\}_{\lambda\in\mathcal{R}}$ where $\mathcal{R} \subset \mathcal{S}$, P_i generates a new message $\overline{m}_i = \mathsf{alg}_i(m_i, \{G_\lambda\}_{\lambda\in\mathcal{R}})$ of trustworthiness $\overline{t}_i = \mathsf{tru}_i(t_i, \{G_\lambda\}_{\lambda\in\mathcal{R}})$, where the specification of algorithms alg_i and tru_i is application-dependent and beyond the scope of the paper. Finally, P_i outputs a provenance subgraph $G_i = ((\{G_\lambda\}_{\lambda\in\mathcal{R}}), a_i)$ for its newly produced message $\overline{m}_i$, where $a_i = (\mathsf{id}_i, \mathsf{alg}_i, \overline{m}_i, m_i, \mathsf{tru}_i, \overline{t}_i, t_i)$ is the "end" node in G_i. Note that if $\{G_\lambda\} = \emptyset$, then $((G_\lambda), a_i) = (a_i)$.

$\mathsf{PSign}(pp, sk_i, \mathsf{loc}, \{\Sigma_\lambda\}_{\lambda\in\mathcal{R}})$: on input of public parameters pp, local information $\mathsf{loc} = (\mathsf{id}_i, m_i, t_i)$ of message m_i of trustworthiness t_i, a private key sk_i of P_i, and provenance signatures $\{\Sigma_\lambda\}_{\lambda\in\mathcal{R}}$ on respective provenance subgraphs $\{G_\lambda\}_{\lambda\in\mathcal{R}}$ received from P_i's upstream nodes belonging to $\mathcal{R} \subset \mathcal{S}$, P_i executes $\mathsf{PVrf}(pp, \Sigma_\lambda)$ to verify the individual provenance signatures Σ_λ. If any verification fails, abort; otherwise, set $G_i \leftarrow \mathsf{GraphCom}(pp, \mathsf{loc}, \{G_\lambda\}_{\lambda\in\mathcal{R}})$, set $\omega \leftarrow H(G_i)^{x_i}$, and output $\Sigma_i = (G_i, \sigma_i)$ where $\sigma_i = \omega \prod_{P_\lambda \in \mathcal{R}} \sigma_\lambda$.

$\mathsf{PVrf}(pp, \Sigma)$: given parameters pp, provenance signature $\Sigma = (G, \sigma)$, the algorithm parses G to obtain $\{G_i | i = 1, \cdots, \ell\}$ and the signers' identities $\{\mathsf{id}_i | i = 1, \cdots, \ell\}$, and returns 1 if the following equation holds and 0 otherwise: $e(g, \sigma) \stackrel{?}{=} \prod_{i=1}^{\ell} e(X_i, H(G_i))$.

Theorem 1. *If the $\mathcal{BLS}$ signature is $(\mathrm{T}', q_s, \varepsilon')$-secure under a chosen-message attack, our provenance signature scheme is $(\mathrm{T}, q_p, \varepsilon)$-secure where*

$$\varepsilon \geq \varepsilon', \quad q_p = q_s \quad \textit{and} \quad \mathrm{T} \leq \mathrm{T}' - (q_s + 1)N \cdot \mathrm{T}_e, \tag{1}$$

where q_s, q_p are the numbers of the queries to the $\mathcal{BLS}$ signing oracle and the **PSigning** *oracle, respectively, and T_e is the time cost of exponentiation computation.*

4 Optimal Security Hardening

Given a trustworthiness graph, we want to identify the most "influential" K nodes so as to harden their security. This optimization problem turns out to be related to the *independent cascade model* in the context of social networks [10]. However, there is an important difference. In the model by Kempe at al. [10], the influence passes each *arc* with a probability that is independent of any other arc. In our model, a piece of information passes each *node* with a probability that is independent of other nodes. We now show that the optimal security hardening problem is NP-hard. The reduction is based on the NP-complete Set Cover problem.

Theorem 2. *The optimal hardening problem for trustworthiness graphs is NP-hard.*

We now show that the optimal security hardening problem also has a certain submodular structure. A function $f(\cdot)$ mapping sets to $\mathbb{R}^+$ is said to be submodular if it has the so-called *diminishing returns* property: for all $v \in V$ and all $A \subseteq B$ it holds that

$$f(A \cup \{v\}) - f(A) \geq f(B \cup \{v\}) - f(B).$$

This can be exploited to prove that the greedy algorithm produces a solution within an approximation factor of $(1 - 1/e)$, where e is the base of the natural logarithm [17].

Theorem 3. *The function $\sigma(\cdot)$ incurred by optimal hardening is submodular.*

5 Conclusion

We presented the concept of "information trustworthiness management" in the context of information networks and the abstraction of "trustworthiness graph". We investigated a new cryptographic primitive we call "provenance digital signatures" and investigate the issue of optimal security hardening in information networks.

Acknowledgement. This work was partially supported by AFOSR MURI and State of Texas Emerging Technology Fund.

References

1. Archer, D., Delcambre, L., Maier, D.: A Framework for Fine-grained Data Integration and Curation, with Provenance, in a Dataspace. In: TaPP 2009 (2009)
2. Bellare, M., Namprempre, C., Neven, G.: Unrestricted aggregate signatures. In: Arge, L., Cachin, C., Jurdziński, T., Tarlecki, A. (eds.) ICALP 2007. LNCS, vol. 4596, pp. 411–422. Springer, Heidelberg (2007)
3. Boldyreva, A., Gentry, C., O'Neill, A., Yum, D.: Ordered multisignatures and identity-based sequential aggregate signatures, with applications to secure routing. In: ACM CCS 2007 (2007)
4. Boneh, D., Lynn, B., Shacham, H.: Short signatures from the Weil pairing. In: Boyd, C. (ed.) ASIACRYPT 2001. LNCS, vol. 2248, p. 514. Springer, Heidelberg (2001)
5. Boneh, D., Gentry, C., Lynn, B., Shacham, H.: Aggregate and verifiably encrypted signatures from bilinear maps. In: Biham, E. (ed.) EUROCRYPT 2003. LNCS, vol. 2656, pp. 416–432. Springer, Heidelberg (2003)
6. Dai, C., Lin, D., Bertino, E., Kantarcioglu, M.: Approach to Evaluate Data Trustworthiness Based on Data Provenance. In: Jonker, W., Petković, M. (eds.) SDM 2008. LNCS, vol. 5159, pp. 82–98. Springer, Heidelberg (2008)
7. Denning, D.: A Lattice Model of Secure Information Flow. CACM 19(5), 237–243 (1976)
8. Halevy, A., Franklin, M., Maier, D.: Principles of dataspace systems. In: PODS 2006 (2006)
9. Hasan, R., Sion, R., Winslett, M.: The case of the fake picasso: Preventing history forgery with secure provenance. In: FAST 2009 (2009)
10. Kempe, D., Kleinberg, J., Tardos, E.: Maximizing the Spread of Influence through a Social Network. In: ACM KDD 2003 (2003)
11. Kossinets, G., Kleinberg, J., Watts, D.: The Structure of Information Pathways in a Social Communication Network. In: ACM KDD 2008 (2008)
12. Lamport, L.: Time, clocks, and the ordering of events in a distributed system. CACM 21(7), 558–565 (1978)
13. Lu, S., Ostrovsky, R., Sahai, A., Shacham, H., Waters, B.: Sequential Aggregate Signatures and Multisignatures Without Random Oracles. In: Vaudenay, S. (ed.) EUROCRYPT 2006. LNCS, vol. 4004, pp. 465–485. Springer, Heidelberg (2006)
14. Lysyanskaya, A., Micali, S., Reyzin, L., Shacham, H.: Sequential Aggregate Signatures from Trapdoor Permutations. In: Cachin, C., Camenisch, J.L. (eds.) EUROCRYPT 2004. LNCS, vol. 3027, pp. 74–90. Springer, Heidelberg (2004)
15. Mattern, F.: Virtual time and global states of distributed systems. In: Workshop on Parallel and Distributed Algs. (1989)
16. Muniswamy-Reddy, K., Macko, P., Seltzer, M.: Making a Cloud Provenance-Aware. In: TaPP 2009 (2009)

17. Nemhauser, G., Wolsey, L., Fisher, M.: An analysis of the approximations for maximizing submodular set functions. Mathematical Programming 14, 265–294 (1978)
18. Reilly, C., Naughton, J.: Transparently Gathering Provenance with Provenance Aware Condor. In: TaPP 2009 (2009)
19. Sabefield, A., Myers, A.C.: Language-Based Information-Flow Security. In: IEEE JSAC (2003)
20. Spillane, R., Sears, R., Yalamanchili, C., Gaikwad, S., Chinni, M., Zadok, E.: Story Book: An Efficient Extensible Provenance Framework. In: TaPP 2009 (2009)
21. Xu, S., Sandhu, R., Bertino, E.: TIUPAM: A Framework for Trustworthiness-Centric Information Sharing. In: IFIPTM 2009 (2009)
22. Zhang, J., Chapman, A., Lefevre, K.: Do You Know Where Your Data's Been? — Tamper-Evident Database Provenance. In: SDM 2009 (2009)

How to Design Kansei Retrieval Systems?

Yaokai Feng and Seiichi Uchida

Faculty of Information Science and Electrical Engineering,
Kyushu University, Japan
{fengyk,uchida}@ait.kyushu-u.ac.jp

Abstract. All of the information retrieval (IR) systems try to retrieve the information that users really want. For this purpose, users have to exactly express and submit their requirements to the systems. However, how to reflect user's subjectivities is a hard problem. When a user wants to search for something, for instance a passenger car or a costume, he/she normally has a kind of feeling such as "graceful and looks intelligent, but not so expensive." Many researchers call this feeling as "Kansei" in many researches, which means the user's psychological feeling as well as the physiological issues. Let's see another example. Image retrieval systems having an ability to handle subjective expressions are useful especially when the users, who have no knowledge about contents of the image database, try to use some Kansei words (e.g., " beautiful", "calm", etc.) to retrieve unknown images. Unfortunately, traditional information retrieval systems cannot efficiently deal with the user-given search requests with Kansei words. Thus, in many application systems, how to deal with Kansei words from different users has become an important issue that the system designers have to confront. In this background, "Kansei engineering" has become one of the hot topics in IR field. In addition, many Kansei retrieval systems have been implemented. However, all of the existing Kansei retrieval systems aim at specific applications. Thus, they are very different from each other. In this paper, based on the many investigations and analysis on the existing systems, we propose a general method for designing efficient Kansei retrieval systems, which has not been done in this field. Our proposal mainly includes a general flow for designing Kansei retrieval systems and a discussion on how to speed up the Kansei retrieval processes using multidimensional indexes. We hope that this paper will be able to help the designers who are planning to design Kansei retrieval systems.

1 Introduction

Information retrieval systems are certainly user-oriented, where how to reflect user's subjectivity becomes an important and hard problem. When a user wants to search for something, for instance a passenger car or a costume, he/she normally have a kind of feeling such as "graceful and looks intelligent, but not so expensive." This feeling is called as "Kansei" in Japanese, which means the user's psychological feeling as well as the physiological issues. Unfortunately, traditional information retrieval systems cannot efficiently deal with the user-given search requirements having Kansei words.

L. Chen et al. (Eds.): WAIM 2010, LNCS 6184, pp. 405–416, 2010.

Kansei retrieval systems that can process Kansei information have attracted many attentions. Kansei is usually expressed with emotional words such as beautiful, romantic fantastic, comfortable, calm, and so on. For instance, image retrieval systems having an ability to handle subjective expressions are useful especially when the users, who have no knowledge about contents of the image database, try to use some Kansei words (e.g., " beautiful", "calm", etc.) to retrieve unknown images. However, because the key-words in traditional retrieval systems are registered by operators and they are influenced by the operators' subjectivities, it is difficult to obtain the data based on user's feeling or Kansei by using the traditional key-word retrieving methods. This means that the traditional retrieval systems using key-words or/and other text information cannot deal with sensitive words reflecting user's subjectivity. For this reason, they are not enough in many applications.

In this paper, after some existing Kansei retrieval systems being briefly introduced in Section 2 is our proposal, including a general flow for designing Kansei retrieval systems (in Section 3) and a discussion on how to speed up the Kansei retrieval processes using multidimensional indexes (in Section 4). Finally, Section 5 will briefly summarize this paper.

2 Some Existing Kansei Retrieval Systems

Many Kansei retrieval systems aiming at specific applications have been proposed in the last two decades. Some selected examples are briefly introduced here.

The works [8, 9] proposed a method for a textile-design image database system. In this method, a relationship was built between Kansei words and the features of the images (e.g., the color or the pattern shape). In addition, a new human interface based on "Kansei" retrieval method using user models was developed for a distributed image database systems of textile designing. This method provided an easy and flexible access to the image database by specifying certain Kansei words that make users satisfied in his/her perceptional retrieval. Furthermore, the user model would be updated after evaluating the difference between his/her Kansei and objective model on knowledge-base.

The work [11] proposed a method for retrieving the relevance between Kansei words and the shape features of images. Its purpose is to study a methodology for building an image data retrieval system. The system can accept natural language sentences that contain subjective expressions. In this method, images are retrieved interactively using comparative sentences. In order to interpret sentences including subjective expressions and match the result with each image, a space that binds subjective expressions and image features is introduced. The conditions that the space should satisfy and a method to construct such a space are discussed. As an example, a process for constructing and evaluating the shape feature space of "chairs" is proposed, and an experimental image retrieval system for office chairs was developed, which can deal with natural language including subjective expressions.

The work [6] implemented a Kansei database for Ise Katagami (one kind of Japanese paper) design using lattices and unit structures. The work [15] proposed a music retrieval system which could estimate individual characteristics of music data based on users' sensibility. It estimates each user's interest (user model) from the history about which data he/she had accessed and it also estimates a characteristic of music data (music title model) from the history about which users have accessed. The work [19] proposed a method to retrieve a building name from the users' impression to the buildings.

The work [13] proposed an image retrieval system based on Kansei of colors, in which natural language was used for Kansei representations even including the image structures. A method for background image retrieval using Kansei words of colors to represent the sensibility of color was proposed.

3 General Flow of Kansei Retrieval Systems

Most of the existing Kansei retrieval systems aim at specific applications and they are very different from each other. In this section, we proposed a general method for designing efficient Kansei retrieval systems, to the best of our knowledge, which has not been done in this field. And, we believe that our proposal will be able to guide the designers who are planning to design such systems. A general structure of Kansei retrieval systems is shown in Figure 1.

This system can be divided into two parts: *registration part* and *query part*. In the registration part, the quantitative features (quantitative pattern) are extracted from every original object (images, videos, music and so on), which is called *pattern extracting* (Fig.1). After that, every original image and its corresponding quantitative features are registered in the database system. There are many kinds of features can be used in this process of pattern extracting. For example, histogram, texture, local auto-correlation features, local contrast, and so on [17].

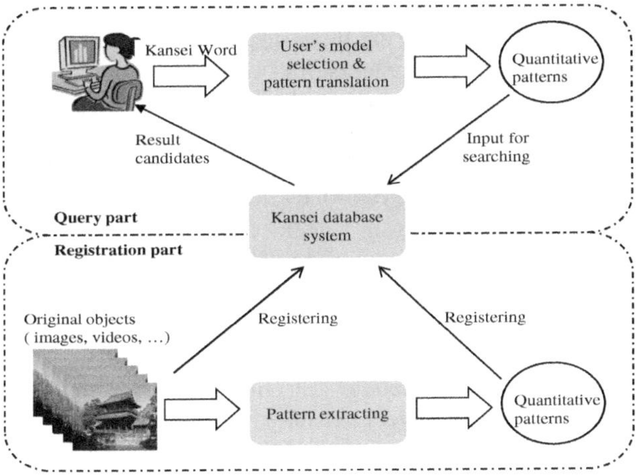

Fig. 1. General flow of designing Kansei retrieval systems

In the query part, as mentioned above, Kansei words vary much for different users even countering the same object. Thus, the *user model selection* (Fig.1) is necessary. That is, after the user gives some Kansei (subjective) words (e.g., calm, romantic, and etc.) to the system for query, a specific user model is selected for this user. Then, the translation function will create a specific quantitative pattern according to the given Kansei words, which is used to implement a specific search in the database system. For the users who have already been known by the system, the corresponding user model can be found easily. For the users who have not been known yet by the system, by asking the user some prepared questions, the system can determine which user group the current user should belong to and which user model should be used for this user.

Obviously, the user models play an important role for the query result. Here, let's see how to build the user models. Although there are actually many specific methods to build the user models, the following four phases are generally needed for building users' models: 1) selecting sample objects and users, 2) collecting primitive Kansei words, 3) clustering users, and 4) learning. The four phases are shown in Figure 2.

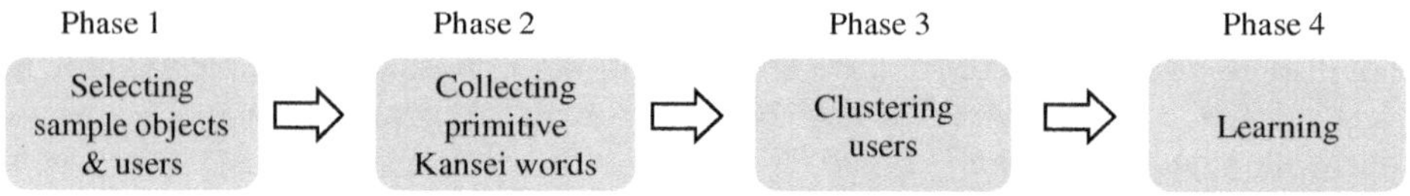

Fig. 2. General flow for building users' models

In Phase 1 of selecting sample objects and users, some typical objects distributed in a broad range are selected as samples. Clustering all the objects in advance may be helpful. At the same time, some potential users (or say, user representatives) having different backgrounds are also selected. In Phase 2 of collecting primitive Kansei words, every selected object is labeled with Kansei words by the selected potential users. There are some different methods to conduct Phase 2. The examples include (1) SD (Semantic Differential) method: a rating scale designed to measure the connotative meaning of objects, events, and concepts. The connotations are used to derive the attitude towards the given objects, events or concepts. The selected potential users are asked to choose where their positions lie, on a scale between two bipolar adjectives. SD method is today one of the most widely used scales in the measurement of attitudes, (2) keyword method. The selected people only need to select one or some of keywords from a decided keyword set for each of such selected objects, and (3) weighted keyword method. This method is extended from the above keyword method. The selected people need to decide a weight for each of their decided keywords to indicate the degree to which the current object meets this keyword.

In Phase 3, all the selected people are clustered according to the Kansei words collected from them about the selected objects. And, all the people having similar Kansei are clustered into the same group. After that, Phase 4 will build a user model for each of the user groups obtained in Phase 3. In this phase, learning is needed to find the relationship for each of user groups between Kansei words and the contents of the objects. The technologies that can be used in this learning phase include regression analysis, particularly multiple regression analysis, canonical correlation analysis, principal components analysis, statistical factor analysis, and so on.

Now, let's see the *query part* in Fig.1. When the user uses this system for Kansei retrieval, he/she only needs to submit to this system some Kansei words or natural language reflecting his/her subjectivity. After that, the part of *users' model selection and Translation* in this system plays the role of transforming the user-given request into corresponding quantitative pattern (quantitative features) that the database system can recognize. The quantitative pattern will be sent to the database system for retrieving. Finally, the retrieval results (actually result candidates) are presented to the user.

The last part is the *Kansei database system* (Fig.1), which should be able to efficiently manage the original objects along with their corresponding quantitative patterns (or say feature vectors), and can answer the query requests using quantitative patterns translated from the Kansei words reflecting the users' real purposes. Most of the relational database management systems (RDBMSs) can be used here. Multidimensional index technologies can be used to speed up the query processing. Since there exist many multidimensional index structures, we must choose one or design a new indexing structure for every specific Kansei retrieval system. This issue will be discussed in the next section.

According to the above discussions, we can know that, the degree of accuracy in *quantitative pattern extraction* of the objects and the degree of accuracy in the *user-model selection and pattern translation* impact much on the satisfaction rate of the Kansei retrieval systems.

4 Indexing Technologies for Speeding Up Kansei Retrieval

Besides the user's satisfaction rate, the response time is also an important factor for any retrieval systems. We will know that the retrievals in Kansei database systems can be regarded as range queries in multidimensional spaces and many multidimensional index structures can be used to Kansei database systems to speed up the retrieval processes.

4.1 Regarding Queries in Kansei Database Systems as Range Queries

In the Kansei database systems, as mentioned above, the quantitative feature vectors (patterns) of the objects are registered. When querying, the user-given Kansei words are also translated into a quantitative feature vector. In Kansei retrieval systems, exact queries trying to find the objects that exactly match the input query quantitative feature vectors are generally unrealistic and unnecessary for most cases. Obviously, all the similar objects to the query quantitative pattern (feature vector) translated from the user-given Kansei words should be reported to the user (Fig. 3). Here, it should be noted that the similar objects will be mapped into neighboring points in the vector space. In this way, the queries in the Kansei database systems become range queries in the multidimensional vector space. That is, all the objects in the feature vector space distributed nearly to the query point (the query feature vector) should be reported to the user.

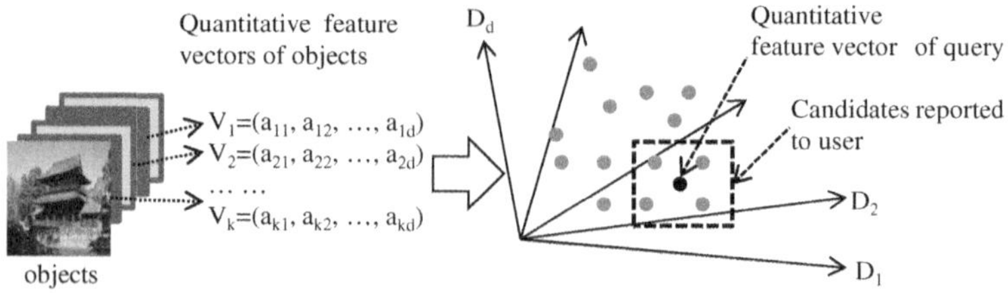

Fig. 3. Every query in Kansei database systems is a range query

4.2 Range Queries in Kansei Retrieval Systems

According to our investigations, the required range queries in Kansei database systems are special. Concretely, the importance degree (or say "weight") of the features (dimensions in the vector space) for each query are perhaps different from each other, which means that the users usually emphasize only part of the features of the objects in each of specific queries. Thus, partial dimensions (not all) of the entire multidimensional feature space are usually enough for actual Kansei retrievals. That is, although the quantitative patterns tend to have many feature values, only part of which is necessary in each of actual retrievals. Such queries are called partially-dimensional (PD) range queries. In these queries, the query ranges are given only in some dimensions (not all) of the feature space. On the contrary, those having query ranges given in all the dimensions of the feature space are called all-dimensional (AD) range queries.

4.3 Using Multidimensional Index Structures to Kansei Retrieval Systems

Since the queries in Kansei database systems can be implemented by multidimensional range queries, the multidimensional indexing technologies can be used to speed up the query process. Surprisingly, no multidimensional indexes are introduced to the existing Kansei retrieval systems.

Many index structures have been proposed in the database community in the recent decades. Examples include R*-tree [2], X-tree [3], SR-tree [14], A-tree [18], and so on. The work [10] conducted a survey on multidimensional indices.

4.3.1 Traditional Multidimensional Indexes for Kansei Retrieval Systems

Among the existing multidimensional index structures, R*-tree is a famous and is efficiently used for many researches and some commercial databases [1, 12]. Here, we take the R*-tree as an example to explain the disadvantage of using the traditional indexing technologies.

Because every node of the R*-tree contains the information of its entries at all of the index dimensions, when R*-tree in the entire n-dimensional index space is used for a PD range query with d ($d < n$) query dimensions, the PD range query can be evaluated by simply extending the query range in each of the other (n-d) irrelevant index dimensions to the entire data range.

The disadvantage of this approach is that, each of the R*-tree nodes contains n-dimensional information of all its entries and only d-dimensional information of them is necessary for a specific PD range query using d ($d < n$) query dimensions. This means that a great deal of unnecessary information, i.e., the information in the irrelevant (*n-d*) dimensions, also has to be read from disk, which obviously degrades the query performance.

4.3.2 Multi-Btree for Kansei Retrieval Systems

In this approach, using the projections of the quantitative feature vectors on each of the index dimensions, one B-tree (or a variant thereof) is constructed for each index dimension. For a *d*-dimensional PD range query, the corresponding *d* B-trees are used individually and their results are intersected to obtain the final query result. In total, *n* B-trees should be constructed in advance for an *n*-dimensional feature space.

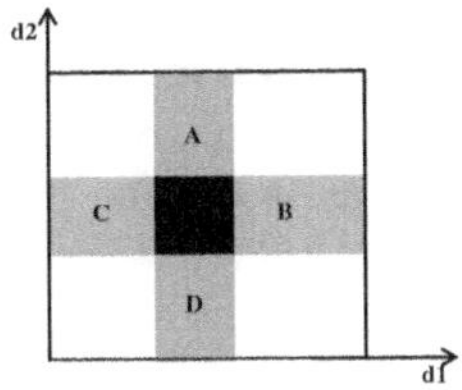

Fig. 4. A PD range query using multi-Btree

Figure 4 is an example of a PD range query evaluated using the multi-Btree, where the two dimensions (d_1 and d_2) are used as query dimensions and the thick shadow region is the given query range. In this example, two B-trees constructed on the dimensions of d_1 and d_2 are used. At first, two range queries are evaluated on the two B-trees, respectively. All of the objects located in the vertical shadow region and the horizontal shadow region are reported as intermediate results. The final result of this range query is given by intersecting them.

The disadvantage of multi-Btree is that queries on different B-trees are evaluated independently without any mutual reference. That is, during searching on each B-tree, the algorithm cannot realize the query ranges in the other index dimensions. Thus, unnecessary checks such as those in regions A, B, C, and D in Figure 5 cannot be pruned. Many unnecessary investigations are thus performed, a great deal of irrelevant information is read from disk and many unnecessary intermediate results are reported by every B-tree. In addition to the unnecessary I/O operations, the intersection phase is also very time-consuming. Considering a dataset having 1,000,000 data points uniformly distributed in a six-dimensional space. Assume that the given PD range query has four query dimensions and the query range in each of the four query dimensions is 1/6 of the entire data range. In this case, the final result of this query has only $1{,}000{,}000/6^4 = 771$ objects. However, the query result on each of the four B-trees has 1,000,100/6=166,666 objects! The total number of intermediate results is 666,666! Even if the query range in each of the query dimensions is decreased to 1/10 of the data range, the above three numbers are 100, 100,000 and 400,000, respectively. That is, although only 100 objects are in the final result, up to 400,000 objects are reported as intermediate results. Another disadvantage of the multi-Btree approach is that managing/updating many disk-resident B-trees requires additional costs.

4.3.3 Multiple Multidimensional Indices for Kansei Retrieval Systems

It is a nature question that "*Why do not we prepare one index for each possible combination of query dimensions*?" Since there are many possible actual combinations of index dimensions (quantitative features) used in the actual retrievals on Kansei database systems, it is not always feasible in applications with large datasets that one index is built for each of such possible combinations. This is because (1) numerous indices have to be constructed and managed, (2) many feature values are repeatedly included in different indices, which is too space-consuming for large datasets and results in a large update cost, and (3) the combinations of index dimensions that are possibly used in the range queries are often unpredictable. Note that, there are a total of (2^n-1) different combinations for n index dimensions.

4.3.4 Adaptive R*-Tree for Kansei Retrieval Systems

We proposed an approach for PD range queries in our previous work [7], which is called Adaptive R*-tree (AR*-tree for short) and it can be efficiently used for Kansei retrieval systems.

General Structure

The key concept of the AR*-tree is that, instead of n-dimensional R*-tree nodes, the AR*-tree consists of *node-groups*, each of which have n one-dimensional nodes. Every node of node-groups holds information of its entries in only one dimension and each node-group holds the information in all the n dimensions. Note that each of the R*-tree nodes holds information of its entries at all of the dimensions. The general structure of the AR*-tree is depicted in Figure 5 and the structure of every node-group is shown in Figure 6. The structure of every node is generally the same as that of the R*-tree and the only difference is that only one-dimensional information is contained in each of the AR*-tree node.

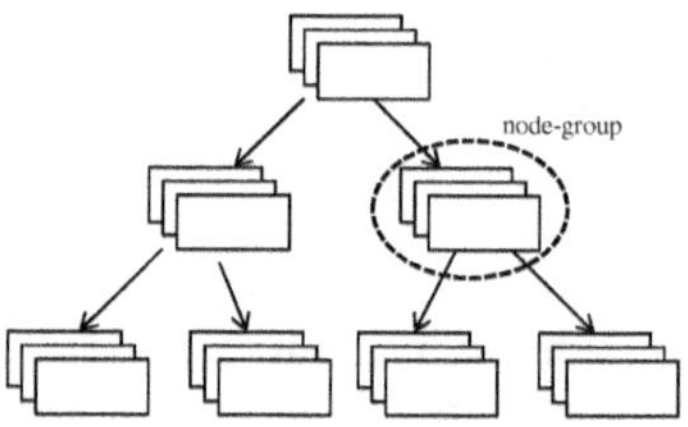

Fig. 5. General structure of AR*-tree

Figure 6 shows the corresponding relationship between the node-group of the AR*-tree and the node of the R*-tree. In the AR*-tree, all of the entries in the same place of the n different nodes of this node-group form a complete n-dimensional MBR in the index space. Whereas every entry in R*-tree nodes includes MBR information in all of the dimensions, every entry in the nodes of the AR*-tree includes only one-dimensional information. This means that every entry of each of AR*-tree nodes only corresponds to an MBR edge. The term *entry of node-group* is used hereinafter, which

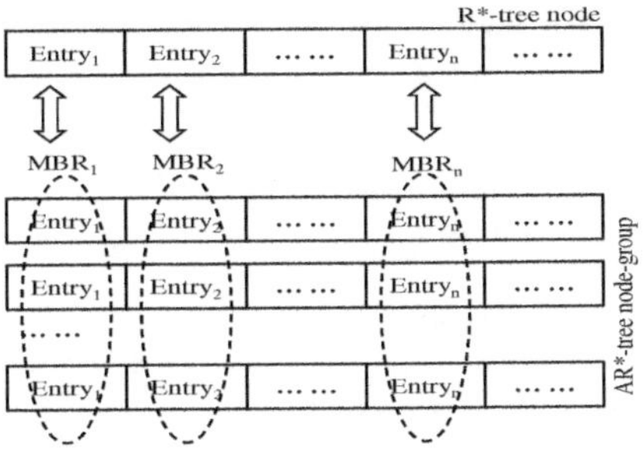

Fig. 6. General structure of node-groups in an n-dimensional AR*-tree

refers to the set of entries having the same index and distributed in all the different nodes of one node-group (see Figure 6). In Figure 6, all of the entries in an ellipse form an entry of this node-group, which corresponds to a complete MBR in the feature space.

The question may arises that whether or not the number of nodes in the AR*-tree increase greatly. The answer is *No*. This is because the maximum number of entries in each node of the AR*-tree increases greatly since only one-dimensional information is contained in each node. According to our experiments the number of nodes increases less than 10%.

Algorithms of AR-tree*

The insert algorithm of the AR*-tree is a simply extensions of the counterparts of the R*-tree. After the new quantitative pattern reaches the leaf node-group, it is divided according to dimensions and stored in different nodes of the leaf node-group. If some node-group must be split, then all of its nodes have to be split at the same time and the split may be up propagated. After a delete operation, if the node-group under-flowed, then all of its nodes should be deleted at the same time and all of its entries are inserted to the AR*-tree again. A range query algorithm is shown in Table 1.

Starting with the root node-group, each entry of the current node-group needs to be checked to decide whether its MBR intersects the query range. If its MBR intersects the query range, and the current node-group is not at the leaf level, then this algorithm is invoked recursively with its child node-groups.

The structure and the algorithm of the AR*-tree guarantees that it can be applied to PD range queries (retrievals in the Kansei retrieval systems) with any combinations of the query dimensions and that only the information in the relevant dimensions is visited. Here we note that the AR*-tree is also able to deal with the retrievals in which all the dimensions of the index space (all the features in the feature vectors) are necessary. Thus, the AR*-tree is suitable for Kansei database systems.

Mathematical Analysis on Performance of R-tree and AR*-tree*

In our previous work [7], we presented a mathematical performance-comparison between the R*-tree and the AR*-tree. Because of the limitation on the space, such analysis is omitted here.

Table 1. Algorithm for range query on the AR*-tree

```
Procedure RangeQuery (rect, node-group)
Input:    rect: query range
  node-group: initial node-group of the query
Output: result: all the tuples in rect
Begin
  For each entry e*) in node-group Do
    If e INTERSECT rect in all the query dimensions**) Then
      If (node-group is not at leaf) Then
        RangeQuery (rect, e.child);
          //e.child: the child node-group corresponding to e
      Else result ← result+e
  EndFor
End
```

*) An entry of a node-group includes all of the entries with the same index in the different nodes of this node-group and it corresponds to a complete MBR.

**) When an entry of a node-group is checked to determine whether it intersects the query range or not, only the nodes in the query dimensions are accessed and the other nodes even in the same node-group are skipped. Moreover, in many cases that an entry of a node-group is checked, even not all of the nodes in the query dimensions need to be checked. This is because that the investigation is done dimension by dimension, so it can stop if the current entry (MBR) is found not to intersect the query range in the current query dimension.

Experimental Comparison on Performance between R-tree and AR*-tree*

A dataset having 200,000 points in a six-dimensional space having Zipf distribution (the constant is 1.5) is used to examine the behavior of the AR*-tree for PD range queries (all the queries in Kansei retrieval systems are PD range queries). The page size of our system is 4096 bytes. Query performance is measured in term of the number of leaf node accesses.

Table 2. Experimental result (comparison of the numbers of leaf node accesses)

Query dimensionality	R*-tree vs AR*-tree	Size of query ranges					
		10%	20%	30%	40%	50%	60%
d=1	R*-tree	1389	2190	2561	3002	3484	4126
	AR*-tree	205	487	498	592	674	793
d=3	R*-tree	509	1480	1590	1924	2506	3498
	AR*-tree	124	412	487	690	996	1479
d=5	R*-tree	118	980	1096	1379	2108	3065
	AR*-tree	204	254	295	496	981	1680

PD range queries are tested with different numbers of query dimensions (query dimensionalities) ranging from 1 to 5. Without loss of generality, the query ranges in all the query dimensions are set equally from 10% to 60% of the whole feature space in increments of 10%. The range query for the range of the same size is repeated 100 times with random locations, and the averages are presented. The experimental result is shown in Table 2, in which *query dimensionality* means the number of dimensions (features) used in the specific retrievals and *size of query ranges* is the size (or say length) of one specific query range in each of the dimensions. Note that, we assume that all of the query ranges in our experiments are hyper-cubes.

The result shows that the AR*-tree has better query performance than the R*-tree. And we can know that the performance of PD range queries on the R*-tree becomes better as the number of query dimensions increases. This is because the search region can be limited in more dimensions as the number of query dimensions increases.

5 Summary and Future Work

In this paper, it was pointed that the traditional multimedia retrieval systems using key-words or/and other text information are not enough in many applications because that they cannot deal with sensitive words reflecting user's subjectivity. After briefly introduced some of the existing Kansei retrieval systems, we proposed a general flow for building Kansei retrieval systems. Also, we discussed how to speed up the retrieval process of Kansei retrieval systems by using multidimensional indexing technologies and we learned that our proposed multidimensional index structure (called AR*-tree) is more suitable to Kansei retrieval systems than other multidimensional index structures. We hope that this paper will be able to help the designers who are planning to design Kansei retrieval systems. In the future, we are going to implement a real Kansei retrieval system.

Acknowledgement

This research was supported in part by the Japan Society for the Promotion of Science through Grants-in-aid for Scientific Research 22500093.

References

1. Adler, D.W.: DB2 Spatial Extender-Spatial Data with the RDBMS. In: Proceedings International Conference on Very Large Data Bases (VLDB), pp. 687–690 (2001)
2. Beckmann, N., Kriegel, H.: The R*-tree: An Efficient and Robust Access Method for Points and Rectangles. In: Proceedings ACM SIGMOD International Conference, pp. 322–331 (1990)
3. Berchtold, S., Keim, D., Kriegel, H.: The X-tree: An Index Structure for High- dimensional data. In: Proceedings the 22nd International Conference on Very large Data Bases (VLDB), pp. 28–39 (1996)
4. Chen, D., Bovik, A.C.: Visual Pattern Image Coding. IEEE Transactions on Communications 38(12), 2137–2146 (1990)
5. Endou, Y.O.: Construction of Kansei Database with Ise Katagami Lattice and Unit Structure: Extraction and Use of Cognitive Characteristics on Pattern Design. Bulletin of Japanese Society for Science of Design 48(3), 119–124 (2001)
6. Feng, Y., Makinouchi, A.: Efficient Evaluation of Partially-Dimensional Range Queries Using Adaptive R*-tree. In: Bressan, S., Küng, J., Wagner, R. (eds.) DEXA 2006. LNCS, vol. 4080, pp. 687–696. Springer, Heidelberg (2006)

7. Fukuda, M., Katsumoto, A., Shibata, Y.: Kansei Retrieve Method based on User Model. Transactions of Information Processing Society of Japan, DPS 95(13), 43–48 (1995)
8. Fukuda, M.: Kansei Retrieval Method Reflecting Shape Pattern of Design Images. Transactions of Information Processing Society of Japan 96(1), 267–274 (1996)
9. Gaede, V., Gunther, O.: Multidimensional Access Methods. ACM Computing Surveys 30(2), 170–231 (1998)
10. Harada, S., Itoh, Y., Nakatani, H.: On Constructing Shape Feature Space for Interpreting Subjective Expressions. Transactions of Information Processing Society of Japan 40(5), 2356–2366 (1999)
11. Informix Spatial DataBlade Module, `http://ww306.ibm.com/software/data/Informix/blades/spatial/rtree.html`
12. Baek, S., Cho, M., Hwang, M., Kim, P.: Kansei-based Image Retrieval Associated with Color. In: Bloch, I., Petrosino, A., Tettamanzi, A.G.B. (eds.) WILF 2005. LNCS (LNAI), vol. 3849, pp. 326–333. Springer, Heidelberg (2006)
13. Katayama, N., Satoh, S.: The SR-tree: An Index Structure for High- Dimensional Nearest Neighbor Queries. In: Proceedings ACM SIGMOD International Conference, pp. 369–380 (1997)
14. Miura, M., Mitsuishi, T., Sasaki, J., Funyu, Y.: A Music Retrieval System which Estimates Characteristics of Data based on Users' Sensibility. Information Processing Society of Japan, SIG Notes 2002(3), 129–136 (2002)
15. Motomura, Y., Yoshida, K., Fujimoto, K.: Generative user models for adaptive Information Retrieval. In: Proceedings IEEE International Conference on System, Man and Cybernetics, pp. 665–670 (2000)
16. Ogino, A., Kato, T.: Kansei System Modeling: Design Method for Kansei Retrieval Systems. Transactions of Information Processing Society of Japan 47(SIG4) (TOD29), 28–39 (2006)
17. Sakurai, Y.: The A-tree: An Index Structure for High-Dimensional Space Using Relative Approximation. In: Proceedings the 26th International Conference on Very Large Data Bases (VLDB), pp. 516–526 (2000)
18. Tsutsumi, K.: A Development of the Building Kansei Information Retrieval System. In: Proceedings the International Conference on Computing in Civil and Building Engineering, pp. 174–181 (2004)
19. Zhang, C.: On Supporting Containment Queries in Relational Database Management Systems. In: Proceedings ACM SIGMOD International Conference, pp. 425–436 (2001)

Detecting Hot Events from Web Search Logs

Yingqin Gu[1,2], Jianwei Cui[1,2], Hongyan Liu[3], Xuan Jiang[1,2],
Jun He[1,2], Xiaoyong Du[1,2], and Zhixu Li[1,2]

[1] Key Labs of Data Engineering and Knowledge Engineering, Ministry of Education, China
[2] School of Information, Renmin University of China, Beijing 100872, China
{guyingqin,cjwruc,jx,hejun,duyong,lizx}@ruc.edu.cn
[3] Department of Management Science and Engineering, Tsinghua University, Beijing 100084, China
hyliu@tsinghua.edu.cn

Abstract. Detecting events from web resources is a challenging task, attracting many attentions in recent years. Web search log is an important data source for event detection because the information it contains reflects users' activities and interestingness to various real world events. There are three major issues for event detection from web search logs: effectiveness, efficiency and the organization of detected events. In this paper, we develop a novel Topic and Event Detection method, *TED*, to address these issues. We first divide the whole data into *topics* for efficiency consideration, and then incorporate link information, temporal information and query content to ensure the quality of detected events. Finally, events detected are organized through the proposed *interestingness measure* as well as topics they belong to. Experiments are conducted on a commercial search engine log. The results demonstrate that our method can effectively and efficiently detect hot events and give a meaningful organization of them.

Keywords: Event detection, click-through data, efficient algorithm.

1 Introduction

As the richness of information on the web grows, more and more researchers are motivated to discover knowledge such as topics and events from web data. The existing approaches of such event detection can be divided into three categories: *content-based* method, *structure-based* method and *log-based* method. In plain terms, the content-based method detects events through analyzing textual information of web resources using techniques such as natural language processing [1]; the structure-based method utilizes website structures and hyperlink structures to discover events [2]; and the log-based method, which is a new research direction in event detection, exploits web search logs (namely, the *click-through data*) to detect events [3] [4].

In [3], the author classifies web data into two types: *author-centric* and *visitor-centric*. Based on this classification, the former two approaches utilize the author-centric data, which are created by web publishers, and the log-based method utilizes the visitor-centric data, which can reflect users' browsing or query activities. Therefore, the log-based method can extract information such as users' activities and

L. Chen et al. (Eds.): WAIM 2010, LNCS 6184, pp. 417–428, 2010.

interestingness to various real world events, and such information may play equally or even more important role in event detection compared with the author-centric data. Besides, the click-through data are collected automatically by web search engine and are easier to obtain. Detecting events from such data has more practical significance. Because of the above reasons, our focus in this paper is to detect events form click-through data.

Table 1 shows an example of click-through data, which record the interactions between users and a web search engine. It can also be represented as a bipartite graph as showed in Fig. 1. From Table 1 we can observe that each record contains three elements: query keywords issued by users, URL of the page clicked by users and the time the query was submitted to the search engine. From the click-through data, three kinds of information can be used for event detection: *link information* (that is indicated by the queries and the corresponding clicked pages), *temporal information*(time) and *query content*(query keywords). Then our task is to utilize the above information to discover groups of click records (or query-page pairs in the bipartite graph) that correspond to real life events.

Table 1. Example of click-through data

Query	URL	Time
q1: David Blaine	p1: http://abcnews.go.com/GMA/.......	2006/5/2
q1: David Blaine	p2: http://www.katu.com/entertain......	2006/5/2
q2: Blaine	p1: http://abcnews.go.com/GMA/.......	2006/5/2
q2: Blaine	p2: http://www.katu.com/entertain......	2006/5/2
q3: David Blaine drowned	p3: http://abclocal.go.com/kabc/story...	2006/5/9

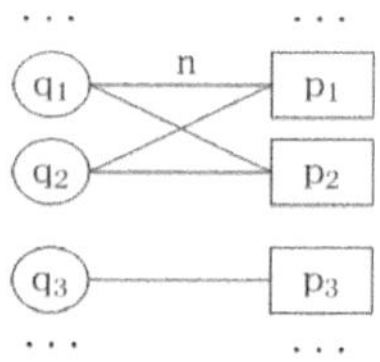

Fig. 1. Bipartite graph

In order to enhance event detection from click-through data, we deem that three issues need to be addressed. First, the click-through data are produced by users' query submission and browsing activities. It is quite noisy and sparse. Therefore, how to discover real life events with high precision and recall is a problem. Second, the web search logs usually contain at least millions of log records. The efficiency of event detection is an important issue. Last but not the least, the detected events need to be organized well so that from the results users can find the real world interesting events conveniently.

This paper aims to address the above three issues. In terms of the effectiveness, we propose a novel notion called *click-through burst region* as the event indicator for event detection and incorporate link information, temporal information and query content simultaneously to ensure the quality of detected events. As for the efficiency, we propose an efficient algorithm, which divides the whole data into several small semantic-relevant subsets, each of which is called a *topic*. Then the event detection is performed in each topic, making the whole process efficient. In order to organize the results orderly, we introduce an *interestingness* measure, which is similar to the work in [4], to rank the detected events. Besides, since we discover topics first, events extracted from one topic can be clustered naturally.

The proposed log-based event detection method is performed on a real life click-through dataset collected from MSN search engine. We also manually labeled a list of events to evaluate the quality of the detected events. The results show that by incorporating the three kinds of information the effectiveness is improved evidently, and from the performance on datasets of different size our algorithm shows high efficiency.

The rest of this paper is organized as follows: Section 2 reviews related work. In Section 3, we introduce our proposed log-based method for event detection. Experimental results on real life data are shown in Section 4. Finally, we draw conclusions and future work in Section 5.

2 Related Work

In this section, we will introduce some previous works in event detection area and discuss difference between previous works and our work.

Event detection is part of a broader area called Topic Detection and Tracking (TDT). TDT is a famous research project which can be divided into two categories [5] as Retrospective Event Detection (RED) [5] [6] and New Event Detection (NED) [7] [8]. At the moment, our work is more related to RED. RED is first proposed in [5] by Yang et al., and an agglomerative clustering algorithm called Group Average Clustering was proposed in that paper. In [6], the author proposed a multi-model RED algorithm, which incorporated both the content and the time information, and an approach was proposed to determine the approximate number of events. Besides TDT, many research works focus on detecting events by identifying burst patterns of content-based features from a text stream [9] [10] [11]. [9] introduced how to extract burst features from text streams, where the text stream is modeled as an infinite state automation and the bursts are modeled as transition states. In [10], the author proposed a parameter-free method to group related busty features into one event. In [11], a mixture density-based approach is proposed to detect bursts of word features for event detection. The difference between our work and above TDT research or content based methods is that we detect events based on different data source. From the visitor-centric data, we may find hotter and more interesting events.

Recently, with the development of search engine and Web2.0 technology, many researches have focused on exploiting web search logs for various purposes such as query expansion [12], named entity mining [13] and web search improvement [14], etc. However, to the best of our knowledge, there are only two of such works focusing on event detection [3] [4]. The work done by Zhao et al. [3] is the first effort, in which two phases of clustering based on semantic and temporal similarity respectively are performed to group similar query-page pairs corresponding to real life events. While in [4], the authors use query session as indicator of event. They first map each query session to a polar space based on content and time similarity, then group query sessions that are similar in content and close in time to represent an event. The general method of our work is different from the above two works. Besides, both the above two works run some time consuming algorithms in the whole click-through data and fail to mention the efficiency in their papers; while the algorithm we propose is quite efficient and applicable.

3 Framework of Our Method

The framework of our method, *TED*, for exploiting web search logs to detect events is presented in Fig. 2.

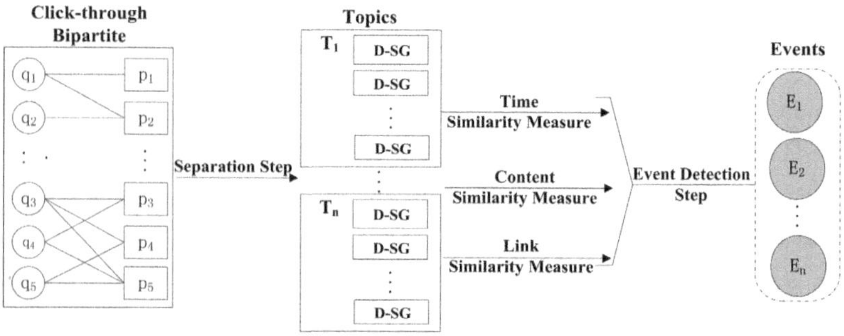

Fig. 2. The framework of exploiting click-through data for event detection

Given the click-through data, which can be represented as a bipartite graph, we first divide this graph into several sub-graphs each of which corresponds to a topic by applying a quite efficient algorithm called *Shingle* and utilizing query content information. Then, we propose a novel notion called *click-through burst region* as event indicator to further detect events from topics. For each topic, the events can be detected by clustering the similar burst regions. Here the link information, temporal information and query content are combined to measure the burst regions' similarity. Finally, we organize the detected events through their interestingness and the topics they belong to.

3.1 Dividing Click-Through Data into Topics

In this step, we tend to divide the whole click-through data into several sub-graphs so that events can be detected efficiently in each small sub-graph. To do this, we implement an algorithm called *Shingle* [15]. The substance of algorithm *Shingle* is to use the Jaccard coefficient to measure similarities of nodes in a graph so that the nodes with similar neighbors tend to be grouped into one dense sub-graph. While its method is based on recursive stages of fingerprinting the graph, which after multiple applications can turn dense sub-graphs of arbitrary size into fingerprints of constant size. It is very efficient and is capable of handling graphs with tens of billions edges [15].

After running the algorithm Shingle, we get dense sub-graphs of click-through bipartite graph only based on the link information. While work in [16] illustrates that using link information alone will produce a high precision at a low recall level, which means that click records belong to one event may be separated into different dense graphs. To solve this problem, we further consider query content of each dense sub-graph and merge the content-similar sub-graphs into one larger sub-graph to reflect *topic* information. It can be done through comparing the similarity of query content in each dense sub-graph, here the classical *tfidf* and *cosine similarity* techniques are used to measure the similarity of queries, and the *inverted indexing* is used to speed up this step. Then a pruning strategy based on an interestingness measure which will be introduced in Section 3.3 is used so that uninteresting topics need not be considered anymore.

3.2 Event Detection

In this section, we will introduce our method to detect events from each topic. From each topic, we first propose a novel event indicator called *click-through burst region* (*burst region* for short). Then link information, temporal information and query content are combined linearly to measure the similarity between burst regions. Finally burst regions can be clustered as events.

3.2.1 Click-Through Burst Region

Based on the intuitive premise used in [9], the appearance of an event can be signaled by a "burst of activity". Therefore, a sharp increase in time series of query-page pair's click-through (the number of click-throughs) tends to indicate a real life event. Based on this, we choose burst region defined below as event indicator.

Definition 1(*click-through burst region*) *click-through burst region* is a period in the time series of a query-page pair's click-through, in which the click through increased sharply than average click-through of the time series.

We calculate a threshold called *cutoff* by adding average and stand derivation of the click-through time series for detecting burst regions. Each of detected burst regions B can be represented by (T_{st}, T_{ed}), where T_{st} and T_{ed} is the start time and the end time of burst region B respectively.

3.2.2 Burst Region Similarity

In this section, we introduce the method to measure the similarity of two *click-through burst regions* by combining link, content and time similarity.

The link-based similarity between two burst regions B_i and B_j is denoted as $linkSim(B_i, B_j)$. We take advantage of the method in [3] to calculate $linkSim(B_i, B_j)$. First, bipartite graph of each topic is converted to a dual graph. Each edge between a query q and an URL p in the bipartite graph is converted to a node $<q, p>$ of the dual graph. Two nodes in the dual graph are linked by an edge if they have the same query or URL. Then, we run algorithm *SimFusion* [17] to calculate the link similarity between different nodes to represent link-based similarity of burst regions as shown in equation (1). In equation (1), P_x is a query-page pair containing burst region B_i, and P_y contains burst region B_j.

$$linkSim(B_i, B_j) = SimFusion(P_x, P_y) \tag{1}$$

The content-based similarity is donated as $contentSim(B_i, B_j)$ and is calculated by the query content similarity as introduced in Section 3.1.

$$conetentSim(B_i, B_j) = Sim(q_x, q_y) \tag{2}$$

The third type similarity we considered is the time-based similarity, which evaluates how near two burst regions happened by Equation (3):

$$timeSim(B_i, B_j) = \begin{cases} \dfrac{-distance(B_i, B_j)}{|B_i| + |B_j| + distance(B_i, B_j)} & \text{if } distance(B_i, B_j) >= 0 \\ \dfrac{1}{2}\left(\dfrac{overlap(B_i, B_j)}{|B_i|} + \dfrac{overlap(B_i, B_j)}{|B_j|}\right) & \text{otherwise} \end{cases} \tag{3}$$

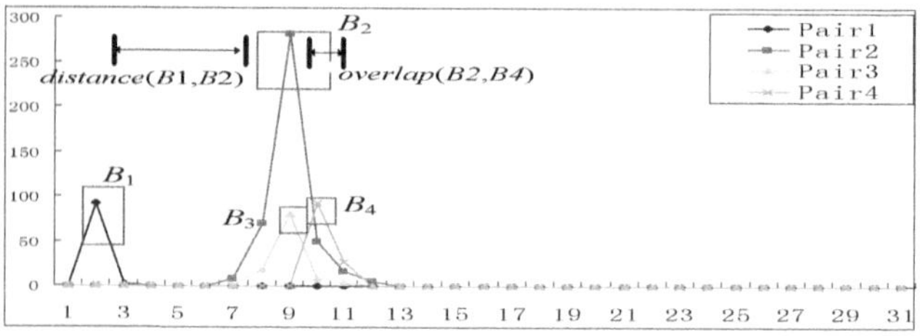

Fig. 3. Time-based similarity of four burst regions

In Equation (3), *distance*(B_i, B_j) describes how far two burst regions B_i and B_j are, which can be measured by the difference between the starting time of B_j and the ending time of B_i as shown in Fig. 3. *overlap*(B_i, B_j) is the time intersection of two burst regions, calculated by the difference between the ending time of B_j and the starting time of B_i. For example, in Fig. 3, *overlap*(B_2, B_4) is equal to T_{ed} of B_2 minus T_{st} of B_4. $|B_i|$ describes how long a burst region lasts. For example, B_1 in Fig.3 lasts four days and so $|B_1|$ equals 4. Therefore, by Equation (3), if two burst regions have overlap, the larger *overlap* they have, the more similar they are. Otherwise, the larger *distance* they have, the less similar they are.

Based on the three type similarity introduced above, the similarity between burst regions B_i and B_j, *Sim*(B_i, B_j), can be calculated by Equation (4):

$$Sim(B_i, B_j) = \alpha \cdot linkSim(B_i, B_j) + \beta \cdot contentSim(B_i, B_j) + \gamma \cdot timeSim(B_i, B_j) \quad (4)$$

α, β and γ are three parameters used to tradeoff the effectiveness of link, content and time similarity. How to set the three parameters will be discussed in the following experimental section. After getting the similarity between *click-through burst regions,* we utilize a parameter free hierarchy-based clustering method [19] to cluster similar burst regions, which uses *silhouette coefficient* [18] to judge when to terminate the clustering procedure. Each cluster obtained after this step corresponds to an event.

3.3 Organizing Detected Events

After detecting the events, effective organization of the detection results is important for improving the utility of our method. To do this, we develop an *interestingness measure* to indicate how hot and interesting a detected event is. An event is assumed to be more interesting if it can attract more users' attention and has a more obvious pattern of "burst of activity". So we introduce the following definition to measure the interestingness.

Definition 2(*attention degree*). Given a query-page pair *p* and event *E* it belongs to, the *attention degree* of *p*, denoted as *ad*(*p*), and the attention degree of *E*, denoted by *ad*(*E*), are defined as:

$$ad(p) = |p| / |E| \quad (5)$$

$$ad(E) = |E| / |D| \quad (6)$$

Here $|p|$ is the click-through count of p, $|E|$ is the click-through count of E to which p belongs to, and $|D|$ is the click-through count of all click-through. So, a higher *attention degree* means this query-page pair or event attracts more people's attention.

Definition 3(*burst rate*) Given a query-page pair p and the event E it belongs to, *burst rate* of p and E are defined as follows:

$$br(p) = \max(|p_i|)/|p| \tag{7}$$

$$br(E) = \sum_i (br(p_i) \cdot ad(p_i)) \tag{8}$$

Where p_i is the ith query-page pair in event E. Based on the above definitions, we give the notion of *interestingness measure*.

Definition 4 (*interestingness measure*) The *interestingness measure* of an event E considers both the attention degree factor and burst rate factor of this event, which is defined as follows:

$$im(E) = ad(E) \cdot br(E) \tag{9}$$

We calculate each event's interestingness measure to rank the detected events so that the more interesting an event is, the topper position it will be in the ranked event list. Furthermore, since we detect event in each topic, events detected from one topic can be organized together and listed by order of the timestamp of each event.

4 Experimental Results

4.1 Dataset

Our experiments are conducted on a real life click-through dataset collected from MSN search engine from May 1 to May 31, 2006. Our click-through dataset contains about 14 million clicks, 3.5 million distinct queries, 4.9 million distinct urls and 6.8 million distinct query-URL(query-page) pairs.

To evaluate effectiveness of our method, we manually labeled 10 real life topics and 13 corresponding events from the dataset. Each labeled topic and event contains a set of query-page pairs. Given a topic, we label query-page pairs to represent the topic and the corresponding events by the following steps:

1. Select a set of queries, denoted as Q, which were frequently submitted and highly correlated to the topic.
2. The click-through data are represented as a bipartite graph, which contain a number of *connected sub-graphs*. From them, a set G of connected sub-graphs that contain the queries in Q are extracted.
3. For each connected sub-graph in G, filter out the queries and URLs whose frequencies are less than a given minimum threshold.
4. For each query-page pair in the filtered G, we manually check whether it belongs to the topic according to its page content. After that, a set of query-page pairs, denoted as T, are chosen to represent the topic.
5. For query-page pairs in T, if there is more than one event for the topic, we further annotate them into several parts to represent different events. Otherwise, there is only one event in T.

Table 2. List of labeled events

Topic	Event	Timestamp
David Blaine	Submerged in an aquarium	May 2, 2006
	Failed to break world record	May 9, 2006
Immigration Bill	Senate reached deal to revive immigration bill	May 11, 2006
	Senate passed immigration bill	May 25, 2006
Charles Barkley	Admit having gambling problem	May 4, 2006
	Called Bryant selfish	May 17, 2006
Chris Daughtry	Eliminated from American Idol	May 10, 2006
Stephen Colbert	"Attack" Bush at a dinner	May 1, 2006
Record Hammerhead	A world-record hammerhead shark caught	May 26, 2006
Ohio Bear Attack	Woman attacked by escaped bear	May 22, 2006
Hoffa Dig	Feds digging for Jimmy Hoffa	May 18, 2006
Pygmy Rabbit	Last male of pygmy rabbit dead	May 18, 2006
Kentucky Derby	Barbaro won the Kentucky Derby	May 6, 2006

Based on the above method, we extract 13 real life events from the click-through dataset. The complete list of topics and corresponding events are shown in Table 2. Then from the labeled click-through records, we randomly choose other unrelated records from the whole datasets to generate larger and noisier data. We extracted four datasets: dataset1, dataset2, dataset3 and dataset4, whose numbers of click-through records are 250k, 350k, 600k and 1,000k respectively.

4.2 Parameter Setting

In this section, we learn how to set parameters in equation (4) and the experiment is performed on dataset1. Methods based on different linear combinations of link information, temporal information and query content are listed in Table 3.

Table 3. Detection schemes based on different combinations of informations

Notation	Explanation
Link	Detection solely based on link information
Time	Detection solely based on temporal information
Content	Detection solely based on query content
Link_Time	Detection based on linear combination of link information and temporal information
Link_Content	Detection based on linear combination of link information and query content
Time_Content	Detection based on linear combination of temporal information and query content
Link_Time_Content	Detection based on linear combination of link information, temporal information and query content

The parameter α, β and γ in equation (4) are set in the following way:

- For Detection based on Link_Content schema, γ is set to zero and α is set to 0.1, 0.3, …, 0.9 and β is set to 0.9, 0.7, …, 0.1 accordingly. It corresponds to five parameter setting cases: para1, para2, para3, para4 and para5 respectively. Parameters of Link_Time schema and Time_Content schema can be set similarly.
- For Link_Time_Content schema, α, β and γ are set according to the values that produce best results for Link_Content and Link_Time schemas.

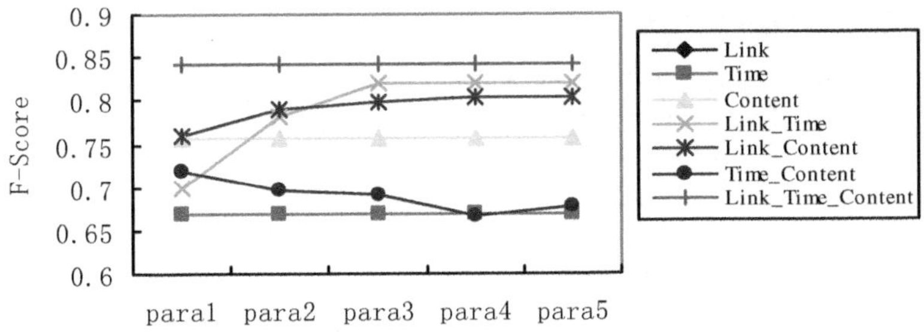

Fig. 4. Performance of different parameters setting

Fig. 4 shows the result of event detection on dataset1. F-score is used to measure the quality of detected events. The F-score of Link schema is quite low and it cannot be shown in the figure. By analyzing the detected events, we find that this is because most events detected by this schema have high precision but very low recall, which is consistent with the observation in [16]. Though the performance of the method *only based on link information* is poor, combining link information with temporal or content information often leads to better performance, and the performance based on the combination of all the three kinds of information is best.

4.3 Efficiency Evaluation

Setting the parameters according to the above experiment, we run our algorithm *TED* on the other three datasets. The experiment is conducted on a HP dc7700 desktop with an Intel Core2 Duo E4400 2.0 GHz CPU and 3.49 GB RAM. Figure 5 and 6 shows the runtime of separation step and F-score of our algorithm on different datasets.

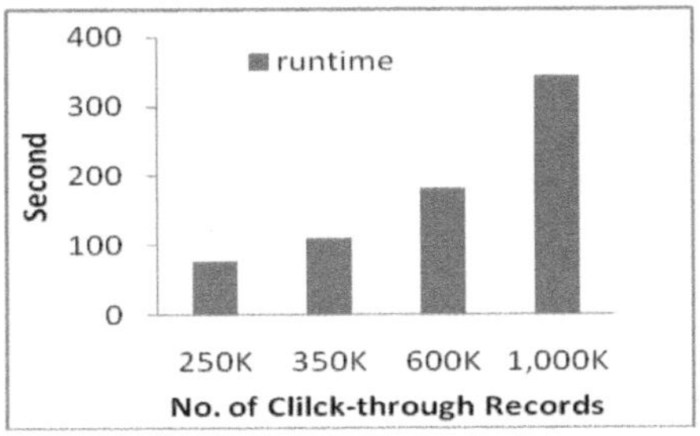

Fig. 5. Efficiency on four datasets

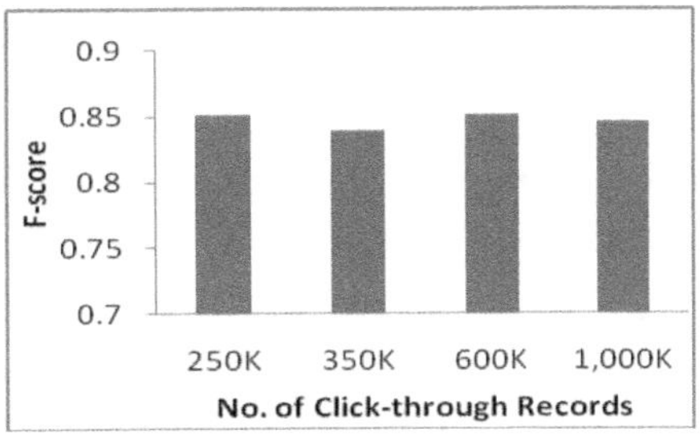

Fig. 6. Effectiveness on four datasets

From Figure 5 we can see that our algorithm is quite efficient. It can be run in minutes. Besides, with the augment of the datasets, the runtime of the algorithm increase linearly. The Figure 6 shows that with the noise data added, there is almost no reduce of the F-score of detected events. These two figures testify that our algorithm has quite high efficiency with good effectiveness.

4.4 Illustrative Examples

By running our algorithm *TED* on the dataset4, we get a list of ranked detected events. Table 4 shows the top 10 ten hot events. And all the labeled events can be found in the top 100 events.

Table 4. List of top 10 hot events

Rank	Events
1	David Blaine submerged in an aquarium
	Failed to break world record
2	Stephen Colbert "attack" Bush
3	No-event
4	Barbaro won in Kentucky Derby
5	Chris Daughtry eliminated from American Idol
6	Holloway case
7	Videotaped killing
8	Michelle Rodriguez
9	Judicial Watch
10	Oprah Winfrey's legend ball

From Table 4 we can find that events of rank 1, 2, 4 and 5 are events in the labeled dataset, and two events about David Blaine are organized together in chronological order. Events of rank 6, 7, 8, 9 and 10 are the newly detected events, among which events of rank 6 and 7 correspond to two criminal case news and event of rank 10 is about a legend ball held by Oprah Winfrey in honor of 25 African-American women in the field of art, while pages related to events of rank 8 and 9 corresponding to a movie star and a government organization are not available now or have been updated, so we have no idea what exactly happened at that time.

By analyzing the result, we find that our algorithm still has some shortcomings. For example, the detected event of rank 3, consists of few click records and it does not correspond to any real life event. This problem may be relieved through a more critical pruning strategy. Besides, although we consider the query content to solve the low-recall problem in separation step, an event may still be possible to be separated into several parts. For instance, we find another event about Kentucky Derby in the top 100 hot events.

4.5 Comparative Experiment

Work in [3], which proposed a two-phase-clustering method, is the one that is most similar to our method for event detection. In this section, we compare our method with it (we call it two-phase-clustering) on efficiency and effectiveness.

Since the two-phase-clustering method runs a time-consuming algorithm *SimFusion* on whole dataset, it cannot process very large click-through data in our experiment environment. To do the comparison, we generate another four smaller datasets: no_noise, noise_2, noise_4 and noise_8, which stand for labeled datasets with no noise, one time noise, three times noise and seven times noise respectively. Dataset of no_noise contains 35k click records.

For efficiency, we compare the runtime of first phase of [3] with the runtime of the separation step of *TED*. Both methods' second steps are performed on subset data and are relatively efficient. Fig. 7 shows the experimental result, where we can see that the runtime of our method increases much slower than that of Two-phase-clustering. In noise_8, our method consume about one minute while First Phase consume four days. So our method is much more efficient than the first phase of [3] in dealing with click-through data. As for effectiveness, Fig. 8 shows the result of F-score for four datasets. We can see that our method has a much higher F-score for each dataset, which means our event detection method performs better than that of [3].

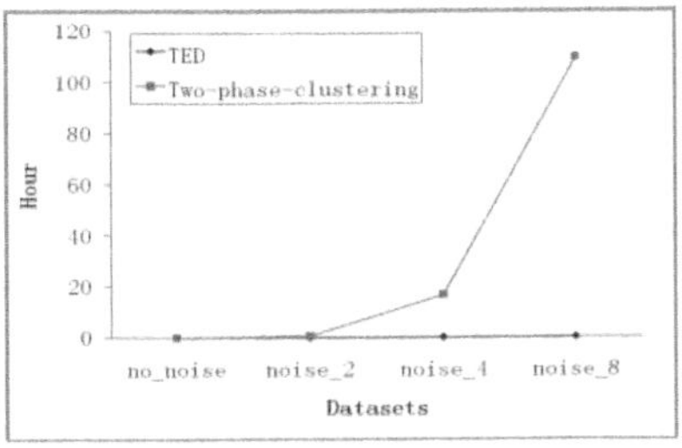

Fig. 7. Efficiency comparison

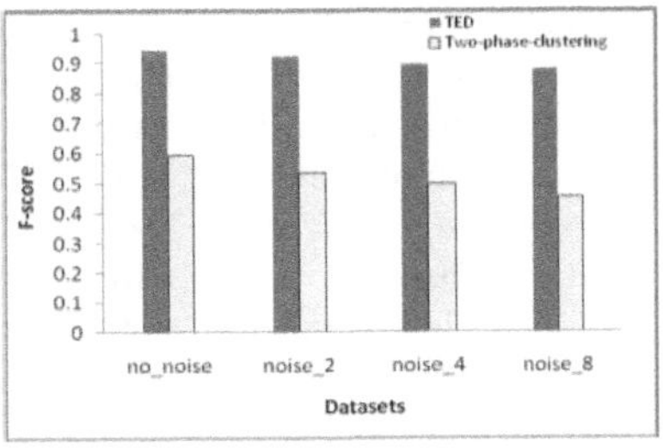

Fig. 8. Effectiveness comparison

5 Conclusion and Future Work

In this paper, we propose an efficient log-based method, *TED*, which incorporates link information, temporal information and query content for topic and event detection. Two major steps are contained in our method. The first is a separation step, in which we use algorithm *Shingle* to divide the whole data into dense sub-graphs and cluster query content similar sub-graphs as topics. Then in each topic, the event detection step is performed, in which we use the burst region as indicator of events and clustering similar burst regions by linearly combing link information, temporal information and query content. The experiments conducted on real life dataset show that our method can detect events effectively and efficiently from click-through data.

Practice asks for online detection of emerging events. For future work, we will extend our Retrospective Event Detection algorithm to New Event Detection. Moreover, we will explore how to utilize the page content to further improve the performance of our method.

Acknowledgments. This work was supported in part by the National Natural Science Foundation of China under Grant No. 70871068, 70621061 and 70890083. We also thank Microsoft Research Asia for providing the real data and funding this research.

References

1. Yang, Y., Zhang, J., Carbonell, J., Jin, C.: Topic-conditioned Novelty Detection. In: 8th ACM SIGKDD International Conference on Knowledge Discovery and Data Mining, pp. 688–693. ACM Press, Edmonton (2002)
2. Sun, A., Lim, E.P.: Web Unit Mining: Finding and Classifying Subgraphs of Web Pages. In: 2003 ACM CIKM International Conference on Information and Knowledge Management, pp. 108–115. ACM Press, New Orleans (2003)

3. Zhao, Q., Liu, T.Y., Bhowmick, S.S., Ma, W.Y.: Event Detection from Evolution of Click-through Data. In: 12th ACM SIGKDD International Conference on Knowledge Discovery and Data Mining, pp. 484–493. ACM Press, Philadelphia (2006)
4. Chen, L., Hu, Y., Nejdl, W.: Deck: Detecting Events from Web Click-through Data. In: 8th IEEE International Conference on Data Mining, pp. 123–132. IEEE Press, Pisa (2008)
5. Yang, Y., Peirce, T., Carbonell, J.: A Study of Retrospective and On-line Event Detection. In: 21st Annual International ACM SIGIR Conference on Research and Development in Information Retrieval, pp. 28–36. ACM Press, Melbourne (1998)
6. Li, Z., Wang, B., Li, M., Ma, W.Y.: A Probabilistic Model for Retrospective News Event Detection. In: 28th Annual International ACM SIGIR Conference on Research and Development in Information Retrieval, pp. 106–113. ACM Press, Salvador (2005)
7. Allan, J., Papka, R., Lavrenko, V.: On-line New Event Detection and Tracking. In: 21st Annual International ACM SIGIR Conference on Research and Development in Information Retrieval, pp. 37–45. ACM Press, Melbourne (1998)
8. Luo, G., Tang, C., Yu, P.S.: Resource-adaptive Real-time New Event Detection. In: ACM SIGMOD International Conference on Management of Data, pp. 497–508. ACM Press, Beijing (2007)
9. Kleinbert, J.: Bursty and Hierarchical Structure in Streams. In: 8th ACM SIGKDD International Conference on Knowledge Discovery and Data Mining, pp. 91–101. ACM Press, Edmonton (2002)
10. Fung, G.P.C., Yu, J.X., Yu, P.S., Lu, H.: Parameter Free Bursty Events Detection in Text Streams. In: 31st International Conference on Very Large Data Bases, pp. 181–192. ACM Press, Trondheim (2005)
11. He, Q., Chang, K., Lim, E.P.: Analyzing Feature Trajectories for Event Detection. In: 30th Annual International ACM SIGIR Conference on Research and Development in Information Retrieval, pp. 207–214. ACM Press, Amsterdam (2007)
12. Cui, H., Wen, J.R., Nie, J.Y., Ma, W.Y.: Probabilistic Query Expansion Using Query Logs. In: 11th international conference on World Wide Web, pp. 325–332. ACM Press, Honolulu (2002)
13. Xu, G., Yang, S.H., Li, H.: Named Entity Mining from Click-Through Data Using Weakly Supervised Latent Dirichlet Allocation. In: 15th ACM SIGKDD International Conference on Knowledge Discovery and Data Mining, pp. 1365–1374. ACM Press, Paris (2009)
14. Zhu, G., Mishne, G.: Mining Rich Session Context to Improve Web Search. In: 15th ACM SIGKDD International Conference on Knowledge Discovery and Data Mining, pp. 1037–1046. ACM Press, Paris (2009)
15. David, G., Ravi, K., Andrew, T.: Discovering Large Dense Subgraphs in Massive Graphs. In: 31st International Conference on Very Large Data Bases, pp. 721–732. ACM Press, Trondheim (2005)
16. Filippo, M.: Combining Link and Content Analysis to Estimate Semantic Similarity. In: 13th international conference on World Wide Web, pp. 452–453. ACM Press, New York (2004)
17. Xi, W., Fox, E., Fan, W., Zhang, B., Chen, Z., Yan, J., Zhuang, D.: SimFusion: Measuring Similarity using Unified Relationship Matix. In: 28th Annual International ACM SIGIR Conference on Research and Development in Information Retrieval, pp. 130–137. ACM Press, Salvador (2005)
18. Leonard, K., Peter, J.R.: Finding Groups in Data: An Introduction to Cluster Analysis. Wiley-Interscience, Hoboken (1990)
19. Cui, J., Li, P., Liu, H., He, J., Du, X.: A Neighborhood Search Method for Link-Based Tag Clustering. In: 5th International Conference on Advanced Data Mining and Application, pp. 91–103. Springer Press, Beijing (2009)

Evaluating Truthfulness of Modifiers Attached to Web Entity Names

Ryohei Takahashi[1], Satoshi Oyama[2], Hiroaki Ohshima[1], and Katsumi Tanaka[1]

[1] Department of Social Informatics, Graduate School of Informatics, Kyoto University
{takahasi,ohshima,tanaka}@dl.kuis.kyoto-u.ac.jp
[2] Division of Synergetic Information Science,
Graduate School of Information Science and Technology, Hokkaido University
oyama@ist.hokudai.ac.jp

Abstract. To make online advertisements or user-generated content more attractive, people often use modifiers such as "authentic," "impressive," "special," and so on. Some of these are exaggerations. That is, sometimes modifiers that are attached to Web entities do not represent the content appropriately. In this paper, we proposed a method to evaluate the truthfulness of modifiers attached to Web entity names by extracting relevant and conflicting terms from the content texts.

1 Introduction

Online advertising services and user-generated content sites make it easy for people to create content on the Web. For example, people can easily advertise their products on the Web or contribute recipes to cooking sites.

When people search websites, they judge whether to read the content by names or snippets. Therefore, to encourage people to read the content, authors try to make the names attractive.

They use various modifiers, some of which are exaggerated. Often, the modifiers in names are not appropriate for the content. For example, there are recipes whose names are "authentic curry" but use roux instead of spices. And there are package tours whose names contain the words "convenient" but require change of airplane or the hotel is far from the city.

This causes problems when people search for content. When people search for content using queries that contain modifiers, precision is reduced because the content that contains the keywords in queries is regarded as relevant by conventional search engines. In addition, people might read content that is not credible.

In this paper, we proposed a method to evaluate the truthfulness of modifiers attached to Web entity names. To do this, we first extract relevant words and conflicting words with modifiers from text that explains the content. Then, we use these terms to evaluate the truthfulness of the names.

L. Chen et al. (Eds.): WAIM 2010, LNCS 6184, pp. 429–440, 2010.

2 Related Works

There have been several studies about the qualities of user-generated contents. For example, Agichtein et al. proposed a method to find high-quality content in question/answering content [1].

Fiore et al. assessed attractiveness in online dating profiles and showed that freely written text is as important as the photo for influencing the overall attractiveness of the profile [2].

Our research extracts evidence of modifiers, so studies about extracting evidence of the Web pages are also relevant. Lee et al. developed a method for finding evidence of real-world events from the Web [3]. Murakami et al. support the evaluation of credibility of online information by gathering agreeing and conflicting opinions [4].

Kobayashi et al. evaluate brand value from text on the Web by collecting attributes describing the quality of a product [5]. This is related to this paper in respect to judging whether names match the content.

Research about searching by modifiers is also relevant. Kato et al. improved the accuracy of image searches in abstract queries by transforming the abstract terms into concrete terms [6]. Yusuf et al. created a system that searches for pictures by onomatopoeia to help people learn Japanese onomatopoeia [7].

Research about folksonomy is also relevant [8] [9]. The modifiers in the names are similar to tag information, but the names of entities are different from tags in that names are attached by only one user.

3 To Evaluate Truthfulness of Modifiers Attached to Web Entities

3.1 Terms Relevant to and Conflicting with Modifiers

To evaluate the truthfulness of modifiers, we extract terms that are relevant to and conflicting with the modifiers from descriptions about the content of the entities.

For example, we consider a recipe whose name is "Japanese style Hamburg steak." If the recipe uses "grated radish" and "soy sauce," we think it is Japanese style. On the other hand, if the recipe uses "red wine" and "mushroom," we consider it not to be Japanese style. Therefore, "grated radish" and "soy sauce" are relevant to "Japanese style," and "red wine" and "mushroom" are conflicting. So, we can judge the modifiers attached to names as true if the entities contain many relevant terms and we can judge them as exaggerated or inaccurate if the entities contain many conflicting terms.

3.2 Differences in Truthfulness due to Range of Comparison

The truthfulness of modifiers differ depending on the range of comparison.

For example, the Hamburg steak recipe using "grated radish" and "soy sauce" is Japanese style when we compare it with other Hamburg steak recipes. So, if the name of this recipe contains "Japanese style," the truthfulness of this modifier is high. However, Hamburg steak is not an original Japanese food, so it conflicts with "Japanese style" if we compare it with all recipes. So, in that comparison, the truthfulness of this modifier is low.

In this way, people judge the truthfulness of modifiers by comparing with some range. We evaluate truthfulness by integrating the comparison with all the categories that the entity belongs to.

3.3 Necessity of Methods without Training

In this problem, we have to evaluate truthfulness of any modifiers. So, we cannot use supervised learning methods because it is impossible to prepare training sets for all the modifiers. That is, we can only use the information of the names and descriptions about the content of entities.

4 Formalization

Each entity e_i consists of the set of modifiers in its name (M_i), the set of categories that the entity belongs to (C_i), and the set of words to describe the content of the entity (W_i). That is,

$$
\begin{aligned}
&e_i = (M_i, C_i, W_i) \\
&M_i \subset M, C_i \subset C, W_i \subset W \\
&M = \{m_1, m_2, \cdots\}, C = \{c_1, c_2, \cdots\}, W = \{w_1, w_2, \cdots\}
\end{aligned}
$$

M is the set of all the modifiers, and m_k is a modifier; C is the set of all the categories, and c_k is a category; and W is the set of all the words, and w_k is a word.

The goal of this research is to calculate the truthfulness of the modifiers attached to each entity. As mentioned in Section 3.2, the truthfulness is the integration of the comparison with all the categories of the entity. That is,

$$Truthfulness(m_j, e_i) = Unite_{c_k \in C_i}(Relevancy(m_j, c_k, e_i)) \tag{1}$$

$Unite$ is the function that unites the relevancy in all the categories that the entity belongs to.

We represent relevancy using probability.

$$Relevancy(m_j, c_k, e_i) = p(c_{jk}|e_i) \tag{2}$$

$p(c_{jk}|e_i)$ is the probability that an entity e_i is in the class that relevant to m_j in c_k .

The set of relevant words (RW_{jk}) and conflicting words (CW_{jk}) are defined as follows.

$$
\begin{aligned}
RW_{jk} &= \{w|p(c_{jk}|w) > p(c_{jk}|\overline{w})\} \\
CW_{jk} &= \{w|p(c_{jk}|w) < p(c_{jk}|\overline{w})\}
\end{aligned}
$$

$\overline{w}$ represents $w \notin W_i$. The set of words that are not in RW_{jk} or CW_{jk} is irrelevant words (IW_{jk}).

$$IW_{jk} = \{w | p(c_{jk}|w) = p(c_{jk}|\overline{w})\} \tag{3}$$

4.1 To Calculate Relevancy in Category

By using Bayes' theorem,

$$p(c_{jk}|e_i) = \frac{p(c_{jk})p(e_i|c_{jk})}{p(e_i)} \tag{4}$$

As mentioned, the content of each entity e_i is represented as the word set W_i. If all the words independently appear with one another, we can transform as follows by using a multi-variate Bernoulli model.

$$p(e_i|c_{jk}) = \prod_{w \in W_i} p(w|c_{jk}) \prod_{w \notin W_i} (1 - p(w|c_{jk})) \tag{5}$$

$$p(e_i) = \prod_{w \in W_i} p(w) \prod_{w \notin W_i} (1 - p(w)) \tag{6}$$

By combining these expressions,

$$p(c_{jk}|e_i) = p(c_{jk}) \prod_{w \in W_i} \frac{p(w|c_{jk})}{p(w)} \prod_{w \notin W_i} \frac{(1 - p(w|c_{jk}))}{(1 - p(w))} \tag{7}$$

In this paper, we assume that

$$w \in RW_{jk} \Leftrightarrow p(m_j \in M_i | w \in W_i, c_k \in C_i) \gg p(m_j \in M_i | w \notin W_i, c_k \in C_i)$$
$$w \in CW_{jk} \Leftrightarrow p(m_j \in M_i | w \in W_i, c_k \in C_i) \ll p(m_j \in M_i | w \notin W_i, c_k \in C_i)$$

$a \gg b$ means a is significantly higher than b.

So, we create the null hypothesis H_0 that

$$p(m_j \in M_i | w \in W_i, c_k \in C_i) = p(m_j \in M_i | w \notin W_i, c_k \in C_i) \tag{8}$$

We treat the terms that reject H_0 and the former probability is significantly higher as relevant words, and that reject H_0 and the latter probability is significantly higher as conflicting words, and that we treat those that do not reject H_0 as irrelevant words.

By Expression (3),

$$\begin{aligned} w \in IW_{jk} &\Leftrightarrow p(c_{jk}|w) = p(c_{jk}|\overline{w}) \\ &\Leftrightarrow p(c_{jk}) = p(c_{jk}|w)p(w) + p(c_{jk}|\overline{w})p(\overline{w}) = p(c_{jk}|w) \\ &\Leftrightarrow \frac{p(w|c_{jk})}{p(w)} = \frac{p(c_{jk}|w)p(w)}{p(c_{jk})p(w)} = 1 \end{aligned}$$

Table 1. Contingency Table

	contain w	not contain w	total
contain m_j in the name	x_{11}	x_{12}	a_1
not contain m_j in the name	x_{21}	x_{22}	a_2
total	b_1	b_2	S

Furthermore, $p(c_{jk})$ is independent of entities, so this do not affect the order of the relevancy. So, Expression (7) can be transformed as

$$p(c_{jk}|e_i) \propto \prod_{w \in W_i \cap (RW_{jk} \cup CW_{jk})} \frac{p(w|c_{jk})}{p(w)} \prod_{w \notin W_i, w \in RW_{jk} \cup CW_{jk}} \frac{1 - p(w|c_{jk})}{1 - p(w)} \quad (9)$$

This expression means that we do not need to consider irrelevant words when we calculate the relevancy.

4.2 Approximation of Probability

As we mentioned in Section 3.3, we do not use training data, so we cannot get the probability of $p(w|c_{jk})$ because we cannot know whether each entity is relevant to the modifiers. In this section, we discuss about methods to approximate the probability. We can generalize Expression (9) as

$$p(c_{jk}|e_i) \propto \prod_{w \in W_i \cap (RW_{jk} \cup CW_{jk})} Score_{in}(w) \prod_{w \notin W_i, w \in RW_{jk} \cup CW_{jk}} Score_{not}(w) \quad (10)$$

The more w is relevant to the modifier, the bigger $Score_{in}(w)$ is.

Ratio of Frequency. In this method, we assume that "most of all the content that contain modifiers m_j are relevant to m_j. " We approximate

$$Score_{in}(w) \approx \frac{p(w|m_j \in M_i)}{p(w)} \quad (11)$$
$$Score_{not}(w) \approx \frac{1 - p(w|m_j \in M_i)}{1 - p(w)}$$

Chi-square Score. Chi-square score also represents the relevancy of word w to c_{jk} . So, this value can be useful.

$$Score_{in}(w) \approx \begin{cases} \chi^2(w) & (w \in RW_{jk}) \\ 1/\chi^2(w) & (w \in CW_{jk}) \end{cases} \quad (12)$$
$$Score_{not}(w) \approx 1$$

In this method, we do not consider about words that is not included in the entity.

4.3 Algorithm to Obtain Relevant Words and Conflicting Words

(1) Divide the entities in the category c_k into two sets — E_{jk} is the set of entities that contain m_j in their names and $\overline{E_{jk}}$ is the set of entities that not contain.

$$E_{jk} = \{e_i | m_j \in M_i, c_k \in C_i\}$$

$$\overline{E_{jk}} = \{e_i | m_j \notin M_i, c_k \in C_i\}$$

(2) Extract all words that appear in E_{jk} or $\overline{E_{jk}}$.

$$W_{jk} = \{w | \mathrm{DF}_{E_{jk}}(w) + \mathrm{DF}_{\overline{E_{jk}}}(w) > 0\}$$

$\mathrm{DF}_{E_{jk}}(w)$ represents the number of elements of $\{e_i | e_i \in E_{jk}, w \in W_i\}$.

(3) For each word w that satisfies $w \in W_{jk}$, we calculate Chi-square score by using following expression.

$$\chi^2_{E_{jk}}(w) = \begin{cases} \sum_{i=1}^{2} \sum_{j=1}^{2} \frac{(x_{ij} - a_i b_j / S)^2}{a_i b_j / S} & (\frac{x_{11}}{a_1} > \frac{x_{21}}{a_2}) \\ -\sum_{i=1}^{2} \sum_{j=1}^{2} \frac{(x_{ij} - a_i b_j / S)^2}{a_i b_j / S} & (\frac{x_{11}}{a_1} < \frac{x_{21}}{a_2}) \end{cases} \tag{13}$$

Table 1. shows the meaning of the symbols.

x_{11}= $\mathrm{DF}_{E_{jk}}(w)$, x_{12}= $|E_{jk}| - \mathrm{DF}_{E_{jk}}(w)$, x_{21}= $\mathrm{DF}_{\overline{E_{jk}}}(w)$, x_{22}= $|\overline{E_{jk}}|- \mathrm{DF}_{\overline{E_{jk}}}(w)$

$a_1 = |E_{jk}|, a_2 = |\overline{E_{jk}}|, b_1 = x_{11} + x_{21}, b_2 = x_{12} + x_{22}, S = b_1 + b_2$

(4) Extract words that satisfy $\chi^2_{E_{jk}}(w) > \chi^2_0(p)$ as the relevant words with m_j in c_k . $\chi^2_0(p)$ represents the Chi-square score at significance level p .

$$RW_{jk} = \{w | w \in W_{jk}, \chi^2_{E_{jk}}(w) > \chi^2_0(p)\}$$

(5) Extract words that satisfy $\chi^2_{E_{jk}}(w) < -\chi^2_0(p)$ as the conflicting words with m_j in c_k .

$$CW_{jk} = \{w | w \in W_{jk}, \chi^2_{E_{jk}}(w) < -\chi^2_0(p)\}$$

(6) Remember $Score_{in}(w)$ and $Score_{not}(w)$ for each word in RW_{jk} and CW_{jk}.

5 Unite the Relevancies in Categories

As we say in Section 3.2, in order to calculate the truthfulness, we unite the relevancy in all the categories that the entity belongs to. This is the Unite function that appears in Expression (1). In this section, we discuss the method used when all the entities belong to two categories and one category is the subcategory of the other. That is, $C_i = \{c_1, c_2\}$ and c_2 is the subcategory of c_1.

Multiply Relevancies. This method multiplies relevancies in two categories.

$$\begin{aligned} &Unite(Relevancy(m_j, c_1, e_i), Relevancy(m_j, c_2, e_i)) \\ &= Relevancy(m_j, c_1, e_i) \times Relevancy(m_j, c_2, e_i) \end{aligned} \tag{14}$$

Use Subcategory Score if Overlap. If $w \in RW_{j1}$ and $w \in RW_{j2}$, we calculate the relevancy of w twice in previous method. In this method and the next, even if $w \in RW_{j1}$ and $w \in RW_{j2}$, we calculate score of w only once. This method only uses the score of subcategory.

$$\begin{aligned} & Unite(Relevancy(m_j, c_1, e_i), Relevancy(m_j, c_2, e_i)) \\ & = Relevancy(m_j, c_2, e_i) \\ & \times \prod_{w \in W_i \cap (RW_{j1} \cup CW_{j1}), w \notin RW_{j2} \cup CW_{j2}} Score_{in}(w) \\ & \times \prod_{w \notin W_i, w \in RW_{j1} \cup CW_{j1}, w \notin RW_{j2} \cup CW_{j2}} Score_{not}(w) \end{aligned} \tag{15}$$

Use Supercategory Score if Overlap. This method only uses the score of supercategory if $w \in RW_{j1}$ and $w \in RW_{j2}$.

$$\begin{aligned} & Unite(Relevancy(m_j, c_1, e_i), Relevancy(m_j, c_2, e_i)) \\ & = Relevancy(m_j, c_1, e_i) \\ & \times \prod_{w \in W_i \cap RW_{j2} \cup CW_{j2}, w \notin RW_{j1} \cup CW_{j1}} Score_{in}(w) \\ & \times \prod_{w \notin W_i, w \in RW_{j2} \cup CW_{j2}, w \notin RW_{j1} \cup CW_{j1}} Score_{not}(w) \end{aligned} \tag{16}$$

6 Experiment

We did two experiments to evaluate the proposed method. The first experiment is about cooking recipes, and the second is about package tours. These two experiments were done in Japanese.

6.1 Cooking Recipe Experiment

We crawled about 16,000 recipes from the cooking site "cookpad"[1] . This is a Japanese site to which people can easily contribute recipes.

Each recipe is an entity e_i. We used the modifiers in the recipe names for M_i. We regarded each recipe as belonging to two categories — the "recipe" category and a category corresponding to the dish's name, such as "curry" or "hamburg steak." So, the number of elements of C_i is two, and the dish name categories are subcategories of the "recipe" category. We did morphological analysis using MeCab[2] and used nouns and verbs for W_i.

We prepared six dish names and four modifiers. We made 24 queries that were combinations of dish names and modifiers. We used 17 queries that the hit

[1] http://cookpad.com/

[2] http://mecab.sourceforge.net/

Table 2. Queries used in cooking recipe experiment

Food	Authentic	Healthy	Japanese style	Plain
Curry	√	√	√	
Hamburg steak		√	√	√
Pasta	√	√	√	√
Omelet containing fried rice			√	
Fried noodles		√	√	√
Fried rice		√	√	√

Table 3. Queries used in package tour experiment

Area	Enjoy fully	Convenient	Elegant	Healing	Impressive
China	√	√	√		√
Korea	√	√	√		
Bali		√	√	√	
Thailand	√	√	√		
Viet Nam	√	√	√	√	
Taiwan	√	√	√		

Table 4. Example of relevant and conflicting words in cooking recipe experiment

Japanese style Hamburg steak		Healthy curry	
RW	CW	RW	CW
grated radish	sauce	tofu	butter
sweetened sake	Worcestershire sauce	half	
soy sauce	tomato	bean-curd refuse	
broth	red wine	enoki mushrooms	
radish	cheese	miso	

counts of the searching results are more than 10. Table 2 shows the queries that used for evaluation. We used 10 recipes for each query.

Table 4 shows the example of relevant words and conflicting words obtained in this experiment.

6.2 Package Tour Experiment

We crawled pages about package tours for Asia from the package tour site "Yahoo! Travel"[3]. There are many overlapping tours, so we use only one package tour when there was overlap, and we used about 13,000 package tours.

Each package tour is an entity e_i. We used the modifiers in the package tour names for M_i. We regarded that each package tour belongs to two categories

[3] http://travel.yahoo.co.jp/

Table 5. Example of relevant and conflicting words in package tour experiment

Korea enjoy fully		China impressive	
RW	CW	RW	CW
the best place	*nothing*	heritage	*nothing*
Bulgogi		world	
food		Quanjude	
factory		The Great Wall	
restaurant		Temple of Heaven	

— the "Asia" category and a category corresponding to the area name, such as "China" or "Korea." We used only nouns for W_i.

We prepared six areas and five modifiers. We made 30 queries that were combinations of areas and modifiers. We used 20 queries that the hit counts of the searching results are more than four. Table 3 shows the queries used for evaluation. We evaluated five package tours for each query.

Table 5 shows the example of relevant words and conflicting words obtained in this experiment.

6.3 Evaluation

Human Ranking. To make the answer set, we had several people score the entities. The higher this score is, the higher the relevancy between the entity and modifier is. We made ranking of each query by using the average scores of each entity and treated this as a "human ranking."

Rank Correlation Coefficient. We evaluated each method by using the Spearman rank correlation coefficient between human ranking and ranking by each method. This is calculated by following expression.

$$\rho = 1 - \frac{6 \sum D^2}{N^3 - N} \tag{17}$$

D means the difference of the rank between two methods. For example, the rank of an entity is one in a method and five in human ranking, D is four. N is the number of entities in each query, so for recipes, $N = 10$, and for package tours, $N = 5$. ρ varies between -1 and 1, and if ρ is near 1, there is a strong correlation between two rankings.

6.4 Comparison of Methods

We compared 11 methods — the combination of { Ratio of Frequency (RF), Chi-square Score (CS) } and { use relevancy of subcategory (only sub), use relevancy of supercategory (only super), multiply the relevancy of two categories (multiply), unite and use subcategory score if overlap (unite sub), unite and use supercategory score if overlap (unite super)} , and classical Naive Bayes without Chi-square test (NB). Fig.1 and Fig.2 show the average of the Spearman rank correlation coefficient of each method and their standard deviation.

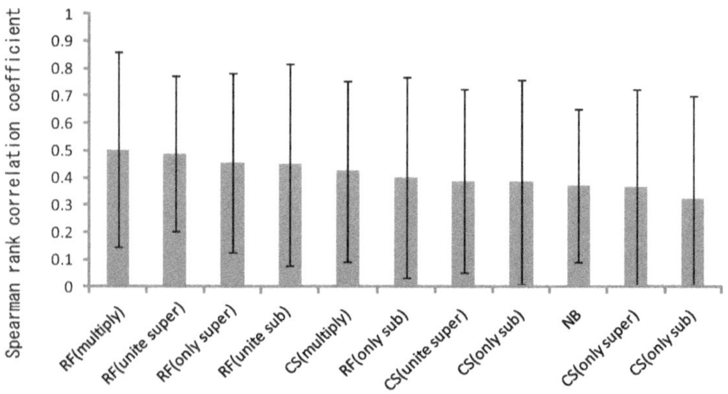

Fig. 1. Average of Spearman rank correlation coefficient in cooking recipe experiment

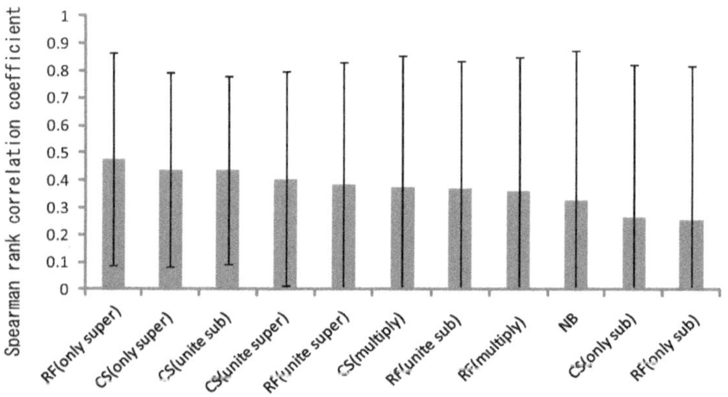

Fig. 2. Average of Spearman rank correlation coefficient in package tour experiment

6.5 Considerations

In cooking recipe experiment, the best and the second best are the methods that unite the relevancy of two categories. This means that relevant words and conflicting words can be extracted from both categories and both are valuable to evaluate truthfulness for modifiers.

On the other hand, in package tour experiment, the best and the second best are the methods that use only the relevancy of the supercategory. The worst and the second worst are the methods that use only the relevancy of the subcategory. This means the extracted words from subcategory are not so valuable for evaluation.

One reason for this is that we can get few entities with modifiers attached to their names in some queries. For example, in the case of query "China impressive," there are only 14 entities that contain "impressive" in their names in

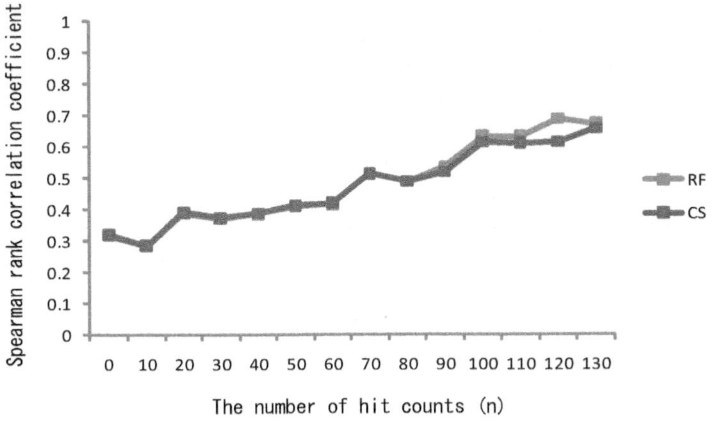

Fig. 3. The correlation between hit counts of modifiers + category name and the Spearman rank correlation coefficient

the "China" category. So, we could not extract valuable terms from the "China" category. Fig.3 shows the average of the Spearman rank correlation coefficient in queries that hit counts of modifiers + category names are more than n. This figure shows that the more the entities that contain modifiers are, the better the the Spearman rank correlation coefficient is.

In addition, in the case of "China impressive," in the human ranking, the package tours that go to Guilin or Jiuzhaigou are highly ranked. However, in the tours that contain "impressive" in their names, there is only one tour that goes to these areas. So, these terms could not reject the null hypothesis H_0, and we could not use these terms. In this way, this method cannot extract terms that are not so popular in the entities that contain modifiers in their names.

We can transform as Expression (7) if all the words independently appear. However, the relevant words and conflicting words that can be obtained include some dependent words. For example, we can get "radish" and "grated radish" as the relevant words in "Japanese-style Hamburg steak." These two words represent almost the same thing, so a recipe that includes these two words have unfairly high score. To improve this problem, it might be useful to regard the dependent words as the same meaning words and remove the word that have lower Chi-square score.

This method might not work well when the modifier is not characteristic, such as "delicious" or "special" because there might be few relevant and conflicting words.

7 Conclusion and Future Work

On the Internet, there are many entities that the modifiers in names are not appropriate for the content. In this paper, we proposed methods to evaluate the truthfulness of modifiers attached to web entity names by extracting relevant and conflicting words from the content texts.

We did cooking recipe experiment and package tour experiment, and compared the each method. There are positive correlation between ranking of each method and human ranking.

We assumed that the majority of the entities that contain the modifiers in their names are relevant to the modifiers. So, this methods might not work well when the majority of the names of entities are exaggerations. In the future, we will try to find a method that can be applied in such a challenging case.

Acknowledgment

This work was supported in part by the following projects and institutions: Grants-in-Aid for Scientific Research (Nos. 18049041, 21700105, 21700106) from MEXT of Japan, a Kyoto University GCOE Program entitled "Informatics Education and Research for Knowledge-Circulating Society," and the National Institute of Information and Communications Technology, Japan.

References

1. Agichtein, E., Castillo, C., Donato, D., Gionis, A., Mishne, G.: Finding high-quality content in social media. In: WSDM 2008, pp. 183–194 (2008)
2. Fiore, A.T., Taylor, L.S., Mendelsohn, G.A., Hearst, M.: Assessing attractiveness in online dating profiles. In: CHI 2008, pp. 797–806 (2008)
3. Lee, R., Kitayama, D., Sumiya, K.: Web-based evidence excavation to explore the authenticity of local events. In: WICOW 2008, pp. 63–66 (2008)
4. Murakami, K., Nichols, E., Matsuyoshi, S., Sumida, A., Masuda, S., Inui, K., Matsumoto, Y.: Statement Map: Assisting Information Credibility Analysis by Visualizing Arguments. In: WICOW 2009, pp. 43–50 (2009)
5. Kobayashi, T., Ohshima, H., Oyama, S., Tanaka, K.: Evaluating brand value on the Web. In: WICOW 2009, pp. 67–74 (2009)
6. Kato, M., Ohshima, H., Oyama, S., Tanaka, K.: Can Social Tagging Improve Web Image Search? In: Bailey, J., Maier, D., Schewe, K.-D., Thalheim, B., Wang, X.S. (eds.) WISE 2008. LNCS, vol. 5175, pp. 235–249. Springer, Heidelberg (2008)
7. Yusuf, M., Asaga, C., Watanabe, C.: Onomatopeta!: Developing a Japanese Onomatopoeia Learning-Support System Utilizing Native Speakers Cooperation. In: Web Intelligence/IAT Workshops 2008, pp. 173–177 (2008)
8. Hotho, A., Jäschke, R., Scgnutz, C., Stumme, G.: Information Retrieval in Folksonomies: Search and Ranking. In: ECWS 2006, pp. 411–426 (2006)
9. Bao, S., Xue, G., Wu, X., Yu, Y., Fei, B., Su, Z.: Optimizing web search using social annotations. In: WWW 2007, pp.501–510 (2007)

Searching the Web for Alternative Answers to Questions on WebQA Sites

Natsuki Takata[1], Hiroaki Ohshima[1], Satoshi Oyama[2], and Katsumi Tanaka[1]

[1] Graduate School of Informatics, Kyoto University, Japan
[2] Graduate School of Information Science and Technology, Hokkaido University, Japan
{takata,ohshima,tanaka}@dl.kuis.kyoto-u.ac.jp, oyama@ist.hokudai.ac.jp

Abstract. We propose a method of discovering alternative answers from the Web that are to a question posted on a Web question & answer (Q&A) site and differ from existing answers to the question on the Q&A site. Our method first automatically generates queries for conventional Web search engines to collect Web pages that can contain answers to the target question. Each collected Web page is evaluated by calculating two kinds of scores: one represents the probability that the page has information that answers a question in the Q&A content and the other represents the possibility that it has an alternative answer. The method is implemented and the system is evaluated using actual Q&A contents.

1 Introduction

In recent years, there has been an increase in the number of users on question & answer (Q&A) sites, such as Yahoo!Answers[1], where users can exchange questions and answers. Because the questions and answers that users have posted are stored on the site, people can use a Q&A site not only to post a question or to answer a question but also to read the pairs of questions and answers posted in the past. According to a survey by REALWORLD Corporation in Japan, many users use Q&A sites to get information from questions and answers that were posted in the past[2]. If you can find questions that are similar in content to things you want to know, you can get useful information by looking at the answers to those questions. However, the Q&A content on Q&A site (a set of a question and one or more answers) has several problems. First, there are relatively much fewer people who can answer questions on a Q&A site because only registered users of the Q&A site can post answers. There may be Q&A content that lacks adequate answers to the question. Second, even if there are users with useful information about a question, they cannot answer the question if they fail to notice that question. In the case of Yahoo!Answers, answers can be posted for only a limited period, so sometimes not enough answers to a question are posted. For Q&A content that does not have enough answers to a question, there may be alternative answers to the question in

[1] http://answers.yahoo.com/
[2] http://japan.internet.com/research/20090909/1.html

L. Chen et al. (Eds.): WAIM 2010, LNCS 6184, pp. 441–452, 2010.

addition to the ones that have already been posted. We think that it would help users who want to get information from Q&A contents if they were shown alternative answers because that would increase the amount of information available to them to resolve their questions. Therefore, we propose a method of finding alternative answers from the Web. Although there exist several researches[1,2] to find similar questions on the same Q&A site and they can be also used to find alternative answers, information on a Q&A site is much more limited than one in the whole Web as we mentioned. Because the Web contains knowledge that is unknown to Q&A sites users, we believe that we can get information that cannot be obtained from Q&A contents by gathering alternative-answer information on the Web from sources other than Q&A sites.

Getting alternative answers involves three steps: generating search queries, calculating a score that represents the probability that a Web page contains information about answers to the question, and calculating a score that represents the probability that the page has different answers from the Q&A content's answers. Finally, we rank pages and present them according to their scores.

In this paper, Section 2 describes related work. Section 3 explains our framework to find alternative answers from the Web. Section 4 presents our implementation. Section 5 describes experimental results using actual data. Section 6 concludes this paper.

2 Related Work

There has been some previous research on Q&A contents on the Web. Berger et al. proposed a method of finding answers from FAQ (frequently asked questions) archives[3]. They said that because there was a gap between the words used in the question and in the answer, answer retrieval had a different behavior from general document retrieval. They proposed a method of retrieving answers by using machine learning and applied it to Q&A pairs to learn which words appear frequently in a question when a word appears in an answer. Research on searching for questions retrieved from a Q&A archive has been described by Jeon et al.[1] and Xue et al.[4], who used a translation-based language model. They treated the problem that it is difficult to search for Q&A content because different words are used in similar questions. So they collected semantically similar questions by using the similarity among their answers and then used machine learning to learn the translation of the questions from the collection. They proposed retrieving many similar questions by using one query on the basis of machine learning results. Another approach to finding similar questions was proposed by Wang et al.[2]. They used a syntactic tree structure to retrieve similar questions. They used the similarity between syntactic parsing trees when calculating the similarity score of questions. These studies[3,1,4,2] retrieved from the target archive questions and answers that were similar to the user's query, so they are different from our study on searching for alternative answers from ordinary Web pages that are not composed of questions and answers. Many researchs about developing Question Answering systems have been described, for example by

Novischi et al.[5] and Harabagiu et al.[6]. Novischi et al. proposed the algorithm for propagating verb arguments in [5] and it could improve the performance of ranking candidate answers in Question Answering system. Harabagiu et al. demonstrated that it was increasing the accuracy of a Q&A system to use textual entailment information for either filtering or ranking answers returned by the system. Although it is the same purpose to look for answers to a question in Q&A systems and our research, our research is different from them because ours aim is to get different answers from existing answers to a question and their aim is to get right answers to factoid questions. There has been some research on evaluating question answering. For example, Fukumoto [7] proposed a system of extracting answers for non-factoid questions and he explained a Q&A evaluation method based on Hovy's BE (basic element) method [8]. He mentioned that an evaluation of non-factoid questions, like why questions, was not easy because the answer string tended to be longer and had many variations. So he proposed evaluating the system's answers automatically by comparing its BEs with the BEs of correct answers. Ko et al. proposed applying a probabilistic graphical model for ranking answers in question answering[9]. Their models could estimate the probability of the correctness of answer candidates. These two studies[7,9] treated the problem of whether the system could output the correct answer to a question rather than whether is could output complementary information.

3 Framework of Finding Alternative Answers

We formulate the problem of finding Web pages that contain alternative answers when a Q&A content is given by a user. First, we assume that each user on the Q&A site is viewing one Q&A content. Ideally, the system we design should output Web pages that include alternative answers even if only Q&A content is given as input. However, all the sentences in a question generally include extra information such as a self-introduction in addition to the question (main topic). It is difficult for the system to find the question part in the sentences automatically. Considering this background, we ask the user to specify the main topic of the question for which they wanted to get alternative answers. Through the following three steps, we can rank Web pages to show the users.

Step 1. On the basis of the entered information, our system collects Web pages by using a conventional Web search engine.

Step 2. The system calculates a score to each Web page; the score indicates the probability of the page having information that answers the question the user has pointed.

Step 3. The system next computes another score, which indicates the probability of the page having alternative answers. Finally, the system ranks the collected Web pages on the basis of these scores.

The input that a user gives at first is the Q&A content and user-selected extracts from the question. We denote the question by q and the set of answers to it by A. In this paper, we denote the individual answers by $a_1, a_2, ...$, so $A = \{a_1, a_2, ...\}$.

The statement that the user selected from part of q is denoted by u. The tuple (u, q, A) is the input.

Step 1. From the input (u, q, A), the system generates queries for Web search engines and gathers Web pages. We denote the collection of the collected Web pages by $P = \{p_1, p_2, ...\}$. This step is expressed as follows.

$$P = CollectPages(u, q, A) \tag{1}$$

Step 2. The system judges whether each Web page collected in Step 1 has information about answers to the question q. In this step, we do not yet consider whether an answer in a page is same as an existing answer in A or not. The scoring function is expressed as follows.

$$IncAns(u, q, A, p_i) \tag{2}$$

The value of the function is calculated for each Web page p_i of P in Step 1. It characterizes p_i as the value representing the probability of a Web page containing answer information.

Step 3. The system should next judge whether or not the page includes alternative answers that do not exist in A. The function that compute the probability of p_i containing an alternative answer if p_i contains an answer to q is expressed as follows.

$$JudgeAlt(u, q, A, p_i) \tag{3}$$

As output to the users, the system ranks the collection of Web pages P and shows these ranked Web pages to the user. In ranking P, it can use both the value of $IncAns(u, Q\&A, p_i)$ and the value of $JudgeAlt(u, Q\&A, p_i)$. The generalized ranking function can represented as follows.

$$Rank(u, q, A, p_i) = \Phi(IncAns(u, q, A, p_i), JudgeAlt(u, q, A, p_i)) \tag{4}$$

Various implementations are possible in each of the above steps. Next section describes our implementations for the steps.

4 An Implementation on Yahoo!Chiebukuro

4.1 Collecting Web Pages That Contain Answers

We targeted Yahoo!Chiebukuro[3], a Japanese Q&A site like Yahoo!Answers, as a Q&A site. The system first makes a query for a Web search engine to gather Web pages that contains alternative answers to q. The query is an AND query consisting of a set of words that express the question q. Therefore, all the words are extracted from either q or u. Here, we need a function to extract a set of words from statements. In our implementation, we perform a morphological analysis of statements by using a Japanese morphological analyzer MeCab[4] and

[3] http://chiebukuro.yahoo.co.jp/

[4] http://mecab.sourceforge.net/

acquire nouns, verbs, and adjectives. A set of words extracted from either q or u is denoted by $ExtractWords(q)$ or $ExtractWords(u)$, respectively. Among the words that appear in q and u, ones that appear frequently in the set of answers A may be more suitable ones that characterize the question q. At the same time, however, q (and even u) contains words that are general words (e.g., "do", "have", etc.) and frequently used especially in question statements (e.g., "question", "tell", etc.). Some of the words can be removed by using a stop-word list. We also try to get words that express the question more accurately by weighting the words in q or u by using the weight TF-IDF. To calculate the TF value, we consider q and A. Here, tf_k (TF value of k), $k \in ExtractWords(q)$ or $k \in ExtractWords(u)$, is calculated by $tf_k = count(k, q) + \sum_{a \in A} count(k, a)$, where $count(k, s)$ indicates the number of times that word k appears in statements s. To get the IDF value, we need to get df_k, the number of documents that contain the target word k, and the total number of documents N. A collection of whole documents must be defined to obtain df_k. We treat all the Q&A contents on Yahoo!Chiebukuro as the collection. Yahoo! offers an API to get search result from Yahoo!Chiebukuro, so we can obtain df_k as the hit count when the word k is issued as a query to the API. $N = 35,108,527$ is the total number of documents on the Yahoo!Chiebukuro on January 9th 2010. Now we have obtained tf_k and df_k, so k's TF-IDF value $v(k)$ is computed using them as follows.

$$v(k) = tf_k \cdot \log\left(\frac{N}{df_k}\right) \tag{5}$$

Words that have high values calculated by (5) are regarded as ones that characterize the question q. The three words k_1, k_2, k_3 that have the highest TF-IDF values are chosen, an AND query for a Web search engine is expressed as $WebQuery = k_1 \wedge k_2 \wedge k_3$.

We can get two queries for a Web search engine according to which set of extracted words is used $ExtractWords(q)$ or $ExtractWords(u)$. We call these two ways **method (Q)** and **method (U)** in this paper. A set of Web pages P is gathered by issuing $WebQuery$ to a Web search engine. We use Yahoo!Japan as a Web search engine through its API.

4.2 Judgment of Pages Containing Answer Information

The system judges whether each page p_n in P includes answer information to q. In case of that the question is "How can I cure a hangover?", the word "alcohol" would be often used in many different answers. Moreover, answers to the question might be to "drink an energy drink with turmeric" and to "drink lots of water", so "drink" can be also used in many different answers. We assumed that answers to a question contain words in common. Such a set of words that appear in common denote is denoted by $C = c_1, c_2, ...$ Ideally, words in C appears often in A, but actually it is often difficult to find common words because answers in A consist of relatively short sentences. We consequently expand an answer in A by gathering similar documents. The way of expansion consists of the following steps.

1. Get a set of words $W_{a_m} = \{w_1^{a_m}, w_2^{a_m}, ...\}$ that characterize a_m, an answer in A.
2. Search for top n search results by issuing query based on W_{a_m}. Statements in the search results (namely snippets) are gathered and a set of them is denoted by S.
3. Extract words that often appear in S as elements of C.

Step 1. To get C, we need to collect the words that characterize each answer in A. To obtain the words that represent an answer, we use an existing method of extracting topic structure proposed by Ma et al.[10]. The method is based on co-occurrence of words. It is possible to extract subject- and content-terms of a text by using the degrees of subject and content. The subject of a Q&A content can be regarded as the content of the question, so Q&A content subject-terms are considered to be the set of words K obtained in 4.1 that characterize the question. A content-term means the words that represent what a text says about its subject. In the case of Q&A content, each answer can be considered to describe the question as the subject of Q&A content. Therefore, the set of content-terms in their study can replace the set of words that characterize the answers W_{a_m}. The degree of content for getting content-terms is computed from the degree of undirected co-occurrence between subject- and content-terms. The degree of undirected co-occurrence $cooc(w_x, w_y)$ between words w_x and w_y is defined as follows.

$$cooc(w_x, w_y) = \frac{df(w_x AND w_y)}{df(w_x) + df(w_y) - df(w_x AND w_y)}. \quad (6)$$

The value expresses the frequency with which words w_x and w_y are used in a document together, and $df(w)$ denotes the number of documents that contain word w. We replace the number of documents by the number of Q&A contents in Yahoo!Chiebukuro and get $df(w)$ by using its API. The degree of content $con(w)$, which means the probability that word w in answer a_m is a content-term of a_m, is calculated by

$$con(w) = \sum_{k_i \in K} cooc(w, k_i), \quad (7)$$

where $w \in ExtractWords(a_m)$. The words that have high evaluation values in (7) are regarded as the elements of the collection of words characterized by a_m (content-terms). We define the two words with the highest values of $con(w)$ ($w \in CollectWords(a_m)$) as elements of W_{a_m}. ($W_{a_m} = \{w_1^{a_m}, w_2^{a_m}\}$).

Step 2. Words appearing in common in the answers are included in the set of documents that have a set of words characterizing the question q together with the set of words characterizing each answer in A. Two kinds of documents sets are available: all the pages on the Web and all the Q&A contents. For each case, we explain how to obtain the collection of words that appear in common in answers $C = \{c_1, c_2, ...\}$.

Case: All pages. We get snippets of Web pages that include K described in 4.1 together with elements of W_{a_m} by step 1. We define a formula for gathering a set of snippets of search results as $CollectSnippets(W)$. Its argument are a set of words, and all the elements are used for AND queries for search engines. We gather snippets for every element in A. The gathered snippets are defined as follows.

$$S = \bigcup_{a_m \in A} \bigcup_{i=1}^{2} CollectSnippets(K \cup w_i^{a_m}) \tag{8}$$

Case: Only Q&A contents. In this case, we collect only answers in Q&A contents that include K and the elements of W_{a_m}. This is because only answers that have common words in the answer expressions for q will appear in the Q&A content answers. We define a formula for gathering answers as $CollectAnswers(W)$, as before, where W denotes the set of words and $CollectAnswers(W)$ returns the collection of answers. W is contained in the Q&A contents that include them. So A'_{a_m}, which is the set of answers in Q&A contents that have K and W_{a_m} together, is represented as follows. We gather answers for every element in A. The gathered ones are defined as follows.

$$A' = \bigcup_{a_m \in A} \bigcup_{i=1}^{2} CollectAnswers(K \cup w_i^{a_m}) \tag{9}$$

Step 3. We define word c, which has a high value of $\sum_{s \in S} count(c, s)$ or $\sum_{a' \in A'} count(c, a')$, as an element of C. We express c's value by v_c and define C as follows.

$$C = \{c | \texttt{c has a high value of } v_c.\} \tag{10}$$

In this study, we collected ten words with high values according to this formula. For each page p_n of page collection P in 4.1, we count the number of elements in C that are contained in p_n. We think that p_n that has answer information will include more elements of C than p'_n that does not. But if p_n has many texts in itself, it contains many elements of C, regardless of whether it has answer information. So we should consider the total number of words in p_n. Therefore, we redefine (2) as follows.

$$IncAns(u, q, A, p_i) = \frac{\sum_{c_i \in C} count(c_i, Nolink(p_n))}{N} \tag{11}$$

$$IncAns(u, q, A, p_i) = \frac{v_{c_i} * \sum_{c_i \in C} count(c_i, Nolink(p_n))}{N}, \tag{12}$$

where N denotes the total number of words in p_n and we express the body text of a page p without links by $Nolink(p)$. Formula(12) means that v_c is regarded as c's weight. Now, the target of the text in p_n is the strings without links. We exclude strings with links in order to judge whether the page itself has the answer. For example, when there is a link string "a good drink for hangovers is here", even though the link contains the word "drink", the advice on what to drink for a hangover is not given on this page itself but on the linked page.

4.3 Judgment and Ranking of Pages Having Alternative Answers

In this section, we explain how to keep the score that represents whether each page has alternative answers, i.e., information that is different from the answer information in Q&A content. So we compute the degree of dissimilarity between each page and A. We use the idea described in [11], which aimed to find pages that have similar themes and dissimilar content to given sample pages. Ohshima et al.[11] proposed computing the dissimilarity between a document and given sample pages by using the unique part of the document and the given pages. We should check how dissimilar each page is to each element of A. Now, we explain how to compute the dissimilarity between a page and A. We treat each page and each element of A as feature vectors represented by a TF. First, we perform morphological analysis of a page's text without its link strings and get the TF vector of page p_i as

$$\mathbf{t_{p_i}}(k) = count(k, Nolink(p_i)). \tag{13}$$

Next, we make a TF vector of each of A's elements. But A's elements are a set of short sentences, as mentioned in 4.2. So we reuse the expansion of A in 4.2. We can regard (10) or (11) as the expansion of the whole A. We represent the expansion of X by $Expand(X)$ and represent the TF vector of a_m as

$$\mathbf{t_{a_m}}(k) = max(count(k, Expand(a_m)) - count(k, Expand(A)), 0). \tag{14}$$

After getting each TF vector, we calculate the cosine similarity between $\mathbf{t_{p_i}}$ and $\mathbf{t_{a_m}}$ as $(cos(\mathbf{t_{p_i}}, \mathbf{t_{a_m}}))$. We repeat this calculation for all elements of A and get the maximum value of their cosine similarities $(Sim(p_i, A))$.

$$Sim(p_i, A) = max(cos(\mathbf{t_{p_i}}, \mathbf{t_{a_1}}), ..., cos(\mathbf{t_{p_i}}, \mathbf{t_{a_m}})) \tag{15}$$

This formula represents the similarity between page p_i and existing answers A. The maximum value of (15) is 1, so we express the dissimilarity between them by

$$Dissim(p_i, A) = 1 - Sim(p_i, A).(= JudgeAlt(u, q, A, p_i)) \tag{16}$$

This formula represents the probability of each page containing alternative answers.

Now, we show the flow of above-mentioned steps at Fig.1. A question q in Q&A site is converted into Web search query K. Each page p_i is connected by the query K in Web like that answer a_i is connected by the question q in Q&A site. The elements of A are expanded to a'_i in Q&A site by the function $Expand(a_i)$. This expansion is possible in the Web, as we explained before. It is used to collect common words C in the expression of answers to q and to calculate (16). Finally, we define the ranking score (4) as

$$Rank(u, q, A, p_i) = IncAns(u, q, A, p_i)^{\alpha} * JudgeAlt(u, q, A, p_i)^{(1-\alpha)}. \tag{17}$$

In the next section, we describe some experiments using our methods.

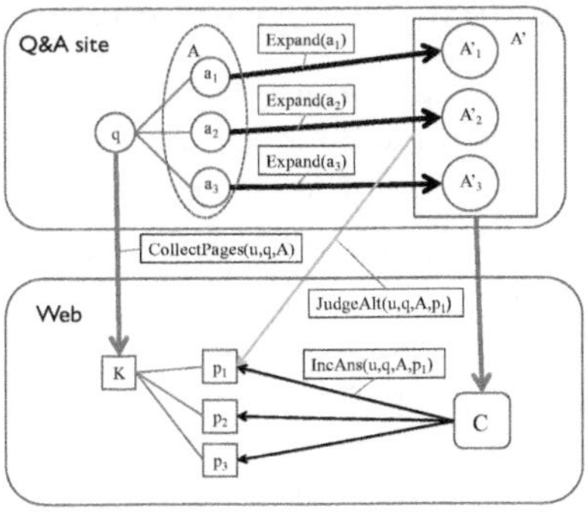

Fig. 1. Abstract of framework

5 Experiments

We evaluated our methods in each step. We prepared 10 Q&A contents for each experiment. The conditions were as follows: first, to make up the number of answers, we chose the number of elements in A to be 3; second, only one thing was asked in q because if it had contained multiple questions, A would have contained a mixture of different answers.

5.1 Making a Web Search Query to Gather Web Pages

We compared methods (Q) and (U) in section 4.1. Our approach needs the user to select parts of question sentences. So in this experiment, we selected one or two sentences that expressed the substance of the question from q. Now, for each of the 10 Q&A contents, we made queries by methods (Q) and (U) and searched the Web with each query. For the top 20 Web pages in the Web search results, we checked whether each page had answer information to q and alternative answer information. We counted how many Web pages out of the 20 had answers and how many had alternative answers. We counted them for each of the 10 Q&A content's results and calculated the average number of Web pages that had answers and alternative answers. The results are given in Table 1. In this table, queries made by method (U) got more answer and alternative-answer pages than method (Q) queries. This means that the user-selected question parts of q were useful for making Web search queries. In subsequent experiments, we used the top 20 pages collected by Web search queries K by method (U).

Table 1. Number of Web pages that had answers or alternative answers

	Average of ans. pages	Average of alt. pages
Method(U)	7.8	6.2
Method(Q)	5.7	4.4

5.2 Checking the Validity of IncAns-Computed Score

We evaluated the validity of score computed by (11) and (12). This score indicates the probability of a Web page having answer information. In section 4.1, we proposed two ways of collecting the elements of C:

(WA) the elements of C are collected in snippets from Web search results by using K and W_{a_m} as queries.
(YA) they are collected in a set of answers from Yahoo!Chiebukuro's search results by using K and W_{a_m} as queries.

In this experiment, we checked two more ways of collecting them as baselines.
(WN) the elements of C are collected in snippets from Web search results by using only K as queries.
(YN) they are collected in a set of answers from Yahoo!Chiebukuro's search results by using only K as queries.

We computed (11) and (12) for the last 20 pages by using C, which was collected in the abovementioned four ways. We represent the ways applied to (11) as (WAN), (WNN), (YAN), and (YNN) and those applied to (12) as (WAW), (WNW), (YAW), and (YNW), where N means normal and W means weighted. After the computations, we arranged the pages in descending order of scores. If there were pages with the same scores, we sorted them in output order of the Web search engine. We ran this operation for the prepared 10 Q&A contents and calculated the recall and precision. Here, we regarded a Web page that had answer information to q as a correct page. We computed the interpolated precision when the recall levels increased from 0 at intervals of 0.1 and computed the 11-point interpolated average precision[12]. In addition the eight methods, we prepare the two data: one is the raw output of the Yahoo! search engine with the query K (we represent this data as Y!-Query), the other is the raw output of it that obtained when we give all nouns and verbs and adjectives (except stopwords we prepared) appearing in u (we represent this as Y!-Base). The results are shown in Figs. 2. From Fig. 2, we can see that method (YAW) was the best of all, and the all methods we proposed exceeded (Y!-Base). Comparing the methods, we found that (WAN, WAW) were better than (WNN, WNW), and that (YAN, YAW) was better than (YNN, YNW). That is to say, we can gather common words C better by using A and q than by using only q. Furthermore, we can gather them better from the answers in Yahoo!Chiebukuro than from Web. However there is a problem: we cannot get the elements of C when the query we use is too complex. Although the problem occurs, we can use (WAW) instead of (YAW). We can almost exceed (Y!-Query) with all of the methods if we take into consideration the weights of C (Fig. 2).

5.3 Checking the Validity of the JudgeAlt-Computed Score

The results in 5.2 show that answers in Yahoo!Chiebukuro are better as the expansion of A than snippets from the Web. So we used (9) to expand A. We computed (17) for method (YAW), which was the best method of the results in 5.2, and re-ranked P on the basis of (17). We tried changing the value of α in

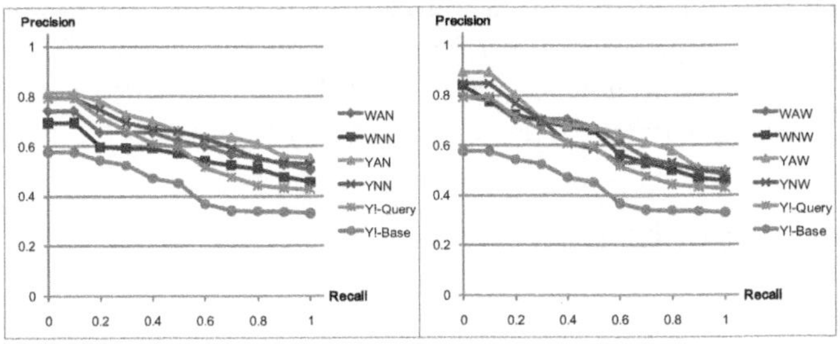

Fig. 2. 11-point interpolated average precision ((11)(12))

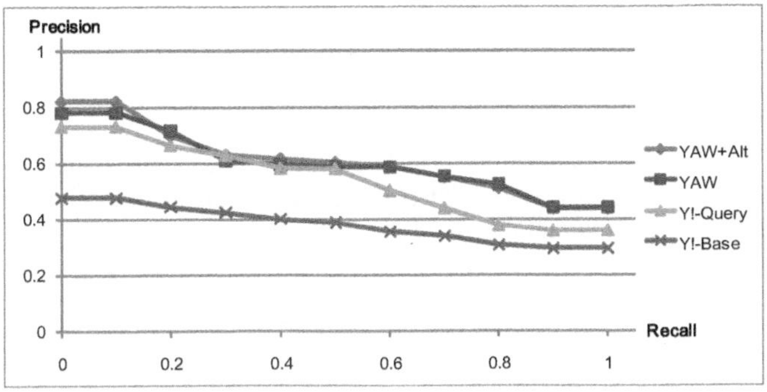

Fig. 3. 11-point interpolated average precision ((17))

(17) and use 0.8 as the value of α empirically. In fact, method (YAW) represents that A is expanded with Yahoo!Chiebukuro's answers and $IncAns(u, q, A, p_i)$ is calculated with (12) considering the weights of C.

We calculated the 11-point interpolated average precision when we reranked the pages on the basis of (17) with (YAW) (we represent this method as YAW+Alt). In this case, pages that have alternative answers are the adapted pages. For comparison, we calculated it when we use the methods (Y!-Base), (Y!-Query), and (YAW). The results are shown in Fig. 3. From Fig. 3, (YAW+alt) almost exceeded all other methods, so the validity of the JudgeAlt-computing score is demonstrated.

6 Conclusion

We proposed methods of collecting Web pages that include alternative answers to a question in Q&A content and of ranking them. Our methods are divided into three main steps. First, we make Web search queries to collect candidate Web pages that contain alternative answers. Then, we judge whether they contain answer information to the question in the Q&A content. Finally, we score them, and the score indicates the probability of each page containing alternative answers. From our experiments, we found that methods exceeded the baseline. In future work, we should get our system to take into consideration the diversity and quality of alternative answers when it ranks Web pages.

Acknowledgements

This work was supported in part by the following projects and institutions: Grants-in-Aid for Scientific Research (Nos. 18049041, 21700105) from MEXT of Japan, a Kyoto University GCOE Program entitled "Informatics Education and Research for Knowledge-Circulating Society," and the National Institute of Information and Communications Technology, Japan.

References

1. Jeon, J., Croft, W.B., Lee, J.H.: Finding similar questions in large question and answer archives. In: Proceedings of the ACM Fourteenth Conference on Information and Knowledge Management, pp. 76–83 (2005)
2. Wang, K., Ming, Z., Chua, T.S.: A syntactic tree matching approach to finding similar questions in community-based qa services. In: SIGIR, pp. 187–194 (2009)
3. Berger, A., Caruana, R., Cohn, D., Freitag, D., Mittal, V.: Bridging the lexical chasm: Statistical approaches to answer-finding. In: Proceedings of the 23rd Annual International ACM SIGIR Conference on Research and Development in Information Retrieval, pp. 192–199 (2000)
4. Xue, X., Jeon, J., Croft, W.B.: Retrieval models for question and answer archives. In: Proceedings of the 31st Annual International ACM SIGIR Conference on Research and Development in Information Retrieval, pp. 475–482 (2008)
5. Novischi, A., Moldovan, D.: Question answering with lexical chains propagating verb arguments. In: ACL (2006)
6. Harabagiu, S., Hickl, A.: Methods for using textual entailment in open-domain question answering. In: ACL, pp. 905–912 (2006)
7. Fukumoto, J.: Question answering system for non-factoid type questions and automatic evaluation based on be method. In: Proceedings of the Sixth NTCIR Workshop, pp. 441–447 (2007)
8. Hovy, E., Lin, C.Y., Zhou, L.: Evaluating duc 2005 using basic elements. In: DUC (2005)
9. Ko, J., Nyberg, E., Si, L.: A probabilistic graphical model for joint answer ranking in question answering. In: SIGIR, pp. 343–350 (2007)
10. Ma, Q., Tanaka, K.: Topic-structure based complementary information retrieval for information augmentation. In: Yu, J.X., Lin, X., Lu, H., Zhang, Y. (eds.) APWeb 2004. LNCS, vol. 3007, pp. 608–619. Springer, Heidelberg (2004)
11. Ohshima, H., Oyama, S., Tanaka, K.: Sibling page search by page examples. In: Sugimoto, S., Hunter, J., Rauber, A., Morishima, A. (eds.) ICADL 2006. LNCS, vol. 4312, pp. 91–100. Springer, Heidelberg (2006)
12. Mannin, C.D., Raghavan, P., Schütze, H.: Introduction to Information Retrieval, Cambridge, pp. 146–147 (2008)

Domain-Independent Classification for Deep Web Interfaces

Yingjun Li[1], Siwei Wang[1], Derong Shen[1], Tiezheng Nie[1], and Ge Yu[1]

[1] College of Information Science and Engineering, Northeastern University, 110004 Shenyang, China
{liyingjun_neu_ise,erhuwang}@163.com,
{shenderong,nietiezheng,yuge}@ise.neu.edu.cn

Abstract. The data sources of Deep Web provide tremendous structured data with high quality. However, classifying these interfaces with domain independent is required since the domains of the huge scale of deep web are hard to predefine. In this paper, we propose a novel approach with three-stage to solve this problem. First, we extract both texts and structure of a query interface by applying FIE algorithm we proposed. Then we construct frequent itemsets by using frequent pattern mining algorithm. Finally, we apply AP clustering algorithm to cluster the frequent itemsets according to similarity measure FGSTD presented in this paper. The experiment demonstrates our approach clusters interfaces well with domain independent.

Keywords: frequent itemset, clustering, domain classification, Deep Web.

1 Introduction

Due to the explosion in the number of Deep Web, how to classify their query interfaces with domain independent for integrating the structured data is still a challenge. In this paper we propose a novel three-stage method to cluster data sources into different domains. We firstly extract the form texts and structure by using FIE algorithm. Secondly, we construct frequent itemsets based on FP growth algorithm. Finally, we apply AP clustering algorithm to cluster these forms according to the similarity measure (FGSTD) we proposed.

Our contributions include: the approach to extract the co-occurrence relation between texts and form structure; the approach to calculate the similarity of forms based on frequent-itemset group of a form; the approach to cluster forms by adopting AP clustering algorithm. Experiments show that the proposed method outperforms existing ones.

2 Related Work

P. Senellart [1] proposed to classify data sources by probing HTML forms guided by domain knowledge and heuristic rules. B.He [2] exploited anchor attributes of query schemas without considering the relation between texts in an interface. What's more,

L. Chen et al. (Eds.): WAIM 2010, LNCS 6184, pp. 453–458, 2010.

we adopt an unsupervised AP clustering algorithm. Luciano Barbosa [3] proposed to classify forms according to texts in forms in a supervised way. Anne H. Ngu [4] proposed a meta-data approach for classifying Web data sources but it was oriented to genomics research. Yiyao Lu [5] utilized the available features on the interface page to clustering e-commerce search engines, however, it applied supervised K-means clustering algorithm which assumed that K is known beforehand.

We focused on the classification of query interfaces of Deep Web data sources with domain independent and propose a classification approach, in which, a new similarity measure evaluating the frequent-itemset group of a form is proposed and an unsupervised AP clustering algorithm is adopted to cluster query interfaces.

3 Motivation

According to B.He's[2] we can obtain two conclusions: First, query schemas are discriminative representatives of structured sources and domain anchor attributes make their domains more distinguishable. Second, the aggregate schema vocabulary of sources of the same domain tends to converge. Here we report another two observations which motivated our approach.

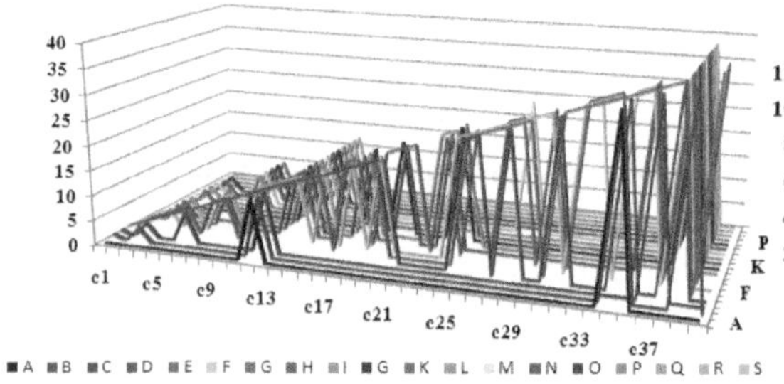

Fig. 1. Texts co-occurrence

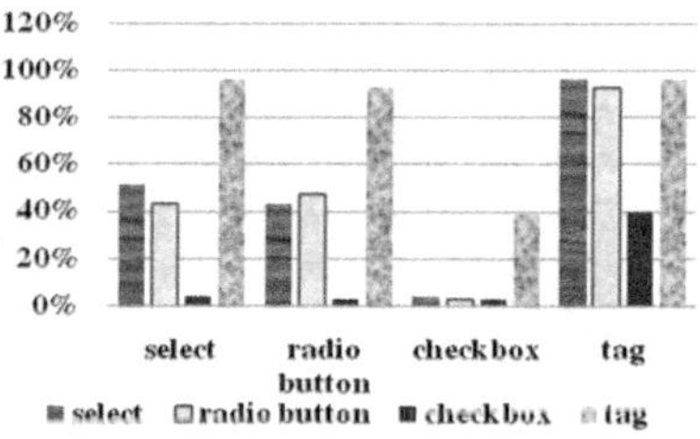

Fig. 2. Text attribute determination

First, we manually collected a dataset. Fig. 1 lists different attributes (z-axis) denoted in letters (A, B…) occurring in 40 data sources (x-axis, y-axis) sampled randomly in one domain while other domains have the similar trend. The testing results manifest that some texts in the same domain tend to co-occur. Second, we can determine it is either an attribute name or an attribute value according to locations of the same text appearing in different interfaces. The statistic is shown in Fig. 2.

4 Query Interfaces Classification

In this section, we elaborate query interface classification method and main components of it: form information extraction, frequent- itemset group generation and similarity computation and forms clustering.

(1) Form information extraction
We call the names of control tags and all texts in forms texts. After extracting all form texts including tags and form structure we do different marks to texts from different

locations. We mark the word from tag as T, one from select control as S, one from checkbox B and one from radio button R. F denotes a query interface form and W represents each word in texts, then we present the definition of query interface item and propose FIE algorithm based on the definition.

Definition 1. A query interface item W_i^C in which $C = T, S, B, R$, i represents the i-th word in texts extracted from the form F. If a form F has n words in texts, F can be denoted as a set of items $IS = < W_1^C, W_2^C ......W_n^C >$.

Algorithm 1. Form Information Extraction algorithm (FIE)

Input: a form F, threshold $\tau 1$, $\tau 2$, $\tau 3$ Output: a set of items IS

For each tag **do**{extract all texts}
For each select **do** {**if** (|<option>| $> \tau 1$) extract the default texts **else** extract all texts }
For each radio or checkbox **do** {
  if (values of <name> are the same and |<name>| $< \tau 2$) extract texts
  else if(values of <name> are different and <name>| $< \tau 3$) extract texts **else** discard}
For each word W in texts of F **do**{
  if (W is composed of {0,1,2,...9} or a stopword) discard it; lowercase(W); Stem(W);
  if (W_i from T) then $W_i \leftarrow W_i^T$; **if**(W_i from S) then $W_i \leftarrow W_i^S$;
  if(W_i from B) then $W_i \leftarrow W_i^B$; **if**(W_i from R) then $W_i \leftarrow W_i^R$; **else** discard it; }
  $IS \leftarrow < W_1^C, W_2^C ......W_k^C >$ // k is the number of words after being disposed($k \geq 1$)

(2) Frequent- itemset group generation and similarity computation
For a form F whose IS is $< W_1^C, W_2^C ......W_k^C >$ its frequent-itemset group (FIG) can be formed as: $FIG = \{< W_i^C >, < W_i^C, W_j^C > ... < W_1^C, W_2^C ... W_m^C >\}$ ($i, j, m \leq k$, $k \geq 1$). We adopt FP-growth to generate frequent itemsets represented as FIS while one of them is represented as FI. If each item in FI_k is in IS_m of F_m, add it to FIG_m. Based on frequent itemsets we use Itemsets Dimensionality (ID) and Group Dimensionality (GD) to represent the number of items in a frequent itemset and maximum ID in a frequent-itemset group respectively.

Due to inconstancy of ID, traditional similarity measure can't work well. Our first method is described as follows:

$$sim(S_1, S_2) = \frac{match(FIG_1, FIG_2)}{\min(|FIG_1|, |FIG_2|)} . \quad (1)$$

Where $match(FIG_1, FIG_2)$ is the number of frequent itemsets appearing in both FIG_1 and FIG_2. $\min(|FIG_1|, |FIG_2|)$ is the minimum number of frequent itemsets in FIG_1 and FIG_2. However, this method doesn't consider complexity of frequent-itemset group.

Data field in physics enlightened us to introduce the interaction of material particles into data space and motivated our FGSTD (Freqent-itemset Group Similarity through Tanimoto Distance). We define space $\Omega \subseteq R^p$ including n datasets (forms) of data object (frequent itemsets). We regard data object as a particle in p dimensionality and the gravitation between particles as similarity between two frequent itemsets.

Given two datasets S_1, S_2, the similarity $\phi(S_1,S_2)$ should satisfy: (1) $\phi(S_1,S_2)$ is a finite function defined in space Ω; (2) $\phi(S_1,S_2)$ is symmetric; (3) $\phi(S_1,S_2)$ is monotonic decreasing function to the distance between their data objects.

In order to give prominence to data clustering we adopt Gaussian function to define $\phi(S_1,S_2)$.

$$\phi(S_1,S_2)=\sum_{i=1}^{k}\left[m_i \times e^{-(d(FI_1,FI_2)/\sigma)^2}\right] \quad (k=\min(GD_1,GD_2))\,. \tag{2}$$

Where $\sigma \in (0,+\infty)$ is a factor to control the interaction force between objects. m_i is the weight of the ith dimensionality frequent itemsets and $\sum_{i=1}^{k} m_i=1$. The similarity $\phi(S_1,S_2)$ is the sum of different dimensionality similarities. For $FI=<W_1^C,W_2^C\ldots>$, we represent each frequent itemset as a vector, and the distance of frequent itemsets in ith dimensionality is defined as:

$$d(FI_1,FI_2)=\max(s(\mathbf{x},\mathbf{y}) \mid j=i, \mathbf{x}\in S_1, \mathbf{y}\in S_2, ID_{\mathbf{x}}=j, ID_{\mathbf{y}}=j)\ . \tag{3}$$

We calculate the similarity of vector $\mathbf{x}$ and $\mathbf{y}$ and develop it in formula (4). We consider not only whether the string is matched ($match(W_{i\mathbf{x}},W_{i\mathbf{y}})$) or not but also where it from ($F(W^{C_\mathbf{x}}{}_{i\mathbf{x}},W^{C_\mathbf{y}}{}_{i\mathbf{y}})$). $p(C_\mathbf{x},C_\mathbf{y})$ denotes the possibility the word is an attribute name according to a text locations appearing in two forms (5).

$$s(\mathbf{x},\mathbf{y})=\frac{\mathbf{x}^t\cdot\mathbf{y}}{\mathbf{x}^t\cdot\mathbf{x}+\mathbf{y}^t\cdot\mathbf{y}-\mathbf{x}^t\cdot\mathbf{y}},\ \mathbf{x}^t\cdot\mathbf{y}=match(W_{i\mathbf{x}},W_{i\mathbf{y}})\times F(W^{C}{}_{i\mathbf{x}},W^{C}{}_{i\mathbf{y}})\,. \tag{4}$$

$$match(W_{i\mathbf{x}},W_{i\mathbf{y}})=\begin{cases}1 & W_{i\mathbf{x}}=W_{i\mathbf{y}}\\ 0 & W_{i\mathbf{x}}\neq W_{i\mathbf{y}}\end{cases} \quad F(W^{C_\mathbf{x}}{}_{i\mathbf{x}},W^{C_\mathbf{y}}{}_{i\mathbf{y}})=p(C_\mathbf{x},C_\mathbf{y})\,. \tag{5}$$

(3) Forms clustering
After obtaining all similarities between each frequent-itemset group, we can generate a *FIG* matrix. Then *FIG* s are clustered by AP cluster method algorithm.

5 Experiments

We adopt the dataset composed of forms in the TEL-8 dataset [6]. As with B.He's, we collected 443 sources over 8 domains (Airfares, Hotels, Car Rentals, Books, Movies, Music Records, Jobs and Automobiles) and totally 1263 frequent itemsets at support threshold s=9. We adopt σ=0.078 according to optimization method based on entropy in physics. We also adopt the conditional entropy ce. Given the number of clusters G $0 \le ce \le \log G$, $\log G$ denotes random clustering result. The closer ce is to 0, the better the result is.

5.1 Experimental Results

We design four group of experiments abbreviated as Af, Ht, Jb, Am, Bk, Cr, Mv and Mr to denote the 8 domains respectively.

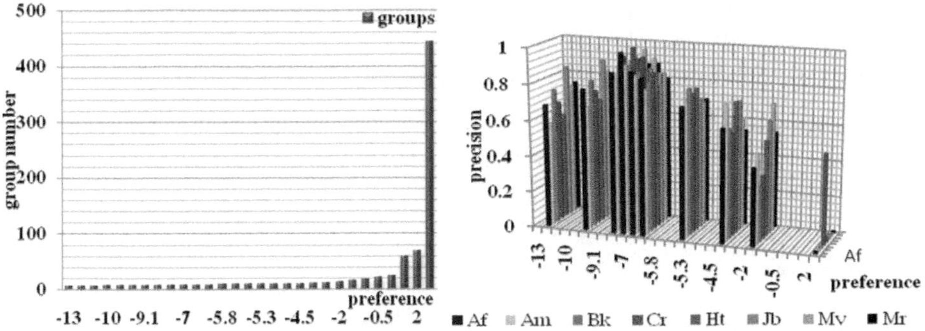

(a) (b)

Fig. 3. Influence of preference on clustering and on precision

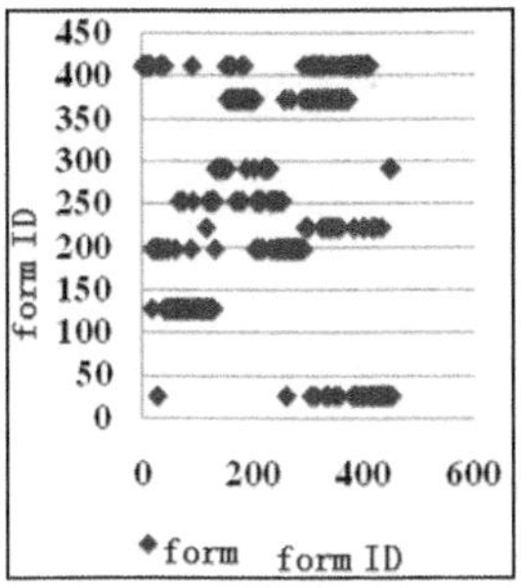

Fig. 4. Our cluster results

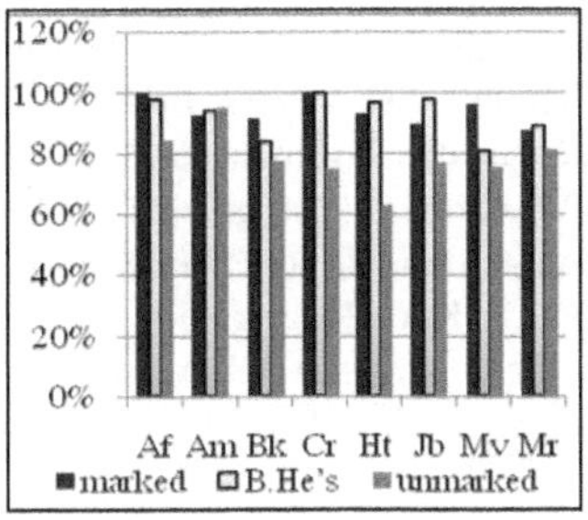

Fig. 5. Precision comparison

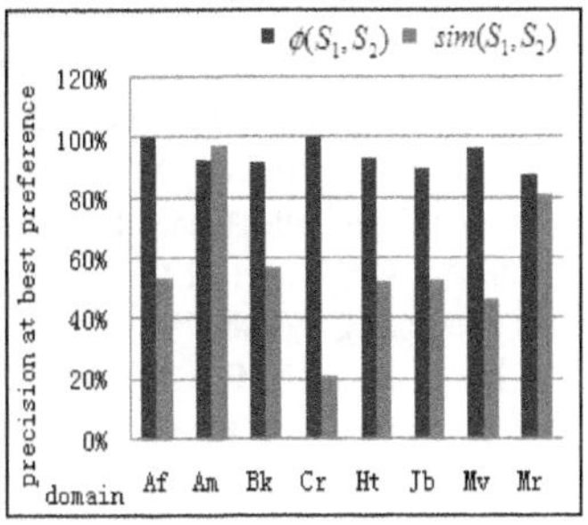

Fig. 6. Similarity comparison

First, we evaluate the influence of preference in AP clustering shown in Fig. 3. The result (a) shows that the higher the preference is, the more clustering groups are. (b) tells us that we obtain the best cluster result at $p = -7$ shown in Fig. 4. Second, we compare the cluster result with B. He's (MD_{hac}). *ce* value (0.29) of our method is much lower than B. He's (0.34) as $p = -7$ (F: $FGSTD_{AP}$, M: MD_{hac}).Third, we compare location-marked cluster result with location-unmarked result in Fig. 5, the precision of $FGSTD_{AP}$ is slightly higher and more stable than B. He's and much higher than location-unmarked method. Finally, we compare similarity measure $\phi(S_1,S_2)$ with $sim(S_1,S_2)$ in Fig. 6 which indicates that the similarity measure is crucial to the cluster and FGSTD greatly improves the precision.

6 Conclusion

In this paper we study data sources classification with domain independent. Motivated by our observations, we propose to class data sources by their interface texts and structure and further mine frequent itemsets to represent forms. Based on frequent itemsets, we develop a novel similarity measure (FGSTD) guided by which, we group forms applying AP algorithm. Experiments show the effectiveness of our extraction of form text co-occurrence relation and structure and FGSTD method.

Acknowledgments. This work is supported by the National Science Foundation (60673139, 60973021), the National High-Tech Development Program (2008AA01Z146).

References

1. Senellart, P., Mittal, A., et al.: Automatic wrapper induction from hidden-web sources with domain knowledge. In: 10th ACM workshop on Web information and data management, pp. 9–16. ACM Press, Napa Valley (2008)
2. He, B., Tao, T., Chang, K.C.-C.: Organizing Structured Web Sources by Query Schemas: A Clustering Approach. In: 13th ACM international conference Information and knowledge management, Washington, DC, USA, pp. 22–31(2004)
3. Barbosa, L., Freire, J.: Combining Classifiers to Identify Online Databases. In: 16th international conference WWW, pp. 431–440. ACM Press, Banff (2007)
4. Ngu, A.H., Rocco, D., et al.: Automatic Discovery and Inferencing of Complex Bioinformatics Web Interfaces. In: WWW, Chiba, Japan, pp. 463–493 (2005)
5. Lu, Y., He, H., et al.: Clustering e-commerce search engines based on their search interface pages using WISE-Cluster. J. Data & Knowledge Engineering 59, 231–246 (2006)
6. Chang, K., He, B., Zhang, Z.: Metaquerier over the deepweb: Shallow integration across holistic sources. In: Proceedings of the VLDB Workshop on Information Integration on the Web Toronto, Canada (2004)

Data Selection for Exact Value Acquisition to Improve Uncertain Clustering

Yu-Chieh Lin[1], De-Nian Yang[2], and Ming-Syan Chen[1,3]

[1] Department of Electrical Engineering, National Taiwan University, Taiwan
[2] Institute of Information Science, Academia Sinica, Taiwan
[3] Research Center for Information Technology Innovation, Academia Sinica, Taiwan

Abstract. In recent years, data uncertainty widely attracts researchers' attention because the amount of imprecise data is growing rapidly. Although data are not known exactly, probability distributions or expected errors are sometimes available. While most researchers on uncertain data mining are looking for methods to extract mining results from uncertain data, which is usually in the form of probability distributions or expected errors, it is also very important to lower the data uncertainty by making a part of data more certain to help get better mining results. For example, input values of some sensors in the sensor network are usually designed to be recorded more frequently than others because they are more important or more likely to change. In this paper, the issue of selecting a part of uncertain data and acquiring their exact values to improve clustering results is explored. Under a general uncertainty model, we propose both global and localized data selection methods, which can be used together with any existing uncertain clustering algorithm. Experimental results show that the quality of clustering improves after the selective exact value acquisition is applied.

1 Introduction

How to handle the uncertainty of data recently becomes an important issue because the quantity of existing uncertain data continuously increases. In the literature, many research results have been reported on the management or mining of uncertain data [1]. The uncertainty might be caused by many factors, including limitation of underlying equipment such as sensors in a sensor network, data modification according to privacy preserving policies, approximation of missing data, and just the nature of data like trajectories, which are the spatiotemporal information of moving objects, to name a few. No matter what the cause of uncertainty is, uncertain data could be stored in a probabilistic database for further usage.

In many applications, clustering is required for better understanding of the database. For most kinds of clustering tasks, traditional algorithms could not be directly applied to uncertain data since their similarity computation is designed only for deterministic values. By modifying traditional ones, clustering algorithms that can be applied to uncertain data are proposed. However, the clustering quality largely depends on how uncertain the database is. For example, if distributed regions of data are quite large, the whole system is with high uncertainty and the clustering result might not be acceptable. In this case, if we can lower the uncertainty of the system, a better clustering result is

L. Chen et al. (Eds.): WAIM 2010, LNCS 6184, pp. 459–470, 2010.

expected to be obtained. Uncertainty of a system is lowered if we get more detailed information of some data. This could be achieved by using better equipments or by increasing sampling frequency.

Motivational Example 1: Climate Information. To forecast weather and to monitor the climate change, lots of equipments are deployed around the world to carry out measurements like temperature and rainfall. Different kinds of equipments have different capabilities and result in different degrees of uncertainty. It is known that simple ombrometers can get rough values of rainfall while a meteorological station can get quite precise values. Not only the nature of equipments but also the location where equipments are installed would affect the degree of uncertainty. For example, the value measured by an ombrometer in an arid area might be different from that measured by an ombrometer in a moist area although the rainfalls of the two areas are actually the same. In this case, if we have a limited set of precise equipments, we should use them to replace the original equipments at the places where the uncertainty is relatively large and with large application-dependent influence.

Motivational Example 2: Summarization of Stream Data. Another example is the sensor network. Sensors read values periodically and upload summarized information following given policies. If a sensor is with more varying readings or is more important than other sensors due to certain reasons (e.g., its location), it should be sampled and be summarized more frequently to represent recent situation.

In this paper, we study the problem of selecting some uncertain data to acquire their exact values to help improve the quality of clustering result as much as possible. The problem is important because no matter how well the uncertain clustering algorithms are designed, the quality of clustering result of uncertain data is usually much worse than that of deterministic data.

It is reasonable to increase the amount of information to decrease database uncertainty. However, in most cases, we can only select a part of data due to the limitation on resource. The problem is quite challenging because it is difficult to leverage all possible factors that might affect the clustering result as a whole.

For the above reasons, we propose a metric to estimate the importance of each uncertain object in an uncertain database. The metric is designed according to how an uncertain object could influence the global clustering result. Sampling process is used to simplify the representation of an object. The metric would be used for selection such that data with the largest metric values are selected. However, computational load of the metric mentioned above has to be taken into consideration, and it could be prohibitively large. To make the selection process more practical, we propose another metric which considers only neighboring objects but not all objects. The utility of localized metric is not much worse than the global one but the computation time is significantly shortened.

Our contributions in this paper are many folds.

- We introduce the concept of exact value acquisition for uncertain data clustering. We discuss what one should do to get most information to improve the quality of clustering results with limited resources.
- We propose an algorithm-independent metric to help decide which uncertain data to be selected for exact value acquisition.

- In view of the efficiency and practicability, a localized metric is proposed.
- We conduct experimental studies to evaluate the proposed ideas. It is shown that the clustering result indeed improves after the exact value acquisition is applied.

The remainder of this paper is organized as follows. Related work is reviewed in Section 2. The problem description is given in Section 3, which contains the probabilistic model used and the detailed problem definition. The uncertain data selection is discussed in Section 4, in view of lots of factors that might be related to the clustering result and also in view of global and local computation. In Section 5, experimental results are shown after the proposed selection algorithm is applied with a density-based uncertain clustering algorithm. Finally, the paper is concluded in Section 6.

2 Related Works

To address the uncertainty of data, many corresponding data mining algorithms are proposed. Explicitly, there are algorithms considering the uncertainty of data for support vector machine classification, frequent pattern mining [14], outlier detection, and clustering [9] [10] [12] [2]. Since the uncertainty of data would affect the results of mining applications, the proposed methods focus on how to handle the uncertainty properly. For example, an attribute would be more important for classification if the uncertainty of it is lower than others.

Since clustering is quite important among mining applications, many clustering algorithms for uncertain data are proposed. In [9], the DBSCAN algorithm [8] is transformed into an uncertain version which can handle the uncertainty well and can find out density-based clusters. Another clustering algorithm focusing on data with uncertainty is [10], which modifies the hierarchical density-based OPTICS algorithm [4]. The well-known K-means algorithm is also modified to an uncertain version [12]. In addition to the case of static data, the problem of clustering uncertain data is extended to the case of streaming data [2]. It follows the concept of microclustering proposed in [3] and modifies the structure of microclusters for additional error information.

In a distributed environment, data collection process is usually designed in view of the characteristic and distribution of data. For example, collection process could be improved by altering sampling strategy [5] [13], doing partial cleaning [6], or modifying data acquisition plan and scheduling [7]. Cheng et al. proposed a method to choose a set of uncertain objects for cleaning to improve the quality of query answers [6]. The PWS-quality metric is proposed to measure the ambiguity of query answers under the possible world semantics, and the improvement of PWS-quality could be viewed as quality improvement of query answers. Deshpande et al. shown that interactive sensor querying is enriched with statistical modeling techniques [7]. Its data acquisition policy is to balance the increase in the confidence of answering queries based on the statistical model and the cost of observation resulting from wireless communication. Different from the works mentioned above, we study how to select data for exact value acquisition to improve the quality of clustering results.

3 Problem Description

In this section, we introduce the model of uncertainty used in this paper. Then, we describe the problem of point selection for exact value acquisition.

3.1 Probabilistic Model

In a probabilistic database, an uncertain object can be represented by all possible instances with their probabilities, where the summation of probabilities is equal to one. However, while dealing with uncertainty in real applications, probabilistic models are usually used for simplified description. In this work, without losing generality, it is assumed that the distribution of each object is known in advance and it could be described using a continuous or discrete probability density function [9] [10].

Definition 1 (Uncertain Object): An uncertain object o_i is a d dimensional tuple where the value of each dimension follows an underlying distribution. The underlying distribution of o_i is described as $[p_{i1}, p_{i2}, \ldots, p_{id}]$, where p_{ij} means the probability density function of object i in the j-th dimension. A probability density funcion $f_o : R^d \rightarrow R_0^+$ which makes the following condition hold: $\int_{o \in R^d} f_o = 1$.

Computation of similarity between two objects is basic and important in most clustering algorithms. With similarity information, relationship of a pair of objects could be decided. The Euclidean distance is usually used to present the similarity because it is easy to compute and usually leads to good performance. However, in an uncertain environment, the value of similarity between two objects would no longer be an exact numerical value but a random variable following a probability density function [9].

Definition 2 (Uncertain Distance)**:** Uncertain distance along an axis between two objects is described by a function $d : R^d \times R^d \rightarrow R_0^+$ which makes the following condition hold: $P(a \leq d(o_1, o_2) \leq b) = \int_a^b p_d(o_1, o_2)(x)dx$, where $P(a \leq d(o_1, o_2) \leq b)$ is the probability that $d(o_1, o_2)$ is between two values a and b, and $p_d : R^d \times R^d \rightarrow R_0^+$ is the distance density function.

3.2 Problem Definition

In this paragraph, definition of the problem is introduced. It is assumed that probabilistic density functions of all objects are available as background knowledge [8] [4] [12]. By selecting an object and doing some further processing, the distribution can be replaced by its exact value. This can be accomplished by replacing a sensor by another one with a higher ability. The problem is to decide which objects to be selected to improve the clustering result most. In reality, the number of selected objects could be constrained in view of the budget issue.

Definition 3 (Object Selection for Exact Value Acquisition)**:** Given n d-dimensional uncertain objects $(o_1, o_2, \ldots, o_n)$ with their probability density functions, denoted as $[p_{11}, p_{12}, \ldots, p_{1d}]$, $[p_{21}, p_{22}, \ldots, p_{2d}]$, ..., we want to select an object o_i for exact value acquisition so that the expected value of the following score is the smallest.

$$Score = \frac{dis(C_{exact}, C_{acqui}(o_i))}{dis(C_{exact}, C_{approx})}.$$

In the above description, C_{exact} and C_{approx} are the results after applying some uncertain clustering algorithm C to deterministic data and to uncertain data, respectively; $C_{acqui}(o_i)$ represents the result after applying C to uncertain data while knowing the exact value of object o_i. The dissimilarity of clustering results between two sets of clusters C_i and C_j is represented as $dis(C_i, C_j)$. It is just a measurement to decide if two sets are similar, and its definition is not restricted. For example, it could be represented by the number of objects that are partitioned into different clusters in the two cluster sets.

4 Selective Exact Value Acquisition for Clustering

As mentioned in the preceding section, adequate objects should be selected for exact value acquisition to improve the quality of clustering result. To decide which object is the most adequate one, characteristics of the distribution of every single object, tendency of all objects, and the result of initial clustering should all be taken into consideration at the same time. This is not easy because it is difficult to consider uncertainty of all objects and it is also difficult to evaluate the quality of clustering result. Moreover, the result of selection might be quite different when considering differenct clustering algorithms due to their different definitions and concepts.

4.1 Influence of Uncertainty

Since the uncertainty is described by probabilistic density functions of objects, the selection should be applied on objects. While selecting objects, several factors should be considered simultaneously. For example, if an object could appear in a large region, uncertainty of the distance between it and another object would be large and it should be selected. However, if the region is far from all other objects, it could be ignored as an outlier. All we have to do is to leverage possible factors, which are listed below, to do a better decision.

Factor: Characteristics of Distribution. Considering the uncertainty of data, a simple idea is to rank the span of all objects and then select the top ones with the highest values. However, the span is not enough to represent the distribution well. In place of the span, variance of an object could be computed and then recorded as a label of the object to show the statistical dispersion. Also, the shape of probabilistic density function could be partitioned into pre-defined classes.

Factor: Relative Position in Feature Space. Not only is the distribution of an object itself considered, the position of the object is also an important factor. If an object is near the border between two clusters, it might be quite important. It is because coverage of the two clusters may change after the exact value of the object is acquired. Also, a centroid object in a k-medians-like algorithm could be important since its value may change or it may become a non-centroid object after the exact value acquisition.

Factor: Position of Initial Clustering Results. For a density-based algorithm, if an object is near the boundary between two clusters, which is the result of an initial clustering, the object is more important than an object surrounded by other objects in the same cluster.

Factor: Algorithm-Dependent Errors. The influence of an object in the clustering process is also important information for selection. Therefore, the expected error incurred in the initial clustering process should be taken into consideration. Since the connectivity of clusters is an important issue when talking about density-based clustering algorithms, the expected error of an object should be computed based not only on the distribution itself but also on distributions of its neighboring objects.

4.2 Metric for Selection

If we want to get better quality of selection, more factors should be taken into consideration. However, it is quite difficult to leverage the influence of different kinds of factors since they are usually described in different ways. How to find a metric that can show the importance of every object and reflect the influence of all factors remains an open problem. Other than using a part of factors to estimate the influence of selecting an object, we try to evaluate the importance of a object according to possible clustering results. The idea is to observe possible clustering results of selecting each object. If the result of selecting an object is quite different from that of selecting no point, the influence of selecting it is large and it should be recognized as an important object.

The flow of data selection is described as follows. First, sampling technique is used to replace the original object representation with a set of samples to remove lots of integration computations. Then, any chosen uncertain clustering algorithm is applied on all samples of each object. Note that there is no restriction on which kind of uncertain clustering algorithm is used. Clustering results of all samples are compared to the original clustering result and the values of dissimilarity are summed up, showing the expected influence of selecting the object. The expected influence of selecting an object is used to represent its importance. It is noted that the dissimilarity is just a measurement between two sets to decide if they are similar, while the way of defining it is not restricted. After all computation is finished, objects could be ranked according to their influence. We can simply do the selection by choosing the object with the top influence. Moreover, if we want to select m objects instead of only one object, we can choose the top-m objects according to the influence ranking.

Take o_i as an example. Assume s_{i1} is selected and o_i is viewed as s_{i1} with a hundred percent probability. Then, the uncertain clustering algorithm is applied and generate C_{i1}, which is the new clustering results. Repeat the process for all samples and we can get a set of clustering results of o_i consisting of $(C_{i1}, C_{i2}, \ldots, C_{ik})$. After the set of clustering results is generated, the influence of selecting an object could be obtained. The influence of selecting object o_i is then defined as I_i, which is the summation of all dissimilarities.

$$I_i = \sum_{1 \leq x,y \leq k} dis(C_{ix}, C_{iy}).$$

4.3 Localized Metric for Selection

Errors in clustering results induced by uncertainty are usually due to misunderstanding of relationship between neighboring objects. Taking density-based clustering as an example, an object would induce severe error only if it is near the boundaries of more than one cluster. The severe error might be the case that two groups of objects are considered as connected while they are not in reality, or the case that two groups of objects are considered as unconnected while they are actually connected. If an object is near the boundary of a single cluster, it would only affect the objects neighboring to it and the number of those objects is restricted. On the other hand, if an object is near the common boundary of at least two clusters, it might affect objects in all neighboring clusters and the number of affected objects could be the total of all those clusters.

Because of the characteristics mentioned above, it is reasonable to find out the influence of an object by observing if the clustering results of neighboring objects change largely. That is, influence is evaluated according to only partial objects.

The clustering results of selecting the j-th sample of object o_i is marked as C_{ij}^L, where there are only r items in C_{ij}^L representing the clustering results of the neighboring r objects. If the dissimilarity of two clustering results is shown as $dis(C_{ix}^L, C_{iy}^L)$, the local influence I_i^L of object o_i is computed as follows.

$$I_i^L = \sum_{1 \leq x,y \leq k} dis(C_{ix}^L, C_{iy}^L).$$

Although the strategy of selection considering local information is similar to that of general case, the localized metric could save a large amount of computation effort. How much computational time to be saved is an issue depending on what kind of the uncertain clustering algorithm is used.

5 Experiments

In this section, experimental results are presented to show the performance of the proposed data selection method for exact value acquisition and the effects of using different input parameters. The FDBSCAN algorithm [9] is chosen to be the uncertain clustering algorithm in our selection algorithm, where all kinds of uncertain clustering algorithm could be used in practical. Although there are lots of uncertain clustering algorithms, the FDBSCAN algorithm is chosen in our work since it can discover arbitrary shape of clusters and it is designed with sampling technique so that it is suitable to be integrated with our algorithm.

5.1 The FDBSCAN Algorithm

The FDBSCAN algorithm is based on the DBSCAN algorithm [8], which clusters deterministic data into groups according to density information. In FDBSCAN, uncertainty of data is taken into consideration by being described by probability density functions, and the distance between two uncertain objects is computed by integration.

To introduce the parameters used in experiments, the FDBSCAN is roughly described as follows. For every two objects, the probability that the distance between them is smaller than ϵ, which is a given threshold, is defined as the probability that two objects are connected. Based on this, the probability that object o_j is density-reachable from o_i could be computed by multiplying the probability that o_i and o_j are connected by the probability that there are more than $(\mu - 1)$ other objects connected to o_i, where μ is a given value describing density. The latter probability could be computed while assuming the probability of connection for every pair of objects is independent of one another. When FDBSCAN is applied, an object is added to the current cluster only if the probability of being density-reachable from the query object exceeds 0.5.

5.2 Quality Evaluation

To evaluate the quality of clustering results, a measurement is designed to compare it with the ground truth, which is obtained when all objects are deterministic. It is to compare the dissimilarity of two sets of clustering result which is computed by summing up the number of object pairs that are not put into the same cluster in two sets of results.

As mentioned in Section 3, the definition of dissimilarity is not restricted. In our experiments, the following formula is used to compute the dissimilarity between two sets of clustering result.

$$dis(C_i, C_j) = n - Match(C_i, C_j),$$

where $Match(C_i, C_j)$ means the number of objects that are partitioned into the same cluster in two sets of clustering results.

To evaluate the effect of our selection strategy, both the qualities of the clustering result after data selection for exact value acquisition and of the clustering result after only the FDBSCAN algorithm are applied. For all of our experiments, the quality of our method and the quality of the FDBSCAN algorithm are shown at the same time for comparison.

Normalized error is used to reflect the quality of a set of clustering results. Computation of the normalized error is defined as follows.

$$NormalizedError = \frac{dis(C_{exact}, C_{acqui}(o_i))}{dis(C_{exact}, C_{approx})}.$$

It could be observed that the smaller the normalized error, the better the quality of clustering results.

To decide if an object is in the same cluster in two sets of clustering results, the mapping of clusters is needed. The concept of mapping process is to conduct minimum weight perfect matching [11]. A perfect matching M is regarded as a minimum weight perfect matching if and only if for any other perfect matching M', the following inequality holds.

$$\sum_{(x,y)\in M} w(x,y) \leq \sum_{(x,y)\in M'} w(x,y).$$

Note that the distance between (x, y) is defined according to the union and intersection of them, and if the numbers of clusters in two sets are different, null clusters are added in.

5.3 Experimental Setup

All experiments are based on a synthetic data set which is generated as follows. There are 1000 objects in the uncertain database. After a set of cluster heads is randomly

Table 1. Experiment Setting

Parameter	Default Setting
# of objects (n)	1000
# of dimensions (d)	2
density (μ)	5
# of samples (k)	5
range per dimension	1.0
connection (ϵ)	0.04
radius	0.04
uncertainty	0.04
neighboring objects (r)	70
# of selected objects(m)	50
threshold	0.5
#of clusters	15

generated, randomly assign each object to one of the cluster, which means its location is near to the cluster head. The location of an object's location is determined based on uniform distribution. Then, one of the three distributions (uniform, normal, and inverse normal distribution) is assigned to each object. Samples of an object are generated based on the above distribution.

The proposed selection algorithm is implemented according to the FDBSCAN algorithm for uncertain clustering. All algorithms are implemented in C++. The experiments were run on a Windows Server with a 3.00 GHz processor and 8.00 GB main memory. The setting of parameters used in the experiments is listed in Table 1. To show the average case of each experiment, each result shown below is the average of 40 runs.

5.4 Experiment Results

Results of experiments are shown below. The results are discussed in view of effectiveness and efficiency.

Effectiveness. Fig. 1 and Fig. 2 are experimental results reflecting the effectiveness. Since the selection is to move a step further from the original uncertain clustering algorithm, the results are compared to the original uncertain clustering algorithm to show the improvement.

In the left part of Fig. 1, the impact of the number of locally selective objects is shown. It is clear to see that the normalized error is quite small when the number is 100. It means that most errors are corrected while selecting 100 objects to calculate the localized metric. However, to balance accuracy and computation overhead, 70 is chosen for the following experiments. The impact of the number of samples for an object is shown in the right part of Fig. 1. The description of an object gets closer to the underlying probability density function when the number of samples becomes larger. However, the number of samples seems not to affect the quality of the selection method. In Fig. 2, the impact of thresholds of both connection and density is shown.

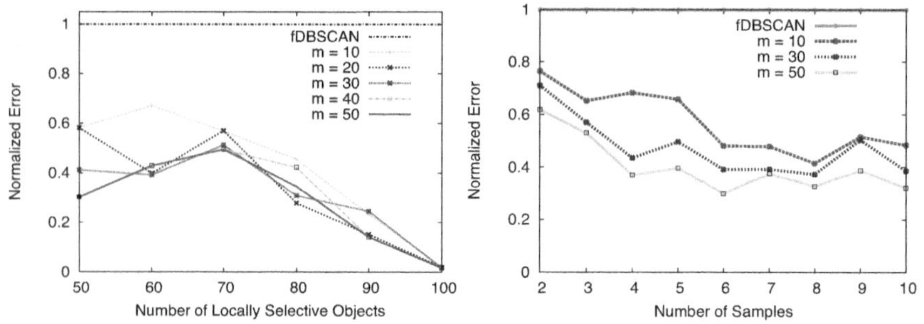

Fig. 1. Normalized Error on Different Number of Locally Selective Objects and Samples

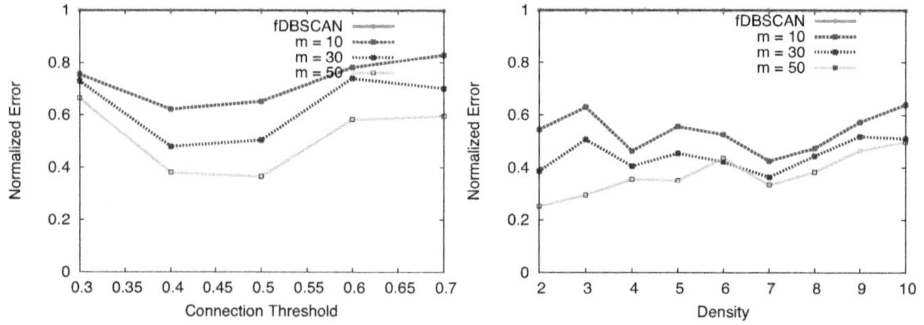

Fig. 2. Normalized Error on Different Thresholds of Connection and Density

It is observed that the impact of the number of locally selective objects is prominent while that of the other parameters is not. The reason is that the number of locally selective objects is directly related to the selection while other parameters are related to the FDBSCAN algorithm.

Efficiency. Time consumption of our methods and the FDBSCAN algorithm according to the number of locally selective objects is shown in Table 2. S-Local refers to the proposed selection method using the localized metric and S-Global refers to the proposed selection method using the original metric. Computation of the S-Global method takes quite long time and it is hence considered impractical. For S-Local , time consumption grows when r grows, where r means the localized metric is computed according to information of only r neighboring objects. If the number of r is set to be a small number, computational load would be acceptable.

In Fig. 3, time consumption related to parameters other than the number of locally selective objects is shown. It is observed that the definition of density would not change the computing overhead while the threshold of connection and the number of samples would. The relationship between time consumption and the threshold of connection is almost linear. The reason might be that if the threshold is high, it is much harder to decide if an object is dense so that most computation tasks could not be pruned.

Table 2. Time Consumption

Algorithm	Time (sec.)	
FDBSCAN		0.453
S-Local	r=50	28.611
	r=100	179.385
	r=150	346.743
	r=200	480.499
S-Global	(r=1000)	2089.946

Moreover, the relationship between time consumption and the number of samples is between linear and square linear. This is reasonable since the computation overhead should be square of the number of samples while there might be some tasks pruned according to too many number of samples.

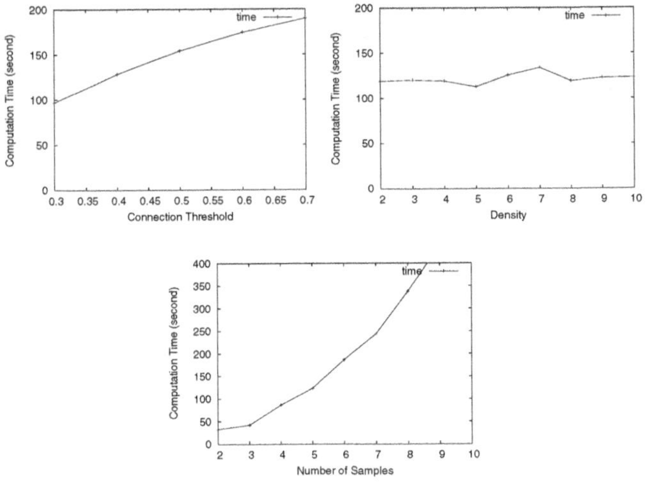

Fig. 3. Time Consumption

6 Conclusion

In this paper, the concept of exact value acquisition for uncertain clustering is introduced. According to the assumption that there are limited resources to acquire more precise values, uncertainty of the system could be lowered and quality of mining results could be improved. In addition to the concept, we propose a method to decide which data to be selected for exact value acquisition. It is based on a proposed algorithm-independent metric representing expected influence of selecting an object. Considering the efficiency and practicability, our method can also be simplified to a localized version by only observing influence on neighboring objects. The selection result could be employed when we do distributed resource planning. Experimental studies are conducted and it is shown that clustering results indeed improve after selective exact value acquisition is applied.

References

1. Aggarwal, C.C., Yu, P.S.: A Survey of Uncertain Data Algorithms and Applications. IEEE Transactions on Knowledge and Data Engineering (2009)
2. Aggarwal, C.C., Yu, P.S.: A Framework for Clustering Uncertain Data Streams. In: Proceedings of the 24th IEEE International Conference on Data Engineering (2008)
3. Aggarwal, C.C., Han, J., Wang, J., Yu, P.S.: A Framework for Clustering Evolving Data Streams. In: Proceedings of the 29th International Conference on Very Large Data Bases (2003)
4. Ankerst, M., Breunig, M.M., Kriegel, H.-P., Sander, J.: OPTICS: Ordering Points to Identify the Clustering Structure. In: Proceedings of the ACM SIGMOD International Conference on Management of Data (1999)
5. Chen, J., Cheng, R.: Quality-Aware Probing of Uncertain Data with Resource Constraints. In: Ludäscher, B., Mamoulis, N. (eds.) SSDBM 2008. LNCS, vol. 5069, pp. 491–508. Springer, Heidelberg (2008)
6. Cheng, R., Chen, J., Xie, X.: Cleaning Uncertain Data with Quality Guarantees. In: Proceedings of the 34th International Conference on Very Large Data Bases (2008)
7. Deshpande, A., Guestrin, C., Madden, S.R., Hellerstein, J.M., Hong, W.: Model-Driven Data Acquisition in Sensor Networks. In: Proceedings of the 34th International Conference on Very Large Data Bases (2004)
8. Ester, M., Kriegel, H.-P., Sander, J., Xu, X.: A Density Based Algorithm for Discovering Clusters in Large Spatial Databases with Noise. In: Proceedings of the 2nd ACM SIGKDD International Conference on Knowledge Discovery and Data Mining (1996)
9. Kriegel, H.-P., Pfeifle, M.: Density-Based Clustering of Uncertain Data. In: Proceedings of the ACM SIGKDD International Conference on Knowledge Discovery and Data Mining (2005)
10. Kriegel, H.-P., Pfeifle, M.: Hierarchical Density Based Clustering of Uncertain Data. In: Proceedings of the 5th IEEE International Conference on Data Mining (2005)
11. Kriegel, H.-P., Pfeifle, M.: Measuring the Quality of Approximated Clusterings. In: BTW (2005)
12. Ngai, W., Kao, B., Chui, C., Cheng, R., Chau, M., Yip, K.Y.: Efficient Clustering of Uncertain Data. In: Proceedings of the 6th IEEE International Conference on Data Mining (2006)
13. Olston, C., Jiang, J., Widom, J.: Adaptive Filters for Continuous Queries over Distributed Data Streams. In: Proceedings of the ACM SIGMOD International Conference on Management of Data (2003)
14. Zhang, Q., Li, F., Yi, K.: Finding Frequent Items in Probailistic Data. In: Proceedings of ACM SIGMOD International Conference on Management of Data (2008)

Exploring the Sentiment Strength of User Reviews

Yao Lu[1,2,3], Xiangfei Kong[2], Xiaojun Quan[2], Wenyin Liu[2,3], and Yinlong Xu[1,3]

[1] Dept. of Computer Sci. and Tech., University of Sci. and Tech. of China, Hefei, China
[2] Department of Computer Science, City University of Hong Kong, HKSAR, China
[3] Joint Research Lab of Excellence, CityU-USTC Advanced Research Institute, Suzhou, China
{luyao2,xfkong,xiaoquan}@student.cityu.edu.hk,
csliuwy@cityu.edu.hk, ylxu@ustc.edu.cn

Abstract. Existing research efforts in sentiment analysis of online user reviews mainly focus on extracting features (such as quality and price) of products/services and classifying users' sentiments into semantic *orientations* (such as positive, negative or neutral). However, few of them take the strength of user sentiments into consideration, which is particularly important in measuring the overall quality of products/services. Intuitively, different reviews for the same feature should have quite different sentiment strength, even though they may express the same polarity of sentiment. This paper presents an approach to estimating the sentiment strength of user reviews according to the strength of adverbs and adjectives expressed by users in their opinion phrases. Experimental result on a hotel review dataset in Chinese shows that the proposed approach is effective in the task of sentiment classification and achieves a good performance on a multi-scale evaluation.

Keywords: opinion mining, sentiment analysis, sentiment strength, text mining.

1 Introduction

With the rapid development and wide popularity of e-commerce application and Web 2.0 technology, more and more users express their experiences or sentiments on certain products through channels on Web, such as product websites, review websites, forums or discussion groups. For example, on the website of Amazon[1], there are a great number of user reviews and comments posted every day for the online goods. These user reviews, regardless of positive or negative, not only reflect users' viewpoints and satisfaction levels, but also have a great impact on other consumers' purchasing behaviors. Hence, sentiment analysis and mining [1] has become an important research issue which benefits manufacturers and managers to obtain users' opinions on their products, as well as other potential customers to make proper decisions.

There have already been extensive studies on sentiment analysis over the past few years [1-6, 9-17]. Most of them can be classified into the following two sub-tasks: (a) features extraction, which aims to extract features of products from reviews. These features are usually important attributes when measuring the quality of certain

[1] http://www.amazon.com

L. Chen et al. (Eds.): WAIM 2010, LNCS 6184, pp. 471–482, 2010.

products, thus they are frequently commented and rated by users; and (b) sentiment classification, which focuses on determining the semantic orientation (usually three values: positive, negative or neutral) of user sentiments on the features. However, the sentiments for each feature with the same polarity might have different sentiment strength reflecting different emotional intensity of users to the products or services. For example, two users may give both positive reviews to the same book, while one says "*This is the most* ***excellent*** *book I have ever read. I love it very much.*" and the other reviews the book as "*That's a* ***good*** *book which is worth reading.*" Even though they both express a positive assessment to the book, the sentiment intensity they convey is different. One can clearly feel that the first one reveals a stronger opinion than the second one from the evidence of the different strengths of adjective word "**excellent**" and "**good**". In spite of lots of existing works on positive and negative sentiment classification, few works were done on exploring the strength of user reviews. It is a new challenging task in opinion mining and sentiment analysis.

In this paper, we propose an approach to assessing the sentiment strength of user reviews. Intuitively, the sentiment strength is reflected by the "strength" of opinion words (words expressing users' positive, neutral or negative opinion) people used when commenting a product. For the above examples, "most excellent" and "good" are the opinion words. Considering that opinion words are mostly composed of adjectives, we measure the sentiment strength according to the strength of adjectives in opinion words. In linguistics, some adverbs (such as "very") are usually used to modify adjectives to enhance the emotional strength of adjectives, especially in user reviews scenario. Therefore, the strength of adverbs is also taken into consideration to accurately measure the sentiment strength. In this paper, we manually mark the strengths of a few frequently used adverbs with values ranging from -1 to +1 based on our intuitions. The strength of adjectives is calculated by a link analysis method based on a generated progressive relation graph of adjectives, in which each node is an adjective and the directed edge between nodes is a kind of progressive relationship obtained through the search engine based on heuristic rules. We apply the proposed approach on a dataset consisting of hotel comments in Chinese in our experiment, and validate it from two aspects (positive & negative review estimation and five-scale estimation[2]). Experimental results show that the proposed approach is effective for sentiment classification and achieves a good performance on the five-scale evaluation.

The rest of this paper is organized as follows. In Section 2, we briefly introduce related works on opinion mining and sentiment analysis. In Section 3, we give a detailed description of our approach to assessing review's sentiment strength. The proposed approach is verified in Section 4. At the same time, an analysis of the experimental results is provided in this section. Finally, we draw the conclusion in Section 5.

2 Related Works

Feature extraction and sentiment classification are two major tasks in the field of opinion mining and sentiment analysis. Specifically, feature extraction aims to identify opinion features (e.g., price and quality) of products, on which users have expressed

[2] The review is scored from 1 to 5 stars, 1 star means worst, 3 stars means medium and 5 stars means best.

their comments. Sentiment classification investigates methods to classify each review text as positive, negative, or neutral based on the extracted opinion features. In this section, we will briefly introduce the related works from the above two aspects.

2.1 Opinion Features Extraction

In customers' reviews, people express their sentiments on certain products by commenting the opinion features of products based on personal experiences. Therefore, extracting opinion features from review text is the first and an important step in opinion mining. It is also the foundation of sentiment classification.

Turney [2] proposes an algorithm to extract phrases containing adjectives or adverbs which are good indicators of sentiment polarity demonstrated by previous works [3, 4]. He firstly tags the words in review text by a part-of-speech (POS) tagger, and then two consecutive words are extracted from the review text based on pre-defined patterns. After that, the semantic orientation of the extracted phrases is derived by calculating the mutual information and classifying the review based on the averaged semantic orientation value of the phrases. An average accuracy of 74% is achieved in his experimental results.

Hu and Liu [5, 6] propose another approach to extracting opinion/product features. Their method, which is based on techniques of data mining and natural language processing, is composed of the following steps: (1) A POS Tagging tool is executed firstly on the review text; (2) Association mining [7] is employed to find out all frequent words or phrases which co-occur in some sentences; (3) Two types of pruning strategies (compactness pruning and redundancy pruning) are used to remove incorrect features. (4) They extract the opinion noun words from the review text according to the frequent features and the nearby adjective words. (5) Finally, they also extract some infrequent features which also reflect the attributes of products/services. At the same time, they use synonyms and antonyms in WordNet [8] to determine the sentiment polarity of words (either positive or negative). Their experiment conducted on customer reviews of electronic products shows that the proposed approach is effective for the opinion features extraction task.

2.2 Sentiment Classification

Unlike traditional topic-based text classification, sentiment classification concerns on the sentiment words and classifies the reviews into sentiment categories of positive or negative (or sometimes neutral). Supervised machine learning methods and unsupervised techniques have been applied for the task of sentiment classification. Pang et al. [9] apply three different machine learning techniques (Naïve Bayes, Maximum Entropy and Support Vector Machine) to classify movie reviews into positive and negative using various features extracted from reviews. Experimental results show that standard machine learning techniques perform well on sentiment classification. Moreover, from the comparison result of the three machine learning methods, Support Vector Machine (SVM) achieves the best performance, while Naïve Bayes tends to be the worst one. Cui et al. [10] also investigate similar task with different machine learning algorithms on huge amount of online review data. A conclusion in their experiment is that a classifier combining with high order n-grams features could achieve better performance. Other related work of using machine learning methods for sentiment classification can be found in [11, 12, 13]. Zagibalov and Carroll [14] propose an unsupervised approach, which just accesses to the raw text without annotated training data, to overcome the problem of domain-dependency in sentiment classification. The experiment results obtained are close to, and sometimes better than those of supervised classifiers.

Apart from the works of binary sentiment classification, there are also some works performed in terms of assigning the star rating to reviews. In [15], Pang et al. predict the star ratings of movie reviews on a five-scale using a meta-algorithm. Their evaluation results show that their method achieves significant improvements over both multi-class and regression of SVM method. Snyder and Barzilay [16] study the reviews on restaurant and predict ratings for various aspects of restaurant, such as the food, ambience and service, on a five-scale. Williams and Anand [17] propose a knowledge-based approach to assign each adjective with polarity strength by measuring semantic distance between words of known polarity (seed words) and the target word according to WordNet [8], which is the most similar work to ours. However, different from theirs, we use the search engine and progressive rules to find progressive relationships between adjectives and measure polarity strength of each adjective based on a link analysis method. NLP-based technique is used to calculate the sentiment strength of each review. Based on the calculated overall sentiment score, each review is graded with 1 to 5 stars according to the predefined interval division.

3 Exploring Review Strength

In this section, we first describe the extraction strategy of opinion phrases from reviews in Section 3.1. The calculation of review strength based on the extracted phrases will be introduced in Section 3.2. After that, the key factors determining the sentiment strength in opinion phrase – adjectives and adverbs, are expounded in Section 3.3 and 3.4 respectively.

3.1 Extracting Opinion Phrases from Reviews

The sentiment strength of a review is determined by the opinion phrases expressing the opinion holder's sentiment. Extracting the proper opinion phrases from review is the crucial step in review sentiment strength estimation. We utilize similar techniques proposed in [6] to deal with the opinion phrases extraction as shown in the following steps.

(1) The ICTCLAS [18] is used to perform the Chinese words segmentation and POS tagging on the review text.
(2) Based on the POS tagging result, we pick out all the *noun* words, and then find the frequent ones as the opinion noun words. We define a noun word as frequent if it appears in more than δ of the review texts.
(3) For each opinion sentence which contains the opinion *noun* words, we extract the nearby *adjective* with or without *adverb* that modifies it. If such an adjective is found, the adjective with or without adverb is considered as an opinion sentiment feature.
(4) We obtain all the opinion phrases from reviews which consist of the opinion *noun* words and the modified opinion sentiment features.

For example, in the customer review "*This is the most excellent book I have ever read.*" We first determine that "book" is an opinion noun word, and then we extract the nearby adjective "excellent" and the adverb "most" which modifies the "excellent" as the opinion sentiment features. Hence, the opinion phrase here is "most excellent book".

3.2 Review Strength Calculation

After extracting all the opinion phrases from review, the overall sentiment strength of a review R is calculated by averaging the strength of opinion phrases as shown in the following formula (1).

$$S(R) = \frac{1}{|OP(R)|} \sum_{i=1}^{|OP(R)|} S(OP_i) \tag{1}$$

In this formula, $OP(R)$ is a set of opinion phrases extracted from the review R, $|OP(R)|$ is the size of the set, and OP_i is the ith opinion phrase in the set. $S(OP_i)$ is denoted as the sentiment strength of ith opinion phrase calculated by the product of adverb strength $S(adv_i)$ and the adjective strength $S(adj_i)$ as formula (2) described.

$$S(OP_i) = S(adv_i) \cdot S(adj_i) \tag{2}$$

The value of $S(adv_i)$ and $S(adj_i)$ ranges from -1 to +1. Sometimes, there is no adverb in the opinion phrase, so the $S(adv_i)$ is set as a default value 0.5. The calculation of those two determined components will be described in details in the following two subsections.

3.3 Strength of Adjectives

To determine the strength of adjective words, we utilize search engine and progressive rules to construct an adjective progressive relationship graph at first. Then, a link analysis method, propagation [19], is performed on the generated graph. The outcome value of each node (representing each adjective word) is treated as the strength. The details of graph construction and the propagation algorithm are described as follows.

3.3.1 Graph Construction

In Chinese, some pairs of adjectives are frequently used in company with to express an emphasized emotion. For example, "*She is very beautiful and very smart*" (她很漂亮很聪明), and "*She is not only beautiful but also smart*" (她不仅漂亮而且聪明), etc. We define such kinds of patterns as progressive relation rules of adjectives. Based on those heuristic rules, we can associate the two adjectives (nodes) with a link, representing one support the other in sentiment strength. For example, if two adjectives Adj_i and Adj_j have once been used as "very Adj_i and very Adj_j", we can build a link from Adj_i to Adj_j.

A total of 3,497 adjective words are collected from the Chinese lexicon. These adjectives are represented as the nodes in the graph. For each pair of adjectives Adj_i and Adj_j ($Adj_i \neq Adj_j$) in the adjective collection, we obtain the progressive relationship between them through the search engine. Three queries of the two adjectives Adj_i and

Adj_j are derived based on three progressive relation rule patterns showed in Table 1. Next, we submit those three queries into the search engine (e.g., Google.com). The sum of returned search results number from search engine for each query is denoted as C_{ij}, which represents the progressive relation from Adj_i to Adj_j. We can also get the relation from Adj_j to Adj_i in the same way.

Table 1. Progressive relationship rules patterns

Progressive relationship rules in Chinese	in English
很Adj_i 很Adj_j	very Adj_i and very Adj_j
既Adj_i 又Adj_j	not only Adj_i but also Adj_j
不仅Adj_i 而且Adj_j	not only Adj_i but also Adj_j

We get in total 306,547 non-zero progressive relationship values for the adjective pairs. The weight of the relational link W_{ij} from Adj_i to Adj_j is calculated as described in formula (3).

$$W_{ij} = \frac{R_{ij}}{\sum_j R_{ij}} = \frac{\log_2(1+C_{ij})}{\sum_j \log_2(1+C_{ij})} \tag{3}$$

The weight of relation W_{ij} between Adj_i and Adj_j is calculated as R_{ij} divided by the sum of all the progressive relation links from adjective Adj_i. R_{ij} represents the progressive relation between Adj_i and Adj_j, which is calculated by the logarithm of the number of search result C_{ij}. The logarithm is taken because the number of search results is not stable and usually varies greatly. Moreover, if the logarithm is not taken, some pairs would take dominant role in the computation as they have large weight.

After obtaining the nodes of adjectives and the relation links with weight between adjectives, we can construct an adjective progressive relationship graph. A sample of this graph is shown in Figure 1. In this figure, we can see that the word "nice" has a progressive support for the word "beautiful", and the progressive relation from "nice" to "beautiful" is captured by the rule patterns based queries described in Table 1 from search engine.

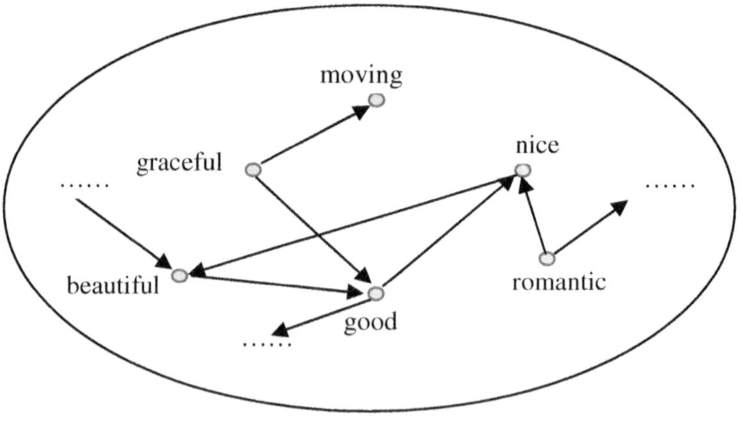

Fig. 1. A sample of adjective progressive relationship graph

3.3.2 Propagation Algorithm

We use the link analysis method called propagation [19] to calculate the strength of each adjective. The basic idea underlying the propagation method in the adjective progressive relationship graph is that: 1) the positive word will enhance the positive strength of words which it points to; 2) the negative word will enhance the negative strength of words which it points to; and 3) the positive and negative strength of a word will be offset if it is pointed by both positive and negative ones.

Therefore, after obtaining the generated adjective progressive relation graph from last step in Section 3.3.1, we choose the nodes with no in-degrees, and mark each of them with the value +1 if they are positive and -1 otherwise[3]. Then, the propagation calculation is iteratively performed according to the following calculation formula (4).

$$S(w_i)^{k+1} = S(w_i)^k + \sum_{w_j \in W} W_{ji} \cdot S(w_j)^k \qquad (4)$$

where W_{ji} is the progressive relationship link weight in the graph form adjective node Adj_i to Adj_j, and W represents all the neighboring nodes of adjective which points to adjective w_i in the graph.

In each iteration, the strength of each adjective is calculated based on the sentiment strength of itself and its neighbors derived from previous iteration. Next, each strength score is normalized by dividing it by the maximal adjective strength score of current iteration.

The terminal condition of the iteration here can be described as two aspects: first, the maximal change of the computing adjective strength value from iteration k to iteration k+1 is smaller than a threshold ε; second, the iteration times is larger than a predefined value η. Base on the propagation theory [20], this approach is convergent.

After performing the propagation algorithm, the sentiment strength of each adjective is obtained, while the positive value of an adjective indicates positive sentiment strength, and the negative value expresses negative sentiment strength. Moreover, higher value means stronger positive sentiment and lower value indicates weaker negative sentiment.

3.4 Strength of Adverbs

The adverb in opinion sentiment feature is used to modify the adjective. An adjective modified by different adverbs may express different emotional intensity. For example, "extremely good" expresses a more powerful sentiment than "very good" does. Both of them express stronger emotion than "good" which receives no modification of the adverb. Therefore, adverb has non-trivial impact on the review sentiment strength of sentiment expression which can not be ignored.

We collect all the adverbs which are used to modify the adjectives from a Chinese lexicon. Based on the different emotional intensity expressed by the adverb, we mark the negative adverbs with a negative score and other positive adverbs with different score in different sentiment level. The score is ranging from -1 to +1 and a higher score expresses a stronger sentiment. For example, we consider that the adverb

[3] If there is no node without in-degrees, we choose 40 seed words (words of known polarity), in which 20 positive adjectives marked by +1 and 20 negative ones marked by -1.

"**extremely**" has higher strength than "**more**" does, but lower than that of "**most**". Consequently, "**most**" is marked with +1, "**extremely**" with +0.9, and "**more**" with +0.6. Negative adverbs, such as "not", "never", "hardly", "seldom", are marked with a negative score -1. There is about 100 such kind of adverbs graded by two people intuitively and we get the average score for each adverb as the final strength score. Table 2 shows examples of adverb and their strength used in our experiments.

Table 2. Example of adverb strength

Adverb	Strength
most (最)	+1
extremely(非常)	+0.9
more (较)	+0.6
little (些许)	+0.2
never (从不)	-1
hardly (几乎不)	-1

4 Experiment Results

4.1 Experiment Setting

We use a real hotel review dataset, collected from Ctrip.com[4] provided by Tan on his website[5]. This dataset contains 2000 positive reviews and 2000 negative reviews in the form of Chinese. We choose 200 positive and 200 negative reviews randomly from the dataset and score each one with five-scale evaluation manually according to the expressed sentiment strength.

As mentioned in the previous part, we get in total 3,497 adjectives and 100 adverbs from the Chinese lexicon. The strength of each adjective and adverb is obtained by the proposed approach as previously described. The parameter δ used in determining the opinion noun word is chosen as 0, 0.01, 0.02, 0.05, 0.1, 0.2 and 0.3 respectively. The threshold ε andη in the terminal condition of propagation are set as 0.001 and 100 respectively.

We evaluate our proposed approach from two aspects – positive & negative sentiment classification and five-scale evaluation. In the first experiment, we use the five-fold cross-validation and evaluate the average classification accuracy. We first choose parameter δ for the best performance on accuracy. Then, we compare our proposed approach which considers the strength of adjectives with method which only considers the positive and negative polarity of adjectives.

In the five-scale estimation, we use two evaluation criterions, namely precision and distance precision, to evaluate the experimental results. The distance precision is calculated as shown in the following formula (5).

[4] http://www.ctrip.com/
[5] http://www.searchforum.org.cn/tansongbo/corpus-senti.htm

$$DP(T) = 1 - \frac{1}{n}\sum_{i=1}^{n}\frac{|ct_i - t_i|}{4} \quad (5)$$

where n is the number of reviews in the test data T, ct_i is the computed five-scale score and t_i is the labeled five-scale score for the ith review.

4.2 Experiment Results

Positive & Negative classification

Positive & Negative classification is also known as the sentiment classification in sentiment analysis. Reviews are classified into two categories – positive and negative based on the expressed sentiment. In our experiment, we calculate the strength score of each review using formula (1) and (2). According to the calculated score, reviews achieved positive scores are considered as positive ones and negative scores are negative ones.

We use the five-fold cross-validation, which divides the 4000 reviews dataset into five parts. This cross-validation process repeats five times and in each times, every single part is rotationally retained as the validation data for testing while the remaining four parts for training. Then, we calculate the average precision for the sentiment classification and present the result in Table 3. As shown in the table the method achieves the highest precision 71.65% when the parameter δ is 0.01.

Table 3. Precision of sentiment classification with different values of parameter δ

δ	0	**0.01**	0.02	0.05	0.1	0.2	0.3
Precision	71.5%	**71.65%**	71.35%	71.1%	71.28%	70.15%	66.13%

We compare the precision of the sentiment classification of our approach with the baseline which doesn't consider the strength but only the positive or negative polarity of adjectives. Figure 2 exhibits the result for the two different approaches. From the figure, we can see that the approach considering the strength of adjective reaches a precision with 5.7% higher than that without considering it in the positive & negative sentiment classification.

Five-Scale Estimation

In five-scale estimation, we grade each review into five levels (stars) according to their sentiment strength scores. 1 star represents the worst, 3 stars denotes medium and 5 stars is the best. Table 4 shows the mapping table between the number of stars a review achieves and its corresponding strength score. For example, if the sentiment strength of a review is calculated as 0.47, it means four stars. We evaluate the precision and distance precision for our approach and show the result in Table 5. From the experiment result, we can see that our approach is very promising on exploring the sentiment strength of review.

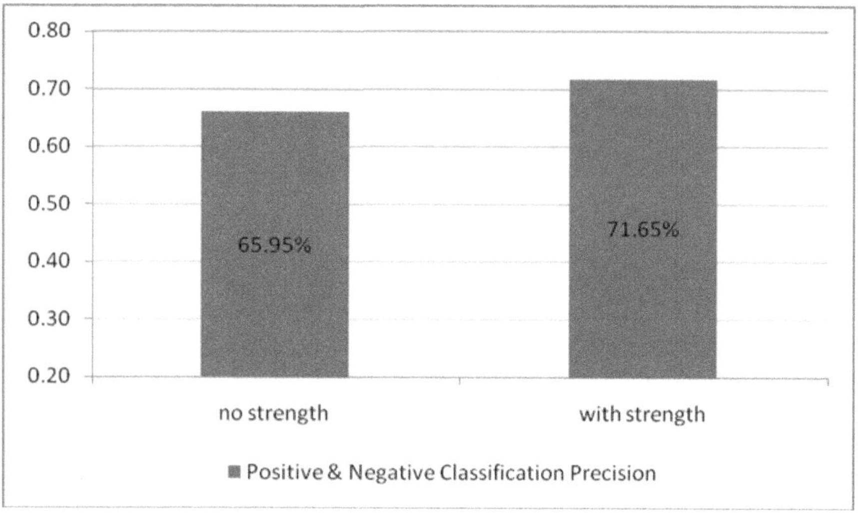

Fig. 2. The Positive & Negative sentiment classification precision with and without considering adjectives strength

Table 4. Achieved stars with corresponding interval

# of Stars	1	2	3	4	5
Interval	(-∞, -0.5]	(-0.5, 0]	(0, 0.2]	(0.2, 0.6]	(0.6, +∞)

Table 5. Precision and distance precision in five-scale estimation

	Precision	Distance Precision
Measurement	38.88%	78.61%

5 Conclusion and Future Works

In this paper, we propose an approach to evaluating the sentiment strength of reviews. We first extract the opinion phrases which consist of the opinion *noun* word and the modified opinion sentiment features from reviews, and then calculate the sentiment strength of review based on the extracted feature phrases. The strength of the opinion phrase is determined by the strength of the adjective word along with the adverb that modifies it. We mark the strength of adverbs manually and employ the link analysis method for calculation of adjective strength based on a progressive relation between adjective words. Experimental results show that our proposed approach is efficient and reaches a precision performance which is 5.7% higher than that without considering the adjective sentiment strength. Our approach also achieves a good performance on five-scale evaluation. The effectiveness and scalability of our approach will be further evaluated on more different review datasets in the future.

Acknowledgments. The work described in this paper was fully supported by a grant from City University of Hong Kong (Project No. 7002488).

The work of Yao Lu and Yinlong Xu was supported by the National Natural Science Foundation of China under Grant No. 60773036.

References

1. Pang, B., Lee, L.: Opinion Mining and Sentiment Analysis. Foundations and Trends in Information Retrieval 2(1-2), 1–135 (2008)
2. Turney, P.D.: Thumbs up or Thumbs down? Semantic Orientation Applied to Unsupervised Classification of Reviews. In: 40th Annual Meeting of the Association for Computational Linguistics, pp. 417–424 (2002)
3. Hatzivassiloglou, V., Wiebe, J.M.: Effects of Adjective Orientation and Gradability on Sentence Subjective. In: 18th International Conference on Computational Linguistics, pp. 299–305 (2000)
4. Wiebe, J.M.: Learning Subjective Adjectives from Corpora. In: 17th National Conference on Artificial Intelligence, pp. 735–740 (2000)
5. Hu, M., Liu, B.: Mining and Summarizing Customer reviews. In: 10th ACM SIGKDD Conference on Knowledge Discovery and Data Mining, pp. 168–177 (2004)
6. Hu, M., Liu, B.: Mining opinion features in customer reviews. In: 19th National Conference on Artificial Intellgience, pp. 755–760 (2004)
7. Agrawal, R., Srikant, R.: Fast Algorithm for Mining Association Rules in Large Database. In: 20th International Conference on Very Large Data Bases, pp. 487–499 (1994)
8. Fellbaum, C.: WordNet: an Electronic Lexical Database. MIT Press, Cambridge (1998)
9. Pang, B., Lee, L., Vaithyanathan, S.: Thumbs up? Sentiment Classification using Machine Learning Techniques. In: 7th Conference on Empirical Methods in Natural Language Processing, pp. 79–86 (2002)
10. Cui, H., Mittal, V., Datar, M.: Comparative experiments on sentiment classification for online product reviews. In: 21st National Conference on Artificial Intelligence, pp. 1265–1270 (2006)
11. Dave, K., Lawrence, S., Pennock, D.M.: Mining the Peanut Gallery: Opinion Extraction and Semantic Classification of Product Reviews. In: 12th International World Wide Web Conference, pp. 519–528 (2003)
12. Esuli, A., Sebastiani, F.: Determining Term Subjectivity and Term Orientation for Opinion Mining. In: 11th Conference of the European Chapter of the Association of Computational Linguistics, pp. 193–200 (2006)
13. Wilson, T., Wiebe, J., Hoffmann, P.: Recognizing Contextual Polarity in Phrase-level Sentiment Analysis. In: Conference on Human Language Technology and Empirical Methods in Natural Language Processing, pp. 347–354 (2005)
14. Zagibalov, T., Carroll, J.: Unsupervised Classification of Sentiment and Objectivity in Chinese text. In: 3rd International Joint Conference on Natural Language Processing, pp. 304–311 (2008)
15. Pang, B., Lee, L.: Seeing Stars: Exploiting Class Relationships for Sentiment Categorization with Respect to Rating Scales. In: 43rd Annual Meeting of the Association for Computational Linguistics, pp. 115–124 (2005)
16. Snyder, B., Barzilay, R.: Multiple Aspect Ranking using the Good Grief Algorithm. In: Annual Conference of the North American Chapter of the Association for Computational Linguistics, pp. 300–307 (2007)

17. Williams, G.K., Anand, S.S.: Predicting the Polarity of Adjecives Using Wordnet. In: 3rd International AAAI Conference on Weblogs and Social Media, pp. 346–349 (2009)
18. Zhang, H., Wang, M., Lv, Z., Zhang, X.: Institute of Computing Technology, Chinese Lexical Analysis System: ICTCLAS 3.0, `http://ictclas.org`
19. Zhang, J., Tang, J., Li, J.Z.: Expert Finding in a Social Network, In: 12th International Conference on Database Systems for Advanced Application, pp. 1066–1069 (2007)
20. Felzenszwalb, P.F., Huttenlocher, D.P.: Efficient Belief Propagation for Early Vision. International Journal of Computer Vision 70(1), 41–54 (2006)

Semantic Entity Detection by Integrating CRF and SVM*

Peng Cai, Hangzai Luo, and Aoying Zhou

Institute of Massive Computing, East China Normal University, China
pengcai2010@gmail.com,
{hzluo,ayzhou}@sei.ecnu.edu.cn

Abstract. Semantic entity detection is very important for extracting and representing the abundant semantic information of multimedia documents. In comparison with other media, e.g. video, image and audio, text expresses semantics more directly and often serves as a bridge in cross-media analysis. However, semantic entity detection from text is still a difficult problem because of the complexity of natural language. In this paper, we propose a novel framework which takes the advantages of both CRF (conditional random fields) and SVM (support vector machines), and present its application to semantic entity detection. Using this framework, context features are represented as the probability of entity boundary and extracted via CRF, and then linguistic and statistical features are extracted via large-scale text document analysis. Finally, all extracted features are integrated and used to perform the classification. As our algorithm systematically integrates the context, linguistic and statistical features, it may outperform traditional algorithms that only adopt part of the features.

1 Introduction

Semantic analysis is the basis of all advanced multimedia applications. As semantic entities, such as persons, products, events etc, carry the most useful semantics, it is essential to detect semantic entities accurately from multimedia documents for semantic analysis. Recently, cross-media analysis approaches have attracted wide attention of researchers because their capability of integrating valuable information of different media (video, image, audio, text)[3,2,12,13,14]. Among which, text is often the most important medium because its semantic analysis technique is more mature than the ones of other media. Researchers focusing on video, image or audio often use the text as semantics directly. However, the semantic analysis of text is still a difficult problem due to the complexity of natural language. As a result, the first problem for cross-media analysis is to extract proper semantic entities from text.

There are two general approaches for semantic entity detection in text. The first approach is based on sequence annotation techniques. In natural language

* This work is supported by NSFC under Grant No. 60925008 and 973 program under Grant No. 2010CB731402.

L. Chen et al. (Eds.): WAIM 2010, LNCS 6184, pp. 483–494, 2010.

analysis area, the similar task, named entity recognition, is resolved by adopting the state-of-the-art sequence model, i.e. CRF, proposed by John Lafferty [11]. As the CRF is the most advanced sequence annotation algorithm, it can catch and utilize the short context feature efficiently and effectively. However, CRF prefers to treat an entity as several labels rather than take it as a whole. It leads that some entity-level and holistic features can't be used effectively.

The second approach for semantic entity detection is to treat it as a classification problem. The most advanced classification algorithm is SVM. By using SVM to detect entity from sequence data, entity-level and holistic features can be integrated efficiently. However, because of the complexity of natural language, it may need millions of dimensions to represent the full information of short context. Due to the curse of dimensionality, classification based approaches can only utilize very limited short context features.

Based on the above observation, the best approach for the semantic entity detection should take the advantages of both CRF and SVM. In this paper, we have developed a novel framework for semantic entity detection via integrating CRF and SVM: (a) short context features are represented as the probability of entity boundary and extracted via CRF; (b) linguistic and statistical features are extracted via large-scale text document analysis; (c) All of extracted features are integrated to perform classification.

The rest of this paper is organized as follows. Related work is reviewed in section 2. In section 3, we introduce some statistical and linguistic features for semantic entity detection, which are ignored in traditional named entity recognition. Section 4 presents the framework which combines CRF and SVM for integrating context, linguistic and statistical features. Experimental results are demonstrated in section 5. Finally, we conclude the paper and give future work in section 6.

2 Related Work

Both CRF and SVM are the state-of-the-art classifiers in sequence label model and traditional classification model respectively. CRF has been extended for different tasks, e.g. Semi-CRF for information extraction [16]. SVM also has been extended for sequence label learning, i.e. structured SVM [17,18]. Although CRF and SVM are based on different philosophy, their performances are very close in sequential prediction if proper feature combination is chosen[10].

Semantic entity detection is similar to named entity recognition, which is the typical application of sequence label model [15]. In this task, CRF has been widely applied in multiple languages[7,1]. The traditional approaches, involving CRF and SVM [9], assume that the short context information provides sufficient evidence for entity detection. For instance, "American International Group" and "LENOVO Co., Ltd" are easy to be recognized, where the first letter of all words is uppercase and "Co., Ltd" is a strong context cue. However, the capitalization can't be guaranteed in web text [19]. Furthermore, in addition to these simple entities, some complex semantic entities such as "AIG bonus", "iPod Nano" and "flying man" are difficult to be detected because of the weak context signal. Thus, the above assumption is feasible only in regular documents, e.g. news report. In the multimedia application , the documents from web usually contain diverse subjects and have different style, which make the performance of traditional method decrease.

Recently, two approaches for combining SVM and CRF were proposed[8,5]. [8] integrated SVM with CRF for handwriting recognition via taking the output of SVM as features for CRF. In handwriting recognition, [8] represented an object with a sequence of data points, and objects were independent to each other. In comparison to [8] , Our framework focuses on detecting entity which embedded in a sequence, i.e. semantic entity in sentence, and take the output of CRF as features for SVM. In [5], CRF and SVM were combined for named entity recognition via majority voting approach. This combination didn't make full use of their respective advantages and couldn't represent the feature of semantic entity by a unified way.

Today, we often need to deal with massive amounts of web pages. Under the circumstances, some statistical information may help for semantic entity detection, which may be extracted via large-scale documents analysis. Especially, when complex entities haven't obvious context cue but they appear frequently in diverse documents, statistical features can complement their short context features. In web-scale document collection, [4] only used a simple n-gram statistics, i.e. point-wise mutual information, for locating complex entities. Although n-gram statistics are useful for detecting complex entities, they need to be integrated with context information so as to achieve better performance. In summary, without effectively integrating all useful features, existing entity detection techniques can't attain the optimal performance.

3 Statistical and Linguistic Features

Statistical and linguistic features provide useful evidence for semantic entity detection from holistic point of view, which ignored in traditional named entity detection. By analyzing large-scale web documents, we observed that some complex semantic entities often appeared frequently in different contexts as a whole. See Table 1, as "iPod Nano" appeared at many websites, its statistical features, such as mutual dependence between "iPod" and "Nano" and context independence of "iPod Nano", significantly differ with common n-gram strings. Based on this observation, statistical features such as mutual dependence in components and entity context independence can help for semantic entity detection. Additionally, from linguistic point of view, some words prefer to serve as the head of entity, e.g. "Michael", but other tend to be located at the front, e.g. "The". Thus, the probability that each word is located at different position of semantic entity can also be used as features for entity detection.

Before diving into the details of these features, we introduce some notations used in this paper. Given a text sentence X^k , let $X^k = \{x_1, x_2, \ldots, x_n\}$, where x_i is the minimal semantic unit, i.e. word. $X^k_{[i,j]} = \{x_i, x_{i+1}, \ldots, x_j\}$, where

Table 1. "iPod Nano" was mentioned in different websites

`http://news.cnet.com/first-look-apple-ipod-nano-4g/`
The only bummer so far regarding the new ***iPod Nano*** is that despite the similarities of screen size and features, Apple is not offering an upgrade path for ***iPod Nano*** 3G users to get their hands on features such as on-device Genius playlist creation or increased accessibility features. Otherwise, sound quality seems to be about on a par with previous iPods, and battery life ratings of 24 hours for music and 4 hours are nearly identical to last year's specs, which promised 24 hours of audio and 5 hours of video. I'll be writing up my full review as soon as possible with more ***iPod Nano*** 4G details to share. Stay tuned....
`http://www.highbeam.com/doc/1G1-135894857.html`
The ***iPod Nano*** features an ultra-portable, lightweight design with a gorgeous color screen, Apple's patent pending Click Wheel and the ability to hold 1,000 songs or 25,000 photos. ***iPod Nano*** works seamlessly with the iTunes(R) Music Store, the world's number one digital music service. The ***iPod Nano*** is available ...
`http://blog.makezine.com/archive/2005/09/how_to_ipod_nano_hacking.html`
The new ***iPod Nano*** is out and while it's not as hackable (yet) as its older cousins, you can do a few things like change the text strings, mod the font and even change the graphics (sorta). Here's HOW TO mod a pod, a work in progress for the ***iPod Nano***....

$1 \le i \le j \le n$, denotes subsequence of X^k. The aim of our framework is to make a decision whether $X^k_{[i,j]}$ is a semantic entity or not.

3.1 Mutual Dependence among Components of Entity

A complex semantic entity often contains several components, and these components always emerge together. For example, "iPod Nano" appeared on many websites when the product came to the market, thus, strong dependence existed between "iPod" and "Nano". A measurement similar to mutual information is used to measure this correlation, defined as follows:

$$MI(X^k_{[i,j]}) = \begin{cases} \frac{C(x_i \ldots x_j)}{\sum_{c=i}^{j} C(x_c)} & (j > i) \\ 1 & (j = i) \end{cases} \tag{1}$$

where the function $C(.)$ denotes the count of n-gram in document collection. Intuitively, if $X^k_{[i,j]}$ is a semantic entity, its components i.e. $x_i, x_{i+1}, \ldots, x_j$ always emerged together in different documents, and then the value of $MI(X^k_{[i,j]})$ usually would be not small. It's noted that $MI(X^k_{[i,j]})$ is used as feature together with the length of $X^k_{[i,j]}$ which has significant influence on the value of $MI(X^k_{[i,j]})$.

3.2 Context Independence of Entity

Semantic entities are often mentioned at all kinds of contexts. See table 1, "iPod Nano" is surrounded by diverse words, which means strong context independence.

Based on this observation, we use the number of distinct words around $X^k_{[i,j]}$ to measure its context independence. Generally speaking, semantic entities have much stronger context independence than non-entity subsequences. In addition, $X^k_{[i,j]}$ may be a semantic entity in local document but not in other documents because of entity disambiguation. For instance, "New York" may be a city name but not if "Times" follows it. Context independence is helpful for resolving this problem, because when "New York" is a city name in local document, its left and right context independence would be strong. However, if the correct entity is "New York Times" in the document, the phrase "New York" will not have strong right context independence, because "Times" always follows it at the right. Therefore, we calculated context independence of $X^k_{[i,j]}$ not only within document collection but also its local document. A measurement similar to access variety [6] was used to calculate context independence. Given $X^k_{[i,j]}$, the *left context independence* in local document can be defined as follows:

$$LCI_{local}(X^k_{[i,j]}) = |L_{X^k_{[i,j]}}| \tag{2}$$

where $L_{X^k_{[i,j]}}=\{x|x, x_i, \ldots, x_j$ is subsequence of X^k, and X^k located in local document$\}$, $|L_{X^k_{[i,j]}}|$ represents the count of distinct words. The right context independence in local document and context independence in document collection can be defined similarly.

3.3 Adjacent Stop Words

Semantic entities are often surrounded by stop words. See table 1, stop words, such as "the", "is" and "new", appear at the left or right of "iPod Nano". Based on this observation, *inverse document frequency* is used to measure this property. Given a word x_{i-1}, which represents the left word to $X^k_{[i,j]}$, $IDF(x_{i-1})$ is defined as follows:

$$IDF(x_{i-1}) = \begin{cases} \log(\frac{N}{N_{x_{i-1}}}) & (i-1 \geq 1) \\ 0 & \text{otherwise} \end{cases} \tag{3}$$

Where N denotes the number of documents and $N_{x_{i-1}}$ represents the number of documents containing x_{i-1}. The definition of $IDF(x_{j+1})$ is similar.

3.4 Linguistic Features

In semantic entity detection, we consider four positions are important, i.e. the left, head, end and right of entity. Give a word w, the probability that w is located at different positions may be calculated via analyzing training set, which defined as follows:

$$P_L(w) = \frac{C(wE)}{C(w)} \tag{4}$$

where $P_L(w)$ represents the probability that w is located at the left of any entity E. The probabilities that w is located at other positions are defined similarly.

4 Integrating CRF and SVM

Although statistical and linguistic information can help semantic entity detection, they can't be directly encoded by CRF , the state-of-the-art model for named entity detection via using short context features. For integrating short context, statistical and linguistic features, we propose the framework that combines CRF and SVM by using CRF to extract the probability of entity boundary , and then taking it as feature for SVM.

4.1 Marginal Probability of Entity Boundary

A tag set is used to annotate each observation variable x_i in CRF model. In this paper, we adopt tag set $L = \{\text{“}S\text{”}, \text{“}B\text{”}, \text{“}I\text{”}, \text{“}E\text{”}, \text{“}O\text{”}\}$, where “S” indicates x_i is a single-word entity , “B”, “I” and “E” indicate x_i located at the beginning, intermediate and end in multi-word entity respectively, and “O” represents x_i out of any entity. $Y^k = \{y_1, y_2, \ldots, y_n\}$ denotes the tag sequence corresponding to $X^k = \{x_1, x_2, \ldots, x_n\}$, where $y_i \in L$ and $1 \leq i \leq n$. Given a training set $D = \{X^k, Y^k\}$, The training goal of CRF is to find distribution $P(Y|X)$ via maximizing conditional log-likelihood [11].

The main difficulty in entity detection is to accurately determine its boundary, especially to multi-word entity. Therefore, the marginal probabilities, i.e. $P(y_i = \text{“}B\text{”}|X^k)$ and $P(y_j = \text{“}E\text{”}|X^k)$, are the most useful information for determining whether $X^k_{[i,j]}$ is entity or not. For combining CRF with SVM, these two marginal probabilities of entity boundary need to be extracted, which are defined as follows:

$$P_B(X^k_{[i,j]}) = P(y_i = \text{“}B\text{”}|X^k) \quad (j > i) \tag{5}$$

$$P_E(X^k_{[i,j]}) = P(y_j = \text{“}E\text{”}|X^k) \quad (j > i) \tag{6}$$

According to CRF, $P(y_i = \text{“}B\text{”}|X^k)$ and $P(y_j = \text{“}E\text{”}|X^k)$ can be derived from equation 7 and 8, which may be calculated effectively via dynamic programming.

$$P(y_i = \text{“}B\text{”}|X^k) = \sum_{\substack{Y' = y_1 \cdots y_i \cdots y_j \cdots y_n \\ \wedge\, y_i = \text{“}B\text{”}}} P(Y'|X^k) \quad (j > i) \tag{7}$$

$$P(y_j = \text{“}E\text{”}|X^k) = \sum_{\substack{Y' = y_1 \cdots y_i \cdots y_j \cdots y_n \\ \wedge\, y_j = \text{“}E\text{”}}} P(Y'|X^k) \quad (j > i) \tag{8}$$

However, it's insufficient only using $P_B(X^k_{[i,j]})$ and $P_E(X^k_{[i,j]})$ to describe the probabilities of entity boundary, because they may provide misguided information sometimes. For example, if two entities exist in one sentence, the corresponding tag sequence may be “B I E O O B E”. Although both $P_B(X^k_{[1,7]})$ and

$P_E(X^k_{[1,7]})$ have high probability , $X^k_{[1,7]}$ is not an entity. To resolve this problem, we use $P_I(X^k_{[i,j]})$ to measure the probability that x_c located at the inside of entity where $i+1 \leq c \leq j-1$, which defined as follows:

$$P_I(X^k_{[i,j]}) = \begin{cases} \frac{\sum_{c=i+1}^{j-1} P(y_c=\text{“}I\text{”}|X^k)}{j-i-1} & (j-i-1>0) \\ \frac{P_B(X^k_{[i,j]})+P_E(X^k_{[i,j]})}{2} & (j-i-1=0) \end{cases} \quad (9)$$

Similarly, $P(y_c = \text{“}I\text{”}|X^k)$ can be extracted via CRF using equation 10:

$$P(y_c = \text{“}I\text{”}|X^k) = \sum_{\substack{Y'=y_1\cdots y_i\cdots y_c\cdots,y_j\cdots,y_n \\ \wedge\, y_c=\text{“}I\text{”}}} P(Y'|X^k) \quad (j>i) \quad (10)$$

To single-word entity, $P_B(X^k_{[i,j]})$, $P_I(X^k_{[i,j]})$ and $P_E(X^k_{[i,j]})$ are represented with $P(y_i = \text{“}S\text{”}|X^k)$. By extracting three marginal probabilities, short context information of $X^k_{[i,j]}$ can be represented in a unified way, and then used as features for SVM.

4.2 Two-Stage Training

For training SVM model, the feature vector of $X^k_{[i,j]}$ can be composed by marginal probabilities, statistical and linguistic features. However, the framework combining CRF and SVM can't be trained on single training set. The reason is that CRF may effectively approximate the distribution of training set. This means if $X^k_{[i,j]}$ in training set is an entity, then its marginal probabilities are always very high. Thus, if the feature vector about $X^k_{[i,j]}$ is constructed by marginal probabilities and other entity-level features, then classification model would only focus on the marginal probability features. To resolve this problem, we propose a two-stage training approach , which is shown in algorithm 1.

The goal of two-stage training is to make improvement on the output of CRF by integrating more features. The first stage of training contains step 1 and 2, which divide single training set D_{AB} into two parts, i.e. D_A and D_B, then train CRF on D_B to get model CRF_B. The second stage includes step 3 to 15, where marginal probabilities , statistical and linguistic features are extracted to construct new training set for SVM. In step 6, $SF(X^k_{[i,j]})$ and $LF(X^k_{[i,j]})$ denote the statistical and linguistic feature set, which discussed in section 3.

Similarly, we may use step 3 to 14 to get another feature vector collection V_B, which contain the information about $X^k \in D_B$, and then merge V_A and V_B to form a larger training set, V_{AB}. Training SVM on V_{AB}, the produced model is denoted by *CRF-SVM++*;

It is noted that although statistical features are unsupervised, they must be calculated on test and training set independently. The reason is that if statistical features are calculated within whole dataset, the framework would belong to transductive learning.

Algorithm 1. Two-Stage Training Algorithm

Input:

Training Set $D_{AB} = \{X^k, Y^k\}$;

Output:

Semantic entity detection model: *CRF-SVM*;

Divide training set D_{AB} into two parts, i.e. D_A and D_B.
Train CRF on D_B, get model CRF_B;
for each $X^k \in D_A$ **do**
  for each $X^k_{[i,j]} \in X^k$ **do**
    Use CRF_B to calculate $P_B(X^k_{[i,j]})$, $P_I(X^k_{[i,j]})$ and $P_E(X^k_{[i,j]})$;
    Calculate statistical and linguistic features i.e. $SF(X^{(k)}_{[i,j]})$, $LF(X^k_{[i,j]})$;
    if $X^k_{[i,j]}$ is entity **then**
      y=+1;
    else
      y=-1;
    end if
    add $\langle P_B(X^k_{[i,j]}), P_I(X^k_{[i,j]}), P_E(X^k_{[i,j]}), LF(X^k_{[i,j]}), SF(X^{(k)}_{[i,j]}), y\rangle$ into V_A ;
  end for
end for
Train SVM on V_A, get model *CRF-SVM*;
return *CRF-SVM*;

5 Experiments

5.1 Dataset and Setup

In our experiments, we used three open datasets: CoNLL 2002 Dutch dataset[1], People's Daily[2] and Lancaster Corpus of Mandarin Chinese (LCMC)[3], where semantic entities such as person, location and organization have been annotated. All documents in CoNLL 2002 Dutch dataset and People's Daily only contain single subject, i.e. news reports. The documents in LCMC cover 15 subjects, including fiction, science, religion, news reports etc. Each corpus except People's Daily is divided into three parts, i.e. D_A, D_B and D_C. D_A and D_B serve as training set and D_C as test set. People's Daily only is used as training set for cross corpus experiment. More details about dataset are shown in table 2.

The framework combining CRF and SVM is trained on D_A and D_B. At first stage, CRF is trained on D_A, D_B, and D_{AB}(the union of D_A and D_B) independently to attain models called as CRF_A,CRF_B, CRF respectively. At second stage, V_A is constructed from D_A, where entity boundary probabilities are extracted via CRF_B, statistical features are calculated from D_A and linguistic features are estimated from D_{AB}. Similarly, V_B can be constructed from D_B and merged with V_A to form larger V_{AB} . Finally, *CRF-SVM* is trained on V_A and *CRF-SVM++* is trained on V_{AB}.

[1] http://lcg-www.uia.ac.be/conll2002/ner.tgz
[2] http://icl.pku.edu.cn/icl_groups/corpus/dwldform1.asp
[3] http://www.lancs.ac.uk/fass/projects/corpus/LCMC/

Table 2. Corpus used in experiments

Corpus	Description	D_A	D_B	D_C(test set)
LCMC	Including 500 articles, covering subjects: fiction, science, religion, news reports etc.	200 articles 11338 entities	150 articles 8279 entities	150 articles 10066 entities
CoNLL 2002 Dutch dataset	Containing 3 files, 480 news report.	File1:ned.train 13354 entities	File2:ned.testa 2618 entities	File3:ned.testb 3950 entities
People's Daily	Including 31 days news reports, from 1,Jan,1998 to 31,Jan,1998	1,Jan-15,Jan 14,778 entities	16,Jan-31,Jan 15,249 entities	

The goal of experiments is to compare the performance of *CRF*, *CRF-SVM* and *CRF-SVM++*, all of which trained on the same annotated dataset i.e. D_{AB}. Several questions need to be answered through performance comparison. Firstly, although the state-of-the-art model CRF has been widely used for named entity detection only using short context features, we want to verify whether statistical and linguistic features can improve entity detection, which integrated via the proposed combination of CRF and SVM framework. Secondly, although *CRF-SVM++* is trained on more samples, it is unknown that whether it outperforms *CRF-SVM* or not. In addition, experiments of traditional named entity detection prefer to use the same corpus for training and test, where good performance can be attained usually. However, there is obvious discrepancy between training and test documents in real multimedia application. Thus, generalization abilities of the three models are also compared by training on one corpus and test on another corpus.

5.2 Comparison among *CRF*, *CRF-SVM* and *CRF-SVM++*

The performance of *CRF*, *CRF-SVM* and *CRF-SVM++* on CoNLL 2002 Dutch dataset and LCMC are presented in figure 1(a) and 1(b). It is shown that both *CRF-SVM* and *CRF-SVM++* outperform *CRF*. This means that statistical and linguistic information can improve traditional entity detection only using short context features.

As figure 1(b) is shown, *CRF-SVM* and *CRF-SVM++* make more improvement on LCMC than CoNLL 2002 Dutch dataset. It implies that the performance of *CRF* may decrease when detecting entity in documents with unseen subject. However, both *CRF-SVM* and *CRF-SVM++* have robust performance. One important reason is that *CRF-SVM* and *CRF-SVM++* integrate many statistical and linguistic features, which are domain independent. Another important reason is that generalization ability of this framework is guaranteed with SVM model.

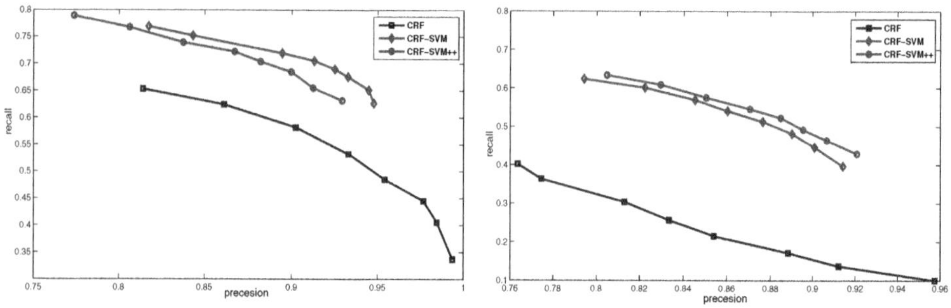

(a) Results on CoNLL 2002 Dutch (b) Results on LCMC

Fig. 1. Results on Dutch and LCMC Dataset

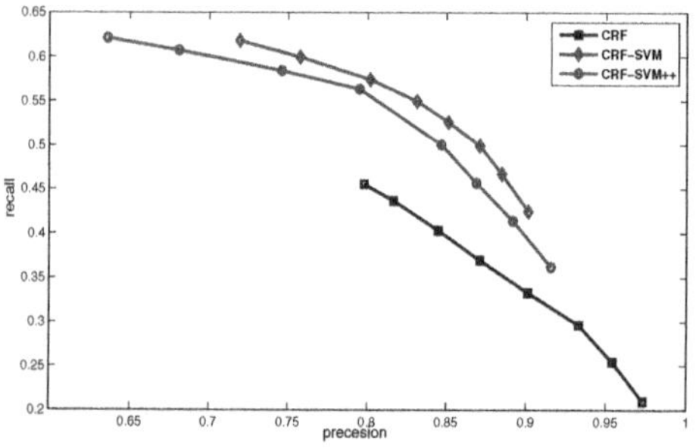

Fig. 2. People' Daily as Training Set, LCMC as Test Set

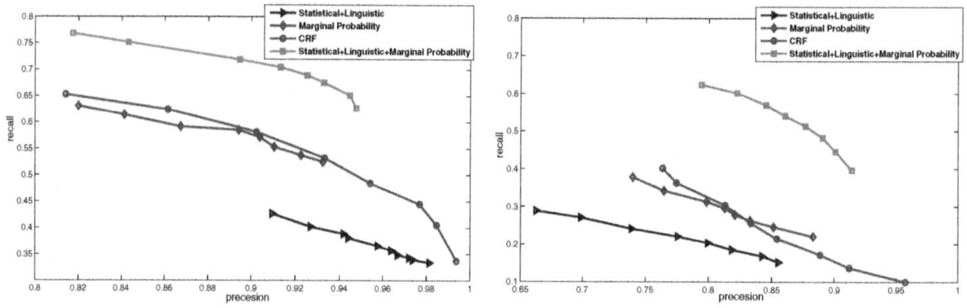

(a) Results on CoNLL 2002 Dutch (b) Results on LCMC

Fig. 3. Results on Dutch and LCMC Dataset under Different Feature Combination

In real applications, e.g. automatic multimedia news recommendation, it is necessary to apply trained model to documents with different style which may not be contained in training corpus. Under this condition, the performance of the three models are evaluated by using People's Daily as training corpus and LCMC as test corpus. Figure 2 presents the results. It's shown that both *CRF-SVM* and *CRF-SVM++* outperform CRF significantly.

Comparing *CRF-SVM* with *CRF-SVM++* from figure 1(a), 1(b) and 2, it's interesting that their performances are very close although *CRF-SVM++* uses more training samples than *CRF-SVM*. The reason is V_B contains the similar information to V_A. Thus, V_{AB} cannot extract extra information by merging them.

5.3 Results under Different Feature Combination

Figure 3(a) and 3(b) present the performance of our framework under different feature combination on CoNLL 2002 Dutch and LCMC dataset. *Marginal Probability* denotes that the framework only adopted short context feature, i.e. marginal probabilities of $X^k_{[i,j]}$, which extracted via CRF. *Statistical+Linguistic* represents that the framework employed statistical and linguistic features, not using marginal probability features. It's obvious that *Statistical+Linguistic* can't outperform *Marginal Probability* and *CRF*, suggesting that short context features are more efficient for entity detection than statistical and linguistic features. However, short context, statistical and linguistic features describe entity from different point of view respectively, which are orthogonal and can complement each other. Thus, *Statistical+Linguistic+Marginal Probability* may get significant improvement via integrating all of them.

Both figure 3(a) and 3(b) illustrate that *Marginal Probability* is very close to *CRF*. This means that almost no information was lost when marginal probability of entity boundary being extracted via CRF. This result indicates that our proposed framework can be extended to other relevant tasks, because more specific features can be integrated with these marginal probabilities.

6 Conclusion and Future Work

In this paper, we present a novel framework to extract the semantic entity by integrating CRF and SVM, which is the basis of deep semantic analysis. The performance of this framework for semantic entity detection was evaluated on different language dataset. The experimental results show that this framework can effectively integrate large amounts of short context features, statistical and linguistic features to semantic entity detection. As a result, it outperforms traditional algorithms that only adopt part of the features.

An object in real world may have many different representations. For instance, a person may have been referenced by distinct names, images and video shots. Therefore, to model the comprehensive semantics of entities, all relevant multimedia information for each semantic entity must be integrated into a multimedia semantic entity. To achieve this goal, we will merge different representations for unique entity in text firstly, and then take the consistent semantic entities as a bridge across other media.

References

1. Chen, W., Zhang, Y., Isahara, H.: Chinese named entity recognition with conditional random fields. In: 5th SIGHAN Workshop on Chinese Language Processing (2006)
2. Christel, M.G., Hauptmann, A.G., Wactlar, H.D., Ng, T.D.: Collages as dynamic summaries for news video. In: ACM Multimedia, pp. 561–569 (2002)
3. Deschacht, K., Moens, M.-F.: Text analysis for automatic image annotation. In: ACL (2007)
4. Downey, D., Broadhead, M., Etzioni, O.: Locating complex named entities in web text. In: IJCAI, pp. 2733–2739 (2007)
5. Ekbal, A., Bandyopadhyay, S.: Bengali named entity recognition using classifier combination. In: ICAPR, pp. 259–262 (2009)
6. Feng, H., Chen, K., Deng, X., Zheng, W.: Accessor variety criteria for chinese word extraction. Computational Linguistics 30(1), 75–93 (2004)
7. Florian, R., Ittycheriah, A., Jing, H., Zhang, T.: Named entity recognition through classifier combination. In: Proceedings of CoNLL 2003, pp. 168–171 (2003)
8. Hoefel, G., Elkan, C.: Learning a two-stage svm/crf sequence classifier. In: CIKM, pp. 271–278 (2008)
9. Isozaki, H., Kazawa, H.: Efficient support vector classifiers for named entity recognition. In: Proceedings of the 19th International Conference on Computational Linguistics (COLING 2002), pp. 390–396 (2002)
10. Keerthi, S.S., Sundararaja, S.: Crf versus svm-struct for sequence labeling. Technical report, Yahoo Research (2007)
11. Lafferty, J.D., McCallum, A., Pereira, F.C.N.: Conditional random fields: Probabilistic models for segmenting and labeling sequence data. In: ICML, pp. 282–289 (2001)
12. Luo, H., Cai, P., Gong, W., Fan, J.: Semantic entity-relationship model for large-scale multimedia news exploration and recommendation. In: Boll, S., Tian, Q., Zhang, L., Zhang, Z., Chen, Y.-P.P. (eds.) MMM 2010. LNCS, vol. 5916, pp. 522–532. Springer, Heidelberg (2010)
13. Luo, H., Fan, J., Keim, D.A., Satoh, S.: Personalized news video recommendation. In: Huet, B., Smeaton, A., Mayer-Patel, K., Avrithis, Y. (eds.) MMM 2009. LNCS, vol. 5371, pp. 459–471. Springer, Heidelberg (2009)
14. Luo, H., Fan, J., Satoh, S., Yang, J., Ribarsky, W.: Integrating multi-modal content analysis and hyperbolic visualization for large-scale news video retrieval and exploration. Image Communication 53, 538–553 (2008)
15. Mccallum, A., Li, W.: Early results for named entity recognition with conditional random fields, feature induction and web-enhanced lexicons. In: CoNLL (2003)
16. Sarawagi, S., Cohen, W.W.: Semi-markov conditional random fields for information extraction. In: NIPS (2004)
17. Taskar, B., Guestrin, C., Koller, D.: Max-margin markov networks. In: NIPS (2003)
18. Tsochantaridis, I., Joachims, T., Hofmann, T., Altun, Y.: Large margin methods for structured and interdependent output variables. Journal of Machine Learning Research 6, 1453–1484 (2005)
19. Whitelaw, C., Kehlenbeck, A., Petrovic, N., Ungar, L.H.: Web-scale named entity recognition. In: CIKM, pp. 123–132 (2008)

An Incremental Method for Causal Network Construction

Hiroshi Ishii, Qiang Ma, and Masatoshi Yoshikawa

Graduate School of Informatics, Kyoto University
Yoshida Honmachi, Sakyo, Kyoto 606-8501, Japan

Abstract. We propose a novel method of constructing causal networks to clarify the relationships among events. Since events and their relationships continually change, our method works in an incremental manner. There are two problems in the conventional methods of constructing causal networks that use keywords representing events: 1) similar events detection to network construction is a time-consuming task, and 2) because the merge operation depends on appearing order of events there is a consistency issue in the incremental construction. In this paper, as the representation model, we propose a Topic-Event Causal network model (TEC model) in which the topic and details of an event are separately represented by using structured keywords. We cluster events by using the topic keyword and then detect similar events per each cluster. This fashion will reduce the comparison times of events. When we compute the similarity of two events in a topic, since we compare the pair of SVO tuples of vertices based on WordNet, we solve the difference in the word used and the lexical ambiguity and keep the consistency with a causal network. We also show experimental results to demonstrate its usefulness.

1 Introduction

Usually, future prediction and decision making require to understand the relationships among events in the real world. Causal network is such a kind of important information which can be used to help us understand the relationships among event. Numerous technologies have been developed to extract causal relations from news articles and documents [1,2,3,4,5,6]. However, conventional methods usually construct causal network in a batch manner and rarely update it. As a result, it is not easy to access the newest causal network and will delay the decision making. In this paper, we propose an incremental method of causal network construction.

Generally, for a causal network, a causal relation is expressed using a directed graph. A source vertex represents the cause event, and a destination vertex represents the result event. To express a chain of causal relation, vertices representing similar event are merged. However, conventional methods using a set of keywords representing an event can't efficiently construct causal networks because of two problems below.

L. Chen et al. (Eds.): WAIM 2010, LNCS 6184, pp. 495–506, 2010.

- Times of comparison for detecting vertices denoting similar event are too many to network construction.
- Because the merging operation is ranked by the appearing order, there is a consistency issue in the incremental construction.

We propose a Topic-Event Causal network model for representing causal relations and a construction method of causal network based on the model. In the TEC model, the topic and details of an event are separately represented by using structured keywords.

- The topic of an event is represented by topic keywords, which are terms appearing frequently in titles of the related news articles. The cause and result vertices of a causal relation contain same topic keywords.
- The detail of an event is represented by a SVO tuple, which consists of a tuple of subject, object, and verb keywords extracted from phrases including causal relation in an article.

Similar vertices of event are detected as follows.

- Step1: we cluster causal relations by using the topic keywords. It is to say, similar event vertices should relate to a same topic. This fashion will reduce the comparison times of vertices in network construction.
- Step2: we compare the details of events per topic to detect similar ones. For each pair of SVO tuples in a same topic, we compare their subject, object and verb phrases respectively by using WordNet. If their subject, object and verb phrases have high relatedness based on WordNet, we say that two SVO tuples are similar, and they may represent same event and should be merged. Because we merge similar event vertices based on their relatedness of concept and we need not to compute the similarity by using vector space model, we can construct causal network without dependency on appearing sequence of events.

The experimental results show that we can reduce the number of times of vertex comparison with no loss of the precision and recall.

2 Related Work

There are various methods [4,5,6] constructing the causal network by using methods of extracting the causal relations[4,5,6].

In another related research described in [7], event threading was used for the construction. This method finds causal relations by clustering and the simulated annealing algorithm. It doesn't need any dictionaries by a method with such statistical approach but need a lot of articles. In case-frame dictionary methods [4,5], a causal network is constructed from documents to form a causal network of common knowledge. In another research [6], a causal network is constructed from web pages. These methods [4,5,6] can find causal relation from only one article. However, in conventional approaches, the similarity of event vertices is not easy to compute because keywords are obtained only from causal phrases. Hence, merge and reduction of vertices becomes difficult. To solve this problem, we extended the types of keyword used.

In case-frame dictionary methods [4,5], there is no method of organizing a causal network. In the research described in [6], there is no method of merging the vertices, and the distance between each pair of vertices represents the similarity between them. However, if the causal network has a lot of vertices and that become complex, users have difficulty in finding and understanding the chain of causal relation. For this, in our research, we organize causal networks incrementally by repeating merging and reducing.

3 TEC Model

We propose a Topic-Event Causal network model to represent and construct network of causal relations. In TEC model, the topic and details of an event are represented separately. A topic is represented by using topic keywords and the details are represented by using a SVO tuple. As we mentioned before, a SVO tuple consists of subject, object and verb keywords for representing an event. In the TEC model, causal relations are represented by an edge-labeled directed graph, i.e., causal network. The source and destination vertices denotes the causal and result events of a causal relation, respectively. There is an importance score labeled on each edge showing the priority of the causal relation. An causal network CN is expressed as follows.

$$CN := (Vs, Ed, L) \tag{1}$$

Vs is the event vertex set. Ed denotes the edge set. L is the set of edge label denoting the importance of that causal relation. v in Vs consists of a pair of topic T and details Ev in the event.

$$v := (T, Ev) \qquad T := \{t_i | i = 1, ...n\} \qquad Ev := (S, V, O)$$

$$S := \{s_j | j = 1, ...x\} \quad V := \{v_k | k = 1, ...y\} \quad O := \{o_l | l = 1, ...z\} \tag{2}$$

Here, k_i is a topic keyword. s_j,v_k and o_l are respective subject, verb and object keywords. Each edge e is expressed as follows.

$$e := (v_{s_e}, v_{d_e}, h_e) \tag{3}$$

v_{s_e} is a source vertex; v_{d_e} is a destination vertex, and h_e is the label denoting the importance score of that edge. The importance score of an edge is determined by the frequency of causal relations. Whenever a causal relation is extracted, the default importance score of the edge is 1. Intuitively, the score becomes larger when the causal relations are extracted frequently. The method of calculating the importance score is described in Section 4.4. Figure 1 shows an example representing a causal relation based on the TEC model.

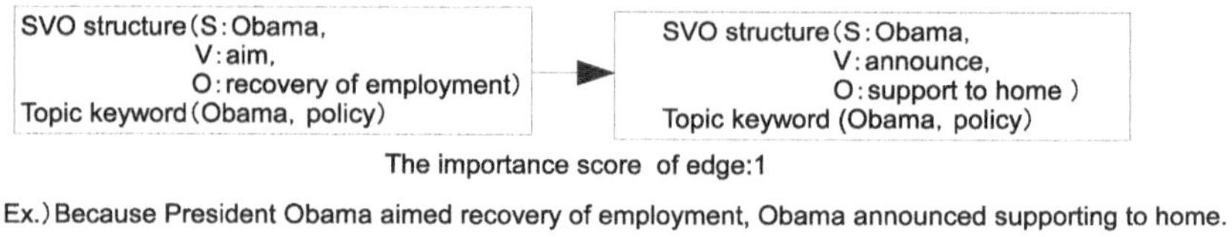

Fig. 1. Causal relation in TEC model

4 Construction of Causal Network Using TEC Model

We construct the causal network based on TEC model. Causal relations are extracted from news articles by using 'clue phrase'. Similar event vertices are detected and merged, and unnecessary causal relations will be deleted in the network constructing process. Since events and relations of them are continuously changing as time goes by, it is required to update the causal network incrementally. In our current work, a causal network is firstly constructed from the articles reported in a certain period. Then we merge the current network with the new one constructed from new articles to update the causal network. Figure 2(a) shows how we extract causal relations (from new articles) in a certain period and make a causal network ((1) (2)). Secondly, we constructs the causal network by performing merging and reduction on the extracted causal network ((3) (4)). Next, the system merges vertices and reduces edges between the new causal network and the previously constructed one. In short, as shown by the cycle in Figure 2, the network is updated by repeating extraction, merging and reduction operations for the causal relations.

The detecting and merging similar event vertices are performed for each topic. At first, we group the vertices of causal relations by using their topic keywords. Then, we compute the similarity of SVO tuples to detect similar event vertices for merging. However, when detecting similar event vertices are performed in a certain period (see also step *a (3)* shown in Figure 2.), article are grouped into topics by using Google News service[1]. As a result, we can perform detecting and merging similar event vertices by just compare the details of vertices because they belong to a same topic.

4.1 Collecting News Articles

As a pretreatment of the network construction, we collect news articles by using of Google News. In Google news, news articles are grouped into topic as related articles. In our collection of the news articles, articles of a certain topic should share the same topic keywords.

4.2 Extracting Causal Relations

For the creation of the event vertices, we extract causal relations as follows.

[1] http://news.google.co.jp

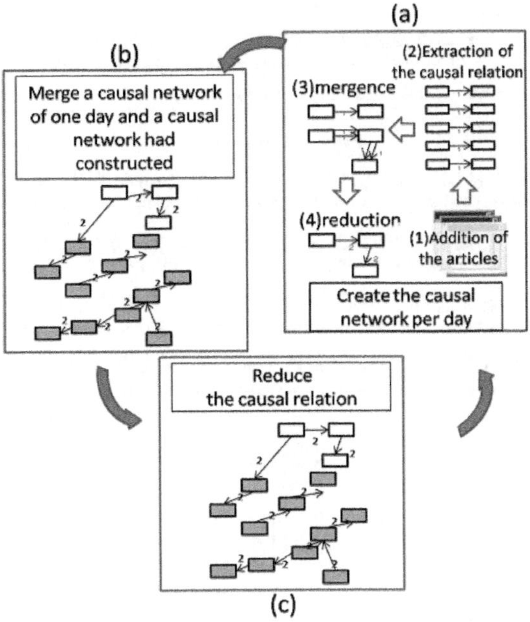

Fig. 2. Incremental Construction of Network

1. Extracting causal relations from news articles
2. Forming event vertices and edges
   a Extracting topic keywords
   b Extracting SVO tuples

Figure 3 shows an example of extracting causal relations from an article.

Extracting Phrase Representing Causal Relations from News Article. To extract causal relations, we used the method based on clue phrases (in Japan) and syntax patterns [3]. A clue phrase is a phrase in a sentence representing a causal relation such as"tame (because)" and "wo haikei ni (behind)". We search the articles for clue phrases and it is supposed that there is a causal relation in the sentence where a clue pharase is detected. Using Cabocha [8], which is a Japanese dependency structure analyzer, we classify the sentences extracted into four syntax patterns.

Pattern A: Both the predicate and subject are effect phrases in a sentence.
"[cause phrase] no tame, [subject of effect phrase] ga [predicate of effect phrase]sita. (Because of [cause phrase], [subject of effect phrase] has [predicate of effect phrase].)"

Pattern B: An effect phrase appears after a cause phrase in a sentence.
"[cause phrase] no tame, [effect phrase] shita. (Because of [cause phrase], it has [effect phrase].)"

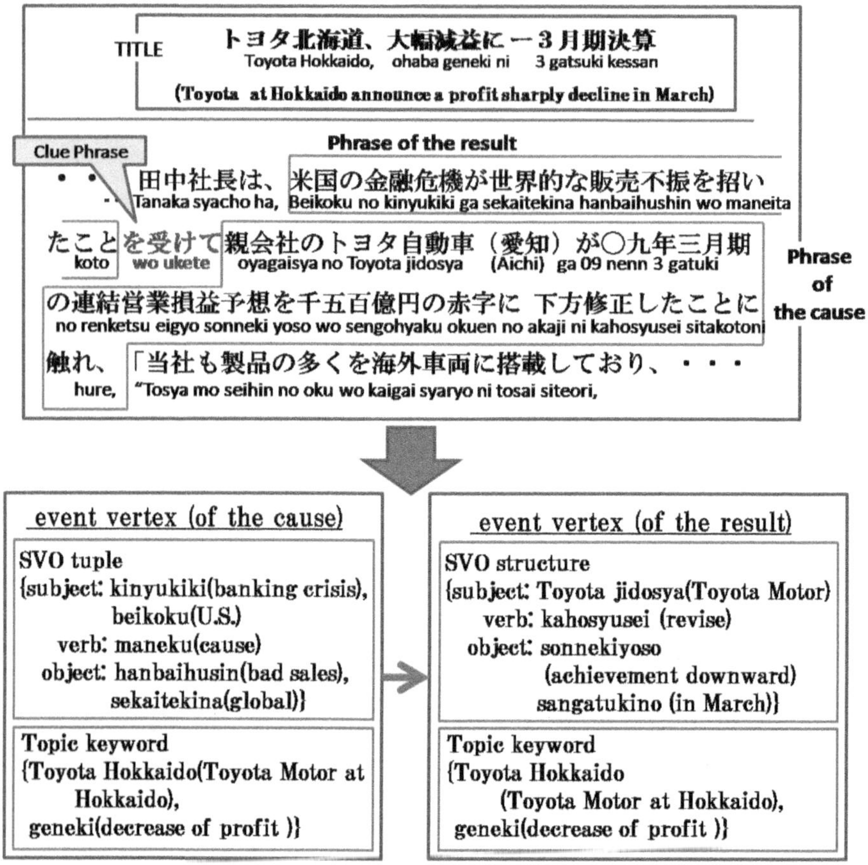

Fig. 3. Extracting Causal Relations from News Article

Pattern C: An effect phrase is the sentence just before a sentence including a clue phrase.
"[effect phrase] shita. [cause phrase] no tame da. (It has [effect phrase]. This is because [cause phrase].)"

Pattern D: A result phrase appears before a cause phrase in a sentence.
"[effect phrase] ha, [cause phrase] tame da. ([effect phrase] was because of [cause phrase].)"

Based on the grammatical features of each syntax pattern, we extract the cause phrase and result phrase from the original sentence. Table 1 shows how we use the main 'clue phrase' currently.

As an example shown in Figure 3, we find a phrase representing a causal relation using the clue phrase "wo ukete(under)". Using Cabocha, the structure we detected is in Pattern A. Here, "Beikoku no kinyukiki ga sekaitekina

Table 1. Clue phrases

Clue phrases
"wo haikei ni(behind)","wo ageru(quoto)","tame(because)","ni tomonau(with)", 'no eikyo ga(effect)","tameda(because)","ni yori(by)","wo ukete(under)", "no koukaga(effect)","no eikyo mo(effect)","ni yotte(by)","kara(because)"

hanbaihusin wo maneita(The Banking crisis in U.S. effected the global sluggish sales)" is the phrase representing the cause event and "Oyagaisya no Toyota jidosya(Aichi) ga 09 nenn 3 gatuki no renketsu eigyo sonneki yoso wo sengo-hyakuokuen no akaji ni kaho syusei sitakoto ni hure("Parent company Toyota Motor (Aichi) revised downward connection operating-profit-or-loss anticipation of the term ended March, 09 to a 150 billion yen deficit" is spoke)" is the phrase representing the result event can be found.

Constructing Event Vertices and Edges from Phrases Representing Causal Relations. As we mentioned before, we use a directed edge to represent a causal relation. Whenever an edge is created, 1 is assigned up to the importance score and topic keywords and SVO tuples of two events are inserted in to each vertex.

(a) Extracting topic keywords k_t
By using Chasen[2], which is a Japanese morphological analyzer, we analyze the titles of related articles and extracted nouns and unknown-words as keywords for further processing. Here, related articles are those in a certain topic obtained from Google News. The words which appear frequently are extracted as the topic keyword T.

(b) Extracting SVO tuples Ev
We use KNP[3] to construct the SVO tuple. We extract keywords of subject, object and verb based on the grammatical frames shown in Table 2. The frames show the relation between noun and verb. As the instances of the extraction, "Beikoku no kinnyukiki ga sekaitekina hanbaihusin wo maneita", "kinyukiki(banking crisis)" are extracted as the subject keywords and "maneita(cause)" are extracted as a verb words according to the "ga"-frame. "sekaitekina(global)" and "hanbaifusin(achievement downward)" as the object kewyords and "maneita(cause)" are extracted as a verb words according to the "wo"-frame.

As shown in Figure 3, the SVO tuple of the vertex of the result event is "Toyota Motor" as the subject, "revise" as the verb and "achievement downward" and "in March" as the object. "Toyota Motor at Hokkaido" and "decrease of profit" in the title are extracted as the topic keywords of the articles.

[2] http://chasen-legacy.sourceforge.jp/
[3] http://nlp.kuee.kyoto-u.ac.jp/nl-resource/knp.html

Table 2. Grammatical frames

grammatical frames
"[object words] + wo + [verb words]"
"[object words] + ni + [verb words]"
"[subject words] + ga + [verb words]"
"[object words] + he + [verb words]"
"[object words] + de + [verb words]"
"[object words] +kara +[verb words]"
"[object words] +to +[verb words]"
"[object words] +yori +[verb words]"

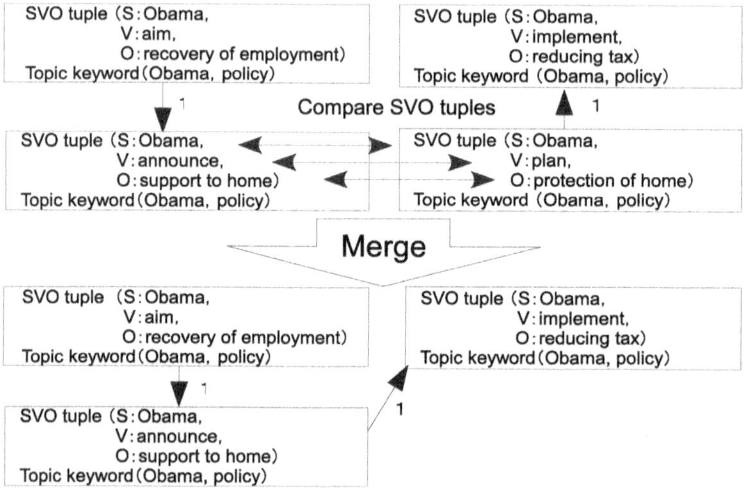

Fig. 4. Merging vertices

4.3 Vertices Merging

To detect similar event vertices, we calculate a topic similarity and a details similarity between each pair of vertices.

- topic similarity: For the calculation of the topic similarities (consine similarities), we represent the topic keywords as vectors based on the vector space model. If the similarity between the pair of topics is larger than the prespecifed threshold, we consider that the articles share a same topic. So we can compute the details similarity between each pair of the SVO tuples in those ariticles.
- details similarity: A details similarity is calculated by the comparison of the pair of SVO tuples of two vertices. Respectively, we calculate the relatedness between their subject, verb and object keywords. Relatedness between two words are computed by using HSO measure [9], in which, WordNet is used

to compute the relatedness score. The details similarity between the details Ev_a and Ev_b of two vertices is calculated as Equation 4.

$$\text{D-sim}(Ev_a, EV_b) = \alpha * relatedness(S_a, S_b) + \beta * relatedness(V_a, V_b) + \gamma * relatedness(O_a, O_b) \quad (4)$$

where, α,β and γ are weight parameters ($\alpha+\beta+\gamma = 1$). If S of a SVO tuples doesn't contain any word, $\alpha = 0$. If O of a SVO tuples doesn't contain any word, $\gamma = 0$. If S and V of a SVO tuples doesn't contain any word, $\gamma = 1$. If O and V of a SVO tuples doesn't contain any word, $\alpha = 1$. If the details similarity is larger than the threshold, we say that two SVO tuples are similar tuples, and they may represent same event and we should merge the vertices represented by them.

Figure 4 shows an example of merging vertices denoting two events: "Obama announced the support to home" and "Obama planed the protection to home". They share the same subject keyword "Obama" and the high relatedness between object keywords ("support" and "protection") and verb keywords ("announce" and "plan") . So we merge the two vertices representing similar event and get a chain of causal relations.

4.4 Reducing the Causal Network

We reduce the size of the causal network for representing a network easy for users to understand. In the reduction method, we compute the sum of the importance scores of duplicative edges when merging similar ones. Based on the importance score of an edge, causal relations with low importance scores are deleted. We call the edges which have similar source and destination vertices duplicative edges. For reduction, we first looks for duplicated edges in the network. If such edges exist, we creates a new edge and gives the sum of the scores of the duplicated edges to the label of the new edge. Finally the original edges are deleted.

5 Experiment

We conducted two experiments: one is the efficiency evaluation of method of separately representing topic and detail keywords; the other is the efficiency evaluation of similarity computation of SVO tuples.

5.1 Experiment I: Evaluation of Separated Representation

We evaluated vertices merging whether we miss pairs of vertices which represent similar events by restrict the calculation for topic using topic keywords. For this experiment, we use 7 set of related articles, 60 articles in Japanese from the economic section of Google News from January 11, 2009 to January 20, 2009. 4 sets, 33 articles related to TOYOTA Motor. Other 3 sets, 27 articles related to

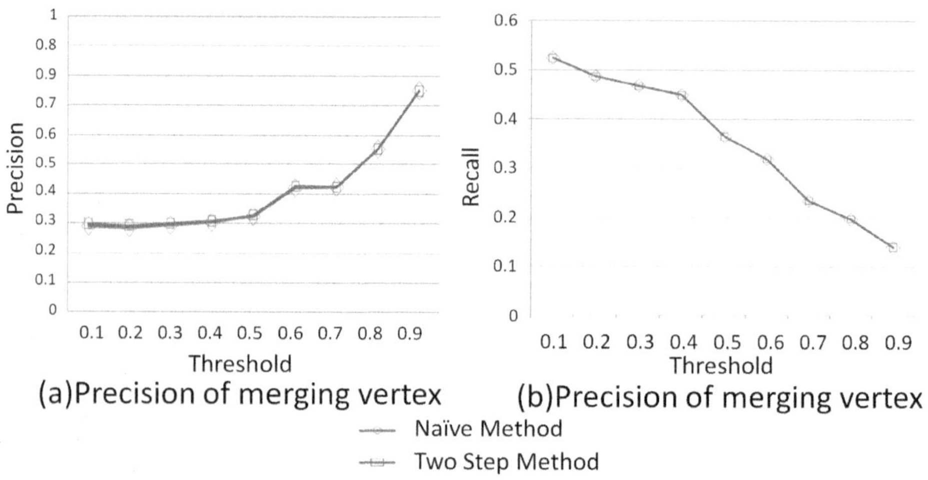

Fig. 5. Results of Experiment I

President Obama. We extracted 43 causal relations, 86 event vertices based on the TEC model from the sets. We calculated the similarity of pairs of vertices for 86 event vertices from the experimental article set. We search the event vertices for the pairs of vertices which represent similar events and 107 pairs of vertices are judged to represent similar events by a human. Precision of vertices merging was defined as in Equation 5.

$$Precision = \frac{\#\ of\ similar\ vertex\ pairs\ judged\ by\ human}{\#\ of\ similar\ vertex\ pairs\ judged\ by\ system} \tag{5}$$

Recall was defined as in Equation 6.

$$Recall = \frac{\#\ of\ vertex\ pair\ judged\ by\ human\ in\ vertex\ pairs\ merged}{\#\ of\ similar\ vertex\ pair\ judged\ by\ human} \tag{6}$$

In the experiment, as the baseline, we use a naïve method which merges vertices based on the similarity of event keywords (keywords contained in the details) based on space vector model. As one variation of our proposed method, a two-step method is used for the experiment. In the two-step method, we first group the news articles into topics and extract causal relations per topic. Then, to merge vertices, we compute the similarity of event keywords as same as that of naïve method.

In Figure 5, there is almost no difference in the results of these two methods. In this experiment, we extracted 84 event vertices. If the process of merging performs for all event vertices (the naïve method), the number of the similarity calculation will be 3486 (=84*83/2). However, If we compute the similarity of topic keywords at first (two-step method), we can split the event vertices into two groups to reduce time of computing event similarity. One group consists

Table 3. Result of vertex merging

threthold	0.50	0.55	0.60	0.65	0.70	0.75
precision	0.40	0.44	0.38	0.38	0.43	0.50
recall	0.5	0.33	0.25	0.25	0.25	0.25

of 50 event vertices about the topic of TOYOTA. The other group consists of 34 event vertices about the topic of USA politics. When the process of merging performs each group, the number of the similarity calculation will be 1786 (=50*49/2+34*33/2). The results show that using that similarity of topics can reduce times of calculation of vertices merging without decreasing precision and recall.

5.2 Experiment II: Evaluation of Similarity Computation of SVO Tuples

For this experiment, we use 19 articles in Japanese which reported about JAL reconstruction from the economic section of Google News from January 09, 2010. The system extracted 25 phrases as those including causal relations. However, 4 phrases didn't include causal phrases. Based on the TEC model, we created 42 event vertices from these 21 causal phrases. We extracted the SVO tuples manually. In the 42 event vertices, the number of pairs of vertex which are manually judged to represent similar event was 11. We calculate the detail similarities between each pair of SVO tuples. At Equation 4, we use $\alpha = 0.4$, $\beta = 0.2$ and $\gamma = 0.4$. If S of a SVO tuples doesn't contain any word, we use $\alpha = 0$, $\beta = 1/3$ and $\gamma = 2/3$. If O doesn't contain any word, we use $\alpha = 2/3$, $\beta = 1/3$ and $\gamma = 0$. Table 3 shows the experimental result. When the similarity threshold of 0.5, our method achieves the best performance. The result shows the chain of causal relations can be found by calculating the details similarities. We need to carry out further experiment with automatic extraction of SVO tuple.

6 Conclusion

We proposed a novel TEC model in which the topic and details of an event are separately represented and propose a incremental causal network construction method based on it. In contrast to conventional causal models, the proposed method can reduce times of calculation of detecting similar events and keep the consistency of the causal network when we incrementally construct it. The experimental results demonstrated the usefulness of our TEC model.

Further study on the construction of the causal network is necessary. We will carry out more experiments and improve the merging and reduction methods based on the results. The time-series features of news articles will be considered to improve construction of the causal network, especially the merge function. The correlation coefficient between cause and result events will also be studied as future work.

Acknowledgment

This research is partly supported by the research for the grant of Scientific Research (No.20700084 and 21013026) made available by MEXT, Japan.

References

1. Girju, R.: Automatic detection of causal relations for question answering. In: Proceedings of the ACL 2003 workshop on Multilingual summarization and question answering, vol. 12, pp. 76–83 (2003)
2. Inui, T., Inui, K., Yuji, M.: Acquiring causal knowledge from text using the connective marker tame (natural-language processing). Transactions of Information Processing Society of Japan 45(3), 919–933 (2004) (in japanese)
3. Sakaji, H., Sekine, S., Masuyama, S.: Extracting causal knowledge using clue phrases and syntactic patterns. In: Yamaguchi, T. (ed.) PAKM 2008. LNCS (LNAI), vol. 5345, pp. 111–122. Springer, Heidelberg (2008)
4. Sato, H., Kasahara, K., Matsuzawa, K.: Transition inferring with simplified causality base. Technical Report of The 56th National Convention of IPSJ (2), 251–252 (1998) (in japanese)
5. Sato, H., Kasahara, K., Matsuzawa, K.: Retrieval of simplified causal knowledge in text and its application. Technical report of IEICE. Thought and language 98, 27–32 (1999)
6. Sato, T., Horita, M.: Assessing the plausibility of inference based on automated construction of causal networks using web-mining. Sociotechnica, 66–74 (2006) (in japanese)
7. Feng, A., Allan, J.: Finding and linking incidents in news. In: Proceedings of the sixteenth ACM Conference on information and knowledge management, pp. 821–830 (2007)
8. Kudo, T., Matsumoto, Y.: Japanese dependency analysis using cascaded chunking, pp. 63–69 (2002)
9. Hirst, G., St Onge, D.: Lexical chains as representations of context for the detection and correction of malapropisms. In: Fellbaum, C. (ed.) WordNet: An Electronic Lexical Database, pp. 305–332. MIT Press, Cambridge (1998)

DCUBE: CUBE on Dirty Databases*

Guohua Jiang, Hongzhi Wang, Shouxu Jiang, Jianzhong Li, and Hong Gao

Institute of Computer Science and Technology, Harbin Institute of Technology,
150001 Harbin, China
marble1@163.com,
{wangzh,jsx,ljz,honggao}@hit.edu.cn

Abstract. In the real world databases, dirty data such as inconsistent data, duplicate data affect the effectiveness of applications with database. It brings new challenges to efficiently process OLAP on the database with dirty data. CUBE is an important operator for OLAP. This paper proposes the CUBE operation based on overlapping clustering, and an effective and efficient storing and computing method for CUBE on the database with dirty data. Based on CUBE, this paper proposes efficient algorithms for answering aggregation queries, and the processing methods of other major operators for OLAP on the database with dirty data. Experimental results show the efficiency of the algorithms presented in this paper.

Keywords: dirty data; CUBE; OLAP.

1 Introduction

Because of the inconsistency of pattern matching in data integration, the inconsistency in information extraction on heterogeneous data, and errors in data gathering, there may be inconsistent data, error data, duplicated data in databases. We define the data which is inconsistent, duplicate or not satisfying integrity constraints as dirty data, and the databases with dirty data as dirty databases. A dirty database system leads to dirty query answers, which will mislead the users and lead them to make wrong decisions. Currently, the major method of dirty data management is data cleaning [1-4], that is to eliminate dirty data from database. However, it will lead to the loss of data, and in some situations, it is impossible to eliminate all dirty data in a database. Therefore, in many cases, it is necessary to perform queries directly on dirty databases. The problem rises how to get the query results with clean degrees on dirty databases. It brings new challenges to the research of database systems. Effective and efficient OLAP on dirty data is one of them.

---

* Supported by the National Science Foundation of China (No 60703012, 60773063), the NSFC-RGC of China (No. 60831160525), National Grant of Fundamental Research 973 Program of China (No. 2006CB303000), National Grant of High Technology 863 Program of China (No. 2009AA01Z149), Key Program of the National Natural Science Foundation of China (No. 60933001), National Postdoctor Foundation of China (No. 20090450126), Development Program for Outstanding Young Teachers in Harbin Institute of Technology (no. HITQNJS. 2009. 052).

L. Chen et al. (Eds.): WAIM 2010, LNCS 6184, pp. 507–512, 2010.

OLAP analysis is an important method of using databases to help users making decisions. There are large amount of dirty data in reality, and they are hard to be eliminated completely. Therefore, it has widely applications to process OLAP analysis on dirty data.

Currently, some techniques about query processing on dirty data have been proposed. [5, 6] adopt the method of filtering out all the suspected dirty results to deal with the queries on dirty data. [7, 8, 9] adopt the method of returning a clean degree which represents the probability of the existing of a result to deal with the queries on dirty data. [10] proposes a method of dealing with star joins on dirty data. However, these methods have never considered about the OLAP analysis on dirty data. [12] proposes a OLAP data model to present data ambiguity, but its model mainly focuses on data imprecision, and does not consider the errors resulted in by data integrity constraint.

CUBE is an important operator of OLAP analysis [11]. Taking advantage of CUBE, the results of aggregation can be maintained off-line, thereby the OLAP analysis can be accelerated. It is natural to use CUBE to speed up the OLAP analysis on dirty data. However, in contrast to the traditional CUBE, the CUBE on dirty data brings new technical challenges. On clean data, the entity of an attribute's value is determinate, so the value can be simply recorded without ambiguity. But on dirty data, one attribute's value maybe belongs to several entities, so the entities and the corresponding clean degrees should be recorded besides the value. This storage feature also makes the CUBE algorithm without considering about ambiguity not effective on dirty data.

To meet these challenges, this paper presents DCUBE, a CUBE operator on dirty data to support the efficient OLAP analysis on dirty data. On dirty data, as the preprocessing, tuples possibly referring to the same entity form a cluster. DCUBE is defined on such clusters. Different from the traditional CUBE, in results of DCUBE, each value is output with a clean degree, which presents the probability that the value is the correct result.

The main contributions of this paper are:

1. In order to support the OLAP analysis on dirty data, the operator DCUBE is proposed, including its definition, efficient storage structure and computation algorithms.
2. The algorithm of performing aggregation queries on dirty data efficiently with DCUBE is proposed.
3. DCUBE is applied to compute several kinds of OLAP operators. With DCUBE, the efficient algorithms for 5 OLAP operators are presented.
4. We test the efficiency of the algorithms proposed in this paper. The experimental results show that the methods proposed by this paper can efficiently process DCUBE on dirty data, and based on DCUBE, OLAP queries on dirty data can be processed efficiently.

2 CUBE on Dirty Data (DCUBE)

Definition 1(MDS): An n dimensional MDS is defined as MDS(D_1, D_2,…, D_n; M_1, M_2,…, M_k), where D_i is the ith dimensional attribute, and M_j is the jth metric attribute. □

Definition 2(DCUBE): Given an MDS(D_1, D_2,…, D_n; M_1, M_2,…, M_k) and a set of attributes $S \subset \{ D_i | 1 \le i \le n \}$, DCUBE on MDS can be represented as DCUBE(MDS, S, f), where f is an aggregation function. And the result Rel of DCUBE(MDS, S, f) is defined as following iterative process.

$\forall sub \subset S$, D={ D_1, D_2,…, D_n }-sub; Rel=Rel ∪ f (MDS, D),

where Rel is in the form of (value, probability) and f(MDS, D) means that f is performed on MDS by the dimensional attributes D. □

In a DCUBE(MDS, S, f), every entity contains a set of elements, which are pairs (cid, prob) for COUNT or triples (cid, vals, prob) for SUM and MAX. cid is the id of a cluster, vals are the values of some metric attributes, prob is the probability that the element is the correct one. A multidimensional array of storing these entities is called an EMA, in which an entity is stored in an item, which has a buffer of size H in the main memory. An EMA is called an aggEMA if it is used to store aggregation results.

If dvals are values of dimensional attributes, mvals are values of metric attributes, the algorithm of distributing data into an EMA is shown in algorithm 1.

Algorithm 1 *Distribute*

```
Input: a relation R, R's overlapping clustering result C
Output: the EMA of R
Flow:
if f=COUNT
    σ_{dvals, cid, prob}(R⋈_{R.tid=C.tid}C)
else if f=SUM or f=MAX
    σ_{dvals, cid, mvals, prob}(R⋈_{R.tid=C.tid}C)
for each tuple in the result of the first step:
use dvals as an index to get an item i of the EMA
    if f=COUNT
        put (cid, prob) into i
    else if f=SUM or f=MAX
        put (cid, mvals, prob) into i
```

Given an EMA M with n dimensions a_1,… , a_n, D_i is the domain of a_i with a threshold h_i. Algorithm 2 shows the way of aggregating M by {a_1,…, a_{i-1}, a_{i+1},…, a_n}.

Algorithm 2 *Aggregate*

```
Input: EMA M, dimension id i
Output: aggEMA A
1. Build a temporary aggEMA T( a_1, …, a_{i-1}, a_{i+1}, …, a_n )
   for ∀d_j∈D_j, j=1, …, n
```

```
        copy all the elements of M[d_1]…[d_n] to T[d_1]...[d_{i-1}]
        [d_{i+1}] …[d_n]
2. Build an aggEMA A( a_1, …, a_{i-1}, a_{i+1}, …, a_n )
     for ∀d_j, d_j' ∈D_j, j=1, …, i-1, i+1, …, n
        if |d_j'-d_j|<r_j
           copy all the elements of T[d_1']…[d_{i-1}'][d_{i+1}']…[d_n']
           to A[d_1]…[d_{i-1}][d_{i+1}]…[d_n]
3. return A
```

3 OLAP Based on DCUBE on Dirty Data

The algorithm of MAX is shown in algorithm 3. The algorithms of COUNT and SUM are omitted for lack of space.

```
Algorithm 3 Qmax

Input: an item g in an aggEMA
Output: a sequence of (value, prob)s
Flow:
1.Group g by cid and the metric attribute and compute
    sum(prob) of each group, sort the grouping result by the
    descending order of the metric attribute.
2.If the number of tuples of the grouping is n, and the cid,
    metric attribute, prob of the ith tuple are separately
    cid_i, m_i and prob_i. M is a map which map a cid to a
    probability with initial value 1. M_i is a item of M, whose
    cid is M_i^cid and prob is M_i^prob:
    for i = 1 to n
       if cid_i∈M
          M[ cid_i ] = M[ cid_i ] + prob_i
       else
          put M[ cid_i ] = prob_i into M
          p = 1
          ∀M_i∈M
             if  M_i^cid≠cid_i
                p = p * ( 1 - M_i^prob )
          p = p * prob_i
          output( m_i , p )
```

In a DCUBE, *slice* is to obtain all the items with values of a specific dimension equaling to a specific value in an EMA; *dice* is to obtain all the entities with values of specific dimension in a specific range in an EMA; *roll-up* and *drill-down* is to find the corresponding results; and *Pivot* is to rearrange the placement of dimensions.

4 Experiments

We take the table *customer* in TPCH[13] as dirty data but neglect the attribute C_CUSTKEY. q1, q2, q3 are 3 queries and the number of dimensional attributes of q1 is bigger than that of q2 and q3. Running time is taken as measure.

Fig. 1 is the result of the scalability of the DCUBE for COUNT. It is observed with the increasing of inputting data, the running time of q1 is longer than that of q2, and the running time of q2 is longer than that of q3. This shows with the increasing of the number of dimensional attributes, the running time of the algorithms increases.

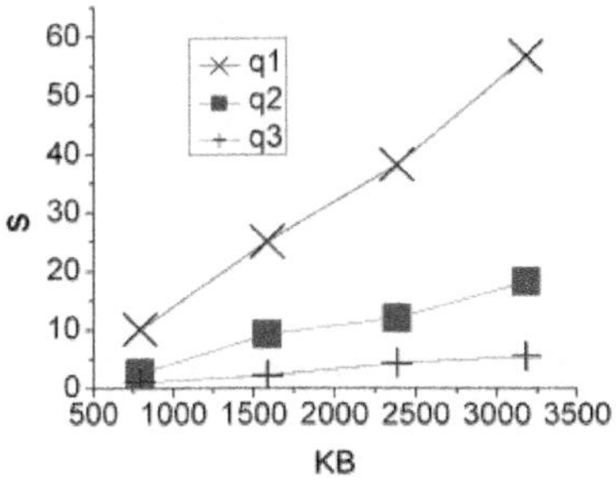

Fig. 1. The result of the DCUBE for COUNT

The result of proceeding MAX is shown in Fig. 2. We can see that the more dimensions a MDS has, the more aggEMAs need to be generated during processing aggregation on DCUBE, the more time it takes.

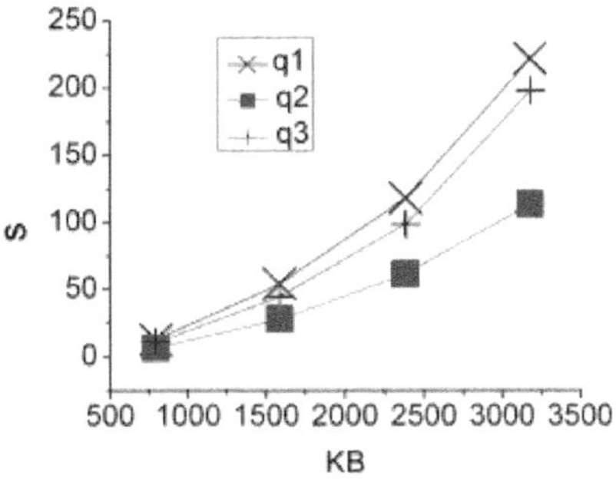

Fig. 2. The result of MAX

5 Conclusion

CUBE is an important operator for OLAP. Effective CUBE on dirty data is one of the key problems to accelerate aggregation queries and to process OLAP analysis on dirty data. Based on overlapping clustering, this paper defines DCUBE, the CUBE on dirty data, and discusses the methods of storing and computing DCUBE on dirty data. With DCUBE, the methods of accelerating aggregation queries on dirty data and the implementation methods of other OLAP operations are proposed in this paper, which can return a sequence of OLAP analysis results with clean degrees' guarantee. The efficiency of the algorithms proposed in this paper is tested by both theoretical analysis and experimental results.

Our future work includes speeding up the methods proposed in this paper and studying the iceberg CUBE on dirty data.

References

1. Xie, J., Yang, J., Chen, J., Wang, H., Yu, P.S.: A sampling-based approach to information recovery. In: ICDE, pp. 476–485. IEEE, Cancún (2008)
2. Qi, Y., Candan, K.S., Sapino, M.L.: Ficsr: Feedback-based nonistency resolution and query processing on misaligned data sources. In: Chan, C.Y., Ooi, B.C., Zhou, A. (eds.) SIGMOD, pp. 151–162. ACM, Beijing (2007)
3. Jeffery, S.R., Garofalakis, M.N., Franklin, M.J.: Adaptive Cleaning for RFID Data Streams. In: Dayal, U., Whang, K.Y., Lomet, D.B., Alonso, G., Lohman, G.M., Kersten, M.L., Cha, S.K., Kim, Y.K. (eds.) VLDB, pp. 163–174. ACM, Seoul (2006)
4. Xiong, H., Pandey, G., Steinbach, M., Kumar, V.: Enhancing Data Analysis with Noise Removal. TKDE 18(2), 304–319 (2006)
5. Fuxman, A., Miller, R.J.: First-order query rewriting for inconsistent databases. Journal of Computer and System Sciences 73(4), 610–635 (2007)
6. Fuxman, A., Fazli, E., Miller, R.J.: ConQuer: Efficient Management of Inconsistent Databases. In: Özcan, F. (ed.) SIGMOD, pp. 155–166. ACM, Baltimore (2005)
7. Andritsos, P., Fuxman, P., Miller, R.J.: Clean Answers over Dirty Databases: A Probabilistic Approach. In: Liu, L., Reuter, A., Whang, K.Y., Zhang, J. (eds.) ICDE, p. 30. IEEE, Atlanta (2006)
8. Gal, A., Martinez, M.V., Simari, G.I., Subrahmanian, V.S.: Aggregate Query Answering under Uncertain Schema Mappings. In: ICDE, pp. 940–951. IEEE, Shanghai (2009)
9. Jiang, G., Wang, H., Li, J., Gao, H.: An Aggregation Query Processing Method of Dirty Database Based on Clustering. Journal of Computer Research and Development (suppl. 46), 140–146 (2009)
10. Sismanis, Y., Wang, L., Fuxman, A., Haas, P.J., Reinwald, B.: Resolution-Aware Query Answering for Business Intelligence. In: ICDE, pp. 976–987. IEEE, Shanghai (2009)
11. Gray, J., Chaudhuri, S., Bosworth, A., Layman, A., Reichart, D., Venkatrao, M., Pellow, F., Pirahesh, H.: Data Cube: A Relational Aggregation Operator Generalizing Group-By, Cross-Tab, and Sub-Totals. The Computing Research Repository, abs/cs/0701155 (2007)
12. Burdick, D., Deshpande, P.M., Jayram, T.S., Ramakrishnan, R., Vaithyanathan, S.: OLAP over uncertain and imprecise data. VLDB J. 16(1), 123–144 (2007)
13. `http://www.tpc.org/tpch/`

An Algorithm for Incremental Maintenance of Materialized XPath View*

Xueyun Jin and Husheng Liao

College of Computer Science and Technology, Beijing University of Technology,
Pingleyuan 100#, Chaoyang District, Beijing 100124, China
{jinxueyun,liaohs}@bjut.edu.cn

Abstract. Cached materialized view has lots of benefits, but it has inconsistency problem when the data source is modified. This paper proposes an incremental maintenance algorithm IMA to implement incremental maintenance of materialized XPath view. The characteristics of IMA are: (1) It can establish an incremental maintenance program automatically; (2) The incremental maintenance program is simple and its function is reassembling the materialized XPath view to obtain a consistent view; (3) The incremental maintenance program is written in XQuery language and can be executed by any XQuery engine; (4) The only auxiliary data used to maintain the materialized XPath view is the incremental maintenance program and its size cost is very small. Experiments have shown that this approach outperforms view recomputation.

Keywords: Incremental Maintenance; Materialized XPath View; XPath; XQuery.

1 Introduction

With the emergence of XML [1] as the standard for representation structured and semi-structured documents, relational databases, and object repositories, more and more distributed applications use XML to represent heterogeneous data sources. Nowadays, W3C has proposed XQuery language [2] as XML query standard and XPath [3] as a language embedded in XQuery to address the nodes of XML trees. In order to improve the query processing on XML data source, cached materialized XQuery view and XPath view can be used. We suppose that XQuery view is a view specified by a query written in XQuery language and XPath view is a view specified by a query written in XPath language. Our work puts its emphasis on XPath view.

Cached materialized view has lots of benefits, but it has inconsistency problem when the data source is modified. View recomputing is a simple method to solve this problem, but it could result in unnecessary overload especially in web environment. Another method is maintaining the view incrementally. Many studies on relational data model have shown that the performance of incremental maintenance of materialized

* This research is supported by: (1) Beijing Municipal Natural Science Foundation (4082003); (2) Discipline and Graduate Students Education Project of Beijing Municipal Commission of Education.

L. Chen et al. (Eds.): WAIM 2010, LNCS 6184, pp. 513–524, 2010.

view is much better than that of view recomputing [4,5,6], but it is still a challenge for incremental maintenance of materialized view on semi-structured data model, such as XML data source.

This paper proposes an incremental maintenance algorithm IMA to implement incremental maintenance of materialized XPath views based on the idea of incremental computation. The characteristics of this algorithm are: (1) It can establish an incremental maintenance program automatically; (2) The incremental maintenance program is simple and its function is reassembling the materialized XPath view to obtain a consistent view; (3) The incremental maintenance program is written in XQuery language and can be executed by any XQuery engine; (4) The only auxiliary data used to maintain the materialized XPath view is the incremental maintenance program and its size cost is very small. This approach can be used in mobile computing environment, heterogeneous system and general C/S system where XML is used as its data source and materialized XPath view is used to improve the performance of refreshed query.

The rest part of this paper is organized as follows. The motivation of our research is given in section 2. Related works are introduced in section 3. Section 4 gives the preliminaries of this research. Section 5 presents the incremental maintenance algorithm IMA. Performance evaluation of our approach is presented in section 6 and section 7 is the conclusion of our work.

2 Motivation

Our approach is inspired by the idea of incremental computation of [7]. It proposes a systematic approach to derive incremental program for a program written in functional programming language. Based on this idea, we use different approach to implement incremental maintenance of materialized view.

Suppose a query named *query* issues to an XML data source *data* is a computation written in XQuery language and its query result is *r*, that is:

$$[query]_{xq}(data) = r \tag{1}$$

In equation (1), the subscript *xq* means this query program *query* is written in XQuery language. In order to improve the performance of refresh query, *r* is cached as a materialized view. When *query* is refreshed, *r* can be obtained from cache directly rather than reissue the query to data source again. However, when $\Delta data$ takes place on *data*, it will result in a change Δr in *r*, and the new query result is called *r'*. Namely:

$$[query]_{xq}(data + \Delta data) = r' = r + \Delta r \tag{2}$$

An incremental maintenance algorithm IMA is used in this research to find what Δr is according to information about *data*, $\Delta data$ and *query*. It generates an incremental maintenance program *imp* written in XQuery as its output. That is:

$$IMA(data, \Delta data, query)=imp \tag{3}$$

imp can be executed on the cached materialized view *r* and guarantee:

$$[imp]_{xq}(r) = r' \tag{4}$$

Motivating example. The example XML document file used in this paper is named *a.xml* and its XML tree is showed in Fig.1. Every node is given a name in form of A_n. The upper-case letter *A* is the label of the node, and subscript *n* is used to distinguish different nodes with the same label. Now we suppose: (1) There is an XPath query *query*, its XPath expression e_q is */D/B/S[1]/P/R[2]* and its query result *r* is cached as a materialized XPath view . *r* is (R_2, R_7, R_{11}, R_{13}); (2) Node S_5 will be deleted and its XPath expression e_m is */D/B[3]/S[1]*. S_5 is called modification node.

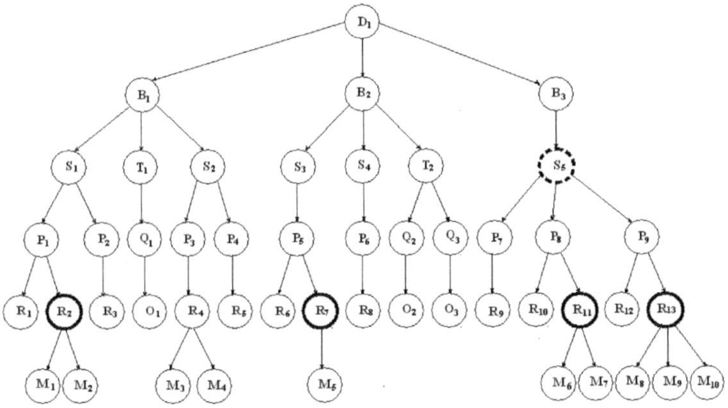

Fig. 1. Example XML tree

```
declare function local:imp($r as item()*) as item()*
{
  subsequence($r, 1, 2),(), subsequence($r, 5)
};
```

Fig. 2. *imp* of motivating example

According to equation (3), incremental maintenance algorithm IMA accepts 3 parameters as input: (1) *data* is the document node of file a.xml: *doc("a.xml")*; (2) *Δdata* is the delete operation on the modification node S_5; (3) *query* is an XPath expression e_q="*/D/B/S[1]/P/R[2]*". In order to generate an incremental maintenance program *imp*, *IMA* obtains 3 values to represent *Δr*: *i*, *k*, r_{new}. Namely, in order to obtain *r'*, in the materialized view *r*, *k* items from the *i*th item will be updated by r_{new}. According to this example, IMA finds that *i* is 3, *k* is 2 and r_{new} is null. Therefore, IMA can generate an incremental maintenance program written in XQuery based on the information of *Δr*. According to equation (4), *imp* is used to execute on *r* and the result is *r'*=(R_2, R_7). The *imp* of the motivating example is shown in Fig. 2. In this program, there is a function *imp* and its only parameter *$r* is used to represent the XPath materialized view *r*. XQuery function *subsequence* is used to reassemble *r* to obtain *r'*.

The following system design strategies are used to improve the performance of our approach: (1) *imp* is established when there is a modification happens, not when the query is refreshed; (2) IMA will check whether the modification is relative to the materialized view. If there is no relation between the materialized view and the modification, IMA needs not to generate any code to maintain materialized view. In practice, the influence of the data source updates on the materialized view is always small because the size of the query result is typically small compared with the original XML source size, and source updates are typically small compared with the original source size, too.

3 Related Works

Article [8] presents an approach for incremental order-preserving maintenance of XQuery views. It is based on a formal algebraic representation of the XQuery view query called XAT and provides a very powerful query processing capability. However, it needs to store the intermediate results as auxiliary data during query processing and there is not any restriction on the size of the auxiliary data.

Another approach is proposed in article [9] to minimize the number and the size of the queries to data source. This approach also uses auxiliary data to maintain the cached materialized views and the size of the auxiliary data depends on the size of the XPath expression and the answer size regardless of the source data size.

A scheme for incremental evaluation of XPath queries is proposed in [10]. It also uses auxiliary data to realize incremental evaluation. However, it gives a restriction that when data is deleted or inserted to data source, only deletion or insertion may occur to query answers. This restriction is too stringent because it is common for a deletion in data source lead to an insertion in query result or an insertion in data source lead to a deletion in query result.

Article [11] proposes an incremental maintenance algorithm of materialized XPath/XSLT views defined by XPath expressions. This scheme needs to maintain an XML Transformation tree to realize the incremental maintenance.

Article [12] studies the incremental evaluation of the result of an XPath query on an XML database under updates. It uses XPath query pattern and maintains an auxiliary data structure to implement incremental evaluation. However, it needs to maintain a complex intermediate data structure.

Different from the approaches listed above, we propose an incremental maintenance algorithm based on the data source, the change in data source and the query. It can generate an incremental maintenance program written in XQuery automatically. As the only auxiliary data, the incremental maintenance program is very small in size and can be executed by any XQuery engine.

4 Preliminaries

Our materialized XPath view model is based on Standard XML [1] and standard XPath [3]. In order to define materialized XPath view, some concepts are defined firstly, on which the materialized XPath view and data modification is defined.

Definition 1: Axis Test, *at,* where *at*∈*{"/"}*, "/" is child test.

Definition 2: Node Test, *nt*, where *nt*∈*{name-test, kind-test}*, *name-test*∈*{QName, "*"}*, *kind-test*∈{*"attribute", "comment", "document", "element", "namespace", "processing-instruction", "text"* }. *QName* is a valid identifier for XML elements and attributes.

Definition 3: Predicate Test, *pt*, where $pt \in \{e_p, \varphi\}$, e_p is an predicate expression in XPath language. φ means *pt* can be null.

Definition 4: XPath step, *s*, is a triple <*at, nt, pt*>, where *at* is an axis test, *nt* is a node test and *pt* is a predicate test. Because *pt* can be φ, it is an optional part of an XPath step. Reference operator "." is used in form of *s.at, s.nt, s.pt* to reference the axis test, node test and predicate test of step *s*.

Definition 5: XPath Expression, *e*, is a sequence $(s_1, s_2, \ldots, s_n)$, where s_i is the *i*th XPath step of *e*.

Definition 6: Materialized XPath view, *R*, is a tuple $<e_q, r>$, where e_q is the *XPath expression* of the XPath query *query*, *r* is the query result of *query*. According to standard XML, *r* is a sequence of XML nodes.

Definition 7: Data Modification, $op_c^{e_m}$, is a modification operation *op* on a node n_m of XML data source. n_m is called **modification node** and it is specified by the XPath expression e_m. *c* is the content of the modification, it is a string. $op_c^{e_m} \in \{IC_c^{e_m}, IA_c^{e_m}, UN_c^{e_m}, UC_c^{e_m}, D_\varphi^{e_m}\}$, where $IC_c^{e_m}$ means inserting *c* as the first child of the n_m; $IA_c^{e_m}$ means inserting *c* as the next sibling of n_m; $UN_c^{e_m}$ means updating the name of n_m to *c*; $UC_c^{e_m}$ means updating the content of n_m to new content *c*; $D_\varphi^{e_m}$ means deleting n_m. In $D_\varphi^{e_m}$, *c* isφ because it is a deleting operation,.

There are 3 constraints in our definitions: (1) Only XPath expression including child test "/" is considered and the situation that DTD of XML file is recursive is not considered. Therefore, an XPath expression including descendant test "//" can be expressed by one or more Xpath expressions which only have child test "/" according to the schema of XML file, and reverse axis test can be transformed into forward axis test in advance; (2) The predicate test is assumed to be about the subtree of the node being test. It is feasible because a node in an XML document is described by its descendants semantically; (3) Our algorithm is based on the modification of one node. If several nodes are modified, the algorithm will deal with these nodes one by one.

Example 1. Consider the motivating example. e_q= *"/D/B/S[1]/P/R[2]"*, it is consists of 5 *XPath steps*: s_1=<*"/", D,φ*>, s_2=<*"/", B,φ*>, s_3=<*"/", S,[1]*>, s_4=<*"/", P,φ*>, and s_5=<*"/", R,[2]*>. *R*=<*"/D/B/S[1]/P/R[2]"*, $(R_2, R_7, R_{11}, R_{13})$>. The modification operation is $D_\varphi^{\text{"/D/B[3]/S[1]"}}$. It means that the node specified by XPath expression *"/D/B[3]/S[1]"* is going to be deleted.

5 Incremental Maintenance Algorithm

IMA is established based on the following facts: (1) Every node in a XML file has document order. Document order is used in this research to find the ancestor node of the modification node; (2) All XPath expressions consist of independent steps. Therefore, all steps can be dealt with independently in our algorithm.

According to equation (3) in section 2, IMA accepts 3 arguments as input: document node of the XML data source n_{doc} is used to represent data source *data*; data modification $op_c^{e_m}$ is used to represent data modification *Δdata*; XPath expression of the XPath query e_q is used to represent the XPath query *query*. IMA tries to obtain 3 values *i*, *k*, r_{new} to represent the change *Δr* in *r*. Namely, in order to obtain *r'*, *k* items from the ith item will be updated by r_{new} in r. Based on that, IMA generates an incremental maintenance program *imp* written in XQuery. In order to obtain i and k, IMA is invoked before the data modification is really took place when a data modification is issued.

5.1 Design Ideas of IMA

There are 5 steps in IMA. The design ideas of these steps are introduced in this section.

1. Separate e_q and e_m

At first, e_q is separated into 2 parts: e_{q1} and e_{q2} ; e_m is separated into 2 parts: e_{m1} and e_{m2}, that is, e_q=*conjunct*(e_{q1}, e_{q2}) and e_m =*conjunct*(e_{m1}, e_{m2}), where function *conjunct* is used to conjunct two XPath expressions into one XPath expression. These 4 parts are very important basic information for the next 4 steps. It is implemented by an algorithm PSA (Path Separate Algorithm). This algorithm will be introduced in section 5.2.

The separation strategy is based on the strategy of determining a very important ancestor node n_a of the modification node n_m. n_a is a very important node because all the modifications can be limited in the subtree of n_a. Therefore, n_a can be used to obtain k and r_{new}. Besides, from the left siblings of this node, i can be acquired.

Suppose there are i steps in e_m, try to find a step e_q.s$_j$ in e_q which have the same name test of e_m.s$_{i-1}$, namely, e_q.s$_j$.*nt* = = e_m.s$_{i-1}$.*nt* and make sure that the first *j-1* steps of e_q do not have any predicate. If it can be found, e_m.s$_{i-1}$ is the criteria step of e_m, and e_q.s$_j$ is the criteria step of e_q. If it can not be found, try to find a step have the same name test of e_m.s$_{i-2}$ in e_q again. This loop will be done until a criteria step of e_q and a criteria step of e_m can be found. After that, path separation can be done according to these 2 criteria steps. If step e_m.s$_j$ is the criteria step of e_m, the first i steps of e_m is e_{m1} and the remaining steps of e_m are e_{m2}; if step $e_q.s_j$ is the criteria step of e_q, the first j steps of e_q is e_{q1} and the remaining steps of e_q is e_{q2}. If the criteria step of e_q and e_m can not be found, e_{q1},e_{q2},e_{m1},e_{m2} will be null. That means that there is no relationship between e_q and e_m and there is no need for IMA to generate *imp* program code for this query.

In the motivation example, e_q is "*/D/B/S[1]/P/R[2]*" and e_m is "*/D/B[3]/S[1]*". According to PSA, there are 3 steps in e_m, and the name test of the second step of e_m is "B". PSA can find a step in e_q that have the same name test, and all steps before that do not have any predicates. Therefore, the second step of e_m is the criteria step of e_m and the second step of e_q is the criteria step of e_q. According to these criteria steps, e_m is separated into two parts: e_{m1} is "*/D/B[3]*", e_{m2} is "*/S[1]*"; e_q is separated into two parts: e_{q1} is "*/D/B*", e_{q2} is "*/S[1]/P/R[2]*".

2. Locate n_a

n_a is an ancestor node of modification node n_m. We use *exeQuery*(n_{doc}, e_{m1}) to locate n_a. Function *exeQuery* is used to invoke the XQuery engine to do an XPath query on a specified node in an XML tree.

In the motivating example, e_{m1} is "*/D/B[3]*", function exeQuery use e_{m1} to address a node on document node n_{doc} to obtain n_a. It is B_3.

3. Obtain *k*

Because all the modifications are limited in the subtree of n_a, IMA uses *count(exeQuery* (n_a, e_{q2})*)* to obtain the value of k. e_{q2} is used to address the items that will be affected by the data modification and XQuery function *count* is used to know the number of these items.

In the motivating example, e_{q2} is "*/S[1]/P/R[2]*", and k is the result of XQuery function *count(exeQuery(*B_3*,"/S[1]/P/R[2]")*. k is 2.

4. Obtain r_{new}

Because IMA is invoked before the data modification is really took place on data source, we must know what n_a is like after the data modification is took place. Algorithm *NUA* is used on n_a, e_{m2} and $op_c^{e_m}$ to construct a new ancestor node n_a' after data modification is took place. This construction is implemented in the memory, not in the data source. After that, e_{m2} can be used on n_a' to obtain r_{new} by *exeQuery(*n_a', e_{q2}*)*. NUA will be introduced in section 5.2.

In the motivating example, n_a is B_3, e_{m2} is "*/S[1]*". Because the modification operation is a delete operation on S_5, n_a' is node B_3 which does not have any children. Therefore, the query result of "*B_3/S[1]*" on n_a' is null. Namely, r_{new} is null.

5. Obtain *i*

Algorithm LA is used to obtain i based on the idea that all nodes in XML file have document order. Therefore, the document order of the left siblings of n_a is less than the document order of n_a. IMA checks all the left siblings of n_a recursively and sum the number of nodes that every left sibling of n_a contributes to r based on e_{q2}. This algorithm will be introduced in section 5.2.

In the motivating example, left siblings of B_3 are B_1 and B_2, their document order is less than the document order of B_3. According to e_{q2}, B_1 contributes 1 node to r, B_2 contributes 1 node to r, and the sum is 2. Therefore, i is 2.

5.2 Incremental Maintenance Algorithm

The incremental maintenance algorithm IMA is introduced in this section. Other algorithms used in IMA are introduced after that.

IMA is showed in Fig.3 and its design ideas have been listed in 5.1. In this algorithm, function *exeQuery(n, e)* is used to invoke XPath query engine with 2 arguments. The first argument is a node n, the second argument is an XPath expression e. It can return the items addressed by the XPath expression e in the subtree of the node n. XQuery function *count(s)* only has one argument s, it is a sequence. Its function is returning the number of items in the sequence s. Function *genCode(*i, k, r_{new}*)* is used to generate an incremental maintenance program *imp* written in XQuery language based on the information of i, k, r_{new}. *imp* can be executed on the materialized view r to obtain r'.

PSA, *NUA* and *LA* are 3 important algorithms used in IMA. Function *count* and *exeQuery* are also used in these algorithms. PSA is showed in Fig.4, NUA is showed in Fig.5, and LA is showed in Fig.6.

Algorithm 1. IMA (Incremental Maintenance Algorithm)

```
    imp=IMA(ndoc, eq, opc^em).
Input:
  ndoc,     document node of the XML data file;
    eq,     XPath expression of the query;
    opc^em, data modification.
Output:
  imp       incremental maintenance program.
Procedure:
  eq1,eq2,em1,em2          <=     PSA( eq, em)
  if eq1!=null and eq2!=null and em1!=null and em2!= null {
     na            <=     exeQuery(ndoc, em1)
     k             <=     count(exeQuery (na, eq2))
     na'           <=     NUA(na,exeQuery(na,em2)
     rnew          <=     exeQuery(na',op, c), eq2)
     if rnew != null or k != 0{
           rr            <=     exeQuery(ndoc, eq1)
           i             <=     LA(rr, na, eq2, 1)
           return genCode(i, k, rnew)
     }
  }
  return null.
```

Fig. 3. Incremental Maintenance Algorithm (IMA)

Algorithm 2. PSA (Path Separation Algorithm)

```
    eq1, eq2, em1, em2 = PSA( eq, em).
Input:
    eq,          XPath expression of the query;
    em,          XPath expression of the modification node.
Output:
  eq1,eq2,em1,em2  subpaths of eq and em
Procedure:
  tm <=    length(em)-1
  while tm>0 {
     if tq = exist(eq, em.stm) {
           em1     <=     subpath(em, tm)
           em2     <=     extract(em, em1)
           eq1     <=     subpath(eq, tq)
           eq2     <=     extract(eq, eq1)
           return
     }
     tm      <=     tm-1
  }
  eq1,eq2,em1,em2   <=     null
  return
```

Fig. 4. Path Separation Algorithm (PSA)

```
Algorithm 3. NUA (Node Update Algorithm)
    na' =NUA(seq , nm , op, c)
Input:
 seq,        a sequence;
 nm,         the modification node;
 op,         the modification operation. op∈{IC,IA,UN,UC,D};
 c,          the content of the modification.
Output:
 na',        the modified na.
Procedure:
 if          empty(seq)
    return null
 x1  <=      seq [1]
 x2  <=      subsequence(seq,2)
 if  nmodify is x1   {
    if       op == IC
       return (element{node-name(x1)}{ x1 /@*, c, x1 /*},x2)
    if       op==IA
       return (x1,c ,x2)
    if       op==UN
       return (element{ c }{ x1 /@*, x1 /*},x2)
    if       op==UC
       return (element{node-name(x1)}{ x1 /@*, c, x1 /*},x2)
    if       op==D
       return (x2)
 }
 if  x2[1] >> nm|| x2[1] is null
    return (element{name(x1)}{x1/@*,NUA(x1/*,nm, c)})
 else
    return ($x1, NUA(x2, nm, c))
```

Fig. 5. Node Update Algorithm (NUA)

In PSA, function *exist(e, st)* returns an integer i to ensure the ith step of e have the same name test of step st, and all steps before step st (including st itself) do not have any predicates. Namely, $e.s_i.nt == st.nt$ is true and $e.s_{1..i}.pt == null$ is true. If function *exist* can not find a step satisfy the condition, it returns *0*. Function *length(e)* returns the number of steps in XPath expression e. Function *subpath(e,t)* can extract a sub-path of e which is consist of first t steps of e. Function *extract* is used on two XPath expressions and *extract*(e_1, e_2) means extract a subpath from e_1 which is consist of steps which are not appeared in e_2.

The first argument of NUA is a sequence. Its initial value is a sequence which has only one node: n_a. The main idea of *NUA* is probing the nodes in the subtree of n_a recursively to construct a new n_a'. If this node is n_m, it is reconstructed according to the modification operation. Otherwise, the document order of the right sibling of this node is used as the criteria to judge whether n_m is in the subtree of this node. According to different condition, different strategies are used to construct node n_a'.

```
Algorithm 4. LA (Locating Algorithm)
      i=LA(rr, na, eq2,  j)
Input:
  rr,        all siblings of na;
  na,        the ancestor node of the modification node;
  j,         an integer, its initial value is 1.
Output:
  i          there will be a change from the ith item in
             the materialized view r.
Procedure:
  if         rr== null
      return j
  x1  <=     rr [1]
  x2  <=     subsequence(rr,2)
  if         x1 << na      {
      jj<= count(exeQuery(x1, eq2))
      return LA(x2, na, j + jj)
  }
```

Fig. 6. Locating Algorithm (LA)

In this algorithm, operator "*[n]*" is used after a sequence q to return the nth item of q. XQuery function *subsequence(q,n)* can return a subsequence of q which is consist of items from the nth item of q to the last item.

In LA, items in *rr* are the siblings of n_a. Algorithm *LA* recursively probes every item in *rr* sequentially until it finds the item whose document order is bigger than that of n_a. During the probing process, this algorithm counts how many items every node in *rr* contributes to the materialized view r. The sum of these numbers is i.

IMA put its attention on the performance in the following cases: (1) IMA tries its best to make n_a located near the modification node n_m to decrease computation; (2) IMA tries to know whether the data modification has no effects on materialized view r in PSA. If there is no relationship between them, there is no need to generate *imp*; (3) IMA should access data source as few as possible because the data source is stored in the I/O device and the speed of I/O is slow. Function *exeQuery* is done in the memory when IMA wants to obtain k and r_{new} because n_a is already in the memory, and it is only done on the data source when we try to obtain n_a and obtain the left sibling of n_a. In order to improve the performance, lazy query technique is used in our system to construct the query result just when the query result is needed by other instructions.

The computational complexity of IMA is $O(n^2)+2log(n)$, where n is the number of steps in an XPath query. However, function *exeQuery* in IMA is used to invoke query engine to execute XPath query and the computational complexity of it is not included in the computational complexity of IMA. Because n is not always a big number in practice, the computational complexity of IMA is actually depend on the computational complexity of *exeQuery*.

6 Performance Evaluation

The performance of our approach is evaluated in this section. Our experimental environment is a C/S system that XPath queries are issued from client to server by the Internet. Qizx/db free engine edition 3.0 [13] is used on client to execute incremental maintenance program *imp* to incrementally maintain the materialized XPath view. All queries are registered at the query agent implemented at server side. IMA is invoked to generate an incremental maintenance program for every query by this query agent when there is a data modification is going to be happened. After all *imp*s for all registered queries are generated, the data modification is really took place on data source.

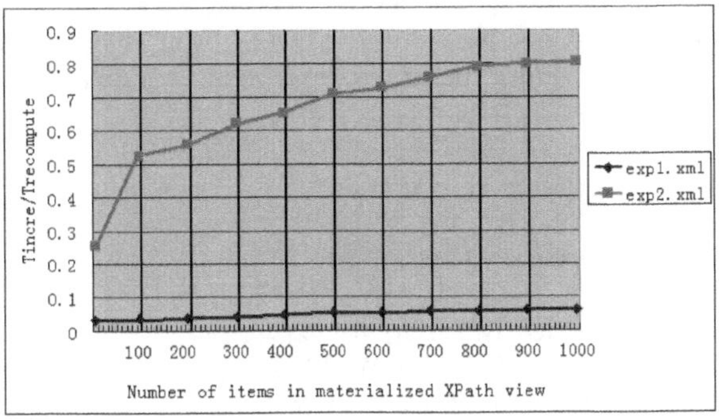

Fig. 7. Experimental results

The XML document files used in this experiment are 2 XML files on the server. One file named *exp1.xml* has information about 81,920 books and another file named *exp2.xml* has information about 1,280 books. The size of *exp1.xml* and *exp2.xml* are *18,257k* and *285k* respectively. $T_{recompute}$ is the time of recomputing materialized view. During this time period, an XPath query is reissued to server, XQuery engine at server executes this query, and the query result is returned to client. T_{increm} is the time of incrementally maintaining materialized view. During this time period, an XPath query is reissued to the query agent, the query agent send back *imp* to the client and the client execute *imp* to obtain new query result. Because algorithm IMA is invoked at the query agent when data modification takes place and *imp* is already generated when the query is refreshed, this experiment ignores the time IMA generate *imp*.

The average value of $T_{increm} / T_{recompute}$ of 30 different XPath query are evaluated according to the number of items in the materialized view *r*. The numbers of items in *r* are range from 10 to 1000. It is feasible because the view is not always very big in practice. The experimental results are showed in Fig.7.

The following conclusions can be drawn from Fig.7: (1) The performance of our approach outperforms view recomputation because all values of $T_{increm} / T_{recompute}$ is less than 1; (2) Suppose |R| is the size of the materialized view and |D| is the size of data source, the smaller |R|/|D| is, the higher the performance of this approach is; (3) Our approach can be used in mobile computing environment, heterogeneous system and general C/S system where XML is used as data source and materialized view is used to improve the performance of refreshed query.

7 Conclusion

This paper presents an incremental maintenance algorithm of materialized XPath views based on the idea of incremental computation. The incremental maintenance program written in XQuery is established automatically and can be executed on materialized view by any XQuery engine. Experiments show that the performance of incremental maintenance of materialized XPath view is better than that of view recomputaion. Our approach can be used in mobile computing environment, heterogeneous system and general C/S system where XML is used as data source and materialized view is used to improve the performance of refreshed query.

For the future work, we intent to apply the idea of incremental computation on the incremental maintenance of materialized XQuery views. It will be more complex than the work we did in this paper because an XQuery program is more complex than an XPath query. We will introduce the future work in other papers.

References

1. W3C. XML, `http://www.w3.org/XML`
2. W3C. XQuery, `http://www.w3.org/XML/xquery`
3. W3C. XPath, `http://www.w3.org/TR/xpath`
4. Blakeley, J.A., Larson, P., Tompa, F.W.: Efficiently Updating Materialized Views. In: Proceedings of the 1993 ACM SIGMOD international conference, pp. 61–71 (1986)
5. Gupta, A., Mumick, I.S.: Maintenance of Materialized Views: Problems and Techniques and Applications. IEEE Data Engineering Bulletin 18(2), 3–18 (1995)
6. Gupta, A., Mumick, I.S., Subrahmanian, V.S.: Maintaining Views Incrementally. In: Proceedings of the 1993 ACM SIGMOD international conference, pp. 157-166 (1993)
7. Liu, Y.A., Teitelbaum, T.: Systematic derivation of incremental programs. Science of Computer Programming 24(1), 1–39 (1995)
8. Dimitrova, K., El-Sayed, M., Rundensteiner, E.A.: Order-Sensitive View Maintenance of Materialized XQuery Views. In: Song, I.-Y., Liddle, S.W., Ling, T.-W., Scheuermann, P. (eds.) ER 2003. LNCS, vol. 2813, pp. 144–157. Springer, Heidelberg (2003)
9. Sawires, A., Tatemura, J., Po, O., Agrawal, D., Candan, K.S.: Incremental Maintenance of Path-Expression Views. In: Proceedings of the 2005 ACM SIGMOD international conference on Management of data, pp. 443–454 (2005)
10. Matsumura, H., Tajima, K.: Incremental Evaluation of a Monotone XPath Fragment. In: Proceedings of the 14th ACM international conference on Information and knowledge management, pp. 245 – 246 (2005)
11. Onizuka, M., Chan, F.Y., Michigami, R., Honishi, T.: Incremental Maintenance for Materialized XPath/XSLT Views. In: Proceedings of the 14th international conference on World Wide Web, pp. 245–246 (2005)
12. Björklund, H., Gelade, W., Marquardt, M., Martens, W.: Incremental XPath evaluation. In: Proceedings of the 12th International Conference on Database Theory, St. Petersburg, Russia, vol. 361, pp. 162–173 (2009)
13. Qizx/db free engine, `http://www.xmlmind.com/qizx`

Query Processing in INM Database System

Jie Hu[1,2], Qingchuan Fu[1], and Mengchi Liu[1]

[1] School of Computer, Wuhan University, China
[2] School of Mathematics and Computer Science, Hubei University, China

Abstract. Real-world objects have various natural and sometimes complex relationships with each other. Via these relationships, they play various roles and then have the corresponding context-dependent properties. To naturally and directly model these situations, we have proposed a novel data model called Information Networking Model (INM). We have also designed information specification language (ISL), information manipulation language (IML) and information query language (IQL) and implemented a database management system based on INM The query language can explore the natural graph structure of INM objects to extract meaningful information in a simple, concise, and compact way. In this paper, we focus on query processing in INM database system. We have used four kinds of search strategies and the system can automatically select an appropriate strategy to efficiently process queries without user's intervention.

Keywords: Query language, query processing, query strategies.

1 Introduction

Real-world objects have various natural and sometimes complex relationships with each other. Via these relationships, they play various roles and then have the corresponding context-dependent properties. To naturally and directly model these situations, we have proposed a novel data model called Information Networking Model (INM) [1], which can directly model real-world organizational structures and represent various kinds of relationships between objects and the corresponding context-dependent properties within the relationships. In INM, all information regarding a real-world entity is represented as single object with a unique object identifier. The object can belong to several classes to reflect the dynamic, many-faceted, and evolutional aspects of the entity and objects are networked through various relationships.

Based on INM, we have designed the corresponding data definition language IDL, data manipulation language IML, and query language IQL. IQL can explore the natural graph structure of objects to extract and construct meaningful results in a concise, natural, and compact way. We have also implemented a novel database management system based on INM that supports IDL, IML and IQL.

In this paper, we mainly focus on the query processing of the INM database system. First, we introduce INM object structure and INM instance database.

L. Chen et al. (Eds.): WAIM 2010, LNCS 6184, pp. 525–536, 2010.

```
Univ WHU[ Faculty →{ Prof: Bob, Lecturer: Amy},
         Student →{ UnderGrad: Ada,
                    GradStudent →{ M.Sc: Ann, PhD: Amy}}]
Univ UCB[ Student→ GradStudent→M.Sc:Bob,
          Faculty→ Professor: Tom]
Univ PKU [ Faculty → Prof: Bev,
         Student →GradStudent→PhD: Ann]
Univ ULB[ Student→ GradStudent→PhD:Bob,
          Faculty→ Professor: Joy]
Univ MIT [ Faculty → Prof: Tom,  Student →UnderGrad:{ Bob, Ann}]
Course ADB [taughtBy: Bob,
           takenBy: {Ann [mark:90], Amy [mark:95]}]
Course DS [ taughtBy: Bob,
           takenBy: Ada [mark:85]]
{UnderGrad, M.Sc, PhD, Prof} Bob [
   age: 45,
   studiesIn: {MIT[status:UnderGrad[startYear:1979]] ,
              UCB[status:M.Sc[startYear:1983, supervisor:Tom]],
              ULB[status:PhD[startYear:1986, supervisor:Joy]]},
   worksIn: WHU[title:Prof [startYear:2001, teaches:{ ADB,DS}, supervises: {Ann, Amy}]]]
{Lecturer, PhD} Amy [
   age:25,
   worksIn:WHU[title:Lecturer[startYear:2004]] ,
   studiesIn: WHU[status:PhD [sno:0501,takes:ADB [mark:95], supervisor:Bob]]]
UnderGrad Ada [studiesIn: WHU[status:UnderGrad [sno:0702, takes: DS [mark:85]]]]
{UnderGrad, M.Sc, PhD} Ann [
   age:23,
   studiesIn: { MIT[status:UnderGrad[sno:9901]],
              WHU[status:M.Sc [sno:0301, takes:ADB [mark:90], supervisor:Bob]],
              PKU[status:PhD [sno:0601, supervisor:Bev]]}]
Prof Bev [ age: 45, worksIn: PKU[title:Prof [supervises:Ann]]]]
Prof Tom [ worksIn: {MIT[title:Prof[startYear:1970]], UCB[title:Prof [startYear:1975, supervises:Bob]] }]
Prof Joy [ worksIn: ULB[title:Prof[startYear:1980, supervises:Bob]]]
```

Fig. 1. Sample Instance Database in INM

Also, we present INM query language and demonstrate how to use it to explore the natural graph structure of INM objects to extract meaningful information in a simple, concise, and compact way. Then we illustrate the architecture of INM database system and elaborate on its query processing.

2 Instance Database

An INM database contains a schema and an instance. The schema contains various class definitions whereas the instance contains various classified objects. We can use IQL to query both schema and instance. However, the instance query is much more complex. Thus, we just introduce the instance database in this section.

In INM, all information regarding a real-world entity is represented as a single object which has a unique oid. An object has one or more object names that may not be unique and may be classified into several classes to reflect the dynamic, many-faceted, and evolutional aspects of the entity. Also, it has various properties, which can be simple attributes, relationship hierarchies to represent real-world organization structures, and context-dependent properties within some relationships. In INM, an object is represented as a tree. The root of the tree is a list of object names associated with the object and each subtree corresponds to a property. An INM instance database is a set of classified objects.

Fig. 1 shows a sample INM instance database which contains information about five universities WHU, PKU, MIT, UCB, and ULB, two courses ADB and DS, and several kinds of people Bob, Amy, Ada, Ann, Bev, Tom, and Joy. Object WHU has two relationship hierarchies with roots Faculty and Student. Relationship Faculty is specialized into Prof with value Bob and Lecturer with value Amy. Relationship Student is specialized into UnderGrad with value Ada and GradStudent which is further specialized into M.Sc with value Ann and PhD with value Amy.

In INM, a relationship hierarchy induces a relationship class hierarchy. Thus we have classes Faculty, Lecturer, Prof, etc. Object Amy belongs to classes Lecturer and PhD. As a Lecturer, Amy has one context-dependent property subtree in which worksIn is a relationship with WHU; she has property title of value Lecturer in the context of worksIn:WHU; she also has property startYear with value 2004 in the context of worksIn:WHU[title:Lecturer]. As a PhD, Amy has one context-dependent property in which studiesIn is a relationship with WHU; she has property status of value PhD in the context of studiesIn:WHU; she also has properties sno, takes, and supervisor with values 0501, ADB, and Bob respectively in the context of studiesIn:WHU[status:PhD].

Fig. 2 shows the tree structure of some objects in Fig. 1.

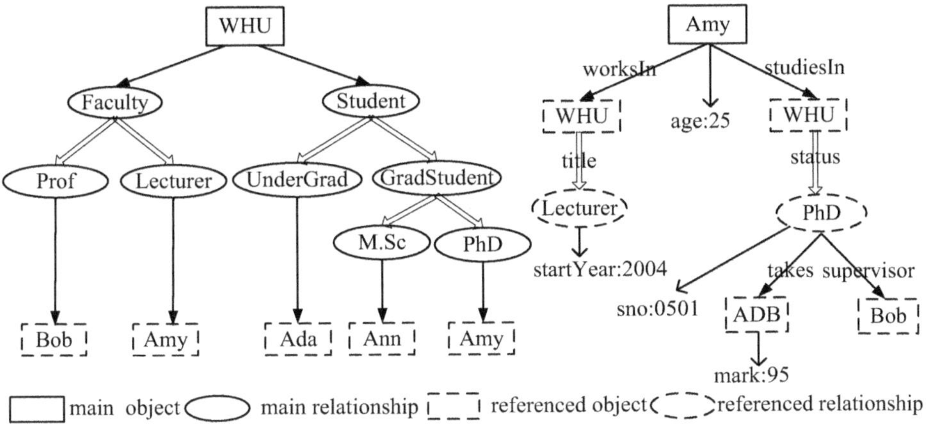

Fig. 2. Object Structures

3 Overview of Information Query Language

A query language normally has a query part and a result part. In SQL3 and OQL [2,3], the SELECT clause can contain nested subqueries to construct complex values and the WHERE clause may also include nested subqueries to form complex conditions. In XQuery [4,5,6,7,8,9], the FLWOR expressions are used to expression queries and construct result. The RETURN clause has the same function as the SELECT clause in SQL and OQL and can have nested FLWOR expressions. Thus, SQL, OQL and XQuery combine the query part and the result part together so that queries are cumbersome to express and difficult to read and comprehend.

In IQL, we take a quite different approach. We separate the query part from the result part strictly. In the query part, we use logical variables to get all the bindings whereas in the result part, we specify how to construct the result using the variables bound to various values. Thus, IQL queries is more concise and compact and easy to understand.

On the other hand, most query languages have different style from their data models. For example, SQL does not use tuple structures to express queries; OQL does not use ODMG object structure to express queries; and XQuery is not XML-like, either. In IQL, the query expressions directly use the object structure and allow variables to appear anywhere in this structure to match any part of objects.

To traverse complex structures in queries, path expressions are normally used. Currently XPath [10] allows most comprehensive path expressions using a slash (i.e, /) and double slashes (i.e, //). Also, predicates which are enclosed by a pair of square brackets (i.e, [ ]) are used in a path expression to filter the results to contain only nodes that meet specific criteria.

In IQL, we use a more general form tree expression in the query part. A tree expression has the same structure as objects but may have variables appear anywhere to bind part of objects and may contain multiple related paths in queries.

Formally, a tree expression has the form $P[P_1, \cdots, P_n]$ with $n \geq 1$ where P is either an object name or a variable, each P_i is a path element of the form $s_i\ E_i$ where s_i is a separator slash (i.e, /) or double-slash (i.e, //), E_i is an element. When $n = 1$, the tree is just a path and can be simplified in to $Ps_1\ E_1$. When $n > 1$ and s_i is a slash, s_i should be omitted. A path element is *ground* if it has no variable, *general* if it just has variables, or *mixed* if otherwise.

Not that constants can be used directly in the tree expression as filtering conditions without using any predicates. In this way, the query expressions are more direct and natural.

For the result part, IQL supports three kinds of patterns: $T : T'$, $T\ [T_1, \cdots, T_n]$, and $[T_1, \cdots, T_n]$. For the first pattern, the values bound to the variable in T' are grouped together for the same value in T. For the second pattern, query output handler uses variables in $T, T_1, \cdots, T_n$ to find nodes in the result graph. Nodes hold the variable in T must be an ancestor of nodes hold variables in $T_1, \cdots, T_n$. Also, $T_1, \cdots, T_n$ are respectively grouped for the same T. Keyword *order by* can be applied to the values bound to the variable. The result expression is a combination of the above three kinds patterns with order by and aggregation.

A query in IQL is an expression of the form:

$$query\ E_1, \cdots, E_n\ construct\ C$$

where $E_1, \cdots, E_n$ with $n \geq 1$ are tree expressions and C is an optional result expression.

In IQL, variables start with \$ followed by an alphanumeric string.

Example 1. The following are examples of queries based on sample instance database in Fig. 1

1. Find professor $\$x$ in WHU, student $\$y$ that $\$x$ supervises, $\$y$'s sno $\$z$, supervisor $\$u$, and age $\$v$. Display professor $\$x$ and for each professor, display student $\$y$ that $\$x$ supervises, the average age of students that $\$y$ supervises. and for each supervised student, display sno, supervisor, and age.
   query WHU//Prof:$\$x$//supervises:$\$y$[//sno:$\$z$, //supervisor:$\$u$, age:$\$v$]
   construct Prof:$\$x$[supervises:$\$y$[sno:$\$z$, supervisor:$\$u$, age:$\$v$], avgAge:avg($\$v$)]
   Here the query expression is the simplification of the query expression WHU[//Prof:$\$x$[//supervises:$\$y$[//sno:$\$z$, //supervisor:$\$u$, age:$\$v$]]] where //Prof:$\$x$, //supervises:$\$y$, //sno:$\$z$, //supervisor:$\$u$, and age:$\$v$ are path elements.
2. Find $\$x$ working in university $\$y$ as a professor. Display $\$x$ and each university $\$y$ that $\$x$ works in as a nested form.
   query person $\$x$/worksIn:$\$y$/title:Prof **construct** Person:$\$x$/worksIn:$\$y$
3. Find $\$u$ that has student Ann and professor $\$x$ whose age is $\$y$ and who supervises student $\$z$. Display $\$u$ order by the number of its professors and each professor order by the number of students supervised and professor's age and student supervised in a nested way.
   query $\$u$[Student: Ann, //Prof:$\$x$[age:$\$y$, //supervises:$\$z$]] **construct** Univ:$\$u$ order by count($\$x$)/Prof:$\$x$ order by count($\$z$)[age:$\$y$, supervises:$\$z$]
4. Find $\$x$, its student $\$y$ and professor $\$f$, $\$y$'s status $\$z$, course $\$w$ that $\$y$ takes and taught by professor $\$f$, $\$y$'s sno $\$v$ in the context of $\$z$, and the mark $\$t$ of courses $\$w$. Display $\$x$, its professor $\$f$ and student $\$y$ in a nested form. For each student $\$y$, display the status $\$z$ and course $\$w$ and the corresponding mark $\$t$ and sno $\$v$.
   query $\$x$[Student:$\$y$//status:$\$z$[//takes:$\$w$/mark:$\$t$, //sno:$\$v$], Prof:$\$f$], $\$w$[taughtBy:$\$f$]
   construct $\$x$[Prof:$\$f$, Student:$\$y$/status:$\$z$[takes:$\$w$/mark:$\$t$, sno:$\$v$]]
5. Find $\$u$ and its graduate student $\$x$, also find $\$y$ whose age is 45 and title is professor. Display $\$u$ and its graduate students. Also display $\$y$.
   query $\$u$//GradStudent:$\$x$, $\$y$[age:45, //title:Prof]
   construct [Univ:$\$u$/GradStudents:$\$x$, Person:$\$y$]

In a query, if the construct expression is not given, then the query is just used check whether or not the query part is true with respect to the instance database. The following example check whether or not WHU has a professor supervising Ann

query WHU//Prof:$\$x$//supervises:Ann

In IQL, separators in path elements of query expressions specify the search scope. From an object or a relationship, single slash (/) denotes going down one level, double slash (//) denotes going down multiple levels within the object structure. For example, WHU//Prof:Bob, Bob//teaches:ADB, ADB/takeBy:Ann are all meaningful. However, WHU//teaches:ADB and Bob//takenBy:Ann are disallowed because double slashes cannot go out of the object structures from WHU into Bob.

4 System Architecture

The INM database management system has been implemented in C using GLib 2.22.3 and Berkeley DB 4.7 on a PC running Linux. The lexical and syntactic analyzer is implemented using Flex 2.5 and Bison 1.25.

The implementation employs a browser-server software architecture as shown in figure 3. The browser provides user interface and ships syntactically correct user query requests to the server for execution. The server performs lexical and syntactical checking and query processing.

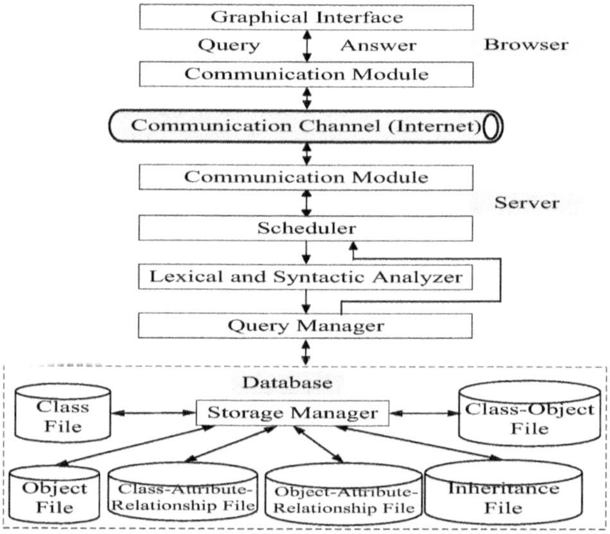

Fig. 3. System Architecture

Browser. The browser is organized into two layers: the graphical interface and the communication module. The graphical interface takes user requests, ships them to the server via communication module, and reformats query results from the server for proper display. The second layer is the communication module. It ships the user requests from the first layer to the server for parsing and execution, and obtains the results from the server and sends them back to the first layer.
Server. The server is organized into five layers. The first layer is the communication module which communicates with the communication module of browsers. It accepts user requests from browsers, sends them to the scheduler, and ships

the results back to the browsers. The second layer is the scheduler. It obtains multiple user requests from the communication module, schedules user requests, and ships them to the lexical and syntactical parser. The third layer is the lexical and syntactical analyzer which performs lexical and syntactical analysis of user requests. It filters out invalid requests, transforms strings of valid requests into standard forms, and sends them to the query manager. The forth layer is query manager which is in charge of query processing. It uses various evaluation strategies for different requests, keeps track of what is in main memory, removes what should be moved from memory to disk after finishing the query processing, and sends the query results to scheduler. The last layer is the storage manager. It is responsible for the management of disk-based data structures and move the data between disk and memory as needed. It is implemented in Berkeley DB and provides rapid access to classes, objects, and other meta information about them on the disk.

5 Query Processing

Query processing mainly involves two modules: parser and execution as shown in Fig. 4. A. We use Flex and Bison to build a bottom-up parser which consists of a lexical analyzer and a semantic analyzer. The lexical analyzer, which takes a query string and breaks it into tokens, is built by Flex. The semantic analyzer, which converts an annotated context-free grammar into an LALR(1) parser, is built by Bison. It obtains sequential tokens from the lexical analyzer, checks the grammar, acts differently according to different grammar statements, and generates a query tree.

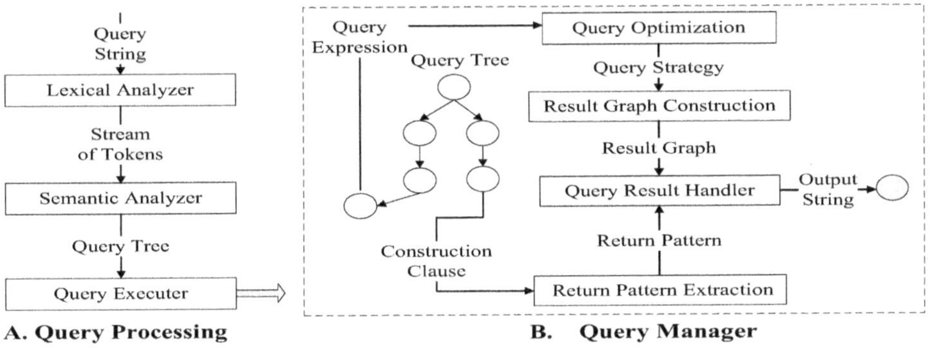

Fig. 4. Query Processing and Query Manager

The query manager is responsible for further processing the query tree. It contains four components: query optimization, result graph construction, return pattern extraction, and query output handler as shown in Fig. 4. B. The query manager takes a query tree from the lexical and syntactic analyzer as an input and generates an output string as query results. It first automatically chooses an evaluation strategy for the query tree during query optimization, then constructs a result graph to hold variable/value bindings, simultaneously extracts variables from construction clause to make sure that the variables also appear in the query tree, and build return patterns. Finally, the query output handler uses the result graph to generate query results in term of return patterns.

Query optimization. In INM system, we have used four kinds of evaluation strategies: *forward chaining search strategy*, *backward chaining search strategy*, *hybrid search strategy*, and *multiple expressions search strategy*. Each strategy supports different query forms and is particularly efficient for some cases, but may not be applicable to or perform relatively poorly on others. The first three kinds of strategies is for queries which just have one query expression whereas the last strategy is for those which have more than one query expression.

Forward chaining search strategy starts with an object name followed by a tree expression to match path elements in a forward manner and binds variable to values. Fig. 5. A is an example of forward chaining search strategy in which WHU is an object name. The query manager first takes WHU as the key to search the index file and retrieves the objects in database. Then it takes WHU as the starting node to match the path element //Prof:$\$x$ and binds variable $\$x$ to the value Bob. Then it takes Bob as the starting node to match the path element //supervises:$\$y$ and binds variable $\$y$ to values Ann and Amy. Then it takes Ann as the starting node to match path elements //sno:$\$z$, //supervisor:$\$u$ and age:$\$v$ respectively and binds variables $\$z$ to values 9901, 0301, and 0601, $\$u$ to values Bob and Bev, and $\$v$ to the value 23. For Amy, the case is similar.

Backward chaining search strategy starts with a path element which is at the end of a tree expression and uses the index of object-attribute-relationship file to match the path elements in reverse. It follows the tree expression to match path elements in a backward manner. Fig. 5. B is an example of backward chaining search strategy in which title:Prof is the last path element. The query manager first generates the search key for title:Prof to search the index and get values WHU, PKU, MIT, UCB, and ULB which are bound to variable $\$y$. Then it generates the search key for worksIn:WHU to search the index and get the value Bob which is bound to variable $\$x$. For worksIn:PKU, worksIn:MIT, worksIn:UCB, and worksIn:ULB, the case is similar.

Hybrid search strategy first selects a starting path element and then explores the path elements before the starting path element with the backward chaining search strategy and the path elements after the starting path element with the backward chaining search strategy. For this strategy, one key problem is how to select the starting path element. We use the following evaluation function:

$$f = \frac{w}{d^k \times n}$$

where w is the weight of the path element partitioned three kinds: ground, mixed, and general and their weights are w_r, w_m, and w_g respectively with

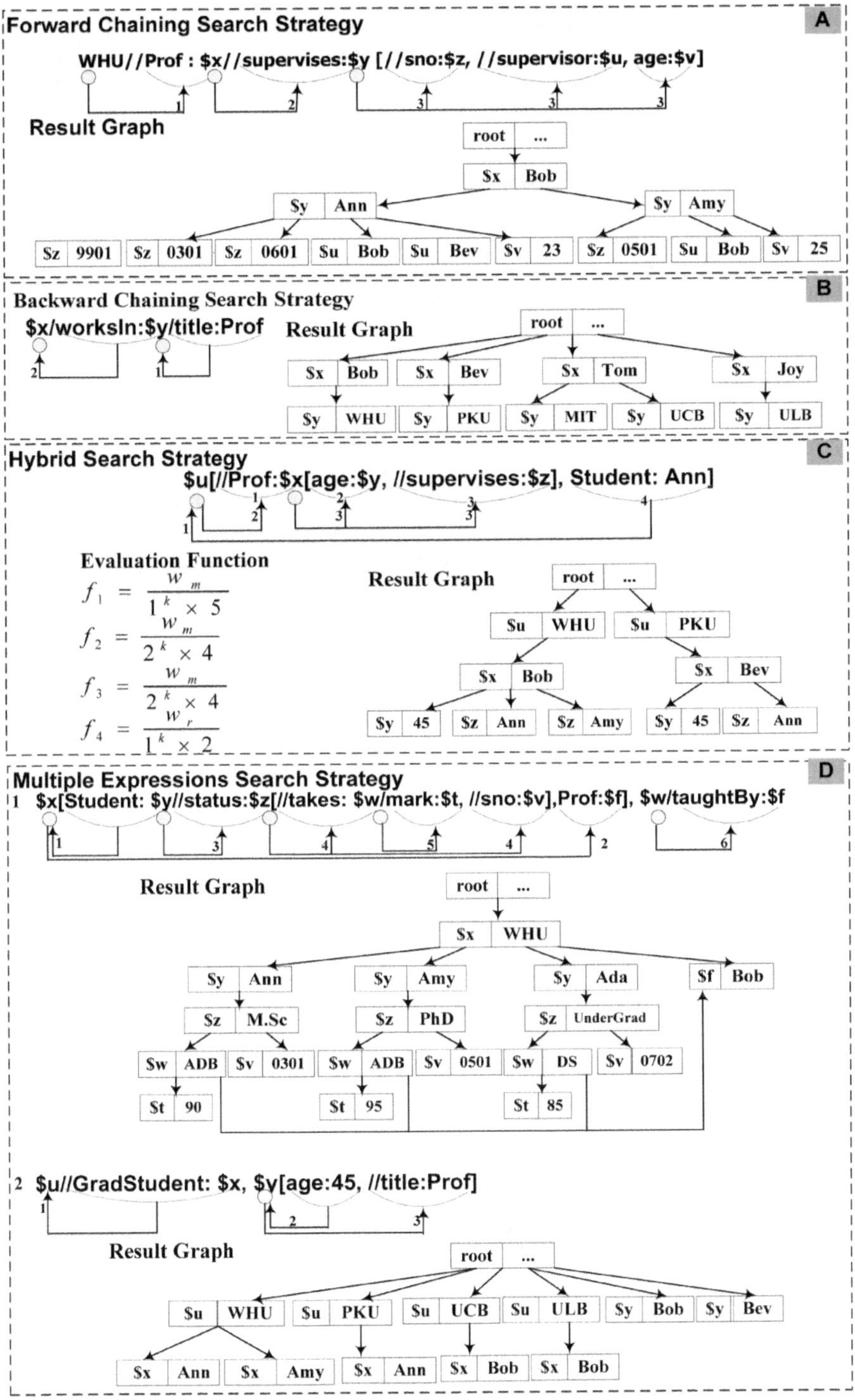

$$f_1 = \frac{w_m}{1^k \times 5}$$
$$f_2 = \frac{w_m}{2^k \times 4}$$
$$f_3 = \frac{w_m}{2^k \times 4}$$
$$f_4 = \frac{w_r}{1^k \times 2}$$

Fig. 5. Search Strategies and Result Graph Examples

$w_r > w_m > w_g$, d is the depth of the path element, k is the coefficient to adjust the impact of d and $k > 1$, n is the number of path element in the database. The path element of the highest evaluation value is selected as the starting one.

Fig. 5. C is an example of hybrid search strategy in which there are four path elements. Query manager select Student:Ann as the starting path element because it has highest evaluation value. The query manager first generates the search key for Student:Ann to search the index and get values WHU and PKU which are bound to variable $\$u$. Then it takes WHU as the starting node to match the path element //Prof:$\$x$ and binds variable $\$x$ to the value Bob. Then it takes Bob as the starting node to match path elements age:$\$y$ and //supervises:$\$z$ and bind variables $\$y$ to the value 45 and $\$z$ to values Ann and Amy respectively. For PKU, the case is similar.

Multiple expressions search strategy is designed for queries which have more than one query expressions. None of the above strategies alone is suitable for this situation. The query manager can automatically select strategies to process queries. Fig. 5. D are examples of multiple expressions search strategy. For the first query, query manager selects Student: $\$y$ as the starting path element and uses hybrid search strategy to process the first query expression. In the second query expression, $\$w$ appears in the first query expression and is bound to values ADB and DS, query manager thus uses forward chaining search strategy to process the second one. For the second query, two query expressions are unrelated. Query manager uses backward chaining search strategy to process the first query expression and hybrid search strategy to process the second one.

Return pattern extraction. It is a preprocessing procedure in query execution before handling query output. It extracts variables from the construction expression in the query tree to check if there exist variables which do not appear in the query expressions. If so, query manager returns an error to the user before getting into executing query expression. It also preprocesses the construct clause so as to make it convenient to execute for query output handler.

Result graph construction. It is a core procedure to build the result graph for the query clause, to hold variable/value bindings and dependency among them, and to maintain hash tables storing them.

Query output handler. It uses result graph to generate query results in terms of return patterns and supports grouping, aggregation, and order by functions.

The following are results of queries in Example 1 in terms of the result graphs as shown in Fig 5:

1. Professors:Bob[supervises:{Ann[sno:{9901,0301,0601},supervisor:{Bob, Bev}, age:23],
   Amy[sno:0501, supervisor:Bob, age:25]},
   avgAge:24]
2. Person:{Bob[worksIn:WHU], Bev[worksIn:PKU],
   Tom[worksIn:{MIT, UCB}], Joy[worksIn:ULB]}
3. Univ:{PKU[Professors:Bev[age:45, supervises:Ann]],
   WHU[Professors:Bob[age:45, supervises:{Ann, Amy}]]}
4. WHU[Students:{Ann[status:M.Sc[takes:ADB[mark:90], sno:0301]],
   Amy[status:PhD[takes:ADB[mark:95], sno:0501]],

Ada[status:UnderGrad[takes:DS[mark:85],sno:0702]]},
Professors:Bob]

5. [Univ:{WHU[GradStudents:{Ann, Amy}], PKU[GradStudents:Ann], UCB[GradStudents:Bob], ULB[GradStudents:Bob]}, Person:{Bob, Bev}]

We evaluate the performance of the proposed strategies on different scale data. All the experiments were run on an Intel Core 2 Duo P8600+2.8GHz machine with 1GB memory running Linux2.6.

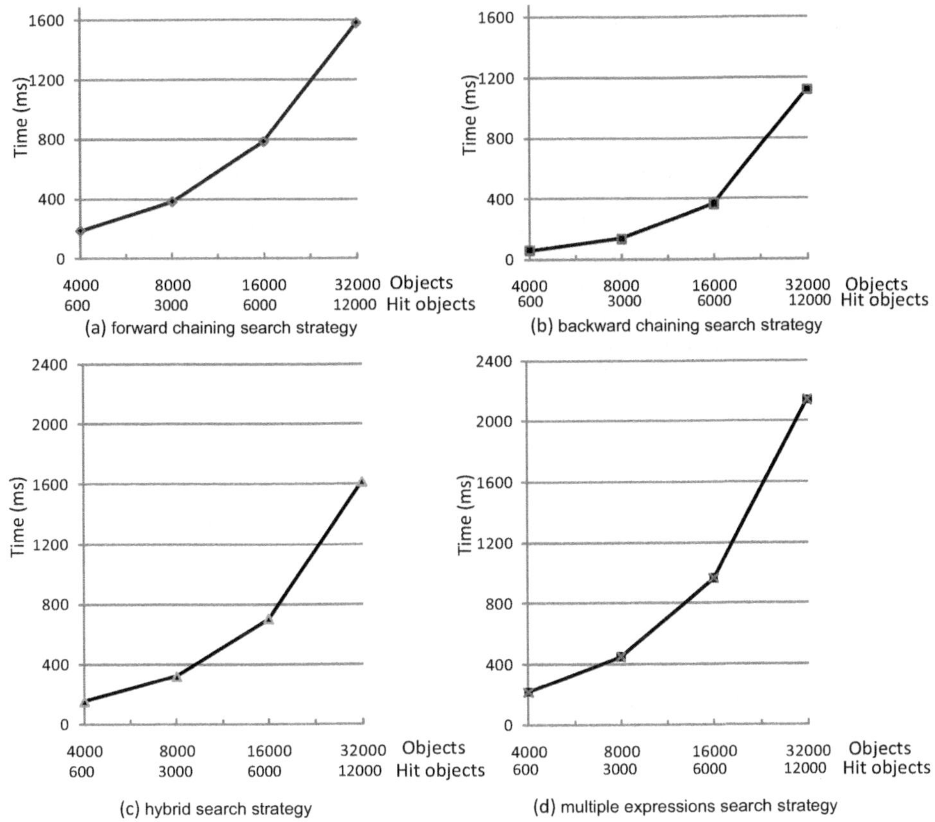

Fig. 6. Query Processing Time for Different Search Strategies Queries

Fig. 6 shows the query processing time for four kinds of strategies with the queries in Example 1 under varying object numbers and hit object numbers. Basically, the query processing time increases linearly with the increases of objects and hit objects. The forth query takes longer time because the query and the result graph is more complex than the others.

6 Conclusion

This paper mainly focuses on query processing in INM database system. We have used four kinds query processing strategies in INM system: forward chaining search strategy, backward chaining search strategy, hybrid search strategy, and multiple expressions search strategy. The system can automatically select an appropriate strategy to efficiently process queries without user's intervention.

The query language we have implemented is primitive. We would like to extend it with quantifiers, predefined functions, and user defined functions, deductive and active rules, formal semantics. We also plan to investigate further query processing and optimization techniques.

References

1. Liu, M., Hu, J.: Information networking model. In: Proceedings of ER, Gramdo, Brazil, pp. 131–144 (November 2009)
2. Alagic, S.: Type-checking oql queries in the odmg type systems. ACM Transactions Database System 24(3), 319–360 (1999)
3. Cattell, R., Barry, D., Berler, M., Eastman, J., Jordan, D., Russel, C., Schadow, O., Stanienda, T., Velez, F. (eds.): The Object Database Standard: ODMG 3.0. Morgan Kaufmann, Los Altos (2000)
4. Walmsley, P.: XQuery. OReilly Media, Inc., Sebastopol (March 2007)
5. Fankhauser, P.: Xquery formal semantics: State and challenges. SIGMOD Record 30(3), 14–19 (2001)
6. Chamberlin, D.D.: Xquery: A query language for xml. In: Proceedings of SIGMOD, San Diego, California, USA, p. 682 (June 2003)
7. Pal, S., Cseri, I., Seeliger, O., Rys, M., Schaller, G., Yu, W., Tomic, D., Baras, A., Berg, B., Churin, D., Kogan, E.: Xquery implementation in a relational database system. In: Proceedings of VLDB, Trondheim, Norway, pp. 1175–1186 (August 2005)
8. Onose, N., Deutsch, A., Papakonstantinou, Y., Curtmola, E.: Rewriting nested xml queries using nested views. In: Proceedings of SIGMOD, Chicago, Illinois, USA, pp. 443–454 (June 2006)
9. Boag, S., Chamberlin, D., Fernandez, M.F., Florescu, D., Robie, J., Simeon, J.: XQuery 1.0: An XML Query Language. Technical report, World Wide Web Consortium (2007), `http://www.w3.org/TR/2007/REC-xquery-20070123`
10. XML Path Language, `http://www.w3.org/TR/xpath20/`

Fragile Watermarking for Color Image Recovery Based on Color Filter Array Interpolation

Zhenxing Qian, Guorui Feng, and Yanli Ren

School of Communication and Information Engineering,
Shanghai University, 200072, Shanghai,
{zxqian,grfeng,renyanli1982123}@shu.edu.cn

Abstract. In this paper, a novel fragile watermarking method is proposed for color image recovery via color filter array interpolation. First we turn a color image into a grey image by color sampling in the form of Bayer patterns. Data of the grey image which is reordered as reference bits are then embedded into the original image along with some authentication bits generated from the image. After the watermarked image is received, authentication bits are extracted to identify which regions are tampered. When the image is detected to be tampered, extracted reference bits are used to reconstruct a color image by color filter array interpolation, which is then used to recover the content of the tampered regions. Experiments show this method has good recovery ability.

Keywords: Self-recovery, fragile watermarking, color filter array interpolation, steganography.

1 Introduction

As editing tools are popular nowadays, digital images can be tampered easily. Data hiding can be used to protect images from tampering, of which fragile watermarking that any modification to the content would be detected is an important branch [1-3]. In recent years, some fragile watermarking methods are developed to have the self-recovery ability to the tampered regions in an image, which is also called self-embedding. The idea was first brought forward by Fridrich in 1999 [4].

Recently, Wang and Tsai propose a method to embed the fractal code of the region of importance (ROI) into the LSBs of the original image to achieve high quality restoration of the ROI when it is inpainted [5]. Cheddad et al. down-sample the half-toning data of the original image and embedded these bits into itself for recovery [6]. In order to increase the restoration area, Lee and Lin propose an effective dual watermark scheme for image tamper detection and recovery, in which two copies of watermark for each non-overlapping block are embedded into bit-planes of the original image [7]. Furthermore, Yang and Shen create an index table for an original image and embed the vector quantization (VQ) of each block into the original image as a basis for recovery, which has higher probability of image recovery with a better quality of recovered images [8]. Zhang et al. expand the secret data and embed them randomly into itself, which can detect errors of any position as long as the tampered areas are not more than 59% [9].

L. Chen et al. (Eds.): WAIM 2010, LNCS 6184, pp. 537–543, 2010.

The above methods have good ability to recover the images that are tampered, especially for the grey images. In this paper, we mainly focus on the recovery of color image. When a color image is generated from a camera, color filter array (CFA) interpolation technology is an important part of imaging [10-12]. According to the theory, we sample the original color image into a grey image in the form of Bayer patterns, which is then embedded into the original image for reference along with the authentication bits. On the receiving side, the authentication bits are extracted to detect the tampered areas. Then the reference data are extracted from the areas that are not tampered, and the tampered areas are recovered via CFA interpolation to the reference data.

2 Watermark Embedding

When embedding the secret bits into the original image for recovery, we first down-sample the original image into a grey image. The imaging procedure in a camera includes the CFA interpolation, which is usually represented by the Bayer pattern [11]. The pattern is shown in Figure 1.

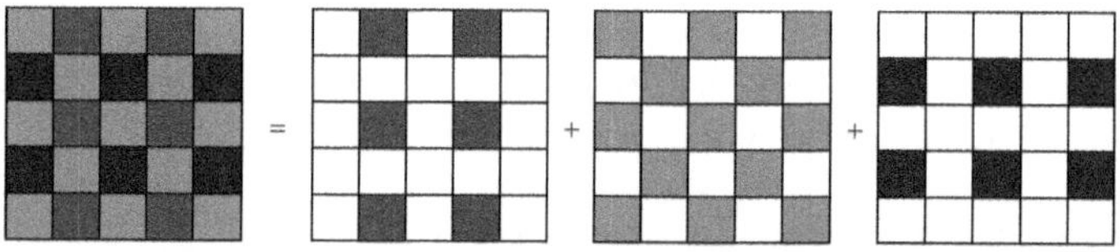

Fig. 1. Bayer pattern used in cameras

Oppositely, we can also generate a grey image from an existing color image. For an existing color image **I** = (**R**, **G**, **B**) composed of $M \times N$ pixels, down-sample each channel according to the model of Bayer pattern [12]:

$$\begin{aligned} \mathbf{D}_R(i,j) &= \frac{1}{4}(1-\cos\pi i)(1+\cos\pi j)\mathbf{R}(i,j) \\ \mathbf{D}_G(i,j) &= \frac{1}{2}(1+\cos\pi i\cos\pi j)\mathbf{G}(i,j) \\ \mathbf{D}_B(i,j) &= \frac{1}{4}(1+\cos\pi i)(1-\cos\pi j)\mathbf{B}(i,j) \end{aligned} \tag{1}$$

where i and j indicate the pixel coordinates of the image. Then a grey image can be generated using Equation (2).

$$\mathbf{D}_I = \mathbf{D}_R + \mathbf{D}_G + \mathbf{D}_B \tag{2}$$

Remove three least significant bit-planes of $\mathbf{D}_I$,

$$\mathbf{D} = \lfloor \mathbf{D}_I / 2^3 \rfloor \tag{3}$$

Rearrange the pixels in **D** to a new map **D**' by two predefined integers p and q, $p \in [1, M)$, $q \in [1, N)$,

$$\mathbf{D}'(i,j) = \mathbf{D}((i+p) \bmod M, (j+q) \bmod N) \tag{4}$$

where p and q will be kept by users as secret keys for self-recovery.

Hence, each pixel of **D'** has 5 bits

$$[d^1_{i,j}, d^2_{i,j}, \ldots, d^5_{i,j}] = \lfloor \mathbf{D}'(i,j)/2^m \rfloor \bmod 2, \quad m = 0,1,\ldots,4 \tag{5}$$

where D' with the total length 5MN will be used as a reference for image recovery.

Divide the image **I** into MN/64 non-overlapping blocks $\{\mathbf{K}_{i,j}$: $i \in [1, M/8]$, $j \in [1, N/8]\}$, each of which has 8×8 pixels. For each block $\mathbf{K}_{i,j}$, calculate the sum of the three channels,

$$\mathbf{S}_{i,j} = \mathbf{K}^r_{i,j} + \mathbf{K}^g_{i,j} + \mathbf{K}^b_{i,j}, \quad 1 \le i \le M/8,\ 1 \le j \le N/8 \tag{6}$$

Input **S** into a hash function to generate some binary bits,

$$[h^1_{i,j}, h^2_{i,j}, \ldots, h^n_{i,j}] = \mathrm{H}(\lfloor \mathbf{S}/4 \rfloor), \quad 1 \le i \le M/8,\ 1 \le j \le N/8 \tag{7}$$

where n is the length of the binary outputs. The hash function must have strong collision resistance that means it's difficult to find any two different inputs correspond to the same output, like the algorithm MD5.

For each block, we divide the binary outputs into 64 segments with the same length, and calculate the parity of each segment. Then we have 64 bits for each block, which will be used as authentication bits. This way, totally we have MN authentication bits for the image **I**.

The watermark is composed of the reference bits from D' and the authentication bits, the total length of which is 6MN. Replace the two LSB layers of the image **I** with these watermark bits, as each LSB of a pixel contains 3 bits in a color image. This way, we obtain a watermarked image.

3 Image Authentication and Recovery

Suppose there are no changes to the size of the watermarked image **W** on the receiving side. Extract the hidden bits from the two LSB layers, from which we separate MN bits for authentication. Divide **W** into MN/64 non-overlapping blocks, calculate the hash bits using Equations (6) and (7), the procedure of which is the same as was described during watermark embedding, and generate 64 new "authentication bits" for each block. If the calculation result is the same as the authentication bits extracted from **W**, the block is judged as "not tampered". Otherwise, the block is "tampered". As the probability of judging a tampered block as "not tampered" is 2^{-64}, the false judgment is virtually impossible.

If some blocks are judged to be tampered, separate the reference bits from the extracted watermark to form a new grey image **X**. Turn **W** to a grey image **F** with the Equations (1) and (2). For the points in **F** that have been judged as tampered, replace them with the points in **X**, as shown in Equation (8).

$$\mathbf{F}'(i,j)=\begin{cases}\mathbf{F}(i,j), & \text{"not tampered" regions}\\ 8\cdot\mathbf{X}((i-p)\bmod M,(j-q)\bmod N), & \text{"tampered" regions}\end{cases} \tag{8}$$

where (i, j) is the coordinate of the image.

With the grey image **F**', regenerate a color image by CFA interpolation as described in the literature [10] and [11]. For example, we consider the case of interpolating the missing green component $g_{i,j}$ from the existing values around. Calculate the horizontal gradient $\Delta H_{i,j}$ and the vertical gradient $\Delta V_{i,j}$ at position (i, j),

$$\Delta H_{i,j}=|G_{i,j-1}-G_{i,j+1}|+|2R_{i,j}-R_{i,j-2}-R_{i,j+2}| \tag{9}$$

$$\Delta V_{i,j}=|G_{i-1,j}-G_{i+1,j}|+|2R_{i,j}-R_{i-2,j}-R_{i+2,j}| \tag{10}$$

where $R_{m,n}$ and $G_{m,n}$ denote the known red and green CFA components at position (m, n). Then the missing green component is interpolated as follows:

$$g_{i,j}=\begin{cases}\dfrac{G_{i,j-1}+G_{i,j+1}}{2}+\dfrac{2R_{i,j}-R_{i,j-2}-R_{i,j+2}}{4}, & \text{if } \Delta H_{i,j}<\Delta V_{i,j}\\ \dfrac{G_{i-1,j}+G_{i+1,j}}{2}+\dfrac{2R_{i,j}-R_{i-2,j}-R_{i+2,j}}{4}, & \text{if } \Delta H_{i,j}>\Delta V_{i,j}\\ \dfrac{G_{i,j-1}+G_{i,j+1}+G_{i-1,j}+G_{i+1,j}}{4}+ & \\ \quad\dfrac{4R_{i,j}-R_{i,j-2}-R_{i,j+2}-R_{i-2,j}-R_{i+2,j}}{8}, & \text{if } \Delta H_{i,j}=\Delta V_{i,j}\end{cases} \tag{11}$$

More details are described in the literature [10]. To achieve more precise interpolation, the horizontal and vertical estimations are multiplied by weights according to their gradients; please refer to [11]. This way, a new color image **C** is generated by CFA interpolated to the grey image **F**'. By replacing the tampered pixels in **W** with **C**, we finally obtain the restored image using Equation (12).

$$\hat{\mathbf{I}}(i,j)=\begin{cases}\mathbf{C}(i,j), & \text{"tampered" regions}\\ \mathbf{W}(i,j), & \text{"not tampered" regions}\end{cases} \tag{12}$$

4 Experimental Results

Some experiments have been implemented to verify the proposed method. We use the test image from the Kodak PhotoCD library (sized by 512×768), one of which is shown in Figure 2 (a). We reconstruct the reference images by the scheme in [9] and the proposed scheme. Figure 2 (b) and (c) are cropped from both reconstructed images for better comparison, where (b) corresponds to the scheme in [9] and (c) corresponds to the proposed scheme. It can be discovered that the image reconstructed from the proposed scheme is significantly clearer.

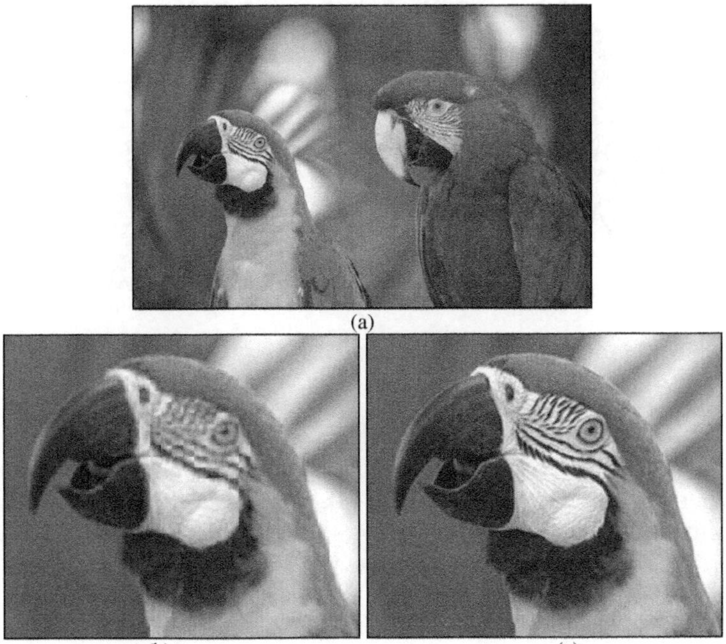

(a)

(b) (c)

Fig. 2. Visions of reconstructed images of two methods are compared, where (a) the original image, (b) is part of the reference image reconstructed by the scheme in [9], and (c) is part of the reference image reconstructed by the proposed scheme.

Figure 3 (a) shows a watermarked image and the value of PSNR compared to the original image is 46.7 dB, which is imperceptible. (b) is the tampered version of the watermarked image, the tamper rate of which is 28.4%, and (c) is the authentication map, in which the white represents the areas "not tampered" while the black represents the "tampered". After self-recovering procedure, PSNR of the restored image shown in (d) is 40.5 dB.

(a) (b)

Fig. 3. Tampered region in the watermarked image is restored, where (a) is a watermarked image, (b) is the tampered image, (c) is the authentication map and (d) is the self-recovered image.

(c) (d)

Fig. 3. *(continued)*

Figure 4 shows the result of an experiment is implemented on the image "Lena" of size 256×256, which is compared with the methods in [7] and [8]. The values of PSNR of the watermarked Lena are 40.7 dB in [7], 40.7 dB in [8], and 46.4 dB in the proposed method, as methods in [7, 8] uses 3 LSBs while we uses 2 LSBs. Values of PSNR of the self-recovered image decrease while the tampering rate gradually increase from 10% to 50%. As the methods uses grey image, we turn our restored image into grey and calculate the PSNR. Results show that our scheme has better recovery quality.

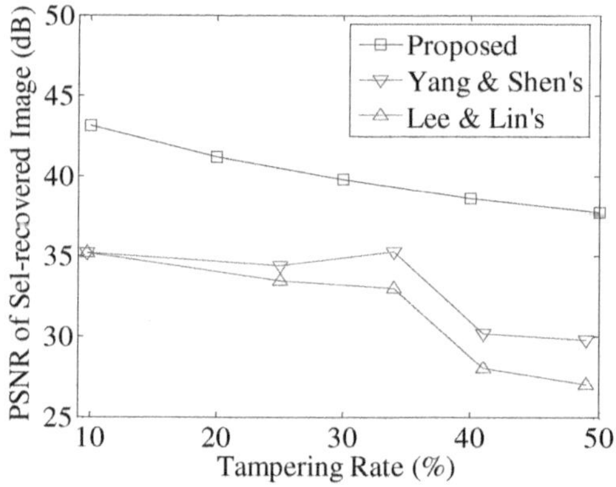

Fig. 4. The proposed method is compared with Lee & Lin's method in [7], and Yang & Shen's method in [8]. Simulations are in the same way as was described [8] using "Lena" of size 256×256. Values of PSNR of the self-recovered image decrease as tampering rate increase. As the proposed method focuses on color images, we turn the restored color image into grey for comparison.

5 Conclusions

In this paper, we propose a fragile watermarking method for color image, in which the original image is sampled to the form of Bayer pattern and embedded into itself accompanied with some hash bits generated from each block. The hash bits can be extracted to authenticate whether the watermarked image is tampered. When regions are tampered, extracted information are used to regenerate a color image by CFA based interpolation, which is then used to recover the lost information of the watermarked image.

Results show the method has better recovery quality, as our method is proposed according to the imaging algorithm of the digital imaging. The proposed scheme can also be used in the digital camera. After CCD catches the view, the Bayer patterns can be embedded into the image while the procedure of CAF interpolation happens.

Acknowledgement

This work was supported by the Natural Science Foundation of China (60872116, 60832010, and 60773079), the Shanghai Natural Science Foundation (09ZR1412400), the Innovation Program of Shanghai Municipal Education Commission (10YZ11), and the Shanghai Postdoctoral Science Foundation (10R21413200).

The authors are with School of Communication and Information Engineering, Shanghai University, China (corresponding author to provide phone: 86-21-56331551; fax: 86-21-56331964; email: zxqian@shu.edu.cn)

References

1. Fridrich, J.: Image watermarking for tamper detection. In: Proceeding of the IEEE International Conference on Image Processing, Chicago, IL, USA, vol. II, pp. 404–408 (1998)
2. Celik, M.U., Sharma, G., Saber, E., Tekalp, A.M.: Hierarchical Watermarking for Secure Image Authentication with Localization. IEEE Transactions on Image Processing 11(6), 585–594 (2002)
3. Suthaharan, S.: Fragile Image Watermarking Using a Gradient Image for Improved Localization and Security. Pattern Recognition Letters 25, 1893–1903 (2004)
4. Fridrich, J., Goljan, M.: Protection of Digital Images Using Self Embedding. In: Proceedings of Symposium on Content Security and Data Hiding in Digital Media (1999)
5. Wang, S.S., Tsai, S.L.: Automatic Image Authentication and Recovery Using Fractal Code Embedding and Image Inpainting. Pattern Recognition 41, 701–712 (2008)
6. Cheddad, A., Condell, J., Curran, K., Mc Kevitt, P.: A Secure and Improved Self-embedding Algorithm to Combat Digital Document Forgery. Signal Processing 89(12), 2324–2332 (2009)
7. Lee, T.Y., Lin, S.D.: Dual Watermark for Image Tamper Detection and Recovery. Pattern Recognition 41, 3497–3506 (2008)
8. Yang, C.W., Shen, J.J.: Recover the Tampered Image Based on VQ Indexing. Signal Processing 90(1), 331–343 (2010)
9. Zhang, X., Wang, S., Feng, G.: Fragile Watermarking Scheme with Extensive Content. In: Ho, A.T.S., Shi, Y.Q., Kim, H.J., Barni, M. (eds.) IWDW 2009. LNCS, vol. 5703, pp. 268–278. Springer, Heidelberg (2009)
10. Hamilton, J.F., Adams, J.E.: Adaptive Color Plane Interpolation in Single Sensor Color Electronic Camera, U.S. Patent 5 629 734 (1997)
11. Zhang, L., Wu, X.: Color Demosaicking via Directional Linear Minimum Mean Square-error Estimation. IEEE Transactions on Image Processing 14, 2167–2178 (2005)
12. Li, X., Gunturk, B., Zhang, L.: Image Demosaicing: A Systematic Survey. In: Proceedings of the SPIE, Visual Communications and Image Processing 2008, San Jose, CA, USA, vol. 6822, pp. 68221J–68221J-15 (2008)

A Hybrid-Feature-Based Efficient Retrieval over Chinese Calligraphic Manuscript Image Repository*

Yi Zhuang and Chengxiang Yuan

College of Computer & Information Engineering, Zhejiang Gongshang University, P.R. China
zhuang@mail.zjgsu.edu.cn

Abstract. In this paper, we propose an interactive indexing scheme to facilitate an efficient search of Chinese calligraphic manuscript images based on hybrid features such as contour points and number of strokes. Different from conventional character retrieval and indexing methods [6], our proposed indexing algorithm allows user to choose other feature such as stroke of character they prefer to as query element. To better facilitate an efficient and unified retrieval, we then propose a *<u>H</u>ybrid-<u>F</u>eature-<u>Tree</u>*(HF-Tree)-based high- dimensional indexing scheme. Comprehensive experiments are conducted to testify its effectiveness and efficiency.

Keywords: hybrid feature, Chinese calligraphic character, high-dimensional index.

1 Introduction

Chinese calligraphic scripts (see Fig. 1) is one of the important parts in Chinese culture[1]. Given a query calligraphic character, retrieving all the similar ones may help studying different written styles of the same character. However, the current approach is to use metadata or indices, which are created manually in a tedious, labor intensive and expensive process. Moreover, so far, although some research efforts have been made in retrieving and indexing the Chinese calligraphic characters images, they all focus on the studies of the shape-similarity- based retrieval and indexing [2,6]. To the best of our knowledge, no one use the number of strokes of a character to facilitate the character retrieval, which are testified to significantly improve the retrieval effectiveness(see Section 3). In our previous work [6], we studied the character retrieval and its indexing algorithms only based on their contour similarity measure. However, although the two characters in Fig.2(a) and Fig.2(b) are similar, their corresponding number of strokes are different. Hence, the number of strokes of a character can also be regarded as an effective pruning criterion(i.e., another feature) to facilitate character retrieval.

* This paper is partially supported by the Program of National Natural Science Foundation of China under Grant No. 60873022, 60903053; The Program of Natural Science Foundation of Zhejiang Province under Grant No. Y1080148, Y1090165; The Key Project of Special Foundation for Young Scholars in Zhejiang Gongshang University under Grant No. G09-7.

L. Chen et al. (Eds.): WAIM 2010, LNCS 6184, pp. 544–550, 2010.

So in this paper, based on the shape-similarity-based character retrieval algorithm [6], we propose an interactive high-dimensional indexing scheme based on hybrid features(e.g., *shape* and *stroke*), called *HF-Tree*. With the aid of the HF-Tree index, a high-dimensional retrieval *of* a character Vq is transformed into a range query in the single dimensional space.

The primary contributions of this paper are as follows:

1. We propose a novel interactive hybrid retrieval method to effectively support the Chinese calligraphic characters retrieval.
2. We introduce a hybrid-feature-tree(*HF-Tree*)-based indexing method to facilitate the interactive and efficient Chinese calligraphic characters retrieval with variable features.

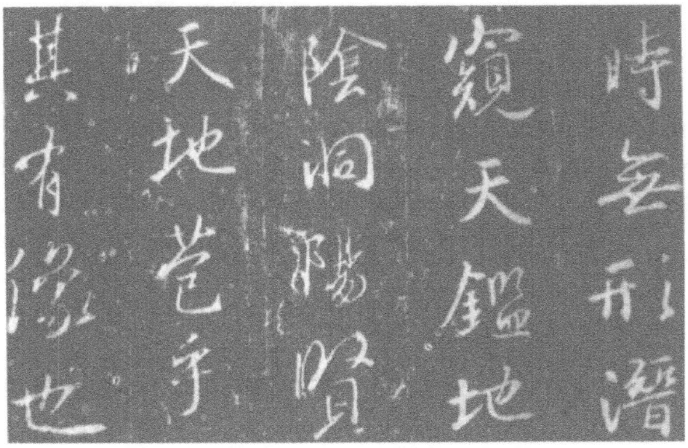

Fig. 1. A calligraphic character images

(a). NS=3

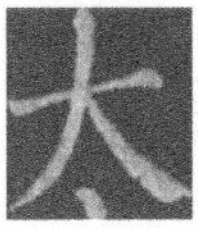

(b). NS=4

Fig. 2. Similar characters with different strokes' number

The rest of this paper is organized as follows. In Section 2, we propose a *Hybrid-Feature- Tree*(HF-Tree)-based high-dimensional indexing scheme to dramatically speed up the retrieval efficiency. In Section 3, we report the results of extensive experiments which are designed to evaluate the efficiency and effectiveness of the proposed approach. Finally, we conclude in Section 4.

2 The HF-Tree Index

In order to improve the retrieval efficiency, in this section, we develop a novel high-dimensional indexing technique, called the *Hybrid-Feature Tree*(HF-Tree for short), to accelerate the retrieval process.

2.1 Preliminaries

Before constructing the HF-Tree, n characters in Ω are first grouped into T clusters(denoted as Cj) by an AP-Cluster algorithm [5], and the centroid(Oj) of each cluster(Cj) can be adaptively selected, where $j \in [1,T]$. Then the centroid distance and the number of strokes of each character are computed. Moreover, its style and the type are identified at the same time. Finally, a uniform index key of a character is obtained, which is inserted by a B+-Tree.

Definition 1 (Cluster Radius). *Given a cluster Cj, the distance between Oj and the character which has the longest distance to Oj is defined as the cluster radius of Cj, denoted as CRj.*

Given a cluster Cj, the cluster sphere of it is denoted as $\Theta(Oj,CRj)$, where Oj is the centroid of cluster Cj, CRj is the cluster radius.

Definition 2 (Centroid Distance). *Given a character V_i, its centroid distance is defined as the distance between V_i and Oj, the centre of cluster that V_i belongs to:*

$$CD(V_i)=d(V_i,Oj) \tag{1}$$

where $d(V_i,Oj)=TMC^1(V_i,Oj), j\in[1,T], i\in[1,\delta]$ *and* δ *is the number of characters in* Cj.

2.2 The Data Structure

In order to effectively prune the search region, we propose the *HF-Tree*, an interactive hybrid- feature indexing scheme in which the high-dimensional index for contour points is based on the iDistance[3]. As mentioned before, all characters are first grouped into T clusters using an AP-Cluster algorithm[4], then the *centroid-distance* and the number of strokes of each character are computed. Thus the character V_i can be modeled as a four-tuple:

$$V_i ::= \langle i, CID, NS, CD \rangle \tag{2}$$

where i refers to the i-th character in Ω; CID is the ID number of the cluster V_i belongs to; NS is the number of strokes of V_i; CD is the centroid distance of V_i;

For each character V_i in a cluster sphere, its index key can be defined as:

$$key(V_i)=CD(V_i) \tag{3}$$

Since the characters are grouped into T clusters, to get a uniform index key of image in different clusters, the index key in Eq. (3) can be rewritten by Eq. (4):

$$key(V_i)=CID+CD(V_i)/MAX \tag{4}$$

where the CID is the ID number of cluster V_i falls in. Note that since $CD(V_i)$ may be larger than one, the value of $CD(V_i)$ should be normalized into the range of [0,1] by being divided a large constant MAX.

To facilitate retrieving characters via submitting an auxiliary information (e.g, the number of strokes) of V_i, its index key can be derived in Eq. (5):

$$key(V_i)=\alpha * NS(V_i)+CID+CD(V_i)/MAX \tag{5}$$

where $NS(V_i)$ refers to the number of strokes of character V_i and α is a stretch constant which is set 10^3 empirically.

For a character, its two values of CD and NS are recorded in the corresponding index key of HF-Tree. Fig. 3 shows the detail steps of constructing a HF-Tree. Note that the routine ***TransValue***(V_i) is a distance transformation function in Eq. (5) and ***BInsert***(key,*bt*) is a B+-tree insert procedure.

---

[1] *TMC* is the similarity function of two characters proposed in [6].

```
Algorithm 1. HF-Tree Index Construction
Input: Ω: the character set;
Output: bt: the index for HF-Tree;
The characters in Ω are grouped into T clusters using the AP cluster algorithm
bt←newFile();                /* create index header file */
for each character Vi∈Ω do
    The CD and NS of Vi are computed;
    key(Vi)=TransValue(Vi); /* Function TransValue() is shown in Eq. (5) */
    BInsert(key(Vi), bt);   /* insert it to B+-tree */
return bt
```

Fig. 3. The index construction algorithm for HF-Tree

2.3 *k*-NN Search Algorithm

In this section, we will study a *k*-NN search of Chinese calligraphic character, which retrieves the *k* most similar characters that are closest in distance to a given character. For example, when user submits a query character "国", its *NS* equals to 8. Then the search range over the HF-Tree is [*left*, *right*], where $left=\alpha*NS(V_i)+CID+(CD(V_i)-r)/MAX$, $right=\alpha*NS(V_i)+CID+CR_j/MAX$.

Fig. 4 details the whole search process which is composed of filtering and refinement stages. First, when a user submits a query, the search starts with a small

```
Algorithm 2. kNN Search
Input: query character Vq, k, NS
Output: query results S
r←0, S←Φ;          // initialization
while (|S|<k)      // |S| refers to the number of candidate characters in S
  r←r+Δr;
  S←RSearch(Vq,r);
  if (|S|>k) then
    for i:=1 to |S|-k do
      Vfar←Farthest(S,Vq);
      S←S-Vfar;
return S;
RSearch(Vq,r)
S1←Φ, S2←Φ;
for i:=1 to T do       // T is the number of clusters
  if Θ(Oi, CRi) contains Θ(Vq,r) then
    S2←Search(Vq,r, i);
    S1←S1∪S2;
    end loop
  else if Θ(Oi, CRi) intersects Θ(Vq,r) then
    S2←Search(Vq,r, i);
    S1←S1∪S2;
return S1;            // return candidate characters
Search(Vq,r, i)
left←α*NS(Vq) +i+(CD(Vq)-r)/MAX;
right←α*NS(Vq) +i+CRj/MAX;
S3←BRSearch[left, right];   // the filtering step
for each character Vj∈S3 do
  if d(Vq,Vj)>r then S3←S3-Vj;  // the refinement stage
return S3;      // return the candidate character set
```

Fig. 4. *k*-NN search algorithm

radius, and step by step, the radius is increased to form a bigger query sphere iteratively (line3), once the number of candidate characters is larger than k (line5), the search stops, then the (|S|-k) characters which are longest to the query one are identified (lines 6-7) and removed from S (line8). In this way, the k nearest neighbor characters of Vq are just returned. Note that, routine ***RSearch***(Vq,r) is the main range search function which returns the candidate characters of range search with centre Vq and radius r and ***Search***(Vq,r) is the implementation of the range search. ***Farthest***(S, Vq) returns the character which is the longest from Vq in S and S is denoted as the candidate character set. ***BRSearch***(*left*,*right*) is a B^+-tree range search function.

3 Experiments

In this section, we present an extensive performance study to evaluate the effectiveness and efficiency of our proposed retrieval and indexing method. The Chinese Calligraphic characters image data we used are from *China-America Academic Digital Library Project* [5] which contains a set of contour point features extracted from the 12,000 character images in which each feature point is composed of a pair of coordinates <*x axis*, *y axis*>.

We implemented the hybrid-based retrieval approach and the HF-Tree index in *C* language. The index page size of B^+-tree is set to 4096 Bytes. All the experiments are run on a Pentium IV CPU at 2.0GHz with 1GB memory. All the following experiments' performances are measured in terms of the average disk page access, and the CPU time over 100 queries.

3.1 Effectiveness of the Retrieval Method

In the first experiment, we have implemented an online interactive & hybrid retrieval system for Chinese calligraphic characters to testify the effectiveness of our proposed retrieval method comparing with the conventional one [6]. As shown in Fig. 5, when user submits an example Chinese calligraphic character by drawing a character "天" and the number of strokes as well, the candidate characters are retrieved by the system with the aid of the HF-Tree. The left part of the figure is the query result by submitting only a character and the right part demonstrates the query results of the hybrid retrieval (e.g., query character and the number of strokes as two query elements).

(a). Query character (b). Query character + strokes

Fig. 5. One retrieval example

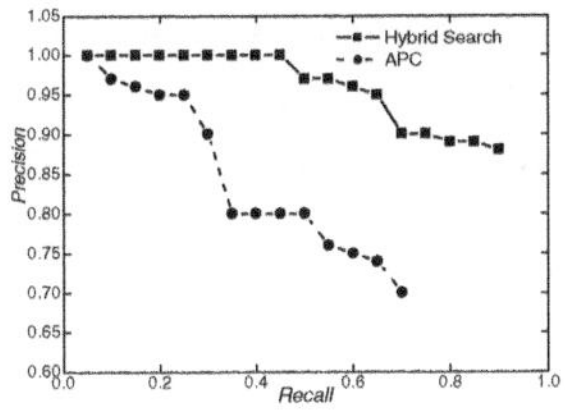

Fig. 6. Recall *vs.* precision

Fig. 6 illustrates a *Recall-Precision* curve for the performance comparisons of the *APC-based* method [6] and our proposed composite search. It compares the average retrieval result (the average precision rate under the average recall rate) of 20 characters queries randomly chosen from the database. Each of them has more than 4 different calligraphic styles and types. The figure shows that the retrieval performance of the composite search is better than that of the APC-based one by a large margin.

3.2 Efficiency of HF-Tree Index

In the following, we test the performance of our proposed indexing method—HF-Tree under different sizes of databases and different k.

3.2.1 Effect of Data Size

In the first experiment, we tested the performance behavior with varying number of characters. Fig. 7a shows the performance of query processing in terms of CPU cost. It is evident that HF-Tree outperforms sequential scan significantly. The CPU cost of HF-Tree increases slowly as the data size grows. It's worth mentioning that the CPU cost of sequential scan is ignored since the computation cost of it is very expensive. In Fig. 7b, the experimental result reveals that the I/O cost of HF-Tree is superior to other three methods. The PDM [6] exhibits a dramatically increase in terms of page access and it finally exceeds the sequential scan when the data size is 8000 because of its I/O intensive operations during query process.

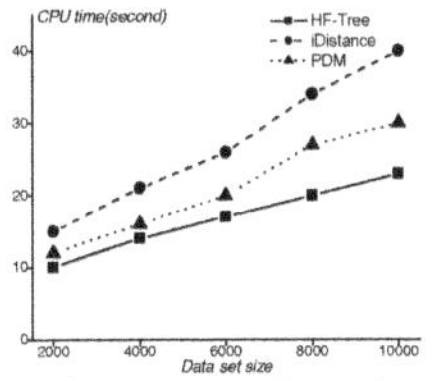

(a) CPU cost *vs.* Data size

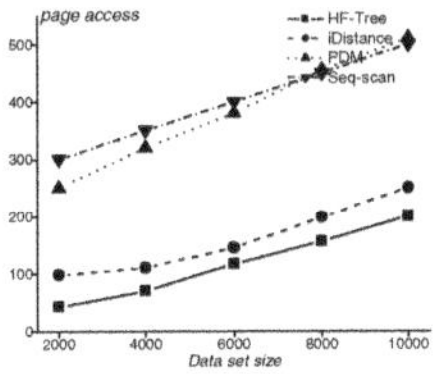

(b) I/O cost *vs.* Data size

Fig. 7. Effect of data size

3.2.2 Effect of *k*

In the final experiment, we evaluate the effect of k on the k-NN search by using the HF-Tree. Figs. 8a and 8b both indicate that when k ranges from 10 to 40, the HF-Tree is superior to other methods in terms of page access and the CPU cost. The results conform to our expectation that the search region of HF-Tree is significantly reduced and the comparison between any two characters is a CPU-intensive task. The CPU cost of sequential scan is ignored due to the expensive computation cost of it.

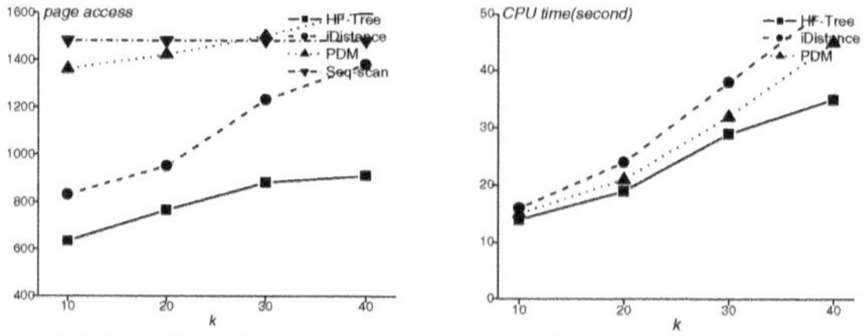

(a) *K vs.* Page Access (b) *K vs.* CPU Cost

Fig. 8. Effect of *k*

4 Conclusions and Future Work

In this paper, we presented an effective approach to retrieving Chinese calligraphic characters by choosing hybrid features; Then a novel hybrid-feature-tree(*HF-Tree*)-based high- dimensional indexing scheme is then proposed to boost the retrieval performance of the large Chinese calligraphic characters. The prototype retrieval system is implemented to demonstrate the applicability and effectiveness of our new approach to Chinese calligraphic character retrieval. It is worth mentioning that the *HF-Tree* can be easily extended to index multiple features such as style and type of a character that will be studied in our future work.

References

[1] Zhang, X.-Z.: Chinese Character Recognition Techniques. Tsinghua University Press, Beijing (1992)

[2] Wu, Y.-S., Ding, X.-Q.: Chinese character recognition: the principles and the implementations. High Education Press, Beijing (1992)

[3] Böhm, C., Berchtold, S., Keim, D.: Searching in High-dimensional Spaces: Index Structures for Improving the Performance of Multimedia Databases. ACM Computing Surveys 33 (3) (2001)

[4] Frey, B.J., Dueck, D.: Clustering by Passing Messages Between Data Points. Science 315, 972–976

[5] The CADAL Project (2005), `http://www.cadal.zju.edu.cn`

[6] Zhuang, Y., Zhuang, Y.-T., Li, Q., Chen, L.: Interactive high-dimensional index for large Chinese calligraphic character databases. ACM Trans. Asian Lang. Inf. Process. 6(2) (2007)

Efficient Filtering of XML Documents with XPath Expressions Containing Ancestor Axis

Bo Ning[1], Chengfei Liu[2], and Guoren Wang[3]

[1] Dalian Maritime University, Dalian, China
ningbo@dlmu.edu.cn
[2] Swinburne University of Technology, Melbourne, Australia
CLiu@groupwise.swin.edu.au
[3] Northeastern University, Shenyang, China
wanggr@mail.neu.edu.cn

Abstract. In this paper, we address the problem of filtering XML documents with large number of XPath expressions, which contain predicates with axes 'ancestor', 'descendant' and 'child'. We propose a novel index structure, called NIndex, to index those complex XPath expressions. Based on NIndex, we proposed a new filtering algorithm with lower complexity for our problem. Our experiment results show that our algorithm performs well across a range of XPath expressions and documents.

1 Introduction

The proliferation of the Internet and intranet, and the exploding volume of information made available on the Internet have fueled the development of a wild range of new applications based on selective dissemination of information. XML allows the encoding of semantic and structural information that can improve delivery accuracy. In an XML filtering system, continuously arriving XML documents are routed to users according to subscriptions specified as queries. Those queries typically specify patterns of selection predicates on multiple elements. However in real applications, XML queries submitted by users are more complex and may contain predicates with ancestor and parent axes.

There has been various work [1,2,3,4,5,6,7] on efficiently filtering XML streams with a collection of XPath expressions (XPEs). The XFilter system [1] handles simple XPath location path expressions by transforming them into a Deterministic Finite Automaton. The YFilter system [2] is an extension of XFilter in which a group of simple XPath location path expressions are combined into a single Nondeterministic Finite Automaton (NFA). The XTrie [3] can handle twig pattern expressions involving predicates which are internally represented as trees called the XTrie-tree. The XPush [4] supports twig pattern with nested predicates and share the common predicates among multiple XPath expressions by using an Alternating Finite Automaton(AFA). The lazy filtering algorithm (LF) [5] handles the univariate XPath which support only 'descendant' and 'child' axes. The algorithms above can handle only forward axes, while can not deal with the XPath expression containing 'ancestor' axis.

L. Chen et al. (Eds.): WAIM 2010, LNCS 6184, pp. 551–557, 2010.

In this paper, we propose a novel index structure named NIndex, which supports the efficient filtering of XML documents based on XPath expressions which contain 'ancestor' axis. Our new index structure offers several novel features that make it especially attractive for large-scale publish/subscribe systems.

2 NIndex: Indexing the XPath Expressions

2.1 PXPE-Tree

We represent an partial XPath expression as a rooted unordered tree, called PXPE-tree, with labeled vertices and edges, T = (V_T, E_T). We use the term PXPE-node to refer to the vertices of a PXPE-tree. Each PXPE-node has a unique incoming edge, which is labeled with the axis. Functions, label: $V_T \rightarrow String$, and axis: $E_T \rightarrow \{ancestor, descendant, parent, child\}$ return the labels associated with the PXPE-nodes and edges respectively.

2.2 Common Sub-pattern

We assume that the symbol $subtree(r)$ express the subtree rooted at PXPE-node r in PXPE-tree T.

Definition 1 (Common Sub-pattern). *Given PXPE-treew T_1 and T_2, if PXPE-tree T_C whose root is n is the subtree(n) of T_1 and T_2, we call the T_C is the Common Sub-pattern of T_1 and T_2.*

Definition 2 (Highest Common Sub-pattern). *Given PXPE-treew T_1 and T_2, S_T=(T_{c_1},...T_{c_n}) is the set of common sub-patterns of T_1 and T_2. We call the T_{c_i} with largest height the Highest Common Sub-pattern of T_1 and T_2.*

Two PXPE-trees may have many common sub-patterns, but there is only one highest common sub-pattern.

2.3 Structure of NIndex

We index PXPE-nodes in NIndex, and we only store one copy of the common sub-patterns. We cluster the PXPE-nodes into the tables by their tag names, and each table T_t stores all PXPE-nodes with the tag t, and each row in T_t corresponds to a PXPE-node which is a root of a sub-pattern of PXPE-trees. For seaching the respective table with certain tag name, a mapping table, implemented in the form of a hash table, is built over all *(tagname, p_table)* pairs for retrieving the pointer to a table of any tag name. We may implement table T_t by using hash table or B+tree for efficient retrieval of row by ID.

Each row in tag table is used to describe a PXPE-node c_n and the sub-pattern rooted at c_n. It includes four kinds of fields: (1) structure of the PXPE-node, including the *axis*, *parent*, *pos*, *p_dc* and *p_a*. The *axis* field records the axis of the current PXPE-node c_n. *desc* and *anc* are respectively short for 'descendant' and 'ancestor'. The *parent* field is the *(tagname, row_num)* pair of the parent node of c_n in PXPE-tree, which is the row_num^{th} row in tag table $T_{tagname}$. The *pos* field denotes the position of c_n among its sibling nodes in PXPE-tree. The *p_dc* field records the set of all children of c_n with 'descendant' and 'child' axes, in which each child is identified by *(tagname, row_num)* pairs. The *p_a* field records the set of all 'ancestor' predicate-node of c_n, in which each node is identified by *(tagname, row_num)* pairs too. (2) A stack for the filtering of 'descendant' and 'child' axes. In the algorithms, one run-time stack is created for each non-leaf query node. Each element e in stack records the depth of e in the data tree and a flag which is a bit array with its size equals to the count of child PXPE-nodes with 'descendant' and 'child' axes of the current node c_n in the PXPE-tree. (3) Field *r_queries*, which includes IDs of those PXPE-tree, that are rooted at the current node c_n. (4) Field *s_times*, which records the shared times of the current row. In addition, for each table T_{tn}, we assign a *a_flag*, which records whether there is the open tag of a element of tag tn during the processing of filtering. It is used for the filtering of 'ancestor' axis, and initialized by zero.

3 The Filtering Algorithm Based on NIndex

Based on NIndex, we propose a filtering algorithm. To process 'descendant'/'child' axes, a stack will be created for c_i when a start tag of an element with tag name n arrives and a bit array for p_{dc} will also be created to check the arrival of its descendant/child elements. To process 'ancestor' axis, *a_flag* is set for the table

Algorithm 1. NIndex::startElement(n)

```
depth = depth + 1;
T_n = mapping(n);
T_n.a_flag++;
if T_n ≠ FAIL then
    for each c_i in T_n do
        c_p = parent[c_i];
        if stack[c_p] is empty then break;
        p = top(stack[c_p]);
        if p.flags[pos[c_i]] == 0 then
            if axis[c_i] == 'desc' or p.depth+1==depth then
                if leaf[c_i] == 'Y' then
                    p.flags[pos[c_i]]=1;
                else
                    s = newElement(stack[c_i],depth);
                    push(stack[c_i],s);

    Function mapping(n)
    if HashTable[n] ≠ NULL then
        return HashTable[n];
    else
        return FAIL
```

T_a when a start tag of an element with tag name a arrives. When an end tag of an element with tag name n arrives, we can check whether D satisfy T as follows: (1) Check 'descendant'/'child' axes of c_i by examing the bit array for p_{dc} to see if all bits of the array are set to 1; (2) Check 'ancestor' axis of c_i by examing, for each tag name a in p_a, whether *a_flag* for the table T_a is set. If both hold, we can immediately send document D to those users who subscribe the request specified in PXPE-tree T.

Given a row c_i of tag name n in table T_n, the basic idea of handling the 'descendant'/'child' axes in *startElement*(n) (as shown in Algorithm 2) is as follows: when a start tag of an element with tag name n arrives, we obtain the parent c_p of c_i first. Nothing needs to be done if the parent element has not arrived (line 7) or c_i under c_p has a match, i.e., line 9 yields a false. Otherwise, if c_i is a non-leaf node, create a stack element s for element c_i with $s.depth = depth$

Algorithm 2. NIndex::endElement(n)

```
1  T_n = mapping(n);
2  if T_n ≠ FAIL then
3      for each c_i in T_n do
4          if leaf[c_i] == 'Y' or stack[c_i] is empty then break;
5          s = top(stack[c_i]);
6          if s.depth == depth then
7              pop(stack[c_i]);
8              q.Flags = q.Flags | s.Flags;
9          AFlag = 1;
10         for each c_j in p_a[c_i] do
11             if T_{c_j.tagname}.aflag == 0 then
12                 AFlag = 0;
13         if evaluate(s.flags ,f[c_i]) == true and AFlag == 1 then
14             c_p = parent(c_i);
15             if c_p == 0 then
16                 add r_queries(c_i) to results set S_result;
17             else
18                 p = top(stack[c_p]);
19                 p.flags[pos[c_i]] = 1;
20                 if axis[c_i]== 'desc' then
21                     clearPredStack(c_i);
22             destroy(s);
23     T_n.a_flag--;
24     depth = depth-1;
25 Procedure clearPredStackS(c_n)
26 if stack[c_n] is not empty then
27     destroy all elements in stack[c_n];
28     for each c_i in p_dc[c_n] do
29         if leaf[c_i] == 'N' then clearPredStackS(c_i);
```

of e and initialize all bits in $s.flags$ to 0 (line 14), and push element s into stack[c_i] (line 15); if c_i is a leaf node, we can immediately to set the flag bit for c_i in c_p (line 12). The basic idea of handling the 'descendant' and 'child' axes in *endElement*(n) (as shown in Algorithm 3) is evaluating the bit array $s.flags$ (line 13) to determine whether a match with *subtree*(c_i) has been found under p (line 19), as well as passing all those bits in $s.flags$ that have been set to 1 down to the new top element of *stack*[c_i] (line 8).

When handling the ancestor axis, given a PXPE-node c_i (with tag name n) which has a child PXPE-node c_j (with tag name m) with 'anc' edge in PXPE-tree, c_i need to check whether the c_j's *a_flag* is non-zero. When *startElement*(m) event happens, we add *a_flag* of T_m by 1 (line 5 in Algorithm 2), and when *endElement*(m) event happens, we subtract *a_flag* of T_m by 1 (line 23 in Algorithm 3). If an element e_m of tag m comes, then *startElement*(m) happens, the *a_flag* of table T_m is non-zero. We can confirm that an element e_n which arrives between the e_m'*startElement*(m) and e_m'*endElement*(m) has an ancesor element e_m in the document. So the relationship between PXPE-nodes c_i and c_j are matched. When *endElement*(n) happens, PXPE-node c_i checks the *a_flag*s of all his child PXPE-nodes with 'anc' edge in PXPE-tree (line 9-12 in Algorithm 3). If all of the *a_flag*s are non-zero, the current element of tag n has all the ancestor elements in the PXPE-tree. If the child and descendant axes are also satisfied (line 13 in Algorithm 3), there is a matching of PXPE-node c_i in the current document. If c_i is the root of PXPE-tree, add the query *ID*s of *r_queries* to the results set (line 16 in Algorithm 3).

4 Performance Evaluation

4.1 Experiment Setup

By using a set of DTDs, we generated a set of XML documents with number of elements varying from 1000 to 5000(size varying from 9K to 400K). We implemented an XPath expression generator with following input parameters. The parameter P controls the size of the set of indexed XPEs . The parameter p_d controls the probability of having a 'descendant' axis at each node. The parameter p_a controls the probability of having a 'ancestor' axis at each node. Three algorithms were compared: (1) YFilter, (2) XTrie, and (3)NIndex.

4.2 Performance Study

Fig. 1 compares the scalability of the algorithms as a function of P, the size of the set of indexed XPEs. The results show that the filtering time increases almost linearly with P, with NIndex being the fastest algorithm. Fig. 2 compares the scalability of the algorithms as a function of the size of the XML documents. The results clearly show that the filtering time increases linearly with the document size for all the algorithms, and the algorithm based on NIndex performs best.

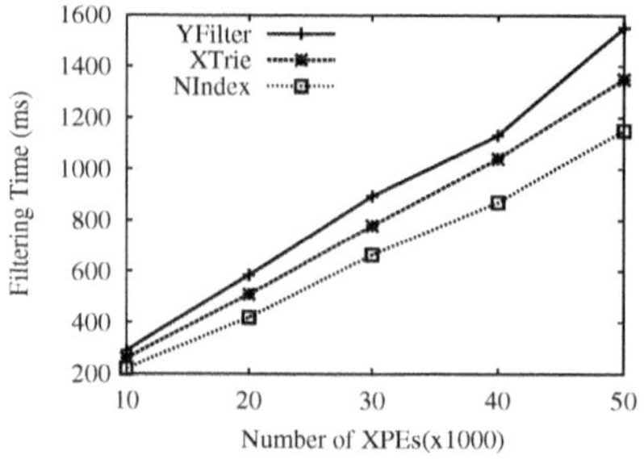

Fig. 1. $P(p_d{=}0.1{,}p_a{=}0)$

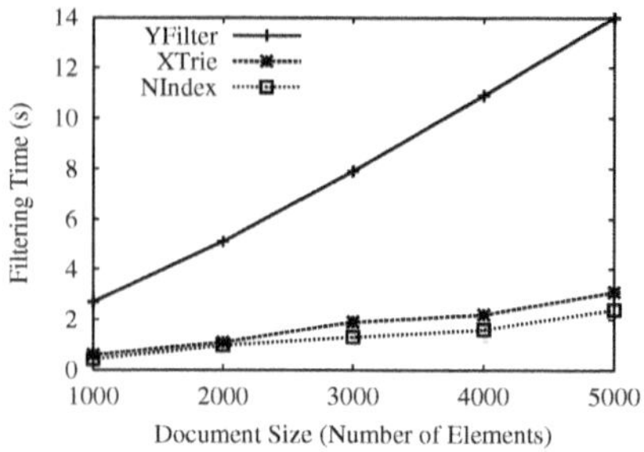

Fig. 2. Size (P=10k, p_d=0.1, p_a=0)

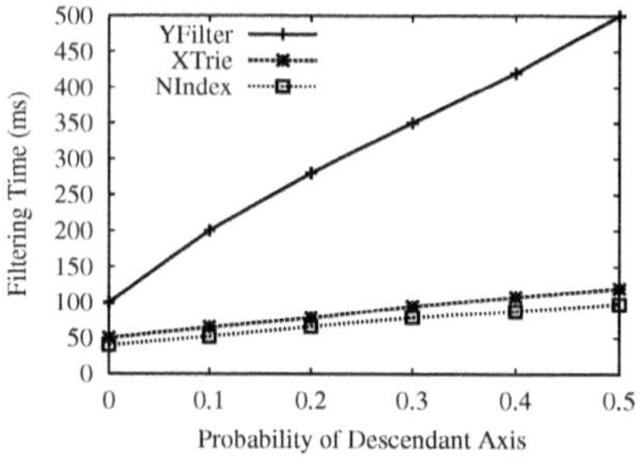

Fig. 3. p_d (P=10k, p_a=0)

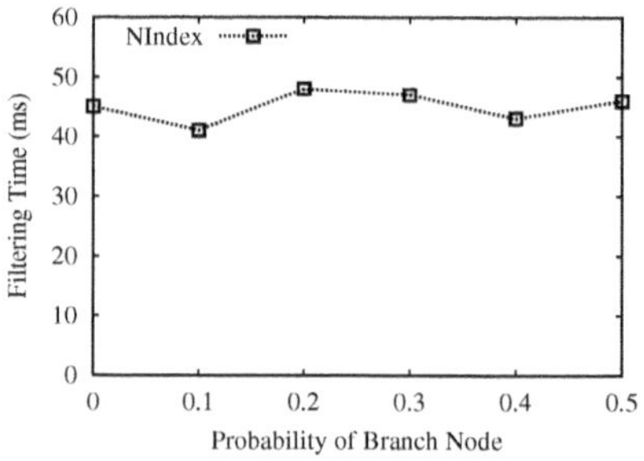

Fig. 4. p_a (P=10k, p_d=0.4)

Fig. 3 shows that increasing p_d, the probability of 'descendant' axis in the XPEs increases the filtering time of all the algorithms. The NIndex performs best and the filtering time increases almost linearly with p_d. In Fig. 4, we tested the effect of the p_a. The results show that the p_a have no effect on our filtering algorithm.

5 Conclusions

In this paper, we addressed the problem of filtering XML documents with large number of user submitted queries in XPath expressions. We proposed a novel index structure, termed NIndex, which is designed to support effective filtering based on complex XPath expressions containing 'ancestor' axis. It is more compact to represent XPath expressions and reduce the number of unnecessary index probes as well as avoid redundant matchings. Then we proposed a new filtering algorithm with lower complexity. Apart from 'child' and 'descendant' axes, our algorithm can also handle the 'ancestor' axis. Our experiment results show that our algorithm performs well across a range of documents and XPEs.

Acknowledgement. This research was supported by the National Natural Science Foundation of China (Grant No. 60773221).

References

1. Altinel, M., Franklin, M.J.: Efficient Filtering of XML Documents for Selective Dissemination of Information. In: Proceeding of VLDB, pp. 53–64 (2000)
2. Diao, Y., Fischer, P., Franklin, M., To, R.: Yfilter: Efficient and scalable filtering of XML documents. In: Proceeding of ICDE (2002)
3. Chan, C.Y., Felber, P., Garofalakis, M.N., Rastogi, R.: Efficient filtering of XML documents with XPath expressions. In: Proceeding of ICDE (2002)
4. Gupta, A.K., Suciu, D.: Stream processing of XPath queries with predicates. In: Proceeding of SIGMOD (2003)
5. Gou, G., Chirkova, R.: Efficient Algorithms for Evaluating XPath over Streams. In: Proceeding of SIGMOD, pp. 269–280 (2007)
6. Tian, F., Reinwald, B., Pirahesh, H., Mayr, T., Myllymaki, J.: Implementing a scalable XML publish/subscribe system using relational database systems. In: Proceeding of SIGMOD, pp. 479–490 (2004)
7. Hou, S., Jacobsen, H.: Predicate-based Filtering of XPath Expressions. In: Proceeding of ICDE, p. 55 (2006)

ACAR: An Adaptive Cost Aware Cache Replacement Approach for Flash Memory

Yanfei Lv, Xuexuan Chen, and Bin Cui

School of Electronics Engineering and Computer Science, Peking University
Key Lab of High Confidence Software Technologies (Ministry of Education), Peking University
{lvyf,xuexuan,bin.cui}@pku.edu.cn

Abstract. Flash memory has been gaining more popularity as a substitution for magnetic disk. However, due to asymmetric IO latency, cache management policy needs to be reconsidered in systems equipped with flash. A novel buffer replacement approach named ACAR, which stands for Adaptive Cost Aware cache Replacement, is proposed in this paper to address this problem. Taking operation cost into consideration, ACAR allocates two pools for clean and dirty pages separately. In addition, dynamical pool size tuning is also performed according to IO pattern evolvement. Furthermore, hot data recognition capacity is realized in an enhanced version of ACAR. Experiments with artificial and real IO traces demonstrate ACAR outperforms the state-of-the-art cache replacement strategies.

1 Introduction

Flash memory has been widely adopted in the portable devices such as PDA, digital camera and MP3 as the durable storage material due to its outstanding characteristics: light weight, power saving and shock resistant. As price drops and volume increases sharply every year, flash based storage devices are expected to be applied to data-intensive systems including database management systems. However, as an EEPROM, flash memory exhibits some totally different IO features compared with traditional disk. How to leverage these features by reconsidering the existing storage technology is one of the main obstacles for the popularization of flash.

Database management systems resort to memory cache to boost the IO performance as there are great speed gap between the memory and disk. However, due to cost and capacity constraints, only the hot data should be loaded into main memory. When it is full, some pages have to be evicted from memory and written back to disk if it is dirty. Which page should be selected as the victim is the key problem for cache replacement strategy. The emergence of flash memory does not essentially change the situation above as there still exists obvious speed gap between flash and main memory. However, a main feature of flash memory is asymmetric speed of read and write, that is, writing a page is several times slower than reading. Consequently, evicting a dirty page from main memory will

L. Chen et al. (Eds.): WAIM 2010, LNCS 6184, pp. 558–569, 2010.

incur significantly higher time cost than a clean page replacement for flash memory while these two costs are similar in traditional disk. Therefore, it is necessary to optimize current disk-oriented cache replacement scheme for flash memory.

Current state-of-the-art works do not fully utilize the read-write cost difference. CFLRU [1] maintains a window on LRU queue. The clean pages in the window will be evicted first even if they are much hotter than the dirty ones. This may deteriorate the overall performance because some obsolete dirty pages tend to occupy the precious main memory resource for a long time. WSR [2] [3] (write sequential reorder) based methods improve the existing disk-oriented cache replacement methods by giving another chance to the dirty pages when they are selected as the victim. But actually, how many "chances" should be given to the dirty pages is depended on the operation cost. In essence, these strategies didn't take quantity of operation cost into consideration. Furthermore, access latency of flash is only a small fraction of magnetic disk, what demands for low complexity online replacement algorithm. Unfortunately, as far as we know, none of existing self-tuning approaches is O(1) in the worst case.

In this paper, we propose a novel cache replacement strategy, named Adaptive Cost Aware cache Replacement (ACAR), based on this read-write cost model. ACAR provides an equal opportunity for clean and dirty pages to compete with each other according to operation cost. To achieve this, we maintain two separate lists for clean and dirty pages, and adjust the length of these two lists dynamically with the workload evolution and operation cost. Our algorithm has the following merits: 1) An operation cost aware cache replacement strategy, 2) Dynamical adjusting structure to the workload, 3) O(1) time complexity for each access in the worst case, and 4) An extension to support hot data recognition.

The rest of this paper is organized as follows: Section 2 introduces background knowledge about flash memory and related work. In Section 3, a new cache replacement method ACAR and its enhancement ACAR+ are presented in detail with analysis. Experimental results are reported in Section 4, and finally we conclude the paper in Section 5.

2 Preliminaries

2.1 Flash Memory

Flash memory is an EEPROM Flash memory which comes into two flavors NOR and NAND. NAND flash is appropriate for data storage while NOR flash is designed for code execute-in-place. Hence, we focus on NAND flash in this paper. There are two kinds of NAND, SLC(Single-Level Cell) and MLC(Multi-Level Cell). MLC has larger capacity compared with SLC at the expense of higher access latency, more energy consumption and lower stability. The read and write unit of NAND is one page (typically 2K). The page with data cannot be rewritten before erased even if it is partially used. Erase performs in a one-time-one-block manner, which contains 64 or 128 pages typically. Furthermore, only sequential page usage is supported in a block. Limited (10000-100000) times of erase can be endured before worn out. Table 1[4] illustrates the access latency of SLC and

Table 1. Access speed of NAND flash and disk

Media	Read	Write	Erase
Magnetic Disk	12.7ms(2KB)	13.7ms(2KB)	N/A
SLC NAND	80μs(2KB)	200μs(2KB)	1.5ms(128KB)
MLC NAND	120μs(2KB)	800μs(2KB)	1.5ms(256KB)

MLC with magnetic disk as comparison. From the table, several IO characteristics can be observed as follows.

Low access latency. As a pure electrical device, flash memory can respond to IO requests quickly even arriving in random pattern. This requires fast cache replacement algorithm.

Asymmetry of IO. The write performs several times slower than read. In addition, potential erase makes the write performance even worse. So cache should allocate low priority to dirty pages on the occasion of eviction.

2.2 Related Work

The cache replacement has been a hot topic for several decades in the database community as well as in the computer architecture area. LRU (Least Recently Used) and LFU (Least Frequently Used) are two classic approaches for cache management. LRU focuses on recency information which reacts quickly to the workload evolution while LFU records frequency which can figure out the long-term pattern of access. After that, many approaches try to combine the merits of LRU and LFU [5] [6] [7] [8]. 2Q [9] is a breakthrough in cache replacement strategy. Many following "advanced" approaches are conducted as improvements based on 2Q. 2Q contains two LRU queues, Q1 and Q2. The pages accessed for the first time are held in Q1; if any page in Q1 is referenced again, it is moved into Q2. Every eviction performs on Q1 first. In this way, 2Q can detect the hot pages and hold them in Q2. LIRS [10], the algorithm integrated into MySQL, divides pages into HIR and LIR corresponding to Q1 and Q2 in 2Q. Differently, LIRS adjusts the length of HIR queue automatically according to the least recent LIR. ARC [11] is a self-tuning strategy without parameter. It accommodates the length of Q1 and Q2 in 2Q dynamically using information of already evicted pages. These disk-oriented cache management strategies are designed to maximize the page hit ratio which may not be suitable for flash-based systems with different I/O characteristics, though the skills they used are helpful to cache design on flash memory.

Many works have been done on developing flash-specific cache management schema. FAB [12] and BPLRU [13] are two block level cache management strategies. However, they are both designed for flash device embedded cache. CFLRU [1] maintains a window on the LRU end of LRU Queue. In this window, clean pages are evicted first. Dirty pages will be evicted unless there does not exist any clean page in the window. However, some cool dirty pages may occupy cache for a long time which decreases the effective size of cache. An improvement of CFLRU with dynamic window-size is also mentioned, but it does not solve this problem in essence. Furthermore, the dynamic window-size CFLRU is not O(1) in the worst case. LIRS-WSR [3] and LRU-WSR [2] are similar methods based on LIRS and LRU separately. They give higher priority to dirty pages by providing another chance to them once they are selected as victim. But this method acts in a fixed manner even when adopted on a device with different operation costs. In addition, WSR methods are not worst-case O(1) algorithm either. A cost aware algorithm is proposed based on CAR[14] in [15]. However, this method is designed for mobile embedded systems and considers compressed pages mainly. In addition, it stores operations which makes it slow to determine victim. CFDC [16] improves CFLRU by clustering the dirty pages in the same block and evicted them as a batch. Recently-Evicted-First Buffer Replacement Policy [17] uses similar technology to improves the overall performance. But this technique is orthogonal to our work as the same method can be integrated into ACAR easily. FlashCache [18] employs flash as a part of main memory for energy-saving purpose which is not the motivation of ours.

3 The ACAR Algorithm

3.1 General Idea

The key idea of ACAR is verification and self-tuning. ACAR can learn the best pool size automatically from the "mistakes" caused by previous decisions. Therefore, we hold previous decisions for mistake detection. Although the cache miss has already occurred, this experience can be adopted as a tip for future decisions. With the assumption of access pattern stability, the knowledge learnt can prevent the same kind of mistake taking place again.

To achieve this, ACAR organizes all the cache-resident pages into two LRU queues named CR (Clean Resident) and DR (Dirty Resident) which contain clean and dirty pages separately. Besides, another two corresponding queues CNR (Clean Non-Resident) and DNR (Dirty Non-Resident) are used to keep the non-resident pages that are evicted from CR and DR. In fact, the pages evicted act as the decisions made by ACAR. If a previously evicted page in non-resident queue is referenced in the future (this is a cache miss that we do not expect), this means the ACAR should have paid more attention to the corresponding queue. Hence, ACAR performs an adjustment by allocating more cache space to this queue. For example, if an access to a page p1 is performed which is in CNR queue, this is definitely a miss as all the pages in CNR are non-resident. Thus, more space is assigned to CR to try to prevent the same thing happening again. The costs of read and write operations are used to decide how much space is allocated to the queue.

We determine the space allocated in each case by analyzing the loss caused by the wrong eviction. There are four cases in total.

1. Read on CNR. This causes a page read. If the page is resident, read can be avoided so the loss is the time of reading a page.
2. Read on DNR. This is the same with case 1.
3. Write on CNR. Since all the read operations are considered in the two cases above, there is no difference between page resident and nonresident. Hence, the loss is 0.
4. Write on DNR. If the page is resident then, these two write can be merged into one, so the loss is the time of write a page.

Once access pattern changes, cache missing is likely to increase accordingly. Consequently, adjustment of ACAR is continuously triggered. The lengths of CR and DR become accommodated to the new workload pattern gradually. Therefore, the ACAR is a self-tuning strategy.

3.2 Implementation

As illustrated in figure 1, all the pages resident in cache are reserved in CR and DR in the way that CR stores the clean pages while DR stores the dirty ones. Thus, we always have that the total size of CR and DR is not larger than cache size. A write on CR page will cause this page moved to DR. Both CR and DR act in LRU manner. ACAR also maintains two auxiliary FIFO queues named CNR and DNR. If a page is evicted from CR or DR, its ID is recorded into CNR or DNR correspondingly. However, the content of that page is freed from cache. Since only page IDs are contained in CNR and DNR, only a little fraction of memory is required and have little effect on the overall performance of cache.

A variable named CRLE (CR Length Expected) of float type is maintained by ACAR which indicates the proper expected length of CR. Once eviction happens, if actual length of CR exceeds CRLE, a page will be selected from CR as the victim by LRU manner. Otherwise, a page in DR is selected. Note that the total length of CR and DR equals cache size when evicting, so there is no need to keep DRLE for DR queue. If any page is hit on CNR or DNR, some adjustment is performed on CRLE. In ACAR, we assume the cost of read as 1, and the cost of write is normalized as $Ratio = writeCost/readCost$. CRLE is

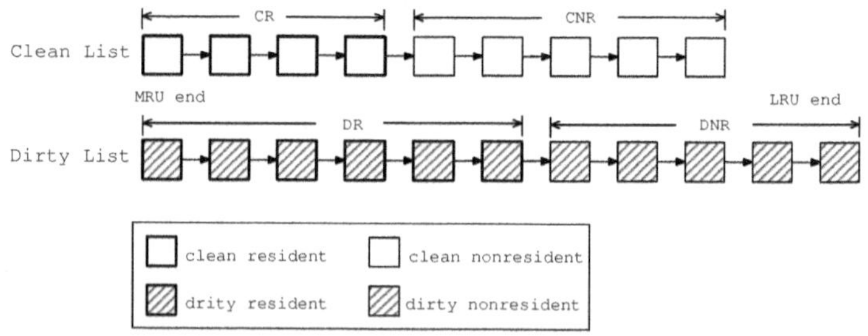

Fig. 1. Data structure of ACAR

Algorithm 1. Acquire free page procedure

```
Output: a free page is returned.
if lengthCR+lengthDR < cache size then    /* There is a free page */
    return any free page in cache;
else
    if CRLE < CR length then
        free a page from CR queue in LRU manner;
        add the page to CNR;
    else
        free a page from DR queue in LRU manner;
        add the page to DNR;
    end
    return the free page;
end
```

increased by 1 if a hit takes place on CNR, decreased by 1 on a read hit on DNR, and decreased by Ratio on a write hit on DNR. In this way, different operations are treated properly in ACAR.

As cache management methods usually do, we keep a hash table of pages in memory to accelerate searching. Pointers to queue entries of the page as well as a pointer to the page data is saved in the hash table. The concrete algorithms are given in algorithm 1 and algorithm 2.

We discuss how to choose the queue lengths of CNR and DNR here. A longer size would incur adjusting of CRLE quickly to help ACAR to be adapted to work load change quickly but too long of CNR and DNR will maintain many obsolete messages that mislead the ACAR. The length is a tuning parameter in our strategy, and we will present experimental results on this factor. The same size is assigned for CNR and DNR, because the weights of write and read operations have already been reflected on Ratio.

The time complexity of ACAR is O(1) in the worst case, so ACAR is very suitable for online processing.

3.3 Algorithm Analysis

In this part, a formal analysis is presented to show some characteristics of ACAR. The variables used in this section is listed in table 2.

Proposition 1. *Under a stable IO pattern, when cache is full, increment of* l_{cr} *will cause CRLE tends to decrease and vice versa.*

The "stable IO pattern" means the access possibility of pages conform to a stable distribution. Note that the decrement of CRLE means pages in CR are more easily to be selected as victim. This will lead to a decrement of l_{cr} which will cause increment of CRLE in turn. For a particular IO pattern, these two phases can arrive at a balance situation as the following proposition shows.

Algorithm 2. ACAR algorithm

```
Input: page address required
Output: page is loaded into cache
get the control information from Hash table;
if page exists in CR or DR then                                /* cache hit */
    perform the operation;
    if page in CR and is write operation then
        move this page to DR;
    end
    perform LRU adjustment in the corresponding queue;
else                                                           /* cache miss */
    if hit on CNR then
        CRLE = min(CRLE + 1, cacheSize);
    end
    if hit on DNR then
        CRLE = max(CRLE − writecost/readcost, 0);
    end
    AcuqireFreePage();
    perform the operation;
    if is write operation then
        move this page to DR.;
    end
    perform LRU adjustment in the corresponding queue;
end
update the information in hash table;
```

Proposition 2. *Under a stable IO pattern, ACAR will come to a stable situation which approximately has*

$$Pw_{dnr} * writeCost + Pr_{dnr} * readCost = Pr_{cnr} * readCost \tag{1}$$

or either l_{wr} *or* l_{cr} *is* $0.Assume$

$$w = \begin{cases} fw * writeCost + fr * readCost, & dirty\ page \\ fr * readCost, & clean\ page \end{cases} \tag{2}$$

ACAR tends to evict the page with lower weight w.

This proposition shows ACAR uses weighted frequency to determine which page to be evicted. Furthermore, the operation cost is reflected in weight. The proofs to these propositions are omitted due to the space limitation.

3.4 Enhanced ACAR with Hot Data Detection

A wise cache management policy should distinguish hot data from cold. For example, scanning of a large file will evict former detected hot pages out of the cache in LRU-based policy. To solve this problem, some existing flash-oriented strategies such as BPLRU [13] and CFDC [16] integrate scan detection approach.

Table 2. Variable list

Variable	Meaning
Pr_{cnr}	Possibility of read on CNR
Pr_{dnr}	Possibility of read on DNR
Pw_{dnr}	Possibility of write on DNR
fw	Write frequency on one page
fr	Read frequency on one page
l_{cr}	Length of CR queue
l_{dr}	Length of DR queue

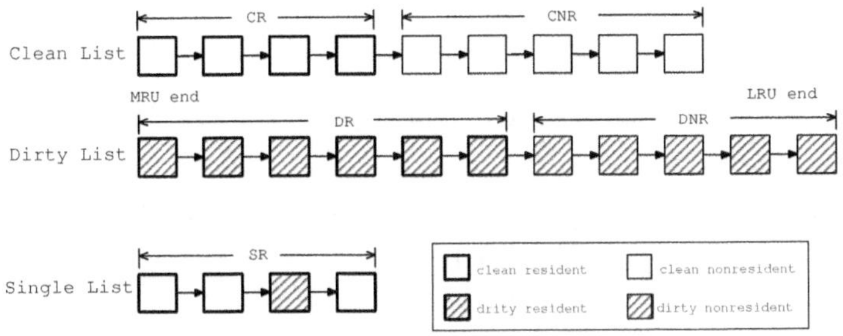

Fig. 2. Data structure of ACAR+

Enhanced ACAR named ACAR+ adds another queue SR(Single List) to deal with this problem. As demonstrated in figure 2, the page referenced for the first time is stored in the single list. If page in single list is accessed again, then it will be elevated into traditional ACAR part. In addition, victim selection is only performed on single list. Thus, once scan takes place, only pages in single list will be evicted. The pages in ACAR part are protected.

4 Experimental Results

In this section, we conduct a trace-driven simulation including artificial and real application workloads. We use the total IO time to the flash in seconds (denoted as Total Cost) as the criterion. Some state-of-the-art algorithms are also implemented for comparison. All experiments are run on a 2.4 GHz Intel Quad CPU with 2 GB of physical memory. The operating system used is Windows 7, and the simulation is developed in Visual Studio 2008 environment using C#.

4.1 Stationary Reference Probability Distribution

A synthetic workload is adopted in this section which has also been used in [9,5]. We generated random references to 1000 pages with a Zipfian distribution. The parameter is configured to simulate 80-20 and 45-20 distributions separately. In addition, we also tune some pages to write-intensive while others read-intensive.

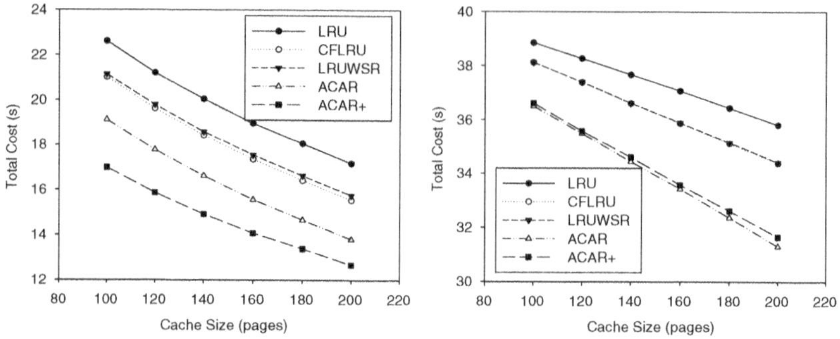

(a) 80-20 distribution on MLC (b) 45-20 distribution on MLC

Fig. 3. Performance of replacement policies on MLC

The number of read is about 65% of the total. Window size of CFLRU is fixed to 30% of cache size as recommended in [1].

At the beginning, we set the operation costs as MLC in table 1. The results are given in figure 3. CFLRU and LRUWSR exceed LRU since they allocated higher priority to dirty pages. ACAR performs better than CFLRU and LRUWSR as it can dynamically adjust to the workload and operation cost. With the help of hot page detection, ACAR+ outperforms all the other strategies in 80-20 distribution. Since the locality in 45-20 distribution is not as obvious as 80-20 distribution, it is harder to predict page accesses in 45-20 distribution. Consequently, each strategy performs worse on 45-20 distribution.

We reconfigure operation costs to simulate SLC. As illustrated in figure 4(a), ACARs also exceed other strategies. It can be observed in figure 4(b) that the number of write operations in SLC is less than that in MLC. Because the write operations in SLC are not so critical as that in MLC, ACAR adjusts the space allocated to clean and dirty pages to achieve better overall performance. However, CFLRU and LRUWSR cannot be aware of this operation cost changes.

We next investigate the effects of parameters of our approach. From figure 5(a), we can see that when the length of CNR and DNR are adjusted, there is no significant change on the overall performance. The ACAR is insensitive to length of NR queues. In the following experiments, we always keep length of CNR and DNR as half of cache size. Figure 5(b) shows the relation between SR length in ACAR+ and its performance. Total cost firstly decreases and then increases with increment of SR. This can be easily understood since ACAR+ performs closer to LRU with larger SR and performs closer to ACAR with smaller SR. We set SR to 10% of cache size in the following experiments.

4.2 Experiments on Real Trace

For our experiments, we collect traces of TPC-C benchmark running on PostgreSQL 8.3.5 and Linux kernel compile using GCC 4.1, and then replay the trace

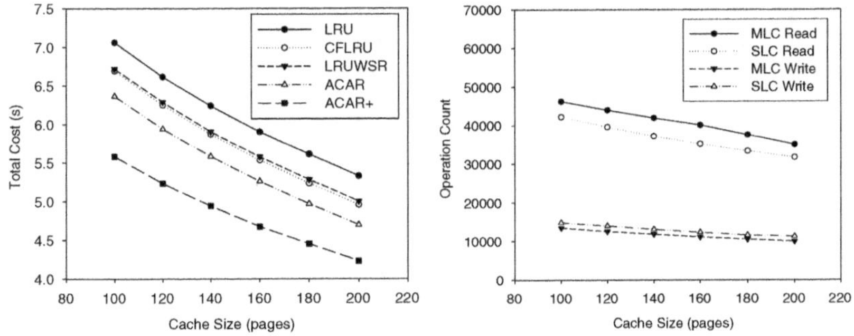

(a) 80-20 distribution on SLC (b) Read and write count comparison

Fig. 4. Performance of replacement policies on SLC for comparison

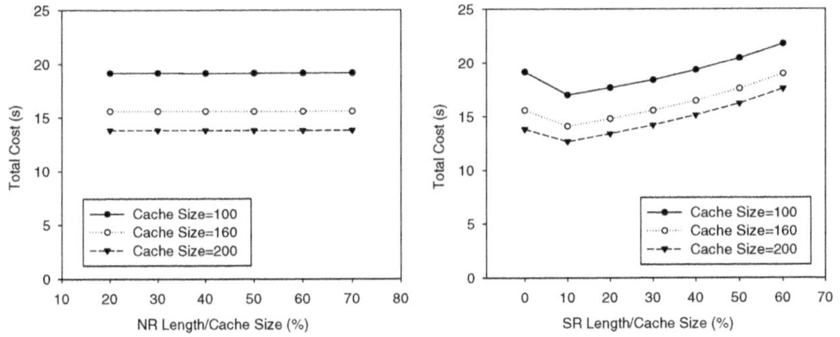

(a) Adjusting length of NR queue (b) Adjusting length of SR queue

Fig. 5. Effects of parameters on performance

with our simulator. The data set of TPC-C is 2GB, and page size of PostgreSQL is 8KB. The version of Linux kernel is 2.6.27. Cache size ranges from 10000 to 20000 in experiment on TPC-C trace. LRU is omitted as CFLRU and LRUWSR are its improvements and show better performance in previous study. We set the costs as SLC in this part, while results are similar to MLC. As demonstrated in figure 6(a), ACAR+ performs much better than other algorithms. This is because the TPC-C is mixed with read and update of the data items, and ACAR methods allocate proper weight to the clean and dirty pages. In addition, the ACAR+ can distinguish cold pages and has the best performance.

The write pattern of Linux kernel compile is mainly sequential. In this case, keeping dirty pages in cache is not a wise decision because they will not likely to be written again. That is why CFLRU and LRUWSR perform worse. But ACAR+ can deal with this problem easily since all the sequential accesses will only occupy cache pages in SR queue. The result is illustrated in figure 6(b).

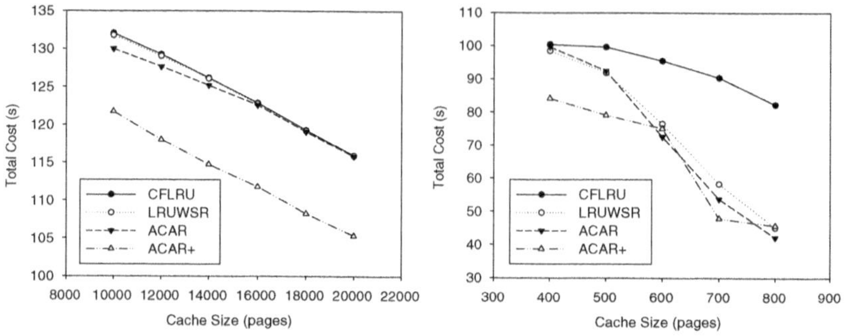

(a) TPC-C (b) Make linux core

Fig. 6. Performance of replacement policies on real trace

5 Conclusion and Future Work

The new features of flash memory pose great challenges for cache management policy. Asymmetric IO speed requires a cost aware strategy, and low access latency sets close restraint on the complexity of the strategy. In this paper, a novel cache replacement policy named ACAR is proposed to deal with this problem. ACAR divides the cache into two pools for clean and dirty pages separately, and dynamically adjusts the size of them according to system workload and operation cost. In addition, ACAR is a worst-case O(1) algorithm suitable for on-line processing. ACAR+ further improves the ACAR by adding another queue for hot data detection.

Next step, we consider to integrate some advanced disk oriented cache replacement strategies, e.g., LIRS, with our ACAR to further boost the performance. We are also interested in working on block-level ACAR which clusters dirty pages in one block together to accelerate write-back performance.

Acknowledgement

This research was supported by the grants of Natural Science Foundation of China (No. 60873063).

References

1. Park, S.Y., Jung, D., Kang, J.U., Kim, J., Lee, J.: Cflru: a replacement algorithm for flash memory. In: CASES, pp. 234–241 (2006)
2. Jung, H., Shim, H., Park, S., Kang, S., Cha, J.: LRU-WSR: Integration of lru and writes sequence reordering for flash memory. IEEE Transactions on Consumer Electronics 54(3), 1215–1223 (2008)

3. Jung, H., Yoon, K., Shim, H., Park, S., Kang, S., Cha, J.: LIRS-WSR: Integration of lirs and writes sequence reordering for flash memory. In: Gervasi, O., Gavrilova, M.L. (eds.) ICCSA 2007, Part I. LNCS, vol. 4705, pp. 224–237. Springer, Heidelberg (2007)
4. Lee, S.W., Moon, B.: Design of flash-based dbms: an in-page logging approach. In: SIGMOD Conference, pp. 55–66 (2007)
5. O'Neil, E.J., O'Neil, P.E., Weikum, G.: The LRU-K page replacement algorithm for database disk buffering. In: Buneman, P., Jajodia, S. (eds.) SIGMOD Conference, pp. 297–306. ACM Press, New York (1993)
6. Lee, D., Choi, J., Kim, J.H., Noh, S.H., Min, S.L., Cho, Y., Kim, C.S.: LRFU: A spectrum of policies that subsumes the least recently used and least frequently used policies. IEEE Trans. Computers 50(12), 1352–1361 (2001)
7. Sokolinsky, L.B.: LFU-K: An effective buffer management replacement algorithm. In: Lee, Y., Li, J., Whang, K.-Y., Lee, D. (eds.) DASFAA 2004. LNCS, vol. 2973, pp. 670–681. Springer, Heidelberg (2004)
8. Robinson, J.T., Devarakonda, M.V.: Data cache management using frequency-based replacement. In: SIGMETRICS, pp. 134–142 (1990)
9. Johnson, T., Shasha, D.: 2Q: A low overhead high performance buffer management replacement algorithm. In: VLDB, pp. 439–450 (1994)
10. Jiang, S., Zhang, X.: LIRS: an efficient low inter-reference recency set replacement policy to improve buffer cache performance. In: SIGMETRICS, pp. 31–42 (2002)
11. Megiddo, N., Modha, D.S.: ARC: A self-tuning, low overhead replacement cache. In: FAST (2003)
12. Jo, H., Kang, J.U., Park, S.Y., Kim, J.S., Lee, J.: FAB: Flash-aware buffer management policy for portable media players. IEEE Transactions on Consumer Electronics 52(2), 485–493 (2006)
13. Kim, H., Ahn, S.: BPLRU: A buffer management scheme for improving random writes in flash storage. In: Baker, M., Riedel, E. (eds.) FAST, pp. 239–252. USENIX (2008)
14. Bansal, S., Modha, D.S.: CAR: Clock with adaptive replacement. In: FAST, pp. 187–200 (2004)
15. Park, J., Lee, H., Hyun, S., Koh, K., Bahn, H.: A cost-aware page replacement algorithm for nand flash based mobile embedded systems. In: Alur, R., Lee, I. (eds.) EMSOFT 2003. LNCS, vol. 2855, pp. 315–324. Springer, Heidelberg (2003)
16. Ou, Y., Härder, T., Jin, P.: CFDC: a flash-aware replacement policy for database buffer management. In: DaMoN, pp.15–20 (2009)
17. Seo, D., Shin, D.: Recently-evicted-first buffer replacement policy for flash storage devices. IEEE Transactions on Consumer Electronics 54(3), 1228–1235 (2008)
18. Kgil, T., Mudge, T.N.: Flashcache: a nand flash memory file cache for low power web servers. In: CASES, pp. 103–112 (2006)

GPU-Accelerated Predicate Evaluation on Column Store

Ren Wu, Bin Zhang, Meichun Hsu, and Qiming Chen

HP Labs, Hewlett-Packard Company,
1501 Page Mill Road, Palo Alto, CA 94304, USA
{ren.wu,bin.zhang2,meichun.hsu,qiming.chen}@hp.com

Abstract. Column scan, or predicate evaluation and filtering over a column of data in a database table, is an important primitive for data mining and data warehousing. In this paper, we present our study on accelerating column scan using a massively parallel accelerator. With a design that takes full advantage of the characteristics of the memory hierarchy and parallel execution in such processors, we have achieved very attractive speedup performance that significantly exceeds previously reported results, making the use of such an accelerator for this type of primitives much more viable. Running on a general purpose graphic processor unit (GPGPU), NVidia GTX 280 GPU, the GPU version is about 5-6 times faster than an implementation on an eight-core CPU, or over 40 times faster than that on a single-core CPU.

Keywords: Parallel Algorithm, Scan, Predicate evaluation, Graphics Processor, GPGPU, Accelerator, Multi-core, Many-core, Data parallelism.

1 Introduction

Graphics processors (GPUs) have developed very rapidly in recent years. GPUs have moved beyond their originally-targeted graphics applications and increasingly become a viable choice for general purpose computing. In fact, with many light-weight data-parallel cores, GPUs can often provide substantial computational power to accelerate general purpose applications at a much lower capital equipment cost and much higher energy efficiency, which means much lower operating cost while contributing to a greener economy.

There have been a number of research works on using GPUs to speed up database management systems (DBMS) and business intelligence analytics [2-7, 13-14]. As the GPGPU technology advances, and as multi-core systems gain popularity, recent studies have begun to focus on measuring how GPGPUs compare with multi-core systems in speeding up data analytics.

This work builds on top of the work recently reported in [11], which specifically addresses the issue of column scan in a main memory on column store-based data warehouse. Column scan refers to predicate evaluation and filtering over a column of data in a database table. In [11], it is reported that a GPU implementation running on Nvidia GeForce 8800 GTX achieved marginally better performance than the CPU

L. Chen et al. (Eds.): WAIM 2010, LNCS 6184, pp. 570–581, 2010.

version running on a quad-core Intel CPU. However, the performance gain is not significant, and, given the higher energy consumption of GPU compared to CPU, it is difficult to conclude that GPGPU has a competitive edge over pure multi-core systems for such tasks.

Recognizing the importance of the column scan primitive, our study aims at exploring design alternatives for GPGPU implementations to determine if one could achieve a much higher level of performance so as to establish a more viable edge for the accelerator approach. Our findings are reported here in this paper. We explore performance impact of various alternative designs that more effectively utilize GPU's thread model, memory hierarchy and bandwidth, and also study the impact of the use of the newer atomic access feature of Nvidia GTX 280's shared memory. Our study confirms that GPUs can deliver a much higher level performance and offer significant speedup over pure multi-core systems.

2 GPU Computing

Graphics processors (GPUs) are originally designed for a very specific domain - to accelerate graphics pipeline. Recognizing the huge potential performance gains from these GPUs, many efforts have been made to use them to perform general purpose computing. With the introduction of Nvidia's CUDA solution, which provides both software support (the CUDA programming language extended from the popular C language), and the CUDA-enabled hardware compute engine (a highly parallel architecture with hundreds of cores and very high memory bandwidth); programming GPUs for general purpose computing has become much easier than before [8].

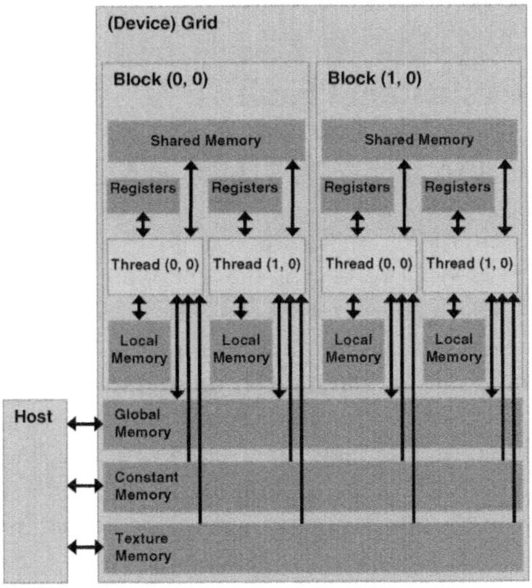

Fig. 1. CUDA memory hierarchy

CUDA extends C by allowing the programmer to define C functions, called kernels, which are executed in parallel by different CUDA threads. From the programmer's point of view, CUDA threads are arranged in a two-level hierarchy. Many threads together form a thread block, and many thread blocks form a thread grid. Threads in the same thread block are run on the same CUDA processor, and can share on-chip memory called shared memory. In addition, all threads have access to the device's global memory.

Figure 1 is a diagram of CUDA's memory hierarchy. Each thread has a private local memory. Each thread block has a shared memory visible to all threads of the block and with the same lifetime as the block. Finally, all threads have access to the same global memory. There are also two read-only memory spaces accessible by all threads: the constant and texture memory.

While CUDA has made it much easier to program GPGPU, the program should be designed with its memory hierarchy in mind to achieve high performance.

The (device) global memory space is not cached, so it is very important to follow the pattern of coalesced memory access to get maximum memory bandwidth. Non-coalesced memory is still allowed but at the cost of wasting memory bandwidth [10].

On the other hand, because it is on-chip, the shared memory is much faster than the global memory. It is a common design pattern to load part of the data from global memory into shared memory first, and then write it back to global memory after processing [10].

Many researchers are now able to use GPUs to accelerate their applications, and many have shown respectable speedup performance compared to CPU-only implementations. Popular commercial applications, such as Adobe's creative suite, Mathematica, etc., have new releases of their GPU-enabled version; researchers have used GPUs in cloud dynamics, N-Body and molecular dynamics simulations, etc, with results that show good promise [8].

3 The Predicate Evaluation Primitive

The column scan primitive has its root in column-based database systems and dictionary based compression. It is one of the critical primitives in analytics processing in such systems [11]. In column scan, the input data is a bit stream, in which every b bits are used to represent the encoded value of a data element in a column of a data table. The scan operator scans the bit stream, extracts the b-bit value and compares it against either a point value or a range of values. The output is also a bit stream, in which one bit is set when the corresponding input data element is found to satisfy the predicate evaluation. Figure 2 illustrates an example, in which 8 bits are used to encode the value of a data element. In this example, the predicate is "equal to 1", and the second data element in the input column is found to satisfy the predicate.

Depending on the size of the dictionary used, it is common to pick the smallest b which is sufficient to encode all values, to reduce the storage and I/O. Because of this, the encoded values are not necessarily byte- or word-aligned, and the scan operator has to process the non-aligned values efficiently.

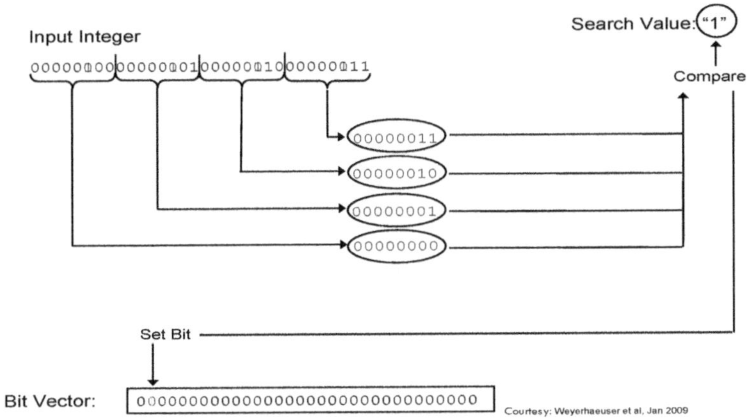

Fig. 2. An example of the scan primitive

3.1 Experiment Design and Hardware

We have implemented the scan primitive discussed in the last section on both CPU and GPU. The CPU version was developed and compiled using Microsoft Visual C++ 2005, with OpenMP enabled for multi-thread support. The GPU version was developed in CUDA 2.0 on top of Microsoft Visual C++ 2005. The machine used in our experiments is an HP XW8400 workstation with dual quad-core Intel Xeon 5345 CPU running at 2.33GHz, Nvidia GeForce GTX 280 graphics board with 1GB onboard device memory, and 20GB of main memory. The operating system is Windows XP x64. The connection between the GPU and the host was via PCIe 1.1 bus, which has 4GB/s of theoretic bandwidth.

Our experiments have shown that the measured bandwidth was about 3GB/s when copying data between the host memory and the pinned global memory on the device. This presented a potential bottleneck for the overall system performance. However, it is noted that the PCIe 2.0, not available in the hardware we used here, has already offered the theoretic maximum bandwidth of 8GB/s. The newer standard, PCIe 3.0, currently under development and will be available at 2010, will double the bandwidth again. Furthermore, there are streaming techniques which allow data transfer and data processing to occur concurrently, effectively hiding the cost of data transfer across PCIe bus [13, 14]. We will briefly discuss this in section 4.8, but the details of such techniques are beyond the scope of this paper.

Since our primary interest is on the performance acceleration ratios by GPUs, we used randomly generated data sets. To make it easier to compare with previously reported results in [11], the selectivity has been fixed at 1/255 unless specially noted, and this is true for both 8-bit and 15-bit cases. The timing reported is the total wall time averaged from 10 experimental runs. The time does not include time to load the data sets from disk to memory, or the time to transfer data from main memory to GPU's device memory. Both CPU- and GPU-versions give identical results and they confirm the algorithmic correctness of our implementations.

3.2 CPU-Only Implementation

The CPU only version was developed as the performance reference. The algorithm itself is straightforward but special attention has been devoted to make it as optimized as possible. It consists of a tight loop of the following steps:

(a) Read a 32-bit input word.
(b) Extract the encoded values in the input word, and, if necessary, the next 32-bit word is fetched as well.
(c) If an extracted value matches the query value, the corresponding bit in the output bitmap is set.

All masks and shifts are calculated on the fly and this helps optimize the use of memory bandwidth since this operation is highly memory bound. Compiler flags and other optimization techniques have also been used here to maximize the performance [9].

Table 1. CPU performance on single core

Encoding	No. of values	Size (MB)	Time (s)	Throughput(GB/s)
8-bit	134,217,728	128	0.416	0.300
15-bit	134,217,728	240	0.503	0.466
8-bit	268,435,456	256	0.828	0.302
15-bit	268,435,456	480	1.005	0.466

Table 1 shows the performance of the CPU version running on a single CPU core. For the 8-bit encoding case, the single CPU core can process 128 MB of data in 0.416 seconds, which translates to a throughput rate of 0.3 GB/s. For the15-bit case, the throughput increases to 0.466 GB/s. It should be pointed out that even with selectivity of 1/255, more than 3/4 of the time has been spent on setting the output bitmap.

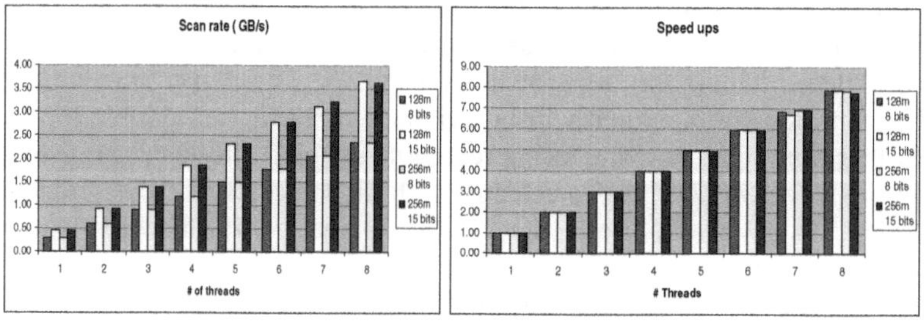

Fig. 3. Scan rate and speedup on multicore

Figure 3 gives the performance of the CPU implementation on multi-cores; up to 8 cores (8 threads) are shown here. The CPU version with 8 cores can process at a rate of 2.4GB/s for the 8-bit case, and 3.7GB/s for the 15-bit cases. The performance of our CPU implementation appears to be comparable to that reported in [11] up to 4 cores. However, our CPU implementation scales largely linearly to the number of

CPU cores up to the 8 cores in our experiments, while [11] reported that in their implementation the speedup is not significant beyond 4 cores due to higher communication overhead between CPUs.

The scan rate achieved did not change much when the dataset size increased from 128 million data values to 256 millions. In the following sections, we have fixed the dataset size to 128 million data elements only.

4 GPU Acceleration

4.1 The Baseline

The first GPU implementation, our baseline, has the following characteristics:

- Both input and output are kept in GPU's device global memory; no other type of memory is used here.
- Every thread works on a data block, which has b * 32 bits, where b is the number of bits per data value.
- Threads are arranged into thread blocks, with t threads per block. We have found that t=128 works the best in this case.
- Each thread will process 32 values of b bits each and generate one 32-bit word as its output. It will be written back to global memory when done. Note that the output from all threads within a thread block use coalesced (i.e., adjacent) memory access. This is one nice property of this algorithm.

Figure 4(a) is an overview of this algorithm and Table 2 shows its performance. For the 8-bit case, the GPU baseline algorithm can process 128m data points in 32 ms, or a throughput rate of 3.91 GB/s. For the 15-bit case, the throughput rate dropped to 2.89 GB/s.

Table 2. GPU Performance - Baseline

Encoding	No. of values	Size (MB)	Time (s)	Throughput(GB/s)
8-bit	134,217,728	128	0.032	3.91
15-bit	134,217,728	240	0.081	2.89

In addition to its simplicity, the main advantage of this algorithm is its coalesced memory access for writing the result bit vector. However, the algorithm does suffer from its non-coalesced memory reads, which prevents the algorithm from utilizing the GPU's memory bandwidth fully. In the following sections, we will discuss various ways for improving this algorithm.

4.2 Bandwidth and Memory Hierarchy

Modern GPUs have very high memory bandwidth. For example, the Nvidia GeForce GTX 280 has the theoretic maximum memory bandwidth of 141.7 GB/s. However, to fully utilize such memory bandwidth, it is crucial to design the data structures and thread structures carefully. The first opportunity for improvement lies in better utilization of the global memory bandwidth by using the "shared" memory of a thread block, and reducing the size of each data block for each thread from 32*b bits to b bits. Since every 32-bit word may contain more than one data element, multiple threads may be accessing the same 32-bit word. While this constitutes bank conflict when accessing the shared memory, it is much cheaper than the non-coalesced access to global memory in our baseline design. Note that the loading from global memory to shared memory is coalesced itself. With this design, each thread works on a single data element, extracts it from the shared memory, compares it to the query value, and sets its output bit if the match is found.

Setting the output bit-vector is a harder problem. The early CUDA device did not support atomic memory writes and it is the algorithm designer's responsibilities to ensure the threads don't write to the same address at the same time; otherwise the race condition may occur.

To avoid the race condition, our implementation allocates a 32-bit temporary output word to each thread, and has each thread write the output to this 32-bit word instead to a single bit only; then a separate process is used to reduce these words into bits. In contrast with writing results directly to global memory, and having a separate kernel to reduce them, we can keep the 32-bit output per thread in the shared memory and merge them in the shared memory right after the predicate evaluation is done.

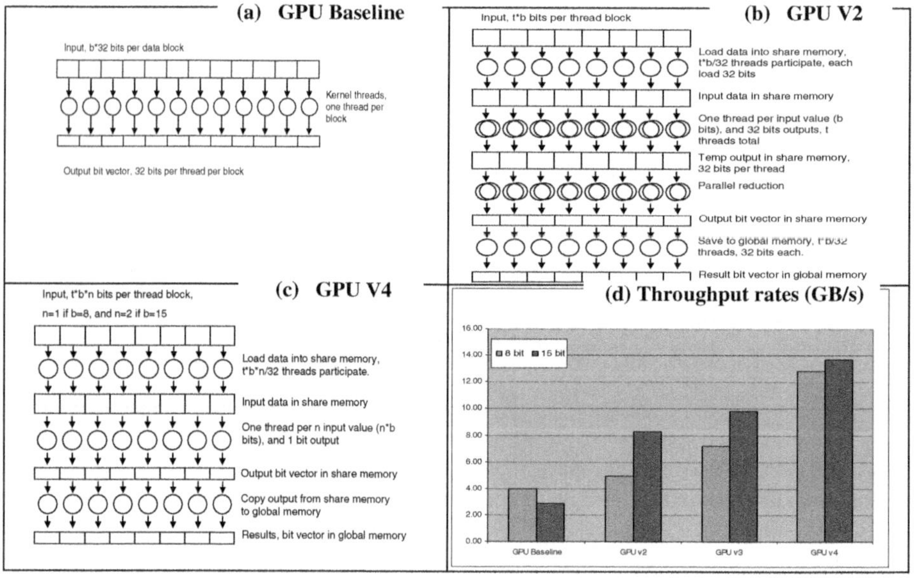

Fig. 4. GPU algorithms and performances

A naïve implementation, in which one loop scans through each of the 32-bit words and sets its corresponding bit in the resulting word, turns out to be very inefficient. In fact, our experiment shows that this merging process is slower than the predicate evaluation processing itself.

We solved this problem by introducing parallel merge. By designing the data structures properly, the parallel reduction is no more than simply OR across 32 words, a much more efficient implementation.

Figure 4(b) contains an illustration of the second algorithm. Double circles are used to indicate threads that may have overlapping access to the same word. The performance results are shown in the GPU V2 column in Figure 4(d).

The throughput rate for the 15-bit case increased dramatically, reaching 8.27 GB/s, almost three times as fast as the previous version. For the 8-bit case, the throughput rate is increased by 25%, to about 5 GB/s.

It is worth noting the difference on throughput rates between 8-bit and 15-bit cases. The reason behind is that memory bandwidth utilization is better in 15-bit case. This can be explained as follow.

Let's say we are processing 8-bit input value. For a thread block of t threads, 8t bits will be processed. To load these 8t bits data from global memory, only 8t/32 threads will be needed for loading, since each thread will load one 32-bit word. This leaves t – 8t/32 threads, or ¾ of threads, idle. In the 15-bit case, only about half of them are idle during the loading phase.

Certainly, this presents another opportunity for further optimizing our algorithm and it is discussed in next section.

4.3 Bandwidth for Copying Data

In the previous section, we have shown that the algorithm is less optimal in the sense that many threads were idle when the data is copied from global to shared memory. To better utilize the memory bandwidth, it is desirable to load a few data elements per thread. In 8-bit case, four elements would be preferred. For 15-bit case, two would be more preferable. By having as many threads participate in loading data as possible, we have a more balanced algorithm and use memory bandwidth better.

Results of this version are shown in the GPU V3 column in Figure 4(d). For 8-bit case, the throughput rate is now about 7.2GB/s, compared to 5GB/s in previous version. For 15-bit case, the throughput rate has reached to 9.2GB/s.

4.4 Utilizing the Newer Atomic Shared Memory Feature

CUDA 1.2 supports atomic shared memory access, which was not supported in previous releases, including GTX 8800 on which [11] was based. For the memory throughput problem we discussed here, this is a particularly useful feature. With atomic shared memory access, we can set the bits inside shared memory directly by each thread, and eliminate the extra effort in parallel reduction. Figure 4(c) illustrates the algorithm that uses atomic shared access, as well as the throughput rate for all GPU algorithms.

The throughput rate for this version was shown in GPU V4 column in Figure 4(d). It confirms that utilizing the atomic shared access feature is more efficient than performing parallel reduction. The throughput rates have now jumped to 12.8 GB/s and 13.7 GB/s for 8-bit and 15-bit data, respectively.

4.5 Analysis of Throughput Performance against Theoretic GPU Bandwidth

The Nvidia GTX 280 GPU used in our experiments has the theoretic maximum bandwidth of 141.7 GB/s, which is a much higher number than the throughput rate that our optimized GPU implementation has achieved. We discuss the gap between the two in the following.

First of all, one should note that the maximum bandwidth quoted above was the theoretic value; the realizable bandwidth is usually smaller than that. Previous works have reported that the best bandwidth achieved in copying within GPU's global memory, on a 8800GTX, was 76GB/s, or 88% of its maximum pin-bandwidth at 86GB/s [12].

On the GTX 280, the best bandwidth we obtained was 113GB/s, or 80% of the theoretic maximum. This was done by utilizing the CUDA's built-in function cudaMemcpy(), as shown in the bandwidthTest sample program shipped with CUDA SDK 2.0. Using custom kernel, instead of the system function, the best bandwidth dropped to 107GB/s, or 75% of the maximum.

Secondly, the raw memory bandwidth is not the most appropriate measure for our purpose of comparing performance. The more appropriate measure is the copy rate, which is defined as the number of bytes copied per second. For memory copy between device's global memory, the best copy rate was 53.3GB/s. Copying from the global memory to device's shared memory is faster, at rate of 78GB/s.

To explain the gap between the copy rate and the throughput rate achieved in our algorithm, a series of experiments was done to measure exactly how the time was spent in the processing. Since there is no profiling tools available at device level, this was done by gradually removing parts of the logic and observing the change in throughput rate. Table 3 shows the results of these experiments. All experiments here are based on GPU V4, on 15-bit dataset with 1/255 of selectivity.

Under the GPU v4 framework, loading the data from global memory to shared memory and initializing the result bit vector on shared memory only, the throughput rate can reach up to 52.4 GB/s. By including writing result bit vector from shared memory to global memory, the throughput rate dropped to 45.5 GB/s. If we want to extract each value and compare it against the targeted value and set the result bit accordingly, even without using atomic operation (and so not guarantee correct result), the throughput rate dropped to 17.1 GB/s. With atomic operation, the throughput rate further dropped to 13.7 GB/s.

Table 3. Performance analysis - Throughput rate

	Throughput rate (GB/s)
V4 Load, Init, and Sync	52.4
V4 Load, Init, Sync and Save	45.5
V4 Non-atomic write	17.1
V4	13.7

Overall the majority of the time was spent on extracting values from the data stream, comparing it again the target value, and set the result bit vector. This is no surprise given that this was the main logic for the algorithm. This is also the reason why the 8-bit throughput is a less than that of the 15-bit case, since for a given data size, the 15-bit case will have less extraction, comparison and bit-setting operations compared to 8-bit case. Also noted by using atomic shared memory write, the performance dropped about 20%. While the overhead is significant, it is still better than performing the parallel reduction step separately.

4.6 Comparison with the CPU Implementation

Figure 5 give the comparison between CPU and GPU implementation. The CPU version running on 4 cores have a throughput rate of 1.2GB/s and 1.9GB/s for 8-bit and 15-bit data respectively. The optimized GPU version, however, can process at the rate of 12.8 GB/s and 13.7GB/s, which are about 10.5x and 7.2x faster than CPU counterpart on 4 cores.

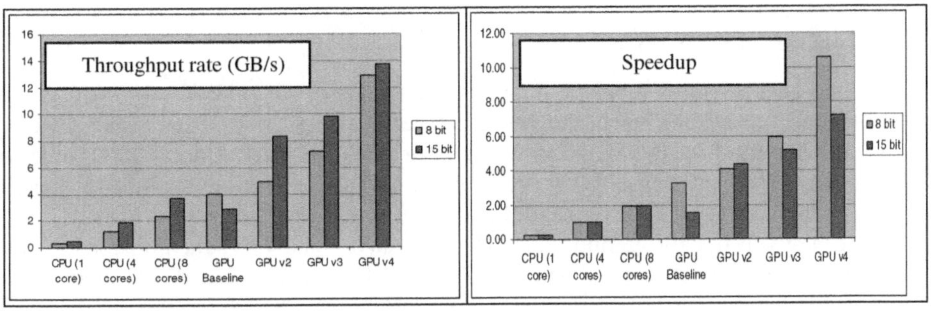

Fig. 5. GPU vs. CPU, Throughput rate and speedup

The speedup is achieved not only due to GPU's massively parallel processing power and its high memory bandwidth, but also due to algorithm and data structure designs that take advantage of the underlying hardware. These experiments indicate that GPU has the potential to deliver considerable performance edge over pure multi-core systems.

4.7 Comparison with Previous Results

Previous work [11] on using GPU for column scan was positive but the performance edge over quad-core CPU systems was not significant enough to clearly justify the investment. Their GPU implementation, running on an Nvidia GeForce 8800 GTX, can process 128MB 8-bit data in 0.091 seconds, or about 1.37GB/s. This is just 29% faster than their CPU version on a quad-core CPU, which was about 1.06GB/s.

The Nvidia Geforce 8800 GTX has 128 cores running at 1.35GHz, and a memory bandwidth of 86.4GB/s. In contrast, the GeForce GTX 280 used in this work has 240 cores running at 1.29GHz, and a memory bandwidth of 141.7 GB/s. GTX 8800 is a CUDA 1.0 device, and does not support atomic share memory access.

Since the hardware we used in this paper is not identical to the one used in [11], it is difficult to have a direct comparison. However, based on extrapolation of the hardware capabilities, we believe that our baseline GPU implementation would deliver comparable or slightly faster performance on comparable hardware than that reported in [11], while our V3 implementation, which does not use the atomic shared memory feature (which was not available in GeForce 8800 GTX) would be about 2-3 times faster than the implementation reported in [11].

Another angle of looking at this is the speed-up obtained over the CPU version. Their CPU version, running on a quad-core Intel CPU Xeon 5355 @ 2.67 GHz, was able to process 120MB of 8-bit data in 0.118 second; a throughput rate of 1.06GB/s. Our CPU implementation, running on a workstation with dual Intel Xeon 2345 @ 2.33 GHz using only four cores, can process the same amount of data within 0.105 seconds, or 1.19GB/s. Since our CPU version is comparable or slightly faster than that reported in [11], it is reasonable to use our own quad-core CPU implementation as a reference point for speedup computation.

4.8 Time for Data Transferring

So far, we have assumed that the data has been transferred to GPU's onboard global memory and our results have showed great performance boost from using GPUs - something that has not been done/proved in prior publication. If we treat GPUs as strict accelerators for existing systems, it is important to include the time for transferring the data from the host to GPU device and the time for transferring the results back.

Table 4 gives the throughput rate when we take time for data transferring into account. The hardware we used here has PCIe 1.1 bus, which provides around 3GB/s of measured bandwidth.

As we discussed in our previous work [13, 14], it is possible to hide some of the data transferring time via streaming – essentially to have CPU, GPU and data transfer all run concurrently. The performance data for both non-streaming and streaming version are presented here.

Table 4. Throughput rate including data transferring

Datasets	Non-streaming (MB/s)	Streaming (MB/s)
8-bit	2245	2680
15-bit	2381	2818

Noted that time for both transferring data from host to device, and transferring results back to host are include here. Still the throughput rate for streaming version has approached the measured bandwidth. In other words, large portion of the calculation have been hide and the throughput rate is limited by the system's PCIe bus which connect the GPU device to the host.

Compare the throughput rate without data transferring time, it is clear that the PCIe bus is still the bottleneck of the system. However, there are a few points we would like to argue here,

- The throughput rate is still much faster than CPU version on four cores, shifting the calculation from CPU to GPU can free these CPU cores for other things and so potential better system-wide performance.
- The machine we used has PCIe 1.1. Modern PC/workstation have commonly equipped with PCIe 2.0, which doubles the bandwidth. The throughput rate on such system will outperform CPU only version on 8 cores.

- In most real world scenarios, the data is most likely stored in disks. And the disk IO is much slower than PCIe bus. It is possible to ship the data to GPU device while doing the disk IO, and make this scan/evaluation essential free.

Designing such system is beyond the scope of this paper, but it is certainly an interesting direction for further research.

5 Conclusions

We have reported our research on using GPU to accelerate column scan in data warehousing and analytics. We have shown that with algorithm and data structure designs that take better advantage of GPU's memory and threading models, we can achieve significant speed-up over pure multi-core implementations, making GPU a more viable alternative to be considered for column scan operations in data intensive analytics than previously reported.

References

1. Chatterjee, S., et al.: Scan primitives for vector computers. In: Proceedings of the 1990 ACM/IEEE conference on Supercomputing, pp. 666–675 (1990)
2. Fang, R., et al.: GPUQP: Query co-processing using graphics processors. In: Proceedings of the 2007 ACM SIGMOD international conference on Management of data, pp. 1061–1063 (2007)
3. Govindaraju, N.K., et al.: Fast computation of database operations using graphics processors. In: Proceedings of the 2004 ACM SIGMOD international conference (2004)
4. Govindaraju, N.K., et al.: Fast and approximate stream mining of quantiles and frequencies using graphics processors. In: Proceedings of the 2005 ACM SIGMOD international conference on Management of data, pp. 611–622 (2005)
5. Harris, M., et al.: Parallel prefix sum (scan) with cuda. In: Nguyen, H. (ed.) GPU Gems 3. Addison Wesley, Reading (2007)
6. He, B., et al.: Mars: A mapreduce framework on graphics processors. In: IEEE International Conference on Parallel Architecture and Compilation Techniques, pp. 1111–1120 (2008)
7. He, B., et al.: Relational joins on graphics processors. In: Proceedings of the 2008 ACM SIGMOD international conference (2008)
8. CUDA Zone, `http://www.nvidia.com/object/cuda_home.html`
9. Intel® 64 and IA-32 Architectures Software Developer's Manuals (2008), `http://www.intel.com/products/processor/manuals/`
10. Nvidia CUDA programming Guide, version 2.0 (2008), `http://developer.download.nvidia.com/compute/cuda/2_0/docs/NVIDIA_CUDA_Programming_Guide_2.0.pdf`
11. Weyerhaeuser, et al.: Exploiting Graphic Card Processor Technology to Accelerate Data Mining Queries in SAP NetWeaver BIA. In: 2008 IEEE International Conference on Data Mining Workshops (2008)
12. Volkov, V., Demmel, J.: LU, QR and Cholesky Factorizations using Vector Capabilities of GPUs. Technical Report No. UCB/EECS-2008-49 (2008)
13. Wu, R., Zhang, B., Hsu, M.: GPU-Accelerated Large Scale Analytics. HP Labs Technical Report, HPL-2009-38
14. Wu, R., Zhang, B., Hsu, M.: Clustering Billions of Data Points Using GPUs. In: ACM UCHPC 2009: Second Workshop on UnConventional High Performance Computing, Italy (2009)

MOSS-DB: A Hardware-Aware OLAP Database

Yansong Zhang[1,2,3], Wei Hu[1,2], and Shan Wang[1,2]

[1] Key Laboratory of the Ministry of Education for Data Engineering and Knowledge Engineering, Renmin University of China, Beijing 100872, China
[2] School of Information, Renmin University of China, Beijing 100872, China
[3] National Survey Research Center at Renmin University of China, Beijing 100872, China
{zhangys_ruc,swang}@ruc.edu.cn

Abstract. The data intensive analytical workload becomes heavy burden for OLAP engine with increasing data volume, user population and query complexity. Large capacity random access memory, multi-level cache and multi-core hardware are main streams of computer. We propose a hardware-aware OLAP model named MOSS-DB which optimizes storage model according to data access features of dimensional tables and fact tables. A hard disk & main memory two-level storage model is employed to support directly dimensional tuple accessing join operator(DDTA-JOIN), DDTA-JOIN simplifies OLAP query processing by replacing traditional join operation with directly accessing dimensional tuple with memory address. So the star schema can be seen as virtual de-normalized table, OLAP query is also simplified to table scan, select and project operations. Query processing on sequence data structure is more suitable for multi-core parallel processing. Our proposal allows massive data DRDB(Disk Resident Database) storage technique to co-operate with MMDB(Main-Memory Database) processing technique, which breaks the main memory capacity limitation. The DDTA-JOIN operation can save cost for index, hash table, etc. For multi-core era, MOSS-DB can flexibly use parallel processing capability of CPU by dynamically dividing fact table into multiple scan partitions and gain maximum cache profit for shared dimensional data. In experiments, we measure that MOSS-DB outperforms conventional DRDB system, and it also outperforms MMDB in SSB testing.

Keywords: hardware-aware query processing, OLAP, memory optimized storage, MOSS-DB, DDTA-JOIN.

1 Introduction

The performance of OLAP is always the most critical issue due to the large data volume which grows from TB level to PB level. Our target is to leverage the big problem of OLAP performance by optimizations with the support of advanced hardware. OLAP performance includes performance for query processing on large data volume, concurrent user query workloads and complex queries. Performance can be improved by three levels: hardware support, optimized storage model and high efficiency query processing algorithms.

Hardware support is once considered as free lunch for databases. Two important factors stopped the free lunch, one is memory wall the other is multi-core architecture. Memory wall is generated by the unbalanced latency of CPU, main memory and hard

L. Chen et al. (Eds.): WAIM 2010, LNCS 6184, pp. 582–594, 2010.

disk. The parallelization of traditional database is limited and multi-core resource can not be automatically utilized by database software without changing inner design.

OLAP is data-intensive application. Storage model decides the physical data layout of database which influences the performance of data retrieval and query processing. Researches of data model can be classified into five types. (1) Row-wise model. It is optimized for update and dense access(width of all accessed attributes/tuple width>λ, e.g. λ>75%). On the contrary, for sparse access, only very small proportion of whole tuple is to be accessed, cache utilization rate is low. (2) Column-wise model. Column-wise model stores data densely and independently, independent columns generate additional joins for correlative accessed attributes in same table, so for dense fact table, too many joins upon large columns affect performance remarkably. Typical analytical DBMSs, e.g., C-Store[1], Sybase IQ[2] and MonetDB[3] employ column-wise model. (3) PAX[4] model. It is tradeoff for I/O and memory bandwidth performance. In each page, data is organized as column-wise model, so PAX acts as row-wise model when updating with only one I/O cost and it acts as column-wise model when accessed in memory. (4) Clustered model[5]. Correlative columns are clustered stored to gain high cache hits and reduce joins between independent columns. This model can be seen as light-weight row-wise model for dense tables. (5) Row-wise simulating column-wise model. [6] proposed that by simulating column-wise model in a row-wise database, the features of compression and column accessing can be achieved without cost of data migration. Most researches focused on data access performance and didn't pay much attention to the OLAP schema and query feature, how to combine OLTP and OLAP system as one is still un-answered.

For the multi-core era, the keys of improving performance are to promote data locality and to simplify query processing, the too complex SQL engine limits the parallelization of OLAP.

So it is time to re-think whether the database should be re-designed according to features of data-intensive workload and characters of advanced hardware.

In this paper, we propose a reduced OLAP engine MOSS-DB(Memory Optimizing Star Schema Database) for star schema OLAP applications. Storage model, data retrieval, query processing and concurrent query workload are all optimized based on star schema features and hardware features. The large but not large enough main-memory is utilized for frequently accessed column-wise dimensional attributes. Large fact table still employs traditional row-wise(N-Array) storage engine, the optimized query processing algorithm named DDTA-JOIN is the key for simplifying complexity of OLAP query processing and optimizing for multi-core scenario.

Our contributions are as follows:

1. We present a hybrid-storage model for optimizing key performance factor and keep compatibility with existed commercial databases;
2. We simplify query processing with the support of memory optimizing dimension tables , which uses DDTA-JOIN to transform complex query plan tree into simple linear table scan and predicate processing;
3. We use light-weight compression and predicate vector to improve predicate processing by decreased size of frequently accessed dimensional column;
4. We develop DDTA-JOIN algorithm for multi-core algorithm, an OLAP engine model for multi-core platform is presented for nowadays OLAP requirements of heavy workloads, greater complexity and growing user populations.

The OLAP model analysis and related work are presented in Sec.2. Algorithms are discussed in Sec.3. Sec.4 shows the results of experiments. Finally, Sec.5 summarizes the paper and discusses future work.

2 Ideal OLAP Model and Related Work

First of all, we analyze the features of data warehouse and OLAP workloads and then discuss the ideal OLAP model with support of state-of-the-art hardware.

In Data Warehouse, star schema and snow-flake schema are typical schemas, snow-flake schema can be considered as extended star schema with more hierarchical dimension tables and more join cost for OLAP query processing. The schema is skewed with a very large fact table and extremely smaller dimension tables. Dimensional attributes in fact table are foreign keys referenced to multiple dimension tables. The workload upon fact table and dimension tables is skewed too. So the ideal storage model is that fact table should be resident in sequential and large capacity storage device and dimension tables should employ small but high performance random access storage device.

Blink[7] used de-normalized schema with machine-word sized banks to simplify query processing and improve performance of predicate processing. [8] explored good parallelization on multi-core CPU for its de-normalized pre-join table scan. In Star schema, dimensional attributes in fact table are all foreign keys referenced to primary key of dimension tables, so join can be considered as retrieval for tuple with equal join keys such as hash join, index join, etc. Join index[9] is a special lookup(join) algorithm with directly accessing tuple to be joined by scanning the join index with physical tuple addresses pairs of each joined tuples. Join index acts as light-weight de-normalized table. Figure 1 illustrates the difference of de-normalized schema and star schema, de-normalized schema is simple for query processing and easily to be parallelized for multi-core CPU, but the space cost is much larger than star schema. Star schema is optimized for storage efficiency but involved more join cost. So the ideal schema should have both good storage performance as normalized star schema and simple but efficient query processing performance as de-normalized schema.

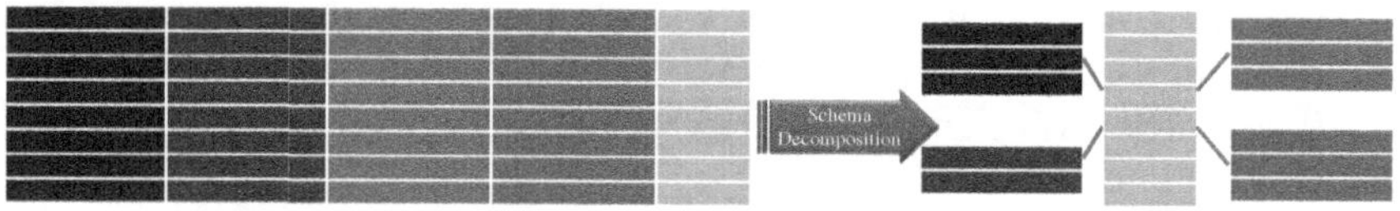

Fig. 1. De-normalized schema and normalized star schema

The ideal storage model in OLAP should be hybrid model in which large sequential correlative attributes in fact table are row-wise stored and the small size but large amount dimensional attributes are column-wise stored. For storage hierarchy, hard disk provides large capacity sequential storage, SSD and RAM can support moderate capacity for random accessing with higher performance, the hierarchical cache levels(L1,L2,L3 caches) provide even higher performance with small capacity. Multi-cores have their private L1 or L2 caches and share the last level cache, so the possible bottlenecks may be shared cache and memory bandwidth which multi-cores may contend same resource simultaneously.

So the ideal strategy is to store small but most frequently accessed data in main memory and make data set even smaller for resident possibility in cache, sequential scanned data should be allocated within small address space and the frequently accessed data set should be allocated within more address space to promote cache hits. Query processing should be simplified as uniform linear processing for maximum parallelization and the large data accessing should be shared for multiple users to reduce conflicts for bandwidth. Most of all, the storage model should keep compatible with traditional commercial DBMS and simplify SQL engine for OLAP processing.

3 MOSS-DB

MOSS-DB(Memory Optimizing Star Schema Database) system employs two-level storage model, the large fact table uses traditional row-wise storage engine to support increasing large data volumes, dimension tables are stored in row-wise tables too but during query processing, dimension tables are loaded into main memory to form compressed column-wise memory dimension tables.

In MOLAP(Multi-dimensional OLAP) model, dimension tables are stored as arrays, the array index is equal to primary key of dimension table in ROLAP(Relational OLAP), measure data of each fact tuple is stored in a multi-dimensional array item, the multi-dimensional array indexes act as dimensional attribute keys of fact tuple in ROLAP. For example, if $D1[m]$, $D2[n]$, $D3[p]$ denote three dimension tables, m, n and p denote boundaries of each dimension table, $F[m][n][p]$ denotes fact table, then any fact tuple $F[i][j][k]$ can be mapped to dimension tuples $D1[i]$, $D2[j]$, $D3[k]$. In MOSS-DB model, we inherit this feature for our column-wise memory dimension table, each dimension table is divided into multiple arrays with same boundary. In SSB dataset, primary keys of 3 dimension tables are all incremental sequences as 0,1,2..., so primary key can be replaced by memory array index. Primary key of dimension table *DWDATE* is incremental sequence as 19920101, 19920102, 19920103..., we can follow two rules:(1) employ a mapping function $D\_Map(x)=date(x)-date(19920101)$. Each primary key can be on-the-fly mapped to array index of dimension table *DWDATE* by *D_Map*;(2) reserve current primary key and use array index as new primary key, replacing dimensional attributes in fact table with array index. The update strategy of column-wise memory dimension table also inherits dimension table in MOLAP model. Fact table is stored with ROLAP model to compress space cost and make MOSS-DB scalable for increasing data volume.

Compared with DRDB such as PostgreSQL, MOSS-DB fully utilizes main memory with more efficient MMDB enabled query processing algorithms. When compared with MMDB such as MonetDB, because of skewed data volume for dimension tables, main memory capacity is no longer limitation for in-memory query processing. For general purpose OLAP workloads, for example SSB [10] (improved TPC-H benchmark with single fact table) and FoodMart benchmark, fact table is dense with narrow fact table width and more correlative attributes. Our hybrid-model can optimize dimensional attribute accessing than row-wise model and can also optimize fact table accessing by eliminating join cost of large fact attributes than column-wise model.

Figure 2 shows the storage architecture of MOSS-DB, for upper level, data size should be even small for better locality.

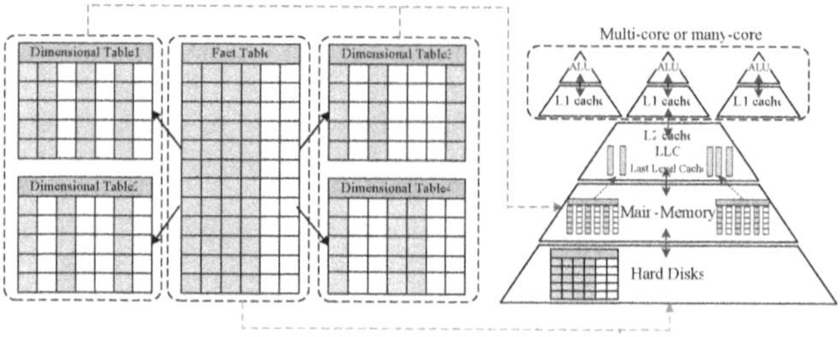

Fig. 2. Architecture of MOSS-DB

3.1 Naïve DDTA-JOIN Algorithm

With array modeled column-wise memory dimension table, join operation of hash probe or index probe is simplified to address access with mapped array index. So the costly hash table or index is no longer needed. The whole query processing is divided into three phases as figure 3.

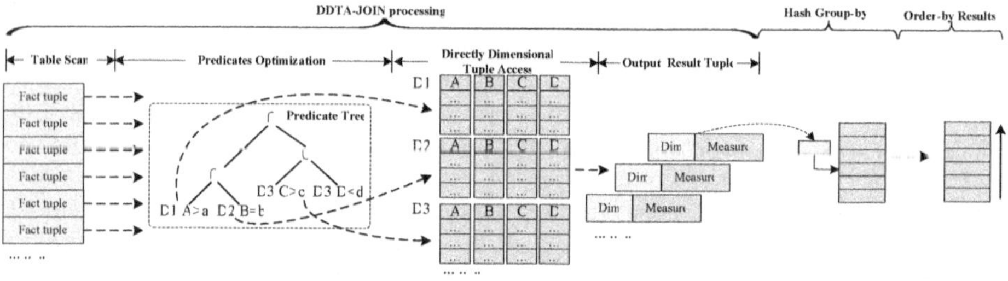

Fig. 3. Query processing in MOSS-DB

In first phase, we define operator DDTA-JOIN(Directly Dimensional Tuple Access JOIN) as following procedure:

(1) sequence scan fact table for each fact tuple;
(2) for each predicate expression in traversal path of predicate tree (optimized predicates order), access dimensional attribute values with mapped dimensional array indexes and process predicate computing, return final predicate result as soon as first TRUE(FALSE) appears in conjunction (disjunction) predicate expressions;
(3) for each fact tuple with TRUE result of predicate expressions, fetch the project attribute data with mapped dimensional array indexes;
(4) produce output tuple for the following operations.

In DDTA-JOIN procedure, star schema tables are used as virtual pre-join table, the order of predicate expressions decides how many dimensional attributes will be accessed. We optimize predicate expression order by predicate tree structure based on cost model with selectivity, data type, data width, predicate computing cost, data padding, etc. The sophisticated cost model will be in our further research.

In second phase, each output tuple is pipelined to hash group-by function for grouped aggregating. For most cases, the group-by result set is very small due to cardinality of group-by attributes.

In third phase, when all the result tuples are aggregated, the order-by function is invoked upon group-by result set to re-order final result set.

3.2 Light-Weight Compression Optimization for DDTA-JOIN

In naïve DDTA-JOIN, for example, in order to process $\delta_{Store\_state='WA'}$*store_state*, each fact tuple maps foreign key of *store_id* to dimensional array index(e.g. *store_id=1→store_state*[*1*]*='Guerrero'*), and then the attribute value is read for predicate computing. The dimensional attribute values are read repeatedly during sequence scan on fact table. Many dimensional attributes of higher hierarchy are long *VARCHAR* data type, so compression on column dimensional attribute can save much space for main memory. Figure 4 illustrates light-weight dictionary compression for in-memory column, it is suitable for low cardinality columns. When each short compression code is read, the dictionary table is probed by this code to get original data for predicate processing. Although compressed column and dictionary table is much smaller for better locality, the additional CPU cost affects the whole performance. [11] discussed the order-preserving string compression for directly processing on compressed data. The *value* and *code* fields in dictionary table have same order, so the equal and range condition can be re-written as condition on compressed data but *LIKE* and many complex condition can't be re-written. We employ order-preserving string compression in MOSS-DB, and compare the performance in experiment section.

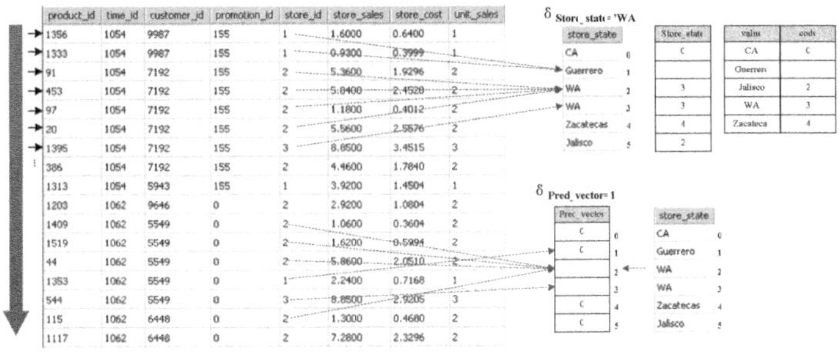

Fig. 4. Predicate vector of DDTA-JOIN in MOSS-DB

[12] proposed *Invisible Join* to reduce join cost for fact table columns. In MOSS-DB, row-wise fact table has no additional join cost for multiple attribute accessing, the main cost is dimensional attribute accessing and predicate processing. We use bitmap as predicate vector to indentify whether certain value satisfies the predicate. In figure 4, *store_state='WA'* is performed on column *store_state* to generate predicate

vector *001100...*, then predicate is re-written as *pred_vector=1*. Without predicate vector, predicate computing is performed over and over, now we perform predicate computing only once and DDTA-JOIN performs simple vector read instead of original complex predicate computing. Predicate vector can be used in any predicate processing, whatever attribute cardinality is high or low. If we store predicate vector with bitmap, space cost is small and cache locality is high, but further CPU cost is consumed for bit operation. Details are discussed in experiment section.

3.3 Parallel DDTA-JOIN for Multi-core System

Parallelization is limited by hardware features and software design. Parallel accessing on sequential storage such as hard disk produces frequently track seek actions which makes performance even poor. Random access storage such as main memory is suitable for parallel accessing, but memory bus is shared for parallel processes.

Now we discuss the parallelization of DDTA-JOIN enabled query processing with three phases, DDTA-JOIN, group-by and order-by.

(1) DDTA-JOIN. DDTA-JOIN is sequence scan based join algorithm, there are two kinds of locality as [13] classified as strong and weak locality. Scan on fact table is weak-locality without tuple re-read, dimensional attribute data is frequent dataset with strong-locality. For complex OLAP queries, DDTA-JOIN has to access multiple dimensional attributes simultaneously, so multiple dimensional columns and fact table contend for shared cache. The ideal strategy is to employ cache partition technique to reduce cache pollution by table scan, which requires support from the OS domain.

(2) Group-by. Group-by merges large amount result tuples to small aggregate tuple set. [14] summarized four methods of enabling parallelism in the writing of tuples to output partitions. For hash group-by operation, independent output buffer can reduce conflicts between threads, it needs additional global group-by result merge procedure and the output buffer must be small to reduce cache misses. If we use single output buffer for concurrent group-by processing, the performance suffers from write conflicts from each thread. In SSB, the group-by result sets vary from 1 to 800, so we select independent output buffer mode to guarantee maximum parallelization.

(3) Order-by. Since the target of order-by is small aggregate result set, we perform order-by operation on hash group-by result set without parallel processing.

In MOSS-DB, large fact table is resident on hard disk as pages as figure 5, when data are loaded into main memory, fact table is transformed into sequential buffered data, the whole data can be divided into partitions based on available cores. Dimensional columns and predicate vectors are shared for different threads. Each thread performs DDTA-JOIN algorithm and generates local group-by result set. Then the group-by result sets are merged together for final aggregate results. Finally, query result set is ordered based on order-by clause. According to Amdahl's law, maximum parallelization must be achieved by minimizing sequential fraction of the process. For DDTA-JOIN, the costly join operations are all

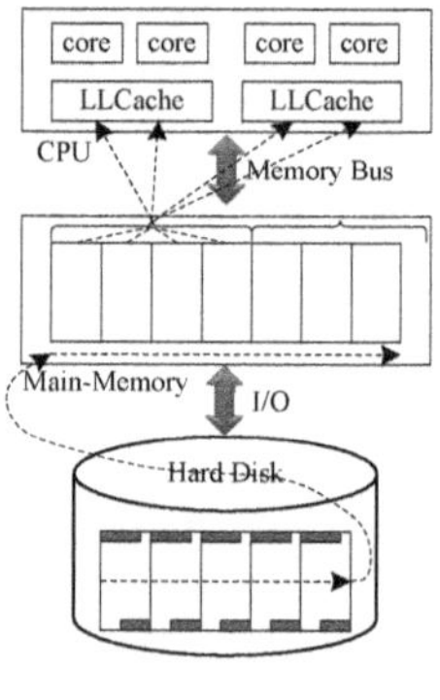

Fig. 5. Parallel DDTA-JOIN

parallelized and only aggregate merge and order-by operation with small result set are sequentially processed, the parallelization can be maximized.

For parallel query processing, another critical performance issue is memory bandwidth, in experiments we find that because of simplified query processing, OLAP query is no longer CPU bound but memory bandwidth bound, when more parallel processes are performed, memory bandwidth becomes bottleneck of system.

For concurrent OLAP workloads, traditional DBMS perform inter-parallel processing, [14] optimized co-runner queries by locality strength of queries for minimum cache conflicts. For intra-parallel processing, cores are dispatched to parallel query processing threads, so we can maintain a queue for concurrent query workloads and submit queries one by one for parallel processing. Table scan of OLAP is a costly procedure due to hard disk latency, memory bandwidth limitation makes CPU latency even larger, the cores have much idle processing resources. To balance memory bandwidth and CPU processing capacity, concurrent queries should be combined into intra-parallel query group. [8] grouped concurrent queries for sharing scan, each tuple serves for multiple queries. [15] serialized query processing to pipelined hash filters, during heavy OLAP workloads, fact table is looped scanned, queries can join processing group dynamically, each fact tuple goes through filters to perform predicate clauses and results are distributed to aggregate processors. Bit-vector is used for identifying queries. In MOSS-DB model, query processing is uniform linear tuple reading and address accessing, concurrent queries can be pushed down to parallel DDTA-JOIN operator with multiple predicate expressions.

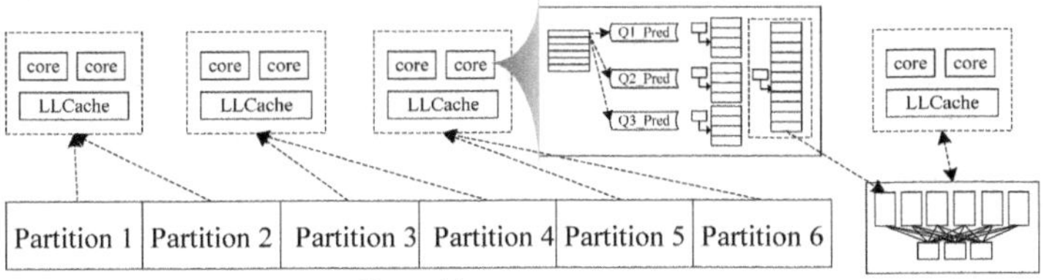

Fig. 6. Concurrent Parallel DDTA-JOIN

Figure 6 illustrates the concurrent parallel DDTA-JOIN processing.

Intra-parallel reduces query processing latency, inter-parallel reduces user response time and improves CPU utilization rate. Static concurrent query task group can be easily pushed down to intra-parallel query processing, but dynamic concurrent query group has to maintain meta data for each processing threads, it is hard to synchronize multiple meta data replicas.

4 Experiments

MOSS-DB supports both MMDB model and DRDB model. With multi-core support, the processing capacity becomes more powerful. To balance the processing power, main memory capacity must be even larger to overlap hard disk latency. So MOSS-DB considers tow typical scenarios, one is MMDB model, the other is DRDB model with large main memory support. We also design experiments for these two models.

4.1 Main Memory MOSS-DB

We perform our experiments on a HP ML350 server with two Intel Xeon Quad-core CPUs of 1.60 GHz, running Ubuntu 4.3.3-5 with 6GB RAM and 80GB hard disk. In each CPU, every two cores share 4MB L2 cache. We use SSB data generator to create 4GB dataset with 24 million fact tuples. There are 17 attributes in fact table and only 7 attributes are utilized in all 13 queries, only 47.26% width of fact tuple is effective for cache reading. So we use two fact tables for experiments one is original fact table, the other is clustered fact table with only 7 accessed attributes in testing queries.

A. Naïve DDTA-JOIN algorithm

We compare our DDTA-JOIN algorithm with open-source column-wise main memory database MonetDB(version:May2009-SuperBall-SP2) which stores each attribute as independent BAT with OID and VALUE pairs, relational algebra is translated into BAT algebra with uniform BAT functions. It outperforms traditional row-wise database for OLAP scenario with sparse attribute accessing, but join cost will increase rapidly with more large fact attributes or higher selectivity of predicate.

Figure 7(a) compares four groups of queries, MonetDB-join represents re-written SSB queries without group-by and order-by clauses which focuses on the most critical performance of join. MonetDB-full represents standard SSB queries, we can see that these two kinds of queries have very tiny difference due to small carnality of group-by result set, so we perform the rest experiments with SSB-J benchmark(join performance test). DDTA-JOIN denotes naïve algorithm with directly dimensional tuple accessing, and clusDDTA-JOIN denotes query process on clustered fact table.

We can see that narrow fact table improves join performance because of better cache performance. In 13 SSB queries, DDTA-JOIN outperforms MonetDB for 10 queries, MonetDB works better in Q3.2~Q3.4 because filer factor for select predicates is extremely low and predicate "(c_city='UNITED KI1' or c_city='UNITED KI5')" produces larger string comparison cost than MonetDB.

B. Compression for DDTA-JOIN algorithm

Figure 7(b) shows the speedup of compression. Light-weight dictionary compression can save space cost for *VARCHAR* type column stored dimensional attributes but additional CPU cost for de-compressing deteriorates the whole performance. We perform process directly on dictionary compressed data for equal and range predicates, in which keys are retrieved on dictionary table first and then re-write query with matched compressed values. The results show that the compressed and frequently accessed dimensional attribute can improve performance very much.

Figure 7(c) tests the predicate vector performance with Q3.4. Predicate vector acts as mediate BAT in MonetDB, the difference is that MonetDB join mediate predicate BAT with other BAT based on equal OIDs while DDTA-JOIN uses predicate vector as directly memory addressed short flags without lookup cost. We design two kinds of predicate vectors, one uses bit for predicate result which costs least space but needs additional CPU cost for parsing certain bit from the whole bit vector. The other uses short data type to store predicate vector, for example *char*[] with values of '*y*' or '*n*', although storage cost is larger, the CPU parsing cost is saved, performance can be further improved. We can see that for SSB workload, predicate vector outperforms other algorithms with compressed columns, clustered fact table and MonetDB.

C. *Parallel DDTA-JOIN algorithm*

DDTA-JOIN is easily parallelized for in-memory sequential fact table, when dividing fact table into required parallel partitions by available cores, each thread performs DDTA-JOIN individually. Figure 7(d) illustrates the parallel performance of Q1.1 for different conditions. Quad-core CPU shares L2 cache between two cores, if parallel tasks are less than total amount of L2 caches, each thread is located for individual core groups, i.e. thread uses the whole L2 cache to minimize cache conflicts. If parallel tasks increase, different threads have to contend the shared L2 cache. We extend Q1.1 to four queries, Simple(reduce predicate expressions), morePred(add more predicate expressions), largePred(maximize predicate complexity), moreComprPred(maximize compressed predicate complexity). Performance curve of AR-largePred is most close to linear acceleration rate, when amount of threads exceeds four, the curve declines because of conflicts in shared L2 caches. The rest four types slowly increase as thread amount increases. We can conclude that, DDTA-JOIN with less complex predicate processing is memory bandwidth bound while with complex predicate processing is CPU bound. CPU bound workload can achieve better parallelization.

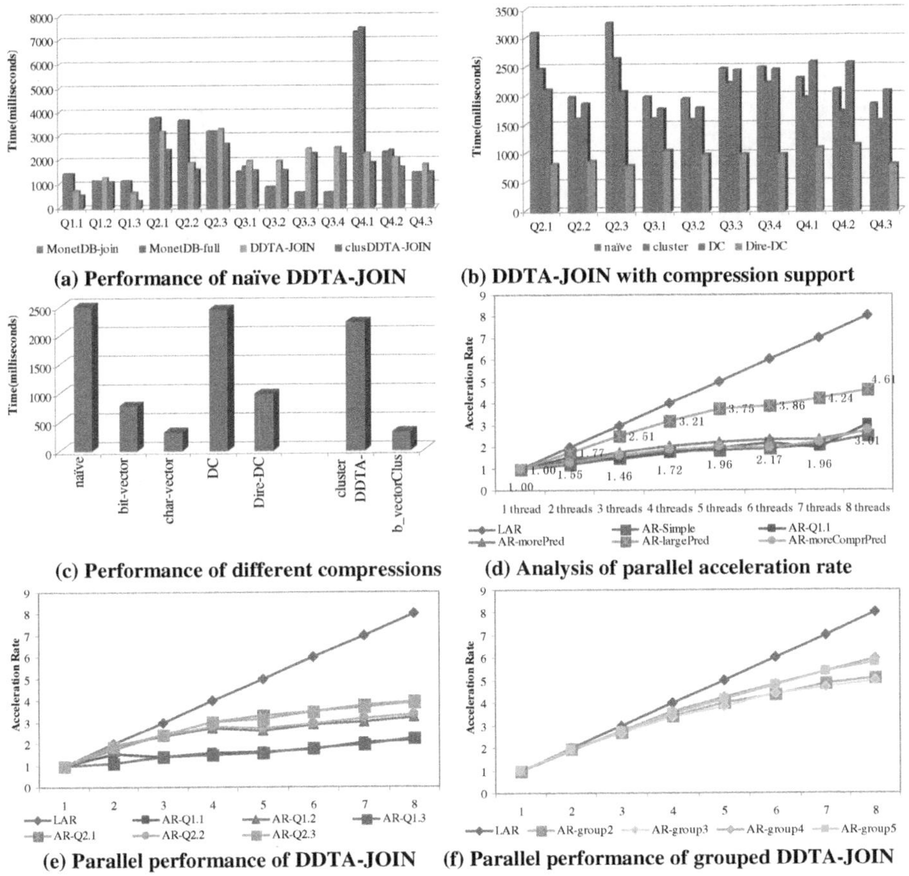

Fig. 7. Naïve, compressed and parallel DDTA-JOIN algorithms

Figure 7(e) measures parallel performance of 6 queries, we observe that queries with more costly predicate processing e.g. Q2.3 achieve better parallel performance. Figure 7(f) illustrates the parallel performance of grouped concurrent queries, we create groups with 2,3,4,5 queries to simulate different concurrent workloads. We can see that parallel performance increases as workload grows. For SSB workload, DDTA-JOIN simplifies complexity of query processing, the memory bandwidth is more critical for parallel performance, grouped concurrent query workload increases CPU cost and balances CPU and memory bandwidth consuming.

4.2 Disk Resident MOSS-DB

For large dataset, we employ tradition row-wise storage engine to store large fact table and dimension tables. Dimension tables are loaded into main memory to form memory column dimension tables and resident in memory during system running. We extend PostgreSQL by embedding our DDTA-JOIN algorithm in table scan module, when tuples are fetched from disk, DDTA-JOIN carries out the rest query processing work. By this, we transform the ordinary SQL engine into memory optimizing OLAP engine by embedding DDTA-JOIN operator for special star schema OLAP workload.

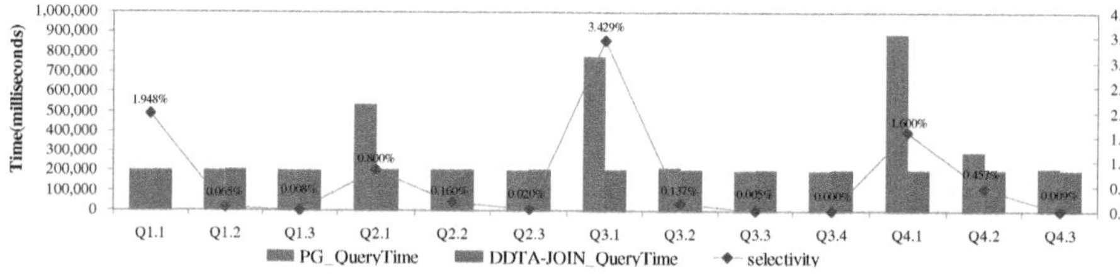

Fig. 8. Disk Resident DDTA-JOIN performance

We use 24GB dataset for performance test in which there are 143999787 fact tuples, the amounts of four dimension tables are 1000000, 720000, 240000 and 2556. Figure 8 compares performance of PostgreSQL and disk resident DDTA-JOIN, the average response time improves 19%, we get maximum acceleration of 76.84% on Q4.1. Predicate vector normalizes different predicate processing cost into equal cost, the performance of DDTA-JOIN is stable even when selectivity is high while PostgtreSQL consumes large space and time cost for hash tables and proves poor performance with high selectivity. I/O latency overlaps time cost of hash join for PostgreSQL, with 4GB dataset, average execution time is also shorten by 13.5% in 10 queries with low selectivity. DDTA-JOIN is stable algorithm for various OLAP workloads even for more complex queries with higher selectivity.

5 Conclusions and Future Work

There are many researches on OLAP performance, main memory and multi-core optimizations, most of these works sound well but hard to realize because of the complexity and efficiency, we often ask ourselves "Why so complex? Can it be simpler?" By analyzing the features of star schema, workload and hardware, we build virtual pre-joined single table for OLAP with DDTA-JOIN support, so the complex query plan tree is transformed into simple tuple reading, addressed accessing and predicate processing with complexity of $O(n)$. Compression and predicate vector further optimize cache performance with less data size by reducing cache conflicts. Furthermore, DDTA-JOIN is easily deployed on multi-core platform by evenly dividing the whole fact tuples into several parallel partitions, only small proportion of global group-by result sets merging and order-by operations are serially processed. We also discuss and measure the concurrent query processing strategy for balanced OLAP engine. We owe our major contribution to the simplicity of star schema OLAP processing which can be easily embedded into SQL engine and make SQL engine qualified for analytical engine. In our future work, we will focus on how to balance performance between hard disk sequential read, memory access and CPU processing.

Acknowledgements

This work is supported by 863 Project of China under Grant No.2009AA01Z149; the joint research of Large Scale Data Management for HP Lab China and Renmin University; the project of Education committee of Beijing(in-memory Online Analytical system); the Graduate Science Foundation of Renmin University of China No.08XNG040 and No. 10XNH096; the Funding of Renmin University of China No. 10XNB053.

References

1. Stonebraker, M., Abadi, D.J., Batkin, A., Chen, X., Cherniack, M., Ferreira, M., Lau, E., Lin, A., Madden, S., O'Neil, E.J., O'Neil, P.E., Rasin, A., Tran, N., Zdonik, S.B.: C-Store: A Column-oriented DBMS. In: Proceedings of VLDB, Trondheim, Norway, pp. 553–564 (2005)
2. MacNicol, R., French, B.: Sybase IQ Multiplex -Designed for analytics. In: Proceedings of VLDB (2004)
3. Boncz, P.A., et al.: Database Architecture Optimized for the New Bottleneck: Memory Access. In: Proceedings of VLDB (1999)
4. Ailamaki, A., DeWitt, D.J., Hill, M.D.: Data page layouts for relational databases on deep memory hierarchies. The VLDB Journal 11(3), 198–215 (2002)
5. Hankins, R.A., Patel, J.M.: Data morphing: an adaptive, cache-conscious storage technique. In: Proceedings of the 29th international conference on Very large data bases, pp. 417–428 (2003)
6. Bruno, N.: Teaching an Old Elephant New Tricks. In: CIDR 2009, Asilomar, California, USA (2009)
7. Johnson, R., Raman, V., Sidle, R., Swart, G.: Row-wise parallel predicate evaluation. In: Proceedings of the 32nd International Conference on Very Large Data Bases, Auckland, New Zealand (2008); VLDB Endowment 1(1), 622–634
8. Qiao, L., Raman, V., Reiss, F., Haas, P.J., Lohman, G.M.: Main-memory scan sharing for multi-core CPUs. PVLDB 1(1), 610–621 (2008)

9. Valduriez, P.: Join indices. ACM Transactions on Database Systems (TODS) 12(2), 218–246 (1987)
10. O'Neil, P., O'Neil, B., Chen, X.: The Star Schema Benchmark (SSB), http://www.cs.umb.edu/~poneil/StarSchemaB.PDF
11. Binnig, C., Hildenbrand, S., Färber, F.: Dictionary-based order-preserving string compression for main memory column stores. In: SIGMOD Conference 2009, pp. 283–296 (2009)
12. Abadi, D.J., Madden, S.R., Hachem, N.: Column-Stores vs. Row-Stores: How Different Are They Really? In: Proceeding of SIGMOD 2008, Vancouvrer, BC, Canada (2008)
13. Lee, R., Ding, X., Chen, F., Lu, Q., Zhang, X.: MCC-DB: Minimizing Cache Conflicts in Multi-core Processors for Databases. PVLDB 2(1), 373–384 (2009)
14. Cieslewicz, J., Ross, K.A.: Data partitioning on chip multiprocessors. In: DaMoN 2008, pp. 25–34 (2008)
15. Candea, G., Polyzotis, N., Vingralek, R.: A Scalable, Predictable Join Operator for Highly Concurrent Data Warehouses. PVLDB 2(1), 277–288 (2009)

Efficient Duplicate Record Detection Based on Similarity Estimation*

Mohan Li, Hongzhi Wang, Jianzhong Li, and Hong Gao

Harbin Institute of Technology, Harbin 150001
limohan.hit@gmail.com

Abstract. In information integration systems, duplicate records bring problems in data processing and analysis. To represent the similarity between two records from different data sources with different schema, the optimal bipartite graph matching is adopted on the attributes of them and the similarity is measured as the weight of such matching. However, the intuitive method has two aspects of shortcomings. The one in efficiency is that it needs to compare all records pairwise. The one in effectiveness is that a strict duplicate records judgment condition results in a low rate of recall. To make the method work in practice, an efficient method is presented in this paper. Based on similarity estimation, the basic idea is to estimate the range of the records similarity in O(1) time, and to determine whether they are duplicate records according to the estimation. Theoretical analysis and experimental results show that the method is effective and efficient.

Keywords: Heterogeneous Records, Duplicate Detection, Record Similarity, Similarity Estimation.

1 Introduction

Information integration systems have been widely used. When integrating data from heterogeneous and autonomous data sources, multiple records representing the same entity are often obtained. Such records are called duplicate records. In an information integration system, duplicate records not only cause data redundancy, resulting in the waste of network bandwidth and storage space, but also provide users too many useless duplicate results. In order to increase the efficient and usability of information integration systems, it is necessary to eliminate duplicate records. Duplicate record detection, which is to partition the record set into clusters each representing the same entity, is the first step of duplicate record elimination.

* Supported by the National Science Foundation of China (No 60703012, 60773063), the NSFC-RGC of China (No. 60831160525), National Grant of Fundamental Research 973 Program of China (No.2006CB303000), National Grant of High Technology 863 Program of China (No. 2009AA01Z149), Key Program of the National Natural Science Foundation of China (No. 60933001), National Post doctor Foundation of China (No. 20090450126), Development Program for Outstanding Young Teachers in Harbin Institute of Technology (no. HITQNJS.2009.052).

L. Chen et al. (Eds.): WAIM 2010, LNCS 6184, pp. 595–607, 2010.

Because of its widely applications, many techniques have been presented to deal with duplicate records detection. [1] is a survey of the early work of duplicate records detection. Some recent work [5, 6, 7, 8] adopt similarity functions of textual similarity, such as edit distance or cosine similarity. Those methods consider that the records corresponding to the same entity are textually similar, and are indeed useful for catching most kinds of typographic errors. The major drawback of textual similarity is that it may be misleading in the conditions of heterogeneous expressions (e.g. J. Smith is short for both John Smith and Jane Smith). Some methods based on segmentation [9, 10, 11] are proposed. Segmentation is to partition a string into its constituent components. Segmentation-based methods can solve the problem of heterogeneous expressions in some degree. There are also some other similarity descriptions are proposed. [12] uses a similarity function to address this problem in this setting. Transformation-based and grammar-based methods are proposed in [13] and [14], respectively. However all these methods does not consider the problem that the records may have various schema or attribute order and not practical for duplicate detection on records from heterogeneous data sources.

To represent the similarity of records with heterogeneous schemas, optimal bipartite graph matching is adopted (naïve Optimal Bipartite Matching Based, OBMAB) [15]. The pair of records is modeled as a bipartite graph with each node as an attribute, each edge as connecting a pair of attributes one from each record. The weights of edges are the similarity between corresponding pair of attributes. With such model, the similarity of two records is defined as the weight of optimal matching in corresponding bipartite graph. Such definition can describe the similarity of any records with different schema. As the comparing records are not necessarily having the same attribute number and order, the method is more suitable for the detection of the duplicate records from heterogeneous data sources effectively. However, each record needs to compare with a large number of records before it is assigned to the appropriate cluster. The method is not suitable for large data set. Moreover, a record will not be classified into a cluster even if only one record and the current record do not meet the requirements of similarity. This makes the method sensitive and results in low recall, which is the ratio of the detected duplicate records to all the duplicate records. Take the following case as an example.

Example 1. Records in {R_1(John Smith, 18), R_2(John Smith, 18, England), R_3(John Smith, England, 18)} all refer to the student named John Smith. While processing R_4 (John Smith, England), with OBMAB, the similarity of R_1 and R_4 is 0.5. However, if the condition that R_4 belongs to the cluster is larger than 0.5, R_4 will not be classified to the cluster, although R_4 has a high similarities with R_2 and R_3. If we reduce the constraint to 0.4, the records as (Jane Smith, 18) can be classified into this cluster. □

To make OBMAB practical, we proposed Similarity Estimating Duplicate Record Detection (SEDRD). For a record R and a cluster C, the upper and lower bounds of the similarity between R and any record in C can be estimated in O(1) time. These bound are used to determine whether R should belong to C. As the result, during the processing of R, the computation of the similarity between R and the records in C is avoided and the processing is accelerated. Another benefit of our method is that the restriction of each cluster is relaxed and the recall is improved.

The contributions of this paper are as follows.

- The optimal-matching-based methods for duplicate record detection are studied in this paper. With the ability of measure the similarity of records with heterogeneous schemas, such methods are suitable for duplicate detection on records from heterogeneous data sources.
- An estimation method of the range of optimal-matching-based similarity is presented based on the properties of edit distance as the base of efficient duplicate record detection method.
- With the estimated ranges of optimal-matching-based similarity, an optimized method for record detection is presented to improve the naïve method in both efficiency and effectiveness.
- Extensive experiments are performed to show that our method outperforms existing methods in both efficiency and effectiveness.

The rest of this paper is organized as follows: Section 2 introduces some background knowledge. Section 3 presents the duplicate record detection method which based on similarity estimation. Experimental results and analysis are reported in Section 4. Section 5 concludes the whole paper.

2 Problem Definition

In this section, we define the problem of detecting duplicate records and introduce the naïve duplicate records detection method based on optimal bipartite graph matching.

2.1 Duplicate Records Detection

With the consideration of transitivity of duplication relationship between records, duplicate record detection is defined as follows.

Definition 1 (Detection of duplicate records on data set *R*). Given a original record set $R = \{R_1,R_2,\ldots,R_m\}$, detection of duplicate records on is defined as follows.

A required similarity ε is given. Divide R into several disjoint subsets $S_1,S_2,\ldots,S_n$, each S_i meet the following 3 properties.

1) For $\forall S_i$, any two records in S_i have a similarity which is not lower than ε;
2) For $\forall S_i,S_j$ $(i\neq j)$, we have $S_i \cap S_j=\emptyset$;
3) For $\forall S_i,S_j$ $(i\neq j)$, $S_i \cup S_j$ does not meet 1).

2.2 The Naïve Duplicate Records Detection Method

The naïve OBMAB method involves three key technologies.

The Similarity of Attributes. The attributes' similarity is defined based on edit distance [2] as it can be applied to a variety of attributes. The edit distance of A_1 and A_2

is $dis(A_1,A_2)$, and the lengths are $len(A_1)$, $len(A_2)$. The similarity of A_1 and A_2 is defined as follows, where m represents the maximal value of $len(A_1)$ and $len(A_2)$.

$$\mathrm{Sim}(A_1, A_2) = 1 - \frac{\mathrm{dis}(A_1, A_2)}{m} \tag{1}$$

The Similarity of Records. Taking the difference of attributes' positions, the loss of some attributes into consideration, the similarity of records is defined based on a bipartite graph as follows.

R_1 and R_2 are two records. A complete bipartite graph $B=(V_1 \cup V_2, E, W)$ is built. Each node u in V_1 and v in V_2 represents R_1's attribute A_{1i} and R_2's attribute A_{2j}, respectively. $E=V_1 \times V_2$, the weight function $W: E \rightarrow [0,1]$ is defined as $W(u,v)=Sim(A_{1i}, A_{2j})$, while $Sim(A_{1i}, A_{2j})$ is the attribute similarity. $M=(V',E')$ is the optimal match of B. $Sim(R_1, R_2)$ denotes similarity of R_1 and R_2.

$$\mathrm{Sim}(R_1, R_2) = \frac{\sum_{e \in E'} W(e)}{\max\{m, n\}} \tag{2}$$

m and n represents the number of attributes of R_1 and R_2, respectively.

Kuhn－Manures algorithm [3,4] (KM algorithm) is a good choice to find the optimal match, so it can be used to compute the similarity of records [15].

Detection of Duplicate Records. The main idea is for each $R_k \in R$, search in the stack to find which cluster R_k belongs to. If R_k does not belong to any existing cluster, build a new cluster for R_k.

The method uses a stack S to store the records (**signature record**) which represents the existing clusters. Each signature record has a bucket to store the records belonging to the cluster. Before a record R_k is classified to a cluster, it should compare with the signature records (denoted by R_s) in S, from the top to the bottom. If the similarity of R_k and R_s is no less than required similarity ε, then R_k is compared with the records in the bucket of R_s. And if all the similarities are no less than ε, R_k enter the bucket of R_s. At the end, each R_s in the stack and the records in R_s's bucket are classified into a cluster. All the clusters form a division satisfying Definition 1. Fig.1 shows the method's framework.

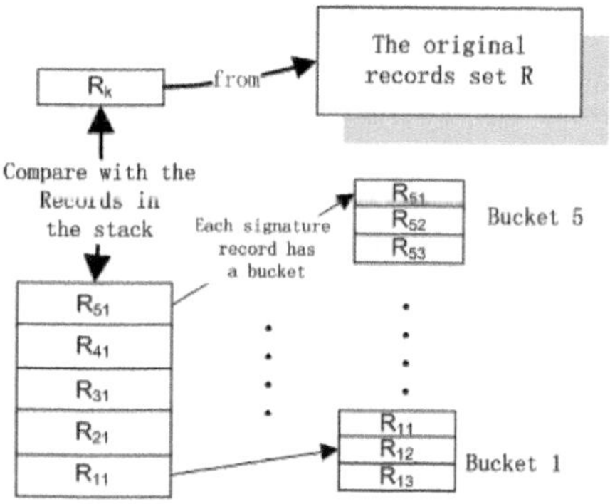

Fig. 1. Framework of the naïve method

The method has two problems. The one is that it needs to compare a large number of records pairwise. The other is that a strict duplicate records judgment condition results in a low rate of recall. An optimized method is to be proposed in section 3.

3 Duplicate Record Detection Based on Similarity Estimation

In this section, we present an efficient duplicate record detection method based on similarity estimation. At first, the basic idea of our method is presented (Section 3.1). Then, we introduce the method's theoretical basis and underlying assumption (Section 3.2). Thirdly, we present the efficient duplicate record detection based on similarity estimation (Section 3.3). At last, detailed discussions are given (section 3.4).

3.1 The Main Idea and Framework

In order to facilitate the following discussion, the symbols to be referred are listed.

Table 1. Symbols and meaning

symbol	Meaning	symbol	Meaning
$Sim(R_i, R_j)$	The similarity of R_i and R_j.	Match(A)	The attributes belonging to the records in R_s.bucket and matching attribute A.
$Sim(R_i, R_j)$.lb	The lower bound of $Sim(R_i, R_j)$.	A_{kl}	The attributes which belong to R_k, and matches attribute A_{si}.
$Sim(R_i, R_j)$.ub	The upper bound of $Sim(R_i, R_j)$.	A_{kl}.ub_dis	The upper bound of the edit distance between A_{kl} and the attributes in $Match(A_{kl})$.
R_s	The signature record in the stack being processing now	A_{kl}.lb_dis	The lower bound of the edit distance between A_{kl} and the attributes in $Match(A_{kl})$.
R_s.bucket	The bucket corresponding to R_s	$Sim(A_{kl},Match(A_{kl}))$.lb	The lower bound of the similarity between A_{kl} and the attributes in $Match(A_{kl})$.
R_b	The records in R_s.bucket	$Sim(A_{kl},Match(A_{kl}))$.ub	The upper bound of the similarity between A_{kl} and the attributes in $Match(A_{kl})$.
R_k	The record being processing now	A_{kl}.max_len	max{A_{si}.max_len, len(A_{kl})}
R_k.lb_sim	The lower bound of the similarities between R_k and $\forall R_b$	A_{kl}.min_len	min{A_{si}.min_len, len(A_{kl})}
		A_{si}	The ith attribute of R_s.
		A_{si}.ub_dis	A_{si}'s upper bound of edit distance
R_k.ub_sim	The upper bound of the similarities between R_k and $\forall R_b$	A_{si}.max_len	The maximal string length of $Match(A_{si})$
		A_{si}.min_len	The minimal string length of $Match(A_{si})$

The framework of our algorithm is shown as follows.

Step 1 Initialize the stack S, ε, **u_con** and **l_con**.
Step 2 Get a record R_k from R,
Step 3 Search in S to find an R_s whose similarity is no less than ε with R_k.

Step 4 IF R_s can not be found, THEN move to step 5.
ELSE estimate R_k.ub_sim and R_k.lb_sim.
IF R_k.ub_sim≥u_con and R_k.lb_sim≥l_con,
THEN R_k enters R_s's bucket and move R_s to the top of the stack.
ELSE move to step 3 to find a new R_s.
Step 5 Push R_k into the stack.
Step 6 IF all the records have been processed, THEN end the algorithm.
ELSE move to step 2.

The basic idea of the acceleration of the comparison is to estimate the upper and lower bounds of the similarities of R_k and records in each cluster (denoted as R_k.*ub_sim* and R_k.*lb_sim*) very efficiently and determine the cluster R_k belonging to with the bounds instead of the real similarities. Given an upper and lower bound (*u_con* and *l_con*, called **required bounds** and considered as the required upper and lower bounds of every bucket). For each R_k, instead of computing the similarities of R_k and all the records in the bucket, an upper and lower bound of the similarities R_k.*ub_sim* and R_k.*lb_sim* are estimated. If R_k.*ub_sim* and R_k.*lb_sim* is no less than *u_con* and *l_con*, respectively, then R_k enter the bucket.

3.2 The Method's Theoretical Basis and Underlying Assumption

In this section we present two properties as the basis of the similarity estimation method. The estimating method in this paper is based on the following property.

Proporty 1. A_1, A_2 and A_3 are three strings. $dis(A_i,A_j)$ is the edit distance of A_i and A_j, let $dis(A_1,A_2)=d_1$, $dis(A_2,A_3)=d_2$, $dis(A_1,A_3)=d_3$. d_1, d_2, d_3 satisfy the inequality:

$$d_1-d_3 \leq d_2 \leq d_1+d_3 \tag{3}$$

Assumption 1 is another useful property for similarity estimation.

Assumption 1. $R_1(A_{11}, A_{12}, A_{13})$, $R_2(A_{21}, A_{22}, A_{23})$, $R_3(A_{31}, A_{32}, A_{33})$ are three records. The matching attributes of R_1 and R_2 are (A_{11}, A_{21}), (A_{12},A_{22}), (A_{13},A_{23}), the matching attributes of R_2 and R_3 are (A_{21},A_{31}), (A_{22},A_{32}), (A_{23},A_{33}). Then, the matching attributes of R_1 and R_3 are (A_{11},A_{31}) (A_{12},A_{32}) (A_{13},A_{33}).

Even though Assumption 1 cannot be proven theoretically, it coincides with the intuition that if the attribute *A* and *B* refer to the same information, and the attribute *B* and *C* refer to the same information, then *A* and *C* also refer to the same information.

3.3 The Method of Similarity Estimation

In this section, we will introduce a simple estimation method first. With it as a component, we introduce the method suitable for large data set.

The Simple Estimation Method. In this subsection, the simple method to estimate the bounds of *Sim(A, C)* with *Sim(A, B)* and *Sim(B, C)*, where all of *A*, *B* and *C* can be attributes or records.

First, consider the case with 3 attributes. A_1, A_2 and A_3 matches with each other. $dis(A_i,A_j)$ represents the edit distance of A_i and A_j. $dis(A_1,A_2)= d_1$, $dis(A_1,A_3)=d_3$. According to Property 1, $dis(A_2,A_3) \in [d_1-d_3, d_1+d_3]$. According to formula (1), $Sim(A_2,A_3) \in [1-(d_1+d_3)/m, 1-(d_1-d_3)/m]$.

For the introduction of the record estimation method, **Perfectly Matched Records Pair (PMRP)** is defined.

Defition 2 (Perfectly Matched Records Pair, PMRP). R_1 and R_2 are two records. If for R_1's attributes set A_1 and R_2's attributes set A_2, there is a one-to-one mapping T: $A_1 \rightarrow A_2$, $T(A_{1i})=A_{2j}$ iff the jth attribute of R_2 (denoted by A_{2j}) matches with the ith attribute of R_1 (denoted by A_{1i}), then (R_1, R_2) is a Perfectly Matched Records Pair. □

(R_1, R_2) being PMRP means that for any R_1's attribute A_{1i}, there is an R_2's attribute A_{2j} matching A_{1i}, and for any R_2's attribute A_{2j}, there is an A_{1i} matching A_{2j}.

For any matching attribute pair (A_{2j}, A_{3k}) with A_{2j} and A_{3k} as attributes in R_2 and R_3, respectively, based on Assumption 1 and the fact that (R_1, R_2) and (R_1,R_3) are both PMRPs, there is a attribute A_{1i} in R_1 satisfies (A_{1i}, A_{2j}) and (A_{1i}, A_{3k}). The upper and lower bound of $Sim(A_{2j}, A_{3k})$ can be estimated from $Sim(A_{1i}, A_{2j})$ and $Sim(A_{1i}, A_{3k})$ in the method discussed above.

With the range of similarity of any matching attribute pair of R_2 and R_3 estimated, $Sim(R_2, R_3)$ is estimated. In the bipartite graph B built on (R_2, R_3), each $W(e)$ $(e=(A_{2j}, A_{3k})\in E')$ is $Sim(A_{2j}, A_{3k})$. The bounds and exact value of $W(e)$ are denoted by $W(e).ub$, $W(e).lb$ and $W(e).val$, respectively. By substituting $W(e).ub$ and $W(e).lb$ into formula (2), $Sim(R_2, R_3).ub$ and $Sim(R_2, R_3).lb$ can be estimated.

$$\mathrm{Sim}(R_2,R_3)\in\left[\frac{\sum_{e\in E'} W(e).lb}{\max\{m,n\}}, \frac{\sum_{e\in E'} W(e).ub}{\max\{m,n\}}\right] \tag{4}$$

The method works well in the records set containing only PMRPs. But in the original records set, records are heterogeneous. To deal with this problem, some preparations are required to make sure that each records pair (R_i, R_j) satisfy the PMRP.

Similarity Estimating Preparations. For the cluster C, a record R_s is in the stack. During the determination of whether a record R_k belongs to the cluster C, R_k should be compared with R_s first. If $\mathrm{Sim}(R_s, R_k)\geq\varepsilon$, as the preparation, a record R_k^* forming PMRP with R_s is generated from R_k using Rule 1. The similarity bound $\mathrm{Sim}(R_k^*, R_s)$.ub and $\mathrm{Sim}(R_k^*, R_s)$.lb are estimated. If the similarity bound satisfy the required bound, then R_k^* enter the bucket of R_s.

Rule 1: For each attribute A_{si} of R_s,

1) If there is an A_{kl} in R_k matching A_{si}, then A_{kl} is the jth attribute of R_k^*.
2) Otherwise the ith attributes of R_k^* is an empty attribute to match A_{si}.

The attributes of R_k matching no attribute of A_{si} are ignored. □

It is easy to see that (R_k^*, R_s) is PMRP.

In R_s.*bucket*, the records are generated using Rule 1 for computation convenience. They all have same attributes number. In order to access original records, each R_k^* has been linked to corresponding R_k. To facilitate our method, we use symbol R_k instead of R_k^* in the following descriptions.

Since (R_k, R_s) is PMRP and for each R_b in R_s.*bucket*, (R_b, R_s) is PMRP, (R_k, R_b) is also PMRP. For each attribute A_{kl} of R_k, since the attribute of R_s matching A_{kl} is A_{si}, $Match(A_{kl})=Match(A_{si})$, where $Match(A_{si})=\{A_{sij} | A_{sij}$ is an attribute of $R_T \in R_s.bucket$ and A_{sij} matches $A_{si}\}$. Therefore, when estimating the similarity bounds of R_k, It needs to estimate the similarity bounds of each attribute A_{kl} and the attributes in $Match(A_{kl})$ ($Sim(A_{kl},Match(A_{kl})).ub$ and $Sim(A_{kl},Match(A_{kl})).lb$) first.

Estimating the Similarity Bounds of Attributes. The estimation is based on the following Theorem.

Theorem 1. For any attribute A_{si} of R_s it is supposed that the attribute in R_k matching A_{si} is A_{kl}. Then,

$$\text{Sim}(A_{kl},\text{Match}(A_{si})).\text{ub} = 1\text{-}(\text{dis}(A_{kl},A_{si})\text{-}A_{si}.\text{ub\_dis})/A_{kl}.\text{max\_len} \quad (5)$$

$$\text{Sim}(A_{kl},\text{Match}(A_{si})).\text{lb} = 1\text{-}(\text{dis}(A_{kl},A_{si})+A_{si}.\text{ub\_dis})/A_{kl}.\text{min\_len} \quad (6)$$

Where $A_{si}.ub\_dis= max(dis(A_{si}, A_{sij}))$, $\forall A_{sij} \in Match(A_{si})=Match(A_{kl})$ $A_{kl}.max\_len$ and $A_{kl}.min\_len$ be the maximum and the minimum string length of A_{kl} and all the attributes in $Match(A_{kl})$. □

Proof. As discussed in the last section, $Match(A_{si})=Match(A_{kl})$. According to Property 1 and formula (3), $\forall A_{sij} \in Match(A_{si})$, $dis(A_{kl}, A_{sij}) \in [dis(A_{kl},A_{si})-dis(A_{si}, A_{sij}), dis(A_{kl},A_{si})+ dis(A_{si}, A_{sij})]$.

$A_{si}.ub\_dis=\max\{dis(A_{si},A_{sij})\}$, then, $dis(A_{kl},A_{sij}) \in [A_{kl}.lb\_dis, A_{kl}.ub\_dis]$, where

$$A_{kl}.\text{ub\_dis} = \text{dis}(A_{kl},A_{si})+A_{si}.\text{ub\_dis} \quad (7)$$

$$A_{kl}.\text{lb\_dis} = \text{dis}(A_{kl},A_{si})\text{-}A_{si}.\text{ub\_dis} \quad (8)$$

According to formula (1), it implies that for $\forall A_{sij} \in Match(A_{si}) = Match(A_{kl})$, $Sim(A_{kl},A_{sij}) \in [1\text{-}A_{kl}.ub\_dis/A_{kl}.min\_len, 1\text{-}A_{kl}.lb\_dis/A_{kl}.max\_len]$. That is,

$$\text{Sim}(A_{kl},A_{sij}).\text{ub}=1\text{-}A_{kl}.\text{lb\_dis}/A_{kl}.\text{max\_len}=1\text{-}(\text{dis}(A_{kl},A_{si})\text{-}A_{si}.\text{ub\_dis})/A_{kl}.\text{max\_len} \quad (10)$$

$$\text{Sim}(A_{kl},A_{sij}).\text{lb}=1\text{-}A_{kl}.\text{ub\_dis}/A_{kl}.\text{min\_len}=1\text{-}(\text{dis}(A_{kl},A_{si})+A_{si}.\text{ub\_dis})/A_{kl}.\text{min\_len} \quad (11)$$

For $\forall A_{sij} \in Match(A_{si})$, $Sim(A_{kl},Match(A_{si})).ub= Sim(A_{kl},A_{sij}).ub$, and $Sim(A_{kl},Match(A_{si})).lb = Sim(A_{kl},A_{sij}).lb$. □

In order to compute the bound, for each attribute A_{si} of a record R_s in the stack, three values, the maximal length of the strings in $Match(A_{Si})$ (denoted by $A_{si}.max\_len$), the minimal length of the strings in $Match(A_{Si})$ (denoted by $A_{si}.min\_len$) and $A_{si}.ub\_dis$ are maintained. The steps of computation are illustrated with an example.

Example 2. Suppose the attribute A_{kl}= "John_Simth", A_{si}= "J.Smith", $Match(A_{kl})$ $=Match(A_{si})$ ={J_Smith, John.Smith}. For A_{si}, $A_{si}.max\_len$=10, $A_{si}.min\_len$=7 and $A_{si}.ub\_dis$=3. It can be computed that $dis(A_{kl},A_{si})$=4, $A_{kl}.min\_len$=10, $A_{kl}.max\_len$=10. Based on these values,

$Sim(A_{kl},Match(A_{si})).ub = 1-(dis(A_{kl},A_{si})-A_{si}.ub\_dis)/A_{kl}.max\_len = 1 - (4-3)/10=0.9$,

$Sim(A_{kl},Match(A_{si})).lb = 1-(dis(A_{kl},A_{si})+A_{si}.ub\_dis)/A_{kl}.min\_len = 1-(4+3)/10=0.3$。

That is, $\forall A_{sij} \in Match(A_{si})$, the similarity of A_{kl} and A_{sij} belongs to [0.3, 0.9]. □

Note that the upper bound may greater than 1, and the lower bound may less than 0. When these happen, the upper bound is set to 1, and the lower bound is set to 0.

Estimating the Similarity Bounds of Records. Intuitively, for each attribute A_{kl} of R_k, substituting W(e) for $Sim(A_{kl},Match(A_{kl})).ub$ and $Sim(A_{kl},Match(A_{kl})).lb$ in formula (2), an upper bound and a lower bound of the similarity of R_k and the records in $R_s.bucket$ is obtained,

$$R_k.ub\_sim = \frac{\sum_{l=1}^{n} Sim(A_{kl}, Match(A_{kl})).ub}{n} \tag{12}$$

$$R_k.lb\_sim = \frac{\sum_{l=1}^{n} Sim(A_{kl}, Match(A_{kl})).lb}{n} \tag{13}$$

where n is the number of attributes in a record.

3.4 Detailed Discussion

The Parameters. It is very important to choose the parameters ε, u_con, l_con when detecting duplication. The chosen of parameters depends on the requirement of precision, efficiency and recall. Parameters with high value will result in high precision but low efficiency and recall. Some techniques of machine learning [16] can be used to choose them. Also, experiences are helpful when choosing them.

Other discussion. SEDRD can compensate the two shortcomings of the naïve method introduced in section 2. Firstly, SEDRD reduces the cost of operations. The method estimates the bounds of the algorithm in O(1) time. A record only needs to compare with the signature records in stack rather than all the records in the buckets. Second, SEDRD improves the recall. When the required bounds are relaxed, it is not as strict as in the naïve method for a record to enter a bucket. The recall is improved.

The worst case of our methods exists in the case without duplicate records in the original record set R. In such case, each record in *R* belongs to a cluster by itself and our method has to spend $O(|R|^2)$ time to search the whole stack for each record in R. However, in general cases, the operation cost is much less, because a record only needs to compare with the signature records in the stack. Especially, for another extreme case with all the records in R belonging to the same cluster, the time complexity of the naïve method is $O(|R|^2)$ while that of our method is $O(|R|)$, because there is always only one record in the stack.

4 Experimental Evaluations

4.1 Experimental Setup

Experiments were run on AMD Sempron 3000+ with 512M memory.

We do the experiment both on real and virtual data set.

For real data set, the records comes from the website of ACM and DBLP are used to test the efficiency and effectiveness.

For the virtual data set, we use the data generator and noises tool to get duplicate records. The differences between two duplicate records are: 1) attributes' positions difference, 2) the loss of some attributes, and 3) typographic errors. Data generator is used to generate some benchmark records randomly, and for each benchmark record, some modify operations are used to modify the benchmarks to get duplicate records.

When generating duplicate records, there are two main parameters: the number of the benchmark records (denoted by N_R), and the number of duplicate records for each benchmark record (denoted by N_D). In order to ensure the accuracy of the experiments, we need to fix N_R first. N_R is set to be 100. That is, we generate a record set which contains 100 benchmark records, and then modify (no more than 50%) the records to generate N_D duplicates. N_D is changed to control the size of R. Since the modification of the benchmark records is no more than 50%, we set ε=0.6, which is a little higher than the lowest similarity.

4.2 Experiments on Virtual Data

Change the Required Upper and Lower Bounds. In this section, the required upper and lower bounds (u_con and l_con) are changed to test their influence of the algorithm. The record set has 100 benchmark records, for each benchmark record, we generate 100 duplicate records. The result is illustrated in Fig.2 and Fig.3.

Fig.2 shows the influence caused by the changing of u_con. In this experiment, l_con is set to 0, so it can be ignored. Fig.3 shows the influence caused by the changing of l_con. In this experiment, u_con is set to 0. Since high required bounds need more compare times, it can be seen that the cost of time is increasing with the increase of the required bounds. In Fig.2, the time cost change gently at first, but when u_con is 0.9, the time needed increases sharply. That is because 0.9 is too high that when a record being processing, it is hard to find the suitable bucket.

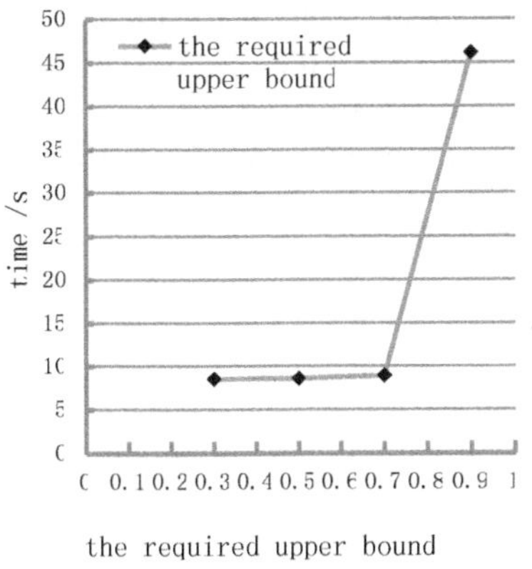

Fig. 2. Change the required upper bound

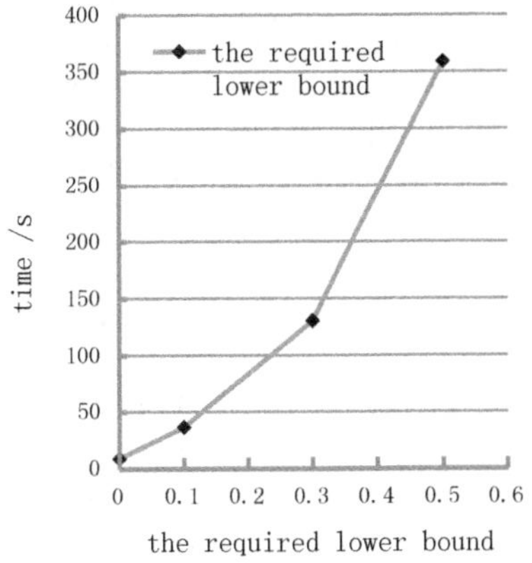

Fig. 3. Change the required lower bound

Change the Size of Original Records Set. By changing the size of original records set, we compare the naïve method and the improved method both on time and recall.

The best values of the required bounds are closely related with the original record set R. Since there are 100 benchmark records, we can infer that the accurate result is 100 subsets after R is divided. We are trying to reduce the influence of bad choice of required bounds. As the result of our test in 4.2, we set the required upper bound and lower bound to be 0.7 and 0.1, respectively. We test different size of original records set by changing N_D. The results are shown in Fig.4 and Fig.5.

The time cost of the two methods is shown in Fig.4, we can see that the time cost of the two methods is both increasing when the original records set are getting larger. But the improved method is increasing much slower than the naïve method.

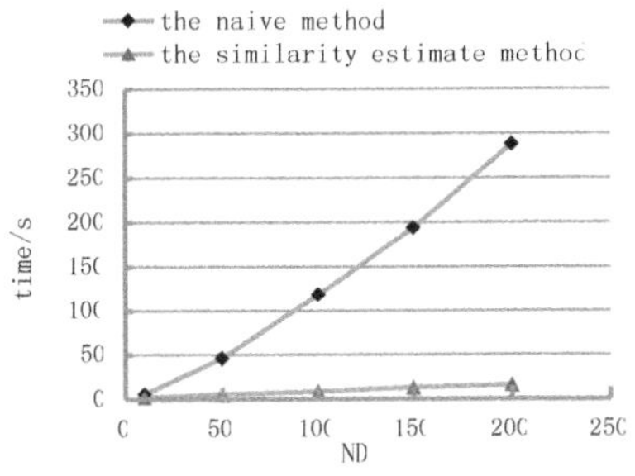

Fig. 4. The time cost of two methods

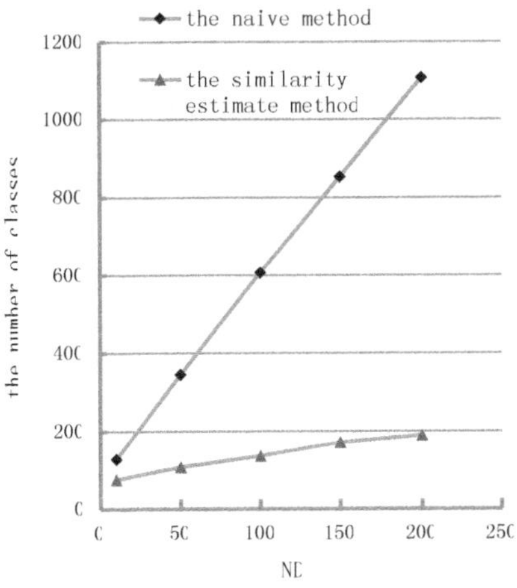

Fig. 5. The result of two methods

The recall of the two methods is shown in Fig.5. We use the number of clusters (subsets) to represent the recall rate. The number which is closer to 100 is better. The numbers of clusters are both increasing with the increase of the size of original records set. But the improved method is increasing much slower than the naïve one. When the original records set contains 20000 records, the improved method get 187 clusters, while the naïve method get 1107 clusters. The recall rate is improved.

4.3 Experiments on Real Data

Original data sets with different size are used to test efficiency, adn ε=0.5, u_con=0.6, l_con=0.5. The result is shown in Fig.6. We put the size of R on X-axis and time cost on Y-axis.

To test the effectiveness, we use a data set with 50 records, and set ε=0.7, u_con=0.8, l_con=0.3. Our algorithm gets 45 clusters. That is quite similar with the divide result of human beings, which is 48 clusters.

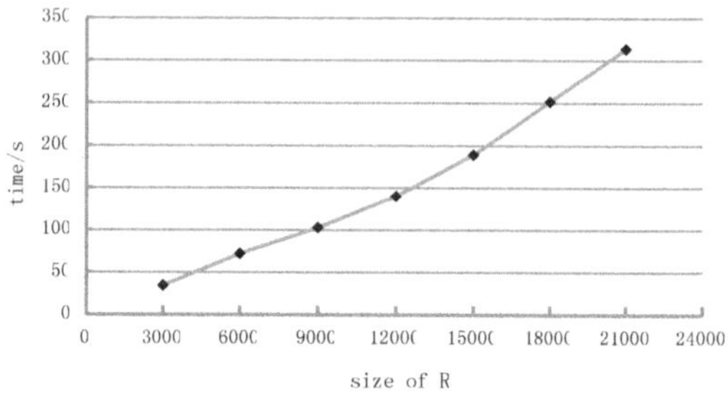

Fig. 6. The efficiency testing

5 Conclusions and Future Work

The duplicate detection method based on optimal bipartite graph matching can deal with record set with attributes' position differences, the loss of some attributes, and typographic errors to a certain extent. The naïve method for such similarity has two shortcomings. First, it costs too much time. Second, the strict classification requirements make a low recall. In this paper, we present an efficient and effective duplicate records detecting method. With the estimation of similarities, such method can efficiently divide the original records set. That not only reduces the times of comparisons, but also improves the recall. Theoretical analysis and experimental results show that the method proposed in this paper is correct and effective.

Our future work includes more accurate estimation of bounds and indices structure for the acceleration of the search in stack.

References

1. Elmagarmid, A.K., Ipeirotis, P.G., Verykios, V.S.: Duplicate record detection: A survey. IEEE Transactions on Knowledge and Data Engineering (2007)
2. Ristad, E.S., Yianilos, P.N.: Learning String-Edit Distance. IEEE Transactions on Pattern Analysis and Machine Intelligence (May 1998)
3. Kuhn, H.W.: The hungarian method for the assignment problem. Naval res. Logist. Quart. (1955)

4. Munkres, J.: Algorithms for the assignment and transportation problems. J. Soc. Indust. Appl. Math. (1957)
5. Bilenko, M., Mooney, R.J.: Adaptive duplicate detection using learnable string similarity measures. In: SIGKDD, pp. 39–48 (August 2003)
6. Chandel, Hassanzadeh, O., Koudas, N., et al.: Benchmarking declarative approximate selection predicates. In: SIGMOD, pp. 353–364 (June 2007)
7. Chaudhuri, S., Ganjam, K., Ganti, V., Motwani, R.: Robust and efficient fuzzy match for online data cleaning. In: SIGMOD, pp. 313–324 (June 2003)
8. Cohen, W.W.: Data integration using similarity joins and a word-based information representation language. ACM Trans. on Information Systems 18(3), 288–321 (2000)
9. Borkar, V.R., Deshmukh, K., Sarawagi, S.: Automatic segmentation of text into structured records. In: SIGMOD, pp. 175–186 (May 2001)
10. Sarawagi, S., Cohen, W.W.: Semi-markov conditional random fields for information extraction. In: NIPS (December 2004)
11. Viola, P.A., Narasimhan, M.: Learning to extract information from semi-structured text using a discriminative context free grammar. In: SIGIR, pp. 330–337 (August 2005)
12. Cohen, W.W., Sarawagi, S.: Exploiting dictionaries in named entity extraction: combining semi-markov extraction processes and data integration methods. In: SIGKDD, pp. 89–98 (August 2004)
13. Arasu, Chaudhuri, S., Kaushik, R.: Transformation-based framework for record matching. In: ICDE, pp. 40-49 (April 2008)
14. Arasu, Kaushik, R.: A Grammar-based Entity Representation Framework for Data Cleaning. In: SIGMOD, pp. 233–244 (June 2009)
15. Mohan, L., Hongzhi, W., Jianzhong, L., Hong, G.: Duplicate Record Detection Method Based on Optimal Bipartite Graph Matching. In: NDBC (October 2009)
16. Alpaydin, E.: Introduction to Machine Learning. MIT Press, Cambridge (2004)

A Novel Composite Kernel for Finding Similar Questions in CQA Services

Jun Wang[1], Zhoujun Li[1], Xia Hu[2], and Biyun Hu[1]

[1] School of Computer Science and Engineering
Beihang University, 100191 Beijing, China
[2] School of Computing, National University of Singapore, 117590, Singapore
wangjun0706149@cse.buaa.edu.cn, lizj@buaa.edu.cn
huxia@comp.nus.edu.sg, hubiyun0706147@cse.buaa.edu.cn

Abstract. Finding similar questions in Community Question Answering (CQA) services plays more and more important role in current web and IR applications. The task aims to retrieve historical questions that are similar or relevant to new questions posed by users. However, traditional "bag-of-words" based models would fail to measure the similarity between question sentences, as they usually ignore sequential and syntactic information. In this paper, we propose a novel composite kernel to improve the accuracy in question matching. Our study illustrate that the composite kernel can efficiently capture both lexical semantics and syntactic information in a question sentence by leveraging word sequence kernel, POS tag sequence kernel and syntactic tree kernel. Experimental results on real world datasets show that our proposed method significantly outperforms the state-of-the-art models.

Keywords: question answering, similarity measure,tree kernel, string kernel.

1 Introduction

One of the emerging trends in Web information services is the growth of social collaborative applications, such as WikiAnswers, Baidu Knows, Yahoo!Answer etc. These applications bring together a network of self-declared "experts" to answer questions posted by other people. Community Question and Answering (CQA) service is one of these collaborative applications, which have attracted a large number of users both seeking and providing answers to a variety of questions on diverse subjects. These CQA services rapidly build up large number of question and answer (Q/A) pairs, and these pairs are valuable as linguistic resources for many researches. In order to analyze these Q/A pairs, there are many situations in which we wish to determine how similar two questions are. For example, "how can I lose weight in a few month?" and "are there any ways of losing pound in a short period?" are two questions asking for ways of losing weight [10], and we wish to determine that there is a high degree of semantic similarity between them, even though they may not share any actual terms in common.

L. Chen et al. (Eds.): WAIM 2010, LNCS 6184, pp. 608–619, 2010.

Existing methods for computing text similarity have focused mainly on either large documents or individual words. However, they are not effective when using such methods to measure similarity between questions. One reason is that users form questions with natural language, where questions are encoded with various lexical, syntactic and semantic features. Some questions have identical meaning but are very different in lexical level, such as the examples given previously. Directly applying traditional document similarity measures based purely on the "bag-of-word"(BOW) may perform unsatisfactory in these cases.

Syntactic or semantic features hence become vital for such task. Syntactic analysis can provide more structured information not readily identified based on sequences of tokens alone. However, a general problem in Natural Language Processing is that as the processing gets deeper, it becomes less accurate. For example, the current accuracy of tokenization, chunking and sentence parsing for English is about 99%, 92%, and 90% respectively [13]. Algorithms based solely on deeper representations inevitably suffer from the errors in computing these representations. On the other hand, low level processing such as tokenization will be more accurate, and may contain useful information missed by deep processing of text. Systems based on a single level of representation are force to choose between shallower representations, which will have fewer errors, and deeper representations, which may be more general.

In this paper, we propose a composite kernel for finding similar questions in CQA archives. First we present a novel weighted tree kernel over full syntactic parsing trees. Based on the kernel proposed in [4], we present two extensions to the original kernel, making it more accurate when processing question sentences and more suitable for our application. Experimental results show that our proposed weighted tree kernel can capture structured syntactic information better and outperforms the original tree kernel. As the tree kernel based methods deeply depend on parsing tree, they inevitably suffer from the errors in parsing. To solve this problem, we combine our proposed weighted tree kernel with another two string kernels and develop a novel composite kernel. There are two reasons of doing so. First, the parsing errors can be compensated by combining with other kernels. Second, we can fully utilize diverse information from both shallow representation and deep representation. Compared with state-of-the-art methods, experiments show that our proposed composite kernel achieve significant improvements.

There are three primary research contributions in this paper:

1. Modified the original tree kernel by presenting two extensions.
2. Proposed a composite kernel by combining the modified tree kernel and two string kernels, and applied it to finding similar questions in CQA archives.
3. Compared the proposed composite kernel with several other methods for similar questions matching problem.

The rest of the paper is organized as follows. Section 2 provides a review of related work. In Section 3 we present a composite kernel by combining a modified tree kernel and two string kernels. Section 4 reports the experiments results and our observation. In section 5, we draw our conclusion in this work.

2 Related Work

Several techniques on similar question matching problem have been proposed in literatures. Representative related work can be classified into four classes: vector space model(VSM) based [1,6], language model(LM) based [2,5], and translation model based [9] and syntactic tree kernel-based [8].

Most of the existing work focuses on addressing the word mismatching problem between user questions and the questions in a QA archive. Burke et al. [1] combined lexical similarity and semantic similarity between questions to rank FAQs, where the lexical similarity was computed using a vector space model(VSM) and the semantic similarity was computed based on WordNet. Jijkoun and Rijke [6] used supervised learning methods to extract QA pairs from FAQ pages, and used a vector space model for QA pair retrieval. Cao et al. [2] used language models to exploit categories of questions for improving question search. Duan et al. [5] searched questions by identifying question topic and question focus with in a language modeling framework. Xue et al. [11] proposed a translation based language model for question search on CQA data.

Prior kernel-based methods for this task focus on using individual tree kernels to exploit tree structure-related features. Wang et al. [9] employed a syntactic tree kernel for finding similar questions in CQA archives. They parsed the questions into syntactic trees and used the similarity of the syntactic trees of the query question and the historical question to rank historical questions. However, as the language processing gets deeper, it becomes less accurate. The method proposed in [9] was solely based on syntactic tree (deeper representation), thus inevitably suffered from the errors in parsing.

In our study, we avoid this problem by using a novel composite kernel to cover more knowledge. Our method has the potential of effectively capturing not only most of the previous flat features, used in [1,2], and also the structured syntactic features, used in [9]. To our best knowledge, this is the first work of using a composite kernel method for finding similar questions in CQA archives.

3 A Novel Composite Kernel

In this section, we define a composite kernel by integrating a modified tree kernel, a word kernel and a POS tag kernel.

3.1 A Modified Tree Kernel

The main underlying idea of tree kernels is to compute the number of common substructures between two trees without explicitly considering the whole fragment space [8]. In order to capture more syntactic information between parsing trees, Collins [4] tried to consider all tree fragments that occur in a syntactic parsing tree. According to his definition, a tree fragment of a syntactic parsing tree, which we call syntactic tree fragments (STFs), is parts of a syntactic parsing tree which include at least one production rule, with the restriction that no production rules can be broken into incomplete parts.

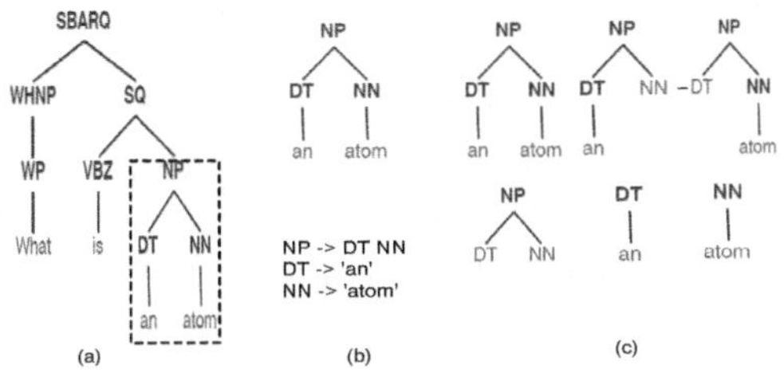

Fig. 1. (a) The syntactic tree of the sample question. (b) One sub-tree and its production rules. (c) All tree fragments in the sub-tree.

Take the question 'What is an atom?' for example. Figure 1(a) depicts the syntactic tree of the sentence, Figure 1(b) is one of its sub-trees and the production rules of the sub-tree, Figure 1(c) lists all tree fragments included in the sub-tree. In the original form of the tree kernel, it relies on mere common tree fragments counts, and lacks feature weighting schemes which have been deemed important by the IR community. In this section, we propose a weighted tree kernel by presenting two extensions to the original tree kernel. The first extension consists in adopting a depth decay factor for each syntactic tree fragments. The second one is that nodes in a tree are set different weight values according to its importance to the tree.

Syntactic Tree Fragment Depth Factor. Based on the original tree kernel framework, we consider a new decay factor: d for the depth of the syntactic tree fragments (STFs). The depth of each special STF tf_i is the level of tf_i root in the entire syntactic tree, with $d_{root} = 1$. Take the question 'what is an atom?' (Figure 1) for example again, the depth of the STF (Figure 1(b)) in the entire syntactic tree (Figure 1(a)) is 3.

Node Weighting Factor. Intuitionally, different parts of the sentence have different importance, and nouns and verbs are considered to be more important than other types of terms such as article, proposition and conjunction. Besides, as the data to be processed in our task are question sentences, we assume that the question *wh*-words have more impact on the performance. The *wh*-word is the question word in given questions. Here, the *wh*-words we considered are *what*, *why*, *where*, *when* and *how*. For example, the *wh*-word of question *'why does the moon turn orange? '* is *why*.

In our weighted tree kernel framework, we set different value for the importance of each none-terminal node in the entire syntactic tree for a special sentence. Particularly, we introduce the node weighting factor δ_i for the importance of node i in the entire syntactic tree. Here, we consider the following three situations:

1.$\delta_i = v_Q$, *where the POS tag label of node i is beginning with W(for question wh-word).*

2.$\delta_i = \upsilon_{\mathrm{NV}}$*, where the POS tag label of node i either beginning with V or N (for verbs or nouns).*
3.$\delta_i = 0.1$*, for all other types of POS tag label.*

where υ_Q is a tuning parameter indicating the importance of the *wh*-words nodes weighting factor and υ_{NV} is a tuning parameter indicating the importance of nouns or verbs nodes weighting factor. For each specific tree fragment i contained in the syntactic tree T, i is weighted by

$$\prod_{j=1}^{s(i)} \sqrt{\delta_j}\sqrt{\mu}^{d(i)}, \tag{1}$$

where $d(i)$ is the depth of i and μ is the weighting factor for the depth, $s(i)$ is the number of none terminal nodes included in i and δ_j is the weighting factor for each none terminal node in the syntactic tree fragment. The number of none terminal nodes included a syntactic tree fragment is equal to the number of production rules it contains.

Weighted Tree Kernel. Based on the above two extensions to the tree kernel, we reformulate the original tree kernel and name the new kernel as weighted tree kernel. Consider a syntactic tree T. Implicitly, we represent it by an m dimensional vector $V(T) = (v_1(T), v_2(T), \ldots, v_m(T))'$, where the i-th element $v_i(T)$ is the weight of the syntactic tree fragment in the i-th dimension if the syntactic tree fragment is in the tree T and zero otherwise.

Let N represent the set of nodes in T. Define the binary indicator function $I_i(n)$ to be 1 if syntactic tree fragment i is seen rooted at node n and 0 otherwise. Let $d(n)$ represent the depth of node n, if syntactic tree fragment i rooted at node n, then $d(i) = d(n)$,and then we can derive that :

$$v_i(T) = \sum_{n \in N} \prod_{j=1}^{s(i)} \sqrt{\delta_j}\sqrt{\mu}^{d(i)} I_i(n) = \sum_{n \in N} \prod_{j=1}^{s(i)} \sqrt{\delta_j}\sqrt{\mu}^{d(n)} I_i(n) \tag{2}$$

Given two syntactic tree T_1 and T_2, the weighted tree kernel function over T_1 and T_2 can be computed as

$$WTK(T_1, T_2) = \sum_i v_i(T_1) v_i(T_2) = \sum_{n_1 \in N_1} \sum_{n_2 \in N_2} \mu^{(d(n_1)+d(n_2))/2} K(n_1, n_2)\ , \tag{3}$$

where

$$K(n_1, n_2) = \sum_i \prod_{j=1}^{s(i)} \delta_j I_i(n_1) I_i(n_2) \tag{4}$$

In order to apply the weighted tree kernel function to measure the similarity of two sentences, we normalize it into the following forms:

$$sim(T_1, T_2) = \frac{WTK(T_1, T_2)}{\sqrt{WTK(T_1, T_1)}\sqrt{WTK(T_2, T_2)}} \tag{5}$$

The value of $K(n_1, n_2)$ can be computed recursively as follows,

1.$K(n_1, n_2) = 0$, *if* $n_1 \neq n_2$*;*
2.$K(n_1, n_2) = \delta_{n_1}$, *if* $n_1 = n_2$ *and* n_1,n_2 *are pre-terminal nodes;*
3.$K(n_1, n_2) = \delta_{n_1} \prod_{j=1}^{nc(n_1)}(1 + K(ch_{n_1}(j), ch_{n_2}(j)))$, *if* $n_1 = n_2$ *and* n_1,n_2 *are neither terminal nodes nor pre-terminal nodes.*

Here $n_1 = n_2$ if and only if the labels and production rules of node n_1 and n_2 are the same. The number of the node n's children is $nc(n)$, so if $n_1 = n_2$ then $nc(n_1) = nc(n_2)$. The j-th child of the node n is $ch_n(j)$. A terminal node means a leaf node, and a pre-terminal node means the immediate predecessor of a leaf node.

According to the dynamic programming idea, we can traverse T_1 and T_2 in post-order, fill in a $|N_1| \times |N_2|$ matrix of $K(n_1, n_2)$, then sum up the matrix entries weighted by $\mu^{(d(n_1)+d(n_2))/2}$. The time complexity of this algorithm turns out to be at most $o(|N_1| \times |N_2|)$.

3.2 POS Tag Kernel and Word Kernel

POS tag kernel (PK) and word kernel (WK) are two string kernels. String kernels [7] are similarity measures between documents seen as sequence of symbols (e.g., possible characters) over an alphabet. In general, similarity is assessed by the number of (possibly non-contiguous) matching subsequences share by two sequences.

Let $\sum$ be a finite alphabet, and $s = s_1 s_2 \ldots s_{|s|}$ a sequence over $\sum$ (i.e.$s_i \in \sum, 1 \leq i \leq |s|$). Let $\mathbf{i} = [i_1, i_2, \ldots, i_n]$, with $1 \leq i_2 \leq \ldots \leq i_n \leq |s|$, be a subset of the indices in s:we will indicate as $s[\mathbf{i}] \in \sum^n$ the subsequence $s_{i_1} s_{i_2} \ldots s_{i_n}$. Note that $s[\mathbf{i}]$does not necessarily from a contiguous subsequence of s. For example, if s is the sequence $CART$ and $\mathbf{i} = [2, 4]$, then $s[\mathbf{i}]$is AT. Let us write $l(\mathbf{i})$ the length spanned by $s[\mathbf{i}]$ in s, that is : $l(\mathbf{i}) = i_n - i_1 + 1$. The sequence kernel of two string s and t over $\sum$ is defined as:

$$K_n(s,t) = \sum_{\mu \in \sum^n} \sum_{\mathbf{i}:s[\mathbf{i}]=\mu} \sum_{\mathbf{j}:t[\mathbf{j}]=\mu} \lambda^{l(\mathbf{i})+l(\mathbf{j})}, \quad (6)$$

where $\lambda \in [0:1]$ is a decay factor used to penalize non-contiguous subsequences and the first sum refers to all possible subsequences of length n. Equation 6 defines a valid kernel as it amounts to performing an inner product in a feature space with one feature per ordered subsequence $\mu \in \sum^n$ with value:

$$\Phi_\mu(s) = \sum_{\mathbf{i}:s[\mathbf{i}]=\mu} \lambda^{l(\mathbf{i})} . \quad (7)$$

Intuitively, this means that we match all possible subsequences of n symbols, even when these subsequences are not consecutive, and with each occurrence "discounted" according to its overall length. Choon et al. provide an efficient method for computing string kernels. For more information the readers may refer to [3].

POS tag kernel (PK) is obtained by applying the string kernel on the sequence of POS tags of a question. For example: given the sentence s_0: *what is autism?*, the associated POS tag sequence is *WP AUX NN?* and some of subsequences extracted by PK are *WP NN* or *WP AUX*. Word kernel (WK) is applied to word sequences of questions. Given s_0, sample substring are *what is autism*, *what is*, *what autism*, *is autism*, etc.

3.3 A Composite Kernel for Finding Similar Questions

Kernel engineering can be carried out by combining basic kernels with additive or multiplicative operators or by designing specific data objects (vectors, sequences and tree structures) for the target tasks. In this section, we define a novel composite kernel by combining a POS tag kernel, a word kernel and our proposed weighted tree kernel.

Kernels applied to new structures produce new kernels. Let $K(t_1, t_2) = \phi(t_1) \cdot \phi(t_2)$ be a basic kernel, where t_1 and t_2 are two trees. If we map t_1 and t_2 into two new structures s_1 and s_2 with a mapping $\phi_M(\cdot)$, we obtain:$K(s_1, s_2) = \phi(s_1) \cdot \phi(s_2) = \phi(\phi_M(t_1)) \cdot \phi(\phi_M(t_2)) = \phi'(t_1) \cdot \phi'(t_2) = K'(t_1, t_2)$, which is a noticeably different kernel induced by the mapping $\phi' = \phi \cdot \phi_M$. In this way, we define a composite kernel by combining three different kernels with linear combination:

$$\begin{aligned} CK(s_1, s_2) &= \alpha_1 WTK(tree(s_1), tree(s_2)) \\ &+ \alpha_2 PK(pos(s_1), pos(s_2)) \\ &+ \alpha_3 WK(word(s_1), word(s_2)) \ , \end{aligned} \tag{8}$$

where s_i means a question sentence, $tree(s_i)$ means mapping a question sentence s_i into a syntactic tree, $pos(s_i)$ means mapping s_i into a POS tag sequence and $word(s_i)$ means mapping s_i into a word sequence. Thus, the combination kernel can explore syntactic features, POS tag sequence features and word sequence features for one question sentence. Some preliminary experiments on a validation set showed that the composite kernel yield the best performance with $\alpha = 0.4_1$, $\alpha_2 = 0.3$ and $\alpha_3 = 0.3$.

4 Experiments

In this section, we present empirical evaluation results to assess the effectiveness of our proposed composite kernel for the similar question matching problem.

4.1 Dataset and Metrics

We selected 50 questions from TREC_10 [1]as query questions. Each query question is submitted to the Yahoo!Answers web services[2] and the 1,000 top-ranked

---

[1] Available at http://l2r.cs.uiuc.edu:80/ cogcomp/Data/QA/QC/TREC_10.label

[2] http://developer.yahoo.com/answers/V1/questionSearch.html

questions according to Yahoo!Answer ranking are collected as candidate questions. Then we re-rank the 1,000 candidate questions according to their similarity to the query. The top 10 candidate questions after being re-ranked are deemed similar or relevant to the query question. Seven methods are used for comparison, 1,213 candidate questions are manully judeged and 199 semantically similar questions are found in total for 50 queries.

Precision@n and Mean Average of Precision(MAP) are used as the performance measures. Precision@n is the fraction of the top-n questions retrieved that are relevant. Mean Average of Precision(MAP)[3] rewards approaches returning relevant questions earlier, and also emphases the rank in returned lists. MAP is defined as the mean of the precision at N values calculated after each relevant answers was retrieved. The final MAP value is defined as the mean average of average precisions of all queries in the test set.

4.2 Weighted Tree Kernel Performance Evaluation

In Section 3.1, we present two extensions to the original tree kernel, weighting factors υ_Q, υ_{NV} and the depth factor μ. If we set $\upsilon_Q = 0.1$, $\upsilon_{\mathrm{NV}} = 0.1$ and $\mu = 1$, our proposed weighted tree kernel (WTK) is equal to the original tree kernel(TK). In this section, we empirically evaluate the individual impact of these factors on the performance. First, we conduct experiment on the weighting factors: wh-word nodes weighting factor and noun or verb nodes weighting factor υ_{NV}. We evaluate the performance by setting υ_Q from 0.5 to 1.9 at increments of 0.1. The results are visually campared in Figure 2 (a) and Figure 2(b) . The *TK* line depicts the performance of the original tree kernel, while the *TK+upsilon_Q*/*TK+upsilon_*NV curve shows the impact of weighting factor $\upsilon_Q/\upsilon_{\mathrm{NV}}$ on the performance in MAP with different parameter settings.

Figure 2(a) shows the performance of $TK+\upsilon_Q$ with different wh-word nodes weighting factor υ_Q values while $\upsilon_{\mathrm{NV}} = 0.1$ and $\mu = 1$. The $TK + \upsilon_Q$ achives the best performance at the value of $\upsilon_Q = 0.05$. As the weight of *wh*-word nodes weighting factor grows, the performance declines. The reason may line in the corpus used in our experiment. We first submit our query question to Yahoo!Answer and the top-ranked 1,000 questions are used as our experiment corpus. The *wh*-word is usually the first word in the query and included in most of retrieved questions returned by Yahoo!Answer. So the *wh*-word has lower discrimination power in this situation. When we decline the impact of *wh*-word nodes weighting factor, The $TK+\upsilon_Q$ performance increases. Figure 2(b) depicts the performance of $TK + \upsilon_{NV}$ with different υ_{NV} values while $\upsilon_Q = 0.1$ and $\mu = 1$. The trend of $TK + \upsilon_{NV}$ reaches a peak at the value of $\upsilon_{\mathrm{NV}} = 0.13$. As the weight of noun or verb nodes grows, the performance of $TK + \upsilon_{\mathrm{NV}}$ declines. When $\upsilon_{\mathrm{NV}} > 0.16$, $TK + \upsilon_{\mathrm{NV}}$ performs worse than *TK*, which means the weighting factor brings in negative impact on performance.

We conducted extensive experiments on different parameter μ settings and found that when $\mu = 0.9$ $TK+\mu$ shows the best results. This parameter value is

[3] MAP_{10}: The MAP calculated on the returned top 10 questions.

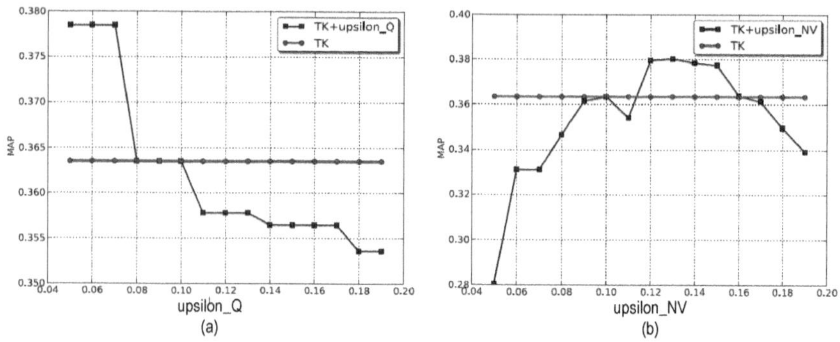

Fig. 2. (a) *wh*-word nodes weighting factor impact on performance. (b) Noun or verb nodes weighting factor impact on performance.

Table 1. Effect of depth factor

Method	Precision@10 (*Impr*)	$\mathbf{MAP}_{10}$ (*Impr*)
$TK_{tree}(baseline)$	0.285 (*N.A*)	0.364 (*N.A*)
$TK_{tree} + depthfactor$	0.346 (+%21.56)	0.372 (+%2.45)

same with [12]. In Table 1 we evaluate the performance of tree kernel(baseline) and our method with depth factor when $\upsilon_Q = 0.1$ and $\upsilon_{\mathrm{NV}} = 0.1$. As compared to baseline, we can achieve 21.56%, and 2.45% improvements in Precision@10, and MAP respectively. The overall performance of our proposed weighted tree kernel is listed in Table 4. Compared to TK, we can achieve 39.64%, and 9.06% improvements in Precision@10, and MAP respectively.

Based on these observations, we can see that our two extensions to the original tree kernel can both achive better performance than original tree kernel. It indicates that our proposed weighted tree kernel can capture structured syntactic information better than the original tree kernel.

4.3 Composite Kernel Performance Evaluation

To evaluate the performance of our composite kernel, we use seven different methods for comparison. Table 2 describes these methods and the parameter settings are listed in Table 3. In TK_{tree}, WTK_{tree},PK_{POS} and $CK_{word+POS+tree}$, question sentences are parsed into syntactic tree and POS tag sequence by using Stanford Parsers[4].

The experimental results are illustrated in Table 4. From the table, we draw the following observation:

- TK_{tree} performs better in *Precision*@10 and worse in MAP than VSM_{BOW}. The reasons may be that TK_{tree} ignores the word sequence information. The parsing error may be another reason that results in disappointed performance.

[4] http://nlp.stanford.edu/software/lex-parser.shtml

Table 2. Methods and description

Method	**Description**
VSM_{BOW}(baseline1)	Traditional vector space model with bag-of-words representation
LM_{BOW}(baseline2)	Language model with bag-of-words representation
TK_{tree}(baseline3)	Tree kernel with parse tree representation
WTK_{tree}	Weighted tree kernel with parse tree representation(proposed)
WK_{word}	Word kernel:String kernel on word sequences
PK_{POS}	POS tag kernel:String kernel on POS tag sequences
$CK_{word+POS+tree}$	Composite kernel(proposed)

Table 3. Methods and parameter setting

Method	**Parameter Setting**
VSM_{BOW}(baseline1)	-
LM_{BOW}(baseline2)	-
TK_{tree}(baseline3)	$\mu = 0.9$
WTK_{tree}	$\mu = 0.9, \upsilon_Q = 0.05, \upsilon_{NV} = 0.13$
WK_{word}	$\lambda = 0.9$, $n = 1$
PK_{POS}	$\lambda = 0.9, n = 3$
$CK_{word+POS+tree}$	$\alpha_1 = 0.4$, $\alpha_2 = 0.3, \alpha_3 = 0.3$

Table 4. Performance of different approaches measured by different metrics

Method	**Precision@10** (*Impr*)	**MAP**$_{10}$ (*Impr*)
VSM_{BOW}	0.268 (*N.A.*)	0.403 (*N.A.*)
LM_{BOW}	0.330 (+%23.13)	0.445 (+%10.37)
TK_{tree}	0.285 (+%6.20)	0.364 (−%9.78)
WTK_{tree}	0.398 (+%48.51)	0.397 (−%1.36)
WK_{word}	0.359 (+%34.33)	0.465 (+%15.45)
PK_{POS}	0.350 (+%30.56)	0.483 (+%19.76)
$CK_{word+POS+tree}$	**0.400 (+%49.25)**	**0.499 (+%24.02)**

• WTK_{tree} performs better than TK_{tree} in all metrics. This suggests that our proposed weighted tree kernel can do better than original tree kernel in capturing structured syntactic information. However, it still performs worse than VSM_{BOW}. The reasons may be the same with TK_{tree}. This suggests that only considering the structured syntactic information does harm performance in finding similar questions.
• WK_{word} and PK_{POS} perform a bit better than VSM_{BOW}. This suggests that word sequence information and POS tag sequence have good predication power for finding similar questions.

• $CK_{word+POS+tree}$ achieves significant performance improvement over all the other mehtods. This indicates that structured syntactic information, word sequence and POS tag sequence information are complementary and the composite kernel can well integrate them: 1) the structured syntactic information captured by WTK_{tree}; 2) word sequence information captured by WK_{word}; 3) POS tag sequence information captured by PK_{POS}.

The main difference between our proposed composite kernel and traditional vector space model or language model lies in the feature represtation and similarity calculation mechanism(kernel function vs. dot-product). In composite kernel, we empoly three feature representation methods: parse tree, POS tag sequence and word sequence. While in traditional vector space model or language model, only bag of words representation is used. Therefore our method has the potential of effectively capturing not only most of the previous word level features but also the ussful syntactic structure features. Moreover, we present two extensions to the original tree kernel according to our application. Experimental results shows that our proposed weighted tree kernel can capture structured syntactic informatin better than original tree kernel and more suitable for processing question sentences in finding similar questions.

5 Conclusion

In this paper, we design a syntactic parsing tree kernel to exploit useful syntactic structure features. We present two extensions to the original tree kernel with a novel weighting scheme and a depth decay factor. A composite kernel is developed by combining our proposed weighted tree kernel, a POS tag kernel and a word kernel. Our study illustrates that the composite kernel could effectively capture both sequential and structured features. Experimental results show that our proposed model significantly outperforms the state-of-the-art methods.

The Stanford Parser is directly used in our experiments. However, this parser, including most off-the-shelf parsers, are not well-trained to parse question sentences. A more targetd parser which is trained on question sets may gain beeter accuracy. Besides, our proposed composite kernel only explores parse tree, POS tag sequence and word sequence information. Capturing more features may gain further improvements and this can be done by including more individual kernels such as WordNet-based semantic kernel and other feature-based kernels.

References

1. Burke, R.D., Hammond, K.J., Kulyukin, V.A., Lytinen, S.L., Tomuro, N., Schoenberg, S.: Question answering from frequently asked question files: Experiences with the faq finder system. AI Magazine 18(2), 57–66 (1997)
2. Cao, X., Cong, G., Cui, B., Jensen, C.S., Zhang, C.: The use of categorization information in language models for question retrieval. In: CIKM 2009, pp. 265–274. ACM, New York (2009)

3. Choon Hui Teo, S.: Fast and space efficient string kernels using suffix arrays. In: ICML 2006, pp. 929–936. ACM, New York (2006)
4. Collins, M., Duffy, N.: New ranking algorithms for parsing and tagging: kernels over discrete structures and the voted perceptron. In: ACL 2002, pp. 263–270. Association for Computational Linguistics (2002)
5. Duan, H., Cao, Y., Lin, C.-Y., Yu, Y.: Searching questions by identifying question topic and question focus. In: Proceedings of ACL 2008: HLT, pp. 156–164. Association for Computational Linguistics (June 2008)
6. Jijkoun, V., de Rijke, M.: Retrieving answers from frequently asked questions pages on the web. In: CIKM 2005, pp. 76–83. ACM, New York (2005)
7. Lodhi, H., Saunders, C., Shawe-Taylor, J., Cristianini, N., Watkins, C.: Text classification using string kernels. J. Mach. Learn. Res. 2, 419–444 (2002)
8. Moschitti, A.: Kernel methods, syntax and semantics for relational text categorization. In: CIKM 2008, pp. 253–262. ACM Press, New York (2008)
9. Wang, K., Ming, Z., Chua, T.-S.: A syntactic tree matching approach to finding similar questions in community-based qa services. In: SIGIR 2009, pp. 187–194. ACM Press, New York (2009)
10. Wang, X.-J., Tu, X., Feng, D., Zhang, L.: Ranking community answers by modeling question-answer relationships via analogical reasoning. In: SIGIR 2009, pp. 179–186. ACM, New York (2009)
11. Xue, X., Jeon, J., Croft, W.B.: Retrieval models for question and answer archives. In: SIGIR 2008, pp. 475–482. ACM, New York (2008)
12. Zhang, D., Lee, W.S.: Question classification using support vector machines. In: SIGIR 2003, pp. 26–32. ACM, New York (2003)
13. Zhao, S., Grishman, R.: Extracting relations with integrated information using kernel methods. In: ACL 2005, pp. 419–426. Association for Computational Linguistics (2005)

Efficient Similarity Query in RFID Trajectory Databases*

Yanqiu Wang, Ge Yu, Yu Gu, Dejun Yue, and Tiancheng Zhang

Northeastern University, China
{wangyanqiu,yuge,guyu,yuedejun,zhangtiancheng}@ise.neu.edu.cn

Abstract. Similarity query is one of the most important operations in trajectory databases and this paper addresses this problem in RFID trajectory databases. Due to the special sensing manner, the model of RFID trajectory is different from the traditional trajectory, leading to the inefficiency of existing techniques. This paper proposes a novel distance function—EDEU(Edit Distance combined with Euclidean Distance), which supports the local time shifting and takes the distance between adjacent logic areas into consideration. We also develop two filter-refinement mechanisms based on Co-occurrence Degree and Length Dispersion Ratio to improve the efficiency of the similarity analysis. Furthermore, we extend our solution to determine the local similarity from the global dissimilarity trajectory pairs. The extensive experiments verify the efficiency of our proposed algorithms.

1 Introduction

With the advances of positioning technologies and computing technologies, a number of interesting applications are being developed based on the similarity query of trajectories. For instance, it is very useful to determine the vehicles with similar moving motion, and to find the migration patterns of some animals by mining the similar trajectories of the animals. The similarity query is an important issue in many application domains and a supporting technique for pattern monitoring, moving object clustering and so on. There are some existing work[12][10][5] focusing on retrieving trajectory pairs from trajectory databases. Specially, as a new technology, the information collected by RFID technology are more and more adopted to describe the movement of objects because of the widely tracking applications, such as supply chain management, visitors tracking and so on[8], while existing work seldom considers the unique characteristics of RFID trajectories. This paper studies the problem of efficient similarity query in RFID trajectory databases.

Due to special sensing manner among readers and tags, the RFID trajectory reflects different features compared to the traditional trajectory. The traditional trajectory usually assumes the availability of GPS-type positioning. The GPS

* The research was supported by the NSF of China under Grants No. 60773220 and the Fundamental Research Funds for the Central Universities No. N090904013.

L. Chen et al. (Eds.): WAIM 2010, LNCS 6184, pp. 620–631, 2010.

receiver continuously reports location and velocity, and the trajectory of a GPS-equipped moving object is usually modelled as a sequence of three-dimensional points. Unlike GPS that continuously reports the coordinates of the moving objects, RFID-based positioning only reports the presences of objects in reader's activation ranges. An RFID reader employs proximity analysis to detect an RFID tag when the tag enters the reader's activation range. The position of each reader is recorded in the database after deployment and each reader's activation range denotes a logic area. Therefore, the RFID trajectory can be modelled as a sequence of symbols representing logic areas. In this paper, we focus on the shape of RFID trajectory because it reflects the activity motion of moving objects, and the time information can be ignored for simplicity. The simplified RFID trajectory is denoted as $T{=}\gamma_1,\gamma_2,\ldots,\gamma_n$, where γ_i represents the logic area.

Given an RFID trajectory database, our target is to search the pairs of moving objects whose similairty are larger than the user specified threshold ε. The similar measurement is highly related to the distance function. There are some available distance functions for trajectories such as Euclidean distance, LCSS, EDR[3], ERP[4] and Edit distance, but none of them considers the unique characteristics of the RFID trajectories analysis. This study proposes a new measurement called EDEU (Edit Distance combined with Euclidean Distance), which integrates the properties of Euclidean distance and Edit distance. The EDEU supports the local time shifting and takes the true distance between logic areas into account, which reflects the difference between RFID trajectories reasonably. Because the huge volume of trajectory databases and the low proportion of similar trajectory pairs, we adopt the filter-refinement mechanism to accelerate the process. We propose the definition of Co-occurrence Degree and Length Dispersion Ratio, which are utilized to quickly filter out the trajectory pairs with low similarity probability, and then refine the much smaller candidate set to get the results. In global dissimilar trajectory pairs, the Co-occurrence Degree sequence is proposed to query the local similarity. Our main contributions are the following:

- We propose a novel measurement EDEU, which satisfies the unique characteristics of RFID trajectory. The similarity of RFID trajectory is defined utilizing this distance function.
- To support fast similarity query, we propose two filtering algorithms based on Co-occurrence Degree and Length Dispersion Ratio, which adopt the filter-refinement framework and improve the efficiency.
- We design efficient ways to search for the local similarity in the global dissimilar trajectory pairs.

The remainder of this paper is organized as follows: section 2 presents the related work of trajectory similarity query. Section 3 introduces the definition of EDEU. Section 4 proposes two efficient filtering algorithms for similar trajectory pairs search. Section 5 presents how to search the local similar regions in global dissimilar pairs. Section 6 shows the experimental results and the last section concludes the full paper.

2 Related Work

Trajectory similarity query has received increasing attention in recent years. Yanagisawa Y. et al. [12] propose an indexing method for processing shape based similarity queries for trajectory databases. This method is based on Euclidean distance and the trajectory is denoted as a directed continuous line with a start and end point. Frentzos E. et al. [5] define a dissimilarity metric (DISSIM) for the measurement of the spatiotemporal dissimilarity between two trajectories, and they propose an efficient approximation method to support k-most-similar-trajectory search in spatiotemporal databases. Chang J. et al.[2] propose spatio-temporal distance(STDist) for computing spatio-temporal similarity between two trajectories of moving objects on road networks. In order to handle the shifts and scaling of data in the detection process, the distance function-Edit distance on Real Sequence (EDR)[4] is introduced. The EDR eliminates the noise effects by quantizing the distance between a pair of items to values of 0 and 1. All these distance functions focus on the trajectories represented as a series of accurate coordinate points, whereas the RFID trajectories are denoted by a series of symbolic points.

As for similarity analysis over symbolic sequences, Mannila H. et al. [7] use Edit distance as the measurement for similarity analysis of event sequences, which is an important form of time series. André-Jönsson H. et al.[1] first transform the numerical time series into symbolic sequences, then search the similarity in symbolic sequences. The data items of symbolic sequences are distinguished by different characters, so the approximate string matching techniques are also helpful for our model. Xiao C. el al. [11] propose an Ed-join algorithm for similarity join with edit distance constraints. They develop two filtering methods by analyzing the locations and contents of mismatching q-grams. Sarawagi S. et al. [9] present an efficient algorithm for performing set joins on predicates involving various similarity measures. However, the semantics of symbolic sequences of the related work is different from ours, in which our symbolic trajectories represent the pattern or activity of moving objects.

RFID has been widely used for monitoring and tracking moving objects, Yang B. et al. [13] design an indoor space for deployment of RFID and propose an query aware continuous range query processing. Chun H. et al. [6] propose an effective path encoding scheme to encode the flow information for products and devise a storage scheme to process tracking queries. Nevertheless the similarity analysis of RFID trajectory is a relatively new topic.

3 Similarity of RFID Trajectory

An important consideration in similarity query is the choice of distance measurement. In this section, we first review why the existing distance functions are not suitable for RFID trajectories analysis. Then a new measurement EDEU is proposed and the definition of similarity is given.

3.1 Reviewing Existing Distance Functions

There have been many distance functions for trajectory analysis, such as Euclidean distance, DTW, LCSS and Edit distance. But none of these distance functions is suitable for RFID trajectories because the unique characteristics of RFID trajectories.

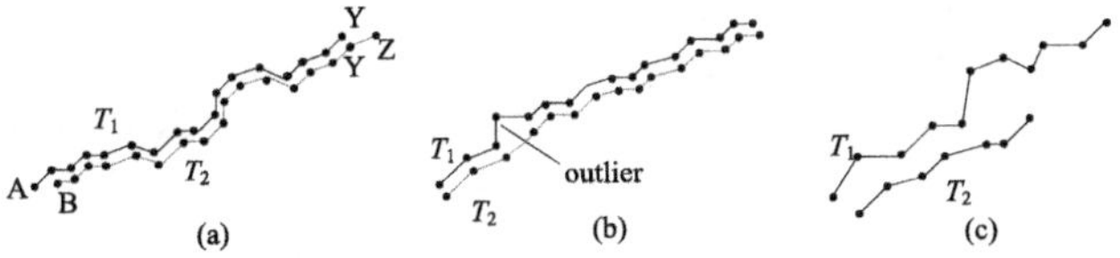

Fig. 1. Three cases of RFID trajectory analysis

We utilize the Euclidean distance and Edit distance to illustrate why these distance functions are not suitable for RFID trajectory analysis. Given trajectories $T_1 = l_1, l_2, \ldots, l_n$ and $T_2 = L_1, L_2, \ldots, L_n$, the Euclidean distance between T_1 and T_2 denotes as

$$EU(T_1, T_2) = \sum_{i=1}^{n} dist(l_i, L_i) \tag{1}$$

where $dist(l_i, L_i)$ is the distance between l_i and L_i. Figure 1(a) exemplifies the local time shifting in trajectories $T_1 = \{A, B, \ldots, Y\}$ and $T_2 = \{B, C, \ldots, Z\}$, and the Euclidean distance accumulates the distance between corresponding location pairs,

$$EU(T_1, T_2) = dist(A, B) + dist(B, C) + \ldots + dist(Y, Z) \tag{2}$$

The value computed by formula (2) is very large, so in this example the similarity of T_1 and T_2 can not be detected by Euclidean distance. As depicted in figure 1(b), we compare T_1 and T_2 where there is an outlier in T_1. In this case the Euclidean distance will fail from the outlier and result in large value. Figure 1(c) shows two trajectories with unequal lengths, the Euclidean distance can not handle this case completely unless the definition is modified. Without supporting the time shifting, outliers and handling the trajectories with unequal lengths, the Euclidean distance is not suitable for similarity analysis of RFID trajectories.

The Edit distance seeks the minimum number of edit operations required to change one trajectory to another, however, the real distance among logic areas

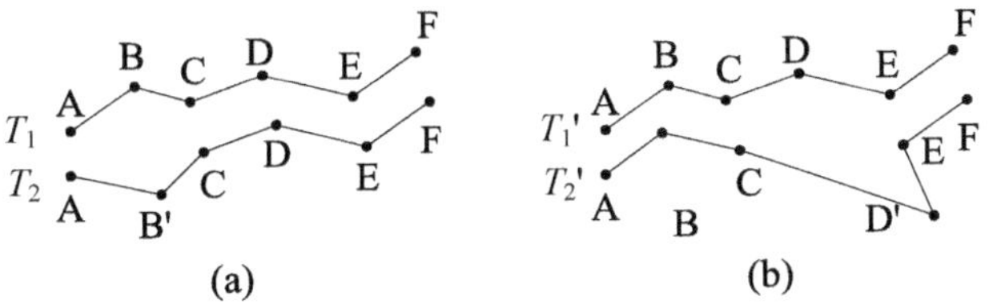

Fig. 2. An example of difference among trajectories

is not taken into consideration. Figure 2 shows two trajectory pairs $< T_1, T_2 >$ and $< T_1', T_2' >$. The T_1 and T_2 are identical except the locations B and B'. The T_1' and T_2' are identical except the locations D and D'. So the Edit distance of T_1 and T_2 is the cost of substituting B for B', and the Edit distance of T_1' and T_2' is the cost of substituting D for D'. The cost of substitution is predefined in Edit distance, thus in this case $ED(T_1, T_2) = ED(T_1', T_2')$. But the locations can not be simply regarded as characters, in practice, the distance between D and D' may be much further than the distance between B and B'. In such case, the pair of $< T_1, T_2 >$ is more similar than $< T_1', T_2' >$. The distances between logic areas have significance to the trajectory analysis, thus the Edit distance is not suitable for RFID trajectories.

3.2 Definitions of EDEU and Similarity

In order to handle the characteristics of RFID trajectories, we propose a new measurement EDEU (Edit Distance combined with Euclidean Distance), which combines the properties of both Edit distance and Euclidean distance.

Definition 1. *(EDEU) Given two trajectories T_u and T_v, EDEU(T_v,T_u) is defined as the minimal cost of transforming T_u to T_v, where the cost of each operation is the distance between adjacent points involved in operation.*

The computing process of EDEU resembles the traditional Edit distance. The "insert", "delete" and "substitution" operations are defined to transform one trajectory to another. The operations here denote the changing of locations in trajectories, and the cost of each operation is the distance between logic areas involved in the operation. For instance, the cost of substituting A with B is the value of $D(A, B)$, and the cost of inserting A before C is the value of $D(A, C)$. $D(L_i, L_j)$ represents the distance between location L_i and L_j, which is denoted by numerical value. We assume there is a reference point O in system, and specify the value of $D(O, L_i)$ for each location. We adopt the dynamic programming method to find the optimization operation sequence. Let $r(i, j)$ denote the cost of transforming the first i locations of trajectory T_1 into the first j locations of trajectory T_2, then $r(m, n)$ is the value of $EDEU(T_1,T_2)$, where m is the length of T_1 and n is the length of T_2. The formula(3) illustrates the computation process.

$$\begin{cases} r(0,0) = 0 \\ r(i,0) = r(i-1,0) + D(L_{i-1}, L_i) \\ r(0,j) = r(0,j-1) + D(L_{i-1}, L_i) \\ r(i,j) = min\{r(i-1,j) + D(L_{i-1}, L_i), \\ \qquad r(i,j-1) + D(l_{i-1}, l_j), r(i-1,j-1) + p(i,j)\} \end{cases} \tag{3}$$

where

$$p(i,j) = \begin{cases} 0 & L_i = l_j \\ D(L_i, l_j) & L_i \neq l_j \end{cases}$$

The EDEU reflects the difference between trajectories in location sequences through transform operations, and it can support the time shifting. EDEU novelly adopts the distance as the cost of an operation, thus the real distance is taken into consideration. EDEU can also handle the trajectories with unequal lengths. Due to these properties, EDEU satisfies the unique requirements of the RFID trajectory analysis. Based on the EDEU, we define the similar function of trajectories as

$$Sim(T_u, T_v) = 1 - \frac{EDEU(T_u, T_v)}{max\{L(T_u), L(T_v)\}} \tag{4}$$

where $L(T_u)$ denotes the summation of distance that is between each adjacent points in trajectory T_u. The similarity between trajectories can be defined as follows:

Definition 2. *Given two trajectories T_u and T_v, T_u and T_v are similar if $Sim(T_u, T_v) > \varepsilon$, where ε is the similar threshold specified by the user.*

With this definition, we can query the similar pairs in trajectory databases.

4 Efficient Similarity Queries over RFID Trajectories

The EDEU can be considered as a variant of Edit distance and it has a time complexity of $O(n^2)$, where n is the length of the longer trajectory. To search for all the similar pairs in trajectory databases, the computation complexity is $O(m^2n^2)$ where m is the trajectory amount in the database. The high time cost of EDEU removes the possibility of pair-wise analysis. Therefore, we propose two filtering algorithms that can reduce the computation cost.

4.1 Co-occurrence Degree Based Filtering Algorithm

Given a trajectory T, a trajectory segment is defined as a subsequence with size q. For instance, "ABC" is a trajectory segment in T="$D, A, B, C, E, F, \ldots$" when q is 3. As a preparatory work, we generate the trajectory segments set for T_u by sliding a window with size q from the beginning,

$$\Phi(T_u) = \{\gamma_1 \ldots \gamma_q \mid \gamma_1, \ldots, \gamma_q \in T_u, q \in \mathbb{N}\} \tag{5}$$

The trajectory segment represents the consecutive locations that passed by some moving object, therefore, the more identical trajectory segments in $\Phi(T_u)$ and $\Phi(T_v)$, the more similarities T_u and T_v have. According to this feature we calculate the proportion of consistent match as Co-occurrence Degree.

Definition 3. *(Co-occurrence Degree) The proportion of co-occurring trajectory segments in two trajectories is defined as Co-occurrence Degree(CoD). Given T_u and T_v,*

$$CoD_{uv} = \mid \Phi(T_u) \cap \Phi(T_v) \mid / \mid \Phi(T_u) \cup \Phi(T_v) \mid \tag{6}$$

where $\Phi(T_u)$, $\Phi(T_v)$ denote the trajectory segments set of T_u and T_v respectively.

The Co-occurrence Degree can be computed in $O(n)$ time, so that we can utilize it to form the candidate set. The details are presented in algorithm 1.

Lines 2-3 of the algorithm calculate the Co-occurrence Degree of the trajectory pair. Next, the filtration is executed according to the Co-occurrence Degree threshold δ and the candidate trajectory pairs are obtained for refinement. The lines 7-9 describe the similarity detection process, which compare the value of $Sim(T_u, T_v)$ with the threshold ε and the result set of similar trajectory pairs is generated. The filtering process by Co-occurrence Degree requires no false dismissals while reducing false candidates. Hence the threshold δ of Co-occurrence Degree is a key issue in this algorithm. Next we will illustrate how to determine the optimal δ.

Algorithm 1. Co-occurrence Degree(Trajectory databases Ω, Similarity threshold ε, Co-occurrence Degree threshold δ)

1 **for** *trajectory pair* $T_u, T_v \in \Omega$ **do**
2   Generate Φ_u, Φ_v
3   /* Φ_u, Φ_v are the TS set of T_u and T_v respectively*/
4   Calculate $CoD_{uv} = \mid \Phi_u \cap \Phi_v \mid$
5   /**Co-occurrence Degree* of T_u and T_v */
6   **if** $CoD_{uv} > \delta$ **then**
7   Calculate $Sim(T_u, T_v)$
8   **if** $Sim(T_u, T_v) > \varepsilon$ **then**
9   Insert $< T_u, T_v >$ into the result set RS
10   **end**
11   **end**
12 **end**
13 Return the trajectory pairs in RS

According to the definition of similar function in formula(4), we can deduce that when the value of $Sim(T_u, T_v)$ is ε, the corresponding value of $EDEU(T_u, T_v)$ is $(1-\varepsilon)*N$, where N is the length of the longer trajectory. The EDEU accumulates the cost of operations that converts T_u to T_v and the cost is the summation of distance between logic areas. We denote the minimum distance between all logic areas as D_{min}, then the maximum number of operations transforming T_u to T_v is $(1-\varepsilon)*N/D_{min}$. If the number of unmatched locations in $< T_u, T_v >$ are no larger than k, the number of co-occurrence trajectory segments in $< T_u, T_v >$ is no less than $N + 1 - (k+1)*q$. Since the number of operations is equal to the number of different logic areas in the trajectory pair $< T_u, T_v >$, the number of Co-occurrence trajectory segments between T_u and T_v is no less than $N+1-((1-\varepsilon)*N/D_{min}+1)*q$ and the *Co-occurrence Degree* of T_u and T_v is

$$CoD^*_{uv} = \frac{N+1-((1-\varepsilon)*N/D_{min}+1)*q}{N+1-q} \tag{7}$$

The CoD^*_{uv} denotes the boundary of *Co-occurrence Degree* corresponding to the similarity threshold ε, that is, CoD^*_{uv} is the minimum value that filters out the false-candidates without false-positive results when executing the algorithm 1.

So when ε is given for similarity query, we calculate δ according to formula(7) as the Co-occurrence Degree threshold.

4.2 Filtering Based on Length Dispersion Ratio

The basic idea of Length Dispersion Ratio is to take advantage of the length information of T_u and T_v when determining whether the similarity of T_u and T_v is within the desired threshold, where the length denotes the number of locations contained in trajectories.

Definition 4. *(Length Dispersion Ratio) The dispersion ratio of two trajectories length,*

$$LDR_{uv} = \frac{|| T_u | - | T_v ||}{max\{| T_u |, | T_v |\}} \tag{8}$$

where $| T_u |$,$| T_v |$ *denote the length of trajectory* T_u,T_v *respectively.*

The Length Dispersion Ratio could be easily obtained by comparing the two trajectories. If trajectory T_u is longer than T_v by k points, at least k operations are needed to transform T_u to T_v when calculating the EDEU. According to the precious analysis, when we execute similarity query with threshold ε, the number of unmatched locations is at most $(1-\varepsilon) * N/D_{min}$, where N is the length of the longer trajectory and D_{min} represents the minimum distance among logic areas. For trajectories T_u and T_v, if $|| T_u | - | T_v ||> (1 - \varepsilon)/D_{min}$, the similarity of T_u and T_v must be smaller than ε. So we can utilize $LDR^*_{uv} = (1 - \varepsilon)/D_{min}$ to quickly filter out the trajectory pairs whose similarity is smaller than ε. The evaluation of Length Dispersion Ratio could be easily computed, so we can utilize it to discard trajectory pairs with large dispersion in length and to generate results without false-positives.

Algorithm 2. Length Dispersion Ratio (Trajectory databases Ω, Similarity threshold ε)

for *each trajectory pair* T_u, $T_v \in \Omega$ **do**
  Calculate LDR_{uv}
  /* LDR_{uv} is the Length Dispersion Ratio of T_u and T_v */
  if $LDR_{uv} > (1 - \varepsilon)/D_{min}$ **then**
    Calculate $Sim(T_u, T_v)$
    if $Sim(T_u, T_v) > \varepsilon$ **then**
      Insert $< T_u, T_v >$ into the result set RS
    end
  end
end
Return the trajectory pairs in RS

Algorithm 1 and 2 provide efficient mechanisms to accelerate the similarity analysis by avoiding the pair-wise way. Since these two methods have no effect on each other, we can combine them to further improve the efficiency. Our experiments in section 6 show that the filtering cost is very low compared with the refinement step.

5 Local Similarity Analysis

Section 3 and 4 propose methods for querying the similar pairs from RFID trajectory databases, however, besides global similarity, the local similarity widely exists in trajectory databases. As shown in figure 4, the trajectory T_1 and T_2 are similar from point P_{start} to P_{end}, while they are not similar in global.

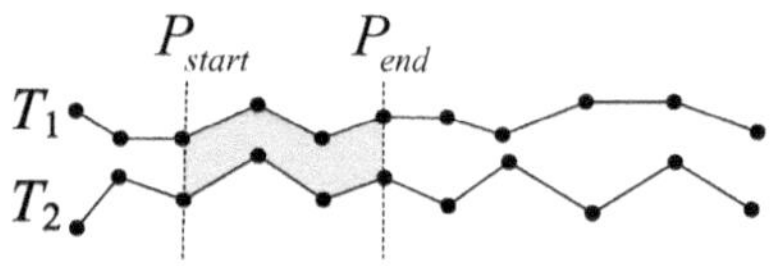

Fig. 3. Local similarity of trajectories

The goal of local similarity analysis is, for each global dissimilar trajectory pair $< T_u, T_v >$, to determine the start and end positions of local similarity if they have. We propose a local similarity analysis algorithm. The details are shown as follows.

Algorithm 3. Local Similarity Analysis (Trajectory pair $< T_u, T_v >$, Similarity threshold ε, Co-occurrence Degree threshold δ, length threshold λ)

$sim \leftarrow 0$ /*similar identification*/
$num \leftarrow 0$ /* number of local similarity in $< T_u, T_v >$*/
Divide T_u and T_v into sub-trajectories $T_{u1}, \ldots, T_{um}, T_{v1}, \ldots, T_{vn}$ with length d
for $i \leftarrow 1$ *to* h **do**
    Calculate $CoD[i] \leftarrow CoD(T_{ui}, T_{vi})$
    if $CoD[i] < \delta$ **then**
        if $Sim == 1$ **then**
            if $(i - P_{start}) * d > \lambda$ **then**
                $P_{end} \leftarrow i$
                Calculate $Sim(T_u, T_v)$ from $(P_{start} * d + 1)$ to $(P_{end} * d + 1)$
                if $Sim > \varepsilon$ **then**
                    Put $(T_u, T_v, P_{start} * d + 1, P_{end} * d + 1)$ into LS
                end
            end
            $sim \leftarrow 0$
        end
        else if $sim == 0$ **then**
            $sim \leftarrow 1$, $p_{start} \leftarrow i$
        end
    end
end
Return the result set LS

The key issue of local similarity detection is finding the start and end positions, which is realized by analysing the Co-occurrence Degree sequence. Lines 3-5 of the algorithm generate the Co-occurrence Degree sequence of T_u and T_v. $CoD[1, \ldots, h]$ denote the Co-occurrence Degree sequence and store the Co-occurrence Degree of each sub-trajectory pair. We aim at finding region P_{start} to P_{end} at Co-occurrence Degree sequence, where the values of $CoD[P_{start}, \ldots, P_{end}]$ are larger than δ and $P_{end} - P_{start} > \lambda$. P_{end} denotes the identifier of the end sub-trajectory, so the corresponding end position in trajectory is $P_{end} * d + 1$. Hence, $T_u[P_{start} * d + 1, \ldots, P_{end} * d + 1]$ and $T_v[P_{start} * d + 1, \ldots, P_{end} * d + 1]$ could be seen as a candidate similar pair, thus we would calculate the local similarity on them.

To fully search for the similarity in RFID trajectory databases, we firstly query the global similar trajectory pairs, and then, query the local similarity from global dissimilar trajectory pairs. The global similar trajectory pairs and the local similarity results are integrated into the final results set.

6 Experiments

In this section, we firstly evaluate the Speedup Ratio and Filtering power of our filtering algorithms compared with the exact method. Speedup ratio is defined as the ratio of the average execution time required by the exact method to the average execution time needed by the filtering techniques. Given a similarity query, the filtering power is defined as the ratio of the candidate set size to the original trajectory pairs size. We then analyse the performance of global similarity query and the local similarity query.

All the experiments were conducted on a PC with Inter core 2 Duo CPU and 3.48G memory. We simulate 1000 trajectories with variant length from 100 to 800, where the length denotes the number of locations contained in trajectories. The trajectories are defined as random arrangement of 50 locations, and the distance between any logic areas are given in advance.

The figures 4 and 5 describe the Speedup Ratio and Filtering power of:

- Mechanism based on Co-occurrence Degree combined with Length Dispersion Ratio, denoted as CoDA + LDR;
- Mechanism based on Co-occurrence Degree, denoted as CoDA;
- Mechanism based on Length Dispersion Ratio, denoted as LDR.

First, we compare the Speedup Ratio of three filtering mechanisms with different number of trajectories and with the different similarity thresholds. As shown in figure 4 , the CoDA + LDR mechanism has the optimal performance compared with CoDA and LDR. The reason is that CoDA + LDR discards more false-candidate trajectory pairs to reduce the computation cost and improve the efficiency.

As shown in figure 5, the candidate set size decreases considerably after the filtering step, in particular, the CoDA + LDR mechanism attains the optimal Filtering power compared with CoDA and LDR.

We also evaluate the performance of local similarity query and the global similarity query. The magnitude of local similarity is relative to the size of the length

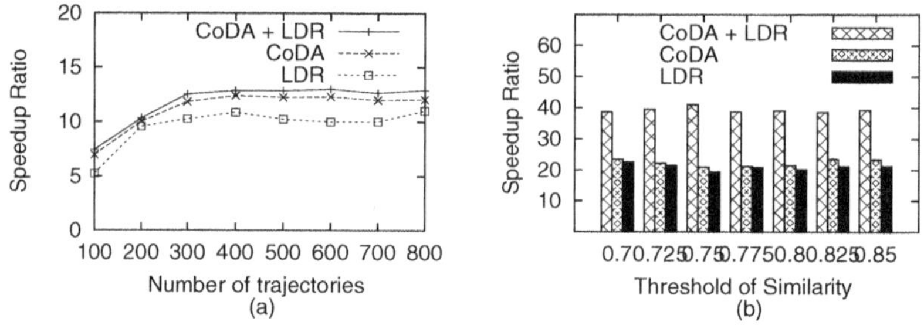

Fig. 4. Comparison of three filtering mechanisms in Speedup Ratio

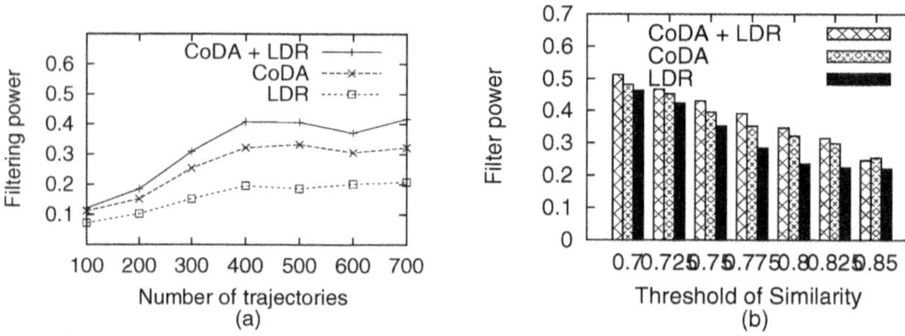

Fig. 5. Comparison of three filtering mechanisms in Filtering power

threshold λ. We show the results when λ is defined as 500. As shown in figure 6(a), there are lots of cases of local similarity existing at the global dissimilar trajectory pairs. Due to the construction of Co-occurrence Degree sequence, the execution time of local similarity query has the same order of magnitude to the global similarity query. And the execution time of both methods increases with the number of trajectories.

In figure 6(b), the execution time of both methods increase with the number of trajectories. Due to the construction of Co-occurrence Degree sequence, the execution time of local similarity query has same magnitude with the global similarity query.

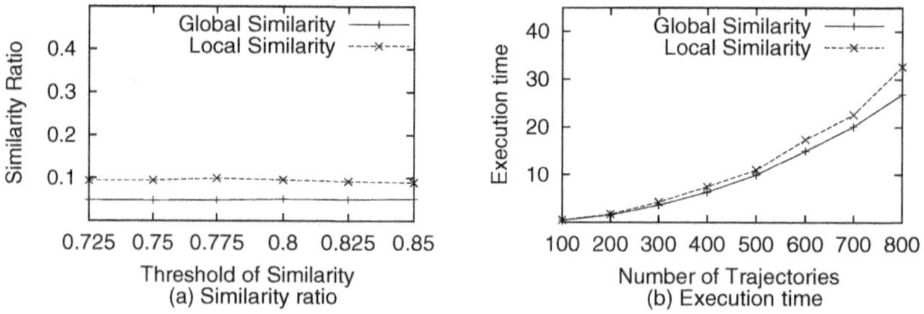

Fig. 6. Comparison of Global and Local similarity

7 Conclusions

This paper addresses the problem of similarity query in RFID trajectory databases. We introduce a novel measurement, the EDEU distance function, which satisfies the special requirements of RFID trajectory analysis. In order to accelerate the query process, we present two filtering algorithms based on Co-occurrence Degree and length desperation ratio, which provide efficient ways to quickly discard dissimilar trajectory pairs without generating false-positives. Then the exact calculation is executed on the much smaller candidate set to obtain the results.

To fully analyse the similarity, we query the local similarity in global dissimilar trajectory pairs. We utilize the sequence of Co-occurrence Degree to rapidly attain the candidate similar region, and then compute the similarity coefficient to get the final results. The extensive experiments confirm the efficiency and quality of our methods.

References

1. André-Jönsson, H., Badal, D.Z.: Using signature files for querying time-series data. In: Komorowski, J., Żytkow, J.M. (eds.) PKDD 1997. LNCS, vol. 1263, Springer, Heidelberg (1997)
2. Chang, J., Bista, R., Kim, J., Kim, Y.: A new trajectory search algorithm based on spatio-temporal similarity on spatial network. In: CIT 2007, pp. 110–115 (2007)
3. Chen, L., Ng, R.: On the marriage of lp-norms and edit distance. In: VLDB '04, pp. 792–803 (2004)
4. Chen, L., Özsu, M., Oria, V.: Robust and fast similarity search for moving object trajectories. In: SIGMOD '05, pp. 491–502 (2005)
5. Frentzos, E., Gratsias, K., Theodoridis, Y.: Index-based most similar trajectory search. In: ICDE '07, pp. 816–825 (2007)
6. Lee, C., Chung, C.: Efficient storage scheme and query processing for supply chain management using rfid. In: SIGMOD '08, pp. 291–302 (2008)
7. Mannila, H., Ronkainen, P.: Similarity of event sequences. In: Temporal Representation and Reasoning '97, pp. 136–139 (1997)
8. Masciari, E.: Rfid data management for effective objects tracking. In: Adams, C., Miri, A., Wiener, M. (eds.) SAC 2007. LNCS, vol. 4876, pp. 457–461. Springer, Heidelberg (2007)
9. Sarawagi, S., Kirpal, A.: Efficient set joins on similarity predicates. In: SIGMOD '04: Proceedings of the 2004 ACM SIGMOD international conference on Management of data, pp. 743–754. ACM, New York (2004)
10. Vlachos, M., Gunopoulos, D., Kollios, G.: Discovering similar multidimensional trajectories. In: ICDE 2002, p. 673 (2002)
11. Xiao, C., Wang, W., Lin, X.: Ed-join: an efficient algorithm for similarity joins with edit distance constraints. Proc. VLDB Endow. 1(1), 933–944 (2008)
12. Yanagisawa, Y., Akahani, T., Satoh, J.: Shape-based similarity query for trajectory of mobile objects. In: Chen, M.-S., Chrysanthis, P.K., Sloman, M., Zaslavsky, A. (eds.) MDM 2003. LNCS, vol. 2574, pp. 63–77. Springer, Heidelberg (2003)
13. Yang, B., Lu, H., Jensen, C.S.: Scalable continuous range monitoring of moving objects in symbolic indoor space. In: CIKM '09, pp. 671–680 (2009)

Context-Aware Basic Level Concepts Detection in Folksonomies

Wen-hao Chen[1], Yi Cai[2], Ho-fung Leung[1], and Qing Li[2]

[1] Department of Computer Science and Engineering
The Chinese University of Hong Kong, Hong Kong, China
whchen@cse.cuhk.edu.hk, lhf@cuhk.edu.hk
[2] Department of Computer Science
City University of Hong Kong, Hong Kong, China
yicai3@cityu.edu.hk, itqli@cityu.edu.hk

Abstract. This paper deals with the problem of exploring implicit semantics in folksonomies. In folksonomies, users create and manage tags to annotate web resources. The collection of user-created tags in folksonomies is a potential semantics source. Much research has been done to extract concepts, and even concepts hierarchy (ontology), which is the important component for knowledge representation (e.g. in semantic web and agent communication), from folksonomies. However, there has been no metric for discovering human acceptable and agreeable concepts, and thus many concepts extracted from folksonomies by existing approaches are not natural for human use. In cognitive psychology, there is a family of concepts named basic level concepts which are frequently used by people in daily life, and most human knowledge is organized by basic level concepts. Thus, extracting basic level concepts from folksonomies is more meaningful for categorizing and organizing web resources than extracting concepts in other granularity. In addition, context plays an important role in basic level concepts detection, as the basic level concepts in the same domain become different in different contexts. In this paper, we propose a method to detect basic level concepts in different contexts from folksonomies. Using Open Directory Project (ODP) as the benchmark, we demonstrate the existence of context effect and the effectiveness of our method.

1 Introduction

Recently, folksonomies have became popular as part of social annotation systems such as social bookmarking (e.g., del.icio.us [1]) and photograph annotation (e.g., flickr [2]), which provide user-friendly interfaces for people to annotate web resources freely, and also enable users to share the annotations on the web. These annotations are known as folksonomy tags, which provide a potential source of user-created metadata. Al-Khalifa et al. [1] demonstrated that folksonomy tags

[1] http://delicious.com/
[2] http://www.flickr.com/

L. Chen et al. (Eds.): WAIM 2010, LNCS 6184, pp. 632–643, 2010.

agreed more closely with human thinking than those automatically extracted from texts. Concepts extracted from these tags may directly represent users' opinions about how web resources should be described. Some research work tried to extract concepts, and even concept hierarchy, from folksonomies. However, there is no metric for discovering human oriented concepts, and thus many concepts extracted from folksonomies by existing work are not natural for human use and the granularity of these extracted concepts are different.

Psychologists find that there is a family of categories named basic level categories which represent the most "natural" level, neither too general nor too specific. People most frequently prefer to use basic level concepts constructed from these categories in daily life and these concepts are the ones first named and understood by children. For example, when people see a car, although we can call it a "vehicle" or a "sedan", most people would call it a "car". What is more, most human knowledge is organized by basic level concepts. Thus, extracting basic level concepts from folksonomies is more meaningful to human users for categorizing and organizing web resources than extracting concepts in other granularity. In addition, contexts play an important role in basic level concept detection. The basic level concepts in the same domain are different in different contexts [2]. For example, for all computer science conferences, people may consider "data mining conferences", "semantic web conference", "graphics conferences" and so on as the basic level concepts in the context of choosing a conference to submit a paper to. However, in the context of assessing a researcher's publications, the basic level concepts for all computer science conferences may be "rank one conferences", "rank two conferences" and so on. Hence, it is necessary to take contexts into consideration while detecting basic level concepts.

In this paper, a metric named contextual category utility is proposed to discover basic level concepts. Based on the contextual category utility, we propose a method to detect basic level concepts in different contexts. To the best of our knowledge, it is the first work on detecting basic level concepts in different contexts from folksonomies. We conduct experiments to evaluate our method using a real-world data set and compare the detected concepts with ODP concepts. Experiment results demonstrate that our method can detect basic level concepts in different contexts effectively. These basic level concepts are more consistent with human thinking than those identified by methods.

2 Preliminaries

2.1 Folksonomy

In our approach, we use the definition of folksonomy given in [3]. In the definition, users are described by their user IDs, and tags are arbitrary strings. The type of resources in a folksonomy depends on the social annotation system[3], and users create tags to annotate resources.

[3] In delicious, for example, resources are web pages while in Flickr resources are images and videos.

Definition 1. *A* **folksonomy** *is a tuple* $\mathbb{F} := (U, T, R, Y)$ *where* U, T *and* R *are finite sets, whose elements are called users, tags and resources, respectively, and* Y *is a ternary relation between them, i.e.* $Y \subseteq U \times T \times R$.

2.2 Basic Level Categories (Concepts) and Category Utility

In cognitive psychology, in a hierarchical category structure such as a taxonomy of plants, there is one level named the basic level at which the categories are cognitively basic. The basic level categories, defined by Rosch et al. [4], carry the most information and are the most differentiated from one another. They are the categories easier than others to learn and recall by humans as concepts. In psychology, generally a concept holds the common features of a category of instances and is the abstraction of that category. Basic level concepts are the abstraction of basic level categories. Objects are identified as belonging to basic level categories and recognized as the basic level concepts faster than others. For example, in classifying life forms, basic level categories tend to be at the level of the genus (maple, dog etc.). If we see a tree, we could call it a "plant", a "maple" and a "sugar maple", but most people will identify it as "maple". The concept "maple" is a basic level concept.

To characterize basic level categories, psychologists give the metric named category utility [5] . Through many experiments, they demonstrate that the character of basic level categories is that they have the highest category utility. It provides a normative information-theoretic measure of the predictive advantage gained by the person who possesses knowledge of the given category structure over the person who does not possess this knowledge:

$$cu(C, F) = \frac{1}{m} \sum_{k=1}^{m} p(c_k) \left[\sum_{i=1}^{n} p(f_i|c_k)^2 - \sum_{i=1}^{n} p(f_i)^2 \right] \tag{1}$$

where C is the set of categories, F is the set of features, f_i is a feature, $p(f_i|c_k)$ is the probability that a member of category c_k has the feature f_i, $p(c_k)$ is the probability that an instance belongs to category c_k, $p(f_i)$ is the probability that an instance has feature f_i, n is the total number of features, m is the total number of categories.

2.3 Contexts and Context Effect

Context refers to the general conditions (circumstances) in which an event or action take place. The context of anything under consideration consists of the ideas, situations, judgments, and knowledge that relate to it. In cognitive psychology [6], the term "context effect" is used to refer to the influence of context in different cognitive tasks. For example, Roth and Shoben [7] investigate the effect of context in categorization, and suggest that, if the prototype view of concepts is applied, contexts should cause a reweighing of the importance of the properties of a concept, thus resulting in a different categorization and concepts. In addition, Tanaka and Taylor [2] find out that the domain knowledge in different context has an effect on finding basic level concepts. The experts has particular domain knowledge tend to treat different concepts as basic level concepts compared with non-experts.

3 Detecting Context-Aware Basic Level Concepts

3.1 Motivation

In folksonomies, tags are given by users to annotate web resources. These tags which naturally express users opinions about the resources constitute a potential semantics source. A good use of this semantics source is to extract concepts from it. Concepts play an important role in knowledge representation (e.g. semantic web and agent communication). Further more concepts are the basic component of ontologies. Many previous researches have been conducted on extracting concepts, and even concepts hierarchy (ontology), from folksonomies. However, there is no metric for discovering human acceptable concepts, and thus many concepts extracted from folksonomies by current works are not natural for human use.

Inspired by studies in cognitive psychology, we try to model human cognitive process in folksonomies so that we can explore the implicit semantics and build more human acceptable and applicable concepts. In cognitive psychology, basic level concepts are frequently used by people in daily life, and most human knowledge is organized by them. In addition, contexts play an important role in concept learning. The basic level concepts will shift based on different contexts. Taking contexts into consideration will make our proposed method more completed and applicable. We also try to demonstrate the effect of context in categorization and concept learning process. As a result, we model instances, concepts and contexts in folksonomies and propose a context-aware method to detect basic level concepts from folksonomies.

3.2 Modeling Instances and Concepts in Folksonomies

In folksonomies, tags are given by users to annotate a resource and describe its characters. Naturally, the tagged resources are considered as instances. For the reason that each resource is described by tags, we consider these tags as properties of instances. Accordingly, an instance is defined as follows:

Definition 2. *An* **instance**, r_i, *is represented by a vector of tag:value pairs,* $r_i = (t_{i,1} : v_{i,1}, t_{i,2} : v_{i,2}, \ldots, t_{i,n} : v_{i,n})$ *with* $t_{i,k} \in T, 0 < v_{i,k} \leq 1, 1 \leq k \leq n$.

where n is the number of the unique tags assigned to resource r_i, $v_{i,k}$ is the weight of tag $t_{i,k}$ in resource r_i. The weight $v_{i,k}$ determines the importance of the tag $t_{i,k}$ to resource r_i. We consider that a tag assigned by more users to a resource is more important because more users think the tag is useful to describe the resource. Accordingly the weight of a tag $t_{i,k}$ is defined as $v_{i,k} = \frac{N_{t_{i,k}}}{N_{r_i}}$, where $N_{t_{i,k}}$ is the number of users using the tag $t_{i,k}$ to annotate the resource r_i and

N_{r_i} is the total number of users assigning tags to r_i. In the case that all users annotate r_i with $t_{i,k}$, the weight $v_{i,k}$ is 1.

A concept is the abstraction of a category of instances and holds the common properties of them [8]. Accordingly, we construct a concept through extracting common tags of a category of instances. These common tags are considered as the properties of the concept. The weights of these tags are their mean values in the category. Accordingly the definition of a concept is as follows.

Definition 3. *A* **concept**, *c_i, is represented by a vector of tag:value pairs, $c_i = (t_{i,1} : v_{i,1}, t_{i,2} : v_{i,2}, \ldots, t_{i,n} : v_{i,n})$ with $t_{i,k} \in T, 0 < v_{i,k} \leq 1, 1 \leq k \leq n$,* where n is the number of unique tags, $t_{i,k}$ is the common tag of a category of resources, $v_{i,k}$ is the mean value of the tag $t_{i,k}$ in the category.

3.3 Modeling Context in Folksonomies

According to the studies in cognitive psychology, contexts plays an important role in human cognitive process. In such a process, there is a set of persons in a context and some subjective aspects of them should be considered as a part of context (e.g. the goal of using a concept, the knowledge of the persons). According to Tananka and Taylor [2], there is one very interesting basic level phenomenon: the shifting of the basic level. People with different domain knowledge have different considerations of basic levels. The domain knowledge has an effect on where the basic level lies. This difference is considered as the effect of contexts. As we mentioned above, a folksonomy consists of a set of resources, a set of tags and a set of users. Users with different domain knowledge annotate the resources with different tags. These tags naturally represent users subjective aspects including purposes and knowledge. Thus, we define a context x as a collection of relevant subjective aspects of users.

Definition 4. *A* **context**, *denoted by x, is a tuple, which consists of a subset of users and tags, $x =< N_u, N_t >$* , where N_u is a set of users and N_t is a set of tags which represents the subjective aspects of users.

In a particular context, some tags are more important than others [8]. In our model, the importance of each tags is indicated by a real number (i.e., importance weight of a tag) between 0 and 1. If a tag is absolutely important for a task in a specific context, then its importance is 1. If a tag is not important at all for a task in specific context, then its importance weight is 0. We define a tag weight vector which reflects importance weights of tags in a context.

Definition 5. *A* **tag weight vector** *in a context x, denoted by V^x, is represented by a vector of tag:value pairs, $V^x = (t_1 : v_1^x, t_2 : v_2^x, \ldots, t_n : v_n^x)$,* $0 \leq v_{i,k} \leq 1$, where n is the number of relevant tags and v_i^x is the importance weight of tag t_i in context x.

Based on subjective aspects, users can form a perspective so as to obtain a set of importance weights for tags in a context. We formally define a perspective as follows:

Definition 6. *A* **perspective**, *denoted by* π^x, *maps a set of users and a set of tags to a tag weight vector,* $\pi^x(N_u, N_t) = V^x$, where V^x is a tag weight vector, N_u is a set of users and N_t is a set of tags.

For the reason that a perspective is formed based on subjective aspects of users, we consider that such a mapping is accomplished by the users in the context and the weight vector is given by the users. For example, people who are interested on programming languages may give a context as: $V^x = (java : 1, ..., css : 0.5)$. It means that the tag "java" is absolutely important and "css" is less important in the context. People may have different perspectives in contexts and give different property weight vectors with respect to their own perspectives.

3.4 Context Effect on Category Utility

In folksonomies, features of instances are represented by tags. Accordingly, in the definition of category utility, the features set F should be changed to the tags set T, and feature f_i should be changed to tag t_i, where $f_i \in F$, $t_i \in T$. In cognitive psychology, under different contexts the basic level concepts are different. Accordingly, we should consider the effect of contexts on category utility. The importance of tags are different in folksonomies under different contexts. To consider the differences in tag importance, we add the tag weight vector V^x of context x to the definition of category utility. Considering the context, the metric of predicting performance should be positively correlated with the tag weight in a certain context. So we change the metric of predicting performance from the correctness $p(t_i)^2$ to $v_i^x \cdot p(t_i)^2$. Furthermore, in folksonomies each resource has different number of tags, and we hope category utility will not be affected by this difference. As a result, we consider the impact of one tag on average in category utility and $\sum_{i=1}^{n} p(f_i)^2$ is changed to $\frac{\sum_{i=1}^{n} v_i^x \cdot p(t_i)^2}{n}$. Accordingly, the contextual category utility is then defined as follows:

$$cu(C, T, x) = \frac{1}{m} \sum_{k=1}^{m} p(c_k) \left[\frac{\sum_{i=1}^{n_k} v_i^x p(t_i|c_k)^2}{n_k} - \frac{\sum_{i=1}^{n} v_i^x p(t_i)^2}{n} \right] \tag{2}$$

where C is the set of categories, T is the set of tags, x is the context. n_k is the number of unique tags in cluster c_k and n is the number of all unique tags. v_i^x is defined as the value of tag t_i in V^x which is the tag weight vector of context x.

3.5 A Context-Aware Basic Level Concepts Detection Algorithm

For the reason that basic level categories (concepts) have the highest category utility, the problem of finding basic level concepts becomes an optimization problem using category utility as the objective function. The value of category utility is influenced by the intra-category similarity which reflects the similarity among members of a category. Categories with high intra-category similarity hold high value of category utility. Accordingly, we put the most similar instances together in every step of our method until the category utility starts to decrease. To compute the similarity, we use the cosine coefficient which is a normally used method of computing similarity between two vectors in information retrieval. In addition, considering the context effect, we add the tag weight into the definition. Accordingly, the similarity metric is defined as follows:

$$sim(a,b,x) = \frac{\sum_{k=1}^{n} v_k^x \cdot v_{a,k} \cdot v_{b,k}}{\sqrt{\sum_{k=1}^{n} v_{a,k}^2} \cdot \sqrt{\sum_{k=1}^{n} v_{b,k}^2}} \qquad (3)$$

where a, b are two concepts, n is the total number of unique tags describing them, and $v_{a,k}$ is the value of tag $t_{a,k}$ in concept a (if a does not have the tag, the value is 0). v_k^x is defined as the value of tag t_k in V^x which is the tag weight vector of context x.

In our algorithm, firstly, we construct concepts from each instance. This type of concept which only includes one instance is considered as the bottom level concepts. Secondly, we compute the similarity between each pair of concepts and build the similarity matrix. Thirdly, the most similar pair in the matrix is generated and merged into a new concept. The new concept contains all instances of the two old concepts and holds their common properties. Then we reconsider the similarity matrix of the remaining concepts. We apply this merging process until only one concept is left, or the similarity between the most similar concepts is 0. In this process we build a dendrogram. We then determine the step where the categories have the highest category utility value. These categories are considered as the basic level categories (concepts). The details of this algorithm are given in algorithm 1, and the time complexity is $O(N^2 \log N)$ where N is the number of resources.

Algorithm 1. Context-aware Basic Level Concepts Detection

```
Input: R, a set of instances (resources); V^x, the tag weight vector of context x
Initialize C, C is an n dimensions vector C = (c_1, c_2, ..., c_n) where its element c_i is the bottom
  level concept. C_size is equal to the number of elements in C. Set sim[n][n] as the similarity
  matrix of C, sim[i][j] = sim(c_i, c_j, x). S = (s_1, s_2, ..., s_n), s_i is used to record the clustering
  result of step i.
Set s_1 = C, step=1,
while C_size > 1 do
    step++
    Find the most similar concepts in C and define a new concept include all instances of them.
    Delete the most similar concepts from C, and add the new concept into C.
    Update the similarity matrix.
    C_size = C_size - 1
    Record the result, s_step = C
    Compute the contextual category utility of this step cu_step
end while
Find the step with the highest category utility cu_max, define the record of this step s_max as
  the basic level categories.
Extract concepts of basic level categories. A concept includes all instances of a category and
  the properties of the concept are the common features (tags) of the instances.
Output these concepts.
```

4 Evaluation

4.1 Data Set and Experiment Setup

Our experiments are conducted on a real world data set: 1087 web pages which are associated with 39475 tags and 57976 users. These web pages are all in the programming domain. Golder [9] demonstrated that, in del.icio.us, in a resource each tag's frequency becomes a nearly fixed proportion of the total frequency of all tags after the resource is bookmarked 100 times. The fixed proportion reflects the real value of a tag in the resource. To make sure that the proportion is nearly fixed, the web pages in our data sets are the ones which are bookmarked more than 100 times in del.icio.us. In addition, the web pages in our data sets must appear in both del.icio.us and Open Directory Project (ODP) [4] because we use ODP as the gold standard. ODP is a user-maintained web directory. Each directory is considered as a concept in ODP. To derive the gold standard concepts from ODP, we first choose a certain directory (e.g. programming) in ODP and then consider all its sub-directories as the gold standard concepts. These concepts in ODP are created, verified and edited by experts around the world and accepted by many users. For evaluation, we apply F1 score which is the aggregation of recall and precision [10] to compare concepts detected by our approach with ODP concepts on their category structures.

Furthermore, to filter the noise tags, we preprocess the data set by (a) removing tags whose weight is less than the threshold q; (b) down casing the obtained tags. Figure 1 presents the F1 scores of the results obtained by using different values of q. We find that if we do not filter any tags ($q = 0$), the clustering results will be the worst (0.011). Among different values of q, 0.02 gives the best result on F1 scores. Accordingly, we set $q = 0.02$ in our experiments.

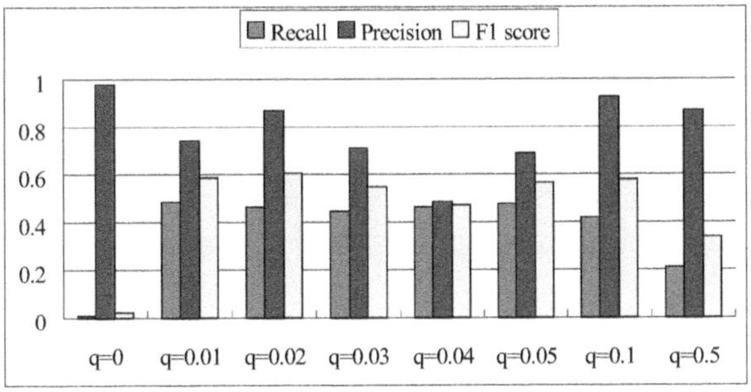

Fig. 1. The impact of threshold q

4.2 Result Analysis

As we mentioned, we model a context in folksonomies through a tag weight vector V^x in which different tags have different values according to their importance in the

[4] http://www.dmoz.org/

context. In our experiments, we use questionnaires to get people's consideration on tag weights in different contexts. In the questionnaire, we ask 20 people to give weights to different tags given the context information (we ask them to give marks to tags where "0" means the tag is not related to the context, "1" means a little bit related to the context, "2" means moderate and "3" means highly related). The value of a tag in the tag weight vector of a context is the average mark of the 20 people after normalizing to the range from 0 to 1. If we are not given any information about the context (i.e., we do not take context into consideration), the weights of all tags are the same and equal to 1. We use two traditional categorization methods as baselines, which are K-means clustering and a concept clustering algorithm named COBWEB [11]. For the reason that the traditional categorization method do not take context into consideration and no information about the context are given, we compare our method with traditional methods without context information first.

In figure 2, we show the results obtained by different methods in our data set without context information. The F1 score of the result using the traditional K-means algorithm (when K is equal to the number of categories in ODP and Euclidean metric is used to determine the distance of two instances) is 0.39. Our approach outperforms K-means by about 50% and the F1 score of our method is 0.59. In addition, our method outperform COBWEB by more on 100% on F1 score. In the results using COBWEB, most of web pages are classified to one concept which is not reasonable so the value of recall is nearly 1 but the precision is only 0.13 and the F1 score is only 0.23. On precision, our proposed method also has the highest value (i.e., 0.46).

In our method, we take context into consideration and make our method to be context-aware for categorization and concept learning. To indicate our method is context-aware, we discuss two contexts (which are denoted by C_{pl} and C_{os} respectively) in our experiments for the same 1087 web pages which are in the programming domain. In the context C_{pl}, people whose interests are on programming languages are trying to classify these web pages. In the context C_{os}, people whose interests are on operation systems are trying to classify these web pages.

Result Analysis for Context C_{pl}. In context C_{pl}, users try to classify web pages based on the interest of themselves. As mentioned, the interest of users in

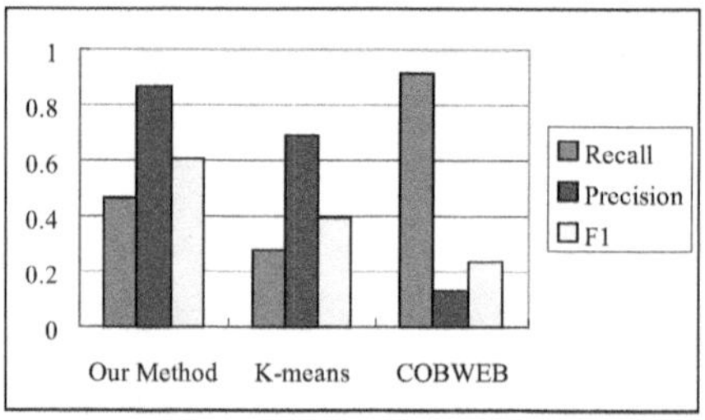

Fig. 2. Comparison of different methods without context information

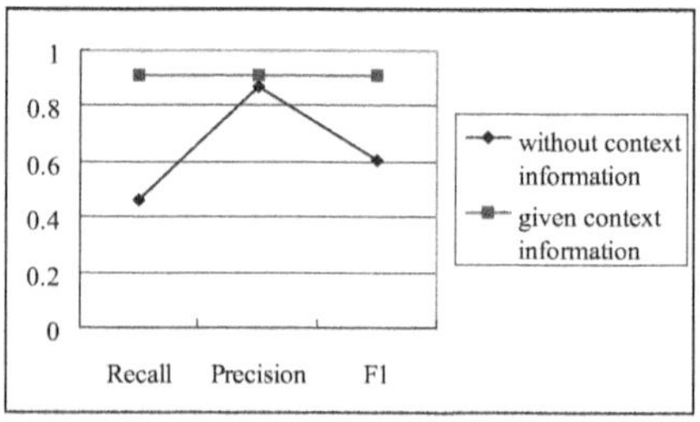

Fig. 3. Results of our method with(out) context information

this context is programming languages. To model this context, we ask 20 students majoring in computer science to give weights to tags based on the interests in C_{pl}. The tag weight vector of this context is as (java: 0.9, mac: 0.1, unix: 0.3, c: 1.0, .net: 0.75, ruby: 0.6, window: 0.3, web: 0.4, blog: 0.0, ...). Tags which are related with programming languages have high weights such as "java" and "c" whose weight are 0.9 and 1.0 respectively.

We compare the detecting basic level concepts using our method in this context with sub-concepts of "programming languages" in ODP. According to figure 3, while we take the context information into consideration, the categorization results and the concepts will be improved. The F1 score is 0.6 without the context information, and while given the information the F1 score increase to 0.91. For our method, the F1 score obtained by given the context information outperform that without context information about 50%. In addition, given the context information, our method also dominate on recall and precision. The detected concepts are almost the same as gold standard concepts which demonstrates our assumption. We show the detected basic level concepts using our method in table 1. In table 1, concepts are represented by the form (tag: value), for example (java: 0.680) where 0.680 is the average weight of the tag "java" in instances of the concept. In addition, we also ask 20 students to evaluate the basic level concepts detected in C_{pl} and the result is shown in table 2. People evaluate the results using the score from 0 to 10 where 10 means that people think the result is perfect under certain context. According to table 2, the average evaluation score given by people on the result of our method in context C_{pl} is 8.16. Such a score means that, given the tag weight vector in C_{pl}, our method can detect the basic level concepts which is consistent with people's expectation. We also can find that the detected concepts are not good with a much smaller evaluation score 4.22 without the context information. Such a result demonstrates the rationality of our context modeling approach and the efficiency of our context-aware basic level concept detection method.

Result Analysis for Context C_{os}. In context C_{os}, users try to classify web pages based on the interest of them and their interest is operation systems. Under this situation, the evaluation results in table 2 show that given the context information (i.e., the tag weight vector), We can build the concepts which is consistent with people's expectation and the F1 score with context information is 7.88 which is much better than the result without the information (2.13).

The experiments demonstrate that our method outperforms previous methods in detecting basic level concepts. The concepts detected by our method are approximate to human's expectation. What is more, our method can detect different basic level concepts in different contexts while previous methods can not.

5 Related Works

Many researches have been conducted on the usage of tags in folksonomies. Ramage et al. [12] compared the clustering results of using traditional words extracted from the text and using tags. Their experiments demonstrated that

Table 1. Basic level concepts detected in different contexts

Context	Basic Level Concepts
context C_{pl}	(xml:0.635), (javascript:0.599), (smalltalk:0.651), (html:0.252), (delphi:0.743), (sql:0.502, database:0.476), (cocoa:0.354, mac:0.213,apple:0.212,osx:0.226), (haskell:0.753), (python:0.812), (basic:0.185), (perl:0.751), (java:0.680), (lisp:0.633), (ruby:0.652), (php:0.651), (c:0.238), (c++:0.687, cpp:0.047), (fortran:0.181)
context C_{os}	(linux:0.406), (windows:0.362), (mac:0.410, osx:0.393, macosx:0.092)

Table 2. Evaluation of basic level concepts in C_{pl} and C_{os}

	C_{pl}	C_{os}
given context information:	8.16	7.88
without context information:	4.22	2.13

using folksonomy tags can improve the clustering result. Au Yeung et al. [13] developed an effective method to disambiguate tags by studying the tripartite structure of folksonomies. He also proposed a k-nearest-neighbor method for classifying web search results based on the data in folksonomies. Specia et al. [14] presented an approach for making explicit the semantics and hierarchy behind the tag space through mapping folksonomies to existent ontologies. Mika [15] extracted broader/narrower tag relations using set theory and proposed an approach to extend the traditional bipartite model of ontologies with the social annotations. Jaschke et al. [16] defined a new data mining task, the mining of frequent tri-concepts, and presented an efficient algorithm to discover these implicit shared conceptualizations.

6 Conclusion and Future Work

This paper presents a novel idea of how implicit semantics in folksonomies can be used to build concepts. For the reason that basic level concepts are considered as cognitive basic and more acceptable and applicable by users, inspired by cognitive psychology, we try to detect basic level concepts in folksonomies. In addition, we consider the effect of context on concept learning and present a context-aware category utility to consider context in folksonomies. Through doing experiments on real world data set, we demonstrate not only the existence of context effect but also the effectiveness of our method on concept learning. These detected concepts can be used in many areas of artificial intelligence, such as recommendation system and semantic web. As an example, based on different contexts of users, systems can recommend different types of web pages and categorization results to them. How to detect users' contexts automatically and apply our method to design recommendation systems is our future research work. In addition, we will try to improve our algorithm and make it more applicable in different data sets in the future.

Acknowledgements

This work presented in this paper is partially supported by a CUHK Direct Grant for Research, and it has been supported, in part, by a research grant from Hong Kong Research Grants Council (RGC) under grant CityU 117608. Finally, we thank the funding support from the Future Network Centre (FNC) of City University of Hong Kong under CityU Applied R&D Centre (Shenzhen), through the grant number 9681001.

References

1. Al-Khalifa, H., Davis, H.: Exploring the value of folksonomies for creating semantic metadata. International Journal on Semantic Web & Information Systems 3(1), 12–38 (2007)
2. Tanaka, J., Taylor, M.: Object categories and expertise: Is the basic level in the eye of the beholder. Cognitive Psychology 23(3), 457–482 (1991)
3. Cattuto, C., Benz, D., Hotho, A., Stumme, G.: Semantic grounding of tag relatedness in social bookmarking systems. In: Sheth, A.P., Staab, S., Dean, M., Paolucci, M., Maynard, D., Finin, T., Thirunarayan, K. (eds.) ISWC 2008. LNCS, vol. 5318, pp. 615–631. Springer, Heidelberg (2008)
4. Rosch, E., Mervis, C.B., Gray, W.D., Johnson, D.M., Boyes-Braem, P.: Basic objects in natural categories. Cognitive Psychology 8(3), 382–439 (1976)
5. Gluck, M., Corter, J.: Information, uncertainty, and the utility of categories. In: Proceedings of the seventh annual conference of the cognitive science society, pp. 283–287 (1985)
6. Galotti, K.M.: Cognitive Psychology In and Out of the Laboratory, 3rd edn. Wadsworth, Belmont (2004)
7. Roth, E.M., Shoben, E.J.: The effect of context on the structure of categories. Cognitive Psychology 15, 346–378 (1983)
8. Murphy, G.L.: The big book of concepts. MIT Press, Cambridge (2002)
9. Golder, S., Huberman, B.: The structure of collaborative tagging systems. Arxiv preprint cs/0508082 (2005)
10. Manning, C., Raghavan, P., Schtze, H.: Introduction to information retrieval. Cambridge University Press, Cambridge (2008)
11. Fisher, D.: Knowledge acquisition via incremental conceptual clustering. Machine learning 2(2), 139–172 (1987)
12. Ramage, D., Heymann, P., Manning, C.D., Molina, H.G.: Clustering the tagged web. In: WSDM 2009: Proceedings of the Second ACM International Conference on Web Search and Data Mining, pp. 54–63. ACM, New York (2009)
13. Au Yeung, C.M., Gibbins, N., Shadbolt, N.: Tag meaning disambiguation through analysis of tripartite structure of folksonomies. In: Web Intelligence and Intelligent Agent Technology Workshops, 2007 IEEE/WIC/ACM International Conferences, pp. 3–6 (2007)
14. Specia, L., Motta, E.: Integrating folksonomies with the semantic web. In: Franconi, E., Kifer, M., May, W. (eds.) ESWC 2007. LNCS, vol. 4519, p. 624. Springer, Heidelberg (2007)
15. Mika, P.: Ontologies are us: A unified model of social networks and semantics. Web Semantics: Science, Services and Agents on the World Wide Web 5(1), 5–15 (2007)
16. Jäschke, R., Hotho, A., Schmitz, C., Ganter, B., Stumme, G.: Discovering shared conceptualizations in folksonomies. Web Semantics: Science, Services and Agents on the World Wide Web 6(1), 38–53 (2008)

Extracting 5W1H Event Semantic Elements from Chinese Online News*

Wei Wang[1,2], Dongyan Zhao[1,3], Lei Zou[1], Dong Wang[1], and Weiguo Zheng[1]

[1]Institute of Computer Science & Technology, Peking University, Beijing, China
[2]Engineering College of Armed Police of People's Republic of China, Xi'an, China
[3]Key Laboratory of Computational Linguistics (Peking University), Ministry of Education, China
{wangwei,zdy,zoulei,wangdong,zhengweiguo}@icst.pku.edu.cn

Abstract. This paper proposes a verb-driven approach to extract 5W1H (**W**ho, **W**hat, **W**hom, **W**hen, **W**here and **H**ow) event semantic information from Chinese online news. The main contributions of our work are two-fold: First, given the usual structure of a news story, we propose a novel algorithm to extract topic sentences by stressing the importance of news headline; Second, we extract event facts (i.e. 5W1H) from these topic sentences by applying a rule-based method (verb-driven) and a supervised machine-learning method (SVM). This method significantly improves the predicate-argument structure used in Automatic Content Extraction (ACE) Event Extraction (EE) task by considering valency (dominant capacity to noun phrases) of a Chinese verb. Extensive experiments on ACE 2005 datasets confirm its effectiveness and it also shows a very high scalability, since we only consider the topic sentences and surface text features. Based on this method, we build a prototype system named Chinese News Fact Extractor (CNFE). CNFE is evaluated on a real world corpus containing 30,000 newspaper documents. Experiment results show that CNFE can extract event facts efficiently.

Keywords: Relationship Extraction, Event Extraction, Verb-driven.

1 Introduction

To relieve information overload, some techniques have been proposed based on Machine Learning (ML) and Natural Language Processing (NLP), such as classification, summarization, recommendation and Information Extraction (IE). These techniques are also used in online news browsing to reduce the pressure of explosive growth of news articles. However, they fail to provide sufficient semantic information for event understanding since they only focus on the document instead of the event itself. In order to get more semantic information about the event, some event-oriented techniques have been proposed, such as Event-based summarization [1,2,3] , Topic Detection and Tracking (TDT) and

* This work is sponsored by Beijing Municipal Science & Technology Commission project "R & D of 3-dimensional risk warning and integrated prevention technology" and China Postdoctoral Science Foundation (No.20080440260).

L. Chen et al. (Eds.): WAIM 2010, LNCS 6184, pp. 644–655, 2010.

so on. However, these event-oriented techniques consider semantic information in a coarse-grained manner.

In this paper, we discuss how to extract structural semantic information from online news corpus, which is the first step to build a large-scale online news semantic knowledge base. In order to address this issue, we consider an important concept in news information gathering, that is 5W1H. The 5W1H originally states that a news story should be considered as complete if it answers a checklist of six questions, what, why, who, when, where, how. The factual answers to these six are considered to be elaborate enough for people to understand the whole story [4]. Recently, 5W1H concept is also utilized in Event Extraction (EE) and Semantic Role Labeling (SRL). However, due to "heavy" linguistic technologies such as dependency parsers and Named-Entity Recognizers (NERs), it is computationally intractable for EE and SRL over a large news corpora [5]. Even though we can use the grid infrastructure, the computational cost is still too high. Therefore, in this paper, we propose a "light" but effective method to extract 5W1H facts from a large news corpora.

We propose a novel news event semantic extracting method to address 5W1H. This method includes three steps: topic sentences extraction, event classification and 5W elements extraction. First, given the importance of news headline, we identify informative sentences which contain the main event's key semantic information in the news article. Second, we combine a rule-based method (verb-driven) and a supervised machine-learning method (SVM) to extract events from these topic sentences. Finally, we recognize 5Ws with the help of specific event templates as well as event trigger's valency and syntactic-semantic rules. We treat the topic sentences, actually a short summarization of the news as "How" of the event and replace "Why" with "Whom" currently. Thus, we obtain a tuple of 5W <Time, Location, Subject, Predicate, Object> and "How".

Based on the proposed method, we implement CNFE (Chinese News Fact Extractor). We evaluate CNFE on a real world corpus containing more than 30,000 newspaper documents to extract ACE events. Experiment results show that CNFE can extract high-quality event facts (i.e. 5W1H) efficiently.

To summarize, we made the following contributions in this paper:

- We propose using 5W1H concept to formulate an event as "[Who] did [What] to [Whom], [When], [Where] and [How]", as these information are essential for people to understand the whole story.
- To extract 5W1H efficiently, given structural characteristics of news stories, we propose a novel algorithm to identify topic sentences from news stories by stressing the importance of headline.
- We propose a novel method to extract events by combining a rule-based (verb-driven) method and a machine-learning method (SVM). The former considers valency of an event trigger. To the best of our knowledge, we are the first to introduce valency grammar into Chinese EE.
- We perform extensive experiments on ACE2005 datasets and a real news corpus, and also compare CNFE with existing methods. Experiment results confirm both effectiveness and efficiency of our approach.

The rest of the paper is organized as follows. In section 2, we discuss some related works in details. The whole flow of proposed event 5W1H semantic elements extraction approach is discussed in section 3. Sequentially in section 4, we demonstrate the results of our experiments on our methods and the prototype system CNFE. Finally, we draw a conclusion in section 5.

2 Related Works

IE refers to the automatic extraction of structured information such as entities, relationships between entities, and attributes describing entities from unstructured sources. Primitively promoted by MUC in 1987-1997 and then developed by ACE since 2000, studies in IE have shifted from NE recognition to binary and multi-way relation extraction. Many research works focus on triple extraction for knowledge base construction, such as Snowball [6], Knowitall [7], Textrunner [5], Leila [8] and StatSnowball [9]. These works confirm the importance of technologies such as pattern matching, light natural-language parsing and feature-based machine learning for large scale practical systems.

Event extraction is actually a multi-way relationship extraction. In MUC-7 [10], event extraction is defined as a domain-dependent scenario template filling task. An ACE [11] event is an event involving zero or more ACE entities, values and time expressions. The goal of the ACE Event Detection and Recognition (VDR) task is to identify all event instances, information about the attributes, and the event arguments of each instance of a pre-specified set of event types. ACE defines the following terminologies related with VDR:

- Event: a specific occurrence involving participants. An ACE event has six attributes (type, subtype, modality, polarity, genericity and tense), zero or more event arguments, and a cluster of event mentions.
- Event trigger: the word that most clearly expresses an event's occurrence.
- Event argument: an entity, or a temporal expression or a value that has a certain role (e.g., Time-Within, Place) in an event.
- Event mention: a sentence (or a text span extent) that mentions an event, including a distinguished trigger and involving arguments.

Driven by ACE VDR task, Heng Ji proposed a serial of schemes on event coreference resolution [12], cross-document [13,14] and cross-lingual [15] event extraction and tracking, these schemes obtained encouraging results. David Ahn decomposed VDR into a series of machine learning sub-tasks (detection of event anchors, assignment of an array of attributes, identification of arguments and assignment of roles, and determination of event coreference) in [16]. Results show that arguments identification has the greatest impact of about 35-40% on ACE value and trigger identification has a high impact of about 20%. Naughton investigated sentence-level statistical techniques for event classification in [17]. The results indicate that SVM consistently outperform the Language Model (LM) technique. An important discovery is that a manual trigger-based classification approach (using WordNet to manually create a list of terms that are synonyms or hyponyms for each event type) is very powerful and outperforms the SVM on three of six event types. However, these works mainly focus on English articles.

Chinese information extraction research starts relatively late, the main research work focused on the Chinese Named Entity Recognition, as well as the mutual relations between these entities. The latest development of Chinese event extraction in the past two years was reported in [18] and [19]. In [18], Yanyan Zhao et. al. proposed a method combining event trigger expansion and a binary classifier in event type recognition and a one-with-multi classification based on Maximum Entropy (ME) in argument recognition. They evaluated the system on ACE2005 corpus and achieved a better performance in comparison with [16]. However, their work left the problem of polysemy unsolved, i.e. some verbs can trigger several ACE events so that they might cause misclassification.

SRL is another example of multi-way semantic relation extraction. Different from full semantic parsing, SRL only labels semantic roles of constituents that have direct relationship with the predicates (verbs) in a sentence. Typical semantic roles include agent, patient, source, goal, and so on, which are core to a predicate, as well as location, time, manner, cause, and so on, which are peripheral [20]. Such semantic information is important in answering 5W1H of a news event. Surdeanu [21] designed a domain-independent IE paradigm, which filled event template slots with predicate and their arguments identified automatically by a SRL parser. However, semantic parsing is still computationally intractable for larger corpus.

Aiming at building a scalable practical system for Chinese online news browsing, we propose a method combining a verb-driven method and a SVM rectifier to identify news event. We also use trigger's valence information and syntactic-semantic rules to help extracting event facts. We keep our research consistent with ACE event extraction in order to compare with other works.

3 Event 5W1H Elements Extraction

3.1 Preliminary

Before the formal discussion of our method, we first give our observations about online news. After observing more than 6000 Chinese news stories in two famous online news services, xinhuanet.cn and people.com.cn, we find that online news stories have three special characteristics: 1) One news story usually tells one important event; 2) Being an eye-catcher, headline often reveals key event information. Furthermore, it contains at least two essential elements such as "*W*ho" and "*W*hat"; 3) Usually, in the first or second paragraph of the story, there is a topic sentence which expands the headline and tells the details of the key event. According to our statistics, the percentages are 74.6% and 9.8% respectively. A feasibility research in [22] also reveals the importance of headlines and topic sentences. Actually, all the characteristics precisely agree with news articles' writing rules. We base our idea of topic sentences extraction on these observations.

We utilize Chinese valency grammar in our 5W1H extraction method. Valency grammar [23,24] was first proposed by French linguist Lucien Tesniere in 1953 and was led into Chinese grammar by Zhu Dexi in 1978. Modern Chinese valency grammar tries to characterize the mapping between semantic predicate-argument relationships and the surface word and phrase configurations by which they are expressed. In a predication which describes an event or an action caused by a verb, arguments (participants of the event) play different roles. Some common accepted semantic roles are agent, patient, dative, instrument, location, time, range, goal, manner and cause. Among them, agent, patient and dative are obligatory arguments, while others are optional. The number of obligatory arguments is valence of a verb, prompting the dominant capacity of a verb to NPs. Research on the valence grammar has lasted for more than 20 years in China, and many progresses have been made. Although the research scope has been extended from verbs to adjectives and nouns, as a feasibility research, verbs are our only concern in this paper. Two example sentences containing a bivalent and a trivalent verb respectively are given below. They demonstrate that a polyseme may have different valencies for different meanings.

- In sentence "我送小王去火车站。(I walk Xiao Wang to the railway station.)", "walk" is a bivalent verb, "I" is subject (agent), "Xiao Wang" is object (patient) and "to the railway station" is a complement (goal). The sentence complies to "NP1+V+NP2" and "walk" dominates two NPs.
- In sentence "小王送我一本书。(Xiao Wang gives me a book.)", "Xiao Wang" is agent, "me" is dative and "a book" is patient. They are obligatory arguments of verb "give". The sentence is not complete if absence any one of them. So valency of "give" is 3. This kind of sentences comply to the syntactic structure "NP1+V+NP2+NP3" or "NP1+PNP2+V+NP3".

According to [25], most verbs in Chinese are bivalent, there are only about 573 trivalent verbs. In [26], a classification and distribution of 2056 meanings of 1223 common verbs in Chinese Verbs Usage Dictionary is investigated. It shows that there are 236 univalent verbs (11.5%), 1641 bivalent verbs (79.8%) and 179 trivalent verbs (8.7%). In order to extract obligatory arguments of an event, we collect syntactic patterns of verbs with different valencies. We use regular expressions coding these syntactic-semantic rules and match them in a sentence to improve the precision of EE. The syntactic-semantic patterns and rules for distinguishing different types of verbs are shown in Table 1.

Table 1. Classification and syntactic-semantic rules of verbal valency

Verb Type	Examples	Rules	Syntactic Patterns
univalent	来,地震,游泳	$(a \vee b) \wedge (\sim (c \wedge d \wedge e \wedge f))$	a: NP1+V, b: V+NP1,
bivalent	泼,喜欢,挥手	$(c \vee d) \wedge (\sim (e \wedge f))$	c: NPl+V+NP2, d: NP1+PNP2+V,
trivalent	打听,供给,存放	$e \vee f$	e: NP1+V+NP2+NP3, f: NP1+PNP2+V+NP3

3.2 Algorithm Overview

Based on the three assumptions and Chinese valency grammar, we defined the 5W1H elements extraction task as: given a headline of a news article, which often contains at least 2Ws (Who & What), find a topic sentence containing the most important event of the story, and extract other Ws from the topic sentences for specified events. The output is 5W1H: a tuple of <Time, Location, Subject, Predicate, Object> and "How" of the event.

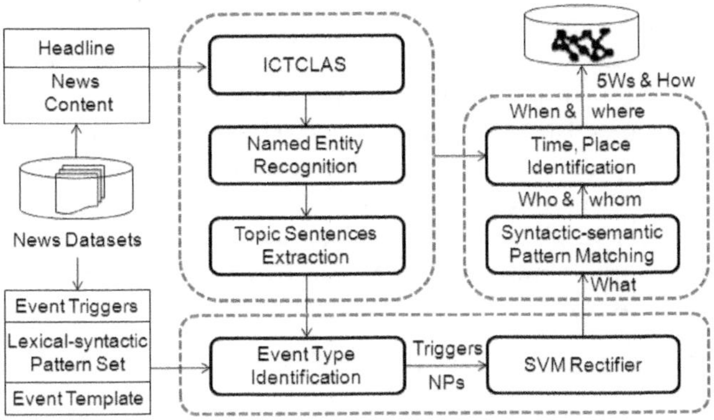

Fig. 1. The framework of event 5W1H semantic elements extraction

Fig. 1 shows the framework of the proposed method. The method consists of three main phases: topic sentence extraction, event type identification and 5W extraction. First, for a given news article, after word segmentation and POS tagging using ICTCLAS[1], we design a novel algorithm to extract topic sentences by stressing the importance of news headlines. Second, we identifies events and their types with the help of a list of trigger words extracted from ACE training corpus and further refines the results using a SVM classifier. In the third phase, we recognize event arguments according to the trigger's valency and its syntactic-semantic rules. At last we output 5W tuples and use the ordered topic sentences as a short summarization to describe "How" of the event.

3.3 Topic Sentences Extraction

Topic sentence identification task is to find an informative sentence which contains key information (5Ws) of a news story. In David Zajic's work of headline generation [22], he directly chose the first sentence as topic sentence based on his observation that a large percentage of headline words are often found in the first sentence. Unfortunately it is not always the case. So we employ extractive automatic text summarization technology to find salient sentences using surface-level features in this work.

According to the linguistic and structural features of a news story, that is, trying to attract readers' eyeballs with a headline or at the beginning of the text, we consider term frequency [27], sentence location in text [28], sentence length [29] and title words overlap rate [30] to select topic sentences. Equation (1) shows the proposed function for sentence importance calculation.

[1] Institute of Computing Technology, Chinese Lexical Analysis System. http://www.ictclas.org/index.html

$$SS_i = \alpha \frac{f(\sum_{w \in S_i} tf(w) \cdot idf(w))}{Length_i} + \beta f(Length_i) + \gamma f(Position_i) + \delta \frac{f(\sum_{w \in S_i} \sum_{w \in T} 1)}{|T| \cdot Length_i} \quad (1)$$

Where α, β, γ, and δ are the parameters (positive integers) for term frequency ($tfidf$), sentence length, sentence location and title's weights, respectively. $f(x)$ is normalization for each parameter. $f(x) = x/(\sum_{S_i \in C} x_i)$

Sentences are ranked by SS_i score. By setting a proper threshold N for the number of selected sentences, we choose the N-Best as the topic sentences and get a sentence set, which is more informative than news headline and shorter than normal summarization. Taking the performance and scalability into account, we believe that it is more simple and effective to deal with a few topic sentences instead of the whole text.

3.4 Event Type Identification

The event type identification module accepts three inputs as shown in Fig. 1: topic sentences with word segmentation and POS tags, a trigger-event-type/subtype table and a set of syntactic-semantic rules of triggers. The list of triggers and their event type/subtype are extracted from ACE05 training dataset. Additionally, event templates of each type/subtype are associated to the triggers. The valency information of each trigger's different meanings and corresponding syntactic-semantic patterns are built based on [25] and [26].

The type identification module searches the topic sentences by examining trigger list and marks each appearance of a trigger as a candidate event. The module also finds chunks using some heuristic rules: 1) Connecting numerals, quantifiers, pronouns, particles with nouns to get max-length NPs; 2) Connecting adjacent characters with same POS tags; 3) Identifying special syntactic patterns in Chinses such as "de(的)", "bei(被)", "ba(把)" structures. After that, the identified trigger, candidate event type/subtype, original sentences with POS tags, NEs and newly identified chunks are input to a SVM rectifier to do fine-grained event type identification. The SVM rectifier is trained on ACE05 Chinese training dataset with deliberately selected features so that it can find out the wrong classification of trigger-based method. By employing lexical and semantic information of a trigger, it can partly solve the polysemy problem and improve the precision of event classification. Features used in the SVM rectifier include:

Trigger's Information: Numbers of a polysemous trigger's meanings, the trigger's frequency on one type of event normalized by its total event frequency, the trigger's total event frequency normalized by its word frequency.

Trigger's NE Context: Presence/absence of two NEs before and behind the trigger with type of Person, Organization and Location.

Trigger's Lexical Context: Presence/absence of POS tags (N, V, A, P and others) of two words before and behind the trigger.

Other Features: Sentence length, the presence/absence of a time-stamp and a location term.

3.5 5W1H Extraction

From the output of event classification, we get headline, topic sentences and a list of 5W candidates of an event, i.e. predicate, event type, NEs, time and location words. Next is to identify semantic elements for the event.

What: Based on our assumptions, we believe that title and topic sentences contain the key event of the news. So we use the event type which is first identified by verb-driven method and then rectified by SVM as "What".

Who, Whom: To identify these two arguments, we analyze the topic sentences in syntactic and semantic planes. In syntactic plane, the NPs and special syntactic structures such as "de(的)", "bei(被)", "ba(把)" are found. In semantic plane, regular expressions are used to match trigger's syntactic-semantic rules. For example, we use an expression "(.*)/n(.*)/trigger(.*?)/n(.*?)/n.*" to match "NP1+V+NP2+NP3". The rules are downward-compatible, i.e., trivalent verbs can satisfy bivalent verb's patterns but not vice versa. So we examine the patterns from trivalent verbs to univalent verbs. We identify obligatory arguments from NEs and NPs of the trigger according to the sentence's syntactic structures. Then we determine their roles (e.g. agent, patient) and associate them with a specific event template.

When, Where: We combine outputs of NER and ICTCLAS to identify time and location arguments. Priority is given to NER. If there is no Time/Location NEs, generated chunks with tags of /nt and /ns are adopted.

How: We use contents of identified <Subject, Predicate, Object> as "How" to describe the process of an event. We first order the triples by examining where they appear in the topic sentences, and then extract the contents between subject and object to describe "Who did What to Whom".

4 Evaluation and Discussion

To evaluate our method, we conduct three experiments. The first experiment is conducted on a self-constructed dataset to evaluate the topic sentence extraction method. The second experiment is conducted on a benchmark dataset to evaluate the effectiveness of our 5W element extraction algorithm. The third experiment is conducted on an open dataset to measure the scalability of CNFE.

4.1 Data Set

DS1 is a self-constructed dataset comprises of 235 Chinese news stories in ACE 2005 training dataset's news wire section and 765 latest news stories collected from xinhuanet.cn. For each story, a topic sentence is labeled manually.

DS2 is the ACE 2005 Chinese training corpus. We extract labeled events from it and there are 2519 sentences in total. These sentences are used to evaluate the verb-driven 5W1H extracter and the SVM rectifier.

DS3 is a whole collection of Beijing Daily's online news in 2009, which contains 30,000 stories. We use this corpus to evaluate the performance of CNFE.

4.2 Evaluation of Topic Sentences Identification

Topic-sentence extraction is the basis of the 5W1H extraction. To identify a topic sentence, as described in equation (1), we consider a sentence's word frequency (*tfidf*), its length, location and word co-occurrence with the headline. To emphasize the weight of title, we fix parameters α, β and γ, and variate parameter δ. We evaluate the precision of topic sentences extraction on DS1 manually. At first we only extract the top scored sentence, but we find some Ws are lost. So we lower the threshold to top three sentences so that more details about the event can be extracted. If the extracted top 3 topic sentences contain the human tagged topic sentence, we mark an extraction as true, otherwise as false.

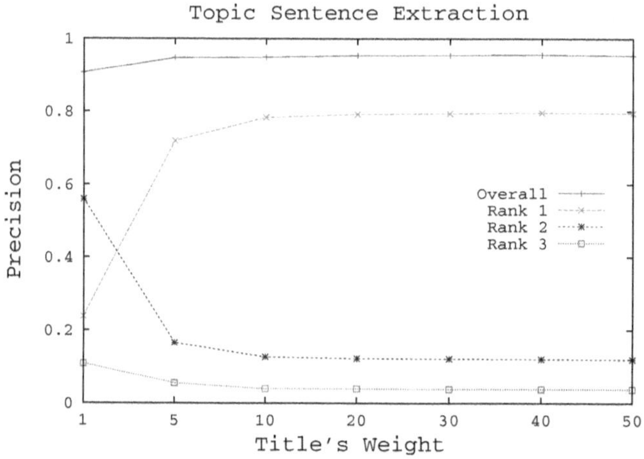

Fig. 2. The precision of topic sentence extraction along with title's weight

Fig. 2 shows the result of topic sentences extraction. With title's weight increases gradually, the precision of topic sentence identification gets a higher value. We choose 40 for parameter δ and achieve a precision of 95.56%. Apparently, the precision of topic sentences extraction on our data set is promising.

4.3 Evaluation of 5W Extraction

In this section, we evaluate our event detection algorithm and the quality of extracted 5W tuples. Our event detection and classification method is verb-driven and enhanced by SVM, as described in 3.4. We extract 621 triggers (verbs) from DS2 and find that only 48 of them are multi-type event triggers. By querying trigger-event-type table, we get candidate event types for each trigger appears in the topic sentences. When a trigger is a polyseme or tagged as a noun, the verb-driven method will not work. Then the SVM classifier, which is implemented on LibSVM[2] and trained on DS2 with deliberately selected features, can make a decision. For evaluation, we use classic F1 score and compare it with [18], which used a similar method. The result is shown in Table 2. For 5W-tuple evaluation, a way

Table 2. Results for event detection and classification

Methods		Recall	Precision	F1
Proposed methods	Verb-driven	74.43%	48.35%	58.62%
	Verb-driven+SVM	68.31%	57.27%	**62.30%**
Yanyan Zhao	trigger expansion+binary classifier	57.14%	64.22%	60.48%

of comparing tuples is needed. To just check whether two tuples are identical would penalize too much those which tuples are almost correct. We extend the idea of triple evaluation defined in [31] to 5W-tuple evaluation, which employs a string similarity measure to compute the similarity between extracted T, L, S, P, O elements and annotated results in DS2. We carefully examined the tuples extracted from "Movement" events (633 event mentions) and "Personnel" events (199 event mentions) from DS2 by hand to find problems of our method. The result is shown in Table 3. We find that the most important factor that affects the correctness of 5W is the complexity of language. Compound sentences and special syntactic structures of Chinese make our extractor error-prone. Wrong segmentation and POS tags, for example, a trigger is segmented into two words and a verb trigger is wrongly tagged as a noun, have a strong impact on the result. The main problems of our method which cause wrong assignment of arguments lie in absence of coreference resolution and wrongly identified NPs.

Table 3. Results of extracted 5Ws on Movement and Personnel events in DS2

ACE Event (number)	Right		Wrong		
	T, L, S, P, O	$T, L, P, (S\|O)$	POS	Structure	Method
Movement(633)	240	161	65	96	71
Personnel(199)	99	25	26	28	21

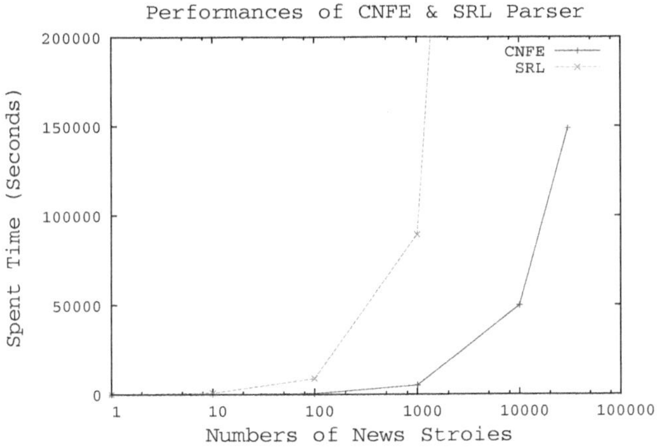

Fig. 3. The performances of CNFE and the SRL baseline system

[2] URL: http://www.csie.ntu.edu.tw/~cjlin/libsvm.

4.4 Evaluation of CNFE

Sine CNFE only use surface text features to extract event facts, it has a better scalability than SRL parser. We implement a baseline system to tag semantic predicate argument structure based on HKUST Chinese Semantic Parser[3]. We run the two systems on DS3 and the performances of them are shown in Fig. 3.

5 Conclusions

In this paper, we propose a novel method to extract 5W1H event semantic information from Chinese online news. We make two main contributions in our work: First, based on a statistic analysis of structural characteristics of 6000 news stories, we propose a novel algorithm to extract topic sentences from news stories by stressing the importance of headline. Second, we propose a method of combining a rule-based method (verb-driven) and a supervised machine-learning method (SVM) to extract 5W1H facts from topic sentences. This method improves predicate-argument structure used in ACE EE task by considering valency of Chinese verbs. Finally, we conduct extensive experiments on a benchmark dataset and an open dataset to confirm the effectiveness of our approach.

Acknowledgments

We would like to thank Sameer Pradhan and Zhaojun WU for offering HKUST Chinese Semantic Parser.

References

1. Filatova, E., Hatzivassiloglou, V.: Event-based Extractive summarization. In: Proceedings of ACL, pp. 104–111 (2004)
2. Li, W., Wu, M., Lu, Q., Xu, W., Yuan, C.: Extractive Summarization using Inter- and Intra- Event Relevance. In: Proceedings of ACL (2006)
3. Liu, M., Li, W., Wu, M., Lu, Q.: Extractive Summarization Based on Event Term Clustering. In: Proceedings of ACL (2007)
4. Carmagnola, F.: The five ws in user model interoperability. In: UbiqUM (2008)
5. Banko, M., Cafarella, M.J., Soderland, S., Broadhead, M., Etzioni, O.: Open Information Extraction from the Web. In: Proceedings of IJCAI, 2670–2676 (2007)
6. Agichtein, E., Gravano, L., Pavel, J., Sokolova, V., Voskoboynik, A.: Snowball: A Prototype System for Extracting Relations from Large Text Collections. In: Proceedings of SIGMOD Conference, pp. 612–612 (2001)
7. Etzioni, O., Cafarella, M.J., Downey, D., Kok, S., Popescu, A., Shaked, T., Soderland, S., Weld, D.S., Yates, A.: Web-scale information extraction in knowitall (preliminary results). In: Proceedings of WWW, pp. 100–110 (2004)
8. Suchanek, F.M., Ifrim, G., Weikum, G.: Combining linguistic and statistical analysis to extract relations from web documents. In: Proceedings of KDD, pp. 712–717 (2006)
9. Zhu, J., Nie, Z., Liu, X., Zhang, B., Wen, J.: StatSnowball: a statistical approach to extracting entity relationships. In: Proceedings of WWW, pp. 101–110 (2009)

[3] http://hlt030.cse.ust.hk/research/c-assert/.

10. Chinchor, N., Marsh, E.: MUC-7 Information Extraction Task Definition (version 5. 1). In: Proceedings of MUC-7 (1998)
11. ACE (Automatic Content Extraction). Chinese Annotation Guidelines for Events. National Institute of Standards and Technology (2005)
12. Chen, Z., Ji, H.: Graph-based Event Coreference Resolution. In: Proceedings of ACL-IJCNLP workshop on TextGraphs-4: Graph-based Methods for Natural Language Processing (2009)
13. Ji, H., Grishman, R.: Refining Event Extraction Through Unsupervised Cross-document Inference. In: Proceedings of ACL (2008)
14. Ji, H., Grishman, R., Chen, Z., Gupta, P.: Cross-document Event Extraction, Ranking and Tracking. In: Proceedings of Recent Advances in Natural Language Processing (2009)
15. Ji, H.: Unsupervised Cross-lingual Predicate Cluster Acquisition to Improve Bilingual Event Extraction. In: Proceedings of HLT-NAACL Workshop on Unsupervised and Minimally Supervised Learning of Lexical Semantics (2009)
16. Ahn, D.: The stages of event extraction. In: Proceedings of the Workshop on Annotations and Reasoning about Time and Events, pp.1–8 (2006)
17. Naughton, M. , Stokes, N., Carthy, J.: Investigating statistical techniques for sentence-level event classification. In: Proceedings of the 22nd International Conference on Computational Linguistics (Coling 2008), pp. 617–624 (2008)
18. Zhao, Y.Y., Qin, B., Che, W.X., Liu, T.: Research on Chinese Event Extraction. Journal of Chinese Information Processing 22(1), 3–8 (2008)
19. Tan, H., Zhao, T., Zheng, J.: Identification of Chinese Event and Their Argument Roles. In: Proceedings of Computer and Information Technology Workshops on IEEE 8th International Conference, pp. 14–19 (2008)
20. Xue, N.: Labeling Chinese Predicates with Semantic Roles. In: Proceedings of Computational Linguistics, pp. 225–255 (2008)
21. Surdeanu, M., Harabagiu, S.M., Williams, J., Aarseth, P.: Using Predicate-Argument Structures for Information Extraction. In: Proceedings of ACL, pp. 8–15 (2003)
22. Dorr, B.J., Zajic, D.M., Schwartz, R.M.: Hedge Trimmer: A Parse-and-Trim Approach to Headline Generation. In: Proceedings of HLT-NAACL, W03-0501 (2003)
23. Tesnière, L.: Esquisse d'une syntaxe structurale. Klincksieck, Paris (1953)
24. Tesnière, L.: Èlṁent de Syntaxe Structurale. Klincksieck, Paris (1959)
25. Feng, X.: Exploration of trivalent verb in modern Chinese (2004)
26. Ningjing, L., Weiguo, Z.: A Study of Verification Principle of Valency of Chinese Verbs and Reclassification of Trivalent Verbs. In: Proceedings of 9th Chinese National Conference on Computational Linguistics (CNCCL 2007), pp. 171–177 (2007)
27. Luhn, H.P.: The Automatic Creation of Literature Abstracts. In: Proceedings of IBM Journal of Research and Development, pp. 159–165 (1958)
28. Edmundson, H.P.: New Methods in Automatic Extracting. Proceedings of J. ACM, 264–285 (1969)
29. Paice, C.D., Jones, P.A.: The Identification of Important Concepts in Highly Structured Technical Papers. In: Proceedings of SIGIR, pp. 69–78 (1993)
30. Paice, C.D.: Constructing literature abstracts by computer: Techniques and prospects. In: Proceedings of Inf. Process. Manage., pp.171–186 (1990)
31. Dali, L., Fortuna, B.: Triplet Extraction From Sentences Using SVM. In: Proceedings of SiKDD (2008)

Automatic Domain Terminology Extraction Using Graph Mutual Reinforcement

Jingjing Kang[1,2], Xiaoyong Du[1,2], Tao Liu[1,2], and He Hu[1,2]

[1] Key Labs of Data Engineering and Knowledge Engineering, Beijing 100872, China
[2] School of Information, Renmin University of China, Beijing 100872, China
{kangjj,duyong,tliu,hehu}@ruc.edu.cn

Abstract. Information Extraction (IE) aims at mining knowledge from unstructured data. Terminology extraction is one of crucial subtasks in IE. In this paper, we propose a novel approach of domain terminology extraction based on ranking, according to linkage of authors, papers and conferences in domain proceedings. Candidate terms are extracted by statistical methods and then ranked by the values of importance derived from mutual reinforcement result in the author-paper-conference graph. Furthermore, we integrate our approach with several classical termhood-based methods including C-value and inverse document frequency. The presented approach does not require any training data, and can be extended to other domains. Experimental results show that our approach outperforms several competitive methods.

Keywords: domain term, terminology extraction, graph mutual reinforcement.

1 Introduction

Domain term [1] refers to a term describing concept which is widely used in domain corpus. Properly managed domain terms can benefit various fields [2], such as automatic thesauri enrichment, ontology construction, keyword extraction, tag suggestion, etc. Though domain terms play a fundamental role in many research areas, it is always hard to obtain them efficiently and precisely.

Traditionally, domain terms are mainly given by domain experts, which is labor-intensive and time-consuming [3]. Experts have sharp eyes and rich knowledge to fulfill the task of the domain dictionary construction, but they may be unfamiliar with some branches of the domain, which results in the low coverage of terminologies in such fields. What's worse, many terminologies recommended according to experts' experience are rarely used by researchers in practice. According to the study on Chinese Classified Thesaurus of the first edition, about 40% of the terms have not been used as keywords or in the title of the corpus. To alleviate the limitation of manual extraction, the importance of ultimate domain term users including the writers and readers should be emphasized. Unfortunately, it is always hard to combine the users' needs with the terminology extraction. One of the solutions to overcome the obstacle is to take the domain corpus into account.

L. Chen et al. (Eds.): WAIM 2010, LNCS 6184, pp. 656–667, 2010.

In this paper, we propose a novel terminology extraction approach integrated with the academic ideas by using the corpus of conference proceedings. In computer science, conference publications are one of the most important criteria to evaluate a researcher's work. Besides the short time to print and the opportunity to describe the work in public [4], conferences are superior in its high innovation and influence. Many technical terms that have a remarkable impact are presented in the conference publications formerly. The proceedings of domain conferences provide a good resource for research on terminology extraction.

We can learn plenty of information from linkage of authors, papers and conferences in domain proceedings. For any paper, the link from an important conference is better than the link from an ordinary one. Similarly, the importance of papers will also interact with the authors. Therefore, we can say that the more important a conference is, the more important the paper it accepts is, and the more important the author is.

Our algorithm takes advantage of graph mutual reinforcement techniques to rank papers, and then use the papers' values of importance to evaluate terms. By applying mutual reinforcement techniques in the graph, important papers will make the importance of the corresponding conferences and authors increase. In turn, conferences will propagate importance to authors and papers, and authors will affect conferences and papers as well. For a paper, the values generated in all the iterations will be summed up as its final value of importance. On the other hand, candidate terms are extracted by statistical methods and then evaluated by the values of importance derived from the paper ranking result. Furthermore, we take into account some termhood-based approaches to enhance the quality of terminologies.

The rest of the paper is organized as follows. Section 2 reviews related study. Section 3 gives an overview about the process of terminology extraction based on graph mutual reinforcement (**GMR-based TE**). Section 4 describes the proposed paper ranking method in domain proceedings in details. After that, we elaborate on the method to evaluate terms in Section 5. Experiment results are discussed in Section 6. Finally, we conclude our work in Section 7.

2 Related Work

To accommodate the explicit demand and implicit requirement of domain terminology acquisition, there is a rise in studies on terminology extraction in recent years. Terminology extraction is defined as the task of extracting domain terminologies from corpus that consists of academic documents. The procedure can be divided into two steps: term selection and term evaluation [8].

(1) Term Selection
In term selection procedure, candidate terms are extracted from corpus. Many automatic term extraction methods have been widely studied in the past few years [9].

Existing approaches can be divided into linguistic techniques and statistical techniques. Linguistic techniques attempt to extract candidate terminologies of certain patterns using linguistic patterns, including part of speech (POS) tagging, lemmatizing, phrase chunking, etc. However, it is hard to collect enough patterns to cover all the terms. Statistical techniques rely on statistical information, such as word frequency, TFIDF, word co-occurrences and n-gram, etc.

(2) Term Evaluation
After the selection step, each extracted term will be assigned with a score calculated by the weighting method and then ranked in the decreasing order of the scores. Finally, the top candidate terms will be recommended.

There are two existing types of feature to evaluate terms: unithood-based techniques and termhood-based ones [10]. Unithood considers the integrity of a term and measures it through the attachment strength of its constituent, while termhood emphasizes the domain-specific feature of a term. Ioannis [9] points out that it is still hard to draw the conclusion that which one performs better.

Most research on domain term extraction takes advantage of machine learning techniques to address the extraction problem. In [11], the author uses graph mutual reinforcement based on bootstrapping to sorts candidate terms and patterns, and learn semantic lexicons from them. A method using Wikipedia as a bilingual corpus for terminology extraction has been recently studied in [3], which has achieved promising results. The approach utilizes the manually labeled training data to train a SVM classifier, which is capable of determining the correctness of unseen term-translation pairs. These studies heavily rely on the quality of annotations on the training data, which can be typically costly to produce when there are huge volumes of data sources.

It is the ranking algorithm that is at the heart of the terminology evaluation. To solve the ranking problem, many link analysis algorithms such as PageRank [5] and HITS [6] have been invented to measure the importance of vertices in the graph. In most of these algorithms, every vertex is treated in the same way. However in our scenario, there are 3 different types of vertices in the graph, i.e. conferences, papers and authors. If we apply the general link analysis algorithms to the conference-paper-author graph, the ranking result will be unreasonable [7], e.g. the larger the number of authors is, the more important the paper will be.

To avoid these potential disadvantages, we propose a novel approach that based on mutual reinforcement on the paper-conference-author graph. Unlike traditional link analysis algorithms, GMR-based TE method treats the author set, the paper set and the conference set separately to produce the score of each vertex. GMR-based TE method does not require a training set, and can be extended to other domains.

3 Overview of Our Approach

Figure 1 shows the procedure of GMR-based TE method. We carry out our approach basically in the two steps, i.e. term selection and term evaluation. In selection step, candidate terms are extracted from corpus by some statistical methods. In the second step, we evaluate the candidate terms by assigning each one with a score, and consider the top ranked candidates as domain terms.

(1)Term Selection
To prepare for the dataset, domain conference papers are crawled from the web. We utilize n-gram model to extract candidate terms, and then use a linguistic filter to restrict them.

(2) Term Evaluation
Since the evaluation algorithm is crucial to terminology extraction, we give much emphasis on this part. We calculate the score of papers based on mutual reinforcement on the conference-paper-author graph. As the candidate term set has been obtained, we calculate the score of each term by combining the ranking scores of papers with some statistical methods. The procedure of graph mutual reinforcement will be discussed in Section 4, and the details of the term evaluation part will be given in Section 5.

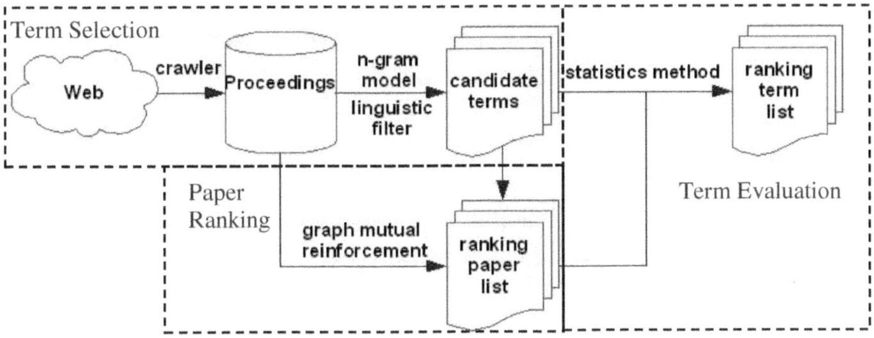

Fig. 1. The block diagram of GMR-based TE method

4 Graph Mutual Reinforcement

In this section, we elaborate on our ranking algorithm based on graph mutual reinforcement. The section starts with the description of the ranking problem in the conference-paper-author graph, followed by the definition of transition probability in the problem, and finished with the process of ranking algorithm.

4.1 Problem Representation

To address the problem of term evaluation, we model the linkage among authors, papers and conferences in the domain proceedings as a tripartite graph:

$$K = (Author,\ Paper,\ Conf;\ E_{AP},\ E_{PC}) \tag{1}$$

where *Author*, *Paper* and *Conf* represent the author set, the paper set and the conference set, respectively. E_{AP} and E_{PC} are edges from *Author* to *Paper* and edges from *Paper* to *Conf*, respectively. Figure 2 is an illustration of the graph.

It's evident that any vertices in the same set are disjoint but may be adjacent to the vertices in the other two sets. For example, an edge that connects a conference and a paper represents that the paper has been accepted by the conference. Similarly, an edge that connects an author and a paper represents the author has written the paper. The tripartite graph can be easily built up from a corpus of conference proceedings.

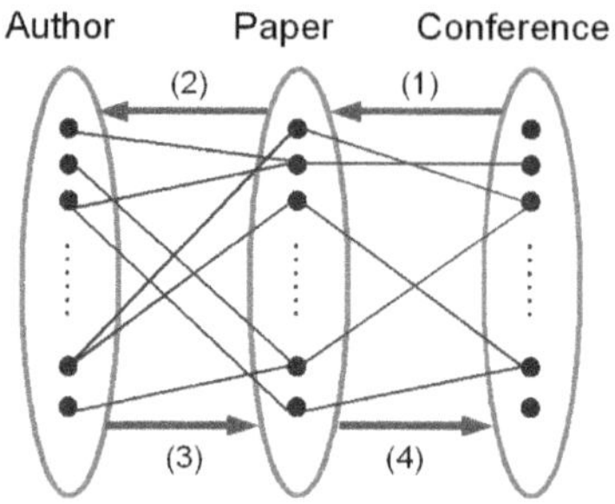

Fig. 2. The tripartite graph K(Author, Paper, Conf; E_{AP}, E_{PC})

4.2 Transition Probability

The one-step transition probability refers to the probability of transitioning from one state to another in a single step [12]. There are 4 types of transition probabilities in our scenario, i.e. transition probabilities from authors to papers, from papers to authors, from conferences to papers and from papers to conferences.

(1) From Authors to Papers
Let T_{AP} denote the transition probability matrix from authors to papers. Suppose T_{AP} is an m×n matrix. The (i, j)th entry of T_{AP}, or $p_{i,j}$ namely, refers to the transition probability from author a_i to paper p_j.

A straightforward implementation of transition probability $p_{i,j}$ is given as: $p_{i,j}=1$ if author a_i has written paper p_j and 0 otherwise. However, it is not suitable in practice because in that case, every author of paper p_j will propagate its score to p_j, which makes the importance of p_j unusually high if p_j has lots of authors.

To overcome the problem, we introduce a normalization step into the calculation. If author a_i and paper p_j share a common edge in the graph, or author a_i has written paper p_j, the transition probability from a_i to p_j is calculated via:

$$p_{i,j} = 1 / \sum_{k=1}^{m} p_{k,j} \tag{2}$$

After normalization, for each column of T_{AP}, the sum of all the probabilities in the column equals to 1. Thus the importance of the papers will be related to the importance of authors, rather than the number of authors.

Figure 3(a) illustrates the relationship between authors and papers. Figure 3(b) represents the transition probability matrix T_{AP} generated by the above method.

(2) From Papers to Authors
Let T_{PA} denote the transition probability matrix from papers to authors. Since T_{AP} is an m×n matrix, T_{PA} should be n×m. Each entry $p_{i,j}$ in T_{PA} is the transition probability from paper p_i to author a_j. Due to the fact that the scores of authors are relevant to quantity of papers, we formalize the transition probability from paper p_i to author a_j by a binary function:

$$p_{i,j} = \begin{cases} 1 & \text{if } p_i \text{ is written by } a_j \\ 0 & \text{else} \end{cases} \quad (3)$$

Figure 3(c) shows the transition probability matrix T_{PA} using this function.

(3) From Conferences to Papers
There is no doubt that the quality of papers has much to do with the ranking of the conference that accepts them. So the transition probabilities from conferences to papers are given just the same as the one in function (3).

(4) From Papers to Conferences
The scale of a conference does not indicate whether or not the conference is important. As a consequence, we handle T_{PC} in the same way as T_{AP} in function (2). The transition probability is normalized so that every column in T_{PC} sums to 1.

4.3 Paper Ranking

We define the value of importance (*VI*) for each vertex as the extent to which the vertex is important. If a paper p_1's *VI* is greater than a paper p_2's, p_1 should be ranked higher than p_2. This is similar to authors and conferences.

Without loss of generality, we propose three assumptions:

Assumption 1. If a conference is important, the papers it accepts are important and the corresponding authors are important.

Assumption 2. If an author is important, the papers that he/she wrote are important and the conferences of these papers are important.

Assumption 3. If a paper is important, the authors who wrote it are important and the conference that accepts it is important.

To assign each paper a *VI*, we apply the mutual reinforcement in the author-paper-conference graph to the ranking problem. In our method, a paper's *VI* is obtained through the iterative process on the tripartite graph. After several iterations, a vertex will propagate its *VI* through the path to another vertex. For instance, in Figure 3(a), although paper p_1 and paper p_3 do not share a common author, *VI* can be propagated from p_1 to p_3 through four steps, i.e. from p_1 to a_1, from a_1 to p_2, from p_2 to a_3 and from a_3 to p_3.

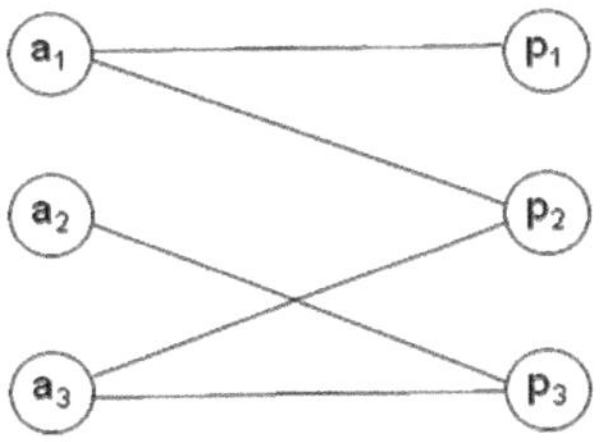

(a)

$$\begin{array}{c} \\ a_1 \\ a_2 \\ a_3 \end{array} \begin{array}{c} \begin{array}{ccc} p_1 & p_2 & p_3 \end{array} \\ \begin{pmatrix} 1 & 0.5 & 0 \\ 0 & 0 & 0.5 \\ 0 & 0.5 & 0.5 \end{pmatrix} \end{array}$$

(b)

$$\begin{array}{c} \\ p_1 \\ p_2 \\ p_3 \end{array} \begin{array}{c} \begin{array}{ccc} a_1 & a_2 & a_3 \end{array} \\ \begin{pmatrix} 1 & 0 & 0 \\ 1 & 0 & 1 \\ 0 & 1 & 1 \end{pmatrix} \end{array}$$

(c)

Fig. 3. (a) Relationships between authors and papers. (b) Transition probability matrix T_{AP}. (c) Transition probability matrix T_{PA}.

Let *Rank(Conf)* denote the domain conference ranking vector. Each entry in *Rank(Conf)* represents a conference's *VI*. To get started, several top conferences in Database area are selected as the seed set $\mathbb{S}$ (in practice, we choose SIGMOD, VLDB and ICDE). At time 0, the *VI* of any conference equals to 0, except for the conferences in the seed set $\mathbb{S}$, which equal 1.

There are 4 steps in each iteration (see Figure 2). At the end of each iteration, the ranking list of papers, authors and conferences will be updated as the *VI* changes.

Step 1: According to *Assumption 1*, important conferences lead to important papers. The scores of conferences will be propagated to their papers with certain transition probabilities at time 1. So we adjust *Rank(Paper)* as:

$$Rank^1(Paper) = Rank^0(Paper) + C \cdot Rank^1(Conf) \cdot T_{CP} \quad (4)$$

where $C \in (0,1)$ is the damping factor which controls the downwards, the contribution from longer path of other vertices.

Step 2: The ranking list of authors will have an effect on the ranking list of papers. This is due to the conclusion drawn in *Assumption 3*: the more important a paper is, the more important its authors will be. So we update *Rank(Author)* as follows:

$$Rank^1(Author) = Rank^0(Author) + C \cdot Rank^0(Paper) \cdot T_{PA} \quad (5)$$

Step 3: As mentioned in *Assumption 2*, a paper's *VI* will also be affected by the author writing it. Authors of higher ranks will have more important papers comparatively.

$$Rank^1(Paper) = Rank^0(Paper) + C \cdot Rank^1(Author) \cdot T_{AP} \quad (6)$$

Step 4: A conference's *VI* will be affected by the papers it accepts, according to *Assumption 3*. Considering the impact that papers propagate to conferences, we update *Rank(Conf)* as follows:

$$Rank^1(Conf) = Rank^0(Conf) + C \cdot Rank^1(Paper) \cdot T_{PC} \quad (7)$$

The impact of each step will be weakened gradually as the time goes. At the end of each iteration, we introduce a normalizing factor that makes all the entries of the ranking vector sum to a constant. After a few iterations, the ranking lists of authors, papers and conferences tend to be convergent.

In summary, we propose the `APCRanking` algorithm to rank papers as follows. The algorithm takes the linkage of authors, papers and conferences as well as the seed set as the input, and produces the ranking values of papers.

```
Algorithm: APCRanking
begin
  Build T_AP, T_PA, T_CP and T_PC as mentioned in 4.2
  Initial Rank^0(Conf) according to seed set S
  repeat
    Rank^n(Paper) ← C·Rank^(n-1)(Conf)·T_CP
    Rank^n(Author) ← C·Rank^(n-1)(Paper)·T_PA
    Rank^n(Paper) ← C·Rank^(n-1)(Author)·T_AP
    Rank^n(Conf) ← C·Rank^(n-1)(Paper)·T_PC
    σ ← |Rank^n(Paper)| - |Rank^(n-1)(Paper)|
    n ← n+1
  until σ<ε
  return Rank^n(Paper)
end
```

Supposing that the number of authors, papers and conferences are m, n and l, respectively, the time complexity of the algorithm is $O(k(nl^2+mn^2+nm^2+ln^2))$ where k is the number of iterations.

5 Term Evaluation

We believe that terminologies that appear in conference papers are important, and terminologies that appear in important papers tend to be more significant than the others. As a consequence, a paper's *VI* can result in an impact on the importance of terminologies appear in them. For example, a terminologies t_1 is more important than t_2 if t_1 appears in more papers and the papers are more important. The impact of t_i from papers can be formulated as:

$$impact(t_i) = \sum_{t_i \in p_j} Rank(p_j) \tag{8}$$

where p_j is the paper that t_i has appeared in it, $Rank(p_j)$ is the entry in *Rank(Paper)*.

Furthermore, we introduce Inverse Document Frequency (IDF) to filter the terms that have low frequencies in the corpus. $IDF(t_i)$ evaluates the importance of term t_i by dividing the number of all papers by the number of papers containing t_i:

$$IDF(t_i) = \log(|D| / df(t_i)) \tag{9}$$

In addition, the scores of terms vary depending on their nestedness as well. Considering the terminology *foreign key*, the *VI* of its substring *key* would be at least as high as *foreign key*, because it will appear where *foreign key* appears. However, *key* is not a terminology in Database domain. Therefore, we need to bias our method towards multi-word terms. One of the most effective approaches that can handle nested term extraction is C-Value [13]. The C-value algorithm is an effective hybrid approach which can extract nested multi-word terms from English corpus by combining linguistic and statistical information together. The C-value of term a is computed as:

$$\text{C-}value(a) = \begin{cases} \log_2 |a| \cdot f(a) & a \text{ is not nested} \\ \log_2 |a| \cdot (f(a) - \dfrac{1}{P(T_a)} \sum_{b \in T_a}^{n} f(b)) & otherwise \end{cases} \tag{10}$$

where a is the candidate string, $f(.)$ is its frequency of occurrence in the corpus, T_a is the set of extracted candidate terms that contain a and $P(T_a)$ is the number of these candidate terms.

In GMR-based TE method, we pre-compute *Rank(Paper)* off-line using the method mentioned in Section 4. Once the task of paper ranking is done, we can evaluate candidates by combining the impact of paper, IDF and C-value together via:

$$value(t_i) = \sum_{t_i \in p_j} Rank(p_j) \cdot IDF(t_i) \cdot C\text{-}value(t_i) \tag{11}$$

6 Experimental Study

6.1 Data Preparation

We conduct the experiments on the domain proceedings corpora, including 39,106 papers from the top-100 conferences in Database domain collected from Libra[1]. Each conference paper contains title, abstract, keywords, conference, authors, etc.

To get possible domain term candidates, we use a trigram word extractor which collects the words appear in the abstracts with length not longer than 3. Terms included in the stop word list are filtered first. Only the terms that have appeared above a given threshold (in practice, we set it 2) can be selected. Finally, we get 19,859 terms as the candidate terms.

6.2 Evaluation of Paper Ranking

As the papers' values of importance will be summed up as part of the importance of terms, the result of paper ranking is pivotal in the term evaluation procedure. Rather than evaluating the paper ranking result directly, we compare the conference ranking results generated in graph mutual reinforcement with several existing methods. This is reasonable because in the process of graph mutual reinforcement, the importance of papers will be propagated to conferences and vice versa. If the conference ranking list is comparable to some known methods, it is obvious that the result of paper ranking is reasonable as well.

We compare our result to other three methods, i.e. EIC [14], NUS [15] and IRank [16]. All of them have the similar ranking results (See Table 1). Furthermore, in GMR-based TE, there is a big gap between the top-3 conferences (SIGMOD, VLDB and ICDE) and others, which is consistent with reality.

Table 1. Comparison of different conference ranking methods

	GMR-based TE		EIC		NUS		IRank
Rank	**Conf**	**Score**	**Conf**	**Score**	**Conf**	**Level**	**Conf**
1	ICDE	1402.95	SIGMOD	0.99	SIGMOD	1	SIGMOD
2	VLDB	1242.21	VLDB	0.99	PODS	1	VLDB
3	SIGMOD	1183.93	ICDE	0.98	VLDB	1	CIKM
4	CIKM	421.44	ICDT	0.97	ICDE	1	ICDE
5	ER(OOER)	419.68	PODS	0.95	ICDT	1	DEXA
6	DEXA	405.73	ER	0.9	DEXA	2	WIDM
7	PODS	387.98	CIKM	0.9	EDBT	2	PODS
8	EDBT	293.49	DEXA	0.88	DASFAA	2	DASFAA
9	DASFAA	275.97	EDBT	0.88	CIKM	2	MobiDE

6.3 Comparison with Other Methods

For comparison, we implemented other two algorithms, i.e. HITS [6] and Session Terms [16]. We use HITS in the bipartite graph of papers and terms. In HITS algorithm,

[1] http://libra.msra.cn

each vertex is assigned an authority value and a hub value. A good paper is a hub that contains many terms, and a good term is an authority that appears in many hub papers. The other method considers a session as several terms conducted in a special form, and splits them properly to get domain terms. We collect session name from DBLP[2], and extract 10,319 domain terms from them using this method. In each method, we rank all the candidates in descending order of assigned scores and select top-N as terminologies.

Not having a complete list of terminologies of database on hand, we cannot evaluate GMR-based TE through a common benchmark. Instead of constructing a domain dictionary from scratch, we propose a new metric which weights each method from the voting of other two. We consider one method is "good" if its top-ranked terms are also in the top-ranked list of other two methods. For instance, if a term t_l is in the top-N list of GMR-based TE and HITS, the scores of both GMR-based TE and HITS will be increased by one. Likewise, if t_l is in the top-N list of all the three methods, each method will get extra two scores. For each method, we calculate its score term by term and then average the score over all terms. The performance of the three methods on top-N candidate terms is demonstrated in Figure 4, where the horizontal axis represents the number of candidates selected as terminologies, and the vertical axis represents the average scores correspondingly. As can be seen, GMR-based TE and HITS agree more on the ranking result, but GMR-based TE achieves higher scores. We only evaluate the terms in the range of top-100 and top-1000, for the reason that the candidates selected as domain terms should not be too many.

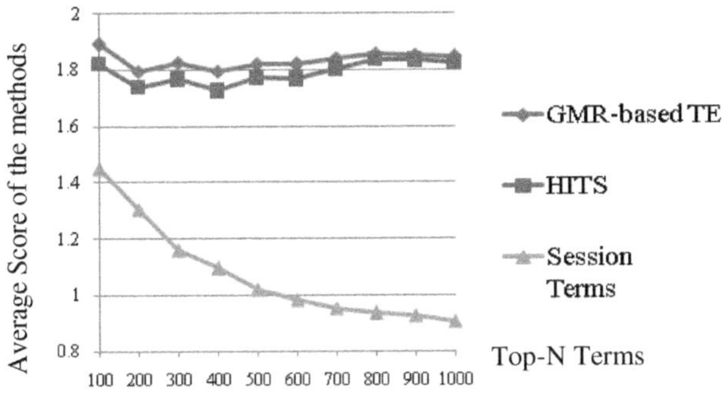

Fig. 4. The average scores of different methods in top-N terminologies

There are three features that affect performance of our approach, i.e. paper impact, IDF and C-value. Words that extracted in the work [15] are taken as the golden standard terms. Figure 5 shows the hitting numbers of GMR-based TE with different features. Proposed method that uses all the three features outperforms the others. Nevertheless, there is no significant improvement by using IDF feature. Thus we need to determine the trade-off between the cost of algorithm and the possible loss of terminologies in practice.

---

[2] http://www.informatik.uni-trier.de/~ley/db/

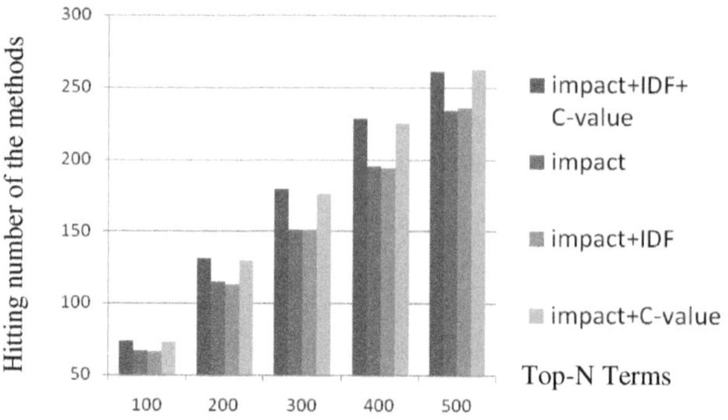

Fig. 5. The top-N terminologies distribution of methods that consist with different features

Table 2 shows the top-20 multi-word terminologies list generated by GMR-based TE method.

Table 2. Top-20 multi-word terminologies

1. Database System	11. Data Warehouse
2. Query Processing	12. Query Optimization
3. Relational Database	13. Business Process
4. Query Language	14. Data Set
5. XML Document	15. Data Management
6. Data Model	16. Data Source
7. Data Mining	17. Concurrency Control
8. Data Stream	18. Distributed Database
9.Experimental Results	19. Data Integration
10. XML Data	20. Data Base

7 Conclusion

Terminology extraction is one of pivotal subtasks in IE. Unlike traditional methods, we introduce a novel approach GMR-based TE, which applies mutual reinforcement in the author-paper-conference graph into the extraction of domain terminologies. Empirical results show that GMR-based TE outperforms several competitive methods, and by using different features, GMR-based TE achieves the best performance.

In conclusion, the contributions of the paper involve:

(1) A method to evaluate papers, authors and conferences in the tripartite graph through the graph mutual reinforcement.

(2) An approach to extract and rank terminologies by combining the impact of papers with several classical methods.

(3) A strategy to compare the results of different methods without having manually labeled golden standard terms.

Acknowledgments

This work was supported by the National Natural Science Foundation of China with Grant No. 60873017 and No. 60773215, and Scientific Research Fund of Renmin University of China with Grant No. 22382074.

References

1. Haiduc, C., Marcus, A.: On the Use of Domain Terms in Source Code. In: 16th IEEE International Conference on Program Comprehension, pp. 113–122. IEEE Press, Amsterdam (2008)
2. Manna, S., Petres, Z., Gedeon, T.: Significant term extraction by Higher Order SVD. In: 7th International Symposium on Applied Machine Intelligence and Informatics, pp. 63–68. IEEE Press, Herl'any (2009)
3. Erdmann, M., Nakayama, K., Hara, T.: Improving the extraction of bilingual terminology from Wikipedia. The ACM Transactions on Multimedia Computing, Communications and Applications 5 (2009)
4. CORPORATE Computer Science and Telecommunications Board: Academic careers for experimental computer scientists and engineers. Communications of the ACM 37, 87–90 (1994)
5. Page, L., Brin, S., Motwani, R., Winograd, T.: The PageRank Citation Ranking: Bringing Order to the Web, `http://ilpubs.stanford.edu:8090/422/`
6. Kleinberg, J.M.: Authoritative sources in a hyperlinked environment. Journal of the ACM (JACM) 46, 604–632 (1999)
7. Nie, Z., Zhang, Y., Wen, J.R., Ma, W.Y.: Object-level ranking: bringing order to Web objects. In: 14th international conference on World Wide Web, Chiba, pp. 567–574 (2005)
8. Nakagawa, H., Mori, T.: Automatic term recognition based on statistics of compound nouns and their components. Terminology, 201–219 (2003)
9. Korkontzelos, I., Klapaftis, I.P., Manandhar, S.: Reviewing and Evaluating Automatic Term Recognition Techniques. In: 6th international conference on Advances in Natural Language Processing, Gothenburg, pp. 248–259 (2008)
10. Kageura, K., Umino, B.: Methods of automatic term recognition: A review. Terminology 3(2), 259–289 (1996)
11. Zhang, Q., Qiu, X., Huang, X., Wu, L.: Learning Semantic Lexicons Using Graph Mutual Reinforcement Based Bootstrapping. Acta Automatica Sinica 34, 1257–1261 (2008)
12. Transition Probabilities, `http://www.utdallas.edu/~jjue/cs6352/markov`
13. Frantzi, K., Ananiadou, S., Mima, H.: Automatic recognition of multi-word terms: the C-value/NC-value method. International Journal on Digital Libraries 3, 115–130 (2000)
14. Computer Science Conference Ranking, `http://www.cs-conference-ranking.org`
15. Computer Science Department Conference Rankings, `http://www.comp.nus.edu.sg/~harishk/mysoc_confs.htm`
16. Li, Z., Du, X., Liu, H., He, J., Zhou, X.: IRank: A Term-based Innovation Ranking System. In: Li, Q., Feng, L., Pei, J., Wang, S.X., Zhou, X., Zhu, Q.-M. (eds.) APWeb/WAIM 2009. LNCS, vol. 5446, pp. 126–137. Springer, Heidelberg (2009)

Semi-supervised Learning from Only Positive and Unlabeled Data Using Entropy

Xiaoling Wang[1], Zhen Xu[2], Chaofeng Sha[2], Martin Ester[3], and Aoying Zhou[1,2]

[1] Software Engineering Institute, East China Normal University, China
[2] Shanghai Key Lab. of Intelligent Information Processing, Fudan University, China
[3] School of Computing Science, Simon Fraser University, Burnaby, Canada
{xlwang,ayzhou}@sei.ecnu.edu.cn
{xuzhen,ayzhou}@fudan.edu.cn

Abstract. The problem of *classification from positive and unlabeled examples* attracts much attention currently. However, when the number of unlabeled negative examples is very small, the effectiveness of former work has been decreased. This paper propose an effective approach to address this problem, and we firstly use entropy to selects the likely positive and negative examples to build a complete training set; and then logistic regression classifier is applied on this new training set for classification. A series of experiments are conducted. The experimental results illustrate that the proposed approach outperforms previous work in the literature.

1 Introduction

The traditional classification task is to construct a classification function $y = \varphi(x)$, which maps any instance $x \in X$(instance space) to one known class label $y \in \{c_1, \cdots, c_n\}$(class label set), based on the labeled training set. This kind of classification method is the *supervised learning*, and it often requires a great deal of labeled instances for training; however, in many real applications, it is impossible to provide enough training examples. As a result, *semi-supervised learning*, i.e. *learning from labeled and unlabeled examples*, is studied, where only a few labeled examples together with large number of available unlabeled ones are given. Different from *learning from positive and negative examples*, another special kind of the problem, namely, *learning from* ***positive*** *and* ***unlabeled*** *examples*, gains more and more attention. It deals with such a case that no labeled negative examples exist in the training set, that is to say, only a few labeled positive examples and lots of unlabeled examples are available, without any information about negative class.

Take email classification for an example. Assuming that there exist 2 different classes of mails: news and entertainment. We can build a classifier according to the content of mails. By this classifier, the incoming mail about the news and entertainment can be classified easily and correctly. However, if the new incoming mail is about job description, it is not belonging to any defined classes. As a result, assigning it to any one of the 2 classes, it is obviously unsuitable.

L. Chen et al. (Eds.): WAIM 2010, LNCS 6184, pp. 668–679, 2010.

Instead, it should be assigned to the negative class, different from the given two positive classes.

This paper addresses the problem of *learning from positive and unlabeled examples*, where the input are multiple(at least 2) labeled positive training classes and unlabeled data. We design an entropy based method to obtain some information of unlabeled examples. For this kind of problem, several related approaches are proposed in recent years. There are mainly two different kinds as follows:

- Completely discarding the unlabeled examples. E.g., one-class SVM[1] constructs a size-suitable area, approximately covering all labeled positive examples, beyond which are negative examples. However, the trained classifier only learns from the labeled positive examples but knows nothing about the negative examples, which easily makes over-fitting.
- Another kind of approaches, e.g., PEBL[2] and Roc-Clu-SVM[3], consider how to find the most likely negative examples, add them to the training dataset, and then apply a classical classification method; LGN[4] is to generate negative examples.

Different from former work, this paper proposes a entropy-based method - **SLE** (**S**emi-supervised **L**earning from only positive and unlabeled data using **E**ntropy). The contribution of this paper is as follows:

1. We study the problem of classifying unlabeled data using positive training set and present an semi-supervised learning method to solve this problem.
2. In order to discover the hidden information in the unlabeled examples, **Entropy** is adopted to find out the most likely positive or negative examples to build a new training set which contains information of unlabeled examples.
3. After constructing the new training set by **Entropy**, a logistic regression classifier is directly used for the classification task. Other traditional classifiers, such as SVM, can also be used for the rest classification task based on new training set.
4. A series of experiments are conducted. We test the effectiveness on two different benchmarks, using F-score as measure. Experimental results verify that our method outperforms previous work.

This paper is organized as follows: Section 2 presents existing related research works; Section 3 introduces the proposed **SLE** approach; Finally, The experimental results are in Section 4, followed by the conclusion in Section 5.

2 Related Work

There are four kinds of approaches for this problem.

1. One simple approach is to completely ignore the unlabeled examples, namely, learning only from the labeled positive examples. E.g., one-class SVM[1] is to construct a suitable area, approximately covering all labeled positive examples. Beyond this region, all examples are viewed as negative. Obviously, it

probably discards very useful information hidden in the unlabeled set, which may make much more contribution to classify or discriminate. Therefore, it easily makes over-fitting.

2. With the unlabeled examples, co-training based on labeled positive ones is one other kind of popular current approach. It usually uses two-phases strategy: (i) extracting likely negative examples from the unlabeled set; (ii) simply using traditional learning methods for the rest classification task. For example, PEBL[2] firstly utilizes 1-DNF[5] to find out quite likely negative examples and secondly employs SVM[6] iteratively for classification. Roc-Clu-SVM[3] uses clustering technique for extraction of likely negative examples in the first step, and sequently SVM[6] is applied for the rest classification task.
3. Quite different from the above ones, B-Pr[7] and W-SVM[8] belong to the probabilistic approaches. Without needing to extract likely negative examples, they transform the original problem $p(y|x)_{y\in\{+,-\}}$ into a simple sample model $p(t|x)_{t\in\{P,U\}}$, where P is the training set and U is the unlabeled data set. But there are several parameters having to be estimated, which directly affect the final performance. Additionally, they can't cope with the extreme case of imbalance existing in the unlabeled set.
4. LGN[4] is based on the assumption that the identical distribution of words belonging to the positive class both in labeled positive examples and unlabeled ones, it generates an artificial negative document for learning. However, in practice, it is very hard or impossible to satisfy this assumption.

Different from the above approaches, we use the entropy's property to reveal the hidden information in the positive instances, and then to find the likely positive and negative instances.

3 The Proposed Approach: SLE

This section introduces the proposed **SLE**(**S**emi-supervised **L**earning method using **E**ntropy) classification method to solve the problem where the training data only contain positive and unlabeled examples. Preliminaries are given in Section 3.1.

3.1 Preliminaries

Feature Extraction. Each document object is modeled as a feature vector with hundreds or thousands of term dimensions. TF-IDF are borrowed from IR to measure the weigh of each term.

$$\text{TF-IDF}_{(t,c_i)} = \frac{\sum_{d\in c_i} n_t}{\sum_{d\in c_i}\sum_{w\in d} n_w} \times \lg \frac{|D|}{|D_t|}$$

where t and w are word features; c_i is the i-th class in training set; n_t and n_w are feature frequency, i.e., times of word t and w occurring in object d respectively; $|D|$ is the number of all objects; $|D_t|$ is the number of objects containing word t.

Over-Sampling. Re-sampling is a commonly used technique in traditional classification method in order to handle the imbalanced examples in different classes. There are two methods: under-sampling and over-sampling. Generally, through under-sampling, the size of major classes decreases to the scale of minor ones; Oppositely, over-sampling makes the number of minor classes' examples approximate to the number of major ones.

Based on the assumption that more examples implies more information, more contribution to classify. Over-sampling are adopted, and original set S and over-sampled set S^o must meet the following relationship: $S^o \supseteq S$.

Entropy $H(x)$. The entropy [9] of the probability distribution $P(x)$ on the set $\{x_1, \cdots, x_n\}$ is defined as:

$$H(x) = -\sum_{i=1}^{n} p(x_i) \lg p(x_i)$$

In this paper, we calculate the entropy of posterior probabilities of every instance d_i in the unlabeled set, and then the revised formula of entropy is defined as follows:

$$H(d_i) = -\sum_{j=1}^{|C|} p(c_j|d_i) \lg p(c_j|d_i)$$

where $p(c_j|d_i)$ is the class posterior probability of instance d_i belonging to the j-th class c_j; $|C|$ is the number of known or predefined class labels appearing in the training set.

For the unlabeled set(labeled as U), the entropy of every instance are calculated, and the instances

$$d_i = \arg\min_{d_i \in \{d_t | \arg\max_{c_k \in C}(p(c_k|d_t))\}} (H(d_i))$$

and

$$d_j = \arg\max_{d_j \in U} (H(d_j))$$

are obtained as the most likely corresponding sub-positive(c_k) and negative examples respectively.

3.2 Problem Description

Given that a training set(P) only containing positive examples, from multiple (at least 2) classes, without negative ones, and one unlabeled set(U) containing both positive and negative examples, our task is to construct a classifier(C), finding all likely negative examples(U_n) hidden in the unlabeled set and it is formulated as follows: input(P, U) $\overset{C}{\Rightarrow}$ *output(U_n).*

3.3 SLE Approach

The detailed algorithm are shown in Algorithm 1, 2 and 3.

Algorithm 1: Find-Positive

Input: training set P, unlabeled set U
Output: positive instances set S_p
$C=\{c_1, \cdots, c_n\}$ are all positive class labels in P;
$S_p = \emptyset$;
for each set B_k,$1 \leq k \leq n$ **do**
    $B_k = \emptyset$;
endfor
for each instance $d_i \in U$ **do**
    $H(d_i) = -\sum_{j=1}^{|C|} p(c_j|d_i) \lg p(c_j|d_i)$;
    $k = \arg\max_{c_k \in C}(p(c_k|d_i))$;
    $B_k = B_k \cup \{d_i\}$;
endfor
$topk = \lambda \times \min_{c_k \in C} |B_k|$;
for each set B_k,$1 \leq k \leq n$ **do**
    while $B_k.size() > topk$ **do**
        $d_i = \arg\max_{d_i \in B_k}(H(d_i))$;
        $B_k.remove(d_i)$;
    endwhile
endfor
for each set B_k,$1 \leq k \leq n$ **do**
    $S_p = S_p \cup B_k$;
endfor
return S_p;

Fig. 1. Finding likely positive examples

- In Algorithm **1**, the original training set(P) is used to learn a classifier(FP) for classifying the unlabeled set(U), and then find all likely positive classes examples(S_p) for further learning, and formulate it as: $input(P, U) \overset{\mathbf{FP}}{\Rightarrow} output(S_p)$, where P and U is the input, S_p is the output.
- In Algorithm **2**, the new training set($P + S_p$) are used to learn a new classifier(FN) for classifying the new unlabeled set($U - S_p$), and then find likely negative examples(S_n) as training data: $input(P + S_p, U - S_p) \overset{\mathbf{FN}}{\Rightarrow} output(S_n)$, where $P + S_p$ and $U - S_p$ is the input, S_n is the output.
- In Algorithm **3**, $P + S_p$ is the positive class and S_n is the negative class for learning, i.e. there exist only two classes(positive and negative) in the training set. Then this new training set is used to learn a logistic classifier(SLE), and to classify the new unlabeled set to find out all negative examples(U_n): $input(\{P + S_p + S_n\}, \{U - S_p - S_n\}) \overset{\mathbf{SLE}}{\Rightarrow} output(U_n)$, where $\{P + S_p + S_n\}$ and $\{U - S_p - S_n\}$ are the input, U_n is the output.

Algorithm 2: Find-Negative

Input: training set P, unlabeled set U
Output: negative instances set S_n
C=$\{c_1, \cdots, c_n\}$ are all positive class labels in P;
$S_n = \emptyset$;
for each set B_k,$1 \leq k \leq n$ **do**
  $B_k = \emptyset$;
endfor
for each instance $d_i \in U$ **do**
  $H(d_i) = -\sum_{j=1}^{|C|} p(c_j|d_i) \lg p(c_j|d_i)$;
  if $S_n.size() < \mu$ **then**
    $S_n = S_n \cup \{d_i\}$;
  else if $H(d_i) > \min_{d_k \in S_n}(H(d_k))$ **then**
      $S_n.remove(d_k)$;
      $S_n = S_n \cup \{d_i\}$;
    endif
  endif
endfor
return S_n;

Fig. 2. Finding likely negative examples

In the above algorithms, we adopt the logistic regression classifier [8,10]. Obviously, other traditional classifiers can also been used in the presented method. In the experiments, we use three standard classifiers published in weka[1], including SVM[11], RLG[12] and LMT[13,14], as the classifiers in the ***Algorithm 3*** of SLE approach.

4 Experimental Evaluation

In this section, we evaluate the performance of our approach. The experiments are conducted on Intel 2.6 GHZ PC with 2 GB of RAM.

The objective of experiments are listed here:

- Firstly, we study the performance of SLE over different data sets including text and nominal data.
- Secondly, we test the robustness of the proposed method for the different number of negative examples, i.e. when the ratio of negative examples varies in the unlabeled data set.
- Thirdly, we verify the importance of *Entropy* to deal with the extremely imbalanced unlabeled set by evaluating Algorithm **1**.

[1] http://www.cs.waikato.ac.nz/ml/weka

```
Algorithm 3: SLE
    Input: training set P, unlabeled set U
    Output: negative instances set U_n
    C={c_1, ··· , c_n} are all positive class labels in P;
    U_n = ∅;
    S_p = Find-Positive(P, U);
    P = P ∪ S_p;
    U = U - S_p;
    S_n = Find-Negative(P, U);
    P = P ∪ S_n;
    U = U - S_n;
    Merge all positive classes into one big positive
    class, i.e, training set has only two classes: one pos-
    itive class("+") and one negative class("-");
    if P is unbalanced then
       over-sample P for making it balanced;
    endif
    for each instance d_i ∈ U do
          if p(-|d_i) > p(+|d_i) then
             U_n = U_n ∪ {d_i};
          endif
    endfor
    return U_n;
```

Fig. 3. SLE classification algorithm

Two representative real benchmarks are used. The two benchmark information is listed in Table 1.

- The first benchmark is 20 Newsgroups[2], where the data covers many different domains, such as **computer**, **science** and **politics**.
- The second benchmark is UCI repository[3]. In this paper, we use the **letter** data set, which identifies each black-and-white rectangular pixel display one of the 26 capital letters in the English alphabet. This benchmark is to test the SLE method for nominal data, not text data type.

We implement the proposed SLE method in Section 3 and three former approaches: LGN[4], NB-E[15] and one class-SVM[1]. As discussed in Section 3.3, SLE consists of **L-SVM**, **L-RLG** and **L-LMT** respectively.

1. L-SVM adopts the standard SVM[11] as a classifier in the Algorithm 3 of SLE method.
2. L-RLG uses a logistic regression classifier RLG[12] in the Algorithm 3, which uses ridge estimators[16] to improve the parameter estimates and to diminish the error of future prediction.

[2] http://people.csail.mit.edu/jrennie/20Newsgroups
[3] http://archive.ics.uci.edu/ml/datasets.html

Table 1. The characters of two benchmark

Benchmark	dataSource	#inst.	#attr.	#class	type
1	20Newsgroups	20,000	>100	20	text
2	UCI Letter	20,000	16	26	not-text

3. L-LMT applies LMT[13,14] as the basic classifier in the Algorithm 3 of SLE method, which combines tree induction methods and logistic regression models for classification.

4.1 Experimental Setting

For two data collections, we define the classification tasks as follows.

- ***Benchmark 1.*** 20 Newsgroups has approximately 20000 documents, divided into 20 different small subgroups respectively, each of which corresponds to a different topic. We firstly choose four subgroups from **computer** topic and two topics from **science** respectively, i.e. {comp.graphics, comp.ibm.hardware, comp.mac.hardware, comp.windows.x}×{sci.crypt, sci.space}, totally $C_4^1 C_2^1 = 8$ pairs of different experiments.

  2-classes problem: For each pair of classes, i.e. selecting one class from {graphics, ibm.hardware, mac.hardware, windows.x}×{crypt, space} respectively as two positive classes, e.g. **graphics×crypt**, a equal part of documents are chosen randomly for training as corresponding positive instances, and the rest as unlabeled positive data in unlabeled set; Then some examples are extracted randomly from the rest 18 subgroups are viewed as unlabeled negative examples in unlabeled set, and the number is $\alpha \times |U|$, where α is a proportion parameter, showing the percentage of negative examples in the unlabeled set, and $|U|$ is the number of all instances in the unlabeled set.

  3-classes problem: Similar to the above 2-classes experiment, except that the third positive class is randomly chosen from the rest 18 classes.

- ***Benchmark 2.*** UCI Letter data is used in the experiment, which contains approximately 20000 instances, divided into 26 different groups, i.e. from **a** to **z**. For simplicity, we divide them into two parts $\{\mathbf{A}, \mathbf{B}, \mathbf{C}, \mathbf{D}\} \times \{\mathbf{O}, \mathbf{P}, \mathbf{Q}\}$, totally $C_4^1 C_3^1 = 12$ pairs.

  2-classes problem: Any pair firstly select one class from $\{\mathbf{A}, \mathbf{B}, \mathbf{C}, \mathbf{D}\} \times \{\mathbf{O}, \mathbf{P}, \mathbf{Q}\}$ respectively as two positive classes, e.g. $\mathbf{A} \times \mathbf{O}$, and the rest settings are the same to the above experiments.

  3-classes problem: It is similar to the above experiments.

4.2 Experimental Result

The experiment randomly runs six times to get the average F-score value as the final result. In the experiments, α is the ratio of the unlabeled negative

Table 2. Performance of 2-classes problem over Benchmark1 ($\alpha = 0.05$)

20newsgroup	**1-SVM**	**LGN**	**NB-E**	**L-SVM**	**L-RLG**	**L-LMT**
graphics - crypt	0.041	0.321	0.55	0.768	0.591	0.73
graphics - space	0.033	0.324	0.464	0.807	0.592	0.835
ibm.hardware - crypt	0.034	0.4	0.421	0.651	0.674	0.715
ibm.hardware - space	0.04	0.366	0.562	0.835	0.723	0.882
mac.hardware - crypt	0.041	0.444	0.557	0.816	0.866	0.856
mac.hardware - space	0.048	0.374	0.604	0.784	0.657	0.83
windows.x - crypt	0.025	0.365	0.422	0.703	0.7	0.788
windows.x - space	0.025	0.264	0.592	0.735	0.531	0.694
average	**0.03**	**0.35**	**0.52**	**0.76**	**0.66**	**0.79**

examples compared to the unlabeled set. E.g. $\alpha = 0.05$ means that the number of the unlabeled negative examples is only 5% of the unlabeled set.

Performance for the 2-classes problem
Table 2 records the F-score values computed by 1-SVM, LGN, NB-E, L-SVM, L-RLG and L-LMT on the benchmark1, i.e., 20Newsgroups dataset. As shown in Table 2, for each row, L-SVM, L-RLG and L-LMT are better than other classifier methods; Meanwhile, NB-E outperforms LGN, but both NB-E and LGN are better than 1-SVM.

From the experimental results, we can see that: (1)When the precondition that the identical distribution of positive words in the training set and unlabeled set is not met, LGN does not perform well; (2)When the number and purity of training examples is not big or high, 1-SVM has unsatisfactory performances, even worse; (3) For both text data and nominal data, L-SVM, L-RLG and L-LMT have much better performance than others approaches.

In Fig.4(C), there are not any positive and negative words existing in UCI letter, completely violating the assumption of LGN, therefor its F-score values are nearly zero. Compared to document data, UCI letter has only 16 attributes, hence the performances of all classifiers are relatively trivially poor, especially 1-SVM, L-SVM and LGN.

Performance for the 3-classes problem
Table 3 records the F-score values of different classification approaches over 3-classes UCI letter data. As shown in Table 3, L-RLG and L-LMT are better than other classifier methods; Meanwhile, F-score values of LGN are zero, but 1-SVM better than NB-E.

The experimental results of 3-classes problem are shown in Fig.4(B) and **(D)**. In the 3-classes experiment, every classifier still remains consistent performance with in the 2-classes experiments.

Effect for dealing with unbalanced data. Algorithm 1 finds the likely positive examples firstly. This is very helpful, especially when the number of unlabeled negative examples is very small in the unlabeled data set, i.e., α is small.

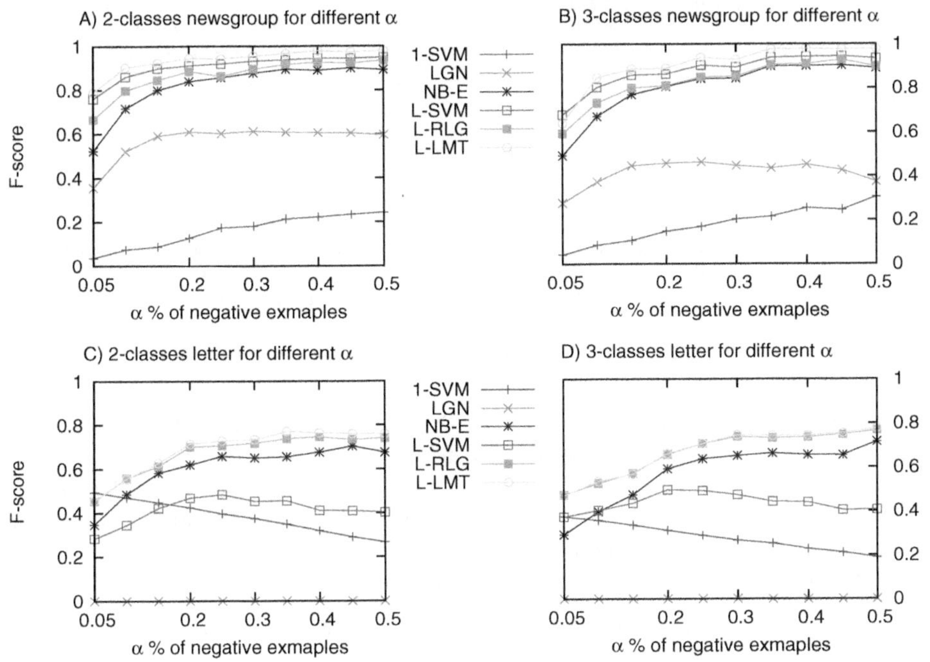

Fig. 4. F-score values for different α

Table 3. Performance of 3-classes problem over Benchmark2($\alpha = 0.05$)

uci-letter	1-SVM	LGN	NB-E	L-SVM	L-RLG	L-LMT
A - O	0.316	0	0.239	0.346	0.392	0.395
A - P	0.449	0	0.343	0.336	0.528	0.548
A - Q	0.38	0	0.248	0.427	0.547	0.54
B - O	0.294	0	0.386	0.413	0.568	0.56
B - P	0.462	0	0.426	0.493	0.549	0.537
B - Q	0.376	0	0.26	0.383	0.52	0.491
C - O	0.305	0	0.328	0.305	0.505	0.481
C - P	0.427	0	0.241	0.417	0.453	0.43
C - Q	0.37	0	0.266	0.358	0.353	0.353
D - O	0.289	0	0.27	0.367	0.455	0.445
D - P	0.44	0	0.259	0.328	0.395	0.419
D - Q	0.387	0	0.257	0.313	0.42	0.453
average	**0.37**	**0**	**0.29**	**0.37**	**0.47**	**0.47**

The reason is Algorithm 1 improves the probability of find the negative examples in the next step. We verify this point in this section.

Fig.5(A) records the results of using Algorithm 1 or not using it. The goal of Algorithm 1 is to find likely positive examples. When $\alpha \leq 0.3$, i.e., the number

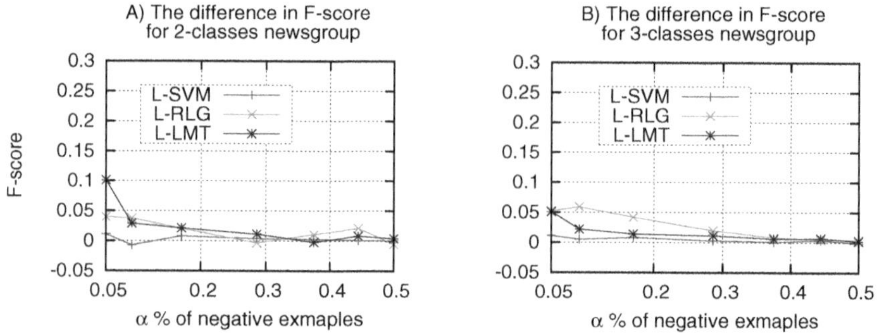

Fig. 5. Effect of Algorithm 1 with unbalanced data

of the unlabeled negative examples is 30% of the unlabeled set, the difference value is bigger than zero, namely, Algorithm 1 improves the final performance, especially for L-LMT and L-RLG. This results verify that Algorithm 1 is helpful to deal with unbalanced unlabeled set. Fig.5(B) shows the similar results in 3-classes document experiments.

From the above experiments, we can draw the following conclusion.

(1) The distribution of positive terms in the training set is often not identical to the distribution in the unlabeled set, obviously it does not meet the assumption of LGN, which is the main reason of lower F-score of LGN classification approach;

(2) NB-E approach classifies the unlabeled set base on entropy maximization, which requires a large number of unlabeled negative examples, therefor, when α grows up, the performance approximates L-RLG.

(3) Compared to other existing methods, the gain degree of SLE is much larger for 20 newsgroups than for letter data. There exists one main cause: for letter data, the number of attributes is only 16, but 20 newsgroups data has hundreds of attribute words, which verify that much more information will give more contribution to the classification results.

In summary, the proposed classification approach SLE outperforms other approaches, including LGN, NB-E and 1-SVM. By adopting Entropy, over-sampling and logistic regression, it almost has no influence on the final classification performance, when the number of positive classes in training set varies.

5 Conclusion

In this paper, we tackle the problem of learning from positive and unlabeled examples and present a novel approach called **SLE**. Different from former work, it firstly finds out likely positive examples and secondly negative ones hidden in unlabeled set, followed by a traditional classifier for the rest task. By a series of experiments, we verify that the proposed approach outperforms former work in the literature. In the further work, we will further study the parameter learning problem and some optimization strategies to improve SLE approach.

Acknowledgments. This work is supported by NSFC grants (No. 60773075 and No. 60925008), National Hi-Tech 863 program under grant 2009AA01Z149, 973 program (No. 2010CB328106), Shanghai International Cooperation Fund Project (Project No.09530708400) and Shanghai Leading Academic Discipline Project (No. B412).

References

1. Manevitz, L.M., Yousef, M., Cristianini, N., Shawe-taylor, J., Williamson, B.: One-class svms for document classification. Journal of Machine Learning Research 2, 139–154 (2001)
2. Yu, H., Han, J., Chang, K.C.C.: Pebl: Positive example based learning for web page classification using svm. In: KDD (2002)
3. Li, X., Liu, B.: Learning to classify texts using positive and unlabeled data. In: IJCAI (2003)
4. Li, X., Liu, B., Ng, S.K.: Learning to identify unexpected instances in the test set. In: IJCAI (2007)
5. Denis, F.: PAC learning from positive statistical queries. In: Richter, M.M., Smith, C.H., Wiehagen, R., Zeugmann, T. (eds.) ALT 1998. LNCS (LNAI), vol. 1501, pp. 112–126. Springer, Heidelberg (1998)
6. Cortes, C., Vapnik, V.: Support vector networks. Machine Learning 20, 273–297 (1995)
7. Zhang, D., Lee, W.S.: A simple probabilistic approach to learning from positive and unlabeled examples. In: UKCI (2005)
8. Elkan, C., Noto, K.: Learing classifiers from only positive and unlabeled data. In: KDD (2008)
9. Cover, T., Thomas, J.: Elements of Information Theory. Wiley Interscience, Hoboken (1991)
10. Guo, Y., Greiner, R.: Optimistic active learning using mutual information. In: IJCAI (2007)
11. Chang, C.C., Lin, C.J.: Libsvm: a library for support vector machines (2001), `http://www.csie.ntu.edu.tw/~cjlin/libsvm`
12. Le Cessie, S., Van Houwelingen, J.C.: Ridge estimators in logistic regression. Applied Statistics 41, 191–201 (1997)
13. Sumner, M., Frank, E., Hall, M.: Speeding up logistic model tree induction. In: Jorge, A.M., Torgo, L., Brazdil, P.B., Camacho, R., Gama, J. (eds.) PKDD 2005. LNCS (LNAI), vol. 3721, pp. 675–683. Springer, Heidelberg (2005)
14. Landwehr, N., Hall, M., Frank, E.: Logistic model trees. In: Lavrač, N., Gamberger, D., Todorovski, L., Blockeel, H. (eds.) ECML 2003. LNCS (LNAI), vol. 2837, pp. 241–252. Springer, Heidelberg (2003)
15. Sha, C., Xu, Z., Wang, X., Zhou, A.: Directly identify unexpected instances in the test set by entropy maximization. In: APWEB-WAIM (2009)
16. Duffy, D.E., Samtmer, T.J.: On the small sample properties of norm-restricted maximum likelihood estimators for logistic regression models. In: Communs Statist. Theory Meth. (1989)

Margin Based Sample Weighting for Stable Feature Selection

Yue Han and Lei Yu

State University of New York at Binghamton
Binghamton, NY 13902, USA
{yhan1,lyu}@binghamton.edu

Abstract. Stability of feature selection is an important issue in knowledge discovery from high-dimensional data. A key factor affecting the stability of a feature selection algorithm is the sample size of training set. To alleviate the problem of small sample size in high-dimensional data, we propose a novel framework of margin based sample weighting which extensively explores the available samples. Specifically, it exploits the discrepancy among local profiles of feature importance at various samples and weights a sample according to the outlying degree of its local profile of feature importance. We also develop an efficient algorithm under the framework. Experiments on a set of public microarray datasets demonstrate that the proposed algorithm is effective at improving the stability of state-of-the-art feature selection algorithms, while maintaining comparable classification accuracy on selected features.

1 Introduction

Various feature selection algorithms have been developed in the past with a focus on improving classification accuracy while reducing dimensionality. A relatively neglected issue is the *stability of feature selection* - the insensitivity of the result of a feature selection algorithm to variations in the training set. The stability issue is particularly critical for applications where feature selection is used as a knowledge discovery tool for identifying characteristic markers to explain the observed phenomena [13]. For example, in microarray analysis, biologists are interested in finding a small number of features (genes or proteins) that explain the mechanisms driving different behaviors of microarray samples. Currently, a feature selection algorithm often selects largely different subsets of features under variations to the training data, although most of these subsets are as good as each other in terms of classification performance [9, 20]. Such instability dampens the confidence of domain experts in experimentally validating the selected features.

A key factor affecting the stability of a feature selection algorithm is the number of samples in the training set, or sample size. Suppose we perform feature selection on a dataset D with n samples and p features. If we randomly split the data into two sets D_1 and D_2 with half of the samples each, and run a feature selection algorithm on them, ideally, we would like to see the same feature selection result (which is likely to happen given unlimited sample size of D).

L. Chen et al. (Eds.): WAIM 2010, LNCS 6184, pp. 680–691, 2010.

However, in reality, due to the limited sample size of D, the results from D_1 and D_2 normally do not agree with each other. When the sample size is very small, the results from D_1 and D_2 could be largely different. For microarray data, the typical number of features (genes) is thousands or tens of thousands, but the number of samples is often less than a hundred. Therefore, a major reason for the instability of feature selection on high-dimensional data is the nature of extremely small sample size compared to the dimensionality (i.e., $p \gg n$). Increasing the number of samples could be very costly or impractical in many applications like microarray analysis.

To tackle the instability problem, a realistic way is to extensively explore the available training samples in order to simulate a training set of larger size. One intuitive approach is to apply the ensemble learning idea to feature selection. Saeys *et al.* introduced ensemble feature selection [17] which aggregates the feature selection results from a conventional feature selection algorithm repeatedly applied on a number of bootstrapped training sets. The bootstrapping procedure used for generating each new training set essentially assigns a weight to each sample randomly (e.g., samples not drawn into the training set have zero weights), without exploiting the data characteristics of the original training set. The effectiveness of this approach in improving the stability of feature selection is limited. Moreover, it is computationally expensive to repeatedly apply the same feature selection algorithm.

In this paper, we propose to extensively explore the available training samples by a novel framework of margin based sample weighting. The framework first weights each sample in a training set according to its influence to the estimation of feature relevance, and then provides the weighted training set to a feature selection method. Inherently, the result of a feature selection algorithm from a given training set is determined by the distribution of samples in the training set. Different samples could have different influence on the feature selection result according to their views (or local profiles) of the importance of all features. If a sample shows quite distinct local profile from the other samples, its absence or presence in the training data will substantially affect the feature selection result. The discrepancy among the local profiles of feature importance at various samples explains why the result of a feature selection algorithm is sensitive to variations in the training data. In order to improve the stability of feature selection result, samples with outlying local profiles need to be weighted differently from the rest of the samples. Therefore, the proposed framework of margin based sample weighting assigns a weight to each sample according to the outlying degree of its local profile of feature importance compared with other samples. In particular, the local profile of feature importance at a given sample is measured based on the hypothesis margin of the sample.

The main contributions of this paper include: (i) introducing the concept of hypothesis-margin feature space; (ii) proposing the framework of margin based sample weighting for stable feature selection; (iii) developing an efficient sample weighting algorithm under the proposed framework. Experiments on a set of public gene expression and protein microarray datasets demonstrate that the proposed algorithm is effective at improving the stability of SVM-RFE algorithm, while maintaining comparable classification accuracy of the selected features. Moreover, the proposed algorithm is more effective and efficient than a recently proposed ensemble feature selection approach.

The rest of the paper is organized as follows. Section 2 reviews related work. Section 3 defines and illustrates the concept of hypothesis-margin feature space and describes the procedure of hypothesis-margin feature space transformation. Section 4 presents the method of sample weighting based on hypothesis-margin feature space and the overall proposed algorithm. Section 5 presents empirical study based on real-world microarray data sets. Section 6 concludes the paper and outlines future research directions.

2 Related Work

Although feature selection is an extensively studied area [11], there exist very limited studies on the stability of feature selection algorithms. Early work in this area mainly focuses on the development of stability measures and empirical evaluation of the stability of existing feature selection algorithms [9, 10].

More recently, two approaches were proposed to improve the stability of feature selection without sacrificing classification accuracy: ensemble feature selection [17] and group based stable feature selection [12, 20]. Saeys *et al.* studied bagging-based ensemble feature selection [17] which aggregates the feature selection results from a conventional feature selection algorithm repeatedly applied on different bootstrapped samples of the same training set. As discussed previously, this approach tackles the instability problem of feature selection by extensively exploring the available training samples; it simulates a training set of larger sample size by creating a number of bootstrapped training sets. Yu *et al.* proposed an alternative approach to tackle the instability problem by exploring the intrinsic correlations among the large number of features. They proposed a group-based stable feature selection framework which identifies groups of correlated features and selects relevant feature groups [12, 20].

In this work, we focus on the approach of exploring the available training samples. However, in contrast with bagging-based ensemble feature selection, our proposed framework does not repeatedly apply a feature selection algorithm on a number of randomly created training sets. It exploits the data characteristics of the training set to weight samples, and then applies a given feature selection algorithm on a single training set of weighted samples.

Another line of research closely related to our work is margin based feature selection. Margins [2] measure the confidence of a classifier w.r.t. its decision, and have been used both for theoretical generalization bounds and as guidelines for algorithm design. There are two natural ways of defining the margin of a sample w.r.t. a hypothesis [3]. Sample-margin (SM) as used by SVMs [2] measures the distance between the sample and the decision boundary of the hypothesis. Hypothesis-margin (HM) as used by AdaBoost [4] measures the distance between the hypothesis and the closest hypothesis that assigns an alternative label to the given sample. Various feature selection algorithms have been developed under the large margin (SM or HM) principles such as SVM-based feature selection [8] and Relief family of algorithms [5]. These algorithms evaluate the importance of features according to their respective contributions to margins, and have exhibited both nice theoretical properties and good generalization performance. However, stability of these algorithms is an issue under small sample size. Compared to margin based feature selection algorithms which use margins to directly evaluate feature importance, our margin based sample weighting framework exploits the discrepancies among the margins at various samples to weight samples and acts as a preprocessing step applicable to any feature selection algorithm.

3 Hypothesis-Margin Feature Space Transformation

In this section, we first formally define hypothesis-margin feature space, then introduce an example to illustrate its effectiveness at capturing the discrepancy among local profiles of feature importance, and then discuss the procedure of transforming the original feature space into the hypothesis margin feature space.

3.1 Definition

Hypothesis-margin (HM) of a sample measures the distance between the hypothesis and the closest hypothesis that assigns an alternative label to the sample [3]. By decomposing the HM of a sample along each dimension, the sample in the original feature space can be represented by a new vector in the hypothesis-margin feature space defined as follows.

Definition 1. *Let* $X = (x_1, ..., x_p)$ *be a sample vector in the original feature space* R^p*, and* X^H *and* X^M *represent the nearest samples to* X *with the same and opposite class labels, respectively. The HM feature space* R'^p *is transformed from the original space* R^p*, such that for each* $X \in R^p$*,* X *is mapped to* $X' \in R'^p$ *according to*

$$x'_i = |x_i - x_i^M| - |x_i - x_i^H| \ , \tag{1}$$

where x'_i is the ith coordinate of X' in the HM feature space. It is easy to prove

$$||X'||_1 = ||X - X^M||_1 - ||X - X^H||_1 \ , \tag{2}$$

where the left part of of Equation (2) represents the L_1-norm of X' in the transformed space and the right part calculates the HM of X based on L_1-norm in the original space. The larger the value of each component x'_i, the more the ith feature contributes to the HM of sample X, which means higher feature importance. In essence, X' captures the local profile of feature importance for all features at X. HM feature space captures local feature profiles for all samples in the original feature space. The overall profile of feature importance over the entire training set can be obtained by aggregating all local feature profiles.

3.2 An Illustrative Example

Figure 1 illustrates the idea of HM feature space through a 2-d example. Each labeled data point (triangle or square) is a sample with two features. Each sample in the original feature space (a) is projected into the HM feature space (b) according to Equation (1) above. We can clearly see that samples labeled with triangles exhibit largely different outlying degrees in the two feature spaces. Specifically, those in the dashed ovals are evenly distributed within the proximity to the rest of the triangles (except the outlier on the leftmost) in the original feature space, but are clearly separated from the majority of the samples in the HM feature space. The outlier triangle in the original space becomes part of the the majority group in the HM feature space.

To decide the overall importance of feature X1 vs. X2, one intuitive idea is to take the average of the local feature profiles over all samples, as adopted by the well-known Relief algorithm [16]. However, since the triangles in the dashed over exhibit distinct local feature profiles from the rest of the samples, the presence or absence of these samples will affect the global decision on which feature is more important. From this illustrative example, we can see that the HM feature space captures the similarity among samples w.r.t. their local profiles of feature importance, and enables the detection of samples that largely deviate from others in this respect, instead of the similarity w.r.t. feature values in the original space. In Section 4, we will further discuss how to exploit such discrepancy to weight samples in order to alleviate the affect of training data variations on feature selection results.

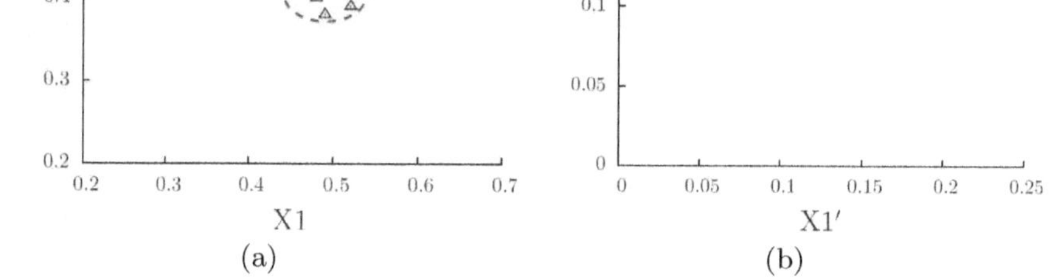

Fig. 1. Hypothesis-margin based feature space transformation: (a) original feature space, and (b) hypothesis-margin (HM) feature space. Each data point in the original space is projected into the new space according to its hypothesis margin in the original space. The class labels of data points are distinguished by triangles and squares.

Algorithm 1. Hypothesis Margin Feature Space Transformation

Input: data $D = \{X_t\}_{t=1}^n$, number of nearest neighbors k
Output: transformed data $D' = \{X_t'\}_{t=1}^n$
for $t = 1$ **to** n **do**
  find nearest hits $\{H_j\}_{j=1}^k$
  find nearest misses $\{M_j\}_{j=1}^k$
  for $i = 1$ **to** p **do**
    apply Equation (3)
  end for
end for

3.3 Procedure

The previous definition and example of HM feature space only consider one nearest neighbor from each class. To reduce the sensitivity of the transformed HM feature space to noise or outliers in the training set, multiple nearest neighbors from each class can be used to compute the HM of a sample. Equation (1) can then be extended to:

$$x_i' = \sum_{j=1}^{k} |x_i - x_i^{M_j}|/k - \sum_{j=1}^{k} |x_i - x_i^{H_j}|/k \tag{3}$$

where $x_i^{H_j}$ or $x_i^{M_j}$ denotes the ith component of the jth nearest neighbor to X with the same (hit) or different (miss) class label respectively; k represents the number of nearest neighbors taken into account. $k = 10$ is the default value.

Algorithm 1 outlines the procedure for transforming the original feature space into the HM feature space given a training set D. The time complexity of this transformation is $O(n^2q)$, where n is the number of samples and q is the dimensionality of D.

4 Margin Based Sample Weighting

The hypothesis margin (HM) feature space introduced in the previous section captures the discrepancy among samples w.r.t. their local profiles of feature importance, and allows us to detect samples that largely deviate from others in this respect. The next step in the framework of margin based sample weighting is to exploit such discrepancy to weight samples in order to alleviate the affect of training data variations on feature selection results. To quantitatively evaluate the outlying degree of each sample X' in the HM feature space, we measure the average distance of X' to all other samples in the HM feature space; greater average distance indicates higher outlying degree. As illustrated in Section 3, the global decision of feature importance is more sensitive to samples that largely deviate from the rest of the samples in the HM feature space than to samples that have low outlying degrees. To improve the stability of a feature selection

Algorithm 2. Margin Based Sample Weighting

Input: data $D = \{X_t\}_{t=1}^n$, number of nearest neighbors k
Output: weight vector for all samples W
Apply **Algorithm 1** to form $D' = \{X'_t\}_{t=1}^n$ in the HM feature space
for $t = 1$ **to** n **do**
  for $j = 1$ **to** n **do**
    if $j \neq t$ **then**
      $d_t += \|X'_t - X'_j\|$
    end if
  end for
  Calculate average distance $\bar{d}_t = d_t/(n-1)$
end for
for $t = 1$ **to** n **do**
  Normalize $\bar{d}_t$ according to Equation (4) to get W_t
end for

algorithm under training data variations, we assign lower weights to samples with higher outlying degrees. Therefore, given the average distance $\bar{d}_t$ of a sample X'_t to all other samples in the HM feature space, the weight for sample X_t in the original feature space is given by the following formula:

$$W_t = -log \frac{\bar{d}_t}{\sum_{i=1}^{n} \bar{d}_i} \quad (4)$$

Algorithm 2 outlines the overall process of margin based sample weighting. Since both the step of HM feature space transformation and the pairwise distance calculation in the transformed space take $O(n^2 q)$, the overall time complexity for Algorithm 2 is still $O(n^2 q)$.

5 Empirical Study

The objective of the empirical study is to evaluate the proposed algorithm in terms of stability and classification performance, and also compare the proposed algorithm with state-of-the-art feature selection algorithms. We first introduce stability measures in Section 5.1, then describe the data sets, comparison algorithms and experimental procedures in Section 5.2, and finally present and discuss the results in Section 5.3.

5.1 Stability Metrics

Evaluating the stability of feature selection algorithms requires some similarity measures for two sets of feature selection results. Let R_1 and R_2 denote two sets of results by a feature selection algorithm from two different training sets, where R_1 and R_2 can be two vectors of feature weights or ranks, or two feature subsets, depending on the output of the algorithm. For feature weighting, the Pearson correlation coefficient can be used to measure the similarity between

R_1 and R_2. For feature ranking, we use Spearman rank correlation coefficient as in [9] and [17]:

$$Sim_R(R_1, R_2) = 1 - 6\sum_{i=1}^{p} \frac{(R_1^i - R_2^i)^2}{p(p^2-1)}, \tag{5}$$

where p is the total number of features, and R_1^i and R_2^i are the ranks of the ith feature in the two rank vectors, respectively. Sim_R takes values in [-1,1]; a value of 1 means that the two rankings are identical and a value of -1 means that they have exactly inverse orders.

For feature subset selection, Jaccard index was used in both [9] and [17].

$$Sim_{ID}(R_1, R_2) = \frac{|R_1 \cap R_2|}{|R_1| + |R_2| - |R_1 \cap R_2|}. \tag{6}$$

Sim_{ID} takes values in [0,1], with 0 meaning that there is no overlap between the two subsets, and 1 that the two subsets are identical.

Sim_{ID} does not take into account the similarity of feature values; two subsets of different features will be considered dissimilar no matter whether the features in one subset are highly correlated with those in the other subset. To capture the similarity in feature values, another similarity measure is proposed in [20], which is defined based on maximum weighted bipartite matching:

$$Sim_V(R_1, R_2) = \frac{\sum_{(\mathrm{X}_i,\mathrm{X}_j)\in M} w_{(\mathrm{X}_i,\mathrm{X}_j)}}{|M|}, \tag{7}$$

where M is a maximum matching in the bipartite graph representing R_1 and R_2. Each weight $w_{(X_i,X_j)}$ is decided by the correlation coefficient between the two features X_i and X_j, where $\mathrm{X}_i \in R_1$ and $\mathrm{X}_j \in R_2$.

Given each measure above, the stability of a feature selection algorithm is then measured as the average of the pair-wise similarity of various feature selection results produced by the same algorithm from different training sets.

5.2 Experimental Setup

In our comparative study, we choose SVM-RFE [8], a highly popular feature selection algorithm in microarray data analysis, as a baseline to represent conventional feature selection algorithms which directly work on a given training set. The main process of SVM-RFE is to recursively eliminate features based on SVM, using the coefficients of the optimal decision boundary to measure the relevance of each feature. At each iteration, it trains a linear SVM classifier, ranks features according to the squared values of feature coefficients assigned by the linear SVM, and eliminates one or more features with the lowest scores. We also evaluate bagging-based ensemble feature selection [17] (introduced in Section 2) and use SVM-RFE as the base algorithm. We refer to this algorithm as **En**-SVM-RFE (**En**-RFE in short). Our proposed framework of margin based sample weighting is also evaluated based on SVM-RFE; instead of the original training set, SVM-RFE is applied on the weighted training set produced according Algorithm 2. We refer to this algorithm as as **IW**-RFE in short.

Table 1. Summary of data sets

Data Set	# Features	# Instances	Source
Colon	2000	62	[1]
Leukemia	7129	72	[6]
Prostate	6034	102	[18]
Lung	12533	181	[7]
Ovarian	15154	253	[14]
JNCI	15154	322	[15]

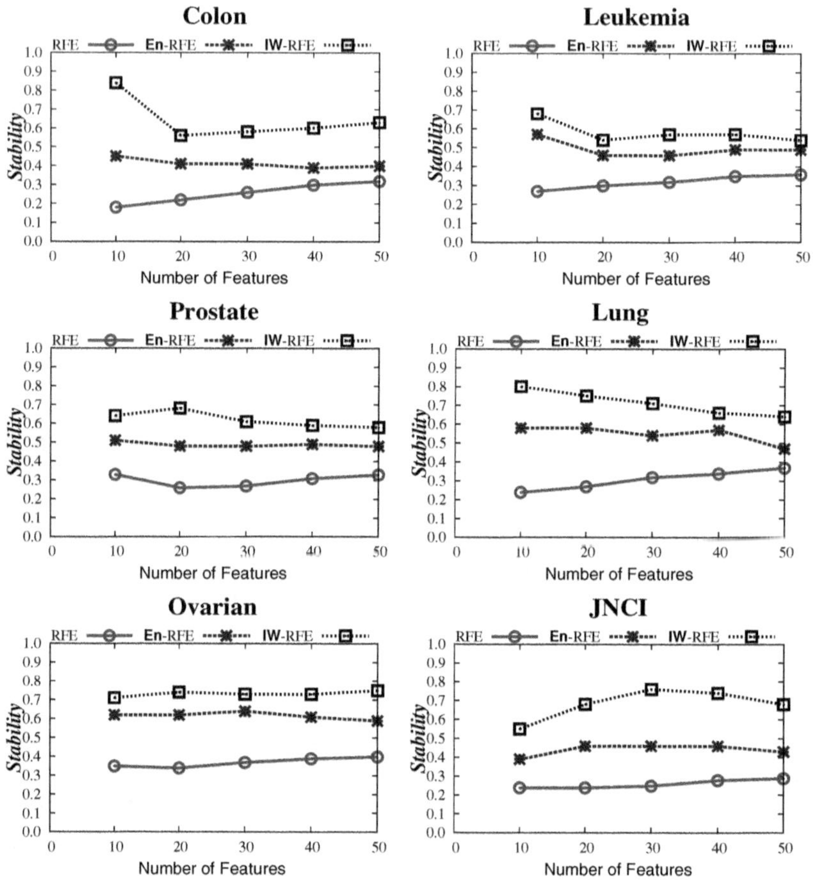

Fig. 2. Comparison of **stability** for original SVM-RFE (RFE), ensemble SVM-RFE (**En**-RFE) and sample weighting SVM-RFE (**IW**-RFE) based on Sim_{ID} measure

We experimented with six frequently studied public gene expression microarray (Colon, Leukemia, Prostate, and Lung) and protein mass spectrometry (Ovarian and JNCI) datasets, characterized in Table 1. For Lung, Ovarian, and

JNCI data sets, we applied t-test to the original data set and only kept the top 5000 features in order to make the experiments more manageable.

To empirically evaluate the stability and accuracy of the above algorithms on a given data set, we apply the 10 fold cross-validation procedure. Each feature selection algorithm is repeatedly applied to 9 out of the 10 folds, while a different fold is hold out each time. Different stability measures are calculated. In addition, a classifier is trained based on the selected features from the same training set and tested on the hold-out fold. The CV accuracies of linear SVM and KNN classification algorithms are calculated. As to algorithm settings, for SVM-RFE, we eliminate 10 percent of remaining features at each iteration. For **En**-RFE, we use 20 bootstrapped training sets to construct the ensemble. For **IW**-RFE, we use $k = 10$ for hypothesis margin transformation. We use Weka's implementation [19] of SVM (linear kernel, default C parameter) and KNN (K=1). Weka's implementation of SVM can directly take weighted samples as input.

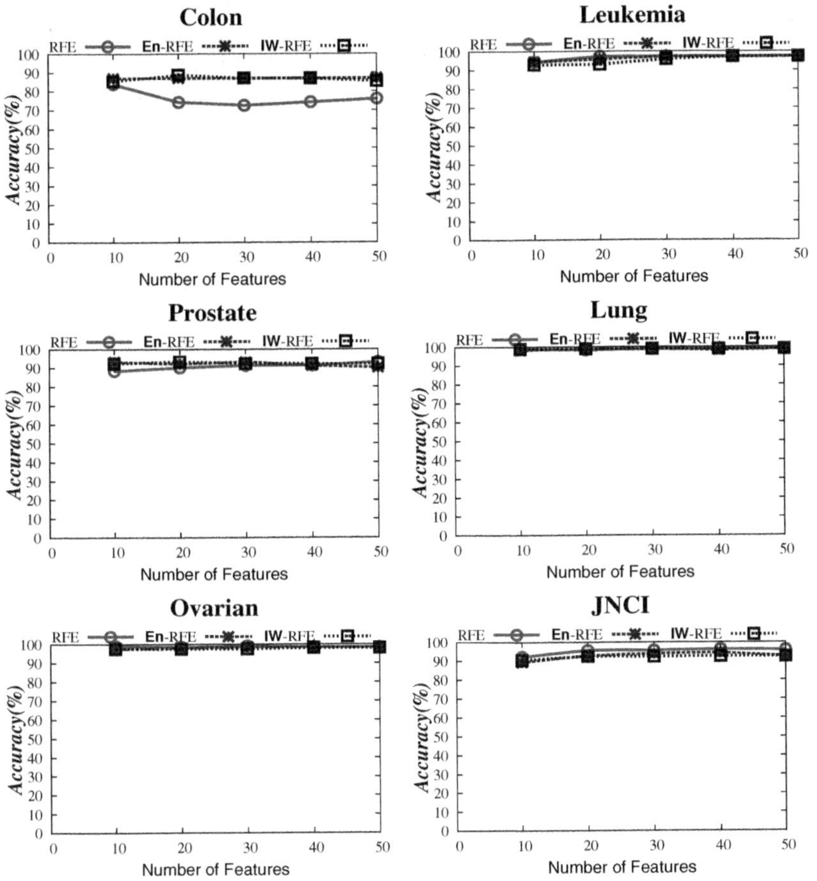

Fig. 3. Comparison of **accuracy** for RFE, **En**-RFE and **IW**-RFE based on average SVM classification accuracies

5.3 Results and Discussion

Figure 2 reports stability profiles (stability scores across different numbers of selected features) of SVM-RFE in three versions (original, Ensemble, and Sample Weighting) based on Sim_{ID} for six data sets. We can clearly observe that stability scores of SVM-RFE based on proposed sample weighting approach (**IW**-RFE) are significantly higher than original SVM-RFE. This observation verifies the effectiveness of proposed approach in alleviating the effect of small sample size on the stability of feature selection. Although the ensemble approach for SVM-RFE (**En**-RFE) also consistently improves the stability of SVM-RFE, the improvement is not as significant as by **IW**-RFE. This can be explained by the bootstrapping procedure used by the ensemble approach which does not exploit the data characteristics of original training data as margin based sample weighting. We also experimented based on the other two stability metrics Sim_V and Sim_R. Since the results based on these measures show very similar trends as Sim_{ID}, these results are not included in Figure 2 for conciseness.

Figure 3 compares the predictive accuracy for SVM classification based on the selected features of SVM-RFE, **En**-RFE, and **IW**-RFE across a range of numbers of selected features from 10 to 50. Among these six data sets, the accuracies resulted from SVM-RFE in three versions are in general very similar under the same size of selected features. This observation illustrates that different feature selection algorithms can lead to similarly good classification results, while their stability can largely vary (as shown in Figure 2). We also evaluated these algorithms based on 1NN classification. Since the predictive accuracies of 1NN show the same trend as Figure 3, they are not included for conciseness.

6 Conclusion

In this paper, we introduced the concept of hypothesis-margin feature space, proposed the framework of margin based sample weighting for stable feature selection, and developed an efficient algorithm under the framework. Experiments on microarray datasets demonstrate that the proposed algorithm is effective at improving the stability of SVM-RFE algorithm, while maintaining comparable classification accuracy. Moreover, it is more effective than the ensemble feature selection approach. We plan to investigate alternative methods of sample weighting based on HM feature space and strategies to combine margin based sample weighting with group-based stable feature selection.

References

[1] Alon, U., Barkai, N., Notterman, D.A., et al.: Broad patterns of gene expression revealed by clustering analysis of tumor and normal colon tissues probed by oligonucleotide arrays. Proc. Natl Acad. Sci. USA 96, 6745–6750 (1999)

[2] Cortes, C., Vapnik, V.: Support vector networks. Machine Learning 20, 273–297 (1995)

[3] Crammer, K., Gilad-Bachrach, R., Navot, A.: Margin analysis of the LVQ algorithm. In: Proceedings of the 17th Conference on Neural Information Processing Systems, pp. 462–469 (2002)

[4] Freund, Y., Schapire, R.E.: A decision-theoretic generalization of on-line learning and an application to boosting. Computer Systems and Science 55(1), 119–139 (1997)

[5] Gilad-Bachrach, R., Navot, A., Tishby, N.: Margin based feature selection: theory and algorithms. In: Proceedings of the 21st International Conference on Machine learning (2004)

[6] Golub, T.R., Slonim, D.K., Tamayo, P., Huard, C., Gaasenbeek, M., Mesirov, J.P., Coller, H., Loh, M.L., Downing, J.R., Caligiuri, M.A., Bloomfield, C.D., Lander, E.S.: Molecular classification of cancer: class discovery and class prediction by gene expression monitoring. Science 286, 531–537 (1999)

[7] Gordon, G.J., Jensen, R.V., Hsiaoand, L., et al.: Translation of microarray data into clinically relevant cancer diagnostic tests using gene expression ratios in lung cancer and mesothelioma. Cancer Research 62, 4963–4967 (2002)

[8] Guyon, I., Weston, J., Barnhill, S., Vapnik, V.: Gene selection for cancer classification using support vector machines. Machine Learning 46, 389–422 (2002)

[9] Kalousis, A., Prados, J., Hilario, M.: Stability of feature selection algorithms: a study on high-dimensional spaces. Knowledge and Information Systems 12, 95–116 (2007)

[10] Krizek, P., Kittler, J., Hlavac, V.: Improving stability of feature selection methods. In: Proceedings of the 12th International Conference on Computer Analysis of Images and Patterns, pp. 929–936 (2007)

[11] Liu, H., Yu, L.: Toward integrating feature selection algorithms for classification and clustering. IEEE Transactions on Knowledge and Data Engineering (TKDE) 17(4), 491–502 (2005)

[12] Loscalzo, S., Yu, L., Ding, C.: Consensus group based stable feature selection. In: Proceedings of the 15th ACM SIGKDD International Conference on Knowledge Discovery and Data Mining (KDD 2009), pp. 567–576 (2009)

[13] Pepe, M.S., Etzioni, R., Feng, Z., Potter, J.D., Thompson, M.L., Thornquist, M., Winget, M., Yasui, Y.: Phases of biomarker development for early detection of cancer. J. Natl. Cancer Inst. 93, 1054–1060 (2001)

[14] Petricoin, E.F., Ardekani, A.M., Hitt, B.A., Levine, P.J., Fusaro, V.A., Steinberg, S.M., Mills, G.B., Simone, C., Fishman, D.A., Kohn, E.C., Liotta, L.A.: Use of proteomic patterns in serum to identify ovarian cancer. Lancet 359, 572–577 (2002)

[15] Petricoin, E.F., et al.: Serum proteomic patterns for detection of prostate cancer. J. Natl. Cancer Inst. 94(20) (2002)

[16] Robnik-Sikonja, M., Kononenko, I.: Theoretical and empirical analysis of Relief and ReliefF. Machine Learning 53, 23–69 (2003)

[17] Saeys, Y., Abeel, T., Peer, Y.V.: Robust feature selection using ensemble feature selection techniques. In: Proceedings of the ECML Confernce, pp. 313–325 (2008)

[18] Singh, D., et al.: Gene expression correlates of clinical prostate cancer behavior. Cancer Cell. 2(2) (2002)

[19] Witten, I.H., Frank, E.: Data Mining - Pracitcal Machine Learning Tools and Techniques. Morgan Kaufmann Publishers, San Francisco (2005)

[20] Yu, L., Ding, C., Loscalzo, S.: Stable feature selection via dense feature groups. In: Proceedings of the 14th ACM International Conference on Knowledge Discovery and Data Mining (KDD 2008), pp. 803–811 (2008)

Associative Classifier for Uncertain Data*

Xiangju Qin[1], Yang Zhang[1,**], Xue Li[2], and Yong Wang[3]

[1] College of Information Engineering, Northwest A&F University, P.R. China
{xiangju,zhangyang}nwsuaf.edu.cn
[2] School of Information Technology and Electrical Engineering,
The University of Queensland, Australia
xueli@itee.uq.edu.au
[3] School of Computer, Northwest Polytechnical University, P.R. China
wangyong@nwpu.edu.cn

Abstract. Associative classifiers are relatively easy for people to understand and often outperform decision tree learners on many classification problems. Existing associative classifiers only work with certain data. However, data uncertainty is prevalent in many real-world applications such as sensor network, market analysis and medical diagnosis. And uncertainty may render many conventional classifiers inapplicable to uncertain classification tasks. In this paper, based on U-Apriori algorothm and CBA algorithm, we propose an associative classifier for uncertain data, uCBA (uncertain Classification Based on Associative), which can classify both certain and uncertain data. The algorithm redefines the support, confidence, rule pruning and classification strategy of CBA. Experimental results on 21 datasets from UCI Repository demonstrate that the proposed algorithm yields good performance and has satisfactory performance even on highly uncertain data.

Keywords: Associative Classification, Uncertain Data, Multiple Rules Classification, Expected Support.

1 Introduction

In recent years, due to advances in technology and deep understanding of data acquisition and processing, uncertain data has attracted more and more attention in the literature. Uncertain data is ubiquitous in many real-world applications, such as environmental monitoring, sensor network, market analysis and medical diagnosis [1]. A number of factors contribute to the uncertainty. It may be caused by imprecision measurements, network latencies, data staling and decision errors [2,3]. Uncertainty can arise in categorical attributes and numeric attributes [1,2]. For example, in cancer diagnosis, it is often very difficult for the doctor to exactly classify a tumor to be benign or malignant due to the experiment precision limitation. Therefore it would be better to represent by probability to be benign or malignant [2].

* This work is supported by the National Natural Science Foundation of China (60873196) and Chinese Universities Scientific Fund (QN2009092).

** Corresponding author.

L. Chen et al. (Eds.): WAIM 2010, LNCS 6184, pp. 692–703, 2010.

Associative classifiers are relatively easy for people to understand and often outperform decision tree learners on many classification problems [5,7,8]. However, data uncertainty may render many conventional classifiers inapplicable to uncertain classification tasks. Consequently, the following adaptations are required to ensure that the extension to CBA [5] can classify uncertain data: Firstly, due to uncertainty, we need to modify the initial definition of *support* and *confidence* of associative rules [11] to mine association rules from uncertain data. Secondly, CBA only utilizes the rule with the highest *confidence* for classification. For uncertain data, an instance may be partially covered by a rule. We define the weight of instance covered by a rule and introduce *multiple rules classification*, and this help to improve the performance of the proposed algorithm. To the best of our knowledge, this is the first work devoted to associative classification of uncertain data.

To sum up, in this paper, based on the *expected support* [4], we extend CBA algorithm [5] and propose an associative classifier, uCBA, for uncertain data. We perform experiments on real datasets with uncertainty, and the experimental results demonstrate that uCBA algorithm perform well even on highly uncertain data.

This paper is organized as follows. In the next section, we survey the related work. Section 3 gives problem statement. Section 4 illustrates the proposed algorithm in detail. The experimental results are shown in Section 5. And finally, we conclude the paper and give future work in Section 6.

2 Related Work

A detailed survey of uncertain data mining techniques may be found in [9].In the case of uncertain data mining, studies include clustering [23,24,25], classification [2,3,10,22], frequent itemsets mining [4,12,13,16,17] and outlier detection [26]. Here, we mainly focus on associative classification of uncertain data.

At present, existing works about classification of uncertain data all fall into extensions to traditional classification algorithms. Qin *et al.* proposed a rule-based algorithm to cope with uncertain data [2]. Later, in [3], Qin *et al.* presented DTU, which based on decision tree algorithm, to deal with uncertain data by extending traditional measurements, such as information entropy and information gain. In [10], Tsang *et al.* extended classical decision tree algorithm and proposed UDT algorithm to handle uncertain data which is represented by probability density function (pdf). In [22], Bi *et al.* proposed Total Support Vector Classification (TSVC), a formulation of support vector classification to handle uncertain data. Associative classifiers for certain dataset have been widely studied [5,7,8]. However, the problem studied in this paper is different from works mentioned above, we consider classification of uncertain data from the perspective of association rule mining and propose an associative classifier for uncertain data, uCBA.

Recently, there have been some studies on frequent itemset mining from uncertain transaction databases. In [4], Chui *et al.* extended Apriori [11] algorithm and proposed U-Apriori algorithm to mine frequent itemsets from uncertain data. U-Apriori computes the *expected support* of itemsets by summing all itemset probabilities. Later, in [12], they additionally proposed a probabilistic filter in order to prune candidates early.

Leung *et al.* proposed the UF-growth algorithm in [13]. Like U-Apriori, UF-growth computes frequent itemsets based on the *expected support*, and it uses the FP-tree [14] approach in order to avoid expensive candidate generation. In [15], Aggarwal *et al.* extended several classical frequent itemset mining algorithms to study their performances when applied to uncertain data. In [16], Zhang *et al.* proposed exact and sampling-based algorithms to find likely frequent items in streaming probabilistic data. In [17], Bernecker *et al.* proposed to find frequent itemsets from uncertain transaction database in a probabilistic way. Different from studies in [4,12,13], work in [17] mined probabilistic frequent itemsets by means of the *probabilistic support*. All the works mentioned above belong to the framework of mining frequent itemsets from uncertain transaction databases, and do not consider mining association rules from uncertain data. In this paper, we apply the *expected support* [4] to mine associative rules from uncertain data, and then perform associative classification for uncertain data.

At present, there are few works about mining associative rules from uncertain data. In [18], Weng *et al.* developed an algorithm to mine fuzzy association rules from uncertain data which is represented by possibility distributions. In their study, there are relations between all the possible values of a categorical attribute,and they provide a similarity matrix to compute the similarity between values of this attribute. While recent studies in the literature about uncertain data management and mining generally base on *possible world model* [6]. In this paper, we integrate *possible world model* [6] into mining association rules from uncertain data.

3 Problem Statement

For simplicity, in this paper, we only consider uncertain categorical attributes, and following studies in [2,3], we also assume the class label is certain.

3.1 A Model for Uncertain Categorical Data

When dealing with uncertain categorical attribute, we utilize the same model as studies in [1,2,3] to represent uncertain categorical data. Under the uncertain categorical model, a dataset can have attributes that are allowed to take uncertain values [2]. And we call these attributes Uncertain Categorical Attributes, UCA. The concept of UCA was introduced in [1]. Let's write $A_i^{u_c}$ for the ith uncertain categorical attribute, and $V_i = \{v_{i1}, v_{i2}, \cdots, v_{i|V_i|}\}$ for its domain. As described in [2], for instance t_j, its attribute value of $A_i^{u_c}$ can be represented by the probability distribution over V_i, and formalized as $P_{ji} = \langle p_{i1}, p_{i2}, \cdots, p_{iV_i}\rangle$, such that $P_{ji}(A_i^{u_c} = v_{ik}) = p_{ik}(1 \leq k \leq |V_i|)$, and $\sum_{k=1}^{|V_i|} p_{ik} = 1.0$, which means $A_i^{u_c}$ takes value of v_{ik} with probability p_{ik}. Certain attribute can be viewed as a special case of uncertain attribute. In this case, the attribute value of $A_i^{u_c}$ for instance t_j can only take one value, v_{ik}, from domain V_i, i.e. $P_{ji}(A_i^{u_c} = v_{ik}) = 1.0(1 \leq k \leq |V_i|)$, $P_{ji}(A_i^{u_c} = v_{ih}) = 0.0(1 \leq h \leq |V_i|, h \neq k)$.

3.2 Associative Rules for Uncertain Data

Let D be the uncertain dataset, Y be the set of class labels, and $y \in Y$ be a class label. Each uncertain instance $t \in D$ follows the scheme $(A_1^{u_c}, A_2^{u_c}, \cdots, A_m^{u_c})$, where

$(A_1^{u_c}, A_2^{u_c}, \cdots, A_m^{u_c})$ are m attributes. Following methods in [5,8], we also map all the possible values of each UCA to a set of attribute-value pairs. With these mappings, we can view an uncertain instance as a set of (attribute, attribute-value) pairs and a class label.

Definition 1. *Let an item x be the (attribute, attribute-value) pair, denoted as $x = (A_i^{u_c}, v_{ik})$, where v_{ik} is a value of attribute $A_i^{u_c}$. Let I be the set of all items in D. An instance t_j satisfies an item $x = (A_i^{u_c}, v_{ik})$ if and only if $P_{ji}(A_i^{u_c} = v_{ik}) > 0.0$, where v_{ik} is the value of ith attribute of t_j.*

Following the definition of rule in [8], we can define a rule for uncertain data:

Definition 2. *An associative rule R for uncertain data, is defined as $R : x_1 \wedge x_2 \wedge \cdots \wedge x_l \rightarrow y$. Here $X = x_1 \wedge x_2 \wedge \cdots \wedge x_l$ is the antecedent of R, and y is the class label of R.*

An uncertain instance t satisfies R if and only if it satisfies every item in R. If t satisfies R, R predicts the class label of t to be y. If a rule contains zero item, then its antecedent is satisfied by any instance.

In U-Apriori [4] algorithm, to handle uncertain data, instead of incrementing the support counts of candidate itemsets by their actual support, the algorithm increments the support counts of candidate itemsets by their expected support under the possible world model.

Definition 3. *The expected support of antecedent, X, of rule R on uncertain dataset D can be defined as [4]:*

$$expSup(X) = \sum_{j=1}^{|D|} \prod_{x \in X} p_{t_j}(x) \tag{1}$$

where $\prod_{x\in X} p_{t_j(x)}$ is the joint probability of antecedent X in instance t_j [4], and $p_{t_j}(x)$ is the existence probability of item x in t_j, $p_{t_j}(x) > 0.0$.

Accordingly, we can compute the expected support of R, $expSup(R)$, as following:

$$expSup(R) = \sum_{j=1}^{|D|} \prod_{x \in X, t_j.class=y} p_{t_j}(x) \tag{2}$$

Rule R is considered to be *frequent* if its expected support exceeds $\rho_s \cdot |D|$, where ρ_s is a user-specified expected support threshold.

Definition 4. *For association rule $R : X \rightarrow y$ on uncertain data, with expected support $expSup(X)$ and $expSup(R)$, its confidence can be formalized as:*

$$confidence(R) = expSup(R)/expSup(X) \tag{3}$$

The intuition behind $confidence(R)$ is to show the expected accuracy of rule R under the possible world model. Rule R is considered to be accurate if and only if its confidence exceeds ρ_c, where ρ_c is a user-specified confidence threshold.

Weight of Uncertain Instance Covered by a Rule. Due to data uncertainty, an instance may be partially covered by a rule. The intuition to define this weight is twofold. On one hand, inspired by pruning rules based on database coverage [7], in classifier builder algorithm, instead of removing one instance from the training data set immediately after it is covered by some selected rule like CBA does, we let it stay there until its covered weight reached 1.0, which ensures that each training instance is covered by at least one rule. This allows us to select more rules. When classifying a new instance, it may have more rules to consult and better chance to be accurately predicted. On the other hand, in *multiple rules classification* algorithm, we utilize this weight to further control the number of matched rules using to predict a test instance. In this paper, we follow the method proposed in [2] to compute the weight of instance covered by rule.

Definition 5. *We define the weight, $w(t_j, R_l)$, of instance t_j covered by the lth rule R_l in the rule sequence as following:*

$$\begin{aligned} w(t_j, R_1) &= 1.0 * P(t_j, R_1) \\ w(t_j, R_2) &= (1.0 - w(t_j, R_1)) * P(t_j, R_2) \\ &\dots \\ w(t_j, R_l) &= (1.0 - \sum_{k=1}^{l-1} w(t_j, R_k)) * P(t_j, R_l) \end{aligned} \quad (4)$$

In formula (4), $P(t_j, R_l)$ is the probability of instance t_j that covered by rule R_l, which can be formalized as following:

$$P(t_j, R_l) = \prod_{x \in R_l.Antecedent} p_{t_j}(x) \quad (5)$$

Multiple Rules Classification. When classifying an uncertain instance, a natural approach is directly following CBA [5], which only utilizes the rule with the highest confidence for classification, i.e. *single rule classification*. However, this direct approach ignores uncertain information in the instance, and hence may decrease the prediction accuracy.

Note that CMAR [7] performs classification based on a weighted χ^2 analysis by using multiple strong associative rules, we can follow the idea of CMAR and modify the formula of weighted χ^2 by using the expected support of rules. In this paper, we refer to methods in [8,10,2] to predict class label, which classifies the test instances by combining multiple rules. Similar to works in [8,10,2], which use the expected accuracy of rules on training dataset [8,10] or the class probability distribution of training instances that follow at the tree leaf to classify the test instance [2], we utilize the confidence of rules to compute the class probability distribution of test instance t to predict the class label, which can be formalized as:

$$y = \arg\max_{y \in Y} \{ \sum_{R_l.class=y} confidence(R_l) * w(t, R_l) | y \in Y, R_l \in rs \} \quad (6)$$

where rs is the set of rules that t matches. This method is also similar to the idea of CMAR.

Pruning Rules based on Pessimistic Error Rate. Since there are strong associations in some datasets, the number of association rules can be huge, and there may be a large number of insignificant association rules, which make no contributions to classification and may even do harm to classification by introducing noise. Consequently, rule pruning is helpful. Following CBA [5], we also utilize pessimistic error rate (PER) based pruning method presented in C4.5 [19] to prune rules, which is formalized as:

$$e = \frac{r + \frac{z^2}{2n} + z\sqrt{\frac{r}{n} - \frac{r^2}{n} + \frac{z^2}{4n}}}{1 + \frac{z^2}{n}} \tag{7}$$

Here under the uncertain data scenario, r is the observed error rate of rule R_l, $r = 1.0 - confidence(R_l)$; n is the expected support of R_l, $n = expSup(R_l)$; $z = \Phi^{-1}(c)$, c is confidence level given by the user.

4 uCBA Algorithm

Based on CBA [5], we propose uCBA algorithm for associative classification of uncertain data. It consists of three parts, a *rule generator* (uCBA-RG), a *classifier builder* (uCBA-CB), and *multiple rules classification* (uCBA-MRC).

4.1 Algorithm for uCBA-RG

Conventional CBA mines associative rules based on Apriori [5] algorithm, while uCBA generates uncertain associative rules based on U-Apriori [4] algorithm. And the general framework of uCBA-RG is the same with that of CBA-RG [5], the differences lie in their ways to accumulate the support counts: if instance t matches R_l, then for CBA-RG, *support* of antecedent X increase incrementally by 1, i.e. $X.condSupCount$++. Furthermore, if R_l and t have the same class label, then *support* of rule also increase incrementally by 1, i.e. $X.ruleSupCount$++ [5]. While for uCBA-RG, if t matches R_l, then the *expected support* of X increase incrementally by probability of t covered by R_l, i.e. $X.expSup$ +=$P(t, R_l)$, $P(t, R_l)$ can be computed following formula (5). *Expected support* of R_l updates similarly. The algorithm is omitted here for lack of space.

4.2 Algorithm for uCBA-CB

Here we give our uCBA-CB algorithm, which is illustrated in Algorithm 1. It has three steps:

Step 1 (Line 1): According to relation '$\succ$' for rules in CBA [5], we sort the set of generated rules R based on *expected support* and *confidence*, which guarantees that we will choose the highest precedence rules for our classifier.

Step 2 (line 2-23): Selecting rules for the classifier from R following the sorted sequence. For each rule R_l, we traverse D to find those instances covered by R_l (line 7) and compute *probability* (line 8) and *weight* (line 9) of instances covered by R_l. If weight of instance covered by R_l is greater than 0, then records the weight and marks R_l if it correctly classifies t_j (line 11). If R_l is marked, then it will be a potential rule in our classifier (line 15,16). Meanwhile, we need to update the weight of instances covered by R_l (line 17,18,19). For uncertain data, we should ensure that the total weight of each

Algorithm 1. Classifier Builder for uCBA

Input:
D : Training Dataset ;
R : A rule set generated by Algorithm uCBA-RG;
Output:
C: The final uCBA Classifier;
1: R=sort(R);
2: $C = \phi$;
3: Initialize $totalWeight[j] = 0, j \in [1, |D|]$;
4: **for** each rule $R_l \in R$ in sequence **do**
5: Initialize $curCoverWeight[j] = 0, j \in [1, |D|]$;
6: **for** each instance $t_j \in D$ **do**
7: **if** $totalWeight[j] \leq 1.0$ && t_j satisfies the antecedent of R_l **then**
8: Compute $P(t_j, R_l)$ following formula (5);
9: Compute $w(t_j, R_l)$ following formula (4);
10: **if** $w(t_j, R_l) > 0$ **then**
11: $curCoverWeight[j] = w(t_j, R_l)$ and mark R_l if it correctly classifies t_j;
12: **end if**
13: **end if**
14: **end for**
15: **if** R_l is marked **then**
16: $C = C \cup \{R_l\}$;
17: **for** $k = 1$ to $|D|$ **do**
18: $totalWeight[k] += curCoverWeight[k]$;
19: **end for**
20: Select a default class for the current C;
21: Compute the total errors of C;
22: **end if**
23: **end for**
24: Find the rule $R_k \in C$ with the lowest total errors and drop all the rules after $R_k \in C$;
25: Add the default class associated with R_k to the end of C;
26: **return** C;

instance covered by all the matching rules is not greater than 1.0 (line 7). Similar to CBA-CB [5], we also select a default class for each potential rule in the classifier (line 20). We then compute and record the total errors that are made by the current C and the default class (line 21). When there is no rule or no training instance left, the rule selection procedure terminates.

Step 3 (line 24-26): Selecting the set of the most predictable rules on training dataset as the final classifier. Same with CBA [5], for our uCBA-CB, the first rule at which there is the least total errors recorded on D is the cutoff rule.

4.3 Algorithm for uCBA-MRC

Here we introduce the algorithm of *multiple rules classification* in uCBA, which is given in Algorithm 2, it has two steps:

Step 1 (line 1-13) : For the test instance t_j, we traverse classifier C to find the matched rules (line 3). Note that, if we use all the matched rules to predict the class label, and do not filter rules with low precedence, it may introduce noise and decrease the prediction accuracy. And we will validate this idea in the experimental study. Therefore, in our uCBA-MRC, under the circumstances of ensuring that the *weight* of each test instance covered by rules is less than 1.0, we further constrain the number of multiple rules not to exceed a user-specified threshold (line 4). When t_j satisfies R_l, we compute the *probability* (line 5) and *weight* (line 6) of instance covered by R_l. If the covered *weight* is greater than 0, then we update the *weight* of instance covered by the matched rules (line 8), and insert R_l into the *multiple rule set* (line 10).

Step 2 (line 14-15): Predict the class label of instance according to formula (6).

Algorithm 2. Multiple-Rule Classification for uCBA

Input:
 C : The final uCBA Classifier generated by Algorithm 1;
 t_j : A testing instance;
 $covThreshold$: The coverage threshold;

Output:
 y : The class label predicted for t_j;

1: $totalWeight = 0$;
2: Initialize the multiple-rule set: $rs = \phi$;
3: **for** each rule $R_l \in C$ in sorted order **do**
4: **if** $totalWeight \leq 1.0$ && $|rs| < coverThreshold$ && t_j satisfies R_l **then**
5: Compute $P(t_j, R_l)$ following formula (5);
6: Compute $w(t_j, R_l)$ following formula (4);
7: **if** $w(t_j, R_l) > 0$ **then**
8: $totalWeight+ = w(t_j, R_l)$;
9: Record $w(t_j, R_l)$ for prediction;
10: $rs = rs \cup \{R_l\}$;
11: **end if**
12: **end if**
13: **end for**
14: Predict the class label, y, of t_j using rs and recorded weights, following formula (6);
15: **return** y;

---

5 Experimental Study

In order to evaluate the classification performance of our uCBA algorithm, we perform experiments on 21 datasets from UCI [20]Repository. At present, for simplicity, our algorithm only consider uncertain categorical attribute. For datasets with numeric attributes, each numeric attribute is first discretized into a categorical one using method as in [5]. At present, there are no standard and public uncertain datasets in the literature. Experiments on uncertain data in the literature all perform on synthetic datasets, which means researchers obtain uncertain dataset via introducing uncertain information into certain dataset [2,3,10].

For all of the experiments in this paper, we utilize the model introduced in Section 3.1 to represent uncertain dataset. For example, as described in [2], when we introduce 20% uncertainty, this attribute will take the original value with 80% probability, and take other values with 20% probability. Meanwhile, we utilize Information Gain, IG, to select the top K attributes with maximum IG values, and transform these top K attributes into uncertain ones. And the uncertain dataset is denoted by Top$K$uA (Top K uncertain Attribute).

Our algorithms are implemented in Java based on the WEKA[1] software packages, and the experiments are conducted on a PC with Core 2 CPU, 2.0GB memory and Windows XP OS. We set *expected support* threshold to 1% and *confidence* threshold to 50%. Following CBA [5], we also set a limit of 80,000 on the total number of candidate rules in memory. As in [2,3,10], we measure the classification performance of the proposed classifier by accuracy. All the experimental results reported here are the average accuracy of 10-fold cross validation.

5.1 Performance of uCBA on Uncertain Datasets

In this group of experiment, we evaluate the performance of uCBA algorithm on different level of uncertain dataset. In the following, UT represents dataset with T% uncertainty, and we denote certain dataset as U0. Note that, uCBA algorithm is equivalent to the traditional CBA when applying to certain dataset, that is to say, when we set $T = 0$, our uCBA algorithm performs the same as CBA does.

Table 1. The Comparison of uCBA for Top2uA on Accuracy

Dataset	CBA	U10		U20		U30		U40	
		Single	Multiple	Single	Multiple	Single	Multiple	Single	Multiple
balance-scale	0.693	0.685	**0.747**	0.685	**0.752**	0.685	**0.722**	0.685	0.685
breast-w	0.959	0.930	**0.961**	0.944	**0.953**	0.956	**0.961**	0.951	**0.960**
credit-a	0.855	0.725	**0.762**	0.761	**0.768**	0.772	**0.775**	0.752	**0.788**
diabetes	0.770	0.699	**0.704**	0.698	**0.699**	0.699	**0.714**	0.699	**0.701**
heart-c	0.792	0.769	**0.795**	0.785	**0.785**	**0.799**	0.782	**0.832**	0.828
heart-h	0.837	**0.827**	0.813	0.813	**0.823**	0.827	0.827	**0.823**	0.816
hepatitis	0.813	**0.826**	0.794	0.819	**0.826**	0.819	**0.839**	0.806	**0.819**
hypothyroid	0.982	0.923	0.923	0.923	**0.923**	0.923	0.923	0.923	0.923
ionosphere	0.929	0.923	**0.929**	0.915	**0.929**	0.915	**0.920**	**0.926**	0.909
labor	0.912	0.860	**0.930**	0.877	**0.912**	0.877	**0.912**	0.877	**0.912**
lymph	0.824	0.797	**0.824**	0.791	**0.818**	**0.804**	0.797	**0.824**	0.797
segment	0.946	0.900	**0.925**	0.904	**0.924**	0.907	**0.926**	0.917	**0.930**
sick	0.976	0.939	**0.939**	0.939	**0.939**	0.939	0.939	0.939	0.939
sonar	0.817	0.822	**0.841**	0.822	**0.837**	0.846	**0.856**	0.841	0.841
soybean	0.893	0.748	**0.792**	0.808	**0.881**	0.865	**0.899**	0.883	**0.895**
breast-cancer	0.654	0.664	**0.692**	**0.696**	0.661	**0.675**	0.668	**0.689**	0.661
car	0.974	0.700	**0.864**	0.700	**0.853**	0.700	**0.825**	0.700	**0.782**
kr-vs-kp	0.975	**0.912**	0.909	**0.859**	0.854	0.819	**0.823**	**0.804**	0.802
mushroom	0.9995	0.998	0.998	0.998	0.998	0.998	0.998	0.998	0.998
nursery	0.935	0.671	**0.675**	0.671	**0.674**	0.671	**0.673**	0.671	**0.667**
vote	0.940	0.883	**0.897**	**0.890**	0.887	0.890	**0.910**	**0.897**	0.890
AveAccuracy	0.880	0.819	**0.844**	0.824	**0.843**	0.828	**0.842**	0.830	**0.835**

[1] http://www.cs.waikato.ac.nz/ml/weka/

Table 1 gives the performance for uCBA on Top2uA and different level of uncertainty (U0-U40) dataset. In Table 1, column *CBA* represents accuracy of CBA on certain datasets; column *Single* represents accuracy of uCBA's *single rule classification*; and column *Multiple* represents accuracy of uCBA's *multiple rules classification*.

As shown in Table 1, with increasing of uncertain level, the accuracy of uCBA degrades to some extent. It can be observed from Table 1 that, in most cases, the accuracy of *Multiple* exceeds that of *Single*; and on all the uncertainty datasets, the averaged accuracy of *Multiple* is higher than that of *Single*. It can be observed from Table 1 that, uCBA performs differently for different datasets. For some datasets, for example, balance-scale, labor and sonar, when introducing uncertainty into the datasets, uCBA-MRC can improve the prediction accuracy comparing with the accuracy of CBA. For most datasets, the performance decrement are within 7%, even when data uncertainty reaches 30%. The worst performance decrement is for the nursery dataset, the classifier has over 94% accuracy on certain data, reduces to around 67.5% when the uncertainty is 10%, to 67.4% when the uncertainty is 20%, and to 67.3% when the uncertainty reaches 30%.

The similar experiment results could be observed when we set K to 1, 3 and other values, and are omitted here for limited space. Overall speaking, the accuracy of uCBA classifier remains relatively stable. Even when the uncertainty level reaches 40% (U40), the average accuracy of uCBA-MRC (83.5%) on 21 datasets is still quite comparable to CBA (88.0%), and only decreases by 4.5% on accuracy. The experiments shows uCBA is quite robust against data uncertainty. Meanwhile, the difference of accuracy of the two methods among different experiment settings is significant on paired-sample t-Test [21], which means *Multiple* is more robust than *Single*.

5.2 Parameter Analysis on *coverThreshold*

In this group of experiment, we analyze the effect of parameter, $coverThreshold$, on accuracy. As discussed earlier, this parameter controls the number of rules for classification. Generally speaking, for uncertain data classification, if we use very few rules for classification, the instance may not be fully covered by rules, and this may lead to bad classification performance; on the other hand, if we use too many rules for classification, we may introduce noise and it may also lead to bad classification performance.

As an example, we analyze the effect of $coverThreshold$ on accuracy over 5 uncertain datasets with different level of uncertainty. From Fig.1, we can see that when the number of rules for classification exceeds 5, the performance of uCBA over the 5 datasets tend to be stable. Therefore, we set this parameter to 5 in all of the experiments in this paper.

5.3 Time and Space Analysis of uCBA

Here we analyze the number of association rules generated and the time token to generate these rules. We select 5 datasets from UCI Repository to perform this experiment, and analyze time and space consumption over Top1uA, Top2uA with U20 uncertain dataset. In Table 2, column *w/o pru* represents without rule pruning, and column *pru* represents rule pruning with PER following fomula (7).

We can see from Table 2 that PER can greatly reduce the number of rules, and prune insignificant rules. Meanwhile, we can also see that the number of association rules on

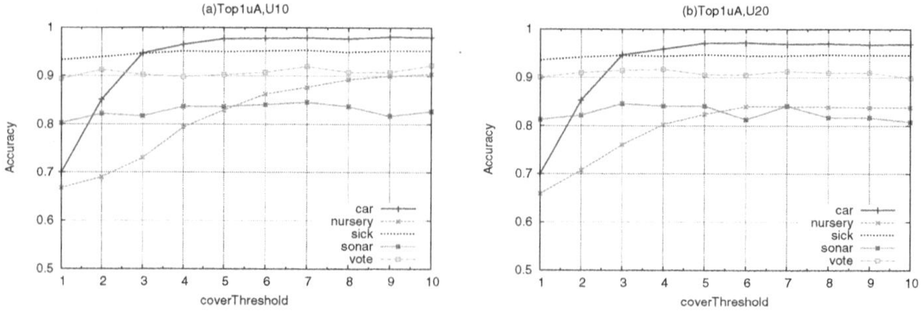

Fig. 1. Experiment with parameter *coverThreshold*

Table 2. Analysis of Time and the Number of Rules

Dataset	CBA		U20,No.of Rules				U20,Run time(s)		U20	
	No. of Rules		Top1uA		Top2uA		uCBA-RG,pru		No. of Rules in C	
	w/o pru	pru	w/o pru	pru	w/o pru	pru	Top1uA	Top2uA	Top1uA	Top2uA
car	1072	118	1063	108	1090	98	0.5	0.6	14	19
nursery	2976	415	2919	402	2842	346	12.9	20.3	178	132
sick	15037	6279	15360	6073	16165	5862	23.4	25.6	242	317
sonar	3307	2795	3303	2783	3306	2796	1.0	1.0	28	27
vote	25590	2033	26620	2197	27525	2221	3.8	4.4	88	243
Average	9596	2328	9853	2312	10186	2265	8	10	110	148

uncertain data is larger than that on certain data, this is because there are many uncertain information in uncertain data. It is shown that under the same level of uncertainty, the more the number of uncertain attributes, the longer it takes to mine association rules.

6 Conclusion and Future Work

Data uncertainty is prevalent in many real-world applications. In this paper, based on the *expected support*, we extend CBA algorithm and propose an associative classifier, uCBA, for uncertain data classification task. We redefine the support, confidence, rule pruning and classification strategy of CBA to build uncertain associative classifier. Experimental results on 21 datasets from UCI Repository demonstrate that the proposed algorithm yields good performance and has satisfactory performance even on highly uncertain data.

At present, our proposed algorithm only considers uncertain categorical attributes. We will consider uncertain numeric attributes in our future work.

References

1. Singh, S., Mayfield, C., Prabhakar, S., Shah, R., Hambrusch, S.: Indexing Uncertain Categorical Data. In: Proc. of ICDE 2007, pp. 616–625 (2007)
2. Qin, B., Xia, Y., Prbahakar, S., Tu, Y.: A Rule-based Classification Algorithm for Uncertain Data. In: The Workshop on Management and Mining of Uncertain Data, MOUND (2009)

3. Qin, B., Xia, Y., Li, F.: DTU: A Decision Tree for Uncertain Data. In: Theeramunkong, T., Kijsirikul, B., Cercone, N., Ho, T.-B. (eds.) PAKDD 2009. LNCS, vol. 5476, pp. 4–15. Springer, Heidelberg (2009)
4. Chui, C.K., Kao, B., Hung, E.: Mining frequent itemsets from uncertain data. In: Zhou, Z.-H., Li, H., Yang, Q. (eds.) PAKDD 2007. LNCS (LNAI), vol. 4426, pp. 47–58. Springer, Heidelberg (2007)
5. Liu, B., Hsu, W., Ma, Y.: Integrating classification and association rule mining. In: KDD, pp. 80–86 (1998)
6. Zimányi, E., Pirotte, A.: Imperfect information in relational databases. In: Uncertainty Management in Information Systems, pp. 35–88 (1996)
7. Li, W., Han, J., Pei, J.: CMAR: Accurate and Efficient Classification Based on Multiple Class-Association Rules. In: Proc. of ICDM 2001, pp. 369–380 (2001)
8. Yin, X., Han, J.: CPAR: Classification based on Predictive Association Rules. In: Proc. of SDM 2003, pp. 331–335 (2003)
9. Aggarwal, C.C., Yu, P.S.: A survey of Uncertain Data Algorithms and Applications. IEEE Transactions on Knowledge and Data Engineering 21(5), 609–623 (2009)
10. Tsang, S., Kao, B., Yip, K.Y., Ho, W.-S., Lee, S.D.: Decision Trees for Uncertain Data. In: Proc. of ICDE 2009, pp. 441–444 (2009)
11. Agrawal, R., Srikant, R.: Fast algorithms for mining association rules in large databases. In: Proc. of 20th VLDB, pp. 487–499. Morgan Kaufmann, San Francisco (1994)
12. Chui, C., Kao, B.: A decremental approach for mining frequent itemsets from uncertain data. In: Washio, T., Suzuki, E., Ting, K.M., Inokuchi, A. (eds.) PAKDD 2008. LNCS (LNAI), vol. 5012, pp. 64–75. Springer, Heidelberg (2008)
13. Leung, C.K.-S., Carmichael, C.L., Hao, B.: Efficient mining of frequent patterns from uncertain data. In: Proc. of ICDM Workshops, pp. 489–494 (2007)
14. Han, J., Pei, J., Yin, Y.: Mining frequent patterns without candidate generation. In: ACM SIGMOD Record, pp. 1–12 (2000)
15. Aggarwal, C.C., Li, Y., Wang, J., Wang, J.: Frequent pattern mining with uncertain data. In: Proc. of KDD 2009, pp. 29–38 (2009)
16. Zhang, Q., Li, F., Yi, K.: Finding Frequent Items in Probabilistic Data. In: Proc. of SIGMOD 2008, pp. 819–832 (2008)
17. Bernecker, T., Kriegel, H.P., Renz, M., Verhein, F., Zuefle, A.: Probabilistic frequent itemset mining in uncertain databases. In: Proc. of SIGKDD 2009, pp. 119–128 (2009)
18. Weng, C.-H., Chen, Y.-L.: Mining fuzzy association rules from uncertain data. Knowledge and Information Systems (2009)
19. Quinlan, J.R.: C4.5: Programs for Machine Learning. Morgan Kaufman Publishers, San Francisco (1993)
20. `http://archive.ics.uci.edu/ml/datasets.html`
21. Dietterich, T.: Approximate Statistical Tests for Comparing Supervised Classification Learning Algorithms. Neural Computation 10(7), 1895–1923 (1998)
22. Bi, J., Zhang, T.: Support Vector Classification with Input Data Uncertainty. In: NIPS, pp. 161–168 (2004)
23. Ngai, W.K., Kao, B., Chui, C.K., Cheng, R., Chau, M., Yip, K.Y.: Efficient clustering of uncertain data. In: Perner, P. (ed.) ICDM 2006. LNCS (LNAI), vol. 4065, pp. 436–445. Springer, Heidelberg (2006)
24. Lee, S.D., Kao, B., Cheng, R.: Reducing UK-means to K-means. In: Proc. of ICDM Workshops, pp. 483–488 (2007)
25. Cormode, G., McGregor, A.: Approximation Algorithms for Clustering Uncertain Data. In: PODS 2008, pp. 191–200 (2008)
26. Aggarwal, C.C., Yu, P.S.: Outlier Detection with Uncertain Data. In: Jonker, W., Petković, M. (eds.) SDM 2008. LNCS, vol. 5159, pp. 483–493. Springer, Heidelberg (2008)

Automatic Multi-schema Integration Based on User Preference

Guohui Ding[1,2], Guoren Wang[1,2], Junchang Xin[1,2], and Huichao Geng[2]

[1] Key Laboratory of Medical Image Computing (NEU), Ministry of Education
[2] College of Information Science & Engineering, Northeastern University, China
dgh_acheng@sina.com, wanggr@mail.neu.edu.cn, xinjunchang@ise.neu.edu.cn

Abstract. Schema integration plays a central role in numerous database applications, such as Deep Web, DataSpaces and Ontology Merging. Although there have been many researches on schema integration, they all neglect user preference which is a very important factor for improving the quality of mediated schemas. In this paper, we propose the automatic multi-schema integration based on user preference. A new concept named reference schema is introduced to represent user preference. This concept can guide the process of integration to generate mediated schemas according to user preference. Different from previous solutions, our approach employs F-measure and "attribute density" to measure the similarity between schemas. Based on this similarity, we design a top-k ranking algorithm that retrieves k mediate schemas which users really expect. The key component of the algorithm is a pruning strategy which makes use of Divide and Conquer to narrow down the search space of the candidate schemas. Finally, the experimental study demonstrates the effectiveness and good performance of our approach.

1 Introduction

The goal of schema integration is to merge a set of existing source schemas, which are related to each other and developed independently by different people, to one or more mediated schemas by correspondences between attributes of schemas. The reason for integrating source schemas is that they are closely related, and have much overlapping information associated with the same real-world concepts, but often represented in different ways and different formats.

There have already existed many researches on schema integration. However, the existing techniques ignore user preference which is a very important factor for improving the quality of schema integration. We use an example in Figure 1 to show the utility of user preference. Consider two schemas to be integrated, S_1 and S_2, which belong to corporation A and B respectively. For simplicity, we consider only two integrating strategies, one is merging "staff" and "employee", while the other is merging "employee", "manager" and "staff". This will generate two mediated schemas M_1 and M_2 respectively. For corporation A, M_2 may invalidate some applications based on S_1, because it destroys the schema structure of S_1. Meanwhile, compared to M_2, the structure of M_1 is

L. Chen et al. (Eds.): WAIM 2010, LNCS 6184, pp. 704–716, 2010.

more similar to that of S_1. As a result, users in corporation A may prefer M_1 to M_2. However, B may be a very small corporation and, therefore, there is no need to design two different schemas for "employee" and "manager" respectively (a unified representation "staff" may be convenient). By contrast with M_1, the structure of M_2 is more similar to that of S_2. Consequently, users in corporation B may prefer M_2 to M_1. As the example shows, different users expect different integration results; so, user preference is able to improve the quality of results of schema integration. Thus, we make use of user preference to guide the integration process to generate more reasonable mediated schemas for different users. User preference can be materialized through a given source schema, namely S_1 for users in corporation A and S_2 for users in B. We call these source schemas reference schemas. This motivates our work in this paper.

To the best of our knowledge, there is no prior work discussing user preference in schema integration. In this paper, we propose an automatic multi-schema integration approach based on user preference. Different from previous solutions, our approach uses F-measure and "attribute density" to measure the similarity between schemas based on correspondences, which can be user-specified or discovered through the automatic schema matching tools [9], between attributes. Then, we design a top-k ranking algorithm for retrieving k mediated schemas which are most similar to the reference schema. The algorithm employs Divide and Conquer to narrow down the search space of the candidate mediated schemas. At the beginning, the user can select a reference schema rs as the template that conforms to user preference; then, rs will guide the integration process to generate mediated schemas according to this template.

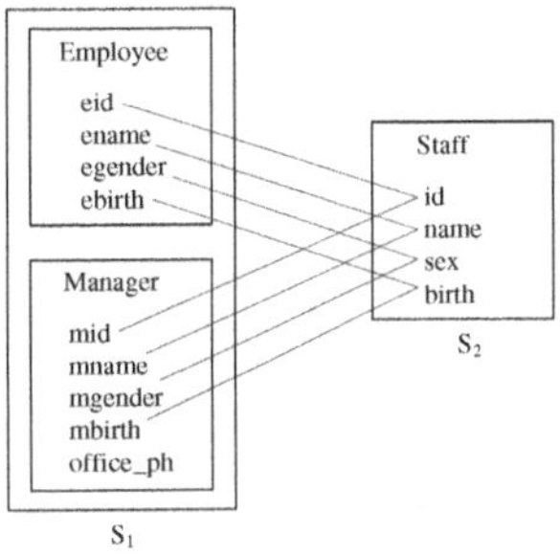

(a) Source Schemas

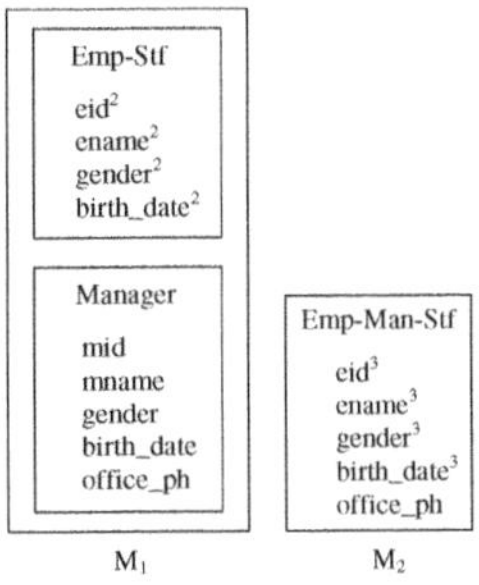

(b) Mediated Schemas

Fig. 1. The Example of Our Motivation

This paper makes the following contributions:

1. We develop an automatic multi-schema integration approach based on user preference, and use the reference schema to materialize the preference.
2. A new concept "attribute density" is introduced to measure the integrated degree of a mediated schema, and together with F-measure to measure the similarity between schemas.

3. The top-k ranking algorithm is developed to retrieve k mediated schemas which users really expect.

2 Preliminaries

In this section, the concept graph model is first introduced to represent the input schemas, followed by correspondences among multiple concepts, and finally, the search space of the candidate schemas is presented.

2.1 Concept Graphs

The input source schemas may have many kinds of representation forms, such as XML and relational models. As a result, a logical view which is used to abstract the concrete physical layout of schemas from different kinds of models is urgently needed. As in [1], we use concept graphs with edges depicting *has-a* relationships to represent, at a higher-level of abstraction, the input schemas.

A concept graph is a pair (V, has) where V is a set of concept nodes and has is a set of directed and labeled edges between concepts. A node of the graph represents a concept of a schema. An edge of the graph depicts a directional reference relation between concepts. The whole S_1 and S_2 and their corresponding concept graphs are shown in Figure 2.

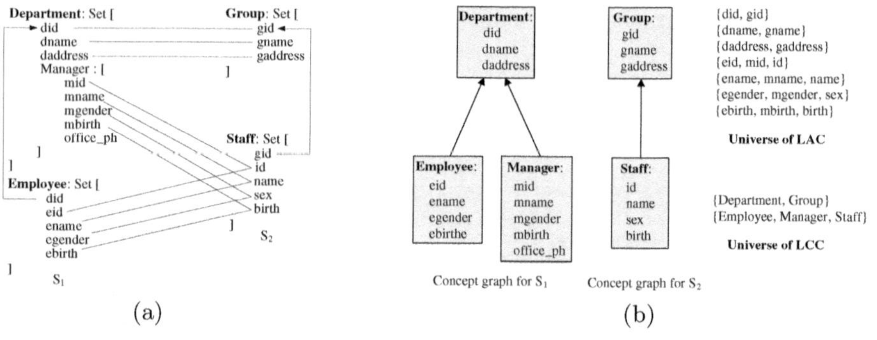

Fig. 2. The Whole Schema S_1 and S_2, and their Concept Graphs

2.2 Correspondences

The traditional correspondence is a binary relationship. To tackle multiple input schemas, we introduce the multivariate correspondence. In this paper, the multivariate correspondence contains the attribute correspondence and the concept correspondence. The former represents an attribute set where each element has the same semantics. The latter represents a concept set where overlapping information exists among different concepts.

Definition 1. *Let u be a universe of attributes of input schemas. Let $ac = \{a_1, ..., a_i, ..., a_n\}$ be an attribute set and $ac \subset u$. If all attributes in ac have the same semantics, we call ac the attribute correspondence.*

Definition 2. *Let $acs = \{ac_1, ..., ac_i, ..., ac_q, ..., ac_n\}$ be a universe of the attribute correspondences of the input schemas. If $ac_q \not\subset ac_i$ and $q \neq i$ for $1 \leq i \leq n$, we call ac_q the largest attribute correspondence, LAC for short.*

Definition 3. *Let $ac = \{a_1, ..., a_i, ..., a_n\}$ be the LAC. If $cc = \{c_1, ..., c_i, ..., c_n\}$ is a concept set and a_i is an attribute of c_i for $1 \leq i \leq n$, we call cc the largest concept correspondence, LCC for short.*

The instances of the *LAC* and *LCC* are shown in the right Figure 2(b).

2.3 Merging Concept Graphs

After recasting a schema into the graph of concepts, the problem of schema integration is transformed to the problem of merging concept graphs.

Definition 4. *Let $cs = \{c_1, ..., c_i, ..., c_n\}$ be a concept set where $n \geq 2$. If cs belongs to some LCC, we say that cs is matched. Then, cs can be consolidated into a single one, cc. We call cc the composite concept, c_i the single concept and say that cc contains c_i.*

For the concepts which are matched, the merging task contains two parts: first, merging the attributes in the same *LAC*; second, reserving the *has-a* relationships. A superscript is attached to the attribute name to show the number of the attributes (duplicates) being merged. For example, the whole concept graphs of M_1 and M_2 are shown in Figure 3.

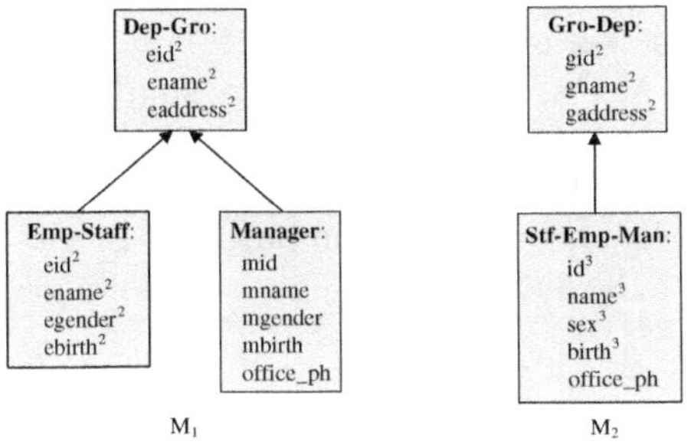

Fig. 3. The Whole Graphs of M_1 and M_2

2.4 Search Space of Mediated Schemas

Theorem 1. *Let $cs = \{c_1, ..., c_i, ..., c_n\}$ be a concept set. Let cs' be any subset of cs, and $|cs'| \geq 2$. If cs is matched, then cs' is also matched.*

Now, we can consider the space of the possible mediated schemas. Theorem 1 shows we can merge any subset of *LCC* to a composite concept, as one concept of the mediated schema, so, one partition of the LCC is a candidate solution. For example, let $lcc = \{c_1, c_2, c_3\}$ be a LCC. For lcc, we can obtain five partitions: $\{\{c_1, c_2, c_3\}\}$, $\{\{c_1, c_2\}, \{c_3\}\}$, $\{\{c_1, c_3\}, \{c_2\}\}$, $\{\{c_2, c_3\}, \{c_1\}\}$, $\{\{c_1\}, \{c_2\}, \{c_3\}\}$. Each partition generates some composite concepts that are a part of the mediated schema. The Cartesian products of the partitions of each LCC compose the space of the possible mediated schemas which are called the candidate schemas. Obviously, the space exhibits exponential growth in size of the LCC. Our task is to find k candidate schemas from the huge space.

3 Scoring Function for Concepts

Given a reference schema rs, we can get a standard schema corresponding to rs.

Definition 5. *Given reference schema rs, let $c = (a_1, ..., a_i, ..., a_n)$ be a concept of rs. If $s = \{l_1, ..., l_i, ..., l_n\}$ is the set of the $LACs$ and $a_i \in l_i$ for $1 \leq i \leq n$, we call $sc = (a_1^{|l_1|}, ..., a_i^{|l_i|}, ..., a_n^{|l_n|})$ the standard concept corresponding to c.*

The standard schema consists of a set of standard concepts. For simplicity, the prefixes "r-" and "s-" are attached to the associated components of the reference schema and the standard schema respectively. Definition 5 shows the s-schema is the same as the r-schema, except the superscript which depicts the number of duplicates of the r-attribute. The s-schema represents the ideal integration scenario that all the input schemas are the duplicates of the r-schema, and need to be combined to a single one, namely the s-schema. As a result, the integration results that users really expect, are the s-schema. The higher the similarity between the candidate schema and the s-schema is, the more popular the candidate schema is for users. Our task is to find k candidate schemas which are most similar to the s-schema.

We take advantage of F-measure to measure similarity between the composite concept and the s-concept. Further, we derive similarity between the candidate schema and the s-schema in Section 4. In the following, we call similarity function scoring function, as all the similarity computation is relative to the s-schema or s-concept. The higher the score is, the higher the similarity is.

Definition 6. *Let cc be a composite concept which contains only one r-concept rc. Let c_{cc} and c_{rc} be the number of attributes of cc and rc respectively. The precision of the cc is defined as follows:*

$$pre = \frac{c_{rc}}{c_{cc}} \tag{1}$$

Definition 7. *Let $cc = (a_1^{c_1}, ..., a_i^{c_i}, ..., a_n^{c_n}, ..., a_z^{c_z})$ be a composite concept which contains only one r-concept rc. Let $sc = (a_1^{d_1}, ..., a_i^{d_i}, ..., a_n^{d_n})$ be the s-concept corresponding to rc. Then, the recall of cc is defined as follows:*

$$rec = \frac{\sum_{i=1}^{n} c_i}{\sum_{i=1}^{n} d_i} \tag{2}$$

With the precision and recall, F-measure is written as follows:

$$fm = \frac{2 \times pre \times rec}{pre + rec} \tag{3}$$

Now, we complete the above definition. Intuitively, if the composite concept cc contains no s-concepts, we set $fm(cc) = 0$. If cc contains more than one s-concept, we also set $fm(cc) = 0$, because cc destroys the structure of the s-schema that these s-concepts exist independently. The precision definition describes the proportion that the number of r-attributes contained by cc accounts for of the total number of attributes of cc. The recall describes how many attribute duplicates are returned from the s-concepts. In contrast to recall, precision is coarse-grained, because the number of duplicates of a composite attribute has no influence on the structure of a concept.

Consider two composite concepts: $cc = (a_1^2, a_2^2, b^2)$, $cc' = (a_1^2, a_2^2, b^1)$, where a_1 and a_2 are r-attributes. Although $fm(cc)$ is equal to $fm(cc')$, cc is better than cc', because attribute b includes more duplicates and reduces more redundancy. The attribute density is introduced to deal with this problem.

Definition 8. *Let $cc = (a_1^{c_1}, ..., a_i^{c_i}, ..., a_z^{c_z})$ be a composite concept containing n single concepts. The attribute density after normalization is defined as follows:*

$$ad = \frac{1}{n} \frac{\sum_{i=1}^{z} c_i}{z} \qquad 2 \leq n \tag{4}$$

The fraction in the right of the equation is the attribute density that describes the average number of duplicates in each attribute. Number n is the upper bound to the value of the attribute density of cc, and we use it to normalize the attribute density. The bigger the attribute density is, the more compact the composite concept is. If $n = 1$, we set the attribute density of a single concept to the constant δ whose utility is explained in Section 4.

Based on Equations (3) and (4), we present scoring function for a concept c which includes n single concepts, described as follows:

$$CSF(c) = \begin{cases} \lambda_1 \times fm(c) + \lambda_2 \times ad(c) & n \geq 2, \lambda_1 + \lambda_2 = 1 \\ \delta \quad n = 1 \end{cases} \tag{5}$$

The above proportionality constants λ_1 and λ_2 are weighting factors of the two measurements, and users can tune them to get more appropriate values for specific applications. In our experiments, we set $\lambda_1 = \lambda_2 = 0.5$.

4 Generation of *K* Best Candidate Schemas

We now describe the algorithm searching k candidate schemas. The algorithm includes two stages: first, finding the best candidate; second, according to results of the former stage, finding the rest $k - 1$ results.

4.1 The Best Candidate Schema

One partition of the LCC is a merging strategy which generates a set of composite concepts as a portion of the candidate schema, and we call this portion the partial candidate schema (PS for short). One candidate schema is obtained by combining one PS of each LCC. Thus, the problem of searching the best candidate schema can be transformed to the problem of searching the best PS of each LCC. Then, we combine them together to a complete schema.

Definition 9. *Let* $ps = \{c_1, ..., c_i, ..., c_n\}$ *be a* PS *of a* LCC*. We define scoring function for* ps *to be:*

$$PSSF(ps) = \frac{1}{n}\sum_{i=1}^{n} CSF(c_i) \tag{6}$$

The search space of PS is exponential in size of LCC. We use the thought of greedy algorithm, that makes the best decision in the current context, to find the best PS. The score of PS is the average of the scores of concepts included in PS. As a result, we hope that the best PS contains less concepts, however, each of them with higher score. Based on this heuristic, in a LCC, we would like to merge a pair of concepts that the score of their merging result is higher than other pairs, and merge concepts as many as possible. The process of generating the best PS is shown in Algorithm 1. The algorithm is an iterative process, and each iteration generates a new PS which is better than the previous one. Finally, the algorithm will terminate, if a new better PS can't be generated.

Algorithm 1. Derive the Best Candidate Schema

input : lcc: the LCC, namely the initial PS;
c_a, c_b, c_{new}: variables of the concept;
th: the threshold in Theorem 2;

repeat
    float $maxScore = 0.0$;
    for *each concept* c_i *in* lcc **do**
        for *each concept* c_j *in* lcc **do**
            $concept\ cc = merging(c_i, c_j);\ //i \neq j$
            if $maxScore < CSF(cc)$ **then**
                $maxScore = CSF(cc)$;
                $c_a = c_i$; $c_b = c_j$; $c_{new} = cc$;
    if $maxScore > th$ **then**
        $lcc.push(c_{new})$; $lcc.remove(c_a)$; $lcc.remove(c_b)$; save lcc;
until $maxScore \leq th$

Let $ps = \{c_1, ..., c_i, ..., c_j, ..., c_n\}$ be a PS where c_i and c_j are any two concepts. The threshold th used in Algorithm 1 is equal to $CSF(c_i)+CSF(c_j)-PSSF(ps)$. For each iteration, the threshold can guarantee that the score of the new PS in the next iteration is higher than the current one. Based on this threshold, our algorithm is able to evolve gradually to the optimal solution with each iteration. The following theorem shows the theory used here.

Theorem 2. *Let* $ps = \{c_1, ..., c_i, ...c_j, ..., c_n\}$ *be a* PS *where* c_i *and* c_j *are any two concepts. We merge* c_i *and* c_j *to a composite concept* cc*, further form a new* PS $ps' = \{c_1, ..., c_{i-1}, cc, ..., c_{n-1}\}$*. If* $CSF(cc) > CSF(c_i) + CSF(c_j) - PSSF(ps)$*, we can conclude that* $PSSF(ps') > PSSF(ps)$*.*

Proof. Let $sum = \sum_{i=1}^{n} CSF(c_i)$, $sc_i = CSF(c_i)$, $sc_j = CSF(c_j)$ and $scc = CSF(cc)$. Because of $PSSF(ps) = \frac{1}{n}sum$, the premise can be rewrote as : $n \times scc > n \times (sc_1 + sc_2) - sum$, and then we transform the formula as follows:

$$n \times scc > n \times (sc_1 + sc_2) - sum$$
$$\Rightarrow n \times scc > n \times (sc_1 + sc_2) - (sum - sc_1 - sc_2 + sc_1 + sc_2)$$
$$\Rightarrow n \times scc > (n-1) \times (sc_1 + sc_2) - n \times (sum - sc_1 - sc_2) + (n-1) \times (sum - sc_1 - sc_2)$$
$$\Rightarrow n \times (scc + sum - sc_1 - sc_2) > (n-1)sum$$
$$\Rightarrow \frac{1}{n-1}(scc + (sum - sc_1 - sc_2)) > \frac{1}{n}sum$$
$$\Rightarrow PSSF(ps') > PSSF(ps)$$
□

We combine the best PSs of each LCC to generate the top-one candidate.

4.2 The Rest Candidate Schemas

Because of the exponential growth of the PSs, it is impossible to enumerate all the PSs of the LCC. Here, we use the approximate but meaningful method to narrow down the space of the candidate schemas. During obtaining the best candidate schema, we found that the PSs generated in the iterations proceed to the optimal objective step by step. All these PSs embody the evolvement of the input schemas from multiple individual schemas to the best unified mediated schema. Consequently, they are more representative and meaningful. We combine them to generate the space of candidate schemas. Then, our algorithm is to find the k results (including the top-one from this space).

Definition 10. *Let $cs = (ps_1, ..., ps_i, ..., ps_n)$ be a candidate schema where ps_i is a PS. Scoring function for cs is defined as follows:*

$$CSSF(cs) = \frac{1}{n}\sum_{i=1}^{n} PSSF(ps_i) \tag{7}$$

We aim to find the top-k candidate schemas with the highest scores. Given a set of input schemas, the variable n of Definition 10 is a constant denoting the number of the LCCs, so we just consider the sum. As in Section 2.4, the space of candidate schemas is Cartesian products of the PSs of each LCC. If there exist n $LCCs$ and each holds m representative PSs, the size of the space is $(c_m^1 \times c_m^1 \times ... \times c_m^1)_n = m^n$. The naive enumeration is not feasible.

Theorem 3. *Let $cs = (ps_1, ..., ps_i, ..., ps_n)$ be a candidate schema where ps_i is a PS. Here, we regard cs as a vector. If cs is in the top-k results, then $cs' = (ps_1, ..., ps_i, ..., ps_{n-1})$ also belongs to the set of top-k results in $n-1$ dimensions.*

Proof. Here, we use the reduction to absurdity. Let $lccs_n = \{lcc_1, ..., lcc_i, ..., lcc_n\}$ be the set of the LCCs. Let $css_k = \{cs_1, ..., cs_i, ..., cs_k\}$ be the top-k results where $cs_i = (ps_{i1}, ..., ps_{ij}, ..., ps_{in})$ is the ith candidate schema and ps_{ij} is a PS of lcc_i. Let $sv_i = (s_{i1}, ..., s_{ij}, ..., s_{in})$ be the score vector of cs_i where $s_{ij} = PSSF(ps_{ij})$. So, $svs_k = \{sv_1, ..., sv_i, ..., sv_k\}$ is the set of the score vectors of css_k. We remove the nth dimension of each sv_i of svs_k to get the set $svs'_k = \{sv'_1, ..., sv'_i, ..., sv'_k\}$ where $sv'_i = (s_{i1}, ..., s_{ij}, ..., s_{i(n-1)})$. Let $svs''_k = \{sv''_1, ..., sv''_i, ..., sv''_k\}$ be the set of the top-k score vectors with respect to $lccs_{n-1} = \{lcc_1, ..., lcc_i, ..., lcc_{n-1}\}$, and $sv''_i = (s''_{i1}, ..., s''_{ij}, ..., s''_{i(n-1)})$ is the ith highest score vector. Let $sum(sv_i) = \sum_{j=1}^{n} s_{ij}$. Assume $(\exists sv'_i) sv'_i \notin svs''_k$, then we get $(\exists sv''_i) sv''_i \in svs''_k \wedge sv''_i \notin svs'_k \Rightarrow (\exists nsv_i)(nsv_i = (s''_{i1}, ..., s''_{ij}, ..., s''_{i(n-1)}, s_{in})) \wedge nsv_i \notin svs_k$. Because $sv'_i \notin svs''_k$, we can get $sum(s_{i1}, ..., s_{ij}, ..., s_{i(n-1)}) < sum(s''_{i1}, ..., s''_{ij}, ..., s''_{i(n-1)}) \Rightarrow sum(s_{i1}, ..., s_{ij}, ..., s_{in}) < sum(s''_{i1}, ..., s''_{ij}, ..., s''_{i(n-1)}, s_{in})$, namely $sum(sv_i) < sum(nsv_i)$. Because of $nsv_i \notin svs_k$ and $sum(nsv_i) > sum(sv_i)$, the nsv_i should be inserted into svs_k and rank in front of sv_i. We get a conclusion that sv_i is the $(i+1)$th highest score vector. However, this conclusion is contrary to our precondition that sv_i is the ith highest score vector, so the theorem 3 is true. □

Let $lccs_n = \{lcc_1, ..., lcc_i, ..., lcc_n\}$ be a LCC set. Based on Theorem 3, we can get a recursive equation for finding the top-k results, as follows:

$$top\text{-}k(lccs_n) = top\text{-}k(top\text{-}k(lccs_{n-1}) \times PS(lcc_n)) \quad (8)$$

where the $PS(lcc_n)$ represents the set of the representative PSs of lcc_n. The recursion will terminate at top-$k(PS(lcc_1))$, so we just need to find the top-k PSs of lcc_1, then perform the contrary recursive process to get the top-k candidate schemas. The details of the algorithm are shown in Algorithm 2. An example for top-3 candidate schemas over 3 LCCs is shown in Figure 4[1].

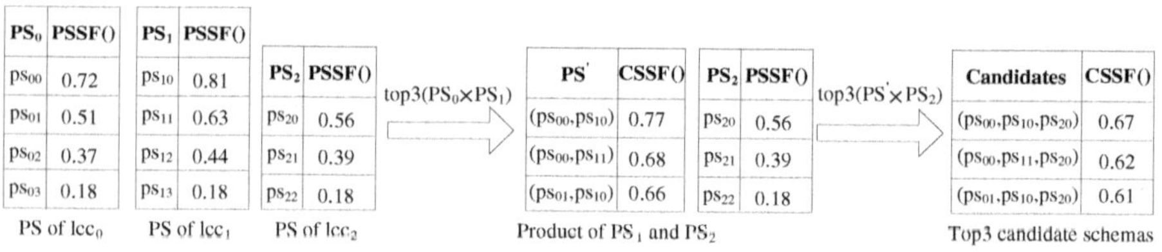

Fig. 4. Example of the Top-k Ranking Algorithm

Algorithm 2. Top-k Ranking Algorithm

input : $lccs[]$: the set of the LCCs of the input schemas;
rs: the given reference schema;
$ps[]$: the set of the PS of $lccs[i]$;
$k[]$: the top-k results;

```
for each element in lccs[] do
    k[]=combine(k[], ps[]); //combine the ps[] of each lccs[i] to a whole schema;
    CSSF(k[]);
    rank(k[]); //rank k[] decendingly according to PSSF()
    k[]=getTopK(k[]); //save the top k schemas;
```

[1] Omit the first step due to the limited space.

4.3 Tuning the Constant δ

The constant δ which is the score of the single concept is monotonic with the threshold in Section 4.1; so, it controls whether to merge two concepts to some extend. Let c and c' be two concepts. As δ decreases, the possibility for merging them increases; in contrast, the possibility will decrease. Thus, increasing δ will resulting in more compact mediated schemas, while reducing δ will result in more normalized mediated schemas with leaving more schemas alone. For example, we consider the extreme case, if $\delta = 1$, no pairs of concepts can be merged, because the threshold in Algorithm 1 holds the upper bound 1.

5 Experimental Evaluation

In this section, we evaluate the performance of our integration approach in synthetic integration scenarios. First, we present how to generate the synthetic input source schemas via the random method. Then, we show the experimental results evaluating the performance of our top-k ranking algorithm along three dimensions: the number of the input schemas, the number k of candidate schemas retrieved, and the parameter δ which controls whether to merge concepts. Our algorithm is implemented using C++ language and the experiments were carried on a PC compatible machine, with Intel Core Duo processor (2.33GHz).

For one input schema, we randomly generate n concepts and $n \in [2...6]$, then, we randomly assign m attributes to a given concept where $m \in [3...8]$. In what follows we focus on simulating the correspondences (LAC) of the input schemas. The ideal integration scenario is that all the input schemas are the duplicates of some schema. The number of LACs for this scenario is the number of attributes of a schema, and each LAC contains all the duplicates of an attribute. In order to simulate the real-world schemas, we assume that a fraction of the input schemas are similar, and set the proportion p to 80% or 40% in our experiment, respectively. When $p = 80\%$, it means that 8 of 10 attributes from different schemas have the same semantics. So, we get the computation for the number of LACs in our synthetic scenario, denoted as $\frac{aver}{p}$, where $aver$ represents the average of the attribute number in each schema. Based on the LAC generated, we randomly distribute the attributes to any LAC. For each time of running the algorithm, we randomly generate a set of synthetic schemas. All the experimental results are the average performance of running the algorithm for many times.

The first experimental results are shown in Figure 5 ($p = 80\%$). This experiment tests the change in the running times as the effect of varying the number of the input schemas. As it can be seen, the times increase with the variation in the number of the input schemas from 10 to 100. Our algorithm performs well, less than one second for retrieving 60 candidate schemas from 100 input source schemas. We also observe that the times for $\delta = 0.15$ are higher than $\delta = 0.45$ all the time. The reason for this behavior is that the increase of δ reduces the possibility of merging concepts, further, decreases the number of the PSs of each LCC. This is consistent with the analysis in subsection 4.3.

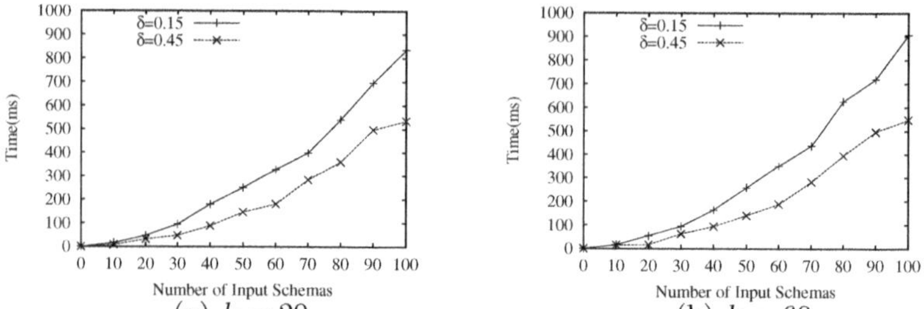

(a) $k = 20$ (b) $k = 60$

Fig. 5. Time Cost Vs. Input Schemas With $p = 80\%$

The experiment in Figure 6 studies the effect of increasing the number k on the performance. We observe that the running times remain unchanged almost and wave around some values as k increases. This is because the main cost of our algorithm is the time of generating the representative PSs to form the candidate schemas, and the time of retrieving the k candidate schemas is less relatively, when $k < 100$. We perform another test for $k > 1000$, and the results show that the cost varies significantly as k increases. However, so large value of k is meaningless for users in practice, so we don't present this results.

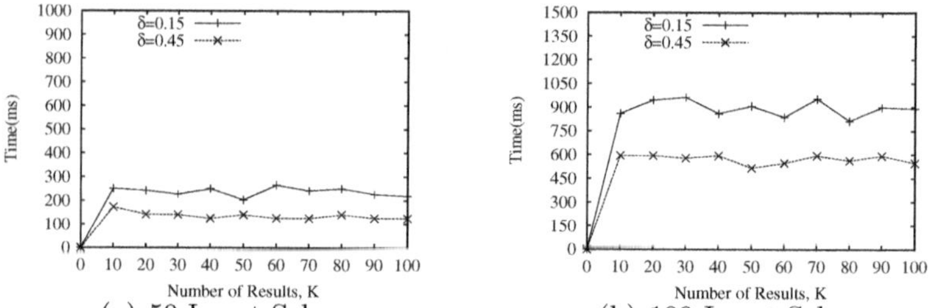

(a) 50 Input Schemas (b) 100 Input Schemas

Fig. 6. Time Cost Vs. Results Retrieved With $p = 80\%$

In the following experiments, we set $p = 40\%$ to simulate the scenario that a less portion of the input schemas are similar. In Figure 7, the variation of the cost is similar to the cost in Figure 5 as the number of the input schemas increases from 10 to 100. However, the running times for $p = 40\%$ are less than the times for $p = 80\%$. The overall similarity of the input schemas decreases when diminishing the value of p; this results in the reduction of the number of the concepts in each LCC. Further, the size of the iterations for generating the representative PSs will be reduced. As a result, the running times decrease with the reduction of the proportion factor p.

The study in Figure 8 is similar to the experiment which tests the effect of the number k on the performance in Figure 6. We observe that the curves for the cost almost parallel to the x-axis, but they are all under the corresponding curves in Figure 6. The reasons have been presented in the above experiment.

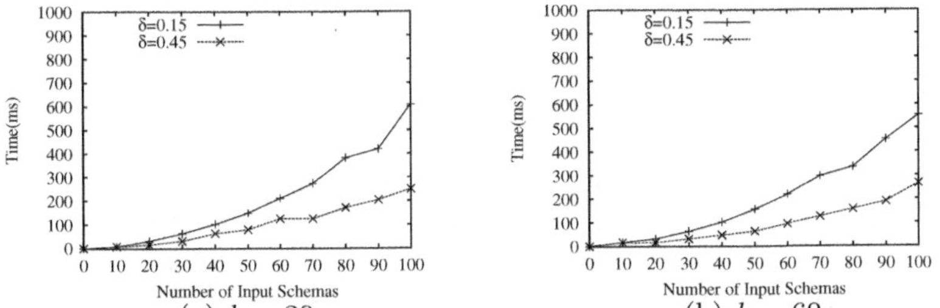

(a) $k = 20$ (b) $k = 60$

Fig. 7. Time Cost Vs. Input Schemas With $p = 40\%$

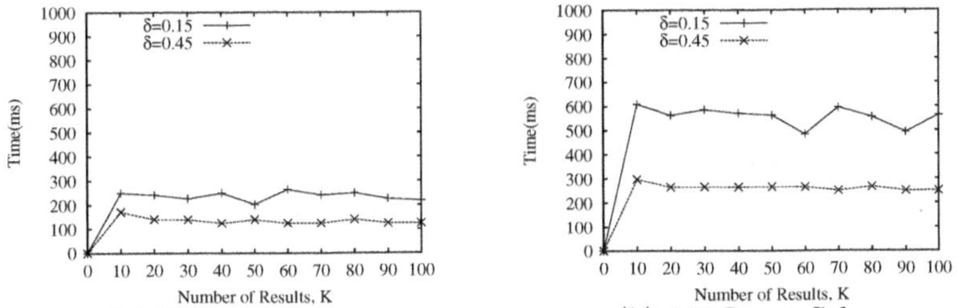

(a) 50 Input Schemas (b) 100 Input Schemas

Fig. 8. Time Cost Vs. Results Retrieved With $p = 40\%$

6 Related Work

Schema integration has been an active research field for a long time [4, 6, 7, 8, 5]. Given a set of source schemas and correspondences ,the recent work [1] systematically enumerates multiple mediated schemas. But their approach relies heavily on user's interaction; thus, it is time consuming and labor intensive. Another recent work [5] proposes an automatic approach to schema integration. Then, they developed an algorithm for the automatic generation of multiple mediated schemas, but the number of the input schemas is restricted to two in their work.

The work [6] develops a generic framework that can be used to merge models in all these contexts. A formalism-independent algorithm for ontology merging and alignment, named PROMPT, is developed in [3]. An ontology merging system FCA-Merge [2] is developed, following the bottom-up techniques which offer a structural description of the merging process.

The attribute correspondence used in our approach can be seen as schema matching, which is another long-standing research problem [9, 10, 11, 12]. The automatic schema matching is summarized in [9]. Recently, the possible mapping is introduced to the schema matching [10, 11], which provide another research thought for schema matching and data integration.

7 Conclusion

In this paper, we introduce user preference to schema integration. Then, we propose automatic multi-schema integration based on user preference. The key component of our approach is the top-k ranking algorithm for automatically retrieving the k mediated schemas which are most similar to the given reference schema (standard schema). The algorithm employs dynamic programming technique to narrow down the space of candidate schemas. Different from previous solutions, our algorithm makes use of the "attribute density" and F-measure to measure the similarity between the candidate schema and the standard schema. Another feature that distinguishes our approach from existing work is that we generate multiple integration results over a set of source schemas.

Acknowledgments

This research was supported by the National Natural Science Foundation of China (Grant No. 60873011, 60773221, 60803026), the 863 Program (Grant No. 2009AA01Z131), and Ph.D. Programs Foundation (Young Teacher) of Ministry of Education of China (Grant No. 20070145112).

References

1. Chiticariu, L., Kolaitis, P.G., Popa, L.: Interactive Generation of Integrated Schemas. In: Proc. of SIGMOD, pp. 833–846 (2008)
2. Stumme, G., Maedche, A.: FCA-MERGE: Bottom-up merging of ontologies. In: Proc. of IJCAI, pp. 225–234 (2001)
3. Noy, N.F., Musen, M.A.: PROMPT: Algorithm and Tool for Automated Ontology Merging and Alignment. In: Proc. of AAAI/IAAI, pp. 450–455 (2000)
4. Udrea, O., Getoor, L., Miller, R.J.: Leveraging Data and Structure in Ontology Integration. In: Proc. of SIGMOD, pp. 449–460 (2007)
5. Radwan, A., Popa, L., Stanoi, I.R., Younis, A.: Top-K Generation of Integrated Schemas Based on Directed and Weighted Correspondences. In: Proc. of SIGMOD, pp. 641–654 (2009)
6. Pottinger, R., Bernstein, P.A.: Merging Models Based on Given Correspondences. In: Proc. of VLDB, pp. 826–873 (2003)
7. Pottinger, R., Bernstein, P.A.: Schema Merging and Mapping Creation for Relational Sources. In: Proc. of EDBT, pp. 73–84 (2008)
8. Franklin, M., Halevy, A., Maier, D.: From Databases to Dataspaces: A New Abstraction for Information Management. In: Proc. of SIGMOD, pp. 1–7 (2005)
9. Rahm, E., Bernstein, P.A.: A survey of approaches to automatic schema matching. VLDB Journal 10(4), 334–350 (2001)
10. Sarma, A.D., Dong, X., Halevy, A.: Bootstrapping Pay-As-You-Go Data Integration Systems. In: Proc. of SIGMOD, pp. 861–874 (2008)
11. Dong, X., Halevy, A.Y., Yu, C.: Data integration with uncertainty. In: Proc. of VLDB, pp. 687–698 (2007)
12. Chan, C., Elmeleegy, H., Ouzzani, M., Elmagarmid, A.: Usage-Based Schema Matching. In: Proc. of ICDE, pp. 20–29 (2008)

EIF: A Framework of Effective Entity Identification*

Lingli Li, Hongzhi Wang, Hong Gao, and Jianzhong Li

Department of Computer Science and Engineering, Harbin Institute of Technology, China
lwsbrr@gmail.com, {wangzh,honggao,lijzh}@hit.edu.cn

Abstract. Entity identification, that is to build corresponding relationships between objects and entities in dirty data, plays an important role in data cleaning. The confusion between entities and their names often results in dirty data. That is, different entities may share the identical name and different names may correspond to the identical entity. Therefore, the major task of entity identification is to distinguish entities sharing the same name and recognize different names referring to the same entity. However, current research focuses on only one aspect and cannot solve the problem completely. To address this problem, in this paper, EIF, a framework of entity identification with the consideration of the both kinds of confusions, is proposed. With effective clustering techniques, approximate string matching algorithms and a flexible mechanism of knowledge integration, EIF can be widely used to solve many different kinds of entity identification problems. In this paper, as an application of EIF, we solved the author identification problem. The effectiveness of this framework is verified by extensive experiments.

Keywords: entity identification, data cleaning, graph partition.

1 Introduction

In many applications, entities are often queried by their names. For example, e-commerce players such as Amazon.com helps people search books by inputting book names; movies can be found on imdb.com by inputting movie names, and researchers are often queried by their names on dblp. Unfortunately, dirty data often lead to incomplete or duplicated results for such queries. From different aspects, there are two major problems. On the one hand, a name may have different spellings and one entity can be represented by multiple names. For example, the name of a researcher "Wei Wang" can be both written as "Wei Wang" and "W. Wei". Another example of this confusion is movie names. Such as the movie called "Hong lou ment" can also be represented as "A Dream in Red Mansions". On the other hand, one name can represent multiple entities. For example, when querying an author named "Wei Wang"

* Supported by the National Science Foundation of China (No 60703012, 60773063), the NSFC-RGC of China(No. 60831160525), National Grant of Fundamental Research 973 Program of China (No.2006CB303000), National Grant of High Technology 863 Program of China (No. 2009AA01Z149), Key Program of the National Natural Science Foundation of China (No. 60933001), National Postdoctor Foundtaion of China (No. 20090450126), Development Program for Outstanding Young Teachers in Harbin Institute of Technology (no. HITQNJS.2009.052).

L. Chen et al. (Eds.): WAIM 2010, LNCS 6184, pp. 717–728, 2010.

in dblp, the database system will output seven different authors all named "Wei Wang". In this paper, the former problem is called *name diversity* for brief and the latter is called *tautonomy*.

Entity identification techniques are to deal with these problems. This is a basic operation in data cleaning and query processing with quality assurance. Given a set of objects with name and other properties, the goal of this operation is to split the set into clusters, such that each cluster corresponds to one real-world entity.

Some techniques for entity identification have been proposed. However, each of these techniques focuses on one of the two problems. The techniques for the first problem are often called "duplicate detection"[1]. These techniques usually find duplicate records by measuring the similarity of individual fields (e.g. objects with similar names). Different approaches are used to compare the similarity. These techniques are based on the assumption that duplicate records should have equal or similar values. With the second problem existing simultaneity, records with the same name referring to different entity cannot be distinguished. As far as we know, the only technique for the second problem is presented in [2]. It identifies entities using linkage information and clustering method. From the experiment in [2], it takes a long time for object distinction; therefore it is not suitable for entity identification on large datasets. Besides, this method distinguishes objects by assuming that the objects have identical names. If this method is used to solve entity identification problem, in which the assumption is unsatisfied, the results might be inaccurate. In summary, when these two aspects of problems both exist, current techniques can not distinguish objects effectively.

For entity identification in general cases, new techniques with the ability of dealing with both these problems are in demand. For effective entity identification, this paper proposes EIF, an entity identification framework. With effective clustering techniques, approximate string matching algorithms and a flexible mechanism of knowledge integration, EIF can deal with both the two aspects of the problems. Given a set of objects, EIF split them into clusters, such that each cluster corresponds to one entity. In this paper, as an application of EIF, we process an author identification algorithm for identifying authors from the database with dirty data. For the simplicity of discussion, in this paper, we only focus on relational data. The techniques in this paper can also be applied to semi-structured data or data in OO-DBMS by representing each object as a tuple of attributes.

The contributions of this paper can be summarized as following:

- EIF, a general entity identification framework by using name and other attributes of objects, is presented in this paper. Both approximate string matching and clustering techniques can be effectively embedded into EIF, domain knowledge integration mechanism as well. This framework can deal with both *name diversity* and *tautonomy* problems. As we know, it is the first strategy with the consideration of both problems.
- As an application of EIF, an author identification algorithm is proposed by using the information of author name and co-authors to solve author identification problem. It shows that by adding proper domain information, EIF is suitable to process problems in practice.
- The effectiveness of this framework is verified by extensive experiments. The experimental results show that the author identification algorithm based on EIF outperforms the existing author identification approaches both in precision and recall.

The rest of this paper is organized as follows. The entity identification framework EIF is introduced in Section 2. In Section 3, we demonstrate how to apply EIF on author identification. Related work is introduced in Section 4. In Section 5, the effectiveness of the algorithm based on EIF is evaluated by experiments. Section 6 concludes the whole paper.

2 The Entity Identification Framework: EIF

In this section, we propose an entity identification framework EIF. EIF consists of two parts. The first is a classifier based on object name to put the objects whose names might refer to the same name in one class, vice versa. The second part is to partition objects in each class and combine these partitions to generate a global partition. This global partition is the final result. In the final result, objects in the same cluster correspond to one entity, vice versa.

2.1 The Introduction to the Framework

The input of EIF is a set of objects, denoted by N. N can be represented as a graph $G = (V, E)$ with $\forall v \in V$ corresponding to an element in N. The initialization of E is null. Firstly, EIF classifies the objects by their names. If the names of two objects are similar, they are classified in one class. Note that one object can be classified into multiple classes. Secondly, EIF generates edges in G. $sim(u, v)$ is defined to be the similarity function of objects u and v according to the domain knowledge. It can be computed from name and other attributes of u and v. Edge (u, v) is added if the value of $sim(u, v) \geq \Delta$ (the determine of threshold Δ will be discussed later). Thirdly, induced subgraph of each class is generated and is partitioned into clusters by domain knowledge. Finally, the global partition is obtained from local partitions generated; the objects belonging to each cluster in the final partition refer to the same entity. The flow of EIF is shown in Algorithm 1.

Algorithm 1. The EIF
Input: a set of objects N with each object consisting of a name and some other attributes.
Ouput: a partition of N, $R = \{G_1, G_2, ..., G_t\}$ $G_1 \cup G_2 \cup ... \cup G_t = N$, $G_i \cap G_j = \varnothing$, $1 \leq i < j \leq t$. Objects in the same cluster refer to the same entity.

1. Initialization: $G_N = (V, E)$, $V = N$, $E = \varnothing$.
2. Classify N into $N_1, N_2, ..., N_k$ by comparing the names of objects, satisfying $N = N_1 \cup N_2 \cup ... \cup N_k$, $\forall a, b \in N_i$, the names of a and b are similar; $\forall a \in N_i$, $b \in N_j$ $(i \neq j)$, the names of a and b are not similar.
3. Define the similarity function sim and the threshold Δ by using the domain knowledge or machine learning approaches. Given $u, v \in N_i$, $1 \leq i \leq k$, the larger $sim(u, v)$ is, the more similar u and v are. $\forall u, v \in V$, if $sim(u, v) \geq \Delta$ insert edge (u, v) to G_N.
4. The subgraph of G_N induced by node set N_i is denoted by $G_N[N_i]$. That is $G_N[N_i] = G_N - \overline{N_i}$, where $\overline{N_i} = V(G_N) - N_i$, $(1 \leq i \leq k)$. A partition of each induced subgraph $G_N[N_i]$, denoted by R_i $(1 \leq i \leq k)$, is obtained by domain knowledge. $\forall a \in G_N[N_i]$, the class object a belongs to in the partition R_i is denoted by $R_i(a)$.

5. The global partition $R = \{G_1, G_2, \ldots, G_t\}$ is combined from the partitions of all the induced subgraphs: R_1, R_2, .., R_k, satisfying $\forall a, b \in V$, if $\exists R_i$ $R_i(a) \neq R_i(b)$ (a and b are not in the same cluster in the partition R_i), then $R(a) \neq R(b)$; otherwise, $R(a) = R(b)$.
6. Return R.

Both *sim* and Δ can be obtained by domain knowledge. For example, if at least two names occur simultaneously in two publications as authors, by the domain knowledge, we know that these authors with the identical name in these two publications are very likely to refer to the same author. Therefore, the similarity function can be defined as the size of intersection of co-author sets, and Δ can be set to 2.

2.2 Induced Subgraph Partition Method

Step 4 is to partition the objects in induced subgraph. Effective clustering approaches are applied to perform such partition, domain knowledge as well. In this paper, an iteration method is used. In iteration, nodes u and v satisfying one of these two conditions are found: 1)$N(u) \subseteq S(v)$ or $N(v) \subseteq S(u)$; 2)$|N(u) \cap N(v)| \geq \lambda \times |N(u) \cup N(v)|$, where for any node v, we denote the set of neighbours of v (including v) in G_N as $N(v)$ and the initial node set of v as $S(v)$.

For each edge $e = (u, v) \in E$ in the induced subgraph $G_N[N_i]$, if e satisfies one of the above conditions, u and v are considered to refer to one entity in N_i and should be partitioned into the same cluster. Once u and v are considered to refer to one entity, (u, v) is contracted and u, v are merged to one node u', where the original node set of u' is denoted as $S(u')$, $S(u') = S(u) \cup S(v)$ and $N(u')$ is denoted as the union of neighbours of u and v, $N(u') = N(u) \cup N(v)$.

The iteration terminates when no more nodes can be merged. The result is the partition of N_i. Each node $u \in N_i$ represents an entity in N_i and $S(u)$ represents the set of objects referring to this entity.The algorithm of this method is shown in algorithm 2.

Algorithm 2. Author Identification with Similar Names Algorithm
Input: $G_N[N_i] = (V', E')$ ($V' = N_i \subseteq V$, $E' \subseteq E$)
Output: G_N' (each node in G_N' corresponds to the objects referring to the same entity)

```
GN' = GN[Ni];
for each v ∈ V do
    S(v) = {v};
for each e = (u, v) ∈ E do
    if |N(u) ∩ N(v)| / |N(u) ∪ N(v)| > λ then
            replace u and v with u';
            N(u') = N(u) ∪ N(v);
            S(u') = S(u) ∪ S(v);
            UpDate = true;
    if UpDate = true then
            goto 2;
return GN'
```

Since the time complexity of *step 1-3* of EIF depends on domain knowledge, we only focus on *step 4-5*. According to our analysis, in the worst case, the time complexity of *step 4* is $O(|V'||E'|)$ and the time complexity of *step 5* is $O(|V'|)$.

2.3 Example

In this subsection, we demonstrate the flow of EIF with Example 1.

Example 1. There are six publications each with a list of authors, and each publication has an author named "Wei Wang" or "Wang Wei". By domain knowledge, it is known that these two names might refer to an identical name. For simplicity, the task of entity identification in this example is to distinguish the authors named "Wei Wang" or "Wang Wei". The information is shown in Table 1. In EIF, the entity identification consists of the following steps.

Table 1. Objects in publications

Obj_ID	Pub_ID	Object Name	Co-Auhtos	Obj_ID	Pub_ID	Object Name	Co-Auhtos
A	1	Wei Wang	Dylan	D	4	Wang Wei	Bob, Mike
B	2	Wei Wang	Bob	E	5	Wang Wei	Dylan
C	3	Wei Wang	Dylan, Mike	F	6	Wang Wei	Bob

Step 1(Fig. 1(a)): generate the corresponding graph G_N of N. Each node in G_N corresponds an author (for simplicity, objects *A*-*F* with name "Wang Wei" or "Wei Wang" are considered).
Step 2(Fig. 1(b)): classify the objects by comparing their names. Since we only distinguish the objects with similar names "Wei Wang" or "Wang Wei", all nodes in G_N belongs to the same class N_1.
Step 3(Fig. 1(c)): Suppose the similarity function is defined as the size of intersection (including the author himself) of co-author set and the threshold Δ is set to be 2. Therefore, for any two objects u and v, if the intersection of their co-author sets is in size of at least 2, an edge (u, v) is inserted into G_N.
Step 4(Fig. 1(d)(e)): partition the objects in the induced subgraph with $\lambda = 1/2$. Since $N(A)\cap N(C)=\{A, C, E\}$, $N(A)\cup N(C)=\{A, C, D, E\}$, so $|N(A)\cap N(C)|=3$, $|N(A)\cup N(C)|=4$, and $|N(A)\cap N(C)|/|N(A)\cup N(C)| = 3/4 \geq \lambda = 0.5$. The condition 2) is satisfied, *A* and *C* are considered to refer to one entity. *A* and *C* are merged into *A'*. $N(A') = N(A)\cup N(C)$, and $S(A') = S(A)\cup S(C) = \{A, C\}$. In the same way, *A'* and *E* are merged into *A''* with $N(A'') = N(A')\cup N(E) =\{A, C, D, E\}$ and $S(A'') = S(A')\cup S(E) = \{A, C, E\}$. For *A''* and *D*, since $N(D) = \{C, B, D, F\}\not\subset S(A'')$ and $N(A'') = \{A, C, D, E\} \not\subset S(D)$, condition 1) is not satisfied. Moreover, $N(A'')\cap N(D) = \{C, D\}$, $N(A'')\cup N(D) = \{A, B, C, D, E, F\}$, so $|N(A'')\cap N(D)| / |N(A'')\cup N(D)| = 1/3 < \lambda$. Condition 2) is not satisfied either.

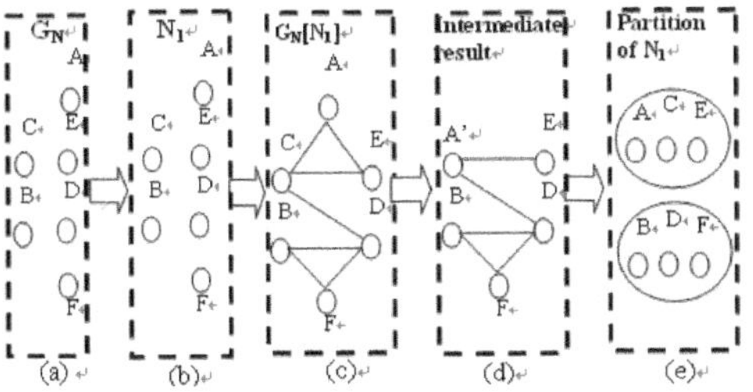

Fig. 1. The flow of EIF applied in author identification

Therefore, A'' and D are not to be merged. *Step 4* of EIF is iterated until no more edge can be contracted. Finally, the partition of N_l is obtained, which is $\{\{A, C, E\}, \{B, D, F\}\}$.

Step 5-6: In *Step 5*, since there is only one class N_l, the final result is the partition of N_l, denoted as R_l. Return R_l in *Step 6*(The algorithm ends).

3 The Author Identification Algorithm Based on EIF (AI-EIF)

Both problems of name diversity and tautonomy exist in author identification of publications. Different authors may share identical or similar names; an author name may also have different spellings in different publications, such as abbreviation, different orders of family name and given name and so on. Therefore, EIF can be applied to the author identification problem. In this section, we will discuss how to apply EIF to design author identification algorithm. Example 1 has shown the major processing of the application of EIF in author identification. In this section, methods based on domain knowledge of publications will be discussed in detail.

3.1 Classification of Objects on Names

According to the EIF, the author identification algorithm should classify the objects by names in *step 2* of Algorithm 1. Objects with similar names should be classified in the same class. Our task is to define the similarity judgement rules between names.

Since author names are in type of string with special formats, rule-based strategies can be used in this step. The matching rules of name in [3] are used as the rules in this paper. These rules enumerate diversities of name spellings.

With these matching rules, we define conditions of classification. An intuitive idea of classification is to make the nodes in the same class match each other, which can be proved to be an NP-Hard problem. Due to limitations on space, we eliminate the proof.

In order to efficiently solve this problem, we propose a heuristic rule-based strategy. The heuristic rules are as follows:

1) *If names a and b are matching, then Class(a) = Class(b),*
2) *If Class(a) = Class(b), and Class(b) = Class(c), then Class(a) = Class(c),*

where for name *a*, we denote the class *a* belongs as *Class(a)*. According to the heuristic rules, we propose the rule-based strategy. This strategy includes the following steps:

1) *Find all matching pairs of name sets by rules in[3]. Each matching pair is considered as a class*
2) *Merge two classes if their intersection is not empty*
3) *Repeat step2) until no more classes can be merged.*
4) *All classes are output.*

When the classes of names are generated, a classification of objects is obtained. However, such classification can not distinguish objects effectively because of *tautonomy*. As a further step, we propose a partition algorithm in the next section to solve the problem of *tautonomy*.

3.2 Partition of Objects Based on Clustering

After authors are classified by names, we implement the 3-5 steps in EIF by entity identification with similar names algorithm.

The first step of this algorithm is to add edges. Each edge $e = (u, v)$ in G_N represents u and v might be the same real-world entity. The rules of whether (u, v) should be added into G_N is determined by domain knowledge and the values of attributes of u, v. The domain knowledge for author identification is as follows.

1) the more similar the research areas are, the more possible the objects with the similar names refer to the same entity

2) the larger the intersection set of co-authors is, the more possible the objects with the similar names refer to the same entity

These rules can be described as similar functions. Before the functions are defined, some basic functions are introduced. Consider two objects *aut1* and *aut2*, *aut1 is in* publication *p1* and *aut2* is in publication *p2*. *aut1* and *aut2* have similar names. It means that after classification, *aut1* and *aut2* are in the same class. Denote the set of citations of publication *p* as *C(p)*, the set of author names of *p* as *A(p)*. The domain similarity function and co-authors similarity function are defined as follows:

1) domain similarity of objects aut1 and aut2: $f((aut1),(aut2)) = |C(p1) \cap C(p2)|$;

2) co-authors similarity of objects aut1 and aut2: $g((aut1),(aut2)) = |A(p1) \cap A(p2)|$

Combining above two similarities, the similarity function ***sim*** is defined as:

$$\mathrm{sim}((\mathrm{aut1}),(\mathrm{aut2})) = a \times f((\mathrm{aut1}),(\mathrm{aut2})) + b \times g((\mathrm{aut1}),(\mathrm{aut2})) \quad (0 \le a, b \le 1, \ \ a+b=1) \qquad (1)$$

Parameters *a, b* can be determined by domain knowledge or machine learning approaches.

According to the similarity function ***sim*** and the threshold Δ, edges are added into G_N in the following rule:

$\forall u, v \in V$, *if* $sim(u, v) \ge \Delta$, *add edge* (u, v) *into* E

Step 3 in EIF for author identification repeats to added edges into *E* in above rule and terminates until no more edge can be added.

4 Related Work

The entity identification problem was first proposed by [1]. Because of its importance, it has been widely studied by researchers from various fields. [16] is a research survey on early work of this problem. Nowadays, there are two kinds of work related to entity identification: definitions of similarity between records and entity identification approaches.

Definitions of similarity between records are the base of entity identification. There are two kinds of similarity definitions: one is based on the similarity of properties of records[4, 5]; the other is based on relations between records [8-10]. These definitions of similarity between entities can be applied in our system and orthogonal with our work.

There are four kinds of entity identification approaches. Approaches based on rules [11, 12] define the conditions of any two records referring to the same entity by rules. Approaches based on statistics identify entities by using statistical techniques, e.g., [15] identify entities by using probability models. Approaches based on machine learning [6, 13-14] solve the problem of entity identification by classification or clustering approaches. Block techniques is to divide records into blocks efficiently, then process each block effectively, so as to reduce as much searching space as possible, e.g., [7] propose an iterative blocking method based on disk.

The techniques proposed usually only focus on some particular part of entity identification problem. Instead, the EIF framework is based on the whole general problem and integrates related techniques by steps. In Step 1, EIF uses approaches of similarity definition of records to define similarity of records; in Step 2, EIF blocks records by using the information of similarity between records obtained in step 1; in Step 3, according to the parameters obtained by statistical techniques and machine learning approaches, EIF identify entities by using entity identification techniques based on rules.

5 Experiments

In order to verify the effectiveness and efficiency of EIF, we perform the extensive experiments. The experimental results and analysis are shown in this section.

5.1 Experimental Settings

1) *Experimental environment*:

We ran experiments on a PC with Pentium Processor 3.20 GHz CPU, 512 RAM. The operation system is Microsoft Window XP. We implemented the algorithms using VC++ 6.0 and SGI's stl library. We have implemented the author identification algorithm based on EIF, called AI-EIF. We evaluate our framework on both real dataset and synthetic data set and show the effectiveness and efficiency of our algorithm.

2) *Data sets*:

In order to test the algorithm in this paper, three datasets are used. The first is the dataset used in [2] for comparisons. The second is the DBLP[17] to test the effectiveness and efficiency of our algorithm on real data. In order to test the impact of parameters on our algorithm, synthetic data is used as well. We designed a data generator for generating publication with authors. The parameters include the number of authors per publications(#aut/per pub), the number of publications(#pub) and the ratio of the number of names to the number of authors(#name/#aut). For each author as an entity, its name is chosen randomly from the name set. To simulate real life situations, the authors forms a scale-free network[18] which models the co-author network among them. For each publication, its authors are a group of randomly selected co-authors in this network.

3) *Measures*:

In order to test the effectiveness of AI-EIF, we compare the entity identification results of EIF with manually identification results. Manually identification is to manually divide the objects into groups according to author's home pages, affiliations and research areas shown on the papers or web pages. According to the definitions in [2], we define the manually partition is C, and the experimental results of AI-EIF is C*. Let TP (true positive) be the number of pairs of objects that are in the same cluster in both C and C*. Let FP (false positive) be the number of pairs of objects in the same cluster in C* but not in C, and FN (false negative) be the number of pairs of references in the same cluster in C but not in C*. Therefore the precision and recall are defined as follows: precision = TP / (TP + FP), recall = TP / (TP + FN).

4) *Parameters setting*:
Since only co-author information is used in the experiments, a = 0, b = 1. For the algorithm, we set $\Delta = 2$ and $\lambda = 0.05$. The default setting of our data generator is that: #name/#aut = 0.9, #pub = 1000, #aut/per pub = 4.

5.2 Experimental Results on Real Data

We test both efficiency and effectiveness of the algorithm on DBLP. We extract information of all 1119K publications for author identification. The processing time of AI-EIF on DBLP is 1.64 hours.

In order to test the effectiveness of AI-EIF, we randomly pick 8 names from all 2074K author names in DBLP and identify them manually. Each of the 8 names corresponds to multiple authors. The basic information of them is shown in Table 2, including the number of authors (#aut) and number of references (#ref). Table 2 also shows the precisions and recalls of each name by AI-EIF. From the result, the precisions are always 100%. It means that AI-EIF always divide objects referring to different authors into different clusters. The average of recall is greater than 90%. It means that in most of time, objects referring to the same entity are in the same cluster.

From the experimental results, it is observed that the recall is affected by the connection between any two authors in the set of authors who cooperated with the author *u*, denoted as *Co(u)*. For any two authors in *Co(u)*, if they cooperated, the connection between them is tight, otherwise it is loose. Take the author named Michael Siegel in Weizmann Institute of Science(WIS) as an example, in all his publications, there are 8 publications he cooperated with some people in WIS, and there are 3 other publications he cooperated with some people in Institut für Informatik and Praktische Mathematik(IIPM). Since the co-operator set in WIS never cooperate with the co-operator set in IIPM, the connection between these two co-operator set is loose. Therefore, in our algorithm, the objects referring to the author Michael Siegel in WIS are partitioned into 2 clusters.

Table 2. Names corresponding to multiple authors and Accuracy of AI-EIF

Name	# aut	# ref	precision	recall	Name	# aut	# ref	precision	recall
Michael Siegel	5	45	1.0	0.804	Hui Xu	13	34	1.0	1.0
Qian Chen	9	39	1.0	0.949	Hai Huang	15	44	1.0	0.780
Dong Liu	12	36	1.0	0.870	Zhi Li	11	32	1.0	1.0
Lin Li	11	30	1.0	0.933	Jian Zhou	12	38	1.0	0.895
Average			1.0	0.904					

5.3 Comparison Experiments

As far as we know, DISTINCT[2] is the best author identification algorithm. Therefore, we compare AI-EIF with DISTINCT. Since DISTINCT only tests its quality for distinguishing references, we compare precision and recall results of AI-EIF with DISTINCT. We test our algorithm using the same test data as [2]. We test AI-EIF on real names in DBLP that correspond to multiple authors. 8 such names are shown in Table 3, together with the number of authors and number of references.

The experimental comparisons of precisions and recalls are also shown in Table 3 respectively. From Table 3, it can be seen that AI-EIF outperforms DISTINCT both in precision and average recall.

Table 3. Names corresponding to multiple authors and Comparison Results

Name	# aut	# ref	Precision DISTINCT	Precision EIF	Recall DISTINCT	Recall EIF
Hui Fang	3	9	1.0	1.0	1.0	1.0
Ajay Gupta	4	16	1.0	1.0	1.0	0.882
Rakesh Kumar	2	38	1.0	1.0	1.0	1.0
Michael Wagner	5	24	1.0	1.0	0.395	0.620
Bing Liu	6	11	1.0	1.0	0.825	1.0
Jim Smith	3	19	0.888	1.0	0.926	0.810
Wei Wang	14	177	0.855	1.0	0.814	0.933
Bin Yu	5	42	1.0	1.0	0.658	0.595
Average			0.94	1.0	0.802	0.871

5.4 Changing Parameters

According to our analysis, the effectiveness and efficiency of AI EIF are influenced by the parameters: λ, #aut/per pub, #name/#aut and #pub. The experimental results are shown in Fig.2 to Fig.7.

We test the impact of λ on real data. For the convenience of observation, only the experimental results of publications of Wei Wang in UNC(entity 0) and Wei Wang in Fudan(entity 1) are shown. The experiment results are shown in Fig. 2. From Fig. 2, it is observed that the recall decreases with the increase of λ. It is because the bigger λ is, the stronger the similarity matching condition of objects is. Therefore, more and more objects referring to the same real-world entity are partitioned into different clusters. This leads to the decrease of recall. Another observation is that in most cases the precision is not affected by λ, while in a few cases, when λ is too small (e.g. λ=0.01 in our experiments), the precisions are no longer 100%. In another word, the larger λ is, the stronger the matching condition is and the higher the precision is, vice versa.

The conclusion drawn from the experiments of changing λ is that the smaller λ is, the lower the recall is and the higher the precision is; vice versa.

In Fig. 3 we test the efficiency by changing #pub from 500 to 5000, #aut = 500. From Fig. 3, it can be seen that the run time is approximately linear to the number of publications. It is because according to the analysis in Section II-D, the run time is approximately linear to the number of objects, which is linear to the number of publications.

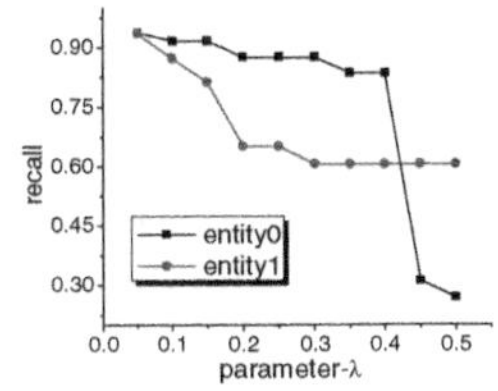

Fig. 2. λ VS recall

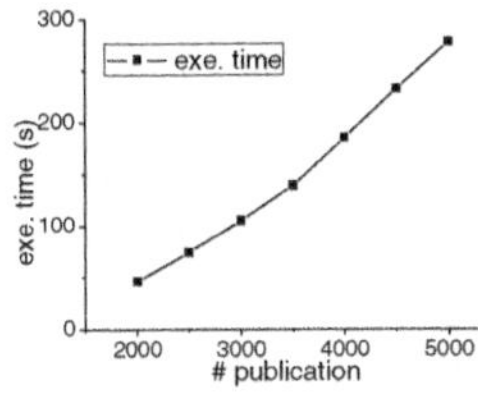

Fig. 3. Exe.time VS #pub

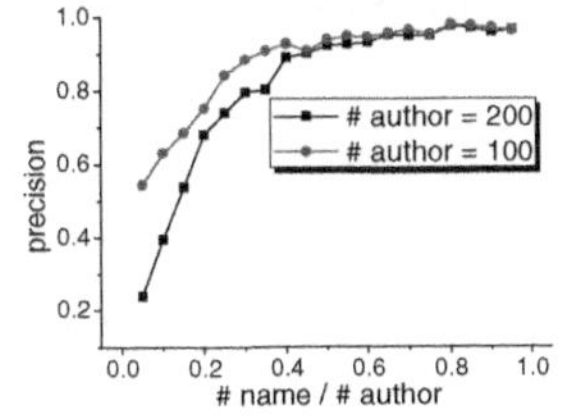

Fig. 4. Precision VS #name/#aut

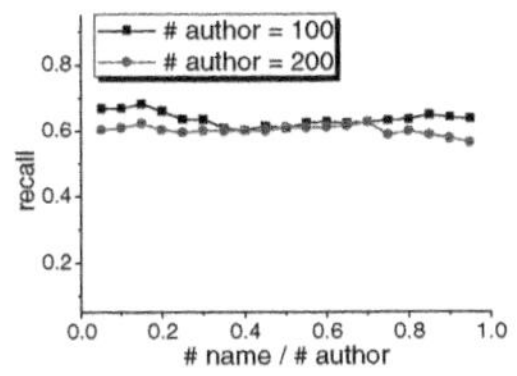

Fig. 5. Recall VS #name/#aut

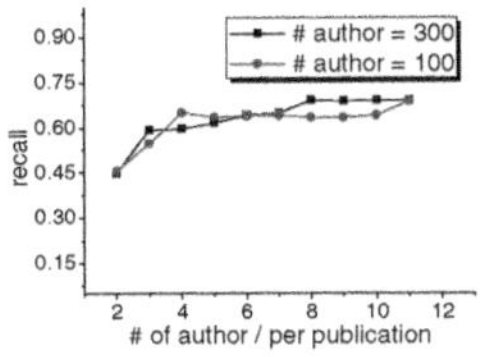

Fig. 6. Recall VS #aut/per pub

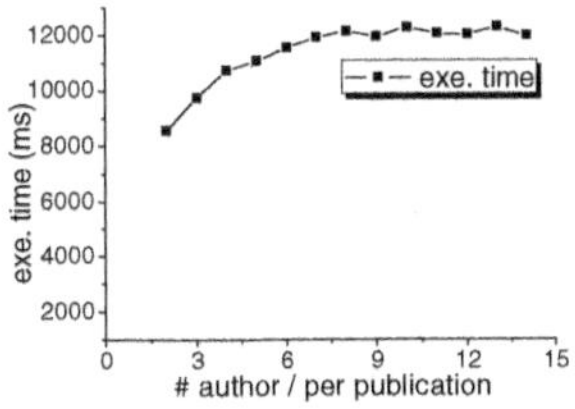

Fig. 7. Exe.time VS # aut/per pub

In Fig. 4 and Fig. 5 we test the impact of the ratio of name number and entity number on effectiveness by changing #name/#aut from 0.05 to 0.95. From Fig.4, it can be seen that the bigger the ratio of the number of names to the number of authors is, the higher the precision is. That is because, the bigger the ratio is, the smaller the probability of different authors having same name is, the less objects referring to different authors are divided into same cluster, the higher precision is. From Fig.5, recalls are insensitive to the ratio of number of names to the number of authors. That is because, FN is insensitive to the probability of different authors having same name.

We test the impact of the number of authors per publication on effectiveness by changing #aut/per pub from 2 to 11. The precision is insensitive to the number of authors in each publication. It shows that the precision of our algorithm is assured. Fig.6 shows the impact of #aut/per pub on recall. Recall increases more and more slowly with the #aut/per pub. The recall increasing with #aut/per pub is because the more number of co-authors in each publication are, the more co-authors are connected by this publication, the higher the connections between co-authors are. Since the connections between co-operators of this author are higher, the recall gets larger. This result is coincident with the analysis of the experimental results of the changing of λ. The reason for the incremental speed getting slower with #aut/per pub is that marginal impact of the number of authors per publication on the recall decreases.

In Fig. 7 we test the efficiency by changing #aut/per pub from 2 to 14. From Fig.7, it can be seen the run time increases more and more slowly with #aut/per pub. The increasing of run time with #aut/per pub is because the more co-authors in each publication, the more information is to be processed. The increment speed of run time becomes slower is because even though the number of co-authors gets larger, the probability of two objects referring to the same author will not get larger in the same scale. It means that the number of objects to process will not increase in the same scale.

6 Conclusions

In this paper, we study the entity identification problem, and propose a general framework of entity identification, EIF. Both clustering techniques and domain knowledge are effectively integrated in EIF, which can process the data with both problems of *name diversity* and *tautonomy*. Both effectiveness and efficiency are verified. The future work includes how to apply EIF into some more complicated applications.

Acknowledgments. Thanks for the help on experiments by Dr. Xiaoxin Yin in Microsoft Research.

References

1. Newcombe, H., Kennedy, J., Axford, S.: Automatic Linkage of Vital Records. Science 130, 954–959 (1959)
2. Yin, X., Han, J., Yu, P.S.: Object Distinction: Distinguishing Objects with Identical Names. In: ICDE 2007 (2007)
3. `http://www.cervantesvirtual.com/research/congresos/jbidi2003/slides/jbidi2003-michael.ley.ppt`
4. Arasu, A., Chaudhuri, S., Kaushik, R.: Transformation-based framework for record matching. In: ICDE 2008 (2008)
5. Arasu, A., Kaushik, R.: A grammar-based entity representation framework for data cleaning. In: SIGMOD, pp. 233–244 (2009)
6. Chen, Z., Kalashnikov, D.V., Mehrotra, S.: Exploiting context analysis for combining multiple entity resolution systems. In: SIGMOD, pp. 207–218 (2009)
7. Whang, S.E., Menestrina, D., Koutrika, G., Theobald, M., Garcia-Molina, H.: Entity resolution with iterative blocking. In: SIGMOD, pp. 219–232 (2009)
8. Culotta, A., McCallum, A.: Joint deduplication of multiple record types in relational data. In: Proc. CIKM 2005, pp. 257–258 (2005)
9. Dong, X., Halevy, A., Madhavan, J.: Reference reconciliation in complex information spaces. In: Proc. SIGMOD 2005, pp. 85–96 (2005)
10. Singla, P., Domingos, P.: Object identification with attribute-mediated dependences. In: Jorge, A.M., Torgo, L., Brazdil, P.B., Camacho, R., Gama, J. (eds.) PKDD 2005. LNCS (LNAI), vol. 3721, pp. 297–308. Springer, Heidelberg (2005)
11. Arasu, A., Re, C., Suciu, D.: Large-scale deduplication with constraints using Dedupalog. In: ICDE 2009 (2009)
12. Koudas, N., Saha, A., Srivastava, D., et al.: Metric functional dependencies In: ICDE (2009)
13. Arasu, A., Chaudhuri, S., Kaushik, R.: Learning string transformations from examples. In: VLDB 2009 (2009)
14. Chaudhuri, S., Chen, B.C., Ganti, V., Kaushik, R.: Example-driven design of efficient record matching queries. In: VLDB 2007 (2007)
15. Milch, B., Marthi, B., Sontag, D., Russell, S., Ong, D.L.: BLOG: Probabilistic models with unknown objects. In: Proc. IJCAI 2005, pp. 1352–1359 (2005)
16. Koudas, N., Sarawagi, S., Srivastava, D.: Record linkage: similarity measures and algorithms. In: SIGMOD Conference, pp. 802–803 (2006)
17. `http://dblp.uni-trier.de/`
18. Barabási, Albert-László, et al.: Scale-Free Networks. Scientific American 288, 50–59 (2003)

A Multilevel and Domain-Independent Duplicate Detection Model for Scientific Database*

Jie Song, Yubin Bao, and Ge Yu

Northeastern University, Shenyang 110004, China
{songjie,baoyb,yuge}@mail.neu.edu.cn

Abstract. The duplicate detection is one of technical difficulties in data cleaning area. At present, the data volume of scientific database is increasing rapidly, bringing new challenges to the duplicate detection. In the scientific database, the duplicate detection model should be suitable for massive and numerical data, should independent from the domains, should well consider the relationships among tables, and should focus on common grounds of the scientific database. In the paper, a multilevel duplicate detection model for scientific database is proposed, which consider numerical data and general usage well. Firstly, the challenges are propose by analyzing duplicate-related characteristics of scientific data; Secondly, similarity measure of the proposed model are defined; Then the details of multilevel detecting algorithms are introduced; At last, some experiments and applications show that the proposed model is more domain-independent and effective, suitable for duplicate detection in scientific database.

1 Introduction

Scientific instruments and computer simulations are obtaining and generating massive data in the domains of astronomy, oceanography, geognosy, meteorology, biomedical and so on, creating an explosion of available data to scientists. The data volumes are approximately doubling each year [1]. How to manage the scientific data is the hot topic which is considered by both industrial and academic world. Data quality is a critical point because the scientific data is always natural and massive, so that data cleaning is adopted to improve the data quality, by detecting and removing the errors and inconsistencies from data [2].

Duplicate detection is the approach that identifies multiple representations of a same real-world object. It is a crucial task in data cleaning, and it has applies in many scenarios such as data integration, customer relationship management, and personal information management [3]. The duplicate problem has been studied extensively under various names, such as merge/purge [4], record linkage [5], entity resolution [6], or reference reconciliation [7], too names but a few. In the scientific database, the duplicate problem is caused by multiple importing or combining same dataset, same numerical value rounding by different scale, or tiny difference of the decimal numbers. Since many works have been done on data de-duplicate in recent years, few of

* This work is supported by National Natural Science Foundation of China (No. 60773222).

L. Chen et al. (Eds.): WAIM 2010, LNCS 6184, pp. 729–741, 2010.

them is suitable for scientific database. Our **motivations** and **related works** are introduced from following aspects:

- **Numerical Data:**

Most of duplicates are approximate duplicate problem, sometimes it is also named as merge/purge, de-duplicate, record linkage problems [4, 8, 5]. In previous domain-independent methods for duplicate detection, the similarity is usually measured by cosine metric[9], Jaccard coefficient[10] or Euclidean distance[11]. It predicts that two vectors whose similarity is greater than a pre-specified similarity threshold are duplicates [4, 5, 8]. However, scientific data mainly consist of numbers and symbols. These approaches are suitable for the textual data well but not the numerical data.

Firstly, the ranges of scientific attributes are quite different, the classical measures will be effected by the attributes with larger value mostly. For example, the Euclidean distance of <*weight*[0-200], *blood_sugar_concentration*[0.00-0.99]> will almost be controlled by the *weight* because its value is great larger than the *blood_sugar_concentration,* the same as other classical measures. The data normalization in data preprocess can fix this problem but not all the data have been preprocessed. Another solution is Mahalanobis distance, but it is only suitable to the attributes in normal distribution[12], and expensive especially dealing with high-dimensions (many attributes). Weighting[13] is also the solution but it is domain-dependent, it is hard to predefine the suitable weights for all kinds of data in different domains.

Secondly, the classical measures are used to measure the vector whose elements are in same data type and meaning. For example, cosine metric is always used to measure the textual similarity, the element of the vector stand for the frequency of each word. In a scientific database, the numerical is the most common type in scientific database, but different numerical attribute has different meaning, dimensionality and significance (detailed explanation in section 2 *C1*). Cosine metric is also not suitable for the high precision numerical data. In this paper, the record with multiple attributes is not treated as a vector, instead that, the similarity of each attribute is calculated separately, and then combine these similarities together by the statistical method. So the problem is shifted to the similarity measuring of the simple attribute.

Thirdly, similarity of a simple attribute can be measured by the diversity in numerical metric. The dissimilarity of the number data is named as distance, $d = | x - y |$. The data is more dissimilar where the distance is more larger. But when the dissimilarities are combined together, the different possibility of duplicate on each attribute should be also considered. Attributes have different contributions to the similarity of the records. Taking <*longitude*, *latitude*, *wind_force*> as an example, the value of *longitude*, *latitude* may contains thousands of possibility if six decimal places is retained, but the *wind-force* may only contain 120 possibility, from 0.0 to 12.0, if one decimal places is retained. Under the same distance, for example 0.1, the *longitude* and *latitude* are more signify than *wind-force* as far as the duplicate issue is concerned.

Fourthly, "loss of precision" is the most common reason which lead to data duplicate, *Scale* is the number of digits to the right of the decimal point, any decimal can be the form of *unscaled_value* × 10^{-scale}, so the *precision* of the data is 10^{-scale}. The same data may be presented in different *scale* because the precision is lost during the data transformation and process, it is also named as "inconsistent precision" problem. For example the *body_temperature* is decimal with maximum two *scale*, data such as 37.5, 37.52 (d=0.2) are possibly duplicate cause they may be the same value in different *precision*, on the contrary, 37.62 and 37.69 (d=0.07) possibly non-duplicate. Based on the distance measure $d = | x - y |$, such situation cannot be satisfied no matter what the distance threshold is assigned. The traditional similarity measure can not deal the duplicate caused by inconsistent precision.

All in all, the classical similarity measures are not suitable to detect the numerical data. In this paper, we will first propose a similarity measure for numerical data in scientific database; then propose an approach to combine similarity of each attribute into the similarity of the records, meanwhile the difference of the range and duplicate possibility of each attribute are also considered.

- **Multilevel Detection:**

Most duplicate detection algorithms apply to a single relation with sufficient attributes in a relational database [2, 4, 14, 15]. However, the relationships between tables should also be well considered. For example, two *patients* even with the same *name*, *sex* and *age* may not duplicate if there *blood sampling* records set are not same. It is more complex than detection in a single table. Some previous works such as [16, 17] considered the relationships between entities in a XML file, but not in database. The challenges are, first, proposing a similarity measuring approach for the record (vector) set; second, proposing a searching algorithm to detect the duplicate in the tables which are connected by *parent-child* or *top-sub* relationships.

Delphi [18] is the most related to this paper. There are several differences between the proposed model and *Delphi*, for example, *Delphi* is general algorithm for textual data. As far as the multilevel detection is concerned, both of this paper and [18] considered the relationships among tables in the detection algorithm, *Delphi* is based on potential rules which are hidden in the relationships between records, such as different state should belong to different country. But in scientific database, such relationships can not be trusted in many cases. Firstly, if primary and foreign keys are surrogate keys, the batch of connected records in parent table and child tables are possibly both duplicate. Secondly, it is common that two records are not duplicate even if their related data are same, such as same results belong to different investigation. At last, what we should do is to detect the duplicates including the relationships, not relying on the relationships.

- **Domain-independent**

Researches in this area mostly focus on the efficiency and effectiveness of algorithms. Treating the various domains of scientific data as a whole, there are many common grounds. It is also important to establish a domain-independent duplicate detection model. In this paper, the generalization of the model is highlight.

All challenges mentioned above are studied in this paper, and the Multilevel Duplicate Detection Model (MD^2M) is proposed. MD^2M is concluded from several projects. It focuses on the domain-independent, proposes the similarity of numerical records and record sets; predefines the threshold of similarity; proposes a multilevel detection algorithm which is more accurate than a single level one. The model has been successfully applied in two projects about the management of oceanographic data and biomedical data. Theories and experiments show that MD^2M is more general, effective and efficient.

2 Preliminaries

In this section, some duplication-related characteristics of the scientific database are summarized as the preliminaries and foundations of MD^2M:

- **C1: Characteristics of the Data.**

The most of scientific data are numerical, there are three kinds of numerical data. **Decimal** values are the mostly common data to present the scientific phenomenon, such as *temperature*, *location* (*longitude*, *latitude*), *concentration* and *density*, they always retain many decimal place for reaching high precision. Some scientific data with less precision are present by **integer** values, such as *year* and *amount*. **Real** value is used to present categorical or boolean data by a finite number of possible values, (e.g., *sex*, *brand*, *color*), it is named as nominal data. There are also some other data types such as string, datetime and binary, but these data types are not popular in scientific database. In MD^2M, only numerical columns are considered in the duplicate detection because they are primary and enough to present the feature of the record. **Nominal** data is the special numerical data, MD^2M will not consider its similarity because it is enumerative and has large possibility to be duplicate.

The scientific database is massive. Firstly, the data volume is enough to shown the statistical and distributed feature of the values. The column is fully filled by the values according to its distribution. On the other hand, the scientific data in database is also high dimensional. In similarity measuring, the record of the table is often treated as a vector, so that values of columns are dimensions of the vector. Records in scientific database are high dimensional vectors even only numerical columns are included. For example, there are more than thirty columns in the *blood_constituent* table in medical database, each column present a constituent of the blood. Even more, the range, dimensionality and duplicate possibility of each column are various. In this case, calculating and combining the similarity of each column is much better than calculating the similarity of record (vector) directly.

In scientific database, there are three kinds of numerical duplicate. The **exactly equal** data are definitely duplicate caused by repeatedly import or mistakes in data integration; **Tiny difference** data are probably duplicate, because the different quality and precision of data-gathering equipments, or the different approaches of data preprocessing, there are slight differences between the values which indicate the same thing. The data with the closed value but **inconsistent precision** are probably duplicate too, it is caused by rounding or losing the precision when gathering, preprocessing and integrating the data.

- **C2: Multilevel Detection**

There are many tables in a scientific database, but the algorithm can not detect the duplicates from all tables together. Generally, some tables which belong to a certain domain will be involved in once detection, these involved tables is organized as a hierarchy.

From the aspect of requirements, when a certain concept is selected to detect the duplicates, it always impliedly refers to the concept itself and its sub-concepts, but not its supra-concepts. For example, if the concept of investigated *ships* is selected to detect duplicate, it also includes the *sails* of each *ship*, the investigated *equipments* of each *sails*, and the *data* collected by each *equipment*, but not include the *nation* which the *ships* belong to. In a scientific database, such concept is presented by a table. So the table hierarchy in once detection is a sub-schema of the whole schema, it satisfies:

- There is one and only one root node, named as top table, which is the selected concept for duplicate detection;
- Because only table and its sub-tables are considered, there are no multiple parents in the hierarchy;
- There are one-to-one or one-to-many relationships among the tables, many-to-many is bidirectional referential relationships, only one-to-many direction is included, not many-to-one direction.
- The uniform algorithm can traverse all involved tables in hierarchies.

Fig. 1 shows an example of hierarchical structure, the right part of Fig. 1 is a simplified schema of scientific database from real project. If table *A* is selected for duplicate detection, four involved tables are shown in left part of Fig. 1 as a hierarchy.

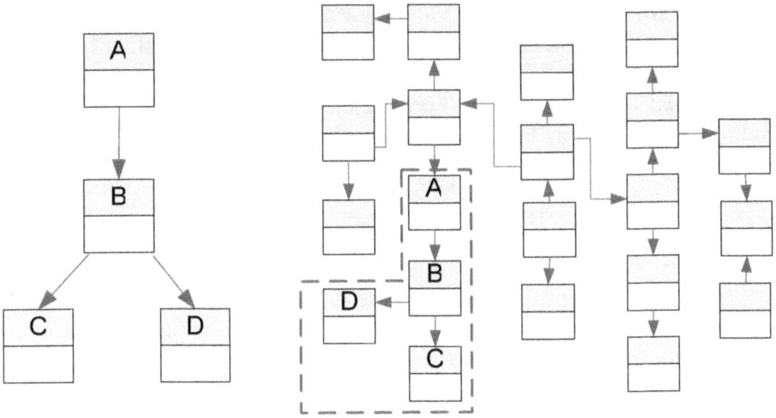

Fig. 1. Example of Hierarchical Structure in Scientific Database

Characteristic *C1* and *C2* are concluded by investigating the scientific data of many domains, they are not exceptions but the common groups. Base on these common characteristics, the duplicate detection model is proposed in the rest of the paper, and finally the experiments analysis and case study proved that the proposed model meet these characteristics well.

3 Similarity Measure

MD^2M includes several elements and algorithms. In the section, the similarities measure of the column, record and record set are proposed, and the threshold selection of these similarity measures are also introduced.

3.1 Similarity

Let *a* and *b* be two records of a table *t* in a scientific database, and the column set of *t* is *t.Col*, $\forall c \in t.Col$, the value of *c* is presented as Va_c, the same as Vb_c. There are some definitions as following:

Definition 1 (Comparison Column). Comparison column is used to test whether two records are duplicate. Let *C* be the *comparison column* set of table *t*, $C \subseteq t.Col$. *n* is the number of *comparison column* in *C*, $C = \{c_i \mid c_i \in t.Col, 1 \le i \le n\}$. ($n \ge 1$). A *comparison column c* includes some attributes:

- *c.max* means the maximum value of *c* in table *t*;
- *c.min* means the minimum value of *c* in table *t*;
- *c.size* means the data amount of *c* in table t;
- *c.scale* means the maximum retained decimal place (number of digits to the right of the decimal point) of *c*.

The *comparison columns* are selected and their attribute values are assigned by querying the metadata of the table and column. It is performed automatically on each table. Based on *C1* in section 2, only numerical column is treated as *comparison column*. But some nominal column are also numerical, the duplicate possibility is evaluated for excluding nominal data. The numerical column is selected as *comparison column* if:

$$p_c = \frac{10^{c.scale}(c.max - c.min)}{c.size} \not\ll 1 \tag{1}$$

In MD^2M, p_c is a coefficient that indicates the duplicate possibility of a column. In the equation 1, the numerator presents the number of possible value of column *c*, and the denominator is number of records in *c*. As we know, the data is more denseness, the potentially duplicate is more great. Coefficient p_c can be treated as density of values if the data is sufficient and fully distributed. It is impossible to evaluate the precise density of every column, so p_c is used as an approximate possibility of the duplicate. The column whose p_c is far less than one is nominal, dense, and/or less precision column, it is excluded from *comparison column* set. For example, the *age* and *sleeping_hour* (0.0 – 24.9) of the *patients* are not suitable to be a *comparison column*.

Definition 2 (Relative Distance). Relative distance is used to measure the distance of the value, If Va_c and Vb_c are two values of the *comparison column c*, *V.scale* means scale of value *V*, *round*(*V*, *n*) ($n \in N$) is the function rounded off value *V* to *n* decimals, the relative distance $Rd(Va_c, Vb_c)$ is calculated by:

$$Rd = \frac{|round(Va_c, k) - round(Vb_c, k)|}{round(c.max, k) - round(c.min, k)} \quad (k = min(Va_c.scale, Vb_c.scale)\ ) \tag{2}$$

It the equitation 2, the numerator is the distance of the two values under the same precision, the denominator is the maximum distance of the values in column *c* under the same precision. So that *relative distance* removes the dimensionality of the distance, and further more, removes the range difference of each *comparison column*. On the other hand, rounding mechanism make sure that the distance is constrained to the same precision, the duplicates caused by "loss of precision" or "inconsistent precision" are include. Equation 2 is simplified as $\frac{|Va_c - Vb_c|}{c.max - c.min}$ when $Va_c.scale = Vb_c.scale = c.scale$.

Definition 3 (Column Similarity). Column similarity measures the similar degree of two values which belong to the same column. The similarity of the Va_c and Vb_c of *comparison column c* is calculated by the following function:

$$Similarity(Va_c, Vb_c) = 1 - Rd(Va_c, Vb_c) \tag{3}$$

Definition 4 (Record Similarity). Record similarity measures the similar degree of two records in the same table. It is combined by the similarity of each *comparison column*. Let *a* and *b* be two records and *C* is *comparison column set* of the table *t*. *C.size* is number of *comparison column* in C, then :

$$\begin{aligned} Similarity(a,b) &= \frac{1}{C.size} \sum_{i=0}^{C.size} P_c \cdot Similarity(Va_{ci}, Vb_{ci}) \\ &= \frac{1}{C.size} \sum_{i=0}^{C.size} P_c \cdot \left(1 - \frac{|round(Va_c, k) - round(Vb_c, k)|}{round(c.max, k) - round(c.min, k)}\right) \\ &\quad (k = min(Va_c.scale, Vb_c.scale)\ ) \end{aligned} \tag{4}$$

Here the mean value is used as the combination of each *column similarity*, it is reasonable because the *column similarity* is the dimensionless value. In fact, the *record similarity* is arithmetic weighted mean of column similarity, P_c (0, 1] is weighting coefficient presenting the duplicate possibility. It is normalized from p_c (0, $+\infty$] by dividing the maximum *p* of *comparison columns*. As a weighting coefficient, it is equivalent by dividing the same number. The range of *column similarity* is $(0,1]$.

Definition 5 (Record Set Similarity). Record set similarity measures the similar degree of two record set in a same table, let *A* and *B* are two record sets which contains *A.size* and *B.size* records. If there are N_A records in set *A* that duplicate with records in set *B*, and N_B records in set *B* that duplicate with records in set *A* (see definition 6). the record set similarity is :

$$Similarity(A,B) = \frac{\frac{N_A}{A.size} + \frac{N_B}{B.size}}{2} \tag{5}$$

Record set similarity is the similarity of two vector arrays, it can be explained as the possibility of "vectors in *A and in B* too" add possibility of "vectors in *B and in A* too". The duplication of two records is defined next. If there is no duplicate in *A* and *B* themselves, then N_A=N_B=N, equation 6 is simplified as :

$$Similarity(A,B) = \frac{N(A.size + B.size)}{2 \cdot A.size \cdot B.size} \tag{6}$$

3.2 Duplication

After the similarity measures are defined, the multilevel duplication is straightforward. Let a and b be two records of a table t in a scientific database, notation "$\cong$" means duplicate, function *Sub*() means getting the referred set:

- *Sub*(*table*) returns the table set that refer to the *table*;
- *Sub*(*record, table*) returns the record set that refer to the *record* in the *table*,

Definition 6 (Record Duplication). Two records a and b are duplicate iff themselves and their sub record sets are all duplicate.

$$\begin{aligned} a \cong b \Leftrightarrow \quad & Similarity(a,b) > \theta_t \quad \text{and} \\ & (\forall t' \in Sub(t), \quad Sub(a,t') \cong Sub(b,t') \quad or \\ & Sub(t) = \varnothing \ ) \end{aligned} \tag{7}$$

Definition 7. Record Set Duplication: Record sets A and B are duplicate iff

$$A \cong B \Leftrightarrow \quad Similarity(A,B) > \delta \tag{8}$$

Noticing the definition 6 is used when *Similarity*(*A*, *B*) is calculated, so that the definition 6 and 7 are recursive definition.

4 Duplicate Detection Algorithms

In this section, the duplicate detection algorithms will be introduced based on the definitions in section 3. Firstly, there are two different approaches of duplicate detection, the one is complete duplicate detection and the other is incremental duplicate detection. The former tries to detect the duplicates from all records; the later can be considered as a search problem, it checks whether the given records duplicate with the existing records or not. Since incremental algorithm is an update of complete algorithm by changing the scope of input data and regroup some process steps, so in the rest of the paper, only complete algorithm is focused.

4.1 Pairs or Cluster

Before the complete algorithm is discussed, let's consider the *pairs* and *cluster*. The final goal of duplicate detection is to identify clusters of duplicates by two approaches: one approach detects duplicates pairwisely and then clusters duplicate pairs by measuring the similarity over these pairs, such as [4]. Another approach applies clustering algorithms to directly identify clusters of duplicate, such as [7, 19], they skip the intermediate step of finding duplicate pairs. Any clustering algorithms can not be used in scientific data duplication.

The "clustering" approach rely on an equivalence relation ∇ of set S. To the duplicate detection model, S is all involved records (R) in a table, relation ∇ should be $\cong$. It can prove that, $\cong$ satisfies the reflexivity, symmetry but not transitivity on R. So duplicate detection can not rely on the approach of "clustering", duplicate records can only be divided into *pairs*. Thereby, MD^2M adopts the pairwise comparison instead any "clustering" approach. So the *record pair* and *candidate set* are defined:

Definition 8. Record Pair: The two records *a*, *b* which *record similarity* is larger than θ_t are combined as a tuple $<a, b>$, named as *record pair.*

Definition 9. Candidate Set: The candidate set *Cs* is the set of *records pairs* in the target table, it is candidate of the next-level duplicate detection.

The *candidate set* of the root table in table hierarchy will be the final results of duplicate detection after contained *records pairs* are proven duplicate by detecting their sub-record sets. Generally, *candidate set* and *record pair* exist in any table of the hierarchy, they are results of current-level detection and inputs of next-level detection.

4.2 Initial Detection

Initial detection intends to find the *candidate set,* in root table of table hierarchy. The pairwise comparison is performed as Algorithm 1.

Algorithm 1. Initial Detection Algorithm

```
Input: Table t
Output: Candidate set Cs
InitialDetection (t)
  a ← first row of t
  While a is not null
     b ←next row of a
     While b is not null
        If Similarity (a, b) >θ_t
           add <a, b > to the Cs
        End If
        b ← next row of b
     End While
     a ← next row of a
  End While
  Return Cs
```

4.3 Multilevel Detection

Multilevel detection is the algorithm to decide whether *record pairs* in *candidate set* are duplicate or not. Taking *record pair* $<a, b>$ in table *t* as a example, $\forall t' \in Sub(t)$, there are two referred record sets *Sub*(*a*, *t*') and *Sub*(*b*, *t*') in sub-table. Let *A* be $Sub(a,t')$ and *B* be $Sub(b,t')$. According to the definition 7, *A* and *B* are duplicate on condition of *Similarity*(*A*, *B*) > φ ,and based on the simulation in section 4.3, it is known that the φ is a very small value. So consuming there is no duplicate data in *A* and *B* themselves:

$$Similarity(A,B) = \frac{N(A.size + B.size)}{2 \cdot A.size \cdot B.size} > \varphi \quad \Rightarrow N > \frac{2\varphi \cdot A.size \cdot B.size}{(A.size + B.size)} \tag{10}$$

According to the equation 10, the record set comparison is simplified as detecting whether there are more than $\frac{2\varphi \cdot A.size \cdot B.size}{(A.size + B.size)}$ records in A that duplicate to any record in B. The input of multilevel detection is a *record pair* <*a*, *b*> and its table *t*:

Algorithm 2. Multilevel Detection Algorithm

```
Input: record pair <a, b> and table t which it belong to
Output: ture or false
MultilevelDetection (a, b, t)
1.  For each table t' in Sub(t)
2.     A = sub(a, t') B = sub(b, t')
3.     x ← first row of A
4.     y ← first row of B
5.     Cs' = ∅
6.     While x is not null
7.        While y is not null
8.           If Similarity (x, y) > φ
9.              add <x, y > to the Cs'
10.          End If
11.          y ← next row of B
12.       End While
13.    x ← next row of A
14.    End While
15.    For each record pair <a', b'> in Cs' of t'
16.       If Cs'.Size ≤ 2φ·A.size·B.size / (A.size + B.size)
17.          Return false
18.       End If
19.       If MultilevelDetection (a', b', t') is false
20.          remove <a', b'> from Cs'
21.       End If
22.    End For
23. End For
24. Return true
```

Line 6 to 14 find all similar *record pairs* by parallel comparison of two records set. Consuming these *record pairs* are all duplicate, the similarity of the *record set* still not satisfies the threshold φ (line 16 and 18), it is obviously no need to recursively invoke multilevel detection to detect sub-tables in next level (line 19). According to the simulation in section 4.3, $Cs'.Size \leq \frac{2\varphi \cdot A.size \cdot B.size}{(A.size + B.size)}$ is satisfied in most cases, it will avoid lots of multilevel detections by checking $Cs'.Size$ before recursive invocation.

5 Experiments

The experiments are performed on a PC server with 2.8 Hz Pentium 4 CPU, windows server 2003 operation system and Oralce10g database. Artificial data is used to compare the proposed similarity measure and other classic measures The experiments are performed on three kinds of duplication: "repeatedly import", "tiny difference" and "inconsistent precision". And the duplicate is detected by three similarity measures: Proposed similarity, Cosine metric and Euclidean distance. Firstly, plenty clean records are prepared, and then the duplicate is introduced by:

- **Repeatedly Import:** all records are copied and re-import to the database;
- **Tiny Difference:** four columns are selected randomly, and a tiny value is added to each column of all records, then re-imported to the database. The new value is calculated as $v_c' = v_c + random[0,4]\times 10^{-vc.scale}$.
- **Inconsistent Precision**: same as the duplicate introduction of "*Tiny Difference*" but $v_c' = round(v_c, random(0, v_c.scale])$.

After introducing the duplicate, the data is doubled. The approximate duplicate rate is 50%. Pairwise duplicate detection is often evaluated using *recall*, *precision* and *f-measure*[2]. After duplicate detection, too many *record pairs* are detected by the cosine metric approach even the threshold is 0.99, the *recall* is large but *precision* is bad, the cosine metric is not suitable to the decimal number. So the comparison between MD^{2}M and Euclidean distance is focused.

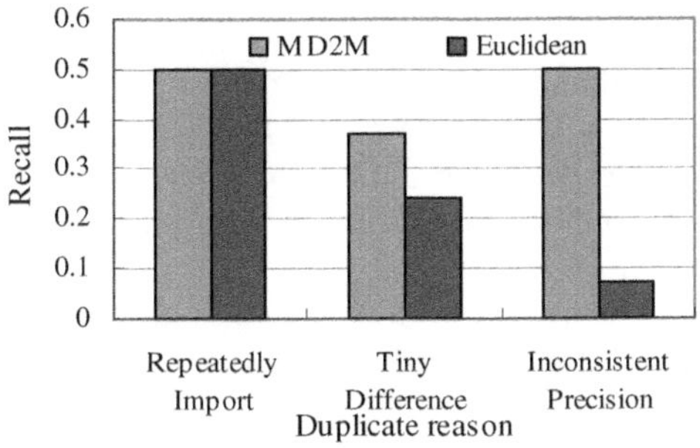

Fig. 3. Recall of MD^{2}M and Euclidean under Different Duplicate Reason

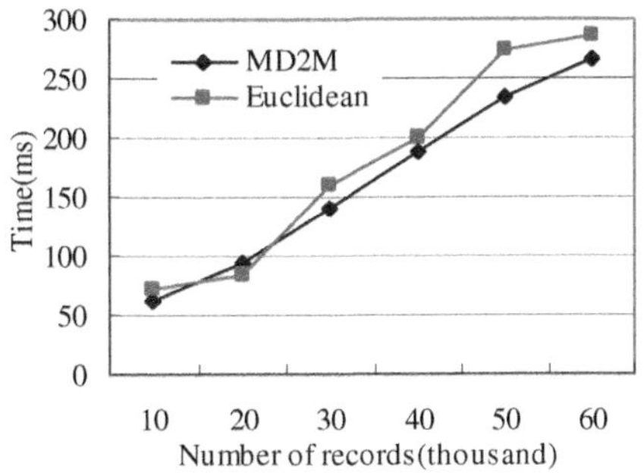

Fig. 4. Performance of MD^{2}M and Euclidean under Different Data Volume

Both two approaches are based on the distance. In Euclidean distance approach, the threshold is also assigned as minimum distance ($10^{-c.scale}$) of *comparison column.* It is difficult to evaluate the *precision* because no one can tell two similar numbers are really duplicate or not in the artificial data. We support all the detected *record pairs* are duplicate and evaluate *recall* instead of *precision*. The results are shown as Fig 3:

- **Repeatedly Import:** Both two approaches successfully detect all the repeatedly import records which are exactly same, *recall* is 0.5;
- **Tiny Difference:** *Recall* of MD^{2}M is about 0.37 because the floating value is $random[0,4]\times 10^{-vc.scale}$, it may probably larger than threshold $10^{-vc.scale}$, some introduced duplicate are missed. But *recall* of Euclidean distance is 0.24. After investigating the results, we find if four randomly selected columns NOT include column *A* and *D* (*A.scale=D.scale* =0), the corresponding records are treated as duplicate no matter how larger the four floating values are. On the contrary, if floating values

of column *A* and *D* are larger than 1, the corresponding records are definitely not duplicate no matter how larger the rest two values are. Obviously, Euclidean distance is controlled by the distance of larger elements, the similarity of small scale columns are hidden by larger scale ones.
- **Inconsistent Precision**: *Recall* of MD^2M is 0.5, MD^2M is designed for detected the duplicate caused by inconsistent precision. *Recall* of Euclidean distance is only 0.07 , it misses most duplicate, except the values are very close and only one scale of precision is lost, for example 54.321 and 54.32, Euclidean distance approach treat these values as "tiny difference" duplicate.

The performance of two approaches is similar (see Fig. 4), the executed time is almost linear to the data volume in both approaches, duplicate rate affect performance a little. MD^2M has good executed performance.

6 Conclusions and Future Work

In this paper, the Multilevel Duplicate Detection Model (MD^2M) for scientific data is presented and implemented. The primary works of this research are following five aspects:

- Analyze and conclude the duplicate related characteristics of scientific database, point out the weakness of classic similarity measures, proposed the challenges.
- Propose the domain-independent duplicate detection model for scientific database, including similarity measures of *comparison column*, *record* and *record set*.
- Propose the algorithms for multilevel duplicate detection in scientific database;
- Prove the model is domain-independent, effective and efficient through some experiments and applications.

Generally, compared with previous studies, MD^2M proposed a domain-independent, multilevel duplicate detection approach and a numerical duplicate detection model for scientific database. Theories and experiments show that MD^2M can assure the quality of the data and further improve the accuracy of data analysis and mining. All of these works are useful for preprocessing and cleaning scientific data. Future works also includes duplicate detection on symbol data, on scientific data storing in XML or other formats, and the duplicate detection based on non-referred tables should be also considered in further.

References

1. Gray, J., Liu, D.T., Nieto-Santisteban, M.A., Szalay, A., et al.: Scientific Data Management in The Coming Decade. SIGMOD Record. 34(4), 34–41 (2005)
2. Rahm, E., Do, H.H.: Data Cleaning: Problem and Current Approaches. IEEE Data Engineering Bulletin 23(3), 1 (2000)
3. Galhardas, H., Florescu, D., Shasha, D., Simon, E., Saita, C.: Declarative Data Cleaning: Language, Model, and Algorithms. In: Proc. of International Conf. on Very Large Databases, pp. 371–380 (2001)

4. Hernandez, M., Stolfo, S.: The Merge/Purge Problem for Large Databases. In: Proc. of the ACM SIGMOD, pp. 127–138 (May 1995)
5. Felligi, I.P., Sunter, A.B.: A Theory for Record Linkage. Journal of the American Statistical Society 64, 1183–1210 (1969)
6. Bhattacharya, I., Getoor, L.: Relational Clustering for Multi-type Entity Resolution. In: Proc. of Workshop on Multi-Relational Data Mining, MRDM (2005)
7. Dong, X., Halevy, A., Madhavan, J.: Reference Reconciliation in Complex Information Spaces. In: Proc. of SIGMOD, pp. 85–96 (2005)
8. Monge, A., Elkan, C.: An Efficient Domain Independent Algorithm for Detecting Approximately Duplicate Database Records. In: Proc. of the SIGMOD Workshop on Data Mining and Knowledge Discovery (May 1997)
9. Garcia, E.: An Information Retrieval Tutorial on Cosine Similarity Measures, Dot Products and Term Weight Calculations, `http://www.miislita.com/information-retrieval-tutorial/cosine-similarity-tutorial.html#Cosim`
10. Rousseau, R.: Jaccard Similarity Leads to the Marczewski-Steinhaus Topology for Information Retrieval. Inf. Process. Manage. (IPM) 34(1), 87–94 (1998)
11. Black, P.E. (ed.): Euclidean Distance, in Dictionary of Algorithms and Data Structures, U.S. National Institute of Standards and Technology, `http://www.itl.nist.gov/div897/sqg/dads/HTML/euclidndstnc.html`
12. Mahalanobis, P.C.: On the generalised distance in statistics. Proceedings of the National Institute of Sciences of India 2 (1), 49–55
13. Xue, Z.-a., Cen, F., Wei, L.-p.: A Weighting Fuzzy Clustering Algorithm Based on Euclidean Distance. In: FSKD 2008, pp. 172–175 (2008)
14. Jin, L., Li, C., Mehrotra, S.: Efficient Record Linkage in Large Data Sets. In: Proc. of International Conf. on Database Systems for Advanced Applications, p. 137 (2003)
15. Lim, E.P., Srivastava, J., Prabhakar, S., Richardson, J.: Entity Identification in Database Integration. In: Proc. of International Conf. on Data Engineering, pp. 294–301 (April 1993)
16. Weis, M.: Fuzzy Duplicate Detection on XML. In: VLDB PhD Workshop (2005)
17. Weis, M., Naumann, F.: Duplicate Detection in XML. In: Proc. of the ACM SIGMOD Workshop on Information Quality in Information Systems, pp. 10–19 (2004)
18. Ananthakrishna, R., Chaudhuri, S., Ganti, V.: Eliminating Fuzzy Duplicates in Data Warehouses. In: Proc. of VLDB, pp. 586–597 (2002)
19. Bhattacharya, I., Getoor, L.: Relational Clustering for Multi-type Entity Resolution. In: Proc. of Workshop on Multi-Relational Data Mining, MRDM (2005)

Generalized UDF for Analytics Inside Database Engine

Meichun Hsu, Qiming Chen, Ren Wu, Bin Zhang, and Hans Zeller*

HP Labs, HP TSG*
Palo Alto, California, USA
Hewlett Packard Co.
{meichun.hsu,qiming.chen,ren.wu,bzhang2,hans.zeller}@hp.com

Abstract. Running analytics computation inside a database engine through the use of UDFs (User Defined Functions) has been investigated, but not yet become a scalable approach due to several technical limitations. One limitation lies in the lack of generality for UDFs to express complex applications and to compose them with relational operators in SQL queries. Another limitation lies in the lack of systematic support for a UDF to cache relations initially for efficient computation in multi-calls. Further, having UDF execution interacted efficiently with query processing requires detailed system programming, which is often beyond the expertise of most application developers.

To solve these problems, we extend the UDF technology in both semantic and system dimensions. We generalize UDF to support scalar, tuple as well as *relation input* and output, allow UDFs to be defined on the entire content of relations and allow the moderate-sized input relations to be cached in initially to avoid repeated retrieval. With such extension the generalized UDFs can be composed with other relational operators and thus integrated into queries naturally. Furthermore, based on the notion of *invocation patterns*, we provide focused system support for efficiently interacting UDF execution with query processing.

We have taken the open-sourced PostgreSQL engine and a commercial and proprietary parallel database engine as our prototyping vehicles; we illustrated the performance, modeling power and usability of the proposed approach with the experimental results on both platforms.

1 Introduction

Pushing data-intensive computation down to the data management layer is the key to fast data access and reduced data transfer. One option for the next generation BI system in the Web age with massively growing data volume and pressing need for low latency is to have the data intensive part of analytics executed inside the DB engine.

There exist two kinds of efforts for integrating applications and data management: as (a) running database programs including stored procedures on server-side but outside the query evaluation process; and (b) wrapping computations by UDFs executed in the query processing environment [1-4,11]. Although both offer the benefit of having computations close to data, compared with the UDF approach, running data-intensive applications on the server-side but outside of the query engine incurs the overhead of ODBC, suffers from the lack of memory sharing, and does not take advantage of the scale-out infrastructure inherent in a parallel database system.

L. Chen et al. (Eds.): WAIM 2010, LNCS 6184, pp. 742–754, 2010.

1.1 Limitations of Existent UDFs

The current UDF technology has several limitations in both expressive power and efficiency. Existing SQL systems offer scalar, aggregate and table functions (table functions are also known as table-valued functions, or TVF), where the input of a scalar or table function can only be bound to the attribute values of a single tuple, and an aggregate function is actually implemented as incremental per-tuple manipulations; these UDFs lack formal support to relational input. However, in addition to per-tuple input (e.g. events), many applications also rely on entire relations (e.g. models). To have the moderately-sized input relations cached in a UDF without repeated retrieval can provide significant performance advantage. In fact, some applications are difficult to implement without the presence of whole relations (such as minimal spanning tree computation). Further, in order to take advantage of data-parallel computation using multi-cores or GPUs, feeding in a UDF a set of tuples initially, rather than one tuple at a time, is important. All these have motivated us to support truly relation-in, relation-out UDFs.

1.2 Related Work

The idea of moving computation closer to database server has been in existence for quite some time. However, many of these efforts are limited to running applications on the database server-side, but not really integrating them with query processing. As a result, the overhead caused by IPC, ODBC, and data copying is still significant.

Integrating applications with query processing with UDFs has been recognized as a way to achieve database extensibility (e.g. [13]). It is also recognized as a solution to data-intensive analytics [1,6] However, the UDF limitations in both performance and modelling power have not been properly addressed so far. The current commercial database engines support scalar, aggregate and table UDFs but has limited such support at the tuple-at-a-time level, and thus does not allow the UDF to reference the entire content of a relation. As memory size increases, caching static relations in UDF closure has become more feasible.

Introducing relation argument is also different from supporting User Defined Aggregate (UDA). With a UDA, an aggregate is calculated incrementally on the per-tuple basis in multiple function calls. In this context, the existing UDA approach is clearly different from loading the entire input relations initially for supporting the applications definable on the entire content of these relations.

Therefore, although user-defined relational and aggregate operators were studied previously [5,13], the notion of relation-in, relation-out UDF has not been supported systematically; and these are the focus of this paper.

1.3 Our Solution

In this work we provide a generalized UDF framework and address the key implementation issues.

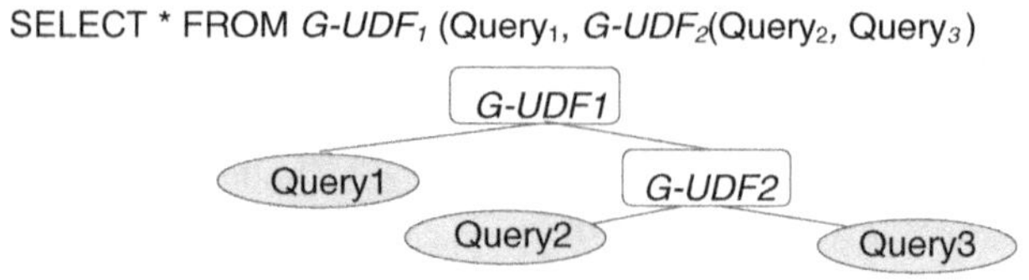

Fig. 1. Integrating applications to query using Generalized UDFs

A *generalized UDF* can have scalar and relation parameters where a scalar parameter may be substituted by a constant or an attribute value from a single tuple; its return value can be scalar, tuple and relation. This notion is the generalization of scalar UDF, aggregate UDF, TVF of SQL Server and Table Function of Oracle. This generalization offers the following benefits:

- Modeling the applications definable on entire relations rather than individual tuples;
- Expressing relational transformations, composing UDFs with other relational operators in a query (Fig. 1) and linking multiple queries in an application dataflow.
- Caching input relations in the UDF's function closure to avoid repeated retrieval; e.g. caching in memory some moderate-sized dimension tables with respect to the per-tuple processing of a sizable fact table.

We then introduce the notion of UDF *invocation pattern* based on the combination of input and output modes. A UDF is invoked within a query; a UDF invocation pattern represents a specific style for applying it to the relation objects passed in from the query processing, such as fed in tuple by tuple, by the entire relation initially, or in a hybrid way. Multiple invocation patterns can be identified and supported accordingly to allow applications to interact with query processing properly. A well-defined pattern underlies the well-understood behaviour and system interface for providing appropriate system support.

We have taken the open-sourced PostgreSQL engine and a commercial and proprietary parallel database engine as our prototyping vehicles for supporting the generalized UDFs. We illustrate the performance, modeling power and usability of the proposed approach with the experimental results on both platforms.

The rest of this paper is organized as follows: Section 2 compares various kinds of UDFs with experimental results; Section 3 describes the generalization of UDFs; Section 4 discusses the implementation issues of generalized UDFs; Section 5 illustrates further experimental results on a parallel database engine; Section 6 concludes the paper.

2 A Comparison of UDFs

In this section we will illustrate the performance problem of the conventional UDFs through expressing the K-Means clustering algorithm in SQL with UDFs. Then we will show how generalized UDFs with various input modes can be used intelligently to alleviate the shortcomings of SQL being cumbersome in expressing data flow logic, and in gaining high performance.

The *k*-means algorithm was developed by J. MacQueen in 1967 and then by J. A. Hartigan and M. A. Wong around 1975; it is used to cluster *n* objects into *k* partitions, $k < n$. The clustering is based on the objects' attributes which form a vector space. The objective is to minimize the total intra-cluster variance.

Let us consider clustering of two-dimensional geographic points. It is an iterative process; in each iteration, the nearest cluster center of each point is identified and the point is assigned as the member of that cluster; then for each center, its coordinates is calculated as the "mean" of the coordinates of its member points. If new locations of the centers are not converged enough from the old ones, the above process is repeated, as illustrated in Fig. 2.

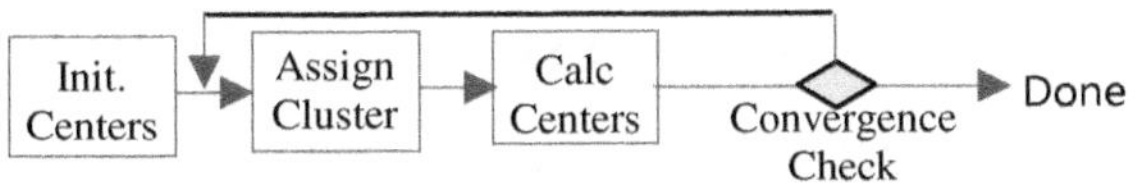

Fig. 2. K-Means clustering

Now let us focus on expressing a single iteration of the K-Means clustering in SQL with UDFs. In the above two phases, the first phase is for each point in relation *Points* [pid, x, y] to compute its distances to all centers in relation *Centers* [cid, x, y], and assign the point to the closest center. The second phase is to re-compute the set of new centers based on the average location of the member points. Let us abbreviate this single iteration as **KM1**.

2.1 Using Scalar UDF

In SQL with a scalar UDF, KM1 can be expressed as

[Query 0: Scalar UDF]

```
SELECT cid, avg(X) AS cx, avg(Y) AS cy FROM
    (SELECT P.x AS X, P.y AS Y, (SELECT cid FROM Centers C WHERE
        dist(P.x, P.y, C.x, C.y) = (SELECT MIN(dist(P2.x, P2.y, C2.x, C2.y))
     FROM Centers C2, Points P2 WHERE P2.x=P.x AND P2.y=P.y) ) AS cid FROM Points P)
GROUP BY cid;
```

The plan of Query 0 is illustrated in Fig 3, where the nearest center for each point is computed wrt all the centers. Since this query uses scalar UDF/expression evaluated on the per-tuple basis, and the UDF is unable to take the entire *Centers* relation as an input argument and cache it initially, the relation Centers has to be retrieved for each point p; furthermore, it has to be retrieved in a nested query as well (Query Optimizer turns it to join) , for the MIN distance from p to centers.

Such *relation fetch overhead* is caused by the lack of relation input argument for UDFs. From the query plan it can be seen that the overhead in fetching the *Centers* relation using scalar UDF is explorative since it is proportional to the number of points.

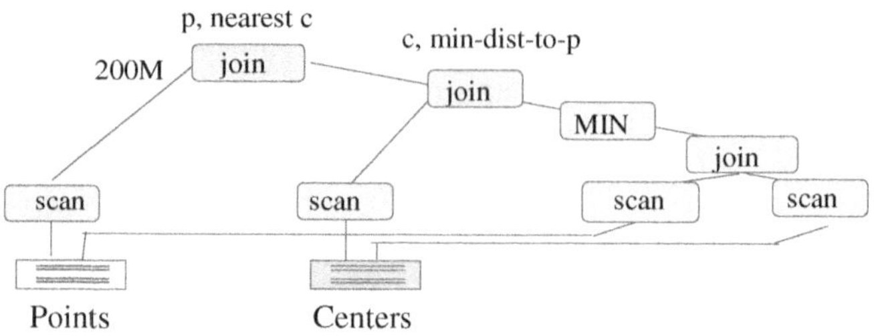

Fig. 3. Query plan for K-Means using conventional UDF

2.2 Using SQL Server TVF/CROSS APPLY

A SQL Server TVF allows table valued return but restricts its input values to be scalar. To apply a TVF to multiple tuples of a relation, a kind of join – CROSS APPLY, is required. With SQL Server CROSS APPLY, KM1 can be expressed as

```
SELECT cid, avg(px) AS cx, avg(py) AS cy FROM (SELECT P.x AS px, P.y AS py,
    (SELECT cd.id FROM Centers AS C CROSS APPLY dist(P.x, P.y, C.x, C.y, C.id) AS cd
     WHERE cd.dist = (SELECT MIN(dist) FROM Centers AS C CROSS APPLY
     dist(P.x, P.y, C.x, C.y, C.id)) ) AS cid FROM Points P) AS pc
GROUP BY cid;
```

where (Centers CROSS APPLY *dist*(C.cid, P.x, P.y, C.x, C.y)) has schema <id, dist>.

Although more general than scalar UDF by table valued output, but without relation input, a TVF has to rely on CROSS APPLY to access the set of tuples in a relation, which in turn, leads to Cartesian product complexity. It can be seen in the above query that the per-point repeated retrieval of relation Centers is not eliminated regardless of using a scalar UDF or a TVF, and the additional join related Cartesian complexity is introduced. As a result, using CROSS APPLY incurs much greater performance penalty.

2.3 Using Oracle TABLE Function

With Oracle TABLE function, KM1 can be expressed as

```
SELECT cid, avg(px) AS cx, avg(py) AS cy FROM (SELECT P.x AS px, P.y AS py,
    (SELECT cd.id FROM TABLE(dist(P.x, P.y, CURSOR(SELECT * FROM Centers))) cd
     WHERE cd.dist = SELECT MIN(dist) FROM
       TABLE(dist(P.x, P.y, CURSOR(SELECT * FROM Centers)))) AS cid FROM Points P)
GROUP BY cid;
```

To the kind of applications like K-Means, this has the same problem as using CROSS APPLY – it also relies on cumbersome Cartesian product operations for pairing tuples thus is also inefficient.

2.4 Using Generalized UDF

Using a generalized UDF with one point-by-point scalar input argument and another relation input argument bound to the entire relation of Centers, KM1 can be expressed by the following query.

```
SELECT cid, avg(px) AS cx, avg(py) AS cy FROM (SELECT P.x AS px, P.y AS py,
   Assign_center (P.x, P.y, "SELECT * FROM Centers") AS cid FROM Points P)
GROUP BY cid;
```

In this query, the relation Centers is retrieved only once in the beginning and cached in the UDF function closure for multiple point-by-point calls. In this way, the shortcoming of SQL being cumbersome in expressing data flow logic is alleviated, and without repeated retrieval of the Centers relation and join operation, the performance gain is significant.

In general, with a generalized UDF, the data of an input relation can be retrieved initially and retained over multiple calls. In this example, all the centers are loaded initially and buffered in the UDF's closure, hence unnecessary to be re-loaded in subsequent calls for each point to find its nearest center. Indeed, this is impossible with a scalar function or SQL expression, where the centers must be retrieved repeatedly for each point, and even worse, repeatedly retrieved for each center to compare its distance to a point with the MIN distance of centers to that point. (since the MIN state cannot be kept in SQL). Such overhead is added to processing each point and is *proportional to the number of points*, which could be very serious if the number of points is large.

2.5 Performance Comparison of Generalized and Conventional UDFs

We first compared the performance of using existing UDFs – Postgres scalar UDF, SQL Server TVF/CROSS APPLY, and Oracle Table Function, in running **KM1** on a single machine with 100 centers and 1M points. The results indicate that due to the differences in query shapes, the performance of using the regular scalar UDF has better performance than using TVF/CROSS APPLY and Oracle Table Function. Therefore we chosen to compare the performance of using the proposed generalized UDF against using the conventional scalar UDF for **KM1** computation.

We use Postgres database engine as our prototyping vehicle to test our approach. The server is HP ProLiant DL360 G4 with 2 x 2.73 Ghz CPUs and 7.74 GB RAM, running Linux 2.6.18-92.1.13.el5 (x86_64). The Performance comparison is illustrated in Fig. 4.

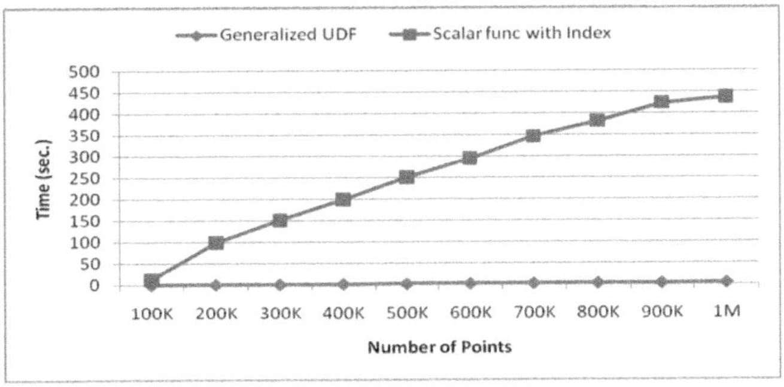

Fig. 4. Performance comparison of generalized UDF and conventional scalar UDF

It can be seen that implementing KM1 using a Generalized UDF significantly over-performs that using a Scalar function. This is not only because the former can intelligently alleviate the shortcomings of SQL being cumbersome in expressing data flow logic, but also because caching the entire *Centers* relation initially can avoid numerous repeated retrievals of that relation on the per-point basis.

We also compared the query performance for other applications using different kinds of UDFs. These experiments have provided the justification for us to generalize the notion of UDF.

3 Generalized UDF

As discussed thus far, we see that a scalar function or a table valued function (TVF of SQL Server or Table Function of Oracle) can only take scalar input arguments corresponding to a single tuple, therefore may be "relation-out" but not "relation-in", which leads to the limitations in both modelling power and performance.

We generalize the existent UDFs to allow the flexible combination of input arguments which may be substituted by constant values, the attribute values of a single tuple, or a entire relation (a table or a query result). A generalized UDF can return a scalar value, a tuple or a relation. From the signature point of view, a generalized UDF may have the following three kinds of argument bindings:

- t-binding: with an input argument bound to an attribute value of a tuple;
- R-binding: with an argument bound to a relation (expressible by a query);
- constant-binding: bound to a constant value.

A scalar argument may fall in either t-binding or constant binding. These are illustrated in Fig.5.

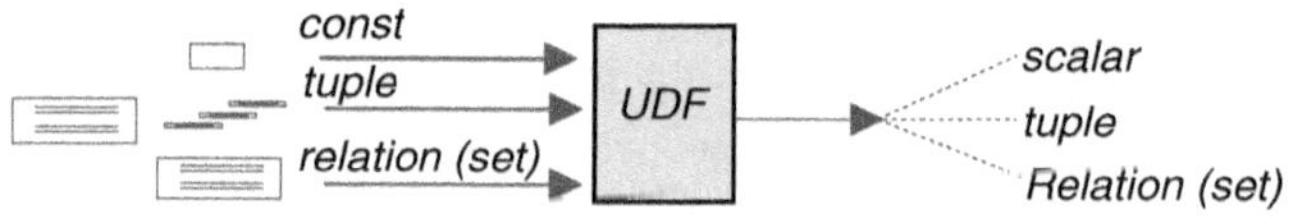

Fig. 5. Input/Output modes of Generalized UDF

By default, if a UDF has any t-binding it is called tuple-by-tuple with respect to that relation. For an R-binding, the corresponding relation is initially fetched, or generated as the result of a query, and retained in the UDF closure for a single call (Fig 6a) or across multiple calls (Fig. 6b). Note that the combination of input/output modes has certain dependency as well as constraint, depending on where the UDF is located in a query, e.g. in the SELECT list, the FROM list, etc.

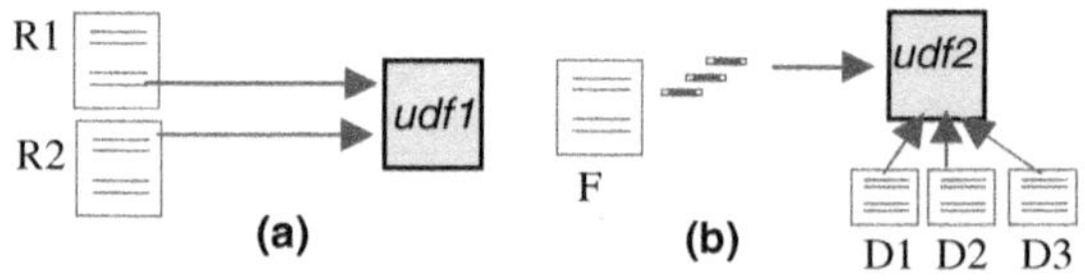

Fig. 6. UDF input parameter passing

This generalization offers the following benefits.

- Modeling the kind of applications definable on the entire contents of some relations;
- Expressing relational transformation. A relation-in, relation-out UDF derives a relation (although it can have database update effects in the function body) just like a standard relational operator, thus is naturally composed with other relational operators or sub-queries in a SQL query, as previously illustrated in Fig 1.
- Caching input relations initially to avoid repeated retrieval.

As the example depicted in Fig. 6(b), the generalized UDF, *udf2*, is defined on a sizable fact table *F* and some moderate-sized dimension tables D_1, D_2, D_3 as below.

```
DEFINE FUNCTION udf2 (id, d1, d2, d3, D1, D2, D3) RETURN t {
int id; float d1, d2, d3;
Tuple t (/*schema of t*/);
Relation D1 (/*schema of D1*/); Relation D2 (/*schema of D2*/); Relation D3 (/*schema of
    D3*/);
PROCEDURE f_shell(/*dll name*/);
}
```

The relation schemas denote the "schema-aware" signature of *udf2*, the actual relation instances or query results compliant to those schemas can be bound to *udf2* as actual parameters.

In the following query on a sizable fact table *F* and moderately-sized dimension table D_1, D_2, D_3, the generalized UDF, *udf2*, is called tuple-by-tuple wrt *F*, with entire D_1, D_2, D_3 retrieved and cached in as static initial values across multiple calls. *udf2* is called multiple times in the query, one for each tuple in *F*.

```
SELECT udf2 (F.id, F.d1, F.d2, F.d3,
  "SELECT * FROM D1", "SELECT * FROM D2", "SELECT * FROM D3").*
FROM F;
```

This generalized UDF, *udf2*, allows both tuple and tuple-set inputs. It has 7 args, the first four correspond to a tuple of relation F, the rest three correspond to the entire relations of D1, D2 and D3. So this UDF is invoked tuple-by-tuple wrt F, but with D1, D2, D3 loaded in the first call as static initial data.

When this UDF is invoked, each tuple of F is manipulated with all the instances of D1, D2 and D3, which are loaded only once initially. As far as the static input relations fit in the memory, repeated retrieval of them can be avoided, which indeed opens the potential for supporting many applications falling in this case; otherwise the correct UDF execution still can be ensured by reusing the database cache management facility.

We also define three return modes: Scalar, Tuple and Set. With the tuple return mode, the function returns one tuple-per-call in multiple calls, typically once for each input tuple. With set return mode, the function returns the entire resulting tuple-set in the end.

Distinguishing these function invocation modes is the key to efficiently integrating function execution with query processing.

Below we express the K-Means calculation in a single iteration (KM1) by two kinds of generalized UDFs, one takes the entire Points and Centers relations as input, another caches in the small-size Centers relation, and applies to the Points on the tuple-by-tuple basis.

In the Query 1 sown below, the UDF *assign_center1* takes the entire Points and Centers relations as input (Fig. 7).

[Query 1: UDF with block input and output]

```
SELECT r.cid, avg(r.x), avg(r.y) FROM assign_center1 (
  "SELECT x,y FROM Points", "SELECT x,y,cid FROM Centers") r
GROUP BY r.cid;
```

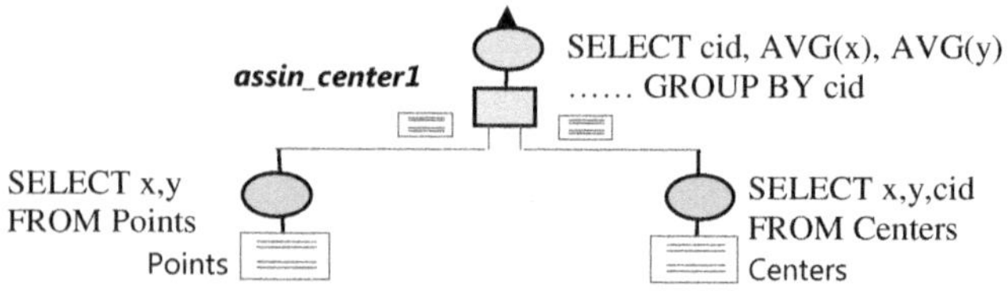

Fig. 7. Query using UDF with only relation input

In the Query 2 sown below, the UDF *assign_center2* caches in the small-size Centers relation, and applies to the Points on the tuple-by-tuple basis (Fig. 8).

[Query 2: UDF with mixed types of inputs]

```
SELECT cid, avg(px) AS cx, avg(py) AS cy FROM
(SELECT P.x AS px, P.y AS py, assign_center2 (P.x, P.y, "SELECT x,y,cid FROM Centers") AS
cid FROM Points P) r
GROUP BY cid;
```

The generalized UDF *assign_center2* (P.x, P.y, "SELECT x,y,cid FROM Centers") allows both tuple and tuple-set inputs. It has 3 args, the first two correspond to a tuple of relation Points, the third arg corresponds to the entire relation of Centers (projected). This UDF is invoked tuple-by-tuple wrt Points, but with Centers loaded in the FIRST_CALL as static initial data. When this UDF is invoked, each point is manipulated with all centers to find the nearest distance. Loading relation Centers in the FIRST_CALL only once as static initial data avoids repeated retrieval of centers in the millions of subsequent calls for per-point processing.

Fig. 8. Query using UDF with per-tuple and block (relation) input

The performance comparison of Query 1 and Query 2 is illustrated in Fig. 9. In case the *Points* relation can fit in the memory, Query 1 that invokes the UDF with both relations cached in actually over-performs, but a sizable *Points* relation may exceed the memory limit, and therefore Query 2 is more scalable.

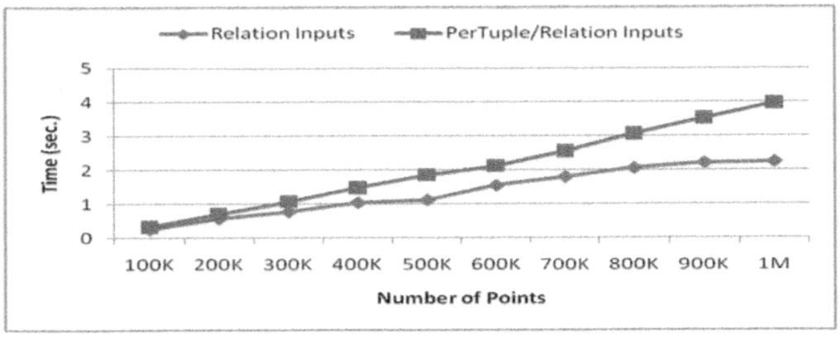

Fig. 9. Query invoking UDF with per-tuple/relation input outperforms that invoking UDF with only relation input

4 Implementation of Generalized UDF

We extended the query engine to support generalized UDFs with relation parameters, in addition to other types of input parameters. Our focus is placed on UDF *invocation pattern*. For example, when any input relation is fed in tuple-by-tuple (analogous to the probe site of hash-join), the UDF is called multiple times with respect to that input during its execution in the host query; when an input relation is to be fed in as a whole (analogous to the build-site of hash-join), that relation must be entirely cached in before any data can be returned. In general, the invocation pattern of a generalized UDF is determined by its input/output characteristics, and in turn, determines the way to handle the input/output data.

Like other relational operators, a function, e.g. a UDF, executed in a query may be called multiple times, one for each returned value. The initial data used for every call and the carry-on data across calls, are handled by the query executor through a function manager. To fit in the above running environment, a function is usually coded with three cases: FIRST_CALL, NORMAL_CALL and LAST_CALL. The FIRST_CALL is executed only once in the first time the UDF is called in the hosting query which provides initial data; the NORMAL_CALL is executed in each call including the first call, for doing the designated application; therefore there would be multiple NORMAL_CALLs if the function is called one tuple at a time. LAST_CALL is made after the last normal call for cleanup purpose. The query executor keeps track the number of calls of the UDF during processing a query, and checks the end-of-data condition for determining the execution. Accordingly, memory spaces allocated for function execution may have different life-spans: e.g. per-query with one call, multi-calls, per-call, etc. When a function interacts with the query executor, switching memory context is often necessary.

Based on this framework, on the extended PostgreSQL engine we handle the input arguments in the following way.

- R-binding is made in the FIRST_CALL where input relations are retrieved through the Postgres internal SPI query interface and cached in the UDF function closure, together with other initial data to be carried-on across multiple calls.

- t-binding is made in each NORMAL_CALL with respect to one input tuple (or other scalar values). Note that if multiple relations are involved in t-binding, the input relation must be the join of these relations.

  The output arguments are handled in the following way.
- *Tuple-Mode* return is handled in each (can be only one) NORMAL_CALL with the first resulting tuple returned.
- *Set-Mode* is handled in the LAST_CALL with the entire result-set returned.

With the above arrangement, a generalized UDF is executed by the extended query engine in the following way.

- When a generalized UDF, say *F*, is defined, the information about its name, arguments, input mode, return mode, dll entry-point, etc, is registered into several meta-tables to be retrieved for executing *F*.
- When *F* is invoked, several handle data structures are provided by extending the corresponding ones (such as Postgres *fcinfo*) used in the query executor. The handle for function execution (***hE***) keeps track, at a minimum, the information about input/output relation argument schemas, input mode, return mode, result set, etc. The handle for invocation context (***hC***) is used to control the execution of the UDF across calls. *hC* keeps track, at a minimum, the information on number of calls, end-of-data status, memory context; it has a pointer to the *hE*, a pointer to user-provided context known as scratchpad for retaining certain application data between calls, and a pointer to *hARG*, a data structure generated from *F*'s definition for keeping actual argument values across calls.
- During function execution, the extended query engine uses several system functions and macros to manipulate these handle structures.

Further, we advocate a "canonical" approach to UDF development: coding the application logic in a single "user-function" rather than mingled with system calls, and making the initial data, if any, accessible to it as external variables. As described in [5], we have developed the UDF-Shell approach to ease users from the burden of dealing with system details. We divide a UDF into a UDF-Shell, as the wrapper for system interaction, and a "*user-function*" that contains the application logic only. The Shell is generated automatically based on the function signature. The system data structures are converted into "common" data structures, which are specified in the generated header files and used in the "*user-function*". The UDF is made by plugging the "*user-function*" to the Shell.

5 Experiments on Parallel Database

We also used a commercial and proprietary parallel database engine (HP Neoview) as a prototyping vehicle to test this innovative extension to UDF. The test environment is set up as a parallel database cluster with 8 server nodes and 16 disks. The support to generalized UDF is extended from the parallel query processors. The dll code of the UDF is made available on each node. Therefore, within a given query execution multiple instances of the function are executing concurrently across the host processes throughout the cluster.

We conducted the experiments using the K-means application. The UDF *assign_center2* is the same as the one used in **query 2** for a single iteration. We compared its performance with the one using a scalar function *dist (p.x, p.y, c.x, c.y)* for computing the distance between a point *p* and a center *c*, shown in **query 0**.

The *Points* relation is partitioned among the nodes. We ran the two queries with different data load (number of points) ranging from 1 million to 200 million, with 2 dimensions and 100 centers. The performance comparison is shown below.

	1M	10M	100M	200M
Generalized UDF	0.3 min	2.7 min	26.8 min	53.3 min
Scalar UDF/ expr	4.5min	41 min	6.8 hr	19.4 hr

The above comparison in the range of 1 million to 100 million points is also depicted in Fig. 10

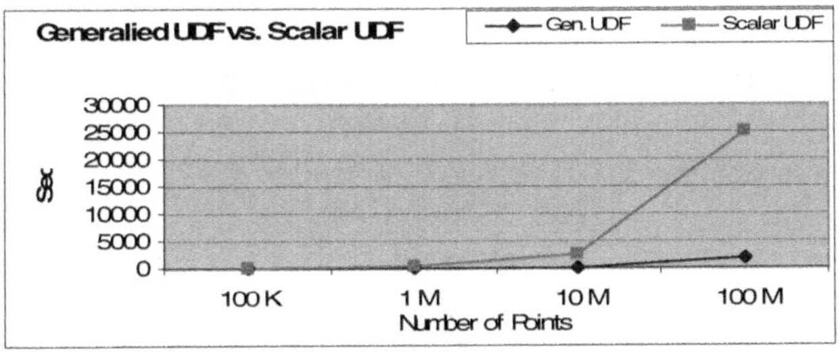

Fig. 10. Using generalized UDF in K-Means query over-performs that using conventional scalar UDF on a parallel database

Our solution scales linearly from 1M to 200M points, and significantly outperforms running K-Means using the conventional UDFs. The reason becomes clear by observing the query plans shown before.

In the conventional UDF-based solution, the inability to access two relations together in the UDF forced the engine to perform multiple joins and send data of *Points* and *Centers* across multiple query processors multiple times. The generalized UDF, in contrast, is executed with a very streamlined data flow, consisting of each node assigning centers locally, performing partial aggregation locally, and then sends the partial aggregation to the global query processor.

We ran the above query using the generalized UDF with different data load (number of points) to observe its linear scalability. As shown in Fig 11. The experiments reveal that our solution scales linearly from 1M to 200M points, which is not possible with the conventional client programming or pure SQL.

Number of points	1M	10M	20M	50M	100M	200M
Time (Sec)	16.9	163	325	814	1610	3200

Fig. 11. Linear scalability using generalized UDF in K-Means clustering

We also compared the performance of the above parallel database engine with the Hadoop MapReduce engine [10,12] and reported some results in [6] which has provided the evidence of using parallel database engine and generalized UDFs for performance gain and scalability.

6 Conclusions

Pushing data-intensive BI analytics down to the database engine with UDFs enables high-performance and secured execution; however, for several technical reasons it has not yet become a scalable approach. This paper proposes a critical extension to UDF – allowing a UDF to input entire relations initially for enhanced expressive power and performance. We also provided focused system support for efficiently integrating UDF execution into the query processing pipeline, based on the notion of *invocation patterns*.

We have taken the open-sourced PostgreSQL engine and a commercial and proprietary parallel database engine as our prototyping vehicles for supporting the generalized UDFs. The value in performance, modeling power and usability of the proposed approach has been proven by the experimental results on both platforms.

We are continuing the development of memory conscious UDF computation that automatically places data in the memory hierarchy including GPU cache, CPU cache, main memory and disk in the way transparent to UDF developers.

References

1. Argyros, T.: How Aster In-Database MapReduce Takes UDF's to the next Level (2008), http://www.asterdata.com/
2. Bryant, R.E.: Data-Intensive Supercomputing: The case for DISC, CMU-CS-07-128 (2007)
3. Chen, Q., Hsu, M.: Data-Continuous SQL Process Model. In: Proc. 16th International Conference on Cooperative Information Systems, CoopIS 2008 (2008)
4. Chen, Q., Hsu, M., Liu, R., Wang, W.: Scaling-up and Speeding-up Video Analytics Inside Database Engine. In: Bhowmick, S.S., Küng, J., Wagner, R. (eds.) DEXA 2009. LNCS, vol. 5690, pp. 244–254. Springer, Heidelberg (2009)
5. Chen, Q., Hsu, M., Liu, R.: Extend UDF Technology for Integrated Analytics. In: Pedersen, T.B., Mohania, M.K., Tjoa, A.M. (eds.) DaWak 2009. LNCS, vol. 5691, pp. 256–270. Springer, Heidelberg (2009)
6. Chen, Q., Therber, A., Hsu, M., Zeller, H., Zhang, B., Wu, R.: Efficiently Support MapReduce alike Computation Models Inside Parallel DBMS. In: IDEAS 2009 (2009)
7. Chen, Q., Hsu, M.: Inter-Enterprise Collaborative Business Process Management. In: Proc. of 17th Int'l Conf. on Data Engineering (ICDE 2001), Germany (2001)
8. Cooper, B.F., et al.: PNUTS: Yahoo!'s Hosted Data Serving Platform. In: VLDB 2008 (2008)
9. Dayal, U., Hsu, M., Ladin, R.: A Transaction Model for Long-Running Activities. In: VLDB 1991 (1991) (received 10 years award in 2001)
10. Dean, J.: Experiences with MapReduce, an abstraction for large-scale computation. In: Int. Conf. on Parallel Architecture and Compilation Techniques. ACM, New York (2006)
11. DeWitt, D.J., Paulson, E., Robinson, E., Naughton, J., Royalty, J., Shankar, S., Krioukov, A.: Clustera: An Integrated Computation and Data Management System. In: VLDB 2008 (2008)
12. HDFS, http://hdf.ncsa.uiuc.edu/HDF5/
13. Jaedicke, M., Mitschang, B.: User-Defined Table Operators: Enhancing Extensibility of ORDBMS. In: VLDB 1999 (1999)

Efficient Continuous Top-*k* Keyword Search in Relational Databases

Yanwei Xu[1,3], Yoshiharu Ishikawa[2,3], and Jihong Guan[1]

[1] Department of Computer Science and Technology, Tongji University, Shanghai, China
[2] Information Technology Center, Nagoya University, Japan
[3] Graduate School of Information Science, Nagoya University, Japan

Abstract. Keyword search in relational databases has been widely studied in recent years. Most of the previous studies focus on how to answer an instant keyword query. In this paper, we focus on how to find the top-*k* answers in relational databases for continuous keyword queries efficiently. As answering a keyword query involves a large number of join operations between relations, reevaluating the keyword query when the database is updated is rather expensive. We propose a method to compute a range for the future relevance score of query answers. For each keyword query, our method computes a state of the query evaluation process, which only contains a small amount of data and can be used to maintain top-*k* answers when the database is continually growing. The experimental results show that our method can be used to solve the problem of responding to continuous keyword searches for a relational database that is updated frequently.

Keywords: Relational databases, keyword search, continuous queries, incremental maintenance.

1 Introduction

As the amount of available text data in relational databases is growing rapidly, the need for ordinary users to be able to search such information effectively is increasing dramatically. Keyword search is the most popular information retrieval method because users need to know neither a query language nor the underlying structure of the data. Keyword search in relational databases has recently emerged as an active research topic [1,2,3,4,5,6,7].

Example 1. In this paper, we use the same running example of database *Complaints* as in [3] (shown in Figure 1). In this example, the database schema is $R = \{Complaints, Products, Customers\}$. There are two foreign key to primary key relationships: *Complaints* $\rightarrow$ *Products* and *Complaints* $\rightarrow$ *Customers*.

If a user gives a keyword query "maxtor netvista", the top-3 answers returned by the keyword search system of [5] are c_3, $c_3 \rightarrow p_2$ and $c_1 \rightarrow p_1$, which are obtained by joining relevant tuples from multiple relations to form a meaningful answer to the query. They are ranked by relevance scores that are computed by a ranking strategy.

Approaches that support keyword search in relational databases can be categorized into two groups: *tuple-based* [1,6,8,9,10] and *relation-based* [2,3,4,5,7]. After a user

L. Chen et al. (Eds.): WAIM 2010, LNCS 6184, pp. 755–767, 2010.

Complaints				
tupleId	*prodId*	*cusId*	*date*	*comments*
c_1	p121	c3232	6.30.02	"disk crashed after just one week of moderate use on an IBM Netvista X41"
c_2	p131	c3131	7.3.02	"lower-end IBM Netvista caught fire, starting apparently with disk"
c_3	p131	c3143	8.3.02	"IBM Netvista unstable with Maxtor HD"
...	...	...	...	...

Products			
tupleId	*prodId*	*manufacturer*	*model*
p_1	p121	"Maxtor"	"D540X"
p_2	p131	"IBM"	"Netvista"
p_3	p141	"Tripplite"	"Smart 700VA"
...	...	...	...

Customers			
tupleId	*cusId*	*name*	*occupation*
u_1	c3232	"John Smith"	"Software Engineer"
u_2	c3131	"Jack Lucas"	"Architect"
u_3	c3143	"John Mayer"	"Student"
...	...	...	...

Fig. 1. A Running Example taken from [3] (Query is "maxtor netvista". Matches are underlined)

inputs a keyword query, the relation-based approaches first enumerate all possible *query plans* (relational algebra expressions) according to the database schema, then these plans are evaluated by sending one or more corresponding SQL statements to the RDBMS to find inter-connected tuples.

In this paper, we study the problem of *continuous* top-k keyword searches in relational databases. Imagine that you are a member of the quality analysis staff at an international computer seller, and you are responsible for analyzing complaints of customers that are collected by customer service offices all over the world. Complaints of customers are arriving continuously, and are stored in the complaints database shown in Example 1. Suppose you want to find the information related to Panasonic Note laptops, then you issue a keyword query "panasonic note" and use one of the existing methods mentioned above to find related information. After observing some answers, you may suspect that some arriving claims will also be related to Panasonic Notes, so you want to search the database continuously using the keyword query. How should the system support such a query?

A naive solution is to issue the keyword query after one or several new related tuples arrive. Existing methods, however, are rather expensive as there might be huge numbers of tuples matched and they require costly join operations between relations. If the database has a high update frequency (as in the situation of the aforementioned example), recomputation will place a heavy workload on the database server.

In this paper we present a method to maintain answers incrementally for a top-k keyword search. Instead of full, non-incremental recomputation, our method performs incremental answer maintenance. Specifically, we retain the state for each query which is obtained through the latest evaluation of the query. A state consists of the current top-k answers, the query plans, and the related statistics. It is used to maintain top-k answers incrementally after the database is updated.

In summary, the main contributions of this paper are as follows:

- We introduce the concept of a continuous keyword query in relational databases. To the best of our knowledge, we are the first to consider the problem of incremental maintenance of top-k answers for keyword queries in relational databases.
- We propose a method for efficiently answering continuous keyword queries. By storing the state of a query evaluation process, our algorithm can handle the insertion of new tuples in most cases without reevaluating the keyword query.

The rest of this paper is organized as follows. In Section 2 the problem is defined. Section 3 briefly introduces the framework for answering continuous keyword search in relational databases. Section 4 presents the details of our method and Section 5 shows our experimental results. Section 6 discusses related work. Conclusions are given in Section 7.

2 Problem Definition

We first briefly define some terms used throughout this paper (detailed definitions can be found in [3,5,7]). A relational database is composed of a set of relations $R_1, R_2, \cdots, R_n$. A *Joint-Tuple-Tree* (*JTT*) T is a joining tree of different tuples. Each node is a tuple in the database, and each pair of adjacent tuples in T is connected via a foreign key to primary key relationship. A JTT is an answer to a keyword query if it contains more than one keyword of the query and each of its leaf tuples contains at least one keyword. Each JTT corresponds to the results produced by a relational algebra expression, which can be obtained by replacing each tuple with its relation name and imposing a full-text selection condition on the relations. Such an algebraic expression is called a *Candidate Network* (*CN*) [3]. For example, Candidate Networks corresponding to the two answers c_3 and $c_3 \rightarrow p_2$ of Example 1 are $Complaints^Q$ and $Complaints^Q \rightarrow Products^Q$, respectively (the notation Q indicates the full-text selection condition). A CN can be easily transformed into an equivalent SQL statement and executed by the RDBMS. Relations in a CN are called *tuple sets* (*TS*). A tuple set R^Q is defined as a set of tuples in relation R that contain at least one keyword in Q.

A *continuous keyword query* consists of (1) a set of distinct keywords, that is, $Q = w_1, w_2, \cdots, w_{|Q|}$, and (2) a parameter k indicating that a user is only interested in the top-k answers ranked by the relevance. The main difference of a continual keyword query to keyword queries in previous work [3,10] is that the user wants to keep the top-k answers list up-to-date while the database is updated continuously. Table 1 summarizes the notation we use in the following discussion.

Table 1. Summary of Notation

Notation	Description	Notation	Description
t	a tuple in a database	T	a joining tree of different tuples
$R(t)$	the relation corresponding to t	$sizeof(T)$	the number of tuples in T
Q	a keyword query	CN	a candidate network
R^Q	the set of tuples in R that contain at least one keyword of Q	$score(T, Q)$	the relevance score of T to Q
		$tscore(t, Q)$	the relevance score of a tuple t to Q

We adopt the IR-style ranking strategy of [3]. The relevance score of a JTT T is computed using the following formulas based on the TF-IDF weighting.

$$score(T, Q) = \frac{\sum_{t \in T}(tscore(t, Q))}{sizeof(T)}$$
$$tscore(t, Q) = \sum_{w \in t \cap Q} \frac{1 + \ln(1 + \ln(tf_{t,w}))}{1 - s + s \cdot \frac{dl_t}{avdl}} \cdot \ln\left(\frac{N+1}{df_w}\right), \quad (1)$$

where $tf_{t,w}$ is the frequency of keyword w in tuple t, df_w is the number of $R(t)$ tuples that contains w ($R(t)$ means the relation that includes t), dl_t is the size (i.e., number of characters) of t, $avdl$ is the average tuple size, N is the total number of $R(t)$ tuples, and s is a constant.

3 Query Processing Framework

Figure 2 shows our framework for continuous keyword query processing in relational databases.

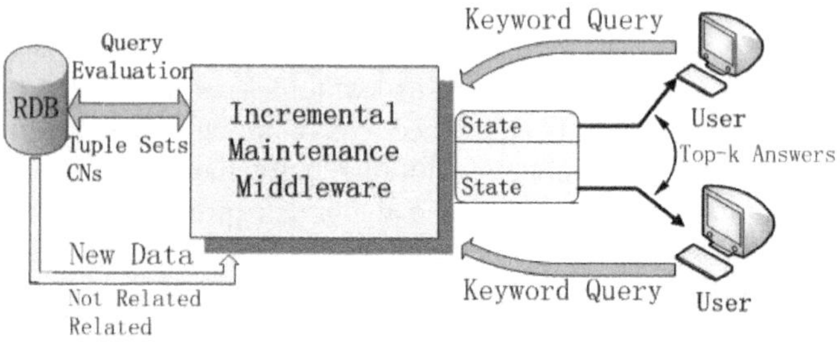

Fig. 2. Continuous Query Processing Framework

Given a keyword query, we first identify the top-k query results. Specifically, we first generate all the non-empty query tuple sets R^Q for each relation R. Then these non-empty query tuple sets and the schema graph are used to generate a set of valid CNs. Finally, the generated CNs are evaluated to identify the top-k answers. For the step of CN evaluation, several query evaluation strategies have been proposed [3,5]. Our method of CN evaluation is based on the method of [3], but can also find the JTTs that have the potential to become top-k answers after some new tuples are inserted.

At the end of the CN evaluation process, the *state* of the process is computed and stored. After being notified of new data, the Incremental Maintenance Middleware (*IMM*) starts the answer maintenance procedure for each continuous keyword query.

The IMM uses some filter conditions to categorize the new data into two types for each keyword query based on their relevance: *not related* and *related*. Then the related new data and the stored state are used by the IMM to start the incremental query evaluation process and compute the new top-k answers. If the variations of the new top-k answers fulfill the update conditions, the new top-k answers are sent to the corresponding users.

4 Continuous Keyword Query Evaluation

In this section, we first present a two-phase CN evaluation method for creating the state for a keyword query. Then we will show how to calculate the effects of new tuples.

4.1 State of a Continuous Keyword Query

Generally speaking, two tasks need to be done after tuples are inserted. New tuples can change the values of df, N and $avdl$ in Eq. (1) and hence change the tuple scores of existing tuples. Therefore, the first task is to check whether some of the current top-k answers can be replaced by other JTTs whose relevance scores have been increased. The new tuples may also lead to new JTTs and new CNs. Therefore, the second task is to compute the new JTTs and check whether any of them can be top-k answers.

For the first task, a naive solution is to compute and store all the JTTs that can be produced by evaluating the CNs generated when the query is evaluated for the first time. After new tuples are inserted, we recompute the relevance score of the stored JTTs and update the top-k answers. This solution is not efficient if the number of existing tuples is large, since it needs to join all the existing tuples in each CN and store a large number of JTTs.

Fortunately, our method only needs to compute and store a small subset of the JTTs. For this purpose, we use the two-phase CN evaluation method shown in Algorithm 1 to evaluate a set of candidate networks *CNSet* for keyword query Q efficiently, and create the state of Q. The first phase (lines 1-11) is for computing the top-k answers, based on the method of [3]. The second phase (lines 15-22) is for finding the JTTs that have the potential to become top-k answers.

The key idea of lines 1-11 is as follows. All CNs of the keyword query are evaluated concurrently following an adaptation of a *priority preemptive, round robin* protocol [12], where the execution of each CN corresponds to a process. Tuples in each tuple set are sorted in descending order of their tuple scores (line 2). There is a *cursor* for each tuple set of all the CNs that indicates the index of the tuple to be checked next (line 3). All the combinations of tuples before the cursor in each tuple set have been joined to find the JTTs. At each loop iteration, the algorithm checks the next tuple of the "most promising" tuple set from the "most promising" CN (lines 8-10). The first phase stops immediately after finding the top-k answers, which can be identified when the score of the current k-th answer is larger than all the priorities of the CNs (line 6). We call the tuples before the cursor of each tuple set the "*checked* tuples", and the tuples with indexes not smaller than the cursor are called "*unchecked* tuples".

Figure 3 shows the main data structure of our CN evaluation method. In order to facilitate discussion, only the CN $Complaints^Q \rightarrow Products^Q$ is considered and we suppose that we want to find the top-2 answers. In Figure 3(a), tuples in the two tuple sets are sorted in descending order of tuple scores and are represented by their primary keys. Arrows between tuples indicate the foreign key to primary key relationship. The top-2 answers discovered are $c1 \rightarrow p1$ and $c3 \rightarrow p2$. All the tuples in the deep background have been joined in order to obtain the top-2 answers. For example, tuple $p1$ has been joined with tuples $c1$, $c2$ and $c3$, and one valid JTT $c1 \rightarrow p1$ has been found. After the execution of phase 1, the two *cursor*s of the two tuple sets are pointing at $c4$ and $p6$, respectively.

The procedure *FindPotentialAnswers* is used to find the potential top-k answers. The basic idea of our method is to compute a range of future tuple scores using the scoring function for computing tuple scores given in Eq. (1):

Algorithm 1. *CNEvaluation(CNSet, k, Q)*

Input: *CNSet*: a set of candidate networks; *k*: an integer; *Q*: a keyword query;

declare *RTemp*: a queue for not-yet-output results ordered by descending *score(T, Q)*; *Results*: a queue for output results ordered by descending *score(T, Q)*
Sort tuples of each tuple set in descending order of *tscore*
Set *cursor* of each tuple set of each CN in *CNSet* to 0
loop
    Compute the priorities of each CN in *CNSet*
    if(the score of the *k*-th answer in *Results* is larger than all the priorities) **then break**
    Output to *Results* the JTTs in *RTemp* with scores larger than all the priorities
    Select the next tuple from the tuple set that has the maximum upper bound score from the CN with the maximum priority for checking
    Add 1 to the *cursor* of the tuple set corresponding to the checked tuple
    Add all the resulting JTTs to *RTemp*
end loop
FindPotentialAnswers(CNSet, Results)
Set *cursor* = *cursor2* for each tuple set of each CN in *CNSet*
Create state for *Q* and return the top-*k* JTTs in *Results*

Procedure *FindPotentialAnswers(CNSet, Results)*
Compute the range of *tscore* for all the tuples in each tuple set of *CNSet* and sort the tuples in each tuple set below the *cursor* in descending order of $tscore^{max}$
lowerBound ← the minimum lower bound of *scores* of the top-*k* answers in *Results*
for all tuple set ts_j of each CN C_i in *CNSet* **do**
    Increase the value of *cursor2* from *cursor* until $max(ts_j[cursor2]) < lowerBound$
for all tuple set ts_j of each CN C_i in *CNSet* **do**
    Join the tuples between *cursor* and *cursor2* of ts_j with the tuples before the *cursor* in the other tuple sets of CN_i
    Add the resulting JTTs to *Results* whose upper bound of *score* is larger than *lowerBound*

$$tscore(t, Q) = \sum_{w \in t \cap Q} \frac{1 + \ln(1 + \ln(tf_{t,w}))}{1 - s + s \cdot \frac{dl_t}{avdl}} \cdot \ln\left(\frac{N+1}{df_w}\right). \quad (2)$$

We consider the situation where (*a*) at most ΔN new tuples are inserted; and (*b*) document frequency changes slightly due to the insertion. Δdf denotes the maximum increased count of the document frequency for every term. Note that the change for a keyword w Δdf_w may be 0. We assume that the average document length (*avdl*) is a *constant* to simplify the problem. Let us use the shorthand notation $A(t, w) = \frac{1+\ln(1+\ln(tf_{t,w}))}{1-s+s\cdot\frac{dl_t}{avdl}}$ and $B(t, w) = \frac{1+\ln(1+\ln(tf_{t,w}))}{1-s+s\cdot\frac{dl_t}{avdl}} \cdot \ln\left(\frac{N+1}{df_w}\right)$. $B(t, w)$ represents the contribution of keyword w to *tscore(t, Q)*.

We derive an upper bound and a lower bound of Eq.(2) which are valid while the two constraints ΔN and Δdf are satisfied. First, we compute the maximum score for the existing tuples t. This situation occurs when all the terms in $t \cap Q$ do not appear in the new documents; hence, we have $tscore(t, Q)^{max} = \sum_{w \in t \cap Q} A(t, w) \cdot \ln\left(\frac{N+1+\Delta N}{df_w}\right)$. For each $B(t, w)$, the minimum value is achieved when the first dt_w new tuples all contain w: $B(t, w)^{min} = A(t, w) \cdot \ln\left(\frac{N+1+\Delta df_w}{df_w+\Delta df_w}\right)$. Therefore, the lower bound of *tscore(t, Q)* is

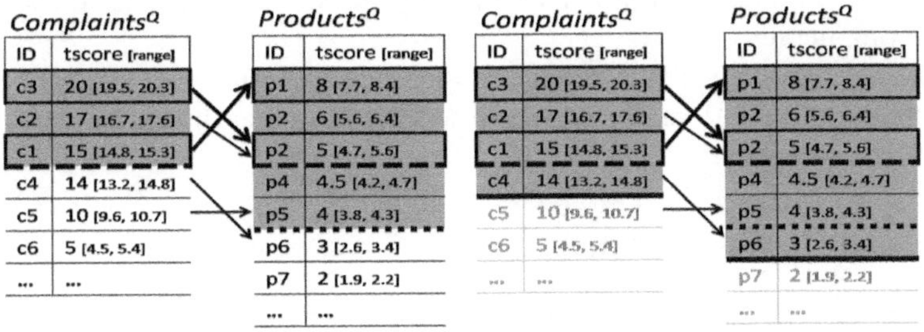

(a) Compute the top-2 answers (b) Find potential top-2 answers

Fig. 3. Two-phase CN evaluation

$tscore(t, Q)^{\min} = \sum_{w \in t \cap Q} A(t, w) \cdot \ln\left(\frac{N+1+\Delta dt_w}{df_w + \Delta df_w}\right)$. Note that this lower bound only can be achieved when all the Δdt_w are equal. Using such ranges, the range of relevance scores of a JTT T can be computed as $[\sum_{t \in T} t.tscore^{\min}, \sum_{t \in T} t.tscore^{\max}] \cdot \frac{1}{sizeof(T)}$.

We continually monitor the change of statistics to determine whether the thresholds ΔN and Δdf are violated. This is not a difficult task: monitoring ΔN is straightforward; for Δdf, we accumulate Δdf_w for all the terms w in the process of handling new tuples. In the following discussion, we consider only the case that the two thresholds ΔN and Δdf are not violated.

For each tuple t in C, we use $max(t) = \left(t.tscore^{\max} + \sum_{t \notin ts_i} \max(ts_i)\right) \cdot \frac{1}{sizeof(C)}$ to indicate the maximum upper bound of *score*s of the possible JTTs that contain t, where $max(ts_i)$ indicates the maximum upper bounds of *tscore*s of tuples in ts_i. If $max(t)$ is larger than the minimum lower bound of *score* of answers in *Results* (*lowerBound* in line 17), t can form some JTTs with the potential to become top-k answers in the future. We find such tuples in lines 18-19, and join them with the tuples before *cursor2* in the other tuple set (line 21). Hence, all the JTTs that are formed by the tuples that have the potential to form top-k answers are computed. However, not all the JTTs computed in line 21 can become top-k answers in the future. In line 22, only the JTTs whose upper bound of score is larger than *lowerBound* are added to *Results*. After the execution of line 12, *Results* contains the top-k answers and the potential top-k answers.

In line 14, the state for Q is created based on the snapshot of *CNEvaluation*. The state contains three kinds of data:

- The keyword statistics: the number of tuples, and document frequencies (i.e., the number of tuples that contain at least one keyword).
- The set of candidate networks: all the checked tuples (checked tuples of multiple instances of one tuple set are merged to reduce the storage space).
- The JTT queue *Results*: each entry contains the tuple ID and the *tscore*.

Note that the tuples before *cursor2* in each tuple set can be considered as highly related to the keyword query and have a high possibility to form JTTs with newly inserted tuples. Hence, they need to be stored in the state for the second task. We need to store the statistic $\sum_{w \in t \cap Q} A(t, w)$ for each tuple t in the state in order to recompute the tuple scores after new tuples are inserted. Fortunately, the value is static and does not change once we compute it.

Figure 3(b) shows the data structure of the CN $Complaints^Q \rightarrow Products^Q$ after the second phase of evaluation. The two tuple sets are further evaluated by checking tuples $c4$ and $p6$, respectively.

4.2 Handling Insertions of Tuples

After receiving a new tuple, the IMM first checks whether the values of df and N still satisfy the assumptions, that is, the differences between the current values of df and N and their values when the state was first created are smaller than Δdf and ΔN, respectively. If the assumptions are satisfies, the algorithm *Insertion* shown in Algorithm 2 is used to incrementally maintain the top-k answers list for a keyword query; if the assumptions are not satisfied, then the query must be reevaluated.

In Algorithm 2, lines 1-3 are for the first task, and lines 5-18 are used to compute the new JTTs that contain the new tuples. In line 1, the values of N and df for the relation $R(t)$ are updated. Then, if it is necessary (line 2), the relevance scores of the JTTs in the JTT queue are updated using the new values of N and df(line 3).

Algorithm 2. *Insertion*(t, Q, S)

Input: t: new tuple; Q: keyword query; S: stored state for Q
Output: New top-k answers of Q

1: update the keyword statistics of $R(t)$
2: **if** there are some tuples of $R(t)$ are contained in the JTT queue of S **then**
3:     recompute the scores of the JTTs in the JTT queue of S
4: **if** t does not contain the keywords of Q **then return**
5: **if** $R(t)^Q$ is a new tuple set **then** generate new CNs
6: compute the value and range for the *tscore* of t
7: *CNSet* $\leftarrow$ CN in S that contains $R(t)^Q \bigcup$ all the new CNs
8: **for all** CN C in *CNSet* **do**
9:     **for all** $R(t)^Q$ of C **do**
10:         **if** $t.tscore^{\max} > \min^C(R(t)^Q)$ **then**
11:             add t to the checked tuples set of $R(t)^Q$
12:             join t with the checked tuples in the other tuple sets of C
13:             **if** $t.tscore^{\max} > max^C(R(t)^Q)$ **then**
14:                 **for all** the other tuple sets ts of C **do**
15:                     query the unchecked tuples of ts from the database
16:                     delete the newly inserted tuples from ts that have not been processed
17:                 call *FindPotentialAnswers*($\{C\}$, *S.Queue*) while replacing $R(t)^Q$ by $\{t\}$
18: **end for**
19: **return** $S.Queue.Top(k)$

If $R(t)^Q$ is a new tuple set, the new CNs that contain $R(t)^Q$ need to be generated (line 5). In line 6, the value of *tscore* for the new tuple is computed using the actual values of df and N; but the values of df and N used for computing the range of *tscore* are the values when the state is created in order to be consistent with the ranges of *tscores* for existing checked tuples of $R(t)^Q$. New tuples can be categorized into two groups by deciding whether each new tuple belongs to the new top-k answers (*related* or *not related*). Generally speaking, new tuples that do not contain any keywords of the query are not related tuples (line 4), and new tuples that contain the keywords may be related. However, a new tuple t that contains the keywords cannot be related is its upper bound of *tscore* is not larger than $min^C(R(t)^Q)$, which is the minimum $tscore^{\max}$s of checked tuples of $R(t)^Q$ (line 10). For the related new tuples, they are processed from line 11 to line 17. In line 12, t is joined with the checked tuples in the other tuple sets of C. Then the algorithm uses another filtering condition, $t.tscore^{\max} > max^C(R(t)^Q)$ in line 13, to determine whether the new tuple t should be joined with the unchecked tuples of the other tuple sets of C. If $t.tscore^{\max} > max^C(R(t)^Q)$, which is the maximum $tscore^{\max}$s of checked tuples of $R(t)^Q$, some $max(ts_i(cursor2))$ may be larger than the minimum lower bound of current top-k answers. Hence, after querying the unchecked tuples from the database in line 15, the procedure *FindPotentialAnswers* of C is called while replacing $R(t)^Q$ by $\{t\}$ (line 17, set of the new tuple). Note that the relevance scores of the new JTTs produced in lines 12 and 17 should be computed using the actual values of dfs and Ns.

The execution of lines 14-17, needed to query unchecked tuples from the database and perform the second phase of the evaluation of C, place a heavy workload on the database. However, our experimental studies show a very low execution frequency for lines 14-17 when maintaining the top-k answers for a keyword query.

5 Experimental Study

For the evaluation, we used the DBLP[1] data set. The downloaded XML file is decomposed into 8 relations, article(articleID, key, title, journalID, crossRef, ⋯), aCite(id, articleID, cite), author(authorID, author), aWrite(id, articleID, authorID), journal(journalID, journal), proc(procID, key, title, ⋯), pEditors(pEditorID, Name), procEditor(id, procEditorID, procID), where underlines and underwaves indicate the keys and foreign keys of the relations, respectively. The numbers of tuples for the 8 relations are, 1092K, 109K, 658K, 2752K, 730, 11K, 12K, 23K. The DBMS used is MySQL (v5.1.44) with the default configurations. Indexes were built for all primary key and foreign key attributes, and full-text indexes were built for all text attributes.

We manually picked a large number of queries for evaluation. We attempted to include a wide variety of keywords and their combinations in the query set, taking into account factors such as the selectivity of keywords, the size of the relevant answers, and the number of potential relevant answers. We focus on the 20 queries with query lengths ranging from 2 to 3, which are listed in Table 2.

Exp-1 (Parameter tuning). In this experiment, we want to study the effects of the two parameters on computing the range of future tuple scores. The number of tuples that need to be joined in the second phase of CN evaluation is determined by ΔN and Δdf. Small values of ΔN and Δdf result in small numbers of tuples be joined, but a large frequency of recomputing the state because the increases of N and df will soon exceed

[1] http://dblp.mpi-inf.mpg.de/dblp-mirror/index.php

Table 2. Queries

QID	Keywords	QID	Keywords	QID	Keywords	QID	Keywords
Q1	bender, p2p	Q6	sigmod, xiaofang	Q11	Hardware, luk, wayne	Q16	Staab, Ontology, Steffen
Q2	Owens, VLSI	Q7	constraint, nikos	Q12	intersection, nikos	Q17	query, Arvind, parametric
Q3	p2p, Steinmetz	Q8	fagin, middleware	Q13	peter, robinson, video	Q18	search, SIGMOD, similarity
Q4	patel, spatial	Q9	fengrong, ishikawa	Q14	ATM, demetres, kouvatsos	Q19	optimal, fagin, middleware
Q5	vldb, xiaofang	Q10	hong, kong, spatial	Q15	Ishikawa, P2P, Yoshiharu	Q20	hongjiang, Multimedia, zhang

ΔN and Δdf, respectively, due to the insertion of tuples. Therefore, the values of ΔN and Δdf represent a tradeoff between the storage space for the state and the efficiency for top-k answer maintenance. In our experiments, the values of ΔN and Δdf are set to be a *fraction* of the values of N and df, respectively. For each query, we run the two-phase CN evaluation algorithm with different values of ΔN and Δdf. The main experimental results for five queries are shown in Figure 4.

We use two metrics to evaluate the effects of the two parameters. The first is *cursor2*/*cursor* where *cursor* and *cursor2* indicate the summation of numbers of checked tuples after the first and second phases of CN evaluation, respectively. Small values of *cursor2*/*cursor* imply a small number of tuples are joined in the second phase for computing the potential top-k answers. The second metric is the size of the state. Figures 4(a) and 4(b) show the changes of *cursor2*/*cursor* for different ΔN and Δdf while fixing the other parameter to 10%. Figure 4(a) and 4(b) show that only a small number of tuples are joined in the second phase of CN evaluation, which implies that the range of tuple scores computed by our method is very tight. The curves in Figure 4(a) and 4(b) are not very steep. Hence, we can use some relatively large value of ΔN and Δdf when creating the state for a continuous keyword query. Note that the values of N in a database are always very large. Therefore, even a small value of ΔN (like 10%) can result in the state being valid until a large number of new tuples (100,000 in our experiment) have been inserted, as long as the Δdfs condition is not violated. Figure 4(c) shows the change of the state size for a query when varying Δdf while keeping ΔN = 10%. The data size of the state of a continuous keyword query is quite small (several MBs at most); hence, the *IMM* can easily load the state of a query for answer maintenance.

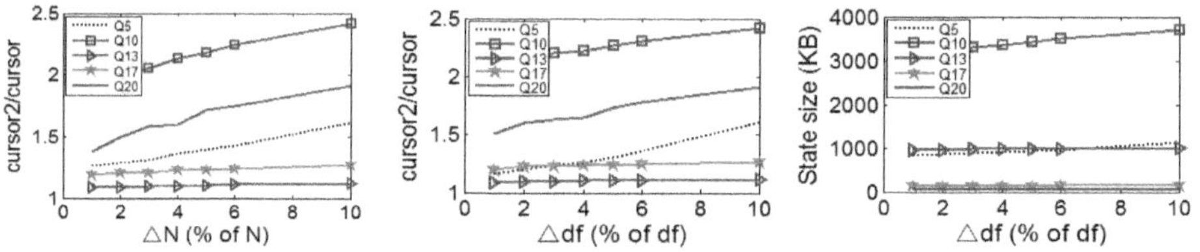

(a) Varying ΔN when Δdf = 10%

(b) Varying Δdf when ΔN = 10%

(c) Change of state size

Fig. 4. Effect of ΔN and Δdf

Exp-2 (Efficiency of answer maintenance). In this experiment, we first create states for the 20 queries. Then we sequentially insert 14,223 new tuples into the database. The CPU times for maintaining the top-k answers for the 20 queries after each new tuples being inserted are recorded. All the experiments are done after the DBMS buffer has been warmed up. The values of ΔN and Δdf are both set to 1%. As the values of ΔN and Δdf are very small, the cost for creating the state of a query is essentially as the cost for the first phase of CN evaluation.

Figure 5(a) shows the time cost to create states (*Create*) and the average time cost of the 20 queries to handle the 14,223 new tuples (*Insert*). Note that the times are displayed using a log scale. From Figure 5(a), we can see that the more time used to create the state of a query, the more time is used to maintain answers for the query. In our experiment, the states of the 20 queries are stored in the database. The states of the queries are read from the database after the IMM receives a new tuple. The time for maintaining the new tuples also contains the time cost of reading the states from database and writing them back to database after handing new tuples. Hence, such time costs represent a large proportion of the total time cost for handling new tuples when they are not related. In order to reveal this relationship, we also plot the state sizes for the 20 queries in Figure 5(a). The cost of reading and writing a state is clearly revealed by the data for Q6. The data of Q6 appears to be an exception because the value of *Insert* is larger than *Create*. The main reason for this is that Q6 is very easy to answer. Hence, the time used to load and write back the state is the majority for handling new tuples for Q6.

Figure 5(b) shows the total time for handing each inserted tuple. In most cases, the time used to handle a new tuple is quite small, which corresponds to the situation that the new tuple does not contain any keyword from the 20 queries. Hence, the algorithm only needs to update the scores of JTTs in the JTT queue of the states. The peaks of the data in Figure 5(b) correspond to the situations in which some queries need to be reevaluated because of violation of the Δdf. Eventually, ΔN is violated, hence several queries need to be reevaluated at the same, this results in the highest peak in Figure 5(b).

(a) Time for creating states and the average time for handling new tuples (b) Total time for handling each new tuple

Fig. 5. Efficiency of maintaining the top-*k* answers

6 Related Work

Keyword search in relational databases has recently emerged as a new research topic [11]. Existing approaches can be broadly classified into two categories: ones based on candidate networks [2,3,7] and others based on Steiner trees [1,8,10].

DISCOVER2 [3] proposed ranking tuple trees according to their IR relevance scores to a query. Our work adopts the *Global Pipelined* algorithm of [3], and can be viewed as a further improvement to the direction of continual keyword search in relational databases. SPARK [5] proposed a new ranking formula by adapting existing IR techniques based on the natural idea of a virtual document. They also proposed two algorithms, based on the algorithm of [3], that minimize the number of accesses to the database. Our method of incremental maintenance of top-k query answers can also be applied to these algorithms, which will be a direction of future work.

7 Conclusion

In this paper, we have studied the problem of finding the top-k answers in relational databases for a continuous keyword query. We proposed storing the state of the CN evaluation process, which can be used to restart the query evaluation after the insertion of new tuples. An algorithm to maintain the top-k answer list on the insertion of new tuples was presented. Our method can efficiently maintain a top-k answers list for a query without recomputing the keyword query. It can, therefore, be used to solve the problem of answering continual keyword searches in a database that is updated frequently.

Acknowledgments

This research is partly supported by the Grant-in-Aid for Scientific Research, Japan (#22300034), the National Natural Science Foundation of China (NSFC) under grant No.60873040, 863 Program under grant No.2009AA01Z135 and Open Research Program of Key Lab of Earth Exploration & Information Techniques of Ministry of China (2008DTKF008). Jihong Guan was also supported by the Program for New Century Excellent Talents in University of China (NCET-06-0376) and the "Shu Guang" Program of Shanghai Municipal Education Commission and Shanghai Education Development Foundation.

References

1. Aditya, B., Bhalotia, G., Chakrabarti, S., Hulgeri, A., Nakhe, C., Parag, Sudarshan, S.: BANKS: Browsing and keyword searching in relational databases. In: VLDB, pp. 1083–1086 (2002)
2. Agrawal, S., Chaudhuri, S., Das, G.: DBXplorer: Enabling keyword search over relational databases. In: ACM SIGMOD, p. 627 (2002)
3. Hristidis, V., Gravano, L., Papakonstantinou, Y.: Efficient IR-style keyword search over relational databases. In: VLDB, pp. 850–861 (2003)
4. Liu, F., Yu, C., Meng, W., Chowdhury, A.: Effective keyword search in relational databases. In: ACM SIGMOD, pp. 563–574 (2006)
5. Luo, Y., Lin, X., Wang, W., Zhou, X.: SPARK: Top-k keyword query in relational databases. In: ACM SIGMOD, pp. 115–126 (2007)
6. Li, G., Zhou, X., Feng, J., Wang, J.: Progressive keyword search in relational databases. In: ICDE, pp. 1183–1186 (2009)

7. Hristidis, V., Papakonstantinou, Y.: DISCOVER: Keyword search in relational databases. In: VLDB, pp. 670–681 (2002)
8. Kacholia, V., Pandit, S., Chakrabarti, S., Sudarshan, S., Desai, R., Karambelkar, H.: Bidirectional expansion for keyword search on graph databases. In: VLDB, pp. 505–516 (2005)
9. He, H., Wang, H., Yang, J., Yu, P.S.: Blinks: Ranked keyword searches on graphs. In: ACM SIGMOD, pp. 305–316. ACM, New York (2007)
10. Li, G., Ooi, B.C., Feng, J., Wang, J., Zhou, L.: EASE: An effective 3-in-1 keyword search method for unstructured, semi-structured and structured data. In: ACM SIGMOD, pp. 903–914 (2008)
11. Wang, S., Zhang, K.: Searching databases with keywords. J. Comput. Sci. Technol. 20(1), 55–62 (2005)
12. Burns, A.: Preemptive priority based scheduling: An appropriate engineering approach. In: Son, S.H. (ed.) Advances in Real Time Systems, pp. 225–248. Prentice Hall, Englewood Cliffs (1994)

V Locking Protocol for Materialized Aggregate Join Views on B-Tree Indices

Gang Luo

IBM T.J. Watson Research Center
luog@us.ibm.com

Abstract. Immediate materialized view maintenance with transactional consistency is highly desirable to support real-time decision making. Nevertheless, due to high deadlock rates, such maintenance can cause significant performance degradation in the database system. To increase concurrency during such maintenance, we previously proposed the V locking protocol for materialized aggregate join views and showed how to implement it on hash indices. In this paper, we address the thorny problem of implementing the V locking protocol on B-tree indices. We also formally prove that our techniques are both necessary and sufficient to ensure correctness (serializability).

1 Introduction

Materialized views are widely used in database systems and Web-based information systems to improve query performance [4]. As real-time decision making is increasingly being needed by enterprises [14], the requirement of immediate materialized view maintenance with transactional consistency is becoming more and more necessary and important for providing consistent and up-to-date query results. Reflecting real world application demands, this requirement has become mandatory in the TPC-R benchmark [13]. Graefe and Zwilling [6] also argued that materialized views are like indexes. Since indexes are always maintained immediately with transactional consistency, materialized views should fulfill the same requirement. A few detailed examples for this requirement on materialized views are provided in [6].

In a materialized aggregate join view *AJV*, multiple tuples are aggregated into one group if they have identical group by attribute values. If generic concurrency control mechanisms are used, immediate maintenance of *AJV* with transactional consistency can cause significant performance degradation in the database system. Since different tuples in a base relation of *AJV* can affect the same aggregated tuple in *AJV*, the addition of *AJV* can introduce many lock conflicts and/or deadlocks that do not arise in the absence of *AJV*. The smaller *AJV* is, the more lock conflicts and/or deadlocks will occur. In practice, this deadlock rate can easily become 50% or higher [9]. A detailed deadlock example is provided in [9].

To address this lock conflict/deadlock issue, we previously proposed the V+W locking protocol [9] for materialized aggregate join views. The key insight is that the *COUNT* and *SUM* aggregate operators are associative and commutative [7]. Hence, during maintenance of the materialized aggregate join view, we can use V locks rather

L. Chen et al. (Eds.): WAIM 2010, LNCS 6184, pp. 768–780, 2010.

than traditional X locks. V locks do not conflict with each other and can increase concurrency, while short-term W locks are used to prevent "split group duplicates" — multiple tuples in the aggregate join view for the same group, as shown in Section 2.2 below. [9] described how to implement the V+W locking protocol on both hash indices and B-tree indices.

It turns out that the W lock solution for the split group duplicate problem can be replaced by a latch (i.e., semaphore) pool solution, which is more efficient because acquiring a latch is much cheaper than acquiring a lock [5]. This leads to the V locking protocol for materialized aggregate join views presented in [10]. There, V locks are augmented with a "value-based" latch pool. Traditionally, latches are used to protect the physical integrity of certain data structures (e.g., the data structures in a page [5]). In our case of materialized view maintenance, no physical data structure would be corrupted if the latch pool were not used. The "value-based" latch pool obtains its name because it is used to protect the logical integrity of aggregate operations rather than the physical integrity of the database. [10] showed how to implement the V locking protocol on hash indices and formally proved the correctness of the implementation method. [10] also performed a simulation study in a commercial RDBMS, demonstrating that the performance of the V locking protocol can be two orders of magnitude higher than that of the traditional X locking protocol.

This paper improves upon our previous work by addressing the particularly thorny problem of implementing the V locking protocol on B-tree indices. Typically, implementing high concurrency locking modes poses special challenges when B-trees are considered, and the V locking protocol is no exception. We make three contributions. First, we present the method of implementing the V locking protocol on B-tree indices. Second, we show that our techniques are all necessary. Third, we formally prove the correctness (serializability) of our implementation method.

In related work, Graefe and Zwilling [6] independently proposed a multi-version concurrency control protocol for materialized aggregate join views. It uses hierarchical escrow locking, snapshot transactions, key-range locking, and system transactions. The key insight of that multi-version concurrency control protocol is similar to that of our V locking protocol. Nevertheless, that multi-version concurrency control protocol cannot avoid split group duplicates in materialized aggregate join views. Instead, special operations have to be performed during materialized aggregate join view query time to address the split group duplicate problem. [6] did not formally show that its proposed techniques are all necessary. [6] also gave no rigorous proof of the correctness of its proposed concurrency control protocol.

Our focus in this paper is materialized aggregate join views. In an extended relational algebra, a general instance of such a view can be expressed as $AJV=\gamma(\pi(\sigma(R_1 \bowtie R_2 \bowtie \ldots \bowtie R_n)))$, where γ is the aggregate operator. SQL allows the aggregate operators *COUNT*, *SUM*, *AVG*, *MIN*, and *MAX*. However, because *MIN* and *MAX* cannot be maintained incrementally (the problem is deletes/updates — e.g., when the *MIN*/*MAX* value is deleted, we need to compute the new *MIN*/*MAX* value using all the values in the aggregate group [3]), we restrict our attention to the three incrementally updateable aggregate operators: *COUNT*, *SUM*, and *AVG*. In practice, *AVG* is computed using *COUNT* and *SUM*, as *AVG*=*SUM*/*COUNT* (*COUNT* and *SUM* are distributive while *AVG* is algebraic [2]). In the rest of the paper, we only discuss *COUNT* and

SUM, whereas our locking techniques for *COUNT* and *SUM* also apply to *AVG*. Moreover, by letting $n=1$ in the definition of *AJV*, we include aggregate views over single relations.

2 V Locks, Latches, and B-Trees

In this section, we present our method of implementing the V locking protocol on B-tree indices. On B-tree indices, we use value locks to refer to key-range locks. To be consistent with the approach advocated by Mohan [11], we use next-key locking to implement key-range locking. We use "key" to refer to the indexed attribute of the B-tree index. We assume that the entry of the B-tree index is of the following format: (key value, row id list).

2.1 The V Locking Protocol

In the V locking protocol for materialized aggregate join views [10], we have three kinds of elementary locks: S, X, and V. The compatibilities among these locks are listed in Table 1, while the lock conversion lattice is shown in Fig. 1.

Table 1. Compatibilities among the elementary locks

	S	X	V
S	yes	no	no
X	no	no	no
V	no	no	yes

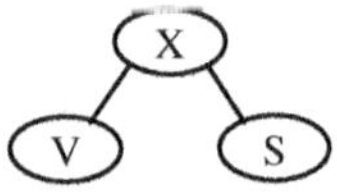

Fig. 1. The lock conversion lattice of the elementary locks

In the V locking protocol for materialized aggregate join views, S locks are used for reads, V locks are used for associative and commutative aggregate update writes, while X locks are used for transactions that do both reads and writes. These locks can be of any granularity, and, like traditional S and X locks, can be physical locks (e.g., tuple, page, or table locks) or value locks.

2.2 Split Groups and B-Trees

We consider how split group duplicates can arise when a B-tree index is declared over the aggregate join view *AJV*. Suppose the schema of *AJV* is (*a*, *b*, *sum*(*c*)), and we build a B-tree index I_B on attribute *a*. Also, assume there is no tuple (1, 2, *X*) in *AJV*, for any *X*. Consider the following two transactions *T* and *T'*. *T* integrates a new join result tuple (1, 2, 3) into *AJV* (by insertion into some base relation *R*). *T'* integrates another new join result tuple (1, 2, 4) into *AJV* (by insertion into *R*). Using standard concurrency control without V locks, to integrate a join result tuple t_1 into *AJV*, a transaction will execute something like the following operations:

(1) Obtain an X value lock for $t_1.a$ on I_B. This value lock is held until the transaction commits/aborts.
(2) Make a copy of the row id list in the entry for $t_1.a$ of I_B.
(3) For each row id in the row id list, fetch the corresponding tuple t_2. Check whether $t_2.a=t_1.a$ and $t_2.b=t_1.b$.
(4) If some tuple t_2 satisfies the condition $t_2.a=t_1.a$ and $t_2.b=t_1.b$, integrate t_1 into t_2 and stop.
(5) If no tuple t_2 satisfies the condition $t_2.a=t_1.a$ and $t_2.b=t_1.b$, insert a new tuple into *AJV* for t_1. Also, insert the row id of this new tuple into I_B.

Suppose now we use V value locks instead of X value locks and the two transactions *T* and *T'* above are executed in the following sequence:

(1) *T* obtains a V value lock for $a=1$ on the B-tree index I_B, searches the row id list in the entry for $a=1$, and finds that no tuple t_2 whose attributes $t_2.a=1$ and $t_2.b=2$ exists in *AJV*.
(2) *T'* obtains a V value lock for $a=1$ on I_B, searches the row id list in the entry for $a=1$, and finds that no tuple t_2 whose attributes $t_2.a=1$ and $t_2.b=2$ exists in *AJV*.
(3) *T* inserts a new tuple t_1=(1, 2, 3) into *AJV*, and inserts the row id of t_1 into the row id list in the entry for $a=1$ of I_B.
(4) *T'* inserts a new tuple t_3=(1, 2, 4) into *AJV*, and inserts the row id of t_3 into the row id list in the entry for $a=1$ of I_B.

Now the aggregate join view *AJV* contains two tuples (1, 2, 3) and (1, 2, 4) instead of a single tuple (1, 2, 7). Hence, we have the split group duplicate problem.

2.3 The Latch Pool

To enable the use of V locks while avoiding split group duplicates, we use the same latch pool for aggregate join views as that described in [10]. The latches in the latch pool guarantee that for each aggregate group, at any time, at most one tuple corresponding to this group exists in the aggregate join view.

For efficiency we pre-allocate a latch pool that contains $N>1$ X (exclusive) latches. We use a hash function *H* that maps key values into integers between 1 and *N*. We use requesting/releasing a latch on key value *v* to mean requesting/releasing the $H(v)$-th latch in the latch pool.

We ensure that the following properties always hold for this latch pool. First, during the period that a transaction holds a latch in the latch pool, this transaction does not request another latch in the latch pool. Second, to request a latch in the latch pool, a transaction must first release all the other latches in the RDBMS (including those latches that are not in the latch pool) that it currently holds. Third, during the period that a transaction holds a latch in the latch pool, this transaction does not request any lock. The first two properties guarantee that there are no deadlocks between latches.

The third property guarantees that there are no deadlocks between latches and locks. These properties are necessary, because in an RDBMS, latches are not considered in deadlock detection.

We define a *false latch conflict* as one that arises due to hash conflicts (i.e., $H(v_1)=H(v_2)$ and $v_1 \neq v_2$). The value of N only influences the efficiency of the V locking protocol – the larger the number N, the smaller the probability of having false latch conflicts. It does not affect the correctness of the V locking protocol. In practice, if we use a good hash function [5] and N is substantially larger than the number of concurrently running transactions in the RDBMS, the probability of having false latch conflicts should be small.

2.4 Implementing V Locking with B-Trees

Implementing a high concurrency locking scheme in the presence of indices is difficult, especially if we consider issues of recoverability. Key-value locking as proposed by Mohan [11] was perhaps the first published description of the issues that arise and their solution. Unfortunately, we cannot directly use the techniques in Mohan [11] to implement V locks as value (key-range) locks. Otherwise as shown in [9], serializability can be violated.

2.4.1 Operations of Interest

To implement V value locks on B-tree indices correctly, we need to combine those techniques in Mohan *et al.* [11, 5] with the technique of logical deletion of keys [12, 8]. In our protocol, there are five operations of interest:

(1) **Fetch**: Fetch the row ids for a given key value v_1.
(2) **Fetch next**: Given the current key value v_1, find the next key value $v_2>v_1$ existing in the B-tree index, and fetch the row id(s) associated with key value v_2.
(3) **Put an X value lock on key value v_1.**
(4) **Put a first kind V value lock on key value v_1.**
(5) **Put a second kind V value lock on key value v_1.**

Transactions use the latches in the latch pool in the following way:

(1) To integrate a new join result tuple *t* into an aggregate join view *AJV* (e.g., due to insertion into some base relation of *AJV*), we first put a second kind V value lock on the B-tree index. Immediately before we start the tuple integration, we request a latch on the group by attribute value of *t*. After integrating *t* into *AJV*, we release the latch on the group by attribute value of *t*.
(2) To remove a join result tuple from *AJV* (e.g., due to deletion from some base relation of *AJV*), we put a first kind V value lock on the B-tree index.

Unlike Mohan *et al.* [11, 5], we do not consider the operations of insert and delete. We show why this is by an example. Suppose a B-tree index is built on attribute *a* of an aggregate join view *AJV*. Assume we insert a tuple into some base relation of *AJV* and generate a new join result tuple *t*. The steps to integrate *t* into *AJV* are as follows:

```
If the aggregate group of t exists in AJV
        Update the aggregate group in AJV;
Else Insert a new aggregate group into AJV for t;
```

Once again, we do not know whether we need to update an existing aggregate group in *AJV* or insert a new aggregate group into *AJV* until we read *AJV*. However, we do know that we need to acquire a second kind V value lock on *t.a* before we can integrate *t* into *AJV*. Similarly, suppose we delete a tuple from some base relation of *AJV*. We compute the corresponding join result tuples. For each such join result tuple *t*, we execute the following steps to remove *t* from *AJV*:

Find the aggregate group of *t* in *AJV*;
Update the aggregate group in *AJV*;
  If all join result tuples have been removed from the aggregate group
    Delete the aggregate group from *AJV*;

In this case, we do not know whether we need to update an aggregate group in *AJV* or delete an aggregate group from *AJV* in advance. However, we do know that we need to acquire a first kind V value lock on *t.a* before we can remove *t* from *AJV*.

The ARIES/KVL method described in Mohan [11] for implementing value locks on a B-tree index requires the insertion/deletion operation to be done immediately after a transaction obtains appropriate locks. Also, in ARIES/KVL, the value lock implementation method is closely tied to the B-tree implementation method, because ARIES/KVL strives to take advantage of both IX locks and instant locks to increase concurrency. In the V locking mechanism, high concurrency has already been guaranteed by the fact that V locks are compatible with themselves. We can exploit this advantage so that our method for implementing value locks for aggregate join views on B-tree indices is more general and flexible than the ARIES/KVL method. Specifically, in our method, after a transaction obtains appropriate locks, we allow it to execute other operations before it executes the insertion/deletion/update/read operation. Also, our value lock implementation method is only loosely tied to the B-tree implementation method.

2.4.2 Operation Implementation Method

Our method for implementing value locks for aggregate join views on B-tree indices is as follows. Consider a transaction *T*.

Op1. Fetch: We first check whether some entry for value v_1 exists in the B-tree index I_B. If such an entry exists, we put an S lock for v_1 on I_B. If no such entry exists, we find the smallest value v_2 in I_B such that $v_2>v_1$. Then we put an S lock for v_2 on I_B.

Op2. Fetch next: We find the smallest value v_2 in I_B such that $v_2>v_1$. Then we put an S lock for v_2 on I_B.

Op3. Put an X value lock on key value v_1: We first put an X lock for value v_1 on I_B. Then we check whether some entry for v_1 exists in I_B. If no such entry exists, we find the smallest value v_2 in I_B such that $v_2>v_1$. Then we put an X lock for v_2 on I_B.

Op4. Put a first kind V value lock on key value v_1: We put a V lock for value v_1 on I_B.

Op5. Put a second kind V value lock on key value v_1: We first put a V lock for value v_1 on I_B. Then we check whether some entry for v_1 exists in I_B. If no entry for v_1 exists, we do the following:

(a) We find the smallest value v_2 in I_B such that $v_2>v_1$. Then we put a short-term V lock for v_2 on I_B. If the V lock for v_2 on I_B is acquired as an X lock, we upgrade the V lock for v_1 on I_B to an X lock. This situation may occur when transaction *T* already holds an S or X lock for v_2 on I_B.

(b) We request a latch on v_2. We insert into I_B an entry for v_l with an empty row id list. (Note that at a later point T will insert a row id into this row id list after T inserts the corresponding tuple into the aggregate join view.) Then we release the latch on v_2.

(c) We release the short-term V lock for value v_2 on I_B.

Table 2 summarizes the locks acquired during different operations.

Table 2. Summary of locking

		current key v_l	next key v_2
fetch	v_l exists	S	
	v_l does not exist		S
fetch next			S
X value lock	v_l exists	X	
	v_l does not exist	X	X
first kind V value lock		V	
second kind V value lock	v_l exists	V	
	v_l does not exist and the V lock on v_2 is acquired as a V lock	V	V
	v_l does not exist and the V lock on v_2 is acquired as an X lock	X	X

During the period that a transaction T holds a first kind V (or second kind V, or X) value lock for value v_l on the B-tree index I_B, if T wants to delete the entry for value v_l, T needs to do a logical deletion of keys [12, 8] instead of a physical deletion. That is, instead of removing the entry for v_l from I_B, it is left there with a *delete_flag* set to 1. If the delete is rolled back, the *delete_flag* is reset to 0. If another transaction inserts an entry for v_l into I_B before the entry for v_l is garbage collected, the *delete_flag* of the entry for v_l is reset to 0. This is to avoid potential write-read conflicts discussed at the beginning of Section 2.4. The physical deletion operations are necessary, otherwise I_B may grow unbounded. To leverage the overhead of the physical deletion operations, we perform them as garbage collection by other operations (of other transactions) that happen to pass through the affected nodes in I_B [8].

In Op4 (put a first kind V value lock on key value v_l), usually an entry for value v_l exists in the B-tree index. However, the situation that no entry for v_l exists in the B-tree index is still possible. To illustrate this, consider an aggregate join view *AJV* that is defined on base relation R and several other base relations. Suppose a B-tree index I_B is built on attribute d of *AJV*. If we insert a new tuple t into R and generate several new join result tuples, we need to acquire the appropriate second kind V value locks on I_B before we can integrate these new join result tuples into *AJV*. If we delete a tuple t from R, to maintain *AJV*, normally we need to first compute the corresponding join result tuples that are to be removed from *AJV*. These join result tuples must have been integrated into *AJV* before. Hence, when we acquire the first kind V value locks for their *d* attribute values, these *d* attribute values must exist in I_B.

However, there is an exception. Suppose attribute *d* of the aggregate join view *AJV* comes from base relation *R*. Consider the following scenario (see [10] for details). There is only one tuple *t* in *R* whose attribute *d*=*v*, but no matching tuple in the other base relations of *AJV* that can be joined with *t*. Hence, there is no tuple in *AJV* whose attribute *d*=*v*. Suppose transaction *T* executes the following SQL statement:

delete from *R* where *R.d*=*v*;

In this case, to maintain *AJV*, there is no need for *T* to compute the corresponding join result tuples that are to be removed from *AJV*. *T* can execute the following "direct propagate" update operation:

delete from *AJV* where *AJV.d*=*v*;

Then when *T* requests a first kind V value lock for *d*=*v* on the B-tree index I_B, *T* will find that no entry for value *v* exists in I_B.

In Op4 (put a first kind V value lock on key value v_1), even if no entry for value v_1 exists in the B-tree index I_B, we still only need to put a V lock for v_1 on I_B. There is no need to put any lock for value v_2 on I_B. That is, no next-key locking is necessary in this case. This is because the first kind V value lock can only be used to remove a join result tuple from the aggregate join view *AJV*. In the case that no entry for v_1 currently exists in I_B, usually no join result tuple for v_1 can be removed from *AJV* (unless another transaction inserts an entry for v_1 into I_B), because no join result tuple currently exists for v_1. Then the first kind V value lock on key value v_1 is used to protect a null operation. Therefore, no next-key locking is necessary. Note: it is possible that after transaction *T* obtains the first kind V value lock for v_1 on I_B, another transaction inserts an entry for v_1 into I_B. Hence, we cannot omit the V lock for v_1 on I_B. This effect is clearer from the correctness proof in Section 4.

3 Necessity of Our Techniques

The preceding section is admittedly dense and intricate, so it is reasonable to ask if all this effort is really necessary. Unfortunately the answer appears to be yes — we use the following aggregate join view *AJV* to illustrate the rationale for the techniques introduced in Section 2.4. The schema of *AJV* is (*a*, *sum*(*b*)). Suppose a B-tree index I_B is built on attribute *a* of *AJV*. We show that if any of the techniques from the previous section are omitted (and not replaced by other equivalent techniques), then we cannot guarantee serializability.

Technique 1. As mentioned above in Op5 (put a second kind V value lock on key value v_1), we need to request a latch on value v_2. The following example illustrates why. Suppose originally the aggregate join view *AJV* contains two tuples that correspond to *a*=*1* and *a*=*4*. Consider three transactions *T*, *T′*, and *T″* on *AJV*. *T* integrates a new join result tuple (3, 5) into *AJV*. *T′* integrates a new join result tuple (2, 6) into *AJV*. *T″* reads those tuples whose attribute *a* is between 1 and 3. Suppose no latch on v_2 is requested. Also, suppose *T*, *T′*, and *T″* are executed as follows:

(1) T puts a V lock for a=*3* and another V lock for a=*4* on *AJV*.

	1			4
T			V	V

(2) T' finds the entries for a=*1* and a=*4* in the B-tree index. T' puts a V lock for a=2 and another V lock for a=*4* on *AJV*.

	1			4
T			V	V
T'		V		V

(3) T inserts the tuple (3, 5) and an entry for a=*3* into *AJV* and the B-tree index I_B, respectively.

	1		3	4
T			V	V
T'		V		V

(4) T commits and releases the V lock for a=*3* and the V lock for a=*4*.

	1		3	4
T'		V		V

(5) Before T' inserts the entry for a=*2* into I_B, T'' finds the entries for a=*1*, a=*3*, and a=*4* in the B-tree index. T'' puts an S lock for a=*1* and another S lock for a=*3* on *AJV*.

	1		3	4
T'		V		V
T''	S		S	

In this way, T'' can start execution even before T' finishes execution. This is incorrect due to the write-read conflict between T' and T'' (on the tuple whose attribute a=2).

Technique 2. As mentioned above in Op5 (put a second kind V value lock on key value v_1), if the V lock for value v_2 on the B-tree index I_B is acquired as an X lock, we need to upgrade the V lock for value v_1 on I_B to an X lock. The following example illustrates why. Suppose originally the aggregate join view *AJV* contains only one tuple that corresponds to a=*4*. Consider two transactions T and T' on *AJV*. T first reads those tuples whose attribute a is between 1 and 4, then integrates a new join result tuple (3, 6) into *AJV*. T' integrates a new join result tuple (2, 5) into *AJV*. Suppose the V lock for v_1 on I_B is not upgraded to an X lock. Also, suppose T and T' are executed as follows:

(1) T finds the entry for a=*4* in the B-tree index I_B. T puts an S lock for a=*4* on *AJV*. T reads the tuple in *AJV* whose attribute a=*4*.

			4
T			S

(2) T puts a V lock for a=*3* and another V lock for a=*4* on *AJV*. Note the V lock for a=*4* is acquired as an X lock because T has already put an S lock for a=*4* on *AJV*.

			4
T		V	X

(3) T inserts the tuple (3, 6) and an entry for a=*3* into *AJV* and I_B, respectively. Then T releases the V lock for a=*4* on *AJV*. Note T still holds an X lock for a=*4* on *AJV*.

		3	4
T		V	X

(4) Before T finishes execution, T' finds the entries for a=*3* and a=*4* in I_B T' puts a V lock for a=2 and another V lock for a=*3* on *AJV*.

		3	4
T		V	X
T'	V	V	

In this way, T' can start execution even before T finishes execution. This is incorrect due to the read-write conflict between T and T' (on the tuple whose attribute a=2).

Technique 3. As mentioned above in Op5 (put a second kind V value lock on key value v_1), if no entry for value v_1 exists in the B-tree index I_B, we need to insert an entry for v_1 into I_B. The following example illustrates why. Suppose originally the aggregate join view *AJV* contains two tuples that correspond to a=*1* and a=*5*. Consider three transactions T, T', and T'' on *AJV*. T integrates two new join result tuples (4, 5) and (2, 6) into *AJV*. T' integrates a new join result tuple (3, 7) into *AJV*. T''

reads those tuples whose attribute a is between 1 and 3. Suppose we do not insert an entry for v_1 into I_B. Also, suppose T, T', and T'' are executed as follows:

(1) T finds the entries for $a=1$ and $a=5$ in the B-tree index I_B. For the new join result tuple (4, 5), T puts a V lock for $a=4$ and another V lock for $a=5$ on AJV.

	1				5
T				V	V

(2) T finds the entries for $a=1$ and $a=5$ in I_B. For the new join result tuple (2, 6), T puts a V lock for $a=2$ and another V lock for $a=5$ on AJV.

	1				5
T		V		V	V

(3) T inserts the tuple (4, 6) and an entry for $a=4$ into AJV and I_B, respectively.

	1			4	5
T		V		V	V

(4) T' finds the entries for $a=1$, $a=4$, and $a=5$ in I_B. T' puts a V lock for $a=3$ and another V lock for $a=4$ on AJV.

	1			4	5
T		V		V	V
T'			V	V	

(5) T' inserts the tuple (3, 7) and an entry for $a=3$ into AJV and I_B, respectively.

	1		3	4	5
T		V		V	V
T'			V	V	

(6) T' commits and releases the two V locks for $a=3$ and $a=4$.

	1		3	4	5
T		V		V	V

(7) Before T inserts the entry for $a=2$ into I_B, T'' finds the entries for $a=1$, $a=3$, $a=4$, and $a=5$ in I_B. T'' puts an S lock for $a=1$ and another S lock for $a=3$ on AJV.

	1		3	4	5
T		V		V	V
T''	S		S		

In this way, T'' can start execution even before T finishes execution. This is incorrect due to the write-read conflict between T and T'' (on the tuple whose attribute $a=2$).

4 Correctness of the Key-Range Locking Protocol

In this section, we prove the correctness (serializability) of our key-range locking strategy for aggregate join views on B-tree indices. Suppose a B-tree index I_B is built on attribute d of an aggregate join view AJV. To prove serializability, for any value v_1 (irrespective of whether an entry for v_1 exists in I_B, i.e., the phantom problem [5] is also considered), we only need to show that there is no read-write, write-read, or write-write conflict between two different transactions on those tuples of AJV whose $d=v_1$ [1, 5]. As shown in Korth [7], write-write conflicts are avoided by the associative and commutative properties of the addition operation. Furthermore, the use of the latches in the latch pool guarantees that for each aggregate group, at any time at most one tuple corresponding to this group exists in AJV. We enumerate all the possible cases to show that write-read and read-write conflicts do not exist. Since we use next-key locking, in the enumeration, we only need to focus on v_1 and the smallest existing value v_2 in I_B such that $v_2>v_1$.

Consider the following two transactions T and T'. T updates (some of) the tuples in the aggregate join view AJV whose attribute d has value v_1. T' reads the tuples in AJV whose attribute d has value v_1 (e.g., through a range query). Suppose v_2 is the smallest existing value in the B-tree index I_B such that $v_2>v_1$. T needs to obtain a first kind V (or second kind V, or X) value lock for $d=v_1$ on I_B. T' needs to obtain an S value lock for $d=v_1$ on I_B. There are four possible cases:

(1) **Case 1:** An entry E for value v_1 already exists in the B-tree index I_B. Also, transaction T' obtains the S value lock for $d=v_1$ on I_B first.

To put an S value lock for $d=v_1$ on I_B, T' needs to put an S lock for $d=v_1$ on AJV. During the period that T' holds the S lock for $d=v_1$ on AJV, the entry E for value v_1 always exists in I_B. Then during this period, transaction T cannot obtain the V (or V, or X) lock for $d=v_1$ on AJV. That is, T cannot obtain the first kind V (or second kind V, or X) value lock for $d=v_1$ on I_B.

(2) **Case 2:** An entry E for value v_1 already exists in the B-tree index I_B. Also, transaction T obtains a first kind V (or second kind V, or X) value lock for $d=v_1$ on I_B first.

To put a first kind V (or second kind V, or X) value lock for $d=v_1$ on I_B, T needs to put a V (or V, or X) lock for $d=v_1$ on AJV. During the period that T holds the V (or V, or X) lock for $d=v_1$ on AJV, the entry E for v_1 always exists in I_B. Note during this period, if some transaction deletes E from I_B, E is only logically deleted. Only after T releases the V (or V, or X) lock for $d=v_1$ on AJV may E be physically deleted from I_B. Hence, during the period that T holds the V (or V, or X) lock for $d=v_1$ on AJV, transaction T' cannot obtain the S lock for $d=v_1$ on AJV. That is, T' cannot obtain the S value lock for $d=v_1$ on I_B.

(3) **Case 3:** No entry for value v_1 exists in the B-tree index I_B. Also, transaction T' obtains the S value lock for $d=v_1$ on I_B first.

To put an S value lock for $d=v_1$ on I_B, T' needs to put an S lock for $d=v_2$ on AJV. During the period that T' holds the S lock for $d=v_2$ on AJV, no other transaction T'' can insert an entry for value v_3 into I_B such that $v_1 \le v_3 < v_2$, because this would require T'' to obtain a V (or X) lock for $d=v_2$ on AJV. Then during the period that T' holds the S lock for $d=v_2$ on AJV, transaction T cannot obtain the second kind V (or X) value lock for $d=v_1$ on I_B, because this would require T to obtain a V (or X) lock for $d=v_2$ on AJV. Note during the period that T' holds the S lock for $d=v_2$ on AJV, T can put a V lock for $d=v_1$ on AJV and then obtain the first kind V value lock for $d=v_1$ on I_B. However, during this period, T cannot use the first kind V value lock for $d=v_1$ on I_B to do any update. This is because no entry for v_1 exists in I_B, and T cannot use the first kind V value lock for $d=v_1$ to insert an entry for v_1 into I_B. Hence, there is no read-write conflict between T and T' on $d=v_1$. Also, if T' itself inserts an entry for value v_3 into I_B such that $v_1 \le v_3 < v_2$, T' will hold an X lock for $d=v_3$ on AJV (see how the second kind V and X value locks are implemented on the B-tree index in Section 2.4). Then T still cannot obtain the second kind V (or X) value lock for $d=v_1$ on I_B before T' finishes execution. (If $v_1=v_3$, then T cannot obtain the first kind V value lock for $d=v_1$ on I_B before T' finishes execution. If $v_1<v_3$, T cannot use the first kind V value lock for $d=v_1$ on I_B to do any update.)

(4) **Case 4:** No entry for value v_1 exists in the B-tree index I_B. Also, transaction T obtains the first kind V (or second kind V, or X) value lock for $d=v_1$ on I_B first. In this case, there are three possible scenarios:

(a) T obtains the first kind V value lock for $d=v_1$ on I_B first. Hence, T puts a V lock for $d=v_1$ on AJV. During the period that T holds the V lock for $d=v_1$ on AJV, another transaction T'' can insert an entry for v_1 into I_B. $T''\neq T$, as T cannot use a first kind V value lock for $d=v_1$ to insert an entry for v_1 into I_B. Before T'' inserts an entry for v_1 into I_B, no such entry exists in I_B. Hence, T cannot use the first kind V value lock for $d=v_1$ to do update and no write-read conflict exists between T and T' on $d=v_1$. After T'' inserts an entry for v_1 into I_B, the entry for v_1 cannot be physically deleted from I_B before T releases the V lock for $d=v_1$ on AJV. Hence, during this period, T' cannot obtain the S value lock for $d=v_1$ on I_B, as T' cannot put an S lock for $d=v_1$ on AJV.

(b) T obtains the second kind V value lock for $d=v_1$ on I_B first. Hence, T puts a V lock for $d=v_1$ and another V lock for $d=v_2$ on AJV. Also, T inserts a new entry for v_1 into I_B. Before T inserts the new entry for v_1 into I_B, T holds the V lock and the latch for $d=v_2$ on AJV. During that period, no other transaction T'' can insert an entry for value v_3 into I_B such that $v_1 \leq v_3 < v_2$, because this would require T'' to obtain a latch (or X lock) for $d=v_2$ on AJV. Then during that period, T' cannot obtain the S value lock for $d=v_1$ on I_B, because this would require T' to obtain an S lock for $d=v_2$ on AJV. After T inserts the new entry for v_1 into I_B, T will hold a V lock for $d=v_1$ on AJV until T finishes execution. Then during this period, T' still cannot obtain the S value lock for $d=v_1$ on I_B, as this would require T' to obtain an S lock for $d=v_1$ on AJV.

(c) T obtains the X value lock for $d=v_1$ on I_B first. Hence, T puts an X lock for $d=v_1$ and another X lock for $d=v_2$ on AJV. During the period that T holds these two X locks, no other transaction T'' can insert an entry for value v_3 into I_B such that $v_1 \leq v_3 < v_2$, as this would require T'' to obtain a V (or X) lock for $d=v_2$ on AJV. Also, T' cannot obtain the S value lock for $d=v_1$ on I_B. This is because to do so, depending on whether T has inserted a new entry for v_1 into I_B or not, T' needs to obtain an S lock for either $d=v_1$ or $d=v_2$ on AJV.

In the above three scenarios, the situation that T itself inserts an entry for value v_3 into I_B such that $v_1 \leq v_3 < v_2$ can be discussed in a way similar to that of Case 3.

Hence, for any value v_1, there is no read-write or write-read conflict between two different transactions on those tuples of the aggregate join view AJV whose attribute d has value v_1. As discussed at the beginning of this section, write-write conflicts do not exist and thus our key-range locking protocol guarantees serializability.

5 The Case of Non-aggregate Join Views with B-Tree Indices

Implementing the V locking protocol for (non-aggregate) join views in the presence of B-tree indices is tricky. For example, suppose we do not use the latches in the latch pool. That is, we only use S, X, and V value locks on join views. Suppose we implement S, X, and V value locks for join views on B-tree indices in the same way as described in Section 2.4. Also, suppose a B-tree index I_B is built on attribute a of a join view $JV=\pi(\sigma(R_1 \bowtie R_2 \bowtie \ldots \bowtie R_n))$. Then to insert a new join result tuple t into JV, we need to first put a V value lock for $t.a$ on I_B. If no entry for $t.a$ exists in I_B, we need to find the smallest value v_2 in I_B such that $v_2 > t.a$ and put a V lock for v_2 on I_B. Unfortunately, this approach does not work. The reason is similar to what is shown for Technique 1 in Section 3. (We can replace the V lock for value v_2 on I_B by an X lock. However, the X lock for v_2 on I_B cannot be downgraded to a V lock. Hence, this X lock greatly reduces concurrency.)

To implement value locks for join views on B-tree indices with high concurrency, we can use the latches in the latch pool and treat join views in the same way as aggregate join views. For join views, we still use four kinds of value locks: S, X, first kind V, and second kind V. For example, suppose a B-tree index I_B is built on attribute a of a join view *JV*. As described in Section 2.4, to insert a new join result tuple t into *JV*, we first put a second kind V value lock for $t.a$ on I_B. To delete a join result tuple t from *JV*, we first put a first kind V value lock for $t.a$ on I_B. For join views, all the four different kinds of value locks (S, X, first kind V, and second kind V) can be implemented on B-tree indices in the same way as described in Section 2.4. The only exception is that we no longer need the latch on the group by attribute value of tuple t. The correctness (serializability) of the implementation can be proved in a way similar to that described in Section 4. Note here, for join views, the latches in the latch pool are used for a different purpose from that for aggregate join views.

References

1. Bernstein, P.A., Hadzilacos, V., Goodman, N.: Concurrency Control and Recovery in Database Systems. Addison-Wesley Publishers, Reading (1987)
2. Gray, J., Bosworth, A., Layman, A., et al.: Data Cube: A Relational Aggregation Operator Generalizing Group-By, Cross-Tab, and Sub-Total. In: ICDE 1996, pp. 152–159 (1996)
3. Gehrke, J., Korn, F., Srivastava, D.: On Computing Correlated Aggregates over Continual Data Streams. In: SIGMOD 2001, pp. 13–24 (2001)
4. Gupta, A., Mumick, I.S.: Materialized Views: Techniques, Implementations, and Applications. MIT Press, Cambridge (1999)
5. Gray, J., Reuter, A.: Transaction Processing: Concepts and Techniques. Morgan Kaufmann Publishers, San Francisco (1993)
6. Graefe G., Zwilling M.J.: Transaction Support for Indexed Views. In: SIGMOD 2004, pp. 323–334 (2004)
7. Korth, H.F.: Locking Primitives in a Database System. JACM 30(1), 55–79 (1983)
8. Kornacker, M., Mohan, C., Hellerstein, J.M.: Concurrency and Recovery in Generalized Search Trees. In: SIGMOD 1997, pp. 62–72 (1997)
9. Luo, G., Naughton, J.F., Ellmann, C.J., Watzke, M.W.: Locking Protocols for Materialized Aggregate Join Views. In: VLDB 2003, pp. 596–607 (2003)
10. Luo, G., Naughton, J.F., Ellmann, C.J., Watzke, M.W.: Locking Protocols for Materialized Aggregate Join Views. TKDE 17(6), 796–807 (2005)
11. Mohan, C.: ARIES/KVL: A Key-Value Locking Method for Concurrency Control of Multiaction Transactions Operating on B-Tree Indexes. In: VLDB 1990, pp. 392–405 (1990)
12. Mohan, C.: Commit_LSN: A Novel and Simple Method for Reducing Locking and Latching in Transaction Processing Systems. In: VLDB 1990, pp. 406–418 (1990)
13. Poess, M., Floyd, C.: New TPC Benchmarks for Decision Support and Web Commerce. SIGMOD Record 29(4), 64–71 (2000)
14. Dver, A.: Real-time Enterprise. Business week (December 2, 2002)

Web Information Credibility

Katsumi Tanaka

Graduate School of Informatics, Kyoto University
Yoshida-Honmachi, Sakyo, Kyoto 606-8501
tanaka@dl.kuis.kyoto-u.ac.jp

Abstract. World Wide Web is the biggest repository of information and knowledge. Such information gives people a framework for organizing their private and professional lives. Research aimed at evaluating the credibility of Web content has recently become increasingly crucial because the Web has started to influence our daily lives. The abundance of content on the Web, the lack of publishing barriers, and poor quality control of Web content raise credibility issues. If users are not aware of the credibility of Web information, they can be easily misled, and sometimes it is dangerous to users.

For example, some researchers reported that there are more than twenty thousand health-related sites on the Web, but more than half of such sites have not been reviewed by medical specialists. Wikipedia has been more popular on the Web, but the risks of Wikipedia are also indicated from the viewpoint of credibility. There are a lot of exaggerated ads and fake images and movies. The importance of the image forensic research also becomes important.

Many dimensions concerned with the information credibility are grouped into two key components: expertise and trustworthiness. Expertise is a factor about the writer's ability to produce correct or fair information and the degree to which the reader can perceive knowledge and skill from the information. The expertise factor is defined by the terms knowledgeable, experienced, competent, and so on. The trustworthiness is a factor about readers' perceptions that the information is true as they know it, and it is the degree to which readers can perceive the goodness or morality of the target information. The trustworthiness factor is defined by the terms well-intentioned, unbiased, reputable, and so on. In the areas of Web search and mining, however, most of conventional research has focused on ranking search results based on popularity by analyzing link structures or on mining useful rules from the Web. They have not focused on the analysis of the credibility of target information.

Consequently, few users perform rigorous evaluations of the credibility of obtained information. Therefore, the exploration of a general framework and automatic tools for supporting users in the judgment of web content credibility are becoming increasingly necessary.

In this talk, we describe a new framework and methods for evaluating the Web information credibility. These include: a bipartite-graph framework for evaluating the credibility of relations, and several methods for analyzing Web information credibility from the viewpoint of (1) content analysis, (2) social support analysis and (3) author analysis.

L. Chen et al. (Eds.): WAIM 2010, LNCS 6184, p. 781, 2010.

Author Index

GPSR Compliance

The European Union's (EU) General Product Safety Regulation (GPSR) is a set of rules that requires consumer products to be safe and our obligations to ensure this.

If you have any concerns about our products, you can contact us on ProductSafety@springernature.com

In case Publisher is established outside the EU, the EU authorized representative is:

Springer Nature Customer Service Center GmbH
Europaplatz 3
69115 Heidelberg, Germany

Batch number: 10712242

Printed by Printforce, the Netherlands